PRINCETON READINGS

IN POLITICAL THOUGHT

Princeton Readings
in Political Thought

Essential Texts

since Plato

Mitchell Cohen and Nicole Fermon,

Editors

PRINCETON UNIVERSITY PRESS · PRINCETON, NEW JERSEY

Library of Congress Cataloging-in-Publication Data

Princeton readings in political thought : essential texts since Plato
  / Mitchell Cohen and Nicole Fermon, editors.
        p. cm.
    Includes bibliographical references.
    ISBN 0-691-03688-8 (cloth : alk. paper). — ISBN 0-691-03689-6
  pbk. : alk. paper)
      1. Political science—History. 2. Political science. I. Cohen,
  Mitchell, 1952-   . II. Fermon, Nicole, 1950-   .
  JA81.P928   1996
  320'.01—dc20   95–23990
                                                          CIP

This book has been composed in Galliard Typeface

Princeton University Press books are printed on acid-free paper and meet the guidelines for
permanence and durability of the Committee on Production Guidelines for Book Longevity of the
Council on Library Resources

http:// pup.princeton.edu

Printed in the United States of America

10   9   8   7   6   5   4   3   2   1

10   9   8   7   6   5   4   3   2
(Pbk.)

Most of the selections in this book have been edited. Footnotes have sometimes been abridged,
rearranged, or deleted by the editors. For full references, readers are directed to the original editions.

Contents

Acknowledgments

Aquinas:
Excerpts from "The Treatise on Law," *Summa Theologica*, from *Thomas Aquinas on Politics and Ethics*, edited by Paul E. Sigmund. © 1985 by W. W. Norton & Company, Inc. Used by permission of the publisher.

Arendt:
Excerpts from *The Origins of Totalitarianism* by Hannah Arendt. Copyright 1951 and renewed 1979 by Mary McCarthy West, reprinted by permission of Harcourt Brace & Company.

Aristotle:
Reprinted from *The Politics of Aristotle* translated by Ernest Barker (1946) by permission of Oxford University Press.

Augustine:
From *The Political Writings of St. Augustine*, edited with an Introduction by Henry Paolucci. Copyright © 1962 by Regnery Gateway, Inc. All rights reserved. Reprinted by permission of Regnery Publishing, Inc., Washington, D.C.

Beauvoir:
From *The Second Sex* by Simone De Beauvoir, trans., H. M. Parshley. Copyright 1952 and renewed 1980 by Alfred A. Knopf, Inc. Reprinted by permission of the publisher.

Bentham:
From Jeremy Bentham, "An Introduction to the Principles of Morals and Legislation," in *John Stuart Mill: Utilitarianism and Other Writings*, Meridian/NAL.

Burke:
From *The Works of the Right Honorable Edmund Burke*, rev. ed., vol. 3, *Reflections on the Revolution in France*, Little, Brown, 1865.

Calvin:
From McNeill, John T., *On God and Political Duty by John Calvin*, © 1956. Reprinted by permission of Prentice Hall, Upper Saddle River, New Jersey.

Cicero:
Reprinted by permission of the publishers and the Loeb Classical Library from Cicero, *De Re Publica De Legibus*, vol. XVI, translated by Clinton Walker Keyes, Cambridge, Mass.: Harvard University Press, 1977.

Declaration of the Rights of Man:
From *The Constitution and Other Documents Illustrative of the History of France, 1789–1907*, 2nd ed., rev., by Frank Maloy Anderson, Wilson, 1908.

Fanon:
From *The Wretched of the Earth* by Franz Fanon, translated by Constance Farrington. Copyright © 1963, 1991 by Presence Africaine. Used by permission of Grove Press, Inc.

Foucault:
From Michel Foucault, *Discipline and Punish*, trans. by Alan Sheridan. Copyright © 1975 by Editions Gallimard. Reprinted by permission of Georges Borchardt, Inc.

Freud:
Reprinted from *Civilization and Its Discontents* by Sigmund Freud, translated from the German by James Strachey, with the permission of W. W. Norton & Company, Inc. Copyright © 1961 by James Strachey, renewed 1989 by Alix Strachey. Also used with permission of Random House UK Ltd.

Reprinted from *Totem and Taboo* by Sigmund Freud, translated from the German by James Strachey, with the permission of W. W. Norton & Company, Inc. Copyright © 1950 by Routledge & Kegan Paul, Ltd. Also used by permission of International Thomson Publishing Services Ltd.

"Why War?" from *The Collected Papers*, volume 5, by Sigmund Freud. Edited by James Strachey. Published by Basic Books, Inc. by arrangement with The Hogarth Press, Ltd. and the Institute of Psycho-Analysis, London. Reprinted by permission of BasicBooks, a division of HarperCollins Publishers, Inc. Also used by permission of Random House UK Ltd.

Goldman:
Emma Goldman, "Victims of Moralty," from *Red Emma Speaks*, ed. by Alix Kates Shulman. Used by permission of Alix Kates Shulman.

Gouges:
Reprinted from *Women, the Family, and Freedom: The Debate in Documents*, Volume One, 1750–1880, edited by Susan Groag Bell and Karen M. Offen with the permission of the publisher, Stanford University Press. © 1983 by the Board of Trustees of the Leland Stanford Junior University.

Habermas:
From *Jurgen Habermas on Society and Politics* by Jurgen Habermas. Copyright © 1989 by Beacon Press. Reprinted by permission of Beacon Press.

Hegel:
Reprinted from Hegel: *The Philosophy of Right* translated by T. M. Knox (1942) by permission of Oxford University Press.

King:
Martin Luther King, Jr., "Letter from Birmingham Jail." Reprinted by arrangement with The Heirs to the Estate of Martin Luther King, Jr., c/o Joan Daves Agency as agent for the proprietor. Copyright 1963, 1964 by Martin Luther King, Jr., copyright renewed 1991, 1992 by Coretta Scott King.

Lenin:
From Lenin, "What Is to Be Done," "State and Revolution," in *The Lenin Reader*, ed. R. C. Tucker, 1975, Norton.

Luther:
Reprinted from *Luther's Works*, Volume 45, edited by Walther L. Brandt, copyright © 1962 Fortress Press. Used by permission of Augsburg Fortress.

Machiavelli:
From Niccolo Machiavelli, *The Prince and Other Discourses*, intro. Max Lerner, Modern Library, 1950.

Malcolm:
From *Malcolm X Speaks*. Copyright © 1965 & 1989 by Betty Shabazz and Pathfinder Press. Reprinted by permission of Pathfinder.

Marx:
Excerpts from "A Contribution to the Critique of Political Economy," "Estranged Labor," "The Communist Manifesto," "After the Revolution," and "Capital," reprinted from *The Marx-Engels Reader*, Second Edition, edited by Robert C. Tucker, with the permission of W. W. Norton & Company, Inc. Copyright © 1978, 1972 by W. W. Norton & Company, Inc.

Michels:
Reprinted with the permission of The Free Press, a Division of Simon & Schuster Inc. from *Political Parties: A Sociological Study of the Oligarchical Tendencies of Modern Democracy*, by Robert Michels, translated by Eden and Cedar Paul. Copyright © 1962 by The Crowell-Collier Publishing Company.

Mill:
Shields, Currin V., *On Liberty by John Stuart Mill*, © 1956. Reprinted by permission of Prentice Hall, Englewood Cliffs, New Jersey.

John Stuart Mill, "On the Subjection of Woman," in *Three Essays*, intro. Richard Wollheim, Oxford.

Mosca:
From Gaetano Mosca, *The Ruling Class*, 1939, McGraw-Hill.

Nietzsche:
From *On the Genealogy of Morals* by Friedrich Nietzsche, translated by Walter Kaufmann. Copyright © 1967 by Random House, Inc. Reprinted by permission of Vintage Books, a division of Random House, Inc.

Nozick:
Selected excerpts from *Anarchy, State and Utopia* by Robert Nozick. Copyright © 1974 by Basic Books, Inc. Reprinted by permission of BasicBooks, a division of HarperCollins Publishers, Inc.

Orwell:

"Politics and the English Language" from *Shooting an Elephant and Other Essays* by George Orwell, copyright 1946 by Sonia Brownell Orwell and renewed 1974 by Sonia Orwell, reprinted by permission of Harcourt Brace & Company. Copyright © The estate of the late Sonia Brownell Orwell and Martin Secker and Warburg Ltd. Used by permission of A. M. Heath & Company Limited, Author's Agents.

Pizan:

Excerpts from *The Book of the City of Ladies* by Christine de Pizan, translated by Earl Jeffrey Richards. Copyright © 1982 by Persea Books, Inc. Reprinted by permission of Persea Books, Inc.

Plato:

From *The Collected Dialogues of Plato*, ed. Edith Hamilton and Huntington Cairns. Bollingen Series LXXI. Copyright © 1961 renewed 1989 by Princeton University Press. "Apology" and "Republic" used with permission of Princeton University Press.

Rawls:

Reprinted by permission of the publishers from *A Theory of Justice* by John Rawls, Cambridge, Mass.: The Belknap Press of Harvard University Press, Copyright © 1971 by the President and Fellows of Harvard College.

Rousseau:

From "Discourse on the Origin and Foundation of Inequality Among Men," in Jean-Jacques Rousseau, *Basic Political Writings*, translated and edited by Donald A. Cress. © 1987. Used by permission of Hackett Publishing Company, Inc. All Rights Reserved.

From Jean-Jacques Rousseau, *On the Social Contract with Geneva Manuscript and Political Economy*, edited by Roger D. Masters and Judith R. Masters. Copyright © 1978 St. Martin's Press, Incorporated. Reprinted with permission of St. Martin's Press, Incorporated.

Strauss:

From Gildin, Hilail, *Political Philosophy: Six Essays by Leo Strauss*, © 1975. Reprinted by permission of Prentice Hall, Upper Saddle River, New Jersey.

Thucydides:

From Thucydides, *The Pelopennesian Wars*, Crowley trans., Modern Library.

Tocqueville:

From Alexis de Tocqueville, *Democracy in America*, ed. Richard Heffner, NAL/Mentor.

Walzer:

Michael Walzer, "In Defense of Equality." © 1973 *Dissent Magazine*. Used by permission of Dissent.

Weber:
From Max Weber, *Selections in Translation*, ed. by W. G. Runciman. © Cambridge University Press 1978. Reprinted with the permission of Cambridge University Press.

Wollstonecraft:
From Mary Wollstonecraft, *A Vindication of the Rights of Woman*, Second Edition, A Norton Critical Edition, ed. by Carol H. Poston.

PRINCETON READINGS

IN POLITICAL THOUGHT

Thinking Politically: An Introduction _____

I

In this anthology you will find selections from important works of political theory that span some 2,500 years, from the ancient Greeks through today. The author of each wrestles, in his or her own time, place, and way, with the most basic questions that human beings can ask about living together—questions about justice, and about relations and institutions of power.

Studying political theory forces us to wrestle with these questions in order to clarify what politics is all about. Indeed, the word "theory" comes from the ancient Greek *theoria*, which means "viewing," "speculation," "contemplation."[1] Here is just a partial list of what political theorists look at, speculate about, and contemplate.

What is power?

What defines a citizen and what are a citizen's obligations?

Who should be "sovereign" in a political community? Who should be included in the community? Who can be excluded?

When does a government become "illegitimate"? When is it legitimate to rebel against political authority? Are there rights with which a government may never tamper?

How far should a government intrude into our private lives?

What should be the role of the state in a just society? What *is* a just society?

What means and what ends are legitimate in politics?

Formulating questions like these can be deceptively simple. Political philosophers frequently find that half their task is defining the very words they use, for how one demarcates terms will affect how one thinks through political problems. Indeed, we can see this throughout the entire history of Western political thought. At its dawn, in *The Republic* (see Chapter 2), we find Plato seeking to answer the question: What is justice? In attempting to explain this basic term, he concluded that justice was to be found in a society with a proper division of labor, in which everybody plays the role for which he or she is naturally best suited. The ideal state, Plato thought, would be a dictatorship of its smartest citizens, "philosopher-kings." The vast majority of the people were simply not competent to govern; they would have other tasks. If we skip ahead—over two millennia ahead—we find the same question still being posed: What is justice? In the 1970s, a Harvard professor, John Rawls, inaugurated a renaissance in political theory with a book entitled *A Theory of Justice* (see Chapter 41). He argued that given "fair" conditions in which to select the principles governing their society, everyone would choose equal liberty, equal opportunity, and the idea that inequalities—socioeconomic differences—would be acceptable provided they are to the benefit of the least advantaged in society.

Plato and Rawls obviously reached different conclusions when trying to define justice. But to grasp their respective contributions—and to see what both of them have to say to us nowadays—we must not just think about their conclusions, but must examine the structure of their arguments as well. What claims do they make and how do they make them? Are they justified? How do they construct their assertions?

II

Now you may be saying to yourself, "Theory, philosophy—it all seems so abstract. Don't these theorists just weave grand webs out of the recesses of their minds? What effect does it all have on the real world anyway?" The impact has been more than you might imagine. Ideas are, of course, only one element of what makes history. Still, how people think politically very much affects how they act politically.

Consider this: When the French Revolution took place in 1789, one powerful influence on leading revolutionaries was the ideas of the Genevan-born political theorist Jean-Jacques Rousseau, even though he had died eleven years earlier. "Man is born free, yet everywhere he is in chains," reads the incendiary first sentence of his book *The Social Contract* (see the selection in Chapter 13). One was completely "free," Rousseau argued, only in a "state of nature" where there was no government or social constraints. Since life in society always requires governance and rules (which, when enforceable, are forms of coercion), and since we will not live in a state of nature, Rousseau asked: Under what conditions can we say that these "chains" are legitimate?

Rousseau wrote that we are politically free when we are subject to laws we have formulated ourselves. So he insisted that "the People" should be "sovereign" and that their "General Will" should be the author of a land's basic laws. These were subversive ideas in prerevolutionary France, a hierarchical society in which the Crown was sovereign and the inhabitants of this realm were the King's subjects, not self-governing citizens. No wonder that *The Social Contract* was banned in Paris and Geneva when it was first published in 1762. Its author had to flee into exile. Yet when the Revolution came, captivated crowds—or so the story goes— listened as the celebrated revolutionary Jean-Paul Marat read Rousseau's book aloud on Paris street corners.

For another example, take a case closer to home. In the late seventeenth century, the British political theorist John Locke articulated a famous theory of revolution in his *Second Treatise of Government* (see Chapter 12). When Thomas Jefferson and his colleagues wrote the Declaration of Independence, shortly after the "shot heard 'round the world" was fired at the British by American farmers in Concord, Massachusetts, they did so with Locke's ideas very much in mind.

Locke argued that there were rights that belonged to human beings by nature— the rights of life, liberty, and property—and that government was entrusted to protect them. Should a government violate this trust, it was no longer legitimate.

Then, citizens had a right to overthrow it and establish a new one. Locke's ideas were tied to the nonviolent "Glorious Revolution of 1688," which established a constitutional monarchy and parliamentary supremacy in Britain: the king was now below, instead of above, the law (although Locke's book was written before this revolution).

Jefferson and the American colonists, facing King George III almost a century later, declared that it was a "self-evident" truth that human beings are "endowed by their Creator with certain inalienable rights," among which were "life, liberty and the pursuit of happiness." Because George III had violated those rights (and others!), Americans no longer owed him fealty. Independence was declared and the colonies became an independent American republic. Later, in 1787, when the delegates assembled in Philadelphia to debate the principles of and then write the U.S. Constitution, among them were men deeply immersed not only in Locke's writings, but in European political theory in general. They read, thought, and talked about political ideas as they fashioned the document that would govern the United States.

III

Early in this anthology, in the section on the ancient world, you will read Aristotle, Plato's pupil. In the fourth century B.C., he asserted, in *The Politics*, that man is a political animal, a being who can fulfill his nature only through participation in a political community. If you didn't live in one, Aristotle asserted, you were either less than human or more than human.

Even if you accepted this in principle, you would probably say it differently nowadays. You would probably say that men and women are political animals. Aristotle, living when he did, didn't accept the equality of women and also believed that slavery was natural. This just gives you a hint at how political ideas get reshaped over centuries. As you read this anthology, you will see that as concepts of human nature and human history change, so do concepts of politics. For one example, Christian thinkers of the Middle Ages didn't accept the idea that we are political animals. For them, religion came first and foremost. They thought religiously and fit politics into their theology. Later, when we enter the modern world, politics reasserts its independence.

But then, in the nineteenth century, we find one of the most important liberal political philosophers, John Stuart Mill, trying to assert the individual's independence from politics by delineating those dimensions of life in which government had no right to intervene—areas that ought to be strictly matters of individual liberty. Government ought not to interfere with acts that are strictly "self-regarding," he argued. Otherwise we will be unable to develop and fulfill ourselves as individuals. At the same time, Mill recognized that despotism comes not only from abusive governments but also from apparently nonpolitical sources. He warned of the "tyranny of majority opinion," of how popular views can have a chilling effect on individual creativity. People are often intimidated by new or unusual ideas. He once declared that "No society in which eccentricity is a matter of reproach can be a wholesome state."

Mill himself took up an unpopular cause in the Britain of his day: feminism. He was an early advocate of women's rights (and as a young man he was once arrested for trying to distribute information about birth control on London streets). This, of course, raises an interesting question: How far does "thinking politically" extend? In various sections of this anthology you will find writings concerning the status of women and the oppression of women. Is this "political"? Certainly, if you define politics in terms of power exercised by and among human beings.

However, some political thinkers contend that we should define politics more narrowly so as to keep an eye on specific features, dynamics, and questions—questions like the nature of the state and different forms of government. Take, for example, Max Weber, a formidable political thinker of the early twentieth century who is often called the "father of sociology." In his brilliant essay "Politics as a Vocation" (see Chapter 26), he defined the "state" as a "human community that (successfully) claims the *monopoly of the legitimate use of physical force* within a given territory." This is a famous definition. Think of all the important questions it raises (and which Weber explored in many writings): what does "legitimate" force mean? Or a "human community" and a "given territory"? Do we specify these on the basis of size? Population?

And again: What about relations of power within this state? Weber's work, it is sometimes said, is a debate with the ghost of Karl Marx. It is easy to see why. Marx insisted that we could never think of "the state" or governments without placing them within a larger socioeconomic totality. He asked: If economic life is dominated by a small part of the population—"the ruling class"—then won't socioeconomic power be translated into political power?

Marx contended that "the state," the organization of political power within a society, was simply a means by which one social class oppresses other classes. Since for him all history is the history of class struggle, governments simply try to keep the have-nots in order on behalf of the haves. Consequently, "the state" is an "executive committee" asserting the interests of the dominant economic class. Marx believed it possible to create a classless society in which the state would eventually vanish. If there is no ruling class and if society is organized cooperatively so that socioeconomic resources benefit all, there would no longer be a need for government as we have known it, he thought. In that case, politics would vanish and, presumably, we'd no longer need to "think politically."

IV

Who is right? Who is wrong? Of course, there is no simple answer. You may find that *even when some political theorists seem very wrong—terribly wrong—you may learn a lot from their errors.* As John Stuart Mill argued in *On Liberty*, even if you believe something to be completely true—absolutely true—unless it is contested and debated and argued, it may well turn into a useless dogma.

So, in opening these pages, we invite you to think politically, to wrestle with great debates about political ideas. Some may lead you to see the world with new eyes, and some of the ideas may simply infuriate you. Frankly, we hope that there is a lot in these pages that will leave you unsettled. Perhaps the arguments will raise for you new questions and open some new horizons about the ways power is exercised. If so, you may want to explore political theory in more depth. We hope that these introductory selections will inspire you to read the full texts.

Mitchell Cohen
Baruch College and the
Graduate School of the
City University of New York

Nicole Fermon
Fordham University

Note

1. F. E. Peters, *Greek Philosophical Terms: A Historical Lexicon* (New York: New York University Press, 1967), 194.

Part One

CLASSICAL POLITICAL THOUGHT

THE ATHENIAN victory over Persia at Marathon (490 B.C.) assured Greek independence from "oriental despotism," and allowed the development of democracy and thus of the culture and politics we know today as European and Western. Ten years later, Athens, a "polis" (city-state), was besieged and burned by Persian King Xerxes in a subsequent invasion. Athenians (acting selflessly as a community) had abandoned their city in order to trap the invaders and destroy their fleet at sea. Their sacrifice allowed the combined Greek forces to defeat the Persian army at Platea. The Athenian navy thus played a crucial role in liberating Greek cities from sixty years of occupation. Athens' leading role in these victories confirmed its power, while its naval hegemony extended over its Greek allies. Once the threat of invasion was eliminated, the Athenian fleet patrolled the Mediterranean to protect it from pirates, securing trade routes and allowing an explosion of commerce, the production of arts, and the development of a civic culture. This era would be the subject of controversy and debate throughout the ages. The political leader of this age, Pericles, was prime minister of Athens for thirty years. He described Athens at the height of its glory, the first year of the great war between Athens and Sparta: "Our constitution does not copy the laws of neighboring states; we are rather a pattern to others than imitators ourselves. Its administration favors the many instead of the few; this is why it is called a democracy."

Direct democracy in Athens developed without the bloodshed that characterized relations between the many (poor) and the few (rich aristocrats) of other Greek cities. Pericles thus spoke in a political context in which all citizens could vote and participate in the Assembly, the legislative body that ruled Athens. The Assembly met regularly as well as for specific emergencies, and functioned with the Council (*Boulé*) of Five Hundred acting as an executive committee for the Assembly. These two institutions, as well as the courts with large juries, were important for popular control of government. Women, slaves, and foreigners ("metics") were barred from politics. As naturalization was very difficult to secure, most people lived in the city without the right to participate in the very institutions which would earn the Athenians political immortality. Perhaps one-tenth of a population of 400,000 or 500,000 were active citizens, either in the huge juries which, sometimes with as many as 1,501 members decided questions of law and politics, or in the civil and military functions decided through lot, election, or through choice. Face-to-face politics was thus possible, with citizens knowing each other and making decisions of war and peace accordingly.

The Greek polis elevated the concept of civic harmony and celebrated the notion of a common life. The Athenian constitution, inaugurated at the end of the sixth century B.C., allowed the realization of this ideal. The experience of constitutional rule was relatively recent by the time Pericles gave his famous funeral oration. The reforms of Solon, and the beginning of democracy, first occurred with the establishment of popular control of the all-important law courts at the beginning of the sixth century, and the elimination of imprisonment for debts which had been instrumental in driving Greek citizens into exile or servitude. Cleisthenes, whose constitutional reforms were adopted in 507 B.C., attacked the principle of aristocratic power by transforming the system of tribes, and initiating a new set of bonds based on locality rather than kinship. Individuals were now citizens on the basis of the *deme* (district) they belonged to, reducing the distinctions that had existed between citizens on the basis of blood ties. The community became more powerful through the gradual process of elevating individual citizen democrats, and the civic community, at the expense of the aristocracy and its interests.

In the city of Pericles and Plato, class structure was thus more fluid, with a growing class of non-noble rich citizens. The positions of slaves, who made up perhaps one-third of the population, and all other noncitizens, was correspondingly more ambiguous. Many slaves were independent small producers who paid a "body rent" to their masters. Slaves occupied the managerial positions which citizens despised. Citizen and slave, freeman and noncitizen, almost all men worked and the traditional division between those who labored and those who had the leisure to be engaged in politics was consequently less absolute.

Despite reforms which emphasized the equality of citizens and the unity of the civic body, the legal status of women in Athens was incompatible with a free life. Neither aristocratic nor laboring women nor slave women could participate in the political life of the city. Although women could inherit property, they could not manage it. Their primary responsibility in addition to domestic labor was to bear citizens for the city. Women's freedom was restricted in all areas of daily life, and those women who had not produced a male heir could legally be compelled to marry a next-of-kin to maintain property within the family. Urban Athens restricted the social and economic role of aristocratic women who were stripped of previous tribal and ancestral familial powers. Although all women found themselves restricted by democratic laws and institutions, women who were not citizens had greater mobility than the wives and daughters of citizens, for restrictions keeping the latter out of the public sphere did not apply to foreigners. Paradoxically, in Sparta, which was a far less democratic agrarian society, women had access to the sphere of production and exchange; they maintained the power to control and manage their property. Democracy, which sought to expand political freedom, had failed to include women. Plato's politics, profoundly hostile to democracy, proposed remarkable freedom and equality for women, and he was able to imagine women rulers and philosophers, and even women warriors, in *The Republic*.

The central character of most of Plato's thirty-five dialogues is Socrates. Socrates was the principal founder of the new discourse of Western philosophy and was spokesman for an antidemocratic ideology. With the exception of what is found in the writings of Xenophon, Aristophanes, and Plato, very little is known with any certainty about Socrates except that he fought in the Peloponnesian War. In 399, he was tried and convicted of impiety and corrupting the youth of Athens. Most of his interlocutors were aristocrats. Although there are speculations that Socrates was a commoner from the most humble class, strong evidence (education, level of military service, and an advantageous marriage) suggests that he belonged to the upper stratum. At his trial he attributed his poverty to preoccupation with the "examination of life" which led him to neglect material affairs.

Socrates was Plato's teacher, as Plato was Aristotle's. They were the originators of the tradition of classical political theory which addressed prevailing questions about the nature of ventures like courage, moderation, piety, friendship, and the possibility of the good life in the just state. They also investigated and interrogated contemporary cultural conventions like tragedy, poetry, and sophistry. Classical political thought not only includes the writings of Plato and Aristotle, but also the later political teachings of the Stoics and Skeptics, and then of the Church Fathers and the Scholastics.

The Apology is Socrates' defense of philosophy and his recommendations for political reform. He is the champion of government by knowledge, and proposes that philosopher-kings (or queens) are the best rulers. *The Apology* presents the account of Socrates' trial by democratic detractors. Told that he could avoid the death penalty by paying a small fine and swearing to remain silent about politics, Socrates replied that the unexamined life was not worth living and he would not accept exile or the injustice of silence. Reason, he also insisted, must be applied to questions of politics and ethics.

In *The Republic*, Plato inquires into the nature of justice and asks what is the best kind of human life. In opposition to the Periclean ideal of versatility, he proposes a Spartan inspired specialization of function. Aristotle would attempt to provide the definitive critique of Plato's political recommendations, claiming in *The Politics* that the arrangements of *The Republic* would make the state too unified. According to Aristotle, the state was an organization which oversaw other organizations, each with its own separate interests. He insisted that constitutional safeguards were essential to the good state and argued against the communism of Plato's *Republic* for a middle class community and for a mixed oligarchic-democratic constitution. The debate between Plato and Aristotle continues today in different guises and arenas. The questions posed are fundamentally the same: How should men, and now women, live in common; what is the best way to order human affairs? What is justice?

1

Thucydides
Pericles' Funeral Oration

(FROM *THE HISTORY OF THE PELOPONNESIAN WAR*)

Thucydides (460?–400? B.C.) was the first Athenian historian to record the contemporary events of his city. He wrote as a soldier and warrior, presenting in the History of the Peloponnesian War *the struggle between the Athenians and the Spartans and their respective allies. The work breaks off in mid-sentence in 411, although the war continued until 404. Thucydides was an adult at the beginning of the war in 431, and he served as a general in 424 until his forced exile in 424/3 as a direct result of his disastrous leadership. Thucydides' historical interpretation owes much to the scientific method in his deliberate gathering of information from a variety of sources, in the style of argumentation, abstract in many aspects, as well as in his theory of causation. The reasons for the war are depicted as mostly psychological, the "truest motive" being Sparta's fear of the growing power of Athens.*

Thucydides is a major surviving representative of the Sophist movement, the first professional intellectuals of Greece, evident in his use of rhetorical devices and in his understanding of history as solely the observable action of humans, deliberately excluding religious or metaphysical explanations. History, and men's lives, are delineated in set speeches, choices clarified in stark and vivid terms, as in Pericles' funeral oration which celebrates Athenian citizens, or in the refusal of discourse which marks the end of politics in the Melian dialogue.

IN THE same winter the Athenians gave a funeral at the public cost to those who had first fallen in this war. It was a custom of their ancestors, and the manner of it is as follows. Three days before the ceremony, the bones of the dead are laid out in a tent which has been erected; and their friends bring to their relatives such offerings as they please. In the funeral procession cypress coffins are borne on wagons, one for each tribe, the bones of the deceased being placed in the coffin of their tribe. Among these is carried one empty bier decked for the missing, that is, for those whose bodies could not be recovered. Any citizen or stranger who pleases joins in the procession: and the female relatives are there to wail at the burial. The dead are laid in the public sepulchre in the most beautiful suburb of the city, in which those who fall in war are always buried—with the exception of those slain at Marathon, who for their singular and extraordinary valour were interred on the spot where they fell. After the bodies have been laid in the earth, a man chosen by the state, of approved wisdom and eminent reputation, pronounces

over them an appropriate panegyric, after which all retire. Such is the manner of
the burying; and throughout the whole of the war, whenever the occasion arose,
the established custom was observed. Meanwhile these were the first that had
fallen, and Pericles, son of Xanthippus, was chosen to pronounce their eulogium.
When the proper time arrived, he advanced from the sepulchre to an elevated
platform in order to be heard by as many of the crowd as possible, and spoke as
follows:

Most of my predecessors in this place have commended him who made this speech
part of the law, telling us that it is well that it should be delivered at the burial of those
who fall in battle. For myself, I should have thought that the worth which had displayed
itself in deeds would be sufficiently rewarded by honours also shown by deeds, such as
you now see in this funeral prepared at the people's cost. And I could have wished that
the reputations of many brave men were not to be imperilled in the mouth of a single
individual, to stand or fall according as he spoke well or ill. For it is hard to speak
properly upon a subject where it is even difficult to convince your hearers that you are
speaking the truth. On the one hand, the friend who is familiar with every fact of the
story may think that some point has not been set forth with that fullness which he wishes
and knows it to deserve; on the other, he who is a stranger to the matter may be led by
envy to suspect exaggeration if he hears anything above his own nature. For men can
endure to hear others praised only so long as they can severally persuade themselves of
their own ability to equal the actions recounted: when this point is passed, envy comes in
and with it incredulity. However, since our ancestors have stamped this custom with their
approval, it becomes my duty to obey the law and to try to satisfy your several wishes
and opinions as best I may.

I shall begin with our ancestors: it is both just and proper that they should have the
honour of the first mention on an occasion like the present. They dwelt in the country
without break in the succession from generation to generation, and handed it down free
to the present time by their valour. And if our more remote ancestors deserved praise,
much more do our own fathers, who added to their inheritance the empire which we now
possess, and spared no pains to be able to leave their acquisitions to us of the present
generation. Lastly, there are few parts of our dominions that have not been augmented by
those of us here, who are still more or less in the vigour of life; and the mother country
has been furnished by us with everything that can enable her to depend on her own
resources whether for war or for peace. That part of our history which tells of the military achievements which gave us our several possessions, or of the ready valour with
which either we or our fathers stemmed the tide of Hellenic or foreign aggression, is a
theme too familiar to my hearers for me to dilate on, and I shall therefore pass it by. But
by what road we reached our position, under what form of government our greatness
grew, out of what national habits it sprang—these are subjects which I may pursue
before I proceed to my panegyric upon these men; for I think them to be themes upon
which on the present occasion a speaker may properly dwell, and to which the whole
assemblage, whether citizens or foreigners, may listen with advantage.

Our constitution does not copy the laws of neighbouring states; we are rather a pattern
to others than imitators ourselves. Its administration favours the many instead of the few;

this is why it is called a democracy. If we look to the laws, they afford equal justice to all in their private differences; if to social standing, advancement in public life falls to reputation for capacity, class considerations not being allowed to interfere with merit; nor again does poverty bar the way: if a man is able to serve the state, he is not hindered by the obscurity of his condition. The freedom which we enjoy in our government extends also to our ordinary life. There, far from exercising a jealous surveillance over each other, we do not feel called upon to be angry with our neighbour for doing what he likes, or even to indulge in those injurious looks which cannot fail to be offensive, although they inflict no positive penalty. But all this ease in our private relations does not make us lawless as citizens. Against this fear is our chief safeguard, teaching us to obey the magistrates and the laws, particularly such as regard the protection of the injured, whether they are actually on the statute book, or belong to that code which, although unwritten, yet cannot be broken without acknowledged disgrace.

Further, we provide plenty of means for the mind to refresh itself from business. We celebrate games and sacrifices all the year round, and the elegance of our private establishments forms a daily source of pleasure and helps to banish our cares; and the magnitude of our city draws the produce of the world into our harbour, so that to the Athenian the fruits of other countries are as familiar a luxury as those of his own.

If we turn to our military policy, there also we differ from our antagonists. We throw open our city to the world, and never by alien acts exclude foreigners from any opportunity of learning or observing, although the eyes of an enemy may occasionally profit by our liberality; we trust less in system and policy than in the native spirit of our citizens; and in education, where our rivals from their very cradles by a painful discipline seek after manliness, at Athens we live exactly as we please, and yet are just as ready to encounter every legitimate danger. In proof of this it may be noticed that the Lacedæmonians do not invade our country alone, but bring with them all their confederates, while we Athenians advance unsupported into the territory of a neighbour, and fighting upon a foreign soil usually vanquish with ease men who are defending their homes. Our united force was never yet encountered by any enemy, because we have at once to attend to our marine and to despatch our citizens by land upon a hundred different services; thus wherever they engage with some such fraction of our strength, a success against a detachment is magnified into a victory over the nation, and a defeat into a reverse suffered at the hands of our entire people. And yet if with habits not of labour but of ease, and courage not of art but of nature, we are still willing to encounter danger, we have the double advantage of escaping the experience of hardships in anticipation and of facing them in the hour of need as fearlessly as those who are never free from them.

Nor are these the only points in which our city is worthy of admiration. We cultivate refinement without extravagance and knowledge without effeminacy; wealth we employ more for use than for show, and place the real disgrace of poverty not in owning to the fact but in declining the struggle against it. Our public men have, besides politics, their private affairs to attend to, and our ordinary citizens, though occupied with the pursuits of industry, are still fair judges of public matters; for, unlike any other nation, regarding him who takes no part in these duties not as unambitious but as useless, we Athenians are able to judge at all events if we cannot originate, and instead of looking on discussion as a stumbling-block in the way of action, we think it an indispensable preliminary to any wise action at all. Again, in our enterprises we present the singular spectacle of daring and deliberation, each carried to its highest point, and both united in the same persons, although usually decision is the fruit of ignorance, hesitation of reflection. But the palm of courage will surely be adjudged most justly to those who best know the difference between hardship and pleasure and yet are never tempted to shrink from danger. In generosity we are equally singular, acquiring our friends by conferring, not by receiving, favours. Yet, of course, the doer of the favour is the firmer friend of the two, in order by continued kindness to keep the recipient in his debt, while the debtor feels less keenly from the very consciousness that the return he makes will be a payment, not a free gift. And it is only the Athenians who, fearless of consequences, confer their benefits not from calculations of expediency, but in the confidence of liberality.

In short, I say that as a city we are the school of Hellas; and I doubt if the world can produce a man, who where he has only himself to depend upon, is equal to so many emergencies, and graced by so happy a versatility as the Athenian. And that this is no mere boast thrown out for the occasion, but plain matter of fact, the power of the state acquired by these habits proves. For Athens alone of her contemporaries is found when tested to be greater than her reputation, and alone gives no occasion to her assailants to blush at the antagonist by whom they have been worsted, or to her subjects to question her title by merit to rule. Rather, the admiration of the present and succeeding ages will be ours, since we have not left our power without witness, but have shown it by mighty proofs; and far from needing a Homer for our panegyrist, or other of his craft whose verses might charm for the moment only for the impression which they gave to melt at the touch of fact, we have forced every sea and land to be the highway of our daring, and everywhere, whether for evil or for good, have left imperishable monuments behind us. Such is the Athens for which these men, in the assertion of their resolve not to lose her, nobly fought and died; and well may every one of their survivors be ready to suffer in her cause.

Indeed if I have dwelt at some length upon the character of our country, it has been to show that our stake in the struggle is not the same as theirs who have no such blessings to lose, and also that the panegyric of the men over whom I am now speaking might be by definite proofs established. That panegyric is now in a great measure complete; for the Athens that I have celebrated is only what the heroism of these and their like have made her, men whose fame, unlike that of most Hellenes, will be found to be only commensurate with their deserts. And if a test of worth be wanted, it is to be found in their closing scene, and this not only in the cases in which it set the final seal upon their merit, but also in those in which it gave the first intimation of their having any. For there is justice in the claim that steadfastness in his country's battles should be as a cloak to cover a man's other imperfections; for the good action has blotted out the bad, and his merit as a citizen more than outweighed his demerits as an individual. But none of these allowed either wealth with its prospect of future enjoyment to unnerve his spirit, or poverty with its hope of a day of freedom and riches to tempt him to shrink from danger. No, holding that vengeance upon their enemies was more to be desired than any personal blessings, and reckoning this to be the most glorious of hazards, they joyfully determined to accept the risk, to make sure of their vengeance and to let their wishes wait; and while committing to hope the uncertainty of final success, in the business before them they thought fit to act boldly and trust in themselves. Thus choosing to die resisting, rather than to live submitting, they fled only from dishonour, but met danger face to face, and after one brief moment, while at the summit of their fortune, escaped, not from their fear, but from their glory.

So died these men as became Athenians. You, their survivors, must determine to have as unaltering a resolution in the field, though you may pray that it may have a happier issue. And not contented with ideas derived only from words of the advantages which were bound up with the defence of your country, though these would furnish a valuable text to a speaker even before an audience so alive to them as the present, you must yourselves realize the power of Athens, and feed your eyes upon her from day to day, till love of her fills your hearts; and then when all her greatness shall break upon you, you must reflect that it was by courage, sense of duty, and a keen feeling of honour in action that men were enabled to win all this, and that no personal failure in an enterprise could make them consent to deprive their country of their valour, but they laid it at her feet as the most glorious contribution that they could offer. For this offering of their lives made in common by them all that each of them individually received that renown which never grows old, and for a sepulchre, not so much that in which their bones have been deposited, but that noblest of shrines wherein their glory is laid up to be eternally remembered upon every occasion on which deed or story shall call for its commemoration. For heroes have the whole earth for their tomb; and in lands far from their own, where the column with its epitaph declares it, there is enshrined in every breast a record unwritten with no tablet to preserve it, except that of the heart. These take as your model, and judging happiness to be the fruit of freedom and freedom of valour, never decline the dangers of war. For it is not the miserable that would most justly be unsparing of their lives; these have nothing to hope for: it is rather they to whom continued life may bring reverses as yet unknown, and to whom a fall, if it came, would be most tremendous in its consequences. And surely, to a man of spirit, the degradation of cowardice must be immeasurably more grievous than the unfelt death which strikes him in the midst of his strength and patriotism!

Comfort, therefore, not condolence, is what I have to offer to the parents of the dead who may be here. Numberless are the chances to which, as they know, the life of man is subject; but fortunate indeed are they who draw for their lot a death so glorious as that which has caused your mourning, and to whom life has been so exactly measured as to terminate in the happiness in which it has been passed. Still I know that this is a hard saying, especially when those are in question of whom you will constantly be reminded by seeing in the homes of others blessings of which once you also boasted: for grief is felt not so much for the want of what we have never known, as for the loss of that to which we have been long accustomed. Yet you who are still of an age to beget children must bear up in the hope of having others in their stead; not only will they help you to forget those whom you have lost, but will be to the state at once a reinforcement and a security; for never can a fair or just policy be expected of the citizen who does not, like his fellows, bring to the decision the interests and apprehensions of a father. And those of you who have passed your prime must congratulate yourselves with the thought that the best part of your life was fortunate, and that the brief span that remains will be cheered by the fame of the departed. For it is only the love of honour that never grows old; and honour it is, not gain, as some would have it, that rejoices the heart of age and helplessness.

Turning to the sons or brothers of the dead, I see an arduous struggle before you. When a man is gone, all are wont to praise him, and should your merit be ever so transcendent, you will still find it difficult not merely to overtake, but even to approach their renown. The living have envy to contend with, while those who are no longer in our path are honoured with a goodwill into which rivalry does not enter. On the other hand, if I must say anything on the subject of female excellence to those of you who will now be in widowhood, it will be all comprised in this brief exhortation. Great will be your glory in not falling short of your natural character; and greatest will be hers who is least talked of among the men whether for good or for bad.

My task is now finished. I have performed it to the best of my ability, and in words, at least, the requirements of the law are now satisfied. If deeds be in question, those who are here interred have received part of their honours already, and for the rest, their children will be brought up till manhood at the public expense: the state thus offers a valuable prize as the garland of victory in this race of valour, for the reward both of those who have fallen and their survivors. And where the rewards for merit are greatest, there are found the best citizens.

And now that you have brought to a close your lamentations for your relatives, you may depart.

2

Plato
Selections

Plato (427?–347 B.C.) was born into a prominent aristocratic family, notable for its antidemocratic politics in Athens. The victory of democracy left Plato and his family without power, and Plato with a predictably poor opinion of the "demagogues," leaders of the democracy. Plato participated in the war against the Spartans, who occupied Athens during the period 404–403, probably in the cavalry. He was a student of Socrates (c. 470–399 B.C.), one of the most influential and controversial figures in Greek thought. Plato's dialogues nearly always have Socrates as a character, and he is made the spokesman of the theory of forms which Aristotle disputes as a Platonic, not a Socratic, theory. In his discussion of justice in The Republic, *Plato first puts forward a theory of ethics. After disposing of the cynical understanding of justice presented by Thrasymachus, a Sophist, the balance of* The Republic *describes justice as an integration of elements of the soul, and as a coordination of three classes of citizens. Members of the Socratic circle, including Plato, took refuge in Megara after Socrates' trial and execution in 399. Plato later traveled extensively, visiting Egypt and making the first of three visits to Syracuse, Sicily. There are thirteen letters attributed to Plato, more than half rejected by modern scholars as forgeries. One letter claims to document Plato's experiment with politics, his relations with the tyrant of Syracuse, Dionysius the Younger, and his opponent, Dion. In his school, the Academy, Plato taught young men the curriculum described in Book VII of* The Republic. *As in many private residences, lecture halls, or gymnasia of the day, these were spaces where listeners and disputants spoke of the nature of truth, of beauty, and of political life.*

THE APOLOGY (SOCRATES' DEFENSE)

I DO NOT know what effect my accusers have had upon you, gentlemen, but for my own part I was almost carried away by them—their arguments were so convincing. On the other hand, scarcely a word of what they said was true. I was especially astonished at one of their many misrepresentations; I mean when they told you that you must be careful not to let me deceive you—the implication being that I am a skillful speaker. I thought that it was peculiarly brazen of them to tell you this without a blush, since they must know that they will soon be effectively confuted, when it becomes obvious that I have not the slightest skill as a speaker—unless, of course, by a skillful speaker they mean one who speaks the truth. If that is what they mean, I would agree that I am an orator, though not after their pattern.

My accusers, then, as I maintain, have said little or nothing that is true, but from me you shall hear the whole truth—not, I can assure you, gentlemen, in flowery language like theirs, decked out with fine words and phrases. No, what you will hear will be a straightforward speech in the first words that occur to me, confident as I am in the justice of my cause, and I do not want any of you to expect anything different. It would hardly be suitable, gentlemen, for a man of my age to address you in the artificial language of a schoolboy orator. One thing, however, I do most earnestly beg and entreat of you. If you hear me defending myself in the same language which it has been my habit to use, both in the open spaces of this city—where many of you have heard me—and elsewhere, do not be surprised, and do not interrupt. Let me remind you of my position. This is my first appearance in a court of law, at the age of seventy, and so I am a complete stranger to the language of this place. Now if I were really from another country, you would naturally excuse me if I spoke in the manner and dialect in which I had been brought up, and so in the present case I make this request of you, which I think is only reasonable, to disregard the manner of my speech—it may be better or it may be worse—and to consider and concentrate your attention upon this one question, whether my claims are fair or not. That is the first duty of the juryman, just as it is the pleader's duty to speak the truth.

The proper course for me, gentlemen of the jury, is to deal first with the earliest charges that have been falsely brought against me, and with my earliest accusers, and then with the later ones. I make this distinction because I have already been accused in your hearing by a great many people for a great many years, though without a word of truth, and I am more afraid of those people than I am of Anytus and his colleagues, although they are formidable enough. But the others are still more formidable. I mean the people who took hold of so many of you when you were children and tried to fill your minds with untrue accusations against me, saying, There is a wise man called Socrates who has theories about the heavens and has investigated everything below the earth, and can make the weaker argument defeat the stronger.

It is these people, gentlemen, the disseminators of these rumors, who are my dangerous accusers, because those who hear them suppose that anyone who inquires into such matters must be an atheist. Besides, there are a great many of these accusers, and they have been accusing me now for a great many years. And what is more, they approached you at the most impressionable age, when some of you were children or adolescents, and they literally won their case by default, because there was no one to defend me. And the most fantastic thing of all is that it is impossible for me even to know and tell you their names, unless one of them happens to be a playwright. All these people, who have tried to set you against me out of envy and love of slander—and some too merely passing on what they have been told by others—all these are very difficult to deal with. It is impossible to bring them here for cross-examination; one simply has to conduct one's defense and argue one's case against an invisible opponent, because there is no one to answer. So I ask you to accept my statement that my critics fall into two classes, on the one hand my immediate accusers, and on the other those earlier ones whom I have mentioned, and you must suppose that I have first to defend myself against the latter. After all, you heard them abusing me longer ago and much more violently than these more recent accusers.

Very well, then, I must begin my defense, gentlemen, and I must try, in the short time that I have, to rid your minds of a false impression which is the work of many years. I should like this to be the result, gentlemen, assuming it to be for your advantage and my own; and I should like to be successful in my defense, but I think that it will be difficult, and I am quite aware of the nature of my task. However, let that turn out as God wills. I must obey the law and make my defense.

Let us go back to the beginning and consider what the charge is that has made me so unpopular, and has encouraged Meletus to draw up this indictment. Very well, what did my critics say in attacking my character? I must read out their affidavit, so to speak, as though they were my legal accusers: Socrates is guilty of criminal meddling, in that he inquires into things below the earth and in the sky, and makes the weaker argument defeat the stronger, and teaches others to follow his example. It runs something like that. You have seen it for yourselves in the play by Aristophanes, where Socrates goes whirling round, proclaiming that he is walking on air, and uttering a great deal of other nonsense about things of which I know nothing whatsoever. I mean no disrespect for such knowledge, if anyone really is versed in it—I do not want any more lawsuits brought against me by Meletus—but the fact is, gentlemen, that I take no interest in it. What is more, I call upon the greater part of you as witnesses to my statement, and I appeal to all of you who have ever listened to me talking—and there are a great many to whom this applies—to clear your neighbors' minds on this point. Tell one another whether any one of you has ever heard me discuss such questions briefly or at length, and then you will realize that the other popular reports about me are equally unreliable.

The fact is that there is nothing in any of these charges, and if you have heard anyone say that I try to educate people and charge a fee, there is no truth in that either. I wish that there were, because I think that it is a fine thing if a man is qualified to teach, as in the case of Gorgias of Leontini and Prodicus of Ceos and Hippias of Elis. Each one of these is perfectly capable of going into any city and actually persuading the young men to leave the company of their fellow citizens, with any of whom they can associate for nothing, and attach themselves to him, and pay money for the privilege, and be grateful into the bargain.

There is another expert too from Paros who I discovered was here on a visit; I happened to meet a man who has paid more in Sophists' fees than all the rest put together—I mean Callias, the son of Hipponicus. So I asked him—he has two sons, you see—Callias, I said, if your sons had been colts or calves, we should have had no difficulty in finding and engaging a trainer to perfect their natural qualities, and this trainer would have been some sort of horse dealer or agriculturalist. But seeing that they are human beings, whom do you intend to get as their instructor? Who is the expert in perfecting the human and social qualities? I assume from the fact of your having sons that you must have considered the question. Is there such a person or not?

Certainly, said he.

Who is he, and where does he come from? said I. And what does he charge?

Evenus of Paros, Socrates, said he, and his fee is five minas.

I felt that Evenus was to be congratulated if he really was a master of this art and taught it at such a moderate fee. I should certainly plume myself and give myself airs if I understood these things, but in fact, gentlemen, I do not.

Here perhaps one of you might interrupt me and say, But what is it that you do, Socrates? How is it that you have been misrepresented like this? Surely all this talk and gossip about you would never have arisen if you had confined yourself to ordinary activities, but only if your behavior was abnormal. Tell us the explanation, if you do not want us to invent it for ourselves.

This seems to me to be a reasonable request, and I will try to explain to you what it is that has given me this false notoriety. So please give me your attention. Perhaps some of you will think that I am not being serious, but I assure you that I am going to tell you the whole truth.

I have gained this reputation, gentlemen, from nothing more or less than a kind of wisdom. What kind of wisdom do I mean? Human wisdom, I suppose. It seems that I really am wise in this limited sense. Presumably the geniuses whom I mentioned just now are wise in a wisdom that is more than human. I do not know how else to account for it. I certainly have no knowledge of such wisdom, and anyone who says that I have is a liar and willful slanderer. Now, gentlemen, please do not interrupt me if I seem to make an extravagant claim, for what I am going to tell you is not my own opinion. I am going to refer you to an unimpeachable authority. I shall call as witness to my wisdom, such as it is, the god at Delphi.

You know Chaerephon, of course. He was a friend of mine from boyhood, and a good democrat who played his part with the rest of you in the recent expulsion and restoration. And you know what he was like, how enthusiastic he was over anything that he had once undertaken. Well, one day he actually went to Delphi and asked this question of the god—as I said before, gentlemen, please do not interrupt—he asked whether there was anyone wiser than myself. The priestess replied that there was no one. As Chaerephon is dead, the evidence for my statement will be supplied by his brother, who is here in court.

Please consider my object in telling you this. I want to explain to you how the attack upon my reputation first started. When I heard about the oracle's answer, I said to myself, What does the god mean? Why does he not use plain language? I am only too conscious that I have no claim to wisdom, great or small. So what can he mean by asserting that I am the wisest man in the world? He cannot be telling a lie; that would not be right of him.

After puzzling about it for some time, I set myself at last with considerable reluctance to check the truth of it in the following way. I went to interview a man with a high reputation for wisdom, because I felt that here if anywhere I should succeed in disproving the oracle and pointing out to my divine authority, You said that I was the wisest of men, but here is a man who is wiser than I am.

Well, I gave a thorough examination to this person—I need not mention his name, but he was one of our politicians that I was studying when I had this experience—and in conversation with him I formed the impression that although in many people's opinion, and especially in his own, he appeared to be wise, in fact he was not. Then when I began to try to show him that he only thought he was wise and was not really so, my efforts were resented both by him and by many of the other people present. However, I reflected as I walked away, Well, I am certainly wiser than this man. It is only too likely that neither of us has any knowledge to boast of, but he thinks that he knows something which he does not know, whereas I am quite conscious of my ignorance. At any rate it seems that I am wiser than he is to this small extent, that I do not think that I know what I do not know.

After this I went on to interview a man with an even greater reputation for wisdom, and I formed the same impression again, and here too I incurred the resentment of the man himself and a number of others.

From that time on I interviewed one person after another. I realized with distress and alarm that I was making myself unpopular, but I felt compelled to put my religious duty first. Since I was trying to find out the meaning of the oracle, I was bound to interview everyone who had a reputation for knowledge. And by dog, gentlemen, for I must be frank with you, my honest impression was this. It seemed to me, as I pursued my investigation at the god's command, that the people with the greatest reputations were almost entirely deficient, while others who were supposed to be their inferiors were much better qualified in practical intelligence.

I want you to think of my adventures as a sort of pilgrimage undertaken to establish the truth of the oracle once and for all. After I had finished with the politicians I turned to the poets, dramatic, lyric, and all the rest, in the belief that here I should expose myself as a comparative ignoramus. I used to pick up what I thought were some of their most perfect works and question them closely about the meaning of what they had written, in the hope of incidentally enlarging my own knowledge. Well, gentlemen, I hesitate to tell you the truth, but it must be told. It is hardly an exaggeration to say that any of the bystanders could have explained those poems better than their actual authors. So I soon made up my mind about the poets too. I decided that it was not wisdom that enabled them to write their poetry, but a kind of instinct or inspiration, such as you find in seers and prophets who deliver all their sublime messages without knowing in the least what they mean. It seemed clear to me that the poets were in much the same case, and I also observed that the very fact that they were poets made them think that they had a perfect understanding of all other subjects, of which they were totally ignorant. So I left that line of inquiry too with the same sense of advantage that I had felt in the case of the politicians.

Last of all I turned to the skilled craftsmen. I knew quite well that I had practically no technical qualifications myself, and I was sure that I should find them full of impressive knowledge. In this I was not disappointed. They understood things which I did not, and to that extent they were wiser than I was. But, gentlemen, these professional experts seemed to share the same failing which I had noticed in the poets. I mean that on the strength of their technical proficiency they claimed a perfect understanding of every other subject, however important, and I felt that this error more than outweighed their positive wisdom. So I made myself spokesman for the oracle, and asked myself whether I would rather be as I was—neither wise with their wisdom nor stupid with their stupidity—or possess both qualities as they did. I replied through myself to the oracle that it was best for me to be as I was.

The effect of these investigations of mine, gentlemen, has been to arouse against me a great deal of hostility, and hostility of a particularly bitter and persistent kind, which has resulted in various malicious suggestions, including the description of me as a professor of wisdom. This is due to the fact that whenever I succeed in disproving another person's claim to wisdom in a given subject, the bystanders assume that I know everything about that subject myself. But the truth of the matter, gentlemen, is pretty certainly this, that real wisdom is the property of God, and this oracle is his way of telling us that human wisdom has little or no value. It seems to me that he is not referring literally to Socrates, but has merely taken my name as an example, as if he would say to us, The wisest of you men is he who has realized, like Socrates, that in respect of wisdom he is really worthless.

That is why I still go about seeking and searching in obedience to the divine command, if I think that anyone is wise, whether citizen or stranger, and when I think that any person is not wise, I try to help the cause of God by proving that he is not. This occupation has kept me too busy to do much either in politics or in my own affairs. In fact, my service to God has reduced me to extreme poverty.

There is another reason for my being unpopular. A number of young men with wealthy fathers and plenty of leisure have deliberately attached themselves to me because they enjoy hearing other people cross-questioned. These often take me as their model, and go on to try to question other persons. Whereupon, I suppose, they find an unlimited number of people who think that they know something, but really know little or nothing. Consequently their victims become annoyed, not with themselves but with me, and they complain that there is a pestilential busybody called Socrates who fills young people's heads with wrong ideas. If you ask them what he does, and what he teaches that has this effect, they have no answer, not knowing what to say. But as they do not want to admit their confusion, they fall back on the stock charges against any philosopher, that he teaches his pupils about things in the heavens and below the earth, and to disbelieve in gods, and to make the weaker argument defeat the stronger. They would be very loath, I fancy, to admit the truth—which is that they are being convicted of pretending to knowledge when they are entirely ignorant. So, jealous, I suppose, for their own reputation, and also energetic and numerically strong, and provided with a plausible and carefully worked-out case against me, these people have been dinning into your ears for a long time past their violent denunciations of myself.

There you have the causes which led to the attack upon me by Meletus and Anytus and Lycon, Meletus being aggrieved on behalf of the poets, Anytus on behalf of the professional men and politicians, and Lycon on behalf of the orators. So, as I said at the beginning, I should be surprised if I were able, in the short time that I have, to rid your minds of a misconception so deeply implanted.

There, gentlemen, you have the true facts, which I present to you without any concealment or suppression, great or small. I am fairly certain that this plain speaking of mine is the cause of my unpopularity, and this really goes to prove that my statements are true, and that I have described correctly the nature and the grounds of the calumny which has been brought against me. Whether you inquire into them now or later, you will find the facts as I have just described them.

So much for my defense against the charges brought by the first group of my accusers. I shall now try to defend myself against Meletus—high-principled and patriotic as he claims to be—and after that against the rest.

Let us first consider their deposition again, as though it represented a fresh prosecution. It runs something like this: Socrates is guilty of corrupting the minds of the young, and of believing in deities of his own invention instead of the gods recognized by the state. Such is the charge. Let us examine its points one by one.

First it says that I am guilty of corrupting the young. But I say, gentlemen, that Meletus is guilty of treating a serious matter with levity, since he summons people to stand their trial on frivolous grounds, and professes concern and keen anxiety in matters about which he has never had the slightest interest. I will try to prove this to your satisfaction.

Come now, Meletus, tell me this. You regard it as supremely important, do you not, that our young people should be exposed to the best possible influence?

I do.

Very well, then, tell these gentlemen who it is that influences the young for the better. Obviously you must know, if you are so much interested. You have discovered the vicious influence, as you say, in myself, and you are now prosecuting me before these gentlemen. Speak up and inform them who it is that has a good influence upon the young. . . . You see, Meletus, that you are tongue-tied and cannot answer. Do you not feel that this is discreditable, and a sufficient proof in itself of what I said, that you have no interest in the subject? Tell me, my friend, who is it that makes the young good?

The laws.

That is not what I mean, my dear sir. I am asking you to name the *person* whose first business it is to know the laws.

These gentlemen here, Socrates, the members of the jury.

Do you mean, Meletus, that they have the ability to educate the young, and to make them better?

Certainly.

Does this apply to all jurymen, or only to some?

To all of them.

Excellent! A generous supply of benefactors. Well, then, do these spectators who are present in court have an improving influence, or not?

Yes, they do.

And what about the members of the Council?

Yes, the councilors too.

But surely, Meletus, the members of the Assembly do not corrupt the young? Or do all of them too exert an improving influence?

Yes, they do.

Then it would seem that the whole population of Athens has a refining effect upon the young, except myself, and I alone demoralize them. Is that your meaning?

Most emphatically, yes.

This is certainly a most unfortunate quality that you have detected in me. Well, let me put another question to you. Take the case of horses. Do you believe that those who improve them make up the whole of mankind, and that there is only one person who has a bad effect on them? Or is the truth just the opposite, that the ability to improve them belongs to one person or to very few persons, who are horse trainers, whereas most people, if they have to do with horses and make use of them, do them harm? Is not this the case, Meletus, both with horses and with all other animals? Of course it is, whether you and Anytus deny it or not. It would be a singular dispensation of fortune for our young people if there is only one person who corrupts them, while all the rest have a beneficial effect. But I need say no more. There is ample proof, Meletus, that you have never bothered your head about the young, and you make it perfectly clear that you have never taken the slightest interest in the cause for the sake of which you are now indicting me.

Here is another point. Tell me seriously, Meletus, is it better to live in a good or in a bad community? Answer my question, like a good fellow; there is nothing difficult about it. Is it not true that wicked people have a bad effect upon those with whom they are in the closest contact, and that good people have a good effect?

Quite true.

Is there anyone who prefers to be harmed rather than benefited by his associates? Answer me, my good man; the law commands you to answer. Is there anyone who prefers to be harmed?

Of course not.

Well, then, when you summon me before this court for corrupting the young and making their characters worse, do you mean that I do so intentionally or unintentionally?

I mean intentionally.

Why, Meletus, are you at your age so much wiser than I at mine? You have discovered that bad people always have a bad effect, and good people a good effect, upon their nearest neighbors. Am I so hopelessly ignorant as not even to realize that by spoiling the character of one of my companions I shall run the risk of getting some harm from him? Because nothing else would make me commit this grave offense intentionally. No, I do not believe it, Meletus, and I do not suppose that anyone else does. Either I have not a bad influence, or it is unintentional, so that in either case your accusation is false. And if I unintentionally have a bad influence, the correct procedure in cases of such involuntary misdemeanors is not to summon the culprit before this court, but to take him aside privately for instruction and reproof, because obviously if my eyes are opened, I shall stop doing what I do not intend to do. But you deliberately avoided my company in the past and refused to enlighten me, and now you bring me before this court, which is the place appointed for those who need punishment, not for those who need enlightenment.

It is quite clear by now, gentlemen, that Meletus, as I said before, has never shown any degree of interest in this subject. However, I invite you to tell us, Meletus, in what sense you make out that I corrupt the minds of the young. Surely the terms of your indictment make it clear that you accuse me of teaching them to believe in new deities instead of the gods recognized by the state. Is not that the teaching of mine which you say has this demoralizing effect?

That is precisely what I maintain.

Then I appeal to you, Meletus, in the name of these same gods about whom we are speaking, to explain yourself a little more clearly to myself and to the jury, because I cannot make out what your point is. Is it that I teach people to believe in some gods—which implies that I myself believe in gods, and am not a complete atheist, so that I am not guilty on that score—but in different gods from those recognized by the state, so that your accusation rests upon the fact that they are different? Or do you assert that I believe in no gods at all, and teach others to do the same?

Yes, I say that you disbelieve in gods altogether.

You surprise me, Meletus. What is your object in saying that? Do you suggest that I do not believe that the sun and moon are gods, as is the general belief of all mankind?

He certainly does not, gentlemen of the jury, since he says that the sun is a stone and the moon a mass of earth.

Do you imagine that you are prosecuting Anaxagoras, my dear Meletus? Have you so poor an opinion of these gentlemen, and do you assume them to be so illiterate as not to know that the writings of Anaxagoras of Clazomenae are full of theories like these? And do you seriously suggest that it is from me that the young get these ideas, when they can buy them on occasion in the market place for a drachma at most, and so have the laugh on Socrates if he claims them for his own, to say nothing of their being so silly? Tell me honestly, Meletus, is that your opinion of me? Do I believe in no god?

No, none at all, not in the slightest degree.

You are not at all convincing, Meletus—not even to yourself, I suspect. In my opinion, gentlemen, this man is a thoroughly selfish bully, and has brought this action against me out of sheer wanton aggressiveness and self-assertion. He seems to be devising a sort of intelligence test for me, saying to himself, Will the infallible Socrates realize that I am contradicting myself for my own amusement, or shall I succeed in deceiving him and the rest of my audience?

It certainly seems to me that he is contradicting himself in this indictment, which might just as well run: Socrates is guilty of not believing in the gods, but believing in the gods. And this is pure flippancy.

I ask you to examine with me, gentlemen, the line of reasoning which leads me to this conclusion. You, Meletus, will oblige us by answering my questions. Will you all kindly remember, as I requested at the beginning, not to interrupt if I conduct the discussion in my customary way?

Is there anyone in the world, Meletus, who believes in human activities, and not in human beings? Make him answer, gentlemen, and don't let him keep on making these continual objections. Is there anyone who does not believe in horses, but believes in horses' activities? Or who does not believe in musicians, but believes in musical activities? No, there is not, my worthy friend. If you do not want to answer, I will supply it for you and for these gentlemen too. But the next question you must answer. Is there anyone who believes in supernatural activities and not in supernatural beings?

No.

How good of you to give a bare answer under compulsion by the court! Well, do you assert that I believe and teach others to believe in supernatural activities? It does not matter whether they are new or old. The fact remains that I believe in them according to your statement; indeed you solemnly swore as much in your affidavit. But if I believe in supernatural activities, it follows inevitably that I also believe in supernatural beings. Is not that so? It is. I assume your assent, since you do not answer. Do we not hold that supernatural beings are either gods or the children of gods? Do you agree or not?

Certainly.

Then if I believe in supernatural beings, as you asseret, if these supernatural beings are gods in any sense, we shall reach the conclusion which I mentioned just now when I said that you were testing my intelligence for your own amusement, by stating first that I do not believe in gods, and then again that I do, since I believe in supernatural beings. If on the other hand these supernatural beings are bastard children of the gods by nymphs or other mothers, as they are reputed to be, who in the world would believe in the children of gods and not in the gods themselves? It would be as ridiculous as to believe in the young of horses or donkeys and not in horses and donkeys themselves. No, Meletus, there is no avoiding the conclusion that you brought this charge against me as a test of my wisdom, or else in despair of finding a genuine offense of which to accuse me. As for your prospect of convincing any living person with even a smattering of intelligence that belief in supernatural and divine activities does not imply belief in supernatural and divine beings, and vice versa, it is outside all the bounds of possibility.

As a matter of fact, gentlemen, I do not feel that it requires much defense to clear myself of Meletus' accusation. What I have said already is enough. But you know very well the truth of what I said in an earlier part of my speech, that I have incurred a great deal of bitter hostility, and this is what will bring about my destruction, if anything does—not Meletus nor Anytus, but the slander and jealousy of a very large section of the people. They have been fatal to a great many other innocent men, and I suppose will continue to be so; there is no likelihood that they will stop at me. But perhaps someone will say, Do you feel no compunction, Socrates, at having followed a line of action which puts you in danger of the death penalty?

I might fairly reply to him, You are mistaken, my friend, if you think that a man who is worth anything ought to spend his time weighing up the prospects of life and death. He has only one thing to consider in performing any action—that is, whether he is acting rightly or wrongly, like a good man or a bad one. On your view the heroes who died at Troy would be poor creatures, especially the son of Thetis. He, if you remember, made light of danger in comparison with incurring dishonor when his goddess mother warned him, eager as he was to kill Hector, in some such words as these, I fancy: My son, if you avenge your comrade Patroclus' death and kill Hector, you will die yourself—'Next after Hector is thy fate prepared.' When he heard this warning, he made light of his death and danger, being much more afraid of an ignoble life and of failing to avenge his friends. 'Let me die forthwith,' said he, 'when I have requited the villain, rather than remain here by the beaked ships to be mocked, a burden on the ground.' Do you suppose that he gave a thought to death and danger?

The truth of the matter is this, gentlemen. Where a man has once taken up his stand, either because it seems best to him or in obedience to his orders, there I believe he is bound to remain and face the danger, taking no account of death or anything else before dishonor.

This being so, it would be shocking inconsistency on my part, gentlemen, if, when the officers whom you chose to command me assigned me my position at Potidaea and Amphipolis and Delium, I remained at my post like anyone else and faced death, and yet afterward, when God appointed me, as I supposed and believed, to the duty of leading the philosophical life, examining myself and others, I were then through fear of death or of any other danger to desert my post. That would indeed be shocking, and then I might really with justice be summoned into court for not believing in the gods, and disobeying the oracle, and being afraid of death, and thinking that I am wise when I am not. For let me tell you, gentlemen, that to be afraid of death is only another form of thinking that one is wise when one is not; it is to think that one knows what one does not know. No one knows with regard to death whether it is not really the greatest blessing that can happen to a man, but people dread it as though they were certain that it is the greatest evil, and this ignorance, which thinks that it knows what it does not, must surely be ignorance most culpable. This, I take it, gentlemen, is the degree, and this the nature of my advantage over the rest of mankind, and if I were to claim to be wiser than my neighbor in any respect, it would be in this—that not possessing any real knowledge of what comes after death, I am also conscious that I do not possess it. But I do know that to do wrong and to disobey my superior, whether God or man, is wicked and dishonorable, and so I shall never feel more fear or aversion for something which, for all I know, may really be a blessing, than for those evils which I know to be evils.

Suppose, then, that you acquit me, and pay no attention to Anytus, who has said that either I should not have appeared before this court at all, or, since I have appeared here, I must be put to death, because if I once escaped your sons would all immediately become utterly demoralized by putting the teaching of Socrates into practice. Suppose that, in view of this, you said to me, Socrates, on this occasion we shall disregard Anytus and acquit you, but only on one condition, that you give up spending your time on this quest and stop philosophizing. If we catch you going on in the same way, you shall be put to death.

Well, supposing, as I said, that you should offer to acquit me on these terms, I should reply, Gentlemen, I am your very grateful and devoted servant, but I owe a greater obedience to God than to you, and so long as I draw breath and have my faculties, I shall never stop practicing philosophy and exhorting you and elucidating the truth for everyone that I meet. I shall go on saying, in my usual way, My very good friend, you are an Athenian and belong to a city which is the greatest and most famous in the world for its wisdom and strength. Are you not ashamed that you give your attention to acquiring as much money as possible, and similarly with reputation and honor, and give no attention or thought to truth and understanding and the perfection of your soul?

And if any of you disputes this and professes to care about these things, I shall not at once let him go or leave him. No, I shall question him and examine him and test him; and if it appears that in spite of his profession he has made no real progress toward goodness, I shall reprove him for neglecting what is of supreme importance, and giving his attention to trivialities. I shall do this to everyone that I meet, young or old, foreigner or fellow citizen, but especially to you, my fellow citizens, inasmuch as you are closer to me in kinship. This, I do assure you, is what my God commands, and it is my belief that no greater good has ever befallen you in this city than my service to my God. For I spend all my time going about trying to persuade you, young and old, to make your first and chief concern not for your bodies nor for your possessions, but for the highest welfare of your souls, proclaiming as I go, Wealth does not bring goodness, but goodness brings wealth and every other blessing, both to the individual and to the state.

Now if I corrupt the young by this message, the message would seem to be harmful, but if anyone says that my message is different from this, he is talking nonsense. And so, gentlemen, I would say, You can please yourselves whether you listen to Anytus or not, and whether you acquit me or not. You know that I am not going to alter my conduct, not even if I have to die a hundred deaths.

Order, please, gentlemen! Remember my request to give me a hearing without interruption. Besides, I believe that it will be to your advantage to listen. I am going to tell you something else, which may provoke a storm of protest, but please restrain yourselves. I assure you that if I am what I claim to be, and you put me to death, you will harm yourselves more than me. Neither Meletus nor Anytus can do me any harm at all; they would not have the power, because I do not believe that the law of God permits a better man to be harmed by a worse. No doubt my accuser might put me to death or have me banished or deprived of civic rights, but even if he thinks—as he probably does, and others too, I dare say— that these are great calamities, I do not think so. I believe that it is far worse to do what he is doing now, trying to put an innocent man to death. For this reason, gentlemen, so far from pleading on my own behalf, as might be supposed, I am really pleading on yours, to save you from misusing the gift of God by condemning me. If you put me to death, you will not easily find anyone to take my place. It is literally true, even if it sounds rather comical, that God has specially appointed me to this city, as though it were a large thoroughbred horse which because of its great size is inclined to be lazy and needs the stimulation of some stinging fly. It seems to me that God has attached me to this city to perform the office of such a fly, and all day long I never cease to settle here, there, and everywhere, rousing, persuading, reproving every one of you. You will not easily find another like me, gentlemen, and if you take my advice you will spare my life. I suspect, however, that before long you will awake from your drowsing, and in your annoyance you will take Anytus' advice and finish me off with a single slap, and then you will go on sleeping till the end of your days, unless God in his care for you sends someone to take my place.

If you doubt whether I am really the sort of person who would have been sent to this city as a gift from God, you can convince yourselves by looking at it in this way. Does it seem natural that I should have neglected my own affairs and endured the humiliation of allowing my family to be neglected for all these years, while I busied myself all the time on your behalf, going like a father or an elder brother to see each one of you privately, and urging you to set your thoughts on goodness? If I had got any enjoyment from it, or if I had been paid for my good advice, there would have been some explanation for my conduct, but as it is you can see for yourselves that although my accusers unblushingly charge me with all sorts of other crimes, there is one thing that they have not had the impudence to pretend on any testimony, and that is that I have ever exacted or asked a fee from anyone. The witness that I can offer to prove the truth of my statement is, I think, a convincing one—my poverty.

It may seem curious that I should go round giving advice like this and busying myself in people's private affairs, and yet never venture publicly to address you as a whole and advise on matters of state. The reason for this is what you have often heard me say before on many other occasions—that I am subject to a divine or supernatural experience, which Meletus saw fit to travesty in his indictment. It began in my early childhood—a sort of voice which comes to me, and when it comes it always dissuades me from what I am proposing to do, and never urges me on. It is this that debars me from entering public life, and a very good thing too, in my opinion, because you may be quite sure, gentlemen, that if I had tried long ago to engage in politics, I should long ago have lost my life, without doing any good either to you or to myself. Please do not be offended if I tell you the truth. No man on earth who conscientiously opposes either you or any other organized democracy, and flatly prevents a great many wrongs and illegalities from taking place in the state to which he belongs, can possibly escape with his life. The true champion of justice, if he intends to survive even for a short time, must necessarily confine himself to private life and leave politics alone.

I will offer you substantial proofs of what I have said—not theories, but what you can appreciate better, facts. Listen while I describe my actual experiences, so that you may know that I would never submit wrongly to any authority through fear of death, but would refuse even at the cost of my life. It will be a commonplace story, such as you often hear in the courts, but it is true.

The only office which I have ever held in our city, gentlemen, was when I was elected to the Council. It so happened that our group was acting as the executive when you decided that the ten commanders who had failed to rescue the men who were lost in the naval engagement should be tried en bloc, which was illegal, as you all recognized later. On this occasion I was the only member of the executive who insisted that you should not act unconstitutionally, and voted against the proposal; and although your leaders were all ready to denounce and arrest me, and you were all urging them on at the top of your voices, I thought that it was my duty to face it out on the side of law and justice rather than support you, through fear of prison or death, in your wrong decision.

This happened while we were still under a democracy. When the oligarchy came into power, the Thirty Commissioners in their turn summoned me and four others to the Round Chamber and instructed us to go and fetch Leon of Salamis from his home for execution. This was of course only one of many instances in which they issued such instructions, their object being to implicate as many people as possible in their wickedness. On this occasion, however, I again made it clear not by my words but by my actions that death did not matter to me at all—if that is not too strong an expression—but that it mattered all the world to me that I should do nothing wrong or wicked. Powerful as it was, that government did not terrify me into doing a wrong action. When we came out of the Round Chamber, the other four went off to Salamis and arrested Leon, and I went home. I should probably have been put to death for this, if the government had not fallen soon afterward. There are plenty of people who will testify to these statements.

Do you suppose that I should have lived as long as I have if I had moved in the sphere of public life, and conducting myself in that sphere like an honorable man, had always upheld the cause of right, and conscientiously set this end above all other things? Not by a very long way, gentlemen; neither would any other man.

You will find that throughout my life I have been consistent in any public duties that I have performed, and the same also in my personal dealings. I have never countenanced any action that was incompatible with justice on the part of any person, including those whom some people maliciously call my pupils. I have never set up as any man's teacher, but if anyone, young or old, is eager to hear me conversing and carrying out my private mission, I never grudge him the opportunity; nor do I charge a fee for talking to him, and refuse to talk without one. I am ready to answer questions for rich and poor alike, and I am equally ready if anyone prefers to listen to me and answer my questions. If any given one of these people becomes a good citizen or a bad one, I cannot fairly be held responsible, since I have never promised or imparted any teaching to anybody, and if anyone asserts that he has ever learned or heard from me privately anything which was not open to everyone else, you may be quite sure that he is not telling the truth.

But how is it that some people enjoy spending a great deal of time in my company? You have heard the reason, gentlemen; I told you quite frankly. It is because they enjoy hearing me examine those who think that they are wise when they are not—an experience which has its amusing side. This duty I have accepted, as I said, in obedience to God's commands given in oracles and dreams and in every other way that any other divine dispensation has ever impressed a duty upon man. This is a true statement, gentlemen, and easy to verify. If it is a fact that I am in the process of corrupting some of the young, and have succeeded already in corrupting others, and if it were a fact that some of the latter, being now grown up, had discovered that I had ever given them bad advice when they were young, surely they ought now to be coming forward to denounce and punish me. And if they did not like to do it themselves, you would expect some of their families—their fathers and brothers and other near relations—to remember it now, if their own flesh and blood had suffered any harm from me. Certainly a great many of them have found their way into this court, as I can see for myself—first Crito over there, my contemporary and near neighbor, the father of this young man Critobulus, and then Lysanias of Sphettus, the father of Aeschines here, and next Antiphon of Cephisus, over there, the father of Epigenes. Then besides there are all those whose brothers have been members of our circle—Nicostratus, the son of Theozotides, the brother of Theodotus, but Theodotus is dead, so he cannot appeal to his brother, and Paralus here, the son of Demodocus, whose brother was Theages. And here is Adimantus, the son of Ariston, whose brother Plato is over there, and Aeantodorus, whose brother Apollodorus is here on this side. I can name many more besides, some of whom Meletus most certainly ought to have produced as witnesses in the course of his speech. If he forgot to do so then, let him do it now—I am willing to make way for him. Let him state whether he has any such evidence to offer. On the contrary, gentlemen, you will find that they are all prepared to help me—the corrupter and evil genius of their nearest and dearest relatives, as Meletus and Anytus say. The actual victims of my corrupting influence might perhaps be excused for helping me; but as for the uncorrupted, their relations of mature age, what other reason can they have for helping me except the right and proper one, that they know Meletus is lying and I am telling the truth?

There, gentlemen, that, and perhaps a little more to the same effect, is the substance of what I can say in my defense. It may be that some one of you, remembering his own case, will be annoyed that whereas he, in standing his trial upon a less serious charge than this, made pitiful appeals to the jury with floods of tears, and had his infant children produced in court to excite the maximum of sympathy, and many of his relatives and friends as well, I on the contrary intend to do nothing of the sort, and that, although I am facing, as it might appear, the utmost danger. It may be that one of you, reflecting on these facts, will be prejudiced against me, and being irritated by his reflections, will give his vote in anger. If one of you is so disposed—I do not expect it, but there is the possibility—I think that I should be quite justified in saying to him, My dear sir, of course I have some relatives. To quote the very words of Homer, even I am not sprung 'from an oak or from a rock,' but from human parents, and consequently I have relatives—yes, and sons too, gentlemen, three of them, one almost grown up and the other two only children—but all the same I am not going to produce them here and beseech you to acquit me.

Why do I not intend to do anything of this kind? Not out of perversity, gentlemen, nor out of contempt for you; whether I am brave or not in the face of death has nothing to do with it. The point is that for my own credit and yours and for the credit of the state as a whole, I do not think that it is right for me to use any of these methods at my age and with my reputation—which may be true or it may be false, but at any rate the view is held that Socrates is different from the common run of mankind. Now if those of you who are supposed to distinguished for wisdom or courage or any other virtue are to behave in this way, it would be a disgrace. I have often noticed that some people of this type, for all their high standing, go to extraordinary lengths when they come up for trial, which shows that they think it will be a dreadful thing to lose their lives—as though they would be immortal if you did not put them to death! In my opinion these people bring disgrace upon our city. Any of our visitors might be excused for thinking that the finest specimens of Athenian manhood, whom their fellow citizens select on their merits to rule over them and hold other high positions, are no better than women. If you have even the smallest reputation, gentlemen, you ought not to descend to these methods; and if we do so, you must not give us license. On the contrary, you must make it clear that anyone who stages these pathetic scenes and so brings ridicule upon our city is far more likely to be condemned than if he kept perfectly quiet.

But apart from all question of appearances, gentlemen, I do not think that it is right for a man to appeal to the jury or to get himself acquitted by doing so; he ought to inform them of the facts and convince them by argument. The jury does not sit to dispense justice as a favor, but to decide where justice lies, and the oath which they have sworn is not to show favor at their own discretion, but to return a just and lawful verdict. It follows that we must not develop in you, nor you allow to grow in yourselves, the habit of perjury; that would be sinful for us both. Therefore you must not expect me, gentlemen, to behave toward you in a way which I consider neither reputable nor moral nor consistent with my religious duty, and above all you must not expect it when I stand charged with impiety by Meletus here. Surely it is obvious that if I tried to persuade you and prevail upon you by my entreaties to go against your solemn oath, I should be teaching you contempt for religion, and by my very defense I should be accusing myself of having no religious belief. But that is very far from the truth. I have a more sincere belief, gentlemen, than any of my accusers, and I leave it to you and to God to judge me as it shall be best for me and for yourselves.

There are a great many reasons, gentlemen, why I am not distressed by this result—I mean your condemnation of me—but the chief reason is that the result was not unexpected. What does surprise me is the number of votes cast on the two sides. I should never have believed that it would be such a close thing, but now it seems that if a mere thirty votes had gone the other way, I should have been acquitted. Even as it is, I feel that so far as Meletus' part is concerned I have been acquitted, and not only that, but anyone can see that if Anytus and Lycon had not come forward to accuse me, Meletus would actually have forfeited his one thousand drachmas for not having obtained one fifth of the votes.

However, we must face the fact that he demands the death penalty. Very good. What alternative penalty shall I propose to you, gentlemen? Obviously it must be adequate. Well, what penalty do I deserve to pay or suffer, in view of what I have done?

I have never lived an ordinary quiet life. I did not care for the things that most people care about—making money, having a comfortable home, high military or civil rank, and all the other activities, political appointments, secret societies, party organizations, which go on in our city. I thought that I was really too strict in my principles to survive if I went in for this sort of thing. So instead of taking a course which would have done no good either to you or to me, I set myself to do you individually in private what I hold to be the greatest possible service. I tried to persuade each one of you not to think more of practical advantages than of his mental and moral well-being, or in general to think more of advantage than of well-being in the case of the state or of anything else. What do I deserve for behaving in this way? Some reward, gentlemen, if I am bound to suggest what I really deserve, and what is more, a reward which would be appropriate for myself. Well, what is appropriate for a poor man who is a public benefactor and who requires leisure for giving you moral encouragement? Nothing could be more appropriate for such a person than free maintenance at the state's expense. He deserves it much more than any victor in the races at Olympia, whether he wins with a single horse or a pair or a team of four. These people give you the semblance of success, but I give you the reality; they do not need maintenance, but I do. So if I am to suggest an appropriate penalty which is strictly in accordance with justice, I suggest free maintenance by the state.

Perhaps when I say this I may give you the impression, as I did in my remarks about exciting sympathy and making passionate appeals, that I am showing a deliberate perversity. That is not so, gentlemen. The real position is this. I am convinced that I never wrong anyone intentionally, but I cannot convince you of this, because we have had so little time for discussion. If it was your practice, as it is with other nations, to give not one day but several to the hearing of capital trials, I believe that you might have been convinced, but under present conditions it is not easy to dispose of grave allegations in a short space of time. So, being convinced that I do no wrong to anybody, I can hardly be expected to wrong myself by asserting that I deserve something bad, or by proposing a corresponding penalty. Why should I? For fear of suffering this penalty proposed by Meletus, when, as I said, I do not know whether it is a good thing or a bad? Do you expect me to choose something which I know very well is bad by making my counter-proposal? Imprisonment? Why should I spend my days in prison, in subjection to the periodically appointed officers of the law? A fine, with imprisonment until it is paid? In my case the effect would be just the same, because I have no money to pay a fine. Or shall I suggest banishment? You would very likely accept the suggestion.

I should have to be desperately in love with life to do that, gentlemen. I am not so blind that I cannot see that you, my fellow citizens, have come to the end of your patience with my discussions and conversations. You have found them too irksome and irritating, and now you are trying to get rid of them. Will any other people find them easy to put up with? That is most unlikely, gentlemen. A fine life I should have if I left this country at my age and spent the rest of my days trying one city after another and being turned out every time! I know very well that wherever I go the young people will listen to my conversation just as they do here, and if I try to keep them off, they will make their elders drive me out, while if I do not, the fathers and other relatives will drive me out of their own accord for the sake of the young.

Perhaps someone may say, But surely, Socrates, after you have left us you can spend the rest of your life in quietly minding your own business.

This is the hardest thing of all to make some of you understand. If I say that this would be disobedience to God, and that is why I cannot 'mind my own business,' you will not believe that I am serious. If on the other hand I tell you that to let no day pass without discussing goodness and all the other subjects about which you hear me talking and examining both myself and others is really the very best thing that a man can do, and that life without this sort of examination is not worth living, you will be even less inclined to believe me. Nevertheless that is how it is, gentlemen, as I maintain, though it is not easy to convince you of it. Besides, I am not accustomed to think of myself as deserving punishment. If I had money, I would have suggested a fine that I could afford, because that would not have done me any harm. As it is, I cannot, because I have none, unless of course you like to fix the penalty at what I could pay. I suppose I could probably afford a mina. I suggest a fine of that amount.

One moment, gentlemen. Plato here, and Crito and Critobulus and Apollodorus, want me to propose thirty minas, on their security. Very well, I agree to this sum, and you can rely upon these gentlemen for its payment.

Well, gentlemen, for the sake of a very small gain in time you are going to earn the reputation—and the blame from those who wish to disparage our city—of having put Socrates to death, 'that wise man'—because they will say I am wise even if I am not, these people who want to find fault with you. If you had waited just a little while, you would have had your way in the course of nature. You can see that I am well on in life and near to death. I am saying this not to all of you but to those who voted for my execution, and I have something else to say to them as well.

No doubt you think, gentlemen, that I have been condemned for lack of the arguments which I could have used if I had thought it right to leave nothing unsaid or undone to secure my acquittal. But that is very far from the truth. It is not a lack of arguments that has caused my condemnation, but a lack of effrontery and impudence, and the fact that I have refused to address you in the way which would give you most pleasure. You would have liked to hear me weep and wail, doing and saying all sorts of things which I regard as unworthy of myself, but which you are used to hearing from other people. But I did not think then that I ought to stoop to servility because I was in danger, and I do not regret now the way in which I pleaded my case. I would much rather die as the result of this defense than live as the result of the other sort. In a court of law, just as in warfare, neither I nor any other ought to use his wits to escape death by any means. In battle it is often obvious that you could escape being killed by giving up your arms and throwing yourself upon the mercy of your pursuers, and in every kind of danger there are plenty of devices for avoiding death if you are unscrupulous enough to stick at nothing. But I suggest, gentlemen, that the difficulty is not so much to escape death; the real difficulty is to escape from doing wrong, which is far more fleet of foot. In this present instance I, the slow old man, have been overtaken by the slower of the two, but my accusers, who are clever and quick, have been overtaken by the faster—by iniquity. When I leave this court I shall go away condemned by you to death, but they will go away convicted by truth herself of depravity and wickedness. And they accept their sentence even as I accept mine. No doubt it was bound to be so, and I think that the result is fair enough.

Having said so much, I feel moved to prophesy to you who have given your vote against me, for I am now at that point where the gift of prophecy comes most readily to men—at the point of death. I tell you my executioners, that as soon as I am dead, vengeance shall fall upon you with a punishment far more painful than your killing of me. You have brought about my death in the belief that through it you will be delivered from submitting your conduct to criticism, but I say that the result will be just the opposite. You will have more critics, whom up till now I have restrained without your knowing it, and being younger they will be harsher to you and will cause you more annoyance. If you expect to stop denunciation of your wrong way of life by putting people to death, there is something amiss with your reasoning. This way of escape is neither possible nor creditable. The best and easiest way is not to stop the mouths of others, but to make yourselves as good men as you can. This is my last message to you who voted for my condemnation.

As for you who voted for my acquittal, I should very much like to say a few words to reconcile you to the result, while the officials are busy and I am not yet on my way to the place where I must die. I ask you, gentlemen, to spare me these few moments. There is no reason why we should not exchange fancies while the law permits. I look upon you as my friends, and I want you to understand the right way of regarding my present position.

Gentlemen of the jury—for *you* deserve to be so called—I have had a remarkable experience. In the past the prophetic voice to which I have become accustomed has always been my constant companion, opposing me even in quite trivial things if I was going to take the wrong course. Now something has happened to me, as you can see, which might be thought and is commonly considered to be a supreme calamity; yet neither when I left home this morning, nor when I was taking my place here in the court, nor at any point in any part of my speech did the divine sign oppose me. In other discussions it has often checked me in the middle of a sentence, but this time it has never opposed me in any part of this business in anything that I have said or done. What do I suppose to be the explanation? I will tell you. I suspect that this thing that has happened to me is a blessing, and we are quite mistaken in supposing death to be an evil. I have good grounds for thinking this, because my accustomed sign could not have failed to oppose me if what I was doing had not been sure to bring some good result.

We should reflect that there is much reason to hope for a good result on other grounds as well. Death is one of two things. Either it is annihilation, and the dead have no consciousness of anything, or, as we are told, it is really a change—a migration of the soul from this place to another. Now if there is no consciousness but only a dreamless sleep, death must be a marvelous gain. I suppose that if anyone were told to pick out the night on which he slept so soundly as not even to dream, and then to compare it with all the other nights and days of his life, and then were told to say, after due consideration, how many better and happier days and nights than this he had spent in the course of his life—well, I think that the Great King himself, to say nothing of any private person, would find these days and nights easy to count in comparison with the rest. If death is like this, then, I call it gain, because the whole of time, if you look at it in this way, can be regarded as no more than one single night. If on the other hand death is a removal from here to some other place, and if what we are told is true, that all the dead are there, what greater blessing could there be than this, gentlemen? If on arrival in the other world, beyond the reach of our so-called justice, one will find there the true judges who are said to preside in those courts, Minos and Rhadamanthus and Aeacus and Triptolemus and all those other half-divinities who were upright in their earthly life, would that be an unrewarding journey? Put it in this way. How much would one of you give to meet Orpheus and Musaeus, Hesiod and Homer? I am willing to die ten times over if this account is true. It would be a specially interesting experience for me to join them there, to meet Palamedes and Ajax, the son of Telamon, and any other heroes of the old days who met their death through an unfair trial, and to compare my fortunes with theirs—it would be rather amusing, I think. And above all I should like to spend my time there, as here, in examining and searching people's minds, to find out who is really wise among them, and who only thinks that he is. What would one not give, gentlemen, to be able to question the leader of that great host against Troy, or Odysseus, or Sisyphus, or the thousands of other men and women whom one could mention, to talk and mix and argue with whom would be unimaginable happiness? At any rate I presume that they do not put one to death there for such conduct, because apart from the other happiness in which their world surpasses ours, they are now immortal for the rest of time, if what we are told is true.

You too, gentlemen of the jury, must look forward to death with confidence, and fix your minds on this one belief, which is certain—that nothing can harm a good man either in life or after death, and his fortunes are not a matter of indifference to the gods. This present experience of mine has not come about mechanically. I am quite clear that the time had come when it was better for me to die and be released from my distractions. That is why my sign never turned me back. For my own part I bear no grudge at all against those who condemned me and accused me, although it was not with this kind intention that they did so, but because they thought that they were hurting me; and that is culpable of them. However, I ask them to grant me one favor. When my sons grow up, gentlemen, if you think that they are putting money or anything else before goodness, take your revenge by plaguing them as I plagued you; and if they fancy themselves for no reason, you must scold them just as I scolded you, for neglecting the important things and thinking that they are good for something when they are good for nothing. If you do this, I shall have had justice at your hands, both I myself and my children.

Now it is time that we were going, I to die and you to live, but which of us has the happier prospect is unknown to anyone but God.

THE REPUBLIC

I went down yesterday to the Piraeus with Glaucon, the son of Ariston, to pay my devotions to the goddess, and also because I wished to see how they would conduct the festival, since this was its inauguration.

I thought the procession of the citizens very fine, but it was no better than the show made by the marching of the Thracian contingent.

After we had said our prayers and seen the spectacle we were starting for town when Polemarchus, the son of Cephalus, caught sight of us from a distance as we were hastening homeward and ordered his boy run and bid us to wait for him, and the boy caught hold of my himation from behind and said, Polemarchus wants you to wait.

And I turned around and asked where his master was.

There he is, he said, behind you, coming this way. Wait for him.

So we will, said Glaucon. And shortly after Polemarchus came up and Adimantus, the brother of Glaucon, and Niceratus, the son of Nicias, and a few others apparently from the procession.

Whereupon Polemarchus said, Socrates, you appear to have turned your faces townward and to be going to leave us.

Not a bad guess, said I.

But you see how many we are? he said.

Surely.

You must either then prove yourselves the better men or stay here.

Why, is there not left, said I, the alternative of our persuading you that you ought to let us go?

But *could* you persuade us, said he, if we refused to listen?

Nohow, said Glaucon.

Well, we won't listen, and you might as well make up your minds to it.

Do you mean to say, interposed Adimantus, that you haven't heard that there is to be a torchlight race this evening on horseback in honor of the goddess?

On horseback? said I. That is a new idea. Will they carry torches and pass them along to one another as they race with the horses, or how do you mean?

That's the way of it, said Polemarchus, and, besides, there is to be a night festival which will be worth seeing. For after dinner we will get up and go out and see the sights and meet a lot of the lads there and have good talk. So stay and do as we ask.

It looks as if we should have to stay, said Glaucon.

Well, said I, if it so be, so be it.

So we went with them to Polemarchus' house, and there we found Lysias and Euthydemus, the brothers of Polemarchus, yes, and Thrasymachus, too, of Chalcedon, and Charmantides of the deme of Paeania, and Clitophon, the son of Aristonymus. And the father of Polemarchus, Cephalus, was also at home.

And I thought him much aged, for it was a long time since I had seen him. He was sitting on a sort of chair with cushions and he had a chaplet on his head, for he had just finished sacrificing in the court. So we went and sat down beside him, for there were seats there disposed in a circle.

As soon as he saw me Cephalus greeted me and said, You are not a very frequent visitor, Socrates. You don't often come down to the Piraeus to see us. That is not right. For if I were still able to make the journey up to town easily there would be no need of your resorting hither, but we would go to visit you. But as it is you should not space too widely your visits here. For I would have you know that, for my part, as the satisfactions of the body decay, in the same measure my desire for the pleasures of good talk and my delight in them increase. Don't refuse then, but be yourself a companion to these lads and make our house your resort and regard us as your very good friends and intimates.

Why, yes, Cephalus, said I, and I enjoy talking with the very aged. For to my thinking we have to learn of them as it were from wayfarers who have preceded us on a road on which we too, it may be, must sometime fare—what it is like. Is it rough and hard-going or easy and pleasant to travel? And so now I would fain learn of you what you think of this thing, now that your time has come to it, the thing that the poets call 'the threshold of old age.' Is it a hard part of life to bear or what report have you to make of it?

Yes, indeed, Socrates, he said, I will tell you my own feeling about it. For it often happens that some of us elders of about the same age come together and verify the old saw of like to like. At these reunions most of us make lament, longing for the lost joys of youth and recalling to mind the pleasures of wine, women, and feasts, and other things thereto appertaining, and they repine in the belief that the greatest things have been taken from them and that then they lived well and now it is no life at all. And some of them complain of the indignities that friends and kinsmen put upon old age and thereto recite a doleful litany of all the miseries for which they blame old age. But in my opinion, Socrates, they do not put the blame on the real cause. For if it were the cause I too should have had the same experience so far as old age is concerned, and so would all others who have come to this time of life. But in fact I have ere now met with others who do not feel in this way, and in particular I remember hearing Sophocles the poet greeted by a fellow who asked, How about your service of Aphrodite, Sophocles—is your natural force still unabated? And he replied, Hush, man, most gladly have I escaped this thing you talk of, as if I had run away from a raging and savage beast of a master. I thought it a good answer then and now I think so still more. For in very truth there comes to old age a great tranquillity in such matters and a blessed release. When the fierce tensions of the passions and desires relax, then is the word of Sophocles approved, and we are rid of many and mad masters. But indeed, in respect of these complaints and in the matter of our relations with kinsmen and friends there is just one cause, Socrates—not old age, but the character of the man. For if men are temperate and cheerful even old age is only moderately burdensome. But if the reverse, old age, Socrates, and youth are hard for such dispositions.

And I was filled with admiration for the man by these words, and desirous of hearing more I tried to draw him out and said, I fancy, Cephalus, that most people, when they hear you talk in this way, are not convinced but think that you bear old age lightly not because of your character but because of your wealth, for the rich, they say, have many consolations.

You are right, he said. They don't accept my view and there is something in their objection, though not so much as they suppose. But the retort of Themistocles comes in pat here, who, when a man from the little island of Seriphus grew abusive and told him that he owed his fame not to himself but to the city from which he came, replied that neither would he himself ever have made a name if he had been born in Seriphus nor the other if he had been an Athenian. And the same principle applies excellently to those who not being rich take old age hard, for neither would the reasonable man find it altogether easy to endure old age conjoined with poverty, nor would the unreasonable man by the attainment of riches ever attain to self-contentment and a cheerful temper.

May I ask, Cephalus, said I, whether you inherited most of your possessions or acquired them yourself?

Acquired, quotha? he said. As a money-maker, I hold a place somewhere half-way between my grandfather and my father. For my grandfather and namesake inherited about as much property as I now possess and multiplied it many times, my father Lysanias reduced it below the present amount, and I am content if I shall leave the estate to these boys not less but by some slight measure more than my inheritance.

The reason I asked, I said, is that you appear to me not to be overfond of money. And that is generally the case with those who have not earned it themselves. But those who have themselves acquired it have a double reason in comparison with other men for loving it. For just as poets feel complacency about their own poems and fathers about their own sons, so men who have made money take this money seriously as their own creation and they also value it for its uses as other people do. So they are hard to talk to since they are unwilling to commend anything except wealth.

You are right, he replied.

I assuredly am, said I. But tell me further this. What do you regard as the greatest benefit you have enjoyed from the possession of property?

Something, he said, which I might not easily bring many to believe if I told them. For let me tell you, Socrates, he said, that when a man begins to realize that he is going to die, he is filled with apprehensions and concern about matters that before did not occur to him. The tales that are told of the world below and how the men who have done wrong here must pay the penalty there, though he may have laughed them down hitherto, then begin to torture his soul with the doubt that there may be some truth in them. And apart from that the man himself either from the weakness of old age or possibly as being now nearer to the things beyond has a somewhat clearer view of them. Be that as it may, he is filled with doubt, surmises, and alarms and begins to reckon up and consider whether he has ever wronged anyone. Now he to whom the ledger of his life shows an account of many evil deeds starts up even from his dreams like a child again and again in affright and his days are haunted by anticipations of worse to come. But on him who is conscious of no wrong that he has done a sweet hope ever attends and a goodly, to be nurse of his old age, as Pindar too says. For a beautiful saying it is, Socrates, of the poet that when a man lives out his days in justice and piety, 'sweet companion with him, to cheer his heart and nurse his old age, accompanieth hope, who chiefly ruleth the changeful mind of mortals.' That is a fine saying and an admirable one. It is for this, then, that I affirm that the possession of wealth is of most value, not it may be to every man but to the good man. Not to cheat any man even unintentionally or play him false, not remaining in debt to a god for some sacrifice or to a man for money, so to depart in fear to that other world—to this result the possession of property contributes not a little. It has also many other uses. But, setting one thing against another, I would lay it down, Socrates, that for a man of sense this is the chief service of wealth.

An admirable sentiment, Cephalus, said I. But speaking of this very thing, justice, are we to affirm thus without qualification that it is truthtelling and paying back what one has received from anyone, or may these very actions sometimes be just and sometimes unjust? I mean, for example, as everyone I presume would admit, if one took over weapons from a friend who was in his right mind and then the lender should go mad and demand them back, that we ought not to return them in that case and that he who did so return them would not be acting justly—nor yet would he who chose to speak nothing but the truth to one who was in that state.

You are right, he replied.

Then this is not the definition of justice—to tell the truth and return what one has received.

Nay, but it is, Socrates, said Polemarchus breaking in, if indeed we are to put any faith in Simonides.

Very well, said Cephalus, indeed I make over the whole argument to you. For it is time for me to attend the sacrifices.

Well, said I, is not Polemarchus the heir of everything that is yours?

Certainly, said he with a laugh, and at the same time went out to the sacred rites.

Tell me, then, you the inheritor of the argument, what it is that you affirm that Simonides says and rightly says about justice.

That it is just, he replied, to render to each his due. In saying this I think he speaks well.

I must admit, said I, that it is not easy to disbelieve Simonides. For he is a wise and inspired man. But just what he may mean by this you, Polemarchus, doubtless know, but I do not. Obviously he does not mean what we were just speaking of, this return of a deposit to anyone whatsoever even if he asks it back when not in his right mind. And yet what the man deposited is due to him in a sense, is it not?

Yes.

But rendered to him it ought not to be by any manner of means when he demands it not being in his right mind.

True, said he.

It is then something other than this that Simonides must, as it seems, mean by the saying that it is just to render back what is due.

Something else in very deed, he replied, for he believes that friends owe it to friends to do them some good and no evil.

I see, said I. You mean that he does not render what is due or owing who returns a deposit of gold if this return and the acceptance prove harmful and the returner and the recipient are friends. Isn't that what you say Simonides means?

Quite so.

But how about this—should one not render to enemies what is their due?

By all means, he said, what is due and owing to them, and there is due and owing from an enemy to an enemy what also is proper for him, some evil.

It was a riddling definition of justice, then, that Simonides gave after the manner of poets, for while his meaning, it seems, was that justice is rendering to each what befits him, the name that he gave to this was 'the due.'

What else do you suppose? said he.

In heaven's name! said I. Suppose someone had questioned him thus. Tell me, Simonides, the art that renders what that is due and befitting to what is called the art of medicine? What do you take it would have been his answer?

Obviously, he said, the art that renders to bodies drugs, foods, and drinks.

And the art that renders to what things what that is due and befitting is called the culinary art?

Seasoning to meats.

Good. In the same way tell me the art that renders what to whom would be denominated justice.

If we are to follow the previous examples, Socrates, it is that which renders benefits and harms to friends and enemies.

To do good to friends and evil to enemies, then, is justice in his meaning?

I think so.

Who then is the most able when they are ill to benefit friends and harm enemies in respect to disease and health?

The physician.

And who navigators in respect of the perils of the sea?

The pilot.

Well then, the just man, in what action and for what work is he the most competent to benefit friends and harm enemies?

In making war and as an ally, I should say.

Very well. But now if they are not sick, friend Polemarchus, the physician is useless to them.

True.

And so to those who are not at sea the pilot.

Yes.

Shall we also say this, that for those who are not at war the just man is useless?

By no means.

There is a use then even in peace for justice?

Yes, it is useful.

But so is agriculture, isn't it?

Yes.

Namely, for the getting of a harvest?

Yes.

But likewise the cobbler's art?

Yes.

Namely, I presume you would say, for the getting of shoes.

Certainly.

Then tell me, for the service and getting of what would you say that justice is useful in time of peace?

In engagements and dealings, Socrates.

And by dealings do you mean associations, partnerships, or something else?

Associations, of course.

Is it the just man, then, who is a good and useful associate and partner in the placing of draughts or the draughts player?

The player.

And in the placing of bricks and stones is the just man a more useful and better associate than the builder?

By no means.

Then what is the association in which the just man is a better partner than the harpist as a harpist is better than the just man for striking the chords?

For money dealings, I think.

Except, I presume, Polemarchus, for the use of money when there is occasion to buy in common or sell a horse. Then, I take it, the man who knows horses, isn't it so?

Apparently.

And again, if it is a vessel, the shipwright or the pilot.

It would seem so.

What then is the use of money in common for which a just man is the better partner?

When it is to be deposited and kept safe, Socrates.

You mean when it is to be put to no use but is to lie idle?

Quite so.

Then it is when money is useless that justice is useful in relation to it?

It looks that way.

And similarly when a scythe is to be kept safe, then justice is useful both in public and private. But when it is to be used, the vinedresser's art is useful?

Apparently.

And so you will have to say that when a shield and a lyre are to be kept and put to no use, justice is useful, but when they are to be made use of, the military art and music.

Necessarily.

And so in all other cases, in the use of each thing, justice is useless but in its uselessness useful?

It looks that way.

Then, my friend, justice cannot be a thing of much worth if it is useful only for things out of use and useless. But let us consider this point. Is not the man who is most skillful to strike or inflict a blow in a fight, whether as a boxer or elsewhere, also the most wary to guard against a blow?

Assuredly.

Is it not also true that he who best knows how to guard against disease is also most cunning to communicate it and escape detection?

I think so.

But again, the very same man is a good guardian of an army who is good at stealing a march upon the enemy in respect of their designs and proceedings generally.

Certainly.

Of whatsoever, then, anyone is a skillful guardian, of that he is also a skillful thief?

It seems so.

If then the just man is an expert in guarding money he is an expert in stealing it.

The argument certainly points that way.

A kind of thief then the just man it seems has turned out to be, and it is likely that you acquired this idea from Homer. For he regards with complacency Autolycus, the maternal uncle of Odysseus, and says, 'he was gifted beyond all men in thievery and perjury.' So justice, according to you and Homer Simonides, seems to be a kind of stealing, with the qualification that it is for the benefit of friends and the harm of enemies. Isn't that what you meant?

No, by Zeus, he replied. I no longer know what I did mean. Yet this I still believe, that justice benefits friends and harms enemies.

May I ask whether by friends you mean those who seem to a man to be worthy or those who really are so, even if they do not seem, and similarly of enemies?

It is likely, he said, that men will love those whom they suppose to be good and dislike those whom they deem bad.

Do not men make mistakes in this matter so that many seem good to them who are not and the reverse?

They do.

For those, then, who thus err the good are their enemies and the bad their friends?

Certainly.

But all the same it is then just for them to benefit the bad and injure the good?

It would seem so.

But again, the good are just and incapable of injustice.

True.

On your reasoning then it is just to wrong those who do no injustice.

Nay, nay, Socrates, he said, the reasoning can't be right.

Then, said I, it is just to harm the unjust and benefit the just.

That seems a better conclusion than the other.

It will work out, then, for many, Polemarchus, who have misjudged men that it is just to harm their friends, for they have got bad ones, and to benefit their enemies, for they are good. And so we shall find ourselves saying the very opposite of what we affirmed Simonides to mean.

Most certainly, he said, it does work out so. But let us change our ground, for it looks as if we were wrong in the notion we took up about the friend and the enemy.

What notion, Polemarchus?

That the man who seems to us good is the friend.

And to what shall we change it now? said I.

That the man who both seems and is good is the friend, but that he who seems but is not really so seems but is not really the friend. And there will be the same assumption about the enemy.

Then on this view it appears the friend will be the good man and the bad the enemy.

Yes.

So you would have us qualify our former notion of the just man by an addition. We then said it was just to do good to a friend and evil to an enemy, but now we are to add that it is just to benefit the friend if he is good and harm the enemy if he is bad?

By all means, he said, that, I think, would be the right way to put it.

Is it then, said I, the part of a good man to harm anybody whatsoever?

Certainly it is, he replied. A man ought to harm those who are both bad and his enemies.

When horses are harmed does it make them better or worse?

Worse.

In respect of the excellence or virtue of dogs or that of horses?

Of horses.

And do not also dogs when harmed become worse in respect of canine and not of equine virtue?

Necessarily.

And men, my dear fellow, must we not say that when they are harmed it is in respect of the distinctive excellence or virtue of man that they become worse?

Assuredly.

And is not justice the specific virtue of man?

That too must be granted.

Then it must also be admitted, my friend, that men who are harmed become more unjust.

It seems so.

Do musicians then make men unmusical by the art of music?

Impossible.

Well, do horsemen by horsemanship unfit men for dealing with horses?

No.

By justice then do the just make men unjust, or in sum do the good by virtue make men bad?

Nay, it is impossible.

It is not, I take it, the function of heat to chill but of its opposite.

Yes.

Nor of dryness to moisten but of its opposite.

Assuredly.

Nor yet of the good to harm but of its opposite.

So it appears.

But the just man is good?

Certainly.

It is not then the function of the just man, Polemarchus, to harm either friend or anyone else, but of his opposite, the unjust.

I think you are altogether right, Socrates.

If, then, anyone affirms that it is just to render to each his due and he means by this that injury and harm is what is due to his enemies from the just man and benefits to his friends, he was no truly wise man who said it. For what he meant was not true. For it has been made clear to us that in no case is it just to harm anyone.

I concede it, he said.

We will take up arms against him, then, said I, you and I together, if anyone affirms that either Simonides or Bias or Pittacus or any other of the wise and blessed said such a thing.

I, for my part, he said, am ready to join in the battle with you.

Do you know, said I, to whom I think the saying belongs—this statement that it is just to benefit friends and harm enemies?

To whom? he said.

I think it was the saying of Periander or Perdiccas or Xerxes or Ismenias the Theban or some other rich man who had great power in his own conceit.

That is most true, he replied.

Very well, said I, since it has been made clear that this too is not justice and the just, what else is there that we might say justice to be?

Now Thrasymachus, even while we were conversing, had been trying several times to break in and lay hold of the discussion but he was restrained by those who sat by him who wished to hear the argument out. But when we came to a pause after I had said this, he couldn't any longer hold his peace. But gathering himself up like a wild beast he hurled himself upon us as if he would tear us to pieces. And Polemarchus and I were frightened and fluttered apart.

He bawled out into our midst, What balderdash is this that you have been talking, and why do you Simple Simons truckle and give way to one another? But if you really wish, Socrates, to know what the just is, don't merely ask questions or plume yourself upon controverting any answer that anyone gives—since your acumen has perceived that it is easier to ask questions than to answer them—but do you yourself answer and tell what you say the just is. And don't you be telling me that it is that which ought to be, or the beneficial or the profitable or the gainful or the advantageous, but express clearly and precisely whatever you say. For I won't take from you any such drivel as that!

And I, when I heard him, was dismayed, and looking upon him was filled with fear, and I believe that if I had not looked at him before he did at me I should have lost my voice. But as it is, at the very moment when he began to be exasperated by the course of the argument I glanced at him first, so that I became capable of answering him, and said with a slight tremor, Thrasymachus, don't be harsh with us. If I, and my friend, have made mistakes in the consideration of the question, rest assured that it is unwillingly that we err. For you surely must not suppose that while, if our quest were for gold, we would never willingly truckle to one another and make concessions in the search and so spoil our chances of finding it, yet that when we are searching for justice, a thing more precious than much fine gold, we should then be so foolish as to give way to one another and not rather do our serious best to have it discovered. You surely must not suppose that, my friend. But you see it is our lack of ability that is at fault. It is pity then that we should far more reasonably receive from clever fellows like you than severity.

And he, on hearing this, gave a great guffaw and laughed sardonically and said, Ye gods! Here we have the well-known irony of Socrates, and I knew it and predicted that when it came to replying you would refuse and dissemble and do anything rather than answer any question that anyone asked you.

That's because you are wise, Thrasymachus, and so you knew very well that if you asked a man how many are twelve, and in putting the question warned him, Don't you be telling me, fellow, that twelve is twice six or three times four or six times two or four times three, for I won't accept any such drivel as that from you as an answer—it was obvious, I fancy, to you that no one could give an answer to a question framed in that fashion. Suppose he had said to you, Thrasymachus, what do you mean? Am I not to give any of the prohibited answers, not even, do you mean to say, if the thing really is one of these, but must I say something different from the truth, or what do you mean?—What would have been your answer to him?

Humph! said he. How very like the two cases are!

There is nothing to prevent it, said I. Yet even granted that they are not alike, yet if it appears to the person asked the question that they are alike, do you suppose that he will any the less answer what appears to him, whether we forbid him or whether we don't?

Is that, then, said he, what you are going to do? Are you going to give one of the forbidden answers?

I shouldn't be surprised, I said, if on reflection that would be my view.

What then, he said, if I show you another answer about justice differing from all these, a better one—what penalty do you think you deserve?

Why, what else, said I, than that which it befits anyone who is ignorant to suffer? It befits him, I presume, to learn from the one who does know. That then is what I propose that I should suffer.

I like your simplicity, said he. But in addition to 'learning' you must pay a fine of money.

Well, I will when I have got it, I said.

It is there, said Glaucon. If money is all that stands in the way, Thrasymachus, go on with your speech. We will all contribute for Socrates.

Oh yes, of course, said he, so that Socrates may contrive, as he always does, to evade answering himself but may cross-examine the other man and refute his replies.

Why, how, I said, my dear fellow, could anybody answer if in the first place he did not know and did not even profess to know, and secondly, even if he had some notion of the matter, he had been told by a man of weight that he mustn't give any of his suppositions as an answer? Nay, it is more reasonable that you should be the speaker. For you do affirm that you know and are able to tell. Don't be obstinate, but do me the favor to reply and don't be chary of your wisdom, and instruct Glaucon here and the rest of us.

When I had spoken thus Glaucon and the others urged him not to be obstinate. It was quite plain that Thrasymachus was eager to speak in order that he might do himself credit, since he believed that he had a most excellent answer to our question. But he demurred and pretended to make a point of my being the respondent. Finally he gave way and then said, Here you have the wisdom of Socrates, to refuse himself to teach, but go about and learn from others and not even pay thanks therefor.

That I learn from others, I said, you said truly, Thrasymachus. But in saying that I do not pay thanks you are mistaken. I pay as much as I am able. And I am able only to bestow praise. For money I lack. But that I praise right willingly those who appear to speak well you will well know forthwith as soon as you have given your answer. For I think that you will speak well.

Hearken and hear then, said he. I affirm that the just is nothing else than the advantage of the stronger. Well, why don't you applaud? Nay, you'll do anything but that.

Provided only I first understand your meaning, said I, for I don't yet apprehend it. The advantage of the stronger is what you affirm the just to be. But what in the world do you mean by this? I presume you don't intend to affirm this, that if Polydamas, the pancratiast, is stronger than we are and the flesh of beef is advantageous for him, for his body, this viand is also for us who are weaker than he both advantageous and just.

You are a buffoon, Socrates, and take my statement in the most detrimental sense.

Not at all, my dear fellow, said I. I only want you to make your meaning plainer.

Don't you know then, said he, that some cities are governed by tyrants, in others democracy rules, in others aristocracy?

Assuredly.

And is not this the thing that is strong and has the mastery in each—the ruling party?

Certainly.

And each form of government enacts the laws with a view to its own advantage, a democracy democratic laws and tyranny autocratic and the others likewise, and by so legislating they proclaim that the just for their subject is that which is for their—the rulers'—advantage and the man who deviates from this law they chastise as a lawbreaker and a wrongdoer. This, then, my good sir, is what I understand as the identical principle of justice that obtains in all states—the advantage of the established government. This I presume you will admit holds power and is strong, so that, if one reasons rightly, it works out that the just is the same thing everywhere, the advantage of the stronger.

A trifling addition perhaps you think it, he said.

It is not yet clear whether it is a big one either, but that we must inquire whether what you say is true is clear. For since I too admit that the just is something that is of advantage—but you are for making an addition and affirm it to be the advantage of the stronger, while I don't profess to know—we must pursue the inquiry.

Inquire away, he said.

I will do so, said I. Tell me, then, you affirm also, do you not, that obedience to rulers is just?

I do.

May I ask whether the rulers in the various states are infallible or capable sometimes of error?

Surely, he said, they are liable to err.

Then in their attempts at legislation they enact some laws rightly and some not rightly, do they not?

So I suppose.

And by rightly we are to understand for their advantage, and by wrongly to their disadvantage? Do you mean that or not?

That.

But whatever they enact must be performed by their subjects and is justice?

Of course.

Then on your theory it is just not only to do what is the advantage of the stronger but also the opposite, what is not to his advantage.

What's that you're saying? he replied.

What you yourself are saying, I think. Let us consider it more closely. Have we not agreed that the rulers in giving orders to the ruled sometimes mistake their own advantage, and that whatever the rulers enjoin it is just for the subjects to perform? Was not that admitted?

I think it was, he replied.

Then you will have to think, I said, that to do what is disadvantageous to the rulers and the stronger has been admitted by you to be just in the case when the rulers unwittingly enjoin what is bad for themselves, while you affirm that it is just for the others to do what they enjoined. In that way does not this conclusion inevitably follow, my most sapient Thrasymachus, that it is just to do the very opposite of what you say? For it is in that case surely the disadvantage of the stronger or superior that the inferior are commanded to perform.

Yes, by Zeus, Socrates, said Polemarchus, nothing could be more conclusive.

Of course, said Clitophon, breaking in, if you are his witness.

What need is there of a witness? Polemarchus said. Thrasymachus himself admits that the rulers sometimes enjoin what is evil for themselves and yet says that it is just for the subjects to do this.

That, Polemarchus, is because Thrasymachus laid it down that it is just to obey the orders of the rulers.

Yes, Clitophon, but he also took the position that the advantage of the stronger is just. And after these two assumptions he again admitted that the stronger sometimes bid the inferior and their subjects do what is to the disadvantage of the rulers. And from these admissions the just would no more be the advantage of the stronger than the contrary.

Oh well, said Clitophon, by the advantage of the superior he meant what the superior supposed to be for his advantage. This was what the inferior had to do, and that this is the just was his position.

That isn't what he said, replied Polemarchus.

Never mind, Polemarchus, said I. But if that is Thrasymachus' present meaning, let us take it from him in that sense. So tell me, Thrasymachus, was this what you intended to say, that the just is the advantage of the superior as it appears to the superior whether it really is or not? Are we to say this was your meaning?

Not in the least, he said. Do you suppose that I call one who is in error a superior when he errs?

I certainly did suppose that you meant that, I replied, when you agreed that rulers are not infallible but sometimes make mistakes.

That is because you argue like a pettifogger, Socrates. Why, to take the nearest example, do you call one who is mistaken about the sick a physician in respect of his mistake or one who goes wrong in a calculation a calculator when he goes wrong and in respect of this error? Yet that is what we say literally—we say that the physician erred, and the calculator and the schoolmaster. But the truth, I take it, is, that each of these in so far as he is that which we entitle him never errs, so that, speaking precisely, since you are such a stickler for precision, no craftsman errs. For it is when his knowledge abandons him that he who goes wrong goes wrong—when he is not a craftsman. So that no craftsman, wise man, or ruler makes a mistake then when he is a ruler, though everybody would use the expression that the physician made a mistake and the ruler erred. It is in this loose way of speaking, then, that you must take the answer I gave you a little while ago. But the most precise statement is that other, that the ruler in so far forth as ruler does not err, and not erring he enacts what is best for himself, and this the subject must do, so that, even as I meant from the start, I say the just is to do what is for the advantage of the stronger.

So then, Thrasymachus, said I, my manner of argument seems to you pettifogging?

It does, he said.

You think, do you, that it was with malice aforethought and trying to get the better of you unfairly that I asked that question?

I don't think it, I know it, he said, and you won't make anything by it, for you won't get the better of me by stealth and, failing stealth, you are not of the force to beat me in debate.

Bless your soul, said I, I wouldn't even attempt such a thing. But that nothing of the sort may spring up between us again, define in which sense you take the ruler and stronger. Do you mean the so-called ruler or that ruler in the precise sense of whom you were just now telling us, and for whose advantage as being the superior it will be just for the inferior to act?

I mean the ruler in the very most precise sense of the word, he said. Now bring on against this your cavils and your shyster's tricks if you are able. I ask no quarter. But you'll find yourself unable.

Why, do you suppose, I said, that I am so mad as to try to beard a lion and try the pettifogger on Thrasymachus?

You did try it just now, he said, paltry fellow though you be.

Something too much of this sort of thing, said I. But tell me, your physician in the precise sense, of whom you were just now speaking, is he a money-maker, an earner of fees, or a healer of the sick? And remember to speak of the physician who is really such.

A healer of the sick, he replied.

And what of the pilot—the pilot rightly so called—is he a ruler of sailors or a sailor?

A ruler of sailors.

We don't, I fancy, have to take into account the fact that he actually sails in the ship, nor is he to be denominated a sailor. For it is not in respect of his sailing that he is called a pilot but in respect of his art and his ruling of the sailors.

True, he said.

Then for each of them is there not a something that is for his advantage?

Quite so.

And is it not also true, said I, that the art naturally exists for this, to discover and provide for each his advantage?

Yes, for this.

Is there, then, for each of the arts any other advantage than to be as perfect as possible?

What do you mean by that question?

Just as if, I said, you should ask me whether it is enough for the body to be the body or whether it stands in need of something else, I would reply, By all means it stands in need. That is the reason why the art of medicine has now been invented, because the body is defective and such defect is unsatisfactory. To provide for this, then, what is advantageous, that is the end for which the art was devised. Do you think that would be a correct answer, or not?

Correct, he said.

But how about this? Is the medical art itself defective or faulty, or has any other art any need of some virtue, quality, or excellence—as the eyes of vision, the ears of hearing—and for this reason is there need of some art over them that will consider and provide what is advantageous for these very ends? Does there exist in the art itself some defect and does each art require another art to consider its advantage and is there need of still another for the considering art and so on ad infinitum, or will the art look out for its own advantage? Or is it fact that it needs neither itself nor another art to consider its advantage and provide against its deficiency? For there is no defect or error at all that dwells in any art. Nor does it befit an art to seek the advantage of anything else than that of its object. But the art itself is free from all harm and admixture of evil, and is right so long as each art is precisely and entirely that which it is. And consider the matter in that 'precise' way of speaking. Is it so or not?

It appears to be so, he said.

Then medicine, said I, does not consider the advantage of medicine but of the body?

Yes.

Nor horsemanship of horsemanship but of horses, nor does any other art look out for itself—for it has no need—but for that of which it is the art.

So it seems, he replied.

But surely, Thrasymachus, the arts do hold rule and are stronger than that of which they are the arts.

He conceded this but it went very hard.

Then no art considers or enjoins the advantage of the stronger but every art that of the weaker which is ruled by it.

This too he was finally brought to admit though he tried to contest it.

Can we deny, then, said I, that neither does any physician in so far as he is a physician seek or enjoin the advantage of the physician but that of the patient? For we have agreed that the physician, 'precisely' speaking, is a ruler and governor of bodies and not a moneymaker. Did we agree on that?

He assented.

And so the 'precise' pilot is a ruler of sailors, not a sailor?

That was admitted.

Then that sort of a pilot and ruler will not consider and enjoin the advantage of the pilot but that of the sailor whose ruler he is.

He assented reluctantly.

Then, said I, Thrasymachus, neither does anyone in any office of rule in so far as he is a ruler consider and enjoin his own advantage but that of the one whom he rules and for whom he exercises his craft, and he keeps his eyes fixed on that and on what is advantageous and suitable to that in all that he says and does.

When we had come to this point in the discussion and it was apparent to everybody that his formula of justice had suffered a reversal of form, Thrasymachus, instead of replying, said, Tell me, Socrates, have you got a nurse?

What do you mean? said I. Why didn't you answer me instead of asking such a question?

Because, he said, she lets her little snotty run about driveling and doesn't wipe your face clean, though you need it badly, if she can't get you to know the difference between the shepherd and the sheep.

And what, pray, makes you think that? said I.

Because you think that the shepherds and the neatherds are considering the good of the sheep and the cattle and fatten and tend them with anything else in view than the good of their masters and themselves. And by the same token you seem to suppose that the rulers in our cities, I mean the real rulers, differ at all in their thoughts of the governed from a man's attitude toward his sheep or that they think of anything else night and day than the sources of their own profit. And you are so far out concerning the just and justice and the unjust and injustice that you don't know that justice and the just are literally the other fellow's good—the advantage of the stronger and the ruler, but a detriment that is all his own of the subject who obeys and serves—while injustice is the contrary and rules those who are simple in every sense of the word and just, and they being thus ruled do what is for his advantage who is the stronger and make him happy by serving him, but themselves by no manner of means. And you must look at the matter, my simple-minded Socrates, in this way, that the just man always comes out at a disadvantage in his relation with the unjust. To begin with, in their business dealings in any joint undertaking of the two you will never find that the just man has the advantage over the unjust at the dissolution of the partnership but that he always has the worst of it. Then again, in their relations with the state, if there are direct taxes or contributions to be paid, the just man contributes more from an equal estate and the other less, and when there is a distribution the one gains much and the other nothing. And so when each holds office, apart from any other loss the just man must count on his own affairs' falling into disorder through neglect, while because of his justice he makes no profit from the state, and thereto he will displease his friends and his acquaintances by his unwillingness to serve them unjustly. But to the unjust man all the opposite advantages accrue. I mean, of course, the one I was just speaking of, the man who has the ability to overreach on a large scale. Consider this type of man, then, if you wish to judge how much more profitable it is to him personally to be unjust than to be just. And the easiest way of all to understand this matter will be to turn to the most consummate form of injustice which makes the man who has done the wrong most happy and those who are wronged and who would not themselves willingly do wrong most miserable. And this is tyranny, which both by stealth and by force takes away what belongs to others, both sacred and profane, both private and public, not little by little but at one swoop. For each several part of such wrongdoing the malefactor who fails to escape detection is fined and incurs the extreme of contumely, for temple robbers, kidnapers, burglars, swindlers, and thieves are the appellations of those who commit these several forms of injustice. But when in addition to the property of the citizens, men kidnap and enslave the citizens themselves, instead of these opprobrious names they are pronounced happy and blessed not only by their fellow citizens but by all who hear the story of the man who has committed complete and entire injustice. For it is not the fear of doing but of suffering wrong that calls forth the reproaches of those who revile injustice. Thus, Socrates, injustice on a sufficiently large scale is a stronger, freer, and more masterful thing than justice, and, as I said in the beginning, it is the advantage of the stronger that is the just, while the unjust is what profits a man's self and is for his advantage.

After this Thrasymachus was minded to depart when like a bathman he had poured his speech in a sudden flood over our ears. But the company would not suffer him and were insistent that he should remain and render an account of what he had said. And I was particularly urgent and said, I am surprised at you, Thrasymachus. After hurling such a doctrine at us, can it be that you propose to depart without staying to teach us properly or learn yourself whether this thing is so or not? Do you think it a small matter that you are attempting to determine and not the entire conduct of life that for each of us would make living most worth while?

Well, do I deny it? said Thrasymachus.

You seem to, said I, or else to care nothing for us and so feel no concern whether we are going to live worse or better lives in our ignorance of what you affirm that you know. Nay, my good fellow, do your best to make the matter clear to us also—it will be no bad investment for you, any benefit that you bestow on such a company as this. For I tell you for my part that I am not convinced; neither do I think that injustice is more profitable than justice, not even if one gives it free scope and does not hinder it of its will. But, suppose, sir, a man to be unjust and to be able to act unjustly either because he is not detected or can maintain it by violence. All the same he does not convince me that it is more profitable than justice. Now it may be that there is someone else among us who feels in this way and that I am not the only one. Persuade us, then, my dear fellow, convince us satisfactorily that we are ill advised in preferring justice to injustice.

And how am I to persuade you? he said. If you are not convinced by what I just now was saying, what more can I do for you? Shall I take the argument and ram it into your head?

Heaven forbid! I said. Don't do that. But in the first place when you have said a thing stand by it, or if you shift your ground change openly and don't try to deceive us. But, as it is, you see, Thrasymachus—let us return to the previous examples—you see that while you began by taking the physician in the true sense of the word, you did not think fit afterward to be consistent and maintain with precision the notion of the true shepherd, but you apparently think that he herds his sheep in his quality of shepherd, not with regard to what is best for the sheep, but as if he were a banqueter about to be feasted with regard to the good cheer, or again with a view to the sale of them, as if he were a money-maker and not a shepherd. But the art of the shepherd surely is concerned with nothing else than how to provide what is best for that over which it is set, since its own affairs, its own best estate, are surely sufficiently provided for so long as it in nowise fails of being the shepherd's art. And in like manner I supposed that we just now were constrained to acknowledge that every form of rule in so far as it is rule considers what is best for nothing else than that which is governed and cared for by it, alike a political and private rule. Why, do you think that the rulers and holders of office in our cities—the true rulers—willingly hold office and rule?

I don't think, he said, I know right well they do.

But what of other forms of rule, Thrasymachus? Do you not perceive that no one chooses of his own will to hold the office of rule? Men demand pay, which implies that not to them will benefit accrue from their holding office but to those whom they rule. Tell me this. We ordinarily say, do we not, that each of the arts is different from others because its power or function is different? And, my dear fellow, in order that we may reach some result, don't answer counter to your real belief.

Well, yes, he said, that is what renders it different.

And does not each art also yield us benefit that is peculiar to itself and not general, as for example medicine health, the pilot's art safety at sea, and the other arts similarly?

Assuredly.

And does not the wage earner's art yield wages? For that is its function. Would you identify medicine and the pilot's art? Or if you please to discriminate 'precisely' as you proposed, none the more if a pilot regains his health because a sea voyage is good for him, no whit the more, I say, for this reason do you call his art medicine, do you?

Of course not, he said.

Neither, I take it, do you call wage earning medicine if a man earning wages is in health.

Surely not.

But what of this? Do you call medicine wage earning, if a man when giving treatment earns wages?

No, he said.

And did we not agree that the benefit derived from each art is peculiar to it?

So be it, he said.

Any common or general benefit that all craftsmen receive, then, they obviously derive from their common use of some further identical thing.

It seems so, he said.

And we say that the benefit of earning wages accrues to the craftsmen from their further exercise of the wage-earning art.

He assented reluctantly.

Then the benefit, the receiving of wages, does not accrue to each from his own art. But if we are to consider it 'precisely,' medicine produces health but the fee-earning art the pay, and architecture a house but the fee-earning art accompanying it the fee, and so with all the others—each performs its own task and benefits that over which it is set. But unless pay is added to it, is there any benefit which the craftsman receives from the craft?

Apparently not, he said.

Does he then bestow no benefit either when he works for nothing?

I'll say he does.

Then, Thrasymachus, is not this immediately apparent, that no art or office provides what is beneficial for itself—but as we said long ago it provides and enjoins what is beneficial to its subject, considering the advantage of that, the weaker, and not the advantage of the stronger? That was why, friend Thrasymachus, I was just now saying that no one of his own will chooses to hold rule and office and take other people's troubles in hand to straighten them out, but everybody expects pay for that, because he who is to exercise the art rightly never does what is best for himself or enjoins it when he gives commands according to the art, but what is best for the subject. That is the reason, it seems, why pay must be provided for those who are to consent to rule, either in the form of money or honor or a penalty if they refuse.

What do you mean by that, Socrates? said Glaucon. The two wages I recognize, but the penalty you speak of and described as a form of wage I don't understand.

Then, said I, you don't understand the wages of the best men for the sake of which the finest spirits hold office and rule when they consent to do so. Don't you know that to be covetous of honor and covetous of money is said to be and is a reproach?

I do, he said.

Well, then, said I, that is why the good are not willing to rule either for the sake of money or of honor. They do not wish to collect pay openly for their service of rule and be styled hirelings, nor to take it by stealth from their office and be called thieves, nor yet for the sake of honor, for they are not covetous of honor. So there must be imposed some compulsion and penalty to constrain them to rule if they are to consent to hold office. That is perhaps why to seek office oneself and not await compulsion is thought disgraceful. But the chief penalty is to be governed by someone worse if a man will not himself hold office and rule. It is from fear of this, as it appears to me, that the better sort hold office when they do, and then they go to it not in the expectation of enjoyment nor as to a good thing, but as to a necessary evil and because they are unable to turn it over to better men than themselves or to their like. For we may venture to say that, if there should be a city of good men only, immunity from office holding would be as eagerly contended for as office is now, and there it would be made plain that in very truth the true ruler does not naturally seek his own advantage but that of the ruled, so that every man of understanding would rather choose to be benefited by another than to be bothered with benefiting him. This point then I by no means concede to Thrasymachus, that justice is the advantage of the superior. But that we will reserve for another occasion. A far weightier matter seems to me Thrasymachus' present statement, his assertion that the life of the unjust man is better than that of the just. Which now do you choose, Glaucon? And which seems to you to be the truer statement?

That the life of the just man is more profitable, I say, he replied.

Did you hear, said I, all the goods that Thrasymachus just now enumerated for the life of the unjust man?

I heard, he said, but I am not convinced.

Do you wish us then to try to persuade him, supposing we can find a way, that what he says is not true?

Of course I wish it, he said.

If then we oppose him in a set speech enumerating in turn the advantages of being just and he replies and we rejoin, we shall have to count up and measure the goods listed in the respective speeches and we shall forthwith be in need of judges to decide between us. But if, as in the preceding discussion, we come to terms with one another as to what we admit in the inquiry, we shall be ourselves both judges and pleaders.

Quite so, he said.

Which method do you like better? said I.

This one, he said.

Come then, Thrasymachus, I said, go back to the beginning and answer us. You affirm that perfect and complete injustice is more profitable than justice that is complete.

I affirm it, he said, and have told you my reasons.

Tell me then how you would express yourself on this point about them. You call one of them, I presume, a virtue and the other a vice?

Of course.

Justice the virtue and injustice the vice?

It is likely, you innocent, when I say that injustice pays and justice doesn't pay.

But what then, pray?

The opposite, he replied.

What! Justice vice?

No, but a most noble simplicity or goodness of heart.

Then do you call injustice badness of heart?

No, but goodness of judgment.

Do you also, Thrasymachus, regard the unjust as intelligent and good?

Yes, if they are capable of complete injustice, he said, and are able to subject to themselves cities and tribes of men. But you probably suppose that I mean those who take purses. There is profit to be sure even in the sort of thing, he said, if it goes undetected. But such things are not worth taking into the account, but only what I just described.

I am not unaware of your meaning in that, I said, but this is what surprised me, that you should range injustice under the head of virtue and wisdom, and justice in the opposite class.

Well, I do so class them, he said.

That, said I, is a stiffer proposition, my friend, and if you are going as far as that it is hard to know what to answer. For if your position were that injustice is profitable yet you conceded it to be vicious and disgraceful as some other disputants do, there would be a chance for an argument on conventional principles. But, as it is, you obviously are going to affirm that it is honorable and strong and you will attach to it all the other qualities that we were assigning to the just, since you don't shrink from putting it in the category of virtue and wisdom.

You are a most veritable prophet, he replied.

Well, said I, I mustn't flinch from following out the logic of the inquiry, so long as I conceive you to be saying what you think. For now, Thrasymachus, I absolutely believe that you are not 'mocking' us but telling us your real opinions about the truth.

What difference does it make to you, he said, whether I believe it or not? Why don't you test the argument?

No difference, said I, but here is something I want you to tell me in addition to what you have said. Do you think the just man would want to overreach or exceed another just man?

By no means, he said. Otherwise he would not be the delightful simpleton that he is.

And would he exceed or overreach or go beyond the just action?

Not that either, he replied.

But how would he treat the unjust man—would he deem it proper and just to outdo, overreach, or go beyond him or would he not?

He would, he said, but he wouldn't be able to.

That is not my question, I said, but whether it is not the fact that the just man does not claim or wish to outdo the just man but only the unjust?

That is the case, he replied.

How about the unjust then? Does he claim to overreach and outdo the just man and the just action?

Of course, he said, since he claims to overreach and get the better of everything.

Then the unjust man will overreach and outdo also both the unjust man and the unjust action, and all his endeavor will be to get the most in everything for himself.

That is so.

Let us put it in this way, I said. The just man does not seek to take advantage of his like but of his unlike, but the unjust man of both.

Admirably put, he said.

But the unjust man is intelligent and good and the just man neither.

That, too, is right, he said.

Is it not also true, I said, that the unjust man is like the intelligent and good and the just man is not?

Of course, he said, being such he will be like to such and the other not.

Excellent. Then each is such as that to which he is like.

What else do you suppose? he said.

Very well, Thrasymachus, but do you recognize that one man is a musician and another unmusical?

I do.

Which is the intelligent and which the unintelligent?

The musician, I presume, is the intelligent and the unmusical the unintelligent.

And is he not good in the things in which he is intelligent and bad in the things in which he is unintelligent?

Yes.

And the same of the physician?

The same.

Do you think then, my friend, that any musician in the tuning of a lyre would want to overreach another musician in the tightening and relaxing of the strings or would claim and think fit to exceed or outdo him?

I do not.

But would he the unmusical man?

Of necessity, he said.

And how about the medical man? In prescribing food and drink would he want to outdo the medical man or the medical procedure?

Surely not.

But he would the unmedical man?

Yes.

Consider then with regard to all forms of knowledge and ignorance whether you think that anyone who knows would choose to do or say other or more than what another who knows would do or say, and not rather exactly what his like would do in the same action.

Why, perhaps it must be so, he said, in such cases.

But what of the ignorant man—of him who does not know? Would he not overreach or outdo equally the knower and the ignorant?

It may be.

But the one who knows is wise?

I'll say so.

And the wise is good?

I'll say so.

Then he who is good and wise will not wish to overreach his like but his unlike and opposite.

It seems so, he said.

But the bad man and the ignoramus will overreach both like and unlike?

So it appears.

And does not our unjust man, Thrasymachus, overreach both unlike and like? Did you not say that?

I did, he replied.

But the just man will not overreach his like but only his unlike?

Yes.

Then the just man is like the wise and good, and the unjust is like the bad and the ignoramus.

It seems likely.

But furthermore we agreed that each is such as that to which he is like.

Yes, we did.

Then the just man has turned out on our hands to be good and wise and the unjust man bad and ignorant.

Thrasymachus made all these admissions not as I now lightly narrate them, but with much balking and reluctance and prodigious sweating, it being summer, and it was then I beheld what I had never seen before—Thrasymachus blushing. But when we did reach our conclusion that justice is virtue and wisdom and injustice vice and ignorance, Good, said I, let this be taken as established. But we were also affirming that injustice is a strong and potent thing. Don't you remember, Thrasymachus?

I remember, he said, but I don't agree with what you are now saying either and I have an answer to it, but if I were to attempt to state it, I know very well that you would say that I was delivering a harangue. Either then allow me to speak at such length as I desire, or, if you prefer to ask questions, go on questioning and I, as we do for old wives telling their tales, will say, 'Very good,' and will nod assent and dissent.

No, no, said I, not counter to your own belief.

Yes, to please you, he said, since you don't allow me freedom of speech. And yet what more do you want?

Nothing, indeed, said I, but if this is what you propose to do, do it, and I will ask the questions.

Ask on, then.

This, then, is the question I ask, the same as before, so that our inquiry may proceed in sequence. What is the nature of injustice as compared with justice? For the statement made, I believe, was that injustice is a more potent and stronger thing than justice. But now, I said, if justice is wisdom and virtue, it will easily, I take it, be shown to be also a stronger thing than injustice, since injustice is ignorance—no one could now fail to recognize that—but what I want is not quite so simple as that. I wish, Thrasymachus, to consider it in some such fashion as this. A city, you would say, may be unjust and try to enslave other cities unjustly, have them enslaved and hold many of them in subjection.

Certainly, he said, and this is what the best state will chiefly do, the state whose injustice is most complete.

I understand, I said, that this was your view. But the point that I am considering is this, whether the city that thus shows itself superior to another will have this power without justice or whether she must of necessity combine it with justice.

If, he replied, what you were just now saying holds good, that justice is wisdom, with justice; if it is as I said, with injustice.

Admirable, Thrasymachus, I said. You not only nod assent and dissent, but give excellent answers.

I am trying to please you, he replied.

Very kind of you. But please me in one thing more and tell me this. Do you think that a city, an army, or bandits, or thieves, or any other group that attempted any action in common, could accomplish anything if they wronged one another?

Certainly not, said he.

But if they didn't, wouldn't they be more likely to?

Assuredly.

For factions, Thrasymachus, are the outcome of injustice, and hatreds and internecine conflicts, but justice brings oneness of mind and love. Is it not so?

So be it, he replied, not to differ from you.

That is good of you, my friend, but tell me this. If it is the business of injustice to engender hatred wherever it is found, will it not, when it springs up either among free men or slaves, cause them to hate and be at strife with one another, and make them incapable of effective action in common?

By all means.

Suppose, then, it springs up between two, will they not be at outs with and hate each other and be enemies both to one another and to the just?

They will, he said.

And then will you tell me that if injustice arises in one it will lose its force and function or will it nonetheless keep it?

Have it that it keeps it, he said.

And is it not apparent that its force is such that wherever it is found in city, family, camp, or in anything else, it first renders the thing incapable of co-operation with itself owing to fraction and difference, and secondly an enemy to itself and to its opposite in every case, the just? Isn't that so?

By all means.

Then in the individual too, I presume, its presence will operate all these effects which it is its nature to produce. It will in the first place make him incapable of accomplishing anything because of inner faction and lack of self-agreement, and then an enemy to himself and to the just. Is it not so?

Yes.

But, my friend, the gods too are just.

Have it that they are, he said.

So to the gods also, it seems, the unjust man will be hateful, but the just man dear.

Revel in your discourse, he said, without fear, for I shall not oppose you, so as not to offend your partisans here.

Fill up the measure of my feast, then, and complete it for me, I said, by continuing to answer as you have been doing. Now that the just appear to be wiser and better and more capable of action and the unjust incapable of any common action, and that if we ever say that any men who are unjust have vigorously combined to put something over, our statement is not altogether true, for they would not have kept their hands from one another if they had been thoroughly unjust, but it is obvious that there was in them some justice which prevented them from wronging at the same time one another too as well as those whom they attacked. And by dint of this they accomplished whatever they did and set out to do injustice only half corrupted by injustice, since utter rascals completely unjust are completely incapable of effective action—all this I understand to be the truth, and not what you originally laid down. But whether it is also true that the just have a better life than the unjust and are happier, which is the question we afterward proposed for examination, is what we now have to consider. It appears even now that they are, I think, from what has already been said. But all the same we must examine it more carefully. For it is no ordinary matter that we are discussing, but the right conduct of life.

Proceed with your inquiry, he said.

I proceed, said I. Tell me then—would you say that a horse has a specific work or function?

I would.

Would you be willing to define the work of a horse or of anything else to be that which one can do only with it or best with it?

I don't understand, he replied.

Well, take it this way. Is there anything else with which you can see except the eyes?

Certainly not.

Again, could you hear with anything but ears?

By no means.

Would you not rightly say that these are the functions of these organs?

By all means.

Once more, you could use a dirk to trim vine branches and a knife and many other instruments.

Certainly.

But nothing so well, I take it, as a pruning knife fashioned for this purpose.

That is true.

Must we not then assume this to be the work or function of that?

We must.

You will now, then, I fancy, better apprehend the meaning of my question when

I asked whether that is not the work of a thing which it only or it better than anything else can perform.

Well, he said, I do understand, and agree that the work of anything is that.

Very good, said I. Do you not also think that there is a specific virtue or excellence of everything for which a specific work or function is appointed? Let us return to the same examples. The eyes we say have a function?

They have.

Is there also a virtue of the eyes?

There is.

And was there not a function of the ears?

Yes.

And so also a virtue?

Also a virtue.

And what of all other things? Is the case not the same?

The same.

Take note now. Could the eyes possibly fulfill their function well if they lacked their own proper excellence and had in its stead the defect?

How could they? he said. For I presume you meant blindness instead of vision.

Whatever, said I, the excellence may be. For I have not yet come to that question, but am only asking whether whatever operates will not do its own work well by its own virtue and badly by its own defect.

That much, he said, you may safely affirm to be true.

Then the ears, too, if deprived of their own virtue will do their work ill?

Assuredly.

And do we then apply the same principle to all things?

I think so.

Then next consider this. The soul, has it a work which you couldn't accomplish with anything else in the world, as for example, management, rule, deliberation, and the like? Is there anything else that soul to which you could rightly assign these and say that they were its peculiar work?

Nothing else.

And again life? Shall we say that too is the function of the soul?

Most certainly, he said.   "αρετε "

And do we not also say that there is an excellence or virtue of the soul?

We do.

Will the soul ever accomplish its own work well if deprived of its own virtue, or is this impossible?

It is impossible.

Of necessity, then, a bad soul will govern and manage things badly while the good soul will in all these things do well.

Of necessity.

And did we not agree that the excellence or virtue of soul is justice and its defect injustice?

Yes, we did.

The just soul and the just man then will live well and the unjust ill?

So it appears, he said, by your reasoning.

But furthermore, he who lives well is blessed and happy, and he who does not the contrary.

Of course.

Then the just is happy and the unjust miserable.

So be it, he said.

But it surely does not pay to be miserable, but to be happy.

Of course not.

Never, then, most worshipful Thrasymachus, can injustice be more profitable than justice.

Let this complete your entertainment, Socrates, at the festival of Bendis.

A feast furnished by you, Thrasymachus, I said, now that you have become gentle with me and are no longer angry. I have not dined well, however—by my own fault, not yours. But just as gluttons snatch at every dish that is handed along and taste it before they have properly enjoyed the preceding, so I, methinks, before finding the first object of our inquiry—what justice is—let go of that and set out to consider something about it, namely whether it is vice and ignorance or wisdom and virtue. And again, when later the view was sprung upon us that injustice is more profitable than justice I could not refrain from turning to that from the other topic. So that for me the present outcome of the discussion is that I know nothing. For if I don't know what the just is, I shall hardly know whether it is a virtue or not, and whether its possessor is or is not happy.

* * * *Ring of Gygeous*

When I had said this I supposed that I was done with the subject, but it all turned out to be only a prelude. For Glaucon, who is always an intrepid, enterprising spirit in everything, would not on this occasion acquiesce in Thrasymachus' abandonment of his case, but said, Socrates, is it your desire to seem to have persuaded us or really to persuade us that it is without exception better to be just than unjust?

Really, I said, if the choice rested with me.

Well, then, you are not doing what you wish. For tell me, do you agree that there is a kind of good which we would choose to possess, not from desire for its aftereffects, but welcoming it for its own sake? As, for example, joy and such pleasures as are harmless and nothing results from them afterward save to have and to hold the enjoyment. — *like, chocolate*

I recognize that kind, said I. *eating*

And again a kind that we love both for its own sake and for its consequences, such as understanding, sight, and health? For these I presume we welcome for both reasons. — *like doing work that you love*

Yes, I said.

And can you discern a third form of good under which fall exercise and being healed when sick and the art of healing and the making of money generally? For of them we would say that they are laborious and painful yet beneficial, and for their own sake we would not accept them, but only for the rewards and other benefits that accrue from them.

Why yes, I said, I must admit this third class also. But what of it?

In which of these classes do you place justice? he said.

In my opinion, I said, it belongs in the fairest class, that which a man who is to be happy must love both for its own sake and for the results.

What, Socrates, do we suppose is the effect of all such sayings about the esteem in which men and gods hold virtue and vice upon the souls that hear them, the souls of young men who are quick-witted and capable of flitting, as it were, from one expression of opinion to another and inferring from them all the character and the path whereby a man would lead the best life? Such a youth would most likely put to himself the question Pindar asks, 'Is it by justice or by crooked deceit that I the higher tower shall scale and so live my life out in fenced and guarded security?' The consequences of my being just are, unless I likewise seem so, not assets, they say, but liabilities, labor, and total loss, but if I am injust and have procured myself a reputation for justice, a godlike life is promised. Then since it is 'the seeming,' as the wise men show me, that 'masters the reality' and is lord of happiness, to this I must devote myself without reserve. For a front and a show I must draw about myself a shadow outline of virtue, but trail behind me the fox of the most sage Archilochus, shifty and bent on gain. Nay, 'tis objected, it is not easy for a wrongdoer always to lie hid. Neither is any other big thing facile, we shall reply. But all the same if we expect to be happy, we must pursue the path to which the footprints of our arguments point. For with a view to lying hid we will organize societies and political clubs, and there are teachers of cajolery who impart the arts of the popular assembly and the courtroom, so that, partly by persuasion, partly by force, we shall contrive to overreach with impunity. But against the gods, it may be said, neither secrecy nor force can avail. Well, if there are no gods, or they do not concern themselves with the doings of men, neither need we concern ourselves with eluding their observation. If they do exist and pay heed, we know and hear of them only from such discourses and from the poets who have described their pedigrees. But these same authorities tell us that the gods are capable of being persuaded and swerved from their course by 'sacrifice and soothing vows' and dedications. We must believe them in both or neither. And if we are to believe them, the thing to do is to commit injustice and offer sacrifice from the fruits of our wrongdoing. For if we are just, we shall, it is true, be unscathed by the gods, but we shall be putting away from us the profits of injustice, but if we are unjust, we shall win those profits, and, by the importunity for our prayers, when we transgress and sin we shall persuade them and escape scot free. Yes, it will be objected, but we shall be brought to judgment in the world below for our unjust deeds here, we or our children's children. Nay, my dear sir, our calculating friend will say, here again the rites for the dead have much efficacy, and the absolving divinities, as the greatest cities declare, and the sons of gods, who became the poets and prophets of the gods, and who reveal that this is the truth.

On what further ground, then, could we prefer justice to supreme injustice? If we combine this with a counterfeit decorum, we shall prosper to our heart's desire, with gods and men, in life and death, as the words of the multitude and of men of the highest authority declare. In consequence, then, of all that has been said, what possibility is there, Socrates, that any man who has the power of any resources of mind, money, body, or family should consent to honor justice and not rather laugh when he hears her praised? In sooth, if anyone is able to show the falsity of these arguments, and has come to know with sufficient assurance that justice is best, he feels much indulgence for the unjust, and is not angry with them, but is aware that except a man by inborn divinity of his nature disdains injustice, or, having won to knowledge, refrains from it, no one else is willing just, but that it is from lack of manly spirit or from old age or some other weakness that men dispraise injustice, lacking the power to practice it. The fact is patent. For no sooner does such a one come into the power than he works injustice to the extent of his ability.

And the sole cause of all this is the fact that was the starting point of this entire plea of my friend here and of myself to you, Socrates, pointing out how strange it is that of all you self-styled advocates of justice, from the heroes of old whose discourses survive to the men of the present day, not one has ever censured injustice or commended justice otherwise than in respect of the repute, the honors, and the gifts that accrue from each. But what each one of them is in itself, by its own inherent force, when it is within the soul of the possessor and escapes the eyes of both gods and men, no one has ever adequately set forth in poetry or prose—the proof that the one is the greatest of all evils that the soul contains within itself, while justice is the greatest good. For if you had all spoken in this way from the beginning and from our youth up had sought to convince us, we should not now be guarding against one another's injustice, but each would be his own best guardian, for fear lest by working injustice he should dwell in communion with the greatest evils.

This, Socrates, and perhaps even more than this, Thrasymachus and haply another might say in pleas for and against justice and injustice, inverting their true potencies, as I believe, grossly. But I—for I have no reason to hide anything from you—am laying myself out to the utmost on the theory, because I wish to hear its refutation from you. Do not merely show us by argument that justice is superior to injustice, but make clear to us what each in and of itself does to its possessor, whereby the one is evil and the other good. But do away with the repute of both, as Glaucon urged. For, unless you take away from either the true repute and attach to each the false, we shall say that it is not justice that you are praising but the semblance, nor injustice that you censure, but the seeming, and that you really are exhorting us to be unjust but conceal it, and that you are at one with Thrasymachus in the opinion that justice is the other man's good, the advantage of the stronger, and that injustice is advantageous and profitable to oneself but disadvantageous to the inferior. Since, then, you have admitted that justice belongs to the class of those highest goods which are desirable both for their consequences and still more for their own sake, as sight, hearing, intelligence, yes and health too, and all other goods that are productive by their very nature and not by opinion, this is what I would have you praise about justice—the benefit which it and the harm which injustice inherently works upon its possessor. But the rewards and the honors that depend on opinion, leave to others to praise. For while I would listen to others who thus commended justice and disparaged injustice, bestowing their praise and their blame on the reputation and the rewards of either, I could not accept that sort of thing from you unless you say I must, because you have passed your entire life in the consideration of this very matter. Do not, then, I repeat, merely prove to us in argument the superiority of justice to injustice, but show us what it is that each inherently does to its possessor—whether he does or does not escape the eyes of gods and men—whereby the one is good and the other evil.

While I had always admired the genius of Glaucon and Adimantus, I was especially pleased by their words on this occasion, and said, It was excellently spoken of you, sons of the man we know, in the beginning of the elegy which the admirer of Glaucon wrote when you distinguished yourselves in the battle of Megara— 'Sons of Ariston, whose race from a glorious sire is godlike.' This, my friends, I think, was well said. For there must indeed be a touch of the godlike in your disposition if you are not convinced that injustice is preferable to justice though you can plead its case in such fashion. And I believe that you are really not convinced. I infer this from your general character, since from your words alone I should have distrusted you. But the more I trust you the more I am at a loss what to make of the matter. I do not know how I can come to the rescue. For I doubt my ability for the reason that you have not accepted the arguments whereby I thought I proved against Thrasymachus that justice is better than injustice. Nor yet again do I know how I can refuse to come to the rescue. For I fear lest it be actually impious to stand idly by when justice is reviled and be fainthearted and not defend her so long as one has breath and can utter his voice. The best thing, then, is to aid her as best I can.

Glaucon, then, and the rest besought me by all means to come to the rescue and not to drop the argument but to pursue to the end the investigation as to the nature of each and the truth about their respective advantages. I said then as I thought, The inquiry we are undertaking is no easy one but calls for keen vision, as it seems to me. So, since we are not clever persons, I think we should employ the method of search that we should use if we, with not very keen vision, were bidden to read small letters from a distance, and then someone had observed that these same letters exist elsewhere larger and on a larger surface. We should have accounted it a godsend, I fancy, to be allowed to read those letters first, and then examine the smaller, if they are the same.

Quite so, said Adimantus, but what analogy to this do you detect in the inquiry about justice?

I will tell you, I said. There is a justice of one man, we say, and, I suppose, also of an entire city?

Assuredly, said he.

Is not the city larger than the man?

It is larger, he said.

Then, perhaps, there would be more justice in the larger object, and more easy to apprehend. If it please you, then, let us first look for its quality in states, and then only examine it also in the individual, looking for the likeness of the greater in the form of the less.

I think that is a good suggestion, he said.

If, then, said I, our argument should observe the origin of a state, we should see also the origin of justice and injustice in it?

It may be, said he.

And if this is done, we may expect to find more easily what we are seeking?

Much more.

Shall we try it, then, and go through with it? I fancy it is no slight task. Reflect, then.

We have reflected, said Adimantus. Proceed and don't refuse.

The origin of the city, then, said I, in my opinion, is to be found in the fact that we do not severally suffice for our own needs, but each of us lacks many things. Do you think any other principle established the state?

No other, said he.

As a result of this, then, one man calling in another for one service and another for another, we, being in need of many things, gather many into one place of abode as associates and helpers, and to this dwelling together we give the name city or state, do we not?

By all means.

And between one man and another there is an interchange of giving, if it so happens, and taking, because each supposes this to be better for himself.

Certainly.

Come, then, let us create a city from the beginning, in our theory. Its real creator, as it appears, will be our needs.

Obviously.

Now the first and chief of our needs is the provision of food for existence and life.

Assuredly.

The second is housing and the third is raiment and that sort of thing.

That is so.

Tell me, then, said I, how our city will suffice for the provision of all these things. Will there not be a farmer for one, and a builder, and then again a weaver? And shall we add thereto a cobbler and some other purveyor for the needs of the body?

Certainly.

The indispensable minimum of a city, then, would consist of four or five men.

Apparently.

What of this, then? Shall each of these contribute his work for the common use of all? I mean, shall the farmer, who is one, provide food for four and spend fourfold time and toil on the production of food and share it with the others, or shall he take no thought for them and provide a fourth portion of the food for himself alone in a quarter of the time and employ the other three-quarters, the one in the provision of a house, the other of a garment, the other of shoes, and not have the bother of associating with other people, but, himself for himself, mind his own affairs?

And Adimantus said, But, perhaps, Socrates, the former way is easier.

It would not, by Zeus, be at all strange, said I, for now that you have mentioned it, it occurs to me myself that, to begin with, our several natures are not all alike but different. One man is naturally fitted for one task, and another for another. Don't you think so?

I do.

Again, would one man do better working at many tasks or one at one?

One at one, he said.

And, furthermore, this, I fancy, is obvious—that if one lets slip the right season, the favorable moment in any task, the work is spoiled.

Obvious.

That, I take it, is because the business will not wait upon the leisure of the workman, but the workman must attend to it as his main affair, and not as a bywork.

He must indeed.

The result, then, is that more things are produced, and better and more easily when one man performs one task according to his nature, at the right moment, and at leisure from other occupations.

By all means.

Then, Adimantus, we need more than four citizens for the provision of the things we have mentioned. For the farmer, it appears, will not make his own plow if it is to be a good one, nor his hoe, nor his other agricultural implements, nor will the builder, who also needs many, and similarly the weaver and cobbler.

True.

Carpenters, then, and smiths and many similar craftsmen, associating themselves with our hamlet, will enlarge it considerably.

Certainly.

Yet it still wouldn't be very large even if we should add to them neatherds and shepherds and other herders, so that the farmers might have cattle for plowing, and the builders oxen to use with the farmers for transportation, and the weavers and cobblers hides and fleeces for their use.

It wouldn't be a small city, either, if it had all these.

But further, said I, it is practically impossible to establish the city in a region where it will not need imports.

It is.

There will be a further need, then, of those who will bring in from some other city what it requires.

There will.

And again, if our servitor goes forth empty-handed, not taking with him any of the things needed by those from whom they procure what they themselves require, he will come back with empty hands, will he not?

I think so.

Then their home production must not merely suffice for themselves but in quality and quantity meet the needs of those of whom they have need.

It must.

So our city will require more farmers and other craftsmen.

Yes, more.

And also of other ministrants who are to export and import the merchandise. These are traders, are they not?

Yes.

We shall also need traders, then.

Assuredly.

And if the trading is carried on by sea, we shall need quite a number of others who are expert in maritime business.

Quite a number.

But again, within the city itself how will they share with one another the products of their labor? This was the very purpose of our association and establishment of a state.

Obviously, he said, by buying and selling.

A market place, then, and money as a token for the purpose of exchange will be the result of this.

By all means.

If, then, the farmer or any other craftsman taking his products to the market place does not arrive at the same time with those who desire to exchange with him, is he to sit idle in the market place and lose time from his own work?

By no means, he said, but there are men who see this need and appoint themselves for this service—in well-conducted cities they are generally those who are weakest in body and those who are useless for any other task. They must wait there in the agora and exchange money for goods with those who wish to sell, and goods for money with as many as desire to buy.

This need, then, said I, creates the class of shopkeepers in our city. Or is not 'shopkeepers' the name we give to those who, planted in the agora, serve us in buying and selling, while we call those who roam from city to city merchants?

Certainly.

And there are, furthermore, I believe, other servitors who in the things of the mind are not altogether worthy of our fellowship, but whose strength of body is sufficient for toil; so they, selling the use of this strength and calling the price wages, are designated, I believe, 'wage earners,' are they not?

Certainly.

Wage earners, then, it seems, are the complement that helps to fill up the state.

I think so.

Has our city, then, Adimantus, reached its full growth, and is it complete?

Perhaps.

Where, then, can justice and injustice be found in it? And along with which of the constituents that we have considered do they come into the state?

I cannot conceive, Socrates, he said, unless it be in some need that those very constituents have of one another.

Perhaps that is a good suggestion, said I. We must examine it and not hold back.

First of all, then, let us consider what will be the manner of life of men thus provided. Will they not make bread and wine and garments and shoes? And they will build themselves houses and carry on their work in summer for the most part unclad and unshod and in winter clothed and shod sufficiently. And for their nourishment they will provide meal from their barley and flour from their wheat, and kneading and cooking these they will serve noble cakes and loaves on some arrangement of reeds or clean leaves. And, reclined on rustic beds strewed with bryony and myrtle, they will feast with their children, drinking of their wine thereto, garlanded and singing hymns to the gods in pleasant fellowship, not begetting offspring beyond their means lest they fall into poverty or war.

Here Glaucon broke in, No relishes apparently, he said, for the men you describe as feasting.

True, said I, I forgot that they will also have relishes—salt, of course, and olives and cheese, and onions and greens, the sort of things they boil in the country, they will boil up together. But for dessert we will serve them figs and chick-peas and beans, and they will toast myrtle berries and acorns before the fire, washing them down with moderate potations. And so, living in peace and health, they will probably die in old age and hand on a like life to their offspring.

And he said, If you were founding a city of pigs, Socrates, what other fodder than this would you provide?

Why, what would you have, Glaucon? said I.

What is customary, he replied. They must recline on couches, I presume, if they are not to be uncomfortable, and dine from tables and have dishes and sweetmeats such as are now in use.

Good, said I. I understand. It is not merely the origin of a city, it seems, that we are considering but the origin of a luxurious city. Perhaps that isn't such a bad suggestion, either. For by observation of such a city it may be we could discern the origin of justice and injustice in states. The true state I believe to be the one we have described—the healthy state, as it were. But if it is your pleasure that we contemplate also a fevered state, there is nothing to hinder. For there are some, it appears, who will not be contented with this sort of fare or with this way of life, but couches will have to be added thereto and tables and other furniture, yes, and relishes and myrrh and incense and girls and cakes—all sorts of all of them. And the requirements we first mentioned, houses and garments and shoes, will no longer be confined to necessities, but we must set painting to work and embroidery, and procure gold and ivory and similar adornments, must we not?

Yes, he said.

Then shall we not have to enlarge the city again? For that healthy state is no longer sufficient, but we must proceed to swell out its bulk and fill it up with a multitude of things that exceed the requirements of necessity in states, as, for example, the entire class of huntsmen, and the imitators, many of them occupied with figures and colors and many with music—the poets and their assistants, rhapsodists, actors, chorus dancers, contractors—and the manufacturers of all kinds of articles, especially those that have to do with women's adornment. And so we shall also want more servitors. Don't you think that we shall need tutors, nurses wet and dry, beauty-shop ladies, barbers, and yet again cooks and chefs? And we shall have need, further, of swineherds; there were none of these creatures in our former city, for we had no need of them, but in this city there will be this further need. And we shall also require other cattle in great numbers if they are to be eaten, shall we not?

Yes.

Doctors, too, are something whose services we shall be much more likely to require if we live thus than as before?

Much.

And the territory, I presume, that was then sufficient to feed the then population, from being adequate will become too small. Is that so or not?

It is.

Then we shall have to cut out a cantle of our neighbor's land if we are to have enough for pasture and plowing, and they in turn of ours if they too abandon themselves to the unlimited acquisition of wealth, disregarding the limit set by our necessary wants.

Inevitably, Socrates.

We shall go to war as the next step, Glaucon—or what will happen?

What you say, he said.

And we are not yet to speak, said I, of any evil or good effect of war, but only to affirm that we have further discovered the origin of war, namely, from those things from which the greatest disasters, public and private, come to states when they come.

Certainly.

Then, my friend, we must still further enlarge our city by no small increment, but by a whole army, that will march forth and fight it out with assailants in defense of all our wealth and the luxuries we have just described.

How so? he said. Are the citizens themselves not sufficient for that?

Not if you, said I, and we all were right in the admission we made when we were molding our city. We surely agreed, if you remember, that it is impossible for one man to do the work of many arts well.

True, he said.

Well, then, said I, don't you think that the business of fighting is an art and a profession?

It is indeed, he said.

Should our concern be greater, then, for the cobbler's art than for the art of war?

By no means.

Can we suppose, then, that while we were at pains to prevent the cobbler from attempting to be at the same time a farmer, a weaver, or a builder instead of just a cobbler, to the end that we might have the cobbler's business well done, and similarly assigned to each and every one man one occupation, for which he was fit and naturally adapted and at which he was to work all his days, at leisure from other pursuits and not letting slip the right moments for doing the work well, and that yet we are in doubt whether the right accomplishment of the business of war is not of supreme moment? Is it so easy that a man who is cultivating the soil will be at the same time a soldier and one who is practicing cobbling or any other trade, though no man in the world could make himself a competent expert at draughts or the dice who did not practice that and nothing else from childhood but treated it as an occasional business? And are we to believe that a man who takes in hand a shield or any other instrument of war springs up on that very day a competent combatant in heavy armor or in any other form of warfare—though no other tool will make a man be an artist or an athlete by his taking it in hand, nor will it be of any service to those who have neither acquired the science of it nor sufficiently practiced themselves in its use?

Great indeed, he said, would be the value of tools in that case!

Then, said I, in the same degree that the task of our guardians is the greatest of all, it would require more leisure than any other business and the greatest science and training.

I think so, said he.

Does it not also require a nature adapted to that very pursuit?

Of course.

It becomes our task, then, it seems, if we are able, to select which and what kind of natures are suited for the guardianship of a state.

Yes, ours.

Upon my word, said I, it is no light task that we have taken upon ourselves. But we must not faint so far as our strength allows.

No, we mustn't.

Do you think, said I, that there is any difference between the nature of a well-bred hound for this watchdog's work and that of a wellborn lad?

What point have you in mind?

I mean that each of them must be keen of perception, quick in pursuit of what it has apprehended, and strong too if it has to fight it out with its captive.

Why, yes, said he, there is need of all these qualities.

And it must, further, be brave if it is to fight well.

Of course.

And will a creature be ready to be brave that is not high-spirited, whether horse or dog or anything else? Have you never observed what an irresistible and invincible thing is spirit, the presence of which makes every soul in the face of everything fearless and unconquerable?

I have.

The physical qualities of the guardian, then, are obvious.

Yes.

And also those of his soul, namely that he must be of high spirit.

Yes, this too.

How then, Glaucon, said I, will they escape being savage to one another and to the other citizens if this is to be their nature?

Not easily, by Zeus, said he.

And yet we must have them gentle to their friends and harsh to their enemies;

otherwise they will not await their destruction at the hands of others, but will be first themselves in bringing it about.

True, he said.

What, then, are we to do? said I. Where shall we discover a disposition that is at once gentle and great-spirited? For there appears to be an opposition between the spirited type and the gentle nature.

There does.

But yet if one lacks either of these qualities, a good guardian he never can be. But these requirements resemble impossibilities, and so the result is that a good guardian is impossible.

It seems likely, he said.

And I was at a standstill, and after reconsidering what we had been saying, I said, We deserve to be at a loss, my friend, for we have lost sight of the comparison that we set before ourselves.

What do you mean?

We failed to note that there are after all such natures as we thought impossible, endowed with these opposite qualities.

Where?

It may be observed in other animals, but especially in that which we likened to the guardian. You surely have observed in well-bred hounds that their natural disposition is to be most gentle to their familiars and those whom they recognize, but the contrary to those whom they do not know.

I am aware of that.

The thing is possible, then, said I, and it is not an unnatural requirement that we are looking for in our guardian.

It seems not.

And does it seem to you that our guardian-to-be will also need, in addition to being high-spirited, the further quality of having the love of wisdom in his nature?

How so? he said. I don't apprehend your meaning.

This too, said I, is something that you will discover in dogs and which is worth our wonder in the creature.

What?

That the sight of an unknown person angers him before he has suffered any injury, but an acquaintance he will fawn upon though he has never received any kindness from him. Have you never marveled at that?

I never paid any attention to the matter before now, but that he acts in some such way is obvious.

But surely that is an exquisite trait of his nature and one that shows a true love of wisdom.

In what respect, pray?

In respect, said I, that he distinguishes a friendly from a hostile aspect by nothing save his apprehension of the one and his failure to recognize the other. How, I ask you, can the love of learning be denied to a creature whose criterion of the friendly and the alien is intelligence and ignorance?

It certainly cannot, he said.

But you will admit, said I, that the love of learning and the love of wisdom are the same?

The same, he said.

Then may we not confidently lay it down, in the case of man too, that if he is to be in some sort gentle to friends and familiars he must be by nature a lover of wisdom and of learning?

Let us so assume, he replied.

The love of wisdom, then, and high spirit and quickness and strength will be combined for us in the nature of him who is to be a good and true guardian of the state.

By all means, he said.

Such, then, I said, would be the basis of his character. But the rearing of these men and their education, how shall we manage that? And will the consideration of this topic advance us in any way toward discerning what is the object of our entire inquiry—the origin of justice and injustice in a state—our aim must be to omit nothing of a sufficient discussion, and yet not to draw it out to tiresome length?

And Glaucon's brother replied, Certainly, I expect that this inquiry will bring us nearer to that end.

Certainly, then, my dear Adimantus, said I, we must not abandon it even if it prove to be rather long.

No, we must not.

Come, then, just as if we were telling stories or fables and had ample leisure, let us educate these men in our discourse.

So we must.

What, then, is our education? Or is it hard to find a better than that which long time has discovered—which is, I suppose, gymnastics for the body, and for the soul, music?

It is.

And shall we not begin education in music earlier than in gymnastics?

Of course.

And under music you include tales, do you not?

I do.

And tales are of two species, the one true and the other false?

Yes.

And education must make use of both, but first of the false?

I don't understand your meaning.

Don't you understand, I said, that we begin by telling children fables, and the fable is, taken as a whole, false, but there is truth in it also? And we make use of fable with children before gymnastics.

That is so.

That, then, is what I meant by saying that we must take up music before gymnastics.

You were right, he said.

Do you not know, then, that the beginning in every task is the chief thing, especially for any creature that is young and tender? For it is then that it is best molded and takes the impression that one wishes to stamp upon it.

Quite so.

Shall we, then, thus lightly suffer our children to listen to any chance stories fashioned by any chance teachers and so to take into their minds opinions for the most part contrary to those that we shall think it desirable for them to hold when they are grown up?

By no manner of means will we allow it.

We must begin, then, it seems, by a censorship over our storymakers, and what they do well we must pass and what not, reject. And the stories on the accepted list we will induce nurses and mothers to tell to the children and so shape their souls by these stories far rather than their bodies by their hands. But most of the stories they now tell we must reject.

What sort of stories? he said.

The example of the greater stories, I said, will show us the lesser also. For surely the pattern must be the same, and the greater and the less must have a like tendency. Don't you think so?

I do, he said, but I don't apprehend which you mean by the greater, either.

Those, I said, that Hesiod and Homer and the other poets related to us. These, methinks, composed false stories which they told and still tell to mankind.

Of what sort? he said. And with what in them do you find fault?

With that, I said, which one ought first and chiefly to blame, especially if the lie is not a pretty one.

What is that?

When anyone images badly in his speech the true nature of gods and heroes, like a painter whose portraits bear no resemblance to his models.

It is certainly right to condemn things like that, he said, but just what do we mean and what particular things?

There is, first of all, I said, the greatest lie about the things of greatest concernment, which was no pretty invention of him who told how Uranus did what Hesiod says he did to Cronus, and how Cronus in turn took his revenge, and then there are the doings and sufferings of Cronus at the hands of his son. Even if they were true I should not think that they ought to be thus lightly told to thoughtless young persons. But the best way would be to bury them in silence, and if there were some necessity for relating them, only a very small audience should be admitted under pledge of secrecy and after sacrificing, not a pig, but some huge and unprocurable victim, to the end that as few as possible should have heard these tales.

Why, yes, said he, such stories are hard sayings.

Yes, and they are not to be told, Adimantus, in our city, nor is it to be said in the hearing of a young man that in doing the utmost wrong he would do nothing to surprise anybody, nor again in punishing his father's wrongdoings to the limit, but would only be following the example of the first and greatest of the gods.

No, by heaven, said he, I do not myself think that they are fit to be told.

. Neither must we admit at all, said I, that gods war with gods and plot against one another and contend—for it is not true either—if we wish our further guardians to deem nothing more shameful than lightly to fall out with one another. Still less must we make battles of gods and giants the subject for them of stories and embroideries, and other enmities many and manifold of gods and heroes toward their kith and kin. But if there is any likelihood of our persuading them that no citizen ever quarreled with his fellow citizen and that the very idea of it is an impiety, that is the sort of thing that ought rather to be said by their elders, men and women, to children from the beginning and as they grow older, and we must compel the poets to keep close to this in their compositions. But Hera's fetterings by her son and the hurling out of heaven of Hephaestus by his father when he was trying to save his mother from a beating, and the battles of the gods in Homer's verse are things that we must not admit into our city either wrought in allegory or without allegory. For the young are not able to distinguish what is and what is not allegory, but whatever opinions are taken into the mind at that age are wont to prove indelible and unalterable. For which reason, maybe, we should do our utmost that the first stories that they hear should be so composed as to bring the fairest lessons of virtue to their ears.

Yes, that is reasonable, he said, but if again someone should ask us to be specific and say what these compositions may be and what are the tales, what could we name?

And I replied, Adimantus, we are not poets, you and I at present, but founders of a state. And to founders it pertains to know the patterns on which poets must compose their fables and from which their poems must not be allowed to deviate, but the founders are not required themselves to compose fables.

*   *   *

. . . . [i]s there any science in the city just founded by us residing in any of its citizens which does not take counsel about some particular thing in the city but about the city as a whole and the betterment of its relations with itself and other states?

Why, yes, there is.

What is it, said I, and in whom is it found?

It is the science of guardianship or government and it is to be found in those rulers to whom we just now gave the name of guardians in the full sense of the word.

And what term then do you apply to the city because of this knowledge?

Well-advised, he said, and truly wise.

Which class, then, said I, do you suppose will be the more numerous in our city, the smiths or these true guardians?

The smiths, by far, he said.

And would not these rulers be the smallest of all the groups of those who possess special knowledge and receive distinctive appellations?

By far.

Then it is by virtue of its smallest class and minutest part of itself, and the wisdom that resides therein, in the part which takes the lead and rules, that a city established on principles of nature would be wise as a whole. And as it appears these are by nature the fewest, the class to which it pertains to partake of the knowledge which alone of all forms of knowledge deserves the name of wisdom.

Most true, he said.

This one of our four, then, we have, I know not how, discovered, the thing itself and its place in the state.

I certainly think, said he, that it has been discovered sufficiently.

But again there is no difficulty in seeing bravery itself and the part of the city in which it resides for which the city is called brave.

How so?

Who, said I, in calling a city cowardly or brave would fix his eyes on any other part of it than that which defends it and wages war in its behalf?

No one at all, he said.

For the reason, I take it, said I, that the cowardice or the bravery of the other inhabitants does not determine for it the one quality or the other.

It does not.

Bravery too, then, belongs to a city by virtue of a part of itself owing to its possession in that part of a quality that under all conditions will preserve the conviction that things to be feared are precisely those which and such as the lawgiver inculcated in their education. Is not that what you call bravery?

I don't altogether understand what you said, he replied, but say it again.

A kind of conservation, I said, is what I mean by bravery.

What sort of a conservation?

The conservation of the conviction which the law has created by education about fearful things—what and what sort of things are to be feared. And by the phrase 'under all conditions' I mean that the brave man preserves it both in pain and pleasures and in desires and fears and does not expel it from his soul. And I may illustrate it by a similitude if you please.

I do.

You are aware that dyers when they wish to dye wool so as to hold the purple hue begin by selecting from the many colors there be the one nature of the white and then give it a careful preparatory treatment so that it will take the hue in the best way, and after the treatment, then and then only, dip it in the dye. And things that are dyed by this process become fast-colored and washing either with or without lyes cannot take away the sheen of their hues. But otherwise you know what happens to them, whether anyone dips other colors or even these without the preparatory treatment.

I know, he said, that they present a ridiculous and washed-out appearance.

By this analogy, then, said I, you must conceive what we too to the best of our ability were doing when we selected our soldiers and educated them in music and exercises of the body. The sole aim of our contrivance was that they should be convinced and receive our laws like a dye as it were, so that their belief and faith might be fast-colored about both the things that are to be feared and all other things because of the fitness of their nature and nurture, and that so their dyes might not be washed out by those lyes that have such dread power to scour our faiths away, pleasure more potent than any detergent or abstergent to accomplish this, and pain and fear, and desire more sure than any lye. This power in the soul, then, this unfailing conservation of right and lawful belief about things to be and not to be feared is what I call and would assume to be courage, unless you have something different to say.

No, nothing, said he, for I presume that you consider mere right opinion about the same matters not produced by education, that which may manifest itself in a beast or a slave, to have little or nothing to do with law and that you would call it by another name than courage.

That is most true, said I.

Well then, he said, I accept this as bravery.

Do so, said I, and you will be right, with the reservation that it is the courage of a citizen. Some other time, if it please you, we will discuss it more fully. At present we were not seeking this but justice, and for the purpose of that inquiry I believe we have done enough.

You are quite right, he said.

Two things still remain, said I, to make out in our city, soberness and the object of the whole inquiry, justice.

Quite so.

If there were only some way to discover justice so that we need not further concern ourselves about soberness.

Well, I, for my part, he said, neither know of any such way nor would I wish justice to be discovered first if that means that we are not to go on to the consideration of soberness. But if you desire to please me, consider this before that.

It would certainly be very wrong of me not to desire it, said I.

Go on with the inquiry then, he said.

I must go on, I replied, and viewed from here it bears more likeness to a kind of concord and harmony than the other virtues did.

How so?

Soberness is a kind of beautiful order and a continence of certain pleasure and appetites, as they say, using the phrase 'master of himself' I know not how, and there are other similar expressions that as it were point us to the same trail. Is that not so?

Most certainly.

Now the phrase 'master of himself' is an absurdity, is it not? For he who is master of himself would also be subject to himself, and he who is subject to himself would be master. For the same person is spoken of in all these expressions.

Of course.

But, said I, the intended meaning of this way of speaking appears to me to be that the soul of a man within him has a better part and a worse part, and the expression self-mastery means the control of the worse by the naturally better part. It is, at any rate, a term of praise. But when, because of bad breeding or some association, the better part, which is the smaller, is dominated by the multitude of the worse, I think that our speech censures this as a reproach, and calls the man in this plight unself-controlled and licentious.

That seems likely, he said.

Turn your eyes now upon our new city, said I, and you will find one of these conditions existent in it. For you will say that it is justly spoken of as master of itself if that in which the superior rules the inferior is to be called sober and self-mastered.

I do turn my eyes upon it, he said, and it is as you say.

And again, the mob of motley appetites and pleasures and pains one would find chiefly in children and women and slaves and in the base rabble of those who are free men in name.

By all means.

But the simple and moderate appetites which with the aid of reason and right opinion are guided by consideration you will find in few and those the best born and best education.

True, he said.

And do you not find this too in your city and a domination there of the desires in the multitude and the rabble by the desires and the wisdom that dwell in the minority of the better sort?

I do, he said.

If, then, there is any city that deserves to be described as master of its pleasures and desires and self-mastered, this one merits that designation.

Most assuredly, he said.

And is it not also to be called sober in all these respects?

Indeed it is, he said.

And yet again, if there is any city in which the rulers and the ruled are of one mind as to who ought to rule, that condition will be found in this. Don't you think so?

I most emphatically do, he said.

In which class of the citizens, then, will you say that the virtue of soberness has its seat when this is their condition? In the rulers or in the ruled?

In both, I suppose, he said.

Do you see then, said I, that our intuition was not a bad one just now that discerned a likeness between soberness and a kind of harmony?

Why so?

Because its operation is unlike that of courage and wisdom, which residing in separate parts respectively made the city, the one wise and the other brave. That is not the way of soberness, but it extends literally through the entire gamut throughout, bringing about the unison in the same chant of the strongest, the weakest, and the intermediate, whether in wisdom or, if you please, in strength, or for that matter in numbers, wealth, or any similar criterion. So that we should be quite right in affirming this unanimity to be soberness, the concord of the naturally superior and inferior as to which ought to rule in both the state and the individual.

I entirely concur, he said.

Very well, said I, we have made out these three forms in our city to the best of our present judgment. What can be the remaining form that would give the city still another virtue? For it is obvious that the remainder is justice.

Obvious.

Now then, Glaucon, is the time for us like huntsmen to surround the covert and keep close watch that justice may not slip through and get away from us and vanish from our sight. It plainly must be somewhere hereable. Keep your eyes open then and do your best to descry it. You may see it before I do and point it out to me.

Would that I could, he said, but I think rather that if you find in me one who can follow you and discern what you point out to him you will be making a very fair use of me.

Pray for success then, said I, and follow along with me.

That I will do, only lead on, he said.

And truly, said I, it appears to be an inaccessible place, lying in deep shadows.

It certainly is a dark covert, not easy to beat up.

But all the same, on we must go.

Yes, on.

And I caught view and gave a halloo and said, Glaucon, I think we have found its trail and I don't believe it will get away from us.

I am glad to hear that, said he.

Truly, said I, we were slackers indeed.

How so?

Why, all the time, bless your heart, the thing apparently was tumbling about our feet from the start and yet we couldn't see it, but were most ludicrous, like people who sometimes hunt for what they hold in their hands. So we did not turn our eyes upon it, but looked off into the distance, which was perhaps the reason it escaped us.

What do you mean? he said.

This, I replied, that it seems to me that though we were speaking of it and hearing about it all the time we did not understand ourselves or realize that we were speaking of it in a sense.

That is a tedious prologue, he said, for an eager listener.

Listen then, said I, and learn if there is anything in what I say. For what we laid down in the beginning as a universal requirement when we were founding our city, this I think, or some form of this, is justice. And what we did lay down, and often said, if you recall, was that each one man must perform one social service in the state for which his nature was best adapted.

Yes, we said that.

And again, that to do one's own business and not to be a busybody is justice is a saying that we have heard from many and have very often repeated ourselves.

We have.

This, then, I said, my friend, if taken in a certain sense appears to be justice, this principle of doing one's own business. Do you know whence I infer this?

No, but tell me, he said.

I think that this is the remaining virtue in the state after our consideration of soberness, courage, and intelligence, a quality which made it possible for them all to grow up in the body politic and which when they have sprung up preserves them as long as it is present. And I hardly need to remind you that we said that justice would be the residue after we had found the other three.

That is an unavoidable conclusion, he said.

But moreover, said I, if we were required to decide what it is whose indwelling presence will contribute most to making our city good, it would be a difficult decision whether it was the unanimity of rulers and ruled or the conservation in the minds of the soldiers of the convictions produced by law as to what things are or are not to be feared, or the watchful intelligence that resides in the guardians, or whether this is the chief cause of its goodness, the principle embodied in child, woman, slave, free, artisan, ruler, and ruled, that each performed his one task as one man and was not a versatile busybody.

Hard to decide indeed, he said.

A thing, then, that in its contribution to the excellence of a state vies with the rivals its wisdom, its soberness, its bravery, is this principle of everyone in it doing his own task.

It is indeed, he said.

And is not justice the name you would have to give to the principle that rivals these as conducting to the virtue of a state?

By all means.

Consider it in this wise too, if so you will be convinced. Will you not assign the conduct of lawsuits in your state to the rulers?

Of course.

Will not this be the chief aim of their decisions, that no one shall have what belongs to others or be deprived of his own?

Nothing else but this.

On the assumption that this is just?

Yes.

From this point of view too, then, the having and doing of one's own and what belongs to oneself would admittedly be justice.

That is so.

Consider now whether you agree with me. A carpenter undertaking to do the work of a cobbler or a cobbler of a carpenter or their interchange of one another's tools or honors or even the attempt of the same man to do both—the confounding of all other functions would not, think you, greatly injure a state, would it?

Not much, he said.

But when, I fancy, one who is by nature an artisan or some kind of money-maker tempted and incited by wealth or command of votes or bodily strength or some similar advantage tries to enter into the class of the soldiers or one of the soldiers into the class of counselors and guardians, for which he is not fitted, and these interchange their tools and their honors or when the same man undertakes all these functions at once, then, I take it, you too believe that this kind of substitution and meddlesomeness is the ruin of a state.

By all means.

The interference with one another's business, then, of three existent classes, and the substitution of the one for the other, is the greatest injury to a state and would most rightly be designated as the thing which chiefly works it harm.

Precisely so.

And the thing that works the greatest harm to one's own state, will you not pronounce to be injustice?

Of course.

This, then, is injustice. Again, let us put it in this way. The proper functioning of the money-makers, the helpers, and the guardians, each doing his own work in the state, being the reverse of that just described, would be justice and would render the city just.

I think the case is thus and no otherwise, said he.

Let us not yet affirm it quite fixedly, I said, but if this form, when applied to the individual man, is accepted there also as a definition of justice, we will then concede the point—for what else will there be to say? But if not, then we will look for something else. But now let us work out the inquiry in which we supposed that, if we found some larger thing that contained justice and viewed it there, we should more easily discover its nature in the individual man. And we agreed that this larger thing is the city, and so we constructed the best city in our power, well knowing that in the good city it would of course be found. What, then, we thought we saw there we must refer back to the individual and, if it is confirmed, all will be well. But if something different manifests itself in the individual, we will return again to the state and test it there and it may be that, by examining them side by side and rubbing them against one another, as it were from the fire sticks we may cause the spark of justice to flash forth, and when it is thus revealed confirm it in our own minds.

Well, he said, that seems a sound method and that is what we must do.

Then, said I, if you call a thing by the same name whether it is big or little, is it unlike in the way in which it is called the same or like?

Like, he said.

Then a just man too will not differ at all from a just city in respect of the very form of justice, but will be like it.

Yes, like.

But now the city was thought to be just because three natural kinds existing in it performed each its own function, and again it was sober, brave, and wise because of certain other affections and habits of these three kinds.

True, he said.

Then, my friend, we shall thus expect the individual also to have these same forms in his soul, and by reason of identical affections of these with those in the city to receive properly the same appellations.

* * *

. . . . [a]fter the completion of the male drama we should in turn go through with the female, especially since you are so urgent.

For men, then, born and bred as we described, there is in my opinion no other right possession and use of children and women than that which accords with the start we gave them. Our endeavor, I believe, was to establish these men in our discourse as the guardians of a flock?

Yes.

Let us preserve the analogy, then, and assign them a generation and breeding answering to it, and see if it suits us or not.

In what way? he said.

In this. Do we expect the females of watchdogs to join in guarding what the males guard and to hunt with them and share all their pursuits or do we expect the females to stay indoors as being incapacitated by the bearing and the breeding of the whelps while the males toil and have all the care of the flock?

They have all things in common, he replied, except that we treat the females as weaker and the males as stronger.

Is it possible, then, said I, to employ any creature for the same ends as another if you do not assign it the same nurture and education?

It is not possible.

If, then, we are to use the women for the same things as the men, we must also teach them the same things.

Yes.

Now music together with gymnastics was the training we gave the men.

Yes.

Then we must assign these two arts to the women also and the offices of war and employ them in the same way.

It would seem likely from what you say, he replied.

Perhaps, then, said I, the contrast with present custom would make much in our proposals look ridiculous if our words are to be realized in fact.

Yes, indeed, he said.

What then, said I, is the funniest thing you note in them? Is it not obviously the women exercising unclad in the palaestra together with the men, not only the young, but even the older, like old men in gymnasiums, when, though wrinkled and unpleasant to look at, they still persist in exercising?

Yes, on my word, he replied, it would seem ridiculous under present conditions.

Then, said I, since we have set out to speak our minds, we must not fear all the gibes with which the wits would greet so great a revolution, and the sort of things they would say about gymnastics and culture, and most of all about the bearing of arms and the bestriding of horses.

You're right, he said.

But since we have begun we must go forward to the rough part of our law, after begging these fellows not to mind their own business but to be serious, and reminding them that it is not long since the Greeks thought it disgraceful and ridiculous, as most of the barbarians do now, for men to be seen naked. And when the practice of athletics began, first with the Cretans and then with the Lacedaemonians, it was open to the wits of that time to make fun of these practices, don't you think so?

I do.

But when, I take it, experience showed that it is better to strip than to veil all things of this sort, then the laughter of the eyes faded away before that which reason revealed to be best, and this made it plain that he talks idly who deems anything else ridiculous but evil, and who tries to raise a laugh by looking to any other pattern of absurdity than that of folly and wrong or sets up any other standard of the beautiful as a mark for his seriousness than the good.

Most assuredly, said he.

Then is not the first thing that we have to agree upon with regard to these proposals whether they are possible or not? And we must throw open the debate to anyone who wishes either in jest or in earnest to raise the question whether female human nature is capable of sharing with the male all tasks or none at all, or some but not others, and under which of these heads this business of war falls. Would not this be that best beginning which would naturally and proverbially lead to the best end?

Far the best, he said.

Shall we then conduct the debate with ourselves in behalf of those others so that the case of the other side may not be taken defenseless and go by default?

Nothing hinders, he said.

Shall we say then in their behalf, There is no need, Socrates and Glaucon, of others disputing against you, for you yourselves at the beginning of the foundation of your city agreed that each one ought to mind as his own business the one thing for which he was fitted by nature? We did so agree, I think, certainly! Can it be denied then that there is by nature a great difference between men and women? Surely there is. Is it not fitting, then, that a different function should be appointed for each corresponding to this difference of nature? Certainly. How, then, can you deny that you are mistaken and in contradiction with yourselves when you turn around and affirm that the men and the women ought to do the same thing, though their natures are so far apart? Can you surprise me with an answer to that question?

Not easily on this sudden challenge, he replied, but I will and do beg you to lend your voice to the plea in our behalf, whatever it may be.

These and many similar difficulties, Glaucon, said I, I foresaw and feared, and so shrank from touching on the law concerning the getting and breeding of women and children.

It does not seem an easy thing, by heaven, he said, no, by heaven.

No, it is not, said I, but the fact is that whether one tumbles into a little diving pool or plump into the great sea he swims all the same.

By all means.

Then we, too, must swim and try to escape out of the sea of argument in the hope that either some dolphin will take us on its back or some other desperate rescue.

So it seems, he said.

Come then, consider, said I, if we can find a way out. We did agree that different natures should have differing pursuits and that the natures of men and women differ. And yet now we affirm that these differing natures should have the same pursuits. That is the indictment?

It is.

What a grand thing, Glaucon, said I, is the power of the art of contradiction!

Why so?

Because, said I, many appear to me to fall into it even against their wills, and to suppose that they are not wrangling but arguing, owing to their inability to apply the proper divisions and distinctions to the subject under consideration. They pursue purely verbal oppositions, practicing eristic, not dialectic on one another.

Yes, this does happen to many, he said, but does this observation apply to us too at present?

Absolutely, said I. At any rate I am afraid that we are unawares slipping into contentiousness.

In what way?

The principle that natures not the same ought not to share in the same pursuits we are following up most manfully and eristically in the literal and verbal sense, but we did not delay to consider at all what particular kind of diversity and identity of nature we had in mind and with reference to what we were trying to define it when we assigned different pursuits to different natures and the same to the same.

No, we didn't consider that, he said.

Wherefore, by the same token, I said, we might ask ourselves whether the natures of bald and long-haired men are the same and not, rather, the contrary. And, after agreeing that they were opposed, we might, if the bald cobbled, forbid the long-haired to do so, or vice versa.

That would be ridiculous, he said.

Would it be so, said I, for any other reason than that we did not then posit likeness and difference of nature in any and every sense, but were paying heed solely to the kind of diversity and homogeneity that was pertinent to the pursuits themselves? We meant, for example, that a man and a woman who have a physician's mind have the same nature. Don't you think so?

I do.

But that a man physician and a man carpenter have different natures?

Certainly, I suppose.

Similarly, then, said I, if it appears that the male and female sex have distinct qualifications for any arts or pursuits, we shall affirm that they ought to be assigned respectively to each. But if it appears that they differ only in just this respect that the female bears and the male begets, we shall say that no proof has yet been produced that the woman differs from the man for our purposes, but we shall continue to think that our guardians and their wives ought to follow the same pursuits.

And rightly, said he.

Then, is it not the next thing to bid our opponent tell us precisely for what art or pursuit concerned with the conduct of a state the woman's nature differs from the man's?

That would be at any rate fair.

Perhaps, then, someone else, too, might say what you were saying a while ago, that it is not easy to find a satisfactory answer on a sudden, but that with time for reflection there is no difficulty.

He might say that.

Shall we, then, beg the raiser of such objections to follow us, if we may perhaps prove able to make it plain to him that there is no pursuit connected with the administration of a state that is peculiar to woman?

By all means.

Come then, we shall say to him, answer our question. Was this the basis of your distinction between the man naturally gifted for anything and the one not so gifted—that the one learned easily, the other with difficulty, that the one with slight instruction could discover much for himself in the matter studied, but the other, after much instruction and drill, could not even remember what he had learned, and that the bodily faculties of the one adequately served his mind, while, for the other, the body was a hindrance? Were there any other points than these by which you distinguish the well-endowed man in every subject and the poorly endowed?

No one, said he, will be able to name any others.

Do you know, then, of anything practiced by mankind in which the masculine sex does not surpass the female on all these points? Must we make a long story of it by alleging weaving and the watching of pancakes and the boiling pot, whereon the sex plumes itself and wherein its defeat will expose it to most laughter?

You are right, he said, that the one sex is far surpassed by the other in everything, one may say. Many women, it is true, are better than many men in many things, but broadly speaking, it is as you say.

Then there is no pursuit of the administrators of a state that belongs to a woman because she is a woman or to a man because he is a man. But the natural capacities are distributed alike among both creatures, and women naturally share in all pursuits and men in all—yet for all the woman is weaker than the man.

Assuredly.

Shall we, then, assign them all to men and nothing to women?

How could we?

We shall rather, I take it, say that one woman has the nature of a physician and another not, and one is by nature musical, and another unmusical?

Surely.

Can we, then, deny that one woman is naturally athletic and warlike and another unwarlike and averse to gymnastics?

I think not.

And again, one a lover, another a hater, of wisdom? And one high-spirited, and the other lacking spirit?

That also is true.

Then it is likewise true that one woman has the qualities of a guardian and another not. Were not these the natural qualities of the men also whom we selected for guardians?

They were.

The women and the men, then, have the same nature in respect to the guardianship of the state, save in so far as the one is weaker, the other stronger.

Apparently.

Women of this kind, then, must be selected to cohabit with men of this kind and to serve with them as guardians since they are capable of it and akin by nature.

By all means.

And to the same natures must we not assign the same pursuits?

The same.

We come round, then, to our previous statement, and agree that it does not run counter to nature to assign music and gymnastics to the wives of the guardians.

By all means.

Our legislation, then, was not impracticable or utopian, since the law we proposed accorded with nature. Rather, the other way of doing things, prevalent today, proves, as it seems, unnatural.

Apparently.

The object of our inquiry was the possibility and the desirability of what we were proposing?

It was.

That it is possible has been admitted.

Yes.

The next point to be agreed upon is that it is the best way.

Obviously.

For the production of a female guardian, then, our education will not be one thing for men and another for women, especially since the nature which we hand over to it is the same.

There will be no difference.

How are you minded, now, in this matter?

In what?

In the matter of supposing some men to be better and some worse, or do you think them all alike?

By no means.

In the city, then, that we are founding, which do you think will prove the better men, the guardians receiving the education which we have described or the cobblers educated by the art of cobbling?

An absurd question, he said.

I understand, said I, and are not these the best of all the citizens?

By far.

And will not these women be the best of all the women?

They, too, by far.

Is there anything better for a state than the generation in it of the best possible women and men?

There is not.

And this, music and gymnastics applied as we described will effect.

Surely.

Then the institution we proposed is not only possible but the best for the state.

That is so.

The women of the guardians, then, must strip, since they will be clothed with virtue as a garment, and must take their part with the men in war and the other duties of civic guardianship and have no other occupation. But in these very duties lighter tasks must be assigned to the women than to the men because of their weakness as a class. But the man who ridicules unclad women, exercising because it is best that they should, 'plucks the unripe fruit' of laughter and does not know, it appears, the end of his laughter nor what he would be at. For the fairest thing that is said or even will be said is this, that the helpful is fair and the harmful foul.

Assuredly.

In this matter, then, of the regulation of women, we may say that we have surmounted one of the waves of our paradox and have not been quite swept away by it in ordaining that our guardians and female guardians must have all pursuits in common, but that in some sort the argument concurs with itself in the assurance that what it proposes is both possible and beneficial.

It is no slight wave that you are thus escaping.

You will not think it a great one, I said, when you have seen the one that follows.

Say on then and show me, said he.

This, said I, and all that precedes has for its sequel, in my opinion, the following law.

What?

That these women shall all be common to all these men, and that none shall cohabit with any privately, and that the children shall be common, and that no parent shall know its own offspring nor any child its parent.

This is a far bigger paradox than the other, and provokes more distrust as to its possibility and its utility.

I presume, said I, that there would be no debate about its utility, no denial that the community of women and children would be the greatest good, supposing it possible. But I take it that its possibility or the contrary would be the chief topic of contention.

Both, he said, would be right sharply debated.

You mean, said I, that I have to meet a coalition of arguments. But I expected to escape from one of them, and that if you agreed that the thing was beneficial, it would remain for me to speak only of its feasibility.

You have not escaped detection, he said, in your attempted flight, but you must render an account of both.

I must pay the penalty, I said, yet do me this much grace. Permit me to take a holiday, just as men of lazy minds are wont to feast themselves on their own thoughts when they walk alone. Such persons, without waiting to discover how their desires may be realized, dismiss that topic to save themselves the labor of deliberating about possibilities and impossibilities, assume their wish fulfilled, and proceed to work out the details in imagination, and take pleasure in portraying what they will do when it is realized, thus making still more idle a mind that is idle without that. I too now succumb to this weakness and desire to postpone and examine later the question of feasibility, but will at present assume that, and will, with your permission, inquire how the rulers will work out the details in practice, and try to show that nothing could be more beneficial to the state and its guardians than the effective operation of our plan. This is what I would try to consider first together with you, and thereafter the other topic, if you allow it.

I do allow it, he said. Proceed with the inquiry.

I think then, said I, that the rulers, if they are to deserve that name, and their helpers likewise, will, the one, be willing to accept orders, and the other, to give them, in some things obeying our laws, and imitating them in others which we leave to their discretion.

Presumably.

You, then, the lawgiver, I said, have picked these men and similarly will select to give over to them women as nearly as possible of the same nature. And they, having houses and meals in common, and no private possessions of that kind, will dwell together, and being commingled in gymnastics and in all their life and education, will be conducted by innate necessity to sexual union. Is not what I say a necessary consequence?

Not by the necessities of geometry, he said, but by those of love, which are perhaps keener and more potent than the other to persuade and constrain the multitude.

They are, indeed, I said. But next, Glaucon, disorder and promiscuity in these unions or in anything else they do would be an unhallowed thing in a happy state and the rulers will not suffer it.

It would not be right, he said.

Obviously, then, we must arrange marriages, sacramental so far as may be. And the most sacred marriages would be those that were most beneficial.

By all means.

How, then, would the greatest benefit result? Tell me this, Glaucon. I see that you have in your house hunting dogs and a number of pedigreed cocks. Have you ever considered something about their unions and procreations?

What? he said.

In the first place, I said, among these themselves, although they are a select breed, do not some prove better than the rest?

They do.

Do you then breed from all indiscriminately, or are you careful to breed from the best?

From the best.

And, again, do you breed from the youngest or the oldest, or, so far as may be, from those in their prime?

From those in their prime.

And if they are not thus bred, you expect, do you not, that your birds' breed and hounds will greatly degenerate?

I do, he said.

And what of horses and other animals? I said. Is it otherwise with them?

It would be strange if it were, said he.

Gracious, said I, dear friend, how imperative, then, is our need of the highest skill in our rulers, if the principle holds also for mankind.

Well, it does, he said, but what of it?

This, said I, that they will have to employ many of those drugs of which we were speaking. We thought that an inferior physician sufficed for bodies that do not need drugs but yield to diet and regimen. But when it is necessary to prescribe drugs we know that a more enterprising and venturesome physician is required.

True, but what is the pertinency?

This, said I. It seems likely that our rulers will have to make considerable use of falsehood and deception for the benefit of their subjects. We said, I believe, that the use of that sort of thing was in the category of medicine.

And that was right, he said.

In our marriages, then, and the procreation of children, it seems there will be no slight need of this kind of 'right.'

How so?

It follows from our former admissions, I said, that the best men must cohabit with the best women in as many cases as possible and the worst with the worst in the fewest, and that the offspring of the one must be reared and that of the other not, if the flock is to be as perfect as possible. And the way in which all this is brought to pass must be unknown to any but the rulers, if, again, the herd of guardians is to be as free as possible from dissension.

Most true, he said.

We shall, then, have to ordain certain festivals and sacrifices, in which we shall bring together the brides and the bridegrooms, and our poets must compose hymns suitable to the marriages that then take place. But the number of the marriages we will leave to the discretion of the rulers, that they may keep the number of the citizens as nearly as may be the same, taking into account wars and diseases and all such considerations, and that, so far as possible, our city may not grow too great or too small.

Right, he said.

Certain ingenious lots, then, I suppose, must be devised so that the inferior man at each conjugation may blame chance and not the rulers.

Yes, indeed, he said.

And on the young men, surely, who excel in war and other pursuits we must bestow honors and prizes, and, in particular, the opportunity of more frequent intercourse with the women, which will at the same time be a plausible pretext for having them beget as many of the children as possible.

Right.

And the children thus born will be taken over by the officials appointed for this, men or women or both, since, I take it, the official posts too are common to women and men.

Yes.

The offspring of the good, I suppose, they will take to the pen or crèche, to certain nurses who live apart in a quarter of the city, but the offspring of the inferior, and any of those of the other sort who are born defective, they will properly dispose of in secret, so that no one will know what has become of them.

That is the condition, he said, of preserving the purity of the guardians' breed.

They will also supervise the nursing of the children, conducting the mothers to the pen when their breasts are full, but employing every device to prevent anyone from recognizing her own infant. And they will provide others who have milk if the mothers are insufficient. But they will take care that the mothers themselves shall not suckle too long, and the trouble of wakeful nights and similar burdens they will devolve upon the nurses, wet and dry.

You are making maternity a soft job for the women of the guardians.

It ought to be, said I, but let us pursue our design. We said that the offspring should come from parents in their prime.

True.

Do you agree that the period of the prime may be fairly estimated at twenty years for a woman and thirty for a man?

How do you reckon it? he said.

The women, I said, beginning at the age of twenty, shall bear for the state to the age of forty, and the man shall beget for the state from the time he passes his prime in swiftness in running to the age of fifty-five.

That is, he said, the maturity and prime for both of body and mind.

Then, if anyone older or younger than the prescribed age meddles with procreation for the state, we shall say that his error is an impiety and an injustice, since he is begetting for the city a child whose birth, if it escapes discovery, will not be attended by the sacrifices and the prayers which the priests and priestesses and the entire city prefer at the ceremonial marriages, that ever better offspring may spring from good sires and from fathers helpful to the state sons more helpful still. But this child will be born in darkness and conceived in foul incontinence.

Right, he said.

And the same rule will apply, I said, if any of those still within the age of procreation goes in to a woman of that age with whom the ruler has not paired him. We shall say that he is imposing on the state a baseborn, uncertified, and unhallowed child.

Most rightly, he said.

But when, I take it, the men and the women have passed the age of lawful procreation, we shall leave the men free to form such relations with whomsoever they please, except daughter and mother and their direct descendants and ascendants, and likewise the women, save with son and father, and so on, first admonishing them preferably not even to bring to light anything whatever thus conceived, but if they are unable to prevent a birth to dispose of it on the understanding that we cannot rear such an offspring.

All that sounds reasonable, he said, but how are they to distinguish one another's fathers and daughters, and the other degrees of kin that you have just mentioned?

They won't, said I, except that a man will call all male offspring born in the tenth and in the seventh month after he became a bridegroom his sons, and all female, daughters, and they will call him father. And, similarly, he will call their offspring his grandchildren and they will call his group grandfathers and grandmothers. And all children born in the period in which their fathers and mothers were procreating will regard one another as brothers and sisters. This will suffice for the prohibitions of intercourse of which we just now spoke. But the law will allow brothers and sisters to cohabit if the lot so falls out and the Delphic oracle approves.

Quite right, said he.

This, then, Glaucon, is the manner of the community of wives and children among the guardians. That it is consistent with the rest of our polity and by far the best way is the next point that we must get confirmed by the argument. Is not that so?

It is, indeed, he said.

Is not the logical first step toward such an agreement to ask ourselves what we could name as the greatest good for the constitution of a state and the proper aim of a lawgiver in his legislation, and what would be the greatest evil, and then to consider whether the proposals we have just set forth fit into the footprints of the good and do not suit those of the evil?

By all means, he said.

Do we know of any greater evil for a state than the thing that distracts it and makes it many instead of one, or a greater good than that which binds it together and makes it one?

We do not.

Is not, then, the community of pleasure and pain the tie that binds, when, so far as may be, all the citizens rejoice and grieve alike at the same births and deaths?

By all means, he said.

But the individualization of these feelings is a dissolvent, when some grieve exceedingly and others rejoice at the same happenings to the city and its inhabitants?

Of course.

And the chief cause of this is when the citizens do not utter in unison such words as 'mine' and 'not mine,' and similarly with regard to the word 'alien'?

Precisely so.

That city, then, is best ordered in which the greatest number use the expression 'mine' and 'not mine' of the same things in the same way.

Much the best.

And the city whose state is most like that of an individual man. For example, if the finger of one of us is wounded, the entire community of bodily connections stretching to the soul for 'integration' with the dominant part is made aware, and all of it feels the pain as a whole, though it is a part that suffers, and that is how we come to say that the man has a pain in his finger. And for any other member of the man the same statement holds, alike for a part that labors in pain or is eased by pleasure.

The same, he said, and, to return to your question, the best-governed state most nearly resembles such an organism.

That is the kind of a state, then, I presume, that, when anyone of the citizens suffers aught of good or evil, will be most likely to speak of the part that suffers as its own and will share the pleasure or the pain as a whole.

Inevitably, he said, if it is well governed.

* * *

Next, said I, compare our nature in respect of education and its lack to such an experience as this. Picture men dwelling in a sort of subterranean cavern with a long entrance open to the light on its entire width. Conceive them as having their legs and necks fettered from childhood, so that they remain in the same spot, able to look forward only, and prevented by the fetters from turning their heads. Picture further the light from a fire burning higher up and at a distance behind them, and between the fire and the prisoners and above them a road along which a low wall has been built, as the exhibitors of puppet shows have partitions before the men themselves, above which they show the puppets.

All that I see, he said.

See also, then, men carrying past the wall implements of all kinds that rise above the wall, and human images and shapes of animals as well, wrought in stone and wood and every material, some of these bearers presumably speaking and others silent.

A strange image you speak of, he said, and strange prisoners.

Like to us, I said. For, to begin with, tell me do you think that these men would have seen anything of themselves or of one another except the shadows cast from the fire on the wall of the cave that fronted them?

How could they, he said, if they were compelled to hold their heads unmoved through life?

And again, would not the same be true of the objects carried past them?

Surely.

If then they were able to talk to one another, do you not think that they would suppose that in naming the things that they saw they were naming the passing objects?

Necessarily.

And if their prison had an echo from the wall opposite them, when one of the passers-by uttered a sound, do you think that they would suppose anything else than the passing shadow to be the speaker?

By Zeus, I do not, said he.

Then in every way such prisoners would deem reality to be nothing else than the shadows of the artificial objects.

Quite inevitably, he said.

Consider, then, what would be the manner of the release and healing from these bonds and this folly if in the course of nature something of this sort should happen to them. When one was freed from his fetters and compelled to stand up suddenly and turn his head around and walk and to lift up his eyes to the light, and in doing all this felt pain and, because of the dazzle and glitter of the light, was unable to discern the objects whose shadows he formerly saw, what do you suppose would be his answer if someone told him that what he had seen before was all a cheat and an illusion, but that now, being nearer to reality and turned toward more real things, he saw more truly? And if also one should point out to him each of the passing objects and constrain him by questions to say what it is, do you not think that he would be at a loss and that he would regard what he formerly saw as more real than the things now pointed out to him?

Far more real, he said.

And if he were compelled to look at the light itself, would not that pain his eyes, and would he not turn away and flee to those things which he is able to discern and regard them as in very deed more clear and exact than the objects pointed out?

It is so, he said.

And if, said I, someone should drag him thence by force up the ascent which is rough and steep, and not let him go before he had drawn him out into the light of the sun, do you not think that he would find it painful to be so haled along, and would chafe at it, and when he came out into the light, that his eyes would be filled with its beams so that he would not be able to see even one of the things that we call real?

Why, no, not immediately, he said.

Then there would be need of habituation, I take it, to enable him to see the things higher up. And at first he would most easily discern the shadows and, after that, the likenesses or reflections in water of men and other things, and later, the things themselves, and from these he would go on to contemplate the appearances in the heavens and heaven itself, more easily by night, looking at the light of the stars and the moon, than by day the sun and the sun's light.

Of course.

And so, finally, I suppose, he would be able to look upon the sun itself and see its true nature, not by reflections in water or phantasms of it in an alien setting, but in and by itself in its own place.

Necessarily, he said.

And at this point he would infer and conclude that this it is that provides the seasons and the courses of the year and presides over all things in the visible region, and is in some sort the cause of all these things that they had seen.

Obviously, he said, that would be the next step.

When then, if he recalled to mind his first habitation and what passed for wisdom there, and his fellow bondsmen, do you not think that he would count himself happy in the change and pity them?

He would indeed.

And if there had been honors and commendations among them which they bestowed on one another and prizes for the man who is quickest to make out the shadows as they pass and best able to remember their customary precedences, sequences, and coexistences, and so most successful in guessing at what was to come, do you think he would be very keen about such rewards, and that he would envy and emulate those who were honored by these prisoners and lorded it among them, or that he would feel with Homer and greatly prefer while living on earth to be serf of another, a landless man, and endure anything rather than opine with them and live that life?

Yes, he said, I think that he would choose to endure anything rather than such a life.

And consider this also, said I. If such a one should go down again and take his old place would he not get his eyes full of darkness, thus suddenly coming out of the sunlight?

He would indeed.

Now if he should be required to contend with these perpetual prisoners in 'evaluating' these shadows while his vision was still dim and before his eyes were accustomed to the dark—and this time required for habituation would not be very short—would he not provoke laughter, and would it not be said of him that he had returned from his journey aloft with his eyes ruined and that it was not worth while even to attempt the ascent? And if it were possible to lay hands on and to kill the man who tried to release them and lead them up, would they not kill him?

They certainly would, he said.

This image then, dear Glaucon, we must apply as a whole to all that has been said, likening the region revealed through sight to the habitation of the prison, and the light of the fire in it to the power of the sun. And if you assume that the ascent and the contemplation of the things above is the soul's ascension to the intelligible region, you will not miss my surmise, since that is what you desire to hear. But the gods know whether it is true. But, at any rate, my dream as it appears to me is that in the region of the known the last thing to be seen and hardly seen is the idea of good, and that when seen it must needs point us to the conclusion that this is indeed the cause for all things of all that is right and beautiful, giving birth in the visible world to light, and the author of light and itself in the intelligible world being the authentic source of truth and reason, and that anyone who is to act wisely in private or public must have caught sight of this.

I concur, he said, so far as I am able.

Come then, I said, and join me in this further thought, and do not be surprised that those who have attained to this height are not willing to occupy themselves with the affairs of men, but their souls ever feel the upward urge and the yearning for that sojourn above. For this, I take it, is likely if in this point too the likeness of our image holds.

Yes, it is likely.

And again, do you think it at all strange, said I, if a man returning from divine contemplations to the petty miseries of men cuts a sorry figure and appears most ridiculous, if, while still blinking through the gloom, and before he has become sufficiently accustomed to the environing darkness, he is compelled in courtrooms or elsewhere to contend about the shadows of justice or the images that cast the shadows and to wrangle in debate about the notions of these things in the minds of those who have never seen justice itself?

It would be by no means strange, he said.

But a sensible man, I said, would remember that there are two distinct disturbances of the eyes arising from two causes, according as the shift is from light to darkness or from darkness to light, and, believing that the same thing happens to the soul too, whenever he saw a soul perturbed and unable to discern something, he would not laugh unthinkingly, but would observe whether coming from a brighter life its vision was obscured by the unfamiliar darkness, or whether the passage from the deeper dark of ignorance into a more luminous world and the greater brightness had dazzled its vision. And so he would deem the one happy in its experience and way of life and pity the other, and if it pleased him to laugh at it, his laughter would be less laughable than that at the expense of the soul that had come down from the light above.

That is a very fair statement, he said.

Then, if this is true, our view of these matters must be this, that education is not in reality what some people proclaim it to be in their professions. What they aver is that they can put true knowledge into a soul that does not possess it, as if they were inserting vision into blind eyes.

They do indeed, he said.

But our present argument indicates, said I, that the true analogy for this indwelling power in the soul and the instrument whereby each of us apprehends is that of an eye that could not be converted to the light from the darkness except by turning the whole body. Even so this organ of knowledge must be turned around from the world of becoming together with the entire soul, like the scene-shifting periactus in the theater, until the soul is able to endure the contemplation of essence and the brightest region of being. And this, we say, is the good, do we not?

Yes.

Of this very thing, then, I said, there might be an art, an art of the speediest and most effective shifting or conversion of the soul, not an art of producing vision in it, but on the assumption that it possesses vision but does not rightly direct it and does not look where it should, an art of bringing this about.

Yes, that seems likely, he said.

Then the other so-called virtues of the soul do seem akin to those of the body. For it is true that where they do not pre-exist, they are afterward created by habit and practice. But the excellence of thought, it seems, is certainly of a more divine quality, a thing that never loses its potency, but, according to the direction of its conversion, becomes useful and beneficent, or, again, useless and harmful. Have you never observed in those who are popularly spoken of as bad, but smart men how keen is the vision of the little soul, how quick it is to discern the things that interest it, a proof that it is not a poor vision which it has, but one forcibly enlisted in the service of evil, so that the sharper its sight the more mischief it accomplishes?

I certainly have, he said.

Observe then, said I, that this part of such a soul, if it had been hammered from childhood, and had thus been struck free of the leaden weights, so to speak, of our birth and becoming, which attaching themselves to it by food and similar pleasures and gluttonies turn downward the vision of the soul—if, I say, freed from these, it had suffered a conversion toward the things that are real and true, that some faculty of the same men would have been most keen in its vision of the higher things, just as it is for the things toward which it is now turned.

It is likely, he said.

Well, then, said I, is not this also likely and a necessary consequence of what has been said, that neither could men who are uneducated and inexperienced in truth ever adequately preside over a state, nor could those who had been permitted to linger on to the end in the pursuit of culture—the one because they have no single aim and purpose in life to which all their actions, public and private, must be directed, and the others, because they will not voluntarily engage in action, believing that while still living they have been transported to the islands of the Blessed?

True, he said.

It is the duty of us, the founders, then, said I, to compel the best natures to attain the knowledge which we pronounced the greatest, and to win to the vision of the good, to scale that ascent, and when they have reached the heights and taken an adequate view, we must not allow what is now permitted.

What is that?

That they should linger there, I said, and refuse to go down again among those bondsmen and share their labors and honors, whether they are of less or of greater worth.

Do you mean to say that we must do them this wrong, and compel them to live an inferior life when the better is in their power?

You have again forgotten, my friend, said I, that the law is not concerned with the special happiness of any class in the state, but is trying to produce this condition in the city as a whole, harmonizing and adapting the citizens to one another by persuasion and compulsion, and requiring them to impart to one another any benefit which they are severally able to bestow upon the community, and that it itself creates such men in the state, not that it may allow each to take what course pleases him, but with a view to using them for the binding together of the commonwealth.

True, he said, I did forget it.

Observe, then, Glaucon, said I, that we shall not be wronging, either, the philosophers who arise among us, but that we can justify our action when we constrain them to take charge of the other citizens and be their guardians. For we will say to them that it is natural that men of similar quality who spring up in other cities should not share in the labors there. For they grow up spontaneously from no volition of the government in the several states, and it is justice that the self-grown, indebted to none for its breeding, should not be zealous either to pay to anyone the price of its nurture. But you we have engendered for yourselves and the rest of the city to be, as it were, king bees and leaders in the hive. You have received a better and more complete education than the others, and you are more capable of sharing both ways of life. Down you must go then, each in his turn, to the habitation of the others and accustom yourselves to the observation of the obscure things there. For once habituated you will discern them infinitely better than the dwellers there, and you will know what each of the 'idols' is and whereof it is a semblance, because you have seen the reality of the beautiful, the just and the good. So our city will be governed by us and you with waking minds, and not, as most cities now which are inhabited and ruled darkly as in a dream by men who fight one another for shadows and wrangle for office as if that were a great good, when the truth is that the city in which those who are to rule are least eager to hold office must needs be best administered and most free from dissension, and the state that gets the contrary type of ruler will be the opposite of this.

By all means, he said.

Will our alumni, then, disobey us when we tell them this, and will they refuse to share in the labors of state each in his turn while permitted to dwell most of the time with one another in that purer world?

Impossible, he said, for we shall be imposing just commands on men who are just. Yet they will assuredly approach office as an unavoidable necessity, and in the opposite temper from that of the present rulers in our cities.

For the fact is, dear friend, said I, if you can discover a better way of life than office holding for your future rulers, a well-governed city becomes a possibility.

For only in such a state will those rule who are really rich, not in gold, but in the wealth that makes happiness—a good and wise life. But if, being beggars and starvelings from lack of goods of their own, they turn to affairs of state thinking that it is thence that they should grasp their own good, then it is impossible. For when office and rule become the prizes of contention, such a civil and internecine strife destroys the office seekers themselves and the city as well.

Most true, he said.

Can you name any other type or ideal of life that looks with scorn on political office except the life of true philosophers? I asked.

No, by Zeus, he said.

But what we require, I said, is that those who take office should not be lovers of rule. Otherwise there will be a contest with rival lovers.

Surely.

What others, then, will you compel to undertake the guardianship of the city than those who have most intelligence of the principles that are the means of good government and who possess distinctions of another kind and a life that is preferable to the political life?

No others, he said.

* * *

We have next to consider, it seems, the origin and nature of democracy, that we may next learn the character of that type of man and range him besides the others for our judgment.

That would at least be a consistent procedure.

Then, said I, is not the transition from oligarchy to democracy effected in some such way as this—by the insatiate greed for that which it set before itself as the good, the attainment of the greatest possible wealth?

In what way?

Why, since its rulers owe their offices to their wealth, they are not willing to prohibit by law the prodigals who arise among the youth from spending and wasting their substance. Their object is, by lending money on the property of such men, and buying it in, to become still richer and more esteemed.

By all means.

And is it not at once apparent in a state that this honoring of wealth is incompatible with a sober and temperate citizenship, but that one or the other of these two ideals is inevitably neglected.

That is pretty clear, he said.

And such negligence and encouragement of licentiousness in oligarchies not infrequently has reduced to poverty men of no ignoble quality.

It surely has.

And there they sit, I fancy, within the city, furnished with stings, that is, arms, some burdened with debt, others disfranchised, others both, hating and conspiring against the acquirers of their estates and the rest of the citizens, and eager for revolution.

'Tis so.

But these money-makers with down-bend heads, pretending not even to see them, but inserting the sting of their money into any of the remainder who do not resist, and harvesting from them in interest as it were a manifold progeny of the parent sum, foster the drone and pauper element in the state.

They do indeed multiply it, he said.

And they are not willing to quench the evil as it bursts into flame either by way of a law prohibiting a man from doing as he likes with his own, or in this way, by a second law that does away with such abuses.

What law?

The law that is next best, and compels the citizens to pay heed to virtue. For if a law commanded that most voluntary contracts should be at the contractor's risk, the pursuit of wealth would be less shameless in the state and fewer of the evils of which we spoke just now would grow up there.

Much fewer, he said.

But as it is, and for all these reasons, this is the plight to which the rulers in the state reduce their subjects, and as for themselves and their offspring, do they not make the young spoiled wantons averse to toil of body and mind, and too soft to stand up against pleasure and pain, and mere idlers?

Surely.

And do they not fasten upon themselves the habit of neglect of everything except the making of money, and as complete an indifference to virtue as the paupers exhibit?

Little they care.

And when, thus conditioned, the rulers and the ruled are brought together on the march, in wayfaring, or in some other common undertaking, either a religious festival, or a campaign, or as shipmates or fellow soldiers or, for that matter, in actual battle, and observe one another, then the poor are not in the least scorned by the rich, but on the contrary, do you not suppose it often happens that when a lean, sinewy, sunburned pauper is stationed in battle beside a rich man bred in the shade, and burdened with superfluous flesh, and sees him panting and helpless— do you not suppose he will think that such fellows keep their wealth by the cowardice of the poor, and that when the latter are together in private, one will pass the word to another, 'our men are good for nothing'?

Nay, I know very well that they do, said he.

And just as an unhealthy body requires but a slight impulse from outside to fall into sickness, and sometimes, even without that, all the man is one internal war, in like manner does not the corresponding type of state need only a slight occasion, the one party bringing in allies from an oligarchic state, or the other from a democratic, to become diseased and wage war with itself, and sometimes even apart from any external impulse faction arises?

Most emphatically.

And a democracy, I suppose, comes into being when the poor, winning the victory, put to death some of the other party, drive out others, and grant the rest of the citizens an equal share in both citizenship and offices—and for the most part these offices are assigned by lot.

Why, yes, he said, that is the constitution of democracy alike whether it is established by force of arms or by terrorism resulting in the withdrawal of one of the parties.

What, then, said I, is the manner of their life and what is the quality of such a constitution? For it is plain that the man of this quality will turn out to be a democratic sort of man.

It is plain, he said.

To begin with, are they not free? And is not the city chock-full of liberty and freedom of speech? And has not every man license to do as he likes?

So it is said, he replied.

And where there is such license, it is obvious that everyone would arrange a plan for leading his own life in the way that pleases him.

Obvious.

All sorts and conditions of men, then, would arise in this polity more than in any other?

Of course.

Possibly, said I, this is the most beautiful of polities; as a garment of many colors, embroidered with all kinds of hues, so this, decked and diversified with every type of character, would appear the most beautiful. And perhaps many would judge it to be the most beautiful, like boys and women when they see bright-colored things.

Yes indeed, he said.

Yes, said I, and it is the fit place, my good friend, in which to look for a constitution.

Why so?

Because, owing to this license, it includes all kinds, and it seems likely that anyone who wishes to organize a state, as we were just now doing, must find his way to a democratic city and select the model that pleases him, as if in a bazaar of constitutions, and after making his choice, establish his own.

Perhaps at any rate, he said, he would not be at a loss for patterns.

And the freedom from all compulsion to hold office in such a city, even if you are qualified, or again, to submit to rule, unless you please, or to make war when the rest are at war, or to keep the peace when the others do so, unless you desire peace, and again, the liberty, in defiance of any law that forbids you, to hold office and sit on juries nonetheless, if it occurs to you to do so, is not all that a heavenly and delicious entertainment for the time being?

Perhaps, he said, for so long.

And is not the placability of some convicted criminals exquisite? Or have you never seen in such a state men condemned to death or exile who nonetheless stay on, and go to and fro among the people, and as if no one saw or heeded him, the man slips in and out like a revenant?

Yes, many, he said.

And the tolerance of democracy, its superiority to all our meticulous requirements, its disdain for our solemn pronouncements made when we were founding our city, that except in the case of transcendent natural gifts no one could ever become a good man unless from childhood his play and all his pursuits were concerned with things fair and good—how superbly it tramples underfoot all such ideals, caring nothing from what practices and way of life a man turns to politics, but honoring him if only he says that he loves the people!

It is a noble polity, indeed! he said.

These and qualities akin to these democracy would exhibit, and it would, it seems, be a delightful form of government, anarchic and motley, assigning a kind of equality indiscriminately to equals and unequals alike!

Yes, he said, everybody knows that.

Observe, then, the corresponding private character. Or must we first, as in the case of the polity, consider the origin of the type?

Yes, he said.

Is not this, then, the way of it? Our thrifty oligarchic man would have a son bred in his father's ways.

Why not?

And he, too, would control by force all his appetites for pleasure that are wasters and not winners of wealth, those which are denominated unnecessary.

Obviously.

And in order not to argue in the dark, shall we first define our distinction between necessary and unnecessary appetites?

Let us do so.

Well, then, desires that we cannot divert or suppress may be properly called necessary, and likewise those whose satisfaction is beneficial to us, may they not? For our nature compels us to seek their satisfaction. Is not that so?

Most assuredly.

Then we shall rightly use the word 'necessary' of them?

Rightly.

And what of the desires from which a man could free himself by discipline from youth up, and whose presence in the soul does no good and in come cases harm? Should we not fairly call all such unnecessary?

Fairly indeed.

Let us select an example of either kind, so that we may apprehend the type.

Let us do so.

Would not the desire of eating to keep in health and condition and the appetite for mere bread and relishes be necessary?

I think so.

The appetite for bread is necessary in both respects, in that it is beneficial and in that if it fails we die.

Yes.

And the desire for relishes, so far as it conduces to fitness?

By all means.

And should we not rightly pronounce unnecessary the appetite that exceeds these and seeks other varieties of food, and that by correction and training from youth up can be got rid of in some cases and is harmful to the body and a hindrance to the soul's attainment of intelligence and sobriety?

Nay, most rightly.

And may we not call the one group the spendthrift desires and the other the profitable, because they help production?

Surely.

And we shall say the same of sexual and other appetites?

The same.

And were we not saying that the man whom we nicknamed the drone is the man who teems with such pleasures and appetites, and who is governed by his unnecessary desires, while the one who is ruled by his necessary appetites is the thrifty oligarchic man?

Why, surely.

To return, then, said I, we have to tell how the democratic man develops from the oligarchic type. I think it is usually in this way.

How?

When a youth, bred in the illiberal and niggardly fashion that we were describing, gets a taste of the honey of the drones and associates with fierce and cunning creatures who know how to purvey pleasures of every kind and variety and condition, there you must doubtless conceive is the beginning of the transformation of the oligarchy in his soul into democracy.

Quite inevitably, he said.

May we not say that just as the revolution in the city was brought about by the aid of an alliance from outside, coming to the support of the similar and corresponding party in the state, so the youth is revolutionized when a like and kindred group of appetites from outside comes to the aid of one of the parties in his soul?

By all means, he said.

And if, I take it, a counteralliance comes to the rescue of the oligarchic part of his soul, either it may be from his father or from his other kin, who admonish and reproach him, then there arise faction and counterfaction and internal strife in the man with himself.

Surely.

And sometimes, I suppose, the democratic element retires before the oligarchic, some of its appetites having been destroyed and others expelled, and a sense of awe and reverence grows up in the young man's soul and order is restored.

That sometimes happens, he said.

And sometimes, again, another brood of desires akin to those expelled are stealthily nurtured to take their place, owing to the father's ignorance of true education, and wax numerous and strong.

Yes, that is wont to be the way of it.

And they tug and pull back to the same associations and in secret intercourse engender a multitude.

Yes indeed.

And in the end, I suppose, they seize the citadel of the young man's soul, finding it empty and unoccupied by studies and honorable pursuits and true discourses, which are the best watchmen and guardians in the minds of men who are dear to the gods.

Much the best, he said.

And then false and braggart words and opinions charge up the height and take their place and occupy that part of such a youth.

They do indeed.

And then he returns, does he not, to those lotus-eaters and without disguise lives openly with them. And if any support comes from his kin to the thrifty element in his soul, those braggart discourses close the gates of the royal fortress within him and refuse admission to the auxiliary force itself, and will not grant audience as to envoys to the words of older friends in private life. And they themselves prevail in the conflict, and naming reverence and awe 'folly' thrust it forth, a dishonored fugitive. And temperance they call 'want of manhood' and banish it with contumely, and they teach that moderation and orderly expenditure are 'rusticity' and 'illiberality,' and they combine with a gang of unprofitable and harmful appetites to drive them over the border.

They do indeed.

And when they have emptied and purged all these the soul of the youth that they have thus possessed and occupied, and whom they are initiating with these magnificent and costly rites, they proceed to lead home from exile insolence and anarchy and prodigality and shamelessness, resplendent in a great attendant choir and crowned with garlands, and in celebration of their praises they euphemistically denominate insolence 'good breeding,' license 'liberty,' prodigality 'magnificence,' and shamelessness 'manly spirit.' And is it not in some such way as this that in his youth the transformation takes place from the restriction to necessary desires in his education to the liberation and release of his unnecessary and harmful desires?

Yes, your description is most vivid, said he.

Then, in his subsequent life, I take it, such a one expends money and toil and time no more on his necessary than on his unnecessary pleasures. But if it is his good fortune that the period of storm and stress does not last too long, and as he grows older the fiercest tumult within him passes, and he receives back a part of the banished elements and does not abandon himself altogether to the invasion of the others, then he establishes and maintains all his pleasures on a footing of equality, forsooth, and so lives turning over the guardhouse of his soul to each as it happens along until it is sated, as if it had drawn the lot for that office, and then in turn to another, disdaining none but fostering them all equally.

Quite so.

And he does not accept or admit into the guardhouse the words of truth when anyone tells him that some pleasures arise from honorable and good desires, and others from those that are base, and that we ought to practice and esteem the one and control and subdue the others, but he shakes his head at all such admonitions and avers that they are all alike and to be equally esteemed.

Such is indeed his state of mind and his conduct.

And does not, said I, also live out his life in this fashion, day by day indulging the appetite of the day, now winebibbing and abandoning himself to the lascivious pleasing of the flute and again drinking only water and dieting, and at one time exercising his body, and sometimes idling and neglecting all things, and at another time seeming to occupy himself with philosophy. And frequently he goes in for politics and bounces up and says and does whatever enters his head. And if military men excite his emulation, thither he rushes, and if moneyed men, to that he turns, and there is no order or compulsion in his existence, but he calls this life of this the life of pleasure and freedom and happiness and cleaves to it to the end.

That is a perfect description, he said, of a devotee of equality.

I certainly think, said I, that he is a manifold man stuffed with most excellent differences, and that like that city he is the fair and many-colored one whom many a man and woman would count fortunate in his life, as containing within himself the greatest number of patterns of constitutions and qualities.

Yes, that is so, he said.

Shall we definitely assert, then, that such a man is to be ranged with democracy and would properly designated as democratic?

Let that be his place, he said.

3

Aristotle
The Politics

Aristotle (384–322 B.C.) was, after Socrates and Plato, the most renowned phi-
losopher of antiquity. He was born in Stagira, a Greek colony near Macedonia.
His father was the physician of the Macedonian king. At age seventeen, Aristotle
went to Athens and studied in Plato's school, the Academy. He stayed until the
death of Plato twenty years later. He then went to Asia Minor, serving for a pe-
riod as tutor of the future Alexander the Great. Aristotle returned to Athens in
335 B.C. to found his own school, the Lyceum, but was compelled to flee Athens
when anti-Macedonian feelings intensified after Alexander's death in 323 B.C.
Aristotle wrote on a vast array of subjects, of which politics is only one—but
one of the most important. His book The Politics *was very much influenced by*
the Athenian ideal of a self-sufficient sovereign political community. He argued
that the state was a natural institution and that man is by nature "a political an-
imal," who finds realization only within a political community.

Political Association and the Theory of the Household

The Ends of Association

Observation shows us, first, that every polis (or state) is a species of association, and, secondly, that all associations are instituted for the purpose of attaining some good—for all men do all their acts with a view to achieving something which is, in their view, a good. We may therefore hold that all associations aim at some good; and we may also hold that the particular association which is the most sovereign of all, and includes all the rest, will pursue this aim most, and will thus be directed to the most sovereign of all goods. This most sovereign and inclusive association is the polis, as it is called, or the political association.

It is a mistake to believe that the 'statesman' [the *politikos*, who handles the affairs of a political association] is the same as the monarch of a kingdom, or the manager of a household, or the master of a number of slaves. Those who hold this view consider that each of these persons differs from the others not with a difference of kind, but according to the number, or the paucity, of the persons with whom he deals. On this view a man who is concerned with few persons is a master: one who is concerned with more is the manager of a household: one who is concerned with still more is a 'statesman,' or a monarch. This view abolishes any real difference between a large household and a small polis; and it also reduces the difference between the 'statesman' and the monarch to the one fact that the latter has an uncontrolled and sole authority, while the former exercises his authority in conformity with the rules imposed by the art of statesmanship and as one who rules and is ruled in turn. But this is a view which cannot be accepted as correct.

Man and Polis

If, accordingly, we begin at the beginning, and consider things in the process of their growth, we shall best be able, in this as in other fields, to attain scientific conclusions by the method we employ. First of all, there must necessarily be a union or pairing of those who cannot exist without one another. Male and female must unite for the reproduction of the species—not from deliberate intention, but from the natural impulse, which exists in animals generally as it also exists in plants, to leave behind them something of the same nature as themselves. Next, there must necessarily be a union of the naturally ruling element with the element which is naturally ruled, for the preservation of both. The element which is able, by virtue of its intelligence, to exercise forethought, is naturally a ruling and master element; the element which is able, by virtue of its bodily power, to do what the other element plans, is a ruled element, which is naturally in a state of slavery; and master and slave have accordingly a common interest. . . . The female and the slave are naturally distinguished from one another. Nature makes nothing in a spirit of stint, as smiths do when they make the Delphic knife to serve a number of purposes: she makes each separate thing for a separate end; and she does so because each instrument has the finest finish when it serves a single purpose and not a variety of purposes.

Among the barbarians, however, the female and the slave occupy the same position—the reason being that no naturally ruling element exists among them, and conjugal union thus comes to be a union of a female who is a slave with a male who is also a slave. This is why our poets have said,

> Meet it is that barbarous peoples should be governed
>   by the Greeks

—the assumption being that barbarian and slave are by nature one and the same. . . .

The first result of these two elementary associations is the household or family. Hesiod spoke truly in the verse,

> First house, and wife, and ox to draw the plough,

for oxen serve the poor in lieu of household slaves. The first form of association naturally instituted for the satisfaction of daily recurrent needs is thus the family; and the members of the family are accordingly termed by Charondas 'associates of the breadchest,' as they are also termed by Epimenides the Cretan 'associates of the manager.' The next form of association—which is also the *first* to be formed from more households than one, and for the satisfaction of something more than daily recurrent needs—is the village.

The most natural form of the village appears to be that of a colony or offshoot from a family; and some have thus called the members of the village by the name of 'sucklings of the same milk,' or, again, of 'sons and the sons of sons.' . . . This, it may be noted, is the reason why each Greek polis was originally ruled— as the peoples of the barbarian world still are—by kings. They were formed of persons who were already monarchically governed, and households are always monarchically governed by the eldest of the kin, just as villages, when they are offshoots from the household, are similarly governed in virtue of the kinship between their members. This primitive kinship is what Homer describes, [in speaking of the Cyclopes]:

> Each of them ruleth
> Over his children and wives,

a passage which shows that they lived in scattered groups, as indeed men generally did in ancient times. The fact that men generally were governed by kings in ancient times, and that some still continue to be governed in that way, is the reason that leads us all to assert that the gods are also governed by a king. We make the lives of the gods in the likeness of our own—as we also make their shapes. . . .

When we come to the final and perfect association, formed from a number of villages, we have already reached the polis—an association which may be said to have reached the height of full self-sufficiency; or rather we may say that while it *grows* for the sake of mere life, it *exists* for the sake of a good life.

Because it is the completion of associations existing by nature, every polis exists by nature, having itself the same quality as the earlier associations from which it grew. It is the end or consummation to which those associations move, and the 'nature' of things consists in their end or consummation; for what each thing is when its growth is completed we call the nature of that thing, whether it be a man or a horse or a family. Again the end, or final cause, is the best. Now self-sufficiency is the end, and so the best.

From these considerations it is evident that the polis belongs to the class of things that exist by nature, and that man is by nature an animal intended to live in a polis. He who is without a polis, by reason of his own nature and not of some accident, is either a poor sort of being, or a being higher than man: he is like the man of whom Homer wrote in denunciation:

> Clanless and lawless and hearthless is he.

The man who is such by nature at once plunges into a passion for war; he is in the position of a solitary advanced piece in a game of draughts.

The reason why man is a being meant for political association, in a higher degree than bees or other gregarious animals can ever associate, is evident. Nature, according to our theory, makes nothing in vain; and man alone of the animals is furnished with the faculty of language. The mere making of sounds serves to indicate pleasure and pain, and is thus a faculty that belongs to animals in general: their nature enables them to attain the point at which they have perceptions of pleasure and pain, and can signify those perceptions to one another. But language serves to declare what is advantageous and what is the reverse, and it therefore serves to declare what is just and what is unjust. It is the peculiarity of man, in comparison with the rest of the animal world, that he alone possesses a perception of good and evil, of the just and the unjust, and of other similar qualities; and it is association in these things which makes a family and a polis.

We may now proceed to add that the polis is prior in the order of nature to the family and the individual. The reason for this is that the whole is necessarily prior to the part. If the whole body be destroyed, there will not be a foot or a hand, except in that ambiguous sense in which one uses the same word to indicate a different thing, as when one speaks of a 'hand' made of stone; for a hand, when destroyed will be no better than a stone 'hand.' All things derive their essential character from their function and their capacity; and it follows that if they are no longer fit to discharge their function, we ought not to say that they are still the same things, but only that, by an ambiguity, they still have the same names.

We thus see that the polis exists by nature and that it is prior to the individual. Not being self-sufficient when they are isolated, all individuals are so many parts all equally depending on the whole. The man who is isolated—who is unable to share in the benefits of political association, or has no need to share because he is already self-sufficient—is no part of the polis, and must therefore be either a beast or a god.

There is therefore an immanent impulse in all men towards an association of this order. But the man who first *constructed* such as association was none the less the greatest of benefactors. Man, when perfected, is the best of animals; but if he be isolated from law and justice he is the worst of all. Injustice is all the graver when it is armed injustice; and man is furnished from birth with arms which are intended to serve the purposes of moral prudence and virtue, but which may be used in preference for opposite ends. That is why, if he be without virtue, he is a most unholy and savage being, and worse than all others in the indulgence of lust and gluttony. Justice belongs to the polis; for justice, which is the determination of what is just, is an ordering of the political association.

Slavery

We may make the assumption that property is part of the household, and that the art of acquiring property is a part of household-management; and we may do so because it is impossible to live well, or indeed to live at all, unless the necessary conditions are present. We may further assume that, just as each art which has a definite sphere must necessarily be furnished with the appropriate instruments if its function is to be discharged, so the same holds good in the sphere of household management. Finally, we may also assume that instruments are partly inanimate and partly animate: the pilot, for instance, has an inanimate instrument in the rudder, and an animate instrument (for all subordinates, in every art, are of the nature of instruments) in the look-out man. On the basis of these assumptions we may conclude that each article of property is an instrument for the purpose of life; that property in general is the sum of such instruments; that the slave is an animate article of property; and that subordinates, or servants, in general may be described as instruments which are prior to other instruments.

There is only one condition on which we can imagine managers not needing subordinates, and masters not needing slaves. This condition would be that each instrument could do its own work, at the word of command or by intelligent anticipation, like the statues of Daedalus or the tripods made by Hephaestus, of which Homer relates that

> Of their own motion they centered the conclave of Gods on
> Olympus,

as if a shuttle should weave of itself, and a plectrum should do its own harp-playing. The instruments of which we have just been speaking are instruments of *production*; but articles of household property are instruments of *action*. From the shuttle there issues something which is different, and exists apart, from the immediate act of its use; but from garments or beds, there only comes the one fact of their use. We may add that, since production and action are different in kind, and both of them need their own proper instruments, those instruments must also show a corresponding difference. Life is action and not production; and therefore the slave is a servant in the sphere of action.

Rule and Subordination

We have next to consider whether there are, or are not, persons who are by nature such as are here defined; whether, in other words, there are persons for whom slavery is the better and just condition, or whether the reverse is the case and all slavery is contrary to nature. The issue is not difficult, whether we study it philosophically in the light of reason, or consider it empirically on the basis of the actual facts. Ruling and being ruled not only belongs to the category of things necessary, but also to that of things expedient; and there are species in which a distinction is already marked, immediately at birth, between those of its members who are intended for being ruled and those who are intended to rule. . . . There are also many kinds both of ruling and ruled elements. This being the case, the rule which is exercised over the better sort of ruled elements is a better sort of rule—as, for example, rule exercised over a man is better than rule over an animal. The reason is that a function is a higher and better function when the elements which go to its discharge are higher and better elements; and where one element rules and another is ruled, we may speak of those elements as going together to discharge a function. . . . In *all* cases where there is a compound, constituted of more than one part but forming one common entity—whether the parts be continuous or discrete—a ruling element and a ruled can always be traced. This characteristic is present in animate beings by virtue of the whole constitution of nature, inanimate as well as animate; for even in things which are inanimate there is a sort of ruling principle, such as is to be found, for example, in a musical harmony. But such considerations perhaps belong to a more popular method of inquiry; and we may content ourselves here with saying that animate beings are the first to be composed of soul and body, with the former naturally ruling and the latter naturally ruled. Dealing with such animate beings, we must fix our attention, in order to discover what nature intends, not on those which are in a corrupt, but on those which are in a natural condition. It follows that we must consider the man who is in the best state both of body and soul, and in whom the rule of soul over body is accordingly evident; for in those who are bad, or who are in a bad condition, the reverse would often appear to be true—the body ruling the soul as the result of their evil and unnatural condition.

Whatever may be said of inanimate things, it is certainly possible, as we have said, to observe in animate beings—and to observe there first—the presence of a ruling authority, both of the sort exercised by a master over slaves and of the sort exercised by a statesman over fellow citizens. The soul rules the body with the sort of authority of a master: mind rules the appetite with the sort of authority of a statesman or a monarch. In this sphere it is clearly natural and beneficial to the body that it should be ruled by the soul, and again it is natural and beneficial to the affective part of the soul that it should be ruled by the mind and the rational part; whereas the equality of the two elements, or their reverse relation, is always detrimental. What holds good in man's inner life also holds good outside it; and the same principle is true of the relation of man to animals as is true of the relation of his soul to his body. Tame animals have a better nature than wild, and it is better for all such animals that they should be ruled by man because they then get the benefit of preservation. Again, the relation of male to female is naturally that of the superior to the inferior—of the ruling to the ruled. This general principle must similarly hold good of all human beings generally.

We may thus conclude that all men who differ from others as much as the body differs from the soul, or an animal from a man (and this is the case with all whose function is bodily service, and who produce their best when they supply such service)—all such are by nature slaves, and it is better for them, on the very same principle as in the other cases just mentioned, to be ruled by a master. A man is thus by nature a slave if he is capable of becoming (and this is the reason why he also actually becomes) the property of another, and if he participates in reason to the extent of apprehending it in another, though destitute of it himself. Herein he differs from animals, which do not apprehend reason, but simply obey their instincts. But the use which is made of the slave diverges but little from the use made of tame animals; both he and they supply their owner with bodily help in meeting his daily requirements.

But it is nature's intention also to erect a physical difference between the body of the freeman and that of the slave, giving the latter strength for the menial duties of life, but making the former upright in carriage and (though useless for physical labour) useful for the various purposes of civic life—a life which tends, as it develops, to be divided into military service and the occupations of peace. The contrary of nature's intention, however, often happens: there are some slaves who have the bodies of freemen—as there are others who have a freeman's soul. But if nature's intention were realized—if men differed from one another in bodily form as much as the statues of the gods—it is obvious that we should all agree that the inferior class ought to be the slaves of the superior. And if this principle is true when the difference is one of the body, it may be affirmed with still greater justice when the difference is one of the soul; though it is not as easy to see the beauty of the soul as it is to see that of the body.

It is thus clear that, just as some are by nature free, so others are by nature slaves, and for these latter the condition of slavery is both beneficial and just.

Citizenship and Constitutions

Who Is a Citizen?

When we are dealing with the subject of polity [i.e. constitutions or forms of government], and seeking to discover the essence and the attributes of each form, our first investigation may well be directed to the polis itself; and we may begin by asking, 'What is the nature of the polis?' In the first place, the nature of the 'polis,' or state, is at present a disputed question; and while some affirm, 'It was the *state* that did such and such an act,' others reply, 'It was not the state, but the *government*—the governing oligarchy or tyrant.' In the second place, all the activity of the statesman and the lawgiver is obviously concerned with the state. Finally, a polity or constitution is a scheme established among the inhabitants of a polis.

A polis or state belongs to the order of 'compounds,' in the same way as all other things which form a single 'whole,' but a 'whole' composed, none the less, of a number of different parts. This being the case, it clearly follows that we must inquire into the nature of the citizen before inquiring into the nature of the state. In other words, a state is a compound made up of citizens; and this compels us to consider who should properly be called a citizen and what a citizen really is. The nature of citizenship, like that of the state, is a question which is often disputed: there is no general agreement on a single definition: the man who is a citizen in a democracy is often not one in an oligarchy. We may leave out of consideration those who enjoy the name and title of citizen in some other than the strict sense— for example, naturalized citizens. A citizen proper is not one by virtue of residence in a given place: resident aliens and slaves share a common place of residence. Nor can the name of citizen be given to those who share in civic rights only to the extent of being entitled to sue and be sued in the courts. This is a right which belongs also to aliens who share its enjoyment by virtue of a treaty; though it is to be noted that there are many places where resident aliens do not enjoy even this limited right to the full—being obliged to choose a legal protector, so that they only share to a limited extent in the common enjoyment of the right. [We may thus dismiss those who have only the right to sue and be sued from our consideration], just as we may also dismiss children who are still too young to be entered on the roll of citizens, or men who are old enough to have been excused from civic duties. There is a sense in which the young and the old may both be called citizens, but it is not altogether an unqualified sense: we must add the reservation that the young are undeveloped, and the old superannuated citizens, or we must use some other qualification; the exact term we apply does not matter, for the meaning is clear.

What we have to define is the citizen in the strict and unqualified sense, who has no defect that has to be made good before he can bear the name—no defect such as youth or age, or such as those attaching to disfranchised or exiled citizens (about whom similar questions have also to be raised and answered). The citizen in this strict sense is best defined by the one criterion, 'a man who shares in the administration of justice and in the holding of office. . . .' We may thus conclude that the citizen of our definition is particularly and especially the citizen of a democracy. Citizens living under other kinds of constitution *may* possibly, but do not necessarily, correspond to the definition. There are some states, for example, in which there is no popular element: such states have no regular meetings of the assembly, but only meetings specially summoned; and they remit the decision of cases to special bodies.

But our definition of citizenship can be amended. We have to note that in constitutions other than the democratic, members of the assembly and the courts do not hold that office for an indeterminate period. They hold it for a limited term; and it is to persons with such a tenure (whether they be many or few) that the citizen's function of deliberating and judging (whether on all issues or only a few) is assigned in these constitutions. The nature of citizenship in general emerges clearly from these considerations; and our final definitions will accordingly be: (1) 'he who enjoys the right of sharing in deliberative or judicial office [for any period, fixed or unfixed] attains thereby the status of a citizen of his state,' and (2) 'a state, in its simplest terms, is a body of such persons adequate in number for achieving a self-sufficient existence.'

The Good Man and the Good Citizen

A question connected with those which have just been discussed is the question whether the excellence of a good man and that of a good citizen are identical or different. If this question is to be properly investigated, we must first describe the excellence of the citizen in some sort of outline. Just as a sailor is a member of an association, so too is a citizen. Sailors differ from one another in virtue of the different capacities in which they act: one is a rower, another a pilot, another a look-out man; and others again will have other names in the same sort of way. This being the case, it is clear that the most accurate definition of the excellence of each sailor will be special to the man concerned; but it is also clear that a common definition of excellence will apply to all, inasmuch as safety in navigation is the common end which all must serve and the object at which each must aim. What is true of sailors is also true of citizens. Though they differ, the end which they all serve is safety in the working of their association; and this association consists in the constitution. The conclusion to which we are thus led is that the excellence of the citizen must be an excellence relative to the constitution. It follows on this that if there are several different kinds of constitution there cannot be a single absolute excellence of the good citizen. But the good man is a man so called in virtue of a single absolute excellence.

It is thus clear that it is possible to be a good citizen without possessing the excellence which is the quality of the good man. But we may reach the same conclusion in another way, by discussing the question with particular reference to the best or ideal constitution. If it is impossible for a polis to be composed entirely and only of good men; if, none the less, each citizen of a polis must discharge *well* the function belonging to him; if his good discharge of his function involves, as it must, his excellence—then, as it is impossible for all the citizens to be alike, the excellence of a good citizen cannot be identical with that of a good man. The excellence of being a good citizen must belong to all citizens indifferently, because that is the condition necessary for the state being the best state; but the excellence of being a good man cannot possibly belong to all—unless, indeed, we hold that every citizen of a good state must also be a good man. . . . There is a further point to be made. The polis is composed of unlike elements. Just as a living being is composed of soul and body, or the soul of the different elements of reason and appetite, or the household of man and wife, or property of master and slave, so the polis too is composed of different and unlike elements—among them not only the various elements already mentioned, but also others in addition. It follows upon this difference between the elements of which the polis is composed that there cannot be a single excellence common to all the citizens, any more than there can be a single excellence common to the leader of a dramatic chorus and his assistants.

It is clear from these considerations that the excellence of the good citizen and that of the good man are not in *all* cases identical. But the question may still be raised whether there are not *some* cases in which there is identity. We call a good ruler a 'good' and 'prudent' man, and we say of the statesman that he ought to be 'prudent.' Indeed there are some who hold that the very training of the ruler should be, from the first, of a different kind; and it is a matter of observation that the sons of kings are specially trained in riding and the art of war. Thus Euripides makes a king say

No subtleties for me,
But what the state most needs,

which implies a special training for the ruler. We may thus assume that, in the case of the ruler, the excellence of the good citizen is identical with that of the good man. But we have to remember that subjects too are citizens. It therefore follows that the excellence of the good citizen cannot be identical with that of the good man in all cases, though it may be so in a particular case. The excellence of the ordinary citizen is different from that of the ruler; and this may well be the reason why Jason, the tyrant of Pherae, said that 'he was a hungry man except when he was tyrant,' meaning that he did not know how to live in a private station.

On the other hand, men hold in esteem the double capacity which consists in knowing both how to rule and how to obey, and they regard the excellence of a worthy citizen as consisting in a good exercise of this double capacity. Now if the excellence of the good man is in the one order of ruling, while that of the good citizen is in both orders these two excellences cannot be held in the same esteem. The position thus being that we find men holding (1) the ruler and ruled should have different sorts of knowledge, and not one identical sort, and (2) that the citizen should have both sorts of knowledge, and share in both, we can now see the next step which our argument has to take.

There is rule of the sort which is exercised by a master and by this we mean the sort of rule connected with menial duties. Here it is not necessary for the ruler to know how to do but only to know how to use: indeed the former kind of knowledge (by which we mean an ability to do menial services personally) has a servile character. There are a number of forms of servile position, because there are a number of forms of menial service which have to be rendered. One of these forms of service is that which is rendered by manual labourers. These, as their very name signifies, are men who live by the work of their hands; and the menial craftsman, or mechanic, belongs to this class. This is the reason why in some states the working classes were once upon a time excluded from office, in the days before the institution of the extreme form of democracy. The occupations pursued by men who are subject to rule of the sort just mentioned need never be studied by the good man, or by the statesman, or by the good citizen—except occasionally and in order to satisfy some personal need, in which case there ceases to be any question of the relation of master and servant.

But there is also rule of the sort which is exercised over persons who are similar in birth to the ruler, and are similarly free. Rule of this sort is what we call political rule; and this is the sort of rule which the ruler must begin to learn by being ruled and by obeying—just as one learns to be a commander of cavalry by serving under another commander, or to be a general of infantry by serving under another general and by acting first as colonel and, even before that, as captain. This is why it is a good saying that 'you cannot be a ruler unless you have first been ruled.' Ruler and ruled have indeed different excellences; but the fact remains that the good citizen must possess the knowledge and the capacity requisite for ruling as well as for being ruled, and the excellence of a citizen may be defined as consisting in 'a knowledge of rule over free men from both points of view.'

A good man, like a good citizen, will need knowledge from both points of view. Accordingly, on the assumption that the temperance and justice required for ruling have a special quality, and equally that the temperance and justice required for being a subject in a free state have *their* special quality, the excellence of the good man (e.g. his justice) will not be one sort of excellence. It will include different sorts—one sort which fits him to act as a ruler, and one which fits him to act as a subject. . . . We may note that the temperance and the courage of a man differ from those of a woman in much the same sort of way. A man would be thought to be cowardly if his courage were only the same as that of a courageous woman; and conversely a woman would be thought to be forward if her modesty were no greater than that which becomes a good man. The function of the man in the household is different from that of the woman: it is the function of the one to acquire, and of the other to keep and store. . . .

'Prudence' is the only form of goodness which is peculiar to the ruler. The other forms [temperance, justice, and courage] must, it would seem, belong equally to rulers and subjects. The form of goodness peculiar to subjects cannot be 'prudence,' and may be defined as 'right opinion.' The ruled may be compared to flute-makers: rulers are like flute-players who use what the flute-makers make.

These considerations will suffice to show whether the excellence of the good man and that of the good citizen are identical or different—or in what sense they are identical and in what sense they are different.

Classifying Constitutions

Citizenship has now been defined and determined. We have next to consider the subject of constitutions. Is there a single type, or are there a number of types? If there are a number of types, what are these types; how many of them are there; and how do they differ? A constitution (or polity) may be defined as 'the organization of a polis, in respect of its offices generally, but especially in respect of that particular office which is sovereign in all issues.' The civic body is everywhere the sovereign of the state; in fact the civic body is the polity (or constitution) itself. In democratic states, for example, the people is sovereign: in oligarchies, on the other hand, the few have that position; and this difference of the sovereign bodies is the reason why we say that the two types of constitution differ—as we may equally apply the same reasoning to other types besides these.

[It is thus evident that there are a number of types of constitution, but before we discuss their nature] we must first ascertain two things—the nature of the end for which the state exists, and the various kinds of authority to which men and their associations are subject. So far as the first of these things is concerned, it has already been stated, in our first book (where we were concerned with the management of the household and the control of slaves), that 'man is an animal impelled by his nature to live in a polis.' A *natural impulse* is thus one reason why men desire to live a social life even when they stand in no need of mutual succour; but they are also drawn together by a *common interest*, in proportion as each attains a share in good life. The good life is the chief end, both for the community as a whole and for each of us individually. But men also come together, and form and maintain political associations, merely for the sake of life; for perhaps there is some element of the good even in the simple act of living, so long as the evils of existence do not preponderate too heavily. It is an evident fact that most men cling hard enough to life to be willing to endure a good deal of suffering, which implies that life has in it a sort of healthy happiness and a natural quality of pleasure.

It is easy enough to distinguish the various kinds of rule or authority of which men commonly speak; and indeed we have often had occasion to define them ourselves in works intended for the general public. The rule of a master is one kind; and here, though there is really a common interest which unites the natural master and the natural slave, the fact remains that the rule is primarily exercised with a view to the master's interest, and only incidentally with a view to that of the slave, who must be preserved in existence if the rule itself is to remain.

Rule over wife and children, and over the household generally, is a second kind of rule, which we have called by the name of household management. Here the rule is either exercised in the interest of the ruled or for the attainment of some advantage common to both ruler and ruled. Essentially it is exercised in the interest of the ruled, as is also plainly the case with other arts besides that of ruling, such as medicine and gymnastics—though an art may incidentally be exercised for the benefit of its practitioner, and there is nothing to prevent (say) a trainer from becoming occasionally a member of the class he instructs, in the same sort of way as a steersman is always one of the crew. Thus a trainer or steersman primarily considers the good of those who are subject to his authority; but when he becomes one of them personally, he incidentally shares in the benefit of that good—the steersman thus being also a member of the crew, and the trainer (though still a trainer) becoming also a member of the class which he instructs.

This principle also applies to a third kind of rule—that exercised by the holders of political office. When the constitution of a state is constructed on the principle that its members are equals and peers, the citizens think it proper that they should hold office by turns [which implies that the office of ruler is primarily intended for the benefit of the ruled and is therefore a duty to be undertaken by each in turn, though incidentally the ruler shares in the general benefit by virtue of being himself a member of the citizen body]. At any rate this is the natural system, and the system which used to be followed in the days when men believed that they ought to serve by turns, and each assumed that others would take over the duty of considering his benefit, just as he had himself, during his term of office, considered the interest of others. To-day the case is altered. Moved by the profits to be derived from office and the handling of public property, men want to hold office continuously. It is as if the holders of office were sick men, who got the benefit of permanent health: at any rate their ardour for office is just what it would be if that were the case. The conclusion which follows is clear. Those constitutions which consider the common interest are *right* constitutions, judged by the standard of absolute justice. Those constitutions which consider only the personal interest of the rulers are all *wrong* constitutions, or *perversions* of the right forms. Such perverted forms are despotic; whereas the polis is an association of freemen.

Economic Classification

. . . Tyranny, as has just been said, is single-person government of the political association on the lines of despotism [i.e., treating the citizens as a master treats slaves]: oligarchy exists where those who have property are the sovereign authority of the constitution; and conversely democracy exists where the sovereign authority is composed of the poorer classes, and not of the owners of property. The first difficulty which arises concerns the definition just given [of democracy and oligarchy]. We have defined democracy as the sovereignty of numbers; but we can conceive a case in which the majority who hold the sovereignty in a state are the well-to-do. Similarly oligarchy is generally stated to be the sovereignty of a small number; but it might conceivably happen that the poorer classes were fewer in number than the well-to-do, and yet—in virtue of superior vigour—were the sovereign authority of the constitution. In neither case could the definition previously given of these constitutions be regarded as true. We might attempt to overcome the difficulty by combining both of the factors—wealth with paucity of numbers, and poverty with mass. On this basis oligarchy might be defined as the constitution under which the rich, being also few in number, hold the offices of the state; and similarly democracy might be defined as the constitution under which the poor, being also many in number, are in control. But this involves us in another difficulty. If our new definition is exhaustive, and there are no forms of oligarchy and democracy other than those enumerated in that definition, what names are we to give to the constitutions just suggested as conceivable—those where the wealthy form a majority and the poor a minority, and where the wealthy majority in the one case, and the poor minority in the other, are the sovereign authority of the constitution? The course of the argument thus appears to show that the factor of number—the small number of the sovereign body in oligarchies, or the large number in democracies—is an accidental attribute, due to the simple fact that the wealthy are generally few and the poor are generally numerous. Therefore the causes originally mentioned are not in fact the real causes of the difference between oligarchies and democracies. The real ground of the difference between oligarchy and democracy is poverty and riches. It is inevitable that any constitution should be an oligarchy if the rulers under it are rulers in virtue of riches, whether they are few or many; and it is equally inevitable that a constitution under which the poor rule should be a democracy.

It happens, however, as we have just remarked, that the rich are few and the poor are numerous. It is only a few who have riches, but all alike share in free status; and these are the real grounds on which the two parties [the oligarchical and the democratic] dispute the control of the constitution.

Actual Constitutions and Their Varieties

The Best Constitution

We have now to consider what is the best constitution and the best way of life for the *majority* of states and men. In doing so we shall not employ a standard of excellence above the reach of ordinary men, or a standard of education requiring exceptional endowments and equipment, or the standard of a constitution which attains an ideal height. We shall only be concerned with the sort of life which most men are able to share and the sort of constitution which it is possible for most states to enjoy. The 'aristocracies,' so called, of which we have just been treating, either lie, at one extreme, beyond the reach of most states, or they approach, at the other, so closely to the constitution called 'polity' that they need not be considered separately and must be treated as identical with it. The issues we have just raised can all be decided in the light of one body of fundamental principles. If we adopt as true the statements (1) that a truly happy life is a life of goodness lived in freedom from impediments, and (2) that goodness consists in a mean—it follows that the best way of life of is one which consists in a mean, and a mean of the kind attainable by every individual. Further, the same criteria which determine whether the citizen-body have a good or bad way of life must also apply to the constitution; for a constitution is the way of life of a citizen-body. In all states there may be distinguished three parts, or classes, of the citizen-body—the very rich; the very poor; and the middle class which forms the mean. Now it is admitted, as a general principle, that moderation and the mean are always best. We may therefore conclude that in the ownership of all gifts of fortune a middle condition will be the best. Men who are in this condition are the most ready to listen to reason. Those who belong to either extreme—the over-handsome, the over-strong, the over-noble, the over-wealthy; or at the opposite end the over-poor, the over-weak, the utterly ignoble—find it hard to follow the lead of reason. Men in the first class tend more to violence and serious crime: men in the second tend too much to roguery and petty offences; and most wrongdoing arises either from violence or roguery. It is a further merit of the middle class that its members suffer least from ambition, which both in the military and the civil sphere is dangerous to states. It must also be added that those who enjoy too many advantages—strength, wealth, connexions, and so forth—are both unwilling to obey and ignorant how to obey. This is a defect which appears in them from the first, during childhood and in home-life: nurtured in luxury, they never acquire a habit of discipline, even in the matter of lessons. But there are also defects in those who suffer from the opposite extreme of a lack of advantages: they are far too mean and poor-spirited. We have thus, on the one hand, people who are ignorant how to rule and only know how to obey, as if they were so many slaves, and, on the other hand, people who are ignorant how to obey any sort of authority and only know how to rule as if they were masters of slaves. The result is a state, not of freemen, but only of slaves and masters: a state of envy on the one side and on the other contempt. Nothing could be further removed from the spirit of friendship or the temper of a political community. Community depends on friendship; and when there is enmity instead of friendship, men will not even share the same path. A state aims at being, as far as it can be, a society composed of equals and peers, and the middle class, more than any other, has this sort of composition. It follows that a state which is based on the middle class is bound to be the best constituted in respect of the elements of which, on our view, a state is naturally composed. The middle classes enjoy a greater security themselves than any other class. They do not, like the poor, covet the goods of others; nor do others covet their possessions, as the poor covet those of the rich. Neither plotting against others, not plotted against themselves, they live in freedom from danger; and we may well approve the prayer of Phocylides

Many things are best for the middling:
Fain would I be of the state's middle class.

It is clear from our argument, first, that the best form of political society is one where power is vested in the middle class, and, secondly, that good government is attainable in those states where there is a large middle class—large enough, if possible, to be stronger than both of the other classes, but at any rate large enough to be stronger than either of them singly; for in that case its addition to either will suffice to turn the scale, and will prevent either of the opposing extremes from becoming dominant. It is therefore the greatest of blessings for a state that its members should possess a moderate and adequate property. Where some have great possessions, and others have nothing at all, the result is either an extreme democracy or an unmixed oligarchy; or it may even be—indirectly, and as a reaction against both of these extremes—a tyranny. Tyranny is a form of government which may grow out of the headiest type of democracy, or out of oligarchy; but it is much less likely to grow out of constitutions of the middle order, or those which approximate to them. We shall explain the reason later, when we come to treat of revolutions and constitutional change.

Meanwhile, it is clear that the middle type of constitution is best. It is the one type free from faction; where the middle class is large, there is least likelihood of faction and dissension among the citizens. Large states are generally more free from faction just because they have a large middle class. In small states, on the other hand, it is easy for the whole population to be divided into only two classes; nothing is left in the middle, and all—or almost all—are either poor or rich. The reason why democracies are generally more secure and more permanent than oligarchies is the character of their middle class, which is more numerous, and is allowed a larger share in the government, than it is in oligarchies. Where democracies have no middle class, and the poor are greatly superior in number, trouble ensues, and they are speedily ruined. It must also be considered a proof of its value that the best legislators have come from the middle class. Solon was one, as his own poems prove: Lycurgus was another (and not, as is sometimes said, a member of the royal family); and the same is true of Charondas and most of the other legislators.

What has just been said also serves to explain why most constitutions are either democratic or oligarchical. In the first place, the middle class is in most states generally small; and the result is that as soon as one or other of the two main classes—the owners of property and the masses—gains the advantage, it oversteps the mean, and drawing the constitution in its own direction it institutes, as the case may be, either a democracy or an oligarchy. In the second place, factious disputes and struggles readily arise between the masses and the rich; and no matter which side may win the day, it refuses to establish a constitution based on the common interest and the principle of equality, but, preferring to exact as the prize of victory a greater share of constitutional rights, it institutes, according to its principles, a democracy or an oligarchy. Thirdly, the policy of the two states which have held the ascendancy in Greece [i.e. Athens and Sparta] has also been to blame. Each has paid an exclusive regard to its own type of constitution; the one has instituted democracies in the states under its control, and the other has set up oligarchies: each has looked to its own advantage, and neither to that of the states it controlled. These three reasons explain why a middle or mixed type of constitution has never been established—or, at the most, has only been established on a few occasions and in a few states. . . . One man, and one only, of all who have hitherto been in a position of ascendancy, has allowed himself to be persuaded to agree to the setting up of such a type. And now it has also become the habit in each individual state not even to want a system of equality, but, instead of that, either to try to dominate or, if beaten, just to submit to the victor.

It is clear, from the argument, which is the best constitution, and what are the reasons why it is so. Once we have thus settled which is the best, it becomes easy to take all the others (including the different varieties, both of democracy and of oligarchy, which we have already distinguished), and to arrange them in an order of merit—first, second, and so on in turn—according as their quality is a better or a worse quality. The nearest to the best must always be better than all the rest, and the one which is farthest removed from the mean must always be worse, if we are judging not in relation to particular circumstances. I use the words 'in relation to particular circumstances' for this reason: one sort of constitution may be intrinsically preferable, but there is nothing to prevent another sort from being more suitable in the given case; and indeed this may often happen.

Causes of Revolution and Constitutional Change

Origins of Revolution

Since we have to consider the various reasons which lead to the rise of seditions and changes in the general run of constitutions, we had better begin with a general view of their origins and causes. They may be said to be three in number; and we must begin by giving a brief outline of each of them separately. The three things we have to investigate are (1) the state of mind which leads to sedition; (2) the objects which are at stake; and (3) the occasions which serve to start political disturbance and mutual dissension.

The principal and general cause of an attitude of mind which disposes men towards change is the cause of which we have just spoken. There are some who stir up sedition because their minds are filled by a passion for equality, which arises from their thinking that they have the worst of the bargain in spite of being the equals of those who have got the advantage. There are others who do it because their minds are filled with a passion for inequality (i.e. superiority), which arises from their conceiving that they get no advantage over others (but only an equal amount, or even a smaller amount) although they are really more than equal to others. (Either of these passions may have some justification; and either may be without any.) Thus inferiors become revolutionaries in order to be equals, and equals in order to be superiors.

This is the state of mind which creates sedition. The objects which are at stake are profit and honour. They are also their opposites—loss and disgrace; for the authors of political sedition may be simply seeking to avert some disgrace, or a fine, from themselves or their friends.

The occasions and origins of disturbances—occasions which encourage the attitude of mind, and lead to the pursuit of the objects, which have just been mentioned—may be counted, from one point of view, as seven, but from another as more than that number. Two of these occasions (profit and honour) are identical with two of the objects which have just been mentioned; but when considered as occasions they act in a different way. As objects, profit and honour provoke dissension because (as we have just noted) men want to get them themselves: as occasions, they lead to dissension because men see other persons getting a larger share—some justly and some unjustly—than they themselves get. Other occasions, besides profit and honour, are insolence; fear; the presence of some form of superiority; contempt; or a disproportionate increase in some part of the state. Four other occasions leading to dissension—but in a different way—are election intrigues; wilful negligence; trifling changes; and dissimilarity of elements.

4

Cicero
On The Republic

Marcus Tullius Cicero, (106–43 B.C.) was a Roman orator and statesman, who wrote philosophy during periods of enforced retirement from politics. Cicero was a student of Greek philosophy, identified with the Academy from which he appropriated a framework for his own views. He was committed to a union of rhetoric and philosophy to form a humanistic ideal. Philosophy would enable man to understand what had to be done, and rhetoric would persuade him of its effectiveness. Rome needed a statesman who possessed both. A free society for Cicero was defined by the victory of persuasion over violence. Among Cicero's many works on physics, ethics, and logic are two dialogues on politics with titles taken from Plato. In On The Republic *(51 B.C.), the famous "Dream of Scipio" presents the virtuous soul after death, and* The Laws, *(date unknown) discusses Roman law, presenting it as an almost perfect example of Greek theory.*

Scipio: [A] commonwealth is the property of a people. But a people is not any collection of human beings brought together in any sort of way, but an assemblage of people in large numbers associated in an agreement with respect to justice and a partnership for the common good. The first cause of such an association is not so much the weakness of the individual as a certain social spirit which nature has implanted in man. For man is not a solitary or unsocial creature, but born with such a nature that not even under conditions of great prosperity of every sort [is he willing to be isolated from his fellow men.] . . .

About fifteen lines are lost. The following fragment may be part of the missing passage.

. . . In a short time a scattered and wandering multitude had become a body of citizens by mutual agreement. . . .

. . . certain seeds, as we may call them, for [otherwise] no source for the other virtues nor for the State itself could be discovered. Such an assemblage of men, therefore, originating for the reason I have mentioned, established itself in a definite place, at first in order to provide dwellings; and this place being fortified by its natural situation and by their labours, they called such a collection of dwellings a town or city, and provided it with shrines and gathering places which were common property. Therefore every people, which is such a gathering of large numbers as I have described, every city, which is an orderly settlement of a people, every commonwealth, which, as I said, is "the property of a people," must be governed by some deliberative body if it is to be permanent. And this deliberative body must, in the first place, always owe its beginning to the same cause as that which produced the State itself. In the second place, this function must either be granted to one man, or to certain selected citizens, or must be assumed by the whole body of citizens. And so when the supreme authority is in the hands of one man, we call him a king, and the form of this State a kingship. When selected citizens hold this power, we say that the State is ruled by an aristocracy. But a popular government (for so it is called) exists when all the power is in the hands of the people. And any one of these three forms of government (if only the bond which originally joined the citizens together in the partnership of the State holds fast), though not perfect or in my opinion the best, is tolerable, though one of them may be superior to another. For either a just and wise king, or a select number of leading citizens, or even the people itself, though this is the least commendable type, can nevertheless, as it seems, form a government that is not unstable, provided that no elements of injustice or greed are mingled with it. . . .

[S]ince law is the bond which unites the civic association, and the justice enforced by law is the same for all, by what justice can an association of citizens be held together when there is no equality among the citizens? For if we cannot agree to equalize men's wealth, and equality of innate ability is impossible, the legal rights at least of those who are citizens of the same commonwealth ought to be equal. For what is a State except an association or partnership in justice? . . .

About fifteen lines are lost. There is no change of topic.

. . . True law is right reason in agreement with nature; it is of universal application, unchanging and everlasting; it summons to duty by its commands, and averts from wrongdoing by its prohibitions. And it does not lay its commands or prohibitions upon good men in vain, though neither have any effect on the wicked. It is a sin to try to alter this law, nor is it allowable to attempt to repeal any part of it, and it is impossible to abolish it entirely. We cannot be freed from its obligations by senate or people, and we need not look outside ourselves for an expounder or interpreter of it. And there will not be different laws at Rome and at Athens, or different laws now and in the future, but one eternal and unchangeable law will be valid for all nations and all times, and there will be one master and ruler, that is, God, over us all, for he is the author of this law, its promulgator, and its enforcing judge. Whoever is disobedient is fleeing from himself and denying his human nature, and by reason of this very fact he will suffer the worst penalties, even if he escapes what is commonly considered punishment. . . .

M: . . . [T]hat animal which we call man, endowed with foresight and quick intelligence, complex, keen, possessing memory, full of reason and prudence, has been given a certain distinguished status by the supreme God who created him; for he is the only one among so many different kinds and varieties of living beings who has a share in reason and thought, while all the rest are deprived of it. But what is more divine, I will not say in man only, but in all heaven and earth, than reason? And reason, when it is full grown and perfected, is rightly called wisdom. Therefore, since there is nothing better than reason, and since it exists both in man and God, the first common possession of man and God is reason. But those who have reason in common must also have right reason in common. And since right reason is Law, we must believe that men have Law also in common with the gods. Further, those who share Law must also share Justice; and those who share these are to be regarded as members of the same commonwealth. If indeed they obey the same authorities and powers, this is true in a far greater degree; but as a matter of fact they do obey this celestial system, the divine mind, and the God of transcendent power. Hence we must now conceive of this whole universe as one commonwealth of which both gods and men are members. . . .

But the most foolish notion of all is the belief that everything is just which is found in the customs or laws of nations. Would that be true, even if these laws had been enacted by tyrants? If the well-known Thirty had desired to enact a set of laws at Athens, or if the Athenians without exception were delighted by the tyrants' laws, that would not entitle such laws to be regarded as just, would it? No more, in my opinion, should that law be considered just which a Roman interrex proposed, to the effect that a dictator might put to death with impunity any citizen he wished, even without a trial. For Justice is one; it binds all human society, and is based on one Law, which is right reason applied to command and prohibition. Whoever knows not this Law, whether it has been recorded in writing anywhere or not, is without Justice.

But if Justice is conformity to written laws and national customs, and if, as the same persons claim, everything is to be tested by the standard of utility, then anyone who thinks it will be profitable to him will, if he is able, disregard and violate the laws. It follows that Justice does not exist at all, if it does not exist in Nature, and if that form of it which is based on utility can be overthrown by that very utility itself. And if Nature is not to be considered the foundation of Justice, that will mean the destruction [of the virtues on which human society depends]. For where then will there be a place for generosity, or love of country, or loyalty, or the inclination to be of service to others or to show gratitude for favours received? For these virtues originate in our natural inclination to love our fellowmen, and this is the foundation of Justice. . . .

M: You understand, then, that the function of a magistrate is to govern, and to give commands which are just and beneficial and in conformity with the law. For as the laws govern the magistrate, so the magistrate governs the people, and it can truly be said that the magistrate is a speaking law, and the law a silent magistrate. Nothing, moreover, is so completely in accordance with the principles of justice and the demands of Nature (and when I use these expressions, I wish it understood that I mean Law) as is government, without which existence is impossible for a household, a city, a nation, the human race, physical nature, and the universe itself. For the universe obeys God; seas and lands obey the universe, and human life is subject to the decrees of supreme Law.

Part Two

THE MIDDLE AGES

IN THE Middle Ages, it was virtually impossible to think about politics without thinking about theology. This is because medieval Europe was a religious civilization. It was born upon the decline and collapse of the Roman Empire, which was concurrent with the ascendence of the Church. In the fourth century A.D., Christianity, which had previously been persecuted, was first given equal status with other religions and then became Rome's state religion. A whole new set of circumstances was created for Christians: what was previously an alien, pagan institution—the state—had embraced their faith. Inevitably, the relation between religion and politics took on novel, complicated dimensions.

The complications are evident if we glance at some of the passages in the New Testament that are relevant to politics. "Render . . . unto Caesar the things which are Caesar's and unto God the things that are God's," says Jesus (Luke 20:25). There were, consequently, two realms: the temporal one (where politics takes place) and that of God. Moreover, Jesus declared that "My kingdom is not of this world" (John 18:36). There was, of course, no question as to which kingdom had priority. Pagan Rome's entwining of its religion with the state as well as any conception of civic affairs as the embodiment of "the good life" (such as in Aristotle) were alien to these pronouncements. However, to say "Render . . . unto Caesar" what was due him implies that obedience was indeed due by Christians to constituted—even antagonistic—authorities, as long as the latter did not contravene God's ordinances. Even then active resistance was unacceptable. After all, what was truly important was not of this world. And this was so even though it was God who gave power to all political masters. In his "Letter to the Romans," St. Paul declares:

> Let every soul be subject unto the higher powers. For there is no power but of God: the powers that be are ordained of God. Whosoever therefore resisteth the power, resisteth the ordinance of God; and they that resist shall receive to themselves damnation. For rulers are not a terror to good works, but to the evil. Wilt thou then not be afraid of the power? Do that which is good, and thou shalt have praise of the same: For he is the minister of God to thee for the good, But if thou do that which is evil, be afraid; for he beareth not the sword in vain. . . . Wherefore ye must needs be subject, not only for wrath, but also for conscience sake. (Romans 13)

All this still presumed that there were two kingdoms: the temporal one and the heavenly one. As viewed by the early church fathers, especially St. Augustine (see our first reading in this section), humanity stands condemned by original sin. The temporal world is therefore inhabited by sinners. Government must keep them in check as we cannot know in this life who is and who isn't saved by God's grace. The state is a necessity because of the fallen nature of men and women.

The Roman Empire eventually divided into two parts. The West was overrun by

Germanic "barbarian" tribes, but the Church survived, based in Rome, whose bishop became pope. The East became the Byzantine Empire, with its capital in Constantinople (today's Istanbul). A form of state-church evolved there, with a patriarch appointed by the emperor. However, the final, official separation of the churches of Rome and Byzantium didn't occur until A.D. 1054: the former became the Roman Catholic church, the latter the Orthodox Catholic church.

The Roman church was the only centralized, organized authority across medieval (western and central) Europe. Also, the only literate members of society were the clergy. Not surprisingly, religion became the touchstone of virtually all discourse, including political discussions. It is also important to remember that this was the world of feudalism, an agrarian civilization in which serfs worked on, were exploited by, and bound to the estates of feudal lords. Towns were few and small. Political and military power was in the hands of the local lords. Indeed, there were no centralized states as we know them today. Monarchs tended to be weak and significantly dependent on the lords. In fact, feudal Europe was the result of a mixture of Roman Christianity and the communal folk customs of the Germanic tribes, whose key institution was the "Comitas"—the king and his associates. The king was below, not above, the law which could not be altered save by consent of the nobles. But it was a hierarchical world in which all people knew their place in this world and hoped for their place in the next. Politics was not perceived as an autonomous realm. When one asked political questions, one asked them in light of God's scheme of things.

By the eighth and ninth centuries A.D., however, local kingdoms were growing. The more his own power developed, the more a monarch found himself in conflicts both with the society's major organized authority, the Church, and local nobles, each protecting their respective turfs. Perhaps the most famous encounter was the Investiture Contest of the eleventh century. Pope Gregory IV and the German Emperor Henry IV clashed over whether a temporal power (Henry) had the right to "invest," that is to authorize, local bishops, thereby making them beholden to the rising, local secular ruler, and not solely to the more distant religious authority in Rome.

Questions of politics were also reposed dramatically for Christianity after the rise of Islam in the Arabian peninsula, beginning in the seventh century A.D. Both faiths insisted on their universality, and their ensuing conflicts took place both on the battlefield and on intellectual terrain. Among other things, there was a revival of Aristotelianism due to the work of medieval Moslem and Jewish thinkers. Previously, Aristotle's work had been little known in the Christian world. But the Arab philosopher Averroes (1126–1198), for one example, tried to deploy Aristotle against Christianity.

The Dominican order was eventually asked to study and come to grips with the ancient Greek philosopher on behalf of the Vatican. One of their friars was Thomas Aquinas, the most important thinker of late medieval Christianity. When it came to political questions, he saw his task as reconciling the Christian (particularly Augustinian) belief that true justice is not of this world, with Aristotle's view that man was by nature a political being who realized the "good life" in political community. Political theory was, of course, subordinate to theology for Aquinas, who contended that "grace perfects nature." Still, in his theory of the different types and levels of law (see the selection in chapter 6 from his "Treatise on Law"), politics begins to carve out something of its own sphere.

Concepts of the separation of religion and politics did develop in the late Middle Ages. For example, Marsilius of Padua, in the early fourteenth century, went so far as to assert that the pope should be subordinate to the temporal ruler in secular affairs, and that a prince was the instrument of the people's will. The emergence of such ideas indicated that something fundamental was changing in the world. The result may be seen in the writings of Machiavelli in early sixteenth-century Florence. He is often called the first modern political thinker. He was only interested in religion to the extent that it could be used to fortify the state. He began to think politically in a new way, posing only secular questions about power. He asked not where the state fit into God's universe, but what made a ruler stronger or weaker. He once wrote in a letter that he loved his homeland more than his soul. When we read Machiavelli, we know we have left the Middle Ages.

5

St. Augustine
City of God

St. Augustine (A.D 354–430) was the bishop of Hippo. He spent most of his life in what is today Algeria, which was then a province of the collapsing Roman Empire. It was a time of great transformation, from the classical world of Roman antiquity to the Christian Middle Ages. Emperor Constantine gave Christianity equal status with other religions in the empire in the Edict of Milan (AD. 313), and Emperor Theodosius, in A.D 395, made Christianity the state religion. Augustine's City of God, from which the following selection is taken, was written between A.D. 413 and 425, and is one of the classical texts of Christian thought. It argues that the human race was condemned by original sin and that salvation is by God's grace alone. Since in this life it is impossible to know who is saved, government must always be obeyed since it restrains a world of sinners. In the earthly city, there can only be the "peace of Babylon." True justice and peace belong to the "City of God," not to this world.

Fallen Nature and the Two Cities

God, desiring not only that the human race might be able by their similarity of nature to associate with one another, but also that they might be bound together in harmony and peace by the ties of relationship, was pleased to derive all men from one individual. And He created men with such a nature that the members of the race should not have died, had not the first two (of whom one was created out of nothing, and the other out of him) merited this with their disobedience; for by them so great a sin was committed, that by it the human nature was altered for the worse, and was transmitted also to their posterity.

That the whole human race has been condemned in its first origin, this life itself, if life it is to be called, bears witness by the host of cruel ills with which it is filled. Is not this proved by the profound and dreadful ignorance which produces all the errors that enfold the children of Adam, and from which no man can be delivered without toil, pain, and fear? Is it not proved by his love of so many vain and hurtful things, which produces gnawing cares, disquiet, griefs, fears, wild joys, quarrels, law-suits, wars, treasons, angers, hatreds, deceit, flattery, fraud, theft, robbery, perfidy, pride, ambition, envy, murders, parricides, cruelty, ferocity, wickedness, luxury, insolence, impudence, shamelessness, fornications, adulteries, incests, and the numberless uncleannesses and unnatural acts of both sexes, which it is shameful so much as to mention; sacrileges, heresies, blasphemies, perjuries, oppression of the innocent, calumnies, plots, falsehoods, false witnessings, unrighteous judgments, violent deeds, plunderings, and innumerable other crimes that do not easily come to mind, but that never absent themselves from the actuality of human existence? These are indeed the crimes of wicked men, yet they spring from that root of error and misplaced love which is born with every son of Adam. For who is there that has not observed with what profound ignorance, manifesting itself even in infancy, and with what superfluity of foolish desires, beginning to appear in boyhood, man comes into this life, so that, were he left to live as he pleased, and to do whatever he pleased, he would plunge into all, or certainly into many of those crimes and iniquities which I mentioned, and could not mention?

But because God does not wholly desert those whom He condemns, nor shuts up in His anger His tender mercies, the human race is restrained by law and education, which keep guard against the ignorance that besets us, and oppose the assaults of vice, but are themselves full of labour and sorrow. For what mean those multifarious threats which are used to restrain the folly of children? What mean pedagogues, masters, the birch, the strap, the cane, the schooling which Scripture says must be given a child, "beating him on the sides lest he wax stubborn," and it be hardly possible or not possible at all to subdue him? Why all these punishments, save to overcome ignorance and bridle evil desires—these evils with which we come into the world? For why is it that we remember with difficulty, and without difficulty forget? learn with difficulty, and without difficulty remain ignorant? are diligent with difficulty, and without difficulty are indolent? Does not this show what vitiated nature inclines and tends to by its own weight, and what succour it needs if it is to be delivered? Inactivity, sloth, laziness, negligence, are vices which shun labour, since labour, though useful, is itself a punishment.

But, besides the punishments of childhood, without which there would be no learning of what the parents wish—and the parents rarely wish anything useful to be taught—who can describe, who can conceive the number and severity of the punishments which afflict the human race—pains which are not only the accompaniment of the wickedness of godless men, but are a part of the human condition and the common misery—what fear and what grief are caused by bereavement and mourning, by losses and condemnations, by fraud and falsehood, by false suspicions, and all the crimes and wicked deeds of other men? For at their hands we suffer robbery, captivity, chains, imprisonment, exile, torture, mutilation, loss of sight, the violation of chastity to satisfy the lust of the oppressor, and many other dreadful evils. What numberless casualties threaten our bodies from without—extremes of heat and cold, storms, floods, inundations, lightning, thunder, hail, earthquakes, houses falling; or from the stumbling, or shying, or vice of horses; from countless poisons in fruits, water, air, animals; from the painful or even deadly bites of wild animals; from the madness which a mad dog communicates, so that even the animal which of all others is most gentle and friendly to its own master, becomes an object of intenser fear than a lion or dragon, and the man whom it has by chance infected with this pestilential contagion becomes so rabid, that his parents, wife, children, dread him more than any wild beast! What disasters are suffered by those who travel by land or sea! What man can go out of his

own house without being exposed on all hands to unforeseen accidents? Returning
home sound in limb, he slips on his own door-step, breaks his leg, and never
recovers. What can seem safer than a man sitting in his chair? Eli the priest fell
from his, and broke his neck. How many accidents do farmers, or rather all men,
fear that the crops may suffer from the weather, or the soil, or the ravages of
destructive animals? Commonly they feel safe when the crops are gathered and
housed. Yet, to my certain knowledge, sudden floods have driven the labourers
away, and swept the barns clean of the finest harvest. Is innocence a sufficient
protection against the various assaults of demons? That no man might think so,
even baptized infants, who are certainly unsurpassed in innocence, are sometimes
so tormented, that God, who permits it, teaches us hereby to bewail the calamities
of this life, and to desire the felicity of the life to come. As to bodily diseases,
they are so numerous that they cannot all be contained even in medical books.
And in very many, or almost all of them, the cures and remedies are themselves
tortures, so that men are delivered from a pain that destroys by a cure that pains.
Has not the madness of thirst driven men to drink human urine, and even their
own? Has not hunger driven men to eat human flesh, and that the flesh not of
bodies found dead, but of bodies slain for the purpose? Have not the fierce pangs
of famine driven mothers to eat their own children, incredibly savage as it seems?
In fine, sleep itself, which is justly called repose, how little of repose there sometimes is in it when disturbed with dreams and visions; and with what terror is the
wretched mind overwhelmed by the appearances of things which are so presented,
and which, as it were, so stand out before the senses, that we cannot distinguish
them from realities! How wretchedly do false appearances distract men in certain
diseases! With what astonishing variety of appearances are even healthy men
sometimes deceived by evil spirits, who produce these delusions for the sake of
perplexing the senses of their victims, if they cannot succeed in seducing them to
their side!

From this hell upon earth, the deserved penalty of sin would have hurled all
headlong even into the second death, of which there is no end, had not the unde-
served grace of God saved some therefrom. And thus it has come to pass, that
though there are very many and great nations all over the earth, whose rites and
customs, speech, arms, and dress, are distinguished by marked differences, yet
there are no more than two kinds of human society, which we may justly call two
cities, according to the language of our Scriptures. The one consists of those who
wish to live after the flesh, the other of those who wish to live after the spirit.

First, we must see what it is to live after the flesh, and what to live after the
spirit. For any one who either does not recollect, or does not sufficiently weigh,
the language of sacred Scripture, may, on first hearing what we have said, suppose that the Epicurean philosophers live after the flesh, because they place man's
highest good in bodily pleasure; and that those others do so who have been of
opinion that in some form or other bodily good is man's supreme good; and that
the mass of men do so who, without dogmatizing or philosophizing on the subject,
are so prone to lust that they cannot delight in any pleasure save such as they
receive from bodily sensations: and he may suppose that the Stoics, who place the

supreme good of men in the soul, live after the spirit; for what is man's soul, if not spirit? But in the sense of the divine Scripture both are proved to live after the flesh. For by flesh it means not only the body of a terrestrial and mortal animal, as when it says, "All flesh is not the same flesh, but there is one kind of flesh of men, another flesh of beasts, another of fishes, another of birds," but it uses this word in many other significations. . . . If we are to ascertain what it is to live after the flesh (which is certainly evil, though the nature of flesh is not itself evil), we must carefully examine that passage of the epistle which the Apostle Paul wrote to the Galatians, in which he says, "Now the works of the flesh are manifest, which are these: adultery, fornication, uncleanness, lasciviousness, idolatry, witchcraft, hatred, variance, emulations, wrath, strife, seditions, heresies, envyings, murders, drunkenness, revellings, and such like: of the which I tell you before, as I have also told you in time past, that they which do such things shall not inherit the kingdom of God." This whole passage of the apostolic epistle being considered, so far as it bears on the matter in hand, will be sufficient to answer the question, what it is to live after the flesh.

In enunciating this proposition of ours, then, that because some live according to the flesh and others according to the spirit there have arisen two diverse and conflicting cities, we might equally well have said, "because some live according to man, others according to God." For Paul says very plainly to the Corinthians, "For whereas there is among you envying and strife, are ye not carnal, and walk according to man?" So that to walk according to man and to be carnal are the same; for by *flesh*, that is, by a part of man, man is meant.

But the character of the human will is of moment; . . . for the man who lives according to God, and not according to man, ought to be a lover of good, and therefore a hater of evil. And since no one is evil by nature, but whosoever is evil is evil by vice, he who lives according to God ought to cherish toward evil men a perfect hatred, so that he shall neither hate the man because of his vice, nor love the vice because of the man. For the vice being cursed, all that ought to be loved, and nothing that ought to be hated, will remain.

He who resolves to love God, and to love his neighbor as himself, not according to man but according to God, is on account of this love said to be of a good will; and this is in Scripture more commonly called charity, but it is also, even in the same books, called love. . . . The right will is, therefore, well-directed love, and the wrong will is ill-directed love. Love yearning to have what is loved, is desire; and having and enjoying it, is joy; fleeing what is opposed to it, is fear; and feeling what is opposed to it, when it has befallen it, is sadness. Now these motions are evil if the love is evil; good if the love is good.

Two cities have been formed, therefore, by two loves: the earthly by love of self, even to contempt of God; the heavenly by love of God, even to contempt of self. The former glories in itself, the latter in the Lord. For the one seeks glory from men; but the greatest glory of the other is God, the witness of conscience. The one lifts up its head in its own glory; the other says to its God, "Thou art my glory, and the lifter up of mine head." In the one, the princes and the nations it subdues are ruled by the love of ruling; in the other, the princes and the subjects serve one another in love, the latter obeying, while the former take thought for all.

The one delights in its own strength, represented in the persons of its rulers; the other says to its God, "I will love Thee, O Lord, my strength." And therefore the wise men of the one city, living according to man, have sought for profit to their own bodies or souls, or both, and those who have known God "glorified Him not as God, neither were thankful, but became vain in their imaginations, and their foolish hearts were darkened; professing themselves to be wise"—that is, glorying in their own wisdom, and being possessed by pride—"they became fools, and changed the glory of the incorruptible God into an image made like to corruptible man, and to birds, and four-footed beasts, and creeping things." For they were either leaders or followers of the people in adoring images, "and worshipped and served the creature more than the Creator, who is blessed for ever." But in the other city there is no human wisdom, but only godliness, which offers due worship to the true God, and looks for its reward in the society of the saints, of holy angels as well as holy men, "that God may be all in all." And when these two cities severally achieve what they wish, they live in peace, each after its kind.

Now peace is a good so great, that even in this earthly and mortal life there is no word we hear with such pleasure, nothing we more strongly desire, or enjoy more thoroughly when it comes. So that if we dwell for a little longer on this subject, we shall not, in my opinion, be wearisome to our readers who will bear with us both for the sake of understanding what is the end of this city of which we speak, and for the sake of the sweetness of peace which is dear to all.

Everyone who has observed the conduct of men's affairs and common human nature will agree with me in this: that just as there is no man who does not long for joy, so there is no man who does not long for peace. Even those who want war, want it really only for victory's sake: that is, they want to attain a glorious peace by fighting. For what is victory if not the subjugation of those who resist us? And when this is done, peace follows.

It is therefore with the desire for peace that wars are waged, even by those who take pleasure in exercising their warlike nature in command and battle. And hence it is obvious that peace is the end sought for by war. For every man seeks peace by waging war, but no man seeks war by making peace. For even they who intentionally interrupt the peace in which they are living have no hatred of peace, but only wish it changed into a peace that suits them better. They do not, therefore, wish to have no peace but only one more to their mind. And in the case of sedition, when men have separated themselves from the community, they yet do not effect what they wish, unless they maintain some kind of peace with their fellow-conspirators. And therefore even robbers take care to maintain peace with their comrades, that they may with greater effect and greater safety invade the peace of other men. And if an individual happen to be of such unrivalled strength, and to be so jealous of partnership, that he trusts himself with no comrades, but makes his own plots, and commits depredations and murders on his own account, yet he maintains some shadow of peace with such persons as he is unable to kill, and from whom he wishes to conceal his deeds. In his own home, too, he makes it his aim to be at peace with his wife and children, and any other members of his household; for unquestionably their prompt obedience to his every look is a source of pleasure to him. And if this be not rendered, he is angry, he chides and punishes; and even by this storm he secures the calm peace of his own home, as occasion demands. For he sees that peace cannot be maintained unless all the members of the same domestic circle be subject to one head, such as he himself is in his own house and therefore if a city or nation offered to submit itself to him, to serve him in the same style as he had made his household serve him, he would no longer lurk in a brigand's hiding-places, but lift his head in open day as a king, though the same covetousness and wickedness should remain in him. And thus all men desire to have peace with their own circle whom they wish to govern as suits themselves. For even those whom they make war against they wish to make their own, and impose on them the laws of their own peace.

But let us suppose a man such as poetry and mythology speak of—a man so insociable and savage as to be called rather a semi-man than a man. Although, then, his kingdom was the solitude of a dreary cave, and he himself was so singularly bad-hearted that he was named Κακός, which is the Greek word for *bad*; though he had no wife to soothe him with endearing talk, no children to play with, no sons to do his bidding, no friend to enliven him with intercourse, not even his father Vulcan (though in one respect he was happier than his father, not having begotten a monster like himself); although he gave to no man, but took as he wished whatever he could, from whomsoever he could, when he could; yet in that solitary den, the floor of which, as Virgil says, was always reeking with recent slaughter, there was nothing else than peace sought, a peace in which no one should molest him, or disquiet him with any assault or alarm. With his own body he desired to be at peace; and he was satisfied only in proportion as he had this peace. For he ruled his members, and they obeyed him; and for the sake of pacifying his mortal nature, which rebelled when it needed anything, and of allaying the sedition of hunger which threatened to banish the soul from the body, he made forays, slew, and devoured, but used the ferocity and savageness he displayed in these actions only for the preservation of his own life's peace. So that, had he been willing to make with other men the same peace which he made with himself in his own cave, he would neither have been called bad, nor a monster, nor a semi-man. Or if the appearance of his body and his vomiting smoky fires frightened men from having any dealings with him, perhaps his fierce ways arose not from a desire to do mischief, but from the necessity of finding a living. But he may have had no existence, or, at least, he was not such as the poets fancifully describe him, for they had to exalt Hercules, and did so at the expense of Cacus. It is better, then, to believe that such a man or semi-man never existed, and that this, in common with many other fancies of the poets, is mere fiction. For the most savage animals (and he is said to have been almost a wild beast) encompass their own species with a ring of protecting peace. They cohabit, beget, produce, suckle, and bring up their young, though very many of them are not gregarious, but solitary—not like sheep, deer, pigeons, starlings, bees, but such as lions, foxes, eagles, bats. For what tigress does not gently purr over her cub, and lay aside her ferocity to fondle them? What kite, solitary as he is when circling over his prey, does not seek a mate, build a nest, hatch the eggs, bring up the young birds, and maintain with the mother of his family as peaceful a domestic alliance as he can? How much more powerfully do the laws of man's nature move him to hold fellowship and maintain peace with all men so far as in him lies, since even wicked men wage war to maintain the peace of their own circle, and wish that, if possible, all men belonged to them, that all men and things might serve but one head, and might, either through love or fear, yield themselves to peace with him!

But the dominion of bad men harms themselves far more than their subjects, for they destroy their own souls in their greater license to exercise their lusts; while those who are put under them in service are not hurt except by their own iniquities. For to the just all the evils imposed on them by unjust rulers are not the punishment of crime, but the test of virtue. Therefore the good man, although he is a slave, is free; but the bad man, even if he reigns, is a slave, and that not of one man, but, what is far more grievous, of as many masters as he has vices; of which vices where the divine Scripture treats, it says: "Of whatsoever a man is overcome, to that he is in bondage."

This earthly city, which shall not be everlasting (for it will no longer be a city when it has been committed to perpetual pains) has all its good in this world, and rejoices in it with such joy as such things can afford. It is spread throughout the world in the most diverse places, and, though united by a common nature, is for the most part divided against itself, and the strongest oppress the others, because all follow after their own interests and lusts, while what is longed for either suffices for none, or not for all, because it is not the true good. Each part of it that arms against another desires to be the world's master, whereas it is itself in bondage to vice. If, when it has conquered, it is inflated with pride, its victory is self-destroying; but if it turns its thoughts upon the common casualties of our mortal condition, and is rather anxious concerning the disasters that may befall it than elated with the successes already achieved, this victory, though of a higher kind, is still only short-lived; for it cannot abidingly rule over those whom it has subjugated by conquest. Yet one cannot say that the things this earthly city desires are not good, since it itself is, of its kind, better than all other human things. For it desires earthly peace for the sake of enjoying earthly goods, and it makes war in order to attain this peace; since, if it has conquered, and there remains no one to resist it, it enjoys a peace which it had not while there were opposing parties to contest it for the enjoyment of those things which were too little to satisfy both.

And the vanquished readily succumb to the victors, preferring any sort of peace and safety to freedom itself; so that they who choose to die rather than be slaves have been greatly wondered at. For nature seems to cry out with one voice through all peoples of the world, that it is better to serve the conqueror than be destroyed by war. Thus it happens (but not without God's providence) that some are endowed with kingdoms and others made subject to kings.

True Justice: Not of This World

Justinus, who wrote Greek or rather foreign history in Latin, and briefly, like Trogus Pompeius whom he followed, begins his work thus: "In the beginning of the affairs of peoples and nations the government was in the hands of kings, who were raised to the height of this majesty not by courting the people, but by the knowledge good men had of their moderation. The people were held bound by no laws; the decisions of the princes were instead of laws. It was the custom to guard rather than to extend the boundaries of the empire; and kingdoms were kept within the bounds of each ruler's native land. Ninus king of the Assyrians first of all, through new lust of empire, changed the old and, as it were, ancestral custom of nations. He first made war on his neighbours, and wholly subdued as far as to the frontiers of Libya the nations as yet untrained to resist." And a little after he says: "Ninus established by constant possession the greatness of the authority he had gained. Having mastered his nearest neighbours, he went on to others, strengthened by the accession of forces, and by making each fresh victory the instrument of that which followed, subdued the nations of the whole East." Now, with whatever fidelity to fact either he or Trogus may in general have written—for that they sometimes told lies is shown by other more trustworthy writers—yet it is agreed among other authors, that the kingdom of the Assyrians was extended far and wide by King Ninus. And it lasted so long, that the Roman empire has not yet attained the same age; for, as those write who have treated of chronological history, this kingdom endured for twelve hundred and forty years from the first year in which Ninus began to reign, until it was transferred to the Medes. But to make war on your neighbours, and thence to proceed to others, and through mere lust of dominion to crush and subdue people who do you no harm, what else is this to be called than great robbery?

Indeed, without justice, what are kingdoms but great robberies? For what are robberies themselves, but little kingdoms? The band itself is made up of men; it is ruled by the authority of a prince, it is knit together by the pact of the confederacy; the booty is divided by the law agreed on. If, by the admittance of abandoned men, this evil increases to such a degree that it holds places, fixes abodes, takes possession of cities, and subdues peoples, it assumes the more plainly the name of a kingdom, because the reality is now manifestly conferred on it, not by the removal of covetousness, but by the addition of impunity. Indeed, that was an apt and true reply which was given to Alexander the Great by a pirate who had been seized. For when that king had asked the man what he meant by keeping hostile possession of the sea, he answered with bold pride, "What thou meanest by seizing the whole earth; but because I do it with a petty ship, I am called a robber, whilst thou who doest it with a great fleet art styled emperor." . . .

. . . [If] we are to accept the definitions laid down by Scipio in [Cicero's] *On the Republic*, there never was a Roman republic; for he briefly defines a republic as the weal of the people. And if this definition be true, there never was a Roman republic, for the people's weal was never attained among the Romans. For the people, according to his definition, is an assemblage associated by a common acknowledgment of right and by a community of interests. And what he means by a common acknowledgment of right he explains at large, showing that a republic cannot be administered without justice. Where, therefore, there is no true justice there can be no right. For that which is done by right is justly done, and what is unjustly done cannot be done by right. For the unjust inventions of men are neither to be considered nor spoken of as rights; for even they themselves say that right is that which flows from the fountain of justice, and deny the definition which is commonly given by those who misconceive the matter, that right is that which is useful to the stronger party. Thus, where there is not true justice there can be no assemblage of men associated by a common acknowledgment of right, and therefore there can be no people, as defined by Scipio or Cicero; and if no people, then no weal of the people, but only of some promiscuous multitude unworthy of the name of people. Consequently, if the republic is the weal of the people, and there is no people if it be not associated by a common acknowledgement of right, and if there is no right where there is no justice, then most certainly it follows that there is no republic where there is no justice.

Further, justice is that virtue which gives every one his due. Where, then, is the justice of man, when he deserts the true God and yields himself to impure demons? Is this to give every one his due? Or is he who keeps back a piece of ground from the purchaser, and gives it to a man who has no right to it, unjust, while he who keeps back himself from the God who made him, and serves wicked spirits, is just?

This same book, *On the Republic*, advocates the cause of justice against injustice with great force and keenness. The pleading for injustice against justice was first heard, and it was asserted (as we noted earlier) that without injustice a republic could neither increase nor even subsist, for it was laid down as an absolutely unassailable position that it is unjust for some men to rule and some to serve; and yet the imperial city to which the republic belongs cannot rule her provinces without having recourse to this injustice. It was replied in behalf of justice, that this ruling of the provinces is just, because servitude may be advantageous to the provincials, and is so when rightly administered—that is to say, when lawless men are prevented from doing harm. And further, as they became worse and worse so long as they were free, they will improve by subjection. To confirm this reasoning, there is added an eminent example drawn from nature: for "why," it is asked, "does God rule man, the soul the body, the reason the passions and other vicious parts of the soul?" This example leaves no doubt that, to some, servitude is useful; and, indeed, to serve God is useful to all. And it is when the soul serves God that it exercises a right control over the body; and in the soul itself the reason must be subject to God if it is to govern as it ought the passions and other vices. Hence, when a man does not serve God, what justice can we ascribe to him, since in this case his soul cannot exercise a just control over the body, nor his reason over his vices? And if there is no justice in such an individual, certainly there can be none in a community composed of such persons. Here, therefore, there is not that common acknowledgment of right which makes an assemblage of men a people whose affairs we call a republic. And why need I speak of the advantageousness, the common participation in which, according to the definition, makes a people? For although, if you choose to regard the matter attentively, you will see that there is nothing advantageous to those who live godlessly, as every one lives who does not serve God but demons, whose wickedness you may measure by their desire to receive the worship of men though they are most impure spirits, yet what I have said of the common acknowledgment of right is enough to demonstrate that, according to the above definition, there can be no people, and therefore no republic, where there is no justice. For if they assert that in their republic the Romans did not serve unclean spirits, but good and holy gods, must we therefore again reply to this evasion, though already we have said enough, and more than enough, to expose it? He must be an uncommonly stupid, or a shamelessly contentious person, who . . . can yet question whether the Romans served wicked and impure demons. But, not to speak of their character, it is written in the law of the true God, "He that sacrificeth unto any god save unto the Lord only, he shall be utterly destroyed." He, therefore, who uttered so menacing a commandment decreed that no worship should be given either to good or bad gods.

And where there is not that justice whereby the one supreme God rules the obedient city according to His grace, so that it sacrifices to none but Him, and whereby, in all the citizens of this obedient city, the soul consequently rules the body and reason the vices in the rightful order, so that, as the individual just man, so also the community and people of the just, live by faith, which works by love, that love whereby man loves God as He ought to be loved, and his neighbour as himself—there, I say, there is not an assemblage associated by a common acknowledgment of right, and by a community of interests. But if there is not this, there is not a people, if our definition be true, and therefore there is no republic; for where there is no people there can be no republic.

But if we discard this definition of a people, and, assuming another, say that a people is an assemblage of reasonable beings bound together by a common agreement as to the objects of their love, then, in order to discover the character of any people, we have only to observe what they love. Yet whatever it loves, if only it is an assemblage of reasonable beings and not of beasts, and is bound together by an agreement as to the objects of love, it is reasonably called a people; and it will be a superior people in proportion as it is bound together by higher interests, inferior in proportion as it is bound together by lower. According to this definition of ours, the Roman people is a people, and its weal is without doubt a commonwealth or republic. But what its tastes were in its early and subsequent days, and how it declined into sanguinary seditions and then to social and civil wars, and so burst asunder or rotted off the bond of concord in which the health of a people consists, history shows. . . . Yet I would not on this account say either that it was not a people, or that its administration was not a republic, so long as there remains an assemblage of reasonable beings bound together by a common agreement as to the objects of love. But what I say of this people and of this republic I must be understood to think and say of the Athenians or any Greek state, of the Egyptians, of the early Assyrian Babylon, and of every other nation, great or small, which had a public government. For, in general, the city of the ungodly, which did not obey the command of God that it should offer no sacrifice save to Him alone, and which, therefore, could not give to the soul its proper command over the body, nor to the reason its just authority over the vices, is void of true justice.

For though the soul may seem to rule the body admirably, and the reason the vices, if the soul and reason do not themselves obey God, as God has commanded them to serve Him, they have no proper authority over the body and the vices. For what kind of mistress of the body and the vices can that mind be which is ignorant of the true God, and which, instead of being subject to His authority, is prostituted to the corrupting influences of the most vicious demons? It is for this reason that the virtues which it seems to itself to possess, and by which it restrains the body and the vices that it may obtain and keep what it desires, are rather vices than virtues so long as there is no reference to God in the matter. For although some suppose that virtues which have a reference only to themselves, and are desired only on their own account, are yet true and genuine virtues, the fact is that even then they are inflated with pride, and are therefore to be reckoned vices rather than virtues.

Thus, in fact, true justice has no existence save in that republic whose founder and ruler is Christ, if at least any choose to call this a republic; and indeed we cannot deny that it is the people's weal. But if perchance this name, which has become familiar in other connections, be considered alien to our common parlance, we may at all events say that in this city is true justice; the city of which Holy Scripture says, "Glorious things are said of thee, O city of God."

6

St. Thomas Aquinas
Politics and Law

St. Thomas Aquinas (1224–1274) was born in Naples and joined the Dominican order over the protests of his family, who were nobles. He was the most important Christian political thinker of the late Middle Ages, although as a theologian politics was only one of his preoccupations. He sought a way to synthesize Christian thought, particularly Augustinianism, with Aristotelianism. For Aristotle, man is essentially a political animal who realizes himself in the political community. For Augustine, salvation of the soul is paramount; the kingdom of true justice is not of this world. In his "Treastise on Law," part of his massive Summa Theologica *(1266–1273), Aquinas tried to discern a positive role for politics in a world of sinners, and to find a way in which reason and faith might work together.*

THE TREATISE ON LAW
(QU. 90–97 FROM SUMMA THEOLOGICA)

The Essence of Law

1. Is Law a Matter of Reason?

Law is a rule or measure of action by which one is led to action or restrained from acting. The word law (*lex*) is derived from *ligare*, to bind, because it binds one to act. The rule and measure of action is the reason, which is the first principle of human action. . . . . Reason has the power to move the will, as explained above, because whenever someone desires an end, reason commands what is to be done to reach it. In order for an act of will that something is to be done to have the character of law, it must be guided by some reason. This is how we should understand the saying [of Roman law] that "the will of the prince has the force of law."[1] Otherwise the will of the prince would be iniquity rather than law. . . .

2. Is Law Always Directed toward the Common Good?

Every part is ordered to the whole as the imperfect is to the perfect. The individual is part of a perfect whole that is the community. Therefore law must concern itself in particular with the happiness of the community. . . .

3. Can Any Person Make Law?

Obj. 1. The Apostle [Paul] says that "since the gentiles who have no law do by nature the things that are of the law, they are a law for themselves."[2] But this is applied to everyone. Therefore anyone can make a law for himself.

Obj. 2. Furthermore as the Philosopher [Aristotle] says in the *Ethics*, "The intention of the legislator is to lead men to virtue."[3] But any man can lead another to virtue. Therefore the reason of any man can make law.

Obj. 3. As the prince in a state (*civitas*) is the ruler of the state so also the father of a family is the ruler of the household. But the prince can make law for the state. Therefore any father of a family can make law in his household.

On the contrary, the *Decretum* quotes Isidore as saying, "As law is an ordination of the people which is sanctioned by the elders and approved by the people."[4] Therefore not any person can make a law.

I answer that properly speaking, law has as its first and foremost purpose the ordering of the common good. To order something to the common good is the responsibility of the whole people, or of someone who represents the whole people. Therefore making law belongs either to the whole people or to the public personage who has the responsibility for the whole people, since, as in all other cases, direction towards an end is the responsibility of the one to whom the end belongs.

Reply to Obj. 1. As is stated above, a law is said to be in someone not only because it involves the participation of the one who makes the law but also that of the one to whom the law applies. And in this way everyone can be said to be a law for himself, because he shares in the action of the legislator. Hence Scripture says in the same place, "they show the work of the law written in their hearts."[5]

Reply to Obj. 2. A private person cannot effectively lead others to virtue. He can only give advice and if that advice is not followed he has no power of compulsion. Law, however, should have the power to lead to virtue as the Philosopher [Aristotle] says.[6] But the power of compulsion belongs to the whole people (*multitudo*) or to the public personage whose duty it is to inflict punishment, as we explain below. Therefore making law belongs only to him. . . .

Reply to Obj. 3. A man is part of a household, and a household is part of a city (*civitas*). Now a city [state] is a perfect community as is stated in Book I of the *Politics*. Therefore the good of one man is not a final end but is directed toward the common good, and the good of a single household is ordered to the good of the state that is a perfect community. Therefore the head of a family can make some rules or regulations but they do not, properly speaking, have the character of law.

4. Is Promulgation Necessary for a Law?

In order for a law to have the binding force that is proper to legislation, it must be applied to those who are to be ruled by it. It is applied by being made known to them through promulgation. Therefore promulgation is necessary for a law to have binding force. From the foregoing articles we can derive a definition of law. Law is nothing else than an ordination of reason for the common good promulgated by the one who is in charge of the community.

The Kinds of Law

1. Is There an Eternal Law?

We have stated above that law is nothing else than a certain dictate of practical reason by a ruler who governs some perfect community. Assuming that the world is governed by divine providence as we argued in Part I, it is evident that the whole community of the universe is governed by the divine reason. Therefore the rational governance of everything on the part of God, as the ruler of the universe, has the quality of law. And since the divine reason's conception of things is not subject to time but is eternal, this kind of law must be called the eternal law.

2. Is There a Natural Law?

Since everything that is subject to divine providence is regulated and measured by the eternal law, as we have shown above, it is evident that all things participate in the eternal law in a certain way because it is imprinted upon them through their respective inclinations to their proper actions and ends. Rational creatures are under divine providence in a more excellent way than the others since by providing for themselves and others they share in the action of providence themselves. They participate in eternal reason in that they have a natural inclination to their proper actions and ends. Such participation in the eternal law by rational creatures is called the natural law.

3. Is There Human Law?

The speculative reason proceeds from naturally known indemonstrable principles to the conclusions of the various sciences which are not innate in us but are acquired by the effort of our reason. In the same way human reason must proceed from the precepts of the natural law as from certain common and indemonstrable principles to other more particular dispositions. Those particular dispositions arrived at by reason are called human laws.

4. Was There a Need for Divine Law?

Besides the natural law and human law it was necessary to have the divine law to direct human life.[7] This is for four reasons: First, law directs man to actions that are appropriately ordered to his final end. If man were destined to an end which did not exceed the natural capacity of mankind, there would be no need for his reason to direct him in any other way than through the natural law and the humanly enacted law that is derived from it. But because man is destined to the end of eternal bliss (*beatitudo*) which exceeds the capacity of the natural human faculties, as explained above, it was necessary for him to be directed to this end by a divinely revealed law, in addition to the natural and human law. Secondly, because of the uncertainty of human judgment, especially in contingent and particular matters, it happens that different decisions are made about different human acts, so that laws are often divergent and even contradictory. For man to know what he should do and not do without any doubt it was necessary for him to be directed in his actions by a law given by God, for it is certain that such a law cannot err. Thirdly, man can make laws about matters that are capable of being judged. But man cannot make a judgment about internal motivations that are hidden, but only about external actions that are public. To be perfectly virtuous, however, man must be upright in both kinds of action. Therefore since human law could not punish or direct interior actions sufficiently, it was necessary for there to be a divine law. Fourthly, as Augustine says, human law cannot punish or prohibit every evil action, because in trying to eliminate evils it may also do away with many good things and the interest of the common good which is necessary for human society may be adversely affected.[8] Therefore in order for no evil to go unforbidden and unpunished, it was necessary for there to be a divine law which forbids all sin.

By the natural law human nature participates in the eternal law in proportion to the capacity of human nature. But man needs to be directed to his supernatural end in a higher way. Hence there is an additional law given by God through which man shares more perfectly in the eternal law.

The Effects of Law

1. Is an Effect of the Law to Make Men Good?

If the intention of the legislator is directed at the true good, i.e., the common good, and regulated according to the principles of divine justice, it follows that the law will make men good absolutely. If however the intention of the legislator is directed not at what is absolutely good but at what is useful or pleasurable for himself or opposed to divine justice, then the law does not make men good absolutely, but only relatively to a particular regime. In this sense good is found even in things that are evil in themselves, such as when one speaks of a good robber because he works in a way that is adapted to his end.

A tyrannical law, since it is not in accordance with reason, is not a law in the strict sense, but rather a perversion of law. However it has something of the character of law to the extent that it intends that the citizens should be good. It only has the character of a law because it is a dictate of a superior over his subjects and is aimed at their obeying law—which is a good that is not absolute but only relative to a specific regime. . . .

Human Law

Was It Useful for Man to Make Human Laws?

Man possesses a natural aptitude for virtue but he needs a certain discipline to perfect that virtue. The man who can develop such discipline by himself is rare. . . . Parental discipline through moral suasion is sufficient for those young people who are inclined to the life of virtue by natural disposition, or custom, or even more because of the help of God. But since there are some who are dissolute and prone to vice who cannot easily be moved by words alone, these have to be restrained from doing evil by force and fear so that they will cease to do evil and leave others in peace, and so that after they become habituated in this way they will do voluntarily what they did earlier out of fear—and become virtuous. Now this kind of discipline through fear of punishment is the discipline of law. Therefore laws are adopted to bring about peace and virtue among men. As the Philosopher [Aristotle] says, "Man is the noblest of animals if he is perfect in virtue, but if he departs from law and justice he is the worst."[9] For unlike other animals man possesses the weapons of reason which he can use to satisfy his passions and base instinct. . . .

The Power of Human Law

Should Law Repress all Vices?

The power or capacity to act results from a habit or interior disposition. Not everything is possible for both the virtuous man and one who does not have the habit of virtue, just as the same thing is not possible for a boy and a full-grown man. Therefore many things are permitted to children which would be punished or at least criticized in adults. Similarly many things are allowed to men who are not advanced in virtue that would not be tolerated in a virtuous man.

Human law is framed for the mass of men, the majority of whom are not perfectly virtuous. Therefore human law does not prohibit every vice from which virtuous men abstain, but only the more serious ones from which the majority can abstain, especially those that harm others and which must be prohibited for human society to survive, such as homicide, theft, and the like.

Does Human Law Oblige in Conscience?

A law may be unjust in two ways. First if it is contrary to human good in the way we have explained—either in its object, for example when a ruler imposes onerous laws on his subjects which are not for the benefit of the community but for his own cupidity and vainglory—or in its author as when someone makes a law that exceeds the power given to him—or in its form, for example, when burdens are placed on the community in an unequal fashion even if they are aimed at the common good. These are acts of violence rather than laws, for as Augustine said, "A law that is unjust is considered to be no law at all."[10] Therefore laws of this kind do not bind in conscience except to avoid scandal or disorder. In such a case a man should give up his right to disobey—as Matthew's Gospel says, "If someone forces you to go a mile, go with him an extra two; if he takes your coat, give him your cloak as well."[11]

Secondly, a law may be unjust because it is contrary to divine goodness. For example, laws enforcing idolatry or another action that is against divine law. Under no circumstance may such laws be obeyed, for as it says in the *Acts [of the Apostles]* "We must obey God rather than men."[12]

Is Everyone Subject to the Law?

Law has two characteristics. First, it is a rule for human actions, and secondly, it has coercive force. . . . A ruler is said to be above the law in its coercive force since properly speaking no one can coerce himself, and the law derives its coercive force only from the power of the ruler. Thus the ruler is said to be above the law because if he violates it there is no one to impose a sentence of condemnation upon him. . . .[13] In the judgment of God (however) the prince is not above the law in its directive force, but should carry out the law of his own free will and without constraint. In addition the prince is above the law because he can change it, if it is expedient, or dispense from it according to the time and place. . . .

The Moral Precepts of the Old Law[14]

1. Do all the Precepts of Morality Belong to the Natural Law?

Moral precepts are distinct from ceremonial and judicial precepts because moral precepts by their very nature are concerned with good morals. Since human moral conduct is directed by reason which is the basic principle of human action, those moral actions that are in accord with reason are called good, and those that depart from reason are called evil. Just as every judgment of the speculative reason proceeds from our natural knowledge of first principles, so every judgment of our practical reason proceeds from certain principles that we know by nature, as we have said earlier. From these principles we can proceed to make practical judgments about different things in different ways. Some human actions are so clearly connected with general first principles that we can approve or reject them immediately with very little reflection. There are other cases in which different circumstances must be taken into account in order to make a decision, which not everyone can do with care, but only the wise—just as not everyone can reach the particular conclusions of the sciences, but only the wise. But there are other matters in which man needs the help of divine instruction—i.e., matters of faith.

The Reason for the Judicial Precepts

1. Did the Old Law Contain Useful Provisions on Government?

Two points should be noted concerning the right ordering of rulers in any city or nation. The first is that all should have a share in the government. In this way peace is preserved among the people and everyone loves and protects the constitution, as is stated in the *Politics*, Book II.[15] The second regards the form of government or constitution. As the Philosopher [Aristotle] tell us in *Politics*, Book III, there are various forms of government.[16] The most outstanding are a kingdom in which one man rules in accordance with virtue, and an aristocracy—that is, government by the best men in which a small number of people rule in accordance with virtue. And so the best constitution for a city or kingdom is one in which one person rules in accordance with virtue, and under him there are others who govern in accordance with virtue, and all have some part in government because they are all eligible to govern and those who govern are chosen by all. This is the best form of polity since it is a judicious combination of kingship—rule by one man, aristocracy—rule by many in accordance with virtue, and democracy—i.e., popular rule in that the rulers can be chosen from the people and the people have the right to choose their rulers.

This was the form of government established by the divine law. Moses and his successors governed the people as sole rulers over all so that there was a kind of kingship. Seventy-two elders were chosen in accordance with their virtue, as Deuteronomy says, "I took out of your tribes wise and noble men and made them rulers" and this was the aristocratic aspect. But it was democratic in that they were elected from all the people, since Exodus says, "Provide wise men from all the people" and also because the people chose them, as Deuteronomy says, "Give me wise men from among you" etc.[17] Therefore it is clear that the constitution that the [Old] Law established was the best.

A kingdom is the best form of government for a people, provided that it does not become corrupt. However because of the great power given to a king, a kingdom can easily degenerate into a tyranny, unless the one who has been given such power is perfect in virtue, because, as the Philosopher [Aristotle] says in *Ethics*, Book IV, "Only the virtuous man acts well in good fortune."[18] Perfect virtue, however is found in few men. The Jews were especially prone to cruelty and avarice—the vices that chiefly incline men to tyranny. Hence at the beginning the Lord did not establish a king with full power over them but appointed a judge and governor to rule them. Later as though in anger he granted their petition for a king, as is clear from what he said to Samuel, "They have not rejected you but me—that I should not reign over them."[19]

The Grace of God—the External Foundation of Human Acts

2. Can Man Will or Do Anything Good without Grace?

Man's nature can be considered in two ways—first, in its integral state as it was before the sin of our first parent, and secondly, corrupted as it is in us, following the sin of our first parent. Now in both states human nature needs the help of God as the Prime [First] Mover to do or will anything good. However in the state of natural integrity man possessed sufficient virtue for action that by his natural powers he could will and do the good that was proportionate to his nature—that is, the good resulting from acquired virtue. However he could not do the good actions that result from infused virtue which exceeded his nature. However in the state of corrupted nature man is deficient even in what he can do by nature since he cannot perform all good actions of this kind by his natural powers. However since human nature is not so completely corrupted by sin as to be totally lacking in natural goodness, it is possible for him in the state of corrupted nature to do some particular good things by virtue of his nature—for example, build houses, plant vineyards, and the like. Yet he cannot do all the good that is natural to him so as never to fall short in any respect. In the same way a sick man can make some movements on his own but to move with the full motion of a man who is healthy he must be cured with the help of medicine.

Therefore in the state of natural integrity the only reason that man needs the power of grace added to the power of nature is to do or will supernatural good, but in the state of corrupted nature he needs it for two reasons—to be healed [of the effects of sin] and also in order to perform acts of supernatural goodness that are meritorious. In addition man needs divine help in both states to move him to good actions.

Notes

1. *Digest*, I, iv, 1.
2. Romans, 2:14.
3. Aristotle, *Nicomachean Ethics*, II, 1.
4. Gratian, *Decretum*, I, ii, 1 quoting Isidore, *Etymologies*, V, 10. The *Decretum* is the authoritative twelfth century canon law collection by the Italian monk, Gratian, who sys-

tematically organized earlier sources in an attempt to harmonize and integrate church law. Isidore of Seville (560–636) was the last of the Fathers of the church.

5. Romans, 2:15.

6. Aristotle, *Nicomachean Ethics*, X, 9.

7. Note that divine law for Aquinas meant God's direct revelation in Scripture. It is to be distinguished from eternal law, God's rational governance of the universe.

8. St. Augustine, *On Free Choice*, I, 51.

9. Aristotle, *Politics*, I, 2.

10. St. Augustine, *On Free Choice*, I, 5.

11. Matthew, 5:40–41.

12. Acts, 5:29.

13. Aquinas is interpreting the Roman law statement, "the prince is free of the law" (*Princeps legibus solutus est*), *Digest* I, ii, 31 (Ulpian).

14. The Old Law—i.e., the legal provisions contained in the Old Testament.

15. Aristotle, *Politics*, II, 1. A better source would be *Politics* III, 1.

16. Aristotle, *Politics*, III, 5–7.

17. Deuteronomy, 1:15; Exodus, 18:21; Deuteronomy, 1:13.

18. Aristotle, *Nicomachean Ethics*, IV, 3.

19. I Samuel, 8:7.

7

Christine de Pizan
The Book of the City of Ladies

Christine de Pizan (1364–1430?) was an Italian-born French poet, essayist, historian, and biographer. One of the most respected authors of her time, de Pizan was a widow who supported herself and her large family and dependents on earnings from her writings. She had been educated despite the widespread belief that learning was dangerous to women, and composed an enormous body of work with the intention of educating and influencing national politics with political, military, and educational writings. De Pizan learned the necessity for women to gain control of their financial destiny when both her husband and her father died, leaving her dependent on corrupt lawyers. She battled for fifteen years to collect a small inheritance, and urged women to understand both national and household economy. De Pizan wrote in praise of women; however, the most notable virtue she extolled was that of self-sacrifice in their relations to their husbands. In The Book of the City of Ladies (1405) she attempted to destroy the myth that women were creatures of great evil or beings of transcendent good.

Here Begins the Book of the City of Ladies, Whose First Chapter Tells Why and for What Purpose This Book Was Written

One day as I was sitting alone in my study surrounded by books on all kinds of subjects, devoting myself to literary studies, my usual habit, my mind dwelt at length on the weighty opinions of various authors whom I had studied for a long time. I looked up from my book, having decided to leave such subtle questions in peace and to relax by reading some light poetry. With this in mind, I searched for some small book. By chance a strange volume came into my hands, not one of my own, but one which had been given to me along with some others. When I held it open and saw from its title page that it was by Mathéolus, I smiled, for though I had never seen it before, I had often heard that like other books it discussed respect for women. I thought I would browse through it to amuse myself. I had not been reading for very long when my good mother called me to refresh myself with some supper, for it was evening. Intending to look at it the next day, I put it down. The next morning, again seated in my study as was my habit, I remembered wanting to examine this book by Mathéolus. I started to read it and went on for a little while. Because the subject seemed to me not very pleasant for people who do not enjoy lies, and of no use in developing virtue or manners, given its lack of integrity in diction and theme, and after browsing here and there and reading the end, I put it down in order to turn my attention to more elevated and useful study. But just the sight of this book, even though it was of no authority, made me wonder how it happened that so many different men—and learned men among them—have been and are so inclined to express both in speaking and in their treatises and writings so many wicked insults about women and their behavior. Not only one or two and not even just this Mathéolus (for this book had a bad name anyway and was intended as a satire) but, more generally, judging from the treatises of all philosophers and poets and from all the orators—it would take too long to mention their names—it seems that they all speak from one and the same mouth. They all concur in one conclusion: that the behavior of women is inclined to and full of every vice. Thinking deeply about these matters, I began to examine my character and conduct as a natural woman and, similarly, I considered other women whose company I frequently kept, princesses, great ladies, women of the middle and lower classes, who had graciously told me of their most private and intimate thoughts, hoping that I could judge impartially and in good conscience whether the testimony of so many notable men could be true. To the best of my knowledge, no matter how long I confronted or dissected the problem, I could not see or realize how their claims could be true when compared to the natural behavior and character of women. Yet I still argued vehemently against women, saying that it would be impossible that so many famous men—such solemn scholars, possessed of such deep and great understanding, so clear-sighted in all things, as it seemed—could have spoken falsely on so many occasions that I could hardly find a book on morals where, even before I had read it in its entirety, I did not find several chapters or certain sections attacking women, no matter who the author was. This reason alone, in short, made me conclude that, although my intellect did not perceive my own great faults and, likewise, those of other women because of its simpleness and ignorance, it was however truly fitting that such was the case. And so I relied more on the judgment of others than on what I myself felt and knew. I was so transfixed in this line of thinking for such a long time that it seemed as if I were in a stupor. Like a gushing fountain, a series of authorities, whom I recalled one after another, came to mind, along with their opinions on this topic. And I finally decided that God formed a vile creature when He made woman, and I wondered how such a worthy artisan could have deigned to make such an abominable work which, from what they say, is the vessel as well as the refuge and abode of every evil and vice. As I was thinking this, a great unhappiness and sadness welled up in my heart, for I detested myself and the entire feminine sex, as though we were monstrosities in nature. And in my lament I spoke these words:

"Oh, God, how can this be? For unless I stray from my faith, I must never doubt that Your infinite wisdom and most perfect goodness ever created anything which was not good. Did You yourself not create women in a very special way and since that time did You not give her all those inclinations which it pleased You for her to have? And how could it be that You could go wrong in anything? Yet look at all these accusations which have been judged, decided, and concluded against women. I do not know how to understand this repugnance. If it is so, fair Lord God, that in fact so many abominations abound in the female sex, for You Yourself say that the testimony of two or three witnesses lends credence, why shall I not doubt that this is true? Alas, God, why did You not let me be born in the world as a man, so that all my inclinations would be to serve You better, and so that I would not stray in anything and would be as perfect as a man is said to be? But since Your kindness has not been extended to me, then forgive my negligence in Your service, most fair Lord God, and may it not displease You, for the servant who receives fewer gifts from his lord is less obliged in his service." I spoke these words to God in my lament and a great deal more for a very long time in sad reflection, and in my folly I considered myself most unfortunate because God had made me inhabit a female body in this world.

Here Christine Describes How Three Ladies Appeared to Her and How the One Who Was in Front Spoke First and Comforted Her in Her Pain

So occupied with these painful thoughts, my head bowed in shame, my eyes filled with tears, leaning on the pommel of my chair's armrest, I suddenly saw a ray of light fall on my lap, as though it were the sun. I shuddered then, as if wakened from sleep, for I was sitting in a shadow where the sun could not have shone at that hour. And as I lifted my head to see where this light was coming from, I saw three crowned ladies standing before me, and the splendor of their bright faces shone on me and throughout the entire room. Now no one would ask whether I was surprised, for my doors were shut and they had still entered. Fearing that some phantom had come to tempt me and filled with great fright, I made the Sign of the Cross on my forehead.

Then she who was the first of the three smiled and began to speak, "Dear daughter, do not be afraid, for we have not come here to harm or trouble you but to console you, for we have taken pity on your distress, and we have come to bring you out of the ignorance which so blinds your own intellect that you shun what you know for a certainty and believe what you do not know or see or recognize except by virtue of many strange opinions. You resemble the fool in the prank who was dressed in women's clothes while he slept; because those who were making fun of him repeatedly told him he was a woman, he believed their false testimony more readily than the certainty of his own identity. Fair daughter, have you lost all sense? Have you forgotten that when fine gold is tested in the furnace, it does not change or vary in strength but becomes purer the more it is hammered and handled in different ways? Do you not know that the best things are the most debated and the most discussed? If you wish to consider the question of the highest form of reality, which consists in ideas or celestial substances, consider whether the greatest philosophers who have lived and whom you support against your own sex have ever resolved whether ideas are false and contrary to the truth.

Notice how these same philosophers contradict and criticize one another, just as you have seen in the *Metaphysics* where Aristotle takes their opinions to task and speaks similarly of Plato and other philosophers. And note, moreover, how even Saint Augustine and the Doctors of the Church have criticized Aristotle in certain passages, although he is known as the prince of philosophers in whom both natural and moral philosophy attained their highest level. It also seems that you think that all the words of the philosophers are articles of faith, that they could never be wrong. As far as the poets of whom you speak are concerned, do you not know that they spoke on many subjects in a fictional way and that often they mean the contrary of what their words openly say? One can interpret them according to the grammatical figure of *antiphrasis*, which means, as you know, that if you call something bad, in fact, it is good, and also vice versa. Thus I advise you to profit from their works and to interpret them in the manner in which they are intended in those passages where they attack women. Perhaps this man, who called himself Mathéolus in his own book, intended it in such a way, for there are many things which, if taken literally, would be pure heresy. As for the attack against the estate of marriage—which is a holy estate, worthy and ordained by God—made not only by Mathéolus but also by others and even by the *Romance of the Rose* where greater credibility is averred because of the authority of its author, it is evident and proven by experience that the contrary of the evil which they posit and claim to be found in this estate through the obligation and fault of women is true. For where has the husband ever been found who would allow his wife to have authority to abuse and insult him as a matter of course, as these authorities maintain? I believe that, regardless of what you might have read, you will never see such a husband with your own eyes, so badly colored are these lies. Thus, in conclusion, I tell you, dear friend, that simplemindedness has prompted you to hold such an opinion. Come back to yourself, recover your senses, and do not trouble yourself anymore over such absurdities. For you know that any evil spoken of women so generally only hurts those who say it, not women themselves."

Against Those Men Who Claim It Is Not Good for Women to Be Educated

Following these remarks, I, Christine, spoke, "My lady, I realize that women have accomplished many good things and that even if evil women have done evil, it seems to me, nevertheless, that the benefits accrued and still accruing because of good women—particularly the wise and literary ones and those educated in the natural sciences whom I mentioned above—outweigh the evil. Therefore, I am amazed by the opinion of some men who claim that they do not want their daughters, wives, or kinswomen to be educated because their mores would be ruined as a result."

She responded, "Here you can clearly see that not all opinions of men are based on reason and that these men are wrong. For it must not be presumed that mores necessarily grow worse from knowing the moral sciences, which teach the virtues, indeed, there is not the slightest doubt that moral education amends and ennobles them. How could anyone think or believe that whoever follows good teaching or doctrine is the worse for it? Such an opinion cannot be expressed or maintained. I do not mean that it would be good for a man or a woman to study the art of divination or those fields of learning which are forbidden—for the holy Church did not remove them from common use without good reason—but it should not be believed that women are the worse for knowing what is good.

"Quintus Hortensius, a great rhetorician and consummately skilled orator in Rome, did not share this opinion. He had a daughter, named Hortensia, whom he greatly loved for the subtlety of her wit. He had her learn letters and study the science of rhetoric, which she mastered so thoroughly that she resembled her father Hortensius not only in wit and lively memory but also in her excellent delivery and order of speech—in fact, he surpassed her in nothing. As for the subject discussed above, concerning the good which comes about through women, the benefits realized by this woman and her learning were, among others, exceptionally remarkable. That is, during the time when Rome was governed by three men, this Hortensia began to support the cause of women and to undertake what no man dared to undertake. There was a question whether certain taxes should be levied on women and on their jewelry during a needy period in Rome. This woman's eloquence was so compelling that she was listened to, no less readily than her father would have been, and she won her case.

"Similarly, to speak of more recent times, without searching for examples in ancient history, Giovanni Andrea, a solemn law professor in Bologna not quite sixty years ago, was not of the opinion that it was bad for women to be educated. He had a fair and good daughter, named Novella, who was educated in the law to such an advanced degree that when he was occupied by some task and not at leisure to present his lectures to his students, he would send Novella, his daughter, in his place to lecture to the students from his chair. And to prevent her beauty from distracting the concentration of her audience, she had a little curtain drawn in front of her. In this manner she could on occasion supplement and lighten her father's occupation. He loved her so much that, to commemorate her name, he wrote a book of remarkable lectures on the law which he entitled *Novella super Decretalium*, after his daughter's name.

"Thus, not all men (and especially the wisest) share the opinion that it is bad for women to be educated. But it is very true that many foolish men have claimed this because it displeased them that women knew more than they did. Your father, who was a great scientist and philosopher, did not believe that women were worth less by knowing science; rather, as you know, he took great pleasure from seeing your inclination to learning. The feminine opinion of your mother, however, who wished to keep you busy with spinning and silly girlishness, following the common custom of women, was the major obstacle to your being more involved in the sciences. But just as the proverb already mentioned above says, 'No one can take away what Nature has given,' your mother could not hinder in you the feeling for the sciences which you, through natural inclination, had nevertheless gathered together in little droplets. I am sure that, on account of these things, you do not think you are worth less but rather that you consider it a great treasure for yourself; and you doubtless have reason to."

And I, Christine, replied to all of this, "Indeed, my lady, what you say is as true as the Lord's Prayer."

Part Three ————————————

MODERN POLITICAL THOUGHT

MACHIAVELLI DESCRIBES himself in the Dedicatory Letter to *The Prince* as a humble, lowly, and obscure man, yet he claims in that text that although those who are low often cannot understand themselves, neither can those who are high and powerful in society. He revives the political concerns of antiquity, developing a secular humanist stance about man's place in the world, in contrast to the religious preoccupations of the Middle Ages. Machiavelli is often referred to as the first modern political theorist because he advocates a science of politics for a world of random movement. Unlike the medievals, he doesn't ask about "legitimate authority" for a stable world, a world where the state is ultimately in God's hands, nor does he discuss the need for personal morality and a society that nurtures it. Machiavelli surrenders the quest for the "good state" for an understanding of the instrumentalities of power. He asks us to recognize the ironies of the political condition: good often leads to evil, order to disorder, culture to terror. Behavior often is dictated by existing conditions and compulsions rather than reason or logic: "[N]ecessity will lead you to do many things which reason does not recommend." Machiavelli invented a new language of politics in order to address the contingencies of daily life, using history to provide an alternative to the Christian discourse of Bible and Revelation. History—especially Roman history—would provide a stable body of knowledge of past experiences from which the lessons could be learned.

The diminished authority of the Church, the emergence of the modern nation state, and the growing power of a commercial class occurred in a climate increasingly more open to scientific questioning and to civic associations. In Italy citizens organized in neighborhood associations, guilds, and militias. The political actor moved in a world circumscribed by the deficiencies of men, and by what Machiavelli called *Fortuna* (Fate), a notoriously capricious adversary that determined at least half the outcome of human affairs. Disorder and instability existed at all levels of human experience. In the cities, there were bloody factional battles, and nationally, there was internecine warfare between popes and princes, between foreign rulers and Italian city-states.

Machiavelli's question was: "How can a state survive in a corrupt world?" Great inequalities in wealth and power, the destruction of peace and justice, disunion, lawlessness, dishonesty, and contempt for moral precepts were the glaring evidence of public and private corruption. The establishment or restoration of order, Machiavelli reasoned, can happen only if a prince, properly advised, governs by despotic power. This legislator, a prince cunning and ferocious, rules alone. The laws made by such a ruler would be able to reconstruct and determine national character. Moral and civic virtue would grow from such good laws, as would social and economic institutions. The prince thus masters an economy of violence, recognizing that "security for man is impossible unless it be conjoined with power." Confronted by conflicting interests competing for access to limited goods, the prince who seizes power must dispense violence in order to "organize everything in the state afresh," to create, as far as Machiavelli is concerned, the conditions for republicanism and for broader civic self-determination.

The Protestant Reformation initiated by Luther's antipapal polemics of 1520 produced an effective theory of resistance, while upholding the power of established rulers. The failure of the Roman Catholic church to conduct an effective reform led to a recognition that such reform was ultimately dependent on princes of the realm. In England, Henry VIII became the champion of the Reformed religion, and consolidated his power in the process. In Germany, Luther supported the savage repression of peasant revolts and the religious persecution of Anabaptists and other radical Protestant reformers. It was not considered appropriate for a Christian to set himself up against his government, according to Luther, "whether that government act justly or unjustly."

The monarchy, the middle strata, and the Protestant church found themselves allies on the question of obedience to authority. Yet, paradoxically, Protestant dissenters struggled for freedom of expression and affirmed the right to resist both secular and religious oppression, even when that meant going against kings or princes. They claimed the historically new right to resist on the ground that kings hold their power from the people, and that this power could be reclaimed in cases of significant abuse.

Luther had established the personal autonomy of the believer as absolute. The Church was the "assembly of all believers in Christ upon earth" and the substance of religion was the inner experience of the believer. It was this spirited affirmation that led to the idea of resisting corruption, what believers saw as the church's, and later, institutional abuses by illegitimate secular rulers.

Civil wars in England and France allowed new forces in society to make unexpected political claims for sovereignty. Hobbes' writings were a response to complete social upheavals caused by years of English civil wars and were intended to support absolute (monarchical) government. *Leviathan* is a book written for masterless men—for those who, although not slaves, are fearful for their lives and suspicious of others. These men, according to Hobbes, desire the same thing and become enemies "and in the way to their end . . . endeavor to destroy or subdue one another." The natural condition of man is a state of war, the war of all against all, and moved by fear or pride man seeks to preserve himself at the expense of any and all of his fellows. All men are equal in their desire to master each other and to be mastered by none, and thus a power must be created which will "overawe" all men. The fearful individual needs to create an awe-inspiring Leviathan capable of establishing peace and allowing individual free activity under his protection. According to Hobbes, the state which manifests the absolute power of the sovereign will protect individuals from each other and from any external threat.

Human anxiety about satisfying needs and appetites finds political expression in the desire for power as well as in the need to resolve conflicts of competing desires. Governments and laws are needed and man "seeks aid by society; for there is no other way by which a man can secure his life and liberty"; man must leave the state of nature. All inhabitants transfer their power to a sovereign. The Leviathan is a "mortal God" who then has the power to use the strength and means of all "as he shall think expedient, for their peace and common defense." The sovereign is authorized by mutual covenant to act in the name of all men, and he alone judges what is necessary for peace and self-defense. The government may be by one man or by an assembly. Hobbes says that only convenience dictates the structure, but he clearly prefers one man. The purpose of absolute rule is to ensure the protection of individuals from internal and external violence. This facilitates a life of competition and acquisition as it guarantees competition without civil war.

Although Locke draws a different picture of the state of nature than Hobbes, the depiction of man as an essentially selfish creature led him to characterize government in the same terms. According to Locke, government was to secure certain rights to property and private self-seeking. Man is no longer driven by the fear and anxiety of self-preservation which Hobbes conjured. Instead, Locke's individual is merely acquisitive and in search of personal pleasures. Man in the state of nature has reason and obeys laws of nature which enjoins him to be well disposed to his neighbors. They form a community and recognize each other's rights to life, liberty, and possessions. Man eventually seeks a government which will keep his neighbor at bay, while granting him a means to socially/politically/commercially interact competitively with him through a variety of established institutions.

Locke's *Two Treatises on Government* was written before the Glorious Revolution of 1688 which established William of Orange (from Holland) and his wife Mary (daughter of James II of England, the deposed Catholic king) as joint monarchs of England. Locke returned from exile on the same boat as the two new rulers. His purpose in the *Two Treatises on Government* was to show that inheritance alone does not confer sovereign power, and that revolution was justified under certain circumstances. After the abdication of James II, Parliament reconvened and drafted a Bill of Rights (1689) which established checks to monarchical power. A king could no longer suspend laws, maintain an army, or tax the people without consent of Parliament. In addition to securing its own arena of power, Parliament also established the right of any male subject to petition the king without prejudice, and the right of any accused person to jury trial and fair punishment.

According to Locke, political power originates from the people who retain the right to revolution in case of significant abuse by the government. If sovereign power acts arbitrarily, or unjustly and unlawfully, the people reserve the right to "appeal to heaven" and take action. Men would be foolish to place themselves under an absolute ruler, argues Locke, and yet agree to themselves abide by laws which enslave them. Men relinquish their right to act as judge and jury in order to be freed of the "inconveniences" of the state of nature, in exchange for settled laws and procedures for enforcement. Locke's version of the social contract, unlike Hobbes', retains man's natural rights, using government to enlarge and enhance those rights. Most important, private property is claimed as a natural right, which the entire force of government protects.

Locke countered the monarchists' claim that a realm was the property of the king by proposing that the right to private property was created when men mix their labor with nature: God gave the earth to all men in common, but he also gave them reason to make good use of the earth. Initially, men are restrained by spoilage and other restrictions to leave behind resources for other men. Later, when men agree to the use of money, accumulation becomes possible, as does the despoilage of nature for reasons of greed. Locke's discussion of property establishes that property is a natural right, not a creation of government as it was for Hobbes. According to Locke, asserting a natural right to property allows further private claims. In effect, his ideas served the transition from a right to use for survival to an entitlement to exclusive use.

Rousseau's political thought represents the culmination of the social contract tradition. He agreed with Hobbes that civil society turns man, "a stupid dim-witted animal," into a human being in the full sense. However, his understanding of man's origins contradicts both Hobbes and Locke. Rousseau wrote that men in earliest times were neither as vicious and fearful as Hobbes believed, nor as acquisitive and self-seeking as Locke imagined them to be. Men were tranquil and lived in solitude. As they came to work together and live in each other's proximity, they became more corrupt. Rousseau's concern in the *Social Contract* is not about how man lost the primeval freedom of nature, but about how the consequent "chains" of government can become legitimate. All societies coerce some men in order to produce freedom for others. Rousseau thought he could imagine one way to enlarge the political community and to empower it.

According to Rousseau, the problem is "to find a form of association which will defend and protect with the whole common force the person and goods of each associate, and in which each, while uniting himself with all, may still obey himself alone, and remain as free as before." Rousseau believes that neither submission, even voluntary, nor force can legitimately obligate men to obey government. He believes that only a contract which protects men from rulers would solve the problem. He proposes a compact which creates neither a sovereign king nor sovereign parliament, but a sovereign people. "The Sovereign, being formed wholly of the individuals who compose it, neither has, nor can have any interest contrary to it." The general will of the people expresses the public interest, which means both the will of all (as the vote might) *and* private interests. It is known as the general will because it is the will for those social goods and all citizens need.

Rousseau valorized the idea of democracy, which had come to be seen as mob rule. Rousseau's theory of popular sovereignty restores the notion of free citizens as those who possess the inalienable right to rule. All forms of governments are revocable by the people. Rousseau argued persuasively for democracy, a political community whose citizens act together to decide the laws of their country. Rousseau's books were banned, ordered to be burned, and he was driven into exile.

John Stuart Mill's political thought was determined by personal experience as much as by intellectual training. Mill's education and socialization at the hands of his father James Mill, and the Benthamites, was an education based on a joyless utilitarianism that denied the vast range of human feelings, and led him to a mental breakdown. Recovering, Mill participated in the politics of women's suffrage, as well as in politics more generally as a member of Parliament. Mill's *On Liberty,* an enduring contribution to liberal thought, extended the discussion of freedom by making a powerful case for the protection of liberties, specifically but not exclusively freedom of thought and self-expression.

Mill argued that freedom was endangered not only by abusive government but by a "tyranny of the majority"—the coercion of public opinion. Mill had adopted Enlightenment teaching that progress, reason, and experience can direct men's actions. This led Mill to assert the importance of free speech and free opinion. Opinions which are suppressed may be true or false, partly true or partly false. Suppressing a true opinion always causes social harm. Mill allows only one exception, that of "clear and present danger" to others, adopted by the United States Supreme Court.

Mill studied socialist writers, even advocating the creation of peasant proprietorships as a remedy to the poverty of Ireland. He rejected socialist solutions but remained an articulate critic of working-class conditions in England. It is in the realm of women's rights that Mill's political activism becomes particularly visionary. Mill is the author of one of the strongest arguments of the nineteenth century regarding women's suffrage. He exposed marriage as being only as consensual as slavery. His confidence that women would choose marriage as a career, if the institution itself was more benevolent, indicates the limits of his egalitarianism. He founded the first women's suffrage society in 1867 with Harriet Taylor and Emily Davis.

Marx and Engels were repelled by the degraded conditions of the English working class, at that time the most advanced and modern working class in history. Engels came from a family of great wealth who owned textile mills in Manchester and Bremen. He wrote *The Condition of the Working Class in England in 1844* while working at the mill in Manchester. Marx's activities as a radical journalist led to his expulsion from France and Brussels, and he was forced to leave Germany when democracy and the newspaper he edited were suppressed. Marx settled in London and although he and Mill lived in that city for twenty years, and wrote about the same kinds of social problems, they never met, and Mill never read Marx.

Marx's view of philosophy was shaped by the idealism of Hegel and the materialism of Feuerbach. But he wrote that ultimately "philosophers have only *interpreted* the world in various ways; the point is to *change* it." Marx did not inspire the great European revolutions of 1848, but he published *The Communist Manifesto* that year. Its concluding exhortation "Workingmen of all countries, unite!" sought to point the way to social justice and unalienated life. Marx believed that from a succession of class-structured societies would come at last a classless society, and the elimination of conflict between exploiter and exploited. History is a dialectic of class struggles, and the latest struggle, pitting bourgeois and proletariat, had "left remaining no other nexus between man and man than naked self-interest, than callous 'cash payment.'" Marx believed that bourgeois society "resolved personal worth into exchange value and, in place of the numberless indefeasible chartered freedoms, set up that single unconscionable freedom—free trade." Marx and Engels believed that democracy could only be fully achieved in a state in which all coercion to produce had been eliminated: "For us it cannot be a question of changing private property but only of destroying it . . . not of improving existing society but of founding a new one."

8

Niccolo Machiavelli
Selections

Niccolo Machiavelli (1469–1527) is often associated with a sinister image—the cynical practitioner of realpolitik *who believes that the end always justifies the means. This tells only part of the story. He is also generally considered the first major "modern" political thinker. Whereas medieval Christians asked how politics and the state suited God's scheme of things, Machiavelli asked questions about the organization and preservation of power. Religion concerned him only inasmuch as it fortified or weakened the state. He was born in 1469 in Florence and lived in the heyday of the Renaissance, when a generation of thinkers cast their eyes back toward antiquity, especially ancient Rome, and away from Church dogma. Machiavelli was an official of the Florentine republic, but lost his job when Spain invaded in 1512, reinstating the de Medici family, who had ruled the city earlier. In 1513, he authored* The Prince, *which describes how a ruler might best preserve and expand his power. Machiavelli probably hoped it would get him a job with the new regime. It didn't. It did lead to the mistaken view that he was a champion of monarchy. But one of his other major works,* The Discourses *(a study of Livy's history of Rome), shows that he was actually a foe of tyranny who preferred a healthy republic based on "good laws and good arms."*

THE PRINCE

Niccolo Machiavelli to Lorenzo the Magnificent, Son of Piero di Medici

It is customary for those who wish to gain the favour of a prince to endeavour to do so by offering him gifts of those things which they hold most precious, or in which they know him to take especial delight. In this way princes are often presented with horses, arms, cloth of gold, gems, and such-like ornaments worthy of their grandeur. In my desire however, to offer to Your Highness some humble testimony of my devotion, I have been unable to find among my possessions anything which I hold so dear or esteem so highly as that knowledge of the deeds of great men which I have acquired through a long experience of modern events and a constant study of the past.

With the utmost diligence I have long pondered and scrutinised the actions of the great, and now I offer the results to Your Highness within the compass of a small volume. . . .

The Various Kinds of Government and the Ways by Which They Are Established

All states and dominions which hold or have held sway over mankind are either republics or monarchies. Monarchies are either hereditary in which the rulers have been for many years of the same family, or else they are of recent foundation. The newly founded ones are either entirely new, as was Milan to Francesco Sforza, or else they are, as it were, new members grafted on to the hereditary possessions of the prince that annexes them, as is the kingdom of Naples to the King of Spain. The dominions thus acquired have either been previously accustomed to the rule of another prince, or else have been free states, and they are annexed either by force of arms of the prince himself, or of others, or else fall to him by good fortune or special ability.

Of Hereditary Monarchies

I will not here speak of republics, having already treated of them fully in another place. I will deal only with monarchies, and will discuss how the various kinds described above can be governed and maintained. In the first place, the difficulty of maintaining hereditary states accustomed to a reigning family is far less than in new monarchies; for it is sufficient not to transgress ancestral usages, and to adapt one's self to unforeseen circumstances; in this way such a prince, if of ordinary assiduity, will always be able to maintain his position, unless some very exceptional and excessive force deprives him of it; and even if he be thus deprived, on the slightest mischance happening to the new occupier, he will be able to regain it. . . .

Of Mixed Monarchies

But it is in the new monarchy that difficulties really exist. First, if it is not entirely new, but a member as it were of a mixed state, its disorders spring at first from a natural difficulty which exists in all new dominions, because men change masters willingly, hoping to better themselves; and this belief makes them take arms against their rulers, in which they are deceived, as experience later proves that they have gone from bad to worse. This is the result of another very natural cause, which is the inevitable harm inflicted on those over whom the prince obtains dominion, both by his soldiers and by an infinite number of other injuries caused by his occupation.

Thus you find enemies in all those whom you have injured by occupying that dominion, and you cannot maintain the friendship of those who have helped you to obtain this possession, as you will not be able to fulfil their expectations, nor can you use strong measures with them, being under an obligation to them; for which reason, however strong your armies may be, you will always need the favour of the inhabitants to take possession of a province.

It is indeed true that, after reconquering rebel territories they are not so easily lost again, for the ruler is now, by the fact of the rebellion, less averse to secure his position by punishing offenders, unmasking suspects, and strengthening himself in weak places. . . . Be it observed, therefore, that those states which on annexation are united to a previously existing state may or may not be of the same nationality and language. If they are, it is very easy to hold them, especially if they are not accustomed to freedom; and to possess them securely it suffices that the family of the princes which formerly governed them be extinct. For the rest, their old condition not being disturbed, and there being no dissimilarity of customs, the people settle down quietly under their new rulers, as is seen in the case of Burgundy, Brittany, Gascony, and Normandy, which have been so long united to France; and although there may be some slight differences of language, the customs of the people are nevertheless similar, and they can get along well together. Whoever obtains possession of such territories and wishes to retain them must bear in mind two things: the one, that the blood of their old rulers be extinct; the other, to make no alteration either in their laws or in their taxes; in this way they will in a very short space of time become united with their old possessions and form one state.

But when dominions are acquired in a province differing in language, laws, and customs, the difficulties to be overcome are great, and it requires good fortune as well as great industry to retain them; one of the best and most certain means of doing so would be for the new ruler to take up his residence there. This would render possession more secure and durable, and it is what the Turk has done in Greece. In spite of all the other measures taken by him to hold that state, it would not have been possible to retain it had he not gone to live there. Being on the spot, disorders can be seen as they arise and can quickly be remedied, but living at a distance, they are only heard of when they get beyond remedy. Besides which, the province is not despoiled by your officials, the subjects being able to obtain satisfaction by direct recourse to their prince; and wishing to be loyal they have more reason to love him, and should they be otherwise inclined they will have greater cause to fear him. Any external power who wishes to assail that state will be less disposed to do so; so that as long as he resides there he will be very hard to dispossess.

The other and better remedy is to plant colonies in one or two of those places which form as it were the keys of the land, for it is necessary either to do this or to maintain a large force of armed men. The colonies will cost the prince little; with little or no expense on his part, he can send and maintain them; he only injures those whose lands and houses are taken to give to the new inhabitants, and these form but a small proportion of the state, and those who are injured, remaining poor and scattered, can never do any harm to him, and all the others are, on the one hand, not injured and therefore easily pacified; and, on the other, are fearful of offending lest they should be treated like those who have been dispossessed. To conclude, these colonies cost nothing, are more faithful, and give less offence; and the injured parties being poor and scattered are unable to do mischief, as I have shown. For it must be noted, that men must either be caressed or else annihilated; they will revenge themselves for small injuries, but cannot do so for great ones; the injury therefore that we do to a man must be such that we need not fear his vengeance. But by maintaining a garrison instead of colonists, one will spend much more, and consume all the revenues of that state in guarding it, so that the acquisition will result in a loss, besides giving much greater offence, since it injures every one in that state with the quartering of the army on it; which being an inconvenience felt by all, every one becomes an enemy, and these are enemies which can do mischief, as, though beaten, they remain in their own homes. In every way, therefore, a garrison is as useless as colonies are useful.

Further, the ruler of a foreign province as described, should make himself the leader and defender of his less powerful neighbours, and endeavour to weaken the stronger ones, and take care that they are not invaded by some foreigner not less powerful than himself. And it will be always the case that he will be invited to intervene at the request of those who are discontented either through ambition or fear, as was seen when the Ætolians invited the Romans into Greece; and in whatever province they entered, it was always at the request of the inhabitants. And the rule is that when a powerful foreigner enters a province, all the less powerful inhabitants become his adherents, moved by the envy they bear to those ruling over them; so much so that with regard to these minor potentates he has no trouble whatever in winning them over, for they willingly join forces with the state that he has acquired. He has merely to be careful that they do not assume too much power and authority, and he can easily with his own forces and their favour put down those that are powerful and remain in everything arbiter of that province. And he who does not govern well in this way will soon lose what he has acquired, and while he holds it will meet with infinite difficulty and trouble.

The Romans in the provinces they took, always followed this policy; they established colonies, inveigled the less powerful without increasing their strength, put down the most powerful and did not allow foreign rulers to obtain influence in them. I will adduce the province of Greece as a sole example. They made friends with the Achæans and the Ætolians, the kingdom of Macedonia was cast down, and Antiochus driven out, nor did they allow the merits of the Achæans or the Ætolians to gain them any increase of territory, nor did the persuasions of Philip induce them to befriend him without reducing his influence, nor could the power of Antiochus make them consent to allow him to hold any state in that province.

For the Romans did in these cases what all wise princes should do, who consider not only present but also future discords and diligently guard against them; for being foreseen they can easily be remedied, but if one waits till they are at hand, the medicine is no longer in time as the malady has become incurable; it happening with this as with those hectic fevers, as doctors say, which at their beginning are easy to cure but difficult to recognise, but in course of time when they have not at first been recognised and treated, become easy to recognise and difficult to cure. Thus it happens in matters of state; for knowing afar off (which it is only given to a prudent man to do) the evils that are brewing, they are easily cured. But when, for want of such knowledge, they are allowed to grow so that every one can recognise them, there is no longer any remedy to be found. Therefore, the Romans, observing disorders while yet remote, were always able to find a remedy, and never allowed them to increase in order to avoid a war; for they knew that war is not to be avoided, and can be deferred only to the advantage of the other side; they therefore declared war against Philip and Antiochus in Greece, so as not to have to fight them in Italy, though they might at the time have avoided either; this they did not choose to do, never caring to do that which is now every day to be heard in the mouths of our wise men, namely to enjoy the advantages of delay, but preferring to trust their own virtue and prudence; for time brings with it all things, and may produce indifferently either good or evil.

The Way to Govern Cities or Dominions That, Previous to Being Occupied, Lived under Their Own Laws

When those states which have been acquired are accustomed to live at liberty under their own laws, there are three ways of holding them. The first is to despoil them; the second is to go and live there in person; the third is to allow them to live under their own laws, taking tribute of them, and creating within the country a government composed of a few who will keep it friendly to you. Because this government, being created by the prince, knows that it cannot exist without his friendship and protection, and will do all it can to keep them. What is more, a city used to liberty can be more easily held by means of its citizens than in any other way, if you wish to preserve it.

There is the example of the Spartans and the Romans. The Spartans held Athens and Thebes by creating within them a government of a few; nevertheless they lost them. The Romans, in order to hold Capua, Carthage, and Numantia, ravaged them, but did not lose them. They wanted to hold Greece in almost the same way as the Spartans held it, leaving it free and under its own laws, but they did not succeed; so that they were compelled to lay waste many cities in that province in order to keep it, because in truth there is no sure method of holding them except by despoiling them. And whoever becomes the ruler of a free city and does not destroy it, can expect to be destroyed by it, for it can always find a motive for rebellion in the name of liberty and of its ancient usages, which are forgotten neither by lapse of time nor by benefits received; and whatever one does or provides, so long as the inhabitants are not separated or dispersed, they do not forget that name and those usages, but appeal to them at once in every emergency, as did Pisa after being so many years held in servitude by the Florentines. But when cities or provinces have been accustomed to live under a prince, and the family of that prince is extinguished, being on the one hand used to obey, and on the other not having their old prince, they cannot unite in choosing one from among themselves, and they do not know how to live in freedom, so that they are slower to take arms, and a prince can win them over with greater facility and establish himself securely. But in republics there is greater life, greater hatred, and more desire for vengeance; they do not and cannot cast aside the memory of their ancient liberty, so that the surest way is either to lay them waste or reside in them.

Of New Dominions Which Have Been Acquired by One's Own Arms and Ability

Let no one marvel if in speaking of new dominions both as to prince and state, I bring forward very exalted instances, for men walk almost always in the paths trodden by others, proceeding in their actions by imitation. Not being always able to follow others exactly, nor attain to the excellence of those he imitates, a prudent man should always follow in the path trodden by great men and imitate those who are most excellent, so that if he does not attain to their greatness, at any rate he will get some tinge of it. He will do as prudent archers, who when the place they wish to hit is too far off, knowing how far their bow will carry, aim at a spot much higher than the one they wish to hit, not in order to reach this height with their arrow, but by help of this high aim to hit the spot they wish to.

I say then that in new dominions, where there is a new prince, it is more or less easy to hold them according to the greater or lesser ability of him who acquires them. And as the fact of a private individual becoming a prince presupposes either great ability or good fortune, it would appear that either of these things would in part mitigate many difficulties. Nevertheless those who have been less beholden to good fortune have maintained themselves best. The matter is also facilitated by the prince being obliged to reside personally in his territory, having no others. But to come to those who have become princes through their own merits and not by fortune, I regard as the greatest, Moses, Cyrus, Romulus, Theseus, and their like. And although one should not speak of Moses, he having merely carried out what was ordered him by God, still he deserves admiration, if only for that grace which made him worthy to speak with God. But regarding Cyrus and others who have acquired or founded kingdoms, they will all be found worthy of admiration; and if their particular actions and methods are examined they will not appear very different from those of Moses, although he had so great a Master. And in examining their life and deeds it will be seen that they owed nothing to fortune but the opportunity which gave them matter to be shaped into what form they thought fit; and without that opportunity their powers would have been wasted, and without their powers the opportunity would have come in vain.

It was thus necessary that Moses should find the people of Israel slaves in Egypt and oppressed by the Egyptians, so that they were disposed to follow him in order to escape from their servitude. It was necessary that Romulus should be unable to remain in Alba, and should have been exposed at his birth, in order that he might become King of Rome and founder of that nation. It was necessary that Cyrus should find the Persians discontented with the empire of the Medes, and the Medes weak and effeminate through long peace. Theseus could not have shown his abilities if he had not found the Athenians dispersed. These opportunities, therefore, gave these men their chance, and their own great qualities enabled them to profit by them, so as to ennoble their country and augment its fortunes.

Those who by the exercise of abilities such as these become princes, obtain their dominions with difficulty but retain them easily, and the difficulties which they have in acquiring their dominions arise in part from the new rules and regulations that they have to introduce in order to establish their position securely. It must be considered that there is nothing more difficult to carry out, nor more doubtful of success, nor more dangerous to handle, than to initiate a new order of things. For the reformer has enemies in all those who profit by the old order, and only lukewarm defenders in all those who would profit by the new order, this lukewarmness arising partly from fear of their adversaries, who have the laws in their favour; and partly from the incredulity of mankind, who do not truly believe in anything new until they have had actual experience of it. Thus it arises that on every opportunity for attacking the reformer, his opponents do so with the zeal of partisans, the others only defend him half-heartedly, so that between them he runs great danger. It is necessary, however, in order to investigate thoroughly this question, to examine whether these innovators are independent, or whether they depend upon others, that is to say, whether in order to carry out their designs they have to entreat or are able to compel. In the first case they invariably succeed ill, and accomplish nothing; but when they can depend on their own strength and are able to use force, they rarely fail. Thus it comes about that all armed prophets have conquered and unarmed ones failed; for besides what has been already said, the character of peoples varies, and it is easy to persuade them of a thing, but difficult to keep them in that persuasion. And so it is necessary to order things so that when they no longer believe, they can be made to believe by force. Moses, Cyrus, Theseus, and Romulus would not have been able to keep their constitutions observed for so long had they been disarmed, as happened in our own time with Fra Girolamo Savonarola, who failed entirely in his new rules when the multitude began to disbelieve in him, and he had no means of holding fast those who had believed nor of compelling the unbelievers to believe. Therefore such men as these have great difficulty in making their way, and all their dangers are met on the road and must be overcome by their own abilities; but when once they have overcome them and have begun to be held in veneration, and have suppressed those who envied them, they remain powerful and secure, honoured and happy. . . .

Of New Dominions Acquired by the Power of Others or by Fortune

Those who rise from private citizens to be princes merely by fortune have little trouble in rising but very much in maintaining their position. They meet with no difficulties on the way as they fly over them, but all their difficulties arise when they are established. Such are they who are granted a state either for money, or by favour of him who grants it, as happened to many in Greece, in the cities of Ionia and of the Hellespont, who were created princes by Darius in order to hold these places for his security and glory; such were also those emperors who from private citizens rose to power by bribing the army. Such as these depend absolutely on the good will and fortune of those who have raised them, both of which are extremely inconstant and unstable. They neither know how to, nor are in a position to maintain their rank, for unless he be a man of great genius it is not likely that one who has always lived in a private position should know how to command, and they are unable to maintain themselves because they possess no forces friendly and faithful to them. Moreover, states quickly founded, like all other things of rapid beginnings and growth, cannot have deep roots and wide ramifications, so that the first storm destroys them, unless, as already said, the man who thus becomes a prince is of such great genius as to be able to take immediate steps for maintaining what fortune has thrown into his lap, and lay afterwards those foundations which others make before becoming princes.

With regard to these two methods of becoming a prince, by ability or by good fortune, I will here adduce two examples which have occurred within our memory, those of Francesco Sforza and Cesare Borgia. Francesco, by appropriate means and through great abilities, from citizen became Duke of Milan, and what he had attained after a thousand difficulties he maintained with little trouble. On the other hand, Cesare Borgia, commonly called Duke Valentine, acquired the state by the influence of his father and lost it when that influence failed, and that although every measure was adopted by him and everything done that a prudent and capable man could do to establish himself firmly in a state that the arms and the favours of others had given him. For, as we have said, he who does not lay his foundations beforehand may by great abilities do so afterwards, although with great trouble to the architect and danger to the building. If, then, one considers the procedure of the duke, it will be seen how firm were the foundations he had laid to his future power, which I do not think it superfluous to examine, as I know of no better precepts for a new prince to follow than may be found in his actions; and if his measures were not successful, it was through no fault of his own but only by the most extraordinary malignity of fortune.

In wishing to aggrandise the duke his son, Alexander VI had to meet very great difficulties both present and future. In the first place, he saw no way of making him ruler of any state that was not a possession of the Church. He knew that the Duke of Milan and the Venetians would not consent in his attempt to take papal cities, because Faenza and Rimini were already under the protection of the Venetians. He saw, moreover, that the military forces of Italy, especially those which might have served him, were in the hands of those who would fear the greatness of the pope, and therefore he could not depend upon them, being all under the command of the Orsini and Colonna and their adherents. It was, therefore, necessary to disturb the existing condition and bring about disorders in the states of Italy in order to obtain secure mastery over a part of them; this was easy, for he found the Venetians, who, actuated by other motives, had invited the French into Italy, which he not only did not oppose, but facilitated by dissolving the first marriage of King Louis. The king came thus into Italy with the aid of the Venetians and the consent of Alexander, and had hardly arrived at Milan before the pope obtained troops from him for his enterprise in the Romagna, which was made possible for him thanks to the reputation of the king. The duke having thus obtained the Romagna and defeated the Colonna, was hindered by two things in maintaining it and proceeding further: the one, his forces, of which he doubted the fidelity; the other the will of France; that is to say, he feared lest the arms of the Orsini of which he had availed himself should fail him, and not only hinder him in obtaining more but take from him what he had already conquered, and he also feared that the king might do the same. He had evidence of this as regards the Orsini when, after taking Faenza, he assaulted Bologna and observed their backwardness in the assault. And as regards the king, he perceived his designs when, after taking the dukedom of Urbino, he attacked Tuscany, and the king made him desist from that enterprise. Whereupon the duke decided to depend no longer on the fortunes and arms of others. The first thing he did was to weaken the parties of the Orsini and Colonna in Rome by gaining all their adherents who were gentlemen and making them his own followers, by granting them large remuneration, and appointing them to commands and offices according to their rank, so that their attachment to their parties was extinguished in a few months, and entirely concentrated on the duke. After this he awaited an opportunity for crushing the chiefs of the Orsini, having already suppressed those of the Colonna family, and when the opportunity arrived he made good use of it, for the Orsini seeing at length that the greatness of the duke and of the Church meant their own ruin, convoked a diet at Magione in the Perugino. Hence sprang the rebellion of Urbino and the tumults in Romagna and infinite dangers to the duke, who overcame them all with the help of the French; and having regained his reputation, neither trusting France nor other foreign forces, in order not to venture on their alliance, he had recourse to stratagem. He dissembled his aims so well that the Orsini made their peace with him, being represented by Signor Paulo whose suspicions the duke disarmed with every courtesy, presenting him with robes, money, and horses, so that in their simplicity they were induced to come to Sinigaglia and fell into his hands. Having thus suppressed these leaders and made their partisans his friends, the duke had laid a very good foundation to his power, having all the Romagna with the duchy of Urbino, and having gained the favour of the inhabitants, who began to feel the benefit of his rule.

And as this part is worthy of note and of imitation by others, I will not omit mention of it. When he took the Romagna, it had previously been governed by weak rulers, who had rather despoiled their subjects than governed them, and given them more cause for disunion than for union, so that the province was a prey to robbery, assaults, and every kind of disorder. He, therefore, judged it necessary to give them a good government in order to make them peaceful and obedient to his rule. For this purpose he appointed Messer Remirro de Orco, a cruel and able man, to whom he gave the fullest authority. This man, in a short time, was highly successful in rendering the country orderly and united, whereupon the duke, not deeming such excessive authority expedient, lest it should become hateful, appointed a civil court of justice in the centre of the province under an excellent president, to which each city appointed its own advocate. And as he knew that the harshness of the past had engendered some amount of hatred, in order to purge the minds of the people and to win them over completely, he resolved to show that if any cruelty had taken place it was not by his orders, but through the harsh disposition of his minister. And having found the opportunity he had him cut in half and placed one morning in the public square at Cesena with a piece of wood and blood-stained knife by his side. The ferocity of this spectacle caused the people both satisfaction and amazement. But to return to where we left off.

The duke being now powerful and partly secured against present perils, being armed himself, and having in a great measure put down those neighbouring forces which might injure him, had now to get the respect of France, if he wished to proceed with his acquisitions, for he knew that the king, who had lately discovered his error, would not give him any help. He began therefore to seek fresh alliances and to vacillate with France on the occasion of the expedition that the French were undertaking towards the kingdom of Naples against the Spaniards, who were besieging Gaeta. His intention was to assure himself of them, which he would soon have succeeded in doing if Alexander had lived.

These were the measures taken by him with regard to the present. As to the future, he feared that a new successor to the states of the Church might not be friendly to him and might seek to deprive him of what Alexander had given him, and he sought to provide against this in four ways. First, by destroying all who were of the blood of those ruling families which he had despoiled, in order to deprive the pope of any opportunity. Secondly, by gaining the friendship of the Roman nobles, so that he might through them hold as it were the pope in check. Thirdly, by obtaining as great a hold on the College as he could. Fourthly, by acquiring such power before the pope died as to be able to resist alone the first onslaught. Of these four things he had at the death of Alexander accomplished three, and the fourth he had almost accomplished. For of the dispossessed rulers he killed as many as he could lay hands on, and very few escaped; he had gained to his party the Roman nobles; and he had a great influence in the College. As to new possessions, he designed to become lord of Tuscany, and already possessed Perugia and Piombino, and had assumed the protectorate over Pisa; and as he had no longer to fear the French (for the French had been deprived of the kingdom of Naples by the Spaniards in such a way that both parties were obliged to buy his friendship) he seized Pisa. After this, Lucca and Siena at once yielded, partly through hate of the Florentines and partly through fear; the Florentines had no resources, so that, had he succeeded as he had done before, in the very year that Alexander died he would have gained such strength and renown as to be able to maintain himself without depending on the fortunes or strength of others, but solely by his own power and ability. But Alexander died five years after Cesare Borgia had first drawn his sword. He was left with only the state of Romagna firmly established, and all the other schemes in mid-air, between two very powerful and hostile armies, and suffering from a fatal illness. But the valour and ability of the duke were such, and he knew so well how to win over men or vanquish them, and so strong were the foundations that he had laid in this short time, that if he had not had those two armies upon him, or else had been in good health, he would have survived every difficulty. And that his foundations were good is seen from the fact that the Romagna waited for him more than a month; in Rome, although half dead, he remained secure, and although the Baglioni, Vitelli, and Orsini entered Rome they found no followers against him. He was able, if not to make pope whom he wished, at any rate to prevent a pope being created whom he did not wish. But if at the death of Alexander he had been well, everything would have been easy. And he told me on the day that Pope Julius II was elected, that he had thought of everything which might happen on the death of his father, and provided against everything, except that he had never thought that at his father's death he would be dying himself.

Reviewing thus all the actions of the duke, I find nothing to blame, on the contrary, I feel bound, as I have done, to hold him up as an example to be imitated by all who by fortune and with the arms of others have risen to power. For with his great courage and high ambition he could not have acted otherwise, and his designs were only frustrated by the short life of Alexander and his own illness. Whoever, therefore, deems it necessary in his new principality to secure himself against enemies, to gain friends, to conquer by force or fraud, to make himself beloved and feared by the people, followed and reverenced by the soldiers, to destroy those who can and may injure him, introduce innovations into old customs, to be severe and kind, magnanimous and liberal, suppress the old militia, create a new one, maintain the friendship of kings and princes in such a way that they are glad to benefit him and fear to injure him, such a one can find no better example than the actions of this man. The only thing he can be accused of is that in the creation of Julius II he made a bad choice; for, as has been said, not being able to choose his own pope, he could still prevent any one individual being made pope, and he ought never to have permitted any of those cardinals to be raised to the papacy whom he had injured, or who when pope would stand in fear of him. For men commit injuries either through fear or through hate. Those whom he had injured were, among others, San Pietro ad Vincula, Colonna, San Giorgio, and Ascanio. All the others, if elected to the pontificate, would have had to fear him except Rohan and the Spaniards; the latter through their relationship and obligations to him, the former from his great power, being related to the King of France. For these reasons the duke ought above all things to have created a Spaniard pope; and if unable, then he should have consented to Rohan being appointed and not San Pietro ad Vincula. And whoever thinks that in high personages new benefits cause old offences to be forgotten, makes a great mistake. The duke, therefore, erred in this choice, and it was the cause of his ultimate ruin.

Of Those Who Have Attained the Position of Prince by Villainy

But as there are still two ways of becoming prince which cannot be attributed entirely either to fortune or to ability, they must not be passed over, although one of them could be more fully discussed if we were treating of republics. These are when one becomes prince by some nefarious or villainous means, or when a private citizen becomes the prince of his country through the favour of his fellow-citizens. And in speaking of the former means, I will give two examples, one ancient, the other modern, without entering further into the merits of this method, as I judge them to be sufficient for any one obliged to imitate them.

Agathocles the Sicilian rose not only from private life but from the lowest and most abject position to be King of Syracuse. The son of a potter, he led a life of the utmost wickedness through all the stages of his fortune. Nevertheless, his wickedness was accompanied by such vigour of mind and body that, having joined the militia, he rose through its ranks to be prætor of Syracuse. Having been appointed to this position, and having decided to become prince, and to hold with violence and without the support of others that which had been constitutionally granted him; and having imparted his design to Hamilcar the Carthaginian, who was fighting with his armies in Sicily, he called together one morning the people and senate of Syracuse, as if he had to deliberate on matters of importance to the republic, and at a given signal had all the senators and the richest men of the people killed by his soldiers. After their death he occupied and held rule over the city without any civil strife. And although he was twice beaten by the Carthaginians and ultimately besieged, he was able not only to defend the city, but leaving a portion of his forces for its defence, with the remainder he invaded Africa, and in a short time liberated Syracuse from the siege and brought the Carthaginians to great extremities, so that they were obliged to come to terms with him, and remain contented with the possession of Africa, leaving Sicily to Agathocles. Whoever considers, therefore, the actions and qualities of this man, will see few if any things which can be attributed to fortune; for, as above stated, it was not by the favour of any person, but through the grades of the militia, in which he had advanced with a thousand hardships and perils, that he arrived at the position of prince, which he afterwards maintained by so many courageous and perilous expedients. It cannot be called virtue to kill one's fellow-citizens, betray one's friends, be without faith, without pity, and without religion; by these methods one may indeed gain power, but not glory. For if the virtues of Agathocles in braving and overcoming perils, and his greatness of soul in supporting and surmounting obstacles be considered, one sees no reason for holding him inferior to any of the most renowned captains. Nevertheless his barbarous cruelty and inhumanity, together with his countless atrocities, do not permit of his being named among the most famous men. We cannot attribute to fortune or virtue that which he achieved without either. . . .

Some may wonder how it came about that Agathocles, and others like him, could, after infinite treachery and cruelty, live secure for many years in their country and defend themselves from external enemies without being conspired against by their subjects; although many others have, owing to their cruelty, been unable to maintain their position in times of peace, not to speak of the uncertain times of war. I believe this arises from the cruelties being exploited well or badly. Well committed may be called those (if it is permissible to use the word well of evil) which are perpetuated once for the need of securing one's self, and which afterwards are not persisted in, but are exchanged for measures as useful to the subjects as possible. Cruelties ill committed are those which, although at first few, increase rather than diminish with time. Those who follow the former method may remedy in some measure their condition, both with God and man; as did Agathocles. As to the others, it is impossible for them to maintain themselves.

Whence it is to be noted, that in taking a state the conqueror must arrange to commit all his cruelties at once, so as not to have to recur to them every day, and so as to be able, by not making fresh changes, to reassure people and win them over by benefiting them. Whoever acts otherwise, either through timidity or bad counsels, is always obliged to stand with knife in hand, and can never depend on his subjects, because they, owing to continually fresh injuries, are unable to depend upon him. For injuries should be done all together, so that being less tasted, they will give less offence. Benefits should be granted little by little, so that they may be better enjoyed. And above all, a prince must live with his subjects in such a way that no accident of good or evil fortune can deflect him from his course; for necessity arising in adverse times, you are not in time with severity, and the good that you do does not profit, as it is judged to be forced upon you, and you will derive no benefit whatever from it. . . .

Of the Civic Principality

But we now come to the case where a citizen becomes prince not through crime or intolerable violence, but by the favour of his fellow-citizens, which may be called a civic principality. To attain this position depends not entirely on worth or entirely on fortune, but rather on cunning assisted by fortune. One attains it by help of popular favour or by the favour of the aristocracy. For in every city these two opposite parties are to be found, arising from the desire of the populace to avoid the oppression of the great, and the desire of the great to command and oppress the people. And from these two opposing interests arises in the city one of the three effects: either absolute government, liberty, or licence. The former is created either by the populace or the nobility, depending on the relative opportunities of the two parties; for when the nobility see that they are unable to resist the people they unite in exalting one of their number and creating him prince, so as to be able to carry out their own designs under the shadow of his authority. The populace, on the other hand, when unable to resist the nobility, endeavour to exalt and create a prince in order to be protected by his authority. He who becomes prince by help of the nobility has greater difficulty in maintaining his power than he who is raised by the populace, for he is surrounded by those who think themselves his equals, and is thus unable to direct or command as he pleases. But one who is raised to leadership by popular favour finds himself alone, and has no one, or very few, who are not ready to obey him. Besides which, it is impossible to satisfy the nobility by fair dealing and without inflicting injury on others, whereas it is very easy to satisfy the mass of the people in this way. For the aim of the people is more honest than that of the nobility, the latter desiring to oppress, and the former merely to avoid oppression. It must also be added that the prince can never insure himself against a hostile populace on account of their number, but he can against the hostility of the great, as they are but few. The worst that a prince has to expect from a hostile people is to be abandoned, but from hostile nobles he has to fear not only desertion but their active opposition, and as they are more far-seeing and more cunning, they are always in time to save themselves and take sides with the one who they expect will conquer. The prince is, moreover, obliged to live always with the same people, but he can easily do without the same nobility, being able to make and unmake them at any time, and improve their position or deprive them of it as he pleases.

And to throw further light on this part of my argument, I would say, that the nobles are to be considered in two different manners; that is, they are either to be ruled so as to make them entirely dependent on your fortunes, or else not. Those that are thus bound to you and are not rapacious, must be honoured and loved; those who stand aloof must be considered in two ways, they either do this through pusillanimity and natural want of courage, and in this case you ought to make use of them, and especially such as are of good counsel, so that they may honour you in prosperity and in adversity you have not to fear them. But when they are not bound to you of set purpose and for ambitious ends, it is a sign that they think more of themselves than of you; and from such men the prince must guard himself and look upon them as secret enemies, who will help to ruin him when in adversity.

One, however, who becomes prince by favour of the populace, must maintain its friendship, which he will find easy, the people asking nothing but not to be oppressed. But one who against the people's wishes becomes prince by favour of the nobles, should above all endeavour to gain the favour of the people; this will be easy to him if he protects them. And as men, who receive good from whom they expected evil, feel under a greater obligation to their benefactor, so the populace will soon become even better disposed towards him than if he had become prince through their favour. The prince can win their favour in many ways, which vary according to circumstances, for which no certain rule can be given, and will therefore be passed over. I will only say, in conclusion, that it is necessary for a prince to possess the friendship of the people; otherwise he has no resource in times of adversity.

Nabis, prince of the Spartans, sustained a siege by the whole of Greece and a victorious Roman army, and defended his country against them and maintained his own position. It sufficed when the danger arose for him to make sure of a few, which would not have sufficed if the populace had been hostile to him. And let no one oppose my opinion in this by quoting the trite proverb, "He who builds on the people, builds on mud"; because that is true when a private citizen relies upon the people and persuades himself that they will liberate him if he is oppressed by enemies or by the magistrates; in this case he might often find himself deceived, as were in Rome the Gracchi and in Florence Messer Georgio Scali. But when it is a prince who founds himself on this basis, one who can command and is a man of courage, and does not get frightened in adversity, and does not neglect other preparations, and one who by his own valour and measures animates the mass of the people, he will not find himself deceived by them, and he will find that he has laid his foundations well.

Usually these principalities are in danger when the prince from the position of a civil ruler changes to an absolute one, for these princes either command themselves or by means of magistrates. In the latter case their position is weaker and more dangerous, for they are at the mercy of those citizens who are appointed magistrates, who can, especially in times of adversity, with great facility deprive them of their position, either by acting against them or by not obeying them. The prince is not in time, in such dangers, to assume absolute authority, for the citizens and subjects who are accustomed to take their orders from the magistrates are not ready in these emergencies to obey his, and he will always in difficult times lack men whom he can rely on. Such a prince cannot base himself on what he sees in quiet times, when the citizens have need of the state; for then every one is full of promises and each one is ready to die for him when death is far off; but in adversity, when the state has need of citizens, then he will find but few. And this experience is the more dangerous, in that it can only be had once. Therefore a wise prince will seek means by which his subjects will always and in every possible condition of things have need of his government, and then they will always be faithful to him.

Of the Things for Which Men, and Especially Princes, Are Praised or Blamed

It now remains to be seen what are the methods and rules for a prince as regards his subjects and friends. And as I know that many have written of this, I fear that my writing about it may be deemed presumptuous, differing as I do, especially in this matter, from the opinions of others. But my intention being to write something of use to those who understand, it appears to me more proper to go to the real truth of the matter than to its imagination; and many have imagined republics and principalities which have never been seen or known to exist in reality; for how we live is so far removed from how we ought to live, that he who abandons what is done for what ought to be done, will rather learn to bring about his own ruin than his preservation. A man who wishes to make a profession of goodness in everything must necessarily come to grief among so many who are not good. Therefore it is necessary for a prince, who wishes to maintain himself, to learn how not to be good, and to use this knowledge and not use it, according to the necessity of the case.

Leaving on one side, then, those things which concern only an imaginary prince, and speaking of those that are real, I state that all men, and especially princes, who are placed at a greater height, are reputed for certain qualities which bring them either praise or blame. Thus one is considered liberal, another *misero* or miserly (using a Tuscan term, seeing that *avaro* with us still means one who is rapaciously acquisitive and *misero* one who makes grudging use of his own); one a free giver, another rapacious; one cruel, another merciful; one a breaker of his word, another trustworthy; one effeminate and pusillanimous, another fierce and high-spirited; one humane, another haughty; one lascivious, another chaste; one frank, another astute; one hard, another easy; one serious, another frivolous; one religious, another an unbeliever, and so on. I know that every one will admit that it would be highly praiseworthy in a prince to possess all the above-named qualities that are reputed good, but as they cannot all be possessed or observed, human conditions not permitting of it, it is necessary that he should be prudent enough to avoid the scandal of those vices which would lose him the state, and guard himself if possible against those which will not lose it him, but if not able to, he can indulge them with less scruple. And yet he must not mind incurring the scandal of those vices, without which it would be difficult to save the state, for if one considers well, it will be found that some things which seem virtues would, if followed, lead to one's ruin, and some others which appear vices result in one's greater security and wellbeing.

Of Cruelty and Clemency, and Whether It Is Better to Be Loved or Feared

Proceeding to the other qualities before named, I say that every prince must desire to be considered merciful and not cruel. He must, however, take care not to misuse this mercifulness. Cesare Borgia was considered cruel, but his cruelty had brought order to the Romagna, united it, and reduced it to peace and fealty. . . .

A prince, therefore, must not mind incurring the charge of cruelty for the purpose of keeping his subjects united and faithful; for, with a very few examples, he will be more merciful than those who, from excess of tenderness, allow disorders to arise, from whence spring bloodshed and rapine; for these as a rule injure the whole community, while the executions carried out by the prince injure only individuals. And of all princes, it is impossible for a new prince to escape the reputation of cruelty, new states being always full of dangers. Wherefore Virgil through the mouth of Dido says: "Hard necessity and the newness of my realm, compel me to do such things and to protect my borders everywhere" (*The Aeneid*).

Nevertheless, he must be cautious in believing and acting, and must not be afraid of his own shadow, and must proceed in a temperate manner with prudence and humanity, so that too much confidence does not render him incautious, and too much diffidence does not render him intolerant.

From this arises the question whether it is better to be loved more than feared, or feared more than loved. The reply is, that one ought to be both feared and loved, but as it is difficult for the two to go together, it is much safer to be feared than loved, if one of the two has to be wanting. For it may be said of men in general that they are ungrateful, voluble, dissemblers, anxious to avoid danger, and covetous of gain; as long as you benefit them, they are entirely yours; they offer you their blood, their goods, their life, and their children, as I have before said, when the necessity is remote; but when it approaches, they revolt. And the prince who has relied solely on their words, without making other preparations, is ruined; for the friendship which is gained by purchase and not through grandeur and nobility of spirit is bought but not secured, and at a pinch is not to be expended in your service. And men have less scruple in offending one who makes himself loved than one who makes himself feared; for love is held by a chain of obligation which, men being selfish, is broken whenever it serves their purpose; but fear is maintained by a dread of punishment which never fails.

Still, a prince should make himself feared in such a way that if he does not gain love, he at any rate avoids hatred; for fear and the absence of hatred may well go together, and will be always attained by one who abstains from interfering with the property of his citizens and subjects or with their women. And when he is obliged to take the life of any one, let him do so when there is a proper justification and manifest reason for it; but above all he must abstain from taking the property of others, for men forget more easily the death of their father than the loss of their patrimony. Then also pretexts for seizing property are never wanting, and one who begins to live by rapine will always find some reason for taking the goods of others, whereas causes for taking life are rarer and more fleeting.

But when the prince is with his army and has a large number of soldiers under his control, then it is extremely necessary that he should not mind being thought cruel; for without this reputation he could not keep an army united or disposed to any duty. Among the noteworthy actions of Hannibal is numbered this, that although he had an enormous army, composed of men of all nations and fighting in foreign countries, there never arose any dissension either among them or against the prince, either in good fortune or in bad. This could not be due to anything but his inhuman cruelty, which together with his infinite other virtues, made him always venerated and terrible in the sight of his soldiers, and without it his other virtues would not have sufficed to produce that effect. Thoughtless writers admire on the one hand his actions, and on the other blame the principal cause of them. . . .

I conclude, therefore, with regard to being feared and loved, that men love at their own free will, but fear at the will of the prince, and that a wise prince must rely on what is in his power and not on what is in the power of others, and he must only contrive to avoid incurring hatred, as has been explained.

In What Way Princes Must Keep Faith

How laudable it is for a prince to keep good faith and live with integrity, and not with astuteness, every one knows. Still the experience of our times shows those princes to have done great things who have had little regard for good faith, and have been able by astuteness to confuse men's brains, and who have ultimately overcome those who have made loyalty their foundation.

You must know, then, that there are two methods of fighting, the one by law, the other by force: the first method is that of men, the second of beasts; but as the first method is often insufficient, one must have recourse to the second. It is therefore necessary for a prince to know well how to use both the beast and the man. This was covertly taught to rulers by ancient writers, who relate how Achilles and many others of those ancient princes were given to Chiron the centaur to be brought up and educated under his discipline. The parable of this semi-animal, semi-human teacher is meant to indicate that a prince must know how to use both natures, and that the one without the other is not durable.

A prince being thus obliged to know well how to act as a beast must imitate the fox and the lion, for the lion cannot protect himself from traps, and the fox cannot defend himself from wolves. One must therefore be a fox to recognise traps, and a lion to frighten wolves. Those that wish to be only lions do not understand this. Therefore, a prudent ruler ought not to keep faith when by so doing it would be against his interest, and when the reasons which made him bind himself no longer exist. If men were all good, this precept would not be a good one; but as they are bad, and would not observe their faith with you, so you are not bound to keep faith with them. Nor have legitimate grounds ever failed a prince who wished to show colourable excuse for the non-fulfilment of his promise. Of this one could furnish an infinite number of modern examples, and show how many times peace has been broken, and how many promises rendered worthless, by the faithlessness of princes, and those that have been best able to imitate the fox have succeeded best. But it is necessary to be able to disguise this character well, and to be a great feigner and dissembler; and men are so simple and so ready to obey present necessities, that one who deceives will always find those who allow themselves to be deceived. . . .

It is not, therefore, necessary for a prince to have all the above-named qualities, but it is very necessary to seem to have them. I would even be bold to say that to possess them and always to observe them is dangerous, but to appear to possess them is useful. Thus it is well to seem merciful, faithful, humane, sincere, religious, and also to be so; but you must have the mind so disposed that when it is needful to be otherwise you may be able to change to the opposite qualities. And it must be understood that a prince, and especially a new prince, cannot observe all those things which are considered good in men, being often obliged, in order to maintain the state, to act against faith, against charity, against humanity, and against religion. And, therefore, he must have a mind disposed to adapt itself according to the wind, and as the variations of fortune dictate, and, as I said before, not deviate from what is good, if possible, but be able to do evil if constrained.

A prince must take great care that nothing goes out of his mouth which is not full of the above-named five qualities, and, to see and hear him, he should seem to be all mercy, faith, integrity, humanity, and religion. And nothing is more necessary than to seem to have this last quality, for men in general judge more by the eyes than by the hands, for every one can see, but very few have to feel. Everybody sees what you appear to be, few feel what you are, and those few will not dare to oppose themselves to the many, who have the majesty of the state to defend them; and in the actions of men, and especially of princes, from which there is no appeal, the end justifies the means. Let a prince therefore aim at

conquering and maintaining the state, and the means will always be judged honourable and praised by every one, for the vulgar is always taken by appearances
and the issue of the event; and the world consists only of the vulgar, and the few
who are not vulgar are isolated when the many have a rallying point in the prince.
A certain prince of the present time, whom it is well not to name, never does
anything but preach peace and good faith, but he is really a great enemy to both,
and either of them, had he observed them, would have lost him state or reputation
on many occasions.

That We Must Avoid Being Despised and Hated

But as I have not spoken of the most important of the qualities in question, I will
now deal briefly and generally with the rest. The prince must, as already stated,
avoid those things which will make him hated or despised; and whenever he succeeds in this, he will have done his part, and will find no danger in other vices. He
will chiefly become hated, as I said, by being rapacious, and usurping the property
and women of his subjects, which he must abstain from doing, and whenever one
does not attack the property or honour of the generality of men, they will live
contented; and one will only have to combat the ambition of a few, who can be
easily held in check in many ways. He is rendered despicable by being thought
changeable, frivolous, effeminate, timid, and irresolute; which a prince must
guard against as a rock of danger, and so contrive that his actions show grandeur,
spirit, gravity, and fortitude; and as to the government of his subjects, let his
sentence be irrevocable, and let him adhere to his decisions so that no one may
think of deceiving or cozening him.

The prince who creates such an opinion of himself gets a great reputation, and it
is very difficult to conspire against one who has a great reputation, and he will not
easily be attacked, so long as it is known that he is capable and reverenced by his
subjects. For a prince must have two kinds of fear: one internal as regards his
subjects, one external as regards foreign powers. From the latter he can defend
himself with good arms and good friends, and he will always have good friends if
he has good arms; and internal matters will always remain quiet, if they are not
perturbed by conspiracy and there is no disturbance from without; and even if
external powers sought to attack him, if he has ruled and lived as I have described, he will always if he stands firm, be able to sustain every shock, as I have
shown that Nabis the Spartan did. But with regard to the subjects, if not acted on
from outside, it is still to be feared lest they conspire in secret, from which the
prince may guard himself well by avoiding hatred and contempt, and keeping the
people satisfied with him, which it is necessary to accomplish, as has been related
at length. And one of the most potent remedies that a prince has against conspiracies, is that of not being hated by the mass of the people; for whoever conspires
always believes that he will satisfy the people by the death of their prince; but if
he thought to offend them by doing this, he would fear to engage in such an

undertaking, for the difficulties that conspirators have to meet are infinite. Experience shows that there have been very many conspiracies, but few have turned out well, for whoever conspires cannot act alone, and cannot find companions except among those who are discontented; and as soon as you have disclosed your intention to a malcontent, you give him the means of satisfying himself, for by revealing it he can hope to secure everything he wants; to such an extent that seeing a certain gain by doing this, and seeing on the other hand only a doubtful one and full of danger, he must either be a rare friend to you or else a very bitter enemy to the prince if he keeps faith with you. And to express the matter in a few words, I say, that on the side of the conspirator there is nothing but fear, jealousy, suspicion, and dread of punishment which frightens him; and on the side of the prince there is the majesty of government, the laws, the protection of friends and of the state which guard him. When to these things is added the goodwill of the people, it is impossible that any one should have the temerity to conspire. For whereas generally a conspirator has to fear before the execution of his plot, in this case, having the people for an enemy, he must also fear after his crime is accomplished, and thus he is not able to hope for any refuge. . . .

I conclude, therefore, that a prince need trouble little about conspiracies when the people are well disposed, but when they are hostile and hold him in hatred, then he must fear everything and everybody. Well-ordered states and wise princes have studied diligently not to drive the nobles to desperation, and to satisfy the populace and keep it contented, for this is one of the most important matters that a prince has to deal with. . . .

How Much Fortune Can Do in Human Affairs and How It May Be Opposed

It is not unknown to me how many have been and are of opinion that worldly events are so governed by fortune and by God, that men cannot by their prudence change them, and that on the contrary there is no remedy whatever, and for this they may judge it to be useless to toil much about them, but let things be ruled by chance. This opinion has been more held in our day, from the great changes that have been seen, and are daily seen, beyond every human conjecture. When I think about them, at times I am partly inclined to share this opinion. Nevertheless, that our free-will may not be altogether extinguished, I think it may be true that fortune is the ruler of half our actions, but that she allows the other half or thereabouts to be governed by us. I would compare her to an impetuous river that, when turbulent, inundates the plains, casts down trees and buildings, removes earth from this side and places it on the other; every one flees before it, and everything yields to its fury without being able to oppose it; and yet though it is of such a kind, still when it is quiet, men can make provision against it by dykes and banks, so that when it rises it will either go into a canal or its rush will not be so wild and dangerous. So it is with fortune, which shows her power where no measures have been taken to resist her, and directs her fury where she knows that no dykes or barriers have been made to hold her.

I conclude then that fortune varying and men remaining fixed in their ways, they are successful so long as these ways conform to circumstances, but when they are opposed then they are unsuccessful. I certainly think that it is better to be impetuous than cautious, for fortune is a woman, and it is necessary, if you wish to master her, to conquer her by force; and it can be seen that she lets herself be overcome by the bold rather than by those who proceed coldly. And therefore, like a woman, she is always a friend to the young, because they are less cautious, fiercer, and master her with greater audacity.

Exhortation to Liberate Italy from the Barbarians

Having now considered all the things we have spoken of, and thought within myself whether at present the time was not propitious in Italy for a new prince, and if there was not a state of things which offered an opportunity to a prudent and capable man to introduce a new system that would do honour to himself and good to the mass of the people, it seems to me that so many things concur to favour a new ruler that I do not know of any time more fitting for such an enterprise. And if, as I said, it was necessary in order that the power of Moses should be displayed that the people of Israel should be slaves in Egypt, and to give scope for the greatness and courage of Cyrus that the Persians should be oppressed by the Medes, and to illustrate the pre-eminence of Theseus that the Athenians should be dispersed, so at the present time, in order that the might of an Italian genius might be recognised, it was necessary that Italy should be reduced to her present condition, and that she should be more enslaved than the Hebrews, more oppressed than the Persians, and more scattered than the Athenians; without a head, without order, beaten, despoiled, lacerated, and overrun, and that she should have suffered ruin of every kind. . . .

This opportunity must not, therefore, be allowed to pass, so that Italy may at length find her liberator. I cannot express the love with which he would be received in all those provinces which have suffered under these foreign invasions, with what thirst for vengeance, with what steadfast faith, with what love, with what grateful tears. What doors would be closed against him? What people would refuse him obedience? What envy could oppose him? What Italian would withhold allegiance? This barbarous domination stinks in the nostrils of every one. May your illustrious house therefore assume this task with that courage and those hopes which are inspired by a just cause, so that under its banner our fatherland may be raised up, and under its auspices be verified that saying of Petrarch:

Valour against fell wrath
Will take up arms; and be the combat quickly sped!
For, sure, the ancient worth,
That in Italians stirs the heart, is not yet dead.

DISCOURSES ON LIVY

Of the Different Kinds of Republics, and of What Kind the Roman Republic Was

I will leave aside what might be said of cities which from their very birth have been subject to a foreign power, and will speak only of those whose origin has been independent, and which from the first governed themselves by their own laws, whether as republics or as principalities, and whose constitution and laws have differed as their origin. Some have had at the very beginning, or soon after, a legislator, who, like Lycurgus with the Lacedæmonians, gave them by a single act all the laws they needed. Others have owed theirs to chance and to events, and have received their laws at different times, as Rome did. It is a great good fortune for a republic to have a legislator sufficiently wise to give her laws so regulated that, without the necessity of correcting them, they afford security to those who live under them. Sparta observed her laws for more than eight hundred years without altering them and without experiencing a single dangerous disturbance. Unhappy, on the contrary, is that republic which, not having at the beginning fallen into the hands of a sagacious and skilful legislator, is herself obliged to reform her laws. More unhappy still is that republic which from the first has diverged from a good constitution. And that republic is furthest from it whose vicious institutions impeded her progress, and make her leave the right path that leads to a good end; for those who are in that condition can hardly ever be brought into the right road. Those republics, on the other hand, that started without having even a perfect constitution, but made a fair beginning, and are capable of improvement—such republics, I say, may perfect themselves by the aid of events. It is very true, however, that such reforms are never effected without danger, for the majority of men never willingly adopt any new law tending to change the constitution of the state, unless the necessity of the change is clearly demonstrated; and as such a necessity cannot make itself felt without being accompanied with danger, the republic may easily be destroyed before having perfected its constitution. That of Florence is a complete proof of this: reorganized after the revolt of Arezzo, in 1502, it was overthrown after the taking of Prato, in 1512.

Having proposed to myself to treat of the kind of government established at Rome, and of the events that led to its perfection, I must at the beginning observe that some of the writers on politics distinguished three kinds of government, viz. the monarchical, the aristocratic, and the democratic; and maintain that the legislators of a people must choose from these three the one that seems to them most suitable. Other authors, wiser according to the opinion of many, count six kinds of governments, three of which are very bad, and three good in themselves, but so liable to be corrupted that they become absolutely bad. The three good ones are those which we have just named; the three bad ones result from the degradation of the other three, and each of them resembles its corresponding original, so that the transition from the one to the other is very easy. Thus monarchy becomes tyranny;

aristocracy degenerates into oligarchy; and the popular government lapses readily into licentiousness. So that a legislator who gives to a state which he founds, either of these three forms of government, constitutes it but for a brief time; for no precautions can prevent either one of the three that are reputed good, from degenerating into its opposite kind; so great are in these the attractions and resemblances between the good and the evil.

Chance has given birth to these different kinds of governments amongst men; for at the beginning of the world the inhabitants were few in number, and lived for a time dispersed, like beasts. As the human race increased, the necessity for uniting themselves for defence made itself felt; the better to attain this object, they chose the strongest and most courageous from amongst themselves and placed him at their head, promising to obey him. Thence they began to know the good and the honest, and to distinguish them from the bad and vicious; for seeing a man injure his benefactor aroused at once two sentiments in every heart, hatred against the ingrate and love for the benefactor. They blamed the first, and on the contrary honored those the more who showed themselves grateful, for each felt that he in turn might be subject to a like wrong; and to prevent similar evils, they set to work to make laws, and to institute punishments for those who contravened them. Such was the origin of justice. This caused them, when they had afterwards to choose a prince, neither to look to the strongest nor bravest, but to the wisest and most just. But when they began to make sovereignty hereditary and non-elective, the children quickly degenerated from their fathers; and, so far from trying to equal their virtues, they considered that a prince had nothing else to do than to excel all the rest in luxury, indulgence, and every other variety of pleasure. The prince consequently soon drew upon himself the general hatred. An object of hatred, he naturally felt fear; fear in turn dictated to him precautions and wrongs, and thus tyranny quickly developed itself. Such were the beginning and causes of disorders, conspiracies, and plots against the sovereigns, set on foot, not by the feeble and timid, but by those citizens who, surpassing the others in grandeur of soul, in wealth, and in courage, could not submit to the outrages and excesses of their princes.

Under such powerful leaders the masses armed themselves against the tyrant, and, after having rid themselves of him, submitted to these chiefs as their liberators. These, abhorring the very name of prince, constituted themselves a new government; and at first, bearing in mind the past tyranny, they governed in strict accordance with the laws which they had established themselves; preferring public interests to their own, and to administer and protect with greatest care both public and private affairs. The children succeeded their fathers, and ignorant of the changes of fortune, having never experienced its reverses, and indisposed to remain content with this civil equality, they in turn gave themselves up to cupidity, ambition, libertinage, and violence, and soon caused the aristocratic government to degenerate into an oligarchic tyranny, regardless of all civil rights. They soon, however, experienced the same fate as the first tyrant; the people, disgusted with their government, placed themselves at the command of whoever was willing to attack them, and this disposition soon produced an avenger, who was sufficiently well seconded to destroy them. The memory of the prince and the wrongs committed by him being still fresh in their minds, and having overthrown the oligarchy, the people were not willing to return to the government of a prince. A popular government was therefore resolved upon, and it was so organized that the authority should not again fall into the hands of a prince or a small number of nobles. And as all governments are at first looked up to with some degree of reverence, the popular state also maintained itself for a time, but which was never of long duration, and lasted generally only about as long as the generation that had established it; for it soon ran into that kind of license which inflicts injury upon public as well as private interests. Each individual only consulted his own passions, and a thousand acts of injustice were daily committed, so that, constrained by necessity, or directed by the counsels of some good man, or for the purpose of escaping from this anarchy, they returned anew to the government of a prince, and from this they generally lapsed again into anarchy, step by step, in the same manner and from the same causes as we have indicated.

Such is the circle which all republics are destined to run through. Seldom, however, do they come back to the original form of government, which results from the fact that their duration is not sufficiently long to be able to undergo these repeated changes and preserve their existence. But it may well happen that a republic lacking strength and good counsel in its difficulties becomes subject after a while to some neighboring state, that is better organized than itself; and if such is not the case, then they will be apt to revolve indefinitely in the circle of revolutions. I say, then, that all kinds of government are defective; those three which we have qualified as good because they are too short-lived, and the three bad ones because of their inherent viciousness. Thus sagacious legislators, knowing the vices of each of these systems of government by themselves, have chosen one that should partake all of them, judging that to be the most stable and solid. In fact, when there is combined under the same constitution a prince, a nobility, and the power of the people, then these three powers will watch and keep each other reciprocally in check.

Amongst those justly celebrated for having established such a constitution, Lycurgus beyond doubt merits the highest praise. He organized the government of Sparta in such manner that, in giving to the king, the nobles, and the people each their portion of authority and duties, he created a government which maintained itself for over eight hundred years in the most perfect tranquillity, and reflected infinite glory upon this legislator. On the other hand, the constitution given by Solon to the Athenians, by which he established only a popular government, was of such short duration that before his death he saw the tyranny of Pisistratus arise. And although forty years afterwards the heirs of the tyrant were expelled, so that Athens recovered her liberties and restored the popular government according to the laws of Solon, yet it did not last over a hundred years; although a number of laws that had been overlooked by Solon were adopted, to maintain the government against the insolence of the nobles and the license of the populace. The fault he had committed in not tempering the power of the people and that of the prince and his nobles, made the duration of the government of Athens very short, as compared with that of Sparta.

But let us come to Rome. Although she had no legislator like Lycurgus, who

constituted her government, at her very origin, in a manner to secure her liberty
for a length of time, yet the disunion which existed between the Senate and the
people produced such extraordinary events, that chance did for her what the laws
had failed to do. Thus, if Rome did not attain the first degree of happiness, she at
least had the second. Her first institutions were doubtless defective, but they were
not in conflict with the principles that might bring her to perfection. For Romulus
and all the other kings gave her many and good laws, well suited even to a free
people; but as the object of these princes was to found a monarchy, and not a
republic, Rome, upon becoming free, found herself lacking all those institutions
that are most essential to liberty, and which her kings had not established. And
although these kings lost their empire, for the reasons and in the manner which we
have explained, yet those who expelled them appointed immediately two consuls
in place of the king; and thus it was found that they had banished the title of king
from Rome, but not the regal power. The government, composed of Consuls and a
Senate, had but two of the three elements of which we have spoken, the monarchical and the aristocratic; the popular power was wanting. In the course of time,
however, the insolence of the nobles, produced by the causes which we shall see
further on, induced the people to rise against the others. The nobility, to save a
portion of their power, were forced to yield a share of it to the people; but the
Senate and the Consuls retained sufficient to maintain their rank in the state. It
was then that the Tribunes of the people were created, which strengthened and
confirmed the republic, being now composed of the three elements of which we
have spoken above. Fortune favored her, so that, although the authority passed
successively from the kings and nobles to the people, by the same degrees and for
the same reasons that we have spoken of, yet the royal authority was never entirely abolished to bestow it upon the nobles; and these were never entirely deprived of their authority to give it to the people; but a combination was formed of
the three powers, which rendered the constitution perfect, and this perfection was
attained by the disunion of the Senate and the people. . . .

In Proportion as the Founders of a Republic or Monarchy Are Entitled to Praise, So Do the Founders of a Tyranny Deserve Execration

Of all men who have been eulogized, those deserve it most who have been the
authors and founders of religions; next come such as have established republics or
kingdoms. After these the most celebrated are those who have commanded
armies, and have extended the possessions of their kingdom or country. To these
may be added literary men, but, as these are of different kinds, they are celebrated
according to their respective degrees of excellence. All others—and their number
is infinite—receive such share of praise as pertains to the exercise of their arts and
professions. On the contrary, those are doomed to infamy and universal execration
who have destroyed religions, who have overturned republics and kingdoms, who
are enemies of virtue, of letters, and of every art that is useful and honorable to
mankind. Such are the impious and violent, the ignorant, the idle, the vile and

degraded. And there are none so foolish or so wise, so wicked or so good, that, in choosing between these two qualities, they do not praise what is praiseworthy and blame that which deserves blame. And yet nearly all men, deceived by a false good and a false glory, allow themselves voluntarily or ignorantly to be drawn towards those who deserve more blame than praise. Such as by the establishment of a republic or kingdom could earn eternal glory for themselves incline to tyranny, without perceiving how much glory, how much honor, security, satisfaction, and tranquillity of mind, they forfeit; and what infamy, disgrace, blame, danger, and disquietude they incur. And it is impossible that those who have lived as private citizens in a republic, or those who by fortune or courage have risen to be princes of the same, if they were to read history and take the records of antiquity for example, should not prefer Scipio to Cæsar; and that those who were (originally) princes should not rather choose to be like Agesilaus, Timoleon, and Dion, than Nabis, Phalaris, and Dionysius; for they would then see how thoroughly the latter were despised, and how highly the former were appreciated. They would furthermore see that Timoleon and the others had no less authority in their country than Dionysius and Phalaris, but that they enjoyed far more security, and for a much greater length of time. Nor let any one be deceived by the glory of that Cæsar who has been so much celebrated by writers; for those who praised him were corrupted by his fortune, and frightened by the long duration of the empire that was maintained under his name, and which did not permit writers to speak of him with freedom. And if anyone wishes to know what would have been said of him if writers had been free to speak their minds, let them read what Catiline said of him. Cæsar is as much more to be condemned, as he who commits an evil deed is more guilty than he who merely has the evil intention. He will also see how highly Brutus was eulogized; for, not being allowed to blame Cæsar on account of his power, they extolled his enemy. Let him also note how much more praise those Emperors merited who, after Rome became an empire, conformed to the laws like good princes, than those who took the opposite course; and he will see that Titus, Nerva, Trajan, Hadrian, Antoninus and Marcus Aurelius did not require the Prætorians nor the multitudinous legions to defend them, because they were protected by their own good conduct, the good will of the people, and by the love of the Senate. He will furthermore see that neither the Eastern nor the Western armies sufficed to save Caligula, Nero, Vitellius, and so many other wicked Emperors, from the enemies which their bad conduct and evil lives had raised up against them.

And if the history of these men were carefully studied, it would prove an ample guide to any prince, and serve to show him the way to glory or to infamy, to security or to perpetual apprehension. For of the twenty-six Emperors that reigned from the time of Cæsar to that of Maximinius, sixteen were assassinated, and ten only died a natural death; and if, amongst those who were killed, there were one or two good ones, like Galba and Pertinax, their death was the consequence of the corruption which their predecessors had engendered amongst the soldiers. And if amongst those who died a natural death there were some wicked ones, like Severus, it was due to their extraordinary good fortune and courage, which two qualities rarely fall to the lot of such men. He will furthermore learn from the lessons of that history how an empire should be organized properly; for all the Emperors that succeeded to the throne by inheritance, except Titus, were bad, and those who became Emperors by adoption were all good, such as the five from Nero to Marcus Aurelius; and when the Empire became hereditary, it came to ruin. Let any prince now place himself in the times from Nerva to Marcus Aurelius, and let him compare them with those that preceded and followed that period, and let him choose in which of the two he would like to have been born, and in which he would like to have reigned. In the period under the good Emperors he will see the prince secure amidst his people, who are also living in security; he will see peace and justice prevail in the world, the authority of the Senate respected, the magistrates honored, the wealthy citizens enjoying their riches, nobility and virtue exalted, and everywhere will he see tranquillity and well-being. And on the other hand he will behold all animosity, license, corruption, and all noble ambition extinct. During the period of the good Emperors he will see that golden age when every one could hold and defend whatever opinion he pleased; in fine, he will see the triumph of the world, the prince surrounded with reverence and glory, and beloved by his people, who are happy in their security. If now he will but glance at the times under the other Emperors, he will behold the atrocities of war, discords and sedition, cruelty in peace as in war, many princes massacred, many civil and foreign wars, Italy afflicted and overwhelmed by fresh misfortunes, and her cities ravaged and ruined; he will see Rome in ashes, the Capitol pulled down by her own citizens, the ancient temples desolate, all religious ties and ceremonies corrupted, and the city full of adultery; he will behold the sea covered with ships full of flying exiles, and the shores stained with blood. He will see innumerable cruelties in Rome, and nobility, riches, and honor, and above all virtue, accounted capital crimes. He will see informers rewarded, servants corrupted against their masters, the freedmen arrayed against their patrons, and those who were without enemies betrayed and oppressed by their friends. And then will he recognize what infinite obligations Rome, Italy, and the whole world owed to Cæsar. And surely, if he be a man, he will be shocked at the thought of re-enacting those evil times, and be fired with an intense desire to follow the example of the good. And truly, if a prince be anxious for glory and the good opinion of the world, he should rather wish to possess a corrupt city, not to ruin it wholly like Cæsar, but to reorganize it like Romulus. For certainly the heavens cannot afford a man a greater opportunity of glory, nor could men desire a better one. And if for the proper organization of a city it should be necessary to abolish the principality, he who had failed to give her good laws for the sake of preserving his rank may be entitled to some excuse; but there would be none for him who had been able to organize the city properly and yet preserve the sovereignty. And, in fine, let him to whom Heaven has vouchsafed such an opportunity reflect that there are two ways open to him; one that will enable him to live securely and insure him glory after death, and the other that will make his life one of constant anxiety, and after death consign him to eternal infamy.

9

Martin Luther
The Christian in Society

Martin Luther (1483–1546) was the initiator of the Protestant Reformation. He was the son of a peasant who became a prosperous copper miner. Luther attended the University of Erfurt, and to please his father, attempted to study law. A violent thunderstorm set the stage for a spiritual crisis which motivated Luther to enter a monastery of Augustinian friars. His studies led to a theological reorientation. He interpreted God's justice not as the divine expression of judgment through reward and punishment, but as God's grace bestowed unconditionally. This put into question the role of a clergy which sold indulgences and pardons, and led Luther to nail his Ninety-five Theses on Indulgences (1517) on the church door at Wittenberg. This act went to the heart of medieval piety, as indulgences were intrinsic to the sacrament of penance. Luther redefined the "church" as the communion of those ruled by Christ's word, questioning hierarchical authority in the Church and asserting instead the priesthood of all believers. After 1521, Luther attacked reformers who demanded more radical changes in the Church. He was particularly hostile to those who wanted to create communities ruled solely by the Sermon on the Mount. Luther argued against them, positing the notion of two "kingdoms," one of Heaven, the other of the Earth, each ruled by God through different forms of laws.

TEMPORAL AUTHORITY: TO WHAT EXTENT IT SHOULD BE OBEYED

. . . First, we must provide a sound basis for the civil law and sword so no one will doubt that it is in the world by God's will and ordinance. The passages which do this are the following: Romans 12, "Let every soul [*seele*] be subject to the governing authority, for there is no authority except from God; the authority which everywhere [*allenthalben*] exists has been ordained by God. He then who resists the governing authority resists the ordinance of God, and he who resists God's ordinance will incur judgment." Again, in I Peter 2 [:13–14], "Be subject to every kind of human ordinance, whether it be to the king as supreme, or to governors, as those who have been sent by him to punish the wicked and to praise the righteous."

The law of this temporal sword has existed from the beginning of the world.

For when Cain slew his brother Abel, he was in such great terror of being killed in turn that God even placed a special prohibition on it and suspended the sword for his sake, so that no one was to slay him [Gen. 4:14–15]. He would not have had this fear if he had not seen and heard from Adam that murderers are to be slain. . . . Hence, it is certain and clear enough that it is God's will that the temporal sword and law be used for the punishment of the wicked and the protection of the upright.

Second. There appear to be powerful arguments to the contrary. Christ says in Matthew 5 [:38–41], "You have heard that it was said to them of old: An eye for an eye, a tooth for a tooth. But I say to you, Do not resist evil; but if anyone strikes you on the right cheek, turn to him the other also. And if anyone would sue you and take your coat, let him have your cloak as well. And if anyone forces you to go one mile, go with him two miles," etc. Likewise Paul in Romans 12 [:19], "Beloved, defend not yourselves, but leave it to the wrath of God; for it is written, 'Vengeance is mine; I will repay, says the Lord.'" And in Matthew 5 [:44], "Love your enemies, do good to them that hate you." And again, in I Peter [3:9], "Do not return evil for evil, or reviling for reviling," etc. These and similar passages would certainly make it appear as though in the New Testament Christians were to have no temporal sword. . . .

Third. Here we must divide the children of Adam and all mankind into two classes, the first belonging to the kingdom of God, the second to the kingdom of the world. Those who belong to the kingdom of God are all the true believers who are in Christ and under Christ, for Christ is King and Lord in the kingdom of God, as Psalm 2 [:6] and all of Scripture says. For this reason he came into the world, that he might begin God's kingdom and establish it in the world. Therefore, he says before Pilate, "My kingdom is not of the world, but every one who is of the truth hears my voice" [John 18:36–37]. In the gospel he continually refers to the kingdom of God, and says, "Amend your ways, the kingdom of God is at hand" [Matt. 4:17, 10:7]; again, "Seek first the kingdom of God and his righteousness" [Matt. 6:33]. He also calls the gospel a gospel of the kingdom of God;[1] because it teaches, governs, and upholds[2] God's kingdom.

Now observe, these people need no temporal law or sword. If all the world were composed of real Christians, that is, true believers, there would be no need for or benefits from prince, king, lord, sword, or law. They would serve no purpose, since Christians have in their heart the Holy Spirit, who both teaches and makes them to do injustice to no one, to love everyone, and to suffer injustice and even death willingly and cheerfully at the hands of anyone. Where there is nothing but the unadulterated doing of right and bearing of wrong, there is no need for any suit, litigation, court, judge, penalty, law, or sword. For this reason it is impossible that the temporal sword and law should find any work to do among Christians, since they do of their own accord much more than all laws and teachings can demand, just as Paul says in I Timothy 1 [:9], "The law is not laid down for the just but for the lawless."

Why is this? It is because the righteous man of his own accord does all and more than the law demands. But the unrighteous do nothing that the law demands;

therefore, they need the law to instruct, constrain, and compel them to do good. . . .

Fourth. All who are not Christians belong to the kingdom of the world and are under the law. There are few true believers, and still fewer who live a Christian life, who do not resist evil and indeed themselves do no evil. For this reason God has provided for them a different government beyond the Christian estate and kingdom of God. He has subjected them to the sword so that, even though they would like to, they are unable to practice their wickedness, and if they do practice it they cannot do so without fear or with success and impunity. In the same way a savage wild beast is bound with chains and ropes so that it cannot bite and tear as it would normally do, even though it would like to; whereas a tame and gentle animal needs no restraint, but is harmless despite the lack of chains and ropes.

If this were not so, men would devour one another, seeing that the whole world is evil and that among thousands there is scarcely a single true Christian. No one could support wife and child, feed himself, and serve God. The world would be reduced to chaos. For this reason God has ordained two governments: the spiritual, by which the Holy Spirit produces Christians and righteous people under Christ; and the temporal, which restrains the un-Christian and wicked so that—no thanks to them—they are obliged to keep still and to maintain an outward peace. Thus does St. Paul interpret the temporal sword in Romans 13 [:3], when he says it is not a terror to good conduct but to bad. And Peter says it is for the punishment of the wicked [I Pet. 2:14].

If anyone attempted to rule the world by the gospel and to abolish all temporal law and sword on the plea that all are baptized and Christian, and that, according to the gospel, there shall be among them no law or sword—or need for either— pray tell me, friend, what would he be doing? He would be loosing the ropes and chains of the savage wild beasts and letting them bite and mangle everyone, meanwhile insisting that they were harmless, tame, and gentle creatures; but I would have the proof in my wounds. Just so would the wicked under the name of Christian abuse evangelical freedom, carry on their rascality, and insist that they were Christians subject neither to law nor sword, as some are already raving and ranting.[3]

To such a one we must say: Certainly it is true that Christians, so far as they themselves are concerned, are subject neither to law nor sword, and have need of neither. But take heed and first fill the world with real Christians before you attempt to rule it in a Christian and evangelical manner. This you will never accomplish; for the world and the masses are and always will be un-Christian, even if they are all baptized and Christian in name. Christians are few and far between (as the saying is). Therefore, it is out of the question that there should be a common Christian government over the whole world, or indeed over a single country or any considerable body of people, for the wicked always outnumber the good. Hence, a man who would venture to govern an entire country or the world with the gospel would be like a shepherd who should put together in one fold wolves, lions, eagles, and sheep, and let them mingle freely with one another, saying, "Help yourselves, and be good and peaceful toward one another. The fold is open, there is plenty of food. You need have no fear of dogs and clubs." The sheep would doubtless keep the peace and allow themselves to be fed and governed peacefully, but they would not live long, nor would one beast survive another.

For this reason one must carefully distinguish between these two governments. Both must be permitted to remain; the one to produce righteousness, the other to bring about external peace and prevent evil deeds. Neither one is sufficient in the world without the other. No one can become righteous in the sight of God by means of the temporal government, without Christ's spiritual government. Christ's government does not extend over all men; rather, Christians are always a minority in the midst of non-Christians. Now where temporal government or law alone prevails, there sheer hypocrisy is inevitable, even though the commandments be God's very own. For without the Holy Spirit in the heart no one becomes truly righteous, no matter how fine the works he does. On the other hand, where the spiritual government alone prevails over land and people, there wickedness is given free rein and the door is open for all manner of rascality, for the world as a whole cannot receive or comprehend it.

Now you see the intent of Christ's words which we quoted above from Matthew 5,[4] that Christians should not go to law or use the temporal sword among themselves. Actually, he says this only to his beloved Christians. . . . If now the whole world were Christian in this sense, then these words would apply to all, and all would act accordingly. Since the world is un-Christian, however, these words do not apply to all; and all do not act accordingly, but are under another government in which those who are not Christian are kept under external constraint and compelled to keep the peace and do what is good. . . .

Fifth. But you say: if Christians then do not need the temporal sword or law, why does Paul say to all Christians in Romans 13 [:1], "Let all souls be subject to the governing authority," and St. Peter, "Be subject to every human ordinance" [I Pet. 2:13], etc., as quoted above? Answer: I have just said that Christians, among themselves and by and for themselves, need no law or sword, since it is neither necessary nor useful for them. Since a true Christian lives and labors on earth not for himself alone but for his neighbor, he does by the very nature of his spirit even what he himself has no need of, but is needful and useful to his neighbor. Because the sword is most beneficial and necessary for the whole world in order to preserve peace, punish sin, and restrain the wicked, the Christian submits most willingly to the rule of the sword, pays his taxes, honors those in authority,[5] serves, helps, and does all he can to assist the governing authority, that it may continue to function and be held in honor and fear. Although he has no need of these things for himself—to him they are not essential—nevertheless, he concerns himself about what is serviceable and of benefit to others, as Paul teaches in Ephesians 5 [:21–6:9].

Just as he performs all other works of love which he himself does not need—he does not visit the sick in order that he himself may be made well, or feed others because he himself needs food—so he serves the governing authority not because he needs it but for the sake of others, that they may be protected and that the

wicked may not become worse. He loses nothing by this; such service in no way
harms him, yet it is of great benefit to the world. If he did not so serve he would
be acting not as a Christian but even contrary to love; he would also be setting a
bad example to others who in like manner would not submit to authority, even
though they were not Christians. In this way the gospel would be brought into
disrepute, as though it taught insurrection and produced self-willed people unwilling to benefit or serve others, when in fact it makes a Christian the servant of all.[6]
Thus in Matthew 17 [:27] Christ paid the half-shekel tax that he might not offend
them, although he had no need to do so.

Thus you observe in the words of Christ quoted above from Matthew 5 that he
clearly teaches that Christians among themselves should have no temporal sword
or law. He does not, however, forbid one to serve and be subject to those who do
have the secular sword and law. Rather, since you do not need it and should not
have it, you are to serve all the more those who have not attained to such heights
as you and who therefore do still need it. Although you do not need to have your
enemy punished, your afflicted neighbor does. You should help him that he may
have peace and that his enemy may be curbed, but this is not possible unless the
governing authority is honored and feared. Christ does not say, "You shall not
serve the governing authority or be subject to it," but rather, "Do not resist evil"
[Matt. 5:39], as much as to say, "Behave in such a way that you bear everything,
so that you may not need the governing authority to help you and serve you or be
beneficial or essential for you, but that you in turn may help and serve it, being
beneficial and essential to it. I would have you be too exalted and far too noble to
have any need of it; it should rather have need of you."

Sixth. You ask whether a Christian too may bear the temporal sword and punish
the wicked, since Christ's words, "Do not resist evil," are so clear and definite
that the sophists have had to make of them a "counsel." Answer: You have now
heard two propositions. One is that the sword can have no place among Christians;
therefore, you cannot bear it among Christians or hold it over them, for they do
not need it. The question, therefore, must be referred to the other group, the non-
Christians, whether you may bear it there in a Christian manner. Here the other
proposition applies, that you are under obligation to serve and assist the sword by
whatever means you can, with body, goods, honor, and soul. For it is something
which you do not need, but which is very beneficial and essential for the whole
world and for your neighbor. Therefore, if you see that there is a lack of hangmen, constables, judges, lords, or princes, and you find that you are qualified, you
should offer your services and seek the position, that the essential governmental
authority may not be despised and become enfeebled or perish. The world cannot
and dare not dispense with it.

Here is the reason why you should do this: In such a case you would be entering
entirely into the service and work of others, which would be of advantage neither
to yourself nor your property or honor, but only to your neighbor and to others.
You would be doing it not with the purpose of avenging yourself or returning evil
for evil, but for the good of your neighbor and for the maintenance of the safety
and peace of others. For yourself, you would abide by the gospel and govern

yourself according to Christ's word [Matt. 5:39–40], gladly turning the other cheek and letting the cloak go with the coat when the matter concerned you and your cause.

In this way the two propositions are brought into harmony with one another: at one and the same time you satisfy God's kingdom inwardly and the kingdom of the world outwardly. You suffer evil and injustice, and yet at the same time you punish evil and injustice; you do not resist evil, and yet at the same time, you do resist it. In the one case, you consider yourself and what is yours; in the other, you consider your neighbor and what is his. In what concerns you and yours, you govern yourself by the gospel and suffer injustice toward yourself as a true Christian; in what concerns the person or property of others, you govern yourself according to love and tolerate no injustice toward your neighbor. The gospel does not forbid this; in fact, in other places it actually commands it.

Notes

1. In Mark 1:14 the King James' Version phrase is more accurate than that of the Revised Standard Version, which omits the term "kingdom." George Arthur Buttrick (commentary ed.), *The Interpreter's Bible* (New York: Abingdon-Cokesbury, 1951–1957), VII, 655.

2. *Enthellt* is here taken to mean *erhält*.

3. The allusion is to the Anabaptists.

4. See the quotation of Matt. 5:38–41.

5. Cf. Rom. 13:6–7.

6. See Luther's 1520 *The Freedom of a Christian* where Romans 13 and Matthew 17 are also cited in illustration of the Christian's willing service to others. Luther's *Werke*, 31, 343–377, especially p. 369.

10 _____

John Calvin
God and Political Duty

John Calvin (1509–1564) was a French Protestant theologian and reformer who studied theology in Paris. He later fulfilled his father's wishes by studying law until he was awarded his doctorate in 1532. A few years later, he left Catholicism and became an engaged Protestant reformer, a teacher and writer on politics and education. He was asked on two separate occasions to organize the reform of politics and mores in Geneva, and his Institutes of the Christian Religion *(1536, with numerous revisions, the last in 1559) presents a systematic exposition of his theories, and a defense of the French Protestants. Although Calvin believed that the Church and State ought to be structurally independent, he noted that magistrates receive their authority from God and are obligated to apply the law of God to the affairs of civil society.*

TO PREVENT anyone from falling into this error, let use therefore consider, in the first place, that man is under two kinds of government—one spiritual, by which the conscience is formed to piety and the service of God; the other political, by which a man is instructed in the duties of humanity and civility, which are to be observed in an intercourse with mankind. They are generally, and not improperly, denominated the spiritual and the temporal jurisdiction, indicating that the former species of government pertains to the life of the soul, and that the latter relates to the concerns of the present state, not only to the provision of food and clothing, but to the enactment of laws to regulate a man's life among his neighbors by the rules of holiness, integrity, and sobriety. For the former has its seat in the interior of the mind, whilst the latter only directs the external conduct; one may be termed a spiritual kingdom, and the other a political one. But these two, as we have distinguished them, always require to be considered separately; and while the one is under discussion, the mind must be abstracted from all consideration of the other. For man contains, as it were, two worlds, capable of being governed by various rulers and various laws. This distinction will prevent what the Gospel inculcates concerning spiritual liberty from being misapplied to political regulations, as though Christians were less subject to the external government of human laws because their consciences have been set at liberty before God, as though their freedom of spirit necessarily exempted them from all carnal servitude. Again, because even in those constitutions which seem to pertain to the spiritual kingdom, there may possibly be some deception, it is necessary to discriminate between these also—which are to be accounted legitimate, as according with the Divine word, and which, on the contrary, ought not to be received among believers. Of civil government I shall treat in another place. Of ecclesiastical laws also I forbear to speak at present, because a full discussion of them will be proper in the Fourth Book, where we shall treat of the power of the Church. But we shall conclude the present argument in the following manner: the question which, as I have observed, is in itself not very obscure or intricate, greatly perplexes many because they do not distinguish with sufficient precision between the external jurisdiction and the court of conscience. The difficulty is increased by Paul's injunction to obey magistrates "not only for wrath, but also for conscience' sake," from which it should follow that the conscience also is bound by political laws. But if this were true, it would supersede all that we have already said, or are now about to say, respecting spiritual government. For the solution of this difficulty it will be of use, first, to know what conscience is. And the definition of it must be derived from the etymology of the word. For as, when men apprehend the knowledge of things in the mind and understanding, they are thence said *scire*, "to know," whence is derived the word *scientia*, "science" or "knowledge," so when they have a sense of Divine justice, as an additional witness, which permits them not to conceal their sins or to elude accusation at the tribunal of the supreme Judge, this sense is termed *conscientia*, "conscience." For it is a kind of medium between God and man, because it does not suffer a man to suppress what he knows within himself, but pursues him till it brings him to conviction. This is what Paul means by "their conscience also bearing witness, and their thoughts accusing, or else excusing, one another." Simple knowledge might remain, as it were, confined within a man. This sentiment, therefore, which places man before the Divine tribunal is appointed, as it were, to watch over man, to observe and examine all his secrets, that nothing may remain enveloped in darkness. Hence the old proverb, "Conscience is as a thousand witnesses." For the same reason Peter speaks of "the answer of a good conscience toward God," to express our tranquility of mind when, persuaded of the favor of Christ, we present ourselves with boldness in the presence of God. And the author of the Epistle to the Hebrews expresses absolution or freedom from every future charge of sin, by "having no more conscience of sin.". . .

On Civil Government

Having already stated that man is the subject of two kinds of government, and having sufficiently discussed that which is situated in the soul, or the inner man, and relates to eternal life—we are, in this chapter, to say something of the other kind which relates to civil justice and the regulation of the external conduct. For, though the nature of this argument seems to have no connection with the spiritual doctrine of faith which I have undertaken to discuss, the sequel will show that I have sufficient reason for connecting them together, and, indeed, that necessity obliges me to it, especially since, on the one hand, infatuated and barbarous men madly endeavor to subvert this ordinance established by God, and, on the other hand, the flatterers of princes, extolling their power beyond all just bounds, hesitate not to oppose it to the authority of God himself. Unless both these errors be resisted, the purity of the faith will be destroyed. Besides, it is of no small importance for us to know what benevolent provision God has made for mankind in this instance, that we may be stimulated by a greater degree of pious zeal to testify our gratitude. In the first place, before we enter on the subject itself, it is necessary for us to recur to the distinction which we have already established, lest we fall into an error very common in the world, and injudiciously confound together these two things the nature of which is altogether different. For some men, when they hear that the Gospel promises a liberty which acknowledges no king or magistrate among them, but submits to Christ alone, think they can enjoy no advantage of their liberty while they see any power exalted above them. They imagine, therefore, that nothing will prosper unless the whole world be modeled in a new form, without any tribunals or laws, or magistrates, or anything of a similar kind which they consider injurious to their liberty. But he who knows how to distinguish between the body and the soul, between this present transitory life and the future eternal one, will find no difficulty in understanding that the spiritual kingdom of Christ and civil government are things very different and remote from each other. Since it is a Jewish folly, therefore, to seek and include the kingdom of Christ under the elements of this world, let us, on the contrary, considering what the Scripture clearly inculcates, that the benefit which is received from the grace of Christ is spiritual—let us, I say, remember to confine within its proper limits all this liberty which is promised and offered to us in him. For why is it that the same apostle who, in one place, exhorts to "stand fast in the liberty wherewith Christ hath made us free and be not entangled again with the yoke of bondage," in another enjoins servants to "care not for" their servile condition, except that spiritual liberty may very well consist with civil servitude? In this sense we are likewise to understand him in these passages: "There is neither Jew nor Greek, there is neither bond nor free, there is neither male nor female." Again: "There is neither Greek nor Jew, circumcision nor uncircumcision, Barbarian, Scythian, bond nor free: but Christ is all, and in all," in which he signifies that it is of no importance what is our condition among men or under the laws of what nation we live, as the kingdom of Christ consists not in these things.

Yet this distinction does not lead us to consider the whole system of civil government as a polluted thing which has nothing to do with Christian men. Some fanatics who are pleased with nothing but liberty, or rather licentiousness without any restraint, do indeed boast and vociferate, That since we are dead with Christ to the elements of this world and, being translated into the kingdom of God, sit among the celestials, it is a degradation to us and far beneath our dignity to be occupied with those secular and impure cares which relate to things altogether uninteresting to a Christian man. Of what use, they ask, are laws without judgments and tribunals? But what have judgments to do with a Christian man? And if it be unlawful to kill, of what use are laws and judgments to us? But as we have just suggested that this kind of government is distinct from that spiritual and internal reign of Christ, so it ought to be known that they are in no respect at variance with each other. For that spiritual reign, even now upon earth, commences within us some preludes of the heavenly kingdom, and in this mortal and transitory life affords us some prelibations of immortal and incorruptible blessedness; but this civil government is designed, as long as we live in this world, to cherish and support the external worship of God, to preserve the pure doctrine of religion, to defend the constitution of the Church, to regulate our lives in a manner requisite for the society of men, to form our manners to civil justice, to promote our concord with each other, and to establish general peace and tranquility—all of which I confess to be superfluous if the kingdom of God, as it now exists in us, extinguishes the present life. But if it is the will of God that while we are aspiring toward our true country, we be pilgrims on the earth, and if such aids are necessary to our pilgrimage, they who take them from man, deprive him of his human nature. They plead that there should be so much perfection in the Church of God that its order would suffice to supply the place of all laws; but they foolishly imagine a perfection which can never be found in any community of men. For since the insolence of the wicked is so great, and their iniquity so obstinate, that it can scarcely be restrained by all the severity of the laws, what may we expect they would do if they found themselves at liberty to perpetuate crimes with impunity whose outrages even the arm of power cannot altogether prevent?

But for speaking of the exercise of civil polity, there will be another place more suitable. At present we only wish it to be understood that to entertain a thought of its extermination is inhuman barbarism; it is equally as necessary to mankind as bread and water, light and air, and far more excellent. For it not only tends to secure the accommodations arising from all these things, that men may breathe, eat, drink, and be sustained in life, though it comprehends all these things while it causes them to live together, yet I say that is not its only tendency; its objects also are that idolatry, sacrileges against the name of God, blasphemies against his truth, and other offenses against religion may not openly appear and be disseminated among the people; that the public tranquility may not be disturbed; that every person may enjoy his property without molestation; that men may transact their business together without fraud or injustice; that integrity and modesty may be cultivated among them; in short, that there may be a public form of religion among Christians, and that humanity may be maintained among men.

[W]e owe these sentiments of affection and reverence to all our rulers, whatever their characters may be; which I the more frequently repeat, that we may learn not to scrutinize the persons themselves, but may be satisfied with knowing that they are invested by the will of the Lord with that function upon which he has impressed an inviolable majesty. But it will be said that rulers owe mutual duties to their subjects. That I have already confessed. But he who infers from this that obedience ought to be rendered to none but just rulers is a very bad reasoner. For husbands owe mutual duties to their wives, and parents to their children. Now, if husbands and parents violate their obligations; if parents conduct themselves with discouraging severity and fastidious moroseness toward their children, whom they are forbidden to provoke to wrath; if husbands despise and vex their wives, whom they are commanded to love and to spare as the weaker vessels—does it follow that children should be less obedient to their parents, or wives to their husbands?

They are still subject even to those who are wicked and unkind. As it is incumbent on all, not to inquire into the duties of one another, but to confine their attention respectively to their own, this consideration ought particularly to be regarded by those who are subject to the authority of others. Wherefore, if we are inhumanly harassed by a cruel prince; if we are rapaciously plundered by an avaricious or luxurious one; if we are neglected by an indolent one; or if we are persecuted, on account of piety, by an impious and sacrilegious one—let us first call to mind our transgressions against God, which he undoubtedly chastises by these scourges. Thus our impatience will be restrained by humility. Let us, in the next place, consider that it is not our province to remedy these evils, and that nothing remains for us but to implore the aid of the Lord, in whose hand are the hearts of kings and the revolutions of kingdoms.

11

Thomas Hobbes
Leviathan

Thomas Hobbes (1588–1679) wrote his classic Leviathan *(1651) at a time of civil war in Britain. He was trained as a classical humanist, but was greatly influenced by Galileo and the scientific revolution. Consequently, he wanted to fashion a "science of politics." While the idea of a social contract ("covenant" for Hobbes) previously had been used to explain the basis and obligations of political life, this was usually with the intention of restraining royal power. Hobbes, in contrast, used the idea to justify absolutism on the grounds that in a state of nature, where there was no government, human beings would engage in a "war of everyone against everyone" so that life would be "nasty, brutish and short." His conclusion: only a sovereign with absolute power could bring and keep the peace.*

Author's Introduction

Nature, the art whereby God hath made and governs the world, is by the *art* of man, as in many other things, so in this also imitated, that it can make an artificial animal. For seeing life is but a motion of limbs, the beginning whereof is in some principal part within; why may we not say, that all *automata* (engines that move themselves by springs and wheels as doth a watch) have an artificial life? For what is the *heart*, but a *spring*; and the *nerves*, but so many *strings*; and the *joints*, but so many *wheels*, giving motion to the whole body, such as was intended by the artificer? *Art* goes yet further, imitating that rational and most excellent work of nature, *man*. For by art is created that great Leviathan called a Commonwealth, or State, in Latin Civitas, which is but an artificial man; though of greater stature and strength than the natural, for whose protection and defence it was intended; and in which the *sovereignty* is an artificial *soul*, as giving life and motion to the whole body; the *magistrates*, and other *officers* of judicature and execution, artificial *joints*; *reward* and *punishment*, by which fastened to the seat of the sovereignty every joint and member is moved to perform his duty, are the *nerves*, that do the same in the body natural; the *strength*; *salus populi*, the *people's safety*, its *business*; *counsellors*, by whom all things needful for it to know are suggested unto it, are the *memory*; *equity*, and *laws*, and artificial *reason* and *will*; *concord*, *health*; *sedition*, *sickness*; and *civil war*, *death*. Lastly, the *pacts* and *convenants*, by which the parts of this body politic were at first made, set together, and united, resemble that *fiat*, or the *let us make man*, pronounced by God in the creation. . . .

Of Power

Power. The power *of a man*, to take it universally, is his present means, to obtain some future apparent good; and is either *original* or *instrumental*.

Natural power, is the eminence of the faculties of body, or mind: as extraordinary strength, form, prudence, arts, eloquence, liberality, nobility. *Instrumental* are those powers, which acquired by these, or by fortune, are means and instruments to acquire more: as riches, reputation, friends, and the secret working of God, which men call good luck. For the nature of power, is in this point, like to fame, increasing as it proceeds; or like the motion of heavy bodies, which the further they go, make still the more haste.

The greatest of human powers, is that which is compounded of the powers of most men, united by consent, in one person, natural, or civil, that has the use of all their powers depending on his will; such as is the power of a commonwealth: or depending on the wills of each particular; such as is the power of a faction or of divers factions leagued. Therefore to have servants, is power; to have friends, is power: for they are strengths united.

Also riches joined with liberality, is power; because it procureth friends, and servants: without liberality, not so; because in this case they defend not; but expose men to envy, as a prey.

Reputation of power, is power; because it draweth with it the adherence of those that need protection.

So is reputation of love of a man's country, called popularity, for the same reason.

Also, what quality soever maketh a man beloved, or feared of many; or the reputation of such quality, is power; because it is a means to have the assistance, and service of many.

Good success is power; because it maketh reputation of wisdom, or good fortune; which makes men either fear him, or rely on him.

Affability of men already in power, is increase of power; because it gaineth love.

Reputation of prudence in the conduct of peace or war, is power; because to prudent men, we commit the government of ourselves, more willingly than to others.

Nobility is power, not in all places, but only in those commonwealths, where it has privileges: for in such privileges, consisteth their power.

Eloquence is power, because it is seeming prudence.

Form is power; because being a promise of good, it recommendeth men to the favour of women and strangers.

The sciences, are small power; because not eminent; and therefore, not acknowledged in any man; nor are at all, but in a few, and in them, but of a few things. For science is of that nature, as none can understand it to be, but such as in a good measure have attained it.

Arts of public use, as fortification, making of engines, and other instruments of war; because they confer to defence, and victory, are power: and though the true mother of them, be science, namely the mathematics; yet, because they are brought into the light, by the hand of the artificer, they be esteemed, the midwife passing with the vulgar for the mother, as his issue.

Of the Natural Condition of Mankind

Nature hath made men so equal, in the faculties of the body, and mind; as that though there be found one man sometimes manifestly stronger in body, or of quicker mind than another; yet when all is reckoned together, the difference between man, and man, is not so considerable, as that one man can thereupon claim to himself any benefit, to which another may not pretend, as well as he. For as to the strength of body, the weakest has strength enough to kill the strongest, either by secret machination, or by confederacy with others, that are in the same danger with himself.

And as to the faculties of the mind, setting aside the arts grounded upon words, and especially that skill of proceeding upon general, and infallible rules, called science; which very few have, and but in few things; as being not a native faculty, born with us; nor attained, as prudence, while we look after somewhat else, I find yet a greater equality amongst men, than that of strength. For prudence, is but experience; which equal time, equally bestows on all men, in those things they equally apply themselves unto. That which may perhaps make such equality incredible, is but a vain conceit of one's own wisdom, which almost all men think they have in a greater degree, than the vulgar; that is, than all men but themselves, and a few others, whom by fame, or for concurring with themselves, they approve. For such is the nature of men, that howsoever they may acknowledge many others to be more witty, or more eloquent, or more learned; yet they will hardly believe there be many so wise as themselves; for they see their own wit at hand, and other men's at a distance. But this proveth rather than men are in that point equal, than unequal. For there is not ordinarily a greater sign of the equal distribution of any thing, than that every man is contented with his share.

From this equality of ability, ariseth equality of hope in the attaining of our ends. And therefore if any two men desire the same thing, which nevertheless they cannot both enjoy, they become enemies; and in the way to their end, which is principally their own conservation, and sometimes their delectation only, endeavour to destroy, or subdue one another. And from hence it comes to pass, that where an invader hath no more to fear, than another man's single power; if one plant, sow, build, or possess a convenient seat, others may probably be expected to come prepared with forces united, to dispossess, and deprive him, not only of the fruit of his labour, but also of his life, or liberty. And the invader again is in the like danger of another.

And from this diffidence of one another, there is no way for any man to secure himself, so reasonable, as anticipation; that is, by force, or wiles, to master the persons of all men he can, so long, till he see no other power great enough to endanger him: and this is no more than his own conservation requireth, and is generally allowed. Also because there be some, that taking pleasure in contemplating their own power in the acts of conquest, which they pursue farther than their security requires; if others, that otherwise would be glad to be at ease within modest bounds, should not by invasion increase their power, they would not be able, long time, by standing only on their defence, to subsist. And by consequence, such augmentation of dominion over men being necessary to a man's conservation, it ought to be allowed him.

Again, men have no pleasure, but on the contrary a great deal of grief, in keeping company, where there is no power able to over-awe them all. For every man looketh that his companion should value him, as the same rate he sets upon himself: and upon all signs of contempt, or undervaluing, naturally endeavours, as far as he dares (which amongst them that have no common power to keep them in quiet, is far enough to make them destroy each other), to extort a greater value from his contemners, by damage; and from others, by the example.

So that in the nature of man, we find three principal causes of quarrel. First, competition; second, diffidence; thirdly, glory.

The first, maketh man invade for gain; the second, for safety; and the third, for reputation. The first use violence, to make themselves masters of other men's persons, wives, children, and cattle; the second, to defend them; the third, for trifles, as a word, a smile, a different opinion, and any other sign of undervalue, either direct in their persons, or by reflection in their kindred, their friends, their nation, their profession, or their name.

Hereby it is manifest, that during the time men live without a common power to keep them all in awe, they are in that condition which is called war; and such a war, as is of every man, against every man. For War, consisteth not in battle only, or the act of fighting; but in a tract of time, wherein the will to contend by battle is sufficiently known: and therefore the notion of *time*, is to be considered in the nature of war; as it is in the nature of weather. For as the nature of foul weather, lieth not in a shower or two of rain; but in an inclination thereto of many days together: so the nature of war, consisteth not in actual fighting; but in the known disposition thereto, during all the time there is no assurance to the contrary. All other time is Peace.

Whatsoever therefore is consequent to a time of war, where every man is enemy to every man; the same is consequent to the time, wherein men live without other security, than what their own strength, and their own invention shall furnish them withal. In such condition, there is no place for industry; because the fruit thereof is uncertain: and consequently no culture of the earth; no navigation, nor use of the commodities that may be imported by sea; no commodious building; no instruments of moving, and removing, such things as require much force; no knowledge of the face of the earth; no account of time; no arts; no letters; no society; and which is worst of all, continual fear, and danger of violent death; and the life of man, solitary, poor, nasty, brutish, and short.

It may seem strange to some man, that has not well weighed these things; that nature should thus dissociate, and render men apt to invade, and destroy one another: and he may therefore, not trusting to this inference, made from the passions, desire perhaps to have the same confirmed by experience. Let him therefore consider with himself, when taking a journey, he arms himself, and seeks to go well accompanied; when going to sleep, he locks his doors; when even in his house he locks his chests; and this when he knows there be laws, and public officers, armed, to revenge all injuries shall be done him; what opinion he has of his fellow-subjects, when he rides armed; of his fellow citizens, when he locks his doors; and of his children, and servants, when he locks his chests. Does he not there as much accuse mankind by his actions, as I do by my words? But neither of us accuse man's nature in it. The desires, and other passions of man, are in themselves no sin. No more are the actions, that proceed from those passions, till they know a law that forbids them: which till laws be made they cannot know: nor can any law be made, till they have agreed upon the person that shall make it.

It may peradventure be thought, there was never such a time, nor condition of war as this; and I believe it was never generally so, over all the world: but there are many places, where they live so now. For the savage people in many places of America, except the government of small families, the concord whereof dependeth on natural lust, have no government at all; and live at this day in that brutish manner, as I said before. Howsoever, it may be perceived what manner of life there would be, where there were no common power to fear, by the manner of life, which men that have formerly lived under a peaceful government, use to degenerate into, in a civil war.

But though there had never been any time, wherein particular men were in a condition of war one against another; yet in all times, kings, and persons of sovereign authority, because of their independency, are in continual jealousies, and in the state and posture of gladiators; having their weapons pointing, and their eyes fixed on one another; that is, their forts, garrisons, and guns upon the frontiers of their kingdoms; and continual spies upon their neighbours; which is a posture of war. But because they uphold thereby, the industry of their subjects; there does not follow from it, that misery, which accompanies the liberty of particular men.

To this war of every man, against every man, this also is consequent; that nothing can be unjust. The notions of right and wrong, justice and injustice have there no place. Where there is no common power, there is no law: where no law, no injustice. Force, and fraud, are in war the two cardinal virtues. Justice, and injustice are none of the faculties neither of the body, nor mind. If they were, they might be in a man that were alone in the world, as well as his senses, and passions. They are qualities, that relate to men in society, not in solitude. It is consequent also to the same condition, that there be no propriety, no dominion, no *mine* and *thine* distinct; but only that to be every man's, that he can get; and for so long, as he can keep it. And thus much for the ill condition, which man by mere nature is actually placed in; though with a possibility to come out of it, consisting partly in the passions, partly in his reason.

The passions that incline men to peace, are fear of death; desire of such things as are necessary to commodious living; and a hope by their industry to obtain them. And reason suggesteth convenient articles of peace, upon which men may be drawn to agreement. These articles, are they, which otherwise are called the Laws of Nature. . . .

Of the First and Second Natural Laws, and of Contracts

The right of nature, which writers commonly call *jus naturale*, is the liberty each man hath, to use his own power, as he will himself, for the preservation of his own nature; that is to say, of his own life; and consequently, of doing anything, which in his own judgment, and reason, he shall conceive to be the aptest means thereunto.

By Liberty, is understood, according to the proper signification of the word, the absence of external impediments: which impediments, may oft take away part of a man's power to do what he would; but cannot hinder him from using the power left him, according as his judgment, and reason shall dictate to him.

A Law of Nature, *lex naturalis*, is a precept or general rule, found out by reason, by which a man is forbidden to do that, which is destructive of his life, or taketh away the means of preserving the same; and to omit that, by which he thinketh it may be best preserved. For though they that speak of this subject, use to confound *jus*, and *lex*, *right* and *law*: yet they ought to be distinguished; because Right, consisteth in liberty to do, or to forbear; whereas Law, determineth, and bindeth to one of them: so that law, and right, differ as much, as obligation, and liberty; which in one and the same matter are inconsistent.

And because the condition of man, as hath been declared in the precedent chapter, is a condition of war of every one against every one; in which case every one is governed by his own reason; and there is nothing he can make use of, that may not be a help unto him, in preserving his life against his enemies; it followeth, that in such a condition, every man has a right to every thing; even to one another's body. And therefore, as long as this natural right of every man to every thing endureth, there can be no security to any man, how strong or wise soever he be, of living out the time, which nature ordinarily alloweth men to live. And consequently it is a precept, or general rule of reason, *that every man, ought to endeavour peace, as far as he has hope of obtaining it; and when he cannot obtain it, that he may seek, and use, all helps, and advantages of war.* The first branch of which rule, containeth the first, and fundamental law of nature; which is, *to seek peace, and follow it.* The second, the sum of the right of nature; which is, *by all means we can, to defend ourselves.*

From this fundamental law of nature, by which men are commanded to endeavour peace, is derived this second law; *that a man be willing, when others are so too, as far forth, as for peace, and defence of himself he shall think it necessary, to lay down this right to all things; and be contented with so much liberty against other men, as he would allow other men against himself.* For as long as every man holdeth this right, of doing any thing he liketh; so long are all men in the condition of war. But if other men will not lay down their right, as well as he; then

TERM PAPER PROJECT
Political Theory
Spring 2001

Compose an essay in which you analyze President George W. Bush's "First 100 Days" in office from the perspectives of at least two of the political philosophers studied in class this semester. Your analysis may take the form of an essay, a dialogue, or a memo to President Bush. You may either focus on how one or two presidential initiatives might be viewed by a number of authors, or offer a much broader critique of his presidency from the perspectives of only two philosophers.

Grades will be based upon both content (originality, the employment of course concepts, incorporation of primary sources), as well as on matters of form (organization, grammar, spelling, syntax, proper citations & etc). The best papers will weave together quotations and concepts by the philosophers (for the purposes of this project, the text by Cohen and Fermon may be cited by page number only) as they apply to the actions, policies, and/or strategies employed by the Bush Administration during its first three months in office. If you employ outside sources (e.g., newspaper accounts of Bush), they should be fully referenced in the essay or in a bibliography.

All papers should be 8-10 pages in length (typed, double-spaced) and are due IN-CLASS on Thursday, April, 12. A severe penalty will be assessed on all late papers.

there is no reason for anyone, to divest himself of his: for that were to expose himself to prey, which no man is bound to, rather than to dispose himself to peace. This is that law of the Gospel; *whatsoever you require that others should do to you, that do ye to them.* And that law of all men, *what you would not have done to you, do not do to others.*

To *lay down* a man's *right* to any thing, is to *divest* himself of the *liberty,* of hindering another of the benefit of his own right to the same. For he that renounceth, or passeth away his right, giveth not to any other man a right which he had not before; because there is nothing to which every man had not right by nature: but only standeth out of his way, that he may enjoy his own original right, without hindrance from him; not without hindrance from another. So that the effect which redoundeth to one man, by another man's defect of right, is but so much diminution of impediments to the use of his own right original.

Right is laid aside, either by simply renouncing it; or by transferring it to another. By *simply* Renouncing; when he cares not to whom the benefit thereof redoundeth. By Transferring; when he intendeth the benefit thereof to some certain person, or persons. And when a man hath in either manner abandoned, or granted away his right; then is he said to be Obliged, or Bound, not to hinder those, to whom such right is granted, or abandoned, from the benefit of it: and that he *ought,* and it is his Duty, not to make void that voluntary act of his own: and that such hindrance is Injustice, and Injury, as being without right; the right being before renounced, or transferred. So that *injury,* or *injustice,* in the controversies of the world, is somewhat like to that, which in the disputations of scholars is called *absurdity.* For as it is there called absurdity, to contradict what one maintained in the beginning: so in the world, it is called injustice, and injury, voluntarily to undo that, which from the beginning he had voluntary done. The way by which a man either simply renounceth, or transferreth his right, is a declaration, or signification, by some voluntary and sufficient sign, or signs, that he doth so renounce, or transfer; or hath to renounced, or transferred the same, to him that accepteth it. And these signs are either words only, or actions only; or, as it happeneth most often, both words, and actions. And the same are the Bonds, by which men are bound, and obliged: bonds, that have their strength, not from their own nature, for nothing is more easily broken than a man's word, but from fear of some evil consequence upon the rupture.

Whensoever a man transferreth his right, or renounceth it; it is either in consideration of some right reciprocally transferred to himself; or for some other good he hopeth for thereby. For it is a voluntary act: and of the voluntary acts of every man, the object is some *good to himself.* And therefore there be some rights, which no man can be understood by any words, or other signs, to have abandoned, or transferred. As first a man cannot lay down the right of resisting them, that assault him by force, to take away his life; because he cannot be understood to aim thereby, at any good to himself. The same may be said of wounds, and chains, and imprisonment; both because there is no benefit consequent to such patience; as there is to be patience of suffering another to be wounded, or imprisoned: as also because a man cannot tell, when he seeth men proceed against him by violence, whether they intend his death or not. And lastly the motive, and end for which this renouncing, and transferring of right is introduced, is nothing else but the security of a man's person, in his life, and in the means of so preserving life, as not to be weary of it. And therefore if a man by words, or other signs, seem to despoil himself of the end, for which those signs were intended; he is not to be understood as if he meant it, or that it was his will; but that he was ignorant of how such words and actions were to be interpreted.

The mutual transferring of right, is that which men call Contract.

There is difference between transferring of right to the thing; and transferring, or tradition, that is delivery of the thing itself. For the thing may be delivered together with the translation of the right; as in buying and selling with ready-money; or exchange of goods, or lands: and it may be delivered some time after.

Again, one of the contractors, may deliver the thing contracted for on his part, and leave the other to perform his part at some determinate time after, and in the mean time be trusted; and then the contract on his part, is called Pact, or Covenant: or both parts may contract now, to perform hereafter: in which cases, he that is to perform in time to come, being trusted, his performance is called *keeping of promise*, or faith; and he failing of performance, if it be voluntary, *violation of faith*.

When the transferring of right, is not mutual: but one of the parties transferreth, in hope to gain thereby friendship, or service from another, or from his friends; or in hope to gain the reputation of charity, or magnanimity; or to deliver his mind from the pain of compassion; or in hope of reward in heaven; this is not contract, but Gift, Free-Gift, Grace: which words signify one and the same thing. . . .

Words alone, if they be of the time to come, and contain a bare promise, are an insufficient sign of a free gift, and therefore not obligatory. For if they be of the time to come, as *to-morrow I will give*, they are a sign I have not given yet, and consequently that my right is not transferred, but remaineth till I transfer it by some other act. But if the words be of the time present, or past, as, *I have given*, or, *do give to be delivered to-morrow*, then is my to-morrow's right given away to-day; and that by the virtue of the words, though there were no other argument of my will. . . .

If a covenant be made, wherein neither of the parties perform presently, but trust one another; in the condition of mere nature, which is a condition of war of every man against every man, upon any reasonable suspicion, it is void: but if there be a common power set over them both, with right and force sufficient to compel performance, it is not void. For he that performeth first, has no assurance the other will perform after; because the bonds of words are too weak to bridle men's ambition, avarice, anger, and other passions, without the fear of some coercive power; which in the condition of mere nature, where all men are equal, and judges of the justness of their own fears, cannot possibly be supposed. And therefore he which performeth first, does but betray himself to his enemy; contrary to the right, he can never abandon, of defending his life, and means of living.

But in a civil estate, where there is a power set up to constrain those that would otherwise violate their faith, that fear is no more reasonable; and for that cause, he which by the covenant is to perform first, is obliged so to do.

The cause of fear, which maketh such a covenant invalid, must be always something arising after the covenant made; as some new fact, or other sign of the will not to perform: else it cannot make the covenant void. For that which could not hinder a man from promising, ought not to be admitted as a hindrance of performing.

He that transferreth any right, transferreth the means of enjoying it, as far as lieth in his power. As he that selleth land, is understood to transfer the herbage, and whatsoever grows upon it: nor can he that sells a mill turn away the stream that drives it. And they that give to a man the right of government in sovereignty, are understood to give him the right of levying money to maintain soldiers; and of appointing magistrates for the administration of justice.

To make covenants with brute beasts, is impossible; because not understanding our speech, they understand not, nor accept of any translation of right; nor can translate any right to another: and without mutual acceptation, there is no covenant.

To make covenant with God, is impossible, but by mediation of such as God speaketh to, either by revelation supernatural, or by his lieutenants that govern under him, and in his name: for otherwise we know now whether our covenants be accepted, or not. And therefore they that vow anything contrary to any law of nature, vow in vain; as being a thing unjust to pay such vow. And if it be a thing commanded by the law of nature, it is not the vow, but the law that binds them.

The matter, or subject of a covenant, is always something that falleth under deliberation; for to covenant, is an act of the will; that is to say, an act, and the last act of deliberation; and is therefore always understood to be something to come; and which is judged possible for him that covenanteth, to perform.

And therefore, to promise that which is known to be impossible, is no covenant. But if that prove impossible afterwards, which before was thought possible, the covenant is valid, and bindeth, though not to the thing itself, yet to the value; or, if that also be impossible, to the unfeigned endeavour of performing as much as is possible: for to more no man can be obliged.

Men are freed of their covenants two ways; by performing; or by being forgiven. For performance, is the natural end of obligation; and forgiveness, the restitution of liberty; as being a retransferring of that right, in which the obligation consisted.

Covenants entered into by fear, in the condition of mere nature, are obligatory. For example, if I covenant to pay a ransom, or service, for my life, to an enemy; I am bound by it: for it is a contract, wherein one receiveth the benefit of life; the other is to receive money, or service for it; and consequently, where no other law, as in the condition of mere nature, forbiddeth the performance, the covenant is valid. Therefore prisoners of war, if trusted with the payment of their ransom, are obliged to pay it: and if a weaker prince, make a disadvantageous peace with a stronger, for fear; he is bound to keep it; unless, as hath been said before, there ariseth some new, and just cause of fear, to renew the war. And even in commonwealths, if I be forced to redeem myself from a thief by promising him money, I am bound to pay it, till the civil law discharge me. For whatsoever I may lawfully do without obligation, the same I may lawfully covenant to do through fear: and what I lawfully covenant, I cannot lawfully break.

A former covenant, makes void a later. For a man that hath passed away his right to one man to-day, hath it not to pass to-morrow to another: and therefore the later promise passeth no right, but is null.

A covenant not to defend myself from force, by force, is always void. For, as I have showed before, no man can transfer, or lay down his right to save himself from death, wounds, imprisonment, the avoiding whereof is the only end of laying down any right; and therefore the promise of not resisting force, in no covenant transferreth any right; nor is obliging. For though a man may covenant thus, *unless I do so, or so, kill me*; he cannot covenant thus, *unless I do so, or so, I will not resist you, when you come to kill me*. For man by nature chooseth the lesser evil, which is danger of death in resisting; rather than the greater, which is certain and present death in not resisting. And this is granted to be true by all men, in that they lead criminals to execution, and prison, with armed men, notwithstanding that such criminals have consented to the law, by which they are condemned. . . .

The force of words, being, as I have formerly noted, too weak to hold men to the performance of their covenants; there are in man's nature, but two imaginable helps to strengthen it. And those are either a fear of the consequence of breaking their word; or a glory, or pride in appearing not to need to break it. This latter is a generosity too rarely found to be presumed on, especially in the pursuers of wealth, command, or sensual pleasure; which are the greatest part of mankind. The passion to be reckoned upon, is fear; whereof there be two very general objects: one, the power of spirits invisible; the other, the power of those men they shall therein offend. Of these two, though the former be the greatest power, yet the fear of the latter is commonly the greater fear. The fear of the former is in every man, his own religion: which hath place in the nature of man before civil society. The latter hath not so; at least not place enough, to keep men to their promises; because in the condition of mere nature, the inequality of power is not discerned, but by the event of battle. So that before the time of civil society, or in the interruption thereof by war, there is nothing can strengthen a covenant of peace agreed on, against the temptations of avarice, ambition, lust, or other strong desire, but the fear of that invisible power, which they every one worship as God; and fear as a revenger of their perfidy. All therefore that can be done between two men not subject to civil power, is to put one another to swear by the God he feareth. . . .

Of Other Laws of Nature

From that law of nature, by which we are obliged to transfer to another, such rights, as being retained, hinder the peace of mankind, there followeth a third; which is this, *that men perform their covenants made*: without which, covenants are in vain, and but empty words; and the right of all men to all things remaining, we are still in the condition of war.

And in this law of nature, consisteth the fountain and original of Justice. For where no covenant hath preceded, there hath no right been transferred, and every man has right to every thing; and consequently, no action can be unjust. But when a covenant is made, then to break it is *unjust*: and the definition of Injustice, is no other than *the not performance of covenant*. And whatsoever is not unjust, is *just*.

But because covenants of mutual trust, where there is a fear of not performance on either part, as hath been said in the former chapter, are invalid; though the original of justice be the making of covenants; yet injustice actually there can be none, till the cause of such fear be taken away; which while men are in the natural condition of war, cannot be done. Therefore before the names of just, and unjust can have place, there must be some coercive power, to compel men equally to the performance of their covenants, by the terror of some punishment, greater than the benefit they expect by the breach of their covenant; and to make good that propriety, which by mutual contract men acquire, in recompense of the universal right they abandon: and such power there is none before the erection of a commonwealth. And this is also to be gathered out of the ordinary definition of justice in the Schools: for they say, that *justice is the constant will of giving to every man his own*. And therefore where there is no *own*, that is no propriety, there is no injustice; and where is no coercive power erected, that is, where there is no commonwealth, there is no propriety; all men having right to all things: therefore where there is no commonwealth, there nothing is unjust. So that the nature of justice, consisteth in keeping of valid covenants: but the validity of covenants begins not but with the constitution of a civil power, sufficient to compel men to keep them: and then it is also that propriety begins.

The fool hath said in his heart, there is no such thing as justice; and sometimes also with his tongue; seriously alleging, that every man's conservation, and contentment, being committed to his own care, there could be no reason, why every man might not do what he thought conduced thereunto: and therefore also to make, or not make; keep, or not keep covenants, was not against reason, when it conduced to one's benefit. He does not therein deny, that there be covenants; and that they are sometimes broken, sometimes kept; and that such breach of them may be called injustice, and the observance of them justice: but he questioneth, whether injustice, taking away the fear of God, for the same fool hath said in his heart there is no God, may not sometimes stand with that reason, which dictateth to every man his own good; and particularly then, when in conduceth to such a benefit, as shall put a man in a condition, to neglect not only the dispraise, and revilings, but also the power of other men. The kingdom of God is gotten by violence: but what if it could be gotten by unjust violence? were it against reason so to get it, when it is impossible to receive hurt by it? and if it be not against reason, it is not against justice; or else justice is not to be approved for good. From such reasoning as this, successful wickedness hath obtained the name of virtue: and some that in all other things have disallowed the violation of faith; yet have allowed it, when it is for the getting of a kingdom. And the heathen that believed, that Saturn was deposed by his son Jupiter, believed nevertheless the same Jupiter to be the avenger of injustice: somewhat like to a piece of law in Coke's *Commentaries on Littleton*; where he says, if the right heir of the crown be attainted of treason; yet the crown shall descend to him, and at that instant the attainder be void: from which instances a man will be very prone to infer; that when the heir apparent of a kingdom, shall kill him that is in possession, though his father; you may call it injustice, or by what other name you will; yet it can never be against reason, seeing all the voluntary actions of men tend to the benefit of themselves; and those actions are most reasonable, that conduce most to their ends. The specious reasoning is nevertheless false.

For the question is not of promises mutual, where there is no security of performance on either side; as when there is no civil power erected over the parties promising; for such promises are no covenants: but either where one of the parties has performed already; or where there is a power to make him perform; there is the question whether it be against reason, that is, against the benefit of the other to perform, or not. And I say it is not against reason. For the manifestation whereof, we are to consider; first, that when a man doth a thing, which notwithstanding any thing can be foreseen, and reckoned on, tendeth to his own destruction, howsoever some accident which he could not expect, arriving may turn it to his benefit; yet such events do not make it reasonably or wisely done. Secondly, that in a condition of war, wherein every man to every man, for want of a common power to keep them all in awe, is an enemy, there is no man who can hope by his own strength, or wit, to defend himself from destruction, without the help of confederates; where every one expects the same defense by the confederation, that any one else does: and therefore he which declares he thinks it reason to deceive those that help him, can in reason expect no other means of safety, than what can be had from his own single power. He therefore that breaketh his covenant, and consequently declareth that he thinks he may with reason do so, cannot be received into any society, that unite themselves for peace and defense, but by the error of them that receive him; nor when he is received, be retained in it, without seeing the danger of their error; which errors a man cannot reasonably reckon upon as the means of his security: and therefore if he be left, or cast out of society, he perisheth; and if he live in society, it is by the errors of other men, which he could not foresee, nor reckon upon; and consequently against the reason of his preservation; and so, as all men that contribute not to his destruction, forbear him only out of ignorance of what is good for themselves.

As for the instance of gaining the secure and perpetual felicity of heaven, by any way; it is frivolous: there being but one way imaginable; and that is not breaking, but keeping of covenant.

And for the other instance of attaining sovereignty by rebellion; it is manifest, that though the event follow, yet because it cannot reasonably be expected, but rather the contrary; and because by gaining it so, others are taught to gain the same in like manner, the attempt thereof is against reason. Justice therefore, that is to say, keeping of covenant, is a rule of reason, by which we are forbidden to do any thing destructive to our life; and consequently a law of nature.

There be some that proceed further; and will not have the law of nature, to be those rules which conduce to the preservation of man's life on earth; but to the attaining of an eternal felicity after death; to which they think the breach of covenant may conduce; and consequently be just and reasonable; such are they that think it a work of merit to kill, or depose, or rebel against, the sovereign power constituted over them by their own consent. But because there is no natural knowledge of man's estate after death; much less of the reward that is then to be given to breach of faith; but only a belief grounded upon other men's saying, that they know it supernaturally, or that they know those, that knew them, that knew others, that knew it supernaturally; breach of faith cannot be called a precept of reason, or nature.

Others, that allow for a law of nature, the keeping of faith, do nevertheless make exception of certain persons; as heretics, and such as use not to perform their covenant to others: and this also is against reason. For if any fault of a man, be sufficient to discharge our covenant made; the same ought in reason to have been sufficient to have hindered the making of it. . . .

As justice dependeth on antecedent covenant; so does Gratitude depend on antecedent grace; that is to say, antecedent free gift: and is the fourth law of nature; which may be conceived in this form, *that a man which receiveth benefit from another of mere grace, endeavour that he which giveth it, have no reasonable cause to repent him of his good will.* For no man giveth, but with intention of good to himself; because gift is voluntary; and of all voluntary acts, the object is to every man his own good; of which if men see they shall be frustrated, there will be no beginning of benevolence, or trust; nor consequently of mutual help; nor of reconciliation of one man to another; and therefore they are to remain still in the condition of *war*; which is contrary to the first and fundamental law of nature, which commandeth men to *seek peace*. The breach of this law, is called *ingratitude*; and hath the same relation to grace, that injustice hath to obligation by covenant.

A fifth law of nature, is Complaisance; that is to say, *that every man strive to accommodate himself to the rest.* For the understanding whereof, we may consider, that there is in men's aptness to society, a diversity of nature, rising from their diversity of affections; not unlike to that we see in stones brought together for building of an edifice. For as that stone which by the asperity, and irregularity of figure, takes more room from others, than itself fills; and for the hardness, cannot be easily made plain, and thereby hindereth the building, is by the builders cast away as unprofitable, and troublesome: so also, a man that by asperity of nature, will strive to retain those things which to himself are superfluous, and to others necessary; and for the stubbornness of his passions, cannot be corrected, is to be left, or cast out of society, as cumbersome thereunto. For seeing every man, not only by right, but also by necessity of nature, is supposed to endeavour all he can, to obtain that which is necessary for his conservation; he that shall oppose himself against it, for things superfluous, is guilty of the war that thereupon is to follow; and therefore doth that, which is contrary to the fundamental law of nature, which commandeth *to seek peace*. The observers of this law, may be called Sociable, the Latins call them *commodi*; the contrary, *stubborn, insociable, froward, intractable.*

A sixth law of nature, is this *that upon caution of the future time, a man ought to pardon the offences past of them that repenting, desire it.* For Pardon, is nothing but granting of peace; which though granted to them that persevere in their hostility, be not peace, but fear; yet not granted to them that give caution of the future time, is sign of an aversion to peace; and therefore contrary to the law of nature.

A seventh is, *that in revenges*, that is, retribution of evil for evil, *men look not at the greatness of the evil past, but the greatness of the good to follow*. Whereby we are forbidden to inflict punishment with any other design, than for correction of the offender, or direction of others. For this law is consequent to the next before it, that commandeth pardon, upon security of the future time. Besides, revenge without respect to the example, and profit to come, is a triumph, or glorying in the hurt of another, tending to no end; for the end is always somewhat to come; and glorying to no end, is vainglory, and contrary to reason, and to hurt without reason, tendeth to the introduction of war; which is against the law of nature; and is commonly styled by the name of *cruelty*.

And because all signs of hatred, or contempt, provoke to fight; insomuch as most men choose rather to hazard their life, than not to be revenged; we may in the eighth place, for a law of nature, set down this precept, *that no man by deed, word, countenance, or gesture, declare hatred, or contempt of another*. The breach of which law, is commonly called *contumely*.

The question who is the better man, has no place in the condition of mere nature; where, as has been shewn before, all men are equal. The inequality that now is, has been introduced by the laws civil. I know that Aristotle in the first book of his *Politics*, for a foundation of his doctrine, maketh men by nature, some more worthy to command, meaning the wiser sort, such as he thought himself to be for his philosophy; others to serve, meaning those that had strong bodies, but were not philosophers as he; as if master and servant were not introduced by consent of men, but by different of wit: which is not only against reason; but also against experience. For there are very few so foolish, that had not rather govern themselves, than be governed by others: nor when the wise in their own conceit, contend by force, with them who distrust their own wisdom, do they always, or often, or almost at any time, get the victory. If nature therefore have made men unequal, that equality is to be acknowledged: or if nature have made men unequal; yet because men that think themselves equal, will not enter into conditions of peace, but upon equal terms, such equality must be admitted. And therefore for the ninth law of nature, I put this, *that every man acknowledge another for his equal by nature*. The breach of this precept is *pride*.

On this law, dependeth another, *that at the entrance into conditions of peace, no man require to reserve to himself any right, which he is not content should be reserved to every one of the rest*. As it is necessary for all men that seek peace, to lay down certain rights of nature; that is to say, not to have liberty to do all they list: so is it necessary for man's life, to retain some; as right to govern their own bodies; enjoy air, water, motion, ways to go from place to place; and all things else, without which a man cannot live, or not live well. If in this case, at the making of peace, men require for themselves, that which they would not have to be granted to others, they do contrary to the precedent law, that commandeth the acknowledgment of natural equality, and therefore also against the law of nature. The observers of this law, are those we call *modest*, and the breakers *arrogant* men. . . .

And because, though men be never so willing to observe these laws, there may nevertheless arise questions concerning a man's action; first, whether it were done, or not done; secondly, if done, whether against the law, or not against the law; the former whereof, is called a question *of fact*; the latter a question *of right*, therefore unless the parties to the question, covenant mutually to stand to the sentence of another, they are as far from peace as ever. This other to whose sentence they submit is called an Arbitrator. And therefore it is of the law of nature, *that they that are at controversy, submit their right to the judgment of an arbitrator.*

And seeing every man is presumed to do all things in order to his own benefit, no man is a fit arbitrator in his own cause; and if he were never so fit; yet equity allowing to each party equal benefit, if one be admitted to be judge, the other is to be admitted also; and so the controversy, that is, the cause of war, remains, against the law of nature.

For the same reason no man in any cause ought to be received for arbitrator, to whom greater profit, or honour, or pleasure apparently ariseth out of the victory of one party, than of the other: for he hath taken, though an unavoidable bribe, yet a bribe; and no man can be obliged to trust him. And thus also the controversy, and the condition of war remaineth, contrary to the law of nature.

And in a controversy of *fact*, the judge being to give more credit to one, than to the other, if there be no other arguments, must give credit to a third; or to a third and fourth; or more: for else the question is undecided, and left to force, contrary to the law of nature.

These are the laws of nature, dictating peace, for a means of the conservation of men in multitudes; and which only concern the doctrine of civil society. There be other things tending to the destruction of particular men; as drunkenness, and all other parts of intemperance; which may therefore also be reckoned amongst those things which the law of nature hath forbidden; but are not necessary to be mentioned, nor are pertinent enough to this place.

And though this may seem too subtle a deduction of the laws of nature, to be taken notice of by all men; whereof the most part are too busy in getting food, and the rest too negligent to understand; yet to leave all men inexcusable, they have been contracted into one easy sum, intelligible even to the meanest capacity; and that is, *Do not that to another, which thou wouldst not have done to thyself*; which sheweth him, that he has no more to do in learning the laws of nature, but, when weighing the actions of other men with his own, they seem too heavy, to put them into the other part of the balance, and his own into their place, that is own passions, and self-love, may add nothing to the weight; and then there is none of these laws of nature that will not appear unto him very reasonable. . . .

Of the Causes, Generation, and Definition of a Commonwealth

The final cause, end, or design of men, who naturally love liberty, and dominion over others, in the introduction of that restraint upon themselves, in which we see them live in commonwealths, is the foresight of their own preservation, and of a more contented life thereby; that is to say, of getting themselves out from that miserable condition of war, which is necessarily consequent, as hath been shown, to the natural passions of men, when there is no visible power to keep them in awe, and tie them by fear of punishment to the performance of their covenants, and observation of those laws of nature set down in the fourteenth and fifteenth chapters.

For the laws of nature, as *justice, equity, modesty, mercy*, and in sum, *doing to others, as we would be done to*, of themselves, without the terror of some power, to cause them to be observed, are contrary to our natural passions, that carry us to partiality, pride, revenge, and the like. And covenants, without the sword, are but words, and of no strength to secure a man at all. Therefore notwithstanding the laws of nature (which every one hath then kept, when he has the will to keep them, when he can do it safely) if there be no power erected, or not great enough for our security; every man will, and may lawfully rely on his own strength and art, for caution against all other men. And in all places, where men have lived by small families, to rob and spoil one another, has been a trade, and so far from being reputed against the law of nature, that the greater spoils they gained, the greater was their honour; and men observed no other laws therein, but the laws of honour; that is, to abstain from cruelty, leaving to men their lives, and instruments of husbandry. And as small families did then; so now do cities and kingdoms which are but greater families, for their own security, enlarge their dominions, upon all pretences of danger, and fear of invasion, or assistance that may be given to invaders, and endeavour as much as they can, to subdue, or weaken their neighbours, by open force, and secret arts, for want of other caution, justly; and are remembered for it in after ages with honour.

Nor is it the joining together of a small number of men, that gives them this security; because in small numbers, small additions on the one side or the other, make the advantage of strength so great, as is sufficient to carry the victory; and therefore gives encouragement to an invasion. The multitude sufficient to confide in for our security, is not determined by any certain number, but by comparison with the enemy we fear; and is then sufficient, when the odds of the enemy is not of so visible and conspicuous moment, to determine the event of war, as to move him to attempt.

And be there never so great a multitude; yet if their actions be directed according to their particular judgments, and particular appetites, they can expect thereby no defence, nor protection, neither against a common enemy, nor against the injuries of one another. For being distracted in opinions concerning the best use and application of their strength, they do not help but hinder one another; and reduce their strength by mutual opposition to nothing: whereby they are easily, not only subdued by a very few that agree together; but also when there is no common enemy, they make war upon each other, for their particular interests. For if we could suppose a great multitude of men to consent in the observation of justice, and other laws of nature, without a common power to keep them all in awe; we might as well suppose all mankind to do the same; and then there neither would be, nor need to be any civil government, or commonwealth at all; because there would be peace without subjection.

Nor is it enough for the security, which men desire should last all the time of their life, that they be governed, and directed by one judgment, for a limited time; as in one battle, or one war. For though they obtain a victory by their unanimous endeavour against a foreign enemy; yet afterwards, when either they have no common enemy, or he that by one part is held for an enemy, is by another part held for a friend, they must needs by the difference of their interests dissolve, and fall again into a war amongst themselves.

It is true, that certain living creatures, as bees, and ants, live sociably one with another, which are therefore by Aristotle numbered amongst political creatures; and yet have no other direction, than their particular judgments and appetites; nor speech, whereby one of them can signify to another, what he thinks expedient for the common benefit: and therefore some man may perhaps desire to know, why mankind cannot do the same. To which I answer,

First, that men are continually in competition for honour and dignity, which these creatures are not; and consequently amongst men there ariseth on that ground, envy and hatred, and finally war; but amongst these not so.

Secondly, that amongst these creatures, the common good differeth not from the private; and being by nature inclined to their private, they procure thereby the common benefit. But man, whose joy consisteth in comparing himself with other men, can relish nothing but what is eminent.

Thirdly, that these creatures, having not, as man, the use of reason, do not see, nor think they see any fault, in the administration of their common business; whereas amongst men, there are very many, that think themselves wiser, and abler to govern the public, better than the rest; and these strive to reform and innovate, one this way, another that way; and thereby bring it into distraction and civil war.

Fourthly, that these creatures, though they have some use of voice, in making known to one another their desires, and other affections; yet they want that art of words, by which some men can represent to others, that which is good, in the likeness of evil; and evil, in the likeness of good; and augment, or diminish the apparent greatness of good and evil; discontenting men, and troubling their peace at their pleasure.

Fifthly, irrational creatures cannot distinguish between *injury*, and *damage*; and therefore as long as they be at ease, they are not offended with their fellows: whereas man is then most troublesome, when he is most at ease: for then it is that he loves to shew his wisdom, and control the actions of them that govern the commonwealth.

Lastly, the agreement of these creatures is natural; that of men, is by covenant only, which is artificial: and therefore it is no wonder if there be somewhat else required, besides covenant, to make their agreement constant and lasting; which is a common power, to keep them in awe, and to direct their actions to the common benefit.

The only way to erect such a common power, as may be able to defend them from the invasion of foreigners, and the injuries of one another, and thereby to secure them in such sort, as that by their own industry, and by the fruits of the earth, they may nourish themselves and live contentedly; is, to confer all their power and strength upon one man, or upon one assembly of men, that may reduce all their wills, by plurality of voices, unto one will; which is as much as to say, to appoint one man, or assembly of men, to bear their person; and every one to own, and acknowledge himself to be author of whatsoever he that so beareth their person, shall act, or cause to be acted, in those things which concern the common peace and safety; and therein to submit their wills, every one to his will, and their judgments, to his judgment. This is more than consent, or concord; it is a real unity of them all, in one and the same person, made by covenant of every man with every man, in such manner, as if every man should say to every man, *I authorize and give up my right of governing myself, to this man, or to this assembly of men, on this condition, that thou give up thy right to him, and authorize all his actions in like manner.* This done, the multitude so united in one person, is called a Commonwealth, in Latin Civitas. This is the generation of that great Leviathan, or rather, to speak more reverently, of that *mortal god*, to which we owe under the *immortal God*, our peace and defence. For by this authority, given him by every particular man in the commonwealth, he hath the use of so much power and strength conferred on him, that by terror thereof, he is enabled to form the wills of them all, to peace at home, and mutual aid against their enemies abroad. And in him consisteth the essence of the commonwealth; which, to define it, is *one person, of whose acts a great multitude, by mutual covenants one with another, have made themselves every one the author, to the end he may use the strength and means of them all, as he shall think expedient, for their peace and common defence.*

And he that carrieth this person is called Sovereign, and said to have *sovereign power*; and every one besides, his Subject.

The attaining to this sovereign power, is by two ways. One by natural force; as when a man maketh his children, to submit themselves, and their children to his government, as being able to destroy them if they refuse; or by war subdueth his enemies to his will, giving them their lives on that condition. The other, is when men agree amongst themselves, to submit to some man, or assembly of men, voluntarily, on confidence to be protected by him against all others. This latter, may be called a political commonwealth, or commonwealth by *institution*; and the former, a commonwealth by *acquisition*. And first, I shall speak of a commonwealth by institution.

Of the Rights of Sovereigns by Institution

A *commonwealth* is said to be *instituted*, when a *multitude* of men do agree, and *covenant, every one, with every one*, that to whatsoever *man*, or *assembly of men*, shall be given by the major part, the *right* to *present* the person of them all, that is to say, to be their *representative*; every one, as well he that *voted for it*, as he that *voted against it*, shall *authorize* all the actions and judgments, of that man, or assembly of men, in the same manner, as if they were his own, to the end, to live peaceably amongst themselves, and be protected against other men.

From this institution of a commonwealth are derived all the *rights*, and *faculties* of him, or them, on whom sovereign power is conferred by the consent of the people assembled.

First, because they covenant, it is to be understood, they are not obliged by former covenant to anything repugnant hereunto. And consequently they that have already instituted a commonwealth, being thereby bound by covenant, to own the actions, and judgments of one, cannot lawfully make a new covenant, amongst themselves, to be obedient to any other, in any thing whatsoever, without his permission. And therefore, they that are subject to a monarch, cannot without his leave cast off monarchy, and return to the confusion of a disunited multitude; nor transfer their person from him that beareth it, to another man, or other assembly of men: for they are bound, every man to every man, to own, and be reputed author of all, that he that already is their sovereign, shall do, and judge fit to be done: so that any one man dissenting, all the rest should break their covenant made to that man, which is injustice: and they have also every man given the sovereignty to him that beareth their person; and therefore if they depose him, they take from him that which is his own, and so again it is injustice. Besides, if he that attempteth to depose his sovereign, be killed, or punished by him for such attempt, he is author of his own punishment, as being by the institution, author of all his sovereign shall do: and because it is injustice for a man to do anything, for which he may be punished by his own authority, he is also upon that title, unjust. And whereas some men have pretended for their disobedience to their sovereign, a new covenant, made, not with men, but with God; this also is unjust: for there is no covenant with God, but by mediation of somebody that representeth God's person; which none doth but God's lieutenant, who hath the sovereignty under God. But this pretence of covenant with God, is so evident a lie, even in the pretenders' own consciences, that it is not only an act of an unjust, but also of a vile and unmanly disposition.

Secondly, because the right of bearing the person of them all, is given to him they make sovereign, by covenant only of one to another, and not of him to any of them; there can happen no breach of covenant on the part of the sovereign; and consequently none of his subjects, by any pretence of forfeiture, can be freed from his subjection. That he which is made sovereign maketh no covenant with his subjects beforehand, is manifest; because either he must make it with the whole multitude, as one party to the covenant; or he must make a several covenant with every man. With the whole, as one party, it is impossible; because as yet they are not one person: and if he make so many several covenants as there be men, those covenants after he hath the sovereignty are void; because what act soever can be pretended by any one of them for breach thereof, is the act both of himself, and of all the rest, because done in the person, and by the right of every one of them in particular. Besides, if any one, or more of them, pretend a breach of the covenant made by the sovereign at his institution; and others, or one other of his subjects, or himself alone, pretend there was no such breach, there is in this case, no judge to decide the controversy; it returns therefore to the sword again; and every man recovereth the right of protecting himself by his own strength, contrary to the design they had in the institution. It is therefore in vain to grant sovereignty by way of precedent covenant. The opinion that any monarch receiveth his power by covenant, that is to say, on condition, proceedeth from want of understanding this easy truth, that covenants being but words and breath, have no force to oblige, contain, constrain, or protect any man, but what it has from the public sword; that is, from the untied hands of that man, or assembly of men that hath the sovereignty, and whose actions are avouched by them all, and performed by the strength of them all, in him united. But when an assembly of men is made sovereign; then no man imagineth any such covenant to have passed in the institution; for no man is so dull as to say, for example, the people of Rome made a covenant with the Romans, to hold the sovereignty on such or such conditions; which not performed, the Romans might lawfully depose the Roman people. That men see not the reason to be alike in a monarchy, and in a popular government, proceedeth from the ambition of some, that are kinder to the government of an assembly, whereof they may hope to participate, than of monarchy, which they despair to enjoy.

Thirdly, because the major part hath by consenting voices declared a sovereign; he that dissented must now consent with the rest; that is, be contented to avow all the actions he shall do, or else justly be destroyed by the rest. For if he voluntarily entered into the congregation of them that were assembled, he sufficiently declared thereby his will, and therefore tacitly covenanted, to stand to what the major part should ordain: and therefore if he refuse to stand thereto, or make protestation against any of their decrees, he does contrary to his covenant, and therefore unjustly. And whether he be of the congregation, or not; and whether his consent be asked, or not, he must either submit to their decrees, or be left in the condition of war he was in before; wherein he might without injustice be destroyed by any man whatsoever.

Fourthly, because every subject is by this institution author of all the actions, and judgments of the sovereign instituted; it follows, that whatsoever he doth, it can be no injury to any of his subjects; nor ought he to be by any of them accused of injustice. For he that doth anything by authority from another, doth therein no injury to him by whose authority he acteth: but by this institution of a commonwealth, every particular man is author of all the sovereign doth: and consequently he that complaineth of injury from his sovereign, complaineth of that whereof he himself is author; and therefore ought not to accuse any man but himself; no nor himself of injury; because to do injury to one's self, is impossible. It is true that they that have sovereign power may commit iniquity, but not injustice, or injury in the proper signification.

Fifthly, and consequently to that which was said last, no man that hath sovereign power can justly be put to death, or otherwise in any manner by his subjects punished. For seeing every subject is author of the actions of his sovereign; he punisheth another for the actions committed by himself.

And because the end of this institution, is the peace and defense of them all; and whosoever has right to the end, has right to the means; it belongeth of right, to whatsoever man, or assembly that hath the sovereignty, to be judge both of the means of peace and defense, and also of the hindrances, and disturbances of the same; and to do whatsoever he shall think necessary to be done, both beforehand, for the preserving of peace and security, by prevention of discord at home, and hostility from abroad; and, when peace and security are lost, for the recovery of the same. And therefore,

Sixthly, it is annexed to the sovereignty, to be judge of what opinions and doctrines are averse, and what conducing to peace; and consequently, on what occasions, how far, and what men are to be trusted withal, in speaking to multitudes of people; and who shall examine the doctrines of all books before they be published. For the actions of men proceed from their opinions; and in the well-governing of opinions, consisteth the well-governing of men's actions, in order to their peace, and concord. And though in matter of doctrine, nothing ought to be regarded but the truth; yet this is not repugnant to regulating the same by peace. For doctrine repugnant to peace, can no more be true, than peace and concord can be against the law of nature. It is true, that in a commonwealth, whereby the negligence, or unskilfulness of governors, and teachers, false doctrines are by time generally received; the contrary truths may be generally offensive. Yet the most sudden, and rough bursting in of a new truth, that can be, does never break the peace, but only sometimes awake the war. For those men that are so remissly governed, that they dare take up arms to defend, or introduce an opinion, are still in war; and their condition not peace, but only a cessation of arms for fear of one another; and they live, as it were, in the precincts of battle continually. It belongeth therefore to him that hath the sovereign power, to be judge, or constitute all judges of opinions and doctrines, as a thing necessary to peace; thereby to prevent discord and civil war.

Seventhly, is annexed to the sovereignty, the whole power of prescribing the rules, whereby every man may know, what goods he may enjoy, and what actions he may do, without being molested by any of his fellow-subjects; and this is it men call *propriety*. For before constitution of sovereign power, as hath already been shown, all men had right to all things; which necessarily causeth war: and therefore this propriety, being necessary to peace, and depending on sovereign power, is the act of that power, in order to the public peace. These rules of propriety, or mine and yours, and of *good, evil, lawful*, and *unlawful* in the actions of subjects, are the civil laws; that is to say, the laws of each commonwealth in particular; though the name of civil law be now restrained to the ancient civil laws of the city of Rome; which being the head of a great part of the world, her laws at that time were in these parts the civil law.

Eighthly, is annexed to the sovereignty, the right of judicature; that is to say, of hearing and deciding all controversies, which may arise concerning law, either civil, or natural; or concerning fact. For without the decision of controversies, there is no protection of one subject, against the injuries of another; the laws concerning mine and yours are in vain; and to every man remaineth, from the natural and necessary appetite of his own conservation, the right of protecting himself by his private strength, which is the condition of war, and contrary to the end for which every commonwealth is instituted.

Ninthly, is annexed to the sovereignty, the right of making war and peace with other nations, and commonwealths; that is to say, of judging when it is for the public good, and how great forces are to be assembled, armed, and paid for that end; and to levy money upon the subjects, to defray the expenses thereof. For the power by which the people are to be defended, consisteth in their armies; and the strength of an army, in the union of their strength under one command; which command the sovereign instituted, therefore hath; because the command of the *militia*, without other institution, maketh him that hath it sovereign. And therefore whosoever is made general of an army, he that hath the sovereign power is always generalissimo.

Tenthly, is annexed to the sovereignty, the choosing of all counsellors, ministers, magistrates, and officers, both in peace and war. For seeing the sovereign is charged with the end, which is the common peace and defense, he is understood to have power to use such means, as he shall think most fit for his discharge.

Eleventhly, to the sovereign is committed the power of rewarding with riches, or honour, and of punishing with corporal or pecuniary punishment, or with ignominy, every subject according to the law he hath formerly made; or if there be no law made, according as he shall judge most to conduce to the encouraging of men to serve the commonwealth, or deterring of them from doing disservice to the same.

Lastly, considering what value men are naturally apt to set upon themselves; what respect they look for from others; and how little they value other men; from whence continually arise amongst them, emulation, quarrels, factions, and at last war, to the destroying of one another, and diminution of their strength against a common enemy; it is necessary that there be laws of honour, and a public rate of the worth of such men as have deserved, or are able to deserve well of the commonwealth; and that there be force in the hands of some or other, to put those laws in execution. But it hath already been shown, that not only the whole *militia*, or forces of the commonwealth; but also the judicature of all controversies, is annexed to the sovereignty. To the sovereign therefore it belongeth also to give titles of honour; and to appoint what order of place, and dignity, each man shall hold; and what signs of respect, in public or private meetings, they shall give to one another.

These are the rights, which make the essence of sovereignty; and which are the marks, whereby a man may discern in what man, or assembly of men, the sovereign power is placed, and resideth. For these are incommunicable, and inseparable. The power to coin money; to dispose of the estate and persons of infant heirs; to have præemption in markets; and all other statute prerogatives, may be transferred by the sovereign; and yet the power to protect his subjects be retained. But if he transfer the *militia*, he retains the judicature in vain, for want of execution of the laws: or if he grant away the power of raising money; the *militia* is in vain; or if he give away the government of doctrines, men will be frighted into rebellion with the fear of spirits. And so if we consider any one of the said rights, we shall presently see, that the holding of all the rest will produce no effect, in the conservation of peace and justice, the end for which all commonwealths are instituted. And this division is it, whereof it is said, a *kingdom divided in itself cannot stand*: for unless this division precede, division into opposite armies can never happen. If there had not first been an opinion received of the greatest part of England, that these powers were divided between the King, and the Lords, and the House of Commons, the people had never been divided and fallen into this civil war; first between those that disagreed in politics; and after between the dissenters about the liberty of religion; which have so instructed men in this point of sovereign right, and there be few now in England that do not see, that these rights are inseparable, and will be so generally acknowledged at the next return of peace; and so continue, till their miseries are forgotten; and no longer, except the vulgar be better taught than they have hitherto been.

And because they are essential and inseparable rights, it follows necessarily, that in whatsoever words any of them seem to be granted away, yet if the sovereign power itself be not in direct terms renounced, and the name of sovereign no more given by the grantees to him that grants them, the grant is void: for when he has granted all he can, if we grant back the sovereignty, all is restored, as inseparably annexed thereunto.

This great authority being indivisible, and inseparably annexed to the sovereignty, there is little ground for the opinion of them, that say of sovereign kings, though they be *singulis majores*, of greater power than every one of their subjects, yet they be *universis minores*, of less power than them all together. For if by *all together*, they mean not the collective body as one person, then *all together*, and *every one*, signify the same; and the speech is absurd. But if by *all together*, they understand them as one person, which person the sovereign bears, then the power of all together, is the same with the sovereign's power; and so again the speech is absurd: which absurdity they see well enough, when the sovereignty is in an assembly of the people; but in a monarch they see it not; and yet the power of sovereignty is the same in whomsoever it be placed.

And as the power, so also the honour of the sovereign, ought to be greater, than that of any, or all the subjects. For in the sovereignty is the fountain of honour. The dignities of lord, earl, duke, and prince are his creatures. As in the presence of the master, the servants are equal, and without any honour at all; so are the subjects, in the presence of the sovereign. And though they shine some more, some less, when they are out of his sight; yet in his presence, they shine no more than the stars in the presence of the sun.

But a man may here object, that the condition of subjects is very miserable; as being obnoxious to the lusts, and other irregular passions of him, or them that have so unlimited a power in their hands. And commonly they that live under a monarch, think it the fault of monarchy; and they that live under the government of democracy, or other sovereign assembly, attribute all the inconvenience to that form of commonwealth; whereas the power in all forms, if they be perfect enough to protect them, is the same: not considering that the state of man can never be without some incommodity or other; and that the greatest, that in any form of government can possibly happen to the people in general, is scarce sensible, in respect to the miseries, and horrible calamities, that accompany a civil war, or that dissolute condition of masterless men, without subjection to laws, and a coercive power to tie their hands from rapine and revenge: nor considering that the greatest pressure of sovereign governors, proceedeth not from any delight, or profit they can expect in the damage or weakening of their subjects, in whose vigour consisteth their own strength and glory; but in the restiveness of themselves, that unwillingly contributing to their own defense, make it necessary for their governors to draw from them what they can in time of peace, that they may have means on any emergent occasion, or sudden need, to resist, or take advantage on their enemies. For all men are by nature provided of notable multiplying glasses, that is their passions and self-love, through which, every little payment appeareth a great grievance; but are destitute of those prospective glasses, namely moral and civil science, to see afar off the miseries that hang over them, and cannot without such payment be avoided. . . .

Of the Several Kinds of Commonwealth by Institution; and of Succession to the Sovereign Power

The difference of commonwealths, consisteth in the difference of the sovereign, or the person representative of all and every one of the multitude. And because the sovereignty is either in one man, or in an assembly of more than one; and into that assembly either every man hath right to enter, or not every one, but certain men distinguished from the rest; it is manifest, there can be but three kinds of commonwealth. For the representative must needs be one man, or more: and if more, then it is the assembly of all, or but of a part. When the representative is one man, then is the commonwealth a Monarchy: when an assembly of all that will come together, then it is a Democracy, or popular commonwealth: when an assembly of a part only, then it is called an Aristocracy. Other kind of commonwealth there can be none: for either one, or more, or all, must have the sovereign power, which I have shown to be indivisible, entire.

There be other names of government, in the histories, and books of policy; as *tyranny*, and *oligarchy*: but they are not the names of other forms of government, but of the same forms misliked, for they that are discontented under *monarchy*, call it *tyranny*; and they that are displeased with *aristocracy*, call it *oligarchy*: so also, they which find themselves grieved under a *democracy*, call it *anarchy*, which signifies want of government; and yet I think no man believes, that want of government, is any new kind of government: nor by the same reason ought they to believe, that the government is of one kind, when they like it, and another, when they mislike it, or are oppressed by the governors.

It is manifest, that men who are in absolute liberty, may, if they please, give authority to one man, to represent them every one; as well as give such authority to any assembly of men whatsoever; and consequently may subject themselves, if they think good, to a monarch, as absolutely, as to any other representative. Therefore, where there is already erected a sovereign power, there can be no other representative of the same people, but only to certain particular ends, by the sovereign limited. For that were to erect two sovereigns; and every man to have his person represented by two actors, that by opposing one another, must needs divide that power, which, if men will live in peace, is indivisible; and thereby reduce the multitude into the condition of war, contrary to the end for which all sovereignty is instituted. And therefore as it is absurd, to think that a sovereign assembly, inviting the people of their dominion, to send up their deputies, with power to make known their advice, or desires, should therefore hold such deputies, rather than themselves, for the absolute representatives of the people: so it is absurd also, to think the same in a monarchy. And I know not how this so manifest a truth, should of late be so little observed; that in a monarchy, he that had the sovereignty from a descent of six hundred years, was alone called sovereign, had the title of Majesty from every one of this subjects, and was unquestionably taken by them for their king, was notwithstanding never considered as their representative; the name without contradiction passing for the title of those men, which at his command were sent up by the people to carry their petitions, and give him, if he permitted it, their advice. Which may serve as an admonition, for those that are the true, and absolute representative of a people, to instruct men in the nature of that office, and to take heed how they admit of any other general representation upon any occasion whatsoever, if they mean to discharge the trust committed to them.

Comparison of monarchy, with sovereign assemblies. The difference between these three kinds of commonwealth, consisteth not in the difference of power; but in the difference of convenience, or aptitude to produce the peace, and security of the people; for which end they were instituted. . . .

Of the Liberty of Subjects

Liberty, or freedom, signifieth, properly, the absence of opposition; by opposition, I mean external impediments of motion; and may be applied no less to irrational, and inanimate creatures, than to rational. For whatsoever is so tied, or environed, as it cannot move but within a certain space, which space is determined by the opposition of some external body, we say it hath not liberty to go further. And so of all living creatures, whilst they are imprisoned, or restrained, with walls, or chains; and of the water whilst it is kept in by banks, or vessels, that otherwise would spread itself into a larger space, we use to say, they are not at liberty, to move in such manner, as without those external impediments they would. But when the impediment of motion, is in the constitution of the thing itself, we use not to say; it wants the liberty; but the power to move; as when a stone lieth still, or a man is fastened to his bed by sickness.

And according to this proper, and generally received meaning of the word, a Freeman, *is he, that in those things, which by his strength and wit he is able to do, is not hindered to do what he has a will to.* But when the words *free* and *liberty*, are applied to any thing but bodies, they are abused; for that which is not subject to motion is not subject to impediment: and therefore, when it is said, for example, the way is free, no liberty of the way is signified, but of those that walk in it without stop. And when we say a gift is free, there is not meant any liberty of the gift, but of the giver, that was not bound by any law or covenant to give it. So when we *speak freely*, it is not the liberty of voice, or pronunciation, but of the man, whom no law hath obliged to speak otherwise than he did. Lastly, from the use of the word *free-will*, no liberty can be inferred of the will, desire, or inclination, but the liberty of the man; which consisteth in this, that he finds no stop, in doing what he has the will, desire, or inclination to do.

Fear and liberty are consistent; as when a man throweth his goods into the sea for *fear* the ship should sink, he doth it nevertheless very willingly, and may refuse to do it if he will; it is therefore the action of one that was *free*: so a man sometimes pays his debt, only for *fear* of imprisonment, which because nobody hindered him from detaining, was the action of a man at *liberty*. And generally all actions which men do in commonwealths, for *fear* of the law, are actions, which the doers had *liberty* to omit.

Liberty, and *necessity* are consistent: as in the water, that hath not only *liberty*, but a *necessity* of descending by the channel; so likewise in the actions which men voluntarily do: which, because they proceed from their will, proceed from *liberty*; and yet, because every act of man's will, and every desire, and inclination proceedeth from some cause, and that from another cause, in a continual chain, whose first link is in the hand of God the first of all causes, proceed from *necessity*. So that to him that could see the connexion of those causes, the *necessity* of all men's voluntary actions would appear manifest. And therefore God, that seeth, and disposeth all things, seeth also that the liberty of man in doing what he will, is accompanied with the *necessity* of doing that which God will, and no more, nor less. For though men may do many things, which God does not command, nor is therefore author of them; yet they can have no passion, nor appetite to anything, of which appetite God's will is not the cause. And did not his will assure the *necessity* of man's will, and consequently of all that on man's will dependeth, the *liberty* of men would be a contradiction, and impediment to the omnipotence and *liberty* of God. And this shall suffice, as to the matter in hand, of that natural *liberty*, which only is properly called *liberty*.

But as men, for the attaining of peace, and conservation of themselves thereby, have made an artificial man, which we call a commonwealth; so also have they made artificial chains, called *civil laws*, which they themselves, by mutual covenants, have fastened at one end, to the lips of that man, or assembly, to whom they have given the sovereign power; and at the other end to their own ears. These bonds, in their own nature but weak, may nevertheless be made to hold, by the danger, though not by the difficulty of breaking them.

In relation to these bonds only it is, that I am to speak now, of the *liberty* of *subjects*. For seeing there is no commonwealth in the world, wherein there be rules enough set down, for the regulating of all the actions, and words of men; as being a thing impossible: it followeth necessarily, that in all kinds of actions by the laws prætermitted, men have the liberty, of doing what their own reasons shall suggest, for the most profitable to themselves. For if we take liberty in the proper sense, for corporal liberty; that is to say, freedom from chains and prison; it were very absurd for men to clamour as they do, for the liberty they so manifestly enjoy. Again, if we take liberty, for an exemption from laws, it is no less absurd, for men to demand as they do, that liberty, by which all other men may be masters of their lives. And yet, as absurd as it is, this is it they demand; not knowing that the laws are of no power to protect them, without a sword in the hands of a man, or men, to cause those laws to be put in execution. The liberty of a subject, lieth therefore only in those things, which in regulating their actions, the sovereign hath prætermitted: such as is the liberty to buy, and sell, and otherwise contract with one another; to choose their own abode, their own diet, their own trade of life, and institute their children as they themselves think fit; and the like.

Nevertheless we are not to understand, that by such liberty, the sovereign power of life and death, is either abolished, or limited. For it has been already shown, that nothing the sovereign representative can do to a subject, on what pretence soever, can properly be called injustice, or injury; because every subject is author of every act the sovereign doth; so that he never wanteth right to any thing, otherwise, than as he himself is the subject of God, and bound thereby to observe the laws of nature. And therefore it may, and doth often happen in commonwealths, that a subject may be put to death, by the command of the sovereign power; and yet neither do the other wrong; as when Jephtha caused his daughter to be sacrificed: in which, and the like cases, he that so dieth, had liberty to do the action, for which he is nevertheless, without injury put to death. And the same holdeth also in a sovereign prince, that putteth to death an innocent subject. For though the action be against the law of nature, as being contrary to equity, as was the killing of Uriah, by David; yet it was not an injury to Uriah, but to God. Not to Uriah, because the right to do what he pleased was given him by Uriah himself: and yet to God, because David was God's subject, and prohibited all iniquity by the law of nature. . . .

The liberty, whereof there is so frequent and honourable mention, in the histories, and philosophy of the ancient Greeks, and Romans, and in the writings, and discourse of those that from them have received all their learning in the politics, is not the liberty of particular men; but the liberty of the commonwealth: which is the same with that which every man then should have, if there were no civil laws, nor commonwealth at all. And the effects of it also be the same. For as amongst masterless men, there is perpetual war, of every man against his neighbor; no inheritance, to transmit to the son, nor to expect from the father; no propriety of goods, or lands; no security; but a full and absolute liberty in every particular man: so in states, and commonwealths not dependent on one another, every commonwealth, not every man, has an absolute liberty, to do what it shall judge, that is to say, what that man, or assembly that representeth it, shall judge most conducing to their benefit. But withal, they live in the condition of a perpetual war, and upon the confines of battle, with their frontiers armed, and cannons planted against their neighbors round about. The Athenians, and Romans were free; that is, free commonwealths: not that any particular men had the liberty to resist their own representative; but that their representative had the liberty to resist, or invade other people. There is written on the turrets of the city of Lucca in great characters at this day, the word Libertas; yet no man can thence infer, that a particular man has more liberty, or immunity from the service of the commonwealth there, than in Constantinople. Whether a commonwealth be monarchical, or popular, the freedom is still the same.

But it is an easy thing, for men to be deceived, by the specious name of liberty; and for want of judgment to distinguish, mistake that for their private inheritance, and birth-right, which is the right of the public only. And when the same error is confirmed by the authority of men in reputation for their writings on this subject, it is no wonder if it produce sedition, and change of government. In these western parts of the world, we are made to receive our opinions concerning the institution, and rights of commonwealths, from Aristotle, Cicero, and other men, Greeks and Romans, that living under popular states, derived those rights, not from the principles of nature, but transcribed them into their books, out of the practice of their own commonwealths, which were popular; as the grammarians describe the rules of language, out of the practice of the time; or the rules of poetry, out of the poems of Homer and Virgil. And because the Athenians were taught, to keep them from desire of changing their government, that they were freemen, and all that lived under monarchy were slaves; therefore Aristotle puts it down in his *Politics*, *In democracy*, Liberty *is to be supposed: for it is commonly held, that no man is Free in any other government*. And as Aristotle; so Cicero, and other writers have grounded their civil doctrine, on the opinions of the Romans, who were taught to hate monarchy, at first, by them that having deposed their sovereign; shared amongst them the sovereignty of Rome; and afterwards by their successors. And by reading of these Greek, and Latin authors, men from their childhood have gotten a habit, under a false show of liberty, of favouring tumults, and of licentious controlling the actions of their sovereigns, and again of controlling those controllers; with the effusion of so much blood, as I think I may truly say, there was never any thing so dearly bought, as these western parts have bought the learning of the Greek and Latin tongues.

To come now to the particulars of the true liberty of a subject; that is to say, what are the things, which though commanded by the sovereign, he may nevertheless, without injustice, refuse to do; we are to consider, what rights we pass away, when we make a commonwealth; or, which is all one, what liberty we deny ourselves, by owning all the actions, without exception, of the man, or assembly, we make our sovereign. For in the act of our *submission*, consisteth both our *obligation*, and our *liberty*; which must therefore be inferred by arguments taken from thence; there being no obligation on any man, which ariseth not from some act of his own; for all men equally, are by nature free. And because such arguments, must either be drawn from the express words, *I authorize all his actions*, or from the intention of him that submitteth himself to his power, which intention is to be understood by the end for which he so submitteth; the obligation, and liberty of the subject, is to be derived, either from those words, or others equivalent; or else from the end of the institution of sovereignty, namely, the peace of the subjects within themselves, and their defense against a common enemy.

First therefore, seeing sovereignty by institution, is by covenant of every one to every one; and sovereignty by acquisition, by covenants of the vanquished to the victor, or child to the parent; it is manifest, that every subject has liberty in all those things, the right whereof cannot by covenant be transferred. I have shewn before in the 14th chapter, that covenants, not to defend a man's own body, are void. Therefore,

If the sovereign command a man, though justly condemned, to kill, wound, or maim himself; or not to resist those that assault him; or to abstain from the use of food, air, medicine, or any other thing, without which he cannot live; yet hath that man the liberty to disobey.

If a man be interrogated by the sovereign, or his authority, concerning a crime done by himself, he is not bound, without assurance of pardon, to confess it; because no man . . . can be obliged by covenant to accuse himself.

Again, the consent of a subject to sovereign power, is contained in these words, *I authorize, or take upon me, all his actions*; in which there is no restriction at all, of his own former natural liberty: for by allowing him to *kill* me, I am not bound to kill myself when he commands me. It is one thing to say, *kill me, or my fellow, if you please*; another thing to say, *I will kill myself, or my fellow*. It followeth therefore, that

No man is bound by the words themselves, either to kill himself, or any other man; and consequently, that the obligation a man may sometimes have, upon the command of the sovereign to execute any dangerous, or dishonourable office, dependeth not on the words of our submission; but on the intention, which is to be understood by the end thereof. When therefore our refusal to obey, frustrates the end for which the sovereignty was ordained; then there is no liberty to refuse: otherwise there is.

Upon this ground, a man that is commanded as a soldier to fight against the enemy, though his sovereign have right enough to punish his refusal with death, may nevertheless in many cases refuse, without injustice; as when he substituteth a sufficient soldier in his place: for in this case he deserteth not the service of the commonwealth. And there is allowance to be made for natural timorousness; not only to women, of whom no such dangerous duty is expected, but also to men of feminine courage. When armies fight, there is on one side, or both, a running away; yet when they do it not out of treachery, but fear, they are not esteemed to do it unjustly, but dishonourably. For the same reason, to avoid battle, is not injustice, but cowardice. But he that inrolleth himself a soldier, or taketh imprest money, taketh away the excuse of a timorous nature; and is obliged, not only to go to the battle, but also not to run from it, without his captain's leave. And when the defense of the commonwealth, required at once the help of all that are able to bear arms, every one is obliged; because otherwise the institution of the common-wealth, which they have not the purpose, or courage to preserve, was in vain.

To resist the sword of the commonwealth, in defense of another man, guilty, or innocent, no man hath liberty; because such liberty, takes away from the sover-eign, the means of protecting us; and is therefore destructive of the very essence of government. But in case a great many men together, have already resisted the sovereign power unjustly, or committed some capital crime, for which every one of them expecteth death, whether have they not the liberty then to join together, and assist, and defend one another? Certainly they have: for they but defend their lives, which the guilty man may as well do, as the innocent. There was indeed injustice in the first breach of their duty; their bearing of arms subsequent to it, though it be to maintain what they have done, is no new unjust act. And if it be only to defend their persons, it is not unjust at all. But the offer of pardon taketh from them, to whom it is offered, the plea of self-defense, and maketh their perseverance in assisting, or defending the rest, unlawful.

As for other liberties, they depend on the silence of the law. In cases where the sovereign has prescribed no rule, there the subject hath the liberty to do, or forbear, according to his own discretion. And therefore such liberty is in some places more, and in some less; and in some times more, in other times less, according as they that have the sovereignty shall think most convenient. As for example, there was a time, when in England a man might enter into his own land, and dispossess such as wrongfully possessed it, by force. But in after times, that liberty of forcible entry, was taken away by a statute made, by the king, in parliament. And in some places of the world, men have the liberty of many wives: in other places, such liberty is not allowed.

If a subject have a controversy with his sovereign, of debt, or of right of possession of lands or goods, or concerning any service required at his hands, or concerning any penalty, corporal, or pecuniary, grounded on a precedent law; he hath the same liberty to sue for his right, as if it were against a subject; and before such judges, as are appointed by the sovereign. For seeing the sovereign demandeth by force of a former law, and not by virtue of his power; he declareth thereby, that he requireth no more, than shall appear to be due by that law. The suit therefore is not contrary to the will of the sovereign; and consequently the subject hath the liberty to demand the hearing of his cause; and sentence, according to that law. But if he demand, or take anything by pretence of his power; there lieth, in that case, no action of law; for all that is done by him in virtue of his power, is done by the authority of every subject, and consequently he that brings an action against the sovereign, brings it against himself.

If a monarch, or sovereign assembly, grant a liberty to all, or any of his subjects, which grant standing, he is disabled to provide for their safety, the grant is void; unless he directly renounce, or transfer the sovereignty to another. For in that he might openly, if it had been his will, and in plain terms, have renounced, or transferred it, and did not; it is to be understood it was not his will, but that the grant proceeded from ignorance of the repugnancy between such a liberty and the sovereign power; and therefore the sovereignty is still retained; and consequently all those powers, which are necessary to the exercising thereof; such as are the power of war, and peace, of judicature, of appointing officers, and councillors, of levying money, and the rest named in the 18th chapter.

The obligation of subjects to the sovereign, is understood to last as long, and no longer, than the power lasteth, by which he is able to protect them. For the right men have by nature to protect themselves, when none else can protect them, can by no covenant be relinquished. The sovereignty is the soul of the commonwealth;

which once departed from the body, the members do no more receive their motion from it. The end of obedience is protection; which, wheresoever a man seeth it, either in his own, or in another's sword, nature applieth his obedience to it, and his endeavour to maintain it. And though sovereignty, in the intention of them that make it, be immortal; yet it is in its own nature, not only subject to violent death, by foreign war; but also through the ignorance, and passions of men, it hath in it, from the very institution, many seeds of a natural mortality, by intestine discord.

If a subject be taken prisoner in war; or his person or his means of life be within the guards of the enemy, and hath his life and corporal liberty given him, on condition to be subject to the victor, he hath liberty to accept the condition; and having accepted it, is the subject of him that took him; because he had no other way to preserve himself. The case is the same, if he be detained on the same terms, in a foreign country. But if a man be held in prison, or bonds, or is not trusted with the liberty of his body; he cannot be understood to be bound by covenant to subjection; and therefore may, if he can, make his escape by any means whatsoever.

If a monarch shall relinquish the sovereignty, both for himself, and his heirs; his subjects return to the absolute liberty of nature; because, though nature may declare who are his sons, and who are the nearest of his kin; yet it dependeth on his own will, as hath been said in the precedent chapter, who shall be his heir. If therefore he will have no heir, there is no sovereignty, nor subjection. The case is the same, if he die without known kindred, and without declaration of his heir. For then there can no heir be known, and consequently no subjection be due.

If the sovereign banish his subject; during the banishment, he is not subject. But he that is sent on a message, or hath leave to travel, is still subject; but it is, by contract between sovereigns, not by virtue of the covenant of subjection. For whosoever entereth into another's dominion, is subject to all the laws thereof; unless he have a privilege of the amity of the sovereigns, or by special licence.

If a monarch subdued by war, render himself subject to the victor; his subjects are delivered from their former obligation, and become obliged to the victor. If he be held prisoner, or have not the liberty of his own body; he is not understood to have given away the right of sovereignty; and therefore his subjects are obliged to yield obedience to the magistrates formerly placed, governing not in their own name, but in his. For, his right remaining, the question is only of the administration; that is to say, of the magistrates and officers; which, if he have not means to name, he is supposed to approve those, which he himself had formerly appointed.

Of Those Things That Weaken, or Tend to the Dissolution of a Commonwealth

Dissolution of commonwealths proceedeth from their imperfect institution. Though nothing can be immortal, which mortals make, yet, if men had the use of reason they pretend to, their commonwealths might be secured, at least from perishing by internal diseases. For by the nature of their institution, they are designed to live, as long as mankind, or as the laws of nature, or as justice itself, which gives them life. Therefore when they come to be dissolved, not by external violence, but intestine disorder, the fault is not in men, as they are the *matter*; but as they are the *makers*, and orderers of them. For men, as they become at last weary of irregular jostling, and hewing one another, and desire with all their hearts, to conform themselves into one firm and lasting edifice: so for want, both of the art of making fit laws, to square their actions by, and also of humility, and patience, to suffer the rude and cumbersome points of their present greatness to be taken off, they cannot without the help of a very able architect, be compiled into any other than a crazy building, such as hardly lasting out their own time, must assuredly fall upon the heads of their posterity.

Amongst the *infirmities* therefore of a commonwealth, I will reckon in the first place, those that arise from an imperfect institution, and resemble the diseases of a natural body, which proceed from a defectuous procreation.

Want of absolute power. Of which, this is one, *that a man to obtain a kingdom, is sometimes content with less power, than to the peace, and defence of the commonwealth is necessarily required.* From whence it cometh to pass, that when the exercise of the power laid by, is for the public safety to be resumed, it hath the resemblance of an unjust act; which disposeth great numbers of men, when occasion is presented, to rebel; in the same manner as the bodies of children, gotten by diseased parents, are subject either to untimely death, or to purge the ill quality, derived from their vicious conception, by breaking out into biles and scabs. And when kings deny themselves some such necessary power, it is not always, though sometimes, out of ignorance of what is necessary to the office they undertake; but many times out of a hope to recover the same again at their pleasure. Wherein they reason not well; because such as will hold them to their promises, shall be maintained against them by foreign commonwealths; who in order to the good of their own subjects let slip few occasions to *weaken* the estate of their neighbours. So was Thomas Beckett, archbishop of Canterbury, supported against Henry the Second, by the Pope; the subjection of ecclesiastics to the commonwealth, having been dispensed with by William the Conqueror at his reception, when he took an oath, not to infringe the liberty of the church. . . .

Nor does this happen in monarchy only. For whereas the style of the ancient Roman commonwealth, was, *The Senate and People of Rome*; neither senate, nor people pretended to the whole power; which first caused the seditions, of Tiberius Gracchus, Caius Gracchus, Lucius Saturninus, and others; and afterwards the wars between the senate and the people, under Marius and Sylla; and again under Pompey and Cæsar, to the extinction of their democracy, and the setting up of monarchy.

The people of Athens bound themselves but from one only action; which was, that no man on pain of death should propound the renewing of the war for the island of Salamis; and yet thereby, if Solon had not caused to be given out he was mad, and afterwards in gesture and habit of a madman, and in verse, propounded it to the people that flocked about him, they had had an enemy perpetually in readiness, even at the gates of their city; such damage, or shifts, are all commonwealths forced to, that have their power never so little limited.

In the second place, I observe the *diseases* of a commonwealth, that proceed from the poison of seditious doctrines, whereof one is, *That every private man is judge of good and evil actions*. This is true in the condition of mere nature, where there are no civil laws; and also under civil government, in such cases as are not determined by the law. But otherwise, it is manifest, that the measure of good and evil actions, is the civil law; and the judge the legislator, who is always representative of the commonwealth. From this false doctrine, men are disposed to debate with themselves, and dispute the commands of the commonwealth; and afterwards to obey, or disobey them, as in their private judgments they shall think fit; whereby the commonwealth is distracted and *weakened*.

Another doctrine repugnant to civil society, is, that *whatsoever a man does against his conscience, is sin*; and it dependeth on the presumption of making himself judge of good and evil. For a man's conscience, and his judgment is the same thing, and as the judgment, so also the conscience may be erroneous. Therefore, though he that is subject to no civil law, sinneth in all he does against his conscience, because he has no other rule to follow but his own reason; yet it is not so with him that lives in a commonwealth; because the law is the public conscience, by which he hath already undertaken to be guided. Otherwise in such diversity, as there is of private consciences, which are but private opinions, the commonwealth must needs be distracted, and no man dare to obey the sovereign power, further than it shall seem good in his own eyes.

It hath been also commonly taught, *that faith and sanctity, are not to be attained by study and reason, but by supernatural inspiration, or infusion*. Which granted, I see not why any man should render a reason of his faith; or why every Christian should not be also a prophet; or why any man should take the law of his country, rather than his own inspiration, for the rule of his action. And thus we fall again in the fault of taking upon us to judge of good and evil; or to make judges of it, such private men as pretend to be supernaturally inspired, to the dissolution of all civil government. Faith comes by hearing, and hearing by those accidents, which guide us into the presence of them that speak to us; which accidents are all contrived by God Almighty; and yet are not supernatural, but only, for the great number of them that concur to every effect, unobservable. Faith and sanctity, are indeed not very frequent; but yet they are not miracles, but brought to pass by education, discipline, correction, and other natural ways, by which God worketh them in his elect, at such times as he thinketh fit. And these three opinions, pernicious to peace and government, have in this part of the world, proceeded chiefly from the tongues, and pens of unlearned divines, who joining the words of Holy Scripture together, otherwise than is agreeable to reason, do what they can, to make men think, that sanctity and natural reason, cannot stand together.

A fourth opinion, repugnant to the nature of a commonwealth, is this, *that he that hath the sovereign power is subject to the civil laws*. It is true, that sovereigns are all subject to the laws of nature; because such laws be divine, and cannot by any man, or commonwealth be abrogated. But to those laws which the sovereign himself, that is, which the commonwealth maketh, he is not subject. For to be subject to laws, is to be subject to the commonwealth, that is to the sovereign representative, that is to himself; which is not subjection, but freedom from the laws. Which error, because it setteth the laws above the sovereign, setteth also a judge above him, and a power to punish him; which is to make a new sovereign; and again for the same reason a third, to punish the second; and so continually without end, to the confusion, and dissolution of the commonwealth.

A fifth doctrine, that tendeth to the dissolution of a commonwealth, is, *that every private man has an absolute propriety in his goods; such, as excludeth the right of the sovereign.* Every man has indeed a propriety that excludes the right of every other subject: and he has it only from the sovereign power; without the protection whereof, every other man should have equal right to the same. But if the right of the sovereign also be excluded, he cannot perform the office they have put him into; which is, to defend them both from foreign enemies, and from the injuries of one another; and consequently there is no longer a commonwealth.

And if the propriety of subjects, exclude not the right of the sovereign representative to their goods; much less to their offices of judicature, or execution, in which they represent the sovereign himself.

There is a sixth doctrine, plainly, and directly against the essence of a commonwealth; and it is this, *that the sovereign power may be divided.* For what is it to divide the power of a commonwealth, but to dissolve it; for powers divided mutually destroy each other. And for these doctrines, men are chiefly beholding to some of those, that making profession of the laws, endeavour to make them depend upon their own learning, and not upon the legislative power.

And as false doctrine, so also oftentimes the example of different government in a neighbouring nation, disposeth men to alteration of the form already settled. So the people of the Jews were stirred up to reject God, and to call upon the prophet Samuel, for a king after the manner of the nations: so also the lesser cities of Greece, were continually disturbed, with seditions of the aristocratical, and democratical factions. . . .

And as to rebellion in particular against monarchy; one of the most frequent causes of it, is the reading of the books of policy, and histories of the ancient Greeks, and Romans; from which, young men, and all others that are unprovided of the antidote of solid reason, receiving a strong, and delightful impression, of the great exploits of war, achieved by the conductors of their armies, receive withal a pleasing idea, of all they have done besides; and imagine their great prosperity, not to have proceeded from the emulation of particular men, but from the virtue of their popular form of government: not considering the frequent seditions, and civil wars, produced by the imperfection of their policy. From the reading, I say, of such books, men have undertaken to kill their kings, because the Greek and Latin writers, in their books, and discourses of policy, make it lawful, and laudable, for any man so to do; provided, before he do it, he call him tyrant. For they say not *regicide*, that is, killing a king, but *tyrannicide*, that is killing of a tyrant is lawful. From the same books, they that live under a monarch conceive an opinion, that the subjects in a popular commonwealth enjoy liberty; but that in a monarchy they are all slaves. I say, they that live under a monarchy conceive such an opinion; not they that live under a popular government: for they find no such matter. In sum, I cannot imagine, how any thing can be more prejudicial to a monarchy, than the allowing of such books to be publicly read, without present applying such correctives of discreet masters, as are fit to take away their venom: which venom I will not doubt to compare to the biting of a mad dog, which is a disease the physicians call *hydrophobia, or fear of water.* For as he that is so bitten, has a continual torment of thirst, and yet abhorreth water; and is in such an estate, as if the poison endeavoured to convert him into a dog: so when a monarchy is once bitten to the quick, by those democratical writers, that continually snarl at the estate; it wanteth nothing more than a strong monarch, which nevertheless out of a certain *tyrannophobia*, or fear of being strongly governed, when they have him, they abhor.

As there have been doctors, that hold there be three souls in a man; so there be also that think there may be more souls, that is, more sovereigns, than one, in a commonwealth; and set up a *supremacy* against the *sovereignty*; *canons* against *laws*; and a *ghostly authority* against the *civil*; working on men's minds, with words and distinctions, that of themselves signify nothing, but bewray by their obscurity; that there walketh, as some think, invisibly another kingdom, as it were a kingdom of fairies, in the dark. Now seeing it is manifest, that the civil power, and the power of the commonwealth is the same thing; and that supremacy, and the power of making canons, and granting faculties, implieth a commonwealth; it followeth, that where one is sovereign, another supreme; where one can make laws, and another make canons; there must needs be two commonwealths, of one and the same subjects; which is a kingdom divided in itself, and cannot stand. For notwithstanding the insignificant distinction of *temporal*, and *ghostly*, they are still two kingdoms, and every subject is subject to two masters. For seeing the *ghostly* power challengeth the right to declare what is sin, it challengeth by consequence to declare what is law, sin being nothing but the transgression of the law; and again, the civil power challenging to declare what is law, every subject must obey two masters, who both will have their commands be observed as law; which is impossible. Or, if it be but one kingdom, either the *civil*, which is the power of the commonwealth, must be subordinate to the *ghostly*, and then there is no sovereignty but the *ghostly*; or the *ghostly* must be subordinate to the *temporal*, and then there is no *supremacy* but the *temporal*. When therefore these two powers oppose one another, the commonwealth cannot but be in great danger of civil war and dissolution. For the *civil* authority being more visible, and standing in the clearer light of natural reason, cannot choose but draw to it in all times a very considerable part of the people: and the *spiritual*, though it stand in the darkness of School distinctions, and hard words, yet because the fear of darkness and ghosts, is greater than other fears, cannot want a party sufficient to trouble, and sometimes to destroy a commonwealth. And this is a disease which not unfitly may be compared to the epilepsy, or falling sickness, which the Jews took to be one kind of possession by spirits, in the body natural. For as in this disease, there is an unnatural spirit, or wind in the head that obstructeth the roots of the nerves, and moving them violently, taketh away the motion which naturally they should have from the power of the soul in the brain, and thereby causeth violent, and irregular motions, which men call convulsions, in the parts; insomuch as he that is seized therewith, falleth down sometimes into the water, and sometimes into the fire, as a man deprived of his senses; so also in the body politic, when the spiritual power, moveth the members of a commonwealth, by the terror of punishments, and hope of rewards, which are the nerves of it, otherwise than by the civil power, which is the soul of the commonwealth, they ought to be moved; and by strange, and hard words suffocates their understanding, it must needs thereby distract the people, and either overwhelm the commonwealth with oppression, or cast it into the fire of a civil war.

Sometimes also in the merely civil government, there be more than one soul; as when the power of levying money, which is the nutritive faculty, has depended on a general assembly; the power of conduct and command, which is the motive faculty, on one man; and the power of making laws, which is the rational faculty, on the accidental consent, not only of those two, but also of a third; this endangereth the commonwealth, sometimes for want of consent to good laws: but most often for want of such nourishment, as is necessary to life, and motion. For although few perceive, that such government, is not government, but division of the commonwealth into three factions, and call it mixed monarchy: yet the truth is, that it is not one independent commonwealth, but three independent factions; nor one representative person, but three. In the kingdom of God, there may be three persons independent, without breach of unity in God that reigneth; but where men reign, that be subject to diversity of opinions, it cannot be so. And therefore if the king bear the person of the people, and the general assembly bear also the person of the people, and another assembly bear the person of a part of the people, they are not one person, nor one sovereign, but three persons, and three sovereigns.

To what disease in the natural body of man, I may exactly compare this irregularity of a commonwealth, I know not. But I have seen a man, that had another man growing out of his side, with a head, arms, breast, and stomach, of his own; if he had had another man growing out of his other side, the comparison might then have been exact.

Hitherto I have named such diseases of a commonwealth, as are of the greatest, and most present danger. There be other not so great; which nevertheless are not unfit to be observed. At first, the difficulty of raising money, for the necessary uses of the commonwealth; especially in the approach of war. This difficulty ariseth from the opinion, that every subject hath a propriety in his lands and goods, exclusive of the sovereign's right to the use of the same. From whence it cometh to pass, that the sovereign power, which foreseeth the necessities and dangers of the commonwealth, finding the passage of money to the public treasury obstructed, by the tenacity of the people, whereas it ought to extend itself, to encounter, and prevent such dangers in their beginnings, contracteth itself as long as it can, and when it cannot longer, struggles with the people by stratagems of law, to obtain little sums, which not sufficing, he is fain at last violently to open the way for present supply, or perish; and being put often to these extremities, at last reduceth the people to their due temper; or else the commonwealth must perish. Insomuch as we may compare this distemper very aptly to an ague; wherein, the fleshly parts being congealed, or by venomous matter obstructed, the veins which by their natural course empty themselves into the heart, are not, as they ought to be, supplied from the arteries, whereby there succeedeth at first a cold contraction, and trembling of the limbs; and afterward a hot, and strong endeavour of the heart, to force a passage for the blood; and before it can do that, contenteth itself with the small refreshments of such things as cool for a time, till, if nature be strong enough, it break at last the contumacy of the parts obstructed, and dissipateth the venom into sweat; or, if nature be too weak, the patient dieth.

Again, there is sometimes in a commonwealth, a disease, which resembleth the pleurisy; and that is, when the treasure of the commonwealth, flowing out of its due course, is gathered together in too much abundance, in one, or a few private men, by monopolies, or by farms of the public revenues; in the same manner as the blood in a pleurisy, getting into the membrane of the breast, breedeth there an inflammation, accompanied with a fever, and painful stitches.

Also, the popularity of a potent subject, unless the commonwealth have very good caution of his fidelity, is a dangerous disease; because the people, which should receive their motion from the authority of the sovereign, by the flattery and by the reputation of an ambitious man are drawn away from their obedience to the laws, to follow a man, of whose virtues, and designs they have no knowledge. And this is commonly of more danger in a popular government, than in a monarchy; because an army is of so great force, and multitude, as it may easily be made believe, they are the people. By this means it was, that Julius Cæsar, who was set up by the people against the senate, having won to himself the affections of his army, made himself master both of senate and people. And this proceeding of popular, and ambitious men, is plain rebellion; and may be resembled to the effects of witchcraft.

Another infirmity of a commonwealth, is the immoderate greatness of a town, when it is able to furnish out of its own circuit, the number, and expense of a great army: as also the great number of corporations; which are as it were many lesser commonwealths in the bowels of a greater, like worms in the entrails of a natural man. To which may be added, the liberty of disputing against absolute power, by pretenders to political prudence; which though bred for the most part in the lees of the people, yet animated by false doctrines, are perpetually meddling with the fundamental laws, to the molestation of the commonwealth; like the little worms, which physicians call *ascarides*.

We may further add, the insatiable appetite of enlarging dominion; with the incurable *wounds* thereby many times received from the enemy; and the *wens*, of ununited conquests, which are many times a burthen, and with less danger lost, than kept; as also the *lethargy* of ease, and *consumption* of riot and vain expense.

Lastly, when in a war, foreign or intestine, the enemies get a final victory; so as, the forces of the commonwealth keeping the field no longer, there is no further protection of subjects in their loyalty; then is the commonwealth Dissolved, and every man at liberty to protect himself by such courses as his own discretion shall suggest unto him. For the sovereign is the public soul, giving life and motion to the commonwealth; which expiring, the members are governed by it no more, than the carcase of a man, by his departed, though immortal, soul. For though the right of a sovereign monarch cannot be extinguished by the act of another; yet the obligation of the members may. For he that wants protection, may seek it anywhere; and when he hath it, is obliged, without fraudulent pretence of having submitted himself out of fear, to protect his protection as long as he is able. But when the power of an assembly is once suppressed, the right of the same perisheth utterly; because the assembly itself is extinct; and consequently, there is no possibility for the sovereignty to re-enter.

12

John Locke
Second Treatise of Government

John Locke (1632–1704) was one of the most influential thinkers in the tradition of Western liberalism. Educated at Oxford, he trained as a physician and became an adviser to the first earl of Shaftesbury. While Locke's Two Treatises of Government *defend the principles of the Glorious Revolution of 1688, which established constitutional monarchy and parliamentary supremacy in Britain, they were actually written some years earlier, during a political debate over the king's prerogatives. At that time, proponents of the king republished Sir Robert Filmer's book* Patriarcha *(originally written in 1640), a book which argued that all political power is patriarchal, dating back to Adam. Locke rebutted this with a social contract theory: government rests on the consent of the governed, who freely leave a state of nature which has proven to be inconvenient for them. Government is created to protect the natural rights of life, liberty, and property, and these are inviolable. Locke's ideas had a great influence on the American revolutionaries, especially Thomas Jefferson. The following selection is from Locke's* Second Treatise of Government.

Of Civil Government

. . . I think it may not be amiss, to set down what I take to be political power; that the power of a *magistrate* over a subject may be distinguished from that of a *father* over his children, a *master* over his servant, a *husband* over his wife, and a *lord* over his slave. All which distinct powers happening sometimes together in the same man, if he be considered under these different relations, it may help us to distinguish these powers one from another, and shew the difference betwixt a ruler of a commonwealth, a father of a family, and a captain of a galley.

Political power, then, I take to be a *right* of making laws with penalties of death, and consequently all less penalties, for the regulating and preserving of property, and of employing the force of the community, in the execution of such laws, and in the defence of the common-wealth from foreign injury; and all this only for the public good.

Of the State of Nature

To understand political power right, and derive it from its original, we must consider, what state all men are naturally in, and that is, a *state of perfect freedom* to order their actions, and dispose of their possessions and persons, as they think fit, within the bounds of the law of nature, without asking leave, or depending upon the will of any other man.

A *state* also *of equality*, wherein all the power and jurisdiction is reciprocal, no one having more than another; there being nothing more evident, than that creatures of the same species and rank, promiscuously born to all the same advantages of nature, and the use of the same faculties, should also be equal one amongst another without subordination or subjection, unless the lord and master of them all should, by any manifest declaration of his will, set one above another, and confer on him, by an evident and clear appointment, an undoubted right to dominion and sovereignty. . . .

But though this be a *state of liberty*, yet *it is not a state of licence*: though man in that state have an uncontroulable liberty to dispose of his person or possessions, yet he has not liberty to destroy himself, or so much as any creature in his possession, but where some nobler use than its bare preservation calls for it. The *state of nature* has a law of nature to govern it, which obliges every one: and reason, which is that law, teaches all mankind, who will but consult it, that being all *equal and independent*, no one ought to harm another in his life, health, liberty, or possessions: for men being all the workmanship of one omnipotent, and infinitely wise maker; all the servants of one sovereign master, sent into the world by his order, and about his business; they are his property, whose workmanship they are, made to last during his, not one another's pleasure: and being furnished with like faculties, sharing all in one community of nature, there cannot be supposed any such *subordination* among us, that may authorize us to destroy one another, as if we were made for one another's uses, as the inferior ranks of creatures are for our's. Every one, as he is *bound to preserve himself*, and not to quit his station wilfully, so by the like reason, when his own preservation comes not in competition, ought he, as much as he can, *to preserve the rest of mankind*, and may not, unless it be to do justice on an offender, take away, or impair the life, or what tends to the preservation of the life, the liberty, health, limb, or goods of another.

And that all men may be restrained from invading others rights, and from doing hurt to one another, and the law of nature be observed, which willeth the peace and *preservation of all mankind*, the *execution* of the law of nature is, in that state, put into every man's hands, whereby every one has a right to punish the transgressors of that law to such a degree, as may hinder its violation: for the *law of nature* would, as all other laws that concern men in this world, be in vain, if there were no body that in the state of nature had a *power to execute* that law, and thereby preserve the innocent and restrain offenders. And if any one in the state of nature may punish another for any evil he has done, every one may do so: for in that *state of perfect equality*, where naturally there is no superiority or jurisdiction of one over another, what any may do in prosecution of that law, every one must needs have a right to do.

And thus, in the state of nature, *one man comes by a power over another*; but yet no absolute or arbitrary power, to use a criminal, when he has got him in his hands, according to the passionate heats, or boundless extravagancy of his own will; but only to retribute to him, so far as calm reason and conscience dictate, what is proportionate to his transgression, which is so much as may serve for *reparation* and *restraint*: for these two are the only reasons, why one man may lawfully do harm to another, which is that we call *punishment*. In transgressing the law of nature, the offender declares himself to live by another rule than that of reason and common equity, which is that measure God has set to the actions of men, for their mutual security; and so he becomes dangerous to mankind, the type, which is to secure them from injury and violence, being slighted and broken by him. Which being a trespass against the whole species, and the peace and safety of it, provided for by the law of nature, every man upon this score, by the right he hath to preserve mankind in general, may restrain, or where it is necessary, destroy things noxious to them, and so may bring such evil on any one, who hath transgressed that law, as may make him repent the doing of it, and thereby deter him, and by his example others, from doing the like mischief. And in the case, and upon this ground, *every man hath a right to punish the offender, and be executioner of the law of nature*.

I doubt not but this will seem a very strange doctrine to some men: but before they condemn it, I desire them to resolve me, by what right any prince or state can put to death, or *punish an alien*, for any crime he commits in their country. It is certain their laws, by virtue of any sanction they receive from the promulgated will of the legislative, reach not a stranger: they speak not to him, nor, if they did, is he bound to hearken to them. The legislative authority, by which they are in force over the subjects of that common-wealth, hath no power over him. Those who have the supreme power of making laws in *England, France* or *Holland*, are to an *Indian*, but like the rest of the world, men without authority: and therefore, if by the law of nature every man hath not a power to punish offences against it, as he soberly judges the case to require, I see not how the magistrates of any community can *punish an alien* of another country; since, in reference to him, they can have no more power than what every man naturally may have over another.

Besides the crime which consists in violating the law, and varying from the right rule of reason, whereby a man so far becomes degenerate, and declares himself to quit the principles of human nature, and to be a noxious creature, there is commonly *injury* done to some person or other, and some other man receives damage by his transgression: in which case he who hath received any damage, has, besides the right of punishment common to him with other men, a particular right to seek *reparation* from him that has done it: and any other person, who finds it just, may also join with him that is injured, and assist him in recovering from the offender so much as may make satisfaction for the harm he has suffered.

From these *two distinct rights*, the one of *punishing* the crime *for restraint*, and preventing the like offence, which right of punishing is in every body; the other of taking *reparation*, which belongs only to the injured party, comes it to pass that the magistrate, who by being magistrate hath the common right of punishing put into his hands, can often, where the public good demands not the execution of the law, *remit* the punishment of criminal offences by his own authority, but yet cannot *remit* the satisfaction due to any private man for the damage he has received. That, he who has suffered the damage has a right to demand in his own name, and he alone can remit: the damnified person has this power of appropriating to himself the goods or service of the offender, *by right of self-preservation*, as every man has a power to punish the crime, to prevent its being committed again, *by the right he has of preserving all mankind*, and doing all reasonable things he can in order to that end: and thus it is, that every man, in the state of nature, has a power to kill a murderer, both *to deter* others from doing the like injury, which no reparation can compensate, by the example of the punishment that attends it from every body, and also to secure men from the attempts of a criminal, who having renounced reason, the common rule and measure God hath given to mankind, hath, by the unjust violence and slaughter he hath committed upon one, declared war against all mankind, and therefore may be destroyed as a *lion* or a *tyger*, one of those wild savage beasts, with whom men can have no society nor security: and upon this is grounded that great law of nature, *Whoso sheddeth man's blood, by man shall his blood be shed*. And *Cain* was so fully convinced, that every one had a right to destroy such a criminal, that after the murder of his brother, he cries out, *Every one that findeth me, shall slay me*; so plain was it writ in the hearts of all mankind.

By the same reason may a man in the state of nature *punish the lesser breaches* of that law. It will perhaps be demanded, with death? I answer, each transgression may be *punished* to that *degree*, and with so much *severity*, as will suffice to make it an ill bargain to the offender, give him cause to repent, and terrify others from doing the like. Every offence, that can be committed in the state of nature, may in the state of nature be also punished equally, and as far forth as it may, in a common-wealth: for though it would be besides my present purpose, to enter here into the particulars of the law of nature, or its *measures of punishment*; yet, it is certain there is such a law, and that too, as intelligible and plain to a rational creature, and a studier of that law, as the positive laws of common-wealths; nay, possibly plainer; as much as reason is easier to be understood, than the fancies and intricate contrivances of men, following contrary and hidden interests put into words; for so truly are a great part of the *municipal laws* of countries, which are only so far right, as they are founded on the law of nature, by which they are to be regulated and interpreted.

To this strange doctrine, *viz.* That *in the state of nature every one has the executive power* of the law of nature, I doubt not but it will be objected, that it is unreasonable for men to be judges in their own cases, that self-love will make men partial to themselves and their friends: and on the other side, that ill nature, passion and revenge will carry them too far in punishing others; and hence nothing but confusion and disorder will follow, and that therefore God hath certainly appointed government to restrain the partiality and violence of men. I easily grant, that *civil government* is the proper remedy for the inconveniences of the state of nature, which must certainly be great, where men may be judges in their own case, since it is easy to be imagined, that he who was so unjust as to do his brother an injury, will scarce be so just as to condemn himself for it: but I shall desire those who make this objection, to remember, that *absolute monarchs* are but men; and if government is to be the remedy of those evils, which necessarily follow from men's being judges in their own cases, and the state of nature is therefore not to be endured, I desire to know what kind of government that is, and how much better it is than the state of nature, where one man, commanding a multitude, has the liberty to be judge in his own case, and may do to all his subjects whatever he pleases, without the least liberty to any one to question or controul those who execute his pleasure? and in whatsoever he doth, whether led by reason, mistake or passion, must be submitted to? much better it is in the state of nature, wherein men are not bound to submit to the unjust will of another: and if he that judges, judges amiss in his own, or any other case, he is answerable for it to the rest of mankind.

It is often asked as a mighty objection, *where are*, or ever were there any *men in such a state of nature*? To which it may suffice as an answer at present, that since all princes and rulers of *independent* governments all through the world, are in a state of nature, it is plain the world never was, nor ever will be, without numbers of men in that state. I have named all governors of *independent communities*, whether they are, or are not, in league with others: for it is not every compact that puts an end to the state of nature between men, but only this one of agreeing together mutually to enter into one community, and make one body politic; other promises, and compacts, men may make one with another, and yet still be in the state of nature. The promises and bargains for truck, &c. between the two men in the desert island, mentioned by *Garcilasso de la Vega*, in his history of *Peru*; or between a *Swiss* and an *Indian*, in the woods of *America*, are binding to them, though they are perfectly in a state of nature, in reference to one another: for truth and keeping of faith belongs to men, as men, and not as members of society.

To those that say, there were never any men in the state of nature, I will not only oppose the authority of the judicious *Hooker, Eccl. Pol. lib. i. sect. 10.* where he says, *The laws which have been hitherto mentioned*, i.e. the laws of nature, *do bind men absolutely, even as they are men, although they have never any settled fellowship, never any solemn agreement amongst themselves what to do, or not to do: but forasmuch as we are not by ourselves sufficient to furnish ourselves with competent store of things, needful for such a life as our nature doth desire, a life fit for the dignity of man; therefore to supply those defects and imperfections which are in us, as living single and solely by ourselves, we are naturally induced to seek communion and fellowship with others: this was the cause of men's uniting themselves at first in politic societies.* But I moreover affirm, that all men are naturally in that state, and remain so, till by their own consents they make themselves members of some politic society; and I doubt not in the sequel of this discourse, to make it very clear.

Of the State of War

The *state of war* is a state of *enmity* and *destruction*: and therefore declaring by word or action, not a passionate and hasty, but a sedate settled design upon another man's life, *puts him in a state of war* with him against whom he has declared such an intention, and so has exposed his life to the other's power to be taken away by him, or any one that joins with him in his defence, and espouses his quarrel; it being reasonable and just, I should have a right to destroy that which threatens me with destruction: for, *by the fundamental law of nature, man being to be preserved* as much as possible, when all cannot be preserved, the safety of the innocent is to be preferred: and one may destroy a man who makes war upon him, or has discovered an enmity to his being, for the same reason that he may kill a *wolf* or a *lion*; because such men are not under the ties of the commonlaw of reason, have no other rule, but that of force and violence, and so may be treated as beasts of prey, those dangerous and noxious creatures, that will be sure to destroy him whenever he falls into their power.

And hence it is, that he who attempts to get another man into his absolute power, does thereby *put himself into a state of war* with him; it being to be understood as a declaration of a design upon his life: for I have reason to conclude, that he who would get me into his power without my consent, would use me as he pleased when he had got me there, and destroy me too when he had a fancy to it; for no body can desire to *have me in his absolute power*, unless it be to compel me by force to that which is against the right of my freedom, *i.e.* make me a slave. To be free from such force is the only security of my preservation; and reason bids me look on him, as an enemy to my preservation, who would take away that *freedom* which is the fence to it; so that he who makes an *attempt to enslave* me, thereby puts himself into a state of war with me. He that, in the state of nature, *would take away the freedom* that belongs to any one in that state, must necessarily be supposed to have a design to take away every thing else, that *freedom* being the foundation of all the rest; as he that, in the state of society, would take away the *freedom* belonging to those of that society or common-wealth, must be supposed to design to take away from them every thing else, and so be looked on as *in a state of war*.

This makes it lawful for a man to *kill a thief*, who has not in the least hurt him, nor declared any design upon his life, any farther than, by the use of force, so to get him in his power, as to take away his money, or what he pleases, from him; because using force, where he has no right, to get me into his power, let his pretence be what it will, I have no reason to suppose, that he, who would *take away my liberty*, would not, when he had me in his power, take away every thing else. And therefore it is lawful for me to treat him as one who has *put himself into a state of war* with me, *i.e.* kill him if I can; for to that hazard does he justly expose himself, whoever introduces a state of war, and is aggressor in it.

And here we have the plain *difference between the state of nature and the state of war*, which however some men have confounded, are as far distant, as a state of peace, good will, mutual assistance and preservation, and a state of enmity, malice, violence and mutual destruction, are one from another. Men living together according to reason, without a common superior on earth, with authority to judge between them, is *properly the state of nature*. But force, or a declared design of force, upon the person of another, where there is no common superior on earth to appeal to for relief, *is the state of war*: and it is the want of such an appeal gives a man the right of war even against an *aggressor*, tho' he be in society and a fellow subject. Thus a *thief*, whom I cannot harm, but by appeal to the law, for having stolen all that I am worth, I may kill, when he sets on me to rob me but of my horse or coat; because the law, which was made for my preservation, where it cannot interpose to secure my life from present force, which, if lost, is capable of no reparation, permits me my own defence, and the right of war, a liberty to kill the aggressor, because the aggressor allows not time to appeal to our common judge, nor the decision of the law, for remedy in a case where the mischief may be irreparable. Want of a common judge with authority, puts all men in a state of nature: force without right, upon a man's person, makes a state of war, both where there is, and is not, a common judge.

But when the actual force is over, the *state of war ceases* between those that are in society, and are equally on both sides subjected to the fair determination of the law; because then there lies open the remedy of appeal for the past injury, and to prevent future harm: but where no such appeal is, as in the state of nature, for want of positive laws, and judges with authority to appeal to, the state of war once begun, continues, with a right to the innocent party to destroy the other whenever he can, until the aggressor offers peace, and desires reconciliation on such terms as may repair any wrongs he has already done, and secure the innocent for the future; nay, where an appeal to the law, and constituted judges, lies open, but the remedy is denied by a manifest perverting of justice, and a barefaced wresting of the laws to protect or indemnify the violence or injuries of some men, or party of men, *there* it is hard to imagine any thing but *a state of war*: for where-ever violence is used, and injury done, though by hands appointed to administer justice, it is still violence and injury, however coloured with the name, pretences, or forms of law, the end whereof being to protect and redress the innocent, by an unbiassed application of it, to all who are under it; where-ever that is not *bona fide* done, *war is made* upon the sufferers, who having no appeal on earth to right them, they are left to the only remedy in such cases, an appeal to heaven.

To avoid this *state of war* (wherein there is no appeal but to heaven, and wherein every the least difference is apt to end, where there is no authority to decide between the contenders) is one great reason of men's putting themselves into society, and quitting the state of nature: for where there is an authority, a power on earth, from which relief can be had by *appeal*, there the continuance of the *state of war* is excluded, and the controversy is decided by that power. Had there been any such court, any superior jurisdiction on earth, to determine the right between *Jephtha* and the *Ammonites*, they had never come to a *state of war*: but we see he was forced to appeal to heaven. . . .

. . . Where there is no judge on earth, the appeal lies to God in heaven.

Of Slavery

The *natural liberty* of man is to be free from any superior power on earth, and not to be under the will or legislative authority of man, but to have only the law of nature for his rule. The *liberty of man*, in society, is to be under no other legislative power, but that established, by consent, in the common-wealth; nor under the dominion of any will, or restraint of any law, but what that legislative shall enact, according to the trust put in it. Freedom then is not what Sir *Robert Filmer* tells us, *Observations, A. 55. a liberty for every one to do what he lists, to live as he pleases, and not to be tied by any laws:* but *freedom of men under government* is, to have a standing rule to live by, common to every one of that society, and made by the legislative power erected in it; a liberty to follow my own will in all things, where the rule prescribes not; and not to be subject to the inconstant, uncertain, unknown, arbitrary will of another man: as *freedom of nature* is, to be under no other restraint but the law of nature.

This *freedom* from absolute, arbitrary power, is so necessary to, and closely joined with a man's preservation, that he cannot part with it, but by what forfeits his preservation and life together: for a man, not having the power of his own life, *cannot*, by compact, or his own consent, *enslave himself* to any one, nor put himself under the absolute, arbitrary power of another, to take away his life, when he pleases. No body can give more power than he has himself; and he that cannot take away his own life, cannot give another power over it. Indeed, having by his fault forfeited his own life, by some act that deserves death; he, to whom he has forfeited it, may (when he has him in his power) delay to take it, and make use of him to his own service, and he does him no injury by it: for, whenever he finds the hardship of his slavery outweigh the value of his life, it is in his power, by resisting the will of his master, to draw on himself the death he desires.

This is the perfect condition of *slavery*, which is nothing else, but *the state of war continued, between a lawful conqueror and a captive*: for, if once *compact* enter between them, and make an agreement for a limited power on the one side, and obedience on the other, the *state of war and slavery* ceases, as long as the compact endures: for as has been said, no man can, by agreement, pass over to another that which he hath not in himself, a power over his own life. . . .

Of Property

Whether we consider natural *reason*, which tells us, that men, being once born, have a right to their preservation, and consequently to meat and drink, and such other things as nature affords for their subsistence: or *revelation*, which gives us an account of those grants God made of the world to *Adam*, and to *Noah*, and his sons, it is very clear, that God, as king *David* says, *Psal.* cxv. 16. *has given the earth to the children of men;* given it to mankind in common. But this being supposed, it seems to some a very great difficulty, how any one should ever come to have a *property* in any thing: I will not content myself to answer, that if it be difficult to make out *property*, upon a supposition that God gave the world to *Adam*, and his posterity in common, it is impossible that any man, but one universal monarch, should have any *property* upon a supposition, that God gave the world to *Adam*, and his heirs in succession, exclusive of all the rest of his posterity. But I shall endeavour to shew, how men might come to have a *property* in several parts of that which God gave to mankind in common, and that without any express compact of all the commoners.

God, who hath given the world to men in common, hath also given them reason to make use of it to the best advantage of life, and convenience. The earth, and all that is therein, is given to men for the support and comfort of their being. And tho' all the fruits it naturally produces, and beasts it feeds, belong to mankind in common, as they are produced by the spontaneous hand of nature; and no body has originally a private dominion, exclusive of the rest of mankind, in any of them, as they are thus in their natural state: yet being given for the use of men, there must of necessity be *a means to appropriate* them some way or other, before they can be of any use, or at all beneficial to any particular man. The fruit, or venison, which nourishes the wild *Indian*, who knows no inclosure, and is still a tenant in common, must be his, and so his, i.e. a part of him, that another can no longer have any right to it, before it can do him any good for the support of his life.

Though the earth, and all inferior creatures, be common to all men, yet every man has a *property* in his own *person*: this no body has any right to but himself. The *labour* of his body, and the *work* of his hands, we may say, are properly his. Whatsoever then he removes out of the state that nature hath provided, and left it in, he hath mixed his *labour* with, and joined to it something that is his own, and thereby makes it his *property*. It being by him removed from the common state nature hath placed it in, it hath by this *labour* something annexed to it, that excludes the common right of other men: for this *labour* being the unquestionable property of the labourer, no man but he can have a right to what that is once joined to, at least where there is enough, and as good, left in common for others.

He that is nourished by the acorns he picked up under an oak, or the apples he gathered from the trees in the wood, has certainly appropriated them to himself. No body can deny but the nourishment is his. I ask then, when did they begin to be his? when he digested? or when he eat? or when he boiled? or when he brought them home? or when he picked them up? and it is plain, if the first gathering made them not his, nothing else could. That *labour* put a distinction between them and common: that added something to them more than nature, the common mother of all, had done; and so they became his private right. And will any one say, he had no right to those acorns or apples, he thus appropriated, because he had not the consent of all mankind to make them his? Was it a robbery thus to assume to himself what belonged to all in common? If such a consent as that was necessary, man had starved, notwithstanding the plenty God had given him. We see in *commons*, which remain so by compact, that it is the taking any part of what is common, and removing it out of the state nature leaves it in, which *begins the property*; without which the common is of no use. And the taking of this or that part, does not depend on the express consent of all the commoners. Thus the grass my horse has bit; the turfs my servant has cut; and the ore I have digged in any place, where I have a right to them in common with others, become my *property*, without the assignation or consent of any body. The *labour* that was mine, removing them out of that common state they were in, hath *fixed* my *property* in them.

By making an explicit consent of every commoner, necessary to any one's appropriating to himself any part of what is given in common, children or servants could not cut the meat, which their father or master had provided for them in

common, without assigning to every one his peculiar part. Though the water running in the fountain be every one's, yet who can doubt, but that in the pitcher is
his only who drew it out? His *labour* hath taken it out of the hands of nature,
where it was common, and belonged equally to all her children, and *hath* thereby
appropriated it to himself.

Thus, this law of reason makes the deer that *Indian*'s who hath killed it; it is
allowed to be his goods, who hath bestowed his labour upon it, though before it
was the common right of every one. . . .

It will perhaps be objected to this, that if gathering the acorns, or other fruits of
the earth, &c. makes a right to them, then any one may *ingross* as much as he
will. To which I answer, Not so. The same law of nature, that does by this means
give us property, does also *bound* that *property* too. *God has given us all things
richly*, 1 Tim. vi. 12. is the voice of reason confirmed by inspiration. But how far
has he given it us? *To enjoy*. As much as any one can make use of to any advantage of life before it spoils, so much he may by his labour fix a property in:
whatever is beyond this, is more than his share, and belongs to others. Nothing
was made by God for man to spoil or destroy. And thus, considering the plenty of
natural provisions there was a long time in the world, and the few spenders; and to
how small a part of that provision the industry of one man could extend itself, and
ingross it to the prejudice of others; especially keeping within the *bounds*, set by
reason, of what might serve for his *use*; there could be then little room for quarrels
or contentions about property so established.

But the *chief matter of property* being now not the fruits of the earth, and the
beasts that subsist on it, but *the earth itself*; as that which takes in and carries with
it all the rest; I think it is plain, that *property* in that too is acquired as the former.
As much land as a man tills, plants, improves, cultivates, and can use the product
of, so much is his *property*. He by his labour does, as it were, inclose it from the
common. Nor will it invalidate his right, to say every body else has an equal title
to it; and therefore he cannot appropriate, he cannot inclose, without the consent
of all his fellow-commoners, all mankind. God, when he gave the world in common to all mankind, commanded man also to labour, and the penury of his condition required it of him. God and his reason commanded him to subdue the earth,
i.e., improve it for the benefit of life, and therein lay out something upon it that
was his own, his labour. He that in obedience to this command of God, subdued,
tilled and sowed any part of it, thereby annexed to it something that was his
property, which another had no title to, nor could without injury take from him.

Nor was this *appropriation* of any parcel of *land*, by improving it, any prejudice to any other man, since there was still enough, and as good left; and more
than the yet unprovided could use. So that, in effect, there was never the less left
for others because of his inclosure for himself: for he that leaves as much as
another can make use of, does as good as take nothing at all. No body could think
himself injured by the drinking of another man, though he took a good draught,
who had a whole river of the same water left him to quench his thirst: and the case
of land and water; where there is enough of both, is perfectly the same.

God gave the world to men in common; but since he gave it them for their benefit, and the greatest conveniencies of life they were capable to draw from it, it cannot be supposed he meant it should always remain common and uncultivated. He gave it to the use of the industrious and rational (and *labour* was to be *his title* to it); not to the fancy or covetousness of the quarrelsome and contentious. He that had as good left for his improvement, as was already taken up, needed not complain, ought not to meddle with what was already improved by another's labour: if he did, it is plain he desired the benefit of another's pains, which he had no right to, and not the ground which God had given him in common with others to labour on, and whereof there was as good left, as that already possessed, and more than he knew what to do with, or his industry could reach to.

It is true, in *land* that is *common* in *England*, or any other country, where there is plenty of people under government, who have money and commerce, no one can inclose or appropriate any part, without the consent of all his fellow-commoners; because this is left common by compact, i.e. by the law of the land, which is not to be violated. And though it be common, in respect of some men, it is not so to all mankind; but is the joint property of this country, or this parish. Besides, the remainder, after such inclosure, would not be as good to the rest of the commoners, as the whole was when they could all make use of the whole; whereas in the beginning and first peopling of the great common of the world, it was quite otherwise. The law man was under, was rather for appropriating. God commanded, and his wants forced him to *labour*. That was his *property* which could not be taken from him where-ever he had fixed it. And hence subduing or cultivating the earth, and having dominion, we see are joined together. The one gave title to the other. So that God, by commanding to subdue, gave authority so far to *appropriate*: and the condition of human life, which requires labour and materials to work on, necessarily introduces private possessions.

The *measure of property* nature has well set by the extent of men's *labour and the conveniencies of life*: no man's labour could subdue, or appropriate all; nor could his enjoyment consume more than a small part; so that it was impossible for any man, this way, to intrench upon the right of another, or acquire to himself a property, to the prejudice of his neighbour, who would still have room for as good, and as large a possession (after the other had taken out his) as before it was appropriated. This *measure* did confine every man's *possession* to a very moderate proportion, and such as he might appropriate to himself, without injury to any body, in the first ages of the world, when men were more in danger to be lost, by wandering from their company, in the then vast wilderness of the earth, than to be straitened for want of room to plant in. And the same *measure* may be allowed still without prejudice to any body, as full as the world seems: for supposing a man, or family, in the state they were at first peopling of the world by the children of *Adam*, or *Noah*; let him plant in some in-land, vacant places of *America*, we shall find that the *possessions* he could make himself, upon the *measures* we have given, would not be very large, nor, even to this day, prejudice the rest of mankind, or give them reason to complain, or think themselves injured by this man's incroachment, though the race of men have now spread themselves to all the corners of the world, and do infinitely exceed the small number was at the beginning. Nay, the extent of *ground* is of so little value, *without labour*, that I have heard it affirmed, that in *Spain* itself a man may be permitted to plough, sow and reap, without being disturbed, upon land he has no other title to, but only his making use of it. But, on the contrary, the inhabitants think themselves beholden to him, who, by his industry on neglected, and consequently waste land, has increased the stock of corn, which they wanted. But be this as it will, which I lay no stress on; this I dare boldly affirm, that the same *rule of propriety*, (*viz.*) that every man should have as much as he could make use of, would hold still in the world, without straitening any body; since there is land enough in the world to suffice double the inhabitants, had not the *invention of money*, and the tacit agreement of men to put a value on it, introduced (by consent) larger possessions, and a right to them; which, how it has done, I shall by and by shew more at large.

This is certain, that in the beginning, before the desire of having more than man needed had altered the intrinsic value of things, which depends only on their usefulness to the life of man; or had *agreed, that a little piece of yellow metal*, which would keep without wasting or decay, should be worth a great piece of flesh, or a whole heap of corn; though men had a right to appropriate, by their labour, each one of himself, as much of the things of nature, as he could use: yet this could not be much, nor to the prejudice of others, where the same plenty was still left to those who would use the same industry. To which let me add, that he who appropriates land to himself by his labour, does not lessen, but increase the common stock of mankind: for the provisions serving to the support of human life, produced by one acre of inclosed and cultivated land, are (to speak much within compass) ten times more than those which are yielded by an acre of land of an equal richness lying waste in common. And therefore he that incloses land, and has a greater plenty of the conveniencies of life from ten acres, than he could have from an hundred left to nature, may truly be said to give ninety acres to mankind: for his labour now supplies him with provisions out of ten acres, which were but the product of an hundred lying in common. I have here rated the improved land very low, in making its product but as ten to one, when it is much nearer an hundred to one: for I ask, whether in the wild woods and uncultivated waste of *America*, left to nature, without any improvement, tillage or husbandry, a thousand acres yield the needy and wretched inhabitants as many conveniencies of life, as ten acres of equally fertile land do in *Devonshire*, where they are well cultivated?

Before the appropriation of land, he who gathered as much or the wild fruit, killed, caught, or tamed, as many of the beasts, as he could; he that so imployed his pains about any of the spontaneous products of nature, as any way to alter them from the state which nature put them in, *by* placing any of his *labour* on them, did thereby *acquire a propriety in them*: but if they perished, in his possession, without their due use; if the fruits rotted, or the venison putrified, before he could spend it, he offended against the common law of nature, and was liable to be punished; he invaded his neighbour's share, for he had *no right, farther than his use* called for any of them, and they might serve to afford him conveniencies of life.

The same *measures* governed the *possession of land* too: whatsoever he tilled and reaped, laid up and made use of, before it spoiled, that was his peculiar right; whatsoever he enclosed, and could feed, and make use of, the cattle and product was also his. But if either the grass of his inclosure rotted on the ground, or the fruit of his planting perished without gathering, and laying up, this part of the earth, notwithstanding his inclosure, was still to be looked on as waste, and might be the possession of any other. Thus, at the beginning, *Cain* might take as much ground as he could till, and make it his own land, and yet leave enough to *Abel's* sheep to feed on; a few acres would serve for both their possessions. But as families increased, and industry inlarged their stocks, their *possessions inlarged* with the need of them; but yet it was commonly *without any fixed property in the ground* they made use of, till they incorporated, settled themselves together, and built cities; and then, by consent, they came in time, to set out the *bounds of their distinct territories*, and agree on limits between them and their neighbours; and by laws within themselves, settled the *properties* of those of the same society: for we see, that in that part of the world which was first inhabited, and therefore like to be best peopled, even as low down as *Abraham's* time, they wandered with their flocks, and their herds, which was their substance, freely up and down; and this *Abraham* did, in a country where he was a stranger. Whence it is plain, that at least a great part of the *land lay in common*; that the inhabitants valued it not, nor claimed property in any more than they made use of. But when there was not room enough in the same place, for their herds to feed together, they by consent, as *Abraham* and *Lot* did, *Gen.* xiii. 5. separated and inlarged their pasture, where it best liked them. . . .

Nor is it so strange, as perhaps before consideration it may appear, that the *property of labour* should be able to over-balance the community of land: for it is *labour* indeed that *puts the difference of value* on every thing; and let any one consider what the difference is between an acre of land planted with tobacco or sugar, sown with wheat or barley, and an acre of the same land lying in common, without any husbandry upon it, and he will find, that the improvement of *labour makes* the far greater part of the value. I think it will be but a very modest computation to say, that of the *products* of the earth useful to the life of man nine tenths are the *effects of labour*: nay, if we will rightly estimate things as they come to our use, and cast up the several expences about them, what in them is purely owing to *nature*, and what to *labour*, we shall find, that in most of them ninety-nine hundredths are wholly to be put on the account of *labour*.

. . . It is *labour* then which *puts the greatest part of value upon land*, without which it would scarcely be worth any thing: it is to that we owe the greatest part of all its useful products; for all that the straw, bran, bread, of that acre of wheat, is more worth than the product of an acre of as good land, which lies waste, is all the effect of labour: for it is not barely the plough-man's pains, the reaper's and thresher's toil, and the baker's sweat, is to be counted into the *bread* we eat; the labour of those who broke the oxen, who digged and wrought the iron and stones, who felled and framed the timber employed about the plough, mill, oven, or any other utensils, which are a vast number, requisite to this corn, from its being feed to be sown to its being made bread, must all be *charged on* the account of labour, and received as an effect of that: nature and the earth furnished only the almost worthless materials, as in themselves. It would be a strange *catalogue of things, that industry provided and made use of, about every loaf of bread*, before it came to our use, if we could trace them; iron, wood, leather, bark, timber, stone, bricks, coals, lime, cloth, dying drugs, pitch, tar, masts, ropes, and all the materials made use of in the ship, that brought any of the commodities made use of by any of the workmen, to any part of the work; all which it would be almost impossible, at least too long, to reckon up.

From all which it is evident, that though the things of nature are given in common, yet man, by being master of himself, and *proprietor of his own person, and the actions or labour of it, had still in himself the great foundation of property*; and that, which made up the great part of what he applied to the support or comfort of his being, when invention and arts had improved the conveniencies of life, was perfectly his own, and did not belong in common to others. Thus *labour*, in the beginning, *gave a right of property*, wherever any one was pleased to employ it upon what was common which remained a long while the far greater part, and is yet more than mankind makes use of. Men, at first, for the most part, contented themselves with what unassisted nature offered to their necessities: and though afterwards, in some parts of the world, (where the increase of people and stock, with the *use of money*, had made land scarce, and so of some value) the several *communities* settled the bounds of their distinct territories, and by laws within themselves regulated the properties of the private men of their society, and so, *by compact* and agreement, *settled the property* which labour and industry began; and the leagues that have been made between several states and kingdoms, either expressly or tacitly disowning all claim and right to the land in the others possession, have, by common consent, given up their pretences to their natural common right, which originally they had to those countries, and so have, by *positive agreement, settled a property* amongst themselves, in distinct parts and parcels of the earth; yet there are still *great tracts of ground* to be found, which (the inhabitants thereof not having joined with the rest of mankind, in the consent of the use of their common money) *lie waste*, and are more than the people who dwell on it do, or can make use of, and so still lie in common; tho' this can scarce happen amongst that part of mankind that have consented to the use of money.

The greatest part of *things really useful* to the life of man, and such as the necessity of subsisting made the first commoners of the world look after, as it doth the *Americans* now, *are* generally things of *short duration*; such as, if they are not consumed by use, will decay and perish of themselves: gold, silver and diamonds, are things that fancy or agreement hath put the value on, more than real use, and the necessary support of life. Now of those good things which nature hath provided in common, every one had a right (as hath been said) to as much as he could use, and *property* in all that he could effect with his labour; all that his *industry* could extend to, to alter from the state nature had put it in, was his. He that *gathered* a hundred bushels of acorns or apples, had thereby a *property* in them, they were his goods as soon as gathered. He was only to look, that he used them before they spoiled, else he took more than his share, and robbed others. And indeed it was a foolish thing, as well a dishonest, to hoard up more than he could make use of. If he gave away a part to any body else, so that it perished not uselessly in his possession, these he also made use of. And if he also bartered away plums, that would have rotted in a week, for nuts that would last good for his eating a whole year, he did no injury; he wasted not the common stock; destroyed no part of the portion of goods that belonged to others, so long as nothing perished uselessly in his hands. Again, if he would give his nuts for a piece of metal, pleased with its colour; or exchange his sheep for shells, or wool for a sparkling pebble or a diamond, and keep those by him all his life, he invaded not the right of others, he might heap up as much of these durable things as he pleased; the *exceeding of the bounds of his just property* not lying in the largeness of his possession, but the perishing of any thing uselessly in it.

And thus *came in the use of money*, some lasting thing that men might keep without spoiling, and that by mutual consent men would take in exchange for the truly useful, but perishable supports of life.

And as different degrees of industry were apt to give men possessions in different proportions, so this *invention of money* gave them the opportunity to continue and enlarge them: for supposing an island, separate from all possible commerce with the rest of the world, wherein there were but an hundred families, but there were sheep, horses and cows, with other useful animals, wholsome fruits, and land enough for corn for a hundred thousand times as many, but nothing in the island, either because of its commonness, or perishableness, fit to supply the place of *money*; what reason could any one have there to enlarge his possessions beyond the use of his family, and a plentiful supply to its *consumption*, either in what their own industry produced, or they could barter for like perishable, useful commodities, with others? Where there is not some thing, both lasting and scarce, and so valuable to be hoarded up, there men will not be apt to enlarge their *possessions of land*, were it never so rich, never so free for them to take: for I ask, what would a man value ten thousand, or an hundred thousand acres of excellent *land*, ready cultivated, and well stocked too with cattle, in the middle of the inland parts of *America*, where he had no hopes of commerce with other parts of the world, to draw *money* to him by the sale of the product? It would not be worth the inclosing, and we should see him give up again to the wild common of nature, whatever was more than would supply the conveniencies of life to be had there for him and his family. Thus in the beginning all the world was *America*, and more so than that is now; for no such thing as *money* was any where known. Find out something that hath the *use and value of money* amongst his neighbours, you shall see the same man will begin presently to enlarge his possessions.

But since gold and silver, being little useful to the life of man in proportion to food, raiment, and carriage, has its *value* only from the consent of men, whereof *labour* yet *makes* in great part, *the measure*, it is plain, that men have agreed to a disproportionate and unequal *possession of the earth*, they having, by a tacit and voluntary consent, found out a way how a man may fairly possess more land than he himself can use the product of, by receiving in exchange for the overplus gold and silver, which may be hoarded up without injury to any one; these metals not spoiling or decaying in the hands of the possessor. This partage of things in an inequality of private possessions, men have made practicable out of the bounds of society, and without compact, only by putting a value on gold and silver, and tacitly agreeing in the use of money: for in governments, the laws regulate the right of property, and the possession of land is determined by positive constitutions. . . .

Of Political or Civil Society

God having made man such a creature, that in his own judgment, it was not good for him to be alone, put him under strong obligations of necessity, convenience, and inclination to drive him into *society* as well as fitted him with understanding and language to continue and enjoy it. . . .

. . . But how a *family*, or any other society of men, differ from that which is properly *political society* we shall best see, by considering wherein *political society* itself consists.

Man being born, as has been proved, with a title to perfect freedom, and an uncontrouled enjoyment of all the rights and privileges of the law of nature, equally with any other man, or number of men in the world, hath by nature a power, not only to preserve his property, that is, his life, liberty and estate, against the injuries and attempts of other men; but to judge of, and punish the breaches of that law in others, as he is persuaded the offence deserves, even with death itself, in crimes where the heinousness of the fact, in his opinion, requires it. But because no *political society* can be, nor subsist, without having in itself the power to preserve the property, and in order thereunto, punish the offences of all those of that society; there, and there only is *political society*, where every one of the members hath quitted this natural power, resigned it up into the hands of the community in all cases that exclude him not from appealing for protection to the law established by it. And thus all private judgment of every particular member being excluded, the community comes to be umpire, by settled standing rules, indifferent, and the same to all parties; and by men having authority from the community, for the execution of those rules, decides all the differences that may happen between any members of that society concerning any matter of right; and punishes those offences which any member hath committed against the society, with such penalties as the law has established: whereby it is easy to discern, who are, and who are not, in *political society* together. Those who are united into one body, and have a common established law and judicature to appeal to, with authority to decide controversies between them, and punish offenders, are in *civil society* one with another: but those who have no such common appeal, I mean on earth, are still in the state of nature, each being, where there is no other, judge for himself, and executioner; which is, as I have before shewed it, the perfect *state of nature*.

And thus the common-wealth comes by a power to set down what punishment shall belong to the several transgressions which they think worthy of it, committed amongst the members of that society (which is the *power of making laws*) as well as it has the power to punish any injury done unto any of its members, by any one that is not of it (which is the *power of war and peace*); and all this for the preservation of the property of all the members of that society, as far as is possible. But though every man who has entered into civil society, and is become a member of any common-wealth, has thereby quitted his power to punish offences, against the law of *nature*, in prosecution of his own private judgment, yet with the judgment of offences, which he has given up to the legislative in all cases, where he can appeal to the magistrate, he has given a right to the common-wealth to employ his force, for the execution of the judgments of the common-wealth, whenever he shall be called to it; which indeed are his own judgments, they being made by himself, or his representative. And herein we have the original of the *legislative* and *executive power* of civil society, which is to judge by standing laws, how far offences are to be punished, when committed within the common-wealth; and also to determine, by occasional judgments founded on the present circumstances of the fact, how far injuries from without are to be vindicated; and in both these to employ all the force of all the members, when there shall be need.

Where-ever therefore any number of men are so united into one society, as to quit every one his executive power of the law of nature, and to resign it to the public, there and there only is a *political, or civil society*. And this is done, where-ever any number of men, in the state of nature, enter into society to make one people, one body politic, under one supreme government; or else when any one joins himself to, and incorporates with any government already made: for hereby he authorizes the society, or which is all one, the legislative thereof, to make laws for him, as the public good of the society shall require; to the execution whereof, his own assistance (as to his own decrees) is due. And this *puts men* out of a state of nature *into* that of a *common-wealth*, by setting up a judge on earth, with authority to determine all the controversies, and redress the injuries that may happen to any member of the common-wealth; which judge is the legislative, or magistrates appointed by it. And where-ever there are any number of men, however associated, that have no such decisive power to appeal to, there they are still in *the state of nature*.

Hence it is evident, that *absolute monarchy*, which by some men is counted the only government in the world, is indeed *inconsistent with civil society*, and so can be no form of civil-government at all: for the *end of civil society*, being to avoid, and remedy those inconveniencies of the state of nature, which necessarily follow from every man's being judge in his own case, by setting up a known authority, to which every one of that society may appeal upon any injury received, or controversy that may arise, and which every one of the society ought to obey; where-ever any persons are, who have not such an authority to appeal to, for the decision of any difference between them, there those persons are still *in the state of nature*; and so is every *absolute prince*, in respect of those who are under his *dominion*. . . .

Of the Beginning of Political Societies

Men being, as has been said, by nature, all free, equal, and independent, no one can be put out of this estate, and subjected to the political power of another, without his own consent. The only way whereby any one divests himself of his natural liberty, and puts on the *bonds of civil society*, is by agreeing with other men to join and unite into a community for their comfortable, safe, and peaceable living one amongst another, in a secure enjoyment of their properties, and a greater security against any, that are not of it. This any number of men may do, because it injures not the freedom of the rest; they are left as they were in the liberty of the state of nature. When any number of men have so *consented to make one community or government*, they are thereby presently incorporated, and make *one body politic*, wherein the *majority* have a right to act and conclude the rest.

For when any number of men have, by the consent of every individual, made a *community*, they have thereby made that *community* one body, with a power to act as one body, which is only by the will and determination of the *majority*: for that which acts any community, being only the consent of the individuals of it, and it being necessary to that which is one body to move one way; it is necessary the body should move that way whither the greater force carries it, which is the *consent of the majority*: or else it is impossible it should act or continue one body, *one community*, which the consent of every individual that united into it, agreed that it should; and so every one is bound by that consent to be concluded by the *majority*. And therefore we see, that in assemblies, impowered to act by positive laws, where no number is set by that positive law which impowers them, the *act of the majority* passes for the act of the whole, and of course determines, as having, by the law of nature and reason, the power of the whole.

And thus every man, by consenting with others to make one body politic under one government, puts himself under an obligation, to every one of that society, to submit to the determination of the *majority*, and to be concluded by it; or else this *original compact*, whereby he with others incorporates into *one society*, would signify nothing, and be no compact, if he be left free, and under no other ties than he was in before in the state of nature. For what appearance would there be of any compact? what new engagement if he were no farther tied by any decrees of the society, than he himself thought fit, and did actually consent to? This would be still as great a liberty, as he himself had before his compact, or any one else in the state of nature hath, who may submit himself, and consent to any acts of it if he thinks fit.

For *if the consent of the majority* shall not, in reason, be received as *the act of the whole*, and conclude every individual; nothing but the consent of every individual can make any thing to be the act of the whole: but such a consent is next to impossible ever to be had, if we consider the infirmities of health, and avocations of business, which in a number, though much less than that of a common-wealth, will necessarily keep many away from the public assembly. . . .

Whosoever therefore out of a state of nature unite into a *community*, must be understood to give up all the power, necessary to the ends for which they unite into society, to the *majority* of the community, unless they expressly agreed in any number greater than the majority. And this is done by barely agreeing to *unite into one political society*, which is *all the compact* that is, or needs be, between the individuals, that enter into, or make up a *common-wealth*. And thus that, which begins and actually *constitutes any political society*, is nothing but the consent of any number of freemen capable of a majority to unite and incorporate into such a society. And this is that, and that only, which did, or could give beginning to any *lawful government* in the world. . . .

Every man being, as has been shewed, *naturally free*, and nothing being able to put him into subjection to any earthly power, but only his own *consent*; it is to be considered, what shall be understood to be a *sufficient declaration* of a man's *consent*, to *make him subject* to the laws of any government. There is a common distinction of an express and a tacit consent, which will concern our present case. No body doubts but an express *consent*, of any man entering into any society, makes him a perfect member of that society, a subject of that government. The difficulty is, what ought to be looked upon as a *tacit consent*, and how far it binds, i.e. how far any one shall be looked on to have consented, and thereby submitted to any government, where he has made no expressions of it at all. And to this I say, that every man, that hath any possessions, or enjoyment, of any part of the dominions of any government, doth thereby give his *tacit consent* and is as far forth obliged to obedience to the laws of that government, during such enjoyment, as any one under it; whether this his possession be of land, to him and his heirs for ever, or a lodging only for a week; or whether it be barely travelling freely on the highway; and in effect, it reaches as far as the very being of any one within the territories of that government.

To understand this the better, it is fit to consider, that every man, when he at first incorporates himself into any common-wealth, he, by his uniting himself thereunto, annexed also, and submits to the community, those possessions, which he has, or shall acquire, that do not already belong to any other government: for it would be a direct contradiction, for any one to enter into society with others for the securing and regulating of property; and yet to suppose his land, whose property is to be regulated by the laws of the society, should be exempt from the jurisdiction of that government, to which he himself, the proprietor of the land, is a subject. By the same act therefore, whereby any one unites his person, which was before free, to any common-wealth, by the same he unites his possessions, which were before free, to it also; and they become, both of them, person and possession, subject to the government and dominion of that common-wealth, as long as it hath a being. Whoever therefore, from thenceforth, by inheritance, purchase, permission, or otherways, *enjoys any part of the land*, so annexed to, and under the government *of that common-wealth, must take it with the condition* it is under; that is, *of submitting to the government of the common-wealth*, under whose jurisdiction it is, as far forth as any subject of it.

But since the government has a direct jurisdiction only over the land, and reaches the possessor of it (before he has actually incorporated himself in the society) only as he dwells upon, and enjoys that; the obligation any one is under, by virtue of such enjoyment, to *submit to the government, begins and ends with the enjoyment*; so that whenever the owner, who has given nothing but such a *tacit consent* to the government, will, by donation, sale, or otherwise, quit the said possession, he is at liberty to go and incorporate himself into any other commonwealth; or to agree with others to begin a new one, *in vacuis locis*, in any part of the world, they can find free and unpossessed: whereas he, that has once, by actual agreement, and any *express* declaration, given his *consent* to be of any common-wealth, is perpetually and indispensibly obliged to be, and remain unalterably a subject to it, and can never be again in the liberty of the state of nature; unless, by any calamity, the government he was under comes to be dissolved; or else by some public act cuts him off from being any longer a member of it.

But submitting to the laws of any country, living quietly, and enjoying privileges and protection under them, *makes not a man a member of that society*: this is only a local protection and homage due to and from all those, who, not being in a state of war, come within the territories belonging to any government, to all parts whereof the force of its laws extends. But this no more *makes a man a member of that society*, a perpetual subject of that common-wealth, than it would make a man a subject to another, in whose family he found it convenient to abide for some time; though, whilst he continued in it, he were obliged to comply with the laws, and submit to the government he found there. And thus we see, that *foreigners*, by living all their lives under another government, and enjoying the privileges and protection of it, though they are bound, even in conscience, to submit to its administration, as far forth as any denison; yet do not thereby come to be *subjects or members of that common-wealth*. Nothing can make any man so, but his actually entering into it by positive engagement, and express promise and compact. This is that, which I think, concerning the beginning of political societies, and that *consent which makes any one a member* of any common-wealth.

Of the Ends of Political Society and Government

If man in the state of nature be so free, as has been said; if he be absolute lord of his own person and possessions, equal to the greatest, and subject to no body, why will he part with his freedom? why will he give up this empire, and subject himself to the dominion and controul of any other power? To which it is obvious to answer, that though in the state of nature he hath such a right, yet the enjoyment of it is very uncertain, and constantly exposed to the invasion of others: for all being kings as much as he, every man his equal, and the greater part no strict observers of equity and justice, the enjoyment of the property he has in this state is very unsafe, very unsecure. This makes him willing to quit a condition, which, however free, is full of fears and continual dangers: and it is not without reason, that he seeks out, and is willing to join in society with others, who are already united, or have a mind to unite, for the mutual *preservation* of their lives, liberties and estates, which I call by the general name, *property*.

The great and *chief end*, therefore, of men's uniting into common-wealths, and putting themselves under government, *is the preservation of their property*. To which in the state of nature there are many things wanting. *First*, There wants an *established*, settled, known law, received and allowed by common consent to be the standard of right and wrong, and the common measure to decide all controversies between them: for though the law of nature be plain and intelligible to all rational creatures; yet men being biassed by their interest, as well as ignorant for want of study of it, are not apt to allow of it as a law binding to them in the application of it to their particular cases. *Secondly*, In the state of nature there wants *a known and indifferent judge*, with authority to determine all differences according to the established law: for every one in that state being both judge and executioner of the law of nature, men being partial to themselves, passion and revenge is very apt to carry them too far, and with too much heat, in their own cases; as well as negligence, and unconcernedness, to make them too remiss in other men's.

Thirdly, In the state of nature there often wants *power* to back and support the sentence when right, and to *give* it due *execution*. They who by any injustice offended, will seldom fail, where they are able, by force to make good their injustice; such resistance many times makes the punishment dangerous, and frequently destructive, to those who attempt it. Thus mankind, notwithstanding all the privileges of the state of nature, being but in an ill condition, while they remain in it, are quickly driven into society. Hence it comes to pass, that we seldom find any number of men live any time together in this state. The inconveniencies that they are therein exposed to, by the irregular and uncertain exercise of the power every man has of punishing the transgressions of others, make them take sanctuary under the established laws of government, and therein seek *the preservation of their property*. It is this makes them so willingly give up every one his single power of punishing, to be exercised by such alone, as shall be appointed to it amongst them; and by such rules as the community, or those authorized by them to that purpose, shall agree on. And in this we have the original *right and rise of both the legislative and executive power*, as well as of the governments and societies themselves.

For in the state of nature, to omit the liberty he has of innocent delights, a man has two powers.

The first is to do whatsoever he thinks fit for the preservation of himself, and others within the permission of the *law of nature*: by which law, common to them all, he and all the rest of *mankind are one community*, make up one society, distinct from all other creatures. And were it not for the corruption and vitiousness of degenerate men, there would be no need of any other; no necessity that men should separate from this great and natural community, and by positive agreements combine into smaller and divided associations.

The other power a man has in the state of nature, is the *power to punish the crimes* committed against that law. Both these he gives up, when he joins in a private, if I may so call it, or particular politic society, and incorporates into any common-wealth, separate from the rest of mankind.

The first *power*, viz. of *doing whatsoever he thought for the preservation of himself*, and the rest of mankind, *he gives up* to be regulated by laws made by the society, so far forth as the preservation of himself, and the rest of that society shall require; which laws of the society in many things confine the liberty he had by the law of nature.

Secondly, The *power of punishing he wholly gives up*, and engages his natural force (which he might before employ in the execution of the law of nature, by his own single authority, as he thought fit) to assist the executive power of the society, as the law thereof shall require: for being now in a new state, wherein he is to enjoy many conveniencies, from the labour, assistance, and society of others in the same community, as well as protection from its whole strength; he is to part also with as much of his natural liberty, in providing for himself, as the good, prosperity, and safety of the society shall require; which is not only necessary, but just, since the other members of the society do the like.

But though men, when they enter into society, give up the equality, liberty, and executive power they had in the state of nature, into the hands of the society, to be so far disposed of by the legislative, as the good of the society shall require; yet it being only with an intention in every one the better to preserve himself, his liberty and property; (for no rational creature can be supposed to change his condition with an intention to be worse) the power of the society, or *legislative* constituted by them, can *never be supposed to extend farther, than the common good*; but is obliged to secure every one's property, by providing against those three defects above mentioned, that made the state of nature so unsafe and uneasy. And so whoever has the legislative or supreme power of any common-wealth, is bound to govern by established *standing laws*, promulgated and known to the people, and not by extemporary decrees; by *indifferent* and upright *judges*, who are to decide controversies by those laws; and to employ the force of the community at home, *only in the execution of such laws*, or abroad to prevent or redress foreign injuries, and secure the community from inroads and invasion. And all this to be directed to no other *end*, but the *peace, safety*, and *public good* of the people.

Of the Extent of the Legislative Power

The great end of men's entering into society, being the enjoyment of their properties in peace and safety, and the great instrument and means of that being the laws established in that society; the *first and fundamental positive law* of all common-wealths *is the establishing of the legislative* power; as the *first and fundamental natural law*, which is to govern even the legislative itself, *is the preservation of the society*, and (as far as will consist with the public good) of every person in it. This *legislative* is not only *the supreme power* to the common-wealth, but sacred and unalterable in the hands where the community have once played it; nor can any edict of any body else, in what form soever conceived, or by what power soever backed, have the force and obligation of a *law*, which has not its *sanction from* that *legislative* which the public has chosen and appointed: for without this the law could not have that, which is absolutely necessary to its being a *law, the consent of the society*, over whom no body can have a power to make laws, but by their own consent, and by authority received from them; and therefore all the *obedience*, which by the most solemn ties any one can be obliged *to* pay, ultimately terminates in this *supreme power*, and is directed by those laws which it enacts: nor can any oaths to any foreign power whatsoever, or any domestic subordinate power, discharge any member of the society from his *obedience to the legislative*, acting pursuant to their trust; nor oblige him to any obedience contrary to the laws so enacted, or farther than they do allow; it being ridiculous to imagine one can be tied ultimately to *obey* any *power* in the society, which is not the *supreme*.

Though the *legislative*, whether placed in one or more, whether it be always in being, or only by intervals, though it be the *supreme* power in every common-wealth; yet,

First, It is *not*, nor can possibly be absolutely *arbitrary* over the lives and fortunes of the people: for it being but the joint power of every member of the society given up to that person, or assembly, which is legislator; it can be no more than those persons had in a state of nature before they entered into society, and gave up to the community: for no body can transfer to another more power than he has in himself; and no body has an absolute arbitrary power over himself, or over any other, to destroy his own life, or take away the life or property of another. A man, as has been proved, cannot subject himself to the arbitrary power of another; and having in the state of nature no arbitrary power over the life, liberty, or possession of another, but only so much as the law of nature gave him for the preservation of himself, and the rest of mankind; this is all he doth, or can give up to the common-wealth, and by it to the *legislative power*, so that the legislative can have no more than this. Their power, in the utmost bounds of it, is *limited to the public good* of the society. It is a power, that hath no other end but preserva-tion, and therefore can never have a right to destroy, enslave, or designedly to impoverish the subjects. The obligations of the law of nature cease not in society, but only in many cases are drawn closer, and have by human laws known penal-ties annexed to them, to inforce their observation. Thus the law of nature stands as an eternal rule to all men, *legislators* as well as others. The *rules* that they make for other men's actions, must, as well as their own and other men's actions, be conformable to the law of nature, i.e. to the will of God, of which that is a declaration, and the *fundamental law of nature being the preservation of mankind*, no human sanction can be good, or valid against it.

Secondly, The *legislative*, or supreme authority, cannot assume to its self a power to rule by extemporary arbitrary decrees, but *is bound to dispense justice*, and decide the rights of the subject *by promulgated standing laws, and known authorized judges*: for the law of nature being unwritten, and so no where to be found but in the minds of men, they who through passion or interest shall miscite, or misapply it, cannot so easily be convinced of their mistake where there is no established judge: and so it serves not, as it ought, to determine the rights, and fence the properties of those that live under it, especially where every one is judge, interpreter, and executioner of it too, and that in his own case: and he that has right on his side, having ordinarily but his own single strength, hath not force enough to defend himself from injuries, or to punish delinquents. To avoid these inconveniences, which disorder men's properties in the state of nature, men unite into societies, that they may have the united strength of the whole society to secure and defend their properties, and may have *standing rules* to bound it, by which every one may know what is his. To this end it is that men give up all their natural power to the society which they enter into, and the community put the legislative power into such hands as they think fit, with this trust, that they shall be governed by *declared laws*, or else their peace, quiet, and property will still be at the same uncertainty, as it was in the state of nature.

Absolute arbitrary power, or governing without *settled standing laws*, can neither of them consist with the ends of society and government, which men would not quit the freedom of the state of nature for, and tie themselves up under, were it not to preserve their lives, liberties and fortunes, and by *stated rules* of right and property to secure their peace and quiet. It cannot be supposed that they should intend, had they a power so to do, to give to any one, or more, an *absolute arbitrary power* over their persons and estates, and put a force into the magistrate's hand to execute his unlimited will arbitrarily upon them. This were to put themselves into a worse condition than the state of nature, wherein they had a liberty to defend their right against the injuries of others, and were upon equal terms of force to maintain it, whether invaded by a single man, or many in combination. . . . And therefore, whatever form the common-wealth is under, the ruling power ought to govern by *declared* and *received laws*, and not by extemporary dictates and undetermined resolutions: for then mankind will be in a far worse condition than in the state of nature, if they shall have armed one, or a few men with the joint power of a multitude, to force them to obey at pleasure the exorbitant and unlimited decrees of their sudden thoughts, or unrestrained, and till that moment unknown wills, without having any measures set down which may guide and justify their actions: for all the power the government has, being only for the good of the society, as it ought not to be *arbitrary* and at pleasure, so it ought to be exercised by *established and promulgated laws*; that both the people may know their duty, and be safe and secure within the limits of the law; and the rulers too kept within their bounds, and not be tempted, by the power they have in their hands, to employ it to such purposes, and by such measures, as they would not have known, and own not willingly.

Thirdly, The *supreme power cannot take* from any man any part of his *property* without his own consent: for the preservation of property being the end of government, and that for which men enter into society, it necessarily supposes and requires, that the people should *have property*, without which they must be supposed to lose that, by entering into society, which was the end for which they entered into it; too gross an absurdity for any man to own. *Men* therefore *in society having property*, they have such a right to the goods, which by the law of the community are their's, that no body hath a right to take their substance or any part of it from them, without their own consent: without this they have no *property* at all; for I have truly no *property* in that, which another can by right take from me, when he pleases, against my consent. Hence it is a mistake to think, that the *supreme or legislative power* of any common-wealth, can do what it will, and dispose of the estates of the subject *arbitrarily*, or take any part of them at pleasure. This is not much to be feared in governments where the *legislative* consists, wholly or in part, in assemblies which are variable, whose members, upon the dissolution of the assembly, are subjects under the common laws of their country, equally with the rest. But in governments, where the *legislative* is in one lasting assembly always in being, or in one man, as in absolute monarchies, there is danger still, that they will think themselves to have a distinct interest from the rest of the community; and so will be apt to increase their own riches and power, by taking what they think fit from the people: for a man's *property* is not at all secure, tho' there be good and equitable laws to set the bounds of it between him and his fellow subjects, if he who commands those subjects have power to take from any private man, what part he pleases of his *property*, and use and dispose of it as he thinks good.

But *government*, into whatsoever hands it is put, being, as I have before shewed, intrusted with this condition, and *for this end*, that men might have and secure their *properties*; the prince, or senate, however it may have power to make laws, for the regulating of *property* between the subjects one amongst another, yet can never have a power to take to themselves the whole, or any part of the subjects *property*, without their own consent: for this would be in effect to leave them no *property* at all. And to let us see, that even *absolute power*, where it is necessary, is *not arbitrary* by being absolute, but is still limited by that reason, and confined to those ends, which required it in some cases to be absolute, we need look no farther than the common practice of martial discipline: for the preservation of the army, and in it of the whole common-wealth, requires an *absolute obedience* to the command of every superior officer, and it is justly death to disobey or dispute the most dangerous or unreasonable of them; but yet we see, that neither the serjeant, that could command a soldier to march up to the mouth of a cannon, or stand in a breach, where he is almost sure to perish, can command that soldier to give him one penny of his money; nor the *general*, that can condemn him to death for deserting his post, or for not obeying the most desperate orders, can yet, with all his *absolute power* of life and death, dispose of one farthing of that soldier's estate, or seize one jot of his goods; whom yet he can command any thing, and hang for the least disobedience; because such a blind obedience is necessary to that end, for which the commander has his power, *viz.* the preservation of the rest; but the disposing of his goods has nothing to do with it.

It is true, governments cannot be supported without great charge, and it is fit every one who enjoys his share of the protection, should pay out of his estate his proportion for the maintenance of it. But still it must be with his own consent, i.e. the consent of the majority, giving it either by themselves, or their representatives chosen by them: for if any one shall claim a *power to lay* and levy *taxes* on the people, by his own authority, and without such consent of the people, he thereby invades the *fundamental law of property*, and subverts the end of government: for what property have I in that, which another may by right take, when he pleases, to himself?

Fourthly, The *legislative cannot transfer the power of making laws* to any other hands: for it being but a delegated power from the people, they who have it cannot pass it over to others. The people alone can appoint the form of the commonwealth, which is by constituting the legislative, and appointing in whose hands that shall be. And when the people have said, We will submit to rules, and be governed by *laws* made by such men, and in such forms, no body else can say other men shall make *laws* for them; nor can the people be bound by any *laws*, but such as are enacted by those whom they have chosen, and authorized to make *laws* for them. The power of the *legislative*, being derived from the people by a positive voluntary grant and institution, can be no other than what that positive grant conveyed, which being only to make *laws*, and not to make *legislators*, the *legislative* can have no power to transfer their authority of making laws, and place it in other hands.

These are the *bounds* which the trust, that is put in them by the society, and the law of God and nature, have *set to the legislative* power of every common-wealth, in all forms of government.

First, They are to given by *promulgated established laws*, not to be varied in particular cases, but to have one rule for rich and poor, for the favourite at court, and the country man at plough.

Secondly, These *laws* also ought to be designed *for* no other end ultimately, but *the good of the people*.

Thirdly, They must *not raise taxes* on the *property of the people, without the consent of the people*, given by themselves, or their deputies. And this properly concerns only such governments where the *legislative* is always in being, or at least where the people have not reserved any part of the legislative to deputies, to be from time to time chosen by themselves.

Fourthly, The *legislative* neither must *nor can transfer the power of making laws* to any body else, or place it any where, but where the people have.

Of the Legislative, Executive, and Federative Power of the Common-wealth

The *legislative* power is that, which has a right *to direct how the force of the common-wealth* shall be employed for preserving the community and the members of it. But because those laws which are constantly to be executed, and whose force is always to continue, may be made in a little time; therefore there is no need, that the *legislative* should be always in being, not having always business to do. And because it may be too great a temptation to human frailty, apt to grasp at power, for the same persons, who have the power of making laws, to have also in their hands the power to execute them, whereby they may exempt themselves from obedience to the laws they make, and suit the law, both in its making, and execution, to their own private advantage, and thereby come to have a distinct interest from the rest of the community, contrary to the end of society and government: therefore in well-ordered common-wealths, where the good of the whole is so considered, as it ought, the *legislative* power is put into the hands of divers persons, who duly assembled, have by themselves, or jointly with others, a power to make laws, which when they have done, being separated again, they are themselves subject to the laws they have made; which is a new and near tie upon them, to take care, that they make them for the public good.

But because the laws, that are at once, and in a short time made, have a constant and lasting force, and need a *perpetual execution*, or an attendance thereunto; therefore it is necessary there should be a *power always in being*, which should see to the *execution* of the laws that are made, and remain in force. And thus the *legislative* and *executive power* come often to be separated.

There is another *power* in every common-wealth, which one may call *natural*, because it is that which answers to the power every man naturally had before he entered into society: for though in a common-wealth the members of it are distinct persons still in reference to one another, and as such are governed by the laws of the society; yet in reference to the rest of mankind, they make one body, which is, as every member of it before was, still in the state of nature with the rest of mankind. Hence it is, that the controversies that happen between any man of the society with those that are out of it, are managed by the public; and an injury done to a member of their body, engages the whole in the reparation of it. So that under this consideration, the whole community is one body in the state of nature, in respect of all other states or persons out of its community.

This therefore contains the power of war and peace, leagues and alliances, and all the transactions, with all persons and communities without the common-wealth, and may be called *Federative*, if one pleases. So the thing be understood, I am indifferent as to the name.

These two powers, *executive* and *federative*, though they be really distinct in themselves, yet one comprehending the *execution* of the municipal laws of the society *within* its self, upon all that are parts of it; the other the management of the *security and interest of the public without*, with all those that it may receive benefit or damage from, yet they are always almost united. And though this *federative power* in the well or ill management of it be of great moment to the common-wealth, yet it is much less capable to be directed by antecedent, standing, positive laws, than the *executive*; and so must necessarily be left to the prudence and wisdom of those, whose hands it is in, to be managed for the public good: for the *laws* that concern subjects one amongst another, being to direct their actions, may well enough *precede* them. But what is to be done in reference to *foreigners*, depending much upon their actions, and the variation of designs and interests, must be *left* in great part *to* the *prudence* of those, who have this power committed to them, to be managed by the best of their skill, for the advantage of the common-wealth. . . .

Of the Subordination of the Powers of the Common-wealth

Though in a constituted common-wealth, standing upon its own basis, and acting according to its own nature, that is, acting for the preservation of the community, there can be but *one supreme power*, which is *the legislative*, to which all the rest are and must be subordinate, yet the legislative being only a fiduciary power to act for certain ends, there remains still *in the people a supreme power to remove or alter the legislative*, when they find the *legislative* act contrary to the trust reposed in them: for all *power given with trust* for the attaining an *end*, being limited by that end, whenever that *end* is manifestly neglected, or opposed, the *trust* must necessarily be *forfeited*, and the power devolve into the hands of those that gave it, who may place it anew where they shall think best for their safety and security. And thus the *community* perpetually *retains a supreme power* of saving themselves from the attempts and designs of any body, even of their legislators, whenever they shall be so foolish, or so wicked, as to lay and carry on designs against the liberties and properties of the subject: for no man or society of men, having a power to deliver up their *preservation*, or consequently the means of it, to the absolute will and arbitrary dominion of another; when ever any one shall go about to bring them into such a slavish condition, they will always have a right to preserve, what they have not a power to part with; and to rid themselves of those, who invade this fundamental, sacred, and unalterable law of *self-preservation*, for which they entered into society. And thus the *community* may be said in this respect to be *always the supreme power*, but not as considered under any form of government, because this power of the people can never take place till the government be dissolved.

In all cases, whilst the government subsists, the *legislative is the supreme power*: for what can give laws to another, must needs be superior to him; and since the legislative is no otherwise legislative of the society, but by the right it has to make laws for all the parts, and for every member of the society, prescribing rules to their actions, and giving power of execution, where they are transgressed, the *legislative* must needs be the *supreme*, and all other powers, in any members or parts of the society, derived from and subordinate to it. . . .

Of Tyranny

As usurpation is the exercise of power, which another hath a right to; so *tyranny is the exercise of power beyond right*, which no body can have a right to. And this is making use of the power any one has in his hands, not for the good of those who are under it, but for his own private separate advantage. When the governor, however intitled, makes not the law, but his will, the rule; and his commands and actions are not directed to the preservation of the properties of his people, but the satisfaction of his own ambition, revenge, covetousness, or any other irregular passion.

If one can doubt this to be truth, or reason, because it comes from the obscure hand of a subject, I hope the authority of a king will make it pass with him. King *James* the first, in his speech to the parliament, 1603, tells them thus, *I will ever prefer the weal of the public, and of the whole commonwealth, in making of good laws and constitutions, to any particular and private ends of mine; thinking ever the wealth and weal of the commonwealth to be my greatest weal and worldly felicity; a point wherein a lawful king doth directly differ from a tyrant: for I do acknowledge, that the special and greatest point of difference that is between a rightful king and an usurping tyrant, is this, that whereas the proud and ambitious tyrant doth think his kingdom and people are only ordained for satisfaction of his desires and unreasonable appetites, the righteous and just king doth by the con-trary acknowledge himself to be ordained for the procuring of the wealth and property of his people.* And again, in his speech to the parliament, 1609, he hath these words, *The king binds himself by a double oath, to the observation of the fundamental laws of his kingdom; tacitly, as by being a king, and so bound to protect as well the people, as the laws of his kingdom; and expressly, by his oath at his coronation; so as every just king, in a settled kingdom, is bound to observe that action made to his people, by his laws, in framing his government agreeable thereunto, according to that paction which God made with* Noah *after the deluge. Hereafter, seed-time and harvest, and cold and heat, and summer and winter, and day and night, shall not cease while the earth remaineth. And therefore a king governing in a settled kingdom, leaves to be a king, and degenerates into a tyrant, as soon as he leaves off to rule according to his laws.* And a little after, *Therefore all kings that are not tyrants, or perjured, will be glad to bound themselves within the limits of their laws; and they that persuade them the contrary, are vipers, and pests both against them and the commonwealth.* Thus that learned king, who well understood the notion of things, makes the difference betwixt a *king* and a *tyrant* to consist only in this, that one makes the laws the bounds of his power, and the good of the public, the end of his government; the other makes all give way to his own will and appetite.

It is a mistake, to think this fault is proper only to monarchies; other forms of government are liable to it, as well as that: for wherever the power, that is put in any hands for the government of the people, and the preservation of their proper-ties, is applied to other ends, and made use of to impoverish, harass, or subdue them to the arbitrary and irregular commands of those that have it; there it pres-ently becomes *tyranny*, whether those that thus use it are one or many. . . .

Where-ever law ends, tyranny begins, if the law be transgressed to another's harm; and whosoever in authority exceeds the power given him by the law, and makes use of the force he has under his command, to compass that upon the subject, which the law allows not, ceases in that to be a magistrate; and, acting without authority, may be opposed, as any other man, who by force invades the right of another. This is acknowledged in subordinate magistrates. He that hath authority to seize my person in the street, may be opposed as a thief and a robber, if he endeavours to break into my house to execute a writ, notwithstanding that I know he has such a warrant, and such a legal authority, as will impower him to arrest me abroad. And why this should not hold in the highest, as well as in the most inferior magistrate, I would gladly be informed. Is it reasonable, that the eldest brother, because he has the greatest part of his father's estate, should thereby have a right to take away any of his younger brothers portions? or that a rich man, who possessed a whole country, should from thence have a right to seize, when he pleased, the cottage and garden of his poor neighbour? The being rightfully possessed of great power and riches, exceedingly beyond the greatest part of the sons of *Adam*, is so far from being an excuse, much less a reason, for rapine and oppression, which the endamaging another without authority is, that it is a great aggravation of it: for the exceeding the bounds of authority is no more a right in a great, than in a petty officer; no more justifiable in a king than a constable; but is so much the worse in him, in that he has more trust put in him, has already a much greater share than the rest of his brethren, and is supposed, from the advantages of his education, employment, and counsellors, to be more knowing in the measures of right and wrong.

May the *commands* then *of a prince be opposed*? may he be resisted as often as any one shall find himself aggrieved, and but imagine he has not right done him? This will unhinge and overturn all polities, and instead of government and order, leave nothing but anarchy and confusion.

To this I answer, that *force* is to be *opposed* to nothing, but to unjust and unlawful *force*; whoever makes any opposition in any other case, draws on himself a just condemnation both from God and man; and so no such danger or confusion will follow. . . .

Of the Dissolution of Government

He that will with any clearness speak of the *dissolution of government*, ought in the first place to distinguish between the *dissolution of the society* and the *dissolution of the government*. That which makes the community, and brings men out of the loose state of nature, into *one politic society*, is the agreement which every one has with the rest to incorporate, and act as one body, and so be one distinct common-wealth. The usual, and almost only way whereby *this union is dissolved*, is the inroad of foreign force making a conquest upon them: for in that case, (not being able to maintain and support themselves, as *one entire* and *independent body*) the union belonging to that body which consisted therein, must necessarily cease, and so every one return to the state he was in before, with a liberty to shift for himself, and provide for his own safety, as he thinks fit, in some other society. Whenever the *society is dissolved*, it is certain the government of that society cannot remain. Thus conquerors swords often cut up governments by the roots, and mangle societies to pieces, separating the subdued or scattered multitude from the protection of, and dependence on, that society which ought to have preserved them from violence. The world is too well instructed in, and too forward to allow of, this way of dissolving of governments, to need any more to be said of it; and there wants not much argument to prove, that where the *society is dissolved*, the government cannot remain; that being as impossible, as for the frame of an house to subsist when the materials of it are scattered and dissipated by a whirl-wind, or jumbled into a confused heap by an earthquake.

Besides this over-turning from without, *governments are dissolved from within*, *First*, When the *legislative is altered*. Civil society being a state of peace, amongst those who are of it, from whom the state of war is excluded by the umpirage, which they have provided in their legislative, for the ending all differences that may arise amongst any of them, it is in their *legislative*, that the members of a common-wealth are united, and combined together into one coherent living body. This *is the soul that gives form, life, and unity*, to the commonwealth: from hence the several members have their mutual influence, sympathy, and connexion: and therefore, when the *legislative* is broken, or *dissolved*, dissolution and death follows: for the *essence and union of the society* consisting in having one will, the legislative, when once established by the majority, has the declaring, and as it were keeping of that will. The *constitution of the legislative* is the first and fundamental act of society, whereby provision is made for the *continuation of their union*, under the direction of persons, and bonds of laws, made by persons authorized thereunto, by the consent and appointment of the people, without which no one man, or number of men, amongst them, can have authority of making laws that shall be binding to the rest. When any one, or more, shall take upon them to make laws, whom the people have not appointed so to do, they make laws without authority, which the people are not therefore bound to obey; by which means they come again to be out of subjection, and may constitute to themselves a *new legislative*, as they think best, being in full liberty to resist the force of those, who without authority would impose any thing upon them. Every one is at the disposure of his own will, when those who had, by the delegation of the society, the declaring of the public will, are excluded from it, and others usurp the place, who have no such authority or delegation.

This being usually brought about by such in the common-wealth who misuse the power they have; it is hard to consider it a right, and know at whose door to lay it, without knowing the form of government in which it happens. Let us suppose then the legislative placed in the concurrence of three distinct persons.

(1.) A single hereditary person, having the constant, supreme, executive power, and with it the power of convoking and dissolving the other two within certain periods of time.

(2.) An assembly of hereditary nobility.

(3.) An assembly of representatives chosen, *pro tempore*, by the people. Such a form of government supposed, it is evident,

First, That when such a single person, or prince, sets up his own arbitrary will in place of the laws, which are the will of the society, declared by the legislative, then the *legislative is changed:* for that being in effect the legislative, whose rules and laws are put in execution, and required to be obeyed; when other laws are set up, and other rules pretended, and inforced, than what the legislative, constituted by the society, have enacted, it is plain that the *legislative is changed.* Whoever introduces new laws, not being thereunto authorized by the fundamental appointment of the society, or subverts the old, disowns and overturns the power by which they were made, and so sets up a *new legislative*.

Secondly, When the prince hinders the legislative from assembling in its due time, or from acting freely, pursuant to those ends for which it was constituted, the *legislative is altered*: for it is not a certain number of men, no, nor their meeting, unless they have also freedom of debating, and leisure of perfecting, what is for the good of the society, wherein the legislative consists: when these are taken away or altered, so as to deprive the society of the due exercise of their power, the *legislative* is truly altered; for it is not names that constitute governments, but the use and exercise of those powers that were intended to accompany them; so that he, who takes away the freedom, or hinders the acting of the legislative in its due seasons, in effect takes *away the legislative*, and *puts an end to the government*.

Thirdly, When, by the arbitrary power of the prince, the electors, or ways of election, are altered, without the consent, and contrary to the common interest of the people, there also the *legislative is altered*: for, if others than those whom the society hath authorized thereunto, do chuse, or in another way than what the society hath prescribed, those chosen are not the legislative appointed by the people.

Fourthly, The delivery also of the people into the subjection of a foreign power, either by the prince, or by the legislative, is certainly a *change of the legislative*, and so a *dissolution of the government*: for the end why people entered into society being to be preserved one intire, free, independent society, to be governed by its own laws; this is lost, whenever they are given up into the power of another.

Why, in such a constitution as this, the *dissolution of the government* in these cases is to be imputed to the prince, is evident; because he, having the force, treasure and offices of the state to employ, and often persuading himself, or being flattered by others, that as supreme magistrate he is uncapable of controul; he alone is in a condition to make great advances toward such changes, under pretence of lawful authority, and has it in his hands to terrify or suppress opposers, as factious, seditious, and enemies to the government: whereas no other part of the legislative, or people, is capable by themselves to attempt any alteration of the legislative, without open and visible rebellion, apt enough to be taken notice of, which, when it prevails, produces effects very little different from foreign conquest. Besides, the prince in such a form of government, having the power of dissolving the other parts of the legislative, and thereby rendering them private persons, they can never in opposition to him, or without his concurrence, alter the legislative by a law, his consent being necessary to give any of their decrees that sanction. But yet, so far as the other parts of the legislative any way contribute to any attempt upon the government, and do either promote, or not, what lies in them, hinder such designs, they are guilty, and partake in this, which is certainly the greatest crime men can be guilty of one towards another.

There is one way more whereby such a government may be dissolved, and that is, when he who has the supreme executive power, neglects and abandons that charge, so that the laws already made can no longer be put in execution. This is demonstratively to reduce all to anarchy, and so effectually *to dissolve the government*: for laws not being made for themselves, but to be, by their execution, the bonds of the society, to keep every part of the body politic in its due place and function; when that totally ceases, the *government* visibly *ceases*, and the people become a confused multitude, without order or connexion. Where there is no longer the administration of justice, for the securing of men's rights, nor any remaining power within the community to direct the force, or provide for the necessities of the public, there certainly is *no government left*. Where the laws cannot be executed, it is all one as if there were no laws; and a government without laws is, I suppose, a mystery in politics, unconceivable to human capacity, and inconsistent with human society.

In these and the like cases, *when the government is dissolved*, the people are at liberty to provide for themselves, by erecting a new legislative, differing from the other, by the change of persons, or form, or both, as they shall find it most for their safety and good: for the *society* can never, by the fault of another, lose the native and original right it has to preserve itself, which can only be done by a settled legislative, and a fair and impartial execution of the laws made by it. But the state of mankind is not so miserable that they are not capable of using this remedy, till it be too late to look for any. To tell *people* they *may provide for themselves*, by erecting a new legislative, when by oppression, artifice, or being delivered over to a foreign power, their old one is gone, is only to tell them, they may expect relief when it is too late, and the evil is past cure. This is in effect no more than to bid them first be slaves, and then to take care of their liberty; and when their chains are on, tell them, they may act like freemen. This, if barely so, is rather mockery than relief; and men can never be secure from tyranny, if there be no means to escape it till they are perfectly under it: and therefore it is, that they have not only a right to get out of it, but to prevent it.

There is therefore, secondly, another way whereby *governments are dissolved*, and that is, when the legislative, or the prince, either of them, act contrary to their trust.

First, The *legislative acts against the trust* reposed in them, when they endeavour to invade the property of the subject, and to make themselves, or any part of the community, masters, or arbitrary disposers of the lives, liberties, or fortunes of the people.

The reason why men enter into society, is the preservation of their property; and the end why they chuse and authorize a legislative, is, that there may be laws made, and rules set, as guards and fences to the properties of all the members of the society, to limit the power, and moderate the dominion, of every part and member of the society: for since it can never be supposed to be the will of the society, that the legislative should have a power to destroy that which every one designs to secure, by entering into society, and for which the people submitted themselves to legislators of their own making; whenever the *legislators endeavour to take away, and destroy the property of the people*, or to reduce them to slavery under arbitrary power, they put themselves into a state of war with the people, who are thereupon absolved from any farther obedience, and are left to the common refuge, which God hath provided for all men, against force and violence. Whensoever therefore the *legislative* shall transgress this fundamental rule of society; and either by ambition, fear, folly or corruption, *endeavour to grasp* themselves, *or put into the hands of any other, an absolute power* over the lives, liberties, and estates of the people; by this breach of trust they *forfeit the power* the people had put into their hands for quite contrary ends, and it devolves to the people, who have a right to resume their original liberty, and, by the establishment of a new legislative (such as they shall think fit) provide for their own safety and security, which is the end for which they are in society. What I have said here, concerning the legislative in general, holds true also concerning the supreme executor, who having a double trust put in him, both to have a part in the legislative, and the supreme execution of the law, acts against both, when he goes about to set up his own arbitrary will as the law of the society. He *acts* also *contrary to his trust*, when he either employs the force, treasure, and offices of the society, to corrupt the *representatives*, and gain them to his purposes; or openly preengages the *electors*, and prescribes to their choice, such, whom he has, by sollicitations, threats, promises, or otherwise, won to his designs; and employs them to bring in such, who have promised before-hand what to vote, and what to enact. Thus to regulate candidates and electors, and new-model the ways of election, what is it but to cut up the government by the roots, and poison the very fountain of public security? for the people having reserved to themselves the choice of their *representatives*, as the fence to their properties, could do it for no other end, but that they might always be freely chosen, and so chosen, freely act, and advise, as the necessity of the common-wealth, and the public good should, upon examination, and mature debate, be judged to require. This, those who give their votes before they hear the debate, and have weighed the reasons on all sides, are not capable of doing. To prepare such an assembly as this, and endeavour to set up the declared abettors of his own will, for the true *representatives* of the people, and the law-makers of the society, is certainly as great a *breach of trust*, and as perfect a declaration of a design to subvert the government, as is possible to be met with. To which, if one shall add rewards and punishments visibly employed to the same end, and all the arts of perverted law made use of, to take off and destroy all that stand in the way of such a design, and will not comply and consent to betray the liberties of their country, it will be past doubt what is doing. What power they ought to have in the society, who thus employ it contrary to the trust went along with it in its first institution, is easy to determine; and one cannot but see, that he, who has once attempted any such thing as this, cannot any longer be trusted.

To this perhaps it will be said, that the people being ignorant, and always discontented, to lay the foundation of government in the unsteady opinion and uncertain humour of the people, is to expose it to certain ruin; and *no government will be able long to subsist*, if the people may set up a new legislative, whenever they take offence at the old one. To this I answer, Quite the contrary. People are not so easily got out of their old forms, as some are apt to suggest. They are hardly to be prevailed with to amend the acknowledged faults in the frame they have been accustomed to. And if there be any original defects, or adventitious ones introduced by time, or corruption; it is not an easy thing to get them changed, even when all the world sees there is an opportunity for it. This slowness and aversion in the people to quit their old constitutions, has, in the many revolutions which have been seen in this kingdom, in this and former ages, still kept us to, or, after some interval of fruitless attempts, still brought us back again to our old legislative of king, lords and commons: and whatever provocations have made the crown be taken from some of our princes heads, they never carried the people so far as to place it in another line.

But it will be said, this *hypothesis* lays a *ferment for* frequent *rebellion*. To which I answer,

First, No more than any other *hypothesis*: for when the people are made miserable, and find themselves *exposed to the ill usage of arbitrary power*, cry up their governors, as much as you will, for sons of *Jupiter*; let them be sacred and divine, descended, or authorized from heaven; give them out for whom or what you please, the same will happen. *The people generally ill treated*, and contrary to right, will be ready upon any occasion to ease themselves of a burden that sits heavy upon them. They will wish, and seek for the opportunity, which in the change, weakness and accidents of human affairs, seldom delays long to offer itself. He must have lived but a little while in the world, who has not seen examples of this in his time; and he must have read very little, who cannot produce examples of it in all sorts of governments in the world.

Secondly, I answer, such *revolutions happen* not upon every little mismanagement in public affairs. *Great mistakes* in the ruling part, many wrong and inconvenient laws, and all the *slips* of human frailty, will be *born by the people* without mutiny or murmur. But if a long train of abuses, prevarications and artifices, all tending the same way, make the design visible to the people, and they cannot but feel what they lie under, and see whither they are going; it is not to be wondered, that they should then rouze themselves, and endeavour to put the rule into such hands which may secure to them the ends for which government was at first erected; and without which, ancient names, and specious forms, are so far from being better, that they are much worse, than the state of nature, or pure anarchy; the inconveniencies being all as great and as near, but the remedy farther off and more difficult.

Thirdly, I answer, that *this doctrine* of a power in the people of providing for their safety a-new, by a new legislative, when their legislators have acted contrary to their trust, by invading their property, is *the best fence against rebellion*, and the probablest means to hinder it: for *rebellion* being an opposition, not to persons, but authority, which is founded only in the constitutions and laws of the government; those, whoever they be, who by force break through, and by force justify their violation of them, are truly and properly *rebels*: for when men, by entering into society and civil-government, have excluded force, and introduced laws for the preservation of property, peace, and unity amongst themselves, those who set up force again in opposition to the laws, do *rebellare*, that is, bring back again the state of war, and are properly rebels: which they who are in power (by the pretence they have to authority, the temptation of force they have in their hands, and the flattery of those about them) being likeliest to do; the properest way to prevent the evil, is to shew them the danger and injustice of it, who are under the greatest temptation to run into it.

In both the fore-mentioned cases, when either the legislative is changed, or the legislators act contrary to the end for which they were constituted; those who are guilty are *guilty of rebellion*: for if any one by force takes away the established legislative of any society, and the laws by them made, pursuant to their trust, he thereby takes away the umpirage, which every one had consented to, for a peaceable decision of all their controversies, and a bar to the state of war amongst them. They, who remove, or change the legislative, take away this decisive power, which no body can have, but by the appointment and consent of the people; and so destroying the authority which the people did, and no body else can set up, and introducing a power which the people hath not authorized, they actually *introduce a state of war*, which is that of force without authority: and thus, by removing the legislative established by the society (in whose decisions the people acquiesced and united, as to that of their own will) they untie the knot, and *expose the people a-new to the state of war*. And if those, who by force take away the legislative, are *rebels*, the *legislators* themselves, as has been shewn, can be no less esteemed so; when they, who were set up for the protection, and preservation of the people, their liberties and properties, shall by force invade and endeavour to take them away; and so they putting themselves into a state of war with those who made them the protectors and guardians of their peace, are properly, and with the greatest aggravation, *rebellantes*, rebels.

But if they, who say *it lays a foundation for rebellion*, mean that it may occasion civil wars, or intestine broils, to tell the people they are absolved from obedience when illegal attempts are made upon their liberties or properties, and may oppose the unlawful violence of those who were their magistrates, when they invade their properties contrary to the trust put in them; and that therefore this doctrine is not to be allowed, being so destructive to the peace of the world: they may as well say, upon the same ground, that honest men may not oppose robbers or pirates, because this may occasion disorder or bloodshed. If any *mischief* come in such cases, it is not to be charged upon him who defends his own right, but *on him that invades* his neighbours. If the innocent honest man must quietly quit all he has, for peace sake, to him who will lay violent hands upon it, I desire it may be considered, what a kind of peace there will be in the world, which consists only in violence and rapine; and which is to be maintained only for the benefit of robbers and oppressors. Who would not think it an admirable peace betwix the mighty and the mean, when the lamb, without resistance, yielded his throat to be torn by the imperious wolf? *Polyphemus*'s den gives us a perfect pattern of such a peace, and such a government, wherein *Ulysses* and his companions had nothing to do, but quietly to suffer themselves to be devoured. And no doubt *Ulysses*, who was a prudent man, preached up *passive obedience*, and exhorted them to a quiet submission, by representing to them of what concernment peace was to mankind; and by shewing the inconveniences might happen, if they should offer to resist *Polyphemus*, who had now the power over them.

The end of government is the good of mankind; and which is *best for mankind*, that the people should be always exposed to the boundless will of tyranny, or that the rulers should be sometimes liable to be opposed, when they grow exorbitant in the use of their power, and employ it for the destruction, and not the preservation of the properties of their people?

Nor let any one say, that mischief can arise from hence, as often as it shall please a busy head, or turbulent spirit, to desire the alteration of the government.

It is true, such men may stir, whenever they please; but it will be only to their own just ruin and perdition: for till the mischief be grown general, and the ill designs of the rulers become visible, or their attempts sensible to the greater part, the people, who are more disposed to suffer than right themselves by resistance, are not apt to stir. The examples of particular injustice, or oppression of here and there an unfortunate man, moves them not. But if they universally have a persuasion, grounded upon manifest evidence, that designs are carrying on against their liberties, and the general course and tendency of things cannot but give them strong suspicions of the evil intention of their governors, who is to be blamed for it? Who can help it, if they, who might avoid it, bring themselves into this suspicion? Are the people to be blamed, if they have the sense of rational creatures, and can think of things no otherwise than as they find and feel them? And is it not rather *their fault*, who put things into such a posture, that they would not have them thought to be as they are? I grant, that the pride, ambition, and turbulency of private men have sometimes caused great disorders in common-wealths, and factions have been fatal to states and kingdoms. But whether *the mischief* hath *oftener* begun *in the peoples wantonness*, and a desire to cast off the lawful authority of their rulers, or *in the rulers insolence*, and endeavours to get and exercise an arbitrary power over their people; whether oppression, or disobedience, gave the first rise to the disorder, I leave it to impartial history to determine. This I am sure, whoever, either ruler or subject, by force goes about to invade the rights of either prince or people, and lays the foundation for *overturning* the constitution and frame of *any just government*, is highly guilty of the greatest crime, I think, a man is capable of, being to answer for all those mischiefs of blood, rapine, and desolation, which the breaking to pieces of governments bring on a country. And he who does it, is justly to be esteemed the common enemy and pest of mankind, and is to be treated accordingly. . . .

To conclude, The *power that every individual gave the society*, when he entered into it, can never revert to the individuals again, as long as the society lasts, but will always remain in the community; because without this there can be no community, no common-wealth, which is contrary to the original agreement: so also when the society hath placed the legislative in any assembly of men, to continue in them and their successors, with direction and authority for providing such successors, *the legislative can never revert to the people* whilst that government lasts; because having provided a legislative with power to continue for ever, they have given up their political power to the legislative, and cannot resume it. But if they have set limits to the duration of their legislative, and made this supreme power in any person, or assembly, only temporary; or else, when by the miscarriages of those in authority, it is forfeited; upon the forfeiture, or at the determination of the time set, *it reverts to the society*, and the people have a right to act as supreme, and continue the legislative in themselves; or erect a new form, or under the old form place it in new hands, as they think good.

13

Jean-Jacques Rousseau
Selections

Jean-Jacques Rousseau (1712–1778) had little formal education but achieved notoriety as a philosopher, novelist, and moralist in an age of social transformation and political upheaval. Rousseau was born in Geneva and grew up in an artisanal milieu which deeply affected his understanding of politics. Following Rousseau's conversion to Roman Catholicism, he briefly served as a tutor, gaining a lifelong interest in education. He set out for Paris in 1742 and quickly became involved with the leading figures of the Enlightenment, such as Diderot, and was a contributor to the Encyclopedie. *Rousseau's political contributions to the debates taking place in Paris were numerous, including* The Discourse on the Sciences and the Arts *(1750), which attacked the idea that learning and virtue were one. Rousseau continued his critique of society in a series of literary and political works, notably* The Discourse on the Origin of Inequality *(1755),* Julie, or The Nouvelle Heloise *(1761), a runaway best seller which purported to tell the aristocracy how to reform itself,* Emile *(1762), a treatise on education, and his* The Social Contract *(1762). Rousseau believed that moral life for man begins with the emergence of society, yet he sees the problem of freedom in society as central, and vigorously denounces tyranny in the public sphere. Rousseau's goal was to find a form of association in which "each one uniting with all obeys, however, only himself and remains as free as before." Rousseau was essentially a radical democrat in that he understood sovereignty as always residing with the people as a whole. He distinguished the supreme political power of citizens from the government, which is power delegated by the people.*

ON THE SOCIAL CONTRACT

Book I

I want to inquire whether there can be a legitimate and reliable rule of administration in the civil order, taking men as they are and laws as they can be. I shall try always to reconcile in this research what right permits with what interest prescribes, so that justice and utility are not at variance.

I start in without proving the importance of my subject. It will be asked if I am a prince or a legislator to write about politics. I reply that I am neither, and that is why I write about politics. If I were a prince or a legislator, I would not waste my time saying what has to be done. I would do it, or keep silent.

Born a citizen of a free State, and a member of the sovereign, the right to vote there is enough to impose on me the duty of learning about public affairs, no matter how feeble the influence of my voice may be. And I am happy, every time I meditate about governments, always to find in my research new reasons to love that of my country!

Subject of This First Book

Man was/is born free, and everywhere he is in chains. One who believes himself the master of others is nonetheless a greater slave than they. How did this change occur? I do not know. What can make it legitimate? I believe I can answer this question.

If I were to consider only force and the effect it produces, I would say that as long as a people is constrained to obey and does so, it does well; as soon as it can shake off the yoke and does so, it does even better. For in recovering its freedom by means of the same right used to steal it, either the people is justified in taking it back, or those who took it away were not justified in doing so. But the social order is a sacred right that serves as a basis for all the others. However, this right does not come from nature; it is therefore based on conventions. The problem is to know what these conventions are. Before coming to that, I should establish what I have just asserted.

On the Social Compact

I assume that men have reached the point where obstacles to their self-preservation in the state of nature prevail by their resistance over the forces each individual can use to maintain himself in that state. Then that primitive state can no longer subsist and the human race would perish if it did not change its way of life.

Now since men cannot engender new forces, but merely unite and direct existing ones, they have no other means of self-preservation except to form, by aggregation, a sum of forces that can prevail over the resistance; set them to work by a single motivation; and make them act in concert.

This sum of forces can arise only from the cooperation of many. But since each man's force and freedom are the primary instruments of his self-preservation, how is he to engage them without harming himself and without neglecting the cares he owes to himself? In the context of my subject, this difficulty can be stated in these terms:

"Find a form of association that defends and protects the person and goods of each associate with all the common force, and by means of which each one, uniting with all, nevertheless obeys only himself and remains as free as before." This is the fundamental problem which is solved by the social contract.

The clauses of this contract are so completely determined by the nature of the act that the slightest modification would render them null and void. So that although they may never have been formally pronounced, they are everywhere the same, everywhere tacitly accepted and recognized, until the social compact is violated, at which point each man recovers his original rights and resumes his natural freedom, thereby losing the conventional freedom for which he renounced it.

Properly understood, all of these clauses come down to a single one, namely the total alienation of each associate, with all his rights, to the whole community. For first of all, since each one gives his entire self, the condition is equal for everyone, and since the condition is equal for everyone, no one has an interest in making it burdensome for the others.

Furthermore, as the alienation is made without reservation, the union is as perfect as it can be, and no associate has anything further to claim. For if some rights were left to private individuals, there would be no common superior who could judge between them and the public. Each man being his own judge on some point would soon claim to be so on all; the state of nature would subsist and the association would necessarily become tyrannical or ineffectual.

Finally, as each gives himself to all, he gives himself to no one; and since there is no associate over whom one does not acquire the same right one grants him over oneself, one gains the equivalent of everything one loses, and more force to preserve what one has.

If, then, everything that is not of the essence of the social compact is set aside, one will find that it can be reduced to the following terms. *Each of us puts his person and all his power in common under the supreme direction of the general will; and in a body we receive each member as an indivisible part of the whole.*

Instantly, in place of the private person of each contracting party, this act of association produces a moral and collective body, composed of as many members as there are voices in the assembly, which receives from this same act its unity, its common *self*, its life, and its will. This public person, formed then, when the voice of duty replaces physical impulse and right replaces appetite, does man, who until that time only considered himself, find himself forced to act upon other principles and to consult his reason before heeding his inclinations. Although in this state he deprives himself of several advantages given him by nature, he gains such great ones, his faculties are exercised and developed, his ideas broadened, his feelings ennobled, and his whole soul elevated to such a point that if the abuses of this new condition did not often degrade him beneath the condition he left, he ought ceaselessly to bless the happy moment that tore him away from it forever, and that changed him from a stupid, limited animal into an intelligent being and a man.

Let us reduce the pros and cons to easily compared terms. What man loses by the social contract is his natural freedom and an unlimited right to everything that tempts him and that he can get; what he gains is civil freedom and the proprietorship of everything he possesses. In order not to be mistaken about these compensations, one must distinguish carefully between natural freedom, which is limited only by the force of the individual, and civil freedom, which is limited by the general will; and between possession, which is only the effect of force or the right of the first occupant, and property, which can only be based on a positive title.

To the foregoing acquisitions of the civil state could be added moral freedom, which alone makes man truly the master of himself. For the impulse of appetite alone is slavery, and obedience to the law one has prescribed for oneself is freedom. But I have already said too much about this topic, and the philosophic meaning of the word *freedom* is not my subject here. . . .

Book II

That Sovereignty Is Inalienable

The first and most important consequence of the principles established above is that the general will alone can guide the forces of the State according to the end for which it was instituted, which is the common good. For if the opposition of private interests made the establishment of societies necessary, it is the agreement of these same interests that made it possible. It is what these different interests have in common that forms the social bond, and if there were not some point at which all the interests are in agreement, no society could exist. Now it is uniquely on the basis of this common interest that society ought to be governed.

I say, therefore, that sovereignty, being only the exercise of the general will, can never be alienated, and that the sovereign, which is only a collective being, can only be represented by itself. Power can perfectly well be transferred, but not will.

Indeed, though it is not impossible for a private will to agree with the general will on a given point, it is impossible, at least, for this agreement to be lasting and unchanging. For the private will tends by its nature toward preferences, and the general will toward equality. It is even more impossible for there to be a guarantee of this agreement even should it always exist. It would not be the result of art, but of chance. The sovereign may well say, "I currently want what a particular man wants, or at least what he says he wants." But it cannot say, "What that man will want tomorrow, I shall still want," since it is absurd for the will to tie itself down for the future and since no will can consent to anything that is contrary to the good of the being that wills. Therefore, if the people promises simply to obey, it dissolves itself by that act; it loses the status of a people. The moment there is a master, there is no longer a sovereign, and from then on the body politic is destroyed.

This is not to say that the commands of leaders cannot pass for expressions of the general will, as long as the sovereign, being free to oppose them, does not do so. In such a case, one ought to presume the consent of the people from universal silence. This will be explained at greater length.

That Sovereignty Is Indivisible

For the same reason that sovereignty is inalienable, it is indivisible. Because either the will is general or it is not. It is the will of the people as a body, or of only a part. In the first case, this declared will is an act of sovereignty and constitutes law. In the second case, it is merely a private will or an act of magistracy; it is at most a decree.

Whether the General Will Can Err

From the foregoing it follows that the general will is always right and always tends toward the public utility. But it does not follow that the people's deliberations always have the same rectitude. One always wants what is good for oneself, but one does not always see it. The people is never corrupted, but it is often fooled, and only then does it appear to want what is bad.

There is often a great difference between the will of all and the general will. The latter considers only the common interest; the former considers private interest, and is only a sum of private wills. But take away from these same wills the pluses and minuses that cancel each other out, and the remaining sum of the difference is the general will.

If, when an adequately informed people deliberates, the citizens were to have no communication among themselves, the general will would always result from the large number of small differences, and the deliberation would always be good. But when factions, partial associations at the expense of the whole, are formed, the will of each of these associations becomes general with reference to its members and particular with reference to the State. One can say, then, that there are no longer as many voters as there are men, but merely as many as there are associations. The differences become less numerous and produce a result that is less general. Finally, when one of these associations is so big that it prevails over all the others, the result is no longer a general will, and the opinion that prevails is merely a private opinion.

In order for the general will to be well expressed, it is therefore important that there be no partial society in the State, and that each citizen give only his own opinion. Such was the unique and sublime system instituted by the great Lycurgus. If there are partial societies, their number must be multiplied and their inequality prevented, as was done by Solon, Numa, and Servius. These precautions are the only valid means of ensuring that the general will is always enlightened and that the people is not deceived.

The engagements that bind us to the social body are obligatory only because they are mutual, and their nature is such that in fulfilling them one cannot work for someone else without also working for oneself. Why is the general will always right and why do all constantly want the happiness of each, if not because there is no one who does not apply this word *each* to himself, and does not think of himself as he votes for all? Which proves that the equality of right, and the concept of justice it produces, are derived from each man's preference for himself and consequently from the nature of man; that the general will, to be truly such, should be general in its object as well as in its essence; that it should come from all to apply to all; and that it loses its natural rectitude when it is directed toward any individual, determinate object. Because then, judging what is foreign to us, we have no true principle of equity to guide us.

Indeed, as soon as it is a matter of fact or a particular right concerning a point that has not been regulated by a prior, general convention, the affair is in dispute. It is a lawsuit where the interested private individuals constitute one party and the public the other, but in which I see neither what law must be followed nor what judge should decide. In this case it would be ridiculous to want to turn to an express decision of the general will, which can only be the conclusion of one of the parties and which, for the other party, is consequently only a foreign, private will, showing injustice on this occasion and subject to error. Thus just as a private will cannot represent the general will, the general will in turn changes its nature when it has a particular object; and as a general will it cannot pass judgment on either a man or a fact. When the people of Athens, for example, appointed or dismissed its leaders, awarded honors to one or imposed penalties on another, and by means of a multitude of particular decrees performed indistinguishably all the acts of government, the people then no longer had a general will properly speaking. It no longer acted as sovereign, but as magistrate. This will appear contrary to commonly held ideas, but you must give me time to present my own.

On Law

[W]hen the entire people enacts something concerning the entire people, it considers only itself, and if a relationship is formed then, it is between the whole object viewed in one way and the whole object viewed in another, without any division of the whole. Then the subject matter of the enactment is general like the will that enacts. It is this act that I call a law.

When I say that the object of the laws is always general, I mean that the law considers the subjects as a body and actions in the abstract, never a man as an individual or a particular action. Thus the law can very well enact that there will be privileges, but it cannot confer them on anyone by name. The law can create several classes of citizens, and even designate the qualities determining who has a right to these classes, but it cannot name the specific people to be admitted to them. It can establish a royal government and hereditary succession, but it cannot elect a king or name a royal family. In short, any function that relates to an individual object does not belong to the legislative power.

Given this idea, one sees immediately that it is no longer necessary to ask who should make laws, since they are acts of the general will; nor whether the prince is above the laws, since he is a member of the State; nor whether the law can be unjust, since no one is unjust toward himself; nor how one is free yet subject to the laws, since they merely record our wills.

Furthermore, one sees that since the law combines the universality of the will and that of the object, what any man, whoever he may be, orders on his own authority is not a law. Whatever is ordered even by the sovereign concerning a particular object is not a law either, but rather a decree; nor is it an act of sovereignty, but of magistracy.

I therefore call every State ruled by laws a republic, whatever the form of administration may be, for then alone the public interest governs and the common-wealth really exists. Every legitimate government is republican. I shall explain later what government is.

On the Legislator

The discovery of the best rules of society suited to nations would require a superior intelligence, who saw all of men's passions yet experienced none of them; who had no relationship at all to our nature yet knew it thoroughly; whose happiness was independent of us, yet who was nevertheless willing to attend to ours; finally one who, preparing for himself a future glory with the passage of time, could work in one century and enjoy the reward in another. Gods would be needed to give laws to men.

The legislator is an extraordinary man in the State in all respects. If he should be so by his genius, he is no less so by his function. It is not magistracy, it is not sovereignty. This function, which constitutes the republic, does not enter into its constitution. It is a particular and superior activity that has nothing in common with human dominion. For if one who has authority over men should not have authority over laws, one who has authority over laws should also not have authority over men. Otherwise his laws, ministers of his passions, would often only perpetuate his injustices, and he could never avoid having private views alter the sanctity of his work.

When Lycurgus gave his homeland laws, he began by abdicating the throne. It was the custom of most Greek cities to entrust the establishment of their laws to foreigners. The modern republics of Italy often imitated this practice. The republic of Geneva did so too, with good results. During its finest period Rome saw all the crimes of tyranny revived in its midst, and nearly perished as a result of combining legislative authority and sovereign power in the same hands.

He who drafts the laws, therefore, does not or should not have any legislative right. And the people itself cannot, even if it wanted to, divest itself of this incommunicable right, because according to the fundamental compact, only the general will obligates private individuals, and one can never be assured that a private will is in conformity with the general will until it has been submitted to the free vote of the people. I have already said this, but it is not useless to repeat it.

Thus one finds combined in the work of legislation two things that seem incompatible: an undertaking beyond human force and, to execute it, an authority that amounts to nothing.

This is what has always forced the fathers of nations to have recourse to the intervention of heaven and to attribute their own wisdom to the Gods; so that the peoples, subjected to the laws of the State as to those of nature, and recognizing the same power in the formation of man and of the City, might obey with freedom and bear with docility the yoke of public felicity.

It is this sublime reason, which rises above the grasp of common men, whose decisions the legislator places in the mouth of the immortals in order to convince by divine authority those who cannot be moved by human prudence. But it is not every man who can make the Gods speak or be believed when he declares himself their interpreter. The legislator's great soul is the true miracle that should prove his mission. Any man can engrave stone tablets, buy an oracle, pretend to have a secret relationship with some divinity, train a bird to talk in his ear, or find other crude ways to impress the people. One who knows only that much might even assemble, by chance, a crowd of madmen, but he will never found an empire, and his extravagant work will soon die along with him. False tricks can form a fleeting bond; wisdom alone can make it durable. The Jewish law, which is still in existence, and the law of the son of Ishmael, which has ruled half the world for ten centuries, still bear witness today to the great men who formulated them. And whereas proud philosophy or blind partisan spirit regards them merely as lucky imposters, the true political theorist admires in their institutions that great and powerful genius which presides over lasting establishments.

One must not conclude from all this, as Warburton does, that politics and religion have a common object for us, but rather that at the origin of nations, one serves as an instrument of the other.

On the People

Just as an architect, before putting up a big building, observes and tests the ground to see whether it can bear the weight, so the wise founder does not start by drafting laws that are good in themselves, but first examines whether the people for whom he intends them is suited to bear them. For this reason, Plato refused to give laws to the Arcadians and Cyrenians, knowing that these two peoples were rich and could not tolerate equality. For this reason, there were good laws and wicked men in Crete, because Minos had disciplined only a people full of vices.

A thousand nations that have flourished on earth could never have tolerated good laws, and even those that could were only so disposed for a very short time during their entire existence. Most peoples, like men, are docile only in their youth. They become incorrigible as they grow older. Once customs are established and prejudices have taken root, it is a dangerous and foolhardy undertaking to want to reform them. The people cannot even tolerate having their ills touched for the purpose of destroying them, like those stupid and cowardly patients who tremble at the sight of a doctor.

To be sure, just as men's minds are unhinged and their memory of the past erased by some illnesses, so there sometimes occur during the lifetime of States violent periods when revolutions have the same effect on peoples as do certain crises on individuals; when horror of the past is equivalent to amnesia, and when the State, set afire by civil wars, is reborn so to speak from its ashes and resumes the vigor of youth by escaping from death's clutches. Sparta in the time of Lycurgus and Rome after the Tarquins were like this, and among us so were Holland and Switzerland after the expulsion of the tyrants.

But these events are rare; they are exceptions that can always be explained by the particular constitution of the exceptional State. They cannot even occur twice for the same people; for it can liberate itself as long as it is merely barbarous, but can no longer do so when the civil machinery is worn out. Then, disturbances can destroy it, but revolutions cannot reestablish it, and as soon as its chains are broken, it falls apart and no longer exists. Henceforth it must have a master and not a liberator. Free peoples, remember this maxim: Freedom can be acquired, but it can never be recovered.

Youth is not childhood. For nations as for men there is a time of youth, or maturity if you prefer, that must be awaited before subjecting them to laws. But the maturity of a people is not always easy to recognize, and if it is anticipated, the work is ruined. One people is capable of discipline at birth, another is not after ten centuries. The Russians will never be truly civilized because they were civilized too early. Peter had the genius of imitation. He did not have true genius, the kind that creates and makes everything from nothing. A few of the things he did were good; most were out of place. He saw that his people was barbarous; he did not see that it was not ripe for a political order. He wanted to make it cultured when it only needed to be made warlike. He wanted first to make Germans and Englishmen, whereas it was necessary to begin by making Russians. He prevented his subjects from ever becoming what they could be by convincing them that they were what they are not. It is like the way a French tutor molds his pupil to shine briefly during his childhood and thereafter never to amount to anything. The Russian empire would like to subjugate Europe and will itself be subjugated. The Tartars, its subjects or its neighbors, will become its masters and ours. This revolution appears inevitable to me. All the kings of Europe are working together to hasten it. . . .

Classification of Laws

Various relations have to be considered in order to organize the whole or give the commonwealth the best possible form. First the action of the entire body acting upon itself—that is, the relationship of the whole to the whole, or of the sovereign to the State; and this relationship is composed of the relationship of intermediary terms, as we shall see later.

The laws that regulate this relationship are named political laws, and are also called fundamental laws, not without a degree of reason if these laws are wise. For if there is only one correct way to organize each State, the people that has found it should abide by it; but if the established order is bad, why should one accept, as fundamental, laws that prevent it from being good? Besides, in any event a people is always the master to change its laws—even the best laws; for if it wishes to do itself harm, who has the right to prevent it from doing so?

The second relation is that of the members to each other or to the entire body. And this relationship should be as small as possible with respect to the former and as large as possible with respect to the latter, so that each citizen is in a position of perfect independence from all the others and of excessive dependence upon the City. This is always achieved by the same means, because only the force of the State creates the freedom of its members. It is from this second relationship that civil laws arise.

It is possible to consider a third type of relation between man and the law, namely that of disobedience and penalty. And this gives rise to the establishment of criminal laws, which are basically not so much a particular type of law as a sanction for all the others.

To these three types of laws is added a fourth, the most important of all; which is not engraved on marble or bronze, but in the hearts of the citizens; which is the true constitution of the State; which gains fresh force each day; which, when other laws age or die out, revives or replaces them, preserves a people in the spirit of its institution, and imperceptibly substitutes the force of habit for that of authority. I am speaking of mores, customs, and especially of opinion—a part of the laws unknown to our political theorists, but on which the success of all the others depends; a part to which the great legislator attends in secret while appearing to limit himself to the particular regulations that are merely the sides of the arch of which mores, slower to arise, form at last the unshakable keystone.

Among these various classes, political laws, which constitute the form of government, are the only ones relevant to my subject. . . .

Book III

Before discussing the various forms of government, let us try to define the precise meaning of this word, which has not yet been very well explained.

On Government in General

. . . We have seen that the legislative power belongs to the people and can belong only to it. It is easy to see, on the contrary, by the principles already established, that the executive power cannot belong to the general public in its legislator's or sovereign capacity, because this power consists solely of particular acts which are not within the jurisdiction of the law, nor consequently of the sovereign, all of whose acts can only be laws.

The public force must therefore have its own agent, which unites it and puts it into operation according to the directions of the general will; which serves as a means of communication between the State and the sovereign; and which does in a sense for the public person what the union of the soul and the body does in man. This is the reason why, in the State, there is government, which has been incorrectly confounded with the sovereign, of which it is only the minister.

What is the government then? An intermediate body established between the subjects and the sovereign for their mutual communication, and charged with the execution of the laws and the maintenance of civil as well as political freedom.

The members of this body are called magistrates or *kings*, that is to say *governors*; and the body as a whole bears the name *prince*. Thus those who claim that the act by which a people subjects itself to leaders is not a contract are entirely right. It is absolutely nothing but a commission, a function in which, as simple officers of the sovereign, they exercise in its name the power that has been entrusted to them by the sovereign, and that the sovereign can limit, modify, and take back whenever it pleases, since the alienation of such a right is incompatible with the nature of the social body and contrary to the goal of the association.

I therefore give the name *government* or supreme administration to the legitimate exercise of the executive power, and Prince or magistrate to the man or the body charged with that administration. . . .

Classification of Governments

In the preceding chapter, we have seen why the various kinds or forms of governments are distinguished by the number of members composing them. It remains to be seen in this chapter how this classification is made.

The sovereign can, in the first place, entrust the government to the entire people or to the majority of people, so that there are more citizens who are magistrates than citizens who are simply private individuals. This form of government is given the name *democracy*.

Or else it can restrict the government to the hands of a small number, so that there are more simple citizens than magistrates; and this form bears the name *aristocracy*.

Finally, it can concentrate the whole government in the hands of a single magistrate from whom all the others derive their power. This third form is the most common, and is called *monarchy* or royal government.

People have always argued a great deal over the best form of government, without considering that each of them is the best in certain cases, and the worst in others.

If the number of supreme magistrates in different States ought to be in inverse proportion to the number of citizens, it follows that in general democratic government is suited to small States, aristocratic to medium-sized ones, and monarchical to large ones. This rule is derived directly from the principle; but countless circumstances can furnish exceptions.

On Democracy

He who makes the law knows better than anyone else how it ought to be executed and interpreted. It therefore seems that there could be no better constitution than one in which the executive power is combined with the legislative. But it is this very thing that makes such a government inadequate in certain respects, because the things that ought to be distinguished are not, and the prince and the sovereign, being nothing but the same person, form so to speak only a government without a government.

It is not good for him who makes the laws to execute them, nor for the body of people to turn its attention away from general considerations to particular objects. Nothing is more dangerous than the influence of private interests on public affairs; and the abuse of laws by the government is a lesser evil than the corruption of the legislator, which is the inevitable consequence of private considerations. Then, the substance of the State being changed, all reform becomes impossible. A people who would never take advantage of government would never take advantage of independence either. A people who would always govern well would not need to be governed.

In the strict sense of the term, a true democracy has never existed and never will exist. It is contrary to the natural order that the majority govern and the minority be governed. It is unimaginable that the people remain constantly assembled to attend to public affairs, and it is obvious that it could not establish commissions to do so without changing the form of administration.

Indeed, I believe it can be stated as a principle that when the functions of the government are divided among several tribunals, those with the fewest members sooner or later acquire the greatest authority, if only because of the facility in expediting business which brings this about naturally.

Besides, consider how many things that are hard to combine are presupposed by this form of government. First, a very small State where the people is easily assembled and where each citizen can easily know all the others. Second, great simplicity of mores, which prevents a multitude of business and knotty discussions. Next, a great equality of ranks and of fortunes, without which equality of rights and authority could not subsist for long. Finally, little or no luxury, because either luxury is the result of wealth, or it makes wealth necessary. It corrupts both rich and poor, the one by possessing, the other by coveting. It sells out the homeland to indolence and vanity; it deprives the State of all of its citizens by enslaving some of them to others and all of them to opinion.

If there were a people of Gods, it would govern itself democratically. Such a perfect government is not suited to men.

On Aristocracy

We have here two quite distinct moral persons, namely the government and the sovereign; and consequently two general wills, one relative to all the citizens, the other solely for the members of the administration. Thus, although the government can regulate its internal policy in whatever way it pleases, it can never speak to the people except in the name of the sovereign, that is in the name of the people itself. This must never be forgotten.

The first societies governed themselves aristocratically. The heads of families

62

deliberated among themselves about public affairs. Young people demurred without difficulty to the authority of experience. This is the source of the names *priests, ancients, senate, elders*. The savages of North America still govern themselves in this manner, and are very well governed.

But as instituted inequality came to predominate over natural inequality, wealth or power was preferred to age, and aristocracy became elective. Finally, when power was passed on together with goods from father to children, creating patrician families, the government was made hereditary, and there were senators only twenty years old.

There are, therefore, three kinds of aristocracy: natural, elective, and hereditary. The first is suited only to simple peoples. The third is the worst of all governments. The second is the best; it is aristocracy properly so-called.

Besides the advantage of distinguishing between the two powers, aristocracy has that of the choice of its members. For in popular government all the citizens are born magistrates, whereas this type limits them to a small number, and they become magistrates only through election, a means by which probity, enlightenment, experience, and all the other reasons for public preference and esteem become so many new guarantees of being well governed.

Moreover, assemblies are more conveniently held, business is better discussed and acted upon in a more orderly and diligent manner, the prestige of the State is better sustained in foreign countries by venerable senators than by an unknown or scorned multitude.

In short, it is the best and most natural order for the wisest to govern the multitude, as long as it is certain that they govern for its benefit and nor for their own. Devices must be multiplied uselessly, nor must twenty thousand men do what one hundred well-chosen men can do still better. But it must be noted that here the corporate interest begins to direct the public force in accordance with the rule of the general will to a lesser degree, and that another unavoidable tendency exempts from the laws a part of the executive power.

With regard to particular matters of expediency, a State must not be so small, nor a people so simple and upright, that the execution of laws follows immediately from the public will, as is the case in a good democracy. Nor must a nation be so large that the leaders, dispersed to govern it, can each make decisions for the sovereign in his own department, and begin by making themselves independent in order to become masters in the long run.

But if aristocracy requires somewhat fewer virtues than popular government, it also requires others which are specific to it, such as moderation among the rich and contentment among the poor. For it seems that rigorous equality would be misplaced in an aristocracy. It was not even adhered to in Sparta.

Besides, if this form includes some inequality of wealth, it is simply in order for the administration of public affairs to be generally confided to those who can best devote all their time to it; but not, as Aristotle claims, for the rich to be always given preference. On the contrary, it is important that an opposite choice should occasionally teach the people that personal merit offers more important reasons for preference than does riches.

DISCOURSE ON THE ORIGIN AND FOUNDATIONS OF INEQUALITY AMONG MEN

QUESTION

Proposed by the Academy of Dijon: What Is the Origin of Inequality Among Men, and Is It Authorized by the Natural Law?

It is of man that I have to speak, and the question I am examining indicates to me that I am going to be speaking to men, for such questions are not proposed by those who are afraid to honor the truth. I will therefore confidently defend the cause of humanity before the wise men who invite me to do so, and I will not be displeased with myself if I make myself worthy of my subject and my judges.

I conceive of two kinds of inequality in the human species: one which I call natural or physical, because it is established by nature and consists in the difference of age, health, bodily strength, and qualities of mind or soul. The other may be called moral or political inequality, because it depends on a kind of convention and is established, or at least authorized, by the consent of men. This latter type of inequality consists in the different privileges enjoyed by some at the expense of others, such as being richer, more honored, more powerful than they, or even causing themselves to be obeyed by them.

There is no point in asking what the source of natural inequality is, because the answer would be found enunciated in the simple definition of the word. There is still less of a point in asking whether there would not be some essential connections between the two inequalities, for that would amount to asking whether those who command are necessarily better than those who obey, and whether strength of body or mind, wisdom or virtue are always found in the same individuals in proportion to power or wealth. Perhaps this is a good question for slaves to discuss within earshot of their masters, but it is not suitable for reasonable and free men who seek the truth.

Precisely what, then, is the subject of this discourse? To mark, in the progress of things, the moment when, right taking the place of violence, nature was subjected to the law. To explain the sequence of wonders by which the strong could resolve to serve the weak, and the people to buy imaginary repose at the price of real felicity.

The philosophers who have examined the foundations of society have all felt the necessity of returning to the state of nature, but none of them has reached it. Some have not hesitated to ascribe to man in that state the notion of just and unjust, without bothering to show that he had to have that notion, or even that it was useful to him. Others have spoken of the natural right that everyone has to preserve what belongs to him, without explaining what they mean by "belonging." Others started out by giving authority to the stronger over the weaker, and immediately brought about government, without giving any thought to the time that had to pass before the meaning of the words "authority" and "government" could exist among men. Finally, all of them, speaking continually of need, avarice, oppression, desires, and pride, have transferred to the state of nature the ideas they acquired in society. They spoke about savage man, and it was civil man they depicted. It did not even occur to most of our philosophers to doubt that the state of nature had existed, even though it is evident from reading the Holy Scriptures that the first man, having received enlightenment and precepts immediately from God, was not himself in that state; and if we give the writings of Moses the credence that every Christian owes them, we must deny that, even before the flood, men were ever in the pure state of nature, unless they had fallen back into it because of some extraordinary event: a paradox that is quite awkward to defend and utterly impossible to prove.

Let us therefore begin by putting aside all the facts, for they have no bearing on the question. The investigations that may be undertaken concerning this subject should not be taken for historical truths, but only for hypothetical and conditional reasonings, better suited to shedding light on the nature of things than on pointing out their true origin, like those our physicists make everyday with regard to the formation of the world. Religion commands us to believe that since God himself drew men out of the state of nature, they are unequal because he wanted them to be so; but it does not forbid us to form conjectures, drawn solely from the nature of man and the beings that surround him, concerning what the human race could have become, if it had been left to itself. That is what I am asked, and what I propose to examine in this discourse. Since my subject concerns man in general, I will attempt to speak in terms that suit all nations, or rather, forgetting times and places in order to think only of the men to whom I am speaking, I will imagine I am in the Lyceum in Athens, reciting the lessons of my masters, having men like Plato and Xenocrates for my judges, and the human race for my audience.

O man, whatever country you may be from, whatever your opinions may be, listen: here is your history, as I have thought to read it, not in the books of your fellowmen, who are liars, but in nature, who never lies. Everything that comes from nature will be true; there will be nothing false except what I have unintentionally added. The times about which I am going to speak are quite remote: how much you have changed from what you were! It is, as it were, the life of your species that I am about to describe to you according to the qualities you have received, which your education and your habits have been able to corrupt but have been unable to destroy. There is, I feel, an age at which an individual man would want to stop. You will seek the age at which you would want your species to have stopped. Dissatisfied with your present state for reasons that portend even greater grounds for dissatisfaction for your unhappy posterity, perhaps you would like to be able to go backwards in time. This feeling should be a hymn in praise of your first ancestors, the criticism of your contemporaries, and the dread of those who have the unhappiness of living after you. . . .

[W]ithout taking note of the changes that must have occurred in the internal as well as the external conformation of man, as he applied his limbs to new purposes and nourished himself on new foods, I will suppose him to have been formed from all time as I see him today: walking on two feet, using his hands as we use ours, directing his gaze over all of nature, and measuring with his eyes the vast expanse of the heavens.

When I strip that being, thus constituted, of all the supernatural gifts he could have received and of all the artificial faculties he could have acquired only through long progress; when I consider him, in a word, as he must have left the hands of nature, I see an animal less strong than some, less agile than others, but all in all, the most advantageously organized of all. I see him satisfying his hunger under an oak tree, quenching his thirst at the first stream, finding his bed at the foot of the same tree that supplied his meal; and thus all his needs are satisfied.

When the earth is left to its natural fertility and covered with immense forests that were never mutilated by the axe, it offers storehouses and shelters at every step to animals of every species. Men, dispersed among the animals, observe and imitate their industry, and thereby raise themselves to the level of animal instinct, with the advantage that, whereas each species has only its own instincts, man, who may perhaps have none that belongs to him, appropriates all of them to himself, feeds himself equally well on most of the various foods which the other animals divide among themselves, and consequently finds his sustenance more easily than any of the rest can.

Accustomed from childhood to inclement weather and the rigors of the seasons, acclimated to fatigue, and forced, naked and without arms, to defend their lives and their prey against other ferocious beasts, or to escape them by taking flight, men develop a robust and nearly unalterable temperament. Children enter the world with the excellent constitution of their parents and strengthen it with the same exercises that produced it, thus acquiring all the vigor that the human race is capable of having. Nature treats them precisely the way the law of Sparta treated the children of its citizens: it renders strong and robust those who are well consti-tuted and makes all the rest perish, thereby differing from our present-day soci-eties, where the state, by making children burdensome to their parents, kills them indiscriminately before their birth.

Since the savage man's body is the only instrument he knows, he employs it for a variety of purposes that, for lack of practice, ours are incapable of serving. And our industry deprives us of the force and agility that necessity obliges him to acquire. If he had had an axe, would his wrists break such strong branches? If he had had a sling, would he throw a stone with so much force? If he had had a ladder, would he climb a tree so nimbly? If he had had a horse, would he run so fast? Give a civilized man time to gather all his machines around him, and un-doubtedly he will easily overcome a savage man. But if you want to see an even more unequal fight, pit them against each other naked and disarmed, and you will soon realize the advantage of constantly having all of one's forces at one's dis-posal, of always being ready for any event, and of always carrying one's entire self, as it were, with one. . . .

So far I have considered only physical man. Let us now try to look at him from a metaphysical and moral point of view.

In any animal I see nothing but an ingenious machine to which nature has given senses in order for it to renew its strength and to protect itself, to a certain point, from all that tends to destroy or disturb it. I am aware of precisely the same things in the human machine, with the difference that nature alone does everything in the operations of an animal, whereas man contributes, as a free agent, to his own operations. The former chooses or rejects by instinct and the latter by an act of freedom. Hence an animal cannot deviate from the rule that is prescribed to it, even when it would be advantageous to do so, while man deviates from it, often to his own detriment. Thus a pigeon would die of hunger near a bowl filled with choice meats, and so would a cat perched atop a pile of fruit or grain, even though both could nourish themselves quite well with the food they disdain, if they were of a mind to try some. And thus dissolute men abandon themselves to excesses which cause them fever and death, because the mind perverts the senses and because the will still speaks when nature is silent.

Every animal has ideas, since it has senses; up to a certain point it even combines its ideas, and in this regard man differs from an animal only in degree. Some philosophers have even suggested that there is a greater difference between two given men than between a given man and an animal. Therefore it is not so much understanding which causes the specific distinction of man from all other animals as it is his being a free agent. Nature commands every animal, and beasts obey. Man feels the same impetus, but he knows he is free to go along or to resist; and it is above all in the awareness of this freedom that the spirituality of his soul is made manifest. For physics explains in some way the mechanism of the senses and the formation of ideas; but in the power of willing, or rather of choosing, and in the feeling of this power, we find only purely spiritual acts, about which the laws of mechanics explain nothing.

But if the difficulties surrounding all these questions should leave some room for dispute on this difference between man and animal, there is another very specific quality which distinguishes them and about which there can be no argument: the faculty of self-perfection, a faculty which, with the aid of circumstances, successively develops all the others, and resides among us as much in the species as in the individual. On the other hand, an animal, at the end of a few months, is what it will be all its life; and its species, at the end of a thousand years, is what it was in the first of those thousand years. Why is man alone subject to becoming an imbecile? Is it not that he thereby returns to his primitive state, and that, while the animal which has acquired nothing and which also has nothing to lose, always retains its instinct, man, in losing through old age or other accidents all that his *perfectibility* has enabled him to acquire, thus falls even lower than the animal itself? It would be sad for us to be forced to agree that this distinctive and almost unlimited faculty is the source of all man's misfortunes; that this is what, by dint of time, draws him out of that original condition in which he would pass tranquil and innocent days; that this is what, through centuries of giving rise to his enlightenment and his errors, his vices and his virtues, eventually makes him a tyrant over himself and nature. It would be dreadful to be obliged to praise as a beneficent being the one who first suggested to the inhabitant on the banks of the Orinoco the use of boards which he binds to his children's temples, and which assure them of at least part of their imbecility and their original happiness.

Savage man, left by nature to instinct alone, or rather compensated for the instinct he is perhaps lacking by faculties capable of first replacing them and then of raising him to the level of instinct, will therefore begin with purely animal functions. Perceiving and feeling will be his first state, which he will have in common with all animals. Willing and not willing, desiring, and fearing will be the first and nearly the only operations of his soul until new circumstances bring about new developments in it.

Whatever the moralists may say about it, human understanding owes much to the passions, which, by common consensus, also owe a great deal to it. It is by their activity that our reason is perfected. We seek to know only because we desire to find enjoyment; and it is impossible to conceive why someone who had neither desires nor fears would go to the bother of reasoning. The passions in turn take their origin from our needs, and their progress from our knowledge. For one can desire or fear things only by virtue of the ideas one can have of them, or from the simple impulse of nature; and savage man, deprived of every sort of enlightenment, feels only the passion of this latter sort. His desires do not go beyond his physical needs. The only goods he knows in the universe are nourishment, a woman and rest; the only evils he fears are pain and hunger. I say pain and not death because an animal will never know what it is to die; and knowledge of death and its terrors is one of the first acquisitions that man has made in withdrawing from the animal condition. . . .

. . . As for myself being shocked by the unending difficulties and convinced of the almost demonstrable impossibility that languages could have arisen and been established by merely human means, I leave to anyone who would undertake it the discussion of the following difficult problem: which was the more necessary: an already formed society for the invention of languages, or an already invented language for the establishment of society?

Whatever these origins may be, it is clear, from the little care taken by nature to bring men together through mutual needs and to facilitate their use of speech, how little she prepared them for becoming habituated to the ways of society, and how little she contributed to all that men have done to establish the bonds of society. In fact, it is impossible to image why, in that primitive state, one man would have a greater need for another man than a monkey or a wolf has for another of its respective species; or, assuming this need, what motive could induce the other man to satisfy it; or even, in this latter instance, how could they be in mutual agreement regarding the conditions. I know that we are repeatedly told that nothing would have been so miserable as man in that state; and if it is true, as I believe I have proved, that it is only after many centuries that men could have had the desire and the opportunity to leave that state, that would be a charge to bring against nature, not against him whom nature has thus constituted. But if we understand the word *miserable* properly, it is a word which is without meaning or which signifies merely a painful privation and suffering of the body or the soul. Now I would very much like someone to explain to me what kind of misery can there be for a free being whose heart is at peace and whose body is in good health? I ask which of the two, civil or natural life, is more likely to become insufferable to those who live it? We see about us practically no people who do not complain about their existence; many even deprive themselves of it to the extent they are able, and the combination of divine and human laws is hardly enough to stop this disorder. I ask if anyone has ever heard tell of a savage who was living in liberty ever dreaming of complaining about his life and of killing himself. Let the judgment therefore be made with less pride on which side real misery lies. On the other hand, nothing would have been so miserable as savage man, dazzled by enlightenment, tormented by passions, and reasoning about a state different from his own. It was by a very wise providence that the latent faculties he possessed should develop only as the occasion to exercise them presents itself, so that they would be neither superfluous nor troublesome to him beforehand, nor underdeveloped and useless in time of need. In instinct alone, man had everything he needed in order to live in the state of nature; in a cultivated reason, he has only what he needs to live in society.

At first it would seem that men in that state, having among themselves no type of moral relations or acknowledged duties, could be neither good nor evil, and had neither vices nor virtues, unless, if we take these words in a physical sense, we call those qualities that can harm an individual's preservation "vices" in him, and those than can contribute to it "virtues." In that case it would be necessary to call the one who least resists the simple impulses of nature the most virtuous. But without departing from the standard meaning of these words, it is appropriate to suspend the judgment we could make regarding such a situation and to be on our guard against our prejudices, until we have examined with scale in hand whether there are more virtues than vices among civilized men; or whether their virtues are more advantageous than their vices are lethal; or whether the progress of their knowledge is sufficient compensation for ills they inflict on one another as they learn of the good they ought to do; or whether, all things considered, they would not be in a happier set of circumstances if they had neither evil to fear nor good to hope for from anyone, rather than subjecting themselves to a universal dependence and obliging themselves to receive everything from those who do not oblige themselves to give them anything.

Above all, let us not conclude with Hobbes that because man has no idea of goodness he is naturally evil; that he is vicious because he does not know virtue; that he always refuses to perform services for his fellow men he does not believe he owes them; or that, by virtue of the right, which he reasonably attributes to himself, to those things he needs, he foolishly imagines himself to be the sole proprietor of the entire universe. Hobbes has very clearly seen the defect of all modern definitions of natural right, but the consequences he draws from his own definition show that he takes it in a sense that is no less false. Were he to have reasoned on the basis of the principles he establishes, this author should have said that since the state of nature is the state in which the concern for our self-preservation is the least prejudicial to that of others, that state was consequently the most appropriate for peace and the best suited for the human race. He says precisely the opposite, because he had wrongly injected into the savage man's concern for self-preservation the need to satisfy a multitude of passions which are the product of society and which have made laws necessary. The evil man, he says, is a robust child. It remains to be seen whether savage man is a robust child. Were we to grant him this, what would we conclude from it? That if this man were as dependent on others when he is robust as he is when he is weak, there is no type of excess to which he would not tend: he would beat his mother if she were too slow in offering him her breast; he would strangle one of his younger brothers, should he find him annoying; he would bite someone's leg, should he be assaulted or aggravated by him. But being robust and being dependent are two contradictory suppositions in the state of nature. Man is weak when he is dependent, and he is emancipated from that dependence before he is robust. Hobbes did not see that the same cause preventing savages from using their reason, as our jurists claim, is what prevents them at the same time from abusing their faculties, as he himself maintains. Hence we could say that savages are not evil precisely because they do not know what it is to be good; for it is neither the development of enlightenment nor the restraint imposed by the law, but the calm of the passions and the ignorance of vice which prevents them from doing evil. *So much more profitable to these is the ignorance of vice than the knowledge of virtue is to those.* Moreover, there is another principle that Hobbes failed to notice, and which, having been given to man in order to mitigate, in certain circumstances, the ferocity of his egocentrism or the desire for self-preservation before this egocentrism of his came into being, tempers the ardor he has for his own well-being by an innate repugnance to seeing his fellow men suffer. I do not believe I have any contradiction to fear in granting the only natural virtue that the most excessive detractor of human virtues was forced to recognize. I am referring to pity, a disposition that is fitting for beings that are as weak and as subject to ills as we are; a virtue all the more universal and all the more useful to man in that it precedes in him any kind of reflection, and so natural that even animals sometimes show noticeable signs of it. Without speaking of the tenderness of mothers for their young and of the perils they have to brave in order to protect them, one daily observes the repugnance that horses have for trampling a living body with their hooves. An animal does not go undisturbed past a dead animal of its own species. There are even some animals that give them a kind of sepulchre; and the mournful lowing of cattle entering a slaughterhouse voices the impression they receive of the horrible spectacle that strikes them. One notes with pleasure the author of *The Fable of the Bees*, having been forced to acknowledge man as a compassionate and sensitive being, departing from his cold and subtle style in the example he gives, to offer us the pathetic image of an imprisoned man who sees outside his cell a ferocious animal tearing a child from its mother's breast, mashing its frail limbs with its murderous teeth, and ripping with its claws the child's quivering entrails. What horrible agitation must be felt by this witness of an event in which he has no personal interest! What anguish must he suffer at this sight, being unable to be of any help to the fainting mother or to the dying child?

Such is the pure movement of nature prior to all reflection. Such is the force of natural pity, which the most depraved mores still have difficulty destroying, since everyday one sees in our theaters someone affected and weeping at the ills of some unfortunate person, and who, were he in the tyrant's place, would intensify the torments of his enemy still more; [like the bloodthirsty Sulla, so sensitive to ills he had not caused, or like Alexander of Pherae, who did not dare attend the performance of any tragedy, for fear of being seen weeping with Andromache and Priam, and yet who listened impassively to the cries of so many citizens who were killed everyday on his orders. *Nature, in giving men tears, bears witness that she gave the human race the softest hearts.*] Mandeville has a clear awareness that, with all their mores, men would never have been anything but monsters, if nature had not given them pity to aid their reason; but he has not seen that from this quality alone flow all the social virtues that he wants to deny in men. In fact, what are generosity, mercy, and humanity, if not pity applied to the weak, to the guilty, or to the human species in general. Benevolence and even friendship are, properly understood, the products of a constant pity fixed on a particular object; for is desiring that someone not suffer anything but desiring that he be happy? Were it true that commiseration were merely a sentiment that puts us in the position of the one who suffers, a sentiment that is obscure and powerful in savage man, developed but weak in man dwelling in civil society, what importance would this idea have to the truth of what I say, except to give it more force? In fact, commiseration will be all the more energetic as the witnessing animal identifies itself more intimately with the suffering animal. Now it is evident that this identification must have been infinitely closer in the state of nature than in the state of reasoning. Reason is what engenders egocentrism, and reflection strengthens it. Reason is what turns man in upon himself. Reason is what separates him from all that troubles him and afflicts him. Philosophy is what isolates him and what moves him to say in secret, at the sight of a suffering man, "Perish if you will; I am safe and sound." No longer can anything but danger to the entire society trouble the tranquil slumber of the philosopher and yank him from his bed. His fellow man can be killed with impunity underneath his window. He has merely to place his hands over his ears and argue with himself a little in order to prevent nature, which rebels within him, from identifying him with the man being assassinated. Savage man does not have this admirable talent, and for lack of wisdom and reason he is always seen thoughtlessly giving in to the first sentiment of humanity. When there is a riot or a street brawl, the populace gathers together; the prudent man withdraws from the scene. It is the rabble, the women of the marketplace, who separate the combatants and prevent decent people from killing one another.

It is therefore quite certain that pity is a natural sentiment, which, by moderating in each individual the activity of the love of oneself, contributes to the mutual preservation of the entire species. Pity is what carries us without reflection to the aid of those we see suffering. Pity is what, in the state of nature, takes the place of laws, mores, and virtue, with the advantage that no one is tempted to disobey its sweet voice. Pity is what will prevent every robust savage from robbing a weak child or an infirm old man of his hard-earned subsistence, if he himself expects to be able to find his own someplace else. Instead of the sublime maxim of reasoned justice, *Do unto others as you would have them do unto you*, pity inspires all men with another maxim of natural goodness, much less perfect but perhaps more useful than the preceding one: *Do what is good for you with as little harm as possible to others.* In a word, it is in this natural sentiment, rather than in subtle arguments that one must search for the cause of the repugnance at doing evil that every man would experience, even independently of the maxims of education. Although it might be appropriate for Socrates and minds of his stature to acquire virtue through reason, the human race would long ago have ceased to exist, if its preservation had depended solely on the reasonings of its members.

With passions so minimally active and such a salutary restraint, being more wild than evil, and more attentive to protecting themselves from the harm they could receive than tempted to do harm to others, men were not subject to very dangerous conflicts. Since they had no sort of intercourse among themselves; since, as a consequence, they knew neither vanity, nor deference, nor esteem, nor contempt; since they had not the slightest notion of mine and thine, nor any true idea of justice; since they regarded the acts of violence that could befall them as an easily redressed evil and not as an offense that must be punished; and since they did not even dream of vengeance except perhaps as a knee-jerk response right then and there, like the dog that bites the stone that is thrown at him, their disputes would rarely have had bloody consequences, if their subject had been no more sensitive than food. . . .

Let us conclude that, wandering in the forests, without industry, without speech, without dwelling, without war, without relationships, with no need for his fellow men, and correspondingly with no desire to do them harm, perhaps never even recognizing any of them individually, savage man, subject to few passions and self-sufficient, had only the sentiments and enlightenment appropriate to that state; he felt only his true needs, took notice of only what he believed he had an interest in seeing; and that his intelligence made no more progress than his vanity. If by chance he made some discovery, he was all the less able to communicate it to others because he did not even know his own children. Art perished with its inventor. There was neither education nor progress; generations were multiplied to no purpose. Since each one always began from the same point, centuries went by with all the crudeness of the first ages; the species was already old, and man remained ever a child. . . .

After having proved that inequality is hardly observable in the state of nature, and that its influence there is almost nonexistent, it remains for me to show its origin and progress in the successive developments of the human mind. After having shown that *perfectibility*, social virtues, and the other faculties that natural man had received in a state of potentiality could never develop by themselves, that to achieve this development they required the chance coming together of several unconnected causes that might never have come into being and without which he would have remained eternally in his primitive constitution, it remains for me to consider and to bring together the various chance happenings that were able to perfect human reason while deteriorating the species, make a being evil while rendering it habituated to the ways of society, and, from so distant a beginning, finally bring man and the world to the point where we see them now. . . .

Part Two

The first person who, having enclosed a plot of land, took it into his head to say *this is mine* and found people simple enough to believe him, was the true founder of civil society. What crimes, wars, murders, what miseries and horrors would the human race have been spared, had someone pulled up the stakes or filled in the ditch and cried out to his fellow men: "Do not listen to this impostor. You are lost if you forget that the fruits of the earth belong to all and the earth to no one!" But it is quite likely that by then things had already reached the point where they could no longer continue as they were. For this idea of property, depending on many prior ideas which could only have arisen successively, was not formed all at once in the human mind. It was necessary to make great progress, to acquire much industry and enlightenment, and to transmit and augment them from one age to another, before arriving at this final stage in the state of nature. Let us therefore take things farther back and try to piece together under a single viewpoint that slow succession of events and advances in knowledge in their most natural order.

Man's first sentiment was that of his own existence; his first concern was that of his preservation. The products of the earth provided him with all the help he needed; instinct led him to make use of them. With hunger and other appetites making him experience by turns various ways of existing, there was one appetite that invited him to perpetuate his species; and this blind inclination, devoid of any sentiment of the heart, produced a purely animal act. Once this need had been satisfied, the two sexes no longer took cognizance of one another, and even the child no longer meant anything to the mother once it could do without her.

Such was the condition of man in his nascent stage; such was the life of an animal limited at first to pure sensations, and scarcely profiting from the gifts nature offered him, far from dreaming of extracting anything from her. But difficulties soon presented themselves to him; it was necessary to learn to overcome them. The height of trees, which kept him from reaching their fruits, the competition of animals that sought to feed themselves on these same fruits, the ferocity of those animals that wanted to take his own life: everything obliged him to apply himself to bodily exercises. It was necessary to become agile, fleet-footed and vigorous in combat. Natural arms, which are tree branches and stones, were soon found ready at hand. He learned to surmount nature's obstacles, combat other animals when necessary, fight for his subsistence even with men, or compensate for what he had to yield to those stronger than himself.

In proportion as the human race spread, difficulties multiplied with the men. Differences in soils, climates and seasons could force them to inculcate these differences in their lifestyles. Barren years, long and hard winters, hot summers that consume everything required new resourcefulness from them. Along the sea-shore and the riverbanks they invented the fishing line and hook, and became fishermen and fish-eaters. In the forests they made bows and arrows, and became hunters and warriors. In cold countries they covered themselves with the skins of animals they had killed. Lightning, a volcano, or some fortuitous chance happening acquainted them with fire: a new resource against the rigors of winter. They learned to preserve this element, then to reproduce it, and finally to use it to prepare meats that previously they devoured raw.

This repeated appropriation of various beings to himself, and of some beings to others, must naturally have engendered in man's mind the perceptions of certain relations. These relationships which we express by the words "large," "small," "strong," "weak," "fast," "slow," "timorous," "bold," and other similar ideas, compared when needed and almost without thinking about it, finally produced in him a kind of reflection, or rather a mechanical prudence which pointed out to him the precautions that were most necessary for his safety.

The new enlightenment which resulted from this development increased his superiority over the other animals by making him aware of it. He trained himself to set traps for them; he tricked them in a thousand different ways. And although several surpassed him in fighting strength or in swiftness in running, of those that could serve him or hurt him, he became in time the master of the former and the scourge of the latter. Thus the first glance he directed upon himself produced within him the first stirring of pride; thus, as yet hardly knowing how to distinguish the ranks, and contemplating himself in the first rank by virtue of his species, he prepared himself from afar to lay claim to it in virtue of his individuality.

Although his fellowmen were not for him what they are for us, and although he had hardly anything more to do with them than with other animals, they were not forgotten in his observations. The conformities that time could make him perceive among them, his female, and himself, made him judge those he did not perceive. And seeing that they all acted as he would have done under similar circumstances, he concluded that their way of thinking and feeling was in complete conformity with his own. And this important truth, well established in his mind, made him follow, by a presentiment as sure as dialectic and more prompt, the best rules of conduct that it was appropriate to observe toward them for his advantage and safety.

Taught by experience that love of well-being is the sole motive of human actions, he found himself in a position to distinguish the rare occasions when common interest should make him count on the assistance of his fellowmen, and those even rarer occasions when competition ought to make him distrust them. In the first case, he united with them in a herd, or at most in some sort of free association, that obligated no one and that lasted only as long as the passing need that had formed it. In the second case, everyone sought to obtain his own advantage, either by overt force, if he believed he could, or by cleverness and cunning, if he felt himself to be the weaker.

This is how men could imperceptibly acquire some crude idea of mutual commitments and of the advantages to be had in fulfilling them, but only insofar as present and perceptible interests could require it, since foresight meant nothing to them, and far from concerning themselves about a distant future, they did not even give a thought to the next day. Were it a matter of catching a deer, everyone was quite aware that he must faithfully keep to his post in order to achieve this purpose; but if a hare happened to pass within reach of one of them, no doubt he would have pursued it without giving it a second thought, and that, having obtained his prey, he cared very little about causing his companions to miss theirs.

It is easy to understand that such intercourse did not require a language much more refined than that of crows or monkeys, which flock together in practically the same way. Inarticulate cries, many gestures, and some imitative noises must for a long time have made up the universal language. By joining to this in each country a few articulate and conventional sounds, whose institution, as I have already said, is not too easy to explain, there were individual languages, but crude and imperfect ones, quite similar to those still spoken by various savage nations today. Constrained by the passing of time, the abundance of things I have to say, and the practically imperceptible progress of the beginnings, I am flying like an arrow over the multitudes of centuries. For the slower events were in succeeding one another, the quicker they can be described.

These first advances enabled man to make more rapid ones. The more the mind was enlightened, the more industry was perfected. Soon they ceased to fall asleep under the first tree or to retreat into caves, and found various types of hatchets made of hard, sharp stones, which served to cut wood, dig up the soil, and make huts from branches they later found it useful to cover with clay and mud. This was the period of a first revolution which formed the establishment of the distinction among families and which introduced a kind of property, whence perhaps there already arose many quarrels and fights. However, since the strongest were probably the first to make themselves lodgings they felt capable of defending, presumably the weak found it quicker and safer to imitate them than to try to dislodge them; and as for those who already had huts, each of them must have rarely sought to appropriate that of his neighbor, less because it did not belong to him than because it was of no use to him, and because he could not seize it without exposing himself to a fierce battle with the family that occupied it.

The first developments of the heart were the effect of a new situation that united the husbands and wives, fathers and children in one common habitation. The habit of living together gave rise to the sweetest sentiments known to men: conjugal love and paternal love. Each family became a little society all the better united because mutual attachment and liberty were its only bonds; and it was then that the first difference was established in the lifestyle of the two sexes, which until then had had only one. Women became more sedentary and grew accustomed to watch over the hut and the children, while the man went to seek their common subsistence. With their slightly softer life the two sexes also began to lose something of their ferocity and vigor. But while each one separately became less suited to combat savage beasts, on the other hand it was easier to assemble in order jointly to resist them.

In this new state, with a simple and solitary life, very limited needs, and the tools they had invented to provide for them, since men enjoyed a great deal of leisure time, they used it to procure for themselves many types of conveniences unknown to their fathers; and that was the first yoke they imposed on themselves without realizing it, and the first source of evils they prepared for their descendants. For in addition to their continuing thus to soften body and mind (those conveniences having through habit lost almost all of their pleasure, and being at the same time degenerated into true needs), being deprived of them became much more cruel than possessing them was sweet, and they were unhappy about losing them without being happy about possessing them.

At this point we can see a little better how the use of speech was established or imperceptibly perfected itself in the bosom of each family; and one can further conjecture how various particular causes could have extended the language and accelerated its progress by making it more necessary. Great floods or earthquakes surrounded the inhabited areas with water or precipices. Upheavals of the globe detached parts of the mainland and broke them up into islands. Clearly among men thus brought together and forced to live together, a common idiom must have been formed sooner than among those who wandered freely about the forests of the mainland. Thus it is quite possible that after their first attempts at navigation, the islanders brought the use of speech to us; and it is at least quite probable that society and languages came into being on islands and were perfected there before they were known on the mainland.

Everything begins to take on a new appearance. Having previously wandered about the forests and having assumed a more fixed situation, men slowly came together and united into different bands, eventually forming in each country a particular nation, united by mores and characteristic features, not by regulations and laws, but by the same kind of life and foods and by the common influence of the climate. Eventually a permanent proximity cannot fail to engender some inter-course among different families. Young people of different sexes live in neighboring huts; the passing intercourse demanded by nature soon leads to another, through frequent contact with one another, no less sweet and more permanent. People become accustomed to consider different objects and to make comparisons. Imperceptibly they acquire the ideas of merit and beauty which produce feelings of preference. By dint of seeing one another, they can no longer get along without seeing one another again. A sweet and tender feeling insinuates itself into the soul and at the least opposition becomes an impetuous fury. Jealousy awakens with love: discord triumphs, and the sweetest passion receives sacrifices of human blood.

In proportion as ideas and sentiments succeed one another and as the mind and heart are trained, the human race continues to be tamed, relationships spread and bonds are tightened. People grew accustomed to gather in front of their huts or around a large tree; song and dance, true children of love and leisure, became the amusement or rather the occupation of idle men and women who had flocked together. Each one began to look at the others and to want to be looked at himself, and public esteem had a value. The one who sang or danced the best, the hand-somest, the strongest, the most adroit or the most eloquent became the most highly regarded. And this was the first step toward inequality and, at the same time, toward vice. From these first preferences were born vanity and contempt on the one hand, and shame and envy on the other. And the fermentation caused by these new leavens eventually produced compounds fatal to happiness and inno-cence.

As soon as men had begun mutually to value one another, and the idea of esteem was formed in their minds, each one claimed to have a right to it, and it was no longer possible for anyone to be lacking it with impunity. From this came the first duties of civility, even among savages; and from this every voluntary wrong became an outrage, because along with the harm that resulted from the injury, the offended party saw in it contempt for his person, which often was more insufferable then the harm itself. Hence each man punished the contempt shown him in a manner proportionate to the esteem in which he held himself; acts of revenge became terrible, and men became bloodthirsty and cruel. This is precisely the stage reached by most of the savage people known to us; and it is for want of having made adequate distinctions among their ideas or of having noticed how far these peoples already were from the original state of nature that many have hastened to conclude that man is naturally cruel, and that he needs civilization in order to soften him. On the contrary, nothing is so gentle as man in his primitive state, when, placed by nature at an equal distance from the stupidity of brutes and the fatal enlightenment of civil man, and limited equally by instinct and reason to protecting himself from the harm that threatens him, he is restrained by natural pity from needlessly harming anyone himself, even if he has been harmed. For according to the axiom of the wise Locke, *where there is no property, there is no injury*.

But it must be noted that society in its beginning stages and the relations already established among men required in them qualities different from those they derived from their primitive constitution; that, with morality beginning to be introduced into human actions, and everyone, prior to the existence of laws, being sole judge and avenger of the offenses he had received, the goodness appropriate to the pure state of nature was no longer what was appropriate to an emerging society; that it was necessary for punishments to become more severe in proportion as the occasions for giving offense became more frequent; and that it was for the fear of vengeance to take the place of the deterrent character of laws. Hence although men had become less forebearing, and although natural pity had already undergone some alteration, this period of the development of human faculties, maintaining a middle position between the indolence of our primitive state and the petulant activity of our egocentrism, must have been the happiest and most durable epoch. The more one reflects on it, the more one finds that this state was the least subject to upheavals and the best for man, and that he must have left it only by virtue of some fatal chance happening that, for the common good, ought never have happened. The example of savages, almost all of whom have been found in this state, seems to confirm that the human race had been made to remain in it always; that this state is the veritable youth of the world; and that all the subsequent progress has been in appearance so many steps toward the perfection of the individual, and in fact toward the decay of the species.

As long as men were content with the rustic huts, as long as they were limited to making their clothing out of skins sewn together with thorns or fish bones, adorning themselves with feathers and shells, painting their bodies with various colors, perfecting or embellishing their bows and arrows, using sharp-edged stones to make some fishing canoes or some crude musical instruments; in a word, as long as they applied themselves exclusively to tasks that a single individual could do and to the arts that did not require the cooperation of several hands, they lived as free, healthy, good and happy as they could in accordance with their nature; and they continued to enjoy among themselves the sweet rewards of independent intercourse. But as soon as one man needed the help of another, as soon as one man realized that it was useful for a single individual to have provisions for two, equality disappeared, property came into existence, labor became necessary. Vast forests were transformed into smiling fields which had to be watered with men's sweat, and in which slavery and misery were soon seen to germinate and grow with the crops.

Metallurgy and agriculture were the two arts whose invention produced this great revolution. For the poet, it is gold and silver; but for the philosopher, it is iron and wheat that have civilized men and ruined the human race. Thus they were both unknown to the savages of America, who for that reason have always remained savages. Other peoples even appear to have remained barbarous, as long as they practiced one of those arts without the other. And perhaps one of the best reasons why Europe has been, if not sooner, at least more constantly and better governed than the other parts of the world, is that it is at the same time the most abundant in iron and the most fertile in wheat.

It is very difficult to guess how men came to know and use iron, for it is incredible that by themselves they thought of drawing the ore from the mine and performing the necessary preparations on it for smelting it before they knew what would result. From another point of view, it is even less plausible to attribute this discovery to some accidental fire, because mines are set up exclusively in arid places devoid of trees and plants, so that one would say that nature had taken precautions to conceal this deadly secret from us. Thus there remains only the extraordinary circumstance of some volcano that, in casting forth molten metal, would have given observers the idea of imitating this operation of nature. Even still we must suppose them to have had a great deal of courage and foresight to undertake such a difficult task and to have envisaged so far in advance the advantages they could derive from it. This is hardly suitable for minds already better trained than theirs must have been.

As for agriculture, its principle was known long before its practice was established, and it is hardly possible that men, constantly preoccupied with deriving their subsistence from trees and plants, did not rather quickly get the idea of the methods used by nature to grow plant life. But their industry probably did not turn in that direction until very late either because trees, which, along with hunting and fishing, provided their nourishment, had no need of their care; or for want of knowing how to use wheat; or for want of tools with which to cultivate it; or for want of foresight regarding future needs; or, finally, for want of the means of preventing others from appropriating the fruits of their labors. Having become more industrious, it is believable that, with sharp stones and pointed sticks, they began by cultivating some vegetables or roots around their huts long before they knew how to prepare wheat and had the tools necessary for large-scale cultivation.

Moreover, to devote oneself to that occupation and to sow the lands, one must be resolved to lose something at first in order to gain a great deal later: a precaution quite far removed from the mind of the savage man, who, as I have said, finds it quite difficult to give thought in the morning to what he will need at night.

The invention of the other arts was therefore necessary to force the human race to apply itself to that of agriculture. Once men were needed in order to smelt and forge the iron, other men were needed in order to feed them. The more the number of workers increased, the fewer hands there were to obtain food for the common subsistence, without there being fewer mouths to consume it; and since some needed foodstuffs in exchange for their iron, the others finally found the secret of using iron to multiply foodstuffs. From this there arose farming and agriculture, on the one hand, and the art of working metals and multiplying their uses, on the other.

From the cultivation of land, there necessarily followed the division of land; and from property once recognized, the first rules of justice. For in order to render everyone what is his, it is necessary that everyone can have something. Moreover, as men began to look toward the future and as they saw that they all had goods to lose, there was not one of them who did not have to fear reprisals against himself for wrongs he might do to another. This origin is all the more natural as it is impossible to conceive of the idea of property arising from anything but manual labor, for it is not clear what man can add, beyond his own labor, in order to appropriate things he has not made. It is labor alone that, in giving the cultivator a right to the product of the soil he has tilled, consequently gives him a right, at least until the harvest, and thus from year to year. With this possession continuing uninterrupted, it is easily transformed into property. When the ancients, says Grotius, gave Ceres the epithet of legislatrix, gave the name Thesmophories to a festival celebrated in her honor, they thereby made it apparent that the division of lands has produced a new kind of right: namely, the right of property, different from that which results from the natural law.

Things in this state could have remained equal, if talents had been equal, and if the use of iron and the consumption of foodstuffs had always been in precise balance. But this proportion, which was not maintained by anything, was soon broken. The strongest did the most work; the most adroit turned theirs to better advantage: the most ingenious found ways to shorten their labor. The farmer had a greater need for iron, or the blacksmith had a greater need for wheat; and in laboring equally, the one earned a great deal while the other barely had enough to live. Thus it is that natural inequality imperceptibly manifests itself together with inequality occasioned by the socialization process. Thus it is that the differences among men, developed by those of circumstances, make themselves more noticeable, more permanent in their effects, and begin to influence the fate of private individuals in the same proportion.

With things having reached this point, it is easy to imagine the rest. I will not stop to describe the successive invention of the arts, the progress of languages, the testing and use of talents, the inequality of fortunes, the use or abuse of wealth, nor all the details that follow these and that everyone can easily supply. I will limit myself exclusively to taking a look at the human race placed in this new order of things.

Thus we find here all our faculties developed, memory and imagination in play, egocentrism looking out for its interests, reason rendered active, and the mind having nearly reached the limit of the perfection of which it is capable. We find here all the natural qualities put into action, the rank and fate of each man established not only on the basis of the quantity of goods and the power to serve or harm, but also on the basis of mind, beauty, strength or skill, on the basis of merit or talents. And since these qualities were the only ones that could attract consideration, he was soon forced to have them or affect them. It was necessary, for his advantage, to show himself to be something other than what he in fact was. Being something and appearing to be something became two completely different things; and from this distinction there arose grand ostentation, deceptive cunning, and all the vices that follow in their wake. On the other hand, although man had previously been free and independent, we find him, so to speak, subject, by virtue of a multitude of fresh needs, to all of nature and particularly to his fellowmen, whose slave in a sense he becomes even in becoming their master; rich, he needs their services; poor, he needs their help; and being midway between wealth and poverty does not put him in a position to get along without them. It is therefore necessary for him to seek incessantly to interest them in his fate and to make them find their own profit, in fact or in appearance, in working for his. This makes him two-faced and crooked with some, imperious and harsh with others, and puts him in the position of having to abuse everyone he needs when he cannot make them fear them and does not find it in his interests to be of useful service to them. Finally, consuming ambition, the zeal for raising the relative level of his fortune, less out of real need than in order to put himself above others, inspires in all men a wicked tendency to harm one another, a secret jealousy all the more dangerous because, in order to strike its blow in greater safety, it often wears the mask of benevolence; in short, competition and rivalry on the one hand, opposition of interest[s] on the other, and always the hidden desire to profit at the expense of someone else. All these ills are the first effect of property and the inseparable offshoot of incipient inequality.

Before representative signs of wealth had been invented, it could hardly have consisted of anything but lands and livestock, the only real goods men can possess. Now when inheritances had grown in number and size to the point of covering the entire landscape and of all bordering on one another, some could no longer be enlarged except at the expense of others; and the supernumeraries, whom weakness or indolence had prevented from acquiring an inheritance in their turn, became poor without having lost anything, because while everything changed around them, they alone had not changed at all. Thus they were forced to receive or steal their subsistence from the hands of the rich. And from that there began to arise, according to the diverse characters of the rich and the poor, domination and servitude, or violence and thefts. For their part, the wealthy had no sooner known the pleasure of domination, than before long they disdained all others, and using their old slaves to subdue new ones, they thought of nothing but the subjugation and enslavement of their neighbors, like those ravenous wolves which, on having once tasted human flesh, reject all other food and desire to devour only men.

Thus, when both the most powerful or the most miserable made of their strength or their needs a sort of right to another's goods, equivalent, according to them, to the right of property, the destruction of equality was followed by the most frightful disorder. Thus the usurpations of the rich, the acts of brigandage by the poor, the unbridled passions of all, stifling natural pity and the still weak voice of justice, made men greedy, ambitious and wicked. There arose between the right of the strongest and the right of the first occupant a perpetual conflict that ended only in fights and murders. Emerging society gave way to the most horrible state of war; since the human race, vilified and desolated, was no longer able to retrace its steps or give up the unfortunate acquisitions it had made, and since it labored only toward its shame by abusing the faculties that honor it, it brought itself to the brink of its ruin. *Horrified by the newness of the ill, both the poor man and the rich man hope to flee from wealth, hating what they once had prayed for.*

It is not possible that men should not have eventually reflected upon so miserable a situation and upon the calamities that overwhelm them. The rich in particular must have soon felt how disadvantageous to them it was to have a perpetual war in which they alone paid all the costs, and in which the risk of losing one's life was common to all and the risk of losing one's goods was personal. Moreover, regardless of the light in which they tried to place their usurpations, they knew full well that they were established on nothing but a precarious and abusive right, and that having been acquired merely by force, force might take them away from them without their having any reason to complain. Even those enriched exclusively by industry could hardly base their property on better claims. They could very well say: "I am the one who built that wall; I have earned this land with my labor." In response to them it could be said: "Who gave you the boundary lines? By what right do you claim to exact payment at our expense for labor we did not impose upon you? Are you unaware that a multitude of your brothers perish or suffer from need of what you have in excess, and that you needed explicit and unanimous consent from the human race for you to help yourself to anything from the common subsistence that went beyond your own?" Bereft of valid reasons to justify himself and sufficient forces to defend himself; easily crushing a private individual, but himself crushed by troops of bandits; alone against all and unable on account of mutual jealousies to unite with his equals against enemies united by the common hope of plunder, the rich, pressed by necessity, finally conceived the most thought-out project that ever entered the human mind. It was to use in his favor the very strength of those who attacked him, to turn his adversaries into his defenders, to instill in them other maxims, and to give them other institutions which were as favorable to him as natural right was unfavorable to him.

With this end in mind, after having shown his neighbors the horror of a situation which armed them all against each other and made their possessions as burdensome as their needs, and in which no one could find safety in either poverty or wealth, he easily invented specious reasons to lead them to his goal. "Let us unite," he says to them, "in order to protect the weak from oppression, restrain the ambitious, and assure everyone of possessing what belongs to him. Let us institute rules of justice and peace to which all will be obliged to conform, which will make special exceptions for no one, and which will in some way compensate for the caprices of fortune by subjecting the strong and the weak to mutual obligations. In short, instead of turning our forces against ourselves, let us gather them into one supreme power that governs us according to wise laws, that protects and defends all the members of the association, repulses common enemies, and maintains us in an eternal concord."

Considerably less than the equivalent of this discourse was needed to convince crude, easily seduced men who also had too many disputes to settle among themselves to be able to get along without arbiters, and too much greed and ambition to be able to get along without masters for long. They all ran to chain themselves, in the belief that they secured their liberty, for although they had enough sense to realize the advantages of a political establishment, they did not have enough experience to foresee its dangers. Those most capable of anticipating the abuses were precisely those who counted on profiting from them; and even the wise saw the need to be resolved to sacrifice one part of their liberty to preserve the other, just as a wounded man has his arm amputated to save the rest of his body.

Such was, or should have been, the origin of society and laws, which gave new fetters to the weak and new forces to the rich, irretrievably destroyed natural liberty, established forever the law of property and of inequality, changed adroit usurpation into an irrevocable right, and for the profit of a few ambitious men henceforth subjected the entire human race to labor, servitude and misery. It is readily apparent how the establishment of a single society rendered indispensable that of all the others, and how, to stand head to head against the united forces, it was necessary to unite in turn. Societies, multiplying or spreading rapidly, soon covered the entire surface of the earth; and it was no longer possible to find a single corner in the universe where someone could free himself from the yoke and withdraw his head from the often ill-guided sword which everyone saw perpetually hanging over his own head. With civil right thus having become the common rule of citizens, the law of nature no longer was operative except between the various societies, when, under the name of the law of nations, it was tempered by some tacit conventions in order to make intercourse possible and to serve as a substitute for natural compassion which, losing between one society and another nearly all the force it had between one man and another, no longer resides anywhere but in a few great cosmopolitan souls, who overcome the imaginary barriers that separate peoples, and who, following the example of the sovereign being who has created them, embrace the entire human race in their benevolence.

Remaining thus among themselves in the state of nature, the bodies politic soon experienced the inconveniences that had forced private individuals to leave it; and that state became even more deadly among these great bodies than that state had among the private individuals of whom they were composed. Whence came the national wars, battles, murders, and reprisals that make nature tremble and offend reason, and all those horrible prejudices that rank the honor of shedding human blood among the virtues. The most decent people learned to consider it one of their duties to kill their fellow men. Finally, men were seen massacring one another by the thousands without knowing why. More murders were committed in a single day of combat and more horrors in the capture of a single city than were committed in the state of nature during entire centuries over the entire face of the earth. Such are the first effects one glimpses of the division of mankind into different societies. . . .

In discovering and following thus the forgotten and lost routes that must have led man from the natural state to the civil state; in reestablishing, with the intermediate positions I have just taken note of, those that time constraints on me have made me suppress or that the imagination has not suggested to me, no attentive reader can fail to be struck by the immense space that separates these two states. It is in this slow succession of things that he will see the solution to an infinity of moral and political problems which the philosophers are unable to resolve. He will realize that, since the human race of one age is not the human race of another age, the reason why Diogenes did not find his man is because he searched among his contemporaries for a man who no longer existed. Cato, he will say, perished with Rome and liberty because he was out of place in his age; and this greatest of men merely astonished the world, which five hundred years earlier he would have governed. In short, he will explain how the soul and human passions are imperceptibly altered and, as it were, change their nature; why, in the long run, our needs and our pleasures change their objects; why, with original man gradually disappearing, society no longer offers to the eyes of the wise man anything but an assemblage of artificial men and factitious passions which are the work of all these new relations and have no true foundation in nature. What reflection teaches us on this subject is perfectly confirmed by observation: savage man and civilized man differ so greatly in the depths of their hearts and in their inclinations, that what constitutes the supreme happiness of the one would reduce the other to despair. Savage man breathes only tranquility and liberty; he wants simply to live and rest easy; and not even the unperturbed tranquility of the Stoic approaches his profound indifference for any other objects. On the other hand, the citizen is always active and in a sweat, always agitated, and unceasingly tormenting himself in order to seek still more laborious occupations. He works until he dies; he even runs to his death in order to be in a position to live, or renounces life in order to acquire immortality. He pays court to the great whom he hates and to the rich whom he scorns. He stops at nothing to obtain the honor of serving them. He proudly crows about his own baseness and their protection; and proud of his slavery, he speaks with disdain about those who do not have the honor of taking part in it. What a spectacle for the Carib are the difficult and envied labors of the European minister! How many cruel deaths would that indolent savage not prefer to the horror of such a life, which often is not mollified even by the pleasure of doing good. But in order to see the purpose of so many cares, the words *power* and *reputation* would have to have a meaning in his mind; he would have to learn that there is a type of men who place some value on the regard the rest of the world has for them, and who know how to be happy and content with themselves on the testimony of others rather than on their own. Such, in fact, is the true cause of all these differences; the savage lives in himself; the man accustomed to the ways of society is always outside himself and knows how to live only in the opinion of others. And it is, as it were, from their judgment alone that he draws the sentiment of his own existence. It is not pertinent to my subject to show how, from such a disposition, so much indifference for good and evil arises, along with such fine discourse on morality; how, with everything reduced to appearances, everything becomes factitious and bogus: honor, friendship, virtue, and often even our vices, about which we eventually find the secret of boasting; how, in a word, always asking others what we are and never daring to question ourselves on this matter, in the midst of so much philosophy, humanity, politeness, and sublime maxims, we have merely a deceitful and frivolous exterior: honor without virtue, reason without wisdom, and pleasure without happiness. It is enough for me to have proved that this is not the original state of man, and that this is only the spirit of society, and the inequality that society engenders, which thus change and alter all our natural inclinations.

I have tried to set forth the origin and progress of inequality, the establishment and abuse of political societies, to the extent that these things can be deduced from the nature of man by the light of reason alone, and independently of the sacred dogmas that give to sovereign authority the sanction of divine right. It follows from this presentation that, since inequality is practically non-existent in the state of nature, it derives its force and growth from the development of our faculties and the progress of the human mind, and eventually becomes stable and legitimate through the establishment of property and laws. Moreover, it follows that moral inequality, authorized by positive right alone, is contrary to natural right whenever it is not combined in the same proportion with physical inequality: a distinction that is sufficient to determine what one should think in this regard about the sort of inequality that reigns among all civilized people, for it is obviously contrary to the law of nature, however it may be defined, for a child to command an old man, for an imbecile to lead a wise man, and for a handful of people to gorge themselves on superfluities while the starving multitude lacks necessities.

14

Adam Smith
The Wealth of Nations

Adam Smith (1723–1790) was a leading figure in the Scottish Enlightenment, and taught moral philosophy in Glasgow. His most famous book, The Wealth of Nations *(1776), is one of the great classics of liberal political economy. Smith believed that there is a natural economic order expressed through competition, self-interest, and individual entrepreneurialism. Through the free market mechanism of supply and demand, he argued, an "invisible hand" brings about a natural equilibrium and harmony. Consequently, he believed in laisser-faire (leave alone)—that is, the idea that government should intrude as little as possible in the socioeconomic realm. However, he did recognize the need for an active government role in some matters of importance, as can be seen in the following passages from* The Wealth of Nations.

Introduction and Plan of the Work

The annual labor of every nation is the fund which originally supplies it with all the necessaries and conveniencies of life which it annually consumes, and which consist always either in the immediate produce of that labor, or in what is purchased with that produce from other nations.

According therefore, as this produce, or what is purchased with it, bears a greater or smaller proportion to the number of those who are to consume it, the nation will be better or worse supplied with all the necessaries and conveniencies for which it has occasion.

But this proportion must in every nation be regulated by two different circumstances: first, by the skill, dexterity, and judgment with which its labor is generally applied; and, secondly, by the proportion between the number of those who are employed in useful labor, and that of those who are not so employed. Whatever be the soil, climate, or extent of territory of any particular nation, the abundance or scantiness of its annual supply must, in that particular situation, depend upon those two circumstances.

The abundance or scantiness of this supply, too, seems to depend more upon the former of those two circumstances than upon the latter. Among the savage nations of hunters and fishers, every individual who is able to work is more or less employed in useful labor, and endeavors to provide, as well as he can, the necessaries and conveniences of life, for himself, or such of his family or tribe as are either too old, or too young, or too infirm to go hunting and fishing. Such nations, however, are so miserably poor that from mere want they are frequently reduced, or at least think themselves reduced, to the necessity sometimes of directly destroying, and sometimes of abandoning, their infants, their old people, and those afflicted with lingering diseases, to perish with hunger, or to be devoured by wild beasts. Among civilized and thriving nations, on the contrary, though a great number of people do not labor at all—many of whom consume the produce of ten times, frequently of a hundred times, more labor than the greater part of those who work—yet the produce of the whole labor of the society is so great that all are often abundantly supplied; and a workman, even of the lowest and poorest order, if he is frugal and industrious, may enjoy a greater share of the necessaries and conveniencies of life than it is possible for any savage to acquire. . . .

Whatever be the actual state of the skill, dexterity, and judgment with which labor is applied in any nation, the abundance or scantiness of its annual supply must depend, during the continuance of that state upon the proportion between the number of those who are annually employed in useful labor, and that of those who are not so employed. The number of useful and productive laborers, it will hereafter appear, is everywhere in proportion to the quantity of capital stock which is employed in setting them to work, and to the particular way in which it is so employed. . . .

Nations tolerably well advanced as to skill, dexterity, and judgment in the application of labor have followed very different plans in the general conduct or direction of it; and those plans have not all been equally favorable to the greatness of its produce. The policy of some nations has given extraordinary encouragement to the industry of the country; that of others to the industry of towns. Scarcely any nation has dealt equally and impartially with every sort of industry. Since the downfall of the Roman Empire, the policy of Europe has been more favorable to arts, manufactures, and commerce—the industry of towns—than to agriculture—the industry of the country. . . .

Though those different plans were, perhaps, first introduced by the private interests and prejudices of particular orders of men, without any regard to, or foresight of, their consequences upon the general welfare of the society; yet they have given occasion to very different theories of political economy, of which some magnify the importance of that industry which is carried on in towns, others of that which is carried on in the country. Those theories have had a considerable influence, not only upon the opinions of men of learning, but upon the public conduct of princes and sovereign states.

Of the Division of Labor

The greatest improvement in the productive powers of labor, and the greater part of the skill, dexterity, and judgment with which it is anywhere directed, or applied, seem to have been the effects of the division of labor.

The effects of the division of labor, in the general business of society, will be more easily understood by considering in what manner it operates in some particular manufactures. It is commonly supposed to be carried furthest in some very trifling ones; not perhaps that it really is carried further in them than in others of

more importance: but in those trifling manufactures which are destined to supply
the small wants of but a small number of people, the whole number of workmen
must necessarily be small; and those employed in every different branch of the
work can often be collected into the same workhouse and place at once under the
view of the spectator. In those great manufactures, on the contrary, which are
destined to supply the great wants of the great body of the people, every different
branch of the work employs so great a number of workmen that it is impossible to
collect them all into the same workhouse. We can seldom see more, at one time,
than those employed in one single branch. Though in such manufactures, therefore, the work may really be divided into a much greater number of parts than in
those of a more trifling nature, the division is not near so obvious, and has accordingly been much less observed.

To take an example, therefore, from a very trifling manufacture; but one in
which the division of labor has been very often taken notice of, the trade of the
pin-maker; a workman not educated to this business (which the division of labor
has rendered a distinct trade), nor acquainted with the use of the machinery employed in it (to the invention of which the same division of labor has probably
given occasion), could scarce, perhaps, with his utmost industry, make one pin in
a day, and certainly could not make twenty. But in the way in which this business
is now carried on, not only the whole work is a peculiar trade, but it is divided
into a number of branches, of which the greater part are likewise peculiar trades.
One man draws out the wire, another straights it, a third cuts it, a fourth points it,
a fifth grinds it at the top for receiving the head; to make the head requires two or
three distinct operations; to put it on is a peculiar business, to whiten the pins is
another; it is even a trade by itself to put them into the paper; and the important
business of making a pin is, in this manner, divided into about eighteen distinct
operations, which, in some manufactories, are all performed by distinct hands,
though in others the same man will sometimes perform two or three of them. I
have seen a small manufactory of this kind where ten men only were employed,
and where some of them consequently performed two or three distinct operations.
But though they were very poor, and therefore but indifferently accommodated
with the necessary machinery, they could, when they exerted themselves, make
among them about twelve pounds of pins in a day. There are in a pound upwards
of four thousand pins of a middling size. Those ten persons, therefore, could make
among them upwards of forty-eight thousand pins in a day. Each person, therefore, making a tenth part of forty-eight thousand pins, might be considered as
making four thousand eight hundred pins in a day. But if they had all wrought
separately and independently, and without any of them having been educated to
this peculiar business, they certainly could not each of them have made twenty,
perhaps not one pin in a day; that is, certainly, not the two hundred and fortieth,
perhaps not the four thousand eight hundredth part, of what they are at present
capable of performing in consequence of a proper division and combination of
their different operations.

In every other art and manufacture, the effects of the division of labor are
similar to what they are in this very trifling one; though in many of them, the labor

can neither be so much subdivided, nor reduced to so great a simplicity of operation. The division of labor, however, so far as it can be introduced, occasions, in every art, a proportionable increase of the productive powers of labor. The separation of different trades and employments from one another seems to have taken place in consequence of this advantage. This separation too is generally carried furthest in those countries which enjoy the highest degree of industry and improvement; what is the work of one man in a rude state of society being generally that of several in an improved one. . . .

It is the great multiplication of the productions of all the different arts, in consequence of the division of labor, which occasions, in a well-governed society, that universal opulence which extends itself to the lowest ranks of the people. Every workman has a great quantity of his own work to dispose of beyond what he himself has occasion for; and every other workman being exactly in the same situation, he is enabled to exchange a great quantity of his own goods for a great quantity, or, what comes to the same thing, for the price of a great quantity of theirs. He supplies them abundantly with what they have occasion for, and they accommodate him as amply with what he has occasion for, and a general plenty diffuses itself through all the different ranks of the society. . . .

Of the Principle Which Gives Occasion to the Division of Labor

This division of labor, from which so many advantages are derived, is not originally the effect of any human wisdom which foresees and intends that general opulence to which it gives occasion. It is the necessary, though very slow and gradual, consequence of a certain propensity in human nature which has in view no such extensive utility: the propensity to truck, barter, and exchange one thing for another.

Whether this propensity be one of those original principles in human nature, of which no further account can be given; or whether, as seems more probable, it be the necessary consequence of the faculties of reason and speech, it belongs not to our present subject to enquire. It is common to all men, and to be found in no other race of animals, which seem to know neither this nor any other species of contracts. Two greyhounds, in running down the same hare, have sometimes the appearance of acting in some sort of concert. Each turns her toward his companion, or endeavors to intercept her when his companion turns her toward himself. This, however, is not the effect of any contract, but of the accidental concurrence of their passions in the same object at that particular time. Nobody ever saw a dog make a fair and deliberate exchange of one bone for another with another dog. Nobody ever saw one animal by its gestures and natural cries signify to another, this is mine, that yours; I am willing to give this for that. When an animal wants to obtain something either of a man or of another animal, it has no other means of persuasion but to gain the favor of those whose service it requires. A puppy fawns upon its dam, and a spaniel endeavors by a thousand attractions to engage the attention of its master who is at dinner, when it wants to be fed by him. Man sometimes uses the same arts with his brethren, and when he has no other means of engaging them to act according to his inclinations, endeavors by every servile and fawning attention to obtain their good will. He has not time, however, to do this upon every occasion. In civilized society he stands at all times in need of the co-operation and assistance of great multitudes, while his whole life is scarce sufficient to gain the friendship of a few persons. In almost every other race of animals each individual, when it is grown up to maturity, is entirely independent, and in its natural state has occasion for the assistance of no other living creature. But man has almost constant occasion for the help of his brethren, and it is in vain for him to expect it from their benevolence only. He will be more likely to prevail if he can interest their self-love in his favor, and show them that it is for their own advantage to do for him what he requires of them. Whoever offers to another a bargain of any kind, proposes to do this. Give me that which I want, and you shall have this which you want, is the meaning of every such offer; and it is in this manner that we obtain from one another the far greater part of those good offices which we stand in need of. It is not from the benevolence of the butcher, the brewer, or the baker, that we expect our dinner, but from their regard to their own interest. We address ourselves, not to their humanity but to their self-love, and never talk to them of our own necessities but of their advantages. Nobody but a beggar chooses to depend chiefly upon the benevolence of his fellow-citizens. Even a beggar does not depend upon it entirely. The charity of well-disposed people, indeed, supplies him with the whole fund of his subsistence. But though this principle ultimately provides him with all the necessaries of life which he has occasion for, it neither does nor can provide him with them as he has occasion for them. The greater part of his occasional wants are supplied in the same manner as those of other people, by treaty, by barter, and by purchase. With the money which one man gives him he purchases food. The old clothes which another bestows upon him he exchanges for other old clothes which suit him better, or for lodging, or for food, or for money, with which he can buy either food, clothes, or lodging, as he has occasion.

As it is by treaty, by barter, and by purchase that we obtain from one another the greater part of those mutual good offices which we stand in need of, so it is this same trucking disposition which originally gives occasion to the division of labor. In a tribe of hunters or shepherds a particular person makes bows and arrows, for example, with more readiness and dexterity than any other. He frequently exchanges them for cattle or for venison with his companions; and he finds at last that he can in this manner get more cattle and venison than if he himself went to the field to catch them. From a regard to his own interest, therefore, the making of bows and arrows grows to be his chief business, and he becomes a sort of armorer. Another excels in making the frames and covers of their little huts or movable houses. He is accustomed to be of use in this way to his neighbors, who reward him in the same manner with cattle and with venison till at last he finds it his interest to dedicate himself entirely to this employment, and to become a sort of house carpenter. In the same manner a third becomes a smith or a brazier; a fourth a tanner or dresser of hides or skins, the principal part of the clothing of savages. And thus the certainty of being able to exchange all that surplus part of the produce of his own labor, which is over and above his own consumption, for such parts of the produce of other men's labor as he may have occasion for, encourages every man to apply himself to a particular occupation, and to cultivate and bring to perfection whatever talent or genius he may possess for that particular species of business.

The difference of natural talents in different men is, in reality, much less than we are aware of; and the very different genius which appears to distinguish men of different professions, when grown up to maturity, is not upon many occasions so much the cause as the effect of the division of labor. The difference between the most dissimilar characters, between a philosopher and a common street porter, for example, seems to arise not so much from nature as from habit, custom, and education. . . .

Of the Real and Nominal Price of Commodities, or of Their Price in Labor and Their Price in Money

Every man is rich or poor according to the degree in which he can afford to enjoy the necessaries, conveniences, and amusements of human life. But after the division of labor has once thoroughly taken place, it is but a very small part of these with which a man's own labor can supply him. The far greater part of them he must derive from the labor of other people, and he must be rich or poor according to the quantity of that labor which he can command or which he can afford to purchase. The value of any commodity, therefore, to the person who possesses it, and who means not to use or consume it himself, but to exchange it for other commodities, is equal to the quantity of labor which it enables him to purchase or command. Labor, therefore, is the real measure of the exchangeable value of all commodities.

The real price of every thing, what every thing really costs to the man who wants to acquire it, is the toil and trouble of acquiring it. What every thing is really worth to the man who has acquired it, and who wants to dispose of it or exchange it for something else, is the toil and trouble which it can save to himself, and which it can impose upon other people. What is bought with money or with goods is purchased by labor, as much as what we acquire by the toil of our own body. That money or those goods indeed save us this toil. They contain the value of a certain quantity of labor which we exchange for what is supposed at the time to contain the value of an equal quantity. Labor was the first price, the original purchase-money, that was paid for all things. It was not by gold or by silver, but by labor, that all the wealth of the world was originally purchased; and its value, to those who possess it, and who want to exchange it for some new productions, is precisely equal to the quantity of labor which it can enable them to purchase or command.

Wealth, as Mr. Hobbes says, is power. But the person who either acquires or succeeds to a great fortune does not necessarily acquire or succeed to any political power, either civil or military. His fortune may, perhaps, afford him the means of acquiring both, but the mere possession of that fortune does not necessarily convey to him either. The power which that possession immediately and directly conveys to him is the power of purchasing; a certain command over all the labor, or over all the produce of labor which is then in the market. His fortune is greater or less precisely in proportion to the extent of this power; or to the quantity either of other men's labor, or, what is the same thing, of the produce of other men's labor which it enables him to purchase or command. The exchangeable value of every thing must always be precisely equal to the extent of this power which it conveys to its owner.

But though labor be the real measure of the exchangeable value of all commodities, it is not that by which their value is commonly estimated. It is often difficult to ascertain the proportion between two different quantities of labor. The time spent in two different sorts of work will not always alone determine this proportion. The different degrees of hardship endured, and of ingenuity exercised, must likewise be taken into account. There may be more labor in an hour's hard work than in two hours easy business; or in an hour's application to a trade which it cost ten years labor to learn than in a month's industry at an ordinary and obvious employment. But it is not easy to find any accurate measure either of hardship or ingenuity. In exchanging indeed the different productions of different sorts of labor for one another, some allowance is commonly made for both. It is adjusted, however, not by any accurate measure, but by the higgling and bargaining of the market, according to that sort of rough equality which, though not exact, is sufficient for carrying on the business of common life.

Every commodity besides, is more frequently exchanged for, and thereby compared with, other commodities than with labor. It is more natural therefore, to estimate its exchangeable value by the quantity of some other commodity than by that of the labor which it can purchase. The greater part of people too understand better what is meant by a quantity of a particular commodity than by a quantity of labor. The one is a plain palpable object; the other an abstract notion, which, though it can be made sufficiently intelligible, is not altogether so natural and obvious.

But when barter ceases, and money has become the common instrument of commerce, every particular commodity is more frequently exchanged for money than for any other commodity. The butcher seldom carries his beef or his mutton to the baker or the brewer, in order to exchange them for bread or for beer; but he carries them to the market where he exchanges them for money, and afterwards exchanges that money for bread and for beer. The quantity of money which he gets for them regulates too the quantity of bread and beer which he can afterwards purchase. It is more natural and obvious to him, therefore, to estimate their value by the quantity of money, the commodity for which he immediately exchanges them, than by that of bread and beer, the commodities for which he can exchange them only by the intervention of another commodity; and rather to say that his butcher's meat is worth threepence or fourpence a pound, than that it is worth three or four pounds of bread, or three or four quarts of small beer. Hence it comes to pass that the exchangeable value of every commodity is more frequently estimated by the quantity of money than by the quantity either of labor or of any other commodity which can be had in exchange for it.

Gold and silver, however, like every other commodity, vary in their value, are sometimes cheaper and sometimes dearer, sometimes of easier and sometimes of more difficult purchase. The quantity of labor which any particular quantity of them can purchase or command, or the quantity of other goods which it will exchange for, depends always upon the fertility or barrenness of the mines which happen to be known about the time when such exchanges are made. The discovery of the abundant mines of America reduced, in the sixteenth century, the value of gold and silver in Europe to about a third of what it had been before. As it cost less labor to bring those metals from the mine to the market, so when they were brought thither they could purchase or command less labor; and this revolution in their value, though perhaps the greatest, is by no means the only one of which history gives some account. But as a measure of quantity, such as the natural foot, fathom, or handful, which is continually varying in its own quantity, can never be an accurate measure of the quantity of other things, so a commodity which is itself continually varying in its own value can never be an accurate measure of the value of other commodities. Equal quantities of labor, at all times and places, may be said to be of equal value to the laborer. In his ordinary state of health, strength, and spirits; in the ordinary degree of his skill and dexterity, he must always lay down the same portion of his ease, his liberty, and his happiness. The price which he pays must always be the same, whatever may be the quantity of goods which he receives in return for it. Of these, indeed, it may sometimes purchase a greater and sometimes a smaller quantity, but it is their value which varies, not that of the labor which purchases them. At all times and places that is dear which it is difficult to come at, or which it costs much labor to acquire; and that cheap which is to be had easily, or with very little labor. Labor alone, therefore, never varying in its own value, is alone the ultimate and real standard by which the value of all commodities can at all times and places be estimated and compared. It is their real price; money is their nominal price only.

But though equal quantities of labor are always of equal value to the laborer, yet to the person who employs him they appear sometimes to be of greater and sometimes of smaller value. He purchases them sometimes with a greater and sometimes with a smaller quantity of goods, and to him the price of labor seems to vary like that of all other things. It appears to him dear in the one case, and cheap in the other. In reality, however, it is the goods which are cheap in the one case, and dear in the other.

In this popular sense, therefore, labor, like commodities, may be said to have a real and a nominal price. Its real price may be said to consist in the quantity of the necessaries and conveniencies of life which are given for it; its nominal price, in the quantity of money. The laborer is rich or poor, is well or ill rewarded, in proportion to the real, not to the nominal, price of his labor. . . .

Of the Wages of Labor

The produce of labor constitutes the natural recompense or wages of labor.

In that original state of things, which precedes both the appropriation of land and the accumulation of stock, the whole produce of labor belongs to the laborer. He has neither landlord nor master to share with him.

Had this state continued, the wages of labor would have augmented with all those improvements in its productive powers to which the division of labor gives occasion. All things would gradually have become cheaper. They would have been produced by a smaller quantity of labor, and as the commodities produced by equal quantities of labor would naturally in this state of things be exchanged for one another, they would have been purchased likewise with the produce of a smaller quantity.

But though all things would have become cheaper in reality, in appearance many things might have become dearer than before, or have been exchanged for a greater quantity of other goods. Let us suppose, for example, that in the greater part of employments the productive powers of labor had been improved to tenfold, or that a day's labor could produce ten times the quantity of work which it had done originally; but that in a particular employment they had been improved only to double, or that a day's labor could produce only twice the quantity of work which it had done before. In exchanging the produce of a day's labor in the greater part of employments for that of a day's labor in this particular one, ten times the original quantity of work in them would purchase only twice the original quantity in it. Any particular quantity in it, therefore, a pound weight, for example, would appear to be five times dearer than before. In reality, however, it would be twice as cheap. Though it required five times the quantity of other goods to purchase it, it would require only half the quantity of labor either to purchase or to produce it. The acquisition, therefore, would be twice as easy as before.

But this original state of things, in which the laborer enjoyed the whole produce of his own labor, could not last beyond the first introduction of the appropriation of land and the accumulation of stock. It was at an end, therefore, long before the most considerable improvements were made in the productive powers of labor, and it would be to no purpose to trace further what might have been its effects upon the recompense or wages of labor.

As soon as land becomes private property, the landlord demands a share of almost all the produce which the laborer can either raise or collect from it. His rent makes the first deduction from the produce of the labor which is employed upon land.

It seldom happens that the person who tills the ground has wherewithal to maintain himself till he reaps the harvest. His maintenance is generally advanced to him from the stock of a master, the farmer who employs him, and who would have no interest to employ him, unless he was to share in the produce of his labor, or unless his stock was to be replaced to him with a profit. This profit makes a second deduction from the produce of the labor which is employed upon land.

The produce of almost all other labor is liable to the like deduction of profit. In all arts and manufactures the greater part of the workmen stand in need of a master to advance them the materials of their work, and their wages and maintenance till it be completed. He shares in the produce of their labor, or in the value which it adds to the materials upon which it is bestowed; and in this share consists his profit.

It sometimes happens, indeed, that a single independent workman has stock sufficient both to purchase the materials of his work, and to maintain himself till it is completed. He is both master and workman, and enjoys the whole produce of his own labor, or the whole value which it adds to the materials upon which it is bestowed. It includes what are usually two distinct revenues, belonging to two distinct persons, the profits of stock, and the wages of labor.

Such cases, however, are not very frequent, and in every part of Europe twenty workmen serve under a master for one that is independent; and the wages of labor are everywhere understood to be, what they usually are, when the laborer is one person, and the owner of the stock which employs him another.

What are the common wages of labor depends everywhere upon the contract usually made between those two parties, whose interests are by no means the same. The workmen desire to get as much, the masters to give as little as possible. The former are disposed to combine in order to raise, the latter in order to lower, the wages of labor.

It is not, however, difficult to foresee which of the two parties must, upon all ordinary occasions, have the advantage in the dispute, and force the other into a compliance with their terms. The masters, being fewer in number, can combine much more easily; and the law, besides, authorizes, or at least does not prohibit their combinations, while it prohibits those of the workmen. We have no acts of Parliament against combining to lower the price of work; but many against combining to raise it. In all such disputes the masters can hold out much longer. A landlord, a farmer, a master manufacturer, or merchant, though they did not employ a single workman, could generally live a year or two upon the stocks which they have already acquired. Many workmen could not subsist a week, few could subsist a month, and scarcely any a year without employment. In the long run the workman may be as necessary to his master as his master is to him, but the necessity is not so immediate.

We rarely hear, it has been said, of the combinations of masters, though frequently of those of workmen. But whoever imagines, upon this account, that masters rarely combine, is as ignorant of the world as of the subject. Masters are always and everywhere in a sort of tacit, but constant and uniform, combination, not to raise the wages of labor above their actual rate. To violate this combination is everywhere a most unpopular action, and a sort of reproach to a master among his neighbors and equals. We seldom, indeed, hear of this combination, because it is the usual and, one may say, the natural state of things which nobody ever hears of. Masters, too, sometimes enter into particular combinations to sink the wages of labor even below this rate. These are always conducted with the utmost silence and secrecy, till the moment of execution, and when the workmen yield, as they sometimes do, without resistance, though severely felt by them, they are never heard of by other people. Such combinations, however, are frequently resisted by a contrary defensive combination of the workmen, who sometimes, too, without any provocation of this kind, combine of their own accord to raise the price of their labor. Their usual pretenses are sometimes the high price of provisions, sometimes the great profit which their masters make by their work. But whether their combinations be offensive or defensive, they are always abundantly heard of.

In order to bring the point to a speedy decision, they have always recourse to the loudest clamor, and sometimes to the most shocking violence and outrage. They are desperate, and act with the folly and extravagance of desperate men, who must either starve or frighten their masters into an immediate compliance with their demands. The masters upon these occasions are just as clamorous upon the other side, and never cease to call aloud for the assistance of the civil magistrate and the rigorous execution of those laws which have been enacted with so much severity against the combinations of servants, laborers, and journeymen. The workmen, accordingly, very seldom derive any advantage from the violence of those tumultuous combinations, which, partly from the interposition of the civil magistrate, partly from the superior steadiness of the masters, partly from the necessity which the greater part of the workmen are under of submitting for the sake of present subsistence, generally end in nothing but the punishment or ruin of the ringleaders.

But though in disputes with their workmen masters must generally have the advantage, there is however a certain rate below which it seems impossible to reduce, for any considerable time, the ordinary wages even of the lowest species of labor.

A man must always live by his work, and his wages must at least be sufficient to maintain him. . . .

Of Restraints upon the Importation from Foreign Countries of Such Goods as Can Be Produced at Home

By restraining, either by high duties, or by absolute prohibitions, the importation of such goods from foreign countries as can be produced at home, the monopoly of the home market is more or less secured to the domestic industry employed in producing them. Thus the prohibition of importing either live cattle or salt provisions from foreign countries secures to the graziers of Great Britain the monopoly of the home market for butcher's meat. The high duties upon the importation of corn, which in times of moderate plenty amount to a prohibition, give a like advantage to the growers of that commodity. The prohibition of the importation of foreign woolens is equally favorable to the woolen manufacturers. The silk manufacture, though altogether employed upon foreign materials, has lately obtained the same advantage. The linen manufacture has not yet obtained it, but is making great strides toward it. Many other sorts of manufacturers have, in the same manner, obtained in Great Britain, either altogether, or very nearly, a monopoly against their countrymen. The variety of goods of which the importation into Great Britain is prohibited, either absolutely, or under certain circumstances, greatly exceeds what can easily be suspected by those who are not well acquainted with the laws of the customs.

That this monopoly of the home market frequently gives great encouragement to that particular species of industry which enjoys it, and frequently turns toward that employment a greater share of both the labor and stock of the society than would otherwise have gone to it, cannot be doubted. But whether it tends either to increase the general industry of the society, or to give it the most advantageous direction, is not, perhaps, altogether so evident.

The general industry of the society never can exceed what the capital of the society can employ. As the number of workmen that can be kept in employment by any particular person must bear a certain proportion to his capital, so the number of those that can be continually employed by all the members of a great society must bear a certain proportion to the whole capital of that society and never can exceed that proportion. No regulation of commerce can increase the quantity of industry in any society beyond what its capital can maintain. It can only divert a part of it into a direction into which it might not otherwise have gone; and it is by no means certain that this artificial direction is likely to be more advantageous to the society than that into which it would have gone of its own accord.

Every individual is continually exerting himself to find out the most advantageous employment for whatever capital he can command. It is his own advantage, indeed, and not that of the society, which he has in view. But the study of his own advantage naturally, nor rather necessarily, leads him to prefer that employment which is most advantageous to the society.

First, every individual endeavors to employ his capital as near home as he can, and consequently as much as he can in the support of domestic industry, provided always that he can thereby obtain the ordinary, or not a great deal less than the ordinary, profits of stock.

Thus, upon equal or nearly equal profits, every wholesale merchant naturally prefers the home trade to the foreign trade of consumption, and the foreign trade of consumption to the carrying trade. In the home trade his capital is never so long out of his sight as it frequently is in the foreign trade of consumption. He can know better the character and situation of the persons whom he trusts, and if he should happen to be deceived, he knows better the laws of the country from which he must seek redress. In the carrying trade, the capital of the merchant is, as it were, divided between two foreign countries, and no part of it is ever necessarily brought home or placed under his own immediate view and command. The capital which an Amsterdam merchant employs in carrying corn from Königsberg to Lisbon, and fruit and wine from Lisbon to Königsberg, must generally be the one half of it at Königsberg and the other half of Lisbon. No part of it need ever come to Amsterdam. The natural residence of such a merchant should either be at Königsberg or Lisbon, and it can only be some very particular circumstances which can make him prefer the residence of Amsterdam. The uneasiness, however, which he feels at being separated so far from his capital generally determines him to bring part both of the Königsberg goods which he destines for the market of Lisbon, and of the Lisbon goods which he destines for that of Königsberg, to Amsterdam; and though this necessarily subjects him to a double charge of loading and unloading, as well as to the payment of some duties and customs, yet for the sake of having some part of his capital always under his own view and command, he willingly submits to this extraordinary charge; and it is in this manner that every country which has any considerable share of the carrying trade becomes always the emporium, or general market, for the goods of all the different countries whose trade it carries on. The merchant, in order to save a second loading and unloading, endeavors always to sell in the home market as much of the goods of all those different countries as he can, and thus, so far as he can, to convert his carrying trade into a foreign trade of consumption. A merchant, in the same manner, who is engaged in the foreign trade of consumption, when he collects goods for foreign markets, will always be glad, upon equal or nearly equal profits, to sell as great a part of them at home as he can. He saves himself the risk and trouble of exportation, when, so far as he can, he thus converts his foreign trade of consumption into a home trade. Home is in this manner the center, if I may say so, around which the capitals of the inhabitants of every country are continually circulating, and toward which they are always tending, though by particular causes they may sometimes be driven off and repelled from it toward more distant employments. But a capital employed in the home trade, it has already been shown, necessarily puts into motion a greater quantity of domestic industry and gives revenue and employment to a greater number of the inhabitants of the country than an equal capital employed in the foreign trade of consumption; and one employed in the foreign trade of consumption has the same advantage over an equal capital employed in the carrying trade. Upon equal, or only nearly equal, profits, therefore, every individual naturally inclines to employ his capital in the manner in which it is likely to afford the greatest support to domestic industry, and to give revenue and employment to the greatest number of people of his own country.

Secondly, every individual who employs his capital in the support of domestic industry necessarily endeavors so to direct that industry that its produce may be of the greatest possible value.

The produce of industry is what it adds to the subject or materials upon which it is employed. In proportion as the value of this produce is great or small, so will likewise be the profits of the employer. But it is only for the sake of profit that any man employs a capital in the support of industry; and he will always, therefore, endeavor to employ it in the support of that industry of which the produce is likely to be of the greatest value, or to exchange for the greatest quantity either of money or of other goods.

But the annual revenue of every society is always precisely equal to the exchangeable value of the whole annual produce of its industry, or rather is precisely the same thing with that exchangeable value. As every individual, therefore, endeavors as much as he can both to employ his capital in the support of domestic industry and so to direct that industry that its produce may be of the greatest value; every individual necessarily labors to render the annual revenue of the society as great as he can. He generally, indeed, neither intends to promote the public interest, nor knows how much he is promoting it. By preferring the support of domestic to that of foreign industry, he intends only his own security; and by directing that industry in such a manner as its produce may be of the greatest value, he intends only his own gain, and he is in this, as in many other cases, led by an invisible hand to promote an end which was no part of his intention. Nor is it always the worse for the society that it was no part of it. By pursuing his own interest he frequently promotes that of the society more effectually than when he really intends to promote it. . . .

The System of Natural Liberty and the Sovereign's Duties

All systems either of preference or of restraint, therefore, being thus completely taken away, the obvious and simple system of natural liberty establishes itself of its own accord. Every man, as long as he does not violate the laws of justice, is left perfectly free to pursue his own interest his own way, and to bring both his industry and capital into competition with those of any other man, or order of men. The sovereign is completely discharged from a duty, in the attempting to perform which he must always be exposed to innumerable delusions, and for the proper performance of which no human wisdom or knowledge could ever be sufficient: the duty of superintending the industry of private people, and of directing it toward the employments most suitable to the interest of the society. According to the system of natural liberty, the sovereign has only three duties to attend to, three duties of great importance, indeed, but plain and intelligible to common understandings: first, the duty of protecting the society from the violence and invasion of other independent societies; secondly, the duty of protecting, as far as possible, every member of the society from the injustice or oppression of every other member of it, or the duty of establishing an exact administration of justice; and, thirdly, the duty of erecting and maintaining certain public works and certain public institutions, which it can never be for the interest of any individual, or small number of individuals, to erect and maintain, because the profit could never repay the expense to any individual or small number of individuals, though it may frequently do much more than repay it to a great society.

The proper performance of those several duties of the sovereign necessarily supposes a certain expense; and this expense again necessarily requires a certain revenue to support it. . . .

Of the Expense of Defense

The first duty of the sovereign, that of protecting the society from the violence and invasion of other independent societies, can be preformed only by means of a military force. But the expense both of preparing this military force in time of peace, and of employing it in time of war, is very different in the different states of society, in the different periods of improvement. . . .

In a more advanced state of society, two different causes contribute to render it altogether impossible that they who take the field should maintain themselves at their own expense. Those two causes are the progress of manufactures, and the improvement in the art of war.

Though a husbandman should be employed in an expedition, provided it begins after seed-time and ends before harvest, the interruption of his business will not always occasion any considerable diminution of his revenue. Without the intervention of his labor, nature does herself the greater part of the work which remains to be done. But the moment that an artificer, a smith, a carpenter, or a weaver, for example, quits his workhouse, the sole source of his revenue is completely dried up. Nature does nothing for him, he does all for himself. When he takes the field, therefore, in defense of the public, as he has no revenue to maintain himself, he must necessarily be maintained by the public. But in a country of which a greater part of the inhabitants are artificers and manufacturers, a great part of the people who go to war must be drawn from those classes, and must therefore be maintained by the public as long as they are employed in its service.

When the art of war too has gradually grown up to be a very intricate and complicated science, when the event of war ceases to be determined, as in the first ages of society, by a single irregular skirmish or battle, but when the contest is generally spun out through several different campaigns, each of which lasts during the greater part of the year; it becomes universally necessary that the public should maintain those who serve the public in war, at least while they are employed in that service. Whatever in time of peace might be the ordinary occupation of those who go to war, so very tedious and expensive a service would otherwise be by far too heavy a burden upon them. . . .

Of the Expense of Justice

The second duty of the sovereign, that of protecting, as far as possible, every member of the society from the injustice or oppression of every other member of it, or the duty of establishing an exact administration of justice, requires two very different degrees of expense in the different periods of society.

Among nations of hunters, as there is scarce any property, or at least none that exceeds the value of two or three days labor; so there is seldom any established magistrate or any regular administration of justice. Men who have no property can injure one another only in their persons or reputations. But when one man kills, wounds, beats, or defames another, though he to whom the injury is done suffers, he who does it receives no benefit. It is otherwise with the injuries to property. The benefit of the person who does the injury is often equal to the loss of him who suffers it. Envy, malice, or resentment are the only passions which can prompt one man to injure another in his person or reputation. But the greater part of men are not very frequently under the influence of those passions; and the very worst men are so only occasionally. As their gratification too, how agreeable soever it may be to certain characters, is not attended with any real or permanent advantage, it is in the greater part of men commonly restrained by prudential considerations. Men may live together in society with some tolerable degree of security, though there is no civil magistrate to protect them from the injustice of those passions. But avarice and ambition in the rich, in the poor the hatred of labor and the love of present ease and enjoyment, are the passions which prompt to invade property, passions much more steady in their operation, and much more universal in their influence. Wherever there is great property, there is great inequality. For one very rich man, there must be at least five hundred poor, and the affluence of the few supposes the indigence of the many. The affluence of the rich excites the indignation of the poor, who are often both driven by want, and prompted by envy, to invade his possessions. It is only under the shelter of the civil magistrate that the owner of the valuable property, which is acquired by the labor of many years, or perhaps of many successive generations, can sleep a single night in security. He is at all times surrounded by unknown enemies, whom, though he never provoked, he can never appease, and from whose injustice he can be protected only by the powerful arm of the civil magistrate continually held up to chastise it. The acquisition of valuable and extensive property, therefore, necessarily requires the establishment of civil government. Where there is no property, or at least none that exceeds the value of two or three days labor, civil government is not so necessary.

Civil government supposed a certain subordination. But as the necessity of civil government gradually grows up with the acquisition of valuable property, so the principal causes which naturally introduce subordination gradually grow up with the growth of that valuable property.

The causes or circumstances which naturally introduce subordination, or which naturally, and antecedent to any civil institution, give some men some superiority over the greater part of their brethren, seem to be four in number.

The first of those causes or circumstances is the superiority of personal qualifications, of strength, beauty, and agility of body; of wisdom, and virtue, of prudence, justice, fortitude, and moderation of mind. The qualifications of the body, unless supported by those of the mind, can give little authority in any period of society. He is a very strong man who, by mere strength of body, can force two weak ones to obey him. The qualifications of the mind can alone give very great authority. They are, however, invisible qualities; always disputable, and generally disputed. No society, whether barbarous or civilized, has ever found it convenient to settle the rules of precedency of rank and subordination according to those invisible qualities; but according to something that is more plain and palpable.

The second of those causes or circumstances is the superiority of age. An old man, provided his age is not so far advanced as to give suspicion of dotage, is everywhere more respected than a young man of equal rank, fortune, and abilities. Among nations of hunters, such as the native tribes of North America, age is the sole foundation of rank and precedency. Among them, father is the appellation of a superior; brother, of an equal; and son, of an inferior. In the most opulent and civilized nations, age regulates rank among those who are in every other respect equal, and among whom, therefore, there is nothing else to regulate it. Among brothers and among sisters, the eldest always take place; and in the succession of the paternal estate every thing which cannot be divided, but must go entire to one person, such as a title of honor, is in most cases given to the eldest. Age is a plain and palpable quality which admits of no dispute.

The third of those causes or circumstances is the superiority of fortune. The authority of riches, however, though great in every age of society, is perhaps greatest in the rudest age of society which admits of any considerable inequality of fortune. A Tartar chief, the increase of whose herds and flocks is sufficient to maintain a thousand men, cannot well employ that increase in any other way than in maintaining a thousand men. The rude state of his society does not afford him any manufactured produce, any trinkets or baubles of any kind, for which he can exchange that part of his rude produce which is over and above his own consumption. The thousand men whom he thus maintains, depending entirely upon him for their subsistence, must both obey his orders in war, and submit to his jurisdiction in peace. He is necessarily both their general and their judge, and his chieftainship is the necessary effect of the superiority of his fortune. In an opulent and civilized society a man may possess a much greater fortune, and yet not be able to command a dozen of people. Though the produce of his estate may be sufficient to maintain, and may perhaps actually maintain, more than a thousand people, yet as those people pay for every thing which they get from him, as he gives scarce anything to anybody but in exchange for an equivalent, there is scarce anybody who considers himself as entirely dependent upon him, and his authority extends only over a few menial servants. The authority of fortune, however, is very great even in an opulent and civilized society. That it is much greater than that either of age or of personal qualities has been the constant complaint of every period of society which admitted of any considerable inequality of fortune. The first period of society, that of hunters, admits of no such inequality. Universal poverty establishes there universal equality, and the superiority either of age or of personal qualities are the feeble, but the sole foundations of authority and subordination. There is therefore little or no authority or subordination in this period of society. The second period of society, that of shepherds, admits of very great inequalities of fortune, and there is no period in which the superiority of fortune gives so great authority to those who possess it. There is no period accordingly in which authority and subordination are more perfectly established. The authority of an Arabian sherif is very great; that of a Tartar khan altogether despotical.

The fourth of those causes or circumstances is the superiority of birth. Superiority of birth supposes an ancient superiority of fortune in the family of the person who claims it. All families are equally ancient; and the ancestors of the prince, though they may be better known, cannot well be more numerous than those of the beggar. Antiquity of family means everywhere the antiquity either of wealth, or of that greatness which is commonly either founded upon wealth, or accompanied with it. Upstart greatness is everywhere less respected than ancient greatness. The hatred of usurpers, the love of the family of an ancient monarch, are, in a great measure, founded upon the contempt which men naturally have for the former, and upon their veneration for the latter. As a military officer submits without reluctance to the authority of a superior by whom he has always been commanded, but cannot bear that his inferior should be set over his head; so men easily submit to a family to whom they and their ancestors have always submitted; but are fired with indignation when another family, in whom they had never acknowledged any such superiority, assumes a dominion over them.

The distinction of birth, being subsequent to the inequality of fortune, can have no place in nations of hunters, among whom all men, being equal in fortune, must likewise be very nearly equal in birth. The son of a wise and brave man may, indeed, even among them, be somewhat more respected than a man of equal merit who has the misfortune to be the son of a fool or a coward. The difference, however, will not be very great; and there never was, I believe, a great family in the world whose illustration was entirely derived from the inheritance of wisdom and virtue.

The distinction of birth not only may but always does take place among nations of shepherds. Such nations are always strangers to every sort of luxury, and great wealth can scarce ever be dissipated among them by improvident profusion. There are no nations accordingly who abound more in families revered and honored on account of their descent from a long race of great and illustrious ancestors; because there are no nations among whom wealth is likely to continue longer in the same families.

Birth and fortune are evidently the two circumstances which principally set one man above another. They are the two great sources of personal distinction, and are therefore the principal causes which naturally establish authority and subordination among men. Among nations of shepherds both those causes operate with their full force. The great shepherd or herdsman, respected on account of his great wealth, and of the great number of those who depend upon him for subsistence, and revered on account of the nobleness of his birth, and of the immemorial antiquity of his illustrious family, has a natural authority over all the inferior shepherds or herdsmen of his horde or clan. He can command the united force of a greater number of people than any of them. His military power is greater than that of any of them. In time of war they are all of them naturally disposed to muster themselves under his banner, rather than under that of any other person, and his birth and fortune thus naturally procure to him some sort of executive power. By commanding too the united force of a greater number of people than any of them, he is best able to compel any one of them who may have injured another to compensate the wrong. He is the person, therefore, to whom all those who are too weak to defend themselves naturally look up for protection. It is to him that they naturally complain of the injuries which they imagine have been done to them, and his interposition in such cases is more easily submitted to, even by the person complained of, than that of any other person would be. His birth and fortune thus naturally procure him some sort of judicial authority.

It is in the age of shepherds, in the second period of society, that the inequality of fortune first begins to take place, and introduces among men a degree of authority and subordination which could not possibly exist before. It thereby introduces some degree of that civil government which is indispensably necessary for its own preservation: and it seems to do this naturally, and even independent of the consideration of that necessity. The consideration of that necessity comes no doubt afterwards to contribute very much to maintain and secure that authority and subordination. The rich, in particular, are necessarily interested to support that order of things, which can alone secure them in the possession of their own advantages.

Men of inferior wealth combine to defend those of superior wealth in the possession of their property, in order that men of superior wealth may combine to defend them in the possession of theirs. All the inferior shepherds and herdsmen feel that the security of their own herds and flocks depends upon the security of those of the great shepherd or herdsman; that the maintenance of their lesser authority depends upon that of his greater authority, and that upon their subordination to him depends his power of keeping their inferiors in subordination to them. They constitute a sort of little nobility, who feel themselves interested to defend the property and to support the authority of their own little sovereign, in order that he may be able to defend their property and to support their authority. Civil government, so far as it is instituted for the security of property, is in reality instituted for the defense of the rich against the poor, or of those who have some property against those who have none at all.

The judicial authority of such a sovereign, however, far from being a cause of expense, was for a long time a source of revenue to him. The persons who applied to him for justice were always willing to pay for it, and a present never failed to accompany a petition. After the authority of the sovereign too was thoroughly established, the person found guilty, over and above the satisfaction which he was obliged to make to the party, was likewise forced to pay an amercement to the sovereign. He had given trouble, he had disturbed, he had broke the peace of his lord the king, and for those offenses an amercement was thought due. In the Tartar governments of Asia, in the governments of Europe which were founded by the German and Scythian nations who overturned the Roman empire, the administration of justice was a considerable source of revenue, both to the sovereign and to all the lesser chiefs or lords who exercised under him any particular jurisdiction, either over some particular tribe or clan, or over some particular territory or district. Originally both the sovereign and the inferior chiefs used to exercise this jurisdiction in their own persons. Afterwards they universally found it convenient to delegate it to some substitute, bailiff, or judge. This substitute, however, was still obliged to account to his principal or constituent for the profits of the jurisdiction. Whoever reads the instructions which were given to the judges of the circuit in the time of Henry II will see clearly that those judges were a sort of itinerant factors, sent round the country for the purpose of levying certain branches of the king's revenue. In those days the administration of justice not only afforded a certain revenue to the sovereign, but to procure this revenue seems to have been one of the principal advantages which he proposed to obtain by the administration of justice.

This scheme of making the administration of justice subservient to the purposes of revenue could scarce fail to be productive of several very gross abuses. The person who applied for justice with a large present in his hand was likely to get something more than justice; while he who applied for it with a small one was likely to get something less. Justice too might frequently be delayed, in order that this present might be repeated. The amercement, besides, of the person complained of, might frequently suggest a very strong reason for finding him in the wrong, even when he had not really been so. That such abuses were far from being uncommon, the ancient history of every country in Europe bears witness.

When the sovereign or chief exercised his judicial authority in his own person, how much soever he might abuse it, it must have been scarce possible to get any redress; because there could seldom be anybody powerful enough to call him to account. When he exercised it by a bailiff, indeed, redress might sometimes be had. If it was for his own benefit only that the bailiff had been guilty of any act of injustice, the sovereign himself might not always be unwilling to punish him, or to oblige him to repair the wrong. But if it was for the benefit of his sovereign, if it was in order to make court to the person who appointed him and who might prefer him, that he had committed any act of oppression, redress would upon most occasions be as impossible as if the sovereign had committed it himself. In all barbarous governments, accordingly, in all those ancient governments of Europe in particular, which were founded upon the ruins of the Roman empire, the administration of justice appears for a long time to have been extremely corrupt; far from being quite equal and impartial even under the best monarchs, and altogether profligate under the worst. . . .

Of the Expense of Public Works and Public Institutions

The third and last duty of the sovereign or commonwealth is that of erecting and maintaining those public institutions and those public works, which, though they may be in the highest degree advantageous to a great society, are, however, of such a nature that the profit could never repay the expense to any individual or small number of individuals and which it therefore cannot be expected that any individual or small number of individuals should erect or maintain. The performance of this duty requires too very different degrees of expense in the different periods of society.

After the public institutions and public works necessary for the defense of the society, and for the administration of justice, both of which have already been mentioned, the other works and institutions of this kind are chiefly those for facilitating the commerce of the society, and those for promoting the instruction of the people. The institutions for instruction are of two kinds: those for the education of the youth, and those for the instruction of people of all ages.

That the erection and maintenance of the public works which facilitate the commerce of any country, such as good roads, bridges, navigable canals, harbors, &c. must require very different degrees of expense in the different periods of society, is evident without any proof. The expense of making and maintaining the public roads of any country must evidently increase with the annual produce of the land and labor of that country, or with the quantity and weight of the goods which it becomes necessary to fetch and carry upon those roads. The strength of a bridge must be suited to the number and weight of the carriages which are likely to pass over it. The depth and the supply of water for a navigable canal must be proportioned to the number and tonnage of the lighters which are likely to carry goods upon it; the extent of a harbor to the number of the shipping which are likely to take shelter in it.

It does not seem necessary that the expense of those public works should be defrayed from that public revenue, as it is commonly called, of which the collection and application are in most countries assigned to the executive power. The greater part of such public works may easily be so managed as to afford a particular revenue sufficient for defraying their own expense, without bringing any burden upon the general revenue of the society.

A highway, a bridge, a navigable canal, for example, may in most cases be both made and maintained by a small toll upon the carriages which make use of them: a harbor, by a moderate port-duty upon the tonnage of the shipping which load or unload in it. The coinage, another institution for facilitating commerce, in many countries not only defrays its own expense, but affords a small revenue or seignorage to the sovereign. The post-office, another institution for the same purpose, over and above defraying its own expense, affords in almost all countries a very considerable revenue to the sovereign. . . .

Of the Expense of the Institutions for the Education of Youth

The institutions for the education of the youth may, in the same manner, furnish a revenue sufficient for defraying their own expense. The fee or honorary which the scholar pays to the master naturally constitutes a revenue of this kind.

Even where the reward of the master does not arise altogether from this natural revenue, it still is not necessary that it should be derived from that general revenue of the society, of which the collection and application are, in most countries, assigned to the executive power. Through the greater part of Europe, accordingly, the endowment of schools and colleges makes either no charge upon that general revenue, or but a very small one. It everywhere arises chiefly from some local or provincial revenue, from the rent of some landed estate, or from the interest of some sum of money allotted and put under the management of trustees for this particular purpose, sometimes by the sovereign himself, and sometimes by some private donor. . . .

15

Publius (James Madison, Alexander Hamilton, and John Jay)
The Federalist Papers

Publius was the joint pseudonym adopted by three of the central figures in the fashioning and ratification of the American Constitution. All of them were to hold high office: Alexander Hamilton became secretary of the Treasury, John Jay became chief justice of the Supreme Court, and James Madison, who is often called "the father of the Constitution," became the fourth president of the United States. For two years after the Constitution was written in Philadelphia in the summer of 1787, political debate about its ratification took place throughout the thirteen states. Publius wrote eighty-five letters defending the Constitution and articulating the key concepts found in it. These included ideas central to America's future political life, such as republicanism, federalism, checks and balances, and the separation of powers.

No. 1. Hamilton

After an unequivocal experience of the inefficacy of the subsisting federal government, you are called upon to deliberate on a new Constitution for the United States of America. The subject speaks its own importance; comprehending in its consequences nothing less than the existence of the Union, the safety and welfare of the parts of which it is composed, the fate of an empire in many respects the most interesting in the world. It has been frequently remarked that it seems to have been reserved to the people of this country, by their conduct and example, to decide the important question, whether societies of men are really capable or not of establishing good government from reflection and choice, or whether they are forever destined to depend for their political constitutions on accident and force. If there be any truth in the remark, the crisis at which we are arrived may with propriety be regarded as the era in which that decision is to be made; and a wrong election of the part we shall act may, in this view, deserve to be considered as the general misfortune of mankind.

This idea will add the inducements of philanthropy to those of patriotism, to heighten the solicitude which all considerate and good men must feel for the event. Happy will it be if our choice should be directed by a judicious estimate of our true interests, unperplexed and unbiased by considerations not connected with the public good. But this is a thing more ardently to be wished than seriously to be expected. The plan offered to our deliberations affects too many particular interests, innovates upon too many local institutions, not to involve in its discussion a variety of objects foreign to its merits, and of views, passions, and prejudices little favorable to the discovery of truth.

Among the most formidable of the obstacles which the new Constitution will have to encounter may readily be distinguished the obvious interest of a certain class of men in every State to resist all changes which may hazard a diminution of the power, emolument, and consequence of the offices they hold under the State establishments; and the perverted ambition of another class of men, who will either hope to aggrandize themselves by the confusions of their country, or will flatter themselves with fairer prospects of elevation from the subdivision of the empire into several partial confederacies than from its union under one government.

It is not, however, my design to dwell upon observations of this nature. I am well aware that it would be disingenuous to resolve indiscriminately the opposition of any set of men (merely because their situations might subject them to suspicion) into interested or ambitious views. Candor will oblige us to admit that even such men may be actuated by upright intentions; and it cannot be doubted that much of the opposition which has made its appearance, or may hereafter make its appearance, will spring from sources, blameless at least if not respectable—the honest errors of minds led astray by preconceived jealousies and fears. So numerous indeed and so powerful are the causes which serve to give a false bias to the judgment, that we, upon many occasions, see wise and good men on the wrong as well as on the right side of questions of the first magnitude to society. This circumstance, if duly attended to, would furnish a lesson of moderation to those who are ever so thoroughly persuaded of their being in the right in any controversy. And a further reason for caution, in this respect, might be drawn from the reflection that we are not always sure that those who advocate the truth are influenced by purer principles than their antagonists. Ambition, avarice, personal animosity, party opposition, and many other motives not more laudable than these, are apt to operate as well upon those who support as those who oppose the right side of a question. Were there not even these inducements to moderation, nothing could be more ill-judged than that intolerant spirit which has at all times characterized political parties. For in politics, as in religion, it is equally absurd to aim at making proselytes by fire and sword. Heresies in either can rarely be cured by persecution.

And yet, however just these sentiments will be allowed to be, we have already sufficient indications that it will happen in this as in all former cases of great national discussion. A torrent of angry and malignant passions will be let loose. To judge from the conduct of the opposite parties, we shall be led to conclude that they will mutually hope to evince the justness of their opinions, and to increase the number of their converts by the loudness of their declamations and by the bitterness of their invectives. An enlightened zeal for the energy and efficiency of government will be stigmatized as the offspring of a temper fond of despotic power and hostile to the principles of liberty. An over-scrupulous jealousy of danger to the rights of the people, which is more commonly the fault of the head than of the heart, will be represented as mere pretense and artifice, the stale bait for popularity at the expense of public good. It will be forgotten, on the one hand, that jealously is the usual concomitant of violent love, and that the noble enthusiasm of liberty is too apt to be infected with a spirit of narrow and illiberal distrust. On the other hand, it will be equally forgotten that the vigor of government is essential to the security of liberty; that, in the contemplation of a sound and well-informed judgment, their interests can never be separated; and that a dangerous ambition more often lurks behind the specious mask of zeal for the rights of the people than under the forbidding appearance of zeal for the firmness and efficiency of government. History will teach us that the former has been found a much more certain road to the introduction of despotism than the latter, and that of those men who have overturned the liberties of republics, the greatest number have begun their career by paying an obsequious court to the people, commencing demagogues and ending tyrants. . . .

No. 6. Hamilton

. . . A man must be far gone in Utopian speculations who can seriously doubt that if these States should either be wholly disunited, or only united in partial confederacies, the subdivisions into which they might be thrown would have frequent and violent contests with each other. To presume a want of motives for such contests as an argument against their existence would be to forget that men are ambitious, vindictive, and rapacious. To look for a continuation of harmony between a number of independent, unconnected sovereignties situated in the same neighborhood would be to disregard the uniform course of human events, and to set at defiance the accumulated experience of ages.

The causes of hostility among nations are innumerable. There are some which have a general and almost constant operation upon the collective bodies of society. Of this description are the love of power or the desire of pre-eminence and dominion—the jealousy of power, or the desire of equality and safety. There are others which have a more circumscribed though an equally operative influence within their spheres. Such are the rivalships and competitions of commerce between commercial nations. And there are others, not less numerous than either of the former, which take their origin entirely in private passions; in the attachments, enmities, interests, hopes, and fears of leading individuals in the communities of which they are members. Men of this class, whether the favorites of a king or of a people, have in too many instances abused the confidence they possessed; and assuming the pretext of some public motive, have not scrupled to sacrifice the national tranquillity to personal advantage or personal gratification. . . .

So far is the general sense of mankind from corresponding with the tenets of those who endeavor to lull asleep our apprehensions of discord and hostility between the States, in the event of disunion, that it has from long observation of the progress of society become a sort of axiom in politics that vicinity, or nearness of situation, constitutes nations natural enemies. An intelligent writer expresses himself on this subject to this effect: "Neighboring Nations [says he] are naturally

Enemies of each other, unless their common weakness forces them to league in a Confederate Republic, and their constitution prevents the differences that neighborhood occasions, extinguishing that secret jealousy which disposes all states to aggrandize themselves at the expense of their neighbors."[1] This passage, at the same time, points out the Evil and suggests the Remedy.

No. 10. Madison

Among the numerous advantages promised by a well-constructed Union, none deserves to be more accurately developed than its tendency to break and control the violence of faction. The friend of popular governments never finds himself so much alarmed for their character and fate as when he contemplates their propensity to this dangerous vice. He will not fail, therefore, to set a due value on any plan which, without violating the principles to which he is attached, provides a proper cure for it. The instability, injustice, and confusion introduced into the public councils have, in truth, been the mortal diseases under which popular governments have everywhere perished, as they continue to be the favorite and fruitful topics from which the adversaries to liberty derive their most specious declamations. The valuable improvements made by the American constitutions on the popular models, both ancient and modern, cannot certainly be too much admired; but it would be an unwarrantable partiality to contend that they have as effectually obviated the danger on this side, as was wished and expected. Complaints are everywhere heard from our most considerate and virtuous citizens, equally the friends of public and private faith and of public and personal liberty, that our governments are too unstable, that the public good is disregarded in the conflicts of rival parties, and that measures are too often decided, not according to the rules of justice and the rights of the minor party, but by the superior force of an interested and overbearing majority. However anxiously we may wish that these complaints had no foundation, the evidence of known facts will not permit us to deny that they are in some degree true. It will be found, indeed, on a candid review of our situation, that some of the distresses under which we labor have been erroneously charged on the operation of our governments; but it will be found, at the same time, that other causes will not alone account for many of our heaviest misfortunes; and, particularly, for that prevailing and increasing distrust of public engagements and alarm for private rights which are echoed from one end of the continent to the other. These must be chiefly, if not wholly, effects of the unsteadiness and injustice with which a factious spirit has tainted our public administration.

By a faction I understand a number of citizens, whether amounting to a majority or minority of the whole, who are united and actuated by some common impulse of passion, or of interest, adverse to the rights of other citizens, or to the permanent and aggregate interests of the community.

There are two methods of curing the mischiefs of faction: the one, by removing its causes; the other, by controlling its effects.

There are again two methods of removing the causes of faction: the one, by destroying the liberty which is essential to its existence; the other, by giving to every citizen the same opinions, the same passions, and the same interests.

It could never be more truly said than of the first remedy that it was worse than the disease. Liberty is to faction what air is to fire, an aliment without which it instantly expires. But it could not be a less folly to abolish liberty, which is essential to political life, because it nourishes faction than it would be to wish the annihilation of air, which is essential to animal life, because it imparts to fire its destructive agency.

The second expedient is as impracticable as the first would be unwise. As long as the reason of man continues fallible, and he is at liberty to exercise it, different opinions will be formed. As long as the connection subsists between his reason and his self-love, his opinions and his passions will have a reciprocal influence on each other; and the former will be objects to which the latter will attach themselves. The diversity in the faculties of men, from which the rights of property originate, is not less an insuperable obstacle to a uniformity of interests. The protection of these faculties is the first object of government. From the protection of different and unequal faculties of acquiring property, the possession of different degrees and kinds of property immediately results; and from the influence of these on the sentiments and views of the respective proprietors ensues a division of the society into different interests and parties.

The latent causes of faction are thus sown in the nature of man; and we see them everywhere brought into different degrees of activity, according to the different circumstances of civil society. A zeal for different opinions concerning religion, concerning government, and many other points, as well of speculation as of practice; an attachment to different leaders ambitiously contending for pre-eminence and power; or to persons of other descriptions whose fortunes have been interesting to the human passions, have, in turn, divided mankind into parties, inflamed them with mutual animosity, and rendered them much more disposed to vex and oppress each other than to co-operate for their common good. So strong is this propensity of mankind to fall into mutual animosities that where no substantial occasion presents itself the most frivolous and fanciful distinctions have been sufficient to kindle their unfriendly passions and excite their most violent conflicts. But the most common and durable source of factions has been the verious and unequal distribution of property. Those who hold and those who are without property have ever formed distinct interests in society. Those who are creditors, and those who are debtors, fall under a like discrimination. A landed interest, a manufacturing interest, a mercantile interest, a moneyed interest, with many lesser interests, grow up of necessity in civilized nations, and divide them into different classes, actuated by different sentiments and views. The regulation of these various and interfering interests forms the principal task of modern legislation and involves the spirit of party and faction in the necessary and ordinary operations of government.

No man is allowed to be a judge in his own cause, because his interest would certainly bias his judgment, and, not improbably, corrupt his integrity. With equal, nay with greater reason, a body of men are unfit to be both judges and parties at the same time; yet what are many of the most important acts of legislation but so many judicial determinations, not indeed concerning the rights of single persons, but concerning the rights of large bodies of citizens? And what are the different classes of legislators but advocates and parties to the causes which they determine? Is a law proposed concerning private debts? It is a question to which the creditors are parties on one side and the debtors on the other. Justice ought to hold the balance between them. Yet the parties are, and must be, themselves the judges; and the most numerous party, or in other words, the most powerful faction must be expected to prevail. Shall domestic manufacturers be encouraged, and in what degree, by restrictions on foreign manufacturers? are questions which would be differently decided by the landed and the manufacturing classes, and probably by neither with a sole regard to justice and the public good. The apportionment of taxes on the various descriptions of property is an act which seems to require the most exact impartiality; yet there is, perhaps, no legislative act in which greater opportunity and temptation are given to a predominant party to trample on the rules of justice. Every shilling with which they overburden the inferior number is a shilling saved to their own pockets.

It is in vain to say that enlightened statesmen will be able to adjust these clashing interests and render them all subservient to the public good. Enlightened statesmen will not always be at the helm. Nor, in many cases, can such an adjustment be made at all without taking into view indirect and remote considerations, which will rarely prevail over the immediate interest which one party may find in disregarding the rights of another or the good of the whole.

The inference to which we are brought is that the *causes* of faction cannot be removed and that relief is only to be sought in the means of controlling its *effects*.

If a faction consists of less than a majority, relief is supplied by the republican principle, which enables the majority to defeat its sinister views by regular vote. It may clog the administration, it may convulse the society; but it will be unable to execute and mask its violence under the forms of the Constitution. When a majority is included in a faction, the form of popular government, on the other hand, enables it to sacrifice to its ruling passion or interest both the public good and the rights of other citizens. To secure the public good and private rights against the danger of such a faction, and at the same time to preserve the spirit and the form of popular government, is then the great object to which our inquiries are directed. Let me add that it is the great desideratum by which alone this form of government can be rescued from the opprobrium under which it has so long labored and be recommended to the esteem and adoption of mankind.

By what means is this object attainable? Evidently by one of two only. Either the existence of the same passion or interest in a majority at the same time must be prevented, or the majority, having such coexistent passion or interest, must be rendered, by their number and local situation, unable to concert and carry into effect schemes of oppression. If the impulse and the opportunity be suffered to coincide, we well know that neither moral nor religious motives can be relied on as an adequate control. They are not found to be such on the injustice and violence of individuals, and lose their efficacy in proportion to the number combined together, that is, in proportion as their efficacy becomes needful.

From this view of the subject it may be concluded that a pure democracy, by which I mean a society consisting of a small number of citizens, who assemble and administer the government in person, can admit of no cure for the mischiefs of faction. A common passion or interest will, in almost every case, be felt by a majority of the whole; a communication and concert results from the form of government itself; and there is nothing to check the inducements to sacrifice the weaker party or an obnoxious individual. Hence it is that such democracies have ever been spectacles of turbulence and contention; have ever been found incompatible with personal security or the rights of property; and have in general been as short in their lives as they have been violent in their deaths. Theoretic politicians, who have patronized this species of government, have erroneously supposed that by reducing mankind to a perfect equality in their political rights, they would at the same time be perfectly equalized and assimilated in their possessions, their opinions, and their passions.

A republic, by which I mean a government in which the scheme of representation takes place, opens a different prospect and promises the cure for which we are seeking. Let us examine the points in which it varies from pure democracy, and we shall comprehend both the nature of the cure and the efficacy which it must derive from the Union.

The two great points of difference between a democracy and a republic are: first, the delegation of the government, in the latter, to a small number of citizens elected by the rest; secondly, the greater number of citizens and greater sphere of country over which the latter may be extended.

The effect of the first difference is, on the one hand, to refine and enlarge the public views by passing them through the medium of a chosen body of citizens, whose wisdom may best discern the true interest of their country and whose patriotism and love of justice will be least likely to sacrifice it to temporary or partial considerations. Under such a regulation it may well happen that the public voice, pronounced by the representatives of the people, will be more consonant to the public good than if pronounced by the people themselves, convened for the purpose. On the other hand, the effect may be inverted. Men of factious tempers, of local prejudices, or of sinister designs, may, by intrigue, by corruption, or by other means, first obtain the suffrages, and then betray the interests of the people. The question resulting is, whether small or extensive republics are most favorable to the election of proper guardians of the public weal; and it is clearly decided in favor of the latter by two obvious considerations.

In the first place it is to be remarked that however small the republic may be the representatives must be raised to a certain number in order to guard against the cabals of a few; and that however large it may be they must be limited to a certain number in order to guard against the confusion of a multitude. Hence, the number of representatives in the two cases not being in proportion to that of the constituents, and being proportionally greatest in the small republic, it follows that if the proportion of fit characters be not less in the large than in the small republic, the former will present a greater option, and consequently a greater probability of a fit choice.

In the next place, as each representative will be chosen by a greater number of citizens in the large than in the small republic, it will be more difficult for unworthy candidates to practise with success the vicious arts by which elections are too often carried; and the suffrages of the people being more free, will be more likely to center on men who possess the most attractive merit and the most diffusive and established characters.

It must be confessed that in this, as in most other cases, there is a mean, on both sides of which inconveniences will be found to lie. By enlarging too much the number of electors, you render the representative too little acquainted with all their local circumstances and lesser interests; as by reducing it too much, you render him unduly attached to these, and too little fit to comprehend and pursue great and national objects. The federal Constitution forms a happy combination in this respect; the great and aggregate interests being referred to the national, the local and particular to the State legislatures.

The other point of difference is the greater number of citizens and extent of territory which may be brought within the compass of republican than of democratic government; and it is this circumstance principally which renders factious combinations less to be dreaded in the former than in the latter. The smaller the society, the fewer probably will be the distinct parties and interests composing it; the fewer the distinct parties and interests, the more frequently will a majority be found of the same party; and the smaller the number of individuals composing a majority, and the smaller the compass within which they are placed, the more easily will they concert and execute their plans of oppression. Extend the sphere and you take in a greater variety of parties and interests; you make it less probable that a majority of the whole will have a common motive to invade the rights of other citizens; or if such a common motive exists, it will be more difficult for all who feel it to discover their own strength and to act in unison with each other. Besides other impediments, it may be remarked that, where there is a consciousness of unjust or dishonorable purposes, communication is always checked by distrust in proportion to the number whose concurrence is necessary.

Hence, it clearly appears that the same advantage which a republic has over a democracy in controlling the effects of faction is enjoyed by a large over a small republic—is enjoyed by the Union over the States composing it. Does this advantage consist in the substitution of representatives whose enlightened views and virtuous sentiments render them superior to local prejudices and to schemes of injustice? It will not be denied that the representation of the Union will be most likely to possess these requisite endowments. Does it consist in the greater security afforded by a greater variety of parties, against the event of any one party being able to outnumber and oppress the rest? In an equal degree does the increased variety of parties comprised within the Union increase this security. Does it, in fine, consist in the greater obstacles opposed to the concert and accomplishment of the secret wishes of an unjust and interested majority? Here again the extent of the Union gives it the most palpable advantage.

The influence of factious leaders may kindle a flame within their particular

States but will be unable to spread a general conflagration through the other States. A religious sect may degenerate into a political faction in a part of the Confederacy; but the variety of sects dispersed over the entire face of it must secure the national councils against any danger from that source. A rage for paper money, for an abolition of debts, for an equal division of property, or for any other improper or wicked project, will be less apt to pervade the whole body of the Union than a particular member of it, in the same proportion as such a malady is more likely to taint a particular county or district than an entire State.

In the extent and proper structure of the Union, therefore, we behold a republican remedy for the diseases most incident to republican government. And according to the degree of pleasure and pride we feel in being republicans ought to be our zeal in cherishing the spirit and supporting the character of federalists.

No. 51. Madison

To what expedient, then, shall we finally resort, for maintaining in practice the necessary partition of power among the several departments as laid down in the Constitution? The only answer that can be given is that as all these exterior provisions are found to be inadequate the defect must be supplied, by so contriving the interior structure of the government as that its several constituent parts may, by their mutual relations, be the means of keeping each other in their proper places. Without presuming to undertake a full development of this important idea I will hazard a few general observations which may perhaps place it in a clearer light, and enable us to form a more correct judgment of the principles and structure of the government planned by the convention.

In order to lay a due foundation for that separate and distinct exercise of the different powers of government, which to a certain extent is admitted on all hands to be essential to the preservation of liberty, it is evident that each department should have a will of its own; and consequently should be so constituted that the members of each should have as little agency as possible in the appointment of the members of the others. Were this principle rigorously adhered to, it would require that all the appointments for the supreme executive, legislative, and judiciary magistracies should be drawn from the same fountain of authority, the people, through channels having no communication whatever with one another. Perhaps such a plan of constructing the several departments would be less difficult in practice than it may in contemplation appear. Some difficulties, however, and some additional expense would attend the execution of it. Some deviations, therefore, from the principle must be admitted. In the constitution of the judiciary department in particular, it might be inexpedient to insist rigorously on the principle: first, because peculiar qualifications being essential in the members, the primary consideration ought to be to select that mode of choice which best secures these qualifications; second, because the permanent tenure by which the appointments are held in that department must soon destroy all sense of dependence on the authority conferring them.

It is equally evident that the members of each department should be as little dependent as possible on those of the others for the emoluments annexed to their offices. Were the executive magistrate, or the judges, not independent of the legislature in this particular, their independence in every other would be merely nominal.

But the great security against a gradual concentration of the several powers in the same department consists in giving to those who administer each department the necessary constitutional means and personal motives to resist encroachments of the others. The provision for defense must in this, as in all other cases, be made commensurate to the danger of attack. Ambition must be made to counteract ambition. The interest of the man must be connected with the constitutional rights of the place. It may be a reflection on human nature that such devices should be necessary to control the abuses of government. But what is government itself but the greatest of all reflections on human nature? If men were angels, no government would be necessary. If angels were to govern men, neither external nor internal controls on government would be necessary. In framing a government which is to be administered by men over men, the great difficulty lies in this: you must first enable the government to control the governed; and in the next place oblige it to control itself. A dependence on the people is, no doubt, the primary control on the government; but experience has taught mankind the necessity of auxiliary precautions.

This policy of supplying, by opposite and rival interests, the defect of better motives, might be traced through the whole system of human affairs, private as well as public. We see it particularly displayed in all the subordinate distributions of power, where the constant aim is to divide and arrange the several offices in such a manner as that each may be a check on the other—that the private interest of every individual may be a sentinel over the public rights. These inventions of prudence cannot be less requisite in the distribution of the supreme powers of the State.

But it is not possible to give to each department an equal power of self-defense. In republican government, the legislative authority necessarily predominates. The remedy for this inconveniency is to divide the legislature into different branches; and to render them, by different modes of election and different principles of action, as little connected with each other as the nature of their common functions and their common dependence on the society will admit. It may even be necessary to guard against dangerous encroachments by still further precautions. As the weight of the legislative authority requires that it should be thus divided, the weakness of the executive may require, on the other hand, that it should be fortified. An absolute negative on the legislature appears, at first view, to be the natural defense with which the executive magistrate should be armed. But perhaps it would be neither altogether safe nor alone sufficient. On ordinary occasions it might not be exerted with the requisite firmness, and on extraordinary occasions it might be perfidiously abused. May not this defect of an absolute negative be supplied by some qualified connection between this weaker department and the weaker branch of the stronger department, by which the latter may be led to support the constitutional rights of the former, without being too much detached from the rights of its own department?

If the principles on which these observations are founded be just, as I persuade myself they are, and they be applied as a criterion to the several State constitutions, and to the federal Constitution, it will be found that if the latter does not perfectly correspond with them, the former are infinitely less able to bear such a test.

There are, moreover, two considerations particularly applicable to the federal system of America, which place that system in a very interesting point of view.

First. In a single republic, all the power surrendered by the people is submitted to the administration of a single government; and the usurpations are guarded against by a division of the government into distinct and separate departments. In the compound republic of America, the power surrendered by the people is first divided between two distinct governments, and then the portion allotted to each subdivided among distinct and separate departments. Hence a double security arises to the rights of the people. The different governments will control each other, at the same time that each will be controlled by itself.

Second. It is of great importance in a republic not only to guard the society against the oppression of its rulers, but to guard one part of the society against the injustice of the other part. Different interests necessarily exist in different classes of citizens. If a majority be united by a common interest, the rights of the minority will be insecure. There are but two methods of providing against this evil: the one by creating a will in the community independent of the majority—that is, of the society itself; the other, by comprehending in the society so many separate descriptions of citizens as will render an unjust combination of a majority of the whole very improbable, if not impracticable. The first method prevails in all governments possessing an hereditary or self-appointed authority. This, at best, is but a precarious security; because a power independent of the society may as well espouse the unjust views of the major as the rightful interests of the minor party, and may possibly be turned against both parties. The second method will be exemplified in the federal republic of the United States. Whilst all authority in it will be derived from and dependent on the society, the society itself will be broken into so many parts, interests and classes of citizens, that the rights of individuals, or of the minority, will be in little danger from interested combinations of the majority. In a free government the security for civil rights must be the same as that for religious rights. It consists in the one case in the multiplicity of interests, and in the other in the multiplicity of sects. The degree of security in both cases will depend on the number of interests and sects; and this may be presumed to depend on the extent of country and number of people comprehended under the same government. This view of the subject must particularly recommend a proper federal system to all the sincere and considerate friends of republican government, since it shows that in exact proportion as the territory of the Union may be formed into more circumscribed Confederacies, or States, oppressive combinations of a majority will be facilitated; the best security, under the republican forms, for the rights of every class of citizen, will be diminished; and consequently the stability and independence of some member of the government, the only other security, must be proportionally increased. Justice is the end of government. It is the end of civil society. It ever has been and ever will be pursued until it be obtained, or until liberty be lost in the pursuit. In a society under the forms of which the stronger faction can readily unite and oppress the weaker, anarchy may as truly be said to reign as in a state of nature, where the weaker individual is not secured against the violence of the stronger; and as, in the latter state, even the stronger individuals are prompted, by the uncertainty of their condition, to submit to a government which may protect the weak as well as themselves; so, in the former state, will the more powerful factions or parties be gradually induced, by a like motive, to wish for a government which will protect all parties, the weaker as well as the more powerful. It can be little doubted that if the State of Rhode Island was separated from the Confederacy and left to itself, the insecurity of rights under the popular form of government within such narrow limits would be displayed by such reiterated oppressions of factious majorities that some power altogether independent of the people would soon be called for by the voice of the very factions whose misrule had proved the necessity of it. In the extended republic of the United States, and among the great variety of interests, parties, and sects which it embraces, a coalition of a majority of the whole society could seldom take place on any other principles than those of justice and the general good; whilst there being thus less danger to a minor from the will of a major party, there must be less pretext, also, to provide for the security of the former, by introducing into the government a will not dependent on the latter, or, in other words, a will independent of the society itself. It is no less certain than it is important, notwithstanding the contrary opinions which have been entertained, that the larger the society, provided it lie within a practicable sphere, the more duly capable it will be of self-government. And happily for the *republican cause*, the practicable sphere may be carried to a very great extent by a judicious modification and mixture of the *federal principle*.

Note

1. Abbé de Mably.

16

Declaration of the Rights of Man and Citizen

The Declaration of the Rights of Man and Citizen *was the work of a committee of more than twenty leaders of the National Assembly of France. It was promulgated in the summer of 1789 and written into the French Constitution of 1793. The Declaration was inspired by Rousseau as well as by the American Declaration of Independence, and the numerous bills of rights of the colonies. This document proclaimed individual rights, serving as inspiration to both liberals and radicals, as well as asserting a commitment to the rights of property. It has served as a model for liberal constitutions and as an inspiration to struggles against tyrants on behalf of human rights.*

The representatives of the French people, organized in National Assembly, considering that ignorance, forgetfulness or contempt of the rights of man, are the sole causes of the public miseries and of the corruption of governments, have resolved to set forth in a solemn declaration the natural, inalienable, and sacred rights of man, in order that this declaration, being ever present to all the members of the social body, may unceasingly remind them of their rights and their duties; in order that the acts of the legislative power and those of the executive power may be each moment compared with the aim of every political institution and thereby may be more respected; and in order that the demands of the citizens, grounded henceforth upon simple and incontestable principles, may always take the direction of maintaining the constitution and the welfare of all.

In consequence, the National Assembly recognizes and declares, in the presence and under the auspices of the Supreme Being, the following rights of man and citizen.

1. Men are born and remain free and equal in rights. Social distinctions can be based only upon public utility.

2. The aim of every political association is the preservation of the natural and imprescriptible rights of man. These rights are liberty, property, security, and resistance to oppression.

3. The source of all sovereignty is essentially in the nation; no body, no individual can exercise authority that does not proceed from it in plain terms.

4. Liberty consists in the power to do anything that does not injure others; accordingly, the exercise of the natural rights of each man has no limits except those that secure to the other members of society the enjoyment of these same rights. These limits can be determined only by law.

5. The law has the right to forbid only such actions as are injurious to society. Nothing can be forbidden that is not interdicted by the law, and no one can be constrained to do that which it does not order.

6. Law is the expression of the general will. All citizens have the right to take part personally, or by their representatives, in its formation. It must be the same for all, whether it protects or punishes. All citizens being equal in its eyes, are equally eligible to all public dignities, places, and employments, according to their capacities, and without other distinction than that of their virtues and their talents.

7. No man can be accused, arrested, or detained, except in the cases determined by the law and according to the forms that it has prescribed. Those who procure, expedite, execute, or cause to be executed arbitrary orders ought to be punished: but every citizen summoned or seized in virtue of the law ought to render instant obedience; he makes himself guilty by resistance.

8. The law ought to establish only penalties that are strictly and obviously necessary, and no one can be punished except in virtue of a law established and promulgated prior to the offence and legally applied.

9. Every man being presumed innocent until he has been pronounced guilty, if it is thought indispensable to arrest him, all severity that may not be necessary to secure his person ought to be strictly suppressed by law.

10. No one should be disturbed on account of his opinions, even religious, provided their manifestation does not derange the public order established by law.

11. The free communication of ideas and opinions is one of the most precious of the rights of man; every citizen then can freely speak, write, and print, subject to responsibility for the abuse of this freedom in the cases determined by law.

12. The guarantee of the rights of man and citizen requires a public force; this force then is instituted for the advantage of *all* and not for the personal benefit of those to whom it is entrusted.

13. For the maintenance of the public force and for the expenses of administration a general tax is indispensable; it ought to be equally apportioned among all the citizens according to their means.

14. All the citizens have the right to ascertain, by themselves or by their representatives, the necessity of the public tax, to consent to it freely, to follow the employment of it, and to determine the quota, the assessment, the collection, and the duration of it.

15. Society has the right to call for an account of his administration from every public agent.

16. Any society in which the guarantee of the rights is not secured, or the separation of powers not determined, has no constitution at all.

17. Property being a *sacred* and inviolable right, no one can be deprived of it, unless a legally established public necessity evidently demands it, under the condition of a just and prior indemnity.

17

Edmund Burke
Reflections on the Revolution in France

*Edmund Burke (1729–1797) was a parliamentarian and political thinker who en-
tered the House of Commons at age 37. Burke is considered one of the "fathers" of modern conservatism. He believed in the inherited wisdom of tradition
and in man's need to accept balance and compromise rather than overthrow the
temporal world order. He was a vociferous critic of the French Revolution, and
in his most celebrated work,* Reflections on the Revolution in France *(1790), he
attacked his contemporaries for a celebration of equality that was contrary to
nature and therefore impossible to attain. Burke wrote that those who advocated
a "leveling" of social and political relations raised "false hopes and vain expectations in those destined to travel in the obscure walk of laborious life." Paradoxically, Burke supported the movement for the independence of Ireland and
the American Revolution, distinguishing these two struggles for independence
from the French Revolution. Burke claimed it was legitimate to restore liberties
which the English government had infringed upon, as opposed to the attempt of
the French revolutionaries to establish "universal rights of men" at the expense
of private property, religion, and the feudal hierarchical order.*

I FLATTER myself that I love a manly, moral, regulated liberty as well as any
gentleman of that society, be he who he will; and perhaps I have given as good
proofs of my attachment to that cause, in the whole course of my public conduct. I
think I envy liberty as little as they do to any other nation. But I cannot stand
forward, and give praise or blame to anything which relates to human actions and
human concerns on a simple view of the object, as it stands stripped of every
relation, in all the nakedness and solitude of metaphysical abstraction. Circumstances (which with some gentlemen pass for nothing) give in reality to every
political principle its distinguishing color and discriminating effect. The circumstances are what render every civil and political scheme beneficial or noxious to
mankind. Abstractedly speaking, government, as well as liberty, is good; yet
could I, in common sense, ten years ago, have felicitated France on her enjoyment
of a government (for she then had a government), without inquiry what the nature
of that government was, or how it was administered? Can I now congratulate the
same nation upon its freedom? Is it because liberty in the abstract may be classed
amongst the blessings of mankind, that I am seriously to felicitate a madman who
has escaped from the protecting restraint and wholesome darkness of his cell on
his restoration to the enjoyment of light and liberty? Am I to congratulate a high-
wayman and murderer who has broke prison upon the recovery of his natural

rights? This would be to act over again the scene of the criminals condemned to the galleys, and their heroic deliverer, the metaphysic Knight of the Sorrowful Countenance.

When I see the spirit of liberty in action, I see a strong principle at work; and this, for a while, is all I can possibly know of it. The wild gas, the fixed air, is plainly broke loose: but we ought to suspend our judgment until the first effervescence is a little subsided, till the liquor is cleared, and until we see something deeper than the agitation of a troubled and frothy surface. I must be tolerably sure, before I venture publicly to congratulate men upon a blessing, that they have really received one. Flattery corrupts both the receiver and the giver; and adulation is not of more service to the people than to kings. I should therefore suspend my congratulations on the new liberty of France, until I was informed how it had been combined with government, with public force, with the discipline and obedience of armies, with the collection of an effective and well-distributed revenue, with morality and religion, with solidity and property, with peace and order, with civil and social manners. All these (in their way) are good things, too; and without them, liberty is not a benefit whilst it lasts, and is not likely to continue long. The effect of liberty to individuals is, that they may do what they please: we ought to see what it will please them to do, before we risk congratulations, which may be soon turned into complaints. Prudence would dictate this in the case of separate, insulated, private men. But liberty, when men act in bodies, is *power*. Considerate people, before they declare themselves, will observe the use which is made of *power*—and particularly of so trying a thing as *new* power in *new* persons, of whose principles, tempers, and dispositions they have little or no experience, and in situations where those who appear the most stirring in the scene may possibly not be the real movers. . . .

It is now sixteen or seventeen years since I saw the queen of France, then the Dauphiness, at Versailles; and surely never lighted on this orb, which she hardly seemed to touch, a more delightful vision. I saw her just above the horizon, decorating and cheering the elevated sphere she just began to move in—glittering like the morning-star, full of life and splendor and joy. Oh! what a revolution! and what an heart must I have, to contemplate without emotion that elevation and that fall! Little did I dream, when she added titles of veneration to those of enthusiastic, distant, respectful love, that she should ever be obliged to carry the sharp antidote against disgrace concealed in that bosom! Little did I dream that I should have lived to see such disasters fallen upon her in a nation of gallant men, in a nation of men of honor, and of cavaliers! I thought ten thousand swords must have leaped from their scabbards to avenge even a look that threatened her with insult. But the age of chivalry is gone. That of sophisters, economists, and calculators has succeeded; and the glory of Europe is extinguished forever. Never, never more, shall we behold that generous loyalty to rank and sex, that proud submission, that dignified obedience, that subordination of the heart, which kept alive, even in servitude itself, the spirit of an exalted freedom! The unbought grace of life, the cheap defence of nations, the nurse of manly sentiment and heroic enterprise, is gone! It is gone, that sensibility of principle, that chastity of honor, which felt a stain like a wound, which inspired courage whilst it mitigated ferocity, which ennobled whatever it touched, and under which vice itself lost half its evil by losing all its grossness!

This mixed system of opinion and sentiment had its origin in the ancient chivalry; and the principle, though varied in its appearance by the varying state of human affairs, subsisted and influenced through a long succession of generations, even to the time we live in. If it should ever be totally extinguished, the loss, I fear, will be great. It is this which has given its character to modern Europe. It is this which has distinguished it under all its forms of government, and distinguished it to its advantage, from the states of Asia, and possibly from those states which flourished in the most brilliant periods of the antique world. It was this, which, without confounding ranks, had produced a noble equality, and handed it down through all the gradations of social life. It was this opinion which mitigated kings into companions, and raised private men to be fellows with kings. Without force or opposition, it subdued the fierceness of pride and power; it obliged sovereigns to submit to the soft collar of social esteem, compelled stern authority to submit to elegance, and gave a domination, vanquisher of laws, to be subdued by manners.

But now all is to be changed. All the pleasing illusions which made power gentle and obedience liberal, which harmonized the different shades of life, and which by a bland assimilation incorporated into politics the sentiments which beautify and soften private society, are to be dissolved by this new conquering empire of light and reason. All the decent drapery of life is to be rudely torn off. All the superadded ideas, furnished from the wardrobe of a moral imagination, which the heart owns and the understanding ratifies, as necessary to cover the defects of our naked, shivering nature, and to raise it to dignity in our own estimation, are to be exploded, as a ridiculous, absurd, and antiquated fashion.

On this scheme of things, a king is but a man, a queen is but a woman, a woman is but an animal—and an animal not of the highest order. All homage paid to the sex in general as such, and without distinct views, is to be regarded as romance and folly. Regicide, and parricide, and sacrilege, are but fictions of superstition, corrupting jurisprudence by destroying its simplicity. The murder of a king, or a queen, or a bishop, or a father, are only common homicide—and if the people are by any chance or in any way gainers by it, a sort of homicide much the most pardonable, and into which we ought not to make too severe a scrutiny.

On the scheme of this barbarous philosophy, which is the offspring of cold hearts and muddy understandings, and which is as void of solid wisdom as it is destitute of all taste and elegance, laws are to be supported only by their own terrors, and by the concern which each individual may find in them from his own private speculations, or can spare to them from his own private interests. In the groves of *their* academy, at the end of every visto, you see nothing but the gallows. Nothing is left which engages the affections on the part of the commonwealth. On the principles of this mechanic philosophy, our institutions can never be embodied, if I may use the expression, in persons—so as to create in us love, veneration, admiration, or attachment. But that sort of reason which banishes the affections is incapable of filling their place. These public affections, combined with manners, are required sometimes as supplements, sometimes as correctives, always as aids to law. The precept given by a wise man, as well as a great critic, for the construction of poems, is equally true as to states:—"*Non satis est pulchra esse poemata, dulcia sunto.*" There ought to be a system of manners in every nation which a well-formed mind would be disposed to relish. To make us love our country, our country ought to be lovely.

But power, of some kind or other, will survive the shock in which manners and opinions perish; and it will find other and worse means for its support. The usurpation, which, in order to subvert ancient institutions, has destroyed ancient principles, will hold power by arts similar to those by which it has acquired it. When the old feudal and chivalrous spirit of *fealty*, which, by freeing kings from fear, freed both kings and subjects from the precautions of tyranny, shall be extinct in the minds of men, plots and assassinations will be anticipated by preventive murder and preventive confiscation, and that long roll of grim and bloody maxims which form the political code of all power not standing on its own honor and the honor of those who are to obey it. Kings will be tyrants from policy, when subjects are rebels from principle.

When ancient opinions and rules of life are taken away, the loss cannot possibly be estimated. From that moment we have no compass to govern us, nor can we know distinctly to what port we steer. Europe, undoubtedly, taken in a mass, was in a flourishing condition the day on which your Revolution was completed. How much of that prosperous state was owning to the spirit of our old manners and opinions is not easy to say; but as such causes cannot be indifferent in their operation, we must presume, that, on the whole, their operation was beneficial.

We are but too apt to consider things in the state in which we find them, without sufficiently adverting to the causes by which they have been produced, and possibly may be upheld. Nothing is more certain than that our manners, our civilization, and all the good things which are connected with manners and with civilization, have, in this European world of ours, depended for ages upon two principles, and were, indeed, the result of both combined: I mean the spirit of a gentleman, and the spirit of religion. The nobility and the clergy, the one by profession, and the other by patronage, kept learning in existence, even in the midst of arms and confusions, and whilst governments were rather in their causes than formed. Learning paid back what it received to nobility and to priesthood, and paid it with usury, by enlarging their ideas, and by furnishing their minds. Happy, if they had all continued to know their indissoluble union, and their proper place! Happy, if learning, not debauched by ambition, had been satisfied to continue the instructor, and not aspired to be the master! Along with its natural protectors and guardians, learning will be cast into the mire and trodden down under the hoofs of a swinish multitude.

If, as I suspect, modern letters owe more than they are always willing to own to ancient manners, so do other interests which we value full as much as they are worth. Even commerce, and trade, and manufacture, the gods of our economical politicians, are themselves perhaps but creatures, are themselves but effects, which, as first causes, we choose to worship. They certainly grew under the same

shade in which learning flourished. They, too, may decay with their natural protecting principles. With you, for the present at least, they all threaten to disappear
together. Where trade and manufactures are wanting to a people, and the spirit of
nobility and religion remains, sentiment supplies, and not always ill supplies, their
place; but if commerce and the arts should be lost in an experiment to try how
well a state may stand without these old fundamental principles, what sort of a
thing must be a nation of gross, stupid, ferocious, and at the same time poor and
sordid barbarians, destitute of religion, honor, or manly pride, possessing nothing
at present, and hoping for nothing hereafter?

I wish you may not be going fast, and by the shortest cut, to that horrible and
disgustful situation. Already there appears a poverty of conception, a coarseness
and vulgarity, in all the proceedings of the Assembly and of all their instructors.
Their liberty is not liberal. Their science is presumptuous ignorance. Their humanity is savage and brutal.

Society is, indeed, a contract. Subordinate contracts for objects of mere occasional interest may be dissolved at pleasure; but the state ought not to be considered as nothing better than a partnership agreement in a trade of pepper and coffee, calico or tobacco, or some other such low concern, to be taken up for a little
temporary interest, and to be dissolved by the fancy of the parties. It is to be
looked on with other reverence; because it is not a partnership in things subservient only to the gross animal existence of a temporary and perishable nature. It is
a partnership in all science, a partnership in all art, a partnership in every virtue
and in all perfection. As the ends of such a partnership cannot be obtained in
many generations, it becomes a partnership not only between those who are living, but between those who are living, those who are dead, and those who are to
be born. Each contract of each particular state is but a clause in the great primeval
contract of eternal society, linking the lower with the higher natures, connecting
the visible and invisible world, according to a fixed compact sanctioned by the
inviolable oath which holds all physical and all moral natures each in their
appointed place. This law is not subject to the will of those who, by an obligation
above them, and infinitely superior, are bound to submit their will to that law. The
municipal corporations of that universal kingdom are not morally at liberty, at
their pleasure, and on their speculations of a contingent improvement, wholly to
separate and tear asunder the bands of their subordinate community, and to dissolve it into an unsocial, uncivil, unconnected chaos of elementary principles. It is
the first and supreme necessity only, a necessity that is not chosen, but chooses, a
necessity paramount to deliberation, that admits no discussion and demands no
evidence, which alone can justify a resort to anarchy. This necessity is no exception to the rule; because this necessity itself is a part, too, of that moral and
physical disposition of things to which man must be obedient by consent or force:
but if that which is only submission to necessity should be made the object of
choice, the law is broken, Nature is disobeyed, and the rebellious are outlawed,
cast forth, and exiled, from this world of reason, and order, and peace, and virtue,
and fruitful penitence, into the antagonist world of madness, discord, vice, confusion, and unavailing sorrow. . . .

Along with the moneyed interest, a new description of men had grown up, with whom that interest soon formed a close and marked union: I mean the political men of letters. Men of letters, fond of distinguishing themselves, are rarely averse to innovation. Since the decline of the life and greatness of Louis the Fourteenth, they were not so much cultivated either by him, or by the Regent, or the successors to the crown; nor were they engaged to the court by favors and emoluments so systematically as during the splendid period of that ostentatious and not impolitic reign. What they lost in the old court protection they endeavored to make up by joining in a sort of incorporation of their own; to which the two academies of France, and afterwards the vast undertaking of the Encyclopædia, carried on by a society of these gentlemen, did not a little contribute.

The literary cabal had some years ago formed something like a regular plan for the destruction of the Christian religion. This object they pursued with a degree of zeal which hitherto had been discovered only in the propagators of some system of piety. They were possessed with a spirit of proselytism in the most fanatical degree—and from thence, by an easy progress, with the spirit of persecution according to their means. What was not to be done towards their great end by any direct or immediate act might be wrought by a longer process through the medium of opinion. To command that opinion, the first step is to establish a dominion over those who direct it. They contrived to possess themselves, with great method and perseverance, of all the avenues to literary fame. Many of them, indeed, stood high in the ranks of literature and science. The world had done them justice, and in favor of general talents forgave the evil tendency of their peculiar principles. This was true liberality; which they returned by endeavoring to confine the reputation of sense, learning, and taste to themselves or their followers. I will venture to say that this narrow, exclusive spirit has not been less prejudicial to literature and to taste than to morals and true philosophy. These atheistical fathers have a bigotry of their own; and they have learnt to talk against monks with the spirit of a monk. But in some things they are men of the world. The resources of intrigue are called in to supply the defects of argument and wit. To this system of literary monopoly was joined an unremitting industry to blacken and discredit in every way, and by every means, all those who did not hold to their faction. To those who have observed the spirit of their conduct it has long been clear that nothing was wanted but the power of carrying the intolerance of the tongue and of the pen into a persecution which would strike at property, liberty, and life.

The desultory and faint persecution carried on against them, more from compliance with form and decency than with serious resentment, neither weakened their strength nor relaxed their efforts. The issue of the whole was, that, what with opposition, and what with success, a violent and malignant zeal, of a kind hitherto unknown in the world, had taken an entire possession of their minds, and rendered their whole conversation, which otherwise would have been pleasing and instructive, perfectly disgusting. A spirit of cabal, intrigue, and proselytism pervaded all their thoughts, words, and actions. And as controversial zeal soon turns its thoughts on force, they began to insinuate themselves into a correspondence with foreign princes—in hopes, through their authority, which at first they flattered, they might bring about the changes they had in view. To them it was indifferent whether these changes were to be accomplished by the thunderbolt of despotism or by the earthquake of popular commotion. The correspondence between this cabal and the late king of Prussia will throw no small light upon the spirit of all their proceedings. For the same purpose for which they intrigued with princes, they cultivated, in a distinguished manner, the moneyed interest of France; and partly through the means furnished by those whose peculiar offices gave them the most extensive and certain means of communication, they carefully occupied all the avenues to opinion.

Writers, especially when they act in a body and with one direction, have great influence on the public mind; the alliance, therefore, of these writers with the moneyed interest had no small effect in removing the popular odium and envy which attended that species of wealth. These writers, like the propagators of all novelties, pretended to a great zeal for the poor and the lower orders, whilst in their satires they rendered hateful, by every exaggeration, the faults of courts, of nobility, and of priesthood. They became a sort of demagogues. They served as a link to unite, in favor of one object, obnoxious wealth to restless and desperate poverty.

As these two kinds of men appear principal leaders in all the late transactions, their junction and politics will serve to account, not upon any principles of law or of policy, but as a *cause*, for the general fury with which all the landed property of ecclesiastical corporations has been attacked, and the great care which, contrary to their pretended principles, has been taken of a moneyed interest originating from the authority of the crown. All the envy against wealth and power was artificially directed against other descriptions of riches. On what other principle than that which I have stated can we account for an appearance so extraordinary and unnatural as that of the ecclesiastical possessions, which had stood so many successions of ages and shocks of civil violences, and were guarded at once by justice and by prejudice, being applied to the payment of debts comparatively recent, invidious, and contracted by a decried and subverted government?

18

Marie-Olympes de Gouges
Declaration of the Rights of Women and Citizens

Marie-Olympes de Gouges (1748–1793) was executed for sedition and, as reported in her obituary, "for having forgotten the virtues which befit her sex." De Gouges was a feminist pamphleteer and a writer, daughter of a butcher and a trinket peddler. Despite slim literary success, de Gouges attracted the hostility of her playwriting colleagues who questioned the authorship of her work. She responded by writing a play, The Philosopher Chastized, *in which she denounced her critics' envy. De Gouges was a political moderate who supported the French monarchy but called for the reform of poor relief and for national workshops. She advocated the creation of a national theater for women, of women's publications, and agitated for greater freedom for women in all social and political arenas: "A woman has the right to mount the scaffold; she must also have the right to mount the tribune." De Gouges' most famous work* The Rights of Women and Citizens, *addressed to Marie Antoinette, asked the queen to declare and defend the rights of women, to lead a revolution.*

MAN, are you capable of being just? It is a woman who asks you this question; at least you will not deny her this right. Tell me! Who has given you the sovereign authority to oppress my sex? Your strength? Your talents? Observe the creator in his wisdom; regard nature in all her grandeur, with which you seem to want to compare yourself; and give me, if you dare, an example of this tyrannical empire.[1] Go back to the animals, consult the elements, study the plants, then glance over all the modifications of organized matter, and cede to the evidence when I offer you the means. Seek, search, and distinguish, if you can, the sexes in the administration of nature. Everywhere you will find them mingled, everywhere they cooperate in harmony with this immortal masterpiece.

Only man has fashioned himself a principle out of this exception. Bizarre, blind, bloated by science and degenerate, in this century of enlightenment and wisdom, he, in grossest ignorance, wishes to exercise the command of a despot over a sex that has received every intellectual faculty; he claims to rejoice in the Revolution and claims his rights to equality, at the very least.

To be decreed by the National Assembly in its last meetings or in those of the next legislature.

Preamble

The mothers, daughters, and sisters, representatives of the nation, demand to be constituted a national assembly. Considering that ignorance, disregard of or contempt for the rights of women are the only causes of public misfortune and of governmental corruption, they have resolved to set forth in a solemn declaration, the natural, inalienable and sacred rights of woman; to the end that this declaration, constantly held up to all members of society, may always remind them of their rights and duties; to the end that the acts based on women's power and those based on the power of men, being constantly measured against the goal of all political institutions, may be more respected; and so that the demands of female citizens, henceforth founded on simple and indisputable principles, may ever uphold the constitution and good morals, and may contribute to the happiness of all.

Consequently, the sex that is superior in beauty as well as in courage of maternal suffering, recognizes and declares, in the presence and under the auspices of the Supreme Being, the following rights of woman and citizen.

Article One. Woman is born free and remains equal in rights to man. Social distinctions can be founded only on general utility.

II. The goal of every political association is the preservation of the natural and irrevocable rights of Woman and Man. These rights are liberty, property, security, and especially resistance to oppression.

III. The principle of all sovereignty resides essentially in the Nation, which is none other than the union of Woman and Man; no group, no individual can exercise any authority that is not derived expressly from it.

IV. Liberty and Justice consist of rendering to persons those things that belong to them; thus, the exercise of woman's natural rights is limited only by the perpetual tyranny with which man opposes her; these limits must be changed according to the laws of nature and reason.

V. The laws of nature and of reason prohibit all acts harmful to society; whatever is not prohibited by these wise and divine laws cannot be prevented, and no one can be forced to do anything unspecified by the law.

VI. The law should be the expression of the general will: all female and male citizens must participate in its elaboration personally or through their representatives. It should be the same for all; all female and male citizens, being equal in the eyes of the law, should be equally admissible to all public offices, places, and employments, according to their capacities and with no distinctions other than those of their virtues and talents.

VII. No woman is immune; she can be accused, arrested, and detained in such cases as determined by law. Women, like men, must obey these rigorous laws.

VIII. Only punishments strictly and obviously necessary may be established by law. No one may be punished except under a law established and promulgated before the offense occurred, and which is legally applicable to women.

IX. If any woman is declared guilty, then the law must be enforced rigorously.

X. No one should be punished for their opinions. Woman has the right to mount the scaffold; she should likewise have the right to speak in public, provided that her demonstrations do not disrupt public order as established by law.

XI. Free communication of thoughts and opinions is one of the most precious rights of woman, since this liberty assures the legitimate paternity of fathers with regard to their children. Every female citizen can therefore freely say: "I am the mother of a child that belongs to you," without a barbaric prejudice forcing her to conceal the truth; she must also answer for the abuse of this liberty in cases determined by law.

XII. Guarantee of the rights of woman and female citizens requires the existence of public services. Such guarantee should be established for the advantage of everyone, not for the personal benefit of those to whom these services are entrusted.

XIII. For the maintenance of public forces and administrative expenses, the contributions of women and men shall be equal; the woman shares in all forced labor and all painful tasks, therefore she should have the same share in the distribution of positions, tasks, assignments, honors, and industry.

XIV. Female and male citizens have the right to determine the need for public taxes, either by themselves or through their representatives. Female citizens can agree to this only if they are admitted to an equal share not only in wealth but also in public administration, and by determining the proportion and extent of tax collection.

XV. The mass of women, allied for tax purposes to the mass of men, has the right to hold every public official accountable for his administration.

XVI. Any society in which the guarantee of rights is not assured, or the separation of powers determined, has no constitution. The constitution is invalid if the majority of individuals who compose the Nation have not cooperated in writing it.

XVII. The right of property is inviolable and sacred to both sexes, jointly or separately. No one can be deprived of it, since it is a true inheritance of nature except when public necessity, certified by law, clearly requires it, subject to just and prior compensation.

Postamble

Woman, wake up! The tocsin of reason is sounding throughout the Universe; know your rights. The powerful empire of nature is no longer surrounded by prejudices, fanaticism, superstition and lies. The torch of truth has dispelled all the clouds of stupidity and usurpation. Man enslaved has multiplied his forces; he has had recourse to yours in order to break his own chains. Having become free, he has become unjust toward his mate. Oh Women! Women! when will you cease to be blind? What advantages have you gained in the Revolution? A more marked scorn, a more signal disdain. During centuries of corruption, you reigned only over the weakness of men. Your empire is destroyed; what then remains for you? The proof of man's injustice. The claim of your patrimony founded on the wise decrees of nature—what have you to fear from such a splendid enterprise? The good word of the legislator at the marriage of Canaan? Do you not fear that our French legislators, who are correcting this morality, which was for such a long time appended to the realm of politics but is no longer fashionable, will again say to you, "Women, what do we have in common with you?" You must answer, "Everything!" If, in their weakness, they are obstinate in drawing this conclusion contrary to their principles, you must courageously invoke the force of reason against their vain pretensions of superiority. Unite yourselves under the banner of philosophy; deploy all the energy of your character, and soon you will see these prideful ones, your adoring servants, no longer grovelling at your feet but proud to share with you the treasures of the Supreme Being. Whatever the obstacles that are put in your way, it is in your power to overturn them; you have only to will it. Let us turn now to the frightful picture of what you have been in society; and since there is currently a question of national education, let us see if our wise legislators will think wisely about the education of women.

Women have done more evil than good. They have had their share in coercion and double-dealings. When forcibly abused, they have countered with stratagems; they have had recourse to all the resources of their charms, and the most blameless among them has not hesitated to use them. They have used poison and irons; they have commanded crime and virtue alike. For centuries, the government of France in particular has depended on the nocturnal administration of women; the cabinet had no secrets from their indiscretion: embassy, military command, ministry, presidency, pontificate, cardinalate—one might say everything profane and sacred subject to the foolishness of man has been subordinated to the greed and ambition of the female sex, which was formerly contemptible and respected but, since the revolution, is respectable and yet contemptible.

What could I not say about this paradox! I have only a moment for offering a few remarks, but this moment will attract the attention of the most remote posterity. Under the Old Regime, all were vicious, all were guilty; but could one not perceive the improvement of things, even in the substance of vice? A woman needed only to be beautiful or lovable; when she possessed these two advantages, she saw a hundred fortunes at her feet. If she did not profit from this situation, she had either a bizarre character or a rare philosophy that led her to despise wealth; in such a case she was relegated to the status of a brainless person; the most indecent woman could make herself respected with enough gold; the buying and selling of women was a kind of industry taken for granted in the first rank of society, which, henceforth, will have no credit. If it did, the revolution would be lost, and under the new order we would remain ever corrupt. Still, can reason hide the fact that all other routes to fortune are closed to woman, whom man buys like a slave on the African coast? The difference is great, as we know. The slave commands the master; but if the master sets her free, without compensation, at an age when the slave has lost all her charms, what becomes of this unfortunate creature? A contemptible toy; even the doors of charity are closed to her; she is poor and old, they say; why didn't she know how to make her fortune? Other more touching examples suggest themselves to reason. A young person without experience, seduced by a man she loves, will abandon her parents to follow him; the ungrateful fellow will leave her after a few years, and the older she has grown with him, the more inhuman will his inconstancy be. If she has children, he will abandon her all the same. If he is rich, he will think himself exempt from sharing his fortune with his noble victims. If some commitment binds him to his duties, he will violate its power by using all legal loopholes. If he is married, other commitments lose their rights. What laws then remain to be made in order to destroy vice down to its very roots? One dealing with the sharing of fortunes between men and women, and another with public administration. It is clear that a woman born to a rich family gains a great deal from equal inheritance. But a woman born to a poor family of merit and virtue—what is her fate? Poverty and shame. If she does not excel in music or painting, she cannot be admitted to any public office, even though she might be quite capable. I wish only to give an overview of things. I will examine them more thoroughly in the new edition of my political works, with notes, which I propose to offer to the public in a few days.

I resume my text with regard to morals. Marriage is the tomb of confidence and love. A married woman can, with impunity, present bastards to her husband and the bastards with the fortune that does not belong to them. An unmarried woman has merely a slim right: ancient and inhuman laws have refused her the right to the name and property of the father of her children, and no new laws on this matter have been passed. If my attempt thus to give my sex an honorable and just stability is now considered a paradox on my part, an attempt at the impossible, I must leave to men yet to come the glory of discussing this matter; but meanwhile, one can pave the way through national education, the restoration of morals, and by conjugal contracts.

Model for a Social Contract between a Man and a Woman

We, N & N, of our own free will, unite ourselves for the remainder of our lives and for the duration of our mutual inclinations, according to the following conditions: We intend and desire to pool our fortunes as community property, while nevertheless preserving the right to divide them on behalf of our own children and those we might have with someone else, mutually recognizing that our fortune belongs directly to our children, from whatever bed they might spring, and that all of them have the right to carry the name of the fathers and mothers who have acknowledged them, and we obligate ourselves to subscribe to the law that punishes the renunciation of one's own flesh and blood. We obligate ourselves equally, in case of separation, to divide our fortune, and to set apart the portion belonging to our children as indicated by the law; and in the case of perfect union, the first to die would assign half the property to their children; and if one of us should die without children, the survivor would inherit everything, unless the dying party had disposed of his half of the common wealth in favor of someone else he might deem appropriate.

Here is the general formula for the conjugal agreement I am proposing. Upon reading this unorthodox piece, I envision all the hypocrites, prudes, clergy, and their gang of diabolic followers rising up against me. But would this plan not offer to the wise a moral means of achieving the perfectibility of a happy government? I shall prove it in a few words. A rich and childless epicurean fervently thinks fit to go to his poor neighbor's house to augment his family. Once a law is passed that will authorize the rich man to adopt the poor woman's children, the bonds of society will be strengthened and its morals purified. This law would perhaps save the wealth of the community and check the disorder that leads so many victims into the refuges of shame, servility, and degeneration of human principles, where nature has so long bemoaned its oppression. May the critics of rational philosophy therefore cease to protest against primitive morals or else go bury themselves in the sources they cite.[2]

I should like a law that protects widows and maidens deceived by the false promises of a man to whom they have become attached; I would like this law to force a fickle-minded man to stand by his agreements or else provide an indemnity proportional to his fortune. Moreover, I would like this law to be rigorous against women, at least against those impudent enough to appeal to a law which they themselves have violated by their own misconduct, if this can be proved. At the same time, I would like prostitutes to be placed in designated quarters, as I discussed in 1788 in *Le Bonheur primitif de l'homme*. It is not the prostitutes who contribute most to the depravation of morals; it is the women of Society. By reeducating the latter, one can modify the former. At first this chain of fraternal union will prove disorderly, but eventually it will result in perfect harmony. I am offering an invincible means of elevating the soul of women; it is for them to join in all the activities of men. If man insists on finding this means impracticable, let him share his fortune with woman, not according to his whim, but according to the wisdom of the law. Prejudice will tumble down; customs and manners will be purified; and nature will recapture all its rights. Add to this the marriage of priests, the reaffirmation of the King on his throne, and the French government will never perish.

Notes

1. From Paris to Peru, from Rome to Japan, the most stupid animal, in my opinion, is man.
2. Abraham had some very [*sic*] legitimate children with Agar, the servant of his wife.

19

Mary Wollstonecraft
A Vindication of the Rights of Woman

Mary Wollstonecraft (1759–1797) leveled a radical critique of patriarchal rule in both its public and private manifestations. An enthusiastic champion of the French Revolution, she took on Burke in her Vindication of the Rights of Men *(1790), and wrote* A Vindication of the Rights of Woman *(1792), making a persuasive argument for women's rights. Wollstonecraft's own domestic circumstances were dominated by a despotic drunken father, a failed gentleman farmer who brutally beat his familial victims. After nursing her mother through a fatal illness, Wollstonecraft left her father's house. Struggling to survive economically without a husband or father, Wollstonecraft opened a school with her two sisters. The school closed but she wrote* Thoughts on the Education of Daughters *(1787), espousing a Rousseauist desire that learning should be pleasurable, and also applying Locke's theories of education to women. She authored the remarkable* Letters Written during a Short Residence in Sweden, Norway and Denmark *(1796).*

Wollstonecraft seemed to have finally found a supportive companion in the English philosopher and novelist William Godwin. Shortly after their marriage in 1797, she conceived her second child, a daughter named Mary who would marry the poet Percy Byssche Shelley, and later write Frankenstein. *Wollstonecraft died of puerperal fever ten days after the birth of her daughter, leaving unfinished her novel* Maria, or the Wrongs of Woman, *which graphically exposed the oppression experienced by women of all classes, miseries which occur due to "the partial laws and customs of society."*

Introduction

After considering the historic page, and viewing the living world with anxious solicitude, the most melancholy emotions of sorrowful indignation have depressed my spirits, and I have sighed when obliged to confess, that either nature has made a great difference between man and man, or that the civilization which has hitherto taken place in the world has been very partial. I have turned over various books written on the subject of education, and patiently observed the conduct of parents and the management of schools; but what has been the result?—a profound conviction that the neglected education of my fellow creatures is the grand source of the misery I deplore; and that women, in particular, are rendered weak and wretched by a variety of concurring causes, originating from one hasty conclusion. The conduct and manners of women, in fact, evidently prove that their minds are not in a healthy state; for, like the flowers which are planted in too rich a soil, strength and usefulness are sacrificed to beauty; and the flaunting leaves, after having pleased a fastidious eye, fade, disregarded on the stalk, long before the season when they ought to have arrived at maturity.—One cause of this barren blooming I attribute to a false system of education, gathered from the books written on this subject by men who, considering females rather as women than human creatures, have been more anxious to make them alluring mistresses than affectionate wives and rational mothers; and the understanding of the sex has been so bubbled by this specious homage, that the civilized women of the present century, with a few exceptions, are only anxious to inspire love, when they ought to cherish a nobler ambition, and by their abilities and virtues exact respect.

In a treatise, therefore, on female rights and manners, the works which have been particularly written for their improvement must not be overlooked; especially when it is asserted, in direct terms, that the minds of women are enfeebled by false refinement; that the books of instruction, written by men of genius, have had the same tendency as more frivolous productions; and that, in the true style of Mahometanism, they are treated as a kind of subordinate beings, and not as a part of the human species, when improveable reason is allowed to be the dignified distinction which raises men above the brute creation, and puts a natural sceptre in a feeble hand.

Yet, because I am a woman, I would not lead my readers to suppose that I mean violently to agitate the contested question respecting the equality or inferiority of the sex; but as the subject lies in my way, and I cannot pass it over without subjecting the main tendency of my reasoning to misconstruction, I shall stop a moment to deliver, in a few words, my opinion.—In the government of the physical world it is observable that the female in point of strength is, in general, inferior to the male. This is the law of nature; and it does not appear to be suspended or abrogated in favour of woman. A degree of physical superiority cannot, therefore, be denied—and it is a noble prerogative! But not content with this natural pre-eminence, men endeavour to sink us still lower, merely to render us alluring objects for a moment; and women, intoxicated by the adoration which men, under the influence of their senses, pay them, do not seek to obtain a durable interest in their hearts, or to become the friends of the fellow creatures who find amusement in their society.

I am aware of an obvious inference:—from every quarter have I heard exclamations against masculine women; but where are they to be found? If by this appellation men mean to inveigh against their ardour in hunting, shooting, and gaming, I shall most cordially join in the cry; but if it be against the imitation of manly virtues, or, more properly speaking, the attainment of those talents and virtues, the exercise of which ennobles the human character, and which raise females in the scale of animal being, when they are comprehensively termed mankind;—all those who view them with a philosophic eye must, I should think, wish with me, that they may every day grow more and more masculine.

This discussion naturally divides the subject. I shall first consider women in the grand light of human creatures, who, in common with men, are placed on this earth to unfold their faculties; and afterwards I shall more particularly point out their peculiar designation.

I wish also to steer clear of an error which many respectable writers have fallen into; for the instruction which has hitherto been addressed to women, has rather been applicable to *ladies*, if the little indirect advice, that is scattered through Sandford and Merton, be excepted; but, addressing my sex in a firmer tone, I pay particular attention to those in the middle class, because they appear to be in the most natural state. Perhaps the seeds of false-refinement, immorality, and vanity, have ever been shed by the great. Weak, artificial beings, raised above the common wants and affections of their race, in a premature unnatural manner, undermine the very foundation of virtue, and spread corruption through the whole mass of society! As a class of mankind they have the strongest claim to pity; the education of the rich tends to render them vain and helpless, and the unfolding mind is not strengthened by the practice of those duties which dignify the human character.—They only live to amuse themselves, and by the same law which in nature invariably produces certain effects, they soon only afford barren amusement.

But as I propose taking a separate view of the different ranks of society, and of the moral character of women, in each, this hint is, for the present, sufficient; and I have only alluded to the subject, because it appears to me to be the very essence of an introduction to give a cursory account of the contents of the work it introduces.

My own sex, I hope, will excuse me, if I treat him like rational creatures, instead of flattering their *fascinating* graces, and viewing them as if they were in a state of perpetual childhood, unable to stand alone. I earnestly wish to point out in what true dignity and human happiness consists—I wish to persuade women to endeavour to acquire strength, both of mind and body, and to convince them that the soft phrases, susceptibility of heart, delicacy of sentiment, and refinement of taste, are almost synonymous with epithets of weakness, and that those beings who are only the objects of pity and that kind of love, which has been termed its sister, will soon become objects of contempt.

Dismissing then those pretty feminine phrases, which the men condescendingly use to soften our slavish dependence, and despising that weak elegancy of mind, exquisite sensibility, and sweet docility of manners, supposed to be the sexual characteristics of the weaker vessel, I wish to shew that elegance is inferior to virtue, that the first object of laudable ambition is to obtain a character as a human being, regardless of the distinction of sex; and that secondary views should be brought to this simple touchstone.

This is a rough sketch of my plan; and should I express my conviction with the energetic emotions that I feel whenever I think of the subject, the dictates of experience and reflection will be felt by some of my readers. Animated by this important object, I shall disdain to cull my phrases or polish my style;—I aim at being useful, and sincerity will render me unaffected; for, wishing rather to persuade by the force of my arguments, than dazzle by the elegance of my language, I shall not waste my time in rounding periods, or in fabricating the turgid bombast of artificial feelings, which, coming from the head, never reach the heart.—I shall be employed about things, not words!—and, anxious to render my sex more respectable members of society, I shall try to avoid that flowery diction which has slided from essays into novels, and from novels into familiar letters and conservation.

These pretty superlatives, dropping glibly from the tongue, vitiate the taste, and create a kind of sickly delicacy that turns away from simple unadorned truth; and a deluge of false sentiments and overstretched feelings, stifling the natural emotions of the heart, render the domestic pleasures insipid, that ought to sweeten the exercise of those severe duties, which educate a rational and immortal being for a nobler field of action.

The education of women has, of late, been more attended to than formerly; yet they are still reckoned a frivolous sex, and ridiculed or pitied by the writers who endeavour by satire or instruction to improve them. It is acknowledged that they spend many of the first years of their lives in acquiring a smattering of accomplishments; meanwhile strength of body and mind are sacrificed to libertine notions of beauty, to the desire of establishing themselves—the only way women can rise in the world—by marriage. And this desire making mere animals of them, when they marry they act as such children may be expected to act:—they dress; they paint, and nickname God's creatures.—Surely these weak beings are only fit for a seraglio!—Can they be expected to govern a family with judgment, or take care of the poor babes whom they bring into the world?

If then it can be fairly deduced from the present conduct of the sex, from the prevalent fondness for pleasure which takes place of ambition and those nobler passions that open and enlarge the soul; that the instruction which women have hitherto received has only tended, with the constitution of civil society, to render them insignificant objects of desire—mere propagators of fools!—if it can be proved that in aiming to accomplish them, without cultivating their understandings, they are taken out of their sphere of duties, and made ridiculous and useless when the short-lived bloom of beauty is over, I presume that *rational* men will excuse me for endeavouring to persuade them to become more masculine and respectable.

Indeed the word masculine is only a bugbear: there is little reason to fear that women will acquire too much courage or fortitude; for their apparent inferiority with respect to bodily strength, must render them, in some degree, dependent on men in the various relations of life; but why should it be increased by prejudices that give a sex to virtue, and confound simple truths with sensual reveries?

Women are, in fact, so much degraded by mistaken notions of female excellence, that I do not mean to add a paradox when I assert, that this artificial weakness produces a propensity to tyrannize, and give birth to cunning, the natural opponent of strength, which leads them to play off those contemptible infantine airs that undermine esteem even whilst they excite desire. Let men become more chaste and modest, and if women do not grow wiser in the same ratio, it will be clear that they have weaker understandings. It seems scarcely necessary to say, that I now speak of the sex in general. Many individuals have more sense than their male relatives; and, as nothing preponderates where there is a constant struggle for an equilibrium, without it has naturally more gravity, some women govern their husbands without degrading themselves, because intellect will always govern.

Observations on the State of Degradation to which Woman Is Reduced by Various Causes

That woman is naturally weak, or degraded by a concurrence of circumstances, is, I think, clear. But this position I shall simply contrast with a conclusion, which I have frequently heard fall from sensible men in favour of an aristocracy: that the mass of mankind cannot be anything, or the obsequious slaves, who patiently allow themselves to be driven forward, would feel their own consequence, and spurn their chains. Men, they further observe, submit every where to oppression, when they have only to lift up their heads to throw off the yoke; yet, instead of asserting their birthright, they quietly lick the dust, and say, let us eat and drink, for to-morrow we die. Women, I argue from analogy, are degraded by the same propensity to enjoy the present moment; and, at last, despise the freedom which they have not sufficient virtue to struggle to attain. But I must be more explicit. . . .

The stamen of immortality, if I may be allowed the phrase, is the perfectibility of human reason; for, were man created perfect, or did a flood of knowledge break in upon him, when he arrived at maturity, the precluded error, I should doubt whether his existence would be continued after the dissolution of the body. But, in the present state of things, every difficulty in morals that escapes from human discussion, and equally baffles the investigation of profound thinking, and the lightning glance of genius, is an argument on which I build my belief of the immortality of the soul. Reason is, consequentially, the simple power of improvement; or, more properly speaking, of discerning truth. Every individual is in this respect a world in itself. More or less may be conspicuous in one being than another; but the nature of reason must be the same in all, if it be an emanation of divinity, the tie that connects the creature with the Creator; for, can that soul be stamped with heavenly image, that is not perfected by the exercise of its own reason? Yet outwardly ornamented with elaborate care, and so adorned to delight man, 'that with honour he may love,' the soul of woman is not allowed to have this distinction, and man, ever placed between her and reason, she is always represented as only created to see through a gross medium, and to take things on trust. But dismissing these fanciful theories, and considering woman as a whole, let it be what it will, instead of a part of man, the inquiry is whether she have reason or not. If she have, which, for a moment, I will take for granted, she was not created merely to be the solace of man, and the sexual should not destroy the human character.

Into this error men have, probably, been led by viewing education in a false light; not considering it as the first step to form a being advancing gradually towards perfection; but only as a preparation for life. . . .

The power of generalizing ideas, of drawing comprehensive conclusions from individual observations, is the only acquirement, for an immortal being, that really deserves the name of knowledge. Merely to observe, without endeavouring to account for any thing, may (in a very incomplete manner) serve as the common sense of life; but where is the store laid up that is to clothe the soul when it leaves the body?

This power has not only been denied to women; but writers have insisted that it is inconsistent, with a few exceptions, with their sexual character. Let men prove this, and I shall grant that woman only exists for man. I must, however, previously remark, that the power of generalizing ideas, to any great extent, is not very common amongst men or women. But this exercise is the true cultivation of the understanding; and every thing conspires to render the cultivation of the understanding more difficult in the female than the male world. . . .

Necessity has been proverbially termed the mother of invention—the aphorism may be extended to virtue. It is an acquirement, and an acquirement to which pleasure must be sacrificed—and who sacrifices pleasure when it is within the grasp, whose mind has not been opened and strengthened by adversity, or the pursuit of knowledge goaded on by necessity?—Happy is it when people have the cares of life to struggle with; for these struggles prevent their becoming a prey to enervating vices, merely from idleness! But, if from their birth men and women be placed in a torrid zone, with the meridian sun of pleasure darting directly upon them, how can they sufficiently brace their minds to discharge the duties of life, or even to relish the affections that carry them out of themselves?

Pleasure is the business of woman's life, according to the present modification of society, and while it continues to be so, little can be expected from such weak beings. Inheriting, in a lineal descent from the first fair defect in nature, the sovereignty of beauty, they have, to maintain their power, resigned the natural rights, which the exercise of reason might have procured them, and chosen rather to be short-lived queens than labour to obtain the sober pleasures that arise from equality. . . .

Lewis the XIVth, in particular, spread factitious manners, and caught, in a specious way, the whole nation in his toils; for, establishing an artful chain of despotism, he made it the interest of the people at large, individually to respect his station and support his power. And women, whom he flattered by a puerile attention to the whole sex, obtained in his reign that prince-like distinction so fatal to reason and virtue.

A king is always a king—and a woman always a woman: his authority and her sex, ever stand between them and rational converse. . . . [I]f, excepting warriors, no great men, of any denomination, have ever appeared amongst the nobility, may it not be fairly inferred that their local situation swallowed up the man, and produced a character similar to that of women, who are *localized*, if I may be allowed the word, by the rank they are placed in, by *courtesy*? Women, commonly called Ladies, are not to be contradicted in company, are not allowed to exert any manual strength; and from them the negative virtues only are expected, when any virtues are expected, patience, docility, good-humour, and flexibility; virtues incompatible with any vigorous exertion of intellect. Besides, by living more with each other, and being seldom absolutely alone, they are more under the influence of sentiments than passions. Solitude and reflection are necessary to give to wishes the force of passions, and to enable the imagination to enlarge the object, and make it the most desirable. The same may be said of the rich; they do not sufficiently deal in general ideas, collected by impassioned thinking, or calm investigation, to acquire that strength of character on which great resolves are built. . . .

In the middle rank of life, to continue the comparison, men, in their youth, are prepared for professions, and marriage is not considered as the grand feature in their lives; whilst women, on the contrary, have no other scheme to sharpen their faculties. It is not business, extensive plans, or any of the excursive flights of ambition, that engross their attention; no, their thoughts are not employed in rearing such noble structures. To rise in the world, and have the liberty of running from pleasure to pleasure, they must marry advantageously, and to this object their time is sacrificed, and their persons often legally prostituted. A man when he enters any profession has his eye steadily fixed on some future advantage (and the mind gains great strength by having all its efforts directed to one point), and, full of his business, pleasure is considered as mere relaxation; whilst women seek for pleasure as the main purpose of existence. In fact, from the education, which they receive from society, the love of pleasure may be said to govern them all; but does this prove that there is a sex in souls? It would be just as rational to declare that the courtiers in France, when a destructive system of despotism had formed their character, were not men, because liberty, virtue, and humanity, were sacrificed to pleasure and vanity.—Fatal passions, which have ever domineered over the *whole* race!

The same love of pleasure, fostered by the whole tendency of their education, gives a trifling turn to the conduct of women in most circumstances. . . .

In short, women, in general, as well as the rich of both sexes, have acquired all the follies and vices of civilization, and missed the useful fruit. It is not necessary for me always to premise, that I speak of the condition of the whole sex, leaving exceptions out of the question. Their senses are inflamed, and their understandings neglected, consequently they become the prey of their senses, delicately termed sensibility, and are blown about by every momentary gust of feeling. Civilized women are, therefore, so weakened by false refinement, that, respecting morals, their condition is much below what it would be were they left in a state nearer to nature. . . . Riches and honours prevent a man from enlarging his understanding, and enervate all his powers by reversing the order of nature, which has ever made true pleasure the reward of labour. Pleasure—enervating pleasure is, likewise, within women's reach without earning it. . . .

Let an enlightened nation[1] then try what effect reason would have to bring them back to nature, and their duty; and allowing them to share the advantages of education and government with man, see whether they will become better, as they grow wiser and become free. They cannot be injured by the experiment; for it is not in the power of man to render them more insignificant than they are at present.

To render this practicable, day schools, for particular ages, should be established by government, in which boys and girls might be educated together. The school for the younger children, from five to nine years of age, ought to be absolutely free and open to all classes.[2] A sufficient number of masters should also be chosen by a select committee, in each parish, to whom any complaint of negligence, &c. might be made, if signed by six of the children's parents.

Ushers would then be unnecessary; for I believe experience will ever prove that this kind of subordinate authority is particularly injurious to the morals of youth. What, indeed, can tend to deprave the character more than outward submission and inward contempt? Yet how can boys be expected to treat an usher with respect, when the master seems to consider him in the light of a servant, and almost to countenance the ridicule which becomes the chief amusement of the boys during the play hours?

But nothing of this kind could occur in an elementary day-school, where boys and girls, the rich and poor, should meet together. And to prevent any of the distinctions of vanity, they should be dressed alike, and all obliged to submit to the same discipline, or leave the school. The school-room ought to be surrounded by a large piece of ground, in which the children might be usefully exercised, for at this age they should not be confined to any sedentary employment for more than an hour at a time. But these relaxations might all be rendered a part of elementary education, for many things improve and amuse the senses, when introduced as a kind of show, to the principles of which, dryly laid down, children would turn a deaf ear. For instance, botany, mechanics, and astronomy. Reading, writing, arithmetic, natural history, and some simple experiments in natural philosophy, might fill up the day; but these pursuits should never encroach on gymnastic plays in the open air. The elements of religion, history, the history of man, and politics, might also be taught by conversations, in the socratic form.

After the age of nine, girls and boys, intended for domestic employments, or mechanical trades, ought to be removed to other schools, and receive instruction, in some measure appropriated to the destination of each individual, the two sexes being still together in the morning; but in the afternoon, the girls should attend a school, where plain-work, mantua-making, millinery, &c. would be their employment.

The young people of superior abilities, or fortune, might now be taught, in another school, the dead and living languages, the elements of science, and continue the study of history and politics, on a more extensive scale, which would not exclude polite literature.

Girls and boys still together? I hear some readers ask: yes. And I should not fear any other consequence than that some early attachment might take place: which, whilst it had the best effect on the moral character of the young people, might not perfectly agree with the views of the parents, for it will be a long time, I fear, before the world will be so far enlightened that parents, only anxious to render their children virtuous, shall allow them to choose companions for life themselves.

Besides, this would be a sure way to promote early marriages, and from early marriages the most salutary physical and moral effects naturally flow. What a different character does a married citizen assume from the selfish coxcomb, who lives, but for himself, and who is often afraid to marry lest he should not be able to live in a certain style. Great emergencies excepted, which would rarely occur in a society of which equality was the basis, a man can only be prepared to discharge the duties of public life, by the habitual practice of those inferiour ones which form the man.

In this plan of education the constitution of boys would not be ruined by the early debaucheries, which now make men so selfish, or girls rendered weak and vain, by indolence, and frivolous pursuits. But, I presuppose, that such a degree of equality should be established between the sexes as would shut out gallantry and coquetry, yet allow friendship and love to temper the heart for the discharge of higher duties.

These would be schools of morality—and the happiness of man, allowed to flow from the pure springs of duty and affection, what advances might not the human mind make? Society can only be happy and free in proportion as it is virtuous; but the present distinctions, established in society, corrode all private, and blast all public virtue.

Notes

1. "France" [Wollstonecraft's note].
2. "Treating this part of the subject, I have borrowed some hints from a very sensible pamphlet, written by the late bishop of Autun on Public Education" [Wollstonecraft's note]. The reference is to Talleyrand's *Rapport sur L'Instruction Publique* (Paris, 1791).

20

Jeremy Bentham
An Introduction to the Principles of Morals and Legislation

*Jeremy Bentham (1748–1832) was one of the founders of "utilitarianism" and
an opponent of theories of natural law, which he called "nonsense on stilts." A
law, he contended, was simply the command of a legislator. So unless "nature"
was a being issuing commands, one could not speak of natural laws. What is
natural to human beings, he thought, is the inclinations to pain and pleasure.
Therefore, Bentham formulated the "Greatest Happiness Principle": something
is good if it augments the greatest happiness of the greatest number of people,
bad if it does the opposite. The following selection comes from his book,* An Introduction to the Principles of Morals and Legislation *(1780). Bentham, who
taught himself to read without teachers and later entered Oxford University at
the age of 12, was in favor of enlightened despotism in his early years, but later
became an advocate of democratic reform.*

Of the Principle of Utility

1. Nature has placed mankind under the governance of two sovereign masters,
pain and *pleasure*. It is for them alone to point out what we ought to do, as well
as to determine what we shall do. On the one hand the standard of right and
wrong, on the other the chain of causes and effects, are fastened to their throne.
They govern us in all we do, in all we say, in all we think: every effort we can
make to throw off our subjection, will serve but to demonstrate and confirm it. In
words a man may pretend to abjure their empire: but in reality he will remain
subject to it all the while. The *principle of utility* recognises this subjection, and
assumes it for the foundation of that system, the object of which is to rear the
fabric of felicity by the hands of reason and of law. Systems which attempt to
question it, deal in sounds instead of senses, in caprice instead of reason, in
darkness instead of light.

But enough of metaphor and declamation: it is not by such means that moral
science is to be improved.

2. The principle of utility is the foundation of the present work: it will be proper
therefore at the outset to give an explicit and determinate account of what is meant
by it. By the principle of utility is meant that principle which approves or disap-
proves of every action whatsoever, according to the tendency which it appears to
have to augment or diminish the happiness of the party whose interest is in ques-

tion: or, what is the same thing in other words, to promote or to oppose that happiness. I say of every action whatsoever; and therefore not only of every action of a private individual, but of every measure of government.

3. By utility is meant that property in any object, whereby it tends to produce benefit, advantage, pleasure, good, or happiness (all this in the present case comes to the same thing) or (what comes again to the same thing) to prevent the happening of mischief, pain, evil, or unhappiness to the party whose interest is considered: if that party be the community in general, then the happiness of the community: if a particular individual, then the happiness of that individual.

4. The interest of the community is one of the most general expressions that can occur in the phraseology of morals: no wonder that the meaning of it is often lost. When it has a meaning, it is this. The community is a fictitious *body*, composed of the individual persons who are considered as constituting as it were its *members*. The interest of the community then is, what?—the sum of the interests of the several members who compose it.

5. It is in vain to talk of the interest of the community, without understanding what is the interest of the individual. A thing is said to promote the interest, or to be *for* the interest, of an individual, when it tends to add to the sum total of his pleasures: or, what comes to the same thing, to diminish the sum total of his pains.

6. An action then may be said to be conformable to the principle of utility, or, for shortness sake, to utility (meaning with respect to the community at large) when the tendency it has to augment the happiness of the community is greater than any it has to diminish it.

7. A measure of government (which is but a particular kind of action, performed by a particular person or persons) may be said to be conformable to or dictated by the principle of utility, when in like manner the tendency which it has to augment the happiness of the community is greater than any which it has to diminish it.

8. When an action, or in particular a measure of government, is supposed by a man to be conformable to the principle of utility, it may be convenient, for the purposes of discourse, to imagine a kind of law or dictate, called a law or dictate of utility; and to speak of the action in question, as being conformable to such law or dictate.

9. A man may be said to be a partisan of the principle of utility, when the approbation or disapprobation he annexes to any action, or to any measure, is determined by and proportioned to the tendency which he conceives it to have to augment or to diminish the happiness of the community: or in other words, to its conformity or uncomformity to the laws or dictates of utility.

10. Of an action that is conformable to the principle of utility one may always say either that it is one that ought to be done, or at least that it is not one that ought not to be done. One may say also, that it is right it should be done; at least that it is not wrong it should be done: that it is a right action; at least that it is not a wrong action. When thus interpreted, the words *ought*, and *right* and *wrong*, and others of that stamp, have a meaning: when otherwise, they have none.

11. Has the rectitude of this principle been ever formally contested? It should seem that it had, by those who have not known what they have been meaning. Is it susceptible of any direct proof? It should seem not: for that which is used to prove every thing else, cannot itself be proved: a chain of proofs must have their commencement somewhere. To give such proof is as impossible as it is needless.

12. Not that there is or ever has been that human creature breathing, however stupid or perverse, who has not on many, perhaps on most occasions of his life, deferred to it. By the natural constitution of the human frame, on most occasions of their lives men in general embrace this principle, without thinking of it: if not for the ordering of their own actions, yet for the trying of their own actions, as well as of those of other men. There have been, at the same time, not many, perhaps, even of the most intelligent, who have been disposed to embrace it purely and without reserve. There are even few who have not taken some occasion or other to quarrel with it, either on account of their not understanding always how to apply it, or on account of some prejudice or other which they were afraid to examine into, or could not bear to part with. For such is the stuff that man is made of: in principle and in practice, in a right track and in a wrong one, the rarest of all human qualities is consistency.

13. When a man attempts to combat the principle of utility, it is with reasons drawn, without his being aware of it, from that very principle itself. His arguments, if they prove any thing, prove not that the principle is *wrong*, but that, according to the applications he supposes to be made of it, it is *misapplied*. Is it possible for a man to move the earth? Yes; but he must first find out another earth to stand upon.

14. To disprove the propriety of it by arguments is impossible; but, from the causes that have been mentioned, or from some confused or partial view of it, a man may happen to be disposed not to relish it. Where this is the case, if he thinks the settling of his opinions on such a subject worth the trouble, let him take the following steps and at length, perhaps, he may come to reconcile himself to it.

1. Let him settle with himself, whether he would wish to discard this principle altogether; if so, let him consider what it is that all his reasonings (in matters of politics especially) can amount to?

2. If he would, let him settle with himself, whether he would judge and act without any principle, or whether there is any other he would judge and act by?

3. If there be, let him examine and satisfy himself whether the principle he thinks he has found is really any separate intelligible principle; or whether it be not a mere principle in words, a kind of phrase, which at bottom expresses neither more nor less than the mere averment of his own unfounded sentiments; that is, what in another person he might be apt to call caprice?

4. If he is inclined to think that his own approbation or disapprobation, annexed to the idea of an act, without any regard to its consequences, is a sufficient foundation for him to judge and act upon, let him ask himself whether his sentiment is to be a standard of right and wrong, with respect to every other man, or whether every man's sentiment has the same privilege of being a standard to itself?

5. In the first case, let him ask himself whether his principle is not despotical, and hostile to all the rest of human race?

6. In the second case, whether it is not anarchical, and whether at this rate there are not as many different standards of right and wrong as there are men? and whether even to the sane man, the same thing, which is right to-day, may not (without the least change in its nature) be wrong to-morrow? and whether the same thing is not right and wrong in the same place at the same time? and in either case, whether all argument is not at an end? and whether, when two men have said, 'I like this,' and 'I don't like it,' they can (upon such a principle) have any thing more to say?

7. If he should have said to himself, No: for that the sentiment which he proposes as a standard must be grounded on reflection, let him say on what particulars the reflection is to turn? if on particulars having relation to the utility of the act, then let him say whether this is not deserting his own principle, and borrowing assistance from that very one in opposition to which he sets it up: or if not on those particulars, on what other particulars?

8. If he should be for compounding the matter, and adopting his own principle in part, and the principle of utility in part, let him say how far he will adopt it?

9. When he has settled with himself where he will stop, then let him ask himself how he justifies to himself the adopting it so far? and why he will not adopt it any farther?

10. Admitting any other principle than the principle of utility to be a right principle, a principle that it is right for a man to pursue; admitting (what is not true) that the word *right* can have a meaning without reference to utility, let him say whether there is any such thing as a *motive* that a man can have to pursue the dictates of it: if there is, let him say what that motive is, and how it is to be distinguished from those which enforce the dictates of utility: if not, then lastly let him say what it is this other principle can be good for?

21

John Stuart Mill
Selections

John Stuart Mill (1806–1873) was an English philosopher and political econo-
mist of note. Mill also was a political activist of great courage and principle on
behalf of women's rights. He was arrested at age seventeen for distributing birth
control information. Mill was one of the most forceful and effective spokesmen
for nineteenth-century liberalism. He was elected to Parliament in 1865, where
his amendment to the 1867 Reform Bill led to the first parliamentary debate on
women's suffrage. Mill was the product of his father's extraordinary education.
James Mill, a Utilitarian reformer, supervised his son's instruction in Greek at
the age of three and Latin at eight. By age fourteen, Mill had done intensive
work in mathematics and logic, having read most of the major Greek and Latin
classics.

In 1826, he suffered a depression so severe it forced him to reconsider the
theories by which he had been raised, believing that he had been emotionally
starved and that his rigid training in analytical thought had left him bereft of
feeling. Most significant in his life was Mill's meeting with Harriet Taylor, the
wife of a rich merchant and mother of several children. Their friendship led to a
lifelong collaboration, and to their eventual marriage in 1858, three years after
the death of Taylor's husband. Mill's essay On Liberty *argued for freedom of*
thought and opinion as the cornerstone of liberal government. He feared for the
tendency of society to silence individuality and override the beliefs of minorities.
Mill believed that representative government was the best form of rule. He ar-
gued for the emancipation of women and their admission to political life in On
the Subjection of Women *(written in 1861, published in 1869). This work was*
published after Harriet Taylor Mill's death along with her own more radical
work, The Emancipation of Women.

ON LIBERTY

Of the Liberty of Thought and Discussion

The time, it is to be hoped, is gone by when any defense would be necessary of
the "liberty of the press" as one of the securities against corrupt or tyrannical
government. No argument, we may suppose, can now be needed against permitting a legislature or an executive, not identified in interest with the people, to
prescribe opinions to them and determine what doctrines or what arguments they

shall be allowed to hear. This aspect of the question, besides, has been so often and so triumphantly enforced by preceding writers that it needs not be specially insisted on in this place. Though the law of England, on the subject of the press, is as servile to this day as it was in the time of the Tudors, there is little danger of its being actually put in force against political discussion except during some temporary panic when fear of insurrection drives ministers and judges from their propriety;[1] and, speaking generally, it is not, in constitutional countries, to be apprehended that the government, whether completely responsible to the people or not, will often attempt to control the expression of opinion, except when in doing so it makes itself the organ of the general intolerance of the public. Let us suppose, therefore, that the government is entirely at one with the people, and never thinks of exerting any power of coercion unless in agreement with what it conceives to be their voice. But I deny the right of the people to exercise such coercion, either by themselves or by their government. The power itself is illegitimate. The best government has no more title to it than the worst. It is as noxious, or more noxious, when exerted in accordance with public opinion than when in opposition to it. If all mankind minus one were of one opinion, mankind would be no more justified in silencing that one person than he, if he had the power, would be justified in silencing mankind. Were an opinion a personal possession of no value except to the owner; if to be obstructed in the enjoyment of it were simply a private injury, it would make some difference whether the injury was inflicted only on a few persons or on many. But the peculiar evil of silencing the expression of an opinion is that it is robbing the human race, posterity as well as the existing generation—those who dissent from the opinion, still more than those who hold it. If the opinion is right, they are deprived of the opportunity of exchanging error for truth; if wrong, they lose, what is almost as great a benefit, the clearer perception and livelier impression of truth produced by its collision with error.

It is necessary to consider separately these two hypotheses, each of which has a distinct branch of the argument corresponding to it. We can never be sure that the opinion we are endeavouring to stifle is a false opinion; and if we were sure, stifling it would be an evil still.

First, the opinion which it is attempted to suppress by authority may possibly be true. Those who desire to suppress it, of course, deny its truth; but they are not infallible. They have no authority to decide the question for all mankind and exclude every other person from the means of judging. To refuse a hearing to an opinion because they are sure that it is false is to assume that *their* certainty is the same thing as *absolute* certainty. All silencing of discussion is an assumption of infallibility. Its condemnation may be allowed to rest on this common argument, not the worse for being common.

Unfortunately for the good sense of mankind, the fact of their fallibility is far from carrying the weight in their practical judgment which is always allowed to it in theory; for while every one well knows himself to be fallible, few think it necessary to take any precautions against their own fallibility, or admit the supposition that any opinion of which they feel very certain may be one of the examples of the error to which they acknowledge themselves to be liable. Absolute princes, or others who are accustomed to unlimited deference, usually feel this complete confidence in their own opinions on nearly all subjects. People more happily situated, who sometimes hear their opinions disputed and are not wholly unused to be set right when they are wrong, place the same unbounded reliance only on such of their opinions as are shared by all who surround them, or to whom they habitually defer; for in proportion to a man's want of confidence in his own solitary judgment does he usually repose, with implicit trust, on the infallibility of "the world" in general. And the world, to each individual, means the part of it with which he comes in contact: his party, his sect, his church, his class of society; the man may be called, by comparison, almost liberal and large-minded to whom it means anything so comprehensive as his own country or his own age. Nor is his faith in the collective authority at all shaken by his being aware that other ages, countries, sects, churches, classes, and parties have thought, and even now think, the exact reverse. He devolves upon his own world the responsibility of being in the right against the dissentient worlds of other people; and it never troubles him that mere accident has decided which of these numerous worlds is the object of his reliance, and that the same causes which make him a churchman in London would have made him a Buddhist or a Confucian in Peking. Yet it is as evident in itself, as any amount of argument can make it, that ages are no more infallible than individuals—every age having held many opinions which subsequent ages have deemed not only false but absurd; and it is as certain that many opinions, now general, will be rejected by future ages, as it is that many, once general, are rejected by the present.

The objection likely to be made to this argument would probably take some such form as the following. There is no greater assumption of infallibility in forbidding the propagation of error than in any other thing which is done by public authority on its own judgment and responsibility. Judgment is given to men that they may use it. Because it may be used erroneously, are men to be told that they ought not to use it at all? To prohibit what they think pernicious is not claiming exemption from error, but fulfilling the duty incumbent on them, although fallible, of acting on their conscientious conviction. If we were never to act on our opinions, because those opinions may be wrong, we should leave all our interests uncared for, and all our duties unperformed. An objection which applies to all conduct can be no valid objection to any conduct in particular. It is the duty of governments, and of individuals, to form the truest opinions they can; to form them carefully, and never impose them upon others unless they are quite sure of being right. But when they are sure (such reasoners may say), it is not conscientiousness but cowardice to shrink from acting on their opinions and allow doctrines which they honestly think dangerous to the welfare of mankind, either in this life or in another, to be scattered abroad without restraint, because other people, in less enlightened times, have persecuted opinions now believed to be true. Let us take care, it may be said, not to make the same mistake; but governments and nations have made mistakes in other things which are not denied to be fit subjects for the exercise of authority: they have laid on bad taxes, made unjust wars. Ought we therefore to lay on no taxes and, under whatever provocation, make no wars? Men and governments must act to the best of their ability. There is no such thing as absolute certainty, but there is assurance sufficient for the purposes of human life. We may, and must, assume our opinion to be true for the guidance of our own conduct; and it is assuming no more when we forbid bad men to pervert society by the propagation of opinions which we regard as false and pernicious.

I answer, that it is assuming very much more. There is the greatest difference between presuming an opinion to be true because, with every opportunity for contesting it, it has not been refuted, and assuming its truth for the purpose of not permitting its refutation. Complete liberty of contradicting and disproving our opinion is the very condition which justifies us in assuming its truth for purposes of action; and on no other terms can a being with human faculties have any rational assurance of being right.

When we consider either the history of opinion or the ordinary conduct of human life, to what is it to be ascribed that the one and the other are no worse than they are? Not certainly to the inherent force of the human understanding, for on any matter not self-evident there are ninety-nine persons totally incapable of judging of it for one who is capable; and the capacity of the hundredth person is only comparative, for the majority of the eminent men of every past generation held many opinions now known to be erroneous, and did or approved numerous things which no one will now justify. Why is it, then, that there is on the whole a preponderance among mankind of rational opinions and rational conduct? If there really is this preponderance—which there must be unless human affairs are, and have always been, in an almost desperate state—it is owing to a quality of the human mind, the source of everything respectable in man either as an intellectual or as a moral being, namely, that his errors are corrigible. He is capable of rectifying his mistakes by discussion and experience. Not by experience alone. There must be discussion to show how experience is to be interpreted. Wrong opinions and practices gradually yield to fact and argument; but facts and arguments, to produce any effect on the mind, must be brought before it. Very few facts are able to tell their own story, without comments to bring out their meaning. The whole strength and value, then, of human judgment depending on the one property, that it can be set right when it is wrong, reliance can be placed on it only when the means of setting it right are kept constantly at hand. In the case of any person whose judgment is really deserving of confidence, how has it become so? Because he has kept his mind open to criticism of his opinions and conduct. Because it has been his practice to listen to all that could be said against him; to profit by as much of it as was just, and to expound to himself, and upon occasion to others, the fallacy of what was fallacious. Because he has felt that the only way in which a human being can make some approach to knowing the whole of a subject is by hearing what can be said about it by persons of every variety of opinion, and studying all modes in which it can be looked at by every character of mind. No wise man ever acquired his wisdom in any mode but this; nor is it in the nature of human intellect to become wise in any other manner. The steady habit of correcting and completing his own opinion by collating it with those of others, so far from causing doubt and hesitation in carrying it into practice, is the only stable foundation for a just reliance on it; for, being cognizant of all that can, at least obviously, be said against him, and having taken up his position against all gainsayers—knowing that he has sought for objections and difficulties instead of avoiding them, and has shut out no light which can be thrown upon the subject from any quarter—he has a right to think his judgment better than that of any person, or any multitude, who have not gone through a similar process.

It is not too much to require that what the wisest of mankind, those who are best entitled to trust their own judgment, find necessary to warrant their relying on it, should be submitted to by that miscellaneous collection of a few wise and many foolish individuals called the public. The most intolerant of churches, the Roman Catholic Church, even at the canonization of a saint admits, and listens patiently to, a "devil's advocate." The holiest of men, it appears, cannot be admitted to posthumous honors until all that the devil could say against him is known and weighed. If even the Newtonian philosophy were not permitted to be questioned, mankind could not feel as complete assurance of its truth as they now do. The beliefs which we have most warrant for have no safeguard to rest on but a standing invitation to the whole world to prove them unfounded. If the challenge is not accepted, or is accepted and the attempt fails, we are far enough from certainty still, but we have done that best that the existing state of human reason admits of: we have neglected nothing that could give the truth a chance of reaching us; if the lists are kept open, we may hope that, if there be a better truth, it will be found when the human mind is capable of receiving it; and in the meantime we may rely on having attained such approach to truth as is possible in our own day. This is the amount of certainty attainable by a fallible being, and this the sole way of attaining it.

Strange it is that men should admit the validity of the arguments for free discussion, but object to their being "pushed to an extreme," not seeing that unless the reasons are good for an extreme case, they are not good for any case. Strange that they should imagine that they are not assuming infallibility when they acknowledge that there should be free discussion on all subjects which can possibly be *doubtful*, but think that some particular principle or doctrine should be forbidden to be questioned because it is so *certain*, that is, because *they are certain* that it is certain. To call any proposition certain, while there is anyone who would deny its certainty if permitted, but who is not permitted, is to assume that we ourselves, and those who agree with us, are the judges of certainty, and judges without hearing the other side.

In the present age—which has been described as "destitute of faith, but terrified at skepticism"—in which people feel sure, not so much that their opinions are true as that they should not know what to do without them—the claims of an opinion to be protected from public attack are rested not so much on its truth as on its importance to society. There are, it is alleged, certain beliefs so useful, not to say indispensable, to well-being that it is as much the duty of governments to uphold those beliefs as to protect any other of the interests of society. In a case of such necessity, and so directly in the line of their duty, something less than infallibility may, it is maintained, warrant, and even bind, governments to act on their own opinion confirmed by the general opinion of mankind. It is also often argued, and still oftener thought, that none but bad men would desire to weaken these salutary beliefs; and there can be nothing wrong, it is thought, in restraining bad men and prohibiting what only such men would wish to practice. This mode of thinking makes the justification of restraints on discussion not a question of the truth of doctrines but of their usefulness, and flatters itself by that means to escape the responsibility of claiming to be an infallible judge of opinions. But those who thus satisfy themselves do not perceive that the assumption of infallibility is merely shifted from one point to another. The usefulness of an opinion is itself matter of opinion—as disputable, as open to discussion, and requiring discussion as much as the opinion itself. There is the same need of an infallible judge of opinions to decide an opinion to be noxious as to decide it to be false, unless the opinion condemned has full opportunity of defending itself. And it will not do to say that the heretic may be allowed to maintain the utility or harmlessness of his opinion, though forbidden to maintain its truth. The truth of an opinion is part of its utility. If we would know whether or not it is desirable that a proposition should be believed, is it possible to exclude the consideration of whether or not it is true? In the opinion, not of bad men, but of the best men, no belief which is contrary to truth can be really useful; and can you prevent such men from urging that plea when they are charged with culpability for denying some doctrine which they are told is useful, but which they believe to be false? Those who are on the side of received opinions never fail to take all possible advantage of this plea; you do not find *them* handling the question of ability as if it could be completely abstracted from that of truth; on the contrary, it is, above all, because their doctrine is "the truth" that the knowledge or the belief of it is held to be so indispensable. There can be no fair discussion of the question of usefulness when an argument so vital may be employed on one side, but not on the other. And in point of fact, when law or public feeling do not permit the truth of an opinion to be disputed, they are just as little tolerant of a denial of its usefulness. The utmost they allow is an extenuation of its absolute necessity, or of the positive guilt of rejecting it.

In order more fully to illustrate the mischief of denying a hearing to opinions because we, in our own judgment, have condemned them, it will be desirable to fix down the discussion to a concrete case; and I choose, by preference, the cases which are least favorable to me—in which the argument against freedom of opinion, both on the score of truth and on that of utility, is considered the strongest. Let the opinions impugned be the belief in a God and in a future state, or any of the commonly received doctrines of morality. To fight the battle on such ground gives a great advantage to an unfair antagonist, since he will be sure to say (and many who have no desire to be unfair will say it internally), Are these the doctrines which you do not deem sufficiently certain to be taken under the protection of law? Is the belief in a God one of the opinions to feel sure of which you hold to be assuming infallibility? But I must be permitted to observe that it is not the feeling sure of a doctrine (be it what it may) which I call an assumption of infallibility. It is the undertaking to decide that question *for others*, without allowing them to hear what can be said on the contrary side. And I denounce and reprobate this pretension not the less if put forth on the side of my most solemn convictions. However positive anyone's persuasion may be, not only of the falsity but of the pernicious consequences—not only of the pernicious consequences, but (to adopt expressions which I altogether condemn) the immorality and impiety of an opinion—yet if, in pursuance of that private judgment, though backed by the public judgment of his country or his contemporaries, he prevents the opinion from being heard in its defense, he assumes infallibility. And so far from the assumption being less objectionable or less dangerous because the opinion is called immoral or impious, this is the case of all others in which it is most fatal. These are exactly the occasions on which the men of one generation commit those dreadful mistakes which excite the astonishment and horror of posterity. It is among such that we find the instances memorable in history, when the arm of the law has been employed to root out the best men and the noblest doctrines; with deplorable success as to the men, though some of the doctrines have survived to be (as if in mockery) invoked in defense of similar conduct toward those who dissent from *them*, or from their received interpretation.

Mankind can hardly be too often reminded that there was once a man called Socrates, between whom and the legal authorities and public opinion of his time there took place a memorable collision. Born in an age and country abounding in individual greatness, this man has been handed down to us by those who best knew both him and the age as the most virtuous man in it; while *we* know him as the head and prototype of all subsequent teachers of virtue, the source equally of the lofty inspiration of Plato and the judicious utilitarianism of Aristotle, "*i maestri di color che sanno*," the two headsprings of ethical as of all other philosophy. This acknowledged master of all the eminent thinkers who have since lived—whose fame, still growing after more than two thousand years, all but outweighs the whole remainder of the names which make his native city illustrious—was put to death by his countrymen, after a judicial conviction, for impiety and immorality. Impiety, in denying the gods recognized by the State; indeed, his accuser asserted (see the *Apologia*) that he believed in no gods at all. Immorality, in being, by his doctrines and instructions, a "corruptor of youth." Of these charges the tribunal, there is every ground for believing, honestly found him guilty, and condemned the man who probably of all then born had deserved best of mankind to be put to death as a criminal. . . .

It still remains to speak of one of the principal causes which make diversity of opinions advantageous, and will continue to do so until mankind shall have entered a stage of intellectual advancement which at present seems at an incalculable distance. We have hitherto considered only two possibilities: that the received opinion may be false, and some other opinion, consequently, true; or that, the received opinion being true, a conflict with the opposite error is essential to a clear apprehension and deep feeling of its truth. But there is a commoner case than either of these: when the conflicting doctrines, instead of being one true and the other false, share the truth between them, and the nonconforming opinion is needed to supply the remainder of the truth of which the received doctrine embodies only a part. Popular opinions, on subjects not palpable to sense, are often true, but seldom or never the whole truth. They are a part of the truth, sometimes a greater, sometimes a smaller part, but exaggerated, distorted, and disjointed from the truths by which they ought to be accompanied and limited. Heretical opinions, on the other hand, are generally some of these suppressed and neglected truths, bursting the bonds which kept them down, and either seeking reconciliation with the truth contained in the common opinion, or fronting it as enemies, and setting themselves up, with similar exclusiveness, as the whole truth. The latter case is hitherto the most frequent, as, in the human mind, one-sidedness has always been the rule, and many-sidedness the exception. Hence, even in revolutions of opinion, one part of the truth usually sets while another rises. Even progress, which ought to superadd, for the most part only substitutes one partial and incomplete truth for another; improvement consisting chiefly in this, that the new fragment of truth is more wanted, more adapted to the needs of the time than that which it displaces. Such being the partial character of prevailing opinions, even when resting on a true foundation, every opinion which embodies somewhat of the portion of truth which the common opinion omits ought to be considered precious, with whatever amount of error and confusion that truth may be blended. No sober judge of human affairs will feel bound to be indignant because those who force on our notice truths which we should otherwise have overlooked, overlook some of those which we see. Rather, he will think that so long as popular truth is one-sided, it is more desirable than otherwise that unpopular truth should have one-sided assertors, too, such being usually the most energetic and the most likely to compel reluctant attention to the fragment of wisdom which they proclaim as if it were the whole.

Thus, in the eighteenth century, when nearly all the instructed, and all those of the uninstructed who were led by them, were lost in admiration of what is called civilization, and of the marvels of modern science, literature, and philosophy, and while greatly overrating the amount of unlikeness between the men of modern and those of ancient times, indulged the belief that the whole of the difference was in their own favor; with what a salutary shock did the paradoxes of Rousseau explode like bombshells in the midst, dislocating the compact mass of one-sided opinion and forcing its elements to recombine in a better form and with additional ingredients. Not that the current opinions were on the whole farther from the truth than Rousseau's were; on the contrary, they were nearer to it; they contained more of positive truth, and very much less of error. Nevertheless there lay in Rousseau's doctrine, and has floated down the stream of opinion along with it, a considerable amount of exactly those truths which the popular opinion wanted; and these are the deposit which was left behind them when the flood subsided. The superior worth of simplicity of life, the enervating and demoralizing effect of the trammels and hypocrisies of artificial society are ideas which have never been entirely absent from cultivated minds since Rousseau wrote; and they will in time produce their due effect, though at present needing to be asserted as much as ever, and to be asserted by deeds; for words, on this subject, have nearly exhausted their power.

In politics, again, it is almost a commonplace that a party of order or stability and a party of progress or reform are both necessary elements of a healthy state of political life, until the one or the other shall have so enlarged its mental grasp as to be a party equally of order and of progress, knowing and distinguishing what is fit to be preserved from what ought to be swept away. Each of these modes of thinking derives its utility from the deficiencies of the other; but it is in a great measure the opposition of the other that keeps each within the limits of reason and sanity. Unless opinions favorable to democracy and to aristocracy, to property and to equality, to cooperation and to competition, to luxury and discipline, and all the other standing antagonisms of practical life, are expressed with equal freedom and enforced and defended with equal talent and energy, there is no chance of both elements obtaining their due; one scale is sure to go up, and the other down. Truth, in the great practical concerns of life, is so much a question of the reconciling and combining of opposites that very few have minds sufficiently capacious and impartial to make the adjustment with an approach to correctness, and it has to be made by the rough process of a struggle between combatants fighting under hostile banners. On any of the great open questions just enumerated, if either of the two opinions has a better claim than the other, not merely to be tolerated, but to be encouraged and countenanced, it is the one which happens at the particular time and place to be in a minority. That is the opinion which, for the time being, represents the neglected interests, the side of human well-being which is in danger of obtaining less than its share. I am aware that there is not, in this country, any intolerance of differences of opinion on most of these topics. They are adduced to show, by admitted and multiplied examples, the universality of the fact that only through diversity of opinion is there, in the existing state of human intellect, a chance of fair play to all sides of the truth. When there are persons to be found who form an exception to the apparent unanimity of the world on any subject, even if the world is in the right, it is always probable that dissentients have something worth hearing to say for themselves, and that truth would lose something by their silence.

It may be objected, "But *some* received principles, especially on the highest and most vital subjects, are more than half-truths. The Christian morality, for instance, is the whole truth on that subject, and if anyone teaches a morality which varies from it, he is wholly in error." As this is of all cases the most important in practice, none can be fitter to test the general maxim. But before pronouncing what Christian morality is or is not, it would be desirable to decide what is meant by Christian morality. If it means the morality of the New Testament, I wonder that any one who derives his knowledge of this from the book itself can suppose that it was announced, or intended, as a complete doctrine of morals. The Gospel always refers to a pre-existing morality and confines its precepts to the particulars in which that morality was to be corrected or superseded by a wider and higher, expressing itself, moreover, in terms most general, often impossible to be interpreted literally, and possessing rather the impressiveness of poetry or eloquence than the precision of legislation. To extract from it a body of ethical doctrine has never been possible without eking it out from the Old Testament, that is, from a system elaborate indeed, but in many respects barbarous, and intended only for a barbarous people. St. Paul, a declared enemy to this Judaical mode of interpreting the doctrine and filling up the scheme of his Master, equally assumes a pre-existing morality, namely that of the Greeks and Romans; and his advice to Christians is in a great measure a system of accommodation to that, even to the extent of giving an apparent sanction to slavery. What is called Christian, but should rather be termed theological, morality was not the work of Christ or the Apostles, but is of much later origin, having been gradually built up by the Catholic Church of the first five centuries, and though not implicitly adopted by moderns and Protestants, has been much less modified by them than might have been expected. For the most part, indeed, they have contented themselves with cutting off the additions which had been made to it in the Middle Ages, each sect supplying the place by fresh additions, adapted to its own character and tendencies. That mankind owe a great debt to this morality, and to its early teachers, I should be the last person to deny, but I do not scruple to say of it that it is, in many important points, incomplete and one-sided, and that, unless ideas and feelings not sanctioned by it had contributed to the formation of European life and character, human affairs would have been in a worse condition than they now are. Christian morality (so called) has all the characters of a reaction; it is, in great part, a protest against paganism. Its ideal is negative rather than positive; passive rather than active; innocence rather than nobleness; abstinence from evil rather than energetic pursuit of good; in its precepts (as has been well said) "thou shalt not" predominates unduly over "thou shalt." In its horror of sensuality, it made an idol of asceticism which has been gradually compromised away into one of legality. It holds out the hope of heaven and the threat of hell as the appointed and appropriate motives to a virtuous life: in this falling far below the best of the ancients, and doing what lies in it to give to human morality an essentially selfish character, by disconnecting each man's feelings of duty from the interests of his fellow creatures, except so far as a self-interested inducement is offered to him for consulting them. It is essentially a doctrine of passive obedience; it inculcates submission to all authorities found established; who indeed are not to be actively obeyed when they command what religion forbids, but who are not to be resisted, far less rebelled against, for any amount of wrong to ourselves. And while, in the morality of the best pagan nations, duty to the State holds even a disproportionate place, infringing on the just liberty of the individual, in purely Christian ethics that grand department of duty is scarcely noticed or acknowledged. It is in the Koran, not the New Testament, that we read the maxim: "A ruler who appoints any man to an office, when there is in his dominions another man better qualified for it, sins against God and against the State." What little recognition the idea of obligation to the public obtains in modern morality is derived from Greek and Roman sources, not from Christian; as, even in the morality of private life, whatever exists of magnanimity, high-mindedness, personal dignity, even the sense of honor, is derived from the purely human, not the religious part of our education, and never could have grown out of a standard of ethics in which the only worth, professedly recognized, is that of obedience.

I am as far as anyone from pretending that these defects are necessarily inherent in the Christian ethics in every manner in which it can be conceived, or that the many requisites of a complete moral doctrine which it does not contain do not admit of being reconciled with it. Far less would I insinuate this out of the doctrines and precepts of Christ himself. I believe that the sayings of Christ are all that I can see any evidence of their having been intended to be; that they are irreconcilable with nothing which a comprehensive morality requires; that everything which is excellent in ethics may be brought within them, with no greater violence to their language than has been done to it by all who have attempted to deduce from them any practical system of conduct whatever. But it is quite consistent with this to believe that they contain, and were meant to contain, only a part of the truth; that many essential elements of the highest morality are among the things which are not provided for, not intended to be provided for, in the recorded deliverances of the Founder of Christianity, and which have been entirely thrown aside in the system of ethics erected on the basis of those deliverances by the Christian Church. And this being so, I think it a greater error to persist in attempting to find in the Christian doctrine that complete rule for our guidance which its Author intended it to sanction and enforce, but only partially to provide. I believe, too, that this narrow theory is becoming a grave practical evil, detracting greatly from the moral training and instruction which so many well-meaning persons are now at length exerting themselves to promote. I much fear that by attempting to form the mind and feelings on an exclusively religious type, and discarding those secular standards (as for want of a better name they may be called) which heretofore coexisted with and supplemented the Christian ethics, receiving some of its spirit, and infusing into it some of theirs, there will result, and is even now resulting, a low, abject, servile type of character which, submit itself as it may to what it deems the Supreme Will, is incapable of rising to or sympathizing in the conception of Supreme Goodness. I believe that other ethics than any which can be evolved form exclusively Christian sources must exist side by side with Christian ethics to produce the moral regeneration of mankind; and that the Christian system is no exception to the rule that in an imperfect state of the human mind the interests of truth require a diversity of opinions. It is not necessary that in ceasing to ignore the moral truths not contained in Christianity men should ignore any of those which it does contain. Such prejudice or oversight, when it occurs, is altogether an evil, but it is one from which we cannot hope to be always exempt, and must be regarded as the price paid for an inestimable good. The exclusive pretension made by a part of the truth to be the whole must and ought to be protested against; and if a reactionary impulse should make the protestors unjust in their turn, this one-sidedness, like the other, may be lamented but must be tolerated. If Christians would teach infidels to be just to Christianity, they should themselves be just to infidelity. It can do truth no service to blink the fact, known to all who have the most ordinary acquaintance with literary history, that a large portion of the noblest and most valuable moral teaching has been the work, not only of men who did not know, but of men who knew and rejected, the Christian faith.

I do not pretend that the most unlimited use of the freedom of enunciating all possible opinions would put an end to the evils of religious or philosophical sectarianism. Every truth which men of narrow capacity are in earnest about is sure to be asserted, inculcated, and in many ways even acted on, as if no other truth existed in the world, or at all events none that could limit or qualify the first. I acknowledge that the tendency of all opinions to become sectarian is not cured by the freest discussion, but is often heightened and exacerbated thereby; the truth which ought to have been, but was not, seen, being rejected all the more violently because proclaimed by persons regarded as opponents. But it is not on the impassioned partisan, it is on the calmer and more disinterested bystander, that this collision of half of it, is the formidable evil; there is always hope when people are forced to listen to both sides; it is when they attend only to one that errors harden into prejudices, and truth itself ceases to have the effect of truth by being exaggerated into falsehood. And since there are few mental attributes more rare than that judicial faculty which can sit in intelligent judgment between two sides of a question, of which only one is represented by an advocate before it, truth has no chance but in proportion as every side of it, every opinion which embodies any fraction of the truth, not only finds advocates, but is so advocated as to be listened to.

We have now recognized the necessity to the mental well-being of mankind (on which all their other well-being depends) of freedom of opinion, and freedom of the expression of opinion, on four distinct grounds, which we will now briefly recapitulate:

First, if any opinion is compelled to silence, that opinion may, for aught we can certainly know, be true. To deny this is to assume our own infallibility.

Secondly, though the silenced opinion be an error, it may, and very commonly does, contain a portion of truth; and since the general or prevailing opinion on any subject is rarely or never the whole truth, it is only by the collision of adverse opinions that the remainder of the truth has any chance of being supplied.

Thirdly, even if the received opinion be not only true, but the whole truth; unless it is suffered to be, and actually is, vigorously and earnestly contested, it will, by most of those who receive it, be held in the manner of a prejudice, with little comprehension or feeling of its rational grounds. And not only this, but, fourthly, the meaning of the doctrine itself will be in danger of being lost or enfeebled, and deprived of its vital effect on the character and conduct: the dogma becoming a mere formal profession, inefficacious for good, but cumbering the ground and preventing the growth of any real and heartfelt conviction from reason or personal experience.

Before quitting the subject of freedom of opinion, it is fit to take some notice of those who say that the free expression of all opinions should be permitted on condition that the manner be temperate, and do not pass the bounds of fair discussion. Much might be said on the impossibility of fixing where these supposed bounds are to be placed; for if the test be offense to those whose opinions are attacked, I think experience testifies that this offense is given whenever the attack is telling and powerful, and that every opponent who pushes them hard, and whom they find it difficult to answer, appears to them, if he shows any strong feeling on the subject, and intemperate opponent. But this, though an important consideration in a practical point of view, merges in a more fundamental objection. Undoubtedly, the manner of asserting an opinion, even though it be a true one, may be very objectionable and may justly incur severe censure. But the principle offenses of the kind are such as it is mostly impossible, unless by accidental self-betrayal, to bring home to conviction. The gravest of them is, to argue sophistically, to suppress facts or arguments, to misstate the elements of the case, or misrepresent the opposite opinion. But all this, even to the most aggravated degree, is so continually done in perfect good faith by persons who are not considered, and in many other respects may not deserve to be considered, ignorant or incompetent, that it is rarely possible, on adequate grounds, conscientiously to stamp the misrepresentation as morally culpable, and still less could law presume to interfere with this kind of controversial misconduct. With regard to what is commonly meant by intemperate discussion, namely invective, sarcasm, personality, and the like, the denunciation of these weapons would deserve more sympathy if it were ever proposed to interdict them equally to both sides; but it is only desired to restrain the employment of them against the prevailing opinion; against the unprevailing they may not only be used without general disapproval, but will be likely to obtain for him who uses them the praise of honest zeal and righteous indignation. Yet whatever mischief arises from their use is greatest when they are employed against the comparatively defenseless; and whatever unfair advantage can be derived by any opinion from this mode of asserting it accrues almost exclusively to received opinions. The worst offense of this kind which can be committed by a polemic is to stigmatize those who hold the contrary opinion as bad and immoral men. To calumny of this sort, those who hold any unpopular opinion are peculiarly exposed, because they are in general few and uninfluential, and nobody but themselves feels much interested in seeing justice done them; but this weapon is, from the nature of the case, denied to those who attack a prevailing opinion: they can neither use it with safety to themselves, nor, if they could, would it do anything but recoil on their own cause. In general, opinions contrary to those commonly received can only obtain a hearing by studied moderation of language and the most cautious avoidance of unnecessary offense, from which they hardly ever deviate even in a slight degree without losing ground, while unmeasured vituperation employed on the side of the prevailing opinion really does deter people from professing contrary opinions and from listening to those who profess them. For the interest, therefore, of truth and justice it is far more important to restrain this employment of vituperative language than the other; and, for example, if it were necessary to choose, there would be much more need to discourage offensive attacks on infidelity than on religion. It is, however, obvious that law and authority have no business with restraining either, while opinion ought, in every instance, to determine its verdict by the circumstances of the individual case—condemning everyone, on whichever side of the argument he places himself, in whose mode of advocacy either want of candor, or malignity, bigotry, or intolerance of feeling manifest themselves; but not inferring these vices from the side which a person takes, though it be the contrary side of the question to our own; and giving merited honor to everyone, whatever opinion he may hold, who has calmness to see and honesty to state what his opponents and their opinions really are, exaggerating nothing to their discredit, keeping nothing back which tells, or can be supposed to tell, in their favor. This is the real morality of public discussion; and if often violated, I am happy to think that there are many controversialists who to a great extent observe it, and a still greater number who conscientiously strive toward it.

Note

1. These words had scarcely been written when, as if to give them an emphatic contradiction, occurred the Government Press Prosecutions of 1858. That ill-judged interference with the liberty of public discussion has not, however, induced me to alter a single word in the text, nor has it at all weakened my conviction that, moments of panic excepted, the era of pains and penalties for political discussion has, in our own country, passed away. For, in the first place, the prosecutions were not persisted in; and, in the second, they were never, properly speaking, political prosecutions. The offense charged was not that of criticizing institutions or the acts or persons of rulers, but of circulating what was deemed an immoral doctrine, the lawfulness of tyrannicide.

If the arguments of the present chapter are of any validity, there ought to exist the fullest liberty of professing and discussing, as a matter of ethical conviction, any doctrine, however immoral it may be considered. It would, therefore, be irrelevant and out of place to examine here whether the doctrine of tyrannicide deserves that title. I shall content myself with saying that the subject has been at all times one of the open questions of morals; that the act of a private citizen in striking down a criminal who, by raising himself above the law, has placed himself beyond the reach of legal punishment or control has been accounted by whole nations, and by some of the best and wisest of men, not a crime but an act of exalted virtue; and that, right or wrong, it is not of the nature of assassination, but of civil war. As such, I hold that the instigation to it, in a specific case, may be a proper subject of punishment, but only if an overt act has followed, and at least a probable connection can be established between the act and the instigation. Even then it is not a foreign government but the very government assailed which alone, in the exercise of self-defense, can legitimately punish attacks directed against its own existence.

ON THE SUBJECTION OF WOMEN

The object of this Essay is to explain, as clearly as I am able, the grounds of an opinion which I have held from the very earliest period when I had formed any opinions at all on social or political matters, and which, instead of being weakened or modified, has been constantly growing stronger by the progress of reflection and the experience of life: That the principle which regulates the existing social relations between the two sexes—the legal subordination of one sex to the other—is wrong in itself, and now one of the chief hindrances to human improvement; and that it ought to be replaced by a principle of perfect equality, admitting no power or privilege on the one side, nor disability on the other. . . .

The generality of a practice is in some cases a strong presumption that it is, or at all events once was, conducive to laudable ends. This is the case, when the practice was first adopted, or afterwards kept up, as a means to such ends, and was grounded on experience of the mode in which they could be most effectually attained. If the authority of men over women, when first established, had been the result of a conscientious comparison between different modes of constituting the government of society; if, after trying various other modes of social organization—the government of women over men, equality between the two, and such mixed and divided modes of government as might be invented—it had been decided, on the testimony of experience, that the mode in which women are wholly under the rule of men, having no share at all in public concerns, and each in private being under the legal obligation of obedience to the man with whom she has associated her destiny, was the arrangement most conducive to the happiness and well-being of both; its general adoption might then be fairly thought to be some evidence that, at the time when it was adopted, it was the best: though even then the considerations which recommended it may, like so many other primeval social facts of the greatest importance, have subsequently, in the course of ages, ceased to exist. But the state of the case is in every respect the reverse of this. In the first place, the opinion in favour of the present system, which entirely subordinates the weaker sex to the stronger, rests upon theory only; for there never has been trial made of any other: so that experience, in the sense in which it is vulgarly opposed to theory, cannot be pretended to have pronounced any verdict. And in the second place, the adoption of this system of inequality never was the result of deliberation, or forethought, or any social ideas, or any notion whatever of what conduced to the benefit of humanity or the good order of society. It arose simply from the fact that from the very earliest twilight of human society, every woman (owing to the value attached to her by men, combined with her inferiority in muscular strength) was found in a state of bondage to some man. Laws and systems of polity always begin by recognizing the relations they find already existing between individuals. They convert what was a mere physical fact into a legal right, give it the sanction of society, and principally aim at the substitution of public and organized means of asserting and protecting these rights, instead of the irregular and lawless conflict of physical strength. Those who had already been compelled to obedience became in this manner legally bound to it. Slavery, from being a mere affair of force between the master and the slave, became regularized and a matter of compact among the masters, who, binding themselves to one another for common protection, guaranteed by their collective strength the private possessions of each, including his slaves. In early times, the great majority of the male sex were slaves, as well as the whole of the female. And many ages elapsed, some of them ages of high cultivation, before any thinker was bold enough to question the rightfulness, and the absolute social necessity, either of the one slavery or of the other. By degrees such thinkers did arise: and (the general progress of society assisting) the slavery of the male sex has, in all the countries of Christian Europe at least (though, in one of them, only within the last few years) been at length abolished, and that of the female sex has been gradually changed into a milder form of dependence. But this dependence, as it exists at present, is not an original institution, taking a fresh start from considerations of justice and social expediency—it is the primitive state of slavery lasting on, through successive mitigations and modifications occasioned by the same causes which have softened the general manners, and brought all human relations more under the control of justice and the influence of humanity. It has not lost the taint of its brutal origin. No presumption in its favour, therefore, can be drawn from the fact of its existence. The only such presumption which it could be supposed to have, must be grounded on its having lasted till now, when so many other things which came down from the same odious source have been done away with. And this, indeed, is what makes it strange to ordinary ears, to hear it asserted that the inequality of rights between men and women has no other source than the law of the strongest. . . .

But, it will be said, the rule of men over women differs from all these others in not being a rule of force: it is accepted voluntarily; women make no complaint, and are consenting parties to it. In the first place, a great number of women do not accept it. Ever since there have been women able to make their sentiments known by their writings (the only mode of publicity which society permits to them), an increasing number of them have recorded protests against their present social condition: and recently many thousands of them, headed by the most eminent women known to the public, have petitioned Parliament for their admission to the Parliamentary Suffrage. The claim of women to be educated as solidly, and in the same branches of knowledge, as men, is urged with growing intensity, and with a great prospect of success; while the demand for their admission into professions and occupations hitherto closed against them, becomes every year more urgent. Though there are not in this country, as there are in the United States, periodical Conventions and an organized party to agitate for the Rights of Women, there is a numerous and active Society organized and managed by women, for the more limited object of obtaining the political franchise. Nor is it only in our own country and in America that women are beginning to protest, more or less collectively, against the disabilities under which they labour. France, and Italy, and Switzerland, and Russia now afford examples of the same thing. How many more women there are who silently cherish similar aspirations, no one can possibly know; but there are abundant tokens how many *would* cherish them, were they not so strenuously taught to repress them as contrary to the proprieties of their sex. It must be remembered, also, that no enslaved class ever asked for complete liberty at once. When Simon de Montfort called the deputies of the commons to sit for the first time in Parliament, did any of them dream of demanding that an assembly, elected by their constituents, should make and destroy ministries, and dictate to the king in affairs of State? No such thought entered into the imagination of the most ambitious of them. The nobility had already these pretensions; the commons pretended to nothing but to be exempt from arbitrary taxation, and from the gross individual oppression of the king's officers. It is a political law of nature that those who are under any power of ancient origin never begin by complaining of the power itself, but only of its oppressive exercise. There is never any want of women who complain of ill usage by their husbands. There would be infinitely more, if complaint were not the greatest of all provocatives to a repetition and increase of the ill usage. It is this which frustrates all attempts to maintain the power but protect the woman against its abuses. In no other case (except that of a child) is the person who has been proved judicially to have suffered an injury, replaced under the physical power of the culprit who inflicted it. Accordingly wives, even in the most extreme and protracted cases of bodily ill usage, hardly ever dare avail themselves of the laws made for their protection: and if, in a moment of irrepressible indignation, or by the interference of neighbours, they are induced to do so, their whole effort afterwards is to disclose as little as they can, and to beg off their tyrant from his merited chastisement.

All causes, social and natural, combine to make it unlikely that women should be collectively rebellious to the power of men. They are so far in a position different from all other subject classes, that their masters require something more from them than actual service. Men do not want solely the obedience of women, they want their sentiments. All men, except the most brutish, desire to have, in the woman most nearly connected with them, not a forced slave but a willing one; not a slave merely, but a favourite. They have therefore put everything in practice to enslave their minds. The masters of all other slaves rely, for maintaining obedience, on fear; either fear of themselves, or religious fears. The masters of women wanted more than simple obedience, and they turned the whole force of education to effect their purpose. All women are brought up from the very earliest years in the belief that their ideal of character is the very opposite to that of men; not self-will, and government by self-control, but submission, and yielding to the control of others. All the moralities tell them that it is the duty of women, and all the current sentimentalities that it is their nature, to live for others; to make complete abnegation of themselves, and to have no life but in their affections. And by their affections are meant the only ones they are allowed to have—those to the men with whom they are connected, or to the children who constitute an additional and indefeasible tie between them and a man. When we put together three things—first, the natural attraction between opposite sexes; secondly, the wife's entire dependence on the husband, every privilege or pleasure she has being either his gift, or depending entirely on his will; and lastly, that the principal object of human pursuit, consideration, and all objects of social ambition, can in general be sought or obtained by her only through him—it would be a miracle if the object of being attractive to men and not become the polar star of feminine education and formation of character. And, this great means of influence over the minds of women having been acquired, an instinct of selfishness made men avail themselves of it to the utmost as a means of holding women in subjection, by representing to them meekness, submissiveness, and resignation of all individual will into the hands of a man, as an essential part of sexual attractiveness. Can it be doubted that any of the other yokes which mankind have succeeded in breaking, would have subsisted till now if the same means had existed, and had been as sedulously used, to bow down their minds to it. . . .

Neither does it avail anything to say that the *nature* of the two sexes adapts them to their present functions and position, and renders these appropriate to them. Standing on the ground of common sense and the constitution of the human mind, I deny that any one knows, or can know, the nature of the two sexes, as long as they have only been seen in their present relation to one another. If men had ever been found in society without women, or women without men, or if there had been a society of men and women in which the women were not under the control of the men, something might have been positively known about the mental and moral differences which may be inherent in the nature of each. What is now called the nature of women is an eminently artificial thing—the result of forced repression in some directions, unnatural stimulation in others. It may be asserted without scruple, that no other class of dependents have had their character so entirely distorted from its natural proportions by their relation with their masters; for, if conquered and slave races have been, in some respects, more forcibly repressed, whatever in them has not been crushed down by an iron heel has generally been let alone, and if left with any liberty of development, it has developed itself according to its own laws: but in the case of women, a hot-house and stove cultivation has always been carried on of some of the capabilities of their nature, for the benefit and pleasure of their masters. Then, because certain products of the general vital force sprout luxuriantly and reach a great development in this heated atmosphere and under this active nurture and watering, while other shoots from the same root, which are left outside in the wintry air, with ice purposely heaped all round them, have a stunted growth, and some are burnt off with fire and disappear; men, with that inability to recognize their own work which distinguishes the unanalytic mind, indolently believe that the tree grows of itself in the way they have made it grow, and that it would die if one half of it were not kept in a vapour bath and the other half in the snow. . . .

The general opinion of men is supposed to be, that the natural vocation of a woman is that of a wife and mother. I say, is supposed to be, because, judging from acts—from the whole of the present constitution of society—one might infer that their opinion was the direct contrary. They might be supposed to think that the alleged natural vocation of women was of all things the most repugnant to their nature; insomuch that if they are free to do anything else—if any other means of living, or occupation of their time and faculties, is open, which has any chance of appearing desirable to them—there will not be enough of them who will be willing to accept the condition said to be natural to them. If this is the real opinion of men in general, it would be well that it should be spoken out. I should like to hear somebody openly enunciating the doctrine (it is already implied in much that is written on the subject)—'It is necessary to society that women should marry and produce children. They will not do so unless they are compelled. Therefore it is necessary to compel them.' The merits of the case would then be clearly defined. It would be exactly that of the slaveholders of South Carolina and Louisiana. 'It is necessary that cotton and sugar should be grown. White men cannot produce them. Negroes will not, for any wages which we choose to give. *Ergo* they must be compelled.'. . . .

It will be well to commence the detailed discussion of the subject by the particular branch of it to which the course of our observations has led us: the conditions which the laws of this and all other countries annex to the marriage contract. Marriage being the destination appointed by society for women, the prospect they are brought up to, and the object which it is intended should be sought by all of them, except those who are too little attractive to be chosen by any man as his companion; one might have supposed that everything would have been done to make this condition as eligible to them as possible, that they might have no cause to regret being denied the option of any other. Society, however, both in this, and, at first, in all other cases, has preferred to attain its object by foul rather than fair means: but this is the only case in which it has substantially persisted in them even to the present day. Originally women were taken by force, or regularly sold by their father to the husband. Until a late period in European history, the father had the power to dispose of his daughter in marriage at his own will and pleasure, without any regard to hers. The Church, indeed, was so far faithful to a better morality as to require a formal 'yes' from the woman at the marriage ceremony; but there was nothing to show that the consent was other than compulsory; and it was practically impossible for the girl to refuse compliance if the father persevered, except perhaps when she might obtain the protection of religion by a determined resolution to take monastic vows. After marriage, the man had anciently (but this was anterior to Christianity) the power of life and death over his wife. She could invoke no law against him; he was her sole tribunal and law. For a long time he could repudiate her, but she had no corresponding power in regard to him. By the old laws of England, the husband was called the *lord* of the wife; he was literally regarded as her sovereign, inasmuch that the murder of a man by his wife was called treason (*petty* as distinguished from *high* treason), and was more cruelly avenged than was usually the case with high treason, for the penalty was burning to death. Because these various enormities have fallen into disuse (for most of them were never formally abolished, or not until they had long ceased to be practised) men suppose that all is now as it should be in regard to the marriage contract; and we are continually told that civilization and Christianity have restored to the woman her just rights. Meanwhile the wife is the actual bond-servant of her husband: no less so, as far as legal obligation goes, than slaves commonly so called. She vows a lifelong obedience to him at the altar, and is held to it all through her life by law. Casuists may say that the obligation of obedience stops short of participation in crime, but it certainly extends to everything else. She can do no act whatever but by his permission, at least tacit. She can acquire no property but for him; the instant it becomes hers, even if by inheritance, it becomes *ipso facto* his. In this respect the wife's position under the common law of England is worse than that of slaves in the laws of many countries: by the Roman law, for example, a slave might have his peculium, which to a certain extent the law guaranteed to him for his exclusive use. The higher classes in this country have given an analogous advantage to their women, through special contracts setting aside the law, by conditions of pin-money, &c.: since parental feeling being stronger with fathers than the class feeling of their own sex, a father generally prefers his own daughter to a son-in-law who is a stranger to him. By means of settlements, the rich usually contrive to withdraw the whole or part of the inherited property of the wife from the absolute control of the husband: but they do not succeed in keeping it under her own control; the utmost they can do only prevents the husband from squandering it, at the same time debarring the rightful owner from its use. The property itself is out of the reach of both; and as to the income derived from it, the form of settlement most favourable to the wife (that called 'to her separate use') only precludes the husband from receiving it instead of her: it must pass through her hands, but if he takes it from her by personal violence as soon as she receives it, he can neither be punished, nor compelled to restitution. This is the amount of the protection which, under the laws of this country, the most powerful nobleman can give his own daughter as respects her husband. In the immense majority of cases there is no settlement: and the absorption of all rights, all property, as well as all freedom of action, is complete. The two are called 'one person in law,' for the purpose of inferring that whatever is hers is his, but the parallel inference is never drawn that whatever is his is hers; the maxim is not applied against the man, except to make him responsible to third parties for her acts, as a master is for the acts of his slaves or of his cattle. I am far from pretending that wives are in general no better treated than slaves; but no slave is a slave to the same lengths, and in so full a sense of the word, as a wife is. Hardly any slave, except one immediately attached to the master's person, is a slave at all hours and all minutes; in general he has, like a soldier, his fixed task, and when it is done, or when he is off duty, he disposes, within certain limits, of his own time, and has a family life into which the master rarely intrudes. 'Uncle Tom' under his first master had his own life in his 'cabin,' almost as much as any man whose work takes him away from home, is able to have in his own family. But it cannot be so with the wife. Above all, a female slave has (in Christian countries) an admitted right, and is considered under a moral obligation, to refuse to her master the last familiarity. Not so the wife: however brutal a tyrant she may unfortunately be chained to—though she may know that he hates her, though it may be his daily pleasure to torture her, and though she may feel it impossible not to loathe him—he can claim from her and enforce the lowest degradation of a human being, that of being made the instrument of an animal function contrary to her inclinations. While she is held in this worst description of slavery as to her own person, what is her position in regard to the children in whom she and her master have a joint interest? They are by law *his* children. He alone has any legal rights over them. Not one act can she do towards or in relation to them, except by delegation from him. Even after he is dead she is not their legal guardian, unless he by will has made her so. He could even send them away from her, and deprive her of the means of seeing or corresponding with them, until this power was in some degree restricted by Serjeant Talfourd's Act. This is her legal state. And from this state she has no means of withdrawing herself. If she leaves her husband, she can take nothing with her, neither her children nor anything which is rightfully her own. If he chooses, he can compel her to return, by law, or by physical force; or he may content himself with seizing for his own use anything which she may earn, or which may be given to her by her relations. It is only legal separation by a decree of a court of justice, which entitles her to live apart, without being forced back into the custody of an exasperated jailer—or which empowers her to apply any earnings to her own use, without fear that a man whom perhaps she has not seen for twenty years will pounce upon her some day and carry all off. This legal separation, until lately, the courts of justice would only give at an expense which made it inaccessible to any one out of the higher ranks. Even now it is only given in cases of desertion, or of the extreme of cruelty; and yet complaints are made every day that it is granted too easily. Surely, if a woman is denied any lot in life but that of being the personal body-servant of a despot, and is dependent for everything upon the chance of finding one who may be disposed to make a favourite of her instead of merely a drudge, it is a very cruel aggravation of her fate that she should be allowed to try this chance only once. The natural sequel and corollary from this state of things would be, that since her all in life depends upon obtaining a good master, she should be allowed to change again and again until she finds one. I am not saying that she ought to be allowed this privilege. That is a totally different consideration. The question of divorce, in the sense involving liberty of remarriage, is one into which it is foreign to my purpose to enter. All I now say is, that to those to whom nothing but servitude is allowed, the free choice of servitude is the only, though a most insufficient, alleviation. Its refusal completes the assimilation of the wife to the slave—and the slave under not the mildest form of slavery: for in some slave codes the slave could, under certain circumstances of ill usage, legally compel the master to sell him. But no amount of ill usage, without adultery superadded, will in England free a wife from her tormentor. . . .

Institutions, books, education, society, all go on training human beings for the old, long after the new has come; much more when it is only coming. But the true virtue of human beings is fitness to live together as equals; claiming nothing for themselves but what they as freely concede to every one else; regarding command of any kind as an exceptional necessity, and in all cases a temporary one; and preferring, whenever possible, the society of those with whom leading and following can be alternate and reciprocal. To these virtues, nothing in life as at present constituted gives cultivation by exercise. The family is a school of despotism, in which the virtues of despotism, but also its vices, are largely nourished. Citizenship, in free countries, is partly a school of society in equality; but citizenship fills only a small place in modern life, and does not come near the daily habits or inmost sentiments. The family, justly constituted, would be the real school of the virtues of freedom. It is sure to be a sufficient one of everything else. It will always be a school of obedience for the children, of command for the parents. What is needed is, that it should be a school of sympathy in equality, of living together in love, without power on one side or obedience on the other. This it ought to be between the parents. It would then be an exercise of those virtues which each requires to fit them for all other association, and a model to the children of the feelings and conduct which their temporary training by means of obedience is designed to render habitual, and therefore natural, to them. The moral training of mankind will never be adapted to the conditions of the life for which all other human progress is a preparation, until they practise in the family the same moral rule which is adapted to the normal constitution of human society. . . .

When the support of the family depends not on property, but on earnings, the common arrangement, by which the man earns the income and the wife superintends the domestic expenditure, seems to me in general the most suitable division of labour between the two persons. If, in addition to the physical suffering of bearing children, and the whole responsibility of their care and education in early years, the wife undertakes the careful and economical application of the husband's earnings to the general comfort of the family; she takes not only her fair share, but usually the larger share, of the bodily and mental exertion required by their joint existence. If she undertakes any additional portion, it seldom relieves her from this, but only prevents her from performing it properly. The care which she is herself disabled from taking of the children and the household, nobody else takes; those of the children who do not die, grow up as they best can, and the management of the household is likely to be so bad, as even in point of economy to be a great drawback from the value of the wife's earnings. In an otherwise just state of things, it is not, therefore, I think, a desirable custom, that the wife should contribute by her labour to the income of the family. In an unjust state of things, her doing so may be useful to her, by making her of more value in the eyes of the man who is legally her master; but, on the other hand, it enables him still farther to abuse his power, by forcing her to work, and leaving the support of the family to her exertions, while he spends most of his time in drinking and idleness. The *power* of earning is essential to the dignity of a woman, if she has not independent property. But if marriage were an equal contract, not implying the obligation of obedience; if the connexion were no longer enforced to the oppression of those to whom it is purely a mischief, but a separation, on just terms (I do not now speak of a divorce), could be obtained by any woman who was morally entitled to it; and if she would then find all honourable employments as freely open to her as to men; it would not be necessary for her protection, that during marriage she should make this particular use of her faculties. Like a man when he chooses a profession, so, when a woman marries, it may in general be understood that she makes choice of the management of a household, and the bringing up of a family, as the first call upon her exertions, during as many years of her life as may be required for the purpose; and that she renounces, not all other objects and occupations, but all which are not consistent with the requirements of this. The actual exercise, in a habitual or systematic manner, of outdoor occupations, or such as cannot be carried on at home, would by this principle be practically interdicted to the greater number of married women. But the utmost latitude ought to exist for the adaptation of general rules to individual suitabilities; and there ought to be nothing to prevent faculties exceptionally adapted to any other pursuit, from obeying their vocation notwithstanding marriage: due provision being made for supplying otherwise any falling-short which might become inevitable, in her full performance of the ordinary functions of mistress of a family. These things, if once opinion were rightly directed on the subject, might with perfect safety be left to be regulated by opinion, without any interference of law. . . .

When we consider the positive evil caused to the disqualified half of the human race by their disqualification—first in the loss of the most inspiriting and elevating kind of personal enjoyment, and next in the weariness, disappointment, and profound dissatisfaction with life, which are so often the substitute for it; one feels that among all the lessons which men require for carrying on the struggle against the inevitable imperfections of their lot on earth, there is no lesson which they more need, than not to add to the evils which nature inflicts, by their jealous and prejudiced restrictions on one another. Their vain fears only substitute other and worse evils for those which they are idly apprehensive of: while every restraint on the freedom of conduct of any of their human fellow creatures (otherwise than by making them responsible for any evil actually caused by it), dries up *pro tanto* the principal fountain of human happiness, and leaves the species less rich, to an inappreciable degree, in all that makes life valuable to the individual human being.

22

Alexis de Tocqueville
Democracy in America

Alexis de Tocqueville (1805–1859) published the two volumes of Democracy in America *in 1835 and 1840, not long after he had returned to his native France from a visit to the United States. He was an aristocrat who served in the French Chamber of Deputies and briefly as foreign minister. His interpretation of the French Revolution,* The Old Regime and the Revolution *(1856), is also a classic. He went to the United States to study the prison system but became preoccupied with American politics in comparison to his European experiences. He believed that America embodied the era of democratic revolutions in which he lived and which was the wave of the future. He emphasized "the general equality of conditions" in America that affected all aspects of politics, economics, customs, and opinions.*

Author's Introduction

Amongst the novel objects that attracted my attention during my stay in the United States, nothing struck me more forcibly than the general equality of condition among the people. I readily discovered the prodigious influence which this primary fact exercises on the whole course of society; it gives a peculiar direction to public opinion, and a peculiar tenor to the laws; it imparts new maxims to the governing authorities, and peculiar habits to the governed.

I soon perceived that the influence of this fact extends far beyond the political character and the laws of the country, and that it has no less empire over civil society than over the government; it creates opinions, gives birth to new sentiments, founds novel customs, and modifies whatever it does not produce. The more I advanced in the study of American society, the more I perceived that this equality of condition is the fundamental fact from which all others seem to be derived, and the central point at which all my observations constantly terminated.

I then turned my thoughts to our own hemisphere, and thought that I discerned there something analogous to the spectacle which the New World presented to me. I observed that equality of condition, though it has not there reached the extreme limit which it seems to have attained in the United States, is constantly approaching it; and that the democracy which governs the American communities appears to be rapidly rising into power in Europe. Hence I conceived the idea of the book which is now before the reader.

It is evident to all alike that a great democratic revolution is going on amongst us; but all do not look at it in the same light. To some it appears to be novel but accidental, and, as such, they hope it may still be checked; to others it seems irresistible, because it is the most uniform, the most ancient, and the most permanent tendency which is to be found in history.

I look back for a moment on the situation of France seven hundred years ago, when the territory was divided amongst a small number of families, who were the owners of the soil and the rulers of the inhabitants; the right of governing descended with the family inheritance from generation to generation; force was the only means by which man could act on man; and landed property was the sole source of power. Soon, however, the political power of the clergy was founded, and began to increase: the clergy opened their ranks to all classes, to the poor and the rich, the vassal and the lord; through the Church, equality penetrated into the Government, and he who as a serf must have vegetated in perpetual bondage took his place as a priest in the midst of nobles, and not unfrequently above the heads of kings.

The different relations of men with each other became more complicated and numerous as society gradually became more stable and civilized. Hence the want of civil laws was felt; and the ministers of law soon rose from the obscurity of the tribunals and their dusty chambers, to appear at the court of the monarch, by the side of the feudal barons clothed in their ermine and their mail. Whilst the kings were ruining themselves by their great enterprises, and the nobles exhausting their resources by private wars, the lower orders were enriching themselves by commerce. The influence of money began to be perceptible in state affairs. The transactions of business opened a new road to power, and the financier rose to a station of political influence in which he was at once flattered and despised.

Gradually the diffusion of intelligence, and the increasing taste for literature and art, caused learning and talent to become a means of government; mental ability led to social power, and the man of letters took a part in the affairs of the state. The value attached to high birth declined just as fast as new avenues to power were discovered. In the eleventh century, nobility was beyond all price; in the thirteenth, it might be purchased. Nobility was first conferred by gift in 1270; and equality was thus introduced into the government by the aristocracy itself.

In the course of these seven hundred years, it sometimes happened that the nobles, in order to resist the authority of the crown, or to diminish the power of their rivals, granted some political influence to the common people. Or, more frequently, the king permitted the lower orders to have a share in the government, with the intention of depressing the aristocracy. In France, the kings have always been the most active and the most constant of levellers. When they were strong and ambitious, they spared no pains to raise the people to the level of the nobles; when they were temperate and feeble, they allowed the people to rise above themselves. Some assisted the democracy by their talents, others by their vices. Louis XI and Louis XIV reduced all ranks beneath the throne to the same degree of subjection; and, finally, Louis XV descended, himself and all his court, into the dust.

As soon as land began to be held on any other than a feudal tenure, and personal property in its turn became able to confer influence and power, every discovery in the arts, every improvement in commerce or manufactures, created so many new elements of equality among men. Henceforward every new invention, every new want which it occasioned, and every new desire which craved satisfaction, was a step towards a general levelling. The taste for luxury, the love of war, the empire of fashion, and the most superficial as well as the deepest passions of the human heart, seemed to co-operate to enrich the poor and to impoverish the rich.

From the time when the exercise of the intellect became a source of strength and of wealth, we see that every addition to science, every fresh truth, and every new idea became a germ of power placed within the reach of the people. Poetry, eloquence, and memory, the grace of the mind, the glow of imagination, depth of thought, and all the gifts which Heaven scatters at a venture, turned to the advantage of the democracy; and even when they were in the possession of its adversaries, they still served its cause by throwing into bold relief the natural greatness of man. Its conquests spread, therefore, with those of civilization and knowledge; and literature became an arsenal open to all, where the poor and the weak daily resorted for arms.

In running over the pages of our history for seven hundred years, we shall scarcely find a single great event which has not promoted equality of condition. The Crusades and the English wars decimated the nobles and divided their possessions: the municipal corporations introduced democratic liberty into the bosom of feudal monarchy; the invention of fire-arms equalized the vassal and the noble on the field of battle; the art of printing opened the same resources to the minds of all classes; the post-office brought knowledge alike to the door of the cottage and to the gate of the palace; and Protestantism proclaimed that all men are alike able to find the road to heaven. The discovery of America opened a thousand new paths to fortune, and led obscure adventurers to wealth and power.

If, beginning with the eleventh century, we examine what has happened in France from one half-century to another, we shall not fail to perceive, at the end of each of these periods, that a twofold revolution has taken place in the state of society. The noble has gone down on the social ladder, and the commoner has gone up; the one descends as the other rises. Every half-century brings them nearer to each other, and they will soon meet.

Nor is this peculiar to France. Whithersoever we turn our eyes, we perceive the same revolution going on throughout the Christian world. The various occurrences of national existence have everywhere turned to the advantage of democracy: all men have aided it by their exertions, both those who have intentionally labored in its cause, and those who have served it unwittingly; those who have fought for it, and those who have declared themselves its opponents, have all been driven along in the same track, have all labored to one end; some ignorantly and some unwillingly, all have been blind instruments in the hands of God.

The gradual development of the principle of equality is, therefore, a Providential fact. It has all the chief characteristics of such a fact: it is universal, it is durable, it constantly eludes all human interference, and all events as well as all men contribute to its progress.

Would it, then, be wise to imagine that a social movement, the causes of which lie so far back, can be checked by the efforts of one generation? Can it be believed that the democracy which has overthrown the feudal system, and vanquished kings, will retreat before tradesman and capitalists? Will it stop now that it has grown so strong, and its adversaries so weak? Whither, then, are we tending? No one can say, for terms of comparison already fail us. The conditions of men are more equal in Christian countries at the present day than they have been at any previous time, or in any part of the world; so that the magnitude of what already has been done prevents us from foreseeing what is yet to be accomplished.

The whole book which is here offered to the public has been written under the impression of a kind of religious terror produced in the author's mind by the view of that irresistible revolution which has advanced for centuries in spite of every obstacle, and which is still advancing in the midst of the ruins it has caused. It is not necessary that God himself should speak in order that we may discover the unquestionable signs of his will. It is enough to ascertain what is the habitual course of nature and the constant tendency of events. I know, without a special revelation, that the planets move in the orbits traced by the Creator's hand.

If the men of our time should be convinced, by attentive observation and sincere reflection, that the gradual and progressive development of social equality is at once the past and future of their history, this discovery alone would confer the sacred character of a Divine decree upon the change. To attempt to check democracy would be in that case to resist the will of God; and the nations would then be constrained to make the best of the social lot awarded to them by Providence.

The Christian nations of our day seem to me to present a most alarming spectacle; the movement which impels them is already so strong that it cannot be stopped, but it is not yet so rapid that it cannot be guided. Their fate is still in their own hands; yet a little while, and it may be so no longer.

The first of the duties which are at this time imposed upon those who direct our affairs, is to educate the democracy; to renovate, if possible, its religious belief; to purify its morals; to regulate its movements; to substitute by degrees a knowledge of business for its inexperience, and an acquaintance with its true interests for its blind instincts; to adapt its government to time and place, and to make it conform to the occurrences and the men of the times. A new science of politics is needed for a new world.

This, however, is what we think of least; placed in the middle of a rapid stream, we obstinately fix our eyes on the ruins which may still be described upon the shore we have left, whilst the current hurries us away, and drags us backward toward the gulf.

In no country in Europe has the great social revolution which I have just described made such rapid progress as in France; but it has always advanced without guidance. The heads of the state have made no preparation for it, and it has advanced without their consent or without their knowledge. The most powerful, the most intelligent, and the most moral classes of the nation have never attempted to take hold of it in order to guide it. The democracy has consequently been abandoned to its wild instincts, and it has grown up like those children who have

ALEXIS DE TOCQUEVILLE

no parental guidance, who receive their education in the public streets, and who are acquainted only with the vices and wretchedness of society. Its existence was seemingly unknown, when suddenly it acquired supreme power. Every one then submitted to its caprices; it was worshipped as the idol of strength; and when afterwards it was enfeebled by its own excesses, the legislator conceived the rash project of destroying it, instead of instructing it and correcting its vices. No attempt was made to fit it to govern, but all were bent on excluding it from the government.

The consequence has been, that the democratic revolution has taken place in the body of society, without that concomitant change in the laws, ideas, customs, and manners, which was necessary to render such a revolution beneficial. Thus we have a democracy, without anything to lessen its vices and bring out its natural advantages; and although we already perceive the evils it brings, we are ignorant of the benefits it may confer.

While the power of the crown, supported by the aristocracy, peaceably governed the nations of Europe, society, in the midst of its wretchedness, had several sources of happiness which can now scarcely be conceived or appreciated. The power of a part of his subjects was an insurmountable barrier to the tyranny of the prince; and the monarch, who felt the almost divine character which he enjoyed in the eyes of the multitude, derived a motive for the just use of his power from the respect which he inspired. The nobles, high as they were placed above the people, could not but take that calm and benevolent interest in their fate which the shepherd feels towards his flock; and without acknowledging the poor as their equals, they watched over the destiny of those whose welfare Providence had intrusted to their care. The people, never having conceived the idea of a social condition different from their own, and never expecting to become equal to their leaders, received benefits from them without discussing their rights. They became attached to them when they were clement and just, and submitted to their exactions without resistance or servility, as to the inevitable visitations of the Deity. Custom and the manners of the time, moreover, had established certain limits to oppression, and put a sort of legal restraint upon violence.

As the noble never suspected that any one would attempt to deprive him of the privileges which he believed to be legitimate, and as the serf looked upon his own inferiority as a consequence of the immutable order of nature, it is easy to imagine that some mutual exchange of good-will took place between two classes so differently gifted by fate. Inequality and wretchedness were then to be found in society; but the souls of neither rank of men were degraded. Men are not corrupted by the exercise of power, or debased by the habit of obedience; but by the exercise of a power which they believe to be illegitimate, and by obedience to a rule which they consider to be usurped and oppressive.

On the one side were wealth, strength, and leisure, accompanied by the refinements of luxury, the elegance of taste, the pleasures of wit, and the cultivation of the arts; on the other, were labor, clownishness, and ignorance. But in the midst of this coarse and ignorant multitude it was not uncommon to meet with energetic passions, generous sentiments, profound religious convictions, and wild virtues.

The social state thus organized might boast of its stability, its power, and, above all, its glory.

But the scene is now changed. Gradually the distinctions of rank are done away; the barriers which once severed mankind are falling down; property is divided, power is shared by many, the light of intelligence spreads, and the capacities of all classes are equally cultivated. The State becomes democratic, and the empire of democracy is slowly and peaceably introduced into the institutions and the manners of the nation.

I can conceive of a society in which all men would feel an equal love and respect for the laws of which they consider themselves as the authors; in which the authority of the government would be respected as necessary, though not as divine; and in which the loyalty of the subject to the chief magistrate would not be a passion, but a quiet and rational persuasion. Every individual being in the possession of rights which he is sure to retain, a kind of manly confidence and reciprocal courtesy would arise between all classes, alike removed from pride and servility. The people, well acquainted with their own true interests, would understand that, in order to profit by the advantages of society, it is necessary to satisfy its requisitions. The voluntary association of the citizens might then take the place of the individual exertions of the nobles, and the community would be alike protected from anarchy and from oppression.

I admit that, in a democratic state thus constituted, society would not be stationary. But the impulses of the social body might there be regulated and made progressive. If there were less splendor than in the midst of an aristocracy, the contrast of misery would also be less frequent; the pleasures of enjoyment might be less excessive, but those of comfort would be more general; the sciences might be less perfectly cultivated, but ignorance would be less common; the impetuosity of the feelings would be repressed, and the habits of the nation softened; there would be more vices and fewer great crimes.

In the absence of enthusiasm and an ardent faith, great sacrifices may be obtained from the members of a commonwealth by an appeal to their understandings and their experience; each individual will feel the same necessity of union with his fellows to protect his own weakness; and as he knows that he can obtain their help only on condition of helping them, he will readily perceive that his personal interest is identified with the interests of the whole community. The nation, taken as a whole, will be less brilliant, less glorious, and perhaps less strong: but the majority of the citizens will enjoy a greater degree of prosperity, and the people will remain quiet, not because they despair of a change for the better, but because they are conscious that they are well off already. If all the consequences of this state of things were not good or useful, society would at least have appropriated all such as were useful and good; and having once and for ever renounced the social advantages of aristocracy, mankind would enter into possession of all the benefits which democracy can afford.

But here it may be asked what we have adopted in the place of those institutions, those ideas, and those customs of our forefathers which we have abandoned. The spell of royalty is broken, but it has not been succeeded by the majesty of the laws. The people have learned to despise all authority, but they still fear it; and fear now extorts more than was formerly paid from reverence and love. I perceive that we have destroyed those individual powers which were able, single-handed, to cope with tyranny; but it is the government that has inherited the privileges of which families, corporations, and individuals have been deprived; to the power of a small number of persons—which, if it was sometimes oppressive, was often conservative—has succeeded the weakness of the whole community.

The division of property has lessened the distance which separated the rich from the poor; but it would seem that the nearer they draw to each other, the greater is their mutual hatred, and the more vehement the envy and the dread with which they resist each other's claims to power; the idea of Right does not exist for either party, and Force affords to both the only argument for the present, and the only guaranty for the future.

The poor man retains the prejudices of his forefathers without their faith, and their ignorance without their virtues; he has adopted the doctrine of self-interest as the rule of his actions, without understanding the science which puts it to use; and his selfishness is no less blind than was formerly his devotedness to others. If society is tranquil, it is not because it is conscious of its strength and its well-being, but because it fears its weakness and its infirmities; a single effort may cost it its life. Everybody feels the evil, but no one has courage or energy enough to seek the cure. The desires, the repinings, the sorrows, and the joys of the present time lead to no visible or permanent result, like the passions of old men, which terminate in impotence.

We have, then, abandoned whatever advantages the old state of things afforded, without receiving any compensation from our present condition; we have destroyed an aristocracy, and we seem inclined to survey its ruins with complacency, and to fix our abode in the midst of them.

The phenomena which the intellectual world presents are not less deplorable. The democracy of France, hampered in its course or abandoned to its lawless passions, has overthrown whatever crossed its path, and has shaken all that it has not destroyed. Its empire has not been gradually introduced, or peaceably established, but it has constantly advanced in the midst of the disorders and the agitations of a conflict. In the heat of the struggle, each partisan is hurried beyond the natural limits of his opinions by the doctrines and the excesses of his opponents, until he loses sight of the end of his exertions, and holds a language which does not express his real sentiments or secret instincts. Hence arises the strange confusion which we are compelled to witness.

I can recall nothing in history more worthy of sorrow and pity, than the scenes which are passing under our eyes. It is as if the natural bond which unites the opinions of man to his tastes, and his actions to his principles, was not broken; the sympathy which has always been observed between the feelings and the ideas of mankind appears to be dissolved, and all the laws of moral analogy to be abolished.

Zealous Christians are still found amongst us, whose minds are nurtured on the thoughts which pertain to a future life, and who readily espouse the cause of human liberty as the source of all moral greatness. Christianity, which has de-

clared that all men are equal in the sight of God, will not refuse to acknowledge
that all citizens are equal in the eye of the law. But, by a singular concourse of
events, religion has been for a time entangled with those institutions which democracy assails; and it is not unfrequently brought to reject the equality which it
loves, and to curse that cause of liberty as a foe, whose efforts it might hallow by
its alliance.

By the side of these religious men, I discern others whose looks are turned to
earth rather than to heaven. These are the partisans of liberty, not only as the
source of the noblest virtues, but more especially as the root of all solid advantages; and they sincerely desire to secure its authority, and to impart its blessings
to mankind. It is natural that they should hasten to invoke the assistance of religion, for they must know that liberty cannot be established without morality, nor
morality without faith. But they have seen religion in the ranks of their adversaries, and they inquire no further; some of them attack it openly, and the re-
minder are afraid to defend it.

In former ages, slavery was advocated by the venal and slavish-minded, whilst
the independent and the warm-hearted were struggling without hope to save the
liberties of mankind. But men of high and generous characters are now to be met
with, whose opinions are at variance with their inclinations, and who praise that
servility which they have themselves never known. Others, on the contrary, speak
of liberty as if they were able to feel its sanctity and its majesty, and loudly claim
for humanity those rights which they have always refused to acknowledge.

There are virtuous and peaceful individuals whose pure morality, quiet habits,
opulence, and talents fit them to be the leaders of the surrounding population.
Their love of country is sincere, and they are ready to make the greatest sacrifices
for its welfare. But civilization often finds them among its opponents; they confound its abuses with its benefits, and the idea of evil is inseparable in their minds
from that of novelty. Near these I find others, whose object is to materialize
mankind, to hit upon what is expedient without heeding what is just, to acquire
knowledge without faith, and prosperity apart from virtue; claiming to be the cham-
pions of modern civilization, they place themselves arrogantly at its head, usurping a
place which is abandoned to them, and of which they are wholly unworthy.

Where are we, then?

The religionists are the enemies of liberty, and the friends of liberty attack
religion; the high-minded and the noble advocate bondage, and the meanest and
most servile preach independence; honest and enlightened citizens are opposed to
all progress, whilst men without patriotism and without principle put themselves
forward as the apostles of civilization and intelligence. Has such been the fate of
the centuries which have preceded our own? and has man always inhabited a
world like the present, where all things are out of their natural connections, where
virtue is without genius, and genius without honor; where the love of order is
confounded with a taste for oppression, and the holy rites of freedom with a
contempt of law; where the light thrown by conscience on human actions is dim,
and where nothing seems to be any longer forbidden or allowed, honorable or
shameful, false or true?

I cannot believe that the Creator made man to leave him in an endless struggle

with the intellectual miseries which surround us. God destines a calmer and a
more certain future to the communities of Europe. I am ignorant of his designs,
but I shall not cease to believe in them because I cannot fathom them, and I had
rather mistrust my own capacity than his justice.

There is a country in the world where the great social revolution which I am
speaking of seems to have nearly reached its natural limits. It has been effected
with ease and quietness; say rather that this country is reaping the fruits of the
democratic revolution which we are undergoing, without having had the revolution itself.

The emigrants who colonized the shores of America in the beginning of the
seventeenth century somehow separated the democratic principle from all the principles which it had to contend with in the old communities of Europe, and trans-
planted it alone to the New World. It has there been able to spread in perfect
freedom, and peaceably to determine the character of the laws by influencing the
manners of the country.

It appears to me beyond a doubt that, sooner or later, we shall arrive, like the
Americans, at an almost complete equality of condition. But I do not conclude
from this, that we shall ever be necessarily led to draw the same political consequences which the Americans have derived from a similar social organization. I
am far from supposing that they have chosen the only form of government which a
democracy may adopt; but as the generative cause of laws and manners in the two
countries is the same, it is of immense interest for us to know what it has produced in each of them.

It is not, then, merely to satisfy a legitimate curiosity that I have examined
America; my wish has been to find there instruction by which we may ourselves
profit. Whoever should imagine that I have intended to write a panegyric would be
strangely mistaken, and on reading this book, he will perceive that such was not
my design: nor has it been my object to advocate any form of government in
particular, for I am of opinion that absolute excellence is rarely to be found in any
system of laws. I have not even pretended to judge whether the social revolution,
which I believe to be irresistible, is advantageous or prejudicial to mankind. I
have acknowledged this revolution as a fact already accomplished, or on the eve
of its accomplishment: and I have selected the nation, from amongst those which
have undergone it, in which its development has been the most peaceful and the
most complete, in order to discern its natural consequences, and to find out, if
possible, the means of rendering it profitable to mankind. I confess that, in America, I saw more than America; I sought there the image of democracy itself, with
its inclinations, its character, its prejudices, and its passions, in order to learn
what we have to fear or to hope from its progress. . . .

Democratic Social Condition of the Anglo-Americans

Social condition, is commonly the result of circumstances, sometimes of laws,
oftener still of these two causes united; but when once established, it may justly be
considered as itself the source of almost all the laws, the usages, and the ideas

which regulate the conduct of nations: whatever it does not produce, it modifies. If we would become acquainted with the legislation and the manners of a nation, therefore, we must begin by the study of its social condition.

The Striking Characteristic of the Social Condition of the Anglo-Americans Is Its Essential Democracy

. . . The social condition of the Americans is eminently democratic; this was its character at the foundation of the colonies, and it is still more strongly marked at the present day. . . . Great equality existed among the emigrants who settled on the shores of New England. Even the germs of aristocracy were never planted in that part of the Union. The only influence which obtained there was that of intellect; the people were used to reverence certain names as the emblems of knowledge and virtue. . . . .

This was the state of things to the east of the Hudson: to the southwest of that river, and as far as the Floridas, the case was different. In most of the States situated to the southwest of the Hudson some great English proprietors had settled, who had imported with them aristocratic principles and the English law of inheritance. I have explained the reasons why it was impossible ever to establish a powerful aristocracy in America; these reasons existed with less force to the southwest of the Hudson. In the South, one man, aided by slaves, could cultivate a great extent of country; it was therefore common to see rich landed proprietors. But their influence was not altogether aristocratic, as that term is understood in Europe, since they possessed no privileges; and the cultivation of their estates being carried on by slaves, they had no tenants depending on them, and consequently no patronage. Still, the great proprietors south of the Hudson constituted a superior class, having ideas and tastes of its own, and forming the centre of political action. This kind of aristocracy sympathized with the body of the people, whose passions and interests it easily embraced; but it was too weak and too short-lived to excite either love or hatred. This was the class which headed the insurrection in the south, and furnished the best leaders of the American Revolution.

At this period, society was shaken to its centre. The people, in whose name the struggle had taken place, conceived the desire of exercising the authority which it had acquired, its democratic tendencies were awakened; and having thrown off the yoke of the mother country, it aspired to independence of every kind. The influence of individuals gradually ceased to be felt, and custom and law united to produce the same result.

But the law of inheritance was the last step to equality. I am surprised that ancient and modern jurists have not attributed to this law a greater influence on human affairs. It is true that these laws belong to civil affairs; but they ought, nevertheless, to be placed at the head of all political institutions; for they exercise an incredible influence upon the social state of a people, whilst political laws only show what this state already is. They have, moreover, a sure and uniform manner of operating upon society, affecting, as it were, generations yet unborn. Through their means, man acquires a kind of preternatural power over the future lot of his fellow-creatures. When the legislator has once regulated the law of inheritance, he may rest from his labor. The machine once put in motion will go on for ages, and advance, as if self-guided, towards a point indicated beforehand. When framed in a particular manner, this law unites, draws together, and vests property and power in a few hands; it causes an aristocracy, so to speak, to spring out of the ground. If formed on opposite principles, its action is still more rapid; it divides, distributes, and disperses both property and power. Alarmed by the rapidity of its progress, those who despair of arresting its motion endeavor, at least, to obstruct it by difficulties and impediments. They vainly seek to counteract its effect by contrary efforts; but it shatters and reduces to powder every obstacle, until we can no longer see anything but a moving and impalpable cloud of dust, which signals the coming of the Democracy. . . .

In virtue of the law of partible inheritance, the death of every proprietor brings about a kind of revolution in the property; not only do his possessions change hands, but their very nature is altered, since they are parcelled into shares, which become smaller and smaller at each division. This is the direct, and as it were the physical, effect of the law. It follows, then, that, in countries where equality of inheritance is established by law, property, and especially landed property, must constantly tend to division into smaller and smaller parts. . . . But the law of equal division exercises its influence not merely upon the property itself, but it affects the minds of the heirs, and brings their passions into play. These indirect consequences tend powerfully to the destruction of large fortunes, and especially of large domains.

Among nations whose law of descent is founded upon the right of primogeniture, landed estates often pass from generation to generation without undergoing division—the consequence of which is, that family feeling is to a certain degree incorporated with the estate. The family represents the estate, the estate the family—whose names, together with its origin, its glory, its power, and its virtues, is thus perpetuated in an imperishable memorial of the past and a sure pledge of the future. When the equal partition of property is established by law, the intimate connection is destroyed between family feeling and the preservation of the paternal estate; the property ceases to represent the family; for, as it must inevitably be divided after one or two generations, it has evidently a constant tendency to diminish, and must in the end be completely dispersed. The sons of the great landed proprietor, if they are few in number, or if fortune befriends them, may indeed entertain the hope of being as wealthy as their father, but not of possessing the same property that he did; their riches must be composed of other elements than his. Now, as soon as you divest the land-owner of that interest in the preservation of his estate which he derives from association, from tradition, and from family pride, you may be certain that, sooner or later, he will dispose of it; for there is a strong pecuniary interest in favor of selling, as floating capital produces higher interest than real property, and is more readily available to gratify the passions of the moment.

Great landed estates which have once been divided never come together again; for the small proprietor draws from his land a better revenue, in proportion, than the large owner does from his; and of course, he sells it at a higher rate. The calculations of gain, therefore, which decide the rich man to sell his domain, will still more powerfully influence him against buying small estates to unite them into a large one. What is called family pride is often founded upon an illusion of self-love. A man wishes to perpetuate and immortalize himself, as it were, in his great-grandchildren. Where family pride ceases to act, individual selfishness comes into play. When the idea of family becomes vague, indeterminate, and uncertain, a man thinks of his present convenience; he provides for the establishment of his next succeeding generation, and no more. Either a man gives up the idea of perpetuating his family, or at any rate, he seeks to accomplish it by other means than by a landed estate.

Thus, not only does the law of partible inheritance render it difficult for families to preserve their ancestral domains entire, but it deprives them of the inclination to attempt it, and compels them in some measure to co-operate with the law in their own extinction. . . . By both these means, the law succeeds in striking at the root of landed property, and dispersing rapidly both families and fortunes. Most certainly it is not for us, Frenchmen of the nineteenth century, who daily witness the political and social changes which the law of partition is bringing to pass, to question its influence. It is perpetually conspicuous in our country, overthrowing the walls of our dwellings, and removing the landmarks of our fields. But although it has produced great effects in France, much still remains for it to do. Our recollections, opinions, and habits present powerful obstacles to its progress.

In the United States, it has nearly completed its work of destruction, and there we can best study its results. The English laws concerning the transmission of property were abolished in almost all the States at the time of the Revolution. The law of entail was so modified as not materially to interrupt the free circulation of property. The first generation having passed away, estates began to be parcelled out; and the change became more and more rapid with the progress of time. And now, after a lapse of a little more than sixty years, the aspect of society is totally altered; the families of the great landed proprietors are almost all commingled with the general mass. . . . The sons of these opulent citizens have become merchants, lawyers, or physicians. Most of them have lapsed into obscurity. The last trace of hereditary ranks and distinctions is destroyed—the law of partition has reduced all to one level.

I do not mean that there is any lack of wealthy individuals in the United States; I know of no country, indeed, where the love of money has taken stronger hold on the affections of men, and where a profounder contempt is expressed for the theory of the permanent equality of property. But wealth circulates with inconceivable rapidity, and experience shows that it is rare to find two succeeding generations in the full enjoyment of it.

This picture, which may, perhaps, be thought to be overcharged, still gives a very imperfect idea of what is taking place in the new States of the West and Southwest. At the end of the last century, a few bold adventurers began to penetrate into the valley of the Mississippi; and the mass of the population very soon began to move in that direction: communities unheard of till then suddenly appeared in the desert. States whose names were not in existence a few years before, claimed their place in the American Union; and in the Western settlements we may behold democracy arrived at its utmost limits. In these States, founded off-hand, and as it were by chance, the inhabitants are but of yesterday. Scarcely known to one another, the nearest neighbors are ignorant of each other's history. In this part of the American continent, therefore, the population has escaped the influence not only of great names and great wealth, but even of the natural aristocracy of knowledge and virtue. None are there able to wield that respectable power which men willingly grant to the remembrance of a life spent in doing good before their eyes. The new States of the West are already inhabited; but society has no existence among them.

It is not only the fortunes of men which are equal in America; even their acquirements partake in some degree of the same uniformity. I do not believe that there is a country in the world where, in proportion to the population, there are so few ignorant, and at the same time so few learned, individuals. Primary instruction is within the reach of everybody; superior instruction is scarcely to be obtained by any. This is not surprising; it is, in fact, the necessary consequence of what we have advanced above. Almost all the Americans are in easy circumstances, and can, therefore, obtain the first elements of human knowledge.

In America, there are but few wealthy persons; nearly all Americans have to take a profession. Now, every profession requires an apprenticeship. The Americans can devote to general education only the early years of life. At fifteen, they enter upon their calling, and thus their education generally ends at the age when ours begins. Whatever is done afterwards is with a view to some special and lucrative object; a science is taken up as a matter of business, and the only branch of it which is attended to is such as admits of an immediate practical application.

In America, most of the rich men were formerly poor; most of those who now enjoy leisure were absorbed in business during their youth; the consequence of which is, that, when they might have had a taste for study, they had no time for it, and when the time is at their disposal, they have no longer the inclination. There is no class, then, in America, in which the taste for intellectual pleasures is transmitted with hereditary fortune and leisure, and by which the labors of the intellect are held in honor. Accordingly, there is an equal want of the desire and the power of application to these objects. A middling standard is fixed in America for human knowledge. All approach as near to it as they can; some as they rise, others as they descend. Of course, a multitude of persons are to be found who entertain the same number of ideas on religion, history, science, political economy, legislation, and government. The gifts of intellect proceed directly from God, and man cannot prevent their unequal distribution. But it is at least a consequence of what we have just said, that although the capacities of men are different, as the Creator intended they should be, Americans find the means of putting them to use are equal.

In America, the aristocratic element has always been feeble from its birth; and if at the present day it is not actually destroyed, it is at any rate so completely disabled, that we can scarcely assign to it any degree of influence on the course of affairs. The democratic principle, on the contrary, has gained so much strength by time, by events, and by legislation, as to have become not only predominant, but all-powerful. There is no family or corporate authority, and it is rare to find even the influence of individual character enjoy any durability. America, then, exhibits in her social state an extraordinary phenomenon. Men are there seen on a greater equality in point of fortune and intellect, or, in other words, more equal in their strength, than in any other country of the world, or in any age of which history has preserved the remembrance.

Political Consequences of Social Democracy

The political consequences of such a social condition as this are easily deducible. It is impossible to believe that equality will not eventually find its way into the political world, as it does everywhere else. To conceive of men remaining forever unequal upon a single point, yet equal on all others, is impossible; they must come in the end to be equal upon all.

Now I know of only two methods of establishing equality in the political world; every citizen must be put in possession of his rights, or rights must be granted to no one. For nations which are arrived at the same stage of social existence as the Anglo-Americans, it is, therefore, very difficult to discover a medium between the sovereignty of all and the absolute power of one man: and it would be vain to deny that the social condition which I have been describing is just as liable to one of these consequences as to the other. There is, in fact, a manly and lawful passion for equality which incites men to wish all to be powerful and honored. This passion tends to elevate the humble to the rank of the great; but there exists also in the human heart a depraved taste for equality, which impels the weak to attempt to lower the powerful to their own level, and reduces men to prefer equality in slavery to inequality with freedom. Not that those nations whose social condition is democratic naturally despise liberty; on the contrary, they have an instinctive love of it. But liberty is not the chief and constant object of their desires; equality is their idol: they make rapid and sudden efforts to obtain liberty, and, if they miss their aim, resign themselves to their disappointment; but nothing can satisfy them without equality, and they would rather perish than lose it.

On the other hand, in a state where the citizens are all nearly on an equality, it becomes difficult for them to preserve their independence against the aggressions of power. No one among them being strong enough to engage in the struggle alone with advantage, nothing but a general combination can protect their liberty. Now, such a union is not always possible. From the same social position, then, nations may derive one or the other of two great political results; these results are extremely different from each other, but they both proceed from the same cause. The Anglo-Americans are the first nation who, having been exposed to this formidable alternative, have been happy enough to escape the dominion of absolute power. They have been allowed by their circumstances, their origin, their intelligence, and especially by their morals, to establish and maintain the sovereignty of the people.

Unlimited Power of the Majority in the United States and Its Consequences

The very essence of democratic government consists in the absolute sovereignty of the majority; for there is nothing in democratic states which is capable of resisting it. Most of the American constitutions have sought to increase this natural strength of the majority by artificial means.

The legislature is, of all political institutions, the one which is most easily swayed by the will of the majority. The Americans determined that the members of the legislature should be elected by the people *directly*, and for a *very brief term*, in order to subject them, not only to the general convictions, but even to the daily passions, of their constituents. The members of both houses are taken from the same classes in society, and nominated in the same manner; so that the movements of the legislative bodies are almost as rapid, and quite as irresistible, as those of a single assembly. It is to a legislature thus constituted, that almost all the authority of the government has been intrusted.

At the same time that the laws increase the strength of those authorities which of themselves were strong, it enfeebled more and more those which were naturally weak. It deprived the representatives of the executive power of all stability and independence; and, by subjecting them completely to the caprices of the legislature, it robbed them of the slender influence which the nature of a democratic government might have allowed them to exercise. In several States, the judicial power was also submitted to the election of the majority; and in all of them, its existence was made to depend on the pleasure of the legislative authority, since the representatives were empowered annually to regulate the stipend of the judges.

Custom has done even more than law. A proceeding is becoming more and more general in the United States, which will, in the end, do away with the guaranties of representative government: it frequently happens that the voters, in electing a delegate, point out a certain line of conduct to him, and impose upon him certain positive obligations which he is pledged to fulfil. With the exception of the tumult, this comes to the same thing as if the majority itself held its deliberations in the market-place.

Several other circumstances concur to render the power of the majority in America not only preponderant, but irresistible. The moral authority of the majority is partly based upon the notion, that there is more intelligence and wisdom in a number of men united than in a single individual, and that the number of the legislators is more important than their equality. The theory of equality is thus applied to the intellects of men; and human pride is thus assailed in its last retreat by a doctrine which the minority hesitate to admit, and to which they will but slowly assent. Like all other powers, and perhaps more than any other, the authority of the many requires the sanction of time in order to appear legitimate. At first, it enforces obedience by constraint; and its laws are not *respected* until they have been long maintained.

The right of governing society, which the majority supposes itself to derive from its superior intelligence, was introduced into the United States by the first settlers; and this idea, which of itself would be sufficient to create a free nation, has now been amalgamated with the manners of the people and the minor incidents of social life.

The French, under the old monarchy, held it for a maxim that the king could do no wrong; and if he did do wrong, the blame was imputed to his advisers. This notion made obedience very easy; it enabled the subject to complain of the law, without ceasing to love and honor the lawgiver. The Americans entertain the same opinion with respect to the majority.

The moral power of the majority is founded upon yet another principle, which is, that the interests of the many are to be preferred to those of the few. It will readily be perceived that the respect here professed for the rights of the greater number must naturally increase or diminish according to the state of parties. When a nation is divided into several great irreconcilable interests, the privilege of the majority is often overlooked, because it is intolerable to comply with its demands.

If there existed in America a class of citizens whom the legislating majority sought to deprive of exclusive privileges which they had possessed for ages, and to bring down from an elevated station to the level of the multitude, it is probable that the minority would be less ready to submit to its laws. But as the United States were colonized by men holding equal rank, there is as yet no natural or permanent disagreement between the interests of its different inhabitants.

There are communities in which the members of the minority can never hope to draw over the majority to their side, because they must then give up the very point which is at issue between them. Thus, an aristocracy can never become a majority whilst it retains its exclusive privileges, and it cannot cede its privileges without ceasing to be an aristocracy.

In the United States, political questions cannot be taken up in so general and absolute a manner; and all parties are willing to recognize the rights of the majority, because they all hope at some time to be able to exercise them to their own advantage. The majority, therefore, in that country, exercise a prodigious actual authority, and a power of opinion which is nearly as great; no obstacles exist which can impede or even retard its progress, so as to make it heed the complaints of those whom it crushes upon its path. This state of things is harmful in itself, and dangerous for the future. . . .

Tyranny of the Majority

I hold it to be an impious and detestable maxim, that, politically speaking, the people have a right to do anything; and yet I have asserted that all authority originates in the will of the majority. Am I, then, in contradiction with myself?

A general law, which bears the name of justice, has been made and sanctioned, not only by a majority of this or that people, but by a majority of mankind. The rights of every people are therefore confined within the limits of what is just. A nation may be considered as a jury which is empowered to represent society at large, and to apply justice, which is its law. Ought such a jury, which represents society, to have more power than the society itself, whose laws it executes?

When I refuse to obey an unjust law, I do not contest the right of the majority to command, but I simply appeal from the sovereignty of the people to the sovereignty of mankind. Some have not feared to assert that a people can never outstep the boundaries of justice and reason in those affairs which are peculiarly its own; and the consequently full power may be given to the majority by which they are represented. But this is the language of a slave.

A majority taken collectively is only an individual, whose opinions, and frequently whose interests, are opposed to those of another individual, who is styled a minority. If it be admitted that a man possessing absolute power may misuse that power by wronging his adversaries, why should not a majority be liable to the same reproach? Men do not change their characters by uniting with each other; nor does their patience in the presence of obstacles increase with their strength. For my own part, I cannot believe it; the power to do everything, which I should refuse to one of my equals, I will never grant to any number of them.

I do not think, for the sake of preserving liberty, it is possible to combine several principles in the same government so as really to oppose them to one another. The form of government which is usually termed *mixed* has always appeared to me a mere chimera. Accurately speaking, there is no such thing as a *mixed government*, in the sense usually given to that word, because, in all communities, some one principle of action may be discovered which preponderates over the others. England, in the last century—which has been especially cited as an example of this sort of government—was essentially an aristocratic state, although it comprised some great elements of democracy; for the laws and customs of the country were such that the aristocracy could not but preponderate in the long run, and direct public affairs according to its own will. The error arose from seeing the interests of the nobles perpetually contending with those of the people, without considering the issue of the contest, which was really the important point. When a community actually has a mixed government—that is to say, when it is equally divided between adverse principles—it must either experience a revolution, or fall into anarchy.

I am therefore of opinion, that social power superior to all others must always be placed somewhere; but I think that liberty is endangered when this power finds no obstacle which can retard its course, and give it time to moderate its own vehemence.

Unlimited power is in itself a bad and dangerous thing. Human beings are not competent to exercise it with discretion. God alone can be omnipotent, because his wisdom and his justice are always equal to his power. There is no power on earth so worthy of honor in itself, or clothed with rights so sacred, that I would admit it uncontrolled and all-predominant authority. When I see that the right and the means of absolute command are conferred on any power whatever, be it called a people or a king, an aristocracy or a democracy, a monarchy or a republic, I say there is the germ of tyranny, and I seek to live elsewhere, under other laws.

In my opinion, the main evil of the present democratic institutions of the United

States does not arise, as is often asserted in Europe, from their weakness, but from their irresistible strength. I am not so much alarmed at the excessive liberty which reigns in that country, as at the inadequate securities which one finds there against tyranny.

When an individual or a party is wronged in the United States, to whom can he apply for redress? If to public opinion, public opinion constitutes the majority; if to the legislature, it represents the majority, and implicitly obeys it; if to the executive power, it is appointed by the majority, and serves as a passive tool in its hands. The public force consists of the majority under arms; the jury is the majority invested with the right of hearing judicial cases; and in certain States, even the judges are elected by the majority. However, iniquitous or absurd the measure of which you complain, you must submit to it as well as you can.

If, on the other hand, a legislative power could be so constituted as to represent the majority without necessarily being the slave of its passions, an executive so as to retain a proper share of authority, and a judiciary so as to remain independent of the other two powers, a government would be formed which would still be democratic, without incurring hardly any risk of tyranny.

I do not say that there is a frequent use of tyranny in America, at the present day; but I maintain that there is no sure barrier against it, and that the causes which mitigate the government there are to be found in the circumstances and the manners of the country, more than in its laws.

Effects of the Omnipotence of the Majority upon the Arbitrary Authority of American Public Officers

A distinction must be drawn between tyranny and arbitrary power. Tyranny may be exercised by means of the law itself, and in that case it is not arbitrary; arbitrary power may be exercised for the public good, in which case it is not tyrannical. Tyranny usually employs arbitrary means, but, if necessary, it can do without them.

In the United States, the omnipotence of the majority, which is favorable to the legal despotism of the legislature, likewise favors the arbitrary authority of the magistrate. The majority has absolute power both to make the law and to watch over its execution; and as it has equal authority over those who are in power, and the community at large, it considers public officers as its passive agents, and readily confides to them the task of carrying out its designs. The details of their office, and the privileges which they are to enjoy, are rarely defined beforehand. It treats them as a master does his servants, since they are always at work in his sight, and he can direct or reprimand them at any instant.

In general, the American functionaries are far more independent within the sphere which is prescribed to them than the French civil officers. Sometimes, even, they are allowed by the popular authority to exceed those bounds; and as they are protected by the opinion, and backed by the power, of the majority, they dare do things which even a European, accustomed as he is to arbitrary power, is astonished at. By this means, habits are formed in the heart of a free country which may some day prove fatal to its liberties.

Power Exercised by the Majority in America upon Opinion

It is in the examination of the exercise of thought in the United States, that we clearly perceive how far the power of the majority surpasses all the powers with which we are acquainted in Europe. Thought is an invisible and subtle power, that mocks all the efforts of tyranny. At the present time, the most absolute monarchs in Europe cannot prevent certain opinions hostile to their authority from circulating in secret through their dominions, and even in their courts. It is not so in America; as long as the majority is still undecided, discussion is carried on; but as soon as its decision is irrevocably pronounced, every one is silent, and the friends as well as the opponents of the measure unite in assenting to its propriety. The reason of this is perfectly clear: no monarch is so absolute as to combine all the powers of society in his own hands, and to conquer all opposition, as a majority is able to do, which has the right both of making and of executing the laws.

The authority of a king is physical, and controls the actions of men without subduing their will. But the majority possesses a power which is physical and moral at the same time, which acts upon the will as much as upon the actions, and represses not only all contest, but all controversy.

I know of no country in which there is so little independence of mind and real freedom of discussion as in America. In any constitutional state in Europe, every sort of religious and political theory may be freely preached and disseminated; for there is no country in Europe so subdued by any single authority, as not to protect the man who raises his voice in the cause of truth from the consequences of his hardihood. If he is unfortunate enough to live under an absolute government, the people are often upon his side; if he inhabits a free country, he can, if necessary, find a shelter behind the throne. The aristocratic part of society supports him in some countries, and the democracy in others. But in a nation where democratic institutions exist, organized like those of the United States, there is but one authority, one element of strength and success, with nothing beyond it.

In America, the majority raises formidable barriers around the liberty of opinion: within these barriers, an author may write what he pleases; but woe to him if he goes beyond them. Not that he is in danger of an *auto-da-fé*, but he is exposed to continued obloquy and persecution. His political career is closed forever, since he has offended the only authority which is able to open it. Every sort of compensation, even that of celebrity, is refused to him. Before publishing his opinions, he imagined that he held them in common with others; but no sooner has he declared them, than he is loudly censured by his opponents, whilst those who think like him, without having the courage to speak out, abandon him in silence. He yields at length, overcome by the daily effort which he has to make, and subsides into silence, as if he felt remorse for having spoken the truth.

Fetters and headsmen were the coarse instruments which tyranny formerly employed; but the civilization of our age has perfected despotism itself, though it seemed to have nothing to learn. Monarchs had, so to speak, materialized oppression: the democratic republics of the present day have rendered it as entirely an affair of the mind, as the will which it is intended to coerce. Under the absolute sway of one man, the body was attacked in order to subdue the soul; but the soul escaped the blows which were directed against it, and rose proudly superior. Such is not the course adopted by tyranny in democratic republics; there the body is left free, and the soul is enslaved. The master no longer says, "You shall think as I do, or you shall die"; but he says, "You are free to think differently from me, and to retain your life, your property, and all that you possess; but you are henceforth a stranger among your people. You may retain your civil rights, but they will be useless to you, for you will never be chosen by your fellow-citizens, if you solicit their votes; and they will affect to scorn you, if you ask for their esteem. You will remain among men, but you will be deprived of the rights of mankind. Your fellow-creatures will shun you like an impure being; and even those who believe in your innocence will abandon you, lest they should be shunned in their turn. Go in peace! I have given you your life, but it is an existence worse than death."

Absolute monarchies had dishonored despotism; let us beware lest democratic republics should reinstate it, and render it less odious and degrading in the eyes of the many, by making it still more onerous to the few.

Works have been published in the proudest nations of the Old World, expressly intended to censure the vices and the follies of the times: Labruyère inhabited the palace of Louis XIV, when he composed his chapter upon the Great, and Molière criticised the courtiers in the pieces which were acted before the court. But the ruling power in the United States is not to be made game of. The smallest reproach irritates its sensibility, and the slightest joke which has any foundation in truth renders it indignant; from the forms of its language up to the solid virtues of its character, everything must be made the subject of encomium. No writer, whatever be his eminence, can escape paying this tribute of adulation to his fellow-citizens. The majority lives in the perpetual utterance of self-applause; and there are certain truths which the Americans can only learn from strangers or from experience.

If America has not as yet had any great writers, the reason is given in these facts; there can be no literary genius without freedom of opinion, and freedom of opinion does not exist in America. The Inquisition has never been able to prevent a vast number of anti-religious books from circulating in Spain. The empire of the majority succeeds much better in the United States, since it actually removes any wish to publish them. Unbelievers are to be met with in America, but there is no public organ of infidelity. Attempts have been made by some governments to protect morality by prohibiting licentious books. In the United States, no one is punished for this sort of books, but no one is induced to write them; not because all the citizens are immaculate in conduct, but because the majority of the community is decent and orderly.

In this case the use of the power is unquestionably good; and I am discussing the nature of the power itself. This irresistible authority is a constant fact, and its judicious exercise is only an accident.

Effects of the Tyranny of the Majority upon the National Character of the Americans

The tendencies which I have just mentioned are as yet but slightly perceptible in political society; but they already exercise an unfavorable influence upon the national character of the Americans. I attribute the small number of distinguished men in political life to the ever-increasing despotism of the majority in the United States.

When the American Revolution broke out, they arose in great numbers; for public opinion then served, not to tyrannize over, but to direct the exertions of individuals. Those celebrated men, sharing the agitation of mind common at that period, had a grandeur peculiar to themselves, which was reflected back upon the nation, but was by no means borrowed from it.

In absolute governments, the great nobles who are nearest to the throne flatter the passions of the sovereign, and voluntarily truckle to his caprices. But the mass of the nation does not degrade itself by servitude; it often submits from weakness, from habit, or from ignorance, and sometimes from loyalty. Some nations have been known to sacrifice their own desires to those of the sovereign with pleasure and pride, thus exhibiting a sort of independence of mind in the very act of submission. These nations are miserable, but they are not degraded. There is a great difference between doing what one does not approve, and feigning to approve what one does; the one is the weakness of a feeble person, the other befits the temper of a lackey.

In free countries, where everyone is more or less called upon to give his opinion on affairs of state—in democratic republics, where public life is incessantly mingled with domestic affairs, where the sovereign authority is accessible on every side, and where its attention can always be attracted by vociferation—more persons are to be met with who speculate upon its weaknesses, and live upon ministering to its passions, than in absolute monarchies. Not because men are naturally worse in these states than elsewhere, but the temptation is stronger and of easier access at the same time. The result is a more extensive debasement of character.

Democratic republics extend the practice of currying favor with the many, and introduce it into all classes at once: this is the most serious reproach that can be addressed to them. This is especially true in democratic states organized like the American republics, where the power of the majority is so absolute and irresistible that one must give up his rights as a citizen, and almost abjure his qualities as a man, if he intends to stray from the track which it prescribes.

In that immense crowd which throngs the avenues to power in the United States, I found very few men who displayed that manly candor and masculine independence of opinion which frequently distinguished the Americans in former times, and which constitutes the leading feature in distinguished characters wheresoever they may be found. It seems, at first sight, as if all the minds of the Americans were formed upon one model, so accurately do they follow the same route. A stranger does, indeed, sometimes meet with Americans who dissent from the rigor of the formularies—with men who deplore the defects of the laws, the mutability and the ignorance of democracy—who even go so far as to observe the evil tendencies which impair the national character, and to point out such remedies as it might be possible to apply; but no one is there to hear them except yourself, and you, to whom these secret reflections are confided, are a stranger and a bird of passage. They are very ready to communicate truths which are useless to you, but they hold a different language in public. . . .

The Greatest Dangers of the American Republics Proceed from the Omnipotence of the Majority

Governments usually perish from impotence or from tyranny. In the former case, their power escapes from them; it is wrested from their grasp in the latter. Many observers who have witnessed the anarchy of democratic states, have imagined that the government of those states was naturally weak and impotent. The truth is, that, when war is once begun between parties, the government loses its control over society. But I do not think that a democratic power is naturally without force or resources; say, rather, that it is almost always by the abuse of its force, and the misemployment of its resources, that it becomes a failure. Anarchy is almost always produced by its tyranny or its mistakes, but not by its want of strength.

It is important not to confound stability with force, or the greatness of a thing with its duration. In democratic republics, the power which directs society is not stable; for it often changes hands, and assumes a new direction. But, whichever way it turns, its force is almost irresistible. The governments of the American republics appear to me to be as much centralized as those of the absolute monarchies of Europe, and more energetic than they are. I do not, therefore, imagine that they will perish from weakness.

If ever the free institutions of America are destroyed, that event may be attributed to the omnipotence of the majority, which may at some future time urge the minorities to desperation, and oblige them to have recourse to physical force. Anarchy will then be the result, but it will have been brought about by despotism.

Mr. Madison expresses the same opinion in the Federalist, No. 51. "It is of great importance in a republic, not only to guard the society against the oppression of its rulers, but to guard one part of the society against the injustice of the other part. Justice is the end of government. It is the end of civil society. It ever has been, and ever will be, pursued until it be obtained, or until liberty be lost in the pursuit. In a society, under the forms of which the stronger faction can readily unite and oppress the weaker, anarchy may as truly be said to reign as in a state of nature, where the weaker individual is not secured against the violence of the stronger: and as, in the latter state, even the stronger individuals are prompted by the uncertainty of their condition to submit to a government which may protect the weak as well as themselves, so, in the former state, will the more powerful factions be gradually induced by a like motive to wish for a government which will protect all parties, the weaker as well as the more powerful. It can be little doubted, that, if the State of Rhode Island was separated from the Confederacy and left to itself, the insecurity of right under the popular form of government within such narrow limits would be displayed by such reiterated oppressions of the factious majorities, that some power altogether independent of the people would soon be called for by the voice of the very factions whose misrule had proved the necessity of it."

Jefferson also said: "The executive power in our government is not the only, perhaps not even the principal, object of my solicitude. The tyranny of the legislature is really the danger most to be feared, and will continue to be so for many years to come. The tyranny of the executive power will come in its turn, but at a more distant period."

I am glad to cite the opinion of Jefferson upon this subject rather than that of any other, because I consider him the most powerful advocate democracy has ever had.

Causes Which Mitigate the Tyranny of the Majority in the United States

Absence of Centralized Administration

. . . But in the United States, the majority, which so frequently displays the tastes and the propensities of a despot, is still destitute of the most perfect instruments of tyranny. In the American republics, the central government has never as yet busied itself but with a small number of objects, sufficiently prominent to attract its attention. The secondary affairs of society have never been regulated by its authority; and nothing has hitherto betrayed its desire of even interfering in them. The majority is become more and more absolute, but has not increased the prerogatives of the central government; those great prerogatives have been confined to a certain sphere; and, although the despotism of the majority may be galling upon one point, it cannot be said to extend to all. However the predominant party in the nation may be carried away by its passions, however ardent it may be in the pursuit of its projects, it cannot oblige all the citizens to comply with its desires in the same manner, and at the same time, throughout the country. When the central government which represents that majority has issued a decree, it must intrust the execution of its will to agents, over whom it frequently has no control, and whom it cannot perpetually direct. The townships, municipal bodies, and counties form so many concealed breakwaters, which check or part the tide of popular determination. If an oppressive law were passed, liberty would still be protected by the mode of executing that law; the majority cannot descend to the details and what may be called the puerilities of administrative tyranny. It does not even imagine that it can do so, for it has not a full consciousness of its authority. It knows only the extent of its natural powers, but is unacquainted with the art of increasing them.

This point deserves attention; for if a democratic republic, similar to that of the United States, were ever founded in a country where the power of one man had previously established a centralized administration, and had sunk it deep into the habits and the laws of the people, I do not hesitate to assert, that, in such a republic, a more insufferable despotism would prevail than in any of the absolute monarchies of Europe; or, indeed, than any which could be found on this side of Asia.

The Profession of the Law Serves to Counterpoise the Democracy

In visiting the Americans and studying their laws, we perceive that the authority they have intrusted to members of the legal profession, and the influence which these individuals exercise in the government, is the most powerful existing security against the excesses of democracy. . . . Men who have made a special study of the laws derive from this occupation certain habits of order, a taste for formalities, and a kind of instinctive regard for the regular connection of ideas, which naturally render them very hostile to the revolutionary spirit and the unreflecting passions of the multitude. . . .

I do not, then, assert that *all* the members of the legal profession are, at *all* times, the friends of order and the opponents of innovation, but merely that most of them are usually so. In a community in which lawyers are allowed to occupy without opposition that high station which naturally belongs to them, their general spirit will be eminently conservative and anti-democratic. When an aristocracy excludes the leaders of that profession from its ranks, it excites enemies who are the more formidable as they are independent of the nobility by their labors, and feel themselves to be their equals in intelligence though inferior in opulence and power. But whenever an aristocracy consents to impart some of its privileges to these same individuals, the two classes coalesce very readily, and assume, as it were, family interests. . . .

Lawyers are attached to public order beyond every other consideration, and the best security of public order is authority. It must not be forgotten, also, that, if they prize freedom much, they generally value legality still more: they are less afraid of tyranny than of arbitrary power; and, provided the legislature undertakes of itself to deprive men of their independence, they are not dissatisfied. . . .

The government of democracy is favorable to the political power of lawyers; for when the wealthy, the noble, and the prince are excluded from the government, the lawyers take possession of it, in their own right, as it were, since they are the only men of information and sagacity, beyond the sphere of the people, who can be the object of the popular choice. If, then, they are led by their tastes toward the aristocracy and the prince, they are brought in contact with the people by their interests. They like the government of democracy, without participating in its propensities and without imitating its weaknesses; whence they derive a twofold authority from it and over it. The people in democratic states do not mistrust the members of the legal profession, because it is known that they are interested to serve the popular cause; and the people listen to them without irritation, because they do not attribute to them any sinister designs. The lawyers do not, indeed, wish to overthrow the institutions of democracy, but they constantly endeavor to turn it away from its real direction by means which are foreign to its nature. Lawyers belong to the people by birth and interest, and to the aristocracy by habit and taste; they may be looked upon as the connecting link of the two great classes of society. . . .

In America, there are no nobles or literary men, and the people are apt to mistrust the wealthy; lawyers consequently form the highest political class, and the most cultivated portion of society. They have therefore nothing to gain by innovation, which adds a conservative interest to their natural taste for public order. If I were asked where I place the American aristocracy, I should reply, without hesitation, that it is not among the rich, who are united by no common tie, but that it occupies the judicial bench and the bar.

The more we reflect upon all that occurs in the United States, the more shall we be persuaded that the lawyers, as a body, form the most powerful, if not the only, counterpoise to the democratic element. In that country, we easily perceive how the legal profession is qualified by its attributes, and even by its faults, to neutralize the vices inherent in popular government. When the American people are intoxicated by passion, or carried away by the impetuosity of their ideas, they are checked and stopped by the almost invisible influence of their legal counsellors. These secretly oppose their aristocratic propensities to the nation's democratic instincts, their superstitious attachment to what is old to its love of novelty, their narrow views to its immense designs, and their habitual procrastination to its ardent impatience.

The courts of justice are the visible organs by which the legal profession is enabled to control the democracy. The judge is a lawyer, who, independently of the taste for regularity and order which he has contracted in the study of law, derives an additional love of stability from the inalienability of his own functions. His legal attainments have already raised him to a distinguished rank amongst his fellows; his political power completes the distinction of his station, and gives him the instincts of the privileged classes. Armed with the power of declaring the laws to be unconstitutional, the American magistrate perpetually interferes in political affairs. He cannot force the people to make laws, but at least he can oblige them not to disobey their own enactments, and not to be inconsistent with themselves. . . .

It must not, moreover, be supposed that the legal spirit is confined, in the United States, to the courts of justice; it extends far beyond them. As the lawyers form the only enlightened class whom the people do not mistrust, they are naturally called upon to occupy most of the public stations. They fill the legislative assemblies, and are at the head of the administration; they consequently exercise a powerful influence upon the formation of the law, and upon its execution. The lawyers are, however, obliged to yield to the current of public opinion, which is too strong for them to resist; but it is easy to find indications of what they would do, if they were free to act. The Americans, who have made so many innovations in their political laws, have introduced very sparing alterations in their civil laws, and that with great difficulty, although many of these laws are repugnant to their social condition. The reason for this is, that, in matters of civil law, the majority are obliged to defer to the authority of the legal profession, and the American lawyers are disinclined to innovate when they are left to their own choice. . . .

Trial by Jury

. . . Trial by jury may be considered in two separate points of view; as a judicial, and as a political institution. . . .

My present purpose is to consider the jury as a political institution. . . . It would be a very narrow view to look upon the jury as a mere judicial institution; for, however great its influence may be upon the decisions of the courts, it is still greater on the destinies of society at large. The jury is, above all, a political institution, and it must be regarded in this light in order to be duly appreciated. By the jury, I mean a certain number of citizens chosen by lot, and invested with a temporary right of judging. Trial by jury, as applied to the repression of crime, appears to me an eminently republican element in the government, for the following reasons.

The institution of the jury may be aristocratic or democratic, according to the class from which the jurors are taken; but it always preserves its republican character, in that it places the real direction of society in the hands of the governed, or of a portion of the governed, and not in that of the government. Force is never more than a transient element of success, and after force, comes the notion of right. A government which should be able to reach its enemies only upon a field of battle would soon be destroyed. The true sanction of political laws is to be found in penal legislation; and if that sanction be wanting, the law will sooner or later lose its cogency. He who punishes the criminal is therefore the real master of society. Now, the institution of the jury raises the people itself, or at least a class of citizens, to the bench of judges. The institution of the jury consequently invests the people, or that class of citizens, with the direction of society. . . . The jury cannot fail to exercise a powerful influence upon the national character. . . . The jury . . . serves to communicate the spirit of the judges to the minds of all the citizens; and this spirit, with the habits which attend it, is the soundest preparation for free institutions. It imbues all classes with a respect of the thing judged, and with the notion of right. If these two elements be removed, the love of independence becomes a mere destructive passion. It teaches men to practise equity; every man learns to judge his neighbor as he would himself be judged. And this is especially true of the jury in civil causes; for, whilst the number of persons who have reason to apprehend a criminal prosecution is small, every one is liable to have a lawsuit. The jury teaches every man not to recoil before the responsibility of his own actions, and impresses him with that manly confidence without which no political virtue can exist. It invests each citizen with a kind of magistracy; it makes them all feel the duties which they are bound to discharge towards society, and the part which they take in its government. By obliging men to turn their attention to other affairs than their own, it rubs off that private selfishness which is the rust of society.

The jury contributes powerfully to form the judgment and to increase the natural intelligence of a people; and this, in my opinion, is its greatest advantage. It may be regarded as a gratuitous public school, ever open, in which every juror learns his rights, enters into daily communication with the most learned and enlightened members of the upper classes, and becomes practically acquainted with the laws, which are brought within the reach of his capacity by the efforts of the bar, the advice of the judge, and even by the passions of the parties. I think that the practical intelligence and political good sense of the Americans are mainly attributable to the long use which they have made of the jury in civil causes. . . .

The jury, then, which seems to restrict the rights of the judiciary, does in reality consolidate its power; and in no country are the judges so powerful as where the people share their privileges. It is especially by means of the jury in civil causes, that the American magistrates imbue even the lower classes of society with the spirit of their profession. Thus the jury, which is the most energetic means of making the people rule, is also the most efficacious means of teaching it how to rule well.

23

G.W.F. Hegel
Philosophy of Right

G.W.F. Hegel (1770–1831) was one of the most challenging and abstract philosophers of modern times. The following selections are from The Philosophy of Right *(1821), his most important book on political philosophy. Hegel argued that history is a rational process propelled by conflicting forces. "Reason is the law of the world," he wrote, believing that the role of reason can be seen in historical progress. "Geist"—the word can be translated from German as both "mind" and "spirit"—works itself out in history. In examining politics, Hegel posits a contradiction between three dimensions of life. The family, based on love, is a form of "particularist altruism." "Civil society," the domain of social and economic interactions between individuals, is based on self-interest. It is "universal egoism." The state resolves the contradiction between these two domains as the embodiment of "universal altruism" and the general will. Hegel has been often misinterpreted as a harbinger of totalitarianism, but he advocated a constitutional monarchy with a quasi-representative assembly and a codified system of law.*

[THE] TRUTH about Right, Ethics, and the state is as old as its public recognition and formulation in the law of the land, in the morality of everyday life, and in religion. What more does this truth require—since the thinking mind is not content to possess it in this ready fashion? It requires to be grasped in thought as well; the content which is already rational in principle must win the *form* of rationality and so appear well-founded to untrammelled thinking. Such thinking does not remain stationary at the given, whether the given be upheld by the external positive authority of the state or the *consensus hominum,* or by the authority of inward feeling and emotion and by the 'witness of the spirit' which directly concurs with it. On the contrary, thought which is free starts out from itself and thereupon claims to know itself as united in its innermost being with the truth.

The unsophisticated heart takes the simple line of adhering with trustful conviction to what is publicly accepted as true and then building on this firm foundation its conduct and its set position in life. Against this simple line of conduct there may at once be raised the alleged difficulty of how it is possible, in an infinite variety of opinions, to distinguish and discover what is universally recognized and valid. This perplexity may at first sight be taken for a right and really serious attitude to the thing, but in fact those who boast of this perplexity are in the position of not being able to see the wood for the trees; the only perplexity and difficulty they are in is one of their own making. Indeed, this perplexity and difficulty of theirs is proof rather that they want as the substance of the right and the ethical not what is universally recognized and valid, but something else. If they had been serious with what is universally accepted instead of busying themselves with the vanity and particularity of opinions and things, they would have clung to what is substantively right, namely to the commands of the ethical order and the state, and would have regulated their lives in accordance with these.

A more serious difficulty arises, however, from the fact that man thinks and tries to find in thinking both his freedom and the basis of ethical life. But however lofty, however divine, the right of thought may be, it is perverted into wrong if it is only this [opining] which passes for thinking and if thinking knows itself to be free only when it diverges from what is *universally* recognized and valid and when it has discovered how to invent for itself some *particular* character.

At the present time, the idea that freedom of thought, and of mind generally, evinces itself only in divergence from, indeed in hostility to, what is publicly recognized, might seem to be most firmly rooted in connexion with the state, and it is chiefly for this reason that a philosophy of the state might seem essentially to have the task of discovering and promulgating still another theory, and a special and original one at that. In examining this idea and the activity in conformity with it, we might suppose that no state or constitution had ever existed in the world at all or was even in being at the present time, but that nowadays—and this 'nowadays' lasts for ever—we had to start all over again from the beginning, and that the ethical world had just been waiting for such present-day projects, proofs, and investigations. So far as nature is concerned, people grant that it is nature as it is which philosophy has to bring within its ken, that the philosopher's stone lies concealed somewhere, somewhere within nature itself, that nature is inherently rational, and that what knowledge has to investigate and grasp in concepts is this actual reason present in it; not the formations and accidents evident to the superficial observer, but nature's eternal harmony, its harmony, however, in the sense of the law and essence immanent within it. The ethical world, on the other hand, the state (i.e. reason as it actualizes itself in the element of self- consciousness), is not allowed to enjoy the good fortune which springs from the fact that it is reason which has achieved power and mastery within that element and which maintains itself and has its home there. The universe of mind is supposed rather to be left to the mercy of chance and caprice, to be God-forsaken, and the result is that if the ethical world is Godless, truth lies outside it, and at the same time, since even so reason is supposed to be in it as well, truth becomes nothing but a problem. But it is this also that is to authorize, nay to oblige, every thinker to take his own road, though not in search of the philosopher's stone, for he is saved this search by the philosophizing of our contemporaries, and everyone nowadays is assured that he has this stone in his grasp as his birthright. Now admittedly it is the case that those who live their lives in the state as it actually exists here and now and find satisfaction there for their knowledge and volition (and of these there are many, more in fact than think or know it, because ultimately this is the position of everybody), or those at any rate who *consciously* find their satisfaction in the state, laugh at these operations and affirmations and regard them as an empty game, sometimes rather funny, sometimes rather serious, now amusing, now dangerous. Thus this restless activity of empty reflection, together with its popularity and the welcome it has received, would be a thing on its own, developing in privacy in its own way, were it not that it is philosophy itself which has earned all kinds of scorn and discredit by its indulgence in this occupation. The worst of these kinds of scorn is this, that, as I said just now, everyone is convinced that his mere birthright puts him in a position to pass judgement on philosophy in general and to condemn it. No other art or science is subjected to this last degree of scorn, to the supposition that we are masters of it without ado. . . .

At the present time, the pettifoggery of caprice has usurped the name of philosophy and succeeded in giving a wide public the opinion that such triflings are philosophy. The result of this is that it has now become almost a disgrace to go on speaking in philosophical terms about the nature of the state, and law-abiding men cannot be blamed if they become impatient so soon as they hear mention of a philosophical science of the state. Still less is it a matter for surprise that governments have at last directed their attention to this kind of philosophy, since, apart from anything else, philosophy with us is not; as it was with the Greeks for instance, pursued in private like an art, but has an existence in the open, in contact with the public, and especially, or even only, in the service of the state. Governments have proved their trust in their scholars who have made philosophy their chosen field by leaving entirely to them the construction and contents of philosophy—though here and there, if you like, it may not have been so much confidence that has been shown as indifference to learning itself, and professorial chairs of philosophy have been retained only as a tradition (in France, for instance, to the best of my knowledge, chairs of metaphysics at least have been allowed to lapse). Their confidence, however, has very often been ill repaid, or alternatively, if you preferred to see indifference, you would have to regard the result, the decay of thorough knowledge, as the penalty of this indifference. Prima facie, superficiality seems to be extremely accommodating, one might say, at least in relation to public peace and order, because it fails to touch or even to guess at the substance of the things; no action, or at least no police action, would thus have been taken against it in the first instance, had it not been that there still existed in the state a need for a deeper education and insight, a need which the state required philosophical science to satisfy. On the other hand, superficial thinking about the ethical order, about right and duty in general, starts automatically from the maxims which constitute superficiality in this sphere, i.e. from the principles of the Sophists which are so clearly outlined for our information in Plato. What is right these principles locate in subjective aims and opinions, in subjective feeling and particular conviction, and from them there follows the ruin of the inner ethical life and a good conscience, of love and right dealing between private persons, no less than the ruin of public order and the law of the land. The significance which such phenomena must acquire for governments is not likely to suffer any diminution as a result of the pretentiousness which has used that very grant of confidence and the authority of a professorial chair to support the demand that the state should uphold and give scope to what corrupts the ultimate source of achievement, namely universal principles, and so even to the defiance of the state as if such defiance were what it deserved. 'If God gives a man an office, he also gives him brains' is an old joke which in these days surely no one will take wholly in earnest. . . .

What is rational is actual and what is actual is rational. On this conviction the plain man like the philosopher takes his stand, and from it philosophy starts in its study of the universe of mind as well as the universe of nature. If reflection, feeling, or whatever form subjective consciousness may take, looks upon the present as something vacuous and looks beyond it with the eyes of superior wisdom, it finds itself in a vacuum, and because it is actually only in the present, it is itself mere vacuity. If on the other hand the Idea passes for 'only an Idea,' for something represented in an opinion, philosophy rejects such a view and shows that nothing is actual except the Idea. Once that is granted, the great thing is to apprehend in the show of the temporal and transient the substance which is immanent and the eternal which is present. For since rationality (which is synonymous with the Idea) enters upon external existence simultaneously with its actualization, it emerges with an infinite wealth of forms, shapes, and appearances. Around its heart it throws a motley covering with which consciousness is at home to begin with, a covering which the concept has first to penetrate before it can find the inward pulse and feel it still beating in the outward appearances. But the infinite variety of circumstance which is developed in this externality by the light of the essence glinting in it—this endless material and its organization—this is not the subject matter of philosophy. . . .

This book, then, containing as it does the science of the state, is to be nothing other than the endeavour to apprehend and portray the state as something inherently rational. As a work of philosophy, it must be poles apart from an attempt to construct a state as it ought to be. The instruction which it may contain cannot consist in teaching the state what it ought to be; it can only show how the state, the ethical universe, is to be understood.

> *Hic* Rhodus, *hic* saltus.
> (Here is the rose, dance thou here.)

To comprehend what is, this is the task of philosophy, because what is, is reason. Whatever happens, every individual is a child of his time; so philosophy too is its own time apprehended in thoughts. It is just as absurd to fancy that a philosophy can transcend its contemporary world as it is to fancy that an individual can overleap his own age, jump over Rhodes. If his theory really goes beyond the world as it is and builds an ideal one as it ought to be, that world exists indeed, but only in his opinions, an unsubstantial element where anything you please may, in fancy, be built.

With hardly an alteration, the proverb just quoted would run: What lies between reason as self-conscious mind and reason as an actual world before our eyes, what separates the former from the latter and prevents it from finding satisfaction in the latter, is the fetter of some abstraction or other which has not been liberated [and so transformed] into the concept. To recognize reason as the rose in the cross of the present and thereby to enjoy the present, this is the rational insight which reconciles us to the actual, the reconciliation which philosophy affords to those in whom there has once arisen an inner voice bidding them to comprehend, not only to dwell in what is substantive while still retaining subjective freedom, but also to possess subjective freedom while standing not in anything particular and accidental but in what exists absolutely.

It is this too which constitutes the more concrete meaning of what was described above rather abstractly as the unity of form and content; for form in its most concrete signification is reason as speculative knowing, and content is reason as the substantial essence of actuality, whether ethical or natural. The known identity of these two is the philosophical Idea. It is a sheer obstinacy, the obstinacy which does honour to mankind, to refuse to recognize in conviction anything not ratified by thought. This obstinacy is the characteristic of our epoch, besides being the principle peculiar to Protestantism. What Luther initiated as faith in feeling and in the witness of the spirit, is precisely what spirit, since become more mature, has striven to apprehend in the concept in order to free and so to find itself in the world as it exists to-day. The saying has become famous that 'a half-philosophy leads away from God'—and it is the same half-philosophy that locates knowledge in an 'approximation' to truth—'while true philosophy leads to God'; and the same is true of philosophy and the state. Just as reason is not content with an approximation which, as something 'neither cold nor hot,' it will 'spue out of its mouth,' so it is just as little content with the cold despair which submits to the view that in this earthly life things are truly bad or at best only tolerable, though here they cannot be improved and that this is the only reflection which can keep us at peace with the world: There is less chill in the peace with the world which knowledge supplies.

One word more about giving instruction as to what the world ought to be. Philosophy in any case always comes on the scene too late to give it. As the thought of the world, it appears only when actuality is already there cut and dried after its process of formation has been completed. The teaching of the concept, which is also history's inescapable lesson, is that it is only when actuality is mature that the ideal first appears over against the real and that the ideal apprehends this same real world in its substance and builds it up for itself into the shape of an intellectual realm. When philosophy paints its grey in grey then has a shape of life grown old. By philosophy's grey in grey it cannot be rejuvenated but only understood. The owl of Minerva spreads its wings only with the falling of the dusk. . . .

The subject-matter of the philosophical science of rights is the Idea of right, i.e. the concept of right together with the actualization of that concept.

Philosophy has to do with Ideas, and therefore not with what are commonly dubbed 'mere concepts.' On the contrary, it exposes such concepts as one-sided and false, while showing at the same time that it is the concept alone (not the mere abstract category of the understanding which we often hear called by the name) which has actuality, and further that it gives this actuality to itself. All else, apart from this actuality established through the working of the concept itself, is ephemeral existence, external contingency, opinion, unsubstantial appearance, falsity, illusion, and so forth. The shapes which the concept assumes in the course of its actualization are indispensable for the knowledge of the concept itself. They are the second essential moment of the Idea, in distinction from the first, i.e. from its form, from its mode of being as concept alone.

The science of right is a section of philosophy. Consequently, its task is to develop the Idea—the Idea being the rational factor in any object of study—out of the concept, or, what is the same thing, to look on at the proper immanent development of the thing itself. . . .

Right is positive in general (*a*) when it has the *form* of being valid in a particular state, and this legal authority is the guiding principle for the knowledge of right in this positive form, i.e. for the science of positive law. (*b*) Right in this positive form acquires a positive element in its *content*

(α) through the particular national character of a people, its stage of historical development, and the whole complex of relations connected with the necessities of nature;

(β) because a system of positive law must necessarily involve the application of the universal concept to particular, externally given, characteristics of objects and cases. This application lies outside speculative thought and the development of the concept, and is the subsumption by the Understanding [of the particular under the universal];

(γ) through the finely detailed provisions requisite for actually pronouncing judgement in court.

If inclination, caprice, and the sentiments of the heart are set up in opposition to positive right and the laws, philosophy at least cannot recognize authorities of that sort.—That force and tyranny may be an element in law is accidental to law and has nothing to do with its nature. . . .

This basis of right is, in general, mind; its precise place and point of origin is the will. The will is free, so that freedom is both the substance of right and its goal, while the system of right is the realm of freedom made actual, the world of mind brought forth out of itself like a second nature.

In correspondence with the stages in the development of the Idea of the absolutely free will, the will is

A. immediate; its concept therefore is abstract, namely personality, and its embodiment is an immediate external thing—the sphere of *Abstract* or *Formal Right*;

B. reflected from its external embodiment into itself—it is then characterized as subjective individuality in opposition to the universal. The universal here is characterized as something inward, the good, and also as something outward, a world presented to the will; both these sides of the Idea are here mediated only by each other. This is the Idea in its division or in its existence as particular; and here we have the right of the subjective will in relation to the right of the world and the right of the Idea, though only the Idea implicit—the sphere of *Morality*;

C. the unity and truth of both these abstract moments—the Idea of the good not only apprehended in thought but so realized both in the will reflected into itself and in the external world that freedom exists as substance, as actuality and necessity, no less than as subjective will; this is the Idea in its absolutely universal existence—*Ethical Life*.

But on the same principle the ethical substance is

(*a*) natural mind, the *Family*;

(*b*) in its division and appearance, *Civil Society*;

(*c*) the *State* as freedom, freedom universal and objective even in the free self-subsistence of the particular will. This actual and organic mind (α) of a single nation (β) reveals and actualizes itself through the inter-relation of the particular national minds until (γ) in the process of world-history it reveals and actualizes itself as the universal world-mind whose right is supreme.

The state is the actuality of the ethical Idea. It is ethical mind *qua* the substantial will manifest and revealed to itself, knowing and thinking itself, accomplishing what it knows and in so far as it knows it. The state exists immediately in custom, mediately in individual self-consciousness, knowledge, and activity, while self-consciousness in virtue of its sentiment towards the state finds in the state, as its essence and the end and product of its activity, its substantive freedom.

The *Penates* are inward gods, gods of the underworld; the mind of a nation (Athene for instance) is the divine, knowing and willing itself. Family piety is feeling, ethical behaviour directed by feeling; political virtue is the willing of the absolute end in terms of thought.

The state is absolutely rational inasmuch as it is the actuality of the substantial will which it possesses in the particular self-consciousness once that consciousness has been raised to consciousness of its universality. This substantial unity is an absolute unmoved end in itself, in which freedom comes into its supreme right. On the other hand this final end has supreme right against the individual, whose supreme duty is to be a member of the state.

If the state is confused with civil society, and if its specific end is laid down as the security and protection of property and personal freedom, then the interest of the individuals as such becomes the ultimate end of their association, and it follows that membership of the state is something optional. But the state's relation to the individual is quite different from this. Since the state is mind objectified, it is only as one of its members that the individual himself has objectivity, genuine individuality, and an ethical life. Unification pure and simple is the true content and aim of the individual, and the individual's destiny is the living of a universal life. His further particular satisfaction, activity, and mode of conduct have this substantive and universally valid life as their starting point and their result.

Rationality, taken generally and in the abstract, consists in the thorough-going unity of the universal and the single. Rationality, concrete in the state, consists (*a*) so far as its content is concerned, in the unity of objective freedom (i.e. freedom of the universal or substantial will) and subjective freedom (i.e. freedom of everyone in his knowing and in his volition of particular ends); and consequently, (*b*) so far as its form is concerned, in self-determining action on laws and principles which are thoughts and so universal. This Idea is the absolutely eternal and necessary being of mind.

The state in and by itself is the ethical whole, the actualization of freedom; and it is an absolute end of reason that freedom should be actual. The state is mind on earth and consciously realizing itself there. In nature, on the other hand, mind actualizes itself only as its own other, as mind asleep. Only when it is present in consciousness, when it knows the starting-point must be not individuality, the single self-consciousness, but only the essence of self-consciousness; for whether man knows it or not, this essence is externally realized as a self-subsistent power in which single individuals are only moments. It is God's way in the world that there is the state. (*Es ist der Gang Gottes in der welt, dass der staat ist.*)[1]

The basis of the state is the power of reason actualizing itself as will. In considering the Idea of the state, we must not have our eyes on particular states or on particular institutions. Instead we must consider the Idea, this actual God, by itself. On some principle or other, any state may be shown to be bad, this or that defect may be found in it; and yet, at any rate if one of the mature states of our epoch is in question, it has in it the moments essential to the existence of the state. But since it is easier to find defects than to understand the affirmative, we may readily fall into the mistake of looking at isolated aspects of the state and so forgetting its inward organic life. The state is no ideal work of art; it stands on earth and so in the sphere of caprice, chance, and error, and bad behaviour may disfigure it in many respects. But the ugliest of men, or a criminal, or an invalid, or a cripple, is still always a living man. The affirmative, life, subsists despite his defects, and it is this affirmative factor which is our theme here. . . .

[The] sanctity of marriage and the institutions in which civil society is an appearance of ethical life constitute the stability of the whole, i.e. stability is secured when universal affairs are the affairs of each member in his particular capacity. What is of the utmost importance is that the law of reason should be shot through and through by the law of particular freedom, and that my particular end should become identified with the universal end, or otherwise the state is left in the air. The state is actual only when its members have a feeling of their own self-hood and it is stable only when public and private ends are identical. If has often been said that the end of the state is the happiness of the citizens. That is perfectly true. If all is not well with them, if their subjective aims are not satisfied, if they do not find that the state as such is the means to their satisfaction, then the footing of the state itself is insecure.

The Idea of the state

(*a*) has immediate actuality and is the individual state as a self-dependent organism—the *Constitution* or *Constitutional Law*;

(*b*) passes over into the relation of one state to other states—*International Law*;

(*c*) is the universal Idea as a genus and as an absolute power over individual states—the mind which gives itself its actuality in the process of *World-History*.

Constitutional Law

The state is the actuality of concrete freedom. But concrete freedom consists in this, that personal individuality and its particular interests not only achieve their complete development and gain explicit recognition for their right (as they do in the sphere of the family and civil society) but, for one thing, they also pass over of their own accord into the interest of the universal, and, for another thing, they know and will the universal; they even recognize it as their own substantive mind; they take it as their end and aim and are active in its pursuit. The result is that the universal does not prevail or achieve completion except along with particular interests and through the co-operation of particular knowing and willing; and individuals likewise do not live as private persons for their own ends alone, but in the very act of willing these they will the universal in the light of the universal, and their activity is consciously aimed at none but the universal end. The principle of modern states has prodigious strength and depth because it allows the principle of subjectivity to progress to its culmination in the extreme of self-subsistent personal particularity, and yet at the same time brings it back to the substantive unity and so maintains this unity in the principle of subjectivity itself.

In contrast with the spheres of private rights and private welfare (the family and civil society), the state is from one point of view an external necessity and their higher authority; its nature is such that their laws and interests are subordinate to it and dependent on it. On the other hand, however, it is the end immanent within them, and its strength lies in the unity of its own universal end and aim with the particular interest of individuals, in the fact that individuals have duties to the state in proportion as they have rights against it. . . .

The constitution is rational in so far as the state inwardly differentiates and determines its activity in accordance with the nature of the concept. The result of this is that each of these powers is in itself the totality of the constitution, because each contains the other moments and has them effective in itself, and because the moments, being expressions of the differentiation of the concept, simply abide in their ideality and constitute nothing but a single individual whole. . . .

The state as a political entity is thus cleft into three substantive divisions:

(a) the power to determine and establish the universal—the Legislature;

(b) the power to subsume single cases and the spheres of particularity under the universal—the Executive;

(c) the power of subjectivity, as the will with the power of ultimate decision—the Crown. In the crown, the different powers are found into an individual unity which is thus at once the apex and basis of the whole, i.e. of constitutional monarchy.

The development of the state to constitutional monarchy is the achievement of the modern world, a world in which the substantial Idea has won the infinite form [of subjectivity]. The history of this inner deepening of the world mind—or in other words this free maturation in course of which the Idea, realizing rationality in the external, releases its moments (and they are only its moments) from itself as totalities, and just for that reason still retains them in the ideal unity of the concept—the history of this genuine formation of ethical life is the content of the whole course of world-history. . . .

Note

1. Translation modified by the editor.

24

Karl Marx
Selections

Karl Marx (1818–1883) was born in Trier, Prussia (in today's Germany) and studied law and philosophy as a young man. He became involved in democratic opposition politics and eventually became an exile in London. His mature theories drew on the dialectical philosophy of G.W.F. Hegel, French utopian socialism, and British political economy to formulate a theory in which history is driven by class conflict. In contemporary capitalism, this was a struggle between the bourgeoisie, the minority of the population who own the means of production of society, and the proletariat, the vast majority of the population who own nothing but their labor power which they sell to the bourgeoisie for what Marx believed necessarily exploitative wages. Marx argued that the proletariat would eventually overthrow capitalism and create a classless, Socialist society governed by the principle, "From each according to his abilities, to each according to his needs." His most famous works are The Communist Manifesto *(1847), written with his lifelong colleague Friedrich Engels, and* Capital, *a three-volume work. (The first volume was published in 1867 and the others after his death.)*

A CONTRIBUTION TO THE CRITIQUE OF POLITICAL ECONOMY (1859)

. . . I am omitting a general introduction which I had jotted down because on closer reflection any anticipation of results still to be proved appears to me to be disturbing, and the reader who on the whole desires to follow me must be resolved to ascend from the particular to the general. A few indications concerning the course of my own politico-economic studies may, on the other hand, appear in place here.

I was taking up law, which discipline, however, I only pursued a subordinate subject along with philosophy and history. In the year 1842–44, as editor of the *Rheinische Zeitung,*[1] I experienced for the first time the embarrassment of having to take part in discussion on so-called material interests. The proceedings of the Rhenish landtag on thefts of wood and parcelling of landed property, the official polemic which Herr von Schaper, then *Oberpräsident* of the Rhine Province, opened against the *Rheinische Zeitung* on the conditions of the Moselle peasantry, and finally debates on free trade and protective tariffs provided the first occasions for occupying myself with economic questions. On the other hand, at that time when the good will "to go further" greatly outweighed knowledge of the subject, a philosophically weakly tinged echo of French socialism and communism made itself audible in the *Rheinische Zeitung*. I declared myself against this amateurism, but frankly confessed at the same time in a controversy with the *Allgemeine Augsburger Zeitung*[2] that my previous studies did not permit me even to venture any judgement on the content of the French tendencies. Instead, I eagerly seized on the illusion of the managers of the *Rheinische Zeitung*, who thought that by a weaker attitude on the part of the paper they could secure a remission of the death sentence passed upon it, to withdraw from the public stage into the study.

The first work which I undertook for a solution of the doubts which assailed me was a critical review of the Hegelian philosophy of right, a work the introduction to which appeared in 1844 in the *Deutsch-Französische Jahrbücher*,[3] published in Paris. My investigation led to the result that legal relations as well as forms of state are to be grasped neither from themselves nor from the so-called general development of the human mind, but rather have their roots in the material conditions of life, the sum total of which Hegel, following the example of the Englishmen and Frenchmen of the eighteenth century, combines under the name of "civil society," that, however, the anatomy of civil society is to be sought in political economy. The investigation of the latter, which I began in Paris, I continued in Brussels, whither I had emigrated in consequence of an expulsion order of M. Guizot. The general result at which I arrived and which, once won, served as a guiding thread for my studies, can be briefly formulated as follows: In the social production of their life, men enter into definite relations that are indispensable and independent of their will, relations of production which correspond to a definite stage of development of their material productive forces. The sum total of these relations of production constitutes the economic structure of society, the real foundation, on which rises a legal and political superstructure and to which correspond definite forms of social consciousness. The mode of production of material life conditions the social, political and intellectual life process in general. It is not the consciousness of men that determines their being, but, on the contrary, their social being that determines their consciousness. At a certain stage of their development, the material productive forces of society come in conflict with the existing relations of production, or—what is but a legal expression for the same thing—with the property relations within which they have been at work hitherto. From forms of development of the productive forces these relations turn into their fetters. Then begins an epoch of social revolution. With the change of the economic foundation the entire immense superstructure is more or less readily transformed. In considering such transformations a distinction should always be made between the material transformation of the economic conditions of production, which can be determined with the precision of natural science, and the legal, political, religious, aesthetic or philosophic—in short, ideological forms in which men become conscious of this conflict and fight it out. Just as our opinion of an individual is not based on what he thinks of himself, so can we not judge of such a period of transformation by its own consciousness; on the contrary, this consciousness must be explained rather from the contradictions of material life, from the existing conflict between the social productive forces and the relations of production. No social order ever perishes before all the productive forces for which there is room in it have developed; and new, higher relations of production never appear before the material conditions of their existence have matured in the womb of the old society itself. Therefore mankind always sets itself only such tasks as it can solve; since, looking at the matter more closely, it will always be found that the task itself arises only when the material conditions for its solution already exist or are at least in the process of formation. In broad outlines Asiatic, ancient, feudal, and modern bourgeois modes of production can be designated as progressive epochs in the economic formation of society. The bourgeois relations of production are the last antagonistic form of the social process of production—antagonistic not in the sense of individual antagonism, but of one arising from the social conditions of life of the individuals; at the same time the productive forces developing in the womb of bourgeois society create the material conditions for the solution of that antagonism. This social formation brings, therefore, the prehistory of human society to a close.

Frederick Engels, with whom, since the appearance of his brilliant sketch on the criticism of the economic categories (in the *Deutsch-Französische Jahrbücher*), I maintained a constant exchange of ideas by correspondence, had by another road (compare his *The Condition of the Working Class in England in 1844*) arrived at the same result as I, and when in the spring of 1845 he also settled in Brussels, we resolved to work out in common the opposition of our view to the ideological view of German philosophy, in fact, to settle accounts with our erstwhile philosophical conscience. The resolve was carried out in the form of a criticism of post-Hegelian philosophy. The manuscript, two large octavo volumes, had long reached its place of publication in Westphalia when we received the news that altered circumstances did not allow of its being printed. We abandoned the manuscript to the gnawing criticism of the mice all the more willingly as we had achieved our main purpose—self-clarification. Of the scattered works in which we put our views before the public at that time, now from one aspect, now from another, I will mention only the *Manifesto of the Communist Party*, jointly written by Engels and myself, and *Discours sur le libre échange* published by me. The decisive points of our view were first scientifically, although only polemically, indicated in my work published in 1847 and directed against Proudhon: *Misère de la Philosophie*, etc. A dissertation written in German on *Wage Labour*, in which I put together my lectures on this subject delivered in the Brussels German Workers' Society, was interrupted, while being printed, by the February Revolution and my consequent forcible removal from Belgium.

The editing of the *Neue Rheinische Zeitung* in 1848 and 1849, and the subsequent events, interrupted my economic studies which could only be resumed in the year 1850 in London. The enormous material for the history of political economy which is accumulated in the British Museum, the favourable vantage point afforded by London for the observation of bourgeois society, and finally the new stage of development upon which the latter appeared to have entered with the discovery of gold in California and Australia, determined me to begin afresh from the very beginning and to work through the new material critically. These studies led partly of themselves into apparently quite remote subjects on which I had to dwell for a shorter or longer period. Especially, however, was the time at my disposal curtailed by the imperative necessity of earning my living. My contributions, during eight years now, to the first English-American newspaper, the *New York Tribune*, compelled an extraordinary scattering of my studies, since I occupy myself with newspaper correspondence proper only in exceptional cases. However, articles on striking economic events in England and on the Continent constituted so considerable a part of my contributions that I was compelled to make myself familiar with practical details which lie outside the sphere of the actual science of political economy.

This sketch of the course of my studies in the sphere of political economy is intended only to show that my views, however they may be judged and however little they coincide with the interested prejudices of the ruling classes, are the results of conscientious investigation lasting many years. But at the entrance to science, as at the entrance to hell, the demand must be posted:

Qui se convien lasciare ogni sospetto;
Ogni viltà convien che qui sia morta.[4]

Notes

1. A radical newpaper Marx edited in the early 1840s.
2. Marx refers to his own article "Communism and the *Augsburg General Journal.*"
3. A revolutionary communist publication Marx published in 1844.
4. Here all mistrust must be abandoned
   And here must perish every craven thought.
                    (Dante, *The Divine Comedy*)

ESTRANGED LABOUR (1844)

We have proceeded from the premises of political economy. We have accepted its language and its laws. We presupposed private property, the separation of labour, capital and land, and of wages, profit of capital and rent of land—likewise division of labour, competition, the concept of exchange-value, etc. On the basis of political economy itself, in its own words, we have shown that the worker sinks to the level of a commodity and becomes indeed the most wretched of commodities; that the wretchedness of the worker is in inverse proportion to the power and magnitude of his production; that the necessary result of competition is the accumulation of capital in a few hands, and thus the restoration of monopoly in a more terrible form; that finally the distinction between capitalist and land-rentier, like that between the tiller of the soil and the factory-worker, disappears and that the whole of society must fall apart into the two classes—the property-*owners* and the propertyless *workers*.

Political economy proceeds from the fact of private property, but it does not explain it to us. It expresses in general, abstract formulae the *material* process through which private property actually passes, and these formulae it then takes for *laws*. It does not *comprehend* these laws—i.e., it does not demonstrate how they arise from the very nature of private property. Political economy does not disclose the source of the division between labour and capital, and between capital and land. When, for example, it defines the relationship of wages to profit, it takes the interest of the capitalists to be the ultimate cause; i.e., it takes for granted what it is supposed to evolve. Similarly, competition comes in everywhere. It is explained from external circumstances. As to how far these external and apparently fortuitous circumstances are but the expression of a necessary course of development, political economy teaches us nothing. We have seen how, to it, exchange itself appears to be a fortuitous fact. The only wheels which political economy sets in motion are *avarice* and the *war amongst the avaricious—competition*.

Precisely because political economy does not grasp the connections within the movement, it was possible to counterpose, for instance, the doctrine of competition to the doctrine of monopoly, the doctrine of craft-liberty to the doctrine of the corporation, the doctrine of the division of landed property to the doctrine of the big estate—for competition, craft-liberty and the division of landed property were explained and comprehended only as fortuitous, premeditated and violent consequences of monopoly, the corporation, and feudal property, not as their necessary, inevitable and natural consequences.

Now, therefore, we have to grasp the essential connection between private property, avarice, and the separation of labour, capital and landed property; between exchange and competition, value and the devaluation of men, monopoly and competition, etc.; the connection between this whole estrangement and the *money*-system.

Do not let us go back to a fictitious primordial condition as the political economist does, when he tries to explain. Such a primordial condition explains nothing. He merely pushes the question away into a grey nebulous distance. He assumes in the form of fact, of an event, what he is supposed to deduce—namely, the necessary relationship between two things—between, for example, division of labour and exchange. Theology in the same way explains the origin of evil by the fall of man: that is, it assumes as a fact, in historical form, what has to be explained.

We proceed from an *actual* economic fact.

The worker becomes all the poorer the more wealth he produces, the more his production increases in power and range. The worker becomes an even cheaper commodity the more commodities he creates. With the *increasing value* of the world of things proceeds in direct proportion the *devaluation* of the world of men. Labour produces not only commodities; it produces itself and the worker as a *commodity*—and does so in the proportion in which it produces commodities generally.

This fact expresses merely that the object which labour produces—labour's product—confronts it as *something alien*, as a *power independent* of the producer. The product of labour is labour which has been congealed in an object, which has become material: it is the *objectification* of labour. Labour's realization is its objectification. In the conditions dealt with by political economy this realization of labour appears as *loss of reality* for the workers; objectification as *loss of the object* and *object-bondage*; appropriation as *estrangement*, as *alienation*.

So much does labour's realization appear as loss of reality that the worker loses reality to the point of starving to death. So much does objectification appear as loss of the object that the worker is robbed of the objects most necessary not only for his life but for his work. Indeed, labour itself becomes an object which he can get hold of only with the greatest effort and with the most irregular interruptions. So much does the appropriation of the object appear as estrangement that the more objects the worker produces the fewer can he possess and the more he falls under the dominion of his product, capital.

All these consequences are contained in the definition that the worker is related to the *product of his labour* as to an *alien* object. For on this premise it is clear that the more the worker spends himself, the more powerful the alien objective world becomes which he creates over-against himself, the poorer he himself—his inner world—becomes, the less belongs to him as his own. It is the same in religion. The more man puts into God, the less he retains in himself. The worker puts his life into the object; but now his life no longer belongs to him but to the object. Hence, the greater this activity, the greater is the worker's lack of objects. Whatever the product of his labour is, he is not. Therefore the greater this product, the less is he himself. The *alienation* of the worker in his product means not only that his labour becomes an object, an *external* existence, but that it exists *outside him*, independently, as something alien to him, and that it becomes a power of its own confronting him; it means that the life which he has conferred on the object confronts him as something hostile and alien.

Let us now look more closely at the *objectification*, at the production of the worker; and therein at the *estrangement*, the *loss* of the object, his product.

The worker can create nothing without *nature*, without the *sensuous external world*. It is the material on which his labor is manifested, in which it is active, from which and by means of which it produces.

But just as nature provides labor with the *means of life* in the sense that labour cannot *live* without objects on which to operate, on the other hand, it also provides the *means of life* in the more restricted sense—i.e., the means for the physical subsistence of the *worker* himself.

Thus the more the worker by his labour *appropriates* the external world, sensuous nature, the more he deprives himself of *means of life* in the double respect: first, that the sensuous external world more and more ceases to be an object belonging to his labour—to be his labour's *means of life*; and secondly, that it more and more ceases to be *means of life* in the immediate sense, means for the physical subsistence of the worker.

Thus in this double respect the worker becomes a slave of his object, first, in that he receives an *object of labour*, i.e., in that he receives *work*; and secondly, in that he receives *means of subsistence*. Therefore, it enables him to exist, first, as a *worker*; and, second, as a *physical subject*. The extremity of this bondage is that it is only as a *worker* that he continues to maintain himself as a *physical subject*, and that it is only as a *physical subject* that he is a *worker*.

(The laws of political economy express the estrangement of the worker in his object thus: the more the worker produces, the less he has to consume; the more values he creates, the more valueless, the more unworthy he becomes; the better formed his product, the more deformed becomes the worker; the more civilized his object, the more barbarous becomes the worker; the mightier labour becomes, the more powerless becomes the worker; the more ingenious labour becomes, the duller becomes the worker and the more he becomes nature's bondsman.)

Political economy conceals the estrangement inherent in the nature of labour by not considering the direct relationship between the worker (labour) *and production*. It is true that labour produces for the rich wonderful things—but for the worker it produces privation. It produces palaces—but for the worker, hovels. It produces beauty—but for the workers, deformity. It replaces labour by machines—but some of the workers it throws back to a barbarous type of labour, and the other workers it turns into machines. It produces intelligence—but for the worker idiocy, cretinism.

The direct relationship of labour to its produce is the relationship of the worker to the objects of his production. The relationship of the man of means to the objects of production and to production itself is only a *consequence* of this first relationship—and confirms it. We shall consider this other aspect later.

When we ask, then, what is the essential relationship of labour we are asking about the relationship of the *worker* to production.

Till now we have been considering the estrangement, the alienation of the worker only in one of its aspects, i.e, the worker's *relationship to the products of his labour*. But the estrangement is manifested not only in the result but in the *act of production*—within the *producing activity* itself. How would the worker come to face the product of his activity as a stranger, were it not that in the very act of production he was estranging himself from himself? The product is after all but the summary of the activity of production. If then the product of labour is alienation, production itself must be active alienation, the alienation of activity, the activity of alienation. In the estrangement of the object of labour is merely summarized the estrangement, the alienation, in the activity of labour itself.

What, then, constitutes the alienation of labour?

First, the fact that labour is *external* to the worker, i.e., it does not belong to his essential being; that in his work, therefore, he does not affirm himself but denies himself, does not feel content but unhappy, does not develop freely his physical and mental energy but mortifies his body and ruins his mind. The worker therefore only feels himself outside his work, and in his work feels outside himself. He is at home when he is not working, and when he is working he is not at home. His labour is therefore not voluntary, but coerced; it is *forced labour*. It is therefore not the satisfaction of a need; it is merely a *means* to satisfy needs external to it. Its alien character emerges clearly in the fact that as soon as no physical or other compulsion exists, labour is shunned like the plague. External labour, labour in which man alienates himself, is a labour of self-sacrifice, of mortification. Lastly, the external character of labour for the worker appears in the fact that it is not his own, but someone else's, that it does not belong to him, that in it he belongs, not to himself, but to another. Just as in religion the spontaneous activity of the human imagination, of the human brain and the human heart, operates independently of the individual—that is, operates on him as an alien, divine or diabolical activity—in the same way the worker's activity is not his spontaneous activity. It belongs to another; it is the loss of his self.

As a result, therefore, man (the worker) no longer feels himself to be freely active in any but his animal functions—eating, drinking, procreating, or at most in his dwelling and in dressing-up, etc.; and in his human functions he no longer feels himself to be anything but an animal. What is animal becomes human and what is human becomes animal.

Certainly eating, drinking, procreating, etc., are also genuinely human functions. But in the abstraction which separates them from the sphere of all other human activity and turns them into sole and ultimate ends, they are animal.

We have considered the act of estranging practical human activity, labour, in two of its aspects. (1) The relation of the worker to the *product of labour* as an alien object exercising power over him. This relation is at the same time the relation to the sensuous external world, to the objects of nature as an alien world antagonistically opposed to him. (2) The relation of labour to the *act of production* within the *labour* process. This relation is the relation of the worker to his own activity as an alien activity not belonging to him; it is activity as suffering, strength as weakness, begetting as emasculating, the worker's *own* physical and mental energy, his personal life or what is life other than activity—as an activity which is turned against him, neither depends on nor belongs to him. Here we have *self-estrangement*, as we had previously the estrangement of the *thing*.

We have yet a third aspect of *estranged labour* to deduce from the two already considered.

Man is a species being, not only because in practice and in theory he adopts the species as his object (his own as well as those of other things), but—and this is only another way of expressing it—but also because he treats himself as the actual, living species; because he treats himself as a *universal* and therefore a free being.

The life of the species, both in man and in animals, consists physically in the fact that man (like an animal) lives on inorganic nature; and the more universal man is compared with an animal, the more universal is the sphere of inorganic nature on which he lives. Just as plants, animals, stones, the air, light, etc., constitute a part of human consciousness in the realm of theory, partly as objects of natural science, partly as objects of art—his spiritual inorganic nature, spiritual nourishment which he must first prepare to make it palatable and digestible—so too in the realm of practice they constitute a part of human life and human activity. Physically man lives only on these products of nature, whether they appear in the form of food, heating, clothes, a dwelling, or whatever it may be. The universality of man is in practice manifested precisely in the universality which makes all nature his *inorganic* body—both inasmuch as nature is (1) his direct means of life, and (2) the material, the object, and the instrument of his life-activity. Nature is man's *inorganic body*—nature, that is, in so far as it is not itself the human body. Man *lives* on nature—means that nature is his *body*, with which he must remain in continuous intercourse if he is not to die. That man's physical and spiritual life is linked to nature means simply that nature is linked to itself, for man is a part of nature.

In estranging from man (1) nature, and (2) himself, his own active functions, his life-activity, estranged labour estranges the *species* from man. It turns for him the *life of the species* into a means of individual life. First it estranges the life of the species and individual life, and secondly it makes individual life in its abstract form the purpose of the life of the species, likewise in its abstract and estranged form.

For in the first place labour, *life-activity*, *productive life* itself, appears to man merely as a *means* of satisfying a need—the need to maintain the physical existence. Yet the productive life is the life of the species. It is life-engendering life. The whole character of a species—its species character—is contained in the character of its life-activity; and free, conscious activity is man's species character. Life itself appears only as *a means to life*.

The animal is immediately identical with its life-activity. It does not distinguish itself from it. It is its *life-activity*. Man makes his life-activity itself the object of his will and of his consciousness. He has conscious life-activity. It is not a determination with which he directly merges. Conscious life-activity directly distinguishes man from animal life-activity. It is just because of this that he is a species being. Or it is only because he is a species being that he is a Conscious Being, i.e., that his own life is an object for him. Only because of that is his activity free activity. Estranged labour reverses this relationship, so that it is just because man is a conscious being that he makes his life-activity, his *essential* being, a mere means to his *existence*.

In creating an *objective world* by his practical activity, in *working-up* inorganic nature, man proves himself a conscious species being, i.e., as a being that treats the species as its own essential being, or that treats itself as a species being. Admittedly animals also produce. They build themselves nests, dwellings, like the bees, beavers, ants, etc. But an animal only produces what it immediately needs for itself or its young. It produces one-sidedly, whilst man produces universally. It produces only under the dominion of immediate physical need, whilst man produces even when he is free from physical need and only truly produces in freedom therefrom. An animal produces only itself, whilst man reproduces the whole of nature. An animal's product belongs immediately to its physical body, whilst man freely confronts his product. An animal forms things in accordance with the standard and the need of the species to which it belongs, whilst man knows how to produce in accordance with the standard of every species, and knows how to apply everywhere the inherent standard to the object. Man therefore also forms things in accordance with the laws of beauty.

It is just in the working-up of the objective world, therefore, that man first really proves himself to be a *species being*. This production is his active species life. Through and because of this production, nature appears as *his* work and his reality. The object of labour is, therefore, the *objectification of man's species life*: for he duplicates himself not only, as in consciousness, intellectually, but also actively, in reality, and therefore he contemplates himself in a world that he has created. In tearing away from man the object of his production, therefore, estranged labour tears from him his *species life*, his real species objectivity, and transforms his advantage over animals into the disadvantage that his inorganic body, nature, is taken from him.

Similarly, in degrading spontaneous activity, free activity, to a means, estranged labour makes man's species life a means to his physical existence.

The consciousness which man has of his species is thus transformed by estrangement in such a way that the species life becomes for him a means.

Estranged labour turns thus:

(3) *Man's species being*, both nature and his spiritual species property, into a being *alien* to him, into a *means* to his *individual existence*. It estranges man's own body from him, as it does external nature and his spiritual essence, his *human* being.

(4) An immediate consequence of the fact that man is estranged from the product of his labour, from his life-activity, from his species being is the *estrangement of man* from *man*. If a man is confronted by himself, he is confronted by the *other* man. What applies to a man's relation to his work, to the product of his labour and to himself, also holds of a man's relation to the other man, and to the other man's labour and object of labour.

In fact, the proposition that man's species nature is estranged from him means that one man is estranged from the other, as each of them is from man's essential nature.

The estrangement of man, and in fact every relationship in which man stands to himself, is first realized and expressed in the relationship in which a man stands to other men.

Hence within the relationship of estranged labour each man views the other in accordance with the standard and the position in which he finds himself as a worker.

We took our departure from a fact of political economy—the estrangement of the worker and his production. We have formulated the concept of this fact—*estranged, alienated* labour. We have analysed this concept—hence analysing merely a fact of political economy.

Let us now see, further, how in real life the concept of estranged, alienated labour must express and present itself.

If the product of labour is alien to me, if it confronts me as an alien power, to whom, then, does it belong?

If my own activity does not belong to me, if it is an alien, a coerced activity, to whom, then, does it belong?

To a being *other* than me.

Who is this being?

The *gods*? To be sure, in the earliest times the principal production (for example, the building of temples, etc., in Egypt, India and Mexico) appears to be in the service of the gods, and the product belongs to the gods. However, the gods on their own were never the lords of labour. No more was *nature*. And what a contradiction it would be if, the more man subjugated nature by his labour and the more the miracles of the gods were rendered superfluous by the miracles of industry, the more man were to renounce the joy of production and the enjoyment of the produce in favour of these powers.

The *alien* being, to whom labour and the produce of labour belongs, in whose service labour is done and for whose benefit the produce of labour is provided, can only be *man* himself.

If the product of labour does not belong to the worker, if it confronts him as an alien power, this can only be because it belongs to some *other man than the worker*. If the worker's activity is a torment to him, to another it must be *delight* and his life's joy. Not the gods, not nature, but only man himself can be this alien power over man.

We must bear in mind the above-stated proposition that man's relation to himself only becomes *objective* and *real* for him through his relation to the other man. Thus, if the product of his labour, his labour *objectified*, is for him an *alien*, hostile, powerful object independent of him, then his position towards it is such that someone else is master of this object, someone who is alien, hostile, powerful, and independent of him. If his own activity is to him an unfree activity, then he is treating it as activity performed in the service, under the dominion, the coercion and the yoke of another man.

Every self-estrangement of man from himself and from nature appears in the relation in which he places himself and nature to men other than and differentiated from himself. For this reason religious self-estrangement necessarily appears in the relationship of the layman to the priest, or again to a mediator, etc., since we are here dealing with the intellectual world. In the real practical world self-estrangement can only become manifest through the real practical relationship to other men. The medium through which estrangement takes place is itself *practical*. Thus through estranged labour man not only engenders his relationship to the object and to the act of production as to powers that are alien and hostile to him; he also engenders the relationship in which other men stand to his production and to his product, and the relationship in which he stands to these other men. Just as he begets his own production as the loss of his reality, as his punishment; just as he begets his own product as a loss, as a product not belonging to him; so he begets the dominion for the one who does not produce over production and over the product. Just as he estranges from himself his own activity, so he confers to the stranger activity which is not his own.

Till now we have only considered this relationship from the standpoint of the worker and later we shall be considering it also from the standpoint of the non-worker.

Through *estranged, alienated labour*, then, the worker produces the relationship to this labour of a man alien to labour and standing outside it. The relationship of the worker to labour engenders the relation to it of the capitalist, or whatever one chooses to call the master of labour. *Private property* is thus the product, the result, the necessary consequence, of *alienated labour*, of the external relation of the worker to nature and to himself.

Private property thus results by analysis from the concept of *alienated labour*—i.e., of *alienated man*, of estranged labour, of estranged life, of *estranged* man.

True, it is as a result of the *movement of private property* that we have obtained the concept of *alienated labour* (of *alienated life*) from political economy. But on analysis of this concept it becomes clear that though private property appears to be the source, the cause of alienated labour, it is really its consequence, just as the gods *in the beginning* are not the cause but the effect of man's intellectual confusion. Later this relationship becomes reciprocal.

Only at the very culmination of the development of private property does this, its secret, re-emerge, namely, that on the one hand it is the *product* of alienated labour, and that secondly it is the *means* by which labour alienates itself, the *realization of this alienation.*

This exposition immediately sheds light on various hitherto unsolved conflicts.

(1) Political economy starts from labour as the real soul of production; yet to labour it gives nothing, and to private property everything. From this contradiction Proudhon has concluded in favour of labour and against private property. We understand, however, that this apparent contradiction is the contradiction of *estranged labour* with itself, and that political economy has merely formulated the laws of estranged labour.

We also understand, therefore, that *wages* and *private property* are identical: where the product, the object of labour pays for labour itself, the wage is but a necessary consequence of labour's estrangement, for after all in the wage of labour, labour does not appear as an end in itself but as the servant of the wage. We shall develop this point later, and meanwhile will only deduce some conclusions.

A *forcing-up of wages* (disregarding all other difficulties, including the fact that it would only be by force, too, that the higher wages, being an anomaly, could be maintained) would therefore be nothing but *better payment for the slave,* and would not conquer either for the worker or for labour their human status and dignity.

Indeed, even the *equality of wages* demanded by Proudhon only transforms the relationships of the present-day worker to his labour into the relationship of all men to labour. Society is then conceived as an abstract capitalist.

Wages are a direct consequence of estranged labour, and estranged labour is the direct cause of private property. The downfall of the one aspect must therefore mean the downfall of the other.

(2) From the relationship of estranged labour to private property it further follows that the emancipation of society from private property, etc., from servitude, is expressed in the *political* form of the *emancipation of the workers*; not that *their* emancipation alone was at stake but because the emancipation of the workers contains universal human emancipation—and it contains this, because the whole

of human servitude is involved in the relation of the worker to production, and every relation of servitude is but a modification and consequence of this relation.

Just as we have found the concept of *private property* from the concept of *estranged, alienated labour* by *analysis*, in the same way every *category* of political economy can be evolved with the help of these two factors; and we shall find again in each category, e.g., trade, competition, capital, money, only a *definite* and *developed expression* of the first foundations.

Before considering this configuration, however, let us try to solve two problems.

(1) To define the general *nature of private property*, as it has arisen as a result of estranged labour, in its relation to *truly human, social property.*

(2) We have accepted the *estrangement of labour, its alienation*, as a fact, and we have analysed this fact. How, we now ask, does *man* come to *alienate*, to estrange, *his labour?* How is this estrangement rooted in the nature of human development? We have already gone a long way to the solution of this problem by *transforming* the question as to the *origin of private property* into the question as to the relation of *alienated labour* to the course of humanity's development. For when one speaks of *private property*, one thinks of being concerned with something external to man. When one speaks of labour, one is directly concerned with man himself. This new formulation of the question already contains its solution.

As to (1): The general nature of private property and its relation to truly human property.

Alienated labour has resolved itself for us into two elements which mutually condition one another, or which are but different expressions of one and the same relationship. *Appropriation* appears as *estrangement*, as *alienation*; and *alienation* appears as *appropriation, estrangement* as true *enfranchisement.*

We have considered the one side—*alienated* labour in relation to the *worker* himself, i.e., the *relation of alienated labour to itself.* The *property-relation of the non-worker to the worker and to labour* we have found as the product, the necessary outcome of this relation of alienated labour. *Private property*, as the material, summary expression of alienated labour, embraces both relations—the *relation of the worker to work, to the product of his labour and to the non-worker*, and the relation of the *non-worker to the worker and to the product of his labour.*

Having seen that in relation to the worker who *appropriates* nature by means of his labour, this appropriation *appears* as estrangement, his own spontaneous activity as activity for another and as activity of another, vitality as a sacrifice of life, production of the object as loss of the object to an alien power, to an *alien* person—we shall now consider the relation to the worker, to labour and its object of this person who is *alien* to labour and the worker.

First it has to be noticed, that everything which appears in the worker as an *activity of alienation, of estrangement*, appears in the non-worker as *a state of alienation, of estrangement.*

Secondly, that the worker's *real, practical attitude* in production and to the product (as a state of mind) appears in the non-worker confronting him as a *theoretical* attitude.

Thirdly, the non-worker does everything against the worker which the worker does against himself; but he does not do against himself what he does against the worker. . . .

THE COMMUNIST MANIFESTO (1848)

A spectre is haunting Europe—the spectre of Communism. All the powers of old Europe have entered into a holy alliance to exorcise this spectre: Pope and Czar, Metternich and Guizot, French Radicals and German police-spies.

Where is the party in opposition that has not been decried as Communistic by its opponents in power? Where the Opposition that has not hurled back the branding reproach of Communism, against the more advanced opposition parties, as well as against its reactionary adversaries?

Two things result from this fact.

I. Communism is already acknowledged by all European Powers to be itself a Power.

II. It is high time that Communists should openly, in the face of the whole world, publish their views, their aims, their tendencies, and meet this nursery tale of the Spectre of Communism with a Manifesto of the party itself.

To this end, Communists of various nationalities have assembled in London, and sketched the following Manifesto, to be published in the English, French, German, Italian, Flemish and Danish languages.

Bourgeois and Proletarians

The history of all hitherto existing society is the history of class struggles.

Freeman and slave, patrician and plebeian, lord and serf, guild-master and journeyman, in a word, oppressor and oppressed, stood in constant opposition to one another, carried on an uninterrupted, now hidden, now open fight, a fight that each time ended, either in a revolutionary re-constitution of society at large, or in the common ruin of the contending classes.

In the earlier epochs of history, we find almost everywhere a complicated arrangement of society into various orders, a manifold gradation of social rank. In ancient Rome we have patricians, knights, plebeians, slaves; in the Middle Ages, feudal lords, vassals, guild-masters, journeymen, apprentices, serfs; in almost all of these classes, again, subordinate gradations.

The modern bourgeois society that has sprouted from the ruins of feudal society has not done away with class antagonisms. It has but established new classes, new conditions of oppression, new forms of struggle in place of the old ones.

Our epoch, the epoch of the bourgeoisie, possesses, however, this distinctive feature: it has simplified the class antagonisms: Society as a whole is more and more splitting up into two great hostile camps, into two great classes directly facing each other: Bourgeoisie and Proletariat.

From the serfs of the Middle Ages sprang the chartered burghers of the earliest towns. From these burgesses the first elements of the bourgeoisie were developed.

The discovery of America, the rounding of the Cape, opened up fresh ground for the rising bourgeoisie. The East-Indian and Chinese markets, the colonisation of America, trade with the colonies, the increase in the means of exchange and in commodities generally, gave to commerce, to navigation, to industry, an impulse never before known, and thereby, to the revolutionary element in the tottering feudal society, a rapid development.

The feudal system of industry, under which industrial production was monopolised by closed guilds, now no longer sufficed for the growing wants of the new markets. The manufacturing system took its place. The guild-masters were pushed on one side by the manufacturing middle class; division of labour between the different corporate guilds vanished in the face of division of labour in each single workshop.

Meantime the markets kept ever growing, the demand ever rising. Even manufacture no longer sufficed. Thereupon, steam and machinery revolutionised industrial production. The place of manufacture was taken by the giant, Modern Industry, the place of the industrial middle class, by industrial millionaires, the leaders of whole industrial armies, the modern bourgeois.

Modern industry has established the world-market, for which the discovery of America paved the way. This market has given an immense development to commerce, to navigation, to communication by land. This development has, in its turn, reacted on the extension of industry; and in proportion as industry, commerce, navigation, railways extended, in the same proportion the bourgeoisie developed, increased its capital, and pushed into the background every class handed down from the Middle Ages.

We see, therefore, how the modern bourgeoisie is itself the product of a long course of development, of a series of revolutions in the modes of production and of exchange.

Each step in the development of the bourgeoisie was accompanied by a corresponding political advance of that class. An oppressed class under the sway of the feudal nobility, an armed and self-governing association in the mediaeval commune, here independent urban republic (as in Italy and Germany), there taxable "third estate" of the monarchy (as in France), afterwards, in the period of manufacture proper, serving either the semi-feudal or the absolute monarchy as a counterpoise against the nobility, and, in fact, corner-stone of the great monarchies in general, the bourgeoisie has at last, since the establishment of Modern Industry and of the world-market, conquered for itself, in the modern representative State, exclusive political sway. The executive of the modern State is but a committee for managing the common affairs of the whole bourgeoisie.

The bourgeoisie, historically, has played a most revolutionary part.

The bourgeoisie, wherever it has got the upper hand, has put an end to all feudal, patriarchal, idyllic relations. It has pitilessly torn asunder the motley feudal ties that bound man to his "natural superiors," and has left remaining no other nexus between man and man than naked self-interest, than callous "cash payment." It has drowned the most heavenly ecstasies of religious fervour, of chivalrous enthusiasm, of philistine sentimentalism, in the icy water of egotistical calculation. It has resolved personal worth into exchange value, and in place of the numberless indefeasible chartered freedoms, has set up that single, unconscionable freedom—Free Trade. In one word, for exploitation, veiled by religious and political illusions, it has substituted naked, shameless, direct, brutal exploitation.

The bourgeoisie has stripped of its halo every occupation hitherto honoured and looked up to with reverent awe. It has converted the physician, the lawyer, the priest, the poet, the man of science, into its paid wage-labourers.

The bourgeoisie has torn-away from the family its sentimental veil, and has reduced the family relation to a mere money relation.

The bourgeoisie has disclosed how it came to pass that the brutal display of vigour in the Middle Ages, which Reactionists so much admire, found its fitting complement in the most slothful indolence. It has been the first to show what man's activity can bring about. It has accomplished wonders far surpassing Egyptian pyramids, Roman aqueducts, the Gothic cathedrals; it has conducted expeditions that put in the shade all former Exoduses of nations and crusades.

The bourgeoisie cannot exist without constantly revolutionising the instruments of production, and thereby the relations of production, and with them the whole relations of society. Conservation of the old modes of production in unaltered form, was, on the contrary, the first condition of existence for all earlier industrial classes. Constant revolutionising of production, uninterrupted disturbance of all social conditions, everlasting uncertainty and agitation distinguish the bourgeois epoch from all earlier ones. All fixed, fast-frozen relations, with their train of ancient and venerable prejudices and opinions, are swept away, all new-formed ones become antiquated before they can ossify. All that is solid melts into air, all that is holy is profaned, and man is at last compelled to face with sober senses, his real conditions of life, and his relations with his kind.

The need of a constantly expanding market for its products chases the bourgeoisie over the whole surface of the globe. It must nestle everywhere, settle everywhere, establish connexions everywhere.

The bourgeoisie has through its exploitation of the world-market given a cosmopolitan character to production and consumption in every country. To the great chagrin of Reactionists, it has drawn from under the feet of industry the national ground on which it stood. All old-established national industries have been destroyed or are daily being destroyed. They are dislodged by new industries, whose introduction becomes a life and death question for all civilised nations, by industries that no longer work up indigenous raw material, but raw material drawn from the remotest zones; industries whose products are consumed, not only at home, but in every quarter of the globe. In place of the old wants, satisfied by the productions of the country, we find new wants, requiring for their satisfaction the products of distant lands and climes. In place of the old local and national seclusion and self-sufficiency, we have intercourse in every direction, universal interdependence of nations. And as in material, so also in intellectual production. The intellectual creations of individual nations become common property. National one-sidedness and narrow-mindedness become more and more impossible, and from the numerous national and local literatures, there arises a world literature.

The bourgeoisie, by the rapid improvement of all instruments of production, by the immensely facilitated means of communication, draws all, even the most barbarian, nations into civilisation. The cheap prices of its commodities are the heavy artillery with which it batters down all Chinese walls, with which it forces the barbarians' intensely obstinate hatred of foreigners to capitulate. It compels all nations, on pain of extinction, to adopt the bourgeois mode of production; it compels them to introduce what it calls civilisation into their midst, *i.e.*, to become bourgeois themselves. In one word, it creates a world after its own image.

The bourgeoisie has subjected the country to the rule of the towns. It has created enormous cities, has greatly increased the urban population as compared with the rural, and has thus rescued a considerable part of the population from the idiocy of rural life. Just as it has made the country dependent on the towns, so it has made barbarian and semi-barbarian countries dependent on the civilised ones, nations and peasants on nations of bourgeois, the East on the West.

The bourgeoisie keeps more and more doing away with the scattered state of the population, of the means of production, and of property. It has agglomerated population, centralised means of production, and has concentrated property in a few hands. The necessary consequence of this was political centralisation. Independent, or but loosely connected provinces, with separate interests, laws, governments and systems of taxation, became lumped together into one nation, with one government, one code of laws, one national class-interest, one frontier and one customs-tariff.

The bourgeoisie, during its rule of scarce one hundred years, has created more massive and more colossal productive forces than have all preceding generations together. Subjection of Nature's forces to man, machinery, application of chemistry to industry and agriculture, steam-navigation, railways, electric telegraphs, clearing of whole continents for cultivation, canalisation of rivers, whole populations conjured out of the ground—what earlier century had even a presentiment that such productive forces slumbered in the lap of social labour?

We see then: the means of production and of exchange, on whose foundation the bourgeoisie built itself up, were generated in feudal society. At a certain stage in the development of these means of production and of exchange, the conditions under which feudal society produced and exchanged, the feudal organisation of agriculture and manufacturing industry, in one word, the feudal relations of property became no longer compatible with the already developed productive forces; they became so many fetters. They had to be burst asunder; they were burst asunder.

Into their place stepped free competition, accompanied by a social and political constitution adapted to it, and by the economical and political sway of the bourgeois class.

A similar movement is going on before our own eyes. Modern bourgeois society with its relations of production, of exchange and of property, a society that has conjured up such gigantic means of production and of exchange, is like the sorcerer, who is no longer able to control the powers of the nether world whom he has called up by his spells. For many a decade past the history of industry and commerce is but the history of the revolt of modern productive forces against modern conditions of production, against the property relations that are the conditions for the existence of the bourgeoisie and of its rule. It is enough to mention the commercial crises that by their periodical return put on its trial, each time more threateningly, the existence of the entire bourgeois society. In these crises a great part not only of the existing products, but also of the previously created productive forces, are periodically destroyed. In these rises there breaks out an epidemic that, in all earlier epochs, would have seemed an absurdity—the epidemic of over-production. Society suddenly finds itself put back into a state of momentary barbarism; it appears as if a famine, a universal war of devastation had cut off the supply of every means of subsistence; industry and commerce seem to be destroyed; and why? Because there is too much civilisation, too much means of subsistence, too much industry, too much commerce. The productive forces at the disposal of society no longer tend to further the development of the conditions of bourgeois property; on the contrary, they have become too powerful for these conditions, by which they are fettered, and so soon as they overcome these fetters, they bring disorder into the whole of bourgeois society, endanger the existence of bourgeois property. The conditions of bourgeois society are too narrow to comprise the wealth created by them. And how does the bourgeoisie get over these crises? On the one hand by enforced destruction of a mass of productive forces; on the other, by the conquest of new markets, and by the more thorough exploitation of the old ones. That is to say, by paving the way for more extensive and more destructive crises, and by diminishing the means whereby crises are prevented.

The weapons with which the bourgeoisie felled feudalism to the ground are now turned against the bourgeoisie itself.

But not only has the bourgeoisie forged the weapons that bring death to itself; it has also called into existence the men who are to wield those weapons—the modern working class—the proletarians.

In proportion as the bourgeoisie, *i.e.*, capital, is developed, in the same proportion is the proletariat, the modern working class, developed—a class of labourers, who live only so long as they find work, and who find work only so long as their labour increases capital. These labourers, who must sell themselves piece-meal, are a commodity, like every other article of commerce, and are consequently exposed to all the vicissitudes of competition, to all the fluctuations of the market.

Owing to the extensive use of machinery and to division of labour, the work of the proletarians has lost all individual character, and consequently, all charm for the workman. He becomes an appendage of the machine, and it is only the most simple, most monotonous, and most easily acquired knack, that is required of him. Hence, the cost of production of a workman is restricted, almost entirely, to the means of subsistence that he requires for his maintenance, and for the propagation of his race. But the price of a commodity, and therefore also of labour, is equal to its cost of production. In proportion, therefore, as the repulsiveness of the work increases, the wage decreases. Nay more, in proportion as the use of machinery and division of labour increases, in the same proportion the burden of toil also increases, whether by prolongation of the working hours, by increase of the work exacted in a given time or by increased speed of the machinery, etc.

Modern industry has converted the little workshop of the patriarchal master into the great factory of the industrial capitalist. Masses of labourers, crowded into the factory, are organised like soldiers. As privates of the industrial army they are placed under the command of a perfect hierarchy of officers and sergeants. Not only are they slaves of the bourgeois class, and of the bourgeois State; they are daily and hourly enslaved by the machine, by the over-looker, and, above all, by the individual bourgeois manufacturer himself. The more openly this despotism proclaims gain to be its end and aim, the more petty, the more hateful and the more embittering it is.

The less the skill and exertion of strength implied in manual labour, in other words, the more modern industry becomes developed, the more is the labour of men superseded by that of women. Differences of age and sex have no longer any distinctive social validity for the working class. All are instruments of labour, more or less expensive to use, according to their age and sex.

No sooner is the exploitation of the labourer by the manufacturer, so far, at an end, that he receives his wage in cash, than he is set upon by the other portions of the bourgeoisie, the landlord, the shopkeeper, the pawnbroker, etc.

The lower strata of the middle class—the small tradespeople, shopkeepers, and retired tradesmen generally, the handicraftsmen and peasants—all these sink gradually into the proletariat, partly because their diminutive capital does not suffice for the scale on which Modern Industry is carried on, and is swamped in the competition with the large capitalists, partly because their specialised skill is rendered worthless by new methods of production. Thus the proletariat is recruited from all classes of the population.

The proletariat goes through various stages of development. With its birth begins its struggle with the bourgeoisie. At first the contest is carried on by individual labourers, then by the workpeople of a factory, then by the operatives of one trade, in one locality, against the individual bourgeois who directly exploits them. They direct their attacks not against the bourgeois conditions of production, but against the instruments of production themselves; they destroy imported wares that compete with their labour, they smash to pieces machinery, they set factories ablaze, they seek to restore by force the vanished status of the workman of the Middle Ages.

At this stage the labourers still form an incoherent mass scattered over the whole country, and broken up by their mutual competition. If anywhere they unite to form more compact bodies, this is not yet the consequence of their own active union, but of the union of the bourgeoisie, which class, in order to attain its own political ends, is compelled to set the whole proletariat in motion, and is moreover yet, for a time, able to do so. At this stage, therefore, the proletarians do not fight their enemies, but the enemies of their enemies, the remnants of absolute monarchy, the landowners, the non-industrial bourgeois, the petty bourgeoisie. Thus the whole historical movement is concentrated in the hands of the bourgeoisie; every victory so obtained is a victory for the bourgeoisie.

But with the development of industry the proletariat not only increases in number; it becomes concentrated in greater masses, its strength grows, and it feels that strength more. The various interests and conditions of life within the ranks of the proletariat are more and more equalised, in proportion as machinery obliterates all distinctions of labour, and nearly everywhere reduces wages to the same low level. The growing competition among the bourgeois, and the resulting commercial crises, make the wages of the workers ever more fluctuating. The unceasing improvement of machinery, ever more rapidly developing, makes their livelihood more and more precarious; the collisions between individual workmen and individual bourgeois take more and more the character of collisions between two classes. Thereupon the workers begin to form combinations (Trades Unions) against the bourgeois; they club together in order to keep up the rate of wages; they found permanent associations in order to make provision beforehand for these occasional revolts. Here and there the contest breaks out into riots.

Now and then the workers are victorious, but only for a time. The real fruit of their battles lies, not in the immediate result, but in the ever-expanding union of the workers. This union is helped on by the improved means of communication that are created by modern industry and that place the workers of different localities in contact with one another. It was just this contact that was needed to centralise the numerous local struggles, all of the same character, into one national struggle between classes. But every class struggle is a political struggle. And that union, to attain which the burghers of the Middle Ages, with their miserable highways, required centuries, the modern proletarians, thanks to railways, achieve in a few years.

This organisation of the proletarians into a class, and consequently into a political party, is continually being upset again by the competition between the workers themselves. But it ever rises up again, stronger, firmer, mightier. It compels legislative recognition of particular interests of the workers, by taking advantage of the divisions among the bourgeoisie itself. Thus the ten-hours' bill in England was carried.

Altogether collisions between the classes of the old society further, in many ways, the course of development of the proletariat. The bourgeoisie finds itself involved in a constant battle. At first with the aristocracy; later on, with those portions of the bourgeoisie itself, whose interests have become antagonistic to the progress of industry; at all times, with the bourgeoisie of foreign countries. In all these battles it sees itself compelled to appeal to the proletariat, to ask for its help, and thus, to drag it into the political arena. The bourgeoisie itself, therefore, supplies the proletariat with its own elements of political and general education, in other words, it furnishes the proletariat with weapons for fighting the bourgeoisie.

Further, as we have already seen, entire sections of the ruling classes are, by the advance of industry, precipitated into the proletariat, or are at least threatened in their conditions of existence. These also supply the proletariat with fresh elements of enlightenment and progress.

Finally, in times when the class struggle nears the decisive hour, the process of dissolution going on within the ruling class, in fact within the whole range of society, assumes such a violent, glaring character, that a small section of the ruling class cuts itself adrift, and joins the revolutionary class, the class that holds the future in its hands. Just as, therefore, at an earlier period, a section of the nobility went over to the bourgeoisie, so now a portion of the bourgeoisie goes over to the proletariat, and in particular, a portion of the bourgeois ideologists, who have raised themselves to the level of comprehending theoretically the historical movement as a whole.

Of all the classes that stand face to face with the bourgeoisie today, the proletariat alone is a really revolutionary class. The other classes decay and finally disappear in the face of Modern Industry; the proletariat is its special and essential product.

The lower middle class, the small manufacturer, the shopkeeper, the artisan, the peasant, all thee fight against the bourgeoisie, to save from extinction their existence as fractions of the middle class. They are therefore not revolutionary, but conservative. Nay more, they are reactionary, for they try to roll back the wheel of history. If by chance they are revolutionary, they are so only in view of their impending transfer into the proletariat, they thus defend not their present, but their future interests, they desert their own standpoint to place themselves at that of the proletariat.

The "dangerous class," the social scum, that passively rotting mass thrown off by the lowest layers of old society, may, here and there, be swept into the movement by a proletarian revolution; its conditions of life, however, prepare it far more for the part of a bribed tool of reactionary intrigue.

In the conditions of the proletariat, those of old society at large are already virtually swamped. The proletarian is without property; his relation to his wife and children has no longer anything in common with the bourgeois family-relations; modern industrial labour, modern subjection to capital, the same in England as in France, in America as in Germany, has stripped him of every trace of national character. Law, morality, religion, are to him so many bourgeois prejudices, behind which lurk in ambush just as many bourgeois interests.

All the preceding classes that got the upper hand, sought to fortify their already acquired status by subjecting society at large to their conditions of appropriation. The proletarians cannot become masters of the productive forces of society, except by abolishing their own previous mode of appropriation, and thereby also every other previous mode of appropriation. They have nothing of their own to secure and to fortify; their mission is to destroy all previous securities for, and insurances of, individual property.

All previous historical movements were movements of minorities, or in the interests of minorities. The proletarian movement is the self-conscious, independent movement of the immense majority, in the interests of the immense majority. The proletariat, the lowest stratum of our present society, cannot stir, cannot raise itself up, without the whole superincumbent strata of official society being sprung into the air.

Though not in substance, yet in form, the struggle of the proletariat with the bourgeoisie is at first a national struggle. The proletariat of each country must, of course, first of all settle matters with its own bourgeoisie.

In depicting the most general phases of the development of the proletariat, we traced the more or less veiled civil war, raging within existing society, up to the point where that war breaks out into open revolution, and where the violent over-throw of the bourgeoisie lays the foundation for the sway of the proletariat.

Hitherto, every form of society has been based, as we have already seen, on the antagonism of oppressing and oppressed classes. But in order to oppress a class, certain conditions must be assured to it under which it can, at least, continue its slavish existence. The serf, in the period of serfdom, raised himself to member-ship in the commune, just as the petty bourgeois, under the yoke of feudal abso-lutism, managed to develop into a bourgeois. The modern labourer, on the con-trary, instead of rising with the progress of industry, sinks deeper and deeper below the conditions of existence of his own class. He becomes a pauper, and pauperism develops more rapidly than population and wealth. And here it be-comes evident, that the bourgeoisie is unfit any longer to be the ruling class in society, and to impose its conditions of existence upon society as an over-riding law. It is unfit to rule because it is incompetent to assure an existence to its slave within his slavery, because it cannot help letting him sink into such a state, that it has to feed him, instead of being fed by him. Society can no longer live under this bourgeoisie, in other words, its existence is no longer compatible with society.

The essential condition for the existence, and for the sway of the bourgeois class, is the formation and augmentation of capital; the condition for capital is wage-labour. Wage-labour rests exclusively on competition between the labourers. The advance of industry, whose involuntary promoter is the bourgeoisie, replaces the isolation of the labourers, due to competition, by their revolutionary combina-tion, due to association. The development of Modern Industry, therefore, cuts from under its feet the very foundation on which the bourgeoisie produces and appropriates products. What the bourgeoisie, therefore, produces, above all, is its own grave-diggers. Its fall and the victory of the proletariat are equally inevitable.

Proletarians and Communists

In what relation do the Communists stand to the proletarians as a whole?

The Communists do not form a separate party opposed to other working-class parties.

They have no interests separate and apart from those of the proletariat as a whole.

They do not set up any sectarian principles of their own, by which to shape and mould the proletarian movement.

The Communists are distinguished from the other working-class parties by this only: (1) In the national struggles of the proletarians of the different countries, they point out and bring to the front the common interests of the entire proletariat, independently of all nationality. (2) In the various stages of development which the struggle of the working class against the bourgeoisie has to pass through, they always and everywhere represent the interests of the movement as a whole.

The Communists, therefore, are on the one hand, practically, the most advanced and resolute section of the working-class parties of every country, that section which pushes forward all others; on the other hand, theoretically, they have over the great mass of the proletariat the advantage of clearly understanding the line of march, the conditions, and the ultimate general results of the proletarian movement.

The immediate aim of the Communists is the same as that of all the other proletarian parties: formation of the proletariat into a class, overthrow of the bourgeois supremacy, conquest of political power by the proletariat.

The theoretical conclusions of the Communists are in no way based on ideas or principles that have been invented, or discovered, by this or that would-be universal reformer.

They merely express, in general terms, actual relations springing from an existing class struggle, from a historical movement going on under our very eyes. The abolition of existing property relations is not at all a distinctive feature of Communism.

All property relations in the past have continually been subject to historical change consequent upon the change in historical conditions.

The French Revolution, for example, abolished feudal property in favour of bourgeois property.

The distinguishing feature of Communism is not the abolition of property generally, but the abolition of bourgeois property. But modern bourgeois private property is the final and most complete expression of the system of producing and appropriating products, that is based on class antagonisms, on the exploitation of the many by the few.

In this sense, the theory of the Communists may be summed up in the single sentence: Abolition of private property.

We Communists have been reproached with the desire of abolishing the right of personally acquiring property as the fruit of a man's own labour, which property is alleged to be the groundwork of all personal freedom, activity and independence.

Hard-won, self-acquired, self-earned property! Do you mean the property of the petty artisan and of the small peasant, a form of property that preceded the bourgeois form? There is no need to abolish that; the development of industry has to a great extent already destroyed it, and is still destroying it daily.

Or do you mean modern bourgeois private property?

But does wage-labour create any property for the labourer? Not a bit. It creates capital, *i.e.*, that kind of property which exploits wage-labour, and which cannot increase except upon condition of begetting a new supply of wage-labour for fresh exploitation. Property, in its present form, is based on the antagonism of capital and wage-labour. Let us examine both sides of this antagonism.

To be a capitalist, is to have not only a purely personal, but a social *status* in production. Capital is a collective product, and only by the united action of many members, nay, in the last resort, only by the united action of all members of society, can it be set in motion.

Capital is, therefore, not a personal, it is a social power.

When, therefore, capital is converted into common property, into the property of all members of society, personal property is not thereby transformed into social property. It is only the social character of the property that is changed. It loses its class-character.

Let us now take wage-labour.

The average price of wage-labour is the minimum wage, *i.e.*, that quantum of the means of subsistence, which is absolutely requisite to keep the labourer in bare existence as a labourer. What, therefore, the wage-labourer appropriates by means of his labour, merely suffices to prolong and reproduce a bare existence. We by no means intend to abolish this personal appropriation of the products of labour, an appropriation that is made for the maintenance and reproduction of human life, and that leaves no surplus wherewith to command the labour of others. All that we want to do away with, is the miserable character of this appropriation, under which the labourer lives merely to increase capital, and is allowed to live only in so far as the interest of the ruling class requires it.

In bourgeois society, living labour is but a means to increase accumulated labour. In Communist society, accumulated labour is but a means to widen, to enrich, to promote the existence of the labourer.

In bourgeois society, therefore, the past dominates the present; in Communist society, the present dominates the past. In bourgeois society capital is independent and has individuality, while the living person is dependent and has no individuality.

And the abolition of this state of things is called by the bourgeois, abolition of individuality and freedom! And rightly so. The abolition of bourgeois individuality, bourgeois independence, and bourgeois freedom is undoubtedly aimed at.

By freedom is meant, under the present bourgeois conditions of production, free trade, free selling and buying.

But if selling and buying disappears, free selling and buying disappears also. This talk about free selling and buying, and all the other "brave words" of our bourgeoisie about freedom in general, have a meaning, if any, only in contrast with restricted selling and buying, with the fettered traders of the Middle Ages, but have no meaning when opposed to the Communistic abolition of buying and selling, of the bourgeois conditions of production, and of the bourgeoisie itself.

You are horrified at our intending to do away with private property. But in your existing society, private property is already done away with for nine-tenths of the population; its existence for the few is solely due to its non-existence in the hands of those nine-tenths. You reproach us, therefore, with intending to do away with a form of property, the necessary condition for whose existence is the non-existence of any property for the immense majority of society.

In one word, you reproach us with intending to do away with your property. Precisely so; that is just what we intend.

From the moment when labour can no longer be converted into capital, money, or rent, into a social power capable of being monopolised, *i.e.*, from the moment when individual property can no longer be transformed into bourgeois property, into capital, from that moment, you say, individuality vanishes.

You must, therefore, confess that by "individual" you mean no other person than the bourgeois, than the middle-class owner of property. This person must, indeed, be swept out of the way, and made impossible.

Communism deprives no man of the power to appropriate the products of society; all that it does is to deprive him of the power to subjugate the labour of others by means of such appropriation.

It has been objected that upon the abolition of private property all work will cease, and universal laziness will overtake us.

According to this, bourgeois society ought long ago to have gone to the dogs through sheer idleness; for those of its members who work, acquire nothing, and those who acquire anything, do not work. The whole of this objection is but another expression of the tautology: that there can no longer be any wage-labour when there is no longer any capital.

All objections urged against the Communistic mode of producing and appropriating material products, have, in the same way, been urged against the Communistic modes of producing and appropriating intellectual products. Just as, to the bourgeois, the disappearance of class property is the disappearance of production itself, so the disappearance of class culture is to him identical with the disappearance of all culture.

That culture, the loss of which he laments, is, for the enormous majority, a mere training to act as a machine.

But don't wrangle with us so long as you apply, to our intended abolition of bourgeois property, the standard of your bourgeois notions of freedom, culture, law, &c. Your very ideas are but the outgrowth of the conditions of your bourgeois production and bourgeois property, just as your jurisprudence is but the will of your class made into a law for all, a will, whose essential character and direction are determined by the economical conditions of existence of your class.

The selfish misconception that induces you to transform into eternal laws of nature and of reason, the social forms springing from your present mode of production and form of property—historical relations that rise and disappear in the progress of production—this misconception you share with every ruling class that has preceded you. What you see clearly in the case of ancient property, what you admit in the case of feudal property, you are of course forbidden to admit in the case of your own bourgeois form of property.

Abolition of the family! Even the most radical flare up at this infamous proposal of the Communists.

On what foundation is the present family, the bourgeois family, based? On capital, on private gain. In its completely developed form this family exists only among the bourgeoisie. But this state of things finds its complement in the practical absence of the family among the proletarians, and in public prostitution.

The bourgeois family will vanish as a matter of course when its complement vanishes, and both will vanish with the vanishing of capital.

Do you charge us with wanting to stop the exploitation of children by their parents? To this crime we plead guilty.

But, you will say, we destroy the most hallowed of relations, when we replace home education by social.

And your education! Is not that also social, and determined by the social conditions under which you educate, by the intervention, direct or indirect, of society, by means of schools, &c.? The Communists have not invented the intervention of society in education; they do but seek to alter the character of that intervention, and to rescue education from the influence of the ruling class.

The bourgeois clap-trap about the family and education, about the hallowed correlation of parent and child, becomes all the more disgusting, the more, by the action of Modern Industry, all family ties among the proletarians are torn asunder, and their children transformed into simple articles of commerce and instruments of labour.

But you Communists would introduce community of women, screams the whole bourgeoisie in chorus.

The bourgeois sees in his wife a mere instrument of production. He hears that the instruments of production are to be exploited in common, and, naturally, can come to no other conclusion than that the lot of being common to all will likewise fall to the women.

He has not even a suspicion that the real point aimed at is to do away with the status of women as mere instruments of production.

For the rest, nothing is more ridiculous than the virtuous indignation of our bourgeois at the community of women which, they pretend, is to be openly and officially established by the Communists. The Communists have no need to introduce community of women; it has existed almost from time immemorial.

Our bourgeois, not content with having the wives and daughters of their proletarians at their disposal, not to speak of common prostitutes, take the greatest pleasure in seducing each other's wives.

Bourgeois marriage is in reality a system of wives in common and thus, at the most, what the Communists might possibly be reproached with, is that they desire to introduce, in substitution for a hypocritically concealed, an openly legalised community of women. For the rest, it is self-evident that the abolition of the present system of production must bring with it the abolition of the community of women springing from that system, *i.e.*, of prostitution both public and private.

The Communists are further reproached with desiring to abolish countries and nationality.

The working men have no country. We cannot take from them what they have not got. Since the proletariat must first of all acquire political supremacy, must rise to be the leading class of the nation, must constitute itself *the* nation, it is, so far, itself national, though not in the bourgeois sense of the word.

National differences and antagonisms between peoples are daily more and more vanishing, owing to the development of the bourgeoisie, to freedom of commerce, to the world-market, to uniformity in the mode of production and in the conditions of life corresponding hereto.

The supremacy of the proletariat will cause them to vanish still faster. United action, of the leading civilised countries at least, is one of the first conditions for the emancipation of the proletariat.

In proportion as the exploitation of one individual by another is put an end to, the exploitation of one nation by another will be put an end to. In proportion as the antagonism between classes within the nation vanishes, the hostility of one nation to another will come to an end.

The charges against Communism made from a religious, a philosophical, and, generally, from an ideological standpoint, are not deserving of serious examination.

Does it require deep intuition to comprehend that man's ideas, views and conceptions, in one word, man's consciousness, changes with every change in the conditions of his material existence, in his social relations and in his social life?

What else does the history of ideas prove, than that intellectual production changes its character in proportion as material production is changed? The ruling ideas of each age have ever been the ideas of its ruling class.

When people speak of ideas that revolutionise society, they do but express the fact, that within the old society, the elements of a new one have been created, and that the dissolution of the old ideas keeps even pace with the dissolution of the old conditions of existence.

When the ancient world was in its last throes, the ancient religions were overcome by Christianity. When Christian ideas succumbed in the 18th century to rationalist ideas, feudal society fought its death battle with the then revolutionary bourgeoisie. The ideas of religious liberty and freedom of conscience merely gave expression to the sway of free competition within the domain of knowledge.

"Undoubtedly," it will be said, "religious, moral, philosophical and juridical ideas have been modified in the course of historical development. But religion, morality, philosophy, political science, and law, constantly survived this change."

"There are, besides, eternal truths, such as Freedom, Justice, etc., that are common to all states of society. But Communism abolishes eternal truths, it abolishes all religion, and all morality, instead of constituting them on a new basis; it therefore acts in contradiction to all past historical experience."

What does this accusation reduce itself to? The history of all past society has consisted in the development of class antagonisms, antagonisms that assumed different forms at different epochs.

But whatever form they may have taken, one fact is common to all past ages, viz., the exploitation of one part of society by the other. No wonder, then, that the social consciousness of past ages, despite all the multiplicity and variety it displays, moves within certain common forms, or general ideas, which cannot completely vanish except with the total disappearance of class antagonisms.

The Communist revolution is the most radical rupture with traditional property relations; no wonder that its development involves the most radical rupture with traditional ideas.

But let us have done with the bourgeois objections to Communism.

We have seen above, that the first step in the revolution by the working class, is to raise the proletariat to the position of ruling class, to win the battle of democracy.

The proletariat will use its political supremacy to wrest, by degrees, all capital from the bourgeoisie, to centralise all instruments of production in the hands of the State, *i.e.*, of the proletariat organised as the ruling class; and to increase the total of productive forces as rapidly as possible.

Of course, in the beginning, this cannot be effected except by means of despotic inroads on the rights of property, and on the conditions of bourgeois production; by means of measures, therefore, which appear economically insufficient and untenable, but which, in the course of the movement, outstrip themselves, necessitate further inroads upon the old social order, and are unavoidable as a means of entirely revolutionising the mode of production.

These measures will of course be different in different countries.

Nevertheless in the most advanced countries, the following will be pretty generally applicable.

1. Abolition of property in land and application of all rents of land to public purposes.

2. A heavy progressive or graduated income tax.

3. Abolition of all right of inheritance.

4. Confiscation of the property of all emigrants and rebels.

5. Centralisation of credit in the hands of the State, by means of a national bank with State capital and an exclusive monopoly.

6. Centralisation of the means of communication and transport in the hands of the State.

7. Extension of factories and instruments of production owned by the State; the bringing into cultivation of waste-lands, and the improvement of the soil generally in accordance with a common plan.

8. Equal liability of all to labour. Establishment of industrial armies, especially for agriculture.

9. Combination of agriculture with manufacturing industries; gradual abolition of the distinction between town and country, by a more equable distribution of the population over the country.

10. Free education for all children in public schools. Abolition of children's factory labour in its present form. Combination of education with industrial production, &c., &c.

When, in the course of development, class distinctions have disappeared, and all production has been concentrated in the hands of a vast association of the whole nation, the public power will lose its political character. Political power, properly so called, is merely the organised power of one class for oppressing another. If the proletariat during its contest with the bourgeoisie is compelled, by the force of circumstances, to organise itself as a class, if, by means of a revolution, it makes itself the ruling class, and, as such, sweeps away by force the old conditions of production, then it will, along with these conditions, have swept away the conditions for the existence of class antagonisms and of classes generally, and will thereby have abolished its own supremacy as a class.

In place of the old bourgeois society, with its classes and class antagonisms, we shall have an association, in which the free development of each is the condition for the free development of all.

Position of the Communists in Relation to the Various Existing Opposition Parties

Section II has made clear the relations of the Communists to the existing working-class parties, such as the Chartists in England and the Agrarian Reformers in America.

The Communists fight for the attainment of the immediate aims, for the enforcement of the momentary interests of the working class; but in the movement of the present, they also represent and take care of the future of that movement. In France the Communists ally themselves with the Social-Democrats, against the conservative and radical bourgeoisie, reserving, however, the right to take up a critical position in regard to phrases and illusions traditionally handed down from the great Revolution.

In Switzerland they support the Radicals, without losing sight of the fact that this party consists of antagonistic elements, partly of Democratic Socialists, in the French sense, partly of radical bourgeois.

In Poland they support the party that insists on an agrarian revolution as the prime condition for national emancipation, that party which fomented the insurrection of Cracow in 1846.

In Germany they fight with the bourgeoisie whenever it acts in a revolutionary way, against the absolute monarchy, the feudal squirearchy, and the petty bourgeoisie.

But they never cease, for a single instant, to instill into the working class the clearest possible recognition of the hostile antagonism between bourgeoisie and proletariat, in order that the German workers may straightway use, as so many weapons against the bourgeoisie, the social and political conditions that the bourgeoisie must necessarily introduce along with its supremacy, and in order that, after the fall of the reactionary classes in Germany, the fight against the bourgeoisie itself may immediately begin.

The Communists turn their attention chiefly to Germany, because that country is on the eve of a bourgeois revolution that is bound to be carried out under more advanced conditions of European civilisation, and with a much more developed proletariat, than that of England was in the seventeenth, and of France in the eighteenth century, and because the bourgeois revolution in Germany will be but the prelude to an immediately following proletarian revolution.

In short, the Communists everywhere support every revolutionary movement against the existing social and political order of things.

In all these movements they bring to the front, as the leading question in each, the property question, no matter what its degree of development at the time.

Finally, they labour everywhere for the union and agreement of the democratic parties of all countries.

The Communists disdain to conceal their views and aims. They openly declare that their ends can be attained only by the forcible overthrow of all existing social conditions. Let the ruling classes tremble at a Communistic revolution. The proletarians have nothing to lose but their chains. They have a world to win.

Working men of all countries, unite!

AFTER THE REVOLUTION

From "Critique of the Gotha Program" (1875)

What we have to deal with here is a communist society, not as it has *developed* on its own foundations, but, on the contrary, just as it *emerges* from capitalist society; which is thus in every respect, economically, morally and intellectually, still stamped with the birth marks of the old society from whose womb it emerges. Accordingly, the individual producer receives back from society—after the deductions have been made—exactly what he gives to it. What he has given to it is his individual quantum of labour. For example, the social working day consists of the sum of the individual hours of work; the individual labour time of the individual producer is the part of the social working day contributed by him, his share in it. He receives a certificate from society that he has furnished such and such an amount of labour (after deducting his labour for the common funds), and with this certificate he draws from the social stock of means of consumption as much as costs the same amount of labour. The same amount of labour which he has given to society in one form he receives back in another.

Here obviously the same principle prevails as that which regulates the exchange of commodities, as far as this is exchange of equal values. Content and form are changed, because under the altered circumstances no one can give anything except his labour, and because, on the other hand, nothing can pass to the ownership of individuals except individual means of consumption. But, as far as the distribution of the latter among the individual producers is concerned, the same principle prevails as in the exchange of commodity equivalents: a given amount of labour in one form is exchanged from an equal amount of labour in another form.

Hence, *equal right* here is still in principle—*bourgeois right*, although principle and practice are no longer at loggerheads, while the exchange of equivalents in commodity exchange only exists *on the average* and not in the individual case.

In spite of this advance, this *equal right* is still constantly stigmatised by a bourgeois limitation. The right of the producers is *proportional* to the labour they supply; the equality consists in the fact that measurement is made with an *equal standard*, labour.

But one man is superior to another physically or mentally and so supplies more labour in the same time, or can labour for a longer time; and labour, to serve as a measure, must be defined by its duration or intensity, otherwise it ceases to be a standard of measurement. This *equal* right is an unequal right for unequal labour. It recognises no class differences, because everyone is only a worker like everyone else; but it tacitly recognises unequal individual endowment and thus productive capacity as natural privileges. *It is, therefore, a right of inequality, in its content, like every right.* Right by its very nature can consist only in the application of an equal standard; but unequal individuals (and they would not be different individuals if they were not unequal) are measurable only by an equal standard in so far as they are brought under an equal point of view, are taken from one *definite* side only, for instance, in the present case, are regarded *only as workers* and nothing more is seen in them, everything else being ignored. Further, one worker is married, another not; one has more children than another, and so on and so forth. Thus, with an equal performance of labour, and hence an equal share in the social consumption fund, one will in fact receive more than another, one will be richer than another, and so on. To avoid all these defects, right instead of being equal would have to be unequal.

But these defects are inevitable in the first phase of communist society as it is when it has just emerged after prolonged birth pangs from capitalist society. Right can never be higher than the economic structure of society and its cultural development conditioned thereby.

In a higher phase of communist society, after the enslaving subordination of the individual to the division of labour, and therewith also the antithesis between mental and physical labour, has vanished; after labour has become not only a means of life but life's prime want; after the productive forces have also increased with the all-round development of the individual, and all the springs of cooperative wealth flow more abundantly—only then can the narrow horizon of bourgeois right be crossed in its entirety and society inscribe on its banner: From each according to his ability, to each according to his needs!

CAPITAL

From Volume 3

In fact, the realm of freedom actually begins only where labour which is determined by necessity and mundane considerations ceases; thus in the very nature of things it lies beyond the sphere of actual material production. Just as the savage must wrestle with Nature to satisfy his wants, to maintain and reproduce life, so must civilized man, and he must do so in all social formations and under all possible modes of production. With his development this realm of physical necessity expands as a result of his wants; but, at the same time, the forces of production which satisfy these wants also increase. Freedom in this field can only consist in socialized man, the associated producers, rationally regulating their interchange with Nature, bringing it under their common control, instead of being ruled by it as by the blind forces of Nature; and achieving this with the least expenditure of energy and under conditions most favourable to, and worthy of, their human nature. But it nonetheless still remains a realm of necessity. Beyond it begins that development of human energy which is an end in itself, the true realm of freedom, which, however, can blossom forth only with the realm of necessity as its basis. The shortening of the working day is its basic prerequisite.

25

Friedrich Nietzsche
On the Genealogy of Morals

Friedrich Nietzsche was born in October 1844 in Rocken, Thuringia, a Saxon region in the east of Germany, and died in Weimar in 1900. Nietzsche's On the Genealogy of Morals *outlines a foundational critique of moral and political social valuation in physiological and historical terms. By describing the difference between master and slave morality (psychologies) and by adumbrating the inexorable rule of the latter morality in the culture of resentment or nihilism, Nietzsche reads the political in terms of the Will to Power. Thus, for Nietzsche, even such political values as equal rights and democratic rule manifest in a covert but essential way the same "lust to rule" that Nietzsche regards as characteristic of every drive or Will to Power. In 1869, Nietzsche was appointed professor of classical philology at the University of Basel, where he taught off and on until ill health forced him to resign altogether in 1879. His first book,* The Birth of Tragedy *(1872), shocked the world of classical studies, inspiring condemnation from his peers. Nietzsche's examination of morality as the basis of culture and society has been formative in contemporary continental traditions of political theory from Weber to Foucault.*

First Essay

10

The slave revolt in morality begins when *ressentiment* itself becomes creative and gives birth to values: the *ressentiment* of natures that are denied the true reaction, that of deeds, and compensate themselves with an imaginary revenge. While every noble morality develops from a triumphant affirmation of itself, slave morality from the outset says No to what is "outside," what is "different," what is "not itself"; and *this* No is its creative deed. This inversion of the value-positing eye—this *need* to direct one's view outward instead of back to oneself—is of the essence of *ressentiment*: in order to exist, slave morality always first needs a hostile external world; it needs, physiologically speaking, external stimuli in order to act at all—its action is fundamentally reaction.

The reverse is the case with the noble mode of valuation: it acts and grows spontaneously, it seeks its opposite only so as to affirm itself more gratefully and triumphantly—its negative concept "low," "common," "bad" is only a subsequently-invented pale, contrasting image in relation to its positive basic concept—filled with life and passion through and through—"we noble ones, we good, beautiful, happy ones!" When the noble mode of valuation blunders and sins against reality, it does so in respect to the sphere with which it is *not* sufficiently familiar, against a real knowledge of which it has indeed inflexibly guarded itself: in some circumstances it misunderstands the sphere it despises, that of the common man, of the lower orders; on the other hand, one should remember that, even supposing that the affect of contempt, of looking down from a superior height, *falsifies* the image of that which it despises, it will at any rate still be a much less serious falsification than that perpetrated on its opponent—*in effigie* of course—by the submerged hatred, the vengefulness of the impotent. There is indeed too much carelessness, too much taking lightly, too much looking away and impatience involved in contempt, even too much joyfulness, for it to be able to transform its object into a real caricature and monster.

One should not overlook the almost benevolent nuances that the Greek nobility, for example, bestows on all the words it employs to distinguish the lower orders from itself; how they are continuously mingled and sweetened with a kind of pity, consideration, and forbearance, so that finally almost all the words referring to the common man have remained as expressions signifying "unhappy," "pitiable" (campore *deilos, deilaios, ponēros, mochthēros*, the last two of which properly designate the common man as workslave and beast of burden)—and how on the other hand "bad," "low," "unhappy" have never ceased to sound to the Greek ear as one note with a tone-color in which "unhappy" preponderates: this as an inheritance from the ancient nobler aristocratic mode of evaluation, which does not belie itself even in its contempt (—philologists should recall the sense in which *oïzyros, anolbos, tlēmōn, dystychein, xymphora* are employed). The "well-born" *felt* themselves to be the "happy"; they did not have to establish their happiness artificially by examining their enemies, or to persuade themselves, *deceive* themselves, that they were happy (as all men of *ressentiment* are in the habit of doing); and they likewise knew, as rounded men replete with energy and therefore *necessarily* active, that happiness should not be sundered from action—being active was with them necessarily a part of happiness (whence *eu prattein* takes its origin)—all very much the opposite of "happiness" at the level of the impotent, the oppressed, and those in whom poisonous and inimical feelings are festering, with whom it appears as essentially narcotic, drug, rest, peace, "sabbath," slackening of tension and relaxing of limbs, in short *passively*.

While the noble man lives in trust and openness with himself (*gennaios* "of noble descent" underlines the nuance "upright" and probably also "naïve"), the man of *ressentiment* is neither upright nor naïve nor honest and straightforward with himself. His soul *squints*; his spirit loves hiding places, secret paths and back doors, everything covert entices him as *his* world, *his* security, *his* refreshment; he understands how to keep silent, how not to forget, how to wait, how to be provisionally self-deprecating and humble. A race of such men of *ressentiment* is bound to become eventually *cleverer* than any noble race; it will also honor cleverness to a far greater degree: namely, as a condition of existence of the first importance; while with noble men cleverness can easily acquire a subtle flavor of luxury and subtlety—for here it is far less essential than the perfect functioning of the regulating *unconscious* instincts or even than a certain imprudence, perhaps a bold recklessness whether in the face of danger or of the enemy; or that enthusiastic impulsiveness in anger, love, reverence, gratitude, and revenge by which noble souls have at all times recognized one another. *Ressentiment* itself, if it should appear in the noble man, consummates and exhausts itself in an immediate reaction, and therefore does not *poison*: on the other hand, it fails to appear at all on countless occasions on which it inevitably appears in the weak and impotent.

To be incapable of taking one's enemies, one's accidents, even one's misdeeds seriously for very long—that is the sign of strong, full natures in whom there is an excess of the power to form, to mold, to recuperate and to forget (a good example of this in modern times is Mirabeau, who had no memory for insults and vile actions done him and was unable to forgive simply because he—forgot). Such a man shakes off with a *single* shrug many vermin that eat deep into others; here alone genuine "love of one's enemies" is possible—supposing it to be possible at all on earth. How much reverence has a noble man for his enemies!—and such reverence is a bridge to love.—For he desires his enemy for himself, as his mark of distinction; he can endure no other enemy than one in whom there is nothing to despise and *very much* to honor! In contrast to this, picture "the enemy" as the man of *ressentiment* conceives him—and here precisely is his deed, his creation: he has conceived "the evil enemy," "*the Evil One*," and this in fact is his basic concept, from which he then evolves, as an afterthought and pendant, a "good one"—himself!

Second Essay

3

. . . "How can one create a memory for the human animal? How can one impress something upon this partly obtuse, partly flighty mind, attuned only to the passing moment, in such a way that it will stay there?"

One can well believe that the answers and methods for solving this primeval problem were not precisely gentle; perhaps indeed there was nothing more fearful and uncanny in the whole prehistory of man than his *mnemotechnics*. "If something is to stay in the memory it must be burned in: only that which never ceases to *hurt* stays in the memory"—this is a main clause of the oldest (unhappily also the most enduring) psychology on earth. One might even say that wherever on earth solemnity, seriousness, mystery, and gloomy coloring still distinguish the life of man and a people, something of the terror that formerly attended all promises, pledges, and vows on earth is *still effective*: the past, the longest, deepest and sternest past, breathes upon us and rises up in us whenever we become "serious." Man could never do without blood, torture, and sacrifices when he felt the need to create a memory for himself; the most dreadful sacrifices and pledges (sacrifices of the first-born among them), the most repulsive mutilations (castration, for example), the cruelest rites of all the religious cults (and all religions are at the deepest level systems of cruelties)—all this has its origin in the instinct that realized that pain is the most powerful aid to mnemonics.

In a certain sense, the whole of asceticism belongs here: a few ideas are to be rendered inextinguishable, ever-present, unforgettable, "fixed," with the aim of hypnotising the entire nervous and intellectual system with these "fixed ideas"— and ascetic procedures and modes of life are means of freeing these ideas from the competition of all other ideas, so as to make them "unforgettable." The worse man's memory has been, the more fearful has been the appearance of his customs; the severity of the penal code provides an especially significant measure of the degree of effort needed to overcome forgetfulness and to impose a few primitive demands of social existence as *present realities* upon these slaves of momentary affect and desire.

We Germans certainly do not regard ourselves as a particularly cruel and hard-hearted people, still less as a particularly frivolous one, living only for the day; but one has only to look at our former codes of punishments to understand what effort it costs on this earth to breed a "nation of thinkers" (which is to say, *the* nation in Europe in which one still finds today the maximum of trust, seriousness, lack of taste, and matter-of-factness—and with these qualities one has the right to breed every kind of European mandarin). These Germans have employed fearful means to acquire a memory, so as to master their basic mob-instinct and its brutal coarseness. Consider the old German punishments; for example, stoning (the sagas already have millstones drop on the head of the guilty), breaking on the wheel (the most characteristic invention and speciality of the German genius in the realm of punishment!), piercing with stakes, tearing apart or trampling by horses ("quartering"), boiling of the criminal in oil or wine (still employed in the four-teenth and fifteenth centuries), the popular flaying alive ("cutting straps"), cutting flesh from the chest, and also the practice of smearing the wrongdoer with honey and leaving him in the blazing sun for the flies. With the aid of such images and procedures one finally remembers five or six "I will not's," in regard to which one had given one's *promise* so as to participate in the advantages of society—and it was indeed with the aid of this kind of memory that one at last came "to reason"! Ah, reason, seriousness, mastery over the affects, the whole somber thing called reflection, all these prerogatives and showpieces of man: how dearly they have been bought! how much blood and cruelty lie at the bottom of all "good things"!

4

But how did that other "somber thing," the consciousness of guilt, the "bad con-science," come into the world?—And at this point we return to the genealogists of morals. To say it again—or haven't I said it yet?—they are worthless. A brief span of experience that is merely one's own, merely modern; no knowledge or will to knowledge of the past; even less of historical instinct, of that "second sight" needed here above all—and yet they undertake history of morality: it stands to reason that their results stay at a more than respectful distance from the truth. Have these genealogists of morals had even the remotest suspicion that, for example, the major moral concept *Schuld* [guilt] has its origin in the very material concept *Schulden* [debts]? Or that punishment, as requital, evolved quite independently of any presupposition concerning freedom or nonfreedom of the will?—to such an extent, indeed, that a *high* degree of humanity had to be attained before the animal "man" began even to make the much more primitive distinctions between "intentional," "negligent," "accidental," "accountable," and their opposites and to take them into account when determining punishments. The idea, now so obvious, apparently so natural, even unavoidable, that had to serve as the explanation of how the sense of justice ever appeared on earth—"the criminal deserves punishment *because* he could have acted differently"—is in fact an extremely late and subtle form of human judgment and inference: whoever transposes it to the beginning is guilty of a crude misunderstanding of the psychology of more primitive mankind. Throughout the greater part of human history punishment was *not* imposed *because* one held the wrongdoer responsible for his deed, thus *not* on the presupposition that only the guilty one should be punished: rather, as parents still punish their children, from anger at some harm or injury, vented on the one who caused it—but this anger is held in check and modified by the idea that every injury has its *equivalent* and can actually be paid back, even if only through the *pain* of the culprit. And whence did this primeval, deeply rooted, perhaps by now ineradicable idea draw its power—this idea of an equivalence between injury and pain? I have already divulged it: in the contractual relationship between *creditor* and *debtor*, which is as old as the idea of "legal subjects" and in turn points back to the fundamental forms of buying, selling, barter, trade, and traffic.

5

When we contemplate these contractual relationships, to be sure, we feel considerable suspicion and repugnance toward those men of the past who created or permitted them. This was to be expected from what we have previously noted. It was here that *promises* were made; it was here that a memory had to be *made* for those who promised; it is here, one suspects, that we shall find a great deal of severity, cruelty, and pain. To inspire trust in his promise to repay, to provide a guarantee of the seriousness and sanctity of his promise, to impress repayment as a duty, an obligation upon his own conscience, the debtor made a contract with the creditor and pledged that if he should fail to repay he would substitute something else that he "possessed," something he had control over; for example, his body, his wife, his freedom, or even his life (or, given certain religious presuppositions, even his bliss after death, the salvation of his soul, ultimately his peace in the grave: thus it was in Egypt, where the debtor's corpse found no peace from the creditor even in the grave—and among the Egyptians such peace meant a great deal). Above all, however, the creditor could inflict every kind of indignity and torture upon the body of the debtor; for example, cut from it as much as seemed commensurate with the size of the debt—and everywhere and from early times one had exact evaluations, *legal* evaluations, of the individual limbs and parts of the body from this point of view, some of them going into horrible and minute detail. I consider it as an advance, as evidence of a freer, more generous, *more Roman* conception of law when the Twelve Tables of Rome decreed it as a matter of indifference how much or how little the creditor cut off in such cases: "*si plus minusve secuerunt, ne fraude esto.*"

Let us be clear as to the logic of this form of compensation: it is strange enough. An equivalence is provided by the creditor's receiving, in place of a literal compensation for an injury (thus in place of money, land, possessions of any kind), a recompense in the form of a kind of *pleasure*—the pleasure of being allowed to vent his power freely upon one who is powerless, the voluptuous pleasure "*de faire le mal pour le plaisir de le faire*," the enjoyment of violation. This enjoyment will be the greater the lower the creditor stands in the social order, and can easily appear to him as a most delicious morsel, indeed as a foretaste of higher rank. In "punishing" the debtor, the creditor participates in a *right of the masters*: at last he, too, may experience for once the exalted sensation of being allowed to despise and mistreat someone as "beneath him"—or at least, if the actual power and administration of punishment has already passed to the "authorities," to *see* him despised and mistreated. The compensation, then, consists in a warrant for and title to cruelty.—

6

It was in *this* sphere then, the sphere of legal obligations, that the moral conceptual world of "guilt," "conscience," "duty," "sacredness of duty" had its origin: its beginnings were, like the beginnings of everything great on earth, soaked in blood thoroughly and for a long time. And might one not add that, fundamentally, this world has never since lost a certain odor of blood and torture? (Not even in good old Kant: the categorical imperative smells of cruelty.) It was here, too, that that uncanny intertwining of the ideas "guilt and suffering" was first effected—and by now they may well be inseparable. To ask it again: to what extent can suffering balance debts or guilt? To the extent that to *make* suffer was in the highest degree pleasurable, to the extent that the injured party exchanged for the loss he had sustained, including the displeasure caused by the loss, an extraordinary counterbalancing pleasure: that of *making* suffer—a genuine *festival*, something which, as aforesaid, was prized the more highly the more violently it contrasted with the rank and social standing of the creditor. This is offered only as a conjecture; for the depths of such subterranean things are difficult to fathom, besides being painful; and whoever clumsily interposes the concept of "revenge" does not enhance his insight into the matter but further veils and darkens it (—for revenge merely leads us back to the same problem: "how can making suffer constitute a compensation?").

It seems to me that the delicacy and even more the tartuffery of tame domestic animals (which is to say modern men, which is to say us) resists a really vivid

comprehension of the degree to which *cruelty* constituted the great festival pleasure of more primitive men and was indeed an ingredient of almost every one of
their pleasures; and how naïvely, how innocently their thirst for cruelty manifested
itself, how, as a matter of principle, they posited "disinterested malice" (or, in
Spinoza's words, *sympathia malevolens*) as a *normal* quality of man—and thus as
something to which the conscience cordially *says Yes!* A more profound eye might
perceive enough of this oldest and most fundamental festival pleasure of man even
in our time; in *Beyond Good and Evil*, section 229 (and earlier in *The Dawn*,
sections 18, 77, 113) I pointed cautiously to the ever-increasing spiritualization
and "deification" of cruelty which permeates the entire history of higher culture
(and in a significant sense actually constitutes it). In any event, it is not long since
princely weddings and public festivals of the more magnificent kind were unthinkable without executions, torturings, or perhaps an auto-da-fé, and no noble household was without creatures upon whom one could heedlessly vent one's malice
and cruel jokes. (Consider, for instance, Don Quixote at the court of the Duchess.
Today we read *Don Quixote* with a bitter taste in our mouths, almost with a
feeling of torment, and would thus seem very strange and incomprehensible to its
author and his contemporaries: they read it with the clearest conscience in the
world as the most cheerful of books, they laughed themselves almost to death over
it). To see others suffer does one good, to make others suffer even more: this is a
hard saying but an ancient, mighty, human, all-too-human principle to which even
the apes might subscribe; for it has been said that in devising bizarre cruelties they
anticipate man and are, as it were, his "prelude." Without cruelty there is no
festival: thus the longest and most ancient part of human history teaches—and in
punishment there is so much that is *festive!*—

7

With this idea, by the way, I am by no means concerned to furnish our pessimists
with more grist for their discordant and creaking mills of life-satiety. On the contrary, let me declare expressly that in the days when mankind was not yet ashamed
of its cruelty, life on earth was more cheerful than it is now that pessimists exist.
The darkening of the sky above mankind has deepened in step with the increase in
man's feeling of shame *at man*. The weary pessimistic glance, mistrust of the
riddle of life, the icy No of disgust with life—these do not characterize the most
evil epochs of the human race: rather do they first step into the light of day as the
swamp weeds they are when the swamp to which they belong comes into being—I
mean the morbid softening and moralization through which the animal "man"
finally learns to be ashamed of all his instincts. On his way to becoming an "angel" (to employ no uglier word) man has evolved that queasy stomach and coated
tongue through which not only the joy and innocence of the animal but life itself
has become repugnant to him—so that he sometimes holds his nose in his own
presence and, with Pope Innocent the Third, disapprovingly catalogues his own
repellent aspects ("impure begetting, disgusting means of nutrition in his mother's

womb, baseness of the matter out of which man evolves, hideous stink, secretion of saliva, urine, and filth").

Today, when suffering is always brought forward as the principal argument *against* existence, as the worst question mark, one does well to recall the ages in which the opposite opinion prevailed because men were unwilling to refrain from *making* suffer and saw in it an enchantment of the first order, a genuine seduction *to* life. Perhaps in those days—the delicate may be comforted by this thought— pain did not hurt as much as it does now; at least that is the conclusion a doctor may arrive at who has treated Negroes (taken as representatives of prehistoric man—) for severe internal inflammations that would drive even the best consti- tuted European to distraction—in the case of Negroes they do *not* do so. (The curve of human susceptibility to pain seems in fact to take an extraordinary and almost sudden drop as soon as one has passed the upper ten thousand or ten million of the top stratum of culture; and for my own part, I have no doubt that the combined suffering of all the animals ever subjected to the knife for scientific ends is utterly negligible compared with *one* painful night of a single hysterical blue- stocking.) Perhaps the possibility may even be allowed that this joy in cruelty does not really have to have died out: if pain hurts more today, it simply requires a certain sublimation and subtilization, that is to say it has to appear translated into the imaginative and psychical and adorned with such innocent names that even the tenderest and most hypocritical conscience is not suspicious of them ("traffic pity" is one such name; "*les nostalgies de la croix*" is another).

What really arouses indignation against suffering is not suffering as such but the senselessness of suffering: but neither for the Christian, who has interpreted a whole mysterious machinery of salvation into suffering, nor for the naïve man of more ancient times, who understood all suffering in relation to the spectator of it or the causer of it, was there any such thing as *senseless* suffering. So as to abolish hidden undetected, unwitnessed suffering from the world and honestly to deny it, one was in the past virtually compelled to invent gods and genii of all the heights and depths, in short something that roams even in secret, hidden places, sees even in the dark, and will not easily let an interesting painful spectacle pass unnoticed. For it was with the aid of such inventions that life then knew how to work the trick which it has always known how to work, that of justifying itself, of justifying its "evil." Nowadays it might require other auxiliary inventions (for example, life as a riddle, life as an epistemological problem). "Every evil the sight of which edifies a god is justified": thus spoke the primitive logic of feeling—and was it, indeed, only primitive? The gods conceived of as the friends of *cruel* spectacles—oh how profoundly this ancient idea still permeates our European hu- manity! Merely consult Calvin and Luther. It is certain, at any rate, that the *Greeks* still knew of no tastier spice to offer their gods to season their happiness than the pleasures of cruelty. With what eyes do you think Homer made his gods look down upon the destinies of men? What was at bottom the ultimate meaning of Trojan Wars and other such tragic terrors? There can be no doubt whatever: they were intended as *festival plays* for the gods; and, insofar as the poet is in these matters of a more "godlike" disposition than other men, no doubt also as festival plays for the poets.

It was in the same way that the moral philosophers of Greece later imagined the eyes of God looking down upon the moral struggle, upon the heroism and self-torture of the virtuous: the "Herakles of duty" was on a stage and knew himself to be; virtue without a witness was something unthinkable for his nation of actors. Surely, that philosophers' invention, so bold and so fateful, which was then first devised for Europe, the invention of "free will," of the absolute spontaneity of man in good and in evil, was devised above all to furnish a right to the idea that the interest of the gods in man, in human virtue, *could never be exhausted.* There must never be any lack of real novelty, of really unprecedented tensions, complications, and catastrophies on the stage of the earth: the course of a completely deterministic world would have been predictable for the gods and they would have quickly grown weary of it—reason enough for those *friends of the gods,* the philosophers, not to inflict such a deterministic world on their gods! The entire mankind of antiquity is full of tender regard for "the spectator," as an essentially public, essentially visible world which cannot imagine happiness apart from spectacles and festivals.—And, as aforesaid, even in great *punishment* there is so much that is festive!

8

To return to our investigation: the feeling of guilt, of personal obligation, had its origin, as we saw, in the oldest and most primitive personal relationship, that between buyer and seller, creditor and debtor: it was here that one person first encountered another person, that one person first *measured himself* against another. No grade of civilization, however low, has yet been discovered in which something of this relationship has not been noticeable. Setting prices, determining values, contriving equivalences, exchanging—these preoccupied the earliest thinking of man to so great an extent that in a certain sense they constitute thinking *as such*: here it was that the oldest kind of astuteness developed; here likewise, we may suppose, did human pride, the feeling of superiority in relation to other animals, have its first beginnings. Perhaps our word "man" (*manas*) still expresses something of precisely *this* feeling of self-satisfaction: man designated himself as the creature that measures values, evaluates and measures, as the "valuating animal as such."

Buying and selling, together with their psychological appurtenances, are older even than the beginnings of any kind of social forms of organization and alliances: it was rather out of the most rudimentary form of personal legal rights that the budding sense of exchange, contract, guilt, right, obligation, settlement, first *transferred* itself to the coarsest and most elementary social complexes (in their relations with other similar complexes), together with the custom of comparing, measuring, and calculating power against power. The eye was now focused on this perspective; and with that blunt consistency characteristic of the thinking of primitive mankind, which is hard to set in motion but then proceeds inexorably in the same direction, one forthwith arrived at the great generalization, "everything has its price; *all* things can be paid for"—the oldest and naïvest moral canon of *justice*, the beginning of all "good-naturedness," all "fairness," all "good will," all "objectivity" on earth. Justice on this elementary level is the good will among parties of approximately equal power to come to terms with one another, to reach an "understanding" by means of a settlement—and to *compel* parties of lesser power to reach a settlement among themselves.—

9

Still retaining the criteria of prehistory (this prehistory is in any case present in all ages or may always reappear): the community, too, stands to its members in that same vital basic relation, that of the creditor to his debtors. One lives in a community, one enjoys the advantages of a communality (oh what advantages! we sometimes underrate them today), one dwells protected, cared for, in peace and trustfulness, without fear of certain injuries and hostile acts to which the man *outside*, the "man without peace," is exposed—a German will understand the original connotations of *Elend*—since one has bound and pledged oneself to the community precisely with a view to injuries and hostile acts. What will happen *if this pledge is broken*? The community, the disappointed creditor, will get what repayment it can, one may depend on that. The direct harm caused by the culprit is here a minor matter; quite apart from this, the lawbreaker is above all a "breaker," a breaker of his contract and his word *with the whole* in respect to all the benefits and comforts of communal life of which he has hitherto had a share. The lawbreaker is a debtor who has not merely failed to make good the advantages and advance payments bestowed upon him but has actually attacked his creditor: therefore he is not only deprived henceforth of all these advantages and benefits, as is fair—he is also reminded *what these benefits are really worth*. The wrath of the disappointed creditor, the community, throws him back again into the savage and outlaw state against which he has hitherto been protected: it thrusts him away—and now every kind of hostility may be vented upon him. "Punishment" at this level of civilization is simply a copy, a *mimus*, of the normal attitude toward a hated, disarmed, prostrated enemy, who has lost not only every right and protection, but all hope of quarter as well; it is thus the rights of war and the victory celebration of the *vae victis*! in all their mercilessness and cruelty—which explains why it is that war itself (including the warlike sacrificial cult) has provided all the *forms* that punishment has assumed throughout history.

10

As its power increases, a community ceases to take the individual's transgressions so seriously, because they can no longer be considered as dangerous and destructive to the whole as they were formerly: the malefactor is no longer "set beyond the pale of peace" and thrust out; universal anger may not be vented upon him as unrestrainedly as before—on the contrary, the whole from now on carefully defends the malefactor against this anger, especially that of those he has directly harmed, and takes him under its protection. A compromise with the anger of those directly injured by the criminal; an effort to localize the affair and to prevent it from causing any further, let alone a general, disturbance; attempts to discover equivalents and to settle the whole matter (*compositio*); above all, the increasingly definite will to treat every crime as in some sense *dischargeable*, and thus at least to a certain extent to *isolate* the criminal and his deed from one another—these traits become more and more clearly visible as the penal law evolves. As the power and self-confidence of a community increase, the penal law always becomes more moderate; every weakening or imperiling of the former brings with it a restoration of the harsher forms of the latter. The "creditor" always becomes more humane to the extent that he has grown richer; finally, how much injury he can endure without suffering from it becomes the actual *measure* of his wealth. It is not unthinkable that a society might attain such a *consciousness of power* that it could allow itself the noblest luxury possible to it—letting those who harm it go *unpunished*. "What are my parasites to me?" it might say. "May they live and prosper: I am strong enough for that!"

The justice which began with, "everything is dischargeable, everything must be discharged," ends by winking and letting those incapable of discharging their debt go free: it ends, as does every good thing on earth, by *overcoming itself*. This self-overcoming of justice: one knows the beautiful name it has given itself—*mercy*; it goes without saying that mercy remains the privilege of the most powerful man, or better, his—beyond the law.

11

Here a word in repudiation of attempts that have lately been made to seek the origin of justice in quite a different sphere—namely in that of *ressentiment*. To the psychologists first of all, presuming they would like to study *ressentiment* close up for once, I would say: this plant blooms best today among anarchists and anti-Semites—where it has always bloomed, in hidden places, like the violet, though with a different odor. And as like must always produce like, it causes us no surprise to see a repetition in such circles of attempts often made before—see above, section 14—to sanctify *revenge* under the name of *justice*—as if justice were at bottom merely a further development of the feeling of being aggrieved—and to rehabilitate not only revenge but all *reactive* affects in general. To the latter as such I would be the last to raise any objection: in respect to the entire biological problem (in relation to which the value of these affects has hitherto been underrated) it even seems to me to constitute a *service*. All I draw attention to is the circumstance that it is the spirit of *ressentiment* itself out of which this new nuance of scientific fairness (for the benefit of hatred, envy, jealousy, mistrust, rancor, and revenge) proceeds. For this "scientific fairness" immediately ceases and gives way to accents of deadly enmity and prejudice once it is a question of dealing with another group of affects, affects that, it seems to me, are of even greater biological value than those reactive affects and consequently deserve even more to be *scientifically* evaluated and esteemed: namely, the truly *active* affects, such as lust for power, avarice, and the like. (E. Dühring: *The Value of Life; A Course in Philosophy*; and, fundamentally, *passim*.)

So much against this tendency in general: as for Dühring's specific proposition that the home of justice is to be sought in the sphere of the reactive feelings, one is obliged for truth's sake to counter it with a blunt antithesis: the *last* sphere to be conquered by the spirit of justice is the sphere of the reactive feelings! When it really happens that the just man remains just even toward those who have harmed him (and not merely cold, temperate, remote, indifferent: being just is always a *positive* attitude), when the exalted, clear objectivity, as penetrating as it is mild, of the eye of justice and *judging* is not dimmed even under the assault of personal injury, derision, and calumny, this is a piece of perfection and supreme mastery on earth—something it would be prudent not to expect or to *believe* in too readily. On the average, a small dose of aggression, malice, or insinuation certainly suffices to drive the blood into the eyes—and fairness out of the eyes—of even the most upright people. The active, aggressive, arrogant man is still a hundred steps closer to justice than the reactive man; for he has absolutely no need to take a false and prejudiced view of the object before him in the way the reactive man does and is bound to do. For that reason the aggressive man, as the stronger, nobler, more courageous, has in fact also had at all times a *freer* eye, a *better* conscience on his side: conversely, one can see who has the invention of the "bad conscience" on his conscience—the man of *ressentiment*!

Finally, one only has to look at history: in which sphere has the entire administration of law hitherto been at home—also the need for law? In the sphere of reactive men, perhaps? By no means: rather in that of the active, strong, spontaneous, aggressive. From a historical point of view, law represents on earth—let it be said to the dismay of the above-named agitator (who himself once confessed: "the doctrine of revenge is the red thread of justice that runs through all my work and efforts")—the struggle *against* the reactive feelings, the war conducted against them on the part of the active and aggressive powers who employed some of their strength to impose measure and bounds upon the excesses of the reactive pathos and to compel it to come to terms. Wherever justice is practiced and maintained one sees a stronger power seeking a means of putting an end to the senseless raging of *ressentiment* among the weaker powers that stand under it (whether they be groups or individuals)—partly by taking the object of *ressentiment* out of the hands of revenge, partly by substituting for revenge the struggle against the enemies of peace and order, partly by devising and in some cases imposing settlements, partly by elevating certain equivalents for injuries into norms to which from then on *ressentiment* is once and for all directed. The most decisive act, however, that the supreme power performs and accomplishes against the predominance of grudges and rancor—it always takes this action as soon as it is in any way strong enough to do so—is the institution of *law*, the imperative declaration of what in general counts as permitted, as just, in its eyes, and what counts as forbidden, as unjust: once it has instituted the law, it treats violence and capricious acts on the part of individuals or entire groups as offenses against the law, as rebellion against the supreme power itself, and thus leads the feelings of its subjects away from the direct injury caused by such offenses; and in the long run it thus attains the reverse of that which is desired by all revenge that is fastened exclusively to the viewpoint of the person injured: from now on the eye is trained to an ever more *impersonal* evaluation of the deed, and this applies even to the eye of the injured person himself (although last of all, as remarked above).

"Just" and "unjust" exist, accordingly, only after the institution of the law (and *not*, as Dühring would have it, after the perpetration of the injury). To speak of just or unjust *in itself* is quite senseless; *in itself*, of course, no injury, assault, exploitation, destruction can be "unjust," since life operates *essentially*, that is in its basic functions, through injury, assault, exploitation, destruction and simply cannot be thought of at all without this character. One must indeed grant something even more unpalatable: that, from the highest biological standpoint, legal conditions can never be other than *exceptional conditions*, since they constitute a partial restriction of the will of life, which is bent upon power, and are subordinate to its total goal as a single means: namely, as a means of creating *greater* units of power. A legal order thought of as sovereign and universal, not as a means in the struggle between power complexes but as a means of *preventing* all struggle in general—perhaps after the communistic cliché of Dühring, that every will must consider every other will its equal—would be a principle *hostile to life*, an agent of the dissolution and destruction of man, an attempt to assassinate the future of man, a sign of weariness, a secret path to nothingness.—

12

Yet a word on the origin and the purpose of punishment—two problems that are separate, or ought to be separate: unfortunately, they are usually confounded. How have previous genealogists of morals set about solving these problems? Naïvely, as has always been their way: they seek out some "purpose" in punishment, for example, revenge of deterrence, then guilelessly place this purpose at the beginning as *causa fiendi* of punishment, and—have done. The "purpose of law," however, is absolutely the last thing to employ in the history of the origin of law: on the contrary, there is for historiography of any kind no more important proposition than the one it took such effort to establish but which really *ought to be* established now: the cause of the origin of a thing and its eventual utility, its actual employment and place in a system of purposes, lie worlds apart; whatever exists, having somehow come into being, is again and again reinterpreted to new ends, taken over, transformed, and redirected by some power superior to it; all events in the organic world are a subduing, a *becoming master*, and all subduing and becoming master involves a fresh interpretation, an adaptation through which any previous "meaning" and "purpose" are necessarily obscured or even obliterated. However well one has understood the *utility* of any physiological organ (or of a legal institution, a social custom, a political usage, a form in art or in a religious cult), this means nothing regarding its origin: however uncomfortable and disagreeable this may sound to older ears—for one had always believed that to understand the demonstrable purpose, the utility of a thing, a form, or an institution, was also to understand the reason why it originated—the eye being made for seeing, the hand being made for grasping.

Thus one also imagined that punishment was devised for punishing. But purposes and utilities are only *signs* that a will to power has become master of something less powerful and imposed upon it the character of a function; and the entire history of a "thing," an organ, a custom can in this way be a continuous sign-chain of ever new interpretations and adaptations whose causes do not even have to be related to one another but, on the contrary, in some cases succeed and alternate with one another in a purely chance fashion. The "evolution" of a thing, a custom, an organ is thus by no means its *progressus* toward a goal, even less a logical *progressus* by the shortest route and with the smallest expenditure of force—but a succession of more or less profound, more or less mutually independent processes of subduing, plus the resistances they encounter, the attempts at transformation for the purpose of defense and reaction, and the results of successful counteractions. The form is fluid, but the "meaning" is even more so.

The case is the same even within each individual organism: with every real growth in the whole, the "meaning" of the individual organs also changes; in certain circumstances their partial destruction, a reduction in their numbers (for example, through the disappearance of intermediary members) can be a sign of increasing strength and perfection. It is not too much to say that even a partial *diminution of utility*, an atrophying and degeneration, a loss of meaning and purposiveness—in short, death—is among the conditions of an actual *progressus*, which always appears in the shape of a will and way to *greater power* and is always carried through at the expense of numerous smaller powers. The magnitude of an "advance" can even be measured by the mass of things that had to be sacrificed to it; mankind in the mass sacrificed to the prosperity of a single *stronger* species of man—that *would* be an advance.

I emphasize this major point of historical method all the more because it is in fundamental opposition to the now prevalent instinct and taste which would rather be reconciled even to the absolute fortuitousness, even the mechanistic senselessness of all events than to the theory that in all events a *will to power* is operating. The democratic idiosyncrasy which opposes everything that dominates and wants to dominate, the modern *misarchism* (to coin an ugly word for an ugly thing) has permeated the realm of the spirit and disguised itself in the most spiritual forms to such a degree that today it has forced its way, has acquired the *right* to force its way into the strictest, apparently most objective sciences; indeed, it seems to me to have already taken charge of all physiology and theory of life—to the detriment of life, as goes without saying, since it has robbed it of a fundamental concept, that of *activity*. Under the influence of the above-mentioned idiosyncrasy, one places instead "adaptation" in the foreground, that is to say, an activity of the second rank, a mere reactivity; indeed, life itself has been defined as a more and more efficient inner adaptation to external conditions (Herbert Spencer). Thus the essence of life, its *will to power*, is ignored; one overlooks the essential priority of the spontaneous, aggressive, expansive, form-giving forces that give new interpretations and directions, although "adaptation" follows only after this; the dominant role of the highest functionaries within the organism itself in which the will to life appears active and form-giving is denied. One should recall what Huxley reproached Spencer with—his "administrative nihilism": but it is a question of rather *more* than mere "administration."

13

To return to our subject, namely *punishment*, one must distinguish two aspects: on the one hand, that in it which is relatively *enduring*, the custom, the act, the "drama," a certain strict sequence of procedures; on the other, that in it which is *fluid*, the meaning, the purpose, the expectation associated with the performance of such procedures. In accordance with the previously developed major point of historical method, it is assumed without further ado that the procedure itself will be something older, earlier than its employment in punishment, that the latter is *projected* and interpreted *into* the procedure (which has long existed but been employed in another sense), in short, that the case is *not* as has hitherto been assumed by our naïve genealogists of law and morals, who have one and all thought of the procedure as *invented* for the purpose of punishing, just as one formerly thought of the hand as invented for the purpose of grasping.

As for the other element in punishment, the fluid element, its "meaning," in a very late condition of culture (for example, in modern Europe) the concept "punishment" possesses in fact not *one* meaning but a whole synthesis of "meanings": the previous history of punishment in general, the history of its employment for the most various purposes, finally crystallizes into a kind of unity that is hard to disentangle, hard to analyze and, as must be emphasized especially, totally *indefinable*. (Today it is impossible to say for certain *why* people are really punished: all concepts in which an entire process is semiotically concentrated elude definition; only that which has no history is definable.) At an earlier stage, on the contrary, this synthesis of "meanings" can still be disentangled, as well as changed; one can still perceive how in each individual case the elements of the synthesis undergo a shift in value and rearrange themselves accordingly, so that now this, now that element comes to the fore and dominates at the expense of the others; and under certain circumstances one element (the purpose of deterrence perhaps) appears to overcome all the remaining elements.

To give at least an idea of how uncertain, how supplemental, how accidental "the meaning" of punishment is, and how one and the same procedure can be employed, interpreted, adapted to ends that differ fundamentally, I set down here the pattern that has emerged from consideration of relatively few chance instances I have noted. Punishment as a means of rendering harmless, of preventing further harm. Punishment as recompense to the injured party for the harm done, rendered in any form (even in that of a compensating affect). Punishment as the isolation of a disturbance of equilibrium, so as to guard against any further spread of the disturbance. Punishment as a means of inspiring fear of those who determine and execute the punishment. Punishment as a kind of repayment for the advantages the criminal has enjoyed hitherto (for example, when he is employed as a slave in the mines). Punishment as the expulsion of a degenerate element (in some cases, of an entire branch, as in Chinese law: thus as a means of preserving the purity of a race or maintaining a social type). Punishment as a festival, namely as the rape and mockery of a finally defeated enemy. Punishment as the making of a memory, whether for him who suffers the punishment—so-called "improvement"—or for those who witness its execution. Punishment as payment of a fee stipulated by the power that protects the wrongdoer from the excesses of revenge. Punishment as a compromise with revenge in its natural state when the latter is still maintained and claimed as a privilege by powerful clans. Punishment as a declaration of war and a war measure against an enemy of peace, of the law, of order, of the authorities, whom, as a danger to the community, as one who has broken the contract that defines the conditions under which it exists, as a rebel, a traitor, and breaker of the peace, one opposes with the means of war.—

14

This list is certainly not complete; it is clear that punishment is overdetermined by utilities of all kinds. All the more reason, then, for deducting from it a *supposed* utility that, to be sure, counts in the popular consciousness as the most essential one—belief in punishment, which for several reasons is tottering today, always finds its strongest support in this. Punishment is supposed to possess the value of awakening the *feeling of guilt* in the guilty person; one seeks in it the actual *instrumentum* of that psychical reaction called "bad conscience," "sting of conscience." Thus one misunderstands psychology and the reality of things even as they apply today: how much more as they applied during the greater part of man's history, his prehistory!

It is precisely among criminals and convicts that the sting of conscience is extremely rare; prisons and penitentiaries are *not* the kind of hotbed in which this species of gnawing worm is likely to flourish: all conscientious observers are agreed on that, in many cases unwillingly enough and contrary to their own inclinations. Generally speaking, punishment makes men hard and cold; it concentrates; it sharpens the feeling of alienation; it strengthens the power of resistance. If it happens that punishment destroys the vital energy and brings about a miserable prostration and self-abasement, such a result is certainly even less pleasant than the usual effects of punishment—characterized by dry and gloomy seriousness.

If we consider those millennia *before* the history of man, we may unhesitatingly assert that it was precisely through punishment that the development of the feeling of guilt was most powerfully *hindered*—at least in the victims upon whom the punitive force was vented. For we must not underrate the extent to which the sight of the judicial and executive procedures prevents the criminal from considering his deed, the type of his action *as such*, reprehensible: for he sees exactly the same kind of actions practiced in the service of justice and approved of and practiced with a good conscience: spying, deception, bribery, setting traps, the whole cunning and underhand art of police and prosecution, plus robbery, violence, defamation, imprisonment, torture, murder, practiced as a matter of principle and without even emotion to excuse them, which are pronounced characteristics of the various forms of punishment—all of them therefore actions which his judges in no way condemn and repudiate *as such*, but only when they are applied and directed to certain particular ends.

The "bad conscience," this most uncanny and most interesting plant of all our earthly vegetation, did *not* grow on this soil; indeed, during the greater part of the past the judges and punishers themselves were *not at all* conscious of dealing with a "guilty person." But with an instigator of harm, with an irresponsible piece of fate. And the person upon whom punishment subsequently descended, again like a piece of fate, suffered no "inward pain" other than that induced by the sudden appearance of something unforeseen, a dreadful natural event, a plunging, crushing rock that one cannot fight.

Third Essay

9

We have seen how a certain asceticism, a severe and cheerful continence with the best will, belongs to the most favorable conditions of supreme spirituality, and is also among its most natural consequences: hence it need be no matter for surprise that philosophers have always discussed the ascetic ideal with a certain fondness. A serious examination of history actually reveals that the bond between philosophy and the ascetic ideal is even much closer and stronger. One might assert that it was only on the leadingstrings of this ideal that philosophy learned to take its first small steps on earth—alas, so clumsily, so unwillingly, so ready to fall on its face and lie on its belly, this timid little toddler and mollycoddle with shaky legs!

Philosophy began as all good things begin: for a long time it lacked the courage for itself; it was always looking round to see if someone would come and help it; yet it was afraid of all who looked at it. Draw up a list of the various propensities and virtues of the philosopher—his bent to doubt, his bent to deny, his bent to suspend judgment (his "ephectic" bent), his bent to analyze, his bent to investigate, seek, dare, his bent to compare and balance, his will to neutrality and objectivity, his will to every "*sine ira et studio*": is it not clear that for the longest time all of them contravened the basic demands of morality and conscience (not to speak of *reason* quite generally, which Luther liked to call "Mistress Clever, the clever whore")—that if a philosopher *had* been conscious of what he was, he would have been compelled to feel himself the embodiment of "*nitimur in vetitum*"—and consequently *guarded* against "feeling himself," against becoming conscious of himself?

It is, to repeat, no different with all the good things of which we are proud today; measured even by the standards of the ancient Greeks, our entire modern way of life, insofar as it is not weakness but power and consciousness of power, has the appearance of sheer *hubris* and godlessness: for the longest time it was precisely the reverse of those things we hold in honor today that had a good conscience on its side and God for its guardian. Our whole attitude toward nature, the way we violate her with the aid of machines and the heedless inventiveness of our technicians and engineers, is *hubris*; our attitude toward God as some alleged spider of purpose and morality behind the great captious web of causality, is *hubris*—we might say, with Charles the Bold when he opposed Louis XI, "*je combats l'universelle araignée*", our attitude toward *ourselves* is *hubris*, for we experiment with ourselves in a way we would never permit ourselves to experiment with animals and, carried away by curiosity, we cheerfully vivisect our souls: what is the "salvation" of the soul to us today? Afterward we cure ourselves: sickness is instructive, we have no doubt of that, even more instructive than health—*those who make sick* seem even more necessary to us today than any medicine men or "saviors." We violate ourselves nowadays, no doubt of it, we nutcrackers of the soul, ever questioning and questionable, as if life were nothing but cracking nuts; and thus we are bound to grow day-by-day more questionable, *worthier* of asking questions; perhaps also worthier—of living?

All good things were formerly bad things; every original sin has turned into an original virtue. Marriage, for example, seemed for a long time a transgression against the rights of the community; one had to make reparation for being so immodest as to claim a woman for oneself (hence, for example, the *jus primae noctis*, which in Cambodia is still the prerogative of the priests, those guardians of all "hallowed customs"). The gentle, benevolent, conciliatory, and compassionate feelings—eventually so highly valued that they almost constitute "the eternal values"—were opposed for the longest time by self-contempt: one was ashamed of mildness as one is today ashamed of hardness (cf. *Beyond Good and Evil*, section 260). Submission to *law*: how the consciences of noble tribes all over the earth resisted the abandonment of vendetta and were loath to bow before the power of the law! "Law" was for a long time a *vetitum*, an outrage, an innovation; it was characterized by violence—it *was* violence to which one submitted, feeling ashamed of oneself. Every smallest step on earth has been paid for by spiritual and physical torture: this whole point of view, "that not only every progressive step, no! every step, movement, and change has required its countless martyrs," sounds utterly strange to us today—I called attention to it in *The Dawn*, section 18.

"Nothing has been bought more dearly," I say there, "than the modicum of human reason and feeling of freedom that are now our pride. It is this pride, however, that makes it almost impossible for us today to empathize with that vast era of the "morality of mores' which preceded 'world history' as the truly decisive history that determined the character of mankind: when suffering was everywhere counted as a virtue, cruelty as a virtue, dissembling as a virtue, revenge as a virtue, slander of reason as a virtue, and when on the other hand well-being was counted as a danger, thirst for knowledge as a danger, peace as a danger, pity as a danger, being pitied as a disgrace, work as a disgrace, madness as divine, *change* as the very essence of immorality and pregnant with disaster."

10

In the same book (section 42) it is explained under what valuation, what *oppression* of valuation, the earliest race of contemplative men had to live: when not feared, they were despised. Contemplation first appeared on earth in disguise, in ambiguous form, with an evil heart and often an anxious head: there is no doubt of that. The inactive, brooding, unwarlike element in the instincts of contemplative men long surrounded them with a profound mistrustfulness: the only way of dispelling it was to arouse a decided *fear* of oneself. And the ancient Brahmins, for instance, knew how to do this! The earliest philosophers knew how to endow their existence and appearance with a meaning, a basis and background, through which others might come to *fear* them: more closely considered, they did so from an even more fundamental need, namely, so as to fear and reverence themselves. For they found all the value judgments within them turned *against* them, they had to fight down every kind of suspicion and resistance against "the philosopher in them." As men of frightful ages, they did this by using frightful means; cruelty toward themselves, inventive self-castigation—this was the principal means these power-hungry hermits and innovators of ideas required to overcome the gods and tradition in themselves, so as to be able to *believe* in their own innovations. I recall the famous story of King Vishvamitra, who through millennia of self-torture acquired such a feeling of power and self-confidence that he endeavored to build a *new heaven*—the uncanny symbol of the most ancient and most recent experience of philosophers on earth: whoever has at some time built a "new heaven" has found the power to do so only in his *own hell.*

Let us compress the facts into a few brief formulas: to begin with, the philosophic spirit always had to use as a mask and cocoon the *previously established* types of the contemplative man—priest, sorcerer, soothsayer, and in any case a religious type—in order to be able to *exist at all: the ascetic ideal* for a long time served the philosopher as a form in which to appear, as a precondition of existence—he had to *represent* it so as to be able to be a philosopher; he had to *believe* in it in order to be able to represent it. The peculiar, withdrawn attitude of the philosopher, world-denying, hostile to life, suspicious of the senses, freed from sensuality, which has been maintained down to the most modern times and has become virtually the *philosopher's pose par excellence*—it is above all a result of the emergency conditions under which philosophy arose and survived at all; for the longest time philosophy would not have been *possible at all* on earth without ascetic wraps and cloak, without an ascetic self-misunderstanding. To put it vividly: the *ascetic priest* provided until the most modern times the repulsive and gloomy caterpillar form in which alone the philosopher could live and creep about.

Has all this really *altered*? Has that many-colored and dangerous winged creature, the "spirit" which this caterpillar concealed, really been unfettered at last and released into the light, thanks to a sunnier, warmer, brighter world? Is there sufficient pride, daring, courage, self-confidence available today, sufficient will of the spirit, will to responsibility, *freedom of will*, for "the philosopher" to be henceforth—*possible* on earth?—

11

Only now that we behold the *ascetic priest* do we seriously come to grips with our problem: what is the meaning of the ascetic ideal?—only now does it become "serious": we are now face to face with the actual *representative of seriousness*. "What is the meaning of all seriousness?"—this even more fundamental question may perhaps be trembling on our lips at this point: a question for physiologists, of course, but one which we must still avoid for the moment. The ascetic priest possessed in this ideal not only his faith but also his will, his power, his interest. His *right* to exist stands or falls with that ideal: no wonder we encounter here a terrible antagonist—supposing we are antagonists of that ideal—one who fights for his existence against those who deny that ideal.

On the other hand, it is inherently improbable that so interested an attitude toward our problem will benefit it: the ascetic priest will hardly provide the best defense of his ideal, just as a woman who tries to defend "woman as such" usually fails—and he certainly will not be the most objective judge of this controversy. Far from fearing he will confute us—this much is already obvious—we shall have to help him defend himself against us.

The idea at issue here is the *valuation* the ascetic priest places on our life: he juxtaposes it (along with what pertains to it: "nature," "world," the whole sphere of becoming and transitoriness) with a quite different mode of existence which it opposes and excludes, *unless* it turn against itself, *deny itself*: in that case, the case of the ascetic life, life counts as a bridge to that other mode of existence. The ascetic treats life as a wrong road on which one must finally walk back to the point where it begins, or as a mistake that is put right by deeds—that we *ought* to put right: for he *demands* that one go along with him; where he can he compels acceptance of *his* evaluation of existence.

What does this mean? So monstrous a mode of valuation stands inscribed in the history of mankind not as an exception and curiosity, but as one of the most widespread and enduring of all phenomena. Read from a distant star, the majuscule script of our earthly existence would perhaps lead to the conclusion that the earth was the distinctively *ascetic planet*, a nook of disgruntled, arrogant, and offensive creatures filled with a profound disgust at themselves, at the earth, at all life, who inflict as much pain on themselves as they possibly can out of pleasure in inflicting pain—which is probably their only pleasure. For consider how regularly and universally the ascetic priest appears in almost every age; he belongs to no one race; he prospers everywhere; he emerges from every class of society. Nor does he breed and propagate his mode of valuation through heredity: the opposite is the case—broadly speaking, a profound instinct rather forbids him to propagate. It must be a necessity of the first order that again and again promotes the growth and prosperity of this *life-inimical* species—it must indeed be in the *interest of life itself* that such a self-contradictory type does not die out. For an ascetic life is a self-contradiction: here rules a *ressentiment* without equal, that of an insatiable instinct and power-will that wants to become master not over something in life but over life itself, over its most profound, powerful, and basic conditions; here an attempt is made to employ force to block up the wells of force; here physiological well-being itself is viewed askance, and especially the outward expression of this well-being, beauty and joy; while pleasure is felt and *sought* in ill-constitutedness, decay, pain, mischance, ugliness, voluntary deprivation, self-mortification, self-flagellation, self-sacrifice. All this is in the highest degree paradoxical: we stand before a discord that *wants* to be discordant, that *enjoys* itself in this suffering and even grows more self-confident and triumphant the more its own presupposition, its physiological capacity for life, *decreases*. "Triumph in the ultimate agony": the ascetic ideal has always fought under this hyperbolic sign; in this enigma of seduction, in this image of torment and delight, it recognized its brightest light, its salvation, its ultimate victory. *Crux, nux, lux*—for the ascetic ideal these three are one.—

13

But let us return to our problem. It will be immediately obvious that such a self-contradiction as the ascetic appears to represent, "life *against* life," is, physiologically considered and not merely psychologically, a simple absurdity. It can only be *apparent*; it must be a kind of provisional formulation, an interpretation and psychological misunderstanding of something whose real nature could not for a long time be understood or described *as it really was*—a mere word inserted into an old *gap* in human knowledge. Let us replace it with a brief formulation of the facts of the matter: *the ascetic ideal springs from the protective instinct of a degenerating life* which tries by all means to sustain itself and to fight for its existence; it indicates a partial physiological obstruction and exhaustion against which the deepest instincts of life, which have remained intact, continually struggle with new expedients and devices. The ascetic ideal is such an expedient; the case is therefore the opposite of what those who reverence this ideal believe: life wrestles in it and through it with death and *against* death; the ascetic ideal is an artifice for the *preservation* of life.

That this ideal acquired such power and ruled over men as imperiously as we find it in history, especially wherever the civilization and taming of man has been carried through, expresses a great fact: the *sickliness* of the type of man we have had hitherto, or at least of the tamed man, and the physiological struggle of man against death (more precisely: against disgust with life, against exhaustion, against the desire for the "end"). The ascetic priest is the incarnate desire to be different, to be in a different place, and indeed this desire at its greatest extreme, its distinctive fervor and passion; but precisely this power of his desire is the chain that holds him captive so that he becomes a tool for the creation of more favorable conditions for being here and being man—it is precisely this *power* that enables him to persuade to existence the whole herd of the ill-constituted, disgruntled, underprivileged, unfortunate, and all who suffer of themselves, by instinctively going before them as their shepherd. You will see my point: this ascetic priest, this apparent enemy of life, this *denier*—precisely, he is among the greatest *conserving* and yes-creating forces of life.

Where does it come from this sickliness? For man is more sick, uncertain, changeable, indeterminate than any other animal, there is no doubt of that—he is *the* sick animal: how has that come about? Certainly he has also dared more, done more new things, braved more and challenged fate more than all the other animals put together: he, the great experimenter with himself, discontented and insatiable, wrestling with animals, nature, and gods for ultimate dominion—he, still unvanquished, eternally directed toward the future, whose own restless energies never leave him in peace, so that his future digs like a spur into the flesh of every present—how should such a courageous and richly endowed animal not also be the most imperiled, the most chronically and profoundly sick of all sick animals?

Man has often had enough; there are actual epidemics of having had enough (as around 1348, at the time of the dance of death); but even this nausea, this weariness, this disgust with himself—all this bursts from him with such violence that it at once becomes a new fetter. The No he says to life brings to light, as if by magic, an abundance of tender Yeses; even when he *wounds* himself, this master of destruction, of self-destruction—the very wound itself afterward compels him *to live.*—

14

The more normal sickliness becomes among men—and we cannot deny its normality—the higher should be the honor accorded the rare cases of great power of soul and body, man's *lucky hits*; the more we should protect the well-constituted from the worst kind of air, the air of the sickroom. Is this done?

The sick represent the greatest danger for the healthy; it is *not* the strongest but the weakest who spell disaster for the strong. Is this known?

Broadly speaking, it is not fear of man that we should desire to see diminished; for this fear compels the strong to be strong, and occasionally terrible—it *maintains* the well-constituted type of man. What is to be feared, what has a more calamitous effect than any other calamity, is that man should inspire not profound fear but profound *nausea*; also not great fear but great *pity*. Suppose these two were one day to unite, they would inevitably beget one of the uncanniest monsters: the "last will" of man, his will to nothingness, nihilism. And indeed a great deal points to this union. Whoever can smell not only with his nose but also with his eyes and ears, scents almost everywhere he goes today something like the air of madhouses and hospitals—I am speaking, of course, of the cultural domain, of every kind of "Europe" on this earth. The *sick* are man's greatest danger; *not* the evil, *not* the "beasts of prey." Those who are failures from the start, downtrodden, crushed—it is they, the *weakest*, who must undermine life among men, who call into question and poison most dangerously our trust in life, in man, and in ourselves. Where does one not encounter that veiled glance which burdens one with a profound sadness, that inward-turned glance of the born failure which betrays how such a man speaks to himself—that glance which is a sigh! "If only I were someone else," sighs this glance: "but there is no hope of that. I am who I am: how could I ever get free of myself? And yet—I *am sick of myself!*"

It is on such soil, on swampy ground, that every weed, every poisonous plant grows, always so small, so hidden, so false, so saccharine. Here the worms of vengefulness and rancor swarm; here the air stinks of secrets and concealment; here the web of the most malicious of all conspiracies is being spun constantly— the conspiracy of the suffering against the well-constituted and victorious, here the aspect of the victorious is *hated*. And what mendaciousness is employed to disguise that this hatred is hatred! What a display of grand words and postures, what an art of "honest" calumny! These failures: what noble eloquence flows from their lips! How much sugary, slimy, humble submissiveness swims in their eyes! What do they really want? At least to *represent* justice, love, wisdom, superiority—that is the ambition of the "lowest," the sick. And how skillfull such an ambition makes them! Admire above all the forger's skill with which the stamp of virtue, even the ring, the golden-sounding ring of virtue, is here counterfeited. They monopolize virtue, these weak, hopelessly sick people, there is no doubt of it: "we alone are the good and just," they say, "we alone are *homines bonae voluntatis.*" They walk among us as embodied reproaches, as warnings to us—as if health, well-constitutedness, strength, pride, and the sense of power were in themselves necessarily vicious things for which one must pay some day, and pay bitterly: how ready they themselves are at bottom to *make* one pay; how they crave to be *hangmen*. There is among them an abundance of the vengeful disguised as judges, who constantly bear the word "justice" in their mouths like poisonous spittle, always with pursed lips, always ready to spit upon all who are not discontented but go their way in good spirits. Nor is there lacking among them that most disgusting species of the vain, the mendacious failures whose aim is to appear as "beautiful souls" and who bring to market their deformed sensuality, wrapped up in verses and other swaddling clothes, as "purity of heart": the species of moral masturbaters and "self-gratifiers." The will of the weak to represent *some* form of superiority, their instinct for devious paths to tyranny over the healthy—where can it not be discovered, this will to power of the weakest!

The sick woman especially: no one can excel her in the wiles to dominate, oppress, and tyrannize. The sick woman spares nothing, living or dead; she will dig up the most deeply buried things (the Bogos say: "woman is a hyena").

Examine the background of every family, every organization, every commonwealth: everywhere the struggle of the sick against the healthy—a silent struggle as a rule, with petty poisons, with pinpricks, with sly long-suffering expressions, but occasionally also with that invalid's Phariseeism of *loud* gestures that likes best to pose as "noble indignation." This hoarse, indignant barking of sick dogs, this rabid mendaciousness and rage of "noble" Pharisees, penetrates even the hallowed halls of science (I again remind readers who have ears for such things of that Berlin apostle of revenge, Eugen Dühring, who employs moral mumbo-jumbo more indecently and repulsively than anyone else in Germany today: Dühring, the foremost moral bigmouth today—unexcelled even among his own ilk, the anti-Semites).

They are all men of *ressentiment*, physiologically unfortunate and worm-eaten, a whole tremulous realm of subterranean revenge, inexhaustible and insatiable in outbursts against the fortunate and happy and in masquerades of revenge and pretexts for revenge: when would they achieve the ultimate, subtlest, sublimest triumph of revenge? Undoubtedly if they succeeded in *poisoning the consciences* of the fortunate with their own misery, with all misery, so that one day the fortunate began to be ashamed of their good fortune and perhaps said one to another: "it is disgraceful to be fortunate: *there is too much misery!*"

But no greater or more calamitous misunderstanding is possible than for the happy, well-constituted, powerful in soul and body, to begin to doubt their *right to happiness* in this fashion. Away with this "inverted world"! Away with this shameful emasculation of feeling! That the sick should *not* make the healthy sick—and this is what such an emasculation would involve—should surely be our supreme concern on earth; but this requires above all that the healthy should be *segregated* from the sick, guarded even from the sight of the sick, that they may not confound themselves with the sick. Or is it their task, perhaps, to be nurses or physicians?

But no worse misunderstanding and denial of *their* task can be imagined: the higher *ought* not to degrade itself to the status of an instrument of the lower, the pathos of distance *ought* to keep their tasks eternally separate! Their right to exist, the privilege of the full-toned bell over the false and cracked, is a thousand times greater: they alone are our *warranty* for the future, they alone are *liable* for the future of man. The sick can never have the ability or obligation to do what *they* can do, what *they* ought to do: but if they are to be able to do what *they* alone ought to do, how can they at the same time be physicians, consolers, and "saviors" of the sick?

And therefore let us have fresh air! fresh air! and keep clear of the madhouses and hospitals of culture! And therefore let us have good company, *our* company! Or solitude, if it must be! But away from the sickening fumes of inner corruption and the hidden rot of disease! . . . So that we may, at least for a while yet, guard ourselves, my friends, against the two worst contagions that may be reserved just for us—against the *great nausea at man!* against *great pity for man!*

Part Four

IN OUR TIMES

THE TWENTIETH century has been a tumultuous, violent century. It was punctuated by war and upheaval affecting millions upon millions of people. A preliminary list of its major events would include two world wars with their bloodshed and genocide, the Bolshevik and Chinese revolutions, decolonization of European empires, and the collapse of the Soviet bloc. Needless to say, thinking politically in the twentieth century entailed contemplating phenomena like these. Some thinkers even inspired some of them—sometimes for better and sometimes very much for worse. It is hardly surprising that the twentieth century is often called a century of contesting "isms"—communism, socialism, liberalism, feminism, conservatism, fascism, totalitarianism.

In this section of the book, you will find a diverse array of theorists writing about a diverse array of subjects. Actually, not all the selections are by people who can properly be characterized as "thinkers." Take, for example, Benito Mussolini, the fascist dictator of Italy from the early 1920s through the 1940s. He propounded an ideology of the extreme right, a series of self-justifying ultranationalist ideas and slogans. They were often not too coherent but they nonetheless composed an ideology which had a major impact, if only because a tyrant proclaiming them ruled an important European country for two decades. Ideas similar to his—and worse—had a considerable following across the continent. So if Mussolini was hardly a philosopher, we can hardly avoid thinking about fascism if we want to think about politics in our times.

At the same time, he is easily contrasted with serious theorists who examined the same era. Take, for one example, Hannah Arendt, who was one of the most influential political philosophers in mid-century America. Arendt, a German Jew, fled fascism—in particular, Hitler's nazism—and eventually became a professor in New York. Her study of *The Origins of Totalitarianism*, published in 1951, tried to think about, to analyze, and to come to grips with "the burden of our times" (the British title of her book). She insisted that something new had come about in the history of tyranny, and that nothing in the past was quite comparable to it. It was embodied especially in the regimes of Hitler and Stalin. Despots in the past aimed to be unchallengeable autocrats; they wanted profit and comfort for themselves and their backers. But the new "totalitarian" regimes aspired to total control of all aspects of life and were responsible for the deaths of millions. They were grounded on ideology and terror, said Arendt.

It was after the carnage of World War II that the phrase "welfare state" came into vogue. It is interesting to note that while, in the 1980s and 1990s, "welfare state" was commonly contrasted to laissez-faire (that is, to governments that allowed the market a "free hand"), the phrase was invented with an entirely different comparison in mind. At the end of the war, a British archbishop, William Temple, contrasted the "power-state" of fascism with the humane "welfare-state" he hoped might be fashioned now that the dictators had fallen. In his country the Labor party won the national elections in 1945 and sought to create a "welfare state" by fashioning a more egalitarian society through extensive social welfare legislation (for example, establishing a national health service) and intervening in the economy.

The ideas of social welfare and "social citizenship" were not new: political theorists have long debated to what extent the state should intervene in social and economic relations. Was laissez-faire—a minimal role for government—the best idea? If so, the market would have autonomy in distributing wealth and services. Or are socioeconomic questions also political in the final analysis? Does the government have a major responsibility to intervene in economic life to alleviate social suffering? What is "justice" and what is a government's relationship to it?

The problem of social equality is prominent in twentieth-century political theory. Only in the late nineteenth and early twentieth centuries was universal suffrage achieved in most Western countries. Before then, only a minority (the upper classes) could vote. Now the question arose: should political democracy—that is, the existence of democratically elected representative governing institutions—be supplemented by some form of social and economic democracy? Was there only political citizenship? What of social or economic citizenship? Some argued that just as the state was concerned with relations of power (between governors and governed), so too were the social and economic realms of life. We get the word democracy from the ancient Greeks: *demos* meant the people and *kratos* meant rule. Democracy was rule by the people. To be true democrats, it was asked, ought we not to extend this principle to all spheres of life? As a wit once quipped, why should control over your life end at the workplace?

As the second half of the twentieth century advanced, the definition of what it meant to have "control over your life" seemed to extend dramatically. Feminists, for example, demanded rights for women, often asserting that "the personal is the political"; minority groups that had been victimized, such as African-Americans, demanded equality and an end to racism; and in the aftermath of decolonization, Third World countries insisted on a new place for themselves, pressing for a fair share of the globe's wealth. In addressing all these cases, what it meant to "think politically"—to think in terms of power relations—went far beyond how to govern a country. It began to cover a wide variety of human relations—sexual, interracial, economic, and social. Could a sexist society be truly democratic? Let alone a racist one? Or one with vast socioeconomic inequalities? Or one run by a colonial power that deemed itself culturally "superior"?

Yet while "democracy" was inscribed on many banners in this century, not all of them led to the establishment of democracy—if by democracy we truly mean rule of the people. The communist regimes imposed on eastern Europe by Moscow after World War II called themselves "People's Democracies," yet rule by the people was to be found nowhere in them. More than one Third World "Liberation Movement" produced brutal dictatorships. Several important political thinkers, especially conservative ones, have argued that the very concept of democracy is a myth, bearing no relation to political reality. Take for example Gaetano Mosca, an

Italian political thinker and parliamentarian. (A selection from his *The Ruling Class* is included in this anthology.) His argument was, in a way, quite simple. He maintained that in all societies throughout history, whatever their actual structure of government, there was, has been, and always will be two classes of people—a minority who rules (he called it the ruling or "political" class) and the vast majority who are ruled. "Democracy" is simply a "political formula," a subterfuge, used by the political class to persuade the vast majority that they really share in power. Even when there is a parliament, an elite—both in it and outside of it—really calls the tune. Hierarchy is unavoidable in political life. Mosca defied his readers to cite one historical example to the contrary. Even in ancient Athens, the "demos," those with the rights and duties of citizenship, composed a minority of the population. Mosca contended that he was making no value judgment: it was a simple fact of political science that there are always elites.

Following Mosca, Robert Michels proposed in his book *Political Parties* that there is an "iron law of oligarchy": wherever there is organization—especially a mass organization—a minority will come to dominate, control, and run it. He took as his example a party famous for its commitment to the creation of a new society based on political, social, and economic democracy—the German Social Democrats. Michels tried to show that, contrary to its own principles, this mass political party was run by elites and that it could not be otherwise: "Who says organization, says oligarchy."

As various commentators have pointed out, neither Mosca nor Michels could have been surprised by the fate of the Bolshevik Revolution in 1917. Karl Marx wrote in *The Communist Manifesto* that in coming to power and becoming the "ruling class," workers would "win the battle of democracy" since they composed the vast majority of society. He insisted that the emancipation of the working class had to be done by the workers themselves, who would be transformed in the process, fashioning a society in which each member would contribute according to his or her abilities and get back what he or she needed. But Lenin, who claimed to be Marx's disciple, maintained that workers could never obtain the necessary "revolutionary consciousness" on their own. Hence, a "vanguard" was needed, a political party that would bring this consciousness to the workers. In power, the Bolsheviks fashioned a one-party state—the bureaucracy became the elite. Later Stalin transmuted it into one of the most oppressive regimes in human history. The working class had no power at all, even though a tyrant and a bureaucracy claimed to rule in its name. (Actually, at the time of the Russian revolution, most of the country's population were peasants, not urban workers.) Undoubtedly, Mosca and Michels would have said: Told you so. Try to make a perfectly equal society, and you will end up, as has everyone else throughout history, with elite rule.

Does this mean that "democracy" or the aspiration to equality are fraudulent ideas? A forceful case to the contrary is made by many democratic thinkers. Among other things they will point out that Mosca based his generalizations partly on his own experiences in the Italian parliament, which was one of the most corrupt in Europe in the late nineteenth and early twentieth centuries. And critics will note that Michels (though not Mosca) became a supporter of Mussolini. Is *that* the alternative to "fraudulent" democracy? Representative democracies may be flawed, but at least elites can be thrown out of office in them. They can be held accountable. Moreover, the more equality and opportunity for all is created in social and economic life, elitism can be tempered. However many their blemishes, usually when European Social Democratic parties came to power they were responsible for an expansion of opportunities and improvement of social conditions for workers and the poor. These parties may not have created perfectly equal or classless societies, and indeed had their own, often self-interested bureaucracies, but they also enlarged the dimension of social rights, served as vehicles by which people who previously had no political voice were able to articulate their needs, and tried to be their representatives, if imperfectly.

Moreover, sophisticated egalitarian democrats don't argue that society should be made "absolutely" equal or that all dimensions of life should be treated as if they were the same. In this section of the book, you will find Michael Walzer, one of America's leading political philosophers and co-editor of the journal *Dissent*, arguing against both right-wing and left-wing caricatures of what equality means. (His immediate target is an American "neoconservative" critic of egalitarianism, Irving Kristol.) Walzer proposes that "equality" must be conceived in an intelligent and differentiated way. He argues for egalitarianism, but contends that because there are different dimensions of human life, equality "cannot be satisfied by a single distributive scheme." It requires "a diversity of principles, which mirrors the diversity of mankind and social goods."

A different track is pursued by Harvard philosopher John Rawls. The publication of his book *A Theory of Justice* in 1971 led to a flowering of debate among political theorists in the United States and abroad. Rawls argues for "justice as fairness." It is important to see precisely what he means. He doesn't mean that justice is simply a matter of being fair. Rawls reinvents a famous tool of social contract theory, which we've already seen in the writings of Hobbes, Locke, and Rousseau. They constructed their respective theories by first placing human beings in a "state of nature" and then describing why they would sign a contract to leave this state and what sort of government they would create upon doing so. Hobbes, Locke, and Rousseau were asking: what types of political institutions are a consequence of human nature and the nature of things?

Instead of a state of nature, Rawls asks us to imagine that we are in an "original position"—circumstances in which we will choose the basic principles governing political and social life. When he speaks of justice as fairness, he means that the conditions in which we choose these principles must be fair. They would be fair, he thinks, if we had general knowledge about politics and society and operated on the basis of enlightened self-interest, but were also under a "veil of ignorance." We wouldn't know our own talents or actual place in society. On the basis of such fair conditions, Rawls thinks, we would choose these principles: everyone must have equal liberty; inequalities—socioeconomic differences—are acceptable if they are to the greatest benefit of the least advantaged (this is Rawls' famous "difference principle"); and there must be equal opportunity for all to achieve positions and offices.

In fact, Rawls has made a case for a liberal democratic welfare state. Besides a selection from *A Theory of Justice*, we have also included a reading from one of his most prominent contemporary critics. Robert Nozick, another Harvard philosopher, maintains in his book *Anarchy, State and Utopia* that anything beyond the most minimal state endangers human liberty and cannot be justified. He opposes redistributing wealth, believing that such an effort must intrude on basic rights that a government dare not touch if there is to be a free society.

All these authors mark out and delimit, in various ways, what it means to "think politically." How far should politics and power extend? Into what domains of life may government legitimately intrude? Into what aspects *must* its presence be felt if there is to be justice? Again: should the social and economic realms be left to themselves? Or should we think of them politically, as these too are realms of power? These questions have been endlessly debated in our times—and undoubtedly will be debated long after.

26

Max Weber
Politics as a Vocation

Max Weber (1864–1920) was one of the most learned and influential thinkers of the late nineteenth and early twentieth centuries. Born in Germany, he identified himself as a "national liberal" and rose to prominence in the 1890s due to his writings on historical political economy. Often hailed as a founder of the discipline of sociology, Weber's analyses of a wide variety of issues and concepts—ranging from modern bureaucracy to the different types of authority—continue to be central to contemporary social science and political science. He was particularly concerned with the "rationalization" of Western society and how that affected the relation between means and ends in social life. Some of his most celebrated works, such as The Protestant Ethic and the Spirit of Capitalism *and* Economy and Society, *are often seen as a "debate with the ghost of Karl Marx." Weber's essays in the philosophy of social science, in which he explored the relation between "value-judgements" and the effort to be "scientific," also have had a formidable impact that lasts through today. The following essay, "Politics as a Vocation," reflects some of his most compelling themes.*

WHAT CAN politics as a vocation offer in the way of inner satisfaction, and which personal qualities does it presuppose in anyone who devotes himself to it?

Well, it offers first of all the sense of power. Even in positions which are, formally speaking, modest, the professional politician can feel himself elevated above the everyday level by the sense of exercising influence over men, of having a share in power over their lives, but above all by the sense of having his finger on the pulse of historically important events. But the question which he has to face is this: through which personal qualities can he hope to do justice to this power (however narrow its limits in his particular case) and so to the responsibility it lays on him? At this point we enter the domain of ethical questions; for it is in this domain that the question arises: what kind of man must one be to venture to lay hands on the spokes of the wheel of history?

Three qualities above all, it might be said, are of decisive importance for the politician: passion, a sense of responsibility and judgment. By 'passion' I mean *realistic* passion—a passionate commitment to a realistic cause, to the god or demon in whose domain it lies. I do not mean 'passion' in the sense of that state of mind which my late friend Georg Simmel used to call 'sterile excitement'—a state which is characteristic of a certain kind of intellectual, especially of Russian intellectuals (though not perhaps all of them!), and which now plays such a large part amongst our own intellectuals in this carnival which is dignified with the proud name of a 'revolution.' It is a kind of 'romanticism of the intellectually interesting' which lacks any realistic sense of responsibility and runs away to nothing. For it is not enough merely to have the passion, however genuinely felt. That alone does not make a politician, unless it is used to further some real cause and so makes a *sense of responsibility* towards this cause the ultimate guide of his behaviour. And that requires the decisive psychological quality of the politician— *judgment*—the ability to contemplate things as they are with inner calm and composure before allowing them to affect one's actions, or in other words, an attitude of *detachment* towards things and people. Lack of detachment, purely as such, is one of the mortal sins for every politician, and one of those qualities which would condemn our rising generation of intellectuals to political impotence if they were to cultivate it. The problem, therefore, is simply how hot passion and cool judgment can be made to combine within the same personality. Politics is made with the head, not with other parts of the body or mind. And dedication to politics can only be born from passion and nourished by it, if it is not to be a frivolous intellectual game but an authentic human activity. But that firm discipline of the personality which is the hallmark of the passionate politician and distinguishes him from the political dilettante who is merely possessed by 'sterile excitement' is achievable only through the habit of detachment, in every sense of that word. The 'strength' of a political 'personality' is to be found above all in the possession of these qualities.

The politician has daily, even hourly, to overcome in himself a wholly banal and all-too-human enemy: the *vanity* which is so common and which is the deadly enemy of all concrete commitment and of all detachment (in this case, detachment towards oneself). Vanity is a very widespread characteristic, and perhaps no one is altogether free of it. In academic and scholarly circles, indeed, it is a kind of occupational disease. But equally, in the case of a scholar, however distasteful its manifestations may be, it is relatively harmless in the sense that it does not, as a rule, interfere with his scholarly activity. In the politician's case, things are quite different. In his work, the urge for *power* plays an inescapable part. The 'power instinct,' as it is often called, belongs therefore among his normal attributes.

The point at which someone in his profession begins to sin against the Holy Ghost, however, is the point at which this urge for power becomes *detached from reality*, and becomes a means of purely personal self-intoxication instead of being applied exclusively in the service of some realistic cause. For there are ultimately only two sorts of mortal sin in the political world: lack of realism and lack of responsibility (which is often, though not always, identical with it). At its most powerful, vanity—the need to occupy the limelight as much as possible—tempts the politician to commit one or both of these sins. The temptation is all the greater, in that the demagogue is forced to take into account the 'effect' which he produces: indeed just because of this he runs a constant risk of becoming a play-actor, making light of the responsibility for the consequences of his actions and asking only what 'impression' he is making. His lack of realism leads him to seek the glittering semblance of power rather than the reality of it, while his lack of responsibility leads him to enjoy power purely for its own sake, without any substantive purpose. For although, or rather precisely *because*, power is the inescapable instrument of all politics, and the urge to power is therefore one of the driving forces behind all politics, there is no more pernicious way to distort the political drive than for a politician to boast of his power like a parvenu and luxuriate conceitedly in the sensation of power—in short, to worship power for its own sake. The pure 'power-politician,' extolled in the cult which has its zealous adherents even in our own society, may operate with impressive effect, but in the event his operations lead only into a meaningless void. In that respect, the critics of 'power-politics' are absolutely right. In the sudden inner collapse of some typical representatives of this way of thinking we have been able to see what inner weakness and impotence is concealed behind their ostentatious but totally empty posturing. It results from an utterly cheap, superficial and *blasé* attitude towards the *meaning* of human activity—an attitude lacking all awareness of the tragic element with which all action, but especially political action, is in fact intertwined.

It is undeniably true, indeed a fundamental truth of all history (though not one to be explored more closely here), that the final result of political activity often, nay, regularly, bears very little relation to the original intention: often, indeed, it is quite the opposite of what was first intended. But, for this very reason, if the activity is to have any kind of inner balance, the intention of serving some real cause must be present. It is a matter for the politician's own fundamental beliefs what *form* this cause, for the sake of which he seeks power and uses power, should take. He can seek to promote national or universal, social-cum-ethical or cultural, secular or religious causes. He can be carried away by enthusiasm for 'progress' (in whatever sense) or he can coolly reject this sort of belief. He can insist on standing firm in the service of an 'ideal,' or he can reject such pretensions on principle and choose to serve the more external goals of everyday life. At all events, some belief or other must always be there. Otherwise, there will weigh on him in the event, it is perfectly correct to point out, the curse of futility to which all finite creatures are subject, even in what seem from the outside to be his greatest successes.

With what has just been said we have already begun to consider the last problem which concerns us this evening: the *ethos* of politics as a 'cause.' What sense of vocation can we find in the profession of politics itself, quite independently of any goals it may serve within the general moral economy of life? In which area of ethics, so to speak, is it at home? Here, to be sure, we find a confrontation of ultimate conceptions of life, between which in the end a *choice* must be made. Let us resolutely approach this problem, which has recently been reopened, although in my view in an extremely distorted form.

But let us first rid the question of an utterly trivial attempt to cloud the issue. Ethics can, of course, first appear on the scene playing a part which, from the moral point of view, is absolutely fatal. Let us consider some examples. You will seldom find a man who has fallen out of love with one woman and in love with another who does not feel the need to justify his action to himself. He will say that the first was not worthy of his love, or that she deceived him, or whatever other 'reasons' of the same general kind there may be. There is a lack of gallantry here; which is still further compounded by the 'justification' which he invents for the unfortunate fact that he doesn't love her any more and that the woman must simply put up with it. In virtue of this justification, he claims to exonerate himself and tries to shift not only the suffering but also the blame on to her. The man who is successful in winning a woman's love behaves in exactly the same way: his rival must be less worthy than himself, otherwise he would not have lost. And of course the case is no different when after a victorious war the victor claims, in an unworthy desire for self-justification: 'I won, because I was in the right.' Or take the case of someone who suffers a mental breakdown because of the sheer horror of war and then, instead of straightforwardly admitting that it was indeed too much for him, feels the need to justify his war-weariness to himself by substituting the feeling that he could not bear the war because he had to fight for a morally evil cause. It is the same with the defeated in war. Instead of looking, like old women, for the 'guilty men' after a war (and, after all, it is the structure of the society which led to the war), it would be more manly and austere to say to the enemy: 'We lost the war, you have won it. All that is now over and done with: now let us talk about the conclusions to be drawn, as far as they concern the *real* interests involved, and, most importantly, in the light of the responsibility towards the *future*, which concerns the victor above all.' Everything else is undignified and one only has to pay for it in the end. Damage to its interests a nation will forgive, but not damage to its honour, least of all when caused by a canting self-righteousness. Every new document which comes to light decades later leads to the revival of the undignified howls, the hatred and the anger, instead of allowing the war and its outcome to be at least *morally* buried. This can be done only if we adopt a realistic and chivalrous, but above all a *dignified* attitude. It cannot be done by insisting on 'morality': that really means no more than a lack of dignity on both sides. Those who do so are occupying themselves not with the true concerns of the politician—the future and his responsibility towards it—but instead with politically sterile, because undecidable, questions of past guilt. It is *here*, if anywhere, that political guilt lies. In so doing, moreover, such people overlook the inevitable distortion of the whole issue by thoroughly material interests—the interest of the victors in extracting the greatest possible advantage, both material and moral, and the hope of the defeated that they may gain some advantage by acknowledging their guilt. If anything is 'vulgar,' that is, and it is the result of using 'morality' in this way as a means of 'getting one's due.'

But what is the nature of the real relation between ethics and politics? Have they, as has sometimes been said, nothing whatever to do with each other? Or, on the contrary, is it correct to say that the *same* ethical standards apply in political life as in every other area of activity? The view has sometimes been taken that these two propositions present us with mutually exclusive alternatives: either the one or the other is correct. But is it true that any ethical system in the world could impose *identical* rules of conduct on sexual, commercial, familial and professional relationships; on one's relations with one's wife, greengrocer, son, competitor, friend and defendant? Should it really matter so little, in deciding on the ethical standards required in politics, that the specific instrument of politics is power, backed up by *violence*? Don't we see that the Bolshevist and Spartacist ideologues achieve exactly the *same* results as any military dictator you care to mention, precisely because they use this essential instrument of politics? What difference is there between domination by the Workers' and Soldiers' Soviets and that by any ruler of the old regime, apart from the persons of the power holders and their dilettantism? What difference is there between the polemics of most of the representatives of the so-called 'new morality' themselves against the opponents whom they criticise and those of any demagogue you care to mention? Someone will say: the nobility of their intentions. Fine! But what we are talking about here is the means which they use; and the opponents whom they attack claim likewise, with equal honesty from their point of view, that their ultimate intentions are noble. 'They that take the sword shall perish with the sword,' and war is war wherever it is fought.

Well then, what about the ethics of the Sermon on the Mount? The Sermon on the Mount, or, in other words, the absolute ethics of the Gospel, is a more serious matter than it is believed to be by those who are nowadays so keen to cite its requirements. It is not something to trifle with. What has been said about the causal principle in science holds equally good of it too: it is not a cab which one can hail at will, to get in or out of as one thinks fit. What it really means, if it is not to be reduced to a set of trivialities, is: all or nothing. Take, for example, the rich young man who 'went away grieved: for he had great possessions.' The commandment of the Gospel is unconditional and clear: give what thou hast—*everything*, categorically. This politician will say that this is a socially meaningless demand, so long as it does not apply to *everyone*. So we must have taxes, tolls, confiscations—in short, compulsion and regulation applied to *everyone*. The ethical commandment simply pays *no* attention to that: that is its very essence. Or what about 'Turn the other cheek'? The commandment is unconditional: we are not to ask questions about the other's right to strike the blow. It is an ethic which denies all self-respect—except for a saint. That is the point: one must be a saint in everything, at least in intention: one must live like Jesus or the Apostles or St. Francis or their like, and *then* this code of ethics will have meaning and express value. Otherwise, it will not. For if the consequence to be drawn from the otherworldly ethics of love is 'Resist not evil with force,' the contrary proposition is true for the politician: 'Thou *shalt* resist evil with force' (otherwise you are *responsible* for the victory of evil). Anyone who wants to act according to the ethics of the Gospel should not go on strike, since strikes are a form of coercion: he should join one of the unaffiliated trades unions. But above all he should not talk about 'revolution.' For the ethic of the Gospel certainly does not teach that civil war is the one legitimate kind of war. The pacifist who lives by the Gospel will refuse to bear arms or will throw them away, as pacifists were recommended to do in Germany, as a moral duty, in order to put an end to the war and so to all wars. The politician will say that the only sure means of discrediting war for all *foreseeable* time would have been to make peace on the basis of the *status quo*. Then the combatant peoples would have asked what the war was all for. It would have been reduced *ad absurdum*—which is not now possible. For there will have been political gains for the victors, or at least for some of them. And the responsibility for that lies with the attitude which made all resistance impossible for us. Now—once the period of exhaustion is past—it will be *peace* which is discredited, *not* war: that is the result of absolute ethics.

Finally, the duty to tell the truth. For absolute ethics this is unconditional. The conclusion has therefore been drawn that all documents should be published, especially those which lay the blame on one's own country, and that on the basis of this one-sided publication guilt should be acknowledged unilaterally, unconditionally, and without regard for the consequences. The politician will find that the result of this is not that truth is advanced, but rather that it is obscured by the misuses to which it is put and the passions which are unleashed; that the only approach which could be fruitful is for impartial umpires methodically to set out the evidence in a way which takes all sides into account. Every other procedure can have consequences for the nation which adopts it which would be impossible to make good even after several decades. But absolute ethics is not even *concerned* with 'consequences.'

That is the decisive point. We must be clear that all activity which is governed by ethical standards can be subsumed under one of two maxims, which are fundamentally different from, and irreconcilably opposed to, each other. The ethical standards may either be based on *intentions* or on *responsibility*. Not that an ethic of intentions is the same as irresponsibility or an ethic of responsibility the same as indifference to intentions. Naturally, there is no question of either of these two things. But there is a profound antithesis between actions governed by the ethics of intention, where to put it in religious language. 'The Christian acts rightly and leaves the outcome to God,' and actions governed by the ethics of responsibility, where one is answerable for the (foreseeable) *consequences* of one's actions. You may put a very plausible case to a Syndicalist who is a convinced believer in the ethics of intention, to the effect that the consequences of his actions will be an increase in the chances for reaction, increased oppression of his class, retardation of its progress; and all this will make not the slightest impression on him. If an action which results from a pure intention has evil consequences, then the responsibility lies not with the man who performed the action but with the world in general, the stupidity of other men—or the will of God who created them as they are. The man who acts according to the ethics of responsibility, on the other hand, takes into account just those ordinary faults in men; he has, as Fichte has justly said, no right whatever to assume their goodness or perfection and doesn't feel himself in any position to shift on to others the consequences of his own action, insofar as he could foresee them. He will say: 'These are the consequences to be imputed to my action.' The man who bases his ethics on intentions feels that he is 'responsible' only for seeing that the flame of pure intention, the flame of protest against the injustice of the social order, is not extinguished. The aim of his action, which, considered from the point of view of its possible consequences, is totally irrational, is to keep fanning this flame; the action can and should have only the value of an example.

But even here we have not finished with the problem. No system of ethics in the world can avoid facing the fact that 'good' ends in many cases can be achieved only at the price of morally dubious or at least dangerous means and the possibility, or even the probability, of evil side-effects. No system of ethics in the world can make it possible to decide when and to what extent the morally good end 'sanctifies' the morally dangerous means and side-effects.

For politics, the essential means is violence. The significance of the tension between means and ends from the ethical point of view can be judged from the fact that, as is well known, the revolutionary Socialists of the Zimmerwald faction, even during the war, professed a principle which could be formulated in the following pregnant words: 'If the choice which faces us is between several more years of war followed by revolution and immediate peace with no revolution, then we choose several more years of war!' If one had gone on to ask what this revolution was supposed to achieve, every scientifically trained Socialist would have replied that there was no question of a transition to an economic order which could be called 'socialist' in *his* sense; rather a bourgeois economy would arise yet again, rid only of its feudal elements and the remains of dynasticism. For this modest result, then, they were willing to face 'several more years of war'! One could well be excused for thinking that even someone with very firm socialist convictions might well reject an end which can only be achieved by such means. Exactly the same applies to Bolshevism and Spartacism, and in general to every kind of revolutionary Socialism. It is, of course, simply ridiculous for those on this side to express *moral* revulsion for the 'power-politicians' of the old regime on account of their use of the same means—however completely justified the rejection of their *ends* may be.

It is on this very problem of the sanctification of the means by the end that the ethics of intention in general seems to have run aground. Indeed, the only logical course open to it is to *repudiate all* activity which involves the use of morally dangerous means. I repeat, this is the only *logical* course. In the real world we do indeed constantly have the experience of seeing the believer in the ethics of intention suddenly turn into a millenarian prophet. For example, those who have just been preaching 'Love against Force,' suddenly urge their followers to use force—for the *last* time, so as to bring about a situation in which *all* violence will be abolished—just as our military commanders said to their men before every offensive, 'This is the last one: it will bring victory and so peace.' The believer in the ethics of intention cannot accept the ethical irrationality of the world. He is a cosmic 'rationalist' in his ethical views. All of you who know your Dostoievsky will remember the scene with the Grand Inquisitor, where this problem is admirably analysed. It is impossible to reconcile the requirements of the ethics of intention and the ethics of responsibility, and equally impossible to lay down a moral rule for deciding which end is to sanctify which means, if one makes any concessions at all to this principle.

My colleague F. W. Foerster, whom I respect very much as a man for the undoubted purity of his intentions, but whose political views, I confess, I totally reject, believes that in his book he has circumvented this difficulty by the simple thesis that from good only good can come and from bad only bad. If this were so, then this whole set of problems would not exist. But it is truly amazing that 2,500 years after the Upanishads such a thesis can still the light of day. Not only the whole course of world history, but every incontrovertible test of everyday experience makes it plain that the opposite is true. The development of all the world religions is due to this fact. The age-old problem of theodicy comes down precisely to this question: how is it that a power which is depicted as being at the same time all-powerful and loving has been able to create an irrational world like this one of unmerited suffering, unpunished injustice and irredeemable folly? Either the omnipotence or the benevolence must be lacking: or else life is governed by wholly different principles of compensation and retribution, principles which we can explain metaphysically or which are even hidden for ever from our understanding. This problem posed by the experience of the irrationality of the world has been the driving force behind all religious development. The Indian doctrine of Karma, Persian Dualism, Original Sin, Predestination and the *deus absconditus* have all grown out of this experience. The ancient Christians, too, knew very well that this world is ruled by demons, and that he who meddles with politics, who in other words makes use of the instruments of power and violence, concludes a pact with the infernal powers. They knew too that for such a man's actions it is *not* the case that from good only good, from bad only bad can come, but that often the opposite holds true. Anyone who cannot see that is indeed politically a child.

Religious ethics have come to terms in various ways with the fact that we are involved in different ways of life, governed by different sets of rules. Hellenic polytheism sacrificed to Aphrodite as well as to Hera, to Dionysus as well as to Apollo, knowing full well that they were not infrequently in conflict with each other. The Hindu way of life made each of the different callings subject to a separate ethical code, a Dharma, and divided them off permanently as castes from each other. These castes were, moreover, organised into a strict hierarchy of rank, from which there was no escape for anyone born into it, except by rebirth in the next life, and by which different castes were placed at varying distances from the highest religious blessings of salvation. This made it possible to cultivate the Dharma of each individual caste, from the ascetics and Brahmins to the thieves and prostitutes, in a manner appropriate to the specific inherent laws of each calling. These included the professions both of war and of politics. You can find a classification of war within the total system of ways of life in the Bhagavadgîtâ, in the dialogue between Krishna and Arjuna. 'Do thou what must be done'—that is, do what is required by the Dharma of the warrior caste and its rules, that which is specifically necessary to achieve the aim of war. In this system of beliefs, work does not obstruct religious salvation but promotes it. From time immemorial, Indra's heaven was as sure a fate for those Indian warriors who met a hero's death as was Valhalla for the Germans. The Indian warrior would, however, have felt as much contempt for Nirvâna as the Germans would have felt for the Christian Heaven with its choirs of angels. This specialisation of ethical codes made it possible for Indian ethics to treat this royal art in a wholly consistent way, by following only the inherent laws of politics and even radically strengthening them. Truly radical 'Machiavellianism,' in the popular sense of that word, is classically expressed in Indian literature in the Arthashâstra of Kautilya (written long before the birth of Christ, ostensibly in the time of Chandragupta): compared to it, Machiavelli's 'Prince' is harmless.

In Catholic ethics, with which Professor Foerster has close connexions, the *consilia evangelica*, as is well known, are recognised as a special code for those blessed with the charisma of the saintly life. A contrast is drawn between the monk on the one hand, who may neither shed blood nor pursue profit, and the pious knight or citizen on the other, of whom the first may shed blood and the second pursue profit. The way in which this ethic is reconciled with, and finds a place in, the system of salvation is less consistent than in India: this is a consequence, indeed a necessary consequence, of the basic presuppositions of the Christian faith. The idea that the world has been corrupted by original sin made it relatively easy to incorporate the use of force into ethics as a corrective against sin and the heretics endangering men's souls. But the purely other-worldly requirements of the Sermon on the Mount, according to which a man's intentions were of supreme importance, and the religious conception of Natural Law as an absolute requirement which was based on it, retained their revolutionary power and emerged with elemental energy at almost all times of social upheaval. They gave rise in particular to the radical pacifist sects. One of these in Pennsylvania made the experiment of a state in which there was no external power; but the outcome was tragic, in that when the War of Independence broke out the Quakers could not take up arms in defence of their own ideals for which the war was being fought.

Ordinarily Protestantism, on the other hand, legitimised the state, and therewith violence as a means, as a divine institution in general and specifically as the legitimate government. Luther took the burden of moral responsibility for war away from the individual and transferred it to the government, which it could never be a sin to obey on any matter other than a question of faith. Calvinism, again, recognised in principle that force might be used in order to defend the faith, and so sanctioned the religious war which was from the beginning a vital element in Islamic life. Evidently, then, the problem of political ethics is definitely *not* simply a modern phenomenon arising out of the rejection of religious belief which originated in the hero-cult of the Renaissance. All religions have grappled with it, with very different degrees of success, and after what has been said it could not have been otherwise. It is the specific use by groups of human beings of the means of legitimate violence as such which determines the particular character of all ethical problems of politics.

Anyone who accepts the use of this means, to whatever ends (and every politician does so) is thereby committed to accepting its specific consequences. This is particularly true of the warrior of faith—religious or revolutionary. Let us steel ourselves to consider the present situation as an example. Anyone who wants to establish absolute justice on earth by *force*, requires for this purpose a following— a human 'apparatus.' To these followers he must hold out the prospect of the necessary internal and external rewards—a reward in heaven or on earth—or else the apparatus will cease to function. Take the internal rewards first: in the conditions of modern class-warfare, these are gratification of hatred and the desire for vengeance, and especially of feelings of resentment and the need for pseudo-moral self-righteousness and therefore of the need to slander and abuse the enemy. The external rewards are adventure, victory, plunder, power and the spoils of office. The leader, once successful, is totally dependent on the functioning of this apparatus which he creates. Thus he is dependent on *its* motives, not his own. And he is dependent therefore on his ability to guarantee these rewards to his followers— the Red Guard, the secret police, the agitators, whom he needs—*over a long period of time*. What he in fact achieves under such conditions is never in his own hands: it is dictated to him by the motives which inspire the actions of his followers, and from the moral point of view these are predominantly vulgar. His followers are only held in check as long as at least some of them (perhaps never, in this world, the majority of them) are moved by an honest belief in his person and his cause. But in the first place, this belief, even where it is sincerely felt, is very often in reality only a means of giving moral 'legitimacy' to the passion for vengeance, power, plunder and office: let us not labour under any illusions about that, for the materialist interpretation of history is also not a cab to be hailed at will, and it does not come to a halt just for revolutionaries! In the second place, and most important of all, emotional revolution is followed by traditionalist routine. The hero of faith, and, even more, faith itself fades away or becomes (which is even more effective) part of the conventional jargon of political philistines and technicians. This development takes place with especial speed in ideological struggles, because it is usually conducted or inspired by true *leaders*, the prophets of the revolution. For, as with every apparatus of leadership, so here, one of the necessary conditions of success is to empty the ideas of all content, to concentrate on matters of fact, and to carry through a process of intellectual 'proletarisation' in the interests of 'discipline.' The followers of a warrior of faith, once they have achieved power, tend to degenerate with particular ease into a thoroughly commonplace class of office-holders.

Anyone who wants to take up politics in general, and especially politics as a vocation, must be conscious of these ethical paradoxes and of his own responsibility for the changes which may be brought about in *himself* under pressure from them. I repeat, he is meddling with the infernal powers which lie in wait for him in every use of violence. The great virtuosi of other-worldly love of mankind and saintliness, whether from Nazareth or Assisi or the castles of Indian kings, have not employed the instrument of politics, force. Their kingdom was 'not of this world,' although they worked and still work in this world: the figures of Platon Karatayev and the saintly characters in Dostoievsky are still the closest approximations to them. The man who is concerned for the welfare of his soul and the salvation of the souls of others does not seek these aims along the path of politics. Politics has quite different goals, which can only be achieved by force. The genius, or demon, of politics lives in a state of inner tension with the God of love, even with the Christian God as the Church depicts Him, and this tension may at any time erupt into irresoluble conflict. This was known to men even in the time when the Church was dominant. The interdict in those days represented an enormously greater power over men and their souls' salvation than the (to use

Fichte's words) 'cold sanction' of Kantian moral judgment: it lay time after time on Florence, but still the citizens of Florence fought against the Papal states. And it is with such situations in mind that Machiavelli, in a beautiful passage in (if I am not mistaken) his *History of Florence*, makes one of his heroes extol those citizens to whom the greatness of their native city is more important than the salvation of their souls.

If, for native city or 'native land,' which not everyone nowadays may consider to represent clear values, you substitute 'the future of Socialism' or even 'international peace,' then you have the problem in its current form. For to seek to achieve all such ends by *political* activity, using force as a means and acting in accordance with the ethics of responsibility, is to endanger the 'welfare of the soul.' But when the goal is pursued in accordance with the pure ethics of intention in a war of faith, it can be damaged and discredited for generations to come, since no one takes responsibility for the consequences. For then the infernal powers which are involved remain unrecognised. These powers are inexorable: they create consequences for a man's activity, even for his own inner personality, to which he is helplessly surrendered if he does not see them. 'The Devil is an old man' (and it is not age in years of life that the proverb refers to), 'so become old in order to understand him.' I have never allowed myself to be trumped in debate by the date on a birth certificate: the sheer fact that someone is twenty, while I am over fifty, can certainly never lead me to think that that alone was an achievement before which I should swoon with awe. It is not age that counts. What matters is the disciplined dispassionateness with which one looks at the realities of life, and the capacity to endure them and inwardly to cope with them.

It is true: politics is made with the head, but certainly not *only* with the head. In that respect those who advocate the ethics of intention are absolutely right. No one can tell anyone else whether they *ought* to act according to the ethics of intention or the ethics of responsibility, or when they should follow the one and when the other. One thing only can be said. In these days of an excitement which, in your opinion, is *not* 'sterile' (though excitement is certainly not always the same thing as genuine passion), when suddenly the politicians of intention come forward *en masse* with the watchword, 'It is the world which is stupid and vulgar, not me; the responsibility for the consequences doesn't concern me, it concerns the others whom I serve and whose stupidity and vulgarity I shall eradicate,' then, I often think, we have to ask first how much *inner strength* lies behind this ethics of intention. I have the impression that, in nine cases out of ten, I have to do with windbags, who do not really feel what they profess to feel, but are simply intoxicating themselves with romantic sensations. This does not interest me very much from the human point of view and impresses me not at all. But it is enormously impressive if a *more mature* man (whether old or young in years) who feels his responsibility for the consequences genuinely and with all his heart and acts according to the ethics of responsibility, says at whatever point it may be: 'Here I stand: I can no other.' That is an expression of authentic humanity and stirs one's feelings. For the *possibility* of this sort of situation occurring at some time or other must indeed exist for *any one* of us who is not inwardly dead. To that extent, the ethics of intention and the ethics of responsibility are not diametrically opposed, but complementary: together they make the true man, the man who can have the 'vocation of politics.'

And now, ladies and gentlemen, let us agree to discuss this point again *ten years from now*. If by that time, as I am sorry to say I cannot help but fear will be the case, for a whole series of reasons, the period of reaction will have long set in and little—perhaps not nothing at all, but at least little that is visible—of what certainly many of you and, as I freely confess, I too have wished and hoped for will have been achieved—if, as is very probable, that is what happens, it will not demoralise me, but it is to be sure an inner burden to be aware of it. In that event, I should very much like to see what has 'become' (inwardly) of those of you who now feel that you are genuine followers of 'the politics of intention' and share in the frenzy which this revolution amounts to. It would be nice if the situation were such that Shakespeare's Sonnet 102 were true:

> Our love was new, and then but in the spring,
> When I was wont to greet it with my lays;
> As Philomel in summer's front doth sing
> And stops her pipe in growth of riper days.

But that is not how things are. It is not 'summer's front' which lies before us, but first of all a Polar night of icy darkness and severity, whichever group may be outwardly victorious at present. For where there is nothing, it is not only the Kaiser but the proletarian too who has lost his rights. When this night begins slowly to fade, who will be left still living of those whose spring has now, to all appearances, been clad in such luxuriant blossom? And what will by then have become of the inner lives of you all? Embitterment or philistinism, simple apathetic acceptance of the world and of one's profession or, third and far from least common, mystical escapism in those who are gifted in that direction or, as is frequently and regrettably the case, force themselves into it to follow the fashion? In every such case I shall conclude that such people were not suited to their field of activity, not able to cope with the world as it really is and with the routine of their daily lives. Objectively and factually, in their innermost hearts, they did not have the vocation for politics which they thought they had. They would have done better to promote brotherly love between man and man in a simple, straightforward way; and for the rest to have worked in a purely down-to-earth way at their everyday tasks.

Politics is a matter of boring down strongly and slowly through hard boards with passion and judgment together. It is perfectly true, and confirmed by all historical experience, that the possible cannot be achieved without continually reaching out towards that which is impossible in this world. But to do that a man must be a leader, and furthermore, in a very straightforward sense of the word, a hero. Even those who are not both must arm themselves with that stoutness of heart which is able to confront even the shipwreck of all their hopes, and they must do this now—otherwise they will not be in a position even to accomplish what is possible today. Only someone who is confident that he will not be shattered if the world, seen from his point of view, is too stupid or too vulgar for what he wants to offer it; someone who can say, in spite of that, 'but still!'—only he has the 'vocation' for politics.

27

Gaetano Mosca
The Ruling Class

Gaetano Mosca (1856–1941) grew up in poverty-stricken Sicily in an upper mid-dle-class family. Three years after his birth, Italy was unified as a nation-state and a parliamentary system was established. He studied political theory as a university student, became editor of the newsletter of the Chamber of Deputies, and was later both deputy and a senator. His firsthand observation of Italy's corrupt political system convinced him that democracy was myth. He developed his own theory of elites in The Ruling Class *(the Italian title was* Elementi di Scienza Politica—Elements of Political Science*) which was first published in 1896 (a revised version came in 1923). Mosca argued that the people never rule, as democrats think. Parliaments simply cover up this fact. Whatever the form of government, there is always a ruling class (the political class) and the ruled. The ruling class legitimizes itself through a "political formula," a justi-fication for the public. The rise of Mussolini and fascism led Mosca to modify his views. He still denied that parliaments were embodiments of democracy, but he now saw them as a useful means for the elite to "circulate" and be re-plenished.*

1. Among the constant facts and tendencies that are to be found in all political organisms, one is so obvious that it is apparent to the most casual eye. In all societies—from societies that are very meagerly developed and have barely attained the dawnings of civilization, down to the most advanced and powerful societies—two classes of people appear—a class that rules and a class that is ruled. The first class, always the less numerous, performs all political functions, monopolizes power and enjoys the advantages that power brings, whereas the second, the more numerous class, is directed and controlled by the first, in a manner that is now more or less legal, now more or less arbitrary and violent, and supplies the first, in appearance at least, with material means of subsistence and with the instrumentalities that are essential to the vitality of the political organism.

In practical life we all recognize the existence of this ruling class (or political class, as we have elsewhere chosen to define it). We all know that, in our own country, whichever it may be, the management of public affairs is in the hands of a minority of influential persons, to which management, willingly or unwillingly, the majority defer. We know that the same thing goes on in neighboring countries, and in fact we should be put to it to conceive of a real world otherwise organized—a world in which all men would be directly subject to a single person without relationships of superiority or subordination, or in which all men would share equally in the direction of political affairs. If we reason otherwise in theory, that is due partly to inveterate habits that we follow in our thinking and partly to the exaggerated importance that we attach to two political facts that loom far larger in appearances than they are in reality.

The first of these facts—and one has only to open one's eyes to see it—is that in every political organism there is one individual who is chief among the leaders of the ruling class as a whole and stands, as we say, at the helm of the state. That person is not always the person who holds supreme power according to law. At times, alongside of the hereditary king or emperor there is a prime minister or a major-domo who wields an actual power that is greater than the sovereign's. At other times, in place of the elected president the influential politician who has procured the president's election will govern. Under special circumstances there may be, instead of a single person, two or three who discharge the functions of supreme control.

The second fact, too, is readily discernible. Whatever the type of political organization, pressures arising from the discontent of the masses who are governed, from the passions by which they are swayed, exert a certain amount of influence on the policies of the ruling, the political, class.

But the man who is at the head of the state would certainly not be able to govern without the support of a numerous class to enforce respect for his orders and to have them carried out; and granting that he can make one individual, or indeed many individuals, in the ruling class feel the weight of his power, he certainly cannot be at odds with the class as a whole or do away with it. Even if that were possible, he would at once be forced to create another class, without the support of which action on his part would be completely paralyzed. On the other hand, granting that the discontent of the masses might succeed in deposing a ruling class, inevitably, as we shall later show, there would have to be another organized minority within the masses themselves to discharge the functions of a ruling class. Otherwise all organization, and the whole social structure, would be destroyed.

2. From the point of view of scientific research the real superiority of the concept of the ruling, or political, class lies in the fact that the varying structure of ruling classes has a preponderant importance in determining the political type, and also the level of civilization, of the different peoples. According to a manner of classifying forms of government that is still in vogue, Turkey and Russia were both, up to a few years ago, absolute monarchies, England and Italy were constitutional, or limited, monarchies and France and the United States were classed as republics. The classification was based on the fact that, in the first two countries mentioned, headship in the state was hereditary and the chief was nominally omnipotent; in the second two, his office is hereditary but his powers and prerogatives are limited; in the last two, he is elected.

That classification is obviously superficial. Absolutisms though they were, there was little in common between the manners in which Russia and Turkey were managed politically, the levels of civilization in the two countries and the organization of their ruling classes being vastly different. On the same basis, the regime in Italy, a monarchy, is much more similar to the regime in France, a republic, than it is to the regime in England, also a monarchy; and there are important differences between the political organizations of the United States and France, though both countries are republics.

As we have already suggested, ingrained habits of thinking have long stood, as they still stand, in the way of scientific progress in this matter. The classification mentioned above, which divides governments into absolute monarchies, limited monarchies and republics, was devised by Montesquieu and was intended to replace the classical categories of Aristotle, who divided governments into monarchies, aristocracies and democracies. What Aristotle called a democracy was simply an aristocracy of fairly broad membership. Aristotle himself was in a position to observe that in every Greek state, whether aristocratic or democratic, there was always one person or more who had a preponderant influence. Between the day of Polybius and the day of Montesquieu, many writers perfected Aristotle's classification by introducing into it the concept of "mixed" governments. Later on the modern democratic theory, which had its source in Rousseau, took its stand upon the concept that the majority of the citizens in any state can participate, and in fact *ought* to participate, in its political life, and the doctrine of popular sovereignty still holds sway over many minds in spite of the fact that modern scholarship is making it increasingly clear that democratic, monarchical and aristocratic principles function side by side in every political organism. We shall not stop to refute this democratic theory here, since that is the task of this work as a whole. Besides, it would be hard to destroy in a few pages a whole system of ideas that has become firmly rooted in the human mind. As Las Casas aptly wrote in his life of Christopher Columbus, it is often much harder to unlearn than to learn.

3. We think it may be desirable, nevertheless, to reply at this point to an objection which might very readily be made to our point of view. If it is easy to understand that a single individual cannot command a group without finding within the group a minority to support him, it is rather difficult to grant, as a constant and natural fact, that minorities rule majorities, rather than majorities minorities. But that is one of the points—so numerous in all the other sciences—where the first impression one has of things is contrary to what they are in reality. In reality the dominion of an organized minority, obeying a single impulse, over the unorganized majority is inevitable. The power of any minority is irresistible as against each single individual in the majority, who stands alone before the totality of the organized minority. At the same time, the minority is organized for the very reason that it is a minority. A hundred men acting uniformly in concert, with a common understanding, will triumph over a thousand men who are not in accord and can therefore be dealt with one by one. Meanwhile it will be easier for the former to act in concert and have a mutual understanding simply because they are a hundred and not a thousand. It follows that the larger the political community, the smaller will the proportion of the governing minority to the governed majority be, and the more difficult will it be for the majority to organize for reaction against the minority.

However, in addition to the great advantage accruing to them from the fact of being organized, ruling minorities are usually so constituted that the individuals who make them up are distinguished from the mass of the governed by qualities that give them a certain material, intellectual or even moral superiority; or else they are the heirs of individuals who possessed such qualities. In other words, members of a ruling minority regularly have some attribute, real or apparent, which is highly esteemed and very influential in the society in which they live.

4. In primitive societies that are still in the early stages of organization, military valor is the quality that most readily opens access to the ruling, or political, class. In societies of advanced civilization, war is the exceptional condition. It may be regarded as virtually normal in societies that are in the initial stages of their development; and the individuals who show the greatest ability in war easily gain supremacy over their fellows—the bravest become chiefs. The fact is constant, but the forms it may assume, in one set of circumstances or another, vary considerably.

As a rule the dominance of a warrior class over a peaceful multitude is attributed to a superposition of races, to the conquest of a relatively unwarlike group by an aggressive one. Sometimes that is actually the case—we have examples in India after the Aryan invasions, in the Roman Empire after the Germanic invasions and in Mexico after the Aztec conquest. But more often, under certain social conditions, we note the rise of a warlike ruling class in places where there is absolutely no trace of a foreign conquest. As long as a horde lives exclusively by the chase, all individuals can easily become warriors. There will of course be leaders who will rule over the tribe, but we will not find a warrior class rising to exploit, and at the same time to protect, another class that is devoted to peaceful pursuits. As the tribe emerges from the hunting stage and enters the agricultural and pastoral stage, then, along with an enormous increase in population and a greater stability in the means of exerting social influence, a more or less clean-cut division into two classes will take place, one class being devoted exclusively to agriculture, the other class to war. In this event, it is inevitable that the warrior class should little by little acquire such ascendancy over the other as to be able to oppress it with impunity.

Poland offers a characteristic example of the gradual metamorphosis of a warrior class into an absolutely dominant class. Originally the Poles had the same organization by rural villages as prevailed among all the Slavic peoples. There was no distinction between fighters and farmers—in other words, between nobles and peasants. But after the Poles came to settle on the broad plains that are watered by the Vistula and the Niemen, agriculture began to develop among them. However, the necessity of fighting with warlike neighbors continued, so that the tribal chiefs, or voivodes, gathered about themselves a certain number of picked men whose special occupation was the bearing of arms. These warriors were distributed among the various rural communities. They were exempt from agricultural duties, yet they received their share of the produce of the soil, along with the other members of the community. In early days their position was not considered very desirable, and country dwellers sometimes waived exemption from agricultural labor in order to avoid going to war. But gradually as this order of things grew stabilized, as one class became habituated to the practice of arms and military organization while the other hardened to the use of the plow and the spade, the warriors became nobles and masters, and the peasants, once companions and brothers, became villains and serfs. Little by little the warrior lords increased their demands to the point where the share they took as members of the community came to include the community's whole produce minus what was absolutely necessary for subsistence on the part of the cultivators; and when the latter tried to escape such abuses they were constrained by force to stay bound to the soil, their situation taking on all the characteristics of serfdom pure and simple.

In the course of this evolution, around the year 1333, King Casimir the Great tried vainly to curb the overbearing insolence of the warriors. When peasants came to complain of the nobles, he contented himself with asking whether they had no sticks and stones. Some generations later, in 1537, the nobility forced all tradesmen in the cities to sell such real estate as they owned, and landed property became a prerogative of nobles only. At the same time the nobility exerted pressure upon the king to open negotiations with Rome, to the end that thenceforward only nobles should be admitted to holy orders in Poland. That barred townsmen and peasants almost completely from honorific positions and stripped them of any social importance whatever.

We find a parallel development in Russia. There the warriors who formed the druzhina, or escort, of the old knezes (princes descended from Rurik) also received a share in the produce of the mirs (rural peasant communities) for their livelihood. Little by little this share was increased. Since land abounded and workers were scarce, the peasants often had an eye to their advantage and moved about. At the end of the sixteenth century, accordingly, the czar Boris Godunov empowered the nobles to hold peasants to their lands by force, so establishing serfdom. However, armed forces in Russia were never composed exclusively of nobles. The muzhiks, or peasants, went to war as common soldiers under the droujina. As early as the sixteenth century, Ivan the Terrible established the order of strelitzes which amounted practically to a standing army, and which lasted until Peter the Great replaced it with regiments organized along western European lines. In those regiments members of the old druzhina, with an intermixture of foreigners, became officers, while the muzhiks provided the entire contingent of privates.

Among peoples that have recently entered the agricultural stage and are relatively civilized, it is the unvarying fact that the strictly military class is the political, or ruling, class. Sometimes the bearing of arms is reserved exclusively to that class, as happened in India and Poland. More often the members of the governed class are on occasion enrolled—always, however, as common soldiers and in the less respected divisions. So in Greece, during the war with the Medes, the citizens belonging to the richer and more influential classes formed the picked corps (the cavalry and the hoplites), the less wealthy fought as peltasts or as slingers, while the slaves, that is the laboring masses, were almost entirely barred from military service. We find analogous arrangements in republican Rome, down to the period of the Punic Wars and even as late as the day of Marius; in Latin and Germanic Europe during the Middle Ages; in Russia, as just explained, and among many other peoples. Caesar notes repeatedly that in his time the backbone of the Gallic armies was formed by cavalrymen recruited from the nobility. The Aedui, for example, could not hold out against Ariovistus after the flower of their cavalry had been killed in battle.

5. Everywhere—in Russia and Poland, in India and medieval Europe—the ruling warrior classes acquire almost exclusive ownership of the land. Land, as we have seen, is the chief source of production and wealth in countries that are not very far advanced in civilization. But as civilization progresses, revenue from land increases proportionately. With the growth of population there is, at least in certain periods, an increase in rent, in the Ricardian sense of the term, largely because great centers of consumption arise—such at all times have been the great capitals and other large cities, ancient and modern. Eventually, if other circumstances permit, a very important social transformation occurs. Wealth rather than military valor comes to be the characteristic feature of the dominant class: the people who rule are the rich rather than the brave.

The condition that in the main is required for this transformation is that social organization shall have concentrated and become perfected to such an extent that the protection offered by public authority is considerably more effective than the protection offered by private force. In other words, private property must be so well protected by the practical and real efficacy of the laws as to render the power of the proprietor himself superfluous. This comes about through a series of gradual alterations in the social structure whereby a type of political organization, which we shall call the "feudal state," is transformed into an essentially different type, which we shall term the "bureaucratic state." We are to discuss these types at some length hereafter, but we may say at once that the evolution here referred to is as a rule greatly facilitated by progress in pacific manners and customs and by certain moral habits which societies contract as civilization advances.

Once this transformation has taken place, wealth produces political power just as political power has been producing wealth. In a society already somewhat mature—where, therefore, individual power is curbed by the collective power—if the powerful are as a rule the rich, to be rich is to become powerful. And, in truth, when fighting with the mailed fist is prohibited whereas fighting with pounds and pence is sanctioned, the better posts are inevitably won by those who are better supplied with pounds and pence.

There are, to be sure, states of a very high level of civilization which in theory are organized on the basis of moral principles of such a character that they seem to preclude this overbearing assertiveness on the part of wealth. But this is a case— and there are many such—where theoretical principles can have no more than a limited application in real life. In the United States all powers flow directly or indirectly from popular elections, and suffrage is equal for all men and women in all the states of the Union. What is more, democracy prevails not only in institutions but to a certain extent also in morals. The rich ordinarily feel a certain aversion to entering public life, and the poor a certain aversion to choosing the rich for elective office. But that does not prevent a rich man from being more influential than a poor man, since he can use pressure upon the politicians who control public administration. It does not prevent elections from being carried on to the music of clinking dollars. It does not prevent whole legislatures and considerable numbers of national congressmen from feeling the influence of powerful corporations and great financiers.

In China, too, down to a few years ago, though the government had not accepted the principle of popular elections, it was organized on an essentially equalitarian basis. Academic degrees gave access to public office, and degrees were conferred by examination without any apparent regard for family or wealth. According to some writers, only barbers and certain classes of boatmen, together with their children, were barred from competing for the various grades of the mandarinate. But though the moneyed class in China was less numerous, less wealthy, less powerful than the moneyed class in the United States is at present, it was none the less able to modify the scrupulous application of this system to a very considerable extent. Not only was the indulgence of examiners often bought with money. The government itself sometimes sold the various academic degrees and allowed ignorant persons, often from the lowest social strata, to hold public office.

In all countries of the world those other agencies for exerting social influence—personal publicity, good education, specialized training, high rank in church, public administration, and army—are always readier of access to the rich than to the poor. The rich invariably have a considerably shorter road to travel than the poor, to say nothing of the fact that the stretch of road that the rich are spared is often the roughest and most difficult.

6. In societies in which religious beliefs are strong and ministers of the faith form a special class a priestly aristocracy almost always arises and gains possession of a more or less important share of the wealth and the political power. Conspicuous examples of that situation would be ancient Egypt (during certain periods), Brahman India and medieval Europe. Oftentimes the priests not only perform religious functions. They possess legal and scientific knowledge and constitute the class of highest intellectual culture. Consciously or unconsciously, priestly hierarchies often show a tendency to monopolize learning and hamper the dissemination of the methods and procedures that make the acquisition of knowledge possible and easy. To that tendency may have been due, in part at least, the painfully slow diffusion of the demotic alphabet in ancient Egypt, though that alphabet was infinitely more simple than the hieroglyphic script. The Druids in Gaul were acquainted with the Greek alphabet but would not permit their rich store of sacred literature to be written down, requiring their pupils to commit it to memory at the cost of untold effort. To the same outlook may be attributed the stubborn and frequent use of dead languages that we find in ancient Chaldea, in India, and in medieval Europe. Sometimes, as was the case in India, lower classes have been explicitly forbidden to acquire knowledge of sacred books.

Specialized knowledge and really scientific culture, purged of any sacred or religious aura, become important political forces only in a highly advanced stage of civilization, and only then do they give access to membership in the ruling class to those who possess them. But in this case too, it is not so much learning in itself that has political value as the practical applications that may be made of learning to the profit of the public or the state. Sometimes all that is required is mere possession of the mechanical processes that are indispensable to the acquisition of a higher culture. This may be due to the fact that on such a basis it is easier to ascertain and measure the skill which a candidate has been able to acquire—it is easier to "mark" or grade him. So in certain periods in ancient Egypt the profession of scribe was a road to public office and power, perhaps because to have learned the hieroglyphic script was proof of long and patient study. In modern China, again, learning the numberless characters in Chinese script has formed the basis of the mandarin's education. In present-day Europe and America the class that applies the findings of modern science to war, public administration, public works and public sanitation holds a fairly important position, both socially and politically, and in our western world, as in ancient Rome, an altogether privileged position is held by lawyers. They know the complicated legislation that arises in all peoples of long-standing civilization, and they become especially powerful if their knowledge of law is coupled with the type of eloquence that chances to have a strong appeal to the taste of their contemporaries.

There are examples in abundance where we see that long-standing practice in directing the military and civil organization of a community creates and develops in the higher reaches of the ruling class a real art of governing which is something better than crude empiricism and better than anything that mere individual experience could suggest. In such circumstances aristocracies of functionaries arise, such as the Roman senate, the Venetian nobility and to a certain extent the English aristocracy. Those bodies all stirred John Stuart Mill to admiration and certainly they all three developed governments that were distinguished for carefully considered policies and for great steadfastness and sagacity in carrying them out. This art of governing is not political science, though it has, at one time or another, anticipated applications of a number of the postulates of political science. However, even if the art of governing has now and again enjoyed prestige with certain classes of persons who have long held possession of political functions, knowledge of it has never served as an ordinary criterion for admitting to public offices persons who were barred from them by social station. The degree of mastery of the art of governing that a person possesses is, moreover, apart from exceptional cases, a very difficult thing to determine if the person has given no practical demonstration that he possesses it.

7. In some countries we find hereditary castes. In such cases the governing class is explicitly restricted to a given number of families, and birth is the one criterion that determines entry into the class or exclusion from it. Examples are exceedingly common. There is practically no country of long-standing civilization that has not had a hereditary aristocracy at one period or another in its history. We find heredi-

tary nobilities during certain periods in China and ancient Egypt, in India, in Greece before the wars with the Medes, in ancient Rome, among the Slavs, among the Latins and Germans of the Middle Ages, in Mexico at the time of the Discovery and in Japan down to a few years ago.

In this connection two preliminary observations are in point. In the first place, all ruling classes tend to become hereditary in fact if not in law. All political forces seem to possess a quality that in physics used to be called the force of inertia. They have a tendency, that is, to remain at the point and in the state in which they find themselves. Wealth and military valor are easily maintained in certain families by moral tradition and by heredity. Qualification for important office—the habit of, and to an extent the capacity for, dealing with affairs of consequence—is much more readily acquired when one has had a certain famil-iarity with them from childhood. Even when academic degrees, scientific training, special aptitudes as tested by examinations and competitions, open the way to public office, there is no eliminating that special advantage in favor of certain individuals which the French call the advantage of *positions déjà prises*. In actual fact, though examinations and competitions may theoretically be open to all, the majority never have the resources for meeting the expense of long preparation, and many others are without the connections and kinships that set an individual promptly on the right road, enabling him to avoid the gropings and blunders that are inevitable when one enters an unfamiliar environment without any guidance or support.

The democratic principle of election by broad-based suffrage would seem at first glance to be in conflict with the tendency toward stability which, according to our theory, ruling classes show. But it must be noted that candidates who are successful in democratic elections are almost always the ones who possess the political forces above enumerated, which are very often hereditary. In the English, French and Italian parliaments we frequently see the sons, grandsons, brothers, nephews and sons-in-law of members and deputies, ex-members and ex-deputies.

In the second place, when we see a hereditary caste established in a country and monopolizing political power, we may be sure that such a status de jure was preceded by a similar status de facto. Before proclaiming their exclusive and he-reditary right to power the families or castes in question must have held the scep-ter of command in a firm grasp, completely monopolizing all the political forces of that country at that period. Otherwise such a claim on their part would only have aroused the bitterest protests and provoked the bitterest struggles.

Hereditary aristocracies often come to vaunt supernatural origins, or at least origins different from, and superior to, those of the governed classes. Such claims are explained by a highly significant social fact, namely that every governing class tends to justify its actual exercise of power by resting it on some universal moral principle. This same sort of claim has come forward in our time in scientific trappings. A number of writers, developing and amplifying Darwin's theories, contend that upper classes represent a higher level in social evolution and are therefore superior to lower classes by organic structure. Gumplowicz we have already quoted. That writer goes to the point of maintaining that the divisions of populations into trade groups and professional classes in modern civilized countries are based on ethnological heterogeneousness.

Now history very definitely shows the special abilities as well as the special defects—both very marked—which have been displayed by aristocracies that have either remained absolutely closed or have made entry into their circles difficult. The ancient Roman patriciate and the English and German nobilities of modern times give a ready idea of the type we refer to. Yet in dealing with this fact, and with the theories that tend to exaggerate its significance, we can always raise the same objection—that the individuals who belong to the aristocracies in question owe their special qualities not so much to the blood that flows in their veins as to their very particular upbringing, which has brought out certain intellectual and moral tendencies in them in preference to others.

Among all the factors that figure in social superiority, intellectual superiority is the one with which heredity has least to do. The children of men of highest mentality often have very mediocre talents. That is why hereditary aristocracies have never defended their rule on the basis of intellectual superiority alone, but rather on the basis of their superiorities in character and wealth.

It is argued, in rebuttal, that education and environment may serve to explain superiorities in strictly intellectual capacities but not differences of a moral order—will power, courage, pride, energy. The truth is that social position, family tradition, the habits of the class in which we live, contribute more than is commonly supposed to the greater or lesser development of the qualities mentioned. If we carefully observe individuals who have changed their social status, whether for better or for worse, and who consequently find themselves in environments different from the ones they have been accustomed to, it is apparent that their intellectual capacities are much less sensibly affected than their moral ones. Apart from a greater breadth of view that education and experience bring to anyone who is not altogether stupid, every individual, whether he remains a mere clerk or becomes a minister of state, whether he reaches the rank of sergeant or the rank of general, whether he is a millionaire or a beggar, abides inevitably on the intellectual level on which nature has placed him. And yet with changes of social status and wealth the proud man often becomes humble, servility changes to arrogance, an honest nature learns to lie, or at least to dissemble, under pressure of need, while the man who has an ingrained habit of lying and bluffing makes himself over and puts on an outward semblance at least of honesty and firmness of character. It is true, of course, that a man fallen from high estate often acquires powers of resignation, self-denial and resourcefulness, just as one who rises in the world sometimes gains in sentiments of justice and fairness. In short, whether a man changes for the better or for the worse, he has to be exceptionally level-headed if he is to change his social status very appreciably and still keep his character unaltered. Mirabeau remarked that, for any man, any great climb on the social ladder produces a crisis that cures the ills he has and creates new ones that he never had before.

Courage in battle, impetuousness in attack, endurance in resistance—such are the qualities that have long and often been vaunted as a monopoly of the higher classes. Certainly there may be vast natural and—if we may say so—innate dif-

ferences between one individual and another in these respects; but more than anything else traditions and environmental influences are the things that keep them
high, low or just average, in any large group of human beings. We generally
become indifferent to danger or, perhaps better, to a given type of danger, when
the persons with whom we daily live speak of it with indifference and remain cool
and imperturbable before it. Many mountaineers or sailors are by nature timid
men, yet they face unmoved, the ones the dangers of the precipice, the others the
perils of the storm at sea. So peoples and classes that are accustomed to warfare
maintain military virtues at the highest pitch.

So true is this that even peoples and social classes which are ordinarily unac-
customed to arms acquire the military virtues rapidly when the individuals who
compose them are made members of organizations in which courage and daring
are traditional, when—if one may venture the metaphor—they are cast into human crucibles that are heavily charged with the sentiments that are to be infused
into their fiber. Mohammed II recruited his terrible Janizaries in the main from
boys who had been kidnapped among the degenerate Greeks of Byzantium. The
much despised Egyptian fellah, unused for long centuries to war and accustomed
to remaining meek and helpless under the lash of the oppressor, became a good
soldier when Mehemet Ali placed him in Turkish or Albanian regiments. The French
nobility has always enjoyed a reputation for brilliant valor, but down to the end of
the eighteenth century that quality was not credited in anything like the same
degree to the French bourgeoisie. However, the wars of the Republic and the
Empire amply proved that nature had been uniformly lavish in her endowments of
courage upon all the inhabitants of France. Proletariat and bourgeoisie both furnished good soldiers and, what is more, excellent officers, though talent for command had been considered an exclusive prerogative of the nobility. Gumplowicz's
theory that differentiation in social classes depends very largely on ethnological
antecedents requires proof at the very least. Many facts to the contrary readily
occur to one—among others the obvious fact that branches of the same family
often belong to widely different social classes.

8. Finally, if we were to keep to the idea of those who maintain the exclusive
influence of the hereditary principle in the formation of ruling classes, we should
be carried to a conclusion somewhat like the one to which we were carried by the
evolutionary principle: The political history of mankind ought to be much simpler
than it is. If the ruling class really belonged to a different race, or if the qualities
that fit it for dominion were transmitted primarily by organic heredity, it is difficult to see how, once the class was formed, it could decline and lose its power.
The peculiar qualities of a race are exceedingly tenacious. Keeping to the evolutionary theory, acquired capacities in the parents are inborn in their children and,
as generation succeeds generation, are progressively accentuated. The descendants
of rulers, therefore, ought to become better and better fitted to rule, and the other
classes ought to see their chances of challenging or supplanting them become
more and more remote. Now the most commonplace experience suffices to assure
one that things do not go in that way at all.

What we see is that as soon as there is a shift in the balance of political forces—when, that is, a need is felt that capacities different from the old should assert themselves in the management of the state, when the old capacities, therefore, lose some of their importance or changes in their distribution occur—then the manner in which the ruling class is constituted changes also. If a new source of wealth develops in a society, if the practical importance of knowledge grows, if an old religion declines or a new one is born, if a new current of ideas spreads, then, simultaneously, far-reaching dislocations occur in the ruling class. One might say, indeed, that the whole history of civilized mankind comes down to a conflict between the tendency of dominant elements to monopolize political power and transmit possession of it by inheritance, and the tendency toward a dislocation of old forces and an insurgence of new forces; and this conflict produces an unending ferment of endosmosis and exosmosis between the upper classes and certain portions of the lower. Ruling classes decline inevitably when they cease to find scope for the capacities through which they rose to power, when they can no longer render the social services which they once rendered, or when their talents and the services they render lose in importance in the social environment in which they live. So the Roman aristocracy declined when it was no longer the exclusive source of higher officers for the army, of administrators for the commonwealth, of governors for the provinces. So the Venetian aristocracy declined when its nobles ceased to command the galleys and no longer passed the greater part of their lives in sailing the seas and in trading and fighting.

In inorganic nature we have the example of our air, in which a tendency to immobility produced by the force of inertia is continuously in conflict with a tendency to shift about as the result of inequalities in the distribution of heat. The two tendencies, prevailing by turn in various regions on our planet, produce now calm, now wind and storm. In much the same way in human societies there prevails now the tendency that produces closed, stationary, crystallized ruling classes, now the tendency that results in a more or less rapid renovation of ruling classes. . . .

28

Robert Michels
Political Parties

Robert Michels (1876–1936) was born in Germany but he lived most of his life as a political sociologist and university teacher in Italy. Michels wrote on political parties and on the forms and functions of power, leadership, bureaucracy, and ruling elites in modern society. His studies of working-class and socialist organization in the late nineteenth and early twentieth centuries argue that a small minority always rules the majority, which he formulated as the "iron law of oligarchy." Michels asserts that "society cannot exist without a dominant class" and that this class struggles above all else to retain power. Michels claimed that democracy is an illusion. In Political Parties *(1911), Michels analyzed the unsuccessful struggle for democracy in the face of tendencies to oligarchic, bureaucratic, and authoritarian leadership which prevail in societies and in social movements.*

WE LIVE in a time in which the idea of cooperation has become so firmly established that even millionaires perceive the necessity of common action. It is easy to understand, then, that organization has become a vital principle of the working class, for in default of it their success is *a priori* impossible. The refusal of the worker to participate in the collective life of his class cannot fail to entail disastrous consequences. In respect of culture and of economic, physical, and physiological conditions, the proletarian is the weakest element of our society. In fact, the isolated member of the working classes is defenseless in the hands of those who are economically stronger. It is only by combination to form a structural aggregate that the proletarians can acquire the faculty of political resistance and attain social dignity. The importance and the influence of the working class are directly proportional to its numerical strength. But for the representation of that numerical strength organization and coordination are indispensable. The principle of organization is an absolutely essential condition for the political struggle of the masses.

Yet this politically necessary principle of organization, while it overcomes that disorganization of forces which would be favorable to the adversary, brings other dangers in its train. We escape Scylla only to dash ourselves on Charybdis. Organization is, in fact, the source from which the conservative currents flow over the plain of democracy, occasioning there disastrous floods and rendering the plain unrecognizable. . . .

Every democratic organization rests, by its very nature, upon a division of labor. But wherever division of labor prevails, there is necessarily specialization, and the specialists become indispensable. This is especially true of such states as Germany, where the Prussian spirit rules, where, in order that the party may be safely steered through all the shoals and breakers that result from police and other official interference and from the threats of the penal laws, the party can be assured of a certain continuity only when a high degree of stability characterizes the leadership.

There is an additional motive in operation. In the working-class organization, whether founded for political or for economic ends, just as much as in the life of the state, it is indispensable that the official should remain in office for a considerable time, so that he may familiarize himself with the work he has to do, may gain practical experience, for he cannot become a useful official until he has been given time to work himself into his new office. Moreover, he will not devote himself zealously to his task, he will not feel himself thoroughly at one with the aim he is intended to pursue, if he is likely to be dismissed at any moment; he needs the sense of security provided by the thought that nothing but circumstances of an unforeseen and altogether extraordinary character will deprive him of his position. Appointment to office for short terms is democratic, but is quite unpractical alike on technical and psychological grounds. Since it fails to arouse in the employee a proper sense of responsibility, it throws the door open to administrative anarchy. In the ministries of lands under a parliamentary regime, where the whole official apparatus has to suffer from its subordination to the continuous changes in majorities, it is well known that neglect and disorder reign supreme. Where the ministers are changed every few months, every one who attains to power thinks chiefly of making a profitable use of that power while it lasts. Moreover, the confusion of orders and regulations which results from the rapid succession of different persons to command renders control extraordinarily difficult, and when abuses are committed it is easy for those who are guilty to shift the responsibility on to other shoulders. "Rotation in office," as the Americans call it, no doubt corresponds to the pure principle of democracy. Up to a certain point it is adapted to check the formation of a bureaucratic spirit of caste. But this advantage is more than compensated by the exploitive methods of ephemeral leaders, with all their disastrous consequences. On the other hand, one of the great advantages of monarchy is that the hereditary prince, having an eye to the interests of his children and his successors, possesses an objective and permanent interest in his position, and almost always abstains from a policy which would hopelessly impair the vital energies of his country, just as the landed proprietor usually rejects methods of cultivation which, while providing large immediate returns, would sterilize the soil to the detriment of his heirs.

Thus, no less in time of peace than in time of war, the relationships between different organizations demand a certain degree of personal and tactical continuity, for without such continuity the political authority of the organization would be impaired. This is just as true of political parties as it is true of states. In international European politics, England has always been regarded as an untrustworthy ally, for her history shows that no other country has ever been able to confide in agreements concluded with England. The reason is to be found in this, that the foreign policy of the United Kingdom is largely dependent upon the party in power, and party changes occur with considerable rapidity. Similarly, the party that changes its leaders too often runs the risk of finding itself unable to contract useful alliances at an opportune moment. The two gravest defects of genuine democracy, its lack of stability (*perpetuum mobile democraticum*) and its difficulty of mobilization, are dependent on the recognized right of the sovereign masses to take part in the management of their own affairs.

In order to bind the leader to the will of the mass and to reduce him to the level of a simple executive organ of the mass, certain primitive democracies have at all times sought to apply, in addition to the means previously enumerated, measures of moral coercion. In Spain, the patriotic revolutionary Junta of 1808 insisted that thirty proletarians should accompany the general who was to negotiate with the French, and these compelled him, in opposition to his own convictions, to reject all Napoleon's proposals. In modern democratic parties, there still prevails the practice, more or less general according to the degree of development these parties have attained, that the rank and file send to the congresses delegates who are fettered by definite instructions, the aim of this being to prevent the delegate from giving upon any decisive question a vote adverse to the opinion of the majority of those whom he represents. This precaution may be efficacious in certain cases, where the questions concerned are simple and clear. But the delegate, since he has no freedom of choice, is reduced to the part of puppet, and cannot allow himself to be influenced by the arguments he hears at the congress or by new matters of fact which are brought to light in the course of the debate. But the result is, that not only is all discussion rendered superfluous in advance, but also that the vote itself is often falsified, since it does not correspond to the real opinions of the delegates. Of late fixed instructions have less often been given to the delegate, for it has become manifest that this practice impairs the cohesion so urgently necessary to every party, and provokes perturbations and uncertainties in its leadership.

In proportion as the chiefs become detached from the mass they show themselves more and more inclined, when gaps in their own ranks have to be filled, to effect this, not by way of popular election, but by cooptation, and also to increase their own effectives wherever possible, by creating new posts upon their own initiative. There arises in the leaders a tendency to isolate themselves, to form a sort of cartel, and to surround themselves, as it were, with a wall, within which they will admit those only who are of their own way of thinking. Instead of allowing their successors to be appointed by the choice of the rank and file, the leaders do all in their power to choose these successors for themselves, and to fill up gaps in their own ranks directly or indirectly by the exercise of their own volition.

This is what we see going on today in all the working-class organizations which are upon a solid foundation. . . .

The logical consequences of these considerations is in direct conflict with the hopes entertained by the founders of the party. Instead of gaining revolutionary energy as the force and solidity of its structure has increased, the precise opposite has occurred; there has resulted, *pari passu* with its growth, a continued increase in the prudence, the timidity even, which inspires its policy. The party, continually threatened by the state upon which its existence depends, carefully avoids (once it has attained to maturity) everything which might irritate the state to excess. The party doctrines are, whenever requisite, attenuated and deformed in accordance with the external needs of the organization.[1] Organization becomes the vital essence of the party. During the first years of its existence, the party did not fail to make a parade of its revolutionary character, not only in respect of its ultimate ends, but also in respect of the means employed for their attainment— although not always in love with these means. But as soon as it attained to political maturity, the party did not hesitate to modify its original profession of faith and to affirm itself revolutionary only "in the best sense of the word," that is to say, no longer on lines which interest the police, but only in theory and on paper. This same party, which at one time did not hesitate, when the triumphant guns of the bourgeois governors of Paris were still smoking, to proclaim with enthusiasm its solidarity with the communards, now announces to the whole world that it repudiates anti-militarist propaganda in any form which may bring its adherents into conflict with the penal code, and that it will not assume any responsibility for the consequences that may result from such a conflict. A sense of responsibility is suddenly becoming active in the Socialist Party. Consequently it reacts with all the authority at its disposal against the revolutionary currents which exist within its own organization, and which it has hitherto regarded with an indulgent eye. In the name of the grave responsibilities attaching to its position it now disavows antimilitarism, repudiates the general strike, and denies all the logical audacities of its past. . . .

Thus, from a means, organization becomes an end. To the institutions and qualities which at the outset were destined simply to ensure the good working of the party machine (subordination, the harmonious cooperation of individual members, hierarchical relationships, discretion, propriety of conduct), a greater importance comes ultimately to be attached than to the productivity of the machine. Henceforward the sole preoccupation is to avoid anything which may clog the machinery. Should the party be attacked, it will abandon valuable positions previously conquered, and will renounce ancient rights rather than reply to the enemy's offensive by methods which might "compromise" its position. Naumann writes sarcastically: "The war-cry 'Proletarians of all countries unite!' has had its due effect. The forces of the organized proletariat have gained a strength which no one believed possible when that war-cry was first sounded. There is money in the treasuries. Is the signal for the final assault never to be given? . . . Is the work of preliminary organization to go on for ever?" As the party's need for tranquility increases, its revolutionary talons atrophy. We have now a finely conservative party which (since the effect survives the cause) continues to employ revolutionary terminology, but which in actual practice fulfils no other function than that of a constitutional opposition.

All this has deviated far from the ideas of Karl Marx, who, were he still alive, ought to be the first to revolt against such a degeneration of Marxism. Yet it is quite possible that, carried away by the spectacle of an army of three million men acting in his name, swearing on solemn occasions *in verba magistri*, he also would find nothing to say in reprobation of so grave a betrayal of his own principles. There were incidents in Marx's life which render such a view possible. He certainly knew how to close his eyes, in public at any rate, to the serious faults committed by the German social democracy in 1876.

In our own day, which may be termed the age of the epigones of Marx, the character of the party as an organization ever greedy for new members, ever seeking to obtain an absolute majority, cooperates with the condition of weakness in which it finds itself vis-à-vis the state, to effect a gradual replacement of the old aim, to demolish the existing state by the new aim, to permeate the state with the men and the ideas of the party. The struggle carried on by the socialists against the parties of the dominant classes is no longer one of principle, but simply one of competition. The revolutionary party has become a rival of the bourgeois parties for the conquest of power. . . . History seems to teach us that no popular movement, however energetic and vigorous, is capable of producing profound and permanent changes in the social organism of the civilized world. The preponderant elements of the movement, the men who lead and nourish it, end by undergoing a gradual detachment from the masses, and are attracted within the orbit of the "political class." They perhaps contribute to this class a certain number of "new ideas," but they also endow it with more creative energy and enhanced practical intelligence, thus providing for the ruling class an ever-renewed youth. The "political class" (continuing to employ Mosca's convenient phrase) has unquestionably an extremely fine sense of its possibilities and its means of defense. It displays a remarkable force of attraction and a vigorous capacity for absorption which rarely fail to exercise and influence even upon the most embittered and uncompromising of its adversaries. From the historical point of view, the anti-romanticists are perfectly right when they sum up their skepticism in such caustic phraseology as this: "What is a revolution? People fire guns in a street; that breaks many windows; scarcely anyone profits but the glaziers. The wind carries away the smoke. Those who stay on top push the others under. . . . It is worth the suffering to turn up so many good paving stones which otherwise could not be moved!"[2] Or we may say, as the song runs in *Madame Angot*: "It's not worth the bother to change the government!" In France, the classic land of social theories and experiments, such pessimism has struck the deepest roots.[3]

Notes

1. A classical example of the extent to which the fear of injuring the socialist organization will lead even the finest intelligences of the party to play tricks with socialist theory is afforded by the history of that celebrated preface which in 1895 Friedrich Engels wrote for a posthumous edition of Marx's book, *Die Klassenkämpfe in Frankreich, 1848–9*. This preface became the subject of great international discussions, and has been justly considered as the first vigorous manifestation of reformism in German socialism. For Engels here declares that socialist tactics will have more success through the use of legal than of illegal and revolutionary means, and thus expressly repudiates the Marxist conception of the socialist revolution. It was not till some years later that Kautsky published a letter from

Engels in which the latter disavowed his preface, saying: "My text had to suffer from the timid legalism of our friends in Berlin, who dreaded a second edition of the anti-socialist laws—a dread to which I was forced to pay attention at the existing political juncture" (Karl Kautsky, *Der Weg zur Macht*, Buchandlung "Vorwärts," 1909, p. 42). From this it would appear that the theory (at that time brand-new) that socialism could attain to its ends by parliamentary methods—and this was the quintessence of Engels' preface—came into existence from a fear lest the socialist party organization (which should be a means, and not an end in itself) might suffer at the hands of the state. Thus Engels was fêted, on the one hand, as a man of sound judgment and one willing to look facts in the face (cf. W. Sombart, *Friedrich Engels, Ein Blatt zur Entwicklungsgeschichte des Sozialismus*, Separat-Abdruck der "Zukunft," Berlin, 1895, p. 32), and was attacked, on the other hand, as a pacifist utopist (cf. Arturo Labriola, *Riforme e Rivoluzione sociale*); whereas in reality Engels would seem to have been the victim of an opportunist sacrifice of principles to the needs of organization, a sacrifice made for love of the party and in opposition to his own theoretical convictions.

2. Trans. from Théophile Gautier, *Les Jeunes-France*, Charpentier, Paris, 1878, p. xv.

3. The disillusionment of the French regarding democracy goes back to the Revolution. Guizot declared that this terrible experiment sufficed "to disgust the liberty-seeking world forever, and to dry up the noblest hopes of the human race at their source." (Trans, from F. Guizot, *Du Gouvernement de la France*, ed. cit., p. 165).

29

V. I. Lenin
Selections

V. I. Lenin (1870–1924) was the leader of the Bolshevik party, which seized power in Russia in 1917 in the first successful Communist revolution. Lenin's real name was Vladimir Ulyanov. His older brother, Alexander, was executed for his role in a plot against the Tsar. As a young man, Lenin studied law and became active in radical politics. The first selection comes from Lenin's book What Is to Be Done? *(1902), which presented his program for Marxists in the Russian empire. In it he substantially revised Marxist theory. Lenin argued that workers would never obtain revolutionary consciousness on their own, and consequently a vanguard party of "professional revolutionaries" was needed. In 1903, the Russian Social Democratic Labor party split between those who supported Lenin's ideas (the Bolsheviks) and those who opposed them (the "Mensheviks," led by Julius Martov) as undemocratic and unfaithful to the spirit of Marx. The second selection is from* State and Revolution *(1917), written in the summer of 1917 when Lenin was in hiding, just before he took power. In it he presents his views about state and society after the Revolution.*

WHAT IS TO BE DONE?

Without revolutionary theory there can be no revolutionary movement. This idea cannot be insisted upon too strongly at a time when the fashionable preaching of opportunism goes hand in hand with an infatuation for the narrowest forms of practical activity. Yet, for Russian Social-Democrats the importance of theory is enhanced by three other circumstances, which are often forgotten: first, by the fact that our Party is only in process of formation, its features are only just becoming defined, and it has as yet far from settled accounts with the other trends of revolutionary thought that threaten to divert the movement from the correct path. On the contrary, precisely the very recent past was marked by a revival of non-Social-Democratic revolutionary trends. . . .

Under these circumstances, what at first sight appears to be an "unimportant" error may lead to most deplorable consequences, and only short-sighted people can consider factional disputes and a strict differentiation between shades of opinion inopportune or superfluous. The fate of Russian Social-Democracy for very many years to come may depend on the strengthening of one or the other "shade."

Secondly, the Social-Democratic movement is in its very essence an international movement. This means, not only that we must combat national chauvinism, but that an incipient movement in a young country can be successful only if it makes use of the experiences of other countries. In order to make use of these experiences it is not enough merely to be acquainted with them, or simply to copy out the latest resolutions. What is required is the ability to treat these experiences critically and to test them independently. He who realises how enormously the modern working-class movement has grown and branched out will understand what a reserve of theoretical forces and political (as well as revolutionary) experience is required to carry out this task.

Thirdly, the national tasks of Russian Social-Democracy are such as have never confronted any other socialist party in the world. We shall have occasion further on to deal with the political and organisational duties which the task of emancipating the whole people from the yoke of autocracy imposes upon us. At this point, we wish to state only that the *role of vanguard fighter can be fulfilled only by a party that is guided by the most advanced theory.* . . .

. . . Strikes occurred in Russia in the seventies and sixties (and even in the first half of the nineteenth century), and they were accompanied by the "spontaneous" destruction of machinery, etc. Compared with these "revolts," the strikes of the nineties might even be described as "conscious," to such an extent do they mark the progress which the working-class movement made in that period. This shows that the "spontaneous element," in essence, represents nothing more nor less than consciousness in an *embryonic form.* Even the primitive revolts expressed the awakening of consciousness to a certain extent. The workers were losing their age-long faith in the permanence of the system which oppressed them and began . . . I shall not say to understand, but to sense the necessity for collective resistance, definitely abandoning their slavish submission to the authorities. But this was, nevertheless, more in the nature of outbursts of desperation and vengeance than of *struggle.* The strikes of the nineties revealed far greater flashes of consciousness; definitive demands were advanced, the strike was carefully timed, known cases and instances in other places were discussed, etc. The revolts were simply the resistance of the oppressed, whereas the systematic strikes represented the class struggle in embryo, but only in embryo. Taken by themselves, these strikes were simply trade union struggles, not yet Social-Democratic struggles. They marked the awakening antagonisms between workers and employers; but the workers were not, and could not be, conscious of the irreconcilable antagonism of their interests to the whole of the modern political and social system, i.e., theirs was not yet Social-Democratic consciousness. In this sense, the strikes of the nineties, despite the enormous progress they represented as compared with the "revolts," remained a purely spontaneous movement.

We have said that *there could not have been* Social-Democratic consciousness among the workers. It would have to be brought to them from without. The history of all countries shows that the working class, exclusively by its own effort, is able to develop only trade union consciousness, i.e., the conviction that it is necessary to combine in unions, fight the employers, and strive to compel the government to pass necessary labour legislation, etc. The theory of socialism, however, grew out of the philosophic, historical, and economic theories elaborated by educated representatives of the propertied classes, by intellectuals. By their social status the founders of modern scientific socialism, Marx and Engels, themselves belonged to the bourgeois intelligentsia. In the very same way, in Russia, the theoretical doctrine of Social-Democracy arose altogether independently of the spontaneous growth of the working-class movement; it arose as a natural and inevitable outcome of the development of thought among the revolutionary socialist intelligentsia. . . .

[All] worship of the spontaneity of the working-class movement, all belittling of the role of "the conscious element," of the role of Social-Democracy, *means, quite independently of whether he who belittles that role desires it or not, a strengthening of the influence of bourgeois ideology upon the workers*. All those who talk about "overrating the importance of ideology," about exaggerating the role of the conscious element, etc., imagine that the labour movement pure and simple can elaborate, and will elaborate, an independent ideology for itself, if only the workers "wrest their fate from the hands of the leaders." But this is a profound mistake. . . .

Since there can be no talk of an independent ideology formulated by the working masses themselves in the process of their movement, the *only* choice is— either bourgeois or socialist ideology. There is no middle course (for mankind has not created a "third" ideology, and, moreover, in a society torn by class antagonisms there can never be a non-class or an above-class ideology). Hence, to belittle the socialist ideology *in any way, to turn aside from it in the slightest degree* means to strengthen bourgeois ideology. There is much talk of spontaneity. But the *spontaneous* development of the working-class movement leads to its subordination to bourgeois ideology, *to its development along the lines of the Credo programme*; for the spontaneous working-class movement is trade-unionism . . . and trade-unionism means the ideological enslavement of the workers by the bourgeoisie. Hence, our task, the task of Social-Democracy, is *to combat spontaneity, to divert* the working-class movement from this spontaneous, trade-unionist striving to come under the wing of the bourgeoisie, and to bring it under the wing of revolutionary Social-Democracy. . . .

The political struggle of Social Democracy is far more extensive and complex than the economic struggle of the workers against the employers and the government. Similarly (indeed for that reason), the organisation of the revolutionary Social-Democratic Party must inevitably be of *a kind different* from the organisation of the workers designed for this struggle. The workers' organisation must in the first place be a trade union organisation; secondly, it must be as broad as possible; and thirdly, it must be as public as conditions will allow (here, and further on, of course, I refer only to absolutist Russia). On the other hand, the organisation of the revolutionaries must consist first and foremost of people who make revolutionary activity their profession (for which reason I speak of the organisation of *revolutionaries*, meaning revolutionary Social-Democrats). In view of this common characteristic of the members of such an organisation, *all distinctions as between workers and intellectuals*, not to speak of distinctions of trade and profession, in both categories, *must be effaced*. Such an organisation must perforce not be very extensive and must be as secret as possible. . . .

In countries where political liberty exists the distinction between a trade union and a political organisation is clear enough, as is the distinction between trade unions and Social-Democracy. The relations between the latter and the former will naturally vary in each country according to historical, legal, and other conditions; they may be more or less close, complex, etc. (in our opinion they should be as close and as little complicated as possible); but there can be no question in free countries of the organisation of trade unions coinciding with the organisation of the Social-Democratic Party. In Russia, however, the yoke of the autocracy appears at first glance to obliterate all distinctions between the Social-Democratic organisation and the workers' associations, since *all* workers' associations and *all* study circles are prohibited, and since the principal manifestation and weapon of the workers' economic struggle—the strike—is regarded as a criminal (and sometimes even as a political!) offence. Conditions in our country, therefore, on the one hand, strongly "impel" the workers engaged in economic struggle to concern themselves with political questions, and, on the other, they "impel" Social-Democrats to confound trade-unionism with Social-Democracy. . . .

The workers organisations for the economic struggle should be trade union organisations. Every Social-Democratic worker should as far as possible assist and actively work in these organisations. But, while this is true, it is certainly not in our interest to demand that only Social-Democrats should be eligible for membership in the "trade" unions, since that would only narrow the scope of our influence upon the masses. Let every worker who understands the need to unite for the struggle against the employers and the government join the trade unions. The very aim of the trade unions would be impossible of achievement, if they did not unite all who have attained at least this elementary degree of understanding, if they were not very *broad* organisations. The broader these organisations, the broader will be our influence over them—an influence due, not only to the "spontaneous" development of the economic struggle, but to the direct and conscious effort of the socialist trade union members to influence their comrades. But a broad organisation cannot apply methods of strict secrecy (since this demands far greater training than is required for the economic struggle). . . .

A small, compact core of the most reliable, experienced, and hardened workers, with responsible representatives in the principal districts and connected by all the rules of strict secrecy with the organisation of revolutionaries, can, with the widest support of the masses and without any formal organisation, perform *all* functions of a trade union organisation, in a manner, moreover, desirable to Social-Democracy. Only in this way can we secure the *consolidation* and development of a *Social-Democratic* trade union movement, despite all the gendarmes.

It may be objected that an organisation which is so *loose* that it is not even definitely formed, and which has not even an enrolled and registered membership, cannot be called an organisation at all. Perhaps so. Not the name is important. What is important is that this "organisation without members" shall do everything that is required, and from the very outset ensure a solid connection between our future trade unions and socialism. Only an incorrigible utopian would have a *broad* organisation of workers, with elections, reports, universal suffrage, etc., under the autocracy.

The moral to be drawn from this is simple. If we begin with the solid foundation of a strong organisation of revolutionaries, we can ensure the stability of the movement as a whole and carry out the aims both of Social-Democracy and of trade unions proper. If, however, we begin with a broad workers' organisation, which is supposedly most "accessible" to the masses (but which is actually most accessible to the gendarmes and makes revolutionaries most accessible to the police), we shall achieve neither the one aim nor the other; we shall not eliminate our rule-of-thumb methods, and, because we remain scattered and our forces are constantly broken up by the police, we shall only make trade unions of the Zubatov and Ozerov type the more accessible to the masses.*

. . . I assert that it is far more difficult to unearth a dozen wise men than a hundred fools. This position I will defend, no matter how much you instigate the masses against me for my "anti-democratic" views, etc. As I have stated repeatedly, by "wise men," in connection with organisation, I mean *professional revolutionaries*, irrespective of whether they have developed from among students or working men. I assert: (1) that no revolutionary movement can endure without a stable organisation of leaders maintaining continuity; (2) that the broader the popular mass drawn spontaneously into the struggle, which forms the basis of the movement and participates in it, the more urgent the need for such an organisation, and the more solid this organisation must be (for it is much easier for all sorts of demagogues to side-track the more backward sections of the masses); (3) that such an organisation must consist chiefly of people professionally engaged in revolutionary activity; (4) that in an autocratic state, the more we *confine* the membership of such as organisation to people who are professionally engaged in revolutionary activity and who have been professionally trained in the art of combating the political police, the more difficult will it be to unearth the organisation; and (5) the *greater* will be the number of people from the working class and from the other social classes who will be able to join the movement and perform active work in it. . . .

Note

* These were workers' organizations dominated by the Tsarist police—Ed.

THE STATE AND REVOLUTION

What Is to Replace the Smashed State Machine?

. . . In 1847, in the *Communist Manifesto*, Marx's answer to this question was as yet a purely abstract one; to be exact, it was an answer that indicated the tasks, but not the ways of accomplishing them. The answer given in the *Communist Mani-*

festo was that this machine was to be replaced by "the proletariat organised as the ruling class," by the "winning of the battle of democracy."

Marx did not indulge in utopias; he expected the *experience* of the mass movement to provide the reply to the question as to the specific forms this organisation of the proletariat as the ruling class would assume and as to the exact manner in which this organisation would be combined with the most complete, most consistent "winning of the battle of democracy."

Marx subjected the experience of the [1871 Paris] commune, meagre as it was, to the most careful analysis in *The Civil War in France*. Let us quote the most important passages of this work. Originating from the Middle Ages, there developed in the nineteenth century "the centralised state power, with its ubiquitous organs of standing army, police, bureaucracy, clergy, and judicature." With the development of class antagonisms between capital and labour, "state power assumed more and more the character of a public force for the suppression of the working class, of a machine of class rule. After every revolution, which marks an advance in the class struggle, the purely coercive character of the state power stands out in bolder and bolder relief." After the revolution of 1848–49, state power became "the national war instrument of capital against labour." The Second Empire consolidated this. "The direct antithesis to the empire was the Commune." It was the "specific form" of "a republic that was not only to remove the monarchical form of class rule, but class rule itself. . . .

What was this "specific form of the proletarian, socialist republic? What was the state it began to create? " . . . The first decree of the Commune . . . was the suppression of the standing army, and its replacement by the armed people. . . . " This demand now figures in the programme of every party calling itself socialist. The real worth of their programmes, however, is best shown by the behavior of our Socialist-Revolutionaries and Mensheviks,* who, right after the revolution of February 27, actually refused to carry out this demand!

> The Commune was formed of the municipal councillors, chosen by universal suffrage in the various wards of Paris, responsible and revocable at any time. The majority of its members were naturally working men, or acknowledged representatives of the working class. . . . The police, which until then had been the instrument of the government, was at once stripped of its political attributes, and turned into the responsible and at all times revocable instrument of the Commune. So were the officials of all other branches of the administration. From the members of the Commune downwards, public service had to be done at *workmen's wages*. The privileges and the representation allowances of the high dignitaries of state disappeared along with the dignitaries themselves. . . . Having once got rid of the standing army and the police, the instruments of the physical force of the old Government, the Commune proceeded at once to break the instrument of spiritual suppression, the power of the priests. . . . The judicial functionaries lost that sham independence . . . they were thenceforward to be elective, responsible, and revocable. . . .

The Commune, therefore, appears to have replaced the smashed state machine "only" by fuller democracy: abolition of the standing army; all officials to be elected and subject to recall. But as a matter of fact this "only" signifies a gigantic replacement of certain institutions by other institutions of a fundamentally different type. This is exactly a case of "quantity being transformed into quality": democracy, introduced as fully and consistently as is at all conceivable, is transformed from bourgeois into proletarian democracy; from the state (= a special force for the suppression of a particular class) into something which is no longer the state proper.

It is still necessary to suppress the bourgeoisie and crush their resistance. This was particularly necessary for the Commune; and one of the reasons for its defeat was that it did not do this with sufficient determination. The organ of suppression, however, is here the majority of the population, and not a minority, as was always the case under slavery, serfdom and wage slavery. And since the majority of the people *itself* suppresses its oppressors, a "special force" for suppression *is no longer necessary*! In this sense, the state *begins to wither away*. Instead of the special institutions of a privileged minority (privileged officaldom, the chiefs of the standing army), the majority itself can directly fulfil all these functions, and the more the functions of state power are performed by the people as a whole, the less need there is for the existence of this power.

In this connection, the following measures of the Commune, emphasised by Marx, are particularly noteworthy: the abolition of all representation allowances, and of all monetary privileges to officials, the reduction of the remuneration of *all* servants of the state to the level of "*workmen's* wages." This shows more clearly than anything else the *turn* from bourgeois to proletarian democracy, from the democracy of the oppressors to that of the oppressed classes, from the state as a "*special force*" for the suppression of a particular class to the suppression of the oppressors by the *general force* of the majority of the people—the workers and the peasants. And it is on this particularly striking point, perhaps the most important as far as the problem of the state is concerned, that the ideas of Marx have been most completely ignored! In popular commentaries, the number of which is legion, this is not mentioned. The thing done is to keep silent about it as if it were a piece of old-fashioned "naïveté," just as Christians, after their religion had been given the status of a state religion, "forgot" the "naïveté" of primitive Christianity with its democratic revolutionary spirit.

The reduction of the remuneration of high state officials seems to be "simply" a demand of naïve, primitive democracy. One of the "founders" of modern opportunism, the ex-Social-Democrat Eduard Bernstein, has more than once repeated the vulgar bourgeois jeers at "primitive" democracy. Like all opportunists, and like the present Kautskyites, he did not understand at all that, first of all, the transition from capitalism to socialism is *impossible* without a certain "reversion" to "primitive" democracy (for how else can the majority, and then the whole population without exception, proceed to discharge state functions?); and that, secondly, "primitive democracy" based on capitalism and capitalist culture is not the same as primitive democracy in prehistoric or precapitalist times. Capitalist culture has *created* large-scale production, factories, railways, the postal service, telephones, etc., and *on this basis* the great majority of the functions of the old "state power" have become so simplified and can be reduced to such exceedingly simple operations of registration, filing and checking that they can be easily performed by every literate person, can quite easily be performed for ordinary "workmen's wages," and that these functions can (and must) be stripped of every shadow of privilege, of every semblance of "official grandeur."

All officials, without exception, elected and subject to recall *at any time*, their salaries reduced to the level of ordinary "workmen's wages"—these simple and "self-evident" democratic measures, while completely uniting the interests of the workers and the majority of the peasants, at the same time serve as a bridge leading from capitalism to socialism. These measures concern the reorganisation of the state, the purely political reorganisation of society; but, of course, they acquire their full meaning and significance only in connection with the "expropriation of the expropriators" either being accomplished or in preparation, i.e, with the transformation of capitalist private ownership of the means of production into social ownership. "The Commune," Marx wrote, "made that catch-word of all bourgeois revolutions, cheap government, a reality, by abolishing the two greatest sources of expenditure—the army and the officialdom."

From the peasants, as from other sections of the petty bourgeoisie, only an insignificant few "rise to the top," "get on in the world" in the bourgeois sense, i.e., become either well-to-do, bourgeois, or officials in secure and privileged positions. In every capitalist country where there are peasants (as there are in most capitalist countries), the vast majority of them are oppressed by the government and long for its overthrow, long for "cheap" government. This can be achieved *only* by the proletariat; and by achieving it, the proletariat at the same time takes a step towards the socialist reorganisation of the state.

Abolition of Parliamentarism

"The Commune," Marx wrote, "was to be a working, not a parliamentary, body, executive and legislative at the same time. . . . Instead of deciding once in three or six years which member of the ruling class was to represent and repress [*ver- und zertreten*] the people in parliament, universal suffrage was to serve the people constituted in communes, as individual suffrage serves every other employer in the search for workers, foremen and accountants for his business."

Owing to the prevalence of social-chauvinism and opportunism, this remarkable criticism of parliamentarism, made in 1871, also belongs now to the "forgotten words" of Marxism. The professional Cabinet Ministers and parliamentarians, the traitors to the proletariat and the "practical" socialists of our day, have left all criticism of parliamentarism to the anarchists, and, on this wonderfully reasonable ground, they denounce *all* criticism of parliamentarism as "anarchism"! It is not surprising that the proletariat of the "advanced" parliamentary countries [is] disgusted with such "socialists." . . .

For Marx, however, revolutionary dialectics was never the empty fashionable phrase, the toy rattle, which Plekhanov, Kautsky and others have made of it. Marx knew how to break with anarchism ruthlessly for its inability to make use even of the "pigsty" of bourgeois parliamentarism, especially when the situation was obviously not revolutionary; but at the same time he knew how to subject parliamentarism to genuinely revolutionary proletarian criticism.

To decide once every few years which member of the ruling class is to repress and crush the people through parliament—this is the real essence of bourgeois parliamentarism, not only in parliamentary-constitutional monarchies, but also in the most democratic republics.

But if we deal with the question of the state, and if we consider parliamentarism as one of the institutions of the state, from the point of view of the tasks of the proletariat in *this* field, what is the way out of parliamentarism? How can it be dispensed with?

Once again we must say: the lessons of Marx, based on the study of the Commune, have been so completely forgotten that the present-day "Social-Democrat" (i.e., present-day traitor to socialism) really cannot understand any criticism of parliamentarism other than anarchist or reactionary criticism.

The way out of parliamentarism is not, of course, the abolition of representative institutions and the elective principle, but the conversion of the representative institutions from talking shops into "working" bodies. "The Commune was to be a working, not a parliamentary, body, executive and legislative at the same time." . . .

The Commune substitutes for the venal and rotten parliamentarism of bourgeois society institutions in which freedom of opinion and discussion does not degenerate into deception, for the parliamentarians themselves have to work, have to execute their own laws, have themselves to test the results achieved in reality, and to account directly to their constituents. Representative institutions remain, but there is *no* parliamentarism here as a special system, as the division of labour between the legislative and the executive, as a privileged position for the deputies. We cannot imagine democracy, even proletarian democracy, without representative institutions, but we can and *must* imagine democracy without parliamentarism, if criticism of bourgeois society is not mere words for us, if the desire to overthrow the rule of the bourgeoisie is our earnest and sincere desire, and not a mere "election" cry for catching workers' votes, as it is with the Mensheviks and Socialist-Revolutionaries. . . .

Abolishing the bureaucracy at once, everywhere and completely, is out of the question. It is a utopia. But to *smash* the old bureaucratic machine at once and to begin immediately to construct a new one that will make possible the gradual abolition of all bureaucracy—this is *not* a utopia, it is the experience of the Commune, the direct and immediate task of the revolutionary proletariat.

Capitalism simplifies the functions of "state" administration; it makes it possible to cast "bossing" aside and to confine the whole matter to the organisation of the proletarians (as the ruling class), which will hire "workers, foremen and accountants" in the name of the whole of society.

We are not utopians, we do not "dream" of dispensing *at once* with all administration, with all subordination. These anarchist dreams, based upon incomprehension of the tasks of the proletarian dictatorship, are totally alien to Marxism, and, as a matter of fact, serve only to postpone the socialist revolution until people are different. No, we want the socialist revolution with people as they are now, with people who cannot dispense with subordination, control and "foremen and accounts."

The subordination, however, must be to the armed vanguard of all the exploited and working people, i.e., to the proletariat. A beginning can and must be made at once, overnight, to replace the specific "bossing" of state officials by the simple functions of "foremen and accountants," functions which are already fully within the ability of the average town dweller and can well be performed for "workmen's wages."

We, the workers, shall organise large-scale production on the basis of what capitalism has already created, relying on our own experience as workers, establishing strict, iron discipline backed up by the state power of the armed workers. We shall reduce the role of state officials to that of simply carrying out our instructions as responsible, revocable, modestly paid "foremen and accountants" (of course, with the aid of technicians of all sorts, types and degrees). This is *our* proletarian task, this is what we can and must *start* with in accomplishing the proletarian revolution. Such a beginning, on the basis of large-scale production, will of itself lead to the gradual "withering away" of all bureaucracy, to the gradual creation of an order—an order without inverted commas, an order bearing no similarity to wage slavery—an order under which the functions of control and accounting, becoming more and more simple, will be performed by each in turn, will then become a habit and will finally die out as the *special* functions of a special section of the population.

A witty German Social-Democrat of the seventies of the last century called the *postal service* an example of the socialist economic system. This is very true. At present the postal service is a business organised on the lines of a state-*capitalist* monopoly. Imperialism is gradually transforming all trusts into organisations of a similar type, in which, standing over the "common" people, who are overworked and starved, one has the same bourgeois bureaucracy. But the mechanism of social management is here already to hand. Once we have overthrown the capitalists, crushed the resistance of these exploiters with the iron hand of the armed workers, and smashed the bureaucratic machine of the modern state, we shall have a splendidly-equipped mechanism, freed from the "parasite," a mechanism which can very well be set going by the united workers themselves, who will hire technicians, foremen and accountants, and pay them *all*, as indeed *all* "state" officials in general, workmen's wages. Here is a concrete, practical task which can immediately be fulfilled in relation to all trusts, a task whose fulfilment will rid the working people of exploitation, a task which takes account of what the Commune had already begun to practice (particularly in building up the state).

To organise the *whole* economy on the lines of the postal service so that the technicians, foremen and accountants, as well as *all* officials, shall receive salaries no higher than "a workman's wage," all under the control and leadership of the armed proletariat—this is our immediate aim. This is the state and this is the economic foundation we need. This is what will bring about the abolition of par-liamentarism and the preservation of representative institutions. This is what will rid the labouring classes of the bourgeoisie's prostitution of these institutions. . . .

The Transition from Capitalism to Communism

Marx continued: "Between capitalist and communist society lies the period of the revolutionary transformation of the one into the other. Corresponding to this is also a political transition period in which the state can be nothing but *the revolutionary dictatorship of the proletariat.*" Marx bases this conclusion on an analysis of the role played by the proletariat in modern capitalist society, on the data concerning the development of this society, and on the irreconcilability of the antagonistic interests of the proletariat and the bourgeoisie.

Previously the question was put as follows: to achieve its emancipation, the proletariat must overthrow the bourgeoisie, win political power and establish its revolutionary dictatorship.

Now the question is put somewhat differently: the transition from capitalist society—which is developing towards communism—to communist society is impossible without a "political transition period," and the state in this period can only be the revolutionary dictatorship of the proletariat.

What, then, is the relation of this dictatorship to democracy?

We have seen that the *Communist Manifesto* simply places side by side the two concepts: "to raise the proletariat to the position of the ruling class" and "to win the battle of democracy." On the basis of all that has been said above, it is possible to determine more precisely how democracy changes in the transition from capitalism to communism.

In capitalist society, providing it develops under the most favourable conditions, we have a more or less complete democracy in the democratic republic. But this democracy is always hemmed in by the narrow limits set by capitalist exploitation, and consequently always remains, in effect, a democracy for the minority, only for the propertied classes, only for the rich. Freedom in capitalist society always remains about the same as it was in the ancient Greek republics: freedom for the slave-owners. Owing to the conditions of capitalist exploitation, the modern wage slaves are so crushed by want and poverty that "they cannot be bothered with democracy," "cannot be bothered with politics"; in the ordinary, peaceful course of events, the majority of the population is debarred from participation in public and political life.

The correctness of this statement is perhaps most clearly confirmed by Germany, because constitutional legality steadily endured there for a remarkably long time—nearly half a century (1871–1914)—and during this period the Social-Democrats were able to achieve far more than in other countries in the way of "utilising legality," and organised a larger proportion of the workers into a political party than anywhere else in the world.

What is this largest proportion of politically conscious and active wage slaves that has so far been recorded in capitalist society? One million members of the Social-Democratic Party—out of fifteen million wage-workers! Three million organised in trade unions—out of fifteen million!

Democracy for an insignificant minority, democracy for the rich—that is the democracy of capitalist society. If we look more closely into the machinery of capitalist democracy, we see everywhere, in the "petty"—supposedly petty—details of the suffrage (residential qualification, exclusion of women, etc.), in the technique of the representative institutions, in the actual obstacles to the right of assembly (public buildings are not for "paupers"!), in the purely capitalist organisation of the daily press, etc., etc.—we see restriction after restriction upon democracy. These restrictions, exceptions, exclusions, obstacles for the poor seem slight, especially in the eyes of one who has never known want himself and has never been in close contact with the oppressed classes in their mass life (and nine out of ten, if not ninety-nine out of a hundred, bourgeois publicists and politicians come under this category); but in their sum total these restrictions exclude and squeeze out the poor from politics, from active participation in democracy.

Marx grasped this *essence* of capitalist democracy splendidly when, in analysing the experience of the Commune, he said that the oppressed are allowed once very few years to decide which particular representatives of the oppressing class shall represent and repress them in parliament!

But from this capitalist democracy—that is inevitably narrow and stealthily pushes aside the poor, and is therefore hypocritical and false through and through—forward development does not proceed simply, directly and smoothly, towards "greater and greater democracy," as the liberal professors and petty-bourgeois opportunists would have us believe. No, forward development, i.e., development towards communism, proceeds through the dictatorship of the proletariat, and cannot do otherwise, for the *resistance* of the capitalist exploiters cannot be *broken* by anyone else or in any other way.

And the dictatorship of the proletariat, i.e., the organisation of the vanguard of the oppressed as the ruling class for the purpose of suppressing the oppressors, cannot result merely in an expansion of democracy. *Simultaneously* with an immense expansion of democracy, which *for the first time* becomes democracy for the poor, democracy for the people, and not democracy for the money-bags, the dictatorship of the proletariat imposes a series of restrictions on the freedom of the oppressors, the exploiters, the capitalists. We must suppress them in order to free humanity from wage slavery, their resistance must be crushed by force; it is clear that there is no freedom and no democracy where there is suppression and where there is violence.

Engels expressed this splendidly in his letter to Bebel when he said, as the reader will remember, that "the proletariat needs the state, not in the interests of freedom but in order to hold down its adversaries, and as soon as it becomes possible to speak of freedom the state as such ceases to exist."

Democracy for the vast majority of the people, and suppression by force, i.e., exclusion from democracy, of the exploiters and oppressors of the people—this is the change democracy undergoes during the *transition* from capitalism to communism.

Only in communist society, when the resistance of the capitalists has been completely crushed, when the capitalists have disappeared, when there are no classes (i.e.,when there is no distinction between the members of society as regards their relation to the social means of production), *only* then "the state . . . ceases to exist," and "*it becomes possible to speak of freedom.*" Only then will a truly complete democracy become possible and be realised, a democracy without any exceptions whatever. And only then will democracy begin to *wither away*, owing to the simple fact that, freed from capitalist slavery, from the untold horrors, savagery, absurdities and infamies of capitalist exploitation, people will gradually *become accustomed* to observing the elementary rules of social intercourse that have been known for centuries and repeated for thousands of years in all copybook maxims. They will become accustomed to observing them without force, without coercion, without subordination, *without the special apparatus* for coercion called the state.

The expression "the state *withers away*" is very well chosen, for it indicates both the gradual and the spontaneous nature of the process. Only habit can, and undoubtedly will, have such an effect; for we see around us on millions of occasions how readily people become accustomed to observing the necessary rules of social intercourse when there is no exploitation, when there is nothing that arouses indignation, evokes protest and revolts, and creates the need for *suppression*.

And so in capitalist society we have a democracy that is curtailed, wretched, false, a democracy only for the rich, for the minority. The dictatorship of the proletariat, the period of transition to communism, will for the first time create democracy for the people, for the majority, along with the necessary suppression of the exploiters, of the minority. Communism alone is capable of providing really complete democracy, and the more complete it is, the sooner it will become unnecessary and wither away of its own accord.

In other words, under capitalism we have the state in the proper sense of the word, that is, a special machine for the suppression of one class by another, and, what is more, of the majority by the minority. Naturally, to be successful, such an undertaking as the systematic suppression of the exploited majority by the exploiting minority calls for the utmost ferocity and savagery in the matter of suppressing, it calls for seas of blood, through which mankind is actually wading its way in slavery, serfdom and wage labour.

Further more, during the *transition* from capitalism to communism suppression is *still* necessary, but it is now the suppression of the exploiting minority by the exploited majority. A special apparatus, a special machine for suppression, the "state," is *still* necessary, but this is now a transitional state. It is no longer a state in the proper sense of the word; for the suppression of the minority of exploiters by the majority of the wage slaves of *yesterday* is comparatively so easy, simple and natural a task that it will entail far less bloodshed than the suppression of the risings of slaves, serfs or wage-labourers, and it will cost mankind far less. And it is compatible with the extension of democracy to such an overwhelming majority of the population that the need for a *special machine* of suppression will begin to disappear. Naturally, the exploiters are unable to suppress the people without a highly complex machine for performing this task, but *the people* can suppress the exploiters even with a very simple "machine," almost without a "machine," without a special apparatus, by the simple *organisation of the armed people* (such as the Soviets of Workers' and Soldiers' Deputies, we would remark, running ahead).

Lastly, only communism makes the state absolutely unnecessary, for there is *nobody* to be suppressed—"nobody" in the sense of a *class*, of a systematic struggle against a definite section of the population. We are not utopians, and do not in the least deny the possibility and inevitability of excesses on the part of *individual persons*, or the need to stop *such* excesses. In the first place, however, no special machine, no special apparatus of suppression, is needed for this; this will be done by the armed people themselves, as simply and as readily as any crowd of civilised people, even in modern society, interferes to put a stop to a scuffle or to prevent a woman from being assaulted. And, secondly, we know that the fundamental social cause of excesses, which consist in the violation of the rules of social intercourse, is the exploitation of the people, their want and their poverty. With the removal of this chief cause, excesses will inevitably begin to "*wither away.*" We do not know how quickly and in what succession, but we do know they will wither away. With their withering away the state will also *wither away*.

Without building utopia, Marx defined more fully what can be defined *now* regarding this future, namely, the difference between the lower and higher places (levels, stages) of communist society.

Note

* *Editor's note*: The Socialist-Revolutionary Party was a peasant-oriented party and the Mensheviks were Lenin's opponents within the Russian Social Democratic Movement.

30

Sigmund Freud
Selections

*Sigmund Freud (1856–1939) was the founder of psychoanalysis and was respon-
sible for a revolution in thought equal to any in the "real" world. Freud was
born in Freiberg (now Czechoslovakia); when he was three years old, his family
moved to Vienna where he studied medicine, participating in the development of
the "talking cure." Freud turned to the psychological aspects of neurology after
studying with J. M. Charcot in Paris. Initially working with J. Breuer, a Viennese colleague, Freud grew convinced of the sexual origin of hysterical symptoms. Freud's* The Interpretation of Dreams *was published in 1899, but it was
not until 1908 that psychoanalysis emerged as a movement at the first International Psycho-analytical Congress. Asserting the centrality of childhood sexuality
to the development of the psyche and the formation of adult neurotic behavior,
Freud claimed that the ego's task was to reconcile the biological instinctual
urges of the* id, *with the demands of the* superego *and reality. Freud's discussion of infantile sexuality violated Victorian morality and the hypocrisy that era
engendered. In particular, Freud documented the traumas suffered by his patients, Viennese girls who seemed to have been seduced as very young children
by older male relatives. He later recanted his initial theory of seduction and developed his theory of early childhood sexuality. He also proposed the theory of
the "Oedipus complex" in which a boy wishes to kill his father and marry his
mother. This substitution has been interpreted by some contemporary critics as a
retraction by Freud of the initial insight regarding widespread sexual abuse of
children in the family. In* Civilization and Its Discontents, *Freud claimed that
cultural achievements are the direct result of constraint and sublimation. Freud
was exiled to London after Austria was occupied by Nazis.*

CIVILIZATION AND ITS DISCONTENTS

I do not think that I have made a complete enumeration of the methods by which
men strive to gain happiness and keep suffering away and I know, too, that the
material might have been differently arranged. One procedure I have not yet mentioned—not because I have forgotten it but because it will concern us later in
another connection. And how could one possibly forget, of all others, this technique in the art of living? It is conspicuous for a most remarkable combination of
characteristic features. It, too, aims of course at making the subject independent of

Fate (as it is best to call it), and to that end it locates satisfaction in internal mental processes, making use, in so doing, of the displaceability of the libido of which we have already spoken. But it does not turn away from the external world; on the contrary, it clings to the objects belonging to that world and obtains happiness from an emotional relationship to them. Nor is it content to aim at an avoidance of unpleasure—a goal, as we might call it, of weary resignation; it passes this by without heed and holds fast to the original, passionate striving for a positive fulfillment of happiness. And perhaps it does in fact come nearer to this goal than any other method. I am, of course, speaking of the way of life which makes love the centre of everything, which looks for all satisfaction in loving and being loved. A psychical attitude of this sort comes naturally enough to all of us; one of the forms in which love manifests itself—sexual love—has given us our most intense experience of an overwhelming sensation of pleasure and has thus furnished us with a pattern for our search for happiness. What is more natural than that we should persist in looking for happiness along the path on which we first encountered it? The weak side of this technique of living is easy to see; otherwise no human being would have thought of abandoning this path to happiness for any other. It is that we are never so defenceless against suffering as when we love, never so helplessly unhappy as when we have lost our loved object or its love. But this does not dispose of the technique of living based on the value of love as a means to happiness. There is much more to be said about it.

We may go on from here to consider the interesting case in which happiness in life is predominantly sought in the enjoyment of beauty, wherever beauty presents itself to our senses and our judgement—the beauty of human forms and gestures, of natural objects and landscapes and of artistic and even scientific creations. This aesthetic attitude to the goal of life offers little protection against the threat of suffering, but it can compensate for a great deal. The enjoyment of beauty has a peculiar, mildly intoxicating quality of feeling. Beauty has no obvious use; nor is there any clear cultural necessity for it. Yet civilization could not do without it. The science of aesthetics investigates the conditions under which things are felt as beautiful, but it has been unable to give any explanation of the nature and origin of beauty, and, as usually happens, lack of success is concealed beneath a flood of resounding and empty words. Psychoanalysis, unfortunately, has scarcely anything to say about beauty either. All that seems certain is its derivation from the field of sexual feeling. The love of beauty seems a perfect example of an impulse inhibited in its aim. 'Beauty' and 'attraction' are originally attributes of the sexual object. It is worth remarking that the genitals themselves, the sight of which is always exciting, are nevertheless hardly ever judged to be beautiful; the quality of beauty seems, instead, to attach to certain secondary sexual characters.

In spite of the incompleteness [of my enumeration], I will venture on a few remarks as a conclusion to our enquiry. The programme of becoming happy, which the pleasure principle imposes on us [cannot be fulfilled; yet we must not— indeed, we cannot—give up our efforts to bring it nearer to fulfilment by some means or other. Very different paths may be taken in that direction, and we may give priority either to the positive aspect of the aim, that of gaining pleasure, or to its negative one, that of avoiding unpleasure. By none of these paths can we attain all that we desire. Happiness, in the reduced sense in which we recognize it as possible, is a problem of the economics of the individual's libido. There is no golden rule which applies to everyone: every man must find out for himself in what particular fashion he can be saved.

Religion restricts this play of choice and adaptation, since it imposes equally on everyone its own path to the acquisition of happiness and protection from suffering. Its technique consists in depressing the value of life and distorting the picture of the real world in a delusional manner—which presupposes an intimidation of the intelligence. At this price, by forcibly fixing them in a state of psychical infantilism and by drawing them into a mass-delusion, religion succeeds in sparing many people an individual neurosis. But hardly anything more. There are, as we have said, many paths which *may* lead to such happiness as is attainable by men, but there is none which does so for certain. Even religion cannot keep its promise. If the believer finally sees himself obliged to speak of God's 'inscrutable decrees', he is admitting that all that is left to him as a last possible consolation and source of pleasure in his suffering is an unconditional submission. And if he is prepared for that, he could probably have spared himself the *détour* he has made. . . .

Our enquiry concerning happiness has not so far taught us much that is not already common knowledge. And even if we proceed from it to the problem of why it is so hard for men to be happy, there seems no greater prospect of learning anything new. We have given the answer already by pointing to the three sources from which our suffering comes: the superior power of nature, the feebleness of our own bodies and the inadequacy of the regulations which adjust the mutual relationships of human beings in the family, the state and society. In regard to the first two sources, our judgement cannot hesitate long. It forces us to acknowledge those sources of suffering and to submit to the inevitable. We shall never completely master nature; and our bodily organism, itself a part of that nature, will always remain a transient structure with a limited capacity for adaptation and achievement. This recognition does not have a paralysing effect. On the contrary, it points the direction for our activity. If we cannot remove all suffering, we can remove some, and we can mitigate some: the experience of many thousands of years has convinced us of that. As regards the third source, the social source of suffering, our attitude is a different one. We do not admit it at all; we cannot see why the regulations made by ourselves should not, on the contrary, be a protection and a benefit for every one of us. And yet, when we consider how unsuccessful we have been in precisely this field of prevention of suffering, a suspicion dawns on us that here, too, a piece of unconquerable nature may lie behind—this time a piece of our own psychical constitution.

When we start considering this possibility, we come upon a contention which is so astonishing that we must dwell upon it. This contention holds that what we call our civilization is largely responsible for our misery, and that we should be much happier if we gave it up and returned to primitive conditions. I call this contention astonishing because, in whatever way we may define the concept of civilization, it is a certain fact that all the things with which we seek to protect ourselves against the threats that emanate from the sources of suffering are part of that very civilization. . . .

Beauty, cleanliness and order obviously occupy a special position among the requirements of civilization. No one will maintain that they are as important for life as control over the forces of nature or as some other factors with which we shall become acquainted. And yet no one would care to put them in the background as trivialities. That civilization is not exclusively taken up with what is useful is already shown by the example of beauty, which we decline to omit from among the interests of civilization. The usefulness of order is quite evident. With regard to cleanliness, we must bear in mind that it is demanded of us by hygiene as well, and we may suspect that even before the days of scientific prophylaxis the connection between the two was not altogether strange to man. Yet utility does not entirely explain these efforts; something else must be at work besides.

No feature, however, seems better to characterize civilization than its esteem and encouragement of man's higher mental activities—his intellectual, scientific and artistic achievements—and the leading role that it assigns to ideas in human life. Foremost among those ideas are the religious systems, on whose complicated structure I have endeavoured to throw light elsewhere. Next come the speculations of philosophy; and finally what might be called man's 'ideals'—his ideas of a possible perfection of individuals, or of peoples or of the whole of humanity, and the demands he sets up on the basis of such ideas. The fact that these creations of his are not independent of one another, but are on the contrary closely interwoven, increases the difficulty not only of describing them but of tracing their psychological derivation. If we assume quite generally that the motive force of all human activities is a striving towards the two confluent goals of utility and a yield of pleasure, we must suppose that this is also true of the manifestations of civilization which we have been discussing here, although this is easily visible only in scientific and aesthetic activities. But it cannot be doubted that the other activities, too, correspond to strong needs in men—perhaps to needs which are only developed in a minority. Nor must we allow ourselves to be misled by judgements of value concerning any particular religion, or philosophic system, or ideal. Whether we think to find in them the highest achievements of the human spirit, or whether we deplore them as aberrations, we cannot but recognize that where they are present, and, in especial, where they are dominant, a high level of civilization is implied.

The last, but certainly not the least important, of the characteristic features of civilization remains to be assessed: the manner in which the relationships of men to one another, their social relationships, are regulated—relationships which affect a person as a neighbour, as a source of help, as another person's sexual object, as a member of a family and of a State. Here it is especially difficult to keep clear of particular ideal demands and to see what is civilized in general. Perhaps we may begin by explaining that the element of civilization enters on the scene with the first attempt to regulate these social relationships. If the attempt were not made, the relationships would be subject to the arbitrary will of the individual: that is to say, the physically stronger man would decide them in the sense of his own interests and instinctual impulses. Nothing would be changed in this if this stronger man should in his turn meet someone even stronger than he. Human life in common is only made possible when a majority comes together which is stronger than any separate individual and which remains united against all separate individuals. The power of this community is then set up as 'right' in opposition to the power of the individual, which is condemned as 'brute force'. This replacement of the power of the individual by the power of a community constitutes the decisive step of civilization. The essence of it lies in the fact that the members of the community restrict themselves in their possibilities of satisfaction, whereas the individual knew no such restrictions. The first requisite of civilization, therefore, is that of justice—that is, the assurance that a law once made will not be broken in favour of an individual. This implies nothing as to the ethical value of such a law. The further course of cultural development seems to tend towards making the law no longer an expression of the will of a small community—a caste or a stratum of the population or a racial group—which, in its turn, behaves like a violent individual towards other, and perhaps more numerous, collections of people. The final outcome should be a rule of law to which all—except those who are not capable of entering a community—have contributed by a sacrifice of their instincts, and which leaves no one—again with the same exception—at the mercy of brute force.

The liberty of the individual is no gift of civilization. It was greatest before there was any civilization, though then, it is true, it had for the most part no value, since the individual was scarcely in a position to defend it. The development of civilization imposes restrictions on it, and justice demands that no one shall escape those restrictions. What makes itself felt in a human community as a desire for freedom may be their revolt against some existing injustice, and so may prove favourable to a further development of civilization; it may remain compatible with civilization. But it may also spring from the remains of their original personality, which is still untamed by civilization and may thus become the basis in them of hostility to civilization. The urge for freedom, therefore, is directed against particular forms and demands of civilization or against civilization altogether. It does not seem as though any influence could induce a man to change his nature into a termite's. No doubt he will always defend his claim to individual liberty against the will of the group. A good part of the struggles of mankind centre round the single task of finding an expedient accommodation—one, that is, that will bring happiness—between this claim of the individual and the cultural claims of the group; and one of the problems that touches the fate of humanity is whether such an accommodation can be reached by means of some particular form of civilization or whether this conflict is irreconcilable.

. . . . We said there that man's discovery that sexual (genital) love afforded him the strongest experiences of satisfaction, and in fact provided him with the prototype of all happiness, must have suggested to him that he should continue to seek the satisfaction of happiness in his life along the path of sexual relations and that he should make genital erotism the central point of his life. We went on to say that in doing so he made himself dependent in a most dangerous way on a portion of the external world, namely, his chosen love-object, and exposed himself to extreme suffering if he should be rejected by that object or should lose it through unfaithfulness or death. For that reason the wise men of every age have warned us most emphatically against this way of life; but in spite of this it has not lost its attraction for a great number of people.

A small minority are enabled by their constitution to find happiness, in spite of everything, along the path of love. But far-reaching mental changes in the function of love are necessary before this can happen. These people make themselves independent of their object's acquiescence by displacing what they mainly value from being loved on to loving; they protect themselves against the loss of the object by directing their love, not to single objects but to all men alike; and they avoid the uncertainties and disappointments of genital love by turning away from its sexual aims and transforming the instinct into an impulse with an *inhibited aim*. What they bring about in themselves in this way is a state of evenly suspended, steadfast, affectionate feeling, which has little external resemblance any more to the stormy agitations of genital love, from which it is nevertheless derived. Perhaps St. Francis of Assisi went furthest in thus exploiting love for the benefit of an inner feeling of happiness. Moreover, what we have recognized as one of the techniques for fulfilling the pleasure principle has often been brought into connection with religion; this connection may lie in the remote regions where the distinction between the ego and objects or between objects themselves is neglected. According to one ethical view, whose deeper motivation will become clear to us presently, this readiness for a universal love of mankind and the world represents the highest standpoint which man can reach. Even at this early stage of the discussion I should like to bring forward my two main objections to this view. A love that does not discriminate seems to me to forfeit a part of its own value, by doing an injustice to its object; and secondly, not all men are worthy of love.

. . . As regards the sexually mature individual, the choice of an object is restricted to the opposite sex, and most extra-genital satisfactions are forbidden as perversions. The requirement, demonstrated in these prohibitions, that there shall be a single kind of sexual life for everyone, disregards the dissimilarities, whether innate or acquired, in the sexual constitution of human beings; it cuts off a fair number of them from sexual enjoyment, and so becomes the source of serious injustice. The result of such restrictive measures might be that in people who are normal—who are not prevented by their constitution—the whole of their sexual interests would flow without loss into the channels that are left open. But heterosexual genital love, which has remained exempt from outlawry, is itself restricted by further limitations, in the shape of insistence upon legitimacy and monogamy. Present-day civilization makes it plain that it will only permit sexual relationships on the basis of a solitary, indissoluble bond between one man and one woman, and that it does not like sexuality as a source of pleasure in its own right and is only prepared to tolerate it because there is so far no substitute for it as a means of propagating the human race.

. . . Men are not gentle creatures who want to be loved, and who at the most can defend themselves if they are attacked; they are, on the contrary, creatures among whose instinctual endowments is to be reckoned a powerful share of aggressiveness. As a result, their neighbour is for them not only a potential helper or sexual object, but also someone who tempts them to satisfy their aggressiveness on him, to exploit his capacity for work without compensation, to use him sexually without his consent, to seize his possessions, to humiliate him, to cause him pain, to torture and to kill him. *Homo homini lupus.*[1] Who, in the face of all his experience of life and of history, will have the courage to dispute this assertion?

The existence of this inclination to aggression, which we can detect in ourselves and justly assume to be present in others, is the factor which disturbs our relations with our neighbour and which forces civilization into such a high expenditure [of energy]. In consequence of this primary mutual hostility of human beings, civilized society is perpetually threatened with disintegration. The interest of work in common would not hold it together; instinctual passions are stronger than reasonable interests. Civilization has to use its utmost efforts in order to set limits to man's aggressive instincts and to hold the manifestations of them in check by psychical reaction-formations. Hence, therefore, the use of methods intended to incite people into identifications and aim-inhibited relationships of love, hence the restriction upon sexual life, and hence too the ideal's commandment to love one's neighbour as oneself—a commandment which is really justified by the fact that nothing else runs so strongly counter to the original nature of man. In spite of every effort, these endeavours of civilization have not so far achieved very much. It hopes to prevent the crudest excesses of brutal violence by itself assuming the right to use violence against criminals, but the law is not able to lay hold of the more cautious and refined manifestations of human aggressiveness. The time comes when each one of us has to give up as illusions the expectations which, in his youth, he pinned upon his fellow-men, and when he may learn how much difficulty and pain has been added to his life by their ill-will. At the same time, it would be unfair to reproach civilization with trying to eliminate strife and competition from human activity. These things are undoubtedly indispensable. But opposition is not necessarily enmity; it is merely misused and made an *occasion* for enmity.

The communists believe that they have found the path to deliverance from our evils. According to them, man is wholly good and is well-disposed to his neighbour; but the institution of private property has corrupted his nature. The ownership of private wealth gives the individual power, and with it the temptation to ill-treat his neighbour; while the man who is excluded from possession is bound to rebel in hostility against his oppressor. If private property were abolished, all wealth held in common, and everyone allowed to share in the enjoyment of it, ill-will and hostility would disappear among men. Since everyone's needs would be satisfied, no one would have any reason to regard another as his enemy; all would willingly undertake the work that was necessary. I have no concern with any economic criticisms of the communist system; I cannot enquire into whether the abolition of private property is expedient or advantageous.[2] But I am able to recognize that the psychological premises on which the system is based are an untenable illusion. In abolishing private property we deprive the human love of aggression of one of its instruments, certainly a strong one, though certainly not the strongest; but we have in no way altered the differences in power and influence which are misused by aggressiveness, nor have we altered anything in its nature. Aggressiveness was not created by property. It reigned almost without limit in primitive times, when property was still very scanty, and it already shows itself in the nursery almost before property has given up its primal, anal form; it forms the basis of every relation of affection and love among people (with the single exception, perhaps, of the mother's relation to her male child). If we do away with personal rights over material wealth, there still remains prerogative in the field of sexual relationships, which is bound to become the source of the strongest dislike and the most violent hostility among men who in other respects are on an equal footing. If we were to remove this factor, too, by allowing complete freedom of sexual life and thus abolishing the family, the germ-cell of civilization, we cannot, it is true, easily foresee what new paths the development of civilization could take; but one thing we can expect, and that is that this indestructible feature of human nature will follow it there.

It is clearly not easy for men to give up the satisfaction of this inclination to aggression. They do not feel comfortable without it. The advantage which a comparatively small cultural group offers of allowing this instinct an outlet in the form of hostility against intruders is not to be despised. It is always possible to bind together a considerable number of people in love, so long as there are other people left over to receive the manifestations of their aggressiveness. . . .

Notes

1. 'Man is a wolf to man.' Derived from Plautus, *Asinaria* II, iv, 88.
2. Anyone who has tasted the miseries of poverty in his own youth and has experienced the indifference and arrogance of the well-to-do, should be safe from the suspicion of having no understanding or good will towards endeavours to fight against the inequality of wealth among men and all that it leads to. To be sure, if an attempt is made to base this fight upon an abstract demand, in the name of justice, for equality for all men, there is a very obvious objection to be made—that nature, by endowing individuals with extremely unequal physical attributes and mental capacities, has introduced injustices against which there is no remedy.

TOTEM AND TABOO

Let us call us the spectacle of a totem meal of the kind we have been discussing, amplified by a few probable features which we have not yet been able to consider. The clan is celebrating the ceremonial occasion by the cruel slaughter of its totem animal and is devouring it raw—blood, flesh and bones. The clansmen are there, dressed in the likeness of the totem and imitating it in sound and movement, as though they are seeking to stress their identity with it. Each man is conscious that he is performing an act forbidden to the individual and justifiable only through the participation of the whole clan; nor may anyone absent himself from the killing and the meal. When the deed is done, the slaughtered animal is lamented and bewailed. The mourning is obligatory, imposed by dread of a threatened retribution. As Robertson Smith (1894) remarks of an analogous occasion, its chief purpose is to disclaim responsibility for the killing.

But the mourning is followed by demonstrations of festive rejoicing: every instinct is unfettered and there is licence for every kind of gratification. Here we have easy access to an understanding of the nature of festivals in general. A festival is a permitted, or rather an obligatory, excess, a solemn breach of a prohibition. It is not that men commit the excesses because they are feeling happy as a result of some injunction they have received. It is rather that excess is of the essence of a festival; the festive feeling is produced by the liberty to do what is as a rule prohibited.

What are we to make, though, of the prelude to this festive joy—the mourning over the death of the animal? If the clansmen rejoice over the killing of the totem—a normally forbidden act—why do they mourn over it as well?

As we have seen, the clansmen acquire sanctity by consuming the totem: they reinforce their identification with it and with one another. Their festive feelings and all that follows from them might well be explained by the fact that they have taken into themselves the sacred life of which the substance of the totem is the vehicle.

Psycho-analysis has revealed that the totem animal is in reality a substitute for the father; and this tallies with the contradictory fact that, though the killing of the animal is as a rule forbidden, yet its killing becomes a festive occasion—the fact that it is killed and yet mourned. The ambivalent emotional attitude, which to this day characterizes the father-complex in our children and which often persists into adult life, seems to extend to the totem animal in its capacity as substitute for the father.

If, now, we bring together the psycho-analytic translation of the totem with the fact of the totem meal and with Darwin's theories of the earliest state of human society, the possibility of a deeper understanding emerges—a glimpse of a hypothesis which may seem fantastic but which offers the advantage of establishing an unsuspected correlation between groups of phenomena that have hitherto been disconnected.

There is, of course, no place for the beginnings of totemism in Darwin's primal horde. All that we find there is a violent and jealous father who keeps all the females for himself and drives away his sons as they grow up. This earliest state of society has never been an object of observation. The most primitive kind of organization that we actually come across—and one that is in force to this day in certain tribes—consists of bands of males; these bands are composed of members with equal rights and are subject to the restrictions of the totemic system, including inheritance through the mother. Can this form of organization have developed out of the other one? and if so along what lines?

If we call the celebration of the totem meal to our help, we shall be able to find an answer. One day¹ the brothers who had been driven out came together, killed and devoured their father and so made an end of the patriarchal horde. United, they had the courage to do and succeeded in doing what would have been impossible for them individually. (Some cultural advance, perhaps, command over some new weapons, had given them a sense of superior strength.) Cannibal savages as they were, it goes without saying that they devoured their victim as well as killing him. The violent primal father had doubtless been the feared and envied model of each one of the company of brothers: and in the act of devouring him they accomplished their identification with him, and each one of them acquired a portion of his strength. The totem meal, which is perhaps mankind's earliest festival, would thus be a repetition and a commemoration of this memorable and criminal deed, which was the beginning of so many things—of social organization, of moral restrictions and of religion.²

In order that these latter consequences may seem plausible, leaving their premises on one side, we need only suppose that the tumultuous mob of brothers were filled with the same contradictory feelings which we can see at work in the ambivalent father-complexes of our children and of our neurotic patients. They hated their father, who presented such a formidable obstacle to their craving for power and their sexual desires; but they loved and admired him too. After they had got rid of him, had satisfied their hatred and had put into effect their wish to identify themselves with him, the affection which had all this time been pushed under was bound to make itself felt.³ It did so in the form of remorse. A sense of guilt made its appearance, which in this instance coincided with the remorse felt by the whole group. The dead father became stronger than the living one had been—for events took the course we so often see them follow in human affairs to this day. What had up to then been prevented by his actual existence was thenceforward prohibited by the sons themselves, in accordance with the psychological procedure so familiar to us in psycho-analyses under the name of 'deferred obedience'. They revoked their deed by forbidding the killing of the totem, the substitute for their father; and they renounced its fruits by resigning their claim to the women who had now been set free. They thus created out of their filial sense of guilt the two fundamental taboos of totemism, which for that very reason inevitably corresponded to the two repressed wishes of the Oedipus complex. Whoever contravened those taboos became guilty of the only two crimes with which primitive society concerned itself.⁴

The two taboos of totemism with which human morality has its beginning, are not on a par psychologically. The first of them, the law protecting the totem animal, is founded wholly on emotional motives: the father had actually been eliminated, and in no real sense could the deed be undone. But the second rule, the prohibition of incest, has a powerful practical basis as well. Sexual desires do not unite men but divide them. Though the brothers had banded together in order to overcome their father, they were all one another's rivals in regard to the women. Each of them would have wished, like his father, to have all the women to himself. The new organization would have collapsed in a struggle of all against all, for none of them was of such overmastering strength as to be able to take on his father's part with success. Thus the brothers had no alternative, if they were to live together, but—not, perhaps, until they had passed through many dangerous crises—to institute the law against incest, by which they all alike renounced the women whom they desired and who had been their chief motive for despatching their father. In this way they rescued the organization which had made them strong—and which may have been based on homosexual feelings and acts, originating perhaps during the period of their expulsion from the horde. Here, too, may perhaps have been the germ of the institution of matriarchy, described by Bachofen [1861], which was in turn replaced by the patriarchal organization of the family.

On the other hand, the claim of totemism to be regarded as a first attempt at a religion is based on the first of these two taboos—that upon taking the life of the totem animal. The animal struck the sons as a natural and obvious substitute for their father; but the treatment of it which they found imposed on themselves expressed more than the need to exhibit their remorse. They could attempt, in their relation to this surrogate father, to allay their burning sense of guilt, to bring about a kind of reconciliation with their father. The totemic system was, as it were, a covenant with their father, in which he promised them everything that a childish imagination may expect from a father—protection, care and indulgence—while on their side they undertook to respect his life, that is to say, not to repeat the deed which had brought destruction on their real father. Totemism, moreover, contained an attempt at self-justification: 'If our father had treated us in the way the totem does, we should never have felt tempted to kill him.' In this fashion totemism helped to smooth things over and to make it possible to forget the event to which it owed its origin.

Features were thus brought into existence which continued thenceforward to have a determining influence on the nature of religion. Totemic religion arose from the filial sense of guilt, in an attempt to allay that feeling and to appease the father by deferred obedience to him. All later religions are seen to be attempts at solving the same problem. They vary according to the stage of civilization at which they arise and according to the methods which they adopt; but all have the same end in view and are reactions to the same great event with which civilization began and which, since it occurred, has not allowed mankind a moment's rest.

There is another feature which was already present in totemism and which has been preserved unaltered in religion. The tension of ambivalence was evidently too great for any contrivance to be able to counteract it; or it is possible that psychological conditions in general are unfavourable to getting rid of these antithetical emotions. However that may be, we find that the ambivalence implicit in the father-complex persists in totemism and in religions generally. Totemic religion not only comprised expressions of remorse and attempts at atonement, it also served as a remembrance of the triumph over the father. Satisfaction over that triumph led to the institution of the memorial festival of the totem meal, in which the restrictions of deferred obedience no longer held. Thus it became a duty to repeat the crime of parricide again and again in the sacrifice of the totem animal, whenever, as a result of the changing conditions of life, the cherished fruit of the crime—appropriation of the paternal attributes—threatened to disappear. We shall not be surprised to find that the element of filial rebelliousness also emerges, in the *later* products of religion, often in the strangest disguises and transformations.

Hitherto we have followed the developments of the *affectionate* current of feeling towards the father, transformed into remorse, as we find them in religion and in moral ordinances (which are not sharply distinguished in totemism). But we must not overlook the fact that it was in the main with the impulses that led to parricide that the victory lay. For a long time afterwards, the social fraternal feelings, which were the basis of the whole transformation, continued to exercise a profound influence on the development of society. They found expression in the sanctification of the blood tie, in the emphasis upon the solidarity of all life within the same clan. In thus guaranteeing one another's lives, the brothers were declaring that no one of them must be treated by another as their father was treated by them all jointly. They were precluding the possibility of a repetition of their father's fate. To the religiously based prohibition against killing the totem was now added the socially based prohibition against fratricide. It was not until long afterwards that the prohibition ceased to be limited to members of the clan and assumed the simple form: 'Thou shalt do no murder.' The patriarchal horde was replaced in the first instance by the fraternal clan, whose existence was assured by the blood tie. Society was now based on complicity in the common crime; religion was based on the sense of guilt and the remorse attaching to it; while morality was based partly on the exigencies of this society and partly on the penance demanded by the sense of guilt.

Thus psycho-analysis, in contradiction to the more recent views of the totemic system but in agreement with the earlier ones, requires us to assume that totemism and exogamy were intimately connected and had a simultaneous origin.

Notes

1. To avoid possible misunderstanding, I must ask the reader to take into account the final sentences of the following footnote as a corrective to this description.

2. This hypothesis, which has such a monstrous air, of the tyrannical father being overwhelmed and killed by a combination of his exiled sons was also arrived at by J. J. Atkinson (*Primal Law*, 1903, 220 f.) as a direct implication of the state of affairs in Darwin's primal horde: 'The patriarch had only one enemy whom he should dread . . . a youthful band of brothers living together in forced celibacy, or at most in polyandrous relation with some single female captive. A horde as yet weak in their impubescence they are, but they would, when strength was gained with time, inevitably wrench by combined attacks, renewed again and again, both wife and life from the paternal tyrant.' Atkinson, who incidentally passed his whole life in New Caledonia and had unusual opportunities for studying the natives, also pointed out that the conditions which Darwin assumed to prevail in the primal horde may easily be observed in herds of wild oxen and horses and regularly lead to the killing of the father of the herd. [Ibid., 222 f.] He further supposed that, after the father had

been disposed of, the horde would be disintegrated by a bitter struggle between the victorious sons. Thus any new organization of society would be precluded: there would be 'an ever-recurring violent succession to the solitary paternal tyrant, by sons whose parricidal hands were so soon again clenched in fratricidal strife.' (Ibid., 228.) Atkinson, who had no psycho-analytic hints to help him and who was ignorant of Robertson Smith's studies, found a less violent transition from the primal horde to the next social stage, at which numbers of males live together in a peaceable community. He believed that through the intervention of maternal love the sons—to begin with only the youngest, but later others as well—were allowed to remain with the horde, and that in return for this toleration the sons acknowledged their father's sexual privilege by renouncing all claim to their mother and sisters. [Ibid., 231 ff.]

Such is the highly remarkable theory put forward by Atkinson. In its essential feature it is in agreement with my own; but its divergence results in its failing to effect a correlation with many other issues.

The lack of precision in what I have written in the text above, its abbreviation of the time factor and its compression of the whole subject matter, may be attributed to the reserve necessitated by the nature of the topic. It would be as foolish to aim at exactitude in such questions as it would be unfair to insist upon certainty.

3. This fresh emotional attitude must also have been assisted by the fact that the deed cannot have given complete satisfaction to those who did it. From one point of view it had been done in vain. Not one of the sons had in fact been able to put his original wish—of taking his father's place—into effect. And, as we know, failure is far more propitious for a moral reaction than satisfaction.

4. 'Murder and incest, or offences of a like kind against the sacred laws of blood, are in primitive society the only crimes of which the community as such takes cognizance.' (Smith, 1894, 419.)

WHY WAR? (1932)

Vienna, September, 1932.

Dear Professor Einstein,

When I heard that you intended to invite me to an exchange of views on some subject that interested you and that seemed to deserve the interest of others besides yourself, I readily agreed. I expected you to choose a problem on the frontiers of what is knowable to-day, a problem to which each of us, a physicist and a psychologist, might have our own particular angle of approach and where we might come together from different directions upon the same ground. You have taken me by surprise, however, by posing the question of what can be done to protect mankind from the curse of war. I was scared at first by the thought of my—I had almost written "our"—incapacity for dealing with what seemed to be a practical problem, a concern for statesmen. But I then realized that you had raised the question not as a natural scientist and physicist but as a philanthropist: you were following the promptings of the League of Nations just as Fridtjof Nansen, the polar explorer, took on the work of bringing help to the starving and homeless victims of the World War. I reflected, moreover, that I was not being asked to make practical proposals but only to set out the problem of avoiding war as it appears to a psychological observer. Here again you yourself have said almost all there is to say on the subject. But though you have taken the wind out of my sails I shall be glad to follow in your wake and content myself with confirming all you have said by amplifying it to the best of my knowledge—or conjecture.

You begin with the relation between Right and Might.[1] There can be no doubt that that is the correct starting-point for our investigation. But may I replace the word "might" by the balder and harsher word "violence"? To-day right and violence appear to us as antitheses. It can easily be shown, however, that the one has developed out of the other; and if we go back to the earliest beginnings and see how that first came about, the problem is easily solved. You must forgive me if in what follows I go over familiar and commonly accepted ground as though it were new, but the thread of my argument requires it.

It is a general principle, then, that conflicts of interest between men are settled by the use of violence. This is true of the whole animal kingdom, from which men have no business to exclude themselves. In the case of men, no doubt, conflicts of *opinion* occur as well which may reach the highest pitch of abstraction and which seem to demand some other technique for their settlement. That, however, is a later complication. To begin with, in a small human horde,[2] it was superior muscular strength which decided who owned things or whose will should prevail. Muscular strength was soon supplemented and replaced by the use of tools: the winner was the one who had the better weapons or who used them the more skillfully. From the moment at which weapons were introduced, intellectual superiority already began to replace brute muscular strength; but the final purpose of the fight remained the same—one side or the other was to be compelled to abandon his claim or his objection by the damage inflicted on him and by the crippling of his strength. That purpose was most completely achieved if the victor's violence eliminated his opponent permanently, that is to say, killed him. This had two advantages: he could not renew his opposition and his fate deterred others from following his example. In addition to this, killing an enemy satisfied an instinctual inclination which I shall have to mention later. The intention to kill might be countered by a reflection that the enemy could be employed in performing useful services if he were left alive in an intimidated condition. In that case the victor's violence was content to subjugate him instead of killing him. This was a first beginning of the idea of sparing an enemy's life, but thereafter the victor had to reckon with his defeated opponent's lurking thirst for revenge and sacrificed some of his own security.

Such, then, was the original state of things: domination by whoever had the greater might—domination by brute violence or by violence supported by intellect. As we know, this régime was altered in the course of evolution. There was a path that led from violence to right or law. What was that path? It is my belief that there was only one: the path which led by way of the fact that the superior strength of a single individual could be rivalled by the union of several ones. *"L'union fait la force."* Violence could be broken by union, and the power of those who were united now represented law in contrast to the violence of the single individual. Thus we see that right is the might of a community. It is still violence, ready to be directed against any individual who resists it; it works by the same methods and follows the same purposes. The only real difference lies in the fact that what prevails is no longer the violence of an individual but that of a community. But in order that the transition from violence to this new right or justice may be effected, one psychological condition must be fulfilled. The union of the majority must be a stable and lasting one. If it were only brought about for the purpose of combating a single domineering individual and were dissolved after his defeat, nothing would have been accomplished. The next person who found himself superior in strength would once more seek to set up a dominion by violence and the game would be repeated *ad infinitum*. The community must be maintained permanently, must be organized, must draw up regulations to anticipate the risk of rebellion and must institute authorities to see that those regulations—the laws—are respected and to superintend the execution of legal acts of violence. The recognition of a community of interests such as these leads to the growth of emotional ties between the members of a united group of people—feelings of unity which are the true source of its strength.

Here, I believe, we already have all the essentials: violence overcome by the transference of power to a large unity, which is held together by emotional ties between its members. What remains to be said is no more than an expansion and a repetition of this.

The situation is simple so long as the community consists only of a number of equally strong individuals. The laws of such an association will determine the extent to which, if the security of communal life is to be guaranteed, each individual must surrender his personal liberty to turn his strength to violent uses. But a state of rest of that kind is only theoretically conceivable. In actuality the position is complicated by the fact that from its very beginning the community comprises elements of unequal strength—men and women, parents and children—and soon, as a result of war and conquest, it also comes to include victors and vanquished, who turn into masters and slaves. The justice of the community then becomes an expression of the unequal degrees of power obtaining within it; the laws are made by and for the ruling members and find little room for the rights of those in subjection. From that time forward there are two factors at work in the community which are sources of unrest over matters of law but tend at the same time to a further growth of law. First, attempts are made by certain of the rulers to set themselves above the prohibitions which apply to everyone—they seek, that is, to go back from a dominion of law to a dominion of violence. Secondly, the oppressed members of the group make constant efforts to obtain more power and to have any changes that are brought about in that direction recognized in the laws— they press forward, that is, from unequal justice to equal justice for all. This second tendency becomes especially important if a real shift of power occurs within a community, as may happen as a result of a number of historical factors. In that case right may gradually adapt itself to the new distribution of power or, as is more frequent, the ruling class is unwilling to recognize the change, and rebellion and civil war follow, with a temporary suspension of law and new attempts at a solution by violence, ending in the establishment of a fresh rule of law. There is yet another source from which modifications of law may arise, and one of which the expression is invariably peaceful: it lies in the cultural transformation of the members of the community. This, however, belongs properly in another connection and must be considered later.

Thus we see that the violent solution of conflicts of interest is not avoided even inside a community. But the everyday necessities and common concerns that are inevitable where people live together in one place tend to bring such struggles to a swift conclusion and under such conditions there is an increasing probability that a peaceful solution will be found. But a glance at the history of the human race reveals an endless series of conflicts between one community and another or several others, between larger and smaller units—between cities, provinces, races, nations, empires—which have almost always been settled by force of arms. Wars of this kind end either in the spoliation or in the complete overthrow and conquest of one of the parties. It is impossible to make any sweeping judgement upon wars of conquest. Some, such as those waged by the Mongols and Turks, have brought nothing but evil. Others, on the contrary, have contributed to the transformation of violence into law by establishing larger units within which the use of violence was made impossible and in which a fresh system of law led to solution of conflicts. In this way the conquests of the Romans gave the countries round the Mediterranean the priceless *pax Romana*, and the greed of the French kings to extend their dominions created a peacefully united and flourishing France. Paradoxical as it may sound, it must be admitted that war might be a far from inappropriate means of establishing the eagerly desired reign of "everlasting" peace, since it is in a position to create the large units within which a powerful central government makes further wars impossible. Nevertheless it fails in this purpose, for the results of conquest are as a rule short-lived: the newly created units fall apart once again, usually owing to a lack of cohesion between the portions that have been united by violence. Hitherto, moreover, the unifications created by conquest, though of considerable extent, have only been *partial*, and the conflicts between these have cried out for violent solution. Thus the result of all these warlike efforts has only been that the human race has exchanged numerous, and indeed unending, minor wars for wars on a grand scale that are rare but all the more destructive.

If we turn to our own times, we arrive at the same conclusion which you have reached by a shorter path. Wars will only be prevented with certainty if mankind unites in setting up a central authority to which the right of giving judgement upon all conflicts of interest shall be handed over. There are clearly two separate requirements involved in this: the creation of a supreme authority and its endowment with the necessary power. One without the other would be useless. The League of Nations is designed as an authority of this kind, but the second condition has not been fulfilled: the League of Nations has no power of its own and can only acquire it if the members of the new union, the separate States, are ready to resign it. And at the moment there seems very little prospect of this. The institution of the

League of Nations would, however, be wholly unintelligible if one ignored the fact that here was a bold attempt such as has seldom (perhaps, indeed, never on such a scale) been made before. It is an attempt to base upon an appeal to certain idealistic attitudes of mind the authority (that is, the coercive influence) which otherwise rests on the possession of power. We have heard that a community is held together by two things: the compelling force of violence and the emotional ties (identifications is the technical name) between its members. If one of the factors is absent, the community may possibly be held together by the other. The ideas that are appealed to can, of course, only have any significance if they give expression to important concerns that are common to the members, and the question arises of how much strength they can exert. History teaches us that they have been to some extent effective. For instance, the Panhellenic idea, the sense of being superior to the surrounding barbarians—an idea which was so powerfully expressed in the Amphictyonies, the Oracles and the Games—was sufficiently strong to mitigate the customs of war among Greeks, though evidently not sufficiently strong to prevent warlike disputes between different sections of the Greek nation or even to restrain a city or confederation of cities from allying itself with the Persian foe in order to gain an advantage over a rival. In the same way, the community of feeling among Christians, powerful though it was, was equally unable at the time of the Renaissance to deter Christian States, whether large or small, from seeking the Sultan's aid in their wars with one another. Nor does any idea exist to-day which could be expected to exert a unifying authority of the sort. Indeed it is all too clear that the national ideals by which nations are at present swayed operate in a contrary direction. Some people are inclined to prophesy that it will not be possible to make an end of war until Communist ways of thinking have found universal acceptance. But that aim is in any case a very remote one to-day, and perhaps it could only be reached after the most fearful civil wars. Thus the attempt to replace actual force by the force of ideas seems at present to be doomed to failure. We shall be making a false calculation if we disregard the fact that law was originally brute violence and that even to-day it cannot do without the support of violence.

I can now proceed to add a gloss to another of your remarks. You express astonishment at the fact that it is so easy to make men enthusiastic about a war and add your suspicion that there is something at work in them—an instinct for hatred and destruction—which goes halfway to meet the efforts of the warmongers. Once again, I can only express my entire agreement. We believe in the existence of an instinct of that kind and have in fact been occupied during the last few years in studying its manifestations. Will you allow me to take this opportunity of putting before you a portion of the theory of the instincts which, after much tentative groping and many fluctuations of opinion, has been reached by workers in the field of psychoanalysis?

According to our hypothesis human instincts are of only two kinds: those which seek to preserve and unite—which we call "erotic," exactly in the sense in which Plato uses the word "Eros" in his *Symposium*, or "sexual," with a deliberate extension of the popular conception of "sexuality"—and those which seek to destroy and kill and which we class together as the aggressive or destructive instinct. As you see, this is in fact no more than a theoretical clarification of the universally familiar opposition between Love and Hate which may perhaps have some fundamental relation to the polarity of attraction and repulsion that plays a part in your own field of knowledge. We must not be too hasty in introducing ethical judgements of good and evil. Neither of these instincts is any less essential than the other; the phenomena of life arise from the operation of both together, whether acting in concert or in opposition. It seems as though an instinct of the one sort can scarcely ever operate in isolation; it is always accompanied—or, as we say, alloyed—with an element from the other side, which modifies its aim or is, in some cases, what enables it to achieve that aim. Thus, for instance, the instinct of self-preservation is certainly of an erotic kind, but it must nevertheless have aggressiveness at its disposal if it is to fulfill its purpose. So, too, the instinct of love, when it is directed towards an object, stands in need of some contribution from the instinct of mastery if it is in any way to possess that object. The difficulty of isolating the two classes of instinct in their actual manifestation is indeed what has so long prevented us from recognizing them.

If you will follow me a little further, you will see that human actions are subject to another complication of a different kind. It is very rarely that an action is the work of a *single* instinctual impulse (which must in itself be compounded of Eros and destructiveness). In order to make an action possible there must be as a rule a *combination* of such compounded motives. This was perceived long ago by a specialist in your own subject, a Professor G. C. Lichtenberg who taught physics at Göttingen during our classical age—though perhaps he was even more remarkable as a psychologist than as a physicist. He invented a Compass of Motives, for he wrote: "The motives that lead us to do anything might be arranged like the thirty-two winds and might be given names on the same pattern: for instance, 'food-food-fame' or 'fame-fame-food.'" So that when human beings are incited to war they may have a whole number of motives for assenting—some noble and some base, some of which they speak openly and others on which they are silent. There is no need to enumerate them all. A lust for aggression and destruction is certainly among them: the countless cruelties in history and in our everyday lives vouch for its existence and its strength. The gratification of these destructive impulses is of course facilitated by their admixture with others of an erotic and idealistic kind. When we read of the atrocities of the past, it sometimes seems as though the idealistic motives served only as an excuse for the destructive appetites; and sometimes—in the case, for instance, of the cruelties of the Inquisition—it seems as though the idealistic motives had pushed themselves forward in consciousness, while the destructive ones lent them an unconscious reinforcement. Both may be true.

I fear I may be abusing your interest, which is after all concerned with the prevention of war and not with our theories. Nevertheless I should like to linger for a moment over our destructive instinct, whose popularity is by no means equal to its importance. As a result of a little speculation, we have come to suppose that this instinct is at work in every living being and is striving to bring it to ruin and to reduce life to its original condition of inanimate matter. Thus it quite seriously deserves to be called a death instinct, while the erotic instincts represent the effort to live. The death instinct turns into the destructive instinct if, with the help of special organs, it is directed outwards, on to objects. The living creature preserves its own life, so to say, by destroying an extraneous one. Some portion of the death instinct, however, remains operative *within* the living being, and we have sought to trace quite a number of normal and pathological phenomena to this internalization of the destructive instinct. We have even been guilty of the heresy of attributing the origin of conscience to this diversion inwards of aggressiveness. You will notice that it is by no means a trivial matter if this process is carried too far: it is positively unhealthy. On the other hand if these forces are turned to destruction in the external world, the living creature will be relieved and the effect must be beneficial. This would serve as a biological justification for all the ugly and dangerous impulses against which we are struggling. It must be admitted that they stand nearer to Nature than does our resistance to them, for which an explanation also needs to be found. It may perhaps seem to you as though our theories are a kind of mythology and, in the present case, not even an agreeable one. But does not every science come in the end to a kind of mythology like this? Cannot the same be said to-day of your own Physics?

For our immediate purpose then, this much follows from what has been said: there is no use in trying to get rid of men's aggressive inclinations. We are told that in certain happy regions of the earth, where nature provides in abundance everything that man requires, there are races whose life is passed in tranquillity and who know neither compulsion nor aggressiveness. I can scarcely believe it and I should be glad to hear more of these fortunate beings. The Russian Communists, too, hope to be able to cause human aggressiveness to disappear by guaranteeing the satisfaction of all material needs and by establishing equality in other respects among all the members of the community. That, in my opinion, is an illusion. They themselves are armed to-day with the most scrupulous care and not the least important of the methods by which they keep their supporters together is hatred of everyone beyond their frontiers. In any case, as you yourself have remarked, there is no question of getting rid entirely of human aggressive impulses: it is enough to try to divert them to such an extent that they need not find expression in war.

Our mythological theory of instincts makes it easy for us to find a formula for *indirect* methods of combating war. If willingness to engage in war is an effect of the destructive instinct, the most obvious plan will be to bring Eros, its antagonist, into play against it. Anything that encourages the growth of emotional ties between men must operate against war. These ties may be of two kinds. In the first place they may be relations resembling those towards a loved object, though without having a sexual aim. There is no need for psychoanalysis to be ashamed to speak of love in this connection, for religion itself uses the same words: "Thou shalt love thy neighbour as thyself." This, however, is more easily said than done. The second kind of emotional tie is by means of identification. Whatever leads men to share important interests produces this community of feeling, these identifications. And the structure of human society is to a large extent based on them.

A complaint which you make about the abuse of authority brings me to another suggestion for the indirect combating of the propensity to war. One instance of the innate and ineradicable inequality of men is their tendency to fall into the two classes of leaders and followers. The latter constitute the vast majority; they stand in need of an authority which will make decisions for them and to which they for the most part offer an unqualified submission. This suggests that more care should be taken than hitherto to educate an upper stratum of men with independent minds, not open to intimidation and eager in the pursuit of truth, whose business it would be to give direction to the dependent masses. It goes without saying that the encroachments made by the executive power of the State and the prohibition laid by the Church upon freedom of thought are far from propitious for the production of a class of this kind. The ideal condition of things would of course be a community of men who had subordinated their instinctual life to the dictatorship of reason. Nothing else could unite men so completely and so tenaciously, even if there were no emotional ties between them. But in all probability that is a Utopian expectation. No doubt the other indirect methods of preventing war are more practicable, though they promise no rapid success. An unpleasant picture comes to one's mind of mills that grind so slowly that people may starve before they get their flour.

The result, as you see, is not very fruitful when an unworldly theoretician is called in to advise on an urgent practical problem. It is a better plan to devote oneself in every particular case to meeting the danger with whatever weapons lie to hand. I should like, however, to discuss one more question, which you do not mention in your letter but which specially interests me. Why do you and I and so many other people rebel so violently against war? Why do we not accept it as another of the many painful calamities of life? After all, it seems quite a natural thing, no doubt it has a good biological basis and in practice it is scarcely avoidable. There is no need to be shocked at my raising this question. For the purpose of an investigation such as this, one may perhaps be allowed to wear a mask of assumed detachment. The answer to my question will be that we react to war in this way because everyone has a right to his own life, because war puts an end to human lives that are full of hope, because it brings individual men into humiliating situations, because it compels them against their will to murder other men, and because it destroys precious material objects which have been produced by the labours of humanity. Other reasons besides might be given, such as that in its present-day form war is no longer an opportunity for achieving the old ideals of heroism and that owing to the perfection of instruments of destruction a future war might involve the extermination of one or perhaps both of the antagonists. All this is true, and so incontestably true that one can only feel astonished that the waging of war has not yet been unanimously repudiated. No doubt debate is possible upon one or two of these points. It may be questioned whether a community ought not to have a right to dispose of individual lives; every war is not open to condemnation to an equal degree; so long as there exist countries and nations that are prepared for the ruthless destruction of others, those others must be armed for war. But I will not linger over any of these issues; they are not what you want to discuss with me, and I have something different in mind. It is my opinion that the main reason why we rebel against war is that we cannot help doing so. We are pacifists because we are obliged to be for organic reasons. And we then find no difficulty in producing arguments to justify our attitude.

No doubt this requires some explanation. My belief is this. For incalculable ages mankind has been passing through a process of evolution of culture. (Some people, I know, prefer to use the term "civilization.") We owe to that process the best of what we have become, as well as a good part of what we suffer from. Though its causes and beginnings are obscure and its outcome uncertain, some of its characteristics are easy to perceive. It may perhaps be leading to the extinction of the human race, for in more than one way it impairs the sexual function; uncultivated races and backward strata of the population are already multiplying more rapidly than highly cultivated ones. The process is perhaps comparable to the domestication of certain species of animals and it is undoubtedly accompanied by physical alterations; but we are still unfamiliar with the notion that the evolution of culture is an organic process of this kind. The psychical modifications that go along with the cultural process are striking and unambiguous. They consist in a progressive displacement of instinctual aims and a restriction of instinctual impulses. Sensations which were pleasurable to our ancestors have become indifferent or even intolerable to ourselves; there are organic grounds for the changes in our ethical and aesthetic ideals. Of the psychological characteristics of culture two appear to be the most important: a strengthening of the intellect, which is beginning to govern instinctual life, and an internalization of the aggressive impulses, with all its consequent advantages and perils. Now war is in the crassest opposition to the psychical attitude imposed on us by the cultural process, and for that reason we are bound to rebel against it; we simply cannot any longer put up with it. This is not merely an intellectual and emotional repudiation; we pacifists have a constitutional intolerance of war, an idiosyncracy magnified, as it were, to the highest degree. It seems, indeed, as though the lowering of aesthetic standards in war plays a scarcely smaller part in our rebellion than do its cruelties.

And how long shall we have to wait before the rest of mankind become pacifists too? There is no telling. But it may not be Utopian to hope that these two factors, the cultural attitude and the justified dread of the consequences of a future war, may result within a measurable time in putting an end to the waging of war. By what paths or by what side-tracks this will come about we cannot guess. But one thing we *can* say: whatever fosters the growth of culture works at the same time against war.

I trust you will forgive me if what I have said has disappointed you, and I remain, with kindest regards,

Yours sincerely,
Sigm. Freud

Notes

Warum Krieg? was the title of an interchange of open letters between Professor Albert Einstein and Freud. This formed one of a series of similar interchanges arranged by the International Institute of Intellectual Co-operation under the auspices of the League of Nations, and was first published simultaneously in German, French and English in Paris in 1933. Freud's letter is in *Gesammelte Werke*, vol. 16. Professor Einstein's, which preceded it, was a short one setting out the problems to be discussed. Present translation by James Strachey.

1. In the original the words *"Recht"* and *"Macht"* are used throughout the essay. It has unfortunately been necessary to sacrifice this stylistic unity in the translation. *"Recht"* has been rendered indifferently by "right," "law" and "justice"; and *"Macht"* by "might," "force" and "power."

2. Freud uses the word "horder" to denote a comparatively small group.

31

Emma Goldman
Victims of Morality

Emma Goldman, (1869–1940) was an anarchist who wrote on issues ranging from syndicalism and free love to homosexual rights and modern drama. From 1906 to 1917, she published a monthly anarchist magazine, Mother Earth, *in which she hoped to combine the American tradition of dissent with that of revolutionary anarchism, mostly an immigrant phenomenon. "Victims of Morality," was published there in 1913. Goldman was born in Lithuania to a family of Russian Jewish shopkeepers. She emigrated to America and became a factory worker in Rochester, New York. Radicalized by the trial and hanging of the Haymarket anarchists in 1886–1887 in Chicago, Goldman emerged as a skillful and compelling speaker who inspired others with her courage before police harassment. She served one year in prison on charges of "inciting to riot" during a hunger demonstration in 1893, and served two weeks in 1916 for her campaign in favor of birth control. Goldman also was jailed in Missouri for two years for opposing the draft during World War I. She always took a book with her when she spoke in public, expecting arrest and incarceration. She was deported to the Soviet Union in 1919, at the height of the Red Scare. Having energetically defended the Bolsheviks while in the United States, Goldman was brutally frank in exposing the disastrous conditions in Russia. She left Russia in 1921.*

Goldman's spirit and enthusiasm opened a new discourse in radical politics, introducing sexual and psychological elements to prevailing theories of liberation. She is celebrated as a feminist heroine by the contemporary women's movement, and is notorious for her denigration of women's suffrage, which she scorned as a deceptive palliative.

NOT so very long ago I attended a meeting addressed by Anthony Comstock, who has for forty years been the guardian of American morals. A more incoherent, ignorant ramble I have never heard from any platform.

The question that presented itself to me, listening to the commonplace, bigoted talk of the man, was, How could anyone so limited and unintelligent wield the power of censor and dictator over a supposedly democratic nation? True, Comstock has the law to back him. Forty years ago, when puritanism was even more rampant than to-day, completely shutting out the light of reason and progress, Comstock succeeded, through shady machination and political wire pulling, to introduce a bill which gave him complete control over the Post Office Department—a control which has proved disastrous to the freedom of the press, as well as the right of privacy of the American citizen.

Since then, Comstock has broken into the private chambers of people, has confiscated personal correspondence, as well as works of art, and has established a system of espionage and graft which would put Russia to shame. Yet the law does not explain the power of Anthony Comstock. There is something else, more terrible than the law. It is the narrow puritanic spirit, as represented in the sterile minds of the Young-Men-and-Old-Maid's Christian Union, Temperance Union, Sabbath Union, Purity League, etc. A spirit which is absolutely blind to the simplest manifestations of life; hence stands for stagnation and decay. As in antebellum days, these old fossils lament the terrible immorality of our time. Science, art, literature, the drama, are at the mercy of bigoted censorship and legal procedure, with the result that America, with all her boastful claims to progress and liberty is still steeped in the densest provincialism.

The smallest dominion in Europe can boast of an art free from the fetters of morality, an art that has the courage to portray the great social problems of our time. With the sharp edge of critical analysis, it cuts into every social ulcer, every wrong, demanding fundamental changes and the transvaluation of accepted values. Satire, wit, humor, as well as the most intensely serious modes of expression, are being employed to lay bare our conventional social and moral lies. In America we would seek in vain for such a medium, since even the attempt at it is made impossible by the rigid régime, by the moral dictator and his clique.

The nearest approach, however, is our muckrakers, who have no doubt rendered great service along economic and social lines. Whether the muckrakers have or have not helped to change conditions, at least they have torn the mask from the lying face of our smug and self-satisfied society.

Unfortunately, the Lie of Morality still stalks about in fine feathers, since no one dares to come within hailing distance of that holy of holies. Yet it is safe to say that no other superstition is so detrimental to growth, so enervating and paralyzing to the minds and hearts of the people, as the superstition of Morality.

The most pathetic, and in a way discouraging, aspect of the situation is a certain element of liberals, and even of radicals, men and women apparently free from religious and social spooks. But before the monster of Morality they are as prostrate as the most pious of their kind—which is an additional proof to the extent to which the morality worm has eaten into the system of its victims and how far-going and thorough the measures must be which are to drive it out again.

Needless to say, society is obsessed by more than one morality. Indeed, every institution of to-day has its own moral standard. Nor could they ever have maintained themselves, were it not for religion, which acts as a shield, and for morality, which acts as the mask. This explains the interest of the exploiting rich in religion and morality. The rich preach, foster, and finance both, as an investment that pays good returns. Through the medium of religion they have paralyzed the mind of the people, just as morality has enslaved the spirit. In other words, religion and morality are a much better whip to keep people in submission than even the club and the gun.

To illustrate: The Property Morality declares that that institution is sacred. Woe to anyone that dares to question the sanctity of Property, or sins against it! Yet everyone knows that Property is robbery; that it represents the accumulated efforts of millions, who themselves are propertyless. And what is more terrible, the more poverty stricken the victim of Property Morality is, the greater his respect and awe for that master. Thus we hear advanced people, even so-called class-conscious workingmen, decry as immoral such methods as sabotage and direct action, because they aim at Property.

Verily, if the victims themselves are so blinded by the Property Morality, what need one expect from the masters? It therefore seems high time to bring home the fact that until the workers will lose respect for the instrument of their material enslavement, they need hope for no relief.

However, it is with the effect of Morality upon women that I am here mostly concerned. So disastrous, so paralyzing has this effect been, that some even of the most advanced among my sisters never thoroughly outgrow it.

It is Morality which condemns woman to the position of a celibate, a prostitute, or a reckless, incessant breeder of hapless children.

First, as to the celibate, the famished and withered human plant. When still a young, beautiful flower, she falls in love with a respectable young man. But Morality decrees that unless he can marry the girl, she must never know the raptures of love, the ecstasy of passion, which reaches its culminating expression in the sex embrace. The respectable young man is willing to marry, but the Property Morality, the Family and Social Moralities decree that he must first make his pile, must save up enough to establish a home and be able to provide for a family. The young people must wait, often many long, weary years.

Meanwhile the respectable young man, excited through the daily association and contact with his sweetheart, seeks an outlet for his nature in return for money. In ninety-nine cases out of a hundred, he will be infected, and when he is materially able to marry, he will infect his wife and possible offspring. And the young flower, with every fiber aglow with the fire of life, with all her being crying out for love and passion? She has no outlet. She develops headaches, insomnia, hysteria; grows embittered, quarrelsome, and soon becomes a faded, withered, joyless being, a nuisance to herself and everyone else. No wonder Stirner preferred the grisette to the maiden grown gray with virtue.

There is nothing more pathetic, nothing more terrible, than this gray-grown victim of a gray-grown Morality. This applies even with greater force to the masses of professional middle-class girls, than to those of the people. Through economic necessity the latter are thrust into life's jungle at an early age; they grow up with their male companions in the factory and shop, or at play and dance. The result is a more normal expression of their physical instincts. Then too, the young men and women of the people are not so hide-bound by externalities, and often follow the call of love and passion regardless of ceremony and tradition.

But the overwrought and oversexed middle-class girl, hedged in her narrow confines with family and social traditions, guarded by a thousand eyes, afraid of her own shadow—the yearning of her inmost being for the man or the child, must turn to cats, dogs, canary birds, or the Bible Class. Such is the cruel dictum of

Morality, which is daily shutting out love, light, and joy from the lives of innumerable victims.

Now, as to the prostitute. In spite of laws, ordinances, persecution, and prisons; in spite of segregation, registration, vice crusades, and other similar devices, the prostitute is the real specter of our age. She sweeps across the plains like a fire burning into every nook of life, devastating, destroying.

After all, she is paying back, in a very small measure, the curse and horrors society has strewn in her path. She, weary with the tramp of ages, harassed and driven from pillar to post, at the mercy of all, is yet the Nemesis of modern times, the avenging angel, ruthlessly wielding the sword of fire. For has she not the man in her power? And, through him, the home, the child, the race. Thus she slays, and is herself the most brutally slain.

What has made her? Whence does she come? Morality, the Morality which is merciless in its attitude to women. Once she dared to be herself, to be true to her nature, to life, there is no return: the woman is thrust out from the pale and protection of society. The prostitute becomes the victim of Morality, even as the withered old maid is its victim. But the prostitute is victimized by still other forces, foremost among them the Property Morality, which compels woman to sell herself as a sex commodity for a dollar per, out of wedlock, or for fifteen dollars a week, in the sacred fold of matrimony. The latter is no doubt safer, more respected, more recognized, but of the two forms of prostitution the girl of the street is the least hypocritical, the least debased, since her trade lacks the pious mask of hypocrisy; and yet she is hounded, fleeced, outraged, and shunned, by the very powers that have made her: the financier, the priest, the moralist, the judge, the jailor, and the detective, not to forget her sheltered, respectably virtuous sister, who is the most relentless and brutal in her persecution of the prostitute.

Morality and its victim, the mother—what a terrible picture! Is there indeed anything more terrible, more criminal, than our glorified sacred function of motherhood? The woman, physically and mentally unfit to be a mother, yet condemned to breed; the woman, economically taxed to the very last spark of energy, yet forced to breed; the woman, tied to a man she loathes, whose very sight fills her with horror, yet made to breed; the woman, worn and used-up from the process of procreation, yet coerced to breed, more, ever more. What a hideous thing, this much-lauded motherhood! No wonder thousands of women risk mutilation, and prefer even death to this curse of the cruel imposition of the spook of Morality. Five thousand are yearly sacrificed upon the altar of this monster, that will not stand for prevention but would cure by abortion. Five thousand soldiers in the battle for their physical and spiritual freedom, and as many thousands more who are crippled and mutilated rather than bring forth life in a society based on decay and destruction.

Is it because the modern woman wants to shirk responsibility, or that she lacks love for her offspring, that she is driven to the most drastic and dangerous means to avoid bearing children? Only shallow, bigoted minds can bring such an accusation. Else they would know that the modern woman has become race-conscious, sensitive to the needs and rights of the child, as the unit of the race, and that therefore the modern woman has a sense of responsibility and humanity, which was quite foreign to her grandmother.

With the economic war raging all around her, with strife, misery, crime, disease, and insanity staring her in the face, with numberless little children ground into gold dust, how can the self- and race-conscious woman become a mother? Morality can not answer this question. It can only dictate, coerce, or condemn— and how many women are strong enough to face this condemnation, to defy the moral dicta? Few, indeed. Hence they fill the factories, the reformatories, the homes for feeble minded, the prisons, the insane asylums, or they die in the attempt to prevent child-birth. Oh, Motherhood, what crimes are committed in thy name! What hosts are laid at your feet, Morality, destroyer of life!

Fortunately, the Dawn is emerging from the chaos and darkness. Woman is awakening, she is throwing off the nightmare of Morality; she will no longer be bound. In her love for the man, she is not concerned in the contents of his pocketbook, but in the wealth of his nature, which alone is the fountain of life and joy. Nor does she need the sanction of the State. Her love is sanction enough for her. Thus she can abandon herself to the man of her choice, as the flowers abandon themselves to dew and light, in freedom, beauty, and ecstasy.

Through her re-born consciousness as a unit, a personality, a race builder, she will become a mother only if she desires the child, and if she can give to the child, even before its birth, all that her nature and intellect can yield: harmony, health, comfort, beauty, and, above all, understanding, reverence, and love, which is the only fertile soil for new life, a new being.

Morality has no terrors for her who has risen beyond good and evil. And though Morality may continue to devour its victims, it is utterly powerless in the face of the modern spirit, that shines in all its glory upon the brow of man and woman, liberated and unafraid.

32

Benito Mussolini
Fascism

Benito Mussolini (1883–1945) ruled Italy for twenty years and was Europe's first Fascist dictator. He seized power in a coup d'etat in 1922 at the head of a Nationalist, anti-Communist party supported by brutal military squads. Mussolini imposed totalitarian rule on Italy and invaded Abyssinia in 1935 as part of his plan of territorial expansion. He intervened on Franco's side in the Spanish Civil War (1936–1939), occupied Albania in 1939, and formed an alliance with Hitler. When his regime collapsed, he was ignominously captured by partisans while hiding among retreating German troops and was executed.

LIKE ALL sound political conceptions, Fascism is action and it is thought; action in which doctrine is immanent, and doctrine arising from a given system of historical forces in which it is inserted, and working on them from within. It has therefore a form correlated to contingencies of time and space; but it has also an ideal content which makes it an expression of truth in the higher region of the history of thought. There is no way of exercising a spiritual influence in the world as a human will dominating the will of others, unless one has a conception both of the transient and the specific reality on which that action is to be exercised, and of the permanent and universal reality in which the transient dwells and has its being. To know men one must know man; and to know man one must be acquainted with reality and its laws. There can be no conception of the State which is not fundamentally a conception of life: philosophy or intuition, system of ideas evolving within the framework of logic or concentrated in a vision or a faith, but always, at least potentially, an organic conception of the world.

Thus many of the practical expressions of Fascism—such as party organisation, system of education, discipline—can only be understood when considered in relation to its general attitude toward life. A spiritual attitude. Fascism sees in the world not only those superficial, material aspects in which man appears as an individual, standing by himself, self-centred, subject to natural law which instinctively urges him toward a life of selfish momentary pleasure; it sees not only the individual but the nation and the country; individuals and generations bound together by a moral law, with common traditions and a mission which suppressing the instinct for life closed in a brief circle of pleasure, builds up a higher life, founded on duty, a life free from the limitations of time and space, in which the individual, by self-sacrifice, the renunciation of self-interest, by death itself, can achieve that purely spiritual existence in which his value as a man consists.

The conception is therefore a spiritual one, arising from the general reaction of the century against the fiacid materialistic positivism of the XIXth century. Anti-positivistic but positive; neither sceptical nor agnostic; neither pessimistic nor supinely optimistic as are, generally speaking, the doctrines (all negative) which place the center of life outside man; whereas, by the exercise of his free will, man can and must create his own world.

Fascism wants man to be active and to engage in action with all his energies; it wants him to be manfully aware of the difficulties besetting him and ready to face them. It conceives of life as a struggle in which it behooves a man to win for himself a really worthy place, first of all by fitting himself (physically, morally, intellectually) to become the implement required for winning it. As for the individual, so for the nation, and so for mankind. Hence the high value of culture in all its forms (artistic, religious, scientific) and the outstanding importance of education. Hence also the essential value of work, by which man subjugates nature and creates the human world (economic, political, ethical, intellectual).

This positive conception of life is obviously an ethical one. It invests the whole field of reality as well as the human activities which master it. No action is exempt from moral judgement; no activity can be despoiled of the value which a moral purpose confers on all things. Therefore life, as conceived of by the Fascist, is serious, austere, religious; all its manifestations are poised in a world sustained by moral forces and subject to spiritual responsibilities. The Fascist disdains an "easy" life.

The Fascist conception of life is a religious one, in which man is viewed in his immanent relation to a higher-law, endowed with an objective will transcending the individual and raising him to conscious membership of a spiritual society. Those who perceive nothing beyond opportunistic considerations in the religious policy of the Fascist régime fail to realise that Fascism is not only a system of government but also and above all a system of thought.

In the Fascist conception of history, man is man only by virtue of the spiritual process to which he contributes as a member of the family, the social group, the nation, and in function of history to which all nations bring their contribution. Hence the great value of tradition in records, in language, in customs, in the rules of social life. Outside history man is a nonentity. Fascism is therefore opposed to all individualistic abstractions based on eighteenth century materialism; and it is opposed to all Jacobinistic utopias and innovations. It does not believe in the possibility of "happiness" on earth as conceived by the economistic literature of the XVIIIth century, and it therefore rejects the teleological notion that at some future time the human family will secure a final settlement of all its difficulties. This notion runs counter to experience which teaches that life is in continual flux and in process of evolution. In politics Fascism aims at realism; in practice it desires to deal only with those problems which are the spontaneous product of historic conditions and which find or suggest their own solutions. Only by entering in to the process of reality and taking possession of the forces at work within it, can man act on man and on nature.

Anti-individualistic, the Fascist conception of life stresses the importance of the State and accepts the individual only in so far as his interests coincide with those of the State, which stands for the conscience and the universal will of man as a historic entity. It is opposed to classical liberalism which arose as a reaction to absolutism and exhausted its historical function when the State became the expression of the conscience and will of the people. Liberalism denied the State in the name of the individual; Fascism reasserts the rights of the State as expressing the real essence of the individual. And if liberty is to be the attribute of living men and not of abstract dummies invented by individualistic liberalism, then Fascism stands for liberty, and for the only liberty worth having, the liberty of the State and of the individual within the State. The Fascist conception of the State is all-embracing; outside of it no human or spiritual values can exist, much less have value. Thus understood, Fascism is totalitarian, and the Fascist State—a synthesis and a unit inclusive of all values—interprets, develops, and potentiates the whole life of a people.

No individuals or groups (political parties, cultural associations, economic unions, social classes) are outside the State. Fascism is therefore opposed to Socialism to which unity within the State (which amalgamates classes into a single economic and ethical reality) is unknown, and which sees in history nothing but the class struggle. Fascism is likewise opposed to trade-unionism as a class weapon. But when brought within the orbit of the State, Fascism recognises the real needs which gave rise to socialism and trade-unionism, giving them due weight in the guild or corporative system in which divergent interests are coordinated and harmonised in the unity of the State.

Grouped according to their several interests, individuals form classes; they form trade-unions when organised according to their several economic activities; but first and foremost they form the State, which is no mere matter of numbers, the sum of the individuals forming the majority. Fascism is therefore opposed to that form of democracy which equates a nation to the majority, lowering it to the level of the largest number; but it is the purest form of democracy if the nation be considered—as it should be—from the point of view of quality rather than quantity, as an idea, the mightiest because the most ethical, the most coherent, the truest, expressing itself in a people as the conscience and will of the few, if not, indeed, of one, and ending to express itself in the conscience and the will of the mass, of the whole group ethnically moulded by natural and historical conditions into a nation, advancing, as one conscience and one will, along the self-same line of development and spiritual formation. Not a race, nor a geographically defined region, but a people, historically perpetuating itself; a multitude unified by an idea and imbued with the will to live, the will to power, self-consciousness, personality.

In so far as it is embodied in a State, this higher personality becomes a nation. It is not the nation which generates the State; that is an antiquated naturalistic concept which afforded a basis for XIXth century publicity in favor of national governments. Rather is it the State which creates the nation, conferring volition and therefore real life on a people made aware of their moral unity.

The right to national independence does not arise from any merely literary and idealistic form of self-consciousness; still less from a more or less passive and unconscious *de facto* situation, but from an active, self-conscious, political will expressing itself in action and ready to prove its rights. It arises, in short, from the existence, at least *in fieri*, of a State. Indeed, it is the State which, as the expression of a universal ethical will, creates the right to national independence.

A nation, as expressed in the State, is a living, ethical entity only in so far as it is progressive. Inactivity is death. Therefore the State is not only Authority which governs and confers legal form and spiritual value on individual wills, but it is also Power which makes its will felt and respected beyond its own frontiers, thus affording practical proof of the universal character of the decisions necessary to ensure its development. This implies organisation and expansion, potential if not actual. Thus the State equates itself to the will of man, whose development cannot be checked by obstacles and which, by achieving self-expression, demonstrates its own infinity.

The Fascist State, as a higher and more powerful expression of personality, is a force, but a spiritual one. It sums up all the manifestations of the moral and intellectual life of man. Its functions cannot therefore be limited to those of enforcing order and keeping the peace, as the liberal doctrine had it. It is no mere mechanical device for defining the sphere within which the individual may duly exercise his supposed rights. The Fascist State is an inwardly accepted standard and rule of conduct, a discipline of the whole person; it permeates the will no less than the intellect. It stands for a principle which becomes the central motive of man as a member of civilised society, sinking deep down into his personality; it dwells in the heart of the man of action and of the thinker, of the artist and of the man of science: soul of the soul.

Fascism, in short, is not only a law-giver and a founder of institutions, but an educator and a promoter of spiritual life. It aims at refashioning not only the forms of life but their content—man, his character, and his faith. To achieve this purpose it enforces discipline and uses authority, entering into the soul and ruling with undisputed sway. Therefore it has chosen as its emblem the Lictor's rods, the symbol of unity, strength, and justice.

33

Hannah Arendt
The Origins of Totalitarianism

Hannah Arendt (1906–1975) was a German Jew who fled the Nazis first to France and then to the United States, where she eventually became a professor of political theory at the New School for Social Research in New York. The Origins of Totalitarianism (1951), from which the following selections are taken, sought to come to grips with the catastrophes brought about by nazism and Stalinism. It is perhaps the most influential book on the subject. She saw totalitarianism as an attempt to impose total domination over all aspects of life, both within countries and beyond their borders (through imperialism). Arendt tried to demonstrate how the Nazi and Stalinist dictatorships were parallel and that at the heart of them was a combination of terror and ideology. Among her other books are The Human Condition *(1958) and* On Revolution *(1963).*

. . . THE TOTALITARIAN movements aim at and succeed in organizing masses—not classes, like the old interest parties of the Continental nation-states; not citizens with opinions about, and interests in, the handling of public affairs, like the parties of Anglo-Saxon countries. While all political groups depend upon proportionate strength, the totalitarian movements depend on the sheer force of numbers to such an extent that totalitarian regimes seem impossible, even under otherwise favorable circumstances, in countries with relatively small populations. After the first World War, a deeply antidemocratic, prodictatorial wave of semitotalitarian and totalitarian movements swept Europe; Fascist movements spread from Italy to nearly all Central and Eastern European countries (the Czech part of Czechoslovakia was one of the notable exceptions); yet even Mussolini, who was so fond of the term "totalitarian state," did not attempt to establish a full-fledged totalitarian regime and contented himself with dictatorship and one-party rule. Similar nontotalitarian dictatorships sprang up in prewar Rumania, Poland, the Baltic states, Hungary, Portugal and Franco Spain. The nazis, who had an unfailing instinct for such differences, used to comment contemptuously on the shortcomings of their Fascist allies while their genuine admiration for the Bolshevik regime in Russia (and the Communist Party in Germany) was matched and checked only by their contempt for Eastern European races. The only man for whom Hitler had "unqualified respect" was "Stalin the genius," and while in the case of Stalin and the Russian regime we do not have (and presumably never will have) the rich documentary material that is available for Germany, we nevertheless know since Khrushchev's speech before the Twentieth Party Congress that Stalin trusted only one man and that was Hitler.

The point is that in all these smaller European countries nontotalitarian dictatorships were preceded by totalitarian movements, so that it appeared that totalitarianism was too ambitious an aim, that although it had served well enough to organize the masses until the movement seized power, the absolute size of the country then forced the would-be totalitarian ruler of masses into the more familiar patterns of class or party dictatorship. The truth is that these countries simply did not control enough human material to allow for total domination and its inherent great losses in population. Without much hope for the conquest of more heavily populated territories, the tyrants in these small countries were forced into a certain old-fashioned moderation lest they lose whatever people they had to rule. This is also why Nazism, up to the outbreak of the war and its expansion over Europe, lagged so far behind its Russian counterpart in consistency and ruthlessness; even the German people were not numerous enough to allow for the full development of this newest form of government. Only if Germany had won the war would she have known a fully developed totalitarian rulership, and the sacrifices this would have entailed not only for the "inferior races" but for the Germans themselves can be gleaned and evaluated from the legacy of Hitler's plans. In any event it was only during the war, after the conquests in the East furnished large masses of people and made the extermination camps possible, that Germany was able to establish a truly totalitarian rule. (Conversely, the chances for totalitarian rule are frighteningly good in the lands of traditional Oriental despotism, in India and China, where there is almost inexhaustible material to feed the power-accumulating and man-destroying machinery of total domination, and where, moreover, the mass man's typical feeling of superfluousness—an entirely new phenomenon in Europe, the concomitant of mass unemployment and the population growth of the last 150 years—has been prevalent for centuries in the contempt for the value of human life.) Moderation or less murderous methods of rule were hardly attributable to the governments' fear of popular rebellion; depopulation in their own country was a much more serious threat. Only where great masses are superfluous or can be spared without disastrous results of depopulation is totalitarian rule, as distinguished from a totalitarian movement, at all possible.

Totalitarian movements are possible wherever there are masses who for one reason or another have acquired the appetite for political organization. Masses are not held together by a consciousness of common interest and they lack that specific class articulateness which is expressed in determined, limited, and obtainable goals. The term masses applies only where we deal with people who either because of sheer numbers, or indifference, or a combination of both, cannot be integrated into any organization based on common interest, into political parties or municipal governments or professional organizations or trade unions. Potentially, they exist in every country and form the majority of those large numbers of neutral, politically indifferent people who never join a party and hardly ever go to the polls.

It was characteristic of the rise of the Nazi movement in Germany and of the Communist movements in Europe after 1930 that they recruited their members from this mass of apparently indifferent people whom all other parties had given up as too apathetic or too stupid for their attention. The result was that the majority of their membership consisted of people who never before had appeared on the political scene. This permitted the introduction of entirely new methods into political propaganda, and indifference to the arguments of political opponents; these movements not only placed themselves outside and against the party system as a whole, they found a membership that had never been reached, never been "spoiled" by the party system. Therefore they did not need to refute opposing arguments and consistently preferred methods which ended in death rather than persuasion, which spelled terror rather than conviction. They presented disagreements as invariably originating in deep natural, social, or psychological sources beyond the control of the individual and therefore beyond the power of reason. This would have been a shortcoming only if they had sincerely entered into competition with other parties; it was not if they were sure of dealing with people who had reason to be equally hostile to all parties.

The success of totalitarian movements among the masses meant the end of two illusions of democratically ruled countries in general and of European nation-states and their party system in particular. The first was that the people in its majority had taken an active part in government and that each individual was in sympathy with one's own or somebody else's party. On the contrary, the movements showed that the politically neutral and indifferent masses could easily be the majority in a democratically ruled country, that therefore a democracy could function according to rules which are actively recognized by only a minority. The second democratic illusion exploded by the totalitarian movements was that these politically indifferent masses did not matter, that they were truly neutral and constituted no more than the inarticulate backward setting for the political life of the nation. Now they made apparent what no other organ of public opinion had ever been able to show, namely, that democratic government had rested as much on the silent approbation and tolerance of the indifferent and inarticulate sections of the people as on the articulate and visible institutions and organizations of the country. Thus when the totalitarian movements invaded Parliament with their contempt for parliamentary government, they merely appeared inconsistent: actually, they succeeded in convincing the people at large that parliamentary majorities were spurious and did not necessarily correspond to the realities of the country, thereby undermining the self-respect and the confidence of governments which also believed in majority rule rather than in their constitutions.

It has frequently been pointed out that totalitarian movements use and abuse democratic freedoms in order to abolish them. This is not just devilish cleverness on the part of the leaders or childish stupidity on the part of the masses. Democratic freedoms may be based on the equality of all citizens before the law; yet they acquire their meaning and function organically only where the citizens belong to and are represented by groups or form a social and political hierarchy. The breakdown of the class system, the only social and political stratification of the European nation-states, certainly was "one of the most dramatic events in recent German history" and as favorable to the rise of Nazism as the absence of social stratification in Russia's immense rural population (this "great flaccid body destitute of political education, almost inaccessible to ideas capable of ennobling action") was to the Bolshevik overthrow of the democratic Kerensky government. Conditions in pre-Hitler Germany are indicative of the dangers implicit in the development of the Western part of the world since, with the end of the second World War, the same dramatic event of a breakdown of the class system repeated itself in almost all European countries, while events in Russia clearly indicate the direction which the inevitable revolutionary changes in Asia may take. Practically speaking, it will make little difference whether totalitarian movements adopt the pattern of Nazism or Bolshevism, organize the masses in the name of race or class, pretend to follow the laws of life and nature or of dialectics and economics. . . .

The means of total domination are not only more drastic. . . . totalitarianism differs essentially from other forms of political oppression known to us such as despotism, tyranny and dictatorship. Wherever it rose to power, it developed entirely new political institutions and destroyed all social, legal and political traditions of the country. No matter what the specifically national tradition or the particular spiritual source of its ideology, totalitarian government always transformed classes into masses, supplanted the party system, not by one-party dictatorships, but by a mass movement, shifted the center of power from the army to the police, and established a foreign policy openly directed toward world domination. Present totalitarian governments have developed from one-party systems; whenever these became truly totalitarian, they started to operate according to a system of values so radically different from all others, that none of our traditional legal, moral, or common sense utilitarian categories could any longer help us to come to terms with, or judge, or predict their course of action.

If it is true that the elements of totalitarianism can be found by retracing the history and analyzing the political implications of what we usually call the crisis of our century, then the conclusion is unavoidable that this crisis is no mere threat from the outside, no mere result of some aggressive foreign policy of either Germany or Russia, and that it will no more disappear with the death of Stalin than it disappeared with the fall of Nazi Germany. It may even be that the true predicaments of our time will assume their authentic form—though not necessarily the cruelest—only when totalitarianism has become a thing of the past.

It is in the line of such reflections to raise the question whether totalitarian government, born of this crisis and at the same time its clearest and only unequivocal symptom, is merely a makeshift arrangement, which borrows its methods of intimidation, its means of organization and its instruments of violence from the well-known political arsenal of tyranny, despotism and dictatorships, and owes its existence only to the deplorable, but perhaps accidental failure of the traditional political forces—liberal or conservative, national or socialist, republican or monarchist, authoritarian or democratic. Or whether, on the contrary, there is such a thing as the *nature* of totalitarian government, whether it has its own essence and can be compared with and defined like other forms of government such as Western thought has known and recognized since the times of ancient philosophy. If this is true, then the entirely new and unprecedented forms of totalitarian organization and course of action must rest on one of the few basic experiences which men can have whenever they live together, and are concerned with public affairs. If there is a basic experience which finds its political expression in totalitarian domination, then, in view of the novelty of the totalitarian form of government, this must be an experience which, for whatever reason, has never before served as the foundation of a body politic and whose general mood—although it may be familiar in every other respect—never before has pervaded, and directed the handling of, public affairs.

If we consider this in terms of the history of ideas, it seems extremely unlikely. For the forms of government under which men live have been very few; they were discovered early, classified by the Greeks and have proved extraordinarily long-lived. If we apply these findings, whose fundamental idea, despite many variations, did not change in the two and a half thousand years that separate Plato from Kant, we are tempted at once to interpret totalitarianism as some modern form of tyranny, that is a lawless government where power is wielded by one man. Arbitrary power, unrestricted by law, wielded in the interest of the ruler and hostile to the interests of the governed, on one hand, fear as the principle of action, namely fear of the people by the ruler and fear of the ruler by the people, on the other—these have been the hallmarks of tyranny throughout our tradition.

Instead of saying that totalitarian government is unprecedented, we could also say that it has exploded the very alternative on which all definitions of the essence of governments have been based in political philosophy, that is the alternative between lawful and lawless government, between arbitrary and legitimate power. That lawful government and legitimate power, on one side, lawlessness and arbitrary power on the other, belonged together and were inseparable has never been questioned. Yet, totalitarian rule confronts us with a totally different kind of government. It defies, it is true, all positive laws, even to the extreme of defying those which it has itself established (as in the case of the Soviet Constitution of 1936, to quote only the most outstanding example) or which it did not care to abolish (as in the case of the Weimar Constitution which the Nazi government never revoked). But it operates neither without guidance of law nor is it arbitrary, for it claims to obey strictly and unequivocally those laws of Nature or of History from which all positive laws always have been supposed to spring.

It is the monstrous, yet seemingly unanswerable claim of totalitarian rule that, far from being "lawless," it goes to the sources of authority from which positive laws received their ultimate legitimation, that far from being arbitrary it is more obedient to these suprahuman forces than any government ever was before, and that far from wielding its power in the interest of one man, it is quite prepared to sacrifice everybody's vital immediate interests to the execution of what it assumes to be the law of History or the law of Nature. Its defiance of positive laws claims to be a higher form of legitimacy which, since it is inspired by the sources themselves, can do away with petty legality. Totalitarian lawfulness pretends to have found a way to establish the rule of justice on earth—something which the legality of positive law admittedly could never attain. The discrepancy between legality and justice could never be bridged because the standards of right and wrong into which positive law translates its own source of authority—"natural law" governing the whole universe, or divine law revealed in human history, or customs and traditions expressing the law common to the sentiments of all men—are necessarily general and must be valid for a countless and unpredictable number of cases, so that each concrete individual case with its unrepeatable set of circumstances somehow escapes it.

Totalitarian lawfulness, defying legality and pretending to establish the direct reign of justice on earth, executes the law of History or of Nature without translating it into standards of right and wrong for individual behavior. It applies the law directly to mankind without bothering with the behavior of men. The law of Nature or the law of History, if properly executed, is expected to produce mankind as its end product; and this expectation lies behind the claim to global rule of all totalitarian governments. Totalitarian policy claims to transform the human species into an active unfailing carrier of a law to which human beings otherwise would only passively and reluctantly be subjected. If it is true that the link between totalitarian countries and the civilized world was broken through the monstrous crimes of totalitarian regimes, it is also true that this criminality was not due to simple aggressiveness, ruthlessness, warfare and treachery, but to a conscious break of that *consensus iuris* which, according to Cicero, constitutes a "people," and which, as international law, in modern times has constituted the civilized world insofar as it remains the foundation-stone of international relations even under the conditions of war. Both moral judgment and legal punishment presuppose this basic consent; the criminal can be judged justly only because he takes part in the *consensus iuris*, and even the revealed law of God can function among men only when they listen and consent to it.

At this point the fundamental difference between the totalitarian and all other concepts of law comes to light. Totalitarian policy does not replace one set of laws with another, does not establish its own *consensus iuris*, does not create, by one revolution, a new form of legality. Its defiance of all, even its own positive laws implies that it believes it can do without any *consensus iuris* whatever, and still not resign itself to the tyrannical state of lawlessness, arbitrariness and fear. It can do without the *consensus iuris* because it promises to release the fulfillment of law from all action and will of man; and it promises justice on earth because it claims to make mankind itself the embodiment of the law.

This identification of man and law, which seems to cancel the discrepancy between legality and justice that has plagued legal thought since ancient times, has nothing in common with the *lumen naturale* or the voice of conscience, by which Nature or Divinity as the sources of authority for the *ius naturale* or the historically revealed commands of God, are supposed to announce their authority in man himself. This never made man a walking embodiment of the law, but on the contrary remained distinct from him as the authority which demanded consent and obedience. Nature or Divinity as the source of authority for positive laws were thought of as permanent and eternal; positive laws were changing and changeable according to circumstances, but they possessed a relative permanence as compared with the much more rapidly changing actions of men; and they derived this permanence from the eternal presence of their source of authority. Positive laws, therefore, are primarily designed to function as stabilizing factors for the ever changing movements of men.

In the interpretation of totalitarianism, all laws have become laws of movement. When the Nazis talked about the law of nature or when the Bolsheviks talk about the law of history, neither nature nor history is any longer the stabilizing source of authority for the actions of mortal men; they are movements in themselves. . . .

Terror is the realization of the law of movement; its chief aim is to make it possible for the force of nature or of history to race freely through mankind, unhindered by any spontaneous human action. As such, terror seeks to "stabilize" men in order to liberate the forces of nature or history. It is this movement which singles out the foes of mankind against whom terror is let loose, and no free action of either opposition or sympathy can be permitted to interfere with the elimination of the "objective enemy" of History or Nature, of the class or the race. Guilt and innocence become senseless notions; "guilty" is he who stands in the way of the natural or historical process which has passed judgment over "inferior races," over individuals "unfit to live," over "dying classes and decadent peoples." Terror executes these judgments, and before its court, all concerned are subjectively innocent: the murdered because they did nothing against the system, and the murderers because they do not really murder but execute a death sentence pronounced by some higher tribunal. The rulers themselves do not claim to be just or wise, but only to execute historical or natural laws; they do not apply laws, but execute a movement in accordance with its inherent law. Terror is lawfulness, if law is the law of the movement of some suprahuman force, Nature or History.

Terror as the execution of a law of movement whose ultimate goal is not the welfare of men or the interest of one man but the fabrication of mankind, eliminates individuals for the sake of the species, sacrifices the "parts" for the sake of the "whole." The suprahuman force of Nature or History has its own beginning and its own end, so that it can be hindered only by the new beginning and the individual end which the life of each man actually is.

Positive laws in constitutional government are designed to erect boundaries and establish channels of communication between men whose community is continually endangered by the new men born into it. With each new birth, a new beginning is born into the world, a new world has potentially come into being. The stability of the laws corresponds to the constant motion of all human affairs, a motion which can never end as long as men are born and die. The laws hedge in each new beginning and at the same time assure its freedom of movement, the potentiality of something entirely new and unpredictable; the boundaries of positive laws are for the political existence of man what memory is for his historical existence: they guarantee the pre-existence of a common world, the reality of some continuity which transcends the individual life span of each generation, absorbs all new origins and is nourished by them.

Total terror is so easily mistaken for a symptom of tyrannical government because totalitarian government in its initial stages must behave like a tyranny and raze the boundaries of man-made law. But total terror leaves no arbitrary lawlessness behind it and does not rage for the sake of some arbitrary will or for the sake of despotic power of one man against all, least of all for the sake of a war of all against all. It substitutes for the boundaries and channels of communication between individual men a band of iron which holds them so tightly together that it is as though their plurality had disappeared into One Man of gigantic dimensions. To abolish the fences of laws between men—as tyranny does—means to take away man's liberties and destroy freedom as a living political reality; for the space between men as it is hedged in by laws, is the living space of freedom. Total terror uses this old instrument of tyranny but destroys at the same time also the lawless, fenceless wilderness of fear and suspicion which tyranny leaves behind. This desert, to be sure, is no longer a living space of freedom, but it still provides some room for the fear-guided movements and suspicion-ridden actions of its inhabitants.

By pressing men against each other, total terror destroys the space between them; compared to the condition within its iron band, even the desert of tyranny, insofar as it is still some kind of space, appears like a guarantee of freedom. Totalitarian government does not just curtail liberties or abolish essential freedoms; nor does it, at least to our limited knowledge, succeed in eradicating the love for freedom from the hearts of man. It destroys the one essential prerequisite of all freedom which is simply the capacity of motion which cannot exist without space.

Total terror, the essence of totalitarian government, exists neither for nor against men. It is supposed to provide the forces of nature or history with an incomparable instrument to accelerate their movement. This movement, proceeding according to its own law, cannot in the long run be hindred; eventually its force will always prove more powerful than the most powerful forces engendered by the actions and the will of men. But it can be slowed down and is slowed down almost inevitably by the freedom of man, which even totalitarian rulers cannot deny, for this freedom—irrelevant and arbitrary as they may deem it— is identical with the fact that men are being born and that therefore each of them *is* a new beginning, begins, in a sense, the world anew. From the totalitarian point of view, the fact that men are born and die can be only regarded as an annoying interference with higher forces. Terror, therefore, as the obedient servant of natural or historical movement has to eliminate from the process not only freedom in any specific sense, but the very source of freedom which is given with the fact of the birth of man and resides in his capacity to make a new beginning. In the iron band of terror, which destroys the plurality of men and makes out of many the One who unfailingly will act as though he himself were part of the course of history or nature, a device has been found not only to liberate the historical and natural forces, but to accelerate them to a speed they never would reach if left to themselves. Practically speaking, this means that terror executes on the spot the death sentences which Nature is supposed to have pronounced on races or individuals who are "unfit to live," or History on "dying classes," without waiting for the slower and less efficient processes of nature or history themselves. . . .

In a perfect totalitarian government, where all men have become One Man, where all action aims at the acceleration of the movement of nature or history, where every single act is the execution of a death sentence which Nature or History has already pronounced, that is, under conditions where terror can be completely relied upon to keep the movement in constant motion, no principle of action separate from its essence would be needed at all. Yet as long as totalitarian rule has not conquered the earth and with the iron band of terror made each single man a part of one mankind, terror in its double function as essence of government and principle, not of action, but of motion, cannot be fully realized. Just as lawfulness in constitutional government is insufficient to inspire and guide men's actions, so terror in totalitarian government is not sufficient to inspire and guide human behavior.

While under present conditions totalitarian domination still shares with other forms of government the need for a guide for the behavior of its citizens in public affairs, it does not need and could not even use a principle of action strictly speaking, since it will eliminate precisely the capacity of man to act. Under conditions of total terror not even fear can any longer serve as an advisor of how to behave, because terror chooses its victims without reference to individual actions or thoughts, exclusively in accordance with the objective necessity of the natural or historical process. Under totalitarian conditions, fear probably is more widespread than ever before; but fear has lost its practical usefulness when actions guided by it can no longer help to avoid the dangers man fears. The same is true for sympathy or support of the regime; for total terror not only selects its victims according to objective standards; it chooses its executioners with as complete a disregard as possible for the candidate's conviction and sympathies. The consistent elimination of conviction as a motive for action has become a matter of record since the great purges in Soviet Russia and the satellite countries. The aim of totalitarian education has never been to instill convictions but to destroy the capacity to form any. The introduction of purely objective criteria into the selective system of the SS troops was Himmler's great organizational invention; he selected the candidates from photographs according to purely racial criteria. Nature itself decided, not only who was to be eliminated, but also who was to be trained as an executioner.

No guiding principle of behavior, taken itself from the realm of human action, such as virtue, honor, fear, is necessary or can be useful to set into motion a body politic which no longer uses terror as a means of intimidation, but whose essence *is* terror. In its stead, it has introduced an entirely new principle into public affairs that dispenses with human will to action altogether and appeals to the craving need for some insight into the law of movement according to which the terror functions and upon which, therefore, all private destinies depend.

The inhabitants of a totalitarian country are thrown into and caught in the process of nature or history for the sake of accelerating its movement; as such, they can only be executioners or victims of its inherent law. The process may decide that those who today eliminate races and individuals or the members of dying classes and decadent peoples are tomorrow those who must be sacrificed. What totalitarian rule needs to guide the behavior of its subjects is a preparation to fit each of them equally well for the role of executioner and the role of victim. This two-sided preparation, the substitute for a principle of action, is the ideology.

Ideologies—isms which to the satisfaction of their adherents can explain everything and every occurence by deducing it from a single premise—are a very recent phenomenon and, for many decades, played a negligible role in political life. Only with the wisdom of hindsight can we discover in them certain elements which have made them so disturbingly useful for totalitarian rule. Not before Hitler and Stalin were the great political potentialities of the ideologies discovered.

Ideologies are known for their scientific character: they combine the scientific approach with results of philosophical relevance and pretend to be scientific philosophy. The word "ideology" seems to imply that an idea can become the subject matter of a science just as animals are the subject matter of zoology, and that the suffix -*logy* in ideology, as in zoology, indicates nothing but the *logoi*, the scientific statements made on it. If this were true, an ideology would indeed be a pseudo-science and a pseudo-philosophy, transgressing at the same time the limitations of science and the limitations of philosophy. Deism, for example, would then be the ideology which treats the idea of God, with which philosophy is concerned, in the scientific manner of theology for which God is a revealed reality. (A theology which is not based on revelation as a given reality but treats God as an idea would be as mad as a zoology which is no longer sure of the physical, tangible existence of animals.) Yet we know that this is only part of the truth. Deism, though it denies divine revelation, does not simply make "scientific" statements on a God which is only an "idea," but uses the idea of God in order to explain the course of the world. The "ideas" of isms—race in racism, God in deism, etc.—never form the subject matter of the ideologies and the suffix -*logy* never indicates simply a body of "scientific" statements.

An ideology is quite literally what its name indicates: it is the logic of an idea. Its subject matter is history, to which the "idea" is applied; the result of this application is not a body of statements about something that *is*, but the unfolding of a process which is in constant change. The ideology treats the course of events as though it followed the same "law" as the logical exposition of its "idea." Ideologies pretend to know the mysteries of the whole historical process—the secrets of the past, the intricacies of the present, the uncertainties of the future—because of the logic inherent in their respective ideas.

Ideologies are never interested in the miracle of being. They are historical, concerned with becoming and perishing, with the rise and fall of cultures, even if they try to explain history by some "law of nature." The word "race" in racism does not signify any genuine curiosity about the human races as a field for scientific exploration, but is the "idea" by which the movement of history is explained as one consistent process. . . .

The *Weltanschauungen* and ideologies of the nineteenth century are not in themselves totalitarian, and although racism and communism have become the decisive ideologies of the twentieth century they were not, in principle, any "more totalitarian" than the others; it happened because the elements of experience on which they were originally based—the struggle between the races for world domination, and the struggle between the classes for political power in the respective countries—turned out to be politically more important than those of other ideologies. In this sense the ideological victory of racism and communism over all other isms was decided before the totalitarian movements took hold of precisely these ideologies. On the other hand, all ideologies contain totalitarian elements, but these are fully developed only by totalitarian movements, and this creates the deceptive impression that only racism and communism are totalitarian in character. The truth is, rather, that the real nature of all ideologies was revealed only in the role that the ideology plays in the apparatus of totalitarian domination. Seen from this aspect, there appear three specifically totalitarian elements that are peculiar to all ideological thinking.

First, in their claim to total explanation, ideologies have the tendency to explain not what is, but what becomes, what is born and passes away. They are in all cases concerned solely with the element of motion, that is, with history in the customary sense of the word. Ideologies are always oriented toward history, even when, as in the case of racism, they seemingly proceed from the premise of nature; here, nature serves merely to explain historical matters and reduce them to matters of nature. The claim to total explanation promises to explain all historical happenings, the total explanation of the past, the total knowledge of the present, and the reliable prediction of the future. Secondly, in this capacity ideological thinking becomes independent of all experience from which it cannot learn anything new even if it is a question of something that has just come to pass. Hence ideological thinking becomes emancipated from the reality that we perceive with our five senses, and insists on a "truer" reality concealed behind all perceptible things, dominating them from this place of concealment and requiring a sixth sense that enables us to become aware of it. The sixth sense is provided by precisely the ideology, that particular ideological indoctrination which is taught by the educational institutions, established exclusively for this purpose, to train the "political soldiers" in the *Ordensburgen* of the Nazis or the schools of the Comintern and the Cominform. The propaganda of the totalitarian movement also serves to emancipate thought from experience and reality; it always strives to inject a secret meaning into every public, tangible event and to suspect a secret intent behind every public political act. Once the movements have come to power, they proceed to change reality in accordance with their ideological claims. The concept of enmity is replaced by that of conspiracy, and this produces a mentality in which reality—real enmity or real friendship—is no longer experienced and understood in its own terms but is automatically assumed to signify something else.

Thirdly, since the ideologies have no power to transform reality, they achieve this emancipation of thought from experience through certain methods of demonstration. Ideological thinking orders facts into an absolutely logical procedure which starts from an axiomatically accepted premise, deducing everything else from it; that is, it proceeds with a consistency that exists nowhere in the realm of reality. The deducing may proceed logically or dialectically; in either case it involves a consistent process of argumentation which, because it thinks in terms of a process, is supposed to be able to comprehend the movement of the suprahuman, natural or historical processes. Comprehension is achieved by the mind's imitating, either logically or dialectically, the laws of "scientifically" established movements with which through the process of imitation it becomes integrated. Ideological argumentation, always a kind of logical deduction, corresponds to the two aforementioned elements of the ideologies—the element of movement and of emancipation from reality and experience—first, because its thought movement does not spring from experience but is self-generated, and, secondly, because it transforms the one and only point that is taken and accepted from experienced reality into an axiomatic premise, leaving from then on the subsequent argumentation process completely untouched from any further experience. Once it has established its premise, its point of departure, experiences no longer interfere with ideological thinking, nor can it be taught by reality.

The device both totalitarian rulers used to transform their respective ideologies into weapons with which each of their subjects could force himself into step with the terror movement was deceptively simple and inconspicuous: they took them dead seriously, took pride the one in his supreme gift for "ice cold reasoning" (Hitler) and the other in the "mercilessness of his dialectics," and proceeded to drive ideological implications into extremes of logical consistency which, to the onlooker, looked preposterously "primitive" and absurd: a "dying class" consisted of people condemned to death; races that are "unfit to live" were to be exterminated. Whoever agreed that there are such things as "dying classes" and did not draw the consequence of killing their members, or that the right to live had something to do with race and did not draw the consequence of killing "unfit races," was plainly either stupid or a coward. This stringent logicality as a guide to action permeates the whole structure of totalitarian movements and governments. It is exclusively the work of Hitler and Stalin who, although they did not add a single new thought to the ideas and propaganda slogans of their movements, for this reason alone must be considered ideologists of the greatest importance.

What distinguished these new totalitarian ideologists from their predecessors was that it was no longer primarily the "idea" of the ideology—the struggle of classes and the exploitation of the workers or the struggle of races and the care for Germanic peoples—which appealed to them, but the logical process which could be developed from it. According to Stalin, neither the idea nor the oratory but "the irresistible force of logic thoroughly overpowered [Lenin's] audience." The power, which Marx thought was born when the idea seized the masses, was discovered to reside, not in the idea itself, but in its logical process which "like a mighty tentacle seizes you on all sides as in a vise and from whose grip you are powerless to tear yourself away; you must either surrender or make up your mind to utter defeat." Only when the realization of the ideological aims, the classless society or the master race, was at stake, could this force show itself. In the process of realization, the original substance upon which the ideologies based themselves as long as they had to appeal to the masses—the exploitation of the workers or the national aspirations of Germany—is gradually lost, devoured as it were by the process itself: in perfect accordance with "ice cold reasoning" and the "irresistible force of logic," the workers lost under Bolshevik rule even those rights they had been granted under Tsarist oppression and the German people suffered a kind of warfare which did not pay the slightest regard to the minimum requirements for survival of the German nation. It is in the nature of ideological politics—and is not simply a betrayal committed for the sake of self-interest or lust for power— that the real content of the ideology (the working class or the Germanic peoples), which originally had brought about the "idea" (the struggle of classes as the law of history or the struggle of races as the law of nature), is devoured by the logic with which the "idea" is carried out. . . .

Totalitarian rulers rely on the compulsion with which we can compel ourselves, for the limited mobilization of people which even they still need; this inner compulsion is the tyranny of logicality against which nothing stands but the great capacity of men to start something new. The tyranny of logicality begins with the mind's submission to logic as a never-ending process, on which man relies in order to engender his thoughts. By this submission, he surrenders his inner freedom as he surrenders his freedom of movement when he bows down to an outward tyranny. Freedom as an inner capacity of man is identical with the capacity to begin, just as freedom as a political reality is identical with a space of movement between men. Over the beginning, no logic, no cogent deduction can have any power, because its chain presupposes, in the form of a premise, the beginning. As terror is needed lest with the birth of each new human being a new beginning arise and raise its voice in the world, so the self-coercive force of logicality is mobilized lest anybody ever start thinking—which as the freest and purest of all human activities is the very opposite of the compulsory process of deduction. Totalitarian government can be safe only to the extent that it can mobilize man's own will power in order to force him into that gigantic movement of History or Nature which supposedly uses mankind as its material and knows neither birth nor death.

The compulsion of total terror on one side, which, with its iron band, presses masses of isolated men together *and* supports them in a world which has become a wilderness for them, and the self-coercive force of logical deduction on the other, which prepares each individual in his lonely isolation against all others, correspond to each other and need each other in order to set the terror-ruled movement into motion and keep it moving. Just as terror, even in its pre-total, merely tyrannical form ruins all relationships between men, so the self-compulsion of ideological thinking ruins all relationships with reality. The preparation has succeeded when people have lost contact with their fellow men as well as the reality around them; for together with these contacts, men lose the capacity of both experience and thought. The ideal subject of totalitarian rule is not the convinced Nazi or the convinced Communist, but people for whom the distinction between fact and fiction (*i.e.*, the reality of experience) and the distinction between true and false (*i.e.*, the standards of thought) no longer exist. . . .

It has frequently been observed that terror can rule absolutely only over men who are isolated against each other and that, therefore, one of the primary concerns of all tyrannical government is to bring this isolation about. Isolation may be the beginning of terror; it certainly is its most fertile ground; it always is its result.

This isolation is, as it were, pretotalitarian; its hallmark is impotence insofar as power always comes from men acting together, "acting in concert" (Burke); isolated men are powerless by definition.

Isolation and impotence, that is the fundamental inability to act at all, have always been characteristic of tyrannies. Political contacts between men are severed in tyrannical government and the human capacities for action and power are frustrated. But not all contacts between men are broken and not all human capacities destroyed. The whole sphere of private life with the capacities for experience, fabrication and thought are left intact. We know that the iron band of total terror leaves no space for such private life and that the self-coercion of totalitarian logic destroys man's capacity for experience and thought just as certainly as his capacity for action. . . .

While isolation concerns only the political realm of life, loneliness concerns human life as a whole. Totalitarian government, like all tyrannies, certainly could not exist without destroying the public realm of life, that is, without destroying, by isolating men, their political capacities. But totalitarian domination as a form of government is new in that it is not content with this isolation and destroys private life as well. It bases itself on loneliness, on the experience of not belonging to the world at all, which is among the most radical and desperate experiences of man.

Loneliness, the common ground for terror, the essence of totalitarian government, and for ideology or logicality, the preparation of its executioners and victims, is closely connected with uprootedness and superfluousness which have been the curse of modern masses since the beginning of the industrial revolution and have become acute with the rise of imperialism at the end of the last century and the break-down of political institutions and social traditions in our own time. To be uprooted means to have no place in the world, recognized and guaranteed by others; to be superfluous means not to belong to the world at all. Uprootedness can be the preliminary condition for superfluousness, just as isolation can (but must not) be the preliminary condition for loneliness. Taken in itself, without consideration of its recent historical causes and its new role in politics, loneliness is at the same time contrary to the basic requirements of the human condition *and* one of the fundamental experiences of every human life. Even the experience of the materially and sensually given world depends upon my being in contact with other men, upon our *common* sense which regulates and controls all other senses and without which each of us would be enclosed in his own particularity of sense data which in themselves are unreliable and treacherous. Only because we have common sense, that is only because not one man, but men in the plural inhabit the earth can we trust our immediate sensual experience. Yet, we have only to remind ourselves that one day we shall have to leave this common world which will go on as before and for whose continuity we are superfluous in order to realize loneliness, the experience of being abandoned by everything and everybody. . . .

Solitude can become loneliness; this happens when all by myself I am deserted by my own self. Solitary men have always been in danger of loneliness, when they can no longer find the redeeming grace of companionship to save them from duality and equivocality and doubt. Historically, it seems as though this danger became sufficiently great to be noticed by others and recorded by history only in the nineteenth century. It showed itself clearly when philosophers, for whom alone solitude is a way of life and a condition of work, were no longer content with the fact that "philosophy is only for the few" and began to insist that nobody "understands" them. Characteristic in this respect is the anecdote reported from Hegel's deathbed which hardly could have been told of any great philosopher before him: "Nobody has understood me except one; and he also misunderstood." Conversely, there is always the chance that a lonely man finds himself and starts the thinking dialogue of solitude. This seems to have happened to Nietzsche in Sils Maria when he conceived *Zarathustra.* In two poems ("Sils Maria" and "Aus hohen Bergen") he tells of the empty expectation and the yearning waiting of the lonely until suddenly *"um Mittag war's, da wurde Eins zu Zwei . ./ Nun feiern wir, vereinten Siegs gewiss,/ das Fest der Feste;/ Freund Zarathustra kam, der Gast der Gäste!"* ("Noon was, when One became Two . . . Certain of united victory we celebrate the feast of feasts; friend Zarathustra came, the guest of guests.")

What makes loneliness so unbearable is the loss of one's own self which can be realized in solitude, but confirmed in its identity only by the trusting and trustworthy company of my equals. In this situation, man loses trust in himself as the partner of his thoughts and that elementary confidence in the world which is necessary to make experiences at all. Self and world, capacity for thought and experience are lost at the same time.

The only capacity of the human mind which needs neither the self nor the other nor the world in order to function safely and which is as independent of experience as it is of thinking is the ability of logical reasoning whose premise is the self-evident. The elementary rules of cogent evidence, the truism that two and two equals four cannot be perverted even under the conditions of absolute loneliness. It is the only reliable "truth" human beings can fall back upon once they have lost the mutual guarantee, the common sense, men need in order to experience and live and know their way in a common world. But this "truth" is empty or rather no truth at all, because it does not reveal anything. (To define consistency as truth as some modern logicians do means to deny the existence of truth.) Under the conditions of loneliness, therefore, the self-evident is no longer just a means of the intellect and begins to be productive, to develop its own lines of "thought." That thought processes characterized by strict self-evident logicality, from which apparently there is no escape, have some connection with loneliness was once noticed by Luther (whose experiences in the phenomena of solitude and loneliness probably were second to no one's and who once dared to say that "there must be a God because man needs one being whom he can trust") in a little-known remark on the Bible text "it is not good that man should be alone": A lonely man, says Luther, "always deduces one thing from the other and thinks everything to the worst." The famous extremism of totalitarian movements, far from having anything to do with true radicalism, consists indeed in this "thinking everything to the worst," in this deducing process which always arrives at the worst possible conclusions.

What prepares men for totalitarian domination in the non-totalitarian world is the fact that loneliness, once a borderline experience usually suffered in certain marginal social conditions like old age, has become an everyday experience of the evergrowing masses of our century. The merciless process into which totalitarianism drives and organizes the masses looks like a suicidal escape from this reality. The "ice-cold reasoning" and the "mighty tentacle" of dialectics which "seizes you as in a vise" appears like a last support in a world where nobody is reliable and nothing can be relied upon. It is the inner coercion whose only content is the strict avoidance of contradictions that seems to confirm a man's identity outside all relationships with others. It fits him into the iron band of terror even when he is alone, and totalitarian domination tries never to leave him alone except in the extreme situation of solitary confinement. By destroying all space between men and pressing men against each other, even the productive potentialities of isolation are annihilated; by teaching and glorifying the logical reasoning of loneliness where man knows that he will be utterly lost if ever he lets go of the first premise from which the whole process is being started, even the slim chances that loneliness may be transformed into solitude and logic into thought are obliterated. If this practice is compared with that of tyranny, it seems as if a way had been found to set the desert itself in motion, to let loose a sand storm that could cover all parts of the inhabited earth.

The conditions under which we exist today in the field of politics are indeed threatened by these devastating sand storms. Their danger is not that they might establish a permanent world. Totalitarian domination, like tyranny, bears the germs of its own destruction. Just as fear and the impotence from which fear springs are antipolitical principles and throw men into a situation contrary to political action, so loneliness and the logical-ideological deducing the worst that comes from it represent an antisocial situation and harbor a principle destructive for all human living together. Nevertheless, organized loneliness is considerably more dangerous than the unorganized impotence of all those who are ruled by the tyrannical and arbitrary will of a single man. Its danger is that it threatens to ravage the world as we know it—a world which everywhere seems to have come to an end—before a new beginning rising from this end has had time to assert itself.

Apart from such considerations—which as predictions are of little avail and less consolation—there remains the fact that the crisis of our time and its central experience have brought forth an entirely new form of government which as a potentiality and an ever-present danger is only too likely to stay with us from now on, just as other forms of government which came about at different historical moments and rested on different fundamental experiences have stayed with mankind regardless of temporary defeats—monarchies, and republics, tyrannies, dictatorships and despotism.

But there remains also the truth that every end in history necessarily contains a new beginning; this beginning is the promise, the only "message" which the end can ever produce. Beginning, before it becomes a historical event, is the supreme capacity of man; politically, it is identical with man's freedom. *Initium ut esset homo creatus est*—"that a beginning be made man was created" said Augustine. This beginning is guaranteed by each new birth; it is indeed every man.

34

George Orwell
Politics and the English Language

*George Orwell (1903–1950) was one of the most prolific and talented writers of the twentieth century. An Englishman born in India, his real name was Eric Blair. He is the author of four volumes of essays, several remarkable books of political reportage—*Homage to Catalonia, *which recounts his experiences in the Spanish Civil War is a classic—and several novels. He was the author of* Animal Farm *and* 1984, *which are among the most acclaimed political novels of the twentieth century. They are both denunciations of totalitarianism—Orwell was a democratic socialist and a fierce opponent of both Soviet communism and German fascism—and among other things, are concerned with the political abuse of language. This is also the theme of the following essay.*

MOST PEOPLE who bother with the matter at all would admit that the English language is in a bad way, but it is generally assumed that we cannot by conscious action do anything about it. Our civilisation is decadent, and our language—so the argument runs—must inevitably share in the general collapse. It follows that any struggle against the abuse of language is a sentimental archaism, like preferring candles to electric light or hansom cabs to aeroplanes. Underneath this lies the half-conscious belief that language is a natural growth and not an instrument which we shape for our own purposes.

Now, it is clear that the decline of a language must ultimately have political and economic causes: it is not due simply to the bad influence of this or that individual writer. But an effect can become a cause, reinforcing the original cause and producing the same effect in an intensified form, and so on indefinitely. A man may take to drink because he feels himself to be a failure, and then fail all the more completely because he drinks. It is rather the same thing that is happening to the English language. It becomes ugly and inaccurate because our thoughts are foolish, but the slovenliness of our language makes it easier for us to have foolish thoughts. The point is that the process is reversible. Modern English, especially written English, is full of bad habits which spread by imitation and which can be avoided if one is willing to take the necessary trouble. If one gets rid of these habits one can think more clearly, and to think clearly is a necessary first step towards political regeneration: so that the fight against bad English is not frivolous and is not the exclusive concern of professional writers. I will come back to this presently, and I hope that by that time the meaning of what I have said here will have become clearer. Meanwhile, here are five specimens of the English language as it is now habitually written.

These five passages have not been picked out because they are especially bad—
I could have quoted far worse if I had chosen—but because they illustrate various
of the mental vices from which we now suffer. They are a little below the average, but are fairly representative samples. I number them so that I can refer back
to them when necessary:

1. I am not, indeed, sure whether it is not true to say that the Milton who once seemed
not unlike a seventeenth-century Shelley had not become, out of an experience ever more
bitter in each year, more alien (sic) to the founder of that Jesuit sect which nothing could
induce him to tolerate.—Professor Harold Laski (Essay in *Freedom of Expression*).

2. Above all, we cannot play ducks and drakes with a native battery of idioms which
prescribes such egregious collocations of vocables as the Basic *put up with* for *tolerate* or
put at a loss for *bewilder*.—Professor Lancelot Hogben (*Interglossa*).

3. On the one side we have the free personality: by definition it is not neurotic, for it
has neither conflict nor dream. Its desires, such as they are, are transparent, for they are
just what institutional approval keeps in the forefront of consciousness; another institutional pattern would alter their number and intensity; there is little in them that is natural,
irreducible, or culturally dangerous. But *on the other side*, the social bond itself is nothing but the mutual reflection of these self-secure integrities. Recall the definition of love.
Is not this the very picture of a small academic? Where is there a place in this hall of
mirrors for either personality or fraternity?—Essay on psychology in *Politics* (New
York).

4. All the "best people" from the gentlemen's clubs, and all the frantic Fascist captains, united in common hatred of Socialism and bestial horror of the rising tide of the
mass revolutionary movement, have turned to acts of provocation, to foul incendiarism,
to medieval legends of poisoned wells, to legalise their own destruction to proletarian
organisations, and rouse the agitated petty-bourgeoisie to chauvinistic fervour on behalf
of the fight against the revolutionary way out of the crisis.—Communist pamphlet.

5. If a new spirit *is* to be infused into this old country, there is one thorny and
contentious reform which must be tackled, and that is the humanisation and galvanisation
of the BBC. Timidity here will bespeak canker and atrophy of the soul. The heart of
Britain may be sound and of strong beat, for instance, but the British lion's roar at
present is like that of Bottom in Shakespeare's *Midsummer Night's Dream*—as gentle as
any sucking dove. A virile new Britain cannot continue indefinitely to be traduced in the
eyes, or rather ears, of the world by the effete languors of Langham Place, brazenly
masquerading as "standard English." When the Voice of Britain is heard at nine o'clock,
better far and infinitely less ludicrous to hear aitches honestly dropped than the present
priggish, inflated, inhibited, school-ma'amish arch braying of blameless bashful mewing
maidens!—Letter in *Tribune*.

Each of these passages has faults of its own, but, quite apart from avoidable
ugliness, two qualities are common to all of them. The first is staleness of imag-
ery: the other is lack of precision. The writer either has a meaning and cannot
express it, or he inadvertently says something else, or he is almost indifferent as to
whether his words mean anything or not. This mixture of vagueness and sheer
incompetence is the most marked characteristic of modern English prose, and

especially of any kind of political writing. As soon as certain topics are raised, the concrete melts into the abstract and no one seems able to think of turns of speech that are not hackneyed: prose consists less and less of *words* chosen for the sake of their meaning, and more of *phrases* tacked together like the sections of a prefabricated hen-house. I list below, with notes and examples, various of the tricks by means of which the work of prose construction is habitually dodged:

Dying metaphors. A newly invented metaphor assists thought by evoking a visual image, while on the other hand a metaphor which is technically "dead" (e.g. *iron resolution*) has in effect reverted to being an ordinary word and can generally be used without loss of vividness. But in between these two classes there is a huge dump of worn-out metaphors which have lost all evocative power and are merely used because they save people the trouble of inventing phrases for themselves. Examples are: *Ring the changes on, take up the cudgels for, toe the line, ride roughshod over, stand shoulder to shoulder with, play into the hands of, no axe to grind, grist to the mill, fishing in troubled waters, rift within the lute, on the order of the day, Achilles' heel, swan song, hotbed.* Many of these are used without knowledge of their meaning (what is a "rift," for instance?), and incompatible metaphors are frequently mixed, a sure sign that the writer is not interested in what he is saying. Some metaphors now current have been twisted out of their original meaning without those who use them even being aware of the fact. For example, *toe the line* is sometimes written *tow the line.* Another example is *the hammer and the anvil*, now always used with the implication that the anvil gets the worst of it. In real life it is always the anvil that breaks the hammer, never the other way about: a writer who stopped to think what he was saying would be aware of this, and would avoid perverting the original phrase.

Operators, or *verbal false limbs.* These save the trouble of picking out appropriate verbs and nouns, and at the same time pad each sentence with extra syllables which give it an appearance of symmetry. Characteristic phrases are: *render inoperative, militate against, prove unacceptable, make contact with, be subjected to, give rise to, give grounds for, have the effect of, play a leading part (rôle) in, make itself felt, take effect, exhibit a tendency to, serve the purpose of*, etc etc. The keynote is the elimination of simple verbs. Instead of being a single word, such as *break, stop, spoil, mend, kill*, a verb becomes a *phrase*, made up of a noun or adjective tacked on to some general-purposes verb such as *prove, serve, form, play, render.* In addition, the passive voice is wherever possible used in preference to the active, and noun constructions are used instead of gerunds (*by examination of* instead of *by examining*). The range of verbs is further cut down by means of the *-ise* and *de-* formations, and banal statements are given an appearance of profundity by means of the *not un-* formation. Simple conjunctions and prepositions are replaced by such phrases as *with respect to, having regard to, the fact that, by dint of, in view of, in the interests of, on the hypothesis that*; and the ends of sentences are saved from anticlimax by such resounding commonplaces as *greatly to be desired, cannot be left out of account, a development to be expected* *in the near future, deserving of serious consideration, brought to a satisfactory conclusion,* and so on and so forth.

Pretentious diction. Words like *phenomenon, element, individual* (as noun), *objective, categorical, effective, virtual, basic, primary, promote, constitute, exhibit, exploit, utilise, eliminate, liquidate,* are used to dress up simple statements and give an air of scientific impartiality to biassed judgements. Adjectives like *epoch-making, epic, historic, unforgettable, triumphant, age-old, inevitable, inexorable, veritable,* are used to dignify the sordid processes of international politics, while writing that aims at glorifying war usually takes on an archaic colour, its characteristic words being: *realm, throne, chariot, mailed fist, trident, sword, shield, buckler, banner, jackboot, clarion.* Foreign words and expressions such as *cul de sac, ancien régime, deus ex machina, mutatis mutandis, status quo, Gleichschaltung, Weltanschauung,* are used to give an air of culture and elegance. Except for the useful abbreviations *i.e., e.g.,* and *etc,* there is no real need for any of the hundreds of foreign phrases now current in English. Bad writers, and especially scientific, political and sociological writers, are nearly always haunted by the notion that Latin or Greek words are grander than Saxon ones, and unnecessary words like *expedite, ameliorate, predict, extraneous, deracinated, clandestine, sub-aqueous* and hundreds of others constantly gain ground from their Anglo-Saxon opposite numbers.[1] The jargon peculiar to Marxist writing (*hyena, hangman, cannibal, petty bourgeois, these gentry, lackey, flunkey, mad dog, White Guard,* etc) consists largely of words and phrases translated from Russian, German or French; but the normal way of coining a new word is to use a Latin or Greek root with the appropriate affix and, where necessary, the *-ise* formation. It is often easier to make up words of this kind (*deregionalise, impermissible, extramarital, non-fragmentatory* and so forth) than to think up the English words that will cover one's meaning. The result, in general, is an increase in slovenliness and vagueness.

Meaningless words. In certain kinds of writing, particularly in art criticism and literary criticism, it is normal to come across long passages which are almost completely lacking in meanings.[2] Words like *romantic, plastic, values, human, dead, sentimental, natural, vitality,* as used in art criticism, are strictly meaningless, in the sense that they not only do not point to any discoverable object, but are hardly even expected to do so by the reader. When one critic writes, "The outstanding features of Mr X's work is its living quality," while another writes, "The immediately striking thing about Mr X's work is its peculiar deadness," the reader accepts this as a simple difference of opinion. If words like *black* and *white* were involved, instead of the jargon words *dead* and *living,* he would see at once that language was being used in an improper way. Many political words are similarly abused. The word *Fascism* has now no meaning except in so far as it signified "something not desirable." The words *democracy, socialism, freedom, patriotic, realistic, justice,* have each of them several different meanings which cannot be reconciled with one another. In the case of a word like *democracy,* not only is there no agreed definition, but the attempt to make one is resisted from all sides. It is almost universally felt that when we call a country democratic we are praising it: consequently the defenders of every kind of régime claim that it is a democracy, and fear that they might have to stop using the word if it were tied down to any one meaning. Words of this kind are often used in a consciously dishonest way. That is, the person who uses them has his own private definition, but allows his hearer to think he means something quite different. Statements *like Marshal Pétain was a true patriot, The Soviet press is the freest in the world, The Catholic Church is opposed to persecution*, are almost always made with intent to deceive. Other words used in variable meanings, in most cases more or less dishonestly, are: *class, totalitarian, science, progressive, reactionary, bourgeois, equality.*

Now that I have made this catalogue of swindles and perversions, let me give another example of the kind of writing that they lead to. This time it must of its nature be an imaginary one. I am going to translate a passage of good English into modern English of the worst sort. Here is a well-known verse from *Ecclesiastes:*

I returned, and saw under the sun, that the race is not to the swift, nor the battle to the strong, neither yet bread to the wise, nor yet riches to men of understanding, nor yet favour to men of skill; but time and chance happeneth to them all.

Here it is in modern English:

Objective consideration of contemporary phenomena compels the conclusion that success or failure in competitive activities exhibits no tendency to be commensurate with innate capacity, but that a considerable element of the unpredictable must invariably be taken into account.

This is a parody, but not a very gross one. Exhibit 3, above, for instance, contains several patches of the same kind of English. It will be seen that I have not made a full translation. The beginning and ending of the sentence follow the original meaning fairly closely, but in the middle the concrete illustrations—race, battle, bread—dissolve into the vague phrase "success or failure in competitive activities." This had to be so, because no modern writer of the kind I am discussing—no one capable of using phrases like "objective consideration of contemporary phenomena"—would ever tabulate his thoughts in that precise and detailed way. The whole tendency of modern prose is away from concreteness. Now analyse these two sentences a little more closely. The first contains 49 words but only 60 syllables, and all its words are those of everyday life. The second contains 38 words of 90 syllables: 18 of its words are from Latin roots, and one from Greek. The first sentence contains six vivid images, and only one phrase ("time and chance") that could be called vague. The second contains not a single fresh, arresting phrase, and in spite of its 90 syllables it gives only a shortened version of the meaning contained in the first. Yet without a doubt it is the second kind of sentence that is gaining ground in modern English. I do not want to exaggerate. This kind of writing is not yet universal, and outcrops of simplicity will occur here and there in the worst-written page. Still, if you or I were told to write a few lines on the uncertainty of human fortunes, we should probably come much nearer to my imaginary sentence than to the one from *Ecclesiastes*.

As I have tried to show, modern writing at its worst does not consist in picking out words for the sake of their meaning and inventing images in order to make the meaning clearer. It consists in gumming together long strips of words which have already been set in order by someone else, and making the results presentable by sheer humbug. The attraction of this way of writing is that it is easy. It is easier—even quicker, once you have the habit—to say *In my opinion it is a not unjustifiable assumption that* than to say *I think*. If you use ready-made phrases, you not only don't have to hunt about for words; you also don't have to bother with the rhythms of your sentences, since these phrases are generally so arranged as to be more or less euphonious. When you are composing in a hurry—when you are dictating to a stenographer, for instance, or making a public speech—it is natural to fall into a pretentious, latinised style. Tags like *a consideration which we should do well to bear in mind* or *a conclusion to which all of us would readily assent* will save many a sentence from coming down with a bump. By using stale metaphors, similes and idioms, you save much mental effort, at the cost of leaving your meaning vague, not only for your reader but for yourself. This is the significance of mixed metaphors. The sole aim of a metaphor is to call up a visual image. When these images clash—as in *The Fascist octopus has sung its swan song, the jackboot is thrown into the melting-pot*—it can be taken as certain that the writer is not seeing a mental image of the objects he is naming; in other words he is not really thinking. Look again at the examples I gave at the beginning of this essay. Professor Laski (1) uses five negatives in 53 words. One of these is superfluous, making nonsense of the whole passage, and in addition there is the slip *alien* for akin, making further nonsense, and several avoidable pieces of clumsiness which increase the general vagueness. Professor Hogben (2) plays ducks and drakes with a battery which is able to write prescriptions, and, while disapproving of the everyday phrase *put up with*, is unwilling to look *egregious* up in the dictionary and see what it means. (3), if one takes an uncharitable attitude towards it, is simply meaningless: probably one could work out its intended meaning by reading the whole of the article in which it occurs. In (4) the writer knows more or less what he wants to say, but an accumulation of stale phrases chokes him like tea-leaves blocking a sink. In (5) words and meaning have almost parted company. People who write in this manner usually have a general emotional meaning—they dislike one thing and want to express solidarity with another—but they are not interested in the detail of what they are saying. A scrupulous writer, in every sentence that he writes, will ask himself at least four questions, thus: What am I trying to say? What words will express it? What image or idiom will make it clearer? Is this image fresh enough to have an effect? And he will probably ask himself two more: Could I put it more shortly? Have I said anything that is avoidably ugly? But you are not obliged to go to all this trouble. You can shirk it by simply throwing your mind open and letting the ready-made phrases come crowding in. They will construct your sentences for you—even think your thoughts for you, to a certain extent—and at need they will perform the important service of partially concealing your meaning even from yourself. It is at this point that the special connection between politics and the debasement of language becomes clear.

In our time it is broadly true that political writing is bad writing. Where it is not true, it will generally be found that the writer is some kind of rebel, expressing his private opinions, and not a "party line." Orthodoxy, of whatever colour, seems to demand a lifeless, imitative style. The political dialects to be found in pamphlets, leading articles, manifestos, White Papers and the speeches of Under-Secretaries do, of course, vary from party to party, but they are all alike in that one almost never finds in them a fresh, vivid, home-made turn of speech. When one watches some tired hack on the platform mechanically repeating the familiar phrases—*bestial atrocities, iron heel, blood-stained tyranny, free peoples of the world, stand shoulder to shoulder*—one often has a curious feeling that one is not watching a live human being but some kind of dummy: a feeling which suddenly becomes stronger at moments when the light catches the speaker's spectacles and turns them into blank discs which seem to have no eyes behind them. And this is not altogether fanciful. A speaker who uses that kind of phraseology has gone some distance towards turning himself into a machine. The appropriate noises are coming out of his larynx, but his brain is not involved as it would be if he were choosing his words for himself. If the speech he is making is one that he is accustomed to make over and over again, he may be almost unconscious of what he is saying, as one is when one utters the responses in church. And this reduced state of consciousness, if not indispensable, is at any rate favourable to political conformity.

In our time, political speech and writing are largely the defence of the indefensible. Things like the continuance of British rule in India, the Russian purges and deportations, the dropping of the atom bombs on Japan, can indeed be defended, but only by arguments which are too brutal for most people to face, and which do not square with the professed aims of political parties. Thus political language has to consist largely of euphemism, question-begging and sheer cloudy vagueness. Defenceless villages are bombarded from the air, the inhabitants driven out into the countryside, the cattle machine-gunned, the huts set on fire with incendiary bullets: this is called *pacification*. Millions of peasants are robbed of their farms and sent trudging along the roads with no more than they can carry: this is called *transfer of population* or *rectification of frontiers*. People are imprisoned for years without trial, or shot in the back of the neck or sent to die of scurvy in Arctic lumber camps: this is called *elimination of unreliable elements*. Such phraseology is needed if one wants to name things without calling up mental pictures of them. Consider for instance some comfortable English professor defending Russian totalitarianism. He cannot say outright, "I believe in killing off your opponents when you can get good results by doing so." Probably, therefore, he will say something like this:

While freely conceding that the Soviet régime exhibits certain features which the humanitarian may be inclined to deplore, we must, I think, agree that a certain curtailment of the right to political opposition is an unavoidable concomitant of transitional periods, and that the rigours which the Russian people have been called upon to undergo have been amply justified in the sphere of concrete achievement.

The inflated style is itself a kind of euphemism. A mass of Latin words falls upon the facts like soft snow, blurring the outlines and covering up all the details. The great enemy of clear language is insincerity. When there is a gap between one's real and one's declared aims, one turns as it were instinctively to long words and exhausted idioms, like a cuttlefish squirting out ink. In our age there is no such thing as "keeping out of politics." All issues are political issues, and politics itself is a mass of lies, evasions, folly, hatred and schizophrenia. When the general atmosphere is bad, language must suffer. I should expect to find—this is a guess which I have not sufficient knowledge to verify—that the Germans, Russian and Italian languages have all deteriorated in the last ten or fifteen years, as a result of dictatorship.

But if thought corrupts language, language can also corrupt thought. A bad usage can spread by tradition and imitation, even among people who should and do know better. The debased language that I have been discussing is in some ways very convenient. Phrases like *a not unjustifiable assumption, leaves much to be desired, would serve no good purpose, a consideration which we should do well to bear in mind*, are a continuous temptation, a packet of aspirins always at one's elbow. Look back through this essay, and for certain you will find that I have again and again committed the very faults I am protesting against. By this morning's post I have received a pamphlet dealing with conditions in Germany. The author tells me that he "felt impelled" to write it. I open it at random, and here is almost the first sentence that I see: "(The Allies) have an opportunity not only of achieving a radical transformation of Germany's social and political structure in such a way as to avoid a nationalistic reaction in Germany itself, but at the same time of laying the foundations of a co-operative and unified Europe." You see, he "feels impelled" to write—feels, presumably, that he has something new to say—and yet his words, like cavalry horses answering the bugle, group themselves automatically into the familiar dreary pattern. This invasion of one's mind by ready-made phrases (*lay the foundations, achieve a radical transformation*) can only be prevented if one is constantly on guard against them, and every such phrase anaesthetises a portion of one's brain.

I said earlier that the decadence of our language is probably curable. Those who deny this would argue, if they produced an argument at all, that language merely reflects existing social conditions, and that we cannot influence its development by any direct tinkering with words and constructions. So far as the general tone or spirit of a language goes, this may be true, but it is not true in detail. Silly words and expressions have often disappeared, not through any evolutionary process but owing to the conscious action of a minority. Two recent examples were *explore every avenue* and *leave no stone unturned*, which were killed by the jeers of a few journalists. There is a long list of fly-blown metaphors which could similarly be got rid of if enough people would interest themselves in the job; and it should also be possible to laugh the *not un-* formation out of existence,[3] to reduce the amount of Latin and Greek in the average sentence, to drive out foreign phrases and strayed scientific words, and, in general, to make pretentiousness unfashionable. But all these are minor points. The defence of the English language implies more than this, and perhaps it is best to start by saying what it does *not* imply.

To begin with, it has nothing to do with archaism, with the salvaging of obsolete words and turns of speech, or with the setting-up of a "standard English" which must never be departed from. On the contrary, it is especially concerned with the scrapping of every word or idiom which has outworn its usefulness. It has nothing to do with correct grammar and syntax, which are of no importance so long as one makes one's meaning clear, or with the avoidance of Americanisms, or with having what is called a "good prose style." On the other hand it is not concerned with fake simplicity and the attempt to make written English colloquial. Nor does it even imply in every case preferring the Saxon word to the Latin one, though it does imply using the fewest and shortest words that will cover one's meaning. What is above all needed is to let the meaning choose the word, and not the other way about. In prose, the worst thing one can do with words is to surrender to them. When you think of a concrete object, you think wordlessly, and then, if you want to describe the thing you have been visualising, you probably hunt about till you find the exact words that seem to fit it. When you think of something abstract you are more inclined to use words from the start, and unless you make a conscious effort to prevent it, the existing dialect will come rushing in and do the job for you, at the expense of blurring or even changing your meaning. Probably it is better to put off using words as long as possible and get one's meaning as clear as one can through pictures or sensations. Afterwards one can choose—not simply *accept*—the phrases that will best cover the meaning, and then switch round and decide what impression one's words are likely to make on another person. This last effort of the mind cuts out all stale or mixed images, all prefabricated phrases, needless repetitions, and humbug and vagueness generally. But one can often be in doubt about the effect of a word or a phrase, and one needs rules that one can rely on when instinct fails. I think the following rules will cover most cases:

   i. Never use a metaphor, simile or other figure of speech which you are used to seeing in print.
   ii. Never use a long word where a short one will do.
   iii. If it is possible to cut a word out, always cut it out.
   iv. Never use the passive where you can use the active.
   v. Never use a foreign phrase, a scientific word or a jargon word if you can think of an everyday English equivalent.
   vi. Break any of these rules sooner than say anything outright barbarous.

These rules sound elementary, and so they are, but they demand a deep change of attitude in anyone who has grown used to writing in the style now fashionable. One could keep all of them and still write bad English, but one could not write the kind of stuff that I quoted in those five specimens at the beginning of this article.

I have not here been considering the literary use of language, but merely language as an instrument for expressing and not for concealing or preventing thought. Stuart Chase and others have come near to claiming that all abstract words are meaningless, and have used this as a pretext for advocating a kind of political quietism. Since you don't know what Fascism is, how can you struggle against Fascism? One need not swallow such absurdities as this, but one ought to recognise that the present political chaos is connected with the decay of language, and that one can probably bring about some improvement by starting at the verbal end. If you simplify your English, you are freed from the worst follies of orthodoxy. You cannot speak any of the necessary dialects, and when you make a stupid remark its stupidity will be obvious, even to yourself. Political language—and with variations this is true of all political parties, from Conservatives to Anarchists—is designed to make lies sound truthful and murder respectable, and to give an appearance of solidity to pure wind. One cannot change this all in a moment, but one can at least change one's own habits, and from time to time one can even, if one jeers loudly enough, send some worn-out and useless phrase—some *jackboot, Achilles' heel, hotbed, melting pot, acid test, veritable inferno* or other lump of verbal refuse—into the dustbin where it belongs.

Notes

1. An interesting illustration of this is the way in which the English flower names which were in use till very recently are being ousted by Greek ones, *snapdragon* becoming *antirrhinum, forget-me-not* becoming *myosotis*, etc. It is hard to see any practical reason for this change of fashion: it is probably due to an instinctive turning-away from the more homely word and a vague feeling that the Greek word is scientific. [Author's footnote.]

2. Example: "Comfort's catholicity of perception and image, strangely Whitmanesque in range, almost the exact opposite in aesthetic compulsion, continues to evoke that trembling atmospheric accumulative hinting at a cruel, an inexorably serene timelessness . . . Wrey Gardiner scores by aiming at simple bullseyes with precision. Only they are not so simple, and through this contented sadness runs more than the surface bitter-sweet of resignation." (*Poetry Quarterly.*) [Author's footnote.]

3. One can cure oneself of the *not un-* formation by memorising this sentence: *A not unblack dog was chasing a not unsmall rabbit across a not ungreen field.* [Author's footnote.]

35

Simone de Beauvoir
The Second Sex

Simone de Beauvoir (Lucie Ernestine Marie Bertrand) (1908–1986) was a central figure in French intellectual life after World War II. De Beauvoir wrote novels and a play, as well as nonfiction ranging from political critiques of contemporary problems and events to autobiography. The Second Sex, published in France in 1949 and in America in 1953, remains her best-known work. Honored and attacked, it is regarded as a cogent and comprehensive work of feminist theory. The work's premise is that "One is not born, but rather, becomes a woman. No biological, psychological or economic fate determines the figure that the human female presents in society; it is civilization as a whole that produces this creature, intermediate between male and eunuch, which is described as feminine." De Beauvoir served as lightning rod and inspiration for the contemporary international feminist movement. Despite a conventional upbringing, she was at the forefront of leftist politics, attempting to live publicly as a liberated woman in a patriarchal society. She disdained marriage as a bourgeois institution and urged women to have a profession. De Beauvoir had a passionate relationship with Jean-Paul Sartre, the existentialist philosopher. Her novels and nonfiction are brilliant expositions of the existentialist assertion that individuals are ultimately responsible for themselves and must act. In 1972, she said "I really am a feminist," allied herself with the Mouvement de la Liberation des Femmes, *and signed the "Manifesto of the 343 Sluts," women who publicly announced that they had broken the law banning abortion and demanded free contraception, free abortion, free motherhood.*

Introduction

For a long time I have hesitated to write a book on woman. The subject is irritating, especially to women; and it is not new. Enough ink has been spilled in the quarreling over feminism, now practically over, and perhaps we should say no more about it. It is still talked about, however, for the voluminous nonsense uttered during the last century seems to have done little to illuminate the problem. After all, is there a problem? And if so, what is it? Are there women, really? Most assuredly the theory of the eternal feminine still has its adherents who will whisper in your ear: "Even in Russia women still are *women*"; and other erudite persons—sometimes the very same—say with a sigh: "Woman is losing her way, woman is lost." One wonders if women still exist, if they will always exist, whether or not it is desirable that they should, what place they occupy in this world, what their place should be. "What has become of women?" was asked recently in an ephemeral magazine.[1]

But first we must ask: what is a woman? "*Tota mulier in utero*," says one, "women is a womb." But in speaking of certain women, connoisseurs declare that they are not women, although they are equipped with a uterus like the rest. All agree in recognizing the fact that females exist in the human species; today as always they make up about one half of humanity. And yet we are told that femininity is in danger; we are exhorted to be women, remain women, become women. It would appear, then, that every female human being is not necessarily a woman; to be so considered she must share in that mysterious and threatened reality known as femininity. Is this attribute something secreted by the ovaries? Or is it a Platonic essence, a product of the philosophic imagination? Is a rustling petticoat enough to bring it down to earth? Although some women try zealously to incarnate this essence, it is hardly patentable. It is frequently described in vague and dazzling terms that seem to have been borrowed from the vocabulary of the seers, and indeed in the times of St. Thomas it was considered an essence as certainly defined as the somniferous virtue of the poppy.

But conceptualism has lost ground. The biological and social sciences no longer admit the existence of unchangeably fixed entities that determine given characteristics, such as those ascribed to woman, the Jew, or the Negro. Science regards any characteristic as a reaction dependent in part upon a *situation*. If today femininity no longer exists, then it never existed. But does the word *woman*, then, have no specific content? This is stoutly affirmed by those who hold to the philosophy of the enlightenment, of rationalism, of nominalism; women, to them, are merely the human beings arbitrarily designated by the word *woman*. Many American women particularly are prepared to think that there is no longer any place for woman as such; if a backward individual still takes herself for a woman, her friends advise her to be psychoanalyzed and thus get rid of this obsession. In regard to a work, *Modern Woman; The Lost Sex*, which in other respects has its irritating features, Dorothy Parker has written: "I cannot be just to books which treat of woman as woman. . . . My idea is that all of us, men as well as women, should be regarded as human beings." But nominalism is a rather inadequate doctrine, and the antifeminists have had no trouble in showing that women simply *are not* men. Surely woman is, like man, a human being; but such a declaration is abstract. The fact is that every concrete human being is always a singular, separate individual. To decline to accept such notions as the eternal feminine, the black soul, the Jewish character, is not to deny that Jews, Negroes, women exist today—this denial does not represent a liberation for those concerned, but rather a flight from reality. Some years ago a well-known woman writer refused to permit her portrait to appear in a series of photographs especially devoted to women writers; she wished to be counted among the men. But in order to gain this privilege she made use of her husband's influence! Women who assert that they are men lay claim none the less to masculine consideration and respect. I recall also a young Trotskyite standing on a platform at a boisterous meeting and getting ready to use her fists, in spite of her evident fragility. She was denying her feminine weakness; but it was for love of a militant male whose equal she wished to be. The attitude of defiance of many American women proves that they are haunted by a sense of their femininity. In truth, to go for a walk with one's eyes open is enough to demonstrate that humanity is divided into two classes of individuals whose clothes, faces, bodies, smiles, gaits, interests, and occupations are manifestly different. Perhaps these differences are superficial, perhaps they are destined to disappear. What is certain is that right now they do most obviously exist.

If her functioning as a female is not enough to define woman, if we decline also to explain her through "the eternal feminine," and if nevertheless we admit, provisionally, that women do exist, then we must face the question: what is a woman?

To state the question is, to me, to suggest, at once, a preliminary answer. The fact that I ask it is in itself significant. A man would never get the notion of writing a book on the peculiar situation of the human male.[2] But if I wish to define myself, I must first of all say: "I am a woman"; on this truth must be based all further discussion. A man never begins by presenting himself as an individual of a certain sex; it goes without saying that he is a man. The terms *masculine* and *feminine* are used symmetrically only as a matter of form, as on legal papers. In actuality the relation of the two sexes is not quite like that of two electrical poles, for man represents both the positive and the neutral, as is indicated by the common use of *man* to designate human beings in general; whereas woman represents only the negative, defined by limiting criteria, without reciprocity. In the midst of an abstract discussion it is vexing to hear a man say: "You think thus and so because you are a woman"; but I know that my only defense is to reply: "I think thus and so because it is true," thereby removing my subjective self from the argument. It would be out of the question to reply: "And you think the contrary because you are a man," for it is understood that the fact of being a man is no peculiarity. A man is in the right in being a man; it is the woman who is in the wrong. It amounts to this: just as for the ancients there was an absolute vertical with reference to which the oblique was defined, so there is an absolute human type, the masculine. Woman has ovaries, a uterus; these peculiarities imprison her in her subjectivity, circumscribe her within the limits of her own nature. It is often said that she thinks with her glands. Man superbly ignores the fact that his anatomy also includes glands, such as the testicles, and that they secrete hormones. He thinks of his body as a direct and normal connection with the world, which he believes he apprehends objectively, whereas he regards the woman as a hindrance, a prison, weighed down by everything peculiar to it. "The female is a female by virtue of a certain *lack* of qualities," said Aristotle; "we should regard the female nature as afflicted with a natural defectiveness." And St. Thomas for his part pronounced woman to be an "imperfect man," an "incidental" being. This is symbolized in Genesis where Eve is depicted as made from what Bossuet called "a supernumerary bone" of Adam.

Thus humanity is male and man defines woman not in herself but as relative to him; she is not regarded as an autonomous being. Michelet writes: "Woman, the relative being. . . . " And Benda is most positive in his *Rapport d'Uriel:* "The body of man makes sense in itself quite apart from that of woman, whereas the

latter seems wanting in significance by itself. . . . Man can think of himself without woman. She cannot think of herself without man." And she is simply what
man decrees; thus she is called "the sex," by which is meant that she appears
essentially to the male as a sexual being. For him she is sex—absolute sex, no
less. She is defined and differentiated with reference to man and not he with
reference to her; she is the incidental, the inessential as opposed to the essential.
He is the Subject, he is the Absolute—she is the Other.[3]

The category of the *Other* is as primordial as consciousness itself. In the most
primitive societies, in the most ancient mythologies, one finds the expression of a
duality—that of the Self and the Other. This duality was not originally attached to
the division of the sexes; it was not dependent upon any empirical facts. It is
revealed in such works as that of Granet on Chinese thought and those of Dumézil
on the East Indies and Rome. The feminine element was at first no more involved
in such pairs as Varuna-Mitra, Uranus-Zeus, Sun-Moon, and Day-Night than it
was in the contrasts between Good and Evil, lucky and unlucky auspices, right
and left, God and Lucifer. Otherness is a fundamental category of human thought.

Thus it is that no group ever sets itself up as the One without at once setting up
the Other over against itself. If three travelers chance to occupy the same compartment, that is enough to make vaguely hostile "others" out of all the rest of the
passengers on the train. In small-town eyes all persons not belonging to the village
are "strangers" and suspect; to the native of a country all who inhabit other countries are "foreigners"; Jews are "different" for the anti-Semite, Negroes are "inferior" for American racists, aborigines are "natives" for colonists, proletarians are
the "lower class" for the privileged.

Lévi-Strauss, at the end of a profound work on the various forms of primitive
societies, reaches the following conclusion: "Passage from the state of Nature to
the state of Culture is marked by man's ability to view biological relations as a
series of contrasts; duality, alternation, opposition, and symmetry, whether under
definite or vague forms, constitute not so much phenomena to be explained as
fundamental and immediately given data of social reality."[4] These phenomena
would be incomprehensible if in fact human society were simply a *Mitsein* or
fellowship based on solidarity and friendliness. Things become clear, on the contrary, if, following Hegel, we find in consciousness itself a fundamental hostility
toward every other consciousness; the subject can be posed only in being opposed—he sets himself up as the essential, as opposed to the other, the inessential, the object.

But the other consciousness, the other ego, sets up a reciprocal claim. The
native traveling abroad is shocked to find himself in turn regarded as a "stranger"
by the natives of neighboring countries. As a matter of fact, wars, festivals, trading, treaties, and contests among tribes, nations, and classes tend to deprive the
concept *Other* of its absolute sense and to make manifest its relativity; willy-nilly,
individuals and groups are forced to realize the reciprocity of their relations. How
is it, then, that this reciprocity has not been recognized between the sexes, that
one of the contrasting terms is set up as the sole essential, denying any relativity
in regard to its correlative and defining the latter as pure otherness? Why is it that

women do not dispute male sovereignty? No subject will readily volunteer to become the object, the inessential; it is not the Other who, in defining himself as the Other, establishes the One. The Other is posed as such by the One in defining himself as the One. But if the Other is not to regain the status of being the One, he must be submissive enough to accept this alien point of view. Whence comes this submission in the case of woman?

There are, to be sure, other cases in which a certain category has been able to dominate another completely for a time. Very often this privilege depends upon inequality of numbers—the majority imposes its rule upon the minority or persecutes it. But women are not a minority, like the American Negroes or the Jews; there are as many women as men on earth. Again, the two groups concerned have often been originally independent; they may have been formerly unaware of each other's existence, or perhaps they recognized each other's autonomy. But a historical event has resulted in the subjugation of the weaker by the stronger. The scattering of the Jews, the introduction of slavery into America, the conquests of imperialism are examples in point. In these cases the oppressed retained at least the memory of former days; they possessed in common a past, a tradition, sometimes a religion or a culture.

The parallel drawn by Bebel between women and the proletariat is valid in that neither ever formed a minority or a separate collective unit of mankind. And instead of a single historical event it is in both cases a historical development that explains their status as a class and accounts for the membership of *particular individuals* in that class. But proletarians have not always existed, whereas there have always been women. They are women in virtue of their anatomy and physiology. Throughout history they have always been subordinated to men,[5] and hence their dependency is not the result of a historical event or a social change—it was not something that *occurred*. The reason why otherness in this case seems to be an absolute is in part that it lacks the contingent or incidental nature of historical facts. A condition brought about at a certain time can be abolished at some other time, as the Negroes of Haiti and others have proved; but it might seem that a natural condition is beyond the possibility of change. In truth, however, the nature of things is no more immutably given, once for all, than is historical reality. If woman seems to be the inessential which never becomes the essential, it is because she herself fails to bring about this change. Proletarians say "We"; Negroes also. Regarding themselves as subjects, they transform the bourgeois, the whites, into "others." But women do not say "We," except at some congress of feminists or similar formal demonstration; men say "women," and women use the same word in referring to themselves. They do not authentically assume a subjective attitude. The proletarians have accomplished the revolution in Russia, the Negroes in Haiti, the Indo-Chinese are battling for it in Indo-China; but the women's effort has never been anything more than a symbolic agitation. They have gained only what men have been willing to grant; they have taken nothing, they have only received.

The reason for this is that women lack concrete means for organizing themselves into a unit which can stand face to face with the correlative unit. They have no past, no history, no religion of their own; and they have no such solidarity of work and interest as that of the proletariat. They are not even promiscuously herded together in the way that creates community feeling among the American Negroes, the ghetto Jews, the workers of Saint-Denis, or the factory hands of Renault. They live dispersed among the males, attached through residence, housework, economic condition, and social standing to certain men—fathers or husbands—more firmly than they are to other women. If they belong to the bourgeoisie, they feel solidarity with men of that class, not with proletarian women; if they are white, their allegiance is to white men, not to Negro women. The proletariat can propose to massacre the ruling class, and a sufficiently fanatical Jew or Negro might dream of getting sole possession of the atomic bomb and making humanity wholly Jewish or black; but woman cannot even dream of exterminating the males. The bond that unites her to her oppressors is not comparable to any other. The division of the sexes is a biological fact, not an event in human history. Male and female stand opposed within a primordial *Mitsein*, and woman has not broken it. The couple is a fundamental unity with its two halves riveted together, and the cleavage of society along the line of sex is impossible. Here is to be found the basic trait of woman: she is the Other in a totality of which the two components are necessary to one another.

One could suppose that this reciprocity might have facilitated the liberation of woman. When Hercules sat at the feet of Omphale and helped with her spinning, his desire for her held him captive; but why did she fail to gain a lasting power? To revenge herself on Jason, Medea killed their children; and this grim legend would seem to suggest that she might have obtained a formidable influence over him through his love for his offspring. In *Lysistrata* Aristophanes gaily depicts a band of women who joined forces to gain social ends through the sexual needs of their men; but this is only a play. In the legend of the Sabine women, the latter soon abandoned their plan of remaining sterile to punish their ravishers. In truth woman has not been socially emancipated through man's need—sexual desire and the desire for offspring—which makes the male dependent for satisfaction upon the female.

Master and slave, also, are united by a reciprocal need, in this case economic, which does not liberate the slave. In the relation of master to slave the master does not make a point of the need that he has for the other; he has in his grasp the power of satisfying this need through his own action; whereas the slave, in his dependent condition, his hope and fear, is quite conscious of the need he has for his master. Even if the need is at bottom equally urgent for both, it always works in favor of the oppressor and against the oppressed. That is why the liberation of the working class, for example, has been slow.

Now, woman has always been man's dependent, if not his slave; the two sexes have never shared the world in equality. And even today woman is heavily handicapped, though her situation is beginning to change. Almost nowhere is her legal status the same as man's, and frequently it is much to her disadvantage. Even when her rights are legally recognized in the abstract, long-standing custom prevents their full expression in the mores. In the economic sphere men and women can almost be said to make up two castes; other things being equal, the former hold the better jobs, get higher wages, and have more opportunity for success than their new competitors. In industry and politics men have a great many more positions and they monopolize the most important posts. In addition to all this, they enjoy a traditional prestige that the education of children tends in every way to support, for the present enshrines the past—and in the past all history has been made by men. At the present time, when women are beginning to take part in the affairs of the world, it is still a world that belongs to men—they have no doubt of it at all and women have scarcely any. To decline to be the Other, to refuse to be a party to the deal—this would be for women to renounce all the advantages conferred upon them by their alliance with the superior caste. Man-the-sovereign will provide woman-the-liege with material protection and will undertake the moral justification of her existence; thus she can evade at once both economic risk and the metaphysical risk of a liberty in which ends and aims must be contrived without assistance. Indeed, along with the ethical urge of each individual to affirm his subjective existence, there is also the temptation to forgo liberty and become a thing. This is an inauspicious road, for he who takes it—passive, lost, ruined— becomes henceforth the creature of another's will, frustrated in his transcendence and deprived of every value. But it is an easy road; on it one avoids the strain involved in undertaking an authentic existence. When man makes of women the *Other*, he may then, expect her to manifest deep-seated tendencies toward complicity. Thus, woman may fail to lay claim to the status of subject because she lacks definite resources, because she feels the necessary bond that ties her to man regardless of reciprocity, and because she is often very well pleased with her role as the *Other*.

But it will be asked at once: how did all this begin? It is easy to see that the duality of the sexes, like any duality, gives rise to conflict. And doubtless the winner will assume the status of absolute. But why should man have won from the start? It seems possible that women could have won the victory; or that the outcome of the conflict might never have been decided. How is it that this world has always belonged to the men and that things have begun to change only recently? Is this change a good thing? Will it bring about an equal sharing of the world between men and women?

These questions are not new, and they have often been answered. But the very fact that women *is the Other* tends to cast suspicion upon all the justifications that men have ever been able to provide for it. These have all too evidently been dictated by men's interest. A little-known feminist of the seventeenth century, Poulain de la Barre, put it this way: "All that has been written about women by men should be suspect, for the men are at once judge and party to the lawsuit." Everywhere, at all times, the males have displayed their satisfaction in feeling that they are the lords of creation. "Blessed be God . . . that He did not make me a woman," say the Jews in their morning prayers, while their wives pray on a note of resignation: "Blessed be the Lord, who created me according to His will." The first among the blessings for which Plato thanked the gods was that he had been created free, not enslaved; the second, a man, not a woman. But the males could not enjoy this privilege fully unless they believed it to be founded on the absolute and the eternal; they sought to make the fact of their supremacy into a right. "Being men, those who have made and compiled the laws have favored their own sex, and jurists have elevated these laws into principles," to quote Poulain de la Barre once more.

Legislators, priests, philosophers, writers, and scientists have striven to show that the subordinate position of woman is willed in heaven and advantageous on earth. The religions invented by men reflect this wish for domination. In the legends of Eve and Pandora men have taken up arms against women. They have made use of philosophy and theology, as the quotations from Aristotle and St. Thomas have shown. Since ancient times satirists and moralists have delighted in showing up the weaknesses of women. We are familiar with the savage indictments hurled against women throughout French literature. Montherlant, for example, follows the tradition of Jean de Meung, though with less gusto. This hostility may at times be well founded, often it is gratuitous; but in truth it more or less successfully conceals a desire for self-justification. As Montaigne says, "It is easier to accuse one sex than to excuse the other." Sometimes what is going on is clear enough. For instance, the Roman law limiting the rights of woman cited "the imbecility, the instability of the sex" just when the weakening of family ties seemed to threaten the interests of male heirs. And in the effort to keep the married woman under guardianship, appeal was made in the sixteenth century to the authority of St. Augustine, who declared that "woman is a creature neither decisive nor constant," at a time when the single woman was thought capable of managing her property. Montaigne understood clearly how arbitrary and unjust was woman's appointed lot: "Women are not in the wrong when they decline to accept the rules laid down for them, since the men make these rules without consulting them. No wonder intrigue and strife abound." But he did not go so far as to champion their cause.

It was only later, in the eighteenth century, that genuinely democratic men began to view the matter objectively. Diderot, among others, strove to show that woman is, like man, a human being. Later John Stuart Mill came fervently to her defense. But these philosophers displayed unusual impartiality. In the nineteenth century the feminist quarrel became again a quarrel of partisans. One of the consequences of the industrial revolution was the entrance of women into productive labor, and it was just here that the claims of the feminists emerged from the realm of theory and acquired an economic basis, while their opponents became the more aggressive. Although landed property lost power to some extent, the bourgeoisie clung to the old morality that found the guarantee of private property in the solidity of the family. Woman was ordered back into the home the more harshly as her emancipation became a real menace. Even within the working class the men endeavored to restrain woman's liberation, because they began to see the women as dangerous competitors—the more so because they were accustomed to work for lower wages.

In proving woman's inferiority, the antifeminists then began to draw not only upon religion, philosophy, and theology, as before, but also upon science—biology, experimental psychology, etc. At most they were willing to grant "equality in difference" to the *other* sex. That profitable formula is most significant; it is precisely like the "equal but separate" formula of the Jim Crow laws aimed at the North American Negroes. As is well known, this so-called equalitarian segregation has resulted only in the most extreme discrimination. The similarity just noted is in no way due to chance, for whether it is a race, a caste, a class, or a sex that is reduced to a position of inferiority, the methods of justification are the same. "The eternal feminine" corresponds to "the black soul" and to "the Jewish character." True, the Jewish problem is on the whole very different from the other two—to the anti-Semite the Jew is not so much an inferior as he is an enemy for whom there is to be granted no place on earth, for whom annihilation is the fate desired. But there are deep similarities between the situation of woman and that of the Negro. Both are being emancipated today from a like paternalism, and the former master class wishes to "keep them in their place"—that is, the place chosen for them. In both cases the former masters lavish more or less sincere eulogies, either on the virtues of "the good Negro" with his dormant, childish, merry soul—the submissive Negro—or on the merits of the woman who is "truly feminine"—that is, frivolous, infantile, irresponsible—the submissive woman. In both cases the dominant class bases its argument on a state of affairs that it has itself created. As George Bernard Shaw puts it, in substance, "The American white relegates the black to the rank of shoeshine boy; and he concludes from this that the black is good for nothing but shining shoes." This vicious circle is met with in all analogous circumstances; when an individual (or a group of individuals) is kept in a situation of inferiority, the fact is that he *is* inferior. But the significance of the verb *to be* must be rightly understood here; it is in bad faith to give it a static value when it really has the dynamic Hegelian sense of "to have become." Yes, women on the whole *are* today inferior to men; that is, their situation affords them fewer possibilities. The question is: should that state of affairs continue?

Many men hope that it will continue; not all have given up the battle. The conservative bourgeoisie still see in the emancipation of women a menace to their morality and their interests. Some men dread feminine competition. Recently a male student wrote in the *Hebdo-Latin:* "Every woman student who goes into medicine or law robs us of a job." He never questioned his rights in this world. And economic interests are not the only ones concerned. One of the benefits that oppression confers upon the oppressors is that the most humble among them is made to *feel* superior; thus, a "poor white" in the South can console himself with the thought that he is not a "dirty nigger"—and the more prosperous whites cleverly exploit this pride.

Similarly, the most mediocre of males feels himself a demigod as compared with women. It was much easier for M. de Montherlant to think himself a hero when he faced women (and women chosen for his purpose) than when he was obliged to act the man among men—something many women have done better than he, for that matter. And in September 1948, in one of his articles in the *Figaro littéraire*, Claude Mauriac—whose great originality is admired by all—could write regarding woman: "*We* listen on a tone [*sic!*] of polite indifference

. . . to the most brilliant among them, well knowing that her wit reflects more or less luminously ideas that come from *us*." Evidently the speaker referred to is not reflecting the ideas of Mauriac himself, for no one knows of his having any. It may be that she reflects ideas originating with men, but then, even among men there are those who have been known to appropriate ideas not their own; and one can well ask whether Claude Mauriac might not find more interesting a conversation reflecting Descartes, Marx, or Gide rather than himself. What is really remarkable is that by using the questionable *we* he identifies himself with St. Paul, Hegel, Lenin, and Nietzsche, and from the lofty eminence of their grandeur looks down disdainfully upon the bevy of women who make bold to converse with him on a footing of equality. In truth, I know of more than one woman who would refuse to suffer with patience Mauriac's "tone of polite indifference."

I have lingered on this example because the masculine attitude is here displayed with disarming ingenuousness. But men profit in many more subtle ways from the otherness, the alterity of women. Here is miraculous balm for those afflicted with an inferiority complex, and indeed no one is more arrogant toward women, more aggressive or scornful, than the man who is anxious about his virility. Those who are not fear-ridden in the presence of their fellow men are much more disposed to recognize a fellow creature in woman; but even to these the myth of woman, the Other, is precious for many reasons.[6] They cannot be blamed for not cheerfully relinquishing all the benefits they derive from the myth, for they realize what they would lose in relinquishing woman as they fancy her to be, while they fail to realize what they have to gain from the woman of tomorrow. Refusal to pose oneself as the Subject, unique and absolute, requires great self-denial. Furthermore, the vast majority of men make no such claim explicitly. They do not *postulate* woman as inferior, for today they are too thoroughly imbued with the ideal of democracy not to recognize all human beings as equals.

In the bosom of the family, woman seems in the eyes of childhood and youth to be clothed in the same social dignity as the adult males. Later on, the young man, desiring and loving, experiences the resistance, the independence of the woman desired and loved; in marriage, he respects woman as wife and mother, and in the concrete events of conjugal life she stands there before him as a free being. He can therefore feel that social subordination as between the sexes no longer exists and that on the whole, in spite of differences, woman is an equal. As, however, he observes some points of inferiority—the most important being unfitness for the professions—he attributes these to natural causes. When he is in a co-operative and benevolent relation with woman, his theme is the principle of abstract equality, and he does not base his attitude upon such inequality as may exist. But when he is in conflict with her, the situation is reversed: his theme will be the existing inequality, and he will even take it as justification for denying abstract equality.[7]

So it is that many men will affirm as if in good faith that women *are* the equals of man and that they have nothing to clamor for, while *at the same time* they will say that woman can never be the equals of man and that their demands are in vain. It is, in point of fact, a difficult matter for man to realize the extreme importance of social discriminations which seem outwardly insignificant but which produce in woman moral and intellectual effects so profound that they appear to spring from her original nature. The most sympathetic of men never fully comprehend woman's concrete situation. And there is no reason to put much trust in the men when they rush to the defense of privileges whose full extent they can hardly measure. We shall not, then, permit ourselves to be intimidated by the number and violence of the attacks launched against women, nor to be entrapped by the self-seeking eulogies bestowed on the "true woman," nor to profit by the enthusiasm for woman's destiny manifested by men who would not for the world have any part of it.

We should consider the arguments of the feminists with no less suspicion, however, for very often their controversial aim deprives them of all real value. If the "woman question" seems trivial, it is because masculine arrogance has made of it a "quarrel"; and when quarreling, one no longer reasons well. People have tirelessly sought to prove that woman is superior, inferior, or equal to man. Some say that, having been created after Adam, she is evidently a secondary being; others say on the contrary that Adam was only a rough draft and that God succeeded in producing the human being in perfection when He created Eve. Woman's brain is smaller; yes, but it is relatively larger. Christ was made a man; yes, but perhaps for his greater humility. Each argument at once suggests its opposite, and both are often fallacious. If we are to gain understanding, we must get out of these ruts; we must discard the vague notions of superiority, inferiority, equality which have hitherto corrupted every discussion of the subject and start afresh.

Very well, but just how shall we pose the question? And, to begin with, who are we to propound it at all? Man is at once judge and party to the case; but so is woman. What we need is an angel—neither man nor woman—but where shall we find one? Still, the angel would be poorly qualified to speak, for an angel is ignorant of all the basic facts involved in the problem. With a hermaphrodite we should be no better off, for here the situation is most peculiar; the hermaphrodite is not really the combination of a whole man and a whole woman, but consists of parts of each and thus is neither. It looks to me as if there are, after all, certain women who are best qualified to elucidate the situation of woman. Let us not be misled by the sophism that because Epimenides was a Cretan he was necessarily a liar; it is not a mysterious essence that compels men and women to act in good or in bad faith, it is their situation that inclines them more or less toward the search for truth. Many of today's women, fortunate in the restoration of all the privileges pertaining to the estate of the human being, can afford the luxury of impartiality—we even recognize its necessity. We are no longer like our partisan elders; by and large we have won the game. In recent debates on the status of women the United Nations has persistently maintained that the equality of the sexes is now becoming a reality, and already some of us have never had to sense in our femininity an inconvenience or an obstacle. Many problems appear to us to be more pressing than those which concern us in particular, and this detachment even allows us to hope that our attitude will be objective. Still, we know the feminine world more intimately than do the men because we have our roots in it, we grasp more immediately than do men what it means to a human being to be feminine; and we are more concerned with such knowledge. I have said that there are more pressing problems, but this does not prevent us from seeing some importance in asking how the fact of being women will affect our lives. What opportunities precisely have been given us and what withheld? What fate awaits our younger sisters, and what directions should they take? It is significant that books by women on women are in general animated in our day less by a wish to demand our rights than by an effort toward clarity and understanding. As we emerge from an era of excessive controversy, this book is offered as one attempt among others to confirm that statement.

But it is doubtless impossible to approach any human problem with a mind free from bias. The way in which questions are put, the points of view assumed, presuppose a relativity of interest; all characteristics imply values, and every objective description, so called, implies an ethical background. Rather than attempt to conceal principles more or less definitely implied, it is better to state them openly at the beginning. This will make it unnecessary to specify on every page in just what sense one uses such words as *superior, inferior, better, worse, progress, reaction,* and the like. If we survey some of the works on woman, we note that one of the points of view most frequently adopted is that of the public good, the general interest; and one always means by this the benefit of society as one wishes it to be maintained or established. For our part, we hold that the only public good is that which assures the private good of the citizens; we shall pass judgment on institutions according to their effectiveness in giving concrete opportunities to individuals. But we do not confuse the idea of private interest with that of happiness, although that is another common point of view. Are not women of the harem more happy than women voters? Is not the housekeeper happier than the working-woman? It is not too clear just what the word *happy* really means and still less what true values it may mask. There is no possibility of measuring the happiness of others, and it is always easy to describe as happy the situation in which one wishes to place them.

In particular those who are condemned to stagnation are often pronounced happy on the pretext that happiness consists in being at rest. This notion we reject, for our perspective is that of existentialist ethics. Every subject plays his part as such specifically through exploits or projects that serve as a mode of transcendence; he achieves liberty only through a continual reaching out toward other liberties. There is no justification for present existence other than its expansion into an indefinitely open future. Every time transcendence falls back into immanence, stagnation, there is a degradation of existence into the *"en-soi"*—the brutish life of subjection to given conditions—and of liberty into constraint and contingence. This downfall represents a moral fault if the subject consents to it; if it is inflicted upon him, it spells frustration and oppression. In both cases it is an absolute evil. Every individual concerned to justify his existence feels that his existence involves an undefined need to transcend himself, to engage in freely chosen projects.

Now, what peculiarly signalizes the situation of woman is that she—a free and autonomous being like all human creatures—nevertheless finds herself living in a world where men compel her to assume the status of the Other. They propose to stabilize her as object and to doom her to immanence since her transcendence is to be overshadowed and forever transcended by another ego (*conscience*) which is essential and sovereign. The drama of woman lies in this conflict between the fundamental aspirations of every subject (ego)—who always regards the self as the essential—and the compulsions of a situation in which she is the inessential. How can a human being in woman's situation attain fulfillment? What roads are open to her? Which are blocked? How can independence be recovered in a state of dependency? What circumstances limit woman's liberty and how can they be overcome? These are the fundamental questions on which I would fain throw some light. This means that I am interested in the fortunes of the individual as defined not in terms of happiness but in terms of liberty.

Quite evidently this problem would be without significance if we were to believe that woman's destiny is inevitably determined by physiological, psychological, or economic forces. Hence I shall discuss first of all the light in which woman is viewed by biology, psychoanalysis, and historical materialism. Next I shall try to show exactly how the concept of the "truly feminine" has been fashioned—why woman has been defined as the Other—and what have been the consequences from man's point of view. Then from woman's point of view I shall describe the world in which women must live; and thus we shall be able to envisage the difficulties in their way as, endeavoring to make their escape from the sphere hitherto assigned them, they aspire to full membership in the human race.

Notes

1. *Franchise*, dead today.
2. The Kinsey Report [Alfred C. Kinsey and others: *Sexual Behavior in the Human Male* (W. B. Saunders Co., 1948)] is no exception, for it is limited to describing the sexual characteristics of American men, which is quite a different matter.
3. E. Lévinas expresses this idea most explicitly in his essay *Temps et l'Autre*. "Is there not a case in which otherness, alterity [*altérité*], unquestionably marks the nature of a being, as its essence, an instance of otherness not consisting purely and simply in the opposition of two species of the same genus? I think that the feminine represents the contrary in its absolute sense, this contrariness being in no wise affected by any relation between it and its correlative and thus remaining absolutely other. Sex is not a certain specific difference . . . no more is the sexual difference a mere contradiction. . . . Nor does this difference lie in the duality of two complementary terms, for two complementary terms imply a pre-existing whole. . . . Otherness reaches its full flowering in the feminine, a term of the same rank as consciousness but of opposite meaning."

I suppose that Lévinas does not forget that woman, too, is aware of her own consciousness, or ego. But it is striking that he deliberately takes a man's point of view, disregarding the reciprocity of subject and object. When he writes that woman is mystery, he implies that she is mystery for man. Thus his description, which is intended to be objective, is in fact an assertion of masculine privilege.

4. See C. Lévi-Strauss: *Les Structures élémentaires de la parenté*. My thanks are due to C. Lévi-Strauss for his kindness in furnishing me with the proofs of his work. . . .

5. With rare exceptions, perhaps, like certain matriarchal rulers, queens, and the like—TR.

6. A significant article on this theme by Michel Carrouges appeared in No. 292 of the *Cahiers du Sud*. He writes indignantly: "Would that there were no woman-myth at all but only a cohort of cooks, matrons, prostitutes, and bluestockings serving functions of pleasure or usefulness!" That is to say, in his view woman has no existence in and for herself; he thinks only of her *function* in the male world. Her reason for existence lies in man. But then, in fact, her poetic "function" as a myth might be more valued than any other. The real problem is precisely to find out why woman should be defined with relation to man.

7. For example, a man will say that he considers his wife in no wise degraded because she has no gainful occupation. The profession of housewife is just as lofty, and so on. But when the first quarrel comes he will exclaim: "Why, you couldn't make your living without me!"

36

Frantz Fanon
The Wretched of the Earth

Frantz Fanon, (1925–1961) was born in Martinique, studied medicine, and be-
came a psychiatrist serving in a government hospital in Algeria (then a French
colony). His experiences led him to resign and join the revolutionary Algerian
National Liberation Front, which he served as the leading ideologist. In his last
work, The Wretched of the Earth *(1961), Fanon asserts that personal liberation*
and decolonialization cannot take place without violence, which he contended
was a preliminary step toward the politicization of the oppressed. Third-world
nationalism itself was for Fanon only a prelude to the worldwide revolution
against colonialism and racism.

LET US return to considering the single combat between native and settler. We
have seen that it takes the form of an armed and open struggle. There is no lack of
historical examples: Indo-China, Indonesia, and of course North Africa. But what
we must not lose sight of is that this struggle could have broken out anywhere, in
Guinea as well as Somaliland, and moreover today it could break out in every
place where colonialism means to stay on, in Angola, for example. The existence
of an armed struggle shows that the people are decided to trust to violent methods
only. He of whom *they* have never stopped saying that the only language he
understands is that of force, decides to give utterance by force. In fact, as always,
the settler has shown him the way he should take if he is to become free. The
argument the native chooses has been furnished by the settler, and by an ironic
turning of the tables it is the native who now affirms that the colonialist understands nothing but force. The colonial regime owes its legitimacy to force and at
no time tries to hide this aspect of things. Every statue, whether of Faidherbe or of
Lyautey, of Bugeaud or of Sergeant Blandan—all these *conquistadors* perched on
colonial soil do not cease from proclaiming one and the same thing: "We are here
by the force of bayonets . . ."[1] the sentence is easily completed. During the phase
of insurrection, each settler reasons on a basis of simple arithmetic. This logic
does not surprise the other settlers, but it is important to point out that it does not
surprise the natives either. To begin with, the affirmation of the principle: "It's
them or us" does not constitute a paradox, since colonialism, as we have seen, is
in fact the organisation of a Manichean world, a world divided up into compartments. And when in laying down precise methods the settler asks each member of
the oppressing minority to shoot down 30 or 100 or 200 natives, he sees that
nobody shows any indignation and that the whole problem is to decide whether it
can be done all at once or by stages.[2]

This chain of reasoning which presumes very arithmetically the disappearance of the colonised people does not leave the native overcome with moral indignation. He has always known that his duel with the settler would take place in the arena. The native loses no time in lamentations, and he hardly ever seeks for justice in the colonial framework. The fact is that if the settler's logic leaves the native unshaken, it is because the latter has practically stated the problem of his liberation in identical terms: "We must form ourselves into groups of two hundred or five hundred, and each group must deal with a settler." It is in this manner of thinking that each of the protagonists begins the struggle.

For the native, this violence represents the absolute line of action. The militant is also a man who works. The questions that the organisation asks the militant bear the mark of this way of looking at things: "Where have you worked? With whom? What have you accomplished?" The group requires that each individual perform an irrevocable action. In Algeria, for example, where almost all the men who called on the people to join in the national struggle were condemned to death or searched for by the French police, confidence was proportional to the hopelessness of each case. You could be sure of a new recruit when he could no longer go back into the colonial system. This mechanism, it seems, had existed in Kenya among the Mau-Mau, who required that each member of the group should strike a blow at the victim. Each one was thus personally responsible for the death of that victim. To work means to work for the death of the settler. This assumed responsibility for violence allows both strayed and outlawed members of the group to come back again and to find their place once more, to become integrated. Violence is thus seen as comparable to a royal pardon. The colonised man finds his freedom in and through violence. This rule of conduct enlightens the agent because it indicates to him the means and the end. The poetry of Césaire takes on in this precise aspect of violence a prophetic significance. We may recall one of the most decisive pages of his tragedy where the Rebel (indeed!) explains his conduct:

THE REBEL *(harshly)*

My name—an offense; my Christian name—humiliation;
my status—a rebel; my age—the stone age.

THE MOTHER

My race—the human race. My religion—brotherhood.

THE REBEL

My race: that of the fallen. My religion . . . but it's not you that will show it to me with your disarmament . . .

'tis I myself, with my rebellion and my poor fists clenched and my woolly head . . .

(Very calm): I remember one November day; it was hardly six months ago . . . The master came into the cabin in a cloud of smoke like an April moon. He was flexing his short muscular arms—he was a very good master—and he was rubbing his little dimpled face with his fat fingers. His blue eyes were smiling and he couldn't get the honeyed words out of his mouth quick enough. "The kid will be a decent fellow," he said looking at me, and he said other pleasant things too, the master—that you had to start very early, that twenty years was not too much to make a good Christian and a good slave, a steady, devoted boy, a good commander's chain-gang captain, sharp-eyed and strong-armed. And all that man saw of my son's cradle was that it was the cradle of a chain-gang captain.

We crept in knife in hand . . .

THE MOTHER

Alas, you'll die for it.

THE REBEL

Killed . . . I killed him with my own hands . . .

Yes, 'twas a fruitful death, a copious death . . .

It was night. We crept among the sugar canes.

The knives sang to the stars, but we did not heed the stars.

The sugar canes scarred our faces with streams of green blades.

THE MOTHER

And I had dreamed of a son to close his mother's eyes.

THE REBEL

But I chose to open my son's eyes upon another sun.

THE MOTHER

O my son, son of evil and unlucky death—

THE REBEL

Mother of living and splendid death,

THE MOTHER

Because he has hated too much.

THE REBEL

Because he has too much loved.

THE MOTHER

Spare me, I am choking in your bonds. I bleed from your wounds.

THE REBEL

And the world does not spare me . . . There is not anywhere in the world a poor creature who's been lynched or tortured in whom I am not murdered and humiliated . . .

THE MOTHER

God of Heaven, deliver him!

THE REBEL

My heart, thou wilt not deliver me from all that I remember . . .

It was an evening in November . . .

And suddenly shouts lit up the silence;

We had attacked, we the slaves; we, the dung underfoot, we the animals with patient hooves,

We were running like madmen; shots rang out . . . We were striking. Blood and sweat cooled and refreshed us. We were striking where the shouts came from, and the shouts became more strident and a great clamour rose from the east: it was the outhouses burning and the flames flickered sweetly on our cheeks.

Then was the assault made on the master's house.

They were firing from the windows.

We broke in the doors.

The master's room was wide open. The master's room was brilliantly lighted, and the master was there, very calm . . . and our people stopped dead . . . it was the master . . . I went in. "It's you," he said, very calm.

It was I, even I, and I told him so, the good slave, the faithful slave, the slave of slaves, and suddenly his eyes were like two cockroaches, frightened in the rainy season . . . I struck, and the blood spurted; that is the only baptism that I remember today.[3]

It is understandable that in this atmosphere, daily life becomes quite simply impossible. You can no longer be a *fellah*, a pimp or an alcoholic as before. The violence of the colonial regime and the counter-violence of the native balance each other and respond to each other in an extraordinary reciprocal homogeneity. This reign of violence will be the more terrible in proportion to the size of the implantation from the mother country. The development of violence among the colonised people will be proportionate to the violence exercised by the threatened colonial regime. In the first phase of this insurrectional period, the home governments are the slaves of the settlers, and these settlers seek to intimidate the natives and their home governments at one and the same time. They use the same methods against both of them. The assassination of the Mayor of Evian, in its method and motivation, is identifiable with the assassination of Ali Boumendjel. For the settlers, the alternative is not between *Algérie algérienne* and *Algéire française* but between an independent Algeria and a colonial Algeria, and anything else is mere talk or attempts at treason. The settler's logic is implacable and one is only staggered by the counter-logic visible in the behaviour of the native insofar as one has not clearly understood beforehand the mechanisms of the settler's ideas. From the moment that the native has chosen the methods of counter-violence, police reprisals automatically call forth reprisals on the side of the nationalists. However, the results are not equivalent, for machine-gunning from aeroplanes and bombardments from the fleet go far beyond in horror and magnitude any answer the natives can make. This recurring terror de-mystifies once and for all the most estranged members of the colonised race. They find out on the spot that all the piles of speeches on the equality of human beings do not hide the commonplace fact that the seven Frenchmen killed or wounded at the Col de Sakamody kindles the indignation of all civilised consciences, whereas the sack of the douars[4] of Guergour and of the dechras of Djerah and the massacre of whole populations—which had merely called forth the Sakamody ambush as a reprisal—all this is of not the slightest importance. Terror, counter-terror, violence, counter-violence: that is what observers bitterly record when they describe the circle of hate, which is so tenacious and so evident in Algeria.

In all armed struggles, there exists what we might call the point of no return. Almost always it is marked off by a huge and all-inclusive repression which engulfs all sectors of the colonised people. This point was reached in Algeria in 1955 with the 12,000 victims of Phillippeville, and in 1956 with Lacoste's instituting of urban and rural militias.[5]

Then it became clear to everybody, including even the settlers, that "things couldn't go on as before." Yet the colonised people do not chalk up the reckoning.

They record the huge gaps made in their ranks as a sort of necessary evil. Since they have decided to reply by violence, they therefore are ready to take all its consequences. They only insist in return that no reckoning should be kept, either, for the others. To the saying "All natives are the same" the colonised person replies "All settlers are the same."[6]

When the native is tortured, when his wife is killed or raped, he complains to no one. The oppressor's government can set up commissions of inquiry and of information daily if it wants to; in the eyes of the native, these commissions do not exist. The fact is that soon we shall have had seven years of crimes in Algeria and there has not yet been a single Frenchman indicted before a French court of justice for the murder of an Algerian. In Indo-China, in Madagascar or in the colonies the native has always known that he need expect nothing from the other side. The settler's work is to make even dreams of liberty impossible for the native. The native's work is to imagine all possible methods for destroying the settler. On the logical plane, the Manicheism of the settler produces a Manicheism of the native. To the theory of the "absolute evil of the native" the theory of the "absolute evil of the settler" replies.

The appearance of the settler has meant in the terms of syncretism the death of the aboriginal society, cultural lethargy, and the petrification of individuals. For the native, life can only spring up again out of the rotting corpse of the settler. This, then is the correspondence, term by term, between the two trains of reasoning.

But it so happens that for the colonised people this violence, because it constitutes their only work, invests their characters with positive and creative qualities. The practice of violence binds them together as a whole, since each individual forms a violent link in the great chain, a part of the great organism of violence which has surged upwards in reaction to the settler's violence in the beginning. The groups recognise each other and the future nation is already indivisible. The armed struggle mobilises the people; that is to say, it throws them in one way and in one direction.

The mobilisation of the masses, when it arises out of the war of liberation, introduces into each man's consciousness the ideas of a common cause, of a national destiny and of a collective history. In the same way the second phase, that of the building-up of the nation, is helped on by the existence of this cement which has been mixed with blood and anger. Thus we come to a fuller appreciation of the originality of the words used in these under-developed countries. During the colonial period the people are called upon to fight against oppression; after national liberation, they are called upon to fight against poverty, illiteracy and under-development. The struggle, they say, goes on. The people realise that life is an unending contest.

We have said that the native's violence unifies the people. By its very structure, colonialism is separatist and regionalist. Colonialism does not simply state the existence of tribes; it also re-inforces it and separates them. The colonial system encourages chieftaincies and keeps alive the old Marabout confraternities. Violence is in action all-inclusive and national. It follows that it is closely involved in the liquidation of regionalism and of tribalism. Thus the national parties show no pity at all towards the caids and the customary chiefs. Their destruction is the preliminary to the unification of the people.

At the level of individuals, violence is a cleansing force. It frees the native from his inferiority complex and from his despair and inaction; it makes him fearless and restores his self-respect. Even if the armed struggle has been symbolic and the nation is demobilised through a rapid movement of decolonisation, the people have the time to see that the liberation has been the business of each and all and that the leader has no special merit. From thence comes that type of aggressive reticence with regard to the machinery of protocol which young governments quickly show. When the people have taken violent part in the national liberation they will allow no one to set themselves up as "liberators". They show themselves to be jealous of the results of their action and take good care not to place their future, their destiny or the fate of their country in the hands of a living god. Yesterday they were completely irresponsible; today they mean to understand everything and make all decisions. Illuminated by violence, the consciousness of the people rebels against any pacification. From now on the demagogues, the opportunists and the magicians have a difficult task. The action which has thrown them into a hand-to-hand struggle confers upon the masses a voracious taste for the concrete. The attempt at mystification becomes, in the long run, practically impossible.

Notes

1. Refers to Mirabeau's famous saying: "I am here by the will of the People; I shall leave only by the force of bayonets." (Transl.)

2. It is evident that this vacuum cleaning destroys the very thing that they want to preserve. Sartre points this out when he says:

In short by the very fact of repealing them (concerning racist ideas) it is revealed that the simultaneous union of all against the natives is unrealisable. Such union only recurs from time to time and moreover it can only come into being as an active groupment in order to massacre the natives—an absurd though perpetual temptation to the settlers, which even if it was feasible would only succeed in abolishing colonisation at one blow. ("*Critique de la Raison Dialectique*," p. 346).

3. Aimé Cesaire: "*Les Armes Miraculeuses.*" (*Et les chiens se taisaient*), pp. 133 to 137. Publ. Gallimard.

4. Temporary village for the use of shepherds. (Transl.)

5. We must go back to this period in order to judge the importance of this decision on the part of the French government in Algeria. Thus we may read in "*Résistance Algérienne*," n° 4, dated 28th March 1957, the following:

In reply to the wish expressed by the General Assembly of the United Nations, the French Government has now decided to create urban militias in Algeria. "Enough blood has been spilled" was what the United Nations said; Lacoste replies "Let us form militias". "Cease fire", advised U.N.A.; Lacoste vociferates, "We must arm the civilians". Whereas the two parties face-to-face with each other were on the recommendation of the United Nations invited to contact each other with a view to coming to an agreement and finding a peaceful and democratic solution, Lacoste decrees that henceforward every European will be armed and should open fire on any person who seems to him suspect. It was then agreed (in the Assembly) that savage and iniquitous repression verging on genocide ought at all costs to be opposed by the authorities: but Lacoste replies "Let us systematise the repression and organise the Algerian man-hunt". And, symbolically, he entrusts the military with civil powers, and gives military powers to civilians. The ring is closed. In the middle, the Algerian, disarmed, famished, tracked down, jostled, struck, lynched, will soon be slaughtered as a suspect. Today, in Algeria, there is not a single Frenchman who is not authorised and even invited to use his weapons. There is not a single Frenchman, in Algeria, one month after the appeal for calm made by U.N.O., who is not permitted, and obliged to search out, investigate and pursue suspects.

One month after the vote on the final motion of the General Assembly of the United Nations, there is not one European in Algeria who is not party to the most frightful work of extermination of modern times. A democratic solution? Right, Lacoste concedes; let's begin by exterminating the Algerians, and to do that, lets arm the civilians and give them *carte blanche*. The Paris press, on the whole, has welcomed the creation of these armed groups with reserve. Fascist militias, they've been called. Yes; but on the individual level, on the plane of human rights, what is fascism if not colonialism when rooted in a traditionally colonialist country? The opinion has been advanced that they are systematically legalised and commended; but does not the body of Algeria bear for the last one hundred and thirty years wounds which gape still wider, more numerous and more deep-seated than ever? "Take care", advises Monsieur Kenne-Vignes, member of parliament for the M.R.P., "do we not by the creation of these militias risk seeing the gap widen between the two communities in Algeria?" Yes; but is not colonial status simply the organised reduction to slavery of a whole people? The Algerian revolution is precisely the affirmed contestation of that slavery and that abyss. The Algerian revolution speaks to the occupying nation and says: "Take your fangs out of the bleeding flesh of Algeria! Let the people of Algeria speak!"

The creation of militias, they say, will lighten the tasks of the Army. It will free certain units whose mission will be to protect the Moroccan and Tunisian borders. In Algeria, the Army is six hundred thousand strong. Almost all the Navy and the Air Force are based there. There is an enormous, speedy police force with a horribly good record since it has absorbed the ex-torturers from Morocco and Tunisia. The territorial units are one hundred thousand strong. The task of the Army, all the same, must be lightened. So let us create urban militias. The fact remains that the hysterical and criminal frenzy of Lacoste imposes them even on clear-sighted French people. The truth is that the creation of militias carries its contradiction even in its justification. The task of the French Army is never-ending. Consequently, when it is given as an objective the gagging of the Algerian people, the door is closed on the future forever. Above all, it is forbidden to analyse, to understand or to measure the depth and the density of the Algerian Revolution: departmental leaders, housing-estate leaders, street leaders, house leaders, leaders who control each landing . . . today, to the surface chequer-board is added an underground network.

In 48 hours two thousand volunteers were enrolled. The Europeans of Algeria responded immediately to Lacoste's call to kill. From now on, each European must check up on all surviving Algerians in his sector; and in addition he will be responsible for information, for a "quick response" to acts of terrorism, for the detection of suspects, for the liquidation of runaways and for the reinforcement of police services. Certainly, the tasks of the Army must be lightened. Today, to the surface mopping-up is added a deeper harrowing. Today, to the killing which is all in the day's work is added planified murder. "Stop the bloodshed", was the advice given by U.N.O. "The best way of doing this", replied Lacoste, "is to make sure there remains no blood to shed". The Algerian people, after having been delivered up to Massu's hordes, is put under the protection of the urban militias. By his decision to create these militias, Lacoste shows quite plainly that he will brook no interference with HIS war. It is a proof that there are no limits once the rot has set in. True, he is at the moment a prisoner of the situation; but what a consolation to drag everyone down in one's fall!

After each of these decisions, the Algerian people tense their muscles still more and fight still harder. After each of these organised, deliberately sought after assassinations, the Algerian people builds up its awareness of self, and consolidates its resistance. Yes; the tasks of the French Army are infinite: for oh, how infinite is the unity of the people of Algeria!

6. This is why there are no prisoners when the fighting first starts. It is only through educating the local leaders politically that those at the head of the movement can make the masses accept (1) that people coming from the mother-country do not always act of their own free will and are sometimes even disgusted by the war; (2) that it is of immediate advantage to the movement that its supporters should show by their actions that they respect certain international conventions; (3) that an army which takes prisoners is an army, and ceases to be considered as a group of wayside bandits; (4) that whatever the circumstances, the possession of prisoners constitutes a means of exerting pressure which must not be overlooked in order to protect our men who are in enemy hands.

37

Martin Luther King, Jr.
Letter from Birmingham Jail

Martin Luther King, Jr. (1929–1968) used the principles of nonviolent struggle and resistance of Satyagraha *(Truth Force), originated by Gandhi, to mobilize the American civil rights struggles of the 1950s and 1960s. King's first pastorate, and his emergence into national leadership, began in Montgomery, Alabama in 1955, when Mrs. Rosa Parks defied the law regulating segregated seating on public transportation. King served as president of the Southern Christian Leadership Conference, attempted to persuade presidential candidates to support civil rights legislation, and traveled widely, speaking for desegregation and southern voter registration. He participated in struggles in Albany, Georgia (1961–1962), in Birmingham, Alabama (1963), and in places too numerous to list. King received the Nobel Peace Prize in 1963. He came to recognize that affirmative action programs without enforcements were useless. On August 28, 1963, he led a March on Washington for Jobs and Freedom. Two hundred thousand people heard King announce that "The whirlwinds of revolt will continue to shake the foundations of our nation until the bright day of justice emerges." King denounced the Vietnam War in 1967, continued organizing, and increasingly focused on exposing economic injustice. In 1968, he announced the birth of the Poor People's Campaign, seeking an "Economic Bill of Rights" from Washington for all the disadvantaged, regardless of race. King was in Memphis, Tennessee, speaking to striking municipal sanitation workers, when he was assassinated by James Earl Ray.*

April 16, 1963

My Dear Fellow Clergymen:

While confined here in the Birmingham city jail, I came across your recent statement calling my present activities "unwise and untimely." Seldom do I pause to answer criticism of my work and ideas. If I sought to answer all the criticisms that cross my desk, my secretaries would have little time for anything other than such correspondence in the course of the day, and I would have no time for constructive work. But since I feel that you are men of genuine good will and that your criticisms are sincerely set forth, I want to try to answer your statement in what I hope will be patient and reasonable terms.

I think I should indicate why I am here in Birmingham, since you have been influenced by the view which argues against "outsiders coming in." I have the honor of serving as president of the Southern Christian Leadership Conference, an organization operating in every southern state, with headquarters in Atlanta, Georgia. We have some eighty-five affiliated organizations across the South, and one of them is the Alabama Christian Movement for Human Rights. Frequently we share staff, educational and financial resources with our affiliates. Several months ago the affiliate here in Birmingham asked us to be on call to engage in a nonviolent direct-action program if such were deemed necessary. We readily consented, and when the hour came we lived up to our promise. So I, along with several members of my staff, am here because I was invited here. I am here because I have organizational ties here.

But more basically, I am in Birmingham because injustice is here. Just as the prophets of the eighth century B.C. left their villages and carried their "thus saith the Lord" far beyond the boundaries of their home towns, and just as the Apostle Paul left his village of Tarsus and carried the gospel of Jesus Christ to the far corners of the Greco-Roman world, so am I compelled to carry the gospel of freedom beyond my own home town. Like Paul, I must constantly respond to the Macedonian call for aid.

Moreover, I am cognizant of the interrelatedness of all communities and states. I cannot sit idly by in Atlanta and not be concerned about what happens in Birmingham. Injustice anywhere is a threat to justice everywhere. We are caught in an inescapable network of mutuality, tied in a single garment of destiny. Whatever affects one directly, affects all indirectly. Never again can we afford to live with the narrow, provincial "outside agitator" idea. Anyone who lives inside the United States can never be considered an outsider anywhere within its bounds.

You deplore the demonstrations taking place in Birmingham. But your statement, I am sorry to say, fails to express a similar concern for the conditions that brought about the demonstrations. I am sure that none of you would want to rest content with the superficial kind of social analysis that deals merely with effects and does not grapple with underlying causes. It is unfortunate that demonstrations are taking place in Birmingham, but it is even more unfortunate that the city's white power structure left the Negro community with no alternative.

In any nonviolent campaign there are four basic steps: collection of the facts to determine whether injustices exist; negotiation; self-purification; and direct action. We have gone through all these steps in Birmingham. There can be no gainsaying the fact that racial injustice engulfs this community. Birmingham is probably the most thoroughly segregated city in the United States. Its ugly record of brutality is widely known. Negroes have experienced grossly unjust treatment in the courts. There have been more unsolved bombings of Negro homes and churches in Birmingham than in any other city in the nation. These are the hard, brutal facts of the case. On the basis of these conditions, Negro leaders sought to negotiate with the city fathers. But the latter consistently refused to engage in good-faith negotiation.

Then, last September, came the opportunity to talk with leaders of Birmingham's economic community. In the course of the negotiations, certain promises were made by the merchants—for example, to remove the stores' humiliating racial signs. On the basis of these promises, the Reverend Fred Shuttlesworth and the leaders of the Alabama Christian Movement for Human Rights agreed to a moratorium on all demonstrations. As the weeks and months went by, we realized that we were the victims of a broken promise. A few signs, briefly removed, returned; the others remained.

As in so many past experiences, our hopes had been blasted, and the shadow of deep disappointment settled upon us. We had no alternative except to prepare for direct action, whereby we would present our very bodies as a means of laying our case before the conscience of the local and the national community. Mindful of the difficulties involved, we decided to undertake a process of self-purification. We began a series of workshops on nonviolence, and we repeatedly asked ourselves: "Are you able to accept blows without retaliating?" "Are you able to endure the ordeal of jail?" We decided to schedule our direct-action program for the Easter season, realizing that except for Christmas, this is the main shopping period of the year. Knowing that a strong economic-withdrawal program would be the by-product of direct action, we felt that this would be the best time to bring pressure to bear on the merchants for the needed change.

Then it occurred to us that Birmingham's mayoralty election was coming up in March, and we speedily decided to postpone action until after election day. When we discovered that the Commissioner of Public Safety, Eugene "Bull" Connor, had piled up enough votes to be in the run-off, we decided again to postpone action until the day after the run-off so that the demonstrations could not be used to cloud the issues. Like many others, we waited to see Mr. Connor defeated, and to this end we endured postponement after postponement. Having aided in this community need, we felt that our direct-action program could be delayed no longer.

You may well ask: "Why direct action? Why sit-ins, marches and so forth? Isn't negotiation a better path?" You are quite right in calling for negotiation. Indeed, this is the very purpose of direct action. Nonviolent direct action seeks to create such a crisis and foster such a tension that a community which has constantly refused to negotiate is forced to confront the issue. It seeks so to dramatize the issue that it can no longer be ignored. My citing the creation of tension as part of the work of the nonviolent-resister may sound rather shocking. But I must confess that I am not afraid of the word "tension." I have earnestly opposed violent tension, but there is a type of constructive, nonviolent tension which is necessary for growth. Just as Socrates felt that it was necessary to create a tension in the mind so that individuals could rise from the bondage of myths and half-truths to the unfettered realm of creative analysis and objective appraisal, so must we see the need for nonviolent gadflies to create the kind of tension in society that will help men rise from the dark depths of prejudice and racism to the majestic heights of understanding and brotherhood.

The purpose of our direct-action program is to create a situation so crisis-packed that it will inevitably open the door to negotiation. I therefore concur with you in your call for negotiation. Too long has our beloved Southland been bogged down in a tragic effort to live in monologue rather than dialogue.

One of the basic points in your statement is that the action that I and my associates have taken in Birmingham is untimely. Some have asked: "Why didn't you give the new city administration time to act?" The only answer that I can give to this query is that the new Birmingham administration must be prodded about as much as the outgoing one, before it will act. We are sadly mistaken if we feel that the election of Albert Boutwell as mayor will bring the millennium to Birmingham. While Mr. Boutwell is a much more gentle person than Mr. Connor, they are both segregationists, dedicated to maintenance of the status quo. I have hope that Mr. Boutwell will be reasonable enough to see the futility of massive resistance to desegregation. But he will not see this without pressure from devotees of civil rights. My friends, I must say to you that we have not made a single gain in civil rights without determined legal and nonviolent pressure. Lamentably, it is an historical fact that privileged groups seldom give up their privileges voluntarily. Individuals may see the moral light and voluntarily give up their unjust posture; but, as Reinhold Niebuhr has reminded us, groups tend to be more immoral than individuals.

We know through painful experience that freedom is never voluntarily given by the oppressor; it must be demanded by the oppressed. Frankly, I have yet to engage in a direct-action campaign that was "well timed" in the view of those who have not suffered unduly from the disease of segregation. For years now I have heard the word "Wait!" It rings in the ear of every Negro with piercing familiarity. This "Wait" has almost always meant "Never." We must come to see, with one of our distinguished jurists, that "justice too long delayed is justice denied."

We have waited for more than 340 years for our constitutional and God-given rights. The nations of Asia and Africa are moving with jetlike speed toward gaining political independence, but we still creep at horse-and-buggy pace toward gaining a cup of coffee at a lunch counter. Perhaps it is easy for those who have never felt the stinging darts of segregation to say, "Wait." But when you have seen vicious mobs lynch your mothers and fathers at will and drown your sisters and brothers at whim; when you have seen hate-filled policemen curse, kick and even kill your black brothers and sisters; when you see the vast majority of your twenty million Negro brothers smothering in an airtight cage of poverty in the midst of an affluent society; when you suddenly find your tongue twisted and your speech stammering as you seek to explain to your six-year-old daughter why she can't go to the public amusement park that has just been advertised on television, and see tears welling up in her eyes when she is told that Funtown is closed to colored children, and see ominous clouds of inferiority beginning to form in her little mental sky, and see her beginning to distort her personality by developing an unconscious bitterness toward white people; when you have to concoct an answer for a five-year-old son who is asking: "Daddy, why do white people treat colored people so mean?"; when you take a cross-country drive and find it necessary to sleep night after night in the uncomfortable corners of your automobile because no motel will accept you; when you are humiliated day in and day out by nagging signs reading "white" and "colored"; when your first name becomes "nigger," your middle name becomes "boy" (however old you are) and your last name becomes "John," and your wife and mother are never given the respected title "Mrs."; when you are harried by day and haunted by night by the fact that you are a Negro, living constantly at tiptoe stance, never quite knowing what to expect next, and are plagued with inner fears and outer resentments; when you are forever fighting a degenerating sense of "nobodiness"—then you will understand why we find it difficult to wait. There comes a time when the cup of endurance runs over, and men are no longer willing to be plunged into the abyss of despair. I hope, sirs, you can understand our legitimate and unavoidable impatience.

You express a great deal of anxiety over our willingness to break laws. This is certainly a legitimate concern. Since we so diligently urge people to obey the Supreme Court's decision of 1954 outlawing segregation in the public schools, at first glance it may seem rather paradoxical for us consciously to break laws. One may well ask: "How can you advocate breaking some laws and obeying others?" The answer lies in the fact that there are two types of laws: just and unjust. I would be the first to advocate obeying just laws. One has not only a legal but a moral responsibility to obey just laws. Conversely, one has a moral responsibility to disobey unjust laws. I would agree with St. Augustine that "an unjust law is no law at all."

Now, what is the difference between the two? How does one determine whether a law is just or unjust? A just law is a man-made code that squares with the moral law or the law of God. An unjust law is a code that is out of harmony with the moral law. To put it in the terms of St. Thomas Aquinas: An unjust law is a human law that is not rooted in eternal law and natural law. Any law that uplifts human personality is just. Any law that degrades human personality is unjust. All segregation statutes are unjust because segregation distorts the soul and damages the personality. It gives the segregator a false sense of superiority and the segregated a false sense of inferiority. Segregation, to use the terminology of the Jewish philosopher Martin Buber, substitutes an "I–it" relationship for an "I–thou" relationship and ends up relegating persons to the status of things. Hence segregation is not only politically, economically and sociologically unsound, it is morally wrong and sinful. Paul Tillich has said that sin is separation. Is not segregation an existential expression of man's tragic separation, his awful estrangement, his terrible sinfulness? Thus it is that I can urge men to obey the 1954 decision of the Supreme Court, for it is morally right; and I can urge them to disobey segregation ordinances, for they are morally wrong.

Let us consider a more concrete example of just and unjust laws. An unjust law is a code that a numerical or power majority group compels a minority group to obey but does not make binding on itself. This is *difference* made legal. By the same token, a just law is a code that a majority compels a minority to follow and that it is willing to follow itself. This is *sameness* made legal.

Let me give another explanation. A law is unjust if it is inflicted on a minority that, as a result of being denied the right to vote, had no part in enacting or devising the law. Who can say that the legislature of Alabama which set up that state's segregation laws was democratically elected? Throughout Alabama all sorts of devious methods are used to prevent Negroes from becoming registered voters, and there are some counties in which, even though Negroes constitute a majority of the population, not a single Negro is registered. Can any law enacted under such circumstances be considered democratically structured?

Sometimes a law is just on its face and unjust in its application. For instance, I have been arrested on a charge of parading without a permit. Now, there is nothing wrong in having an ordinance which requires a permit for a parade. But such an ordinance becomes unjust when it is used to maintain segregation and to deny citizens the First-Amendment privilege of peaceful assembly and protest.

I hope you are able to see the distinction I am trying to point out. In no sense do I advocate evading or defying the law, as would the rabid segregationist. That would lead to anarchy. One who breaks an unjust law must do so openly, lovingly, and with a willingness to accept the penalty. I submit that an individual who breaks a law that conscience tells him is unjust, and who willingly accepts the penalty of imprisonment in order to arouse the conscience of the community over its injustice, is in reality expressing the highest respect for law.

Of course, there is nothing new about this kind of civil disobedience. It was evidenced sublimely in the refusal of Shadrach, Meshach and Abednego to obey the laws of Nebuchadnezzar, on the ground that a higher moral law was at stake. It was practiced superbly by the early Christians, who were willing to face hungry lions and the excruciating pain of chopping blocks rather than submit to certain unjust laws of the Roman Empire. To a degree, academic freedom is a reality today because Socrates practiced civil disobedience. In our own nation, the Boston Tea Party represented a massive act of civil disobedience.

We should never forget that everything Adolf Hitler did in Germany was "legal" and everything the Hungarian freedom fighters did in Hungary was "illegal." It was "illegal" to aid and comfort a Jew in Hitler's Germany. Even so, I am sure that, had I lived in Germany at the time, I would have aided and comforted my Jewish brothers. If today I lived in a Communist country where certain principles dear to the Christian faith are suppressed, I would openly advocate disobeying that country's antireligious laws.

I must make two honest confessions to you, my Christian and Jewish brothers. First, I must confess that over the past few years I have been gravely disappointed with the white moderate. I have almost reached the regrettable conclusion that the Negro's great stumbling block in his stride toward freedom is not the White Citizen's Counciler or the Ku Klux Klanner, but the white moderate, who is more devoted to "order" than to justice; who prefers a negative peace which is the absence of tension to a positive peace which is the presence of justice; who constantly says: "I agree with you in the goal you seek, but I cannot agree with your methods of direct action"; who paternalistically believes he can set the timetable for another man's freedom; who lives by a mythical concept of time and who constantly advises the Negro to wait for a "more convenient season." Shallow understanding from people of good will is more frustrating than absolute misunderstanding from people of ill will. Lukewarm acceptance is much more bewildering than outright rejection.

I had hoped that the white moderate would understand that law and order exist for the purpose of establishing justice and that when they fail in this purpose they become the dangerously structured dams that block the flow of social progress. I had hoped that the white moderate would understand that the present tension in the South is a necessary phase of the transition from an obnoxious negative peace, in which the Negro passively accepted his unjust plight, to a substantive and positive peace, in which all men will respect the dignity and worth of human personality. Actually, we who engage in nonviolent direct action are not the creators of tension. We merely bring to the surface the hidden tension that is already alive. We bring it out in the open, where it can be seen and dealt with. Like a boil that can never be cured so long as it is covered up but must be opened will all its ugliness to the natural medicines of air and light, injustice must be exposed, with all the tension its exposure creates, to the light of human conscience and the air of national opinion before it can be cured.

In your statement you assert that our actions, even though peaceful, must be condemned because they precipitate violence. But is this a logical assertion? Isn't this like condemning a robbed man because his possession of money precipitated the evil act of robbery? Isn't this like condemning Socrates because his unswerving commitment to truth and his philosophical inquiries precipitated the act by the misguided populace in which they made him drink hemlock? Isn't this like condemning Jesus because his unique God-consciousness and never-ceasing devotion to God's will precipitated the evil act of crucifixion? We must come to see that, as the federal courts have consistently affirmed, it is wrong to urge an individual to cease his efforts to gain his basic constitutional rights because the quest may precipitate violence. Society must protect the robbed and punish the robber.

I had also hoped that the white moderate would reject the myth concerning time in relation to the struggle for freedom. I have just received a letter from a white brother in Texas. He writes: "All Christians know that the colored people will receive equal rights eventually, but it is possible that you are in too great a religious hurry. It has taken Christianity almost two thousand years to accomplish what it has. The teachings of Christ take time to come to earth." Such an attitude stems from a tragic misconception of time, from the strangely irrational notion that there is something in the very flow of time that will inevitably cure all ills. Actually, time itself is neutral; it can be used either destructively or constructively. More and more I feel that the people of ill will have used time much more effectively than have the people of good will. We will have to repent in this generation not merely for the hateful words and actions of the bad people but for the appalling silence of the good people. Human progress never rolls in on wheels of inevitability; it comes through the tireless efforts of men willing to be co-workers with God, and without this hard work, time itself becomes an ally of the forces of social stagnation. We must use time creatively, in the knowledge that the time is always ripe to do right. Now is the time to make real the promise of democracy and transform our pending national elegy into a creative psalm of brotherhood. Now is the time to lift our national policy from the quicksand of racial injustice to the solid rock of human dignity.

You speak of our activity in Birmingham as extreme. At first I was rather disappointed that fellow clergymen would see my nonviolent efforts as those of an extremist. I began thinking about the fact that I stand in the middle of two opposing forces in the Negro community. One is a force of complacency, made up in part of Negroes who, as a result of long years of oppression, are so drained of self-respect and a sense of "somebodiness" that they have adjusted to segregation; and in part of a few middle-class Negroes who, because of a degree of academic and economic security and because in some ways they profit by segregation, have become insensitive to the problems of the masses. The other force is one of bitterness and hatred, and it comes perilously close to advocating violence. It is expressed in the various black nationalist groups that are springing up across the nation, the largest and best-known being Elijah Muhammad's Muslim movement. Nourished by the Negro's frustration over the continued existence of racial discrimination, this movement is made up of people who have lost faith in America, who have absolutely repudiated Christianity, and who have concluded that the white man is an incorrigible "devil."

I have tried to stand between these two forces, saying that we need emulate neither the "do-nothingism" of the complacent nor the hatred and despair of the black nationalist. For there is the more excellent way of love and nonviolent protest. I am grateful to God that, through the influence of the Negro church, the way of nonviolence became an integral part of our struggle.

If this philosophy had not emerged, by now many streets of the South would, I am convinced, be flowing with blood. And I am further convinced that if our white brothers dismiss as "rabble-rousers" and "outside agitators" those of us who employ nonviolent direct action, and if they refuse to support our nonviolent efforts, millions of Negroes will, out of frustration and despair, seek solace and security in black-nationalist ideologies—a development that would inevitably lead to a frightening racial nightmare.

Oppressed people cannot remain oppressed forever. The yearning for freedom eventually manifests itself, and that is what has happened to the American Negro. Something within has reminded him of his birthright of freedom, and something without has reminded him that it can be gained. Consciously or unconsciously, he has been caught up by the *Zeitgeist*, and with his black brothers of Africa and his brown and yellow brothers of Asia, South America and the Caribbean, the United States Negro is moving with a sense of great urgency toward the promised land of racial justice. If one recognizes this vital urge that has engulfed the Negro community, one should readily understand why public demonstrations are taking place. The Negro has many pent-up resentments and latent frustrations, and he must release them. So let him march; let him make prayer pilgrimages to the city hall; let him go on freedom rides—and try to understand why he must do so. If his repressed emotions are not released in nonviolent ways, they will seek expression through violence; this is not a threat but a fact of history. So I have not said to my people: "Get rid of your discontent." Rather, I have tried to say that this normal and healthy discontent can be channeled into the creative outlet of nonviolent direct action. And now this approach is being termed extremist.

But though I was initially disappointed at being categorized as an extremist, as I continued to think about the matter I gradually gained a measure of satisfaction from the label. Was not Jesus an extremist for love: "Love your enemies, bless them that curse you, do good to them that hate you, and pray for them which despitefully use you, and persecute you." Was not Amos an extremist for justice:

"Let justice roll down like waters and righteousness like an ever-flowing stream." Was not Paul an extremist for the Christian gospel: "I bear in my body the marks of the Lord Jesus." Was not Martin Luther an extremist: "Here I stand; I cannot do otherwise, so help me God." And John Bunyan: "I will stay in jail to the end of my days before I make a butchery of my conscience." And Abraham Lincoln: "This nation cannot survive half slave and half free." And Thomas Jefferson: "We hold these truths to be self-evident, that all men are created equal . . ." So the question is not whether we will be extremists, but what kind of extremists we will be. Will we be extremists for hate or for love? Will we be extremists for the preservation of injustice or for the extension of justice? In that dramatic scene on Calvary's hill three men were crucified. We must never forget that all three were crucified for the same crime—the crime of extremism. Two were extremists for immorality, and thus fell below their environment. The other, Jesus Christ, was an extremist for love, truth and goodness, and thereby rose above his environment. Perhaps the South, the nation and the world are in dire need of creative extremists.

I had hoped that the white moderate would see this need. Perhaps I was too optimistic; perhaps I expected too much. I suppose I should have realized that few members of the oppressor race can understand the deep groans and passionate yearnings of the oppressed race, and still fewer have the vision to see that injustice must be rooted out by strong, persistent and determined action. I am thankful, however, that some of our white brothers in the South have grasped the meaning of this social revolution and committed themselves to it. They are still all too few in quantity, but they are big in quality. Some—such as Ralph McGill, Lillian Smith, Harry Golden, James McBride Dabbs, Ann Braden and Sarah Patton Boyle—have written about our struggle in eloquent and prophetic terms. Others have marched with us down nameless streets of the South. They have languished in filthy, roach-infested jails, suffering the abuse and brutality of policemen who view them as "dirty nigger-lovers." Unlike so many of their moderate brothers and sisters, they have recognized the urgency of the moment and sensed the need for powerful "action" antidotes to combat the disease of segregation.

Let me take note of my other major disappointment. I have been so greatly disappointed with the white church and its leadership. Of course, there are some notable exceptions. I am not unmindful of the fact that each of you has taken some significant stands on this issue. I commend you, Reverend Stallings, for your Christian stand on this past Sunday, in welcoming Negroes to your worship service on a nonsegregated basis. I commend the Catholic leaders of this state for integrating Spring Hill College several years ago.

But despite these notable exceptions, I must honestly reiterate that I have been disappointed with the church. I do not say this as one of those negative critics who can always find something wrong with the church. I say this as a minister of the gospel, who loves the church; who was nurtured in its bosom; who has been sustained by its spiritual blessings and who will remain true to it as long as the cord of life shall lengthen.

When I was suddenly catapulted into the leadership of the bus protest in Montgomery, Alabama, a few years ago, I felt we would be supported by the white church. I felt that the white ministers, priests and rabbis of the South would be among our strongest allies. Instead, some have been outright opponents, refusing to understand the freedom movement and misrepresenting its leaders; all too many others have been more cautious than courageous and have remained silent behind the anesthetizing security of stained-glass windows.

In spite of my shattered dreams, I came to Birmingham with the hope that the white religious leadership of this community would see the justice of our cause and, with deep moral concern, would serve as the channel through which our just grievances could reach the power structure. I had hoped that each of you would understand. But again I have been disappointed.

I have heard numerous southern religious leaders admonish their worshipers to comply with a desegregation decision because it is the law, but I have longed to hear white ministers declare: "Follow this decree because integration is morally right and because the Negro is your brother." In the midst of blatant injustices inflicted upon the Negro, I have watched white churchmen stand on the sideline and mouth pious irrelevancies and sanctimonious trivialities. In the midst of a mighty struggle to rid our nation of racial and economic injustice, I have heard many ministers say: "Those are social issues, with which the gospel has no real concern." And I have watched many churches commit themselves to a completely other-worldly religion which makes a strange, un-Biblical distinction between body and soul, between the sacred and the secular.

I have traveled the length and breadth of Alabama, Mississippi and all the other southern states. On sweltering summer days and crisp autumn mornings I have looked at the South's beautiful churches with their lofty spires pointing heaven-ward. I have beheld the impressive outlines of her massive religious-education buildings. Over and over I have found myself asking: "What kind of people wor-ship here? Who is their God? Where were their voices when the lips of Governor Barnett dripped with words of interposition and nullification? Where were they when Governor Wallace gave a clarion call for defiance and hatred? Where were their voices of support when bruised and weary Negro men and women decided to rise from the dark dungeons of complacency to the bright hills of creative pro-test?"

Yes, these questions are still in my mind. In deep disappointment I have wept over the laxity of the church. But be assured that my tears have been tears of love. There can be no deep disappointment where there is not deep love. Yes, I love the church. How could I do otherwise? I am in the rather unique position of being the son, the grandson and the great-grandson of preachers. Yes, I see the church as the body of Christ. But, oh! How we have blemished and scarred that body through social neglect and through fear of being nonconformists.

There was a time when the church was very powerful—in the time when the early Christians rejoiced at being deemed worthy to suffer for what they believed. In those days the church was not merely a thermometer that recorded the ideas and principles of popular opinion; it was a thermostat that transformed the mores of society. Whenever the early Christians entered a town, the people in power be-came disturbed and immediately sought to convict the Christians for being "disturbers of the peace" and "outside agitators." But the Christians pressed on, in the conviction that they were "a colony of heaven," called to obey God rather than man. Small in number, they were big in commitment. They were too God-intoxicated to be "astronomically intimidated." By their effort and example they brought an end to such ancient evils as infanticide and gladiatorial contests.

Things are different now. So often the contemporary church is a weak, ineffectual voice with an uncertain sound. So often it is an archdefender of the status quo. Far from being disturbed by the presence of the church, the power structure of the average community is consoled by the church's silent—and often even vocal—sanction of things as they are.

But the judgment of God is upon the church as never before. If today's church does not recapture the sacrificial spirit of the early church, it will lose its authenticity, forfeit the loyalty of millions, and be dismissed as an irrelevant social club with no meaning for the twentieth century. Every day I meet young people whose disappointment with the church has turned into outright disgust.

Perhaps I have once again been too optimistic. Is organized religion too inextricably bound to the status quo to save our nation and the world? Perhaps I must turn my faith to the inner spiritual church, the church within the church, as the true *ekklesia* and the hope of the world. But again I am thankful to God that some noble souls from the ranks of organized religion have broken loose from the paralyzing chains of conformity and joined us as active partners in the struggle for freedom. They have left their secure congregations and walked the streets of Albany, Georgia, with us. They have gone down the highways of the South on tortuous rides for freedom. Yes, they have gone to jail with us. Some have been dismissed from their churches, have lost the support of their bishops and fellow ministers. But they have acted in the faith that right defeated is stronger than evil triumphant. Their witness has been the spiritual salt that has preserved the true meaning of the gospel in these troubled times. They have carved a tunnel of hope through the dark mountain of disappointment.

I hope the church as a whole will meet the challenge of this decisive hour. But even if the church does not come to the aid of justice, I have no despair about the future. I have no fear about the outcome of our struggle in Birmingham, even if our motives are at present misunderstood. We will reach the goal of freedom in Birmingham and all over the nation, because the goal of America is freedom. Abused and scorned though we may be, our destiny is tied up with America's destiny. Before the pilgrims landed at Plymouth, we were here. Before the pen of Jefferson etched the majestic words of the Declaration of Independence across the pages of history, we were here. For more than two centuries our forebears labored in this country without wages; they made cotton king; they built the homes of their masters while suffering gross injustice and shameful humiliation—and yet out of a bottomless vitality they continued to thrive and develop. If the inexpressible cruelties of slavery could not stop us, the opposition we now face will surely fail. We will win our freedom because the sacred heritage of our nation and the eternal will of God are embodied in our echoing demands.

Before closing I feel impelled to mention one other point in your statement that has troubled me profoundly. You warmly commended the Birmingham police force for keeping "order" and "preventing violence." I doubt that you would have so warmly commended the police force if you had seen its dogs sinking their teeth into unarmed, nonviolent Negroes. I doubt that you would so quickly commend the policemen if you were to observe their ugly and inhumane treatment of Negroes here in the city jail; if you were to watch them push and curse old Negro women and young Negro girls; if you were to see them slap and kick old Negro men and young boys; if you were to observe them, as they did on two occasions, refuse to give us food because we wanted to sing our grace together. I cannot join you in your praise of the Birmingham police department.

It is true that the police have exercised a degree of discipline in handling the demonstrators. In this sense they have conducted themselves rather "nonviolently" in public. But for what purpose? To preserve the evil system of segregation. Over the past few years I have consistently preached that nonviolence demands that the means we use must be as pure as the ends we seek. I have tried to make clear that it is wrong to use immoral means to attain moral ends. But now I must affirm that it is just as wrong, or perhaps even more so, to use moral means to preserve immoral ends. Perhaps Mr. Connor and his policemen have been rather nonviolent in public, as was Chief Pritchett in Albany, Georgia, but they have used the moral means of nonviolence to maintain the immoral end of racial injustice. As T. S. Eliot has said: "The last temptation is the greatest treason: To do the right deed for the wrong reason."

I wish you had commended the Negro sit-inners and demonstrators of Birmingham for their sublime courage, their willingness to suffer and their amazing discipline in the midst of great provocation. One day the South will recognize its real heroes. They will be the James Merediths, with the noble sense of purpose that enables them to face jeering and hostile mobs, and with the agonizing loneliness that characterizes the life of the pioneer. They will be old, oppressed, battered Negro women, symbolized in a seventy-two-year-old woman in Montgomery, Alabama, who rose up with a sense of dignity and with her people decided not to ride segregated buses, and who responded with ungrammatical profundity to one who inquired about her weariness: "My feets is tired, but my soul is at rest." They will be the young high school and college students, the young ministers of the gospel and a host of their elders, courageously and nonviolently sitting in at lunch counters and willingly going to jail for conscience' sake. One day the South will know that when these disinherited children of God sat down at lunch counters, they were in reality standing up for what is best in the American dream and for the most sacred values in our Judeo-Christian heritage, thereby bringing our nation back to those great wells of democracy which were dug deep by the founding fathers in their formulation of the Constitution and the Declaration of Independence.

Never before have I written so long a letter. I'm afraid it is much too long to take your precious time. I can assure you that it would have been much shorter if I had been writing from a comfortable desk, but what else can one do when he is alone in a narrow jail cell, other than write long letters, think long thoughts and pray long prayers?

If I have said anything in this letter that overstates the truth and indicates an unreasonable impatience, I beg you to forgive me. If I have said anything that understates the truth and indicates my having a patience that allows me to settle for anything less than brotherhood, I beg God to forgive me.

I hope this letter finds you strong in the faith. I also hope that circumstances will soon make it possible for me to meet each of you, not as an integrationist or a civil-rights leader but as a fellow clergyman and a Christian brother. Let us all hope that the dark clouds of racial prejudice will soon pass away and the deep fog of misunderstanding will be lifted from our fear-drenched communities, and in some not too distant tomorrow the radiant stars of love and brotherhood will shine over our great nation with all their scintillating beauty.

Yours for the cause of Peace and Brotherhood,

MARTIN LUTHER KING, JR.

Note:

AUTHOR'S NOTE: This response to a published statement by eight fellow clergymen from Alabama (Bishop C.C.J. Carpenter, Bishop Joseph A. Durick, Rabbi Hilton L. Grafman, Bishop Paul Hardin, Bishop Holan B. Harmon, the Reverend George M. Murray, the Reverend Edward V. Ramage and the Reverend Earl Stallings) was composed under somewhat constricting circumstances. Begun on the margins of the newspaper in which the statement appeared while I was in jail, the letter was continued on scraps of writing paper supplied by a friendly Negro trusty, and concluded on a pad my attorneys were eventually permitted to leave me. Although the text remains in substance unaltered, I have indulged in the author's prerogative of polishing it for publication.

38

Malcolm X
The Ballot or the Bullet

Malcolm X (1925–1965) was a leading figure within the African American community at the time of his assassination in February 1965 in New York. A militant advocate of black nationalism, he had been born Malcolm Little in Omaha, Nebraska and became a member of the Nation of Islam, a religious sect, while in prison for burglary. After his release, he became a leading figure in that organization, which was led by Elijah Muhammad, and preached a racialist doctrine of black separatism. After trips to Africa and the Mideast, Malcolm X moved away from Elijah Muhammad's racial separatism, all while remaining a black nationalist and a Muslim. His murder came not long after he broke publicly with the Nation of Islam. His ideas and evolution was described in The Autobiography of Malcolm X *(1965). The following is a selection from "The Ballot or the Bullet," a speech Malcolm X gave at the Cory Methodist Church in Cleveland in April 1964.*

THE QUESTION tonight, as I understand it, is "The Negro Revolt, and Where Do We Go From Here?" or "What Next?" In my little humble way of understanding it, it points toward either the ballot or the bullet.

Before we try and explain what is meant by the ballot or the bullet, I would like to clarify something concerning myself. I'm still a Muslim, my religion is still Islam. That's my personal belief. Just as Adam Clayton Powell is a Christian minister who heads the Abyssinian Baptist Church in New York, but at the same time takes part in the political struggles to try and bring about rights to the black people in this country; and Dr. Martin Luther King is a Christian minister down in Atlanta, Georgia, who heads another organization fighting for the civil rights of black people in this country. . . . I myself am a minister, not a Christian minister, but a Muslim minister; and I believe in action on all fronts by whatever means necessary.

Although I'm still a Muslim, I'm not here tonight to discuss my religion. I'm not here to try and change your religion. I'm not here to argue or discuss anything that we differ about, because it's time for us to submerge our differences and realize that it is best for us to first see that we have the same problem, a common problem—a problem that will make you catch hell whether you're a Baptist, or a Methodist, or a Muslim, or a nationalist. Whether you're educated or illiterate, whether you live on the boulevard or in the alley, you're going to catch hell just like I am. We're all in the same boat and we all are going to catch the same hell from the same man. He just happens to be a white man. All of us have suffered here, in this country, political oppression at the hands of the white man, economic exploitation at the hands of the white man, and social degradation at the hands of the white man.

Now in speaking like this, it doesn't mean that we're anti-white, but it does mean we're anti-exploitation, we're anti-degradation, we're anti-oppression. And if the white man doesn't want us to be anti-him, let him stop oppressing and exploiting and degrading us. Whether we are Christians or Muslims or nationalists or agnostics or atheists, we must first learn to forget our differences. If we have differences, let us differ in the closet; when we come out in front, let us not have anything to argue about until we get finished arguing with the man. . . .

If we don't do something real soon, I think you'll have to agree that we're going to be forced either to use the ballot or the bullet. It's one or the other in 1964. It isn't that time is running out—time has run out! 1964 threatens to be the most explosive year America has ever witnessed. The most explosive year. Why? It's also a political year. It's the year when all the white politicians will be back in the so-called Negro community jiving you and me for some votes. The year when all of the white political crooks will be right back in your and my community with their false promises, building up our hopes for a letdown, with their trickery and their treachery, with their false promises which they don't intend to keep. As they nourish these dissatisfactions, it can only lead to one thing, an explosion; and now we have the type of black man on the scene in America today. . . .

Don't let anybody tell you anything about the odds are against you. If they draft you, they send you to Korea and make you face 800 million Chinese. If you can be brave over there, you can be brave right here. These odds aren't as great as those odds. And if you fight here, you will at least know what you're fighting for.

I'm not a politician, not even a student of politics; in fact, I'm not a student of much of anything. I'm not a Democrat, I'm not a Republican, and I don't even consider myself an American. If you and I were Americans, there'd be no problem. Those Hunkies that just got off the boat, they're already Americans; Polacks are already Americans; the Italian refugees are already Americans. Everything that came out of Europe, every blue-eyed thing, is already an American. And as long as you and I have been over here, we aren't Americans yet.

Well, I am one who doesn't believe in deluding myself. I'm not going to sit at your table and watch you eat, with nothing on my plate, and call myself a diner. Sitting at the table doesn't make you a diner, unless you eat some of what's on that plate. Being here in America doesn't make you an American. Being born here in America doesn't make you an American. . . .

I'm one of the 22 million black people who are the victims of Americanism. One of the 22 million black people who are the victims of democracy, nothing but disguised hypocrisy. So, I'm not standing here speaking to you as an American, or a patriot, or a flag-saluter, or a flag-waver—no, not I. I'm speaking as a victim of this American system. And I see America through the eyes of the victim. I don't see any American dream; I see an American nightmare.

These 22 million victims are waking up. Their eyes are coming open. They're beginning to see what they used to only look at. They're becoming politically mature. They are realizing that there are now political trends from coast to coast. As they see these new political trends, it's possible for them to see that every time there's an election the races are so close that they have to have a recount. They had to recount in Massachusetts to see who was going to be governor, it was so close. . . .

And the same with Kennedy and Nixon when they ran for president. It was so close they had to count all over again. Well, what does this mean? It means that when white people are evenly divided, and black people have a bloc of votes of their own, it is left up to them to determine who's going to sit in the White House and who's going to be in the dog house.

It was the black man's vote that put the present administration in Washington, D.C. Your vote, your dumb vote, your ignorant vote, your wasted vote put in an administration in Washington, D.C., that has seen fit to pass every kind of legislation imaginable, saving you until last, then filibustering on top of that. And your and my leaders have the audacity to run around clapping their hands and talk about how much progress we're making. And what a good president we have. If he wasn't good in Texas, he sure can't be good in Washington, D.C. Because Texas is a lynch state. It is in the same breath as Mississippi, no different; only they lynch you in Texas with a Texas accent and lynch you in Mississippi with a Mississippi accent. . . .

In this present administration they have in the House of Representatives 257 Democrats to only 177 Republicans. They control two-thirds of the House vote. Why can't they pass something that will help you and me? In the Senate, there are 67 senators who are of the Democratic Party. Only 33 of them are Republicans. Why, the Democrats have got the government sewed up, and you're the one who sewed it up for them. And what have they given you for it? Four years in office, and just now getting around to some civil-rights legislation. Just now, after everything else is gone, out of the way, they're going to sit down now and play with you all summer long—the same old giant con game that they call filibuster. All those are in cahoots together. Don't you ever think they're not in cahoots together, for the man that is heading the civil-rights filibuster is a man from Georgia named Richard Russell. When Johnson became president, the first man he asked for when he got back to Washington, D.C., was "Dicky"—that's how tight they are. That's his boy, that's his pal, that's his buddy. But they're playing that old con game. One of them makes believe he's for you, and he's got it fixed where the other one is so tight against you, he never has to keep his promise.

So it's time in 1964 to wake up. And when you see them coming up with that kind of conspiracy, let them know your eyes are open. And let them know you got something else that's wide open too. It's got to be the ballot or the bullet. The ballot or the bullet. If you're afraid to use an expression like that, you should get on out of the country, you should get back in the cotton patch, you should get back in the alley. They get all the Negro vote, and after they get it, the Negro gets nothing in return. All they did when they got to Washington was give a few big Negroes big jobs. . . .

I'm not trying to knock out the Democrats for the Republicans, we'll get to them in a minute. But it is true—you put the Democrats first and the Democrats put you last.

Look at it the way it is. What alibis do they use, since they control Congress and the Senate? What alibi do they use when you and I ask, "Well, when are you going to keep your promise?" They blame the Dixiecrats. What is a Dixiecrat? A Democrat. A Dixiecrat is nothing but a Democrat in disguise. The titular head of the Democrats is also the head of the Dixiecrats, because the Dixiecrats are a part of the Democratic Party. The Democrats have never kicked the Dixiecrats out of the party. The Dixiecrats bolted themselves once, but the Democrats didn't put them out. . . .

If the black man in these Southern states had his full voting rights, the key Dixiecrats in Washington, D.C., which means the key Democrats in Washington, D.C., would lose their seats. The Democratic Party itself would lose its power. It would cease to be powerful as a party. When you see the amount of power that would be lost by the Democratic Party if it were to lose the Dixiecrat wing, or branch, or element, you can see where it's against the interests of the Democrats to give voting rights to Negroes in states where the Democrats have been in complete power and authority ever since the Civil War. You just can't belong to that party without analyzing it.

I say again, I'm not anti-Democrat, I'm not anti-Republican, I'm not anti-anything. I'm just questioning their sincerity, and some of the strategy that they've been using on our people by promising them promises that they don't intend to keep. When you keep the Democrats in power, you're keeping the Dixiecrats in power. . . .

In the North, they do it a different way. They have a system that's known as gerrymandering, whatever that means. It means when Negroes become too heavily concentrated in a certain area, and begin to gain too much political power, the white man comes along and changes the district lines. You may say, "Why do you keep saying white man?" Because it's the white man who does it. I haven't ever seen any Negro changing any lines. They don't let him get near the line. It's the white man who does this. And usually, it's the white man who grins at you the most, and pats you on the back, and is supposed to be your friend. He may be friendly, but he's not your friend.

So, what I'm trying to impress upon you, in essence, is this: You and I in America are faced not with a segregationist conspiracy, we're faced with a government conspiracy. . . .

So, where do we go from here? First, we need some friends. We need some new allies. The entire civil-rights struggle needs a new interpretation, a broader interpretation. We need to look at this civil-rights thing from another angle—from the inside as well as from the outside. To those of us whose philosophy is black nationalism, the only way you can get involved in the civil-rights struggle is give it a new interpretation. That old interpretation excluded us. . . .

There's new thinking coming in. There's new strategy coming in. It'll be Molotov cocktails this month, hand grenades next month, and something else next month. It'll be ballots, or it'll be bullets. It'll be liberty, or it will be death. The only difference about this kind of death—it'll be reciprocal.

I don't mean go out and get violent; but at the same time you should never be nonviolent unless you run into some nonviolence. I'm nonviolent with those who are nonviolent with me. But when you drop that violence on me, then you've made me go insane, and I'm not responsible for what I do. And that's the way every Negro should get. Any time you know you're within the law, within your legal rights, within your moral rights, in accord with justice, then die for what you believe in. But don't die alone. Let your dying be reciprocal. This is what is meant by equality. What's good for the goose is good for the gander.

When we begin to get in this area, we need new friends, we need new allies. We need to expand the civil-rights struggle to a higher level—to the level of human rights. Whenever you are in a civil-rights struggle, whether you know it or not, you are confining yourself to the jurisdiction of Uncle Sam. No one from the outside world can speak out in your behalf as long as your struggle is a civil-rights struggle. Civil rights comes within the domestic affairs of this country. All of our African brothers and our Asian brothers and our Latin-American brothers cannot open their mouths and interfere in the domestic affairs of the United States. And as long as it's civil rights, this comes under the jurisdiction of Uncle Sam.

But the United Nations has what's known as the charter of human rights, it has a committee that deals in human rights. You may wonder why all of the atrocities that have been committed in Africa and in Hungary and in Asia and in Latin America are brought before the UN, and the Negro problem is never brought before the UN. This is part of the conspiracy. This old, tricky, blue-eyed liberal who is supposed to be your and my friend, supposed to be in our corner, supposed to be subsidizing our struggle, and supposed to be acting in the capacity of an adviser, never tells you anything about human rights. They keep you wrapped up in civil rights. And you spend so much time barking up the civil-rights tree, you don't even know there's a human-rights tree on the same floor.

When you expand the civil-rights struggle to the level of human rights, you can then take the case of the black man in this country before the nations in the UN. You can take it before the General Assembly. You can take Uncle Sam before a world court. But the only level you can do it on is the level of human rights. Civil rights keeps you under his restrictions, under his jurisdiction. Civil rights keeps you in his pocket. Civil rights means you're asking Uncle Sam to treat you right. Human rights are something you were born with. Human rights are your God-given rights. Human rights are the rights that are recognized by all nations of this earth. And any time any one violates your human rights, you can take them to the world court. Uncle Sam's hands are dripping with blood, dripping with the blood of the black man in this country. He's the earth's number-one hypocrite. He has the audacity—yes, he has—imagine him posing as the leader of the free world. The free world!—and you over here singing "We Shall Overcome." Expand the civil-rights struggle to the level of human rights, take it into the United Nations, where our African brothers can throw their weight on our side, where our Asian brothers can throw their weight on our side, where our Latin-American brothers can throw their weight on our side, and where 800 million Chinamen are sitting there waiting to throw their weight on our side.

Let the world know how bloody his hands are. Let the world know the hypocrisy that's practiced over here. Let it be the ballot or the bullet.

The political philosophy of black nationalism means that the black man should control the politics and the politicians in his own community; no more. The black man in the black community has to be re-educated into the science of politics so he will know what politics is supposed to bring him in return. Don't be throwing out any ballots. A ballot is like a bullet. You don't throw your ballots until you see a target, and if that target is not within your reach, keep your ballot in your pocket. . . .

The economic philosophy of black nationalism is pure and simple. It only means that we should control the economy of our community. Why should white people be running all the stores in our community? Why should white people be running the banks of our community? Why should the economy of our community be in the hands of the white man? Why? If a black man can't move his store into a white community, you tell me why a white man should move his store into a black community. The philosophy of black nationalism involves a re-education program in the black community in regards to economics. . . .

The social philosophy of black nationalism only means that we have to get together and remove the evils, the vices, alcoholism, drug addiction, and other evils that are destroying the moral fiber of our community. We ourselves have to lift the level of our community, the standard of our community to a higher level. . . .

39 _____

Leo Strauss
What Is Political Philosophy?

Leo Strauss (1899–1973) was born in Germany and fled the Nazis in the early 1930s. He established himself in the United States as a critic of dominant trends in social science, particularly the subordination of the study of society and politics to "science." He questioned those who argued that "facts" were the province of "science" and "values" the domain of philosophy. Strauss employed and taught a method of careful reading of original texts, and demonstrated wide-ranging erudition in The Political Philosophy of Hobbes *(1935) and numerous other works of political philosophy. He believed that the best form of rule was one that brought together justice and wisdom.*

The Problem of Political Philosophy

The meaning of political philosophy and its meaningful character is as evident today as it always has been since the time when political philosophy came to light in Athens. All political action aims at either preservation or change. When desiring to preserve, we wish to prevent a change to the worse; when desiring to change, we wish to bring about something better. All political action is then guided by some thought of better and worse. But thought of better or worse implies thought of the good. The awareness of the good which guides all our actions has the character of opinion: it is no longer questioned but, on reflection, it proves to be questionable. The very fact that we can question it directs us towards such a thought of the good as is no longer questionable—towards a thought which is no longer opinion but knowledge. All political action has then in itself a directedness towards knowledge of the good: of the good life, or of the good society. For the good society is the complete political good.

If this directedness becomes explicit, if men make it their explicit goal to acquire knowledge of the good life and of the good society, political philosophy emerges. By calling this pursuit political philosophy, we imply that it forms a part of a larger whole: of philosophy; or that political philosophy is a branch of philosophy. In the expression "political philosophy," "philosophy" indicates the manner of treatment: a treatment which both goes to the roots and is comprehensive; "political" indicates both the subject matter and the function: political philosophy deals with political matters in a manner that it meant to be relevant for political life; therefore its subject must be identical with the goal, the ultimate goal of political action. The theme of political philosophy is mankind's great objectives, freedom and government or empire—objectives which are capable of lifting all men beyond their poor selves. Political philosophy is that branch of philosophy which is closest to political life, to nonphilosophic life, to human life. Only in his *Politics* does Aristotle make use of oaths—the almost inevitable accompaniment of passionate speech.

Since political philosophy is a branch of philosophy, even the most provisional explanation of what political philosophy is cannot dispense with an explanation, however provisional, of what philosophy is. Philosophy, as quest for wisdom, is quest for universal knowledge, for knowledge of the whole. The quest would not be necessary if such knowledge were immediately available. The absence of knowledge of the whole does not mean, however, that men do not have thoughts about the whole: philosophy is necessarily preceded by opinions about the whole. It is, therefore, the attempt to replace opinions about the whole by knowledge of the whole. Instead of "the whole," the philosophers also say "all things": the whole is not a pure ether or an unrelieved darkness in which one cannot distinguish one part from the other, or in which one cannot discern anything. Quest for knowledge of "all things" means quest for knowledge of God, the world, and man—or rather quest for knowledge of the natures of all things: the natures in their totality are "the whole."

Philosophy is essentially not possession of the truth, but quest for the truth. The distinctive trait of the philosopher is that "he knows that he knows nothing," and that his insight into our ignorance concerning the most important things induces him to strive with all his power for knowledge. He would cease to be a philosopher by evading the questions concerning these things or by disregarding them because they cannot be answered. It may be that as regards the possible answers to these questions, the pros and cons will always be in a more or less even balance, and therefore that philosophy will never go beyond the stage of discussion or disputation and will never reach the stage of decision. This would not make philosophy futile. For the clear grasp of a fundamental question requires understanding of the nature of the subject matter with which the question is concerned. Genuine knowledge of a fundamental question, thorough understanding of it, is better than blindness to it, or indifference to it, be that indifference or blindness accompanied by knowledge of the answers to a vast number of peripheral or ephemeral questions or not. *Minimum quod potest haberi de cognitione rerum altissimarum, desiderabilius est quam certissima cognitio quae habetur de minimis rebus.*[1] (Thomas Aquinas, *Summa Theologica*, I, qu. 1a5)

Of philosophy thus understood, political philosophy is a branch. Political philosophy will then be the attempt to replace opinion about the nature of political things by knowledge of the nature of political things. Political things are by their nature subject to approval and disapproval, to choice and rejection, to praise and blame. It is of their essence not to be neutral but to raise a claim to men's obedience, allegiance, decision, or judgment. One does not understand them as what they are, as political things, if one does not take seriously their explicit or implicit claim to be judged in terms of goodness or badness, of justice or injustice, i.e., if one does not measure them by some standard of goodness or justice. To judge soundly one must know the true standards. If political philosophy wishes to do justice to its subject matter, it must strive for genuine knowledge of these standards. Political philosophy is the attempt truly to know both the nature of political things and the right, or the good, political order.

Political philosophy ought to be distinguished from political thought in general. In our times, they are frequently identified. People have gone so far in debasing the name of philosophy as to speak of the philosophies of vulgar impostors. By political thought we understand the reflection on, or the exposition of, political ideas; and by a political idea we may understand any politically significant "phantasm, notion, species, or whatever it is about which the mind can be employed in thinking" concerning the political fundamentals. Hence, all political philosophy is political thought but not all political thought is political philosophy. Political thought is, as such, indifferent to the distinction between opinion and knowledge; but political philosophy is the conscious, coherent, and relentless effort to replace opinions about the political fundamentals by knowledge regarding them. Political thought may not be more, and may not even intend to be more, than the expounding or the defense of a firmly held conviction or of an invigorating myth; but it is essential to political philosophy to be set in motion, and be kept in motion, by the disquieting awareness of the fundamental difference between conviction, or belief, and knowledge. A political thinker who is not a philosopher is primarily interested in, or attached to, a specific order or policy; the political philosopher is primarily interested in, or attached to, the truth. Political thought which is not political philosophy finds its adequate expression in laws and codes, in poems and stories, in tracts and public speeches *inter alia;* the proper form of presenting political philosophy is the treatise. Political thought is as old as the human race; the first man who uttered a word like "father" or an expression like "thou shalt not . . ." was the first political thinker; but political philosophy appeared at a knowable time in the recorded past.

By political theory, people frequently understand today comprehensive reflections on the political situation which lead up to the suggestion of a broad policy. Such reflections appeal in the last resort to principles accepted by public opinion or a considerable part of it; i.e., they dogmatically assure principles which can well be questioned. Works of political theory in this sense would be Pinsker's *Autoemancipation* and Herzl's *Judenstaat.* Pinsker's *Autoemancipation* carries as its motto the words: "If I am not for myself, who will be for me? And if not now, when?" It omits the words: "And if I am only for myself, what am I?" Pinsker's silent rejection of the thought expressed in the omitted words is a crucial premise of the argument developed in his tract. Pinsker does not justify this rejection. For a justification, one would have to turn to the 3rd and 16th chapters of Spinoza's *Tractatus theologico-politicus,* to a work of a political philosopher.

We are compelled to distinguish political philosophy from political theology. By political theory we understand political teachings which are based on divine revelation. Political philosophy is limited to what is accessible to the unassisted human mind. As regards social philosophy, it has the same subject matter as political philosophy, but it regards it from a different point of view. Political philosophy rests on the premise that the political association—one's country or one's nation—is the most comprehensive or the most authoritative association, whereas social philosophy conceives of the political association as a part of a larger whole which it designates by the term "society."

Finally, we must discuss the relation of political philosophy to political science. "Political science" is an ambiguous term: it designates such investigations of political things as are guided by the model of natural science, and it designates the work which is being done by the members of political science departments. As regards the former, or what we may call "scientific" political science, it conceives of itself as *the* way towards genuine knowledge of political things. Just as genuine knowledge of natural things began when people turned from sterile and vain speculation to empirical and experimental study, the genuine knowledge of political things will begin when political philosophy will have given way completely to the scientific study of politics. Just as natural science stands on its own feet, and at most supplies unintentionally materials for the speculations of natural philosophers, political science stands on its own feet, and at most supplies unintentionally materials for the speculations of political philosophers. Considering the contrast between the solidity of the one pursuit and the pitiful pretentiousness characteristic of the other, it is however more reasonable to dismiss the vague and inane speculations of political philosophy altogether than to go on paying lip service to a wholly discredited and decrepit tradition. The sciences, both natural and political, are frankly nonphilosophic. They need philosophy of a kind: methodology or logic. But these philosophic disciplines have obviously nothing in common with political philosophy. "Scientific" political science is in fact incompatible with political philosophy.

The useful work done by the men called political scientists is independent of any aspiration towards "scientific" political science. It consists of careful and judicious collections and analyses of politically relevant data. To understand the meaning of this work, we remind ourselves of our provisional definition of political philosophy. Political philosophy is the attempt to understand the nature of political things. Before one can even think of attempting to understand the nature of political things, one must know political things: one must possess political knowledge. At least every sane adult possesses political knowledge to some degree. Everyone knows something of taxes, police, law, jails, war, peace, armistice. Everyone knows that the aim of war is victory, that war demands the supreme sacrifice and many other deprivations, that bravery deserves praise and cowardice deserves blame. Everyone knows that buying a shirt, as distinguished from casting a vote, is not in itself a political action. The man in the street is supposed to possess less political knowledge than the men who make it their business to supply him with information and guidance regarding political things. He certainly possesses less political knowledge than very intelligent men of long and varied political experience. At the top of the ladder we find the great statesman who possesses political knowledge, political understanding, political wisdom, political skill in the highest degree: political science (*politikē epistēmē*) in the original meaning of the term.

All political knowledge is surrounded by political opinion and interspersed with it. By political opinion we understand here opinion as distinguished from knowledge of political things: errors, guesses, beliefs, prejudices, forecasts, and so on. It is of the essence of political life to be guided by a mixture of political knowledge and political opinion. Hence, all political life is accompanied by more or less coherent and more or less strenuous efforts to replace political opinion by political knowledge. Even governments which lay claim to more than human knowledge are known to employ spies.

The character of political knowledge and of the demands made on it has been profoundly affected by a fairly recent change in the character of society. In former epochs, intelligent men would acquire the political knowledge, the political understanding they needed, by listening to wise old men or, which is the same thing, by reading good historians, as well as by looking around and by devoting themselves to public affairs. These ways of acquiring political knowledge are no longer sufficient because we live in "dynamic mass societies," i.e., in societies which are characterized by both immense complexity and rapid change. Political knowledge is more difficult to come by and it becomes obsolete more rapidly than in former times. Under these conditions it becomes necessary that a number of men should devote themselves entirely to the task of collecting and digesting knowledge of political things. It is this activity which today is frequently called political science. It does not emerge if it has not been realized among other things that even such political matters as have no bearing on the situation of the day deserve to be studied, and that their study must be carried on with the greatest possible care: a specific care which is designed to counteract the specific fallacies to which our judgment on political things is exposed. Furthermore, the men we speak of invest much toil in giving political knowledge the form of teachings which can be transmitted in classrooms. Moreover, while even the most unscrupulous politician must constantly try to replace in his own mind political opinion by political knowledge in order to be successful, the scholarly student of political things will go beyond this by trying to state the results of his investigations in public without any concealment and without any partisanship: he will act the part of the enlightened and patriotic citizen who has no axe of his own to grind. Or, differently expressed, the scholarly quest for political knowledge is essentially animated by a moral impulse, the love of truth. But however one may conceive of the difference between the scholarly and the nonscholarly quest for political knowledge, and however important these differences may be, the scholarly and the nonscholarly quest for political knowledge are identical in the decisive respect: their center of reference is the given political situation, and even in most cases the given political situation in the individual's own country. It is true that a botanist in Israel pays special attention to the flora of Israel, whereas the botanist in Canada pays special attention to the flora of Canada. But his difference, which is not more than the outcome of a convenient and even indispensable division of labor, has an entirely different chapter than the only apparently similar difference between the preoccupation of the Israeli political scientist and the Canadian political scientist. It is only when the Here and Now ceases to be the center of reference that a philosophic or scientific approach to politics can emerge.

All knowledge of political things implies assumptions concerning the nature of political things; i.e., assumptions which concern not merely the given political situation, but political life or human life as such. One cannot know anything about a war going on at a given time without having some notion, however dim and hazy, of war as such and its place within human life as such. One cannot see a policeman as a policeman without having made an assumption about law and government as such. The assumptions concerning the nature of political things, which are implied in all knowledge of political things, have the character of opinions. It is only when these assumptions are made the theme of critical and coherent analysis that a philosophic or scientific approach to politics emerges.

The cognitive status of political knowledge is not different from that of the knowledge possessed by the shepherd, the husband, the general, or the cook. Yet the pursuits of these types of man do not give rise to a pastoral, marital, military, or culinary philosophy because their ultimate goals are sufficiently clear and unambiguous. The ultimate political goal, on the other hand, urgently calls for coherent reflection. The goal of the general is victory, whereas the goal of the statesman is the common good. What victory means is not essentially controversial, but the meaning of the common good is essentially controversial. The ambiguity of the political goal is due to its comprehensive character. Thus the temptation arises to deny, or to evade, the comprehensive character of politics and to treat politics as one compartment among many. But this temptation must be resisted if it is necessary to face our situation as human beings, i.e., the whole situation.

Political philosophy as we have tried to circumscribe it has been cultivated since its beginnings almost without any interruption until a relatively short time ago. Today, political philosophy is in a state of decay and perhaps of putrefaction, if it has not vanished altogether. Not only is there complete disagreement regarding its subject matter, its methods, and its function; its very possibility in any form has become questionable. The only point regarding which academic teachers of political science still agree concerns the usefulness of studying the history of political philosophy. As regards the philosophers, it is sufficient to contrast the work of the four greatest philosophers of the last forty years—Bergson, Whitehead, Husserl, and Heidegger—with the work of Hermann Cohen in order to see how rapidly and thoroughly political philosophy has become discredited. We may describe the present situation as follows. Originally political philosophy was identical with political science, and it was the all-embracing study of human affairs. Today, we find it cut into pieces which behave as if they were parts of a worm. In the first place, one has applied the distinction between philosophy and science to the study of human affairs, and accordingly one makes a distinction between a nonphilosophic political science and a nonscientific political philosophy, a distinction which under present conditions takes away all dignity, all honesty from political philosophy. Furthermore, large segments of what formerly belonged to political philosophy or political science have become emancipated under the names of economics, sociology, and social psychology. The pitiable rump for which honest social scientists do not care is left as prey to philosophers of history and to people who amuse themselves more than others with professions of faith. We hardly exaggerate when we say that today political philosophy does not exist any more, except as matter for burial, i.e., for historical research, or else as a theme of weak and unconvincing protestations.

If we inquire into the reasons for this great change, we receive these answers: political philosophy is unscientific, or it is unhistorical, or it is both. Science and History, those two great powers of the modern world, have finally succeeded in destroying the very possibility of political philosophy.

The rejection of political philosophy as unscientific is characteristic of present-day positivism. Positivism is no longer what it desired to be when Auguste Comte originated it. It still agrees with Comte by maintaining that modern science is the highest form of knowledge, precisely because it aims no longer, as theology and metaphysics did, at absolute knowledge of the Why, but only at relative knowledge of the How. But after having been modified by utilitarianism, evolutionism and neo-Kantianism, it has abandoned completely Comte's hope that a social science modeled on modern natural science would be able to overcome the intellectual anarchy of modern society. In about the last decade of the nineteenth century, social science positivism reached its final form by realizing or decreeing that there is a fundamental difference between facts and values, and that only factual judgments are within the competence of science: scientific social science is incompetent to pronounce value judgments, and must avoid value judgments altogether. As for the meaning of the term "value" in statements of this kind, we can hardly say more than that "values" mean both things preferred and principles of preference.

A discussion of the tenets of social science positivism is today indispensable for explaining the meaning of political philosophy. We reconsider especially the practical consequences of this positivism. Positivistic social science is "value-free" or "ethically neutral": it is neutral in the conflict between good and evil, however good and evil may be understood. This means that the ground which is common to all social scientists, the ground on which they carry on their investigations and discussions, can only be reached through a process of emancipation from moral judgments, or of abstracting from moral judgments: moral obtuseness is the necessary condition for scientific analysis. For to the extent to which we are not yet completely insensitive to moral distinctions, we are forced to make value judgments. The habit of looking at social or human phenomena without making value judgments has a corroding influence on any preferences. The more serious we are as social scientists, the more completely we develop within ourselves a state of indifference to any goal, or of aimlessness and drifting, a state which may be called nihilism. The social scientist is not immune to preferences; his activity is a constant fight against the preferences he has as a human being and a citizen and which threaten to overcome his scientific detachment. He derives the power to counteract these dangerous influences by his dedication to one and only one value—to truth. But according to his principles, truth is not a value which it is necessary to choose: one may reject it as well as choose it. The scientist as scientist must indeed have chosen it. But neither scientists nor science are simply necessary. Social science cannot pronounce on the question of whether social science itself is good. It is then compelled to teach that society can with equal right and with equal reason favor social science as well as suppress it as disturbing, subversive, corrosive, nihilistic. But strangely enough we find social scientists very anxious to "sell" social science, i.e., to prove that social science is necessary. They will argue as follows. Regardless of what our preferences or ends may be, we wish to achieve our ends; to achieve our ends, we must know which means are conducive to our ends; but adequate knowledge of the means conducive to any social ends is the sole function of social science and only of social science; hence social science is necessary for any society or any social movement; social science is then simply necessary; it is a value from every point of view. But once we grant this we are seriously tempted to wonder if there are not a few other things which must be values from every point of view or for every thinking human being. To avoid this inconvenience the social scientist will scorn all considerations of public relations or of private advancement, and take refuge in the virtuous contention that he does not know, but merely believes that quest for truth is good: other men may believe with equal right that quest for truth is bad. But what does he mean by this contention? Either he makes a distinction between noble and ignoble objectives or he refuses to make such a distinction. If he makes a distinction between noble and ignoble objectives, he will say there is a variety of noble objectives or of ideals, and that there is no ideal which is compatible with all other ideals: if one chooses truth as one's ideal, one necessarily rejects other ideals; this being the case, there cannot be a necessity, an evident necessity for noble men to choose truth in preference to other ideals. But as long as the social scientist speaks of ideals, and thus makes a distinction between noble and not noble objectives, or between idealistic integrity and petty egoism, he makes a value judgment which according to his fundamental contention is, as such, no longer necessary. He must then say that it is as legitimate to make the pursuit of safety, income, deference one's sole aim in life as it is to make the quest for truth one's chief aim. He thus lays himself open to the suspicion that his activity as a social scientist serves no other purpose than to increase his safety, his income, and his prestige, or that his competence as a social scientist is a skill which he is prepared to sell to the highest bidder. Honest citizens will begin to wonder whether such a man can be trusted, or whether he can be loyal, especially since he must maintain that it is as defensible to choose loyalty as one's value as it is to reject it. In a word, he will get entangled in the predicament which leads to the downfall of Thrasymachus and his taming by Socrates in the first book of Plato's *Republic*.

It goes without saying that while our social scientist may be confused, he is very far from being disloyal and from lacking integrity. His assertion that integrity and quest for truth are values which one can with equal right choose or reject is a mere movement of his lips and his tongue, to which nothing corresponds in his heart or mind. I have never met any scientific social scientist who apart from being dedicated to truth and integrity was not also wholeheartedly devoted to democracy. When he says that democracy is a value which is not evidently superior to the opposite value, he does not mean that he is impressed by the alternative which he rejects, or that his heart or his mind is torn between alternatives which in themselves are equally attractive. His "ethical neutrality" is so far from being nihilism or a road to nihilism that it is not more than an alibi for thoughtlessness and vulgarity: by saying that democracy and truth are values, he says in effect that one does not have to think about the reasons why these things are good, and that he may bow as well as anyone else to the values that are adopted and respected by his society. Social science positivism fosters not so much nihilism as conformism and philistinism.

It is not necessary to enter here and now into a discussion of the theoretical weaknesses of social science positivism. It suffices to allude to the considerations which speak decisively against this school.

1. It is impossible to study social phenomena, i.e., all important social phenomena, without making value judgments. A man who sees no reason for not despising people whose horizon is limited to their consumption of food and their digestion may be a tolerable econometrist; he cannot say anything relevant about the character of a human society. A man who refuses to distinguish between great statesmen, mediocrities, and insane impostors may be a good bibliographer; he cannot say anything relevant about politics and political history. A man who cannot distinguish between a profound religious thought and a languishing superstition may be a good statistician; he cannot say anything relevant about the sociology of religion. Generally speaking, it is impossible to understand thought or action or work without evaluating it. If we are unable to evaluate adequately, as we very frequently are, we have not yet succeeded in understanding adequately. The value judgments which are forbidden to enter through the front door of political science, sociology, or economics enter these disciplines through the back door; they come from that annex of present-day social science which is called psychopathology. Social scientists see themselves compelled to speak of unbalanced, neurotic, maladjusted people. But these value judgments are distinguished from those used by the great historians, not by greater clarity or certainty, but merely by their poverty: a slick operator is as well adjusted as—he may be better adjusted than—a good man or a good citizen. Finally, we must not overlook the invisible value judgments which are concealed from undiscerning eyes but nevertheless most powerfully present in allegedly purely descriptive concepts. For example, when social scientists distinguish between democratic and authoritarian habits or

types of human beings, what they call "authoritarian" is in all cases known to be a caricature of everything of which they, as good democrats of a certain kind, disapprove. Or when they speak of three principles of legitimacy—rational, traditional, and charismatic—their very expression "routinization of charisma" betrays a Protestant or liberal preference which no conservative Jew and no Catholic would accept: in the light of the notion of "routinization of charisma," the genesis of the Halakah out of biblical prophesy on the one hand, and the genesis of the Catholic Church out of the New Testament teaching, necessarily appear as cases of "routinization of charisma." If the objection should be made that value judgments are indeed inevitable in social science but have a merely conditional character, I would reply as follows: Are the conditions in question not necessarily fulfilled when we are interested in social phenomena? Must the social scientist not necessarily make the assumption that a healthy social life in this world is good, just as medicine necessarily makes the assumption that health and a healthy long life are good? And also are not all factual assertions based on conditions, or assumptions, which however do not become questionable as long as we deal with facts qua facts (e.g., that there are "facts," that events have causes)?

The impossibility of a "value-free" political science can be shown most simply as follows. Political science presupposes a distinction between political things and things which are not political; it presupposes therefore some answer to the question "what is political?" In order to be truly scientific, political science would have to raise this question and to answer it explicitly and adequately. But it is impossible to define the political, i.e., that which is related in a relevant way to the *polis,* the "country" or the "state," without answering the question of what constitutes this kind of society. Now, a society cannot be defined without reference to its purpose. The most well-known attempt to define "the state" without regard to its purpose admittedly led to a definition which was derived from "the modern type of state" and which is fully applicable only to that type; it was an attempt to define the modern state without having first defined the state. But by defining the state, or rather civil society, with reference to its purpose, one admits a standard in the light of which one must judge political actions and institutions: the purpose of civil society necessarily functions as a standard for judging of civil societies.

2. The rejection of value judgments is based on the assumption that the conflicts between different values or value-systems are essentially insoluble for human reason. But this assumption, while generally taken to be sufficiently established, has never been proven. Its proof would require an effort of the magnitude of that which went into the conception and elaboration of the *Critique of Pure Reason;* it would require a comprehensive critique of evaluating reason. What we find in fact are sketchy observations which pretend to prove that this or that specific value conflict is insoluble. It is prudent to grant that there are value conflicts which cannot in fact be settled by human reason. But if we cannot decide which of two mountains whose peaks are hidden by clouds is higher than the other, cannot we decide that a mountain is higher than a molehill? If we cannot decide, regarding a war between two neighboring nations which have been fighting each other for

centuries, which nation's cause is more just, cannot we decide that Jezebel's action against Naboth was inexcusable? The greatest representative of social science positivism, Max Weber, has postulated the insolubility of all value conflicts, because his soul craved a universe in which failure, that bastard of forceful sinning accompanied by still more forceful faith, instead of felicity and serenity, was to be the mark of human nobility. The belief that value judgments are not subject, in the last analysis, to rational control encourages the inclination to make irresponsible assertions regarding right and wrong or good and bad. One evades serious discussion of serious issues by the simple device of passing them off as value problems. One even creates the impression that all important human conflicts are value conflicts, whereas, to say the least, many of these conflicts arise out of men's very agreement regarding values.

3. The belief that scientific knowledge, i.e., the kind of knowledge possessed or aspired to by modern science, is the highest form of human knowledge, implies a depreciation of prescientific knowledge. If one takes into consideration the contrast between scientific knowledge of the world and prescientific knowledge of the world, one realizes that positivism preserves in a scarcely disguised manner Descartes' universal doubt of prescientific knowledge and his radical break with it. It certainly distrusts prescientific knowledge, which it likes to compare to folklore. This superstition fosters all sorts of sterile investigations or complicated idiocies. Things which every ten-year-old child of normal intelligence knows are regarded as being in need of scientific proof in order to become acceptable as facts. And this scientific proof, which is not only not necessary, is not even possible. To illustrate this by the simplest example: all studies in social science presuppose that its devotees can tell human beings from other beings; this most fundamental knowledge was not acquired by them in classrooms; and this knowledge is not transformed by social science into scientific knowledge, but retains its initial status without any modification throughout. If this prescientific knowledge is not knowledge, all scientific studies, which stand or fall with it, lack the character of knowledge. The preoccupation with scientific proof of things which everyone knows well enough, and better, without scientific proof, leads to the neglect of that thinking, or that reflection, which must precede all scientific studies if these studies are to be relevant. The scientific study of politics is often presented as ascending from the ascertainment of political "facts," i.e., of what has happened hitherto in politics, to the formulation of "laws" whose knowledge would permit the prediction of further political events. This goal is taken as a matter of course without a previous investigation as to whether the subject matter with which political science deals admits of adequate understanding in terms of "laws" or whether the universals through which political things can be understood as what they are must not be conceived of in entirely different terms. Scientific concern with political facts, relations of political facts, recurrent relations of political facts, or laws of political behavior, requires isolation of the phenomena which it is studying. But if this isolation is not to lead to irrelevant

or misleading results, one must see the phenomena in question within the whole to which they belong, and one must clarify that whole, i.e., the whole political or politico-social order. One cannot arrive, e.g., at a kind of knowledge of "group politics" which deserves to be called scientific if one does not reflect on what genus of political orders is presupposed if there is to be "group politics" at all, and what kind of political order is presupposed by the specific "group politics" which one is studying. But one cannot clarify the character of a specific democracy, e.g., or of democracy in general, without having a clear understanding of the alternatives to democracy. Scientific political scientists are inclined to leave it at the distinction between democracy and authoritarianism, i.e., they absolutize the given political order by remaining within a horizon which is defined by the given political order and its opposite. The scientific approach tends to lead to the neglect of the primary or fundamental questions and therewith to thoughtless acceptance or received opinion. As regards these fundamental questions our friends of scientific exactness are strangely unexacting. To refer again to the most simple and at the same time decisive example, political science requires clarification of what distinguishes political things from things which are not political; it requires that the question be raised and answered "What is political?" This question cannot be dealt with scientifically but only dialectically. And dialectical treatment necessarily begins from prescientific knowledge and takes it most seriously. Prescientific knowledge, or "common sense" knowledge, is thought to be discredited by Copernicus and the succeeding natural science. But the fact that what we may call telescopic-microscopic knowledge is very fruitful in certain areas does not entitle one to deny that there are things which can only be seen as what they are if they are seen with the unarmed eye; or, more precisely, if they are seen in the perspective of the citizen, as distinguished from the perspective of the scientific observer. If one denies this, one will repeat the experience of Gulliver with the nurse in Brobdingnag and become entangled in the kind of research projects by which he was amazed in Laputa.

4. Positivism necessarily transforms itself into historicism. By virtue of its orientation by the model of natural science, social science is in danger of mistaking peculiarities of, say, mid-twentieth century United States, or more generally of modern Western society, for the essential character of human society. To avoid this danger, it is compelled to engage in "cross-cultural research," in the study of other cultures, both present and past. But in making this effort, it misses the meaning of those other cultures, because it interprets them through a conceptual scheme which originates in modern Western society, which reflects that particular society, and which fits at best only that particular society. To avoid this danger, social science must attempt to understand those cultures as they understand or understood themselves: the understanding primarily required of the social scientist is historical understanding. Historical understanding becomes the basis of a truly empirical science of society. But if one considers the infinity of the task of historical understanding, one begins to wonder whether historical understanding does not

take the place of the scientific study of society. Furthermore, social science is said to be a body of true propositions about social phenomena. The propositions are answers to questions. What valid answers, objectively valid answers, are, may be determined by the rules or principles of logic. But the questions depend on one's direction of interest, and hence on one's values, i.e., on subjective principles. Now it is the direction of interests, and not logic, which supplies the fundamental concepts. It is therefore not possible to divorce from each other the subjective and objective elements of social science: the objective answers receive their meaning from the subjective questions. If one does not relapse into the decayed Platonism which is underlying the notion of timeless values, one must conceive of the values embodied in a given social science as dependent on the society to which the social science is question belongs, i.e., on history. Not only is social science superseded by historical studies; social science itself proves to be "historical." Reflection on social science as a historical phenomenon leads to the relativization of social science and ultimately of modern science generally. As a consequence, modern science comes to be viewed as one historically relative way of understanding things which is not in principle superior to alternative ways of understanding.

It is only at this point that we come face to face with the serious antagonist of political philosophy: historicism. After having reached its full growth, historicism is distinguished from positivism by the following characteristics: (1) It abandons the distinction between facts and values, because every understanding, however, theoretical, implies specific evaluations. (2) It denies the authoritative character of modern science, which appears as only one form among many of man's thinking orientation in the world. (3) It refuses to regard the historical process as fundamentally progressive, or, more generally stated, as reasonable. (4) It denies the relevance of the evolutionist thesis by contending that the evolution of man out of nonman cannot make intelligible man's humanity. Historicism rejects the question of the good society, that is to say, of *the* good society, because of the essentially historical character of society and of human thought: there is no essential necessity for raising the question of the good society; this question is not in principle coeval with man; its very possibility is the outcome of a mysterious dispensation of fate. The crucial issue concerns the status of those permanent characteristics of humanity, such as the distinction between the noble and the base, which are admitted by the thoughtful historicists: can these permanencies be used as criteria for distinguishing between good and bad dispensations of fate? The historicist answers this question in the negative. He looks down on the permanencies in question because of their objective, common, superficial, and rudimentary character: to become relevant, they would have to be completed, and their completion is no longer common but historical. It was the contempt for these permanencies which permitted the most radical historicist in 1933 to submit to, or rather to welcome, as a dispensation of fate, the verdict of the least wise and least moderate part of his nation while it was in its least wise and least moderate mood, and at the same time to speak of wisdom and moderation. The biggest event of 1933 would rather seem to have proved, if such proof was necessary, that man cannot abandon the question of the good society, and that he cannot free himself from the responsibility for answering it by deferring to History or to any other power different from his own reason.

Note

1. "The least knowledge one can have of the highest things is more desirable than the most certain knowledge one has of the lowest things."

40

Michael Walzer
In Defense of Equality

Michael Walzer (1935–   ) is professor of social science at the Institute for Advanced Study, Princeton, and co-editor of the political quarterly Dissent, *where the following article initially appeared in 1973. He is one of America's foremost political thinkers today, and is an advocate of a democratic, egalitarian radicalism in opposition to conservatism. However, he argues for a pluralistic and complex notion of equality. Rather than applying one abstract notion of equality to all aspects of life, making everything the same, Walzer believes that the different spheres of life should have their own autonomy: "What egalitarianism requires is that many bells should ring." Among his books are* Spheres of Justice *(1983),* Radical Principles *(1980),* Just and Unjust Wars *(1977), and* Thick and Thin *(1994).*

I

At the very center of conservative thought lies this idea: that the present division of wealth and power corresponds to some deeper reality of human life. Conservatives don't want to say merely that the present division is what it ought to be, for that would invite a search for some distributive principle—as if it were possible to *make* a distribution. They want to say that whatever the division of wealth and power is, it naturally is, and that all efforts to change it, temporarily successful in proportion to their bloodiness, must be futile in the end. We are then invited, as in Irving Kristol's recent *Commentary* article, to reflect upon the perversity of those who would make the attempt.[1] Like a certain sort of leftist thought, conservative argument seems quickly to shape itself around a rhetoric of motives rather than one of reasons. Kristol is especially adept at that rhetoric and strangely unconcerned about the reductionism it involves. He aims to expose egalitarianism as the ideology of envious and resentful intellectuals. No one else cares about it, he says, except the "new class" of college-educated, professional, most importantly, professorial men and women, who hate their bourgeois past (and present) and long for a world of their own making.

I suppose I should have felt, after reading Kristol's piece, that the decent drapery of my socialist convictions has been stripped away, that I was left naked and shivering, small-minded and self-concerned. Perhaps I did feel a little like that, for my first impulse was to respond in kind, exposing anti-egalitarianism as the ideology of those other intellectuals—"they are mostly professors, of course"—whose spiritual path was sketched some years ago by the editor of *Commentary*. But that would be at best a degrading business, and I doubt that my analysis would be any more accurate than Kristol's. It is better to ignore the motives of these "new men" and focus instead on what they say: that the inequalities we are all familiar with are inherent in our condition, are accepted by ordinary people (like themselves), and are criticized only by the perverse. I think all these assertions are false; I shall try to respond to them in a serious way.

Kristol doesn't argue that we can't possibly have greater equality or greater inequality than we presently have. Both communist and aristocratic societies are possible, he writes, under conditions of political repression or economic under-development and stagnation. But insofar as men and women are set free from the coerciveness of the state and from material necessity, they will distribute themselves in a more natural way, more or less as contemporary Americans have done. The American way is exemplary because it derives from or reflects the real in-equalities of mankind. People don't naturally fall into two classes (patricians and plebeians) as conservatives once thought; nor can they plausibly be grouped into a single class (citizens or comrades) as leftists still believe. Instead, "human talents and abilities . . . distribute themselves along a bell-shaped curve, with most peo-ple clustered around the middle, and with much smaller percentages at the lower and higher ends." The marvels of social science!—this distribution is a demon-strable fact. And it is another "demonstrable fact that in all modern bourgeois societies, the distribution of income is also along a bell-shaped curve. . . ." The second bell echoes the first. Moreover, once this harmony is established, "the political structure—the distribution of political power—follows along the same way. . . ." At this point, Kristol must add, "however slowly and reluctantly," since he believes that the Soviet economy is moving closer every year to its natu-ral shape, and it is admittedly hard to find evidence that nature is winning out in the political realm. But in the United States, nature is triumphant: we are perfectly bell-shaped.

The first bell is obviously the crucial one. The defense of inequality reduces to these two propositions: that talent is distributed unequally and that talent will win out. Clearly, we all want men and women to develop and express their talents, but whenever they are able to do that, Kristol suggests, the bell-shaped curve will appear or reappear, first in the economy, then in the political system. It is a neat argument but also a peculiar one, for there is no reason to think that "human talents and abilities" in fact distribute themselves along a *single* curve, although income necessarily does. Consider the range and variety of human capacities: intelligence, physical strength, agility and grace, artistic creativity, mechanical skill, leadership, endurance, memory, psychological insight, the capacity for hard work—even, moral strength, sensitivity, the ability to express compassion. Let's assume that with respect to all these, most people (but different people in each case) cluster around the middle of whatever scale we can construct, with smaller numbers at the lower and higher ends. Which of these curves is actually echoed by the income bell? Which, if any, ought to be?

There is another talent that we need to consider: the ability to make money, the green thumb of bourgeois society—a secondary talent, no doubt, combining many of the others in ways specified by the immediate environment, but probably also a talent that distributes, if we could graph it, along a bell-shaped curve. Even this curve would not correlate exactly with the income bell because of the intervention of luck, that eternal friend of the untalented, whose most important social expression is the inheritance of property. But the correlation would be close enough, and it might also be morally plausible and satisfying. People who are able to make money ought to make money, in the same way that people who are able to write books ought to write books. Every human talent should be developed and expressed.

The difficulty here is that making money is only rarely a form of self-expression, and the money we make is rarely enjoyed for its intrinsic qualities (at least, economists frown upon that sort of enjoyment). In a capitalist world, money is the universal medium of exchange; it enables the men and women who possess it to purchase virtually every other sort of social good; we collect it for its exchange value. Political power, celebrity, admiration, leisure, works of art, baseball teams, legal advice, sexual pleasure, travel, education, medical care, rare books, sailboats—all these (and much more) are up for sale. The list is as endless as human desire and social invention. Now isn't it odd, and morally implausible and unsatisfying, that all these things should be distributed to people with a talent for making money? And even odder and more unsatisfying that they should be distributed (as they are) to people who have money, whether or not they made it, whether or not they possess any talent at all?

Rich people, of course, always look talented—just as the beautiful people always look beautiful—to the deferential observer. But it is the first task of social science, one would think, to look beyond these appearances. "The properties of money," Marx wrote, "are my own (the possessor's) properties and faculties. What I *am* and *can do* is, therefore, not at all determined by my individuality. I *am* ugly, but I can buy the most beautiful woman for myself. Consequently, I am not ugly, for the effect of ugliness, its power to repel, is annulled by money. . . . I am a detestable, dishonorable, unscrupulous, and stupid man, but money is honored and so also is its possessor."[2]

It would not be any better if we gave people money in direct proportion to their intelligence, their strength, or their moral rectitude. The resulting distributions would each, no doubt, reflect what Kristol calls "the tyranny of the bell-shaped curve," though it is worth noticing again that the populations in the lower, middle, and upper regions of each graph would be radically different. But whether it was the smart, the strong, or the righteous who enjoyed all the things that money can buy, the oddity would remain: why them? Why anybody? In fact, there is no single talent or combination of talents that plausibly entitles a man to every available social good—and there is no single talent or combination of talents that necessarily must win the available goods of a free society. Kristol's bell-shaped curve is tyrannical only in a purely formal sense. Any particular distribution may indeed be bell-shaped, but there are a large number of possible distributions. Nor need there by a single distribution of all social goods, for different goods might well be distributed differently. Nor again need all these distributions follow this or that talent curve, for in the sharing of some social goods, talent does not seem a relevant consideration at all.

Consider the case of medical care: surely it should not be distributed to individuals because they are wealthy, intelligent, or righteous, but only because they are sick. Now, over any given period of time, it may be true that some men and women won't require any medical treatment, a very large number will need some moderate degree of attention, and a few will have to have intensive care. If that is so, then we must hope for the appearance of another bell-shaped curve. Not just any bell will do. It must be the right one, echoing what might be called the susceptibility-to-sickness curve. But in America today, the distribution of medical care actually follows closely the lines of the income graph. It's not how a man feels, but how much money he has that determines how often he visits a doctor. Another demonstrable fact! Does it require envious intellectuals to see that something is wrong?

There are two possible ways of setting things right. We might distribute income in proportion to susceptibility-to-sickness, or we might make sure that medical care is not for sale at all, but is available to those who need it. The second of these is obviously the simpler. Indeed, it is a modest proposal and already has wide support, even among those ordinary men and women who are said to be indifferent to equality. And yet, the distribution of medical care solely for medical reasons would point the way toward an egalitarian society, for it would call the dominance of the income curve dramatically into question.

II

What egalitarianism requires is that many bells should ring. Different goods should be distributed to different people for different reasons. Equality is not a simple notion, and it cannot be satisfied by a single distributive scheme—not even, I hasten to add, by a scheme that emphasizes need. "From each according to his abilities, to each according to his needs" is a fine slogan with regard to medical care. Tax money collected from all of us in proportion to our resources (these will never correlate exactly with our abilities, but that problem I shall leave aside for now) must pay the doctors who care for those of us who are sick. Other people who deliver similar sorts of social goods should probably be paid in the same way—teachers and lawyers, for example. But Marx's slogan doesn't help at all with regard to the distribution of political power, honor and fame, leisure time, rare books, and sailboats. None of these things can be distributed to individuals in proportion to their needs, for they are not things that anyone (strictly speaking) needs. They can't be distributed in equal amounts or given to whoever wants them, for some of them are necessarily scarce, and some of them can't be possessed unless other people agree on the proper name of the possessor. There is no criterion, I think, that will fit them all. In the past they have indeed been distributed on a single principle: men and women have possessed them or their historical equivalents because they were strong or well-born or wealthy. But this only suggests that a society in which any single distributive principle is dominant cannot be an egalitarian society. Equality requires a diversity of principles, which mirrors the diversity both of mankind and of social goods.

Whenever equality in this sense does not prevail, we have a kind of tyranny, for it is tyrannical of the well-born or the strong or the rich to gather to themselves social goods that have nothing to do with their personal qualities. This is an idea beautifully expressed in a passage from Pascal's *Pensées*, which I am going to quote at some length, since it is the source of my own argument.[3]

> The nature of tyranny is to desire power over the whole world and outside its own sphere.
>
> There are different companies—the strong, the handsome, the intelligent, the devout—and each man reigns in his own, not elsewhere. But sometimes they meet, and the strong and the handsome fight for mastery—foolishly, for their mastery is of different kinds. They misunderstand one another, and make the mistake of each aiming at universal dominion. Nothing can win this, not even strength, for it is powerless in the kingdom of the wise. . . .
>
> *Tyranny.* The following statements, therefore, are false and tyrannical: "Because I am handsome, so I should command respect." "I am strong, therefore men should love me. . . ." "I am . . . etc."
>
> Tyranny is the wish to obtain by one means what can only be had by another. We owe different duties to different qualities: love is the proper response to charm, fear to strength, and belief to learning.

Marx makes a very similar argument in one of the early manuscripts; perhaps he had this *pensée* in mind.[4]

> Let us assume man to be man, and his relation to the world to be a human one. Then love can only be exchanged for love, trust for trust, etc. If you wish to enjoy art you must be an artistically cultivated person; if you wish to influence other people, you must be a person who really has a stimulating and encouraging effect upon others. . . . If you love without evoking love in return, i.e., if you are not able, by the manifestation of yourself as a loving person, to make yourself a beloved person, then your love is impotent and a misfortune.

The doctrine suggested by these passages is not an easy one, and I can expound it only in a tentative way. It isn't that every man should get what he deserves—as in the old definition of justice—for dessert is relevant only to some of the exchanges that Pascal and Marx have in mind. Charming men and women don't deserve to be loved: I may love this one or that one, but it can't be the case that I ought to do so. Similarly, learned men don't deserve to be believed: they are believed or not depending on the arguments they make. What Pascal and Marx are saying is that love and belief can't rightly be had in any other way—can't be purchased or coerced, for example. It is wrong to seek them in any way that is alien to their intrinsic character. In its extended form, their argument is that for all our personal and collective resources, there are distributive reasons that are somehow *right,* that are naturally part of our ideas about the things themselves. So nature is re-established as a critical standard, and we are invited to wonder at the strangeness of the existing order.

This new standard is egalitarian, even though it obviously does not require an equal distribution of love and belief. The doctrine of right reasons suggests that we pay equal attention to the "different qualities," and to the "individuality" of every man and woman, that we find ways of sharing our resources that match the variety of their needs, interests, and capacities. The clues that we must follow lie in the conceptions we already have, in the things we already know about love and belief, and also about respect, obedience, education, medical care, legal aid, all the necessities of life—for this is no esoteric doctrine, whatever difficulties it involves. Nor is it a panacea for human misfortune, as Marx's last sentence makes clear: it is only meant to suggest a humane form of social accommodation. There is little we can do, in the best of societies, for the man who isn't loved. But there may be ways to avoid the triumph of the man who doesn't love—who buys love or forces it—or at least of his parallels in the larger social and political world: the leaders, for example, who are obeyed because of their coercive might or their enormous wealth. Our goal should be an end to tyranny, a society in which no human being is master outside his sphere. That is the only society of equals worth having.

But it isn't readily had, for there is no necessity implied by the doctrine of right reasons. Pascal is wrong to say that "strength is powerless in the kingdom of the wise"—or rather, he is talking of an ideal realm and not of the intellectual world as we know it. In fact, wise men and women (at any rate, smart men and women) have often in the past defended the tyranny of the strong, as they still defend the tyranny of the rich. Sometimes, of course, they do this because they are persuaded of the necessity or the utility of tyrannical rule; sometimes for other reasons. Kristol suggests that whenever intellectuals are not persuaded, they are secretly aspiring to a tyranny of their own: they too would like to rule outside their sphere. Again, that's certainly true of some of them, and we all have our own lists. But it's not necessarily true. Surely it is possible, though no doubt difficult, for an intellectual to pay proper respect to the "different companies." I want to argue that in our society the only way to do that, or to begin to do it, is to worry about the tyranny of money.

III

Let's start with some things that money cannot buy. It can't buy the American League pennant: star players can be hired, but victories presumably are not up for sale. It can't buy the National Book Award: writers can be subsidized, but the judges presumably can't be bribed. Nor, it should be added, can the pennant or the award be won by being strong, charming, or ideologically correct—at least we all hope not. In these sorts of cases, the right reasons for winning are built into the very structure of the competition. I am inclined to think that they are similarly built into a large number of social practices and institutions. It's worth focusing again, for example, on the practice of medicine. From ancient times, doctors were required to take an oath to help the sick, not the powerful or the wealthy. That requirement reflects a common understanding about the very nature of medical care. Many professionals don't share that understanding, but the opinion of ordinary men and women, in this case at least, is profoundly egalitarian.

The same understanding is reflected in our legal system. A man accused of a crime is entitled to a fair trial simply by virtue of being an accused man; nothing else about him is a relevant consideration. That is why defendants who cannot afford a lawyer are provided with legal counsel by the state: otherwise justice would be up for sale. And that is why defense counsel can challenge particular jurors thought to be prejudiced: the fate of the accused must hang on his guilt or innocence, not on his political opinions, his social class, or his race. We want different defendants to be treated differently, but only for the right reasons.

The case is the same in the political system, whenever the state is a democracy. Each citizen is entitled to one vote simply because he is a citizen. Men and women who are ambitious to exercise greater power must collect votes, but they can't do that by purchasing them; we don't want votes to be traded in the marketplace, though virtually everything else is traded there, and so we have made it a criminal offense to offer bribes to voters. The only right way to collect votes is to campaign for them, that is, to be persuasive, stimulating, encouraging, and so on. Great inequalities in political power are acceptable only if they result from a political process of a certain kind, open to argument, closed to bribery and coercion. The freely given support of one's fellow citizens is the appropriate criterion for exercising political power and, once again, it is not enough, or it shouldn't be, to be physically powerful, or well-born, or even ideologically correct.

It is often enough, however, to be rich. No one can doubt the mastery of the wealthy in the spheres of medicine, justice, and political power, even though these are not their own spheres. I don't want to say, their unchallenged mastery, for in democratic states we have at least made a start toward restricting the tyranny of money. But we have only made a start: think how different America would have to be before these three companies of men and women—the sick, the accused, the politically ambitious—could be treated in strict accordance with their individual qualities. It would be immediately necessary to have a national health service, national legal assistance, the strictest possible control over campaign contributions. Modest proposals, again, but they represent so many moves toward the realization of that old socialist slogan about the abolition of money. I have always been puzzled by that slogan, for socialists have never, to my knowledge, advocated a return to a barter economy. But it makes a great deal of sense if it is interpreted to mean *the abolition of the power of money outside its sphere.* What socialists want is a society in which wealth is no longer convertible into social goods with which it has no intrinsic connection.

But it is in the very nature of money to be convertible (that's all it is), and I find it hard to imagine the sorts of laws and law enforcement that would be necessary to prevent monied men and women from buying medical care and legal aid over and above whatever social minimum is provided for everyone. In the United

States today, people can even buy police protection beyond what the state provides, though one would think that it is the primary purpose of the state to guarantee equal security to all its citizens, and it is by no means the rich, despite the temptations they offer, who stand in greatest need of protection. But this sort of thing could be prevented only by a very considerable restriction of individual liberty—of the freedom to offer services and to purchase them. The case is even harder with respect to politics itself. One can stop overt bribery, limit the size of campaign contributions, require publicity, and so on. But none of these things will be enough to prevent the wealthy from exercising power in all sorts of ways to which their fellow citizens have never consented. Indeed, the ability to hold or spend vast sums of money is itself a form of power, permitting what might be called preemptive strikes against the political system. And this, it seems to me, is the strongest possible argument for a radical redistribution of wealth. So long as money is convertible outside its sphere, it must be widely and more or less equally held so as to minimize its distorting effects upon legitimate distributive processes.

IV

What is the proper sphere of wealth? What sorts of things are rightly had in exchange for money? The obvious answer is also the right one: all those economic goods and services, beyond what is necessary to life itself, that men and women find useful or pleasing. There is nothing degraded about wanting these things; there is nothing unattractive, boring, debased, or philistine about a society organized to provide them for its members. Kristol insists that a snobbish dislike for the sheer productivity of bourgeois society is a feature of egalitarian argument. I would have thought that a deep appreciation of that productivity has more often marked the work of socialist writers. The question is, how are the products to be distributed? Now, the right way to possess useful and pleasing things is by making them, or growing them, or somehow providing them for others. The medium of exchange is money, and this is the proper function of money and, ideally, its only function.

There should be no way of acquiring rare books and sailboats except by working for them. But this is not to say that workers deserve whatever money they can get for the goods and services they provide. In capitalist society, the actual exchange value of the work they do is largely a function of market conditions over which they exercise no control. It has little to do with the intrinsic value of the work or with the individual qualities of the worker. There is no reason for socialists to respect it, unless it turns out to be socially useful to do so. There are other values, however, that they must respect, for money isn't the only or necessarily the most important thing for which work can be exchanged. A lawyer is surely entitled to the respect he wins from his colleagues and to the gratitude and praise he wins from his clients. The work he has done may also constitute a good reason for making him director of the local legal aid society; it may even be a good reason for making him a judge. It isn't, on the face of it, a good reason for allowing him an enormous income. Nor is the willingness of his clients to pay his fees a sufficient reason, for most of them almost certainly think they should be paying less. The money they pay is different from the praise they give, in that the first is extrinsically determined, the second freely offered.

In a long and thoughtful discussion of egalitarianism in the *Public Interest*, Daniel Bell worries that socialists today are aiming at an "equality of results" instead of the "just meritocracy" (the career open to talents) that he believes was once the goal of leftist and even of revolutionary politics.[5] I confess that I am tempted by "equality of results" in the sphere of money, precisely because it is so hard to see how a person can merit the things that money can buy. On the other hand, it is easy to list cases where merit (of one sort or another) is clearly the right distributive criteria, and where socialism would not require the introduction of any other principle.

> Six people speak at a meeting, advocating different policies, seeking to influence the decision of the assembled group.
> Six doctors are known to aspire to a hospital directorship.
> Six writers publish novels and anxiously await the reviews of the critics.
> Six men seek the company and love of the same woman.

Now, we all know the right reasons for the sorts of decisions, choices, judgments that are in question here. I have never heard anyone seriously argue that the woman must let herself be shared, or the hospital establish a six-man directorate, or the critics distribute their praise evenly, or the people at the meeting adopt all six proposals. In all these cases, the personal qualities of the individuals involved, or the arguments they make, or the work they do (as these appear to the others) should carry the day.

But what sorts of personal qualities are relevant to owning a $20,000 sailboat? A love for sailing, perhaps, and a willingness to build the boat or to do an equivalent amount of work. In America today, it would take a steelworker about two years to earn that money (assuming that he didn't buy anything else during all that time) and it would take a corporation executive a month or two. How can that be right, when the executive also has a rug on the floor, air-conditioning, a deferential secretary, and enormous personal power? He is being paid as he goes, while the steelworker is piling up a kind of moral merit (so we have always been taught) by deferring pleasure. Surely there is no meritocratic defense for this sort of difference. It would seem much better to pay the worker and the executive more or less the same weekly wage and let the sailboat be bought by the person who is willing to forgo other goods and services, that is, by the person who really wants it. Is this "equality of result"? In fact, the results will be different, if the people are, and it seems to me that they will be different for the right reasons.

Against this view, there is a conventional but also very strong argument that can be made on behalf of enterprise and inventiveness. If there is a popular defense of inequality, it is this one, but I don't think it can carry us very far toward the inequalities that Kristol wants to defend. Consider the case of the man who builds a better mousetrap, or opens a restaurant and sells delicious blintzes, or does a little teaching on the side. He has no air-conditioning, no secretary, no power; probably his reward has to be monetary. He has to have a chance, at least, to earn a little more money than his less enterprising neighbors. The market doesn't guarantee that he will in fact earn more, but it does make it possible, and until some other way can be found to do that, market relations are probably defensible under the doctrine of right reasons. Here in the world of the petty-bourgeoisie, it seems appropriate that people able to provide goods or services that are novel, timely, or particularly excellent should reap the rewards they presumably had in mind when they went to work. And that they were right to have in mind: no one would want to feed blintzes to strangers, day after day, merely to win their gratitude.

But one might well want to be a corporation executive, day after day, merely to make all those decisions. It is precisely the people who are paid or who pay themselves vast sums of money who reap all sorts of other rewards too. We need to sort out these different forms of payment. First of all, there are rewards, like the pleasure of exercising power, that are intrinsic to certain jobs. An executive must make decisions—that's what he is there for—and even decisions seriously affecting other people. It is right that he should do that, however, only if he has been persuasive, stimulating, encouraging, and so on, and won the support of a majority of those same people. That he owns the corporation or has been chosen by the owners isn't enough. Indeed, given the nature of corporate power in contemporary society, the following statement (to paraphrase Pascal) is false and tyrannical: because I am rich, so I should make decisions and command obedience. Even in corporations organized democratically, of course, the personal exercise of power will persist. It is more likely to be seen, however, as it is normally seen in political life—as the chief attraction of executive positions. And this will cast a new light on the other rewards of leadership.

The second of these consists in all the side-effects of power: prestige, status, deference, and so on. Democracy tends to reduce these, or should tend that way when it is working well, without significantly reducing the attractions of decision making. The same is true of the third form of reward, money itself, which is owed to work, but not necessarily to place and power. We pay political leaders much less than corporation executives, precisely because we understand so well the excitement and appeal of political office. Insofar as we recognize the political character of corporations, then, we can pay their executives less too. I doubt that there would be a lack of candidates even if we paid them no more than was paid to any other corporation employee. Perhaps there are reasons for paying them more—but not meritocratic reasons, for we give all the attention that is due to their merit when we make them our leaders.

We do not give all due attention to the restaurant owner, however, merely by eating his blintzes. Him we have to pay, and he can ask, I suppose, whatever the market will bear. That's fair enough, and no real threat to equality so long as he can't amass so much money that he becomes a threat to the integrity of the political system and so long as he does not exercise power, tyrannically, over other men and women. Within his proper sphere, he is as good a citizen as any other. His activities recall Dr. Johnson's remark: "There are few ways in which man can be more innocently employed than in getting money."

V

The most immediate occasion of the conservative attack on equality is the reappearance of the quota system—newly designed, or so it is said, to move us closer to egalitarianism rather than to maintain old patterns of religious and racial discrimination. Kristol does not discuss quotas, perhaps because they are not widely supported by professional people (or by professors): the disputes of the last several years do not fit the brazen simplicity of his argument. But almost everyone else talks about them, and Bell worries at some length, and rightly, about the challenge quotas represent to the "just meritocracy" he favors. Indeed, quotas in any form, new or old, establish "wrong reasons" as the basis of important social decisions, perhaps the most important social decisions: who shall be a doctor, who shall be a lawyer, and who shall be a bureaucrat. It is obvious that being black or a woman or having a Spanish surname (any more than being white, male, and Protestant) is no qualification for entering a university or a medical school or joining the civil service. In a sense, then, the critique of quotas consists almost entirely of a series of restatements and reiterations of the argument I have been urging in this essay. One only wishes that the critics would apply it more generally than they seem ready to do. There is more to be said, however, if they consistently refuse to do that.

The positions for which quotas are being urged are, in America today, key entry points to the good life. They open the way, that is, to a life marked above all by a profusion of goods, material and moral: possessions, conveniences, prestige, and deference. Many of these goods are not in any plausible sense appropriate rewards for the work that is being done. They are merely the rewards that upper classes throughout history have been able to seize and hold for their members. Quotas, as they are currently being used, are a way of redistributing these rewards by redistributing the social places to which they conventionally pertain. It is a bad way, because one really wants doctors and (even) civil servants to have certain sorts of qualifications. To the people on the receiving end of medical and bureaucratic services, race and class are a great deal less important than knowledge, competence, courtesy, and so on. I don't want to say that race and class are entirely unimportant: it would be wrong to underestimate the distortions introduced by an inegalitarian society into these sorts of human relations. But if the right reason for receiving medical care is being sick, then the right reason for giving medical care is being able to help the sick. And so medical schools should pay attention, first of all and almost exclusively, to the potential helpfulness of their applicants.

But they may be able to do that only if the usual connections between place and reward are decisively broken. Here is another example of the doctrine of right reasons. If men and women wanted to be doctors primarily because they wanted to be helpful, they would have no reason to object when judgments were made about their potential helpfulness. But so long as there are extrinsic reasons for wanting to be a doctor, there will be pressure to choose doctors (that is, to make medical school places available) for reasons that are similarly extrinsic. So long as the goods that medical schools distribute include more than certificates of competence, include, to be precise, certificates of earning power, quotas are not entirely implausible. I don't see that being black is a worse reason for owning a sailboat than being a doctor. They are equally bad reasons.

Quotas today are a means of lower-class aggrandizement, and they are likely to be resolutely opposed, opposed without guilt and worry, only by people who are entirely content with the class structure as it is and with the present distribution of goods and services. For those of us who are not content, anxiety cannot be avoided. We know that quotas are wrong, but we also know that the present distribution of wealth makes no moral sense, that the dominance of the income curve plays havoc with legitimate distributive principles, and that quotas are a form of redress no more irrational than the world within which and because of which they are demanded. In an egalitarian society, however, quotas would be unnecessary and inexcusable.

VI

I have put forward a difficult argument in very brief form, in order to answer Kristol's even briefer argument—for he is chiefly concerned with the motives of those who advocate equality and not with the case they make or try to make. He is also concerned, he says, with the fact that equality has suddenly been discovered and is now for the first time being advocated as the *chief* virtue of social institutions: as if societies were not complex and values ambiguous. I don't know what discoverers and advocates he has in mind.[6] But it is worth stressing that equality as I have described it does not stand alone, but is closely related to the idea of liberty. The relation is complex, and I cannot say very much about it here. It is a feature of the argument I have made, however, that the right reason for distributing love, belief, and most important for my immediate purposes, political power is the freely given consent of lovers, believers, and citizens. In these sorts of cases, of course, we all have standards to urge upon our fellows: we say that so and so should not be believed unless he offers evidence or that so and so should not be elected to political office unless he commits himself to civil rights. But clearly credence and power are not and ought not to be distributed according to my standards or yours. What is necessary is that everyone else be able to say yes or no. Without liberty, then, there could be no rightful distribution at all. On the other hand, we are not free, not politically free at least, if *his* yes, because of his birth or place or fortune, counts seventeen times more heavily than *my* no. Here the case is exactly as socialists have always claimed it to be: liberty and equality are the two chief virtues of social institutions, and they stand best when they stand together.

(1973)

Notes

1. "About Equality," *Commentary*, November 1972.

2. *Early Writings*, trans. T. B. Bottomore (London, 1963), p. 191.

3. I am also greatly indebted to Bernard Williams, in whose essay "The Idea of Equality" (first published in Laslett and Runciman, *Philosophy, Politics and Society*, second series [Oxford, 1962]) a similar argument is worked out. The example of medical care, to which I recur, is suggested by him. The Pascal quote is from J. M. Cohen's translation of *The Pensées* (London and Baltimore, 1961). no. 244.

4. *Early Writings*, pp. 193–94.

5. "On Meritocracy and Equality," *Public Interest*, Fall 1972.

6. The only writer he mentions is John Rawls, whose *Theory of Justice* (Cambridge, Mass., 1971) Kristol seems entirely to misunderstand. For Rawls explicitly accords priority to the "liberty principle" over those other maxims that point toward greater equality.

41

John Rawls
A Theory of Justice

John Rawls (1921–   ) is professor of philosophy at Harvard University. When his book A Theory of Justice *appeared in 1971, it inaugurated a vigorous debate about political theory, in particular liberal political theory, in the United States and abroad. Few books of political theory have had as much of an impact in recent years. Rawls reinvented social contract theory in order to justify the principles of a liberal democratic welfare state. He asks us to imagine that we are in an "original position" in which we are under a "veil of ignorance." This prevents us from knowing what place or what talents we will have in society. He believes that this establishes the fair conditions in which individuals can choose the basic principles governing society. In these conditions, he believes we would reach the following principles: (1) Each person should have an equal right to the most extensive liberty compatible with the same liberty for others. (2) Social and economic inequalities should be arranged so that they are to the greatest benefit of the least advantaged (the "difference principle"); there will be fair and equal opportunity for all offices.*

Justice as Fairness

In this introductory chapter I sketch some of the main ideas of the theory of justice I wish to develop. The exposition is informal and intended to prepare the way for the more detailed arguments that follow. Unavoidably there is some overlap between this and later discussions. I begin by describing the role of justice in social cooperation and with a brief account of the primary subject of justice, the basic structure of society. I then present the main idea of justice as fairness, a theory of justice that generalizes and carries to a higher level of abstraction the traditional conception of the social contract. The compact of society is replaced by an initial situation that incorporates certain procedural constraints on arguments designed to lead to an original agreement on principles of justice. I also take up, for purposes of clarification and contrast, the classical utilitarian and intuitionist conceptions of justice and consider some of the differences between these views and justice as fairness. My guiding aim is to work out a theory of justice that is a viable alternative to these doctrines which have long dominated our philosophical tradition.

The Role of Justice

Justice is the first virtue of social institutions, as truth is of systems of thought. A theory however elegant and economical must be rejected or revised if it is untrue;

likewise laws and institutions no matter how efficient and well-arranged must be reformed or abolished if they are unjust. Each person possesses an inviolability founded on justice that even the welfare of society as a whole cannot override. For this reason justice denies that the loss of freedom for some is made right by a greater good shared by others. It does not allow that the sacrifices imposed on a few are outweighed by the larger sum of advantages enjoyed by many. Therefore in a just society the liberties of equal citizenship are taken as settled; the rights secured by justice are not subject to political bargaining or to the calculus of social interests. The only thing that permits us to acquiesce in an erroneous theory is the lack of a better one; analogously, an injustice is tolerable only when it is necessary to avoid an even greater injustice. Being first virtues of human activities, truth and justice are uncompromising.

These propositions seem to express our intuitive conviction of the primacy of justice. No doubt they are expressed too strongly. In any event I wish to inquire whether these contentions or others similar to them are sound, and if so how they can be accounted for. To this end it is necessary to work out a theory of justice in the light of which these assertions can be interpreted and assessed. I shall begin by considering the role of the principles of justice. Let us assume, to fix ideas, that a society is a more or less self-sufficient association of persons who in their relations to one another recognize certain rules of conduct as binding and who for the most part act in accordance with them. Suppose further that these rules specify a system of cooperation designed to advance the good of those taking part in it. Then, although a society is a cooperative venture for mutual advantage, it is typically marked by a conflict as well as by an identity of interests. There is an identity of interests since social cooperation makes possible a better life for all than any would have if each were to live solely by his own efforts. There is a conflict of interests since persons are not indifferent as to how the greater benefits produced by their collaboration are distributed, for in order to pursue their ends they each prefer a larger to a lesser share. A set of principles is required for choosing among the various social arrangements which determine this division of advantages and for underwriting an agreement on the proper distributive shares. These principles are the principles of social justice: they provide a way of assigning rights and duties in the basic institutions of society and they define the appropriate distribution of the benefits and burdens of social cooperation.

Now let us say that a society is well-ordered when it is not only designed to advance the good of its members but when it is also effectively regulated by a public conception of justice. That is, it is a society in which (1) everyone accepts and knows that the others accept the same principles of justice, and (2) the basic social institutions generally satisfy and are generally known to satisfy these principles. In this case while men may put forth excessive demands on one another, they nevertheless acknowledge a common point of view from which their claims may be adjudicated. If men's inclination to self-interest makes their vigilance against one another necessary, their public sense of justice makes their secure association together possible. Among individuals with disparate aims and purposes a shared conception of justice establishes the bonds of civic friendship; the general desire for justice limits the pursuit of other ends. One may think of a public conception of justice as constituting the fundamental charter of a well-ordered human association.

Existing societies are of course seldom well-ordered in this sense, for what is just and unjust is usually in dispute. Men disagree about which principles should define the basic terms of their association. Yet we may still say, despite this disagreement, that they each have a conception of justice. That is, they understand the need for, and they are prepared to affirm, a characteristic set of principles for assigning basic rights and duties and for determining what they take to be the proper distribution of the benefits and burdens of social cooperation. Thus it seems natural to think of the concept of justice as distinct from the various conceptions of justice and as being specified by the role which these different sets of principles, these different conceptions, have in common. Those who hold different conceptions of justice can, then, still agree that institutions are just when no arbitrary distinctions are made between persons in the assigning of basic rights and duties and when the rules determine a proper balance between competing claims to the advantages of social life. Men can agree to this description of just institutions since the notions of an arbitrary distinction and of a proper balance, which are included in the concept of justice, are left open for each to interpret according to the principles of justice that he accepts. These principles single out which similarities and differences among persons are relevant in determining rights and duties and they specify which division of advantages is appropriate. Clearly this distinction between the concept and the various conceptions of justice settles no important questions. It simply helps to identify the role of the principles of social justice. . . .

The Subject of Justice

Many different kinds of things are said to be just and unjust: not only laws, institutions, and social systems, but also particular actions of many kinds, including decisions, judgments, and imputations. We also call the attitudes and dispositions of persons, and persons themselves, just and unjust. Our topic, however, is that of social justice. For us the primary subject of justice is the basic structure of society, or more exactly, the way in which the major social institutions distribute fundamental rights and duties and determine the division of advantages from social cooperation. By major institutions I understand the political constitution and the principal economic and social arrangements. Thus the legal protection of freedom of thought and liberty of conscience, competitive markets, private property in the means of production, and the monogamous family are examples of major social institutions. Taken together as one scheme, the major institutions define men's rights and duties and influence their life-prospects, what they can expect to be and how well they can hope to do. The basic structure is the primary subject of justice because its effects are so profound and present from the start. The intuitive notion here is that this structure contains various social positions and that men born into different positions have different expectations of life determined, in part, by the political system as well as by economic and social circumstances. In this way the institutions of society favor certain starting places over others. These are especially deep inequalities. Not only are they pervasive, but they affect men's initial chances in life; yet they cannot possibly be justified by an appeal to the notions of merit or desert. It is these inequalities, presumably inevitable in the basic structure of any society, to which the principles of social justice must in the first instance apply. These principles, then, regulate the choice of a political constitution and the main elements of the economic and social system. The justice of a social scheme depends essentially on how fundamental rights and duties are assigned and on the economic opportunities and social conditions in the various sectors of society. . . .

A conception of social justice, then, is to be regarded as providing in the first instance a standard whereby the distributive aspects of the basic structure of society are to be assessed. This standard, however, is not to be confused with the principles defining the other virtues, for the basic structure, and social arrangements generally, may be efficient or inefficient, liberal or illiberal, and many other things, as well as just or unjust. A complete conception defining principles for all the virtues of the basic structure, together with their respective weights when they conflict, is more than a conception of justice; it is a social ideal. The principles of justice are but a part, although perhaps the most important part, of such a conception. A social ideal in turn is connected with a conception of society, a vision of the way in which the aims and purposes of social cooperation are to be understood. The various conceptions of justice are the outgrowth of different notions of society against the background of opposing views of the natural necessities and opportunities of human life. Fully to understand a conception of justice we must make explicit the conception of social cooperation from which it derives. But in doing this we should not lose sight of the special role of the principles of justice or of the primary subject to which they apply.

The Main Idea of the Theory of Justice

My aim is to present a conception of justice which generalizes and carries to a higher level of abstraction the familiar theory of the social contract as found, say, in Locke, Rousseau, and Kant. In order to do this we are not to think of the original contract as one to enter a particular society or to set up a particular form of government. Rather, the guiding idea is that the principles of justice for the basic structure of society are the object of the original agreement. They are the principles that free and rational persons concerned to further their own interests would accept in an initial position of equality as defining the fundamental terms of their association. These principles are to regulate all further agreements; they specify the kinds of social cooperation that can be entered into and the forms of government that can be established. This way of regarding the principles of justice I shall call justice as fairness.

Thus we are to imagine that those who engage in social cooperation choose together, in one joint act, the principles which are to assign basic rights and duties and to determine the division of social benefits. Men are to decide in advance how they are to regulate their claims against one another and what is to be the foundation charter of their society. Just as each person must decide by rational reflection what constitutes his good, that is, the system of ends which it is rational for him to pursue, so a group of persons must decide once and for all what is to count among them as just and unjust. The choice which rational men would make in this hypothetical situation of equal liberty, assuming for the present that this choice problem has a solution, determines the principles of justice.

In justice as fairness the original position of equality corresponds to the state of nature in the traditional theory of the social contract. This original position is not, of course, thought of as an actual historical state of affairs, much less as a primitive condition of culture. It is understood as a purely hypothetical situation characterized so as to lead to a certain conception of justice. Among the essential features of this situation is that no one knows his place in society, his class position or social status, nor does any one know his fortune in the distribution of natural assets and abilities, his intelligence, strength, and the like. I shall even assume that the parties do not know their conceptions of the good or their special psychological propensities. The principles of justice are chosen behind a veil of ignorance. This ensures that no one is advantaged or disadvantaged in the choice of principles by the outcome of natural chance or the contingency of social circumstances. Since all are similarly situated and no one is able to design principles to favor his particular condition, the principles of justice are the result of a fair agreement or bargain. For given the circumstances of the original position, the symmetry of everyone's relations to each other, this initial situation is fair between individuals as moral persons, that is, as rational beings with their own ends and capable, I shall assume, of a sense of justice. The original position is, one might say, the appropriate initial status quo, and thus the fundamental agreements reached in it are fair. This explains the propriety of the name "justice as fairness": it conveys the idea that the principles of justice are agreed to in an initial situation that is fair. The name does not mean that the concepts of justice and fairness are the same, any more than the phrase "poetry as metaphor" means that the concepts of poetry and metaphor are the same.

Justice as fairness begins, as I have said, with one of the most general of all choices which persons might make together, namely, with the choice of the first principles of a conception of justice which is to regulate all subsequent criticism and reform of institutions. Then, having chosen a conception of justice, we can suppose that they are to choose a constitution and a legislature to enact laws, and so on, all in accordance with the principles of justice initially agreed upon. Our social situation is just if it is such that by this sequence of hypothetical agreements we would have contracted into the general system of rules which defines it. Moreover, assuming that the original position does determine a set of principles (that is, that a particular conception of justice would be chosen), it will then be true that whenever social institutions satisfy these principles those engaged in them can say to one another that they are cooperating on terms to which they would agree if they were free and equal persons whose relations with respect to one another were fair. They could all view their arrangements as meeting the stipulations which they would acknowledge in an initial situation that embodies widely accepted and reasonable constraints on the choice of principles. The general recognition of this fact would provide the basis for a public acceptance of the corresponding principles of justice. No society can, of course, be a scheme of cooperation which men enter voluntarily in a literal sense; each person finds himself placed at birth in some particular position in some particular society, and the nature of this position materially affects his life prospects. Yet a society satisfying the principles of justice as fairness comes as close as a society can to being a voluntary scheme, for it meets the principles which free and equal persons would assent to under circumstances that are fair. In this sense its members are autonomous and the obligations they recognize self-imposed.

One feature of justice as fairness is to think of the parties in the initial situation as rational and mutually disinterested. This does not mean that the parties are egoists, that is, individuals with only certain kinds of interests, say in wealth, prestige, and domination. But they are conceived as not taking an interest in one another's interests. They are to presume that even their spiritual aims may be opposed, in the way that the aims of those of different religions may be opposed. Moreover, the concept of rationality must be interpreted as far as possible in the narrow sense, standard in economic theory, of taking the most effective means to given ends. . . . One must try to avoid introducing into it any controversial ethical elements. The initial situation must be characterized by stipulations that are widely accepted.

In working out the conception of justice as fairness one main task clearly is to determine which principles of justice would be chosen in the original position. . . .

The merit of the contract terminology is that it conveys the idea that principles of justice may be conceived as principles that would be chosen by rational persons, and that in this way conceptions of justice may be explained and justified. The theory of justice is a part, perhaps the most significant part, of the theory of rational choice. Furthermore, principles of justice deal with conflicting claims upon the advantages won by social cooperation; they apply to the relations among several persons or groups. The word "contract" suggests this plurality as well as the condition that the appropriate division of advantages must be in accordance with principles acceptable to all parties. The condition of publicity for principles of justice is also connoted by the contract phraseology. Thus, if these principles are the outcome of an agreement, citizens have a knowledge of the principles that others follow. It is characteristic of contract theories to stress the public nature of political principles. Finally there is the long tradition of the contract doctrine. Expressing the tie with this line of thought helps to define ideas and accords with natural piety. There are then several advantages in the use of the term "contract." With due precautions taken, it should not be misleading. . . .

The Original Position and Justification

I have said that the original position is the appropriate initial status quo which insures that the fundamental agreements reached in it are fair. This fact yields the name "justice as fairness." It is clear, then, that I want to say that one conception of justice is more reasonable than another, or justifiable with respect to it, if rational persons in the initial situation would choose its principles over those of the other for the role of justice. Conceptions of justice are to be ranked by their acceptability to persons so circumstanced. Understood in this way the question of justification is settled by working out a problem of deliberation: we have to ascertain which principles it would be rational to adopt given the contractual situation. This connects the theory of justice with the theory of rational choice.

If this view of the problem of justification is to succeed, we must, of course, describe in some detail the nature of this choice problem. A problem of rational decision has a definite answer only if we know the beliefs and interests of the parties, their relations with respect to one another, the alternatives between which they are to choose, the procedure whereby they make up their minds, and so on. As the circumstances are presented in different ways, correspondingly different principles are accepted. The concept of the original position, as I shall refer to it, is that of the most philosophically favored interpretation of this initial choice situation for the purposes of a theory of justice.

But how are we to decide what is the most favored interpretation? I assume, for one thing, that there is a broad measure of agreement that principles of justice should be chosen under certain conditions. To justify a particular description of the initial situation one shows that it incorporates these commonly shared presumptions. One argues from widely accepted but weak premises to more specific conclusions. Each of the presumptions should by itself be natural and plausible; some of them may seem innocuous or even trivial. The aim of the contract approach is to establish that taken together they impose significant bounds on acceptable principles of justice. The ideal outcome would be that these conditions determine a unique set of principles; but I shall be satisfied if they suffice to rank the main traditional conceptions of social justice.

One should not be misled, then, by the somewhat unusual conditions which characterize the original position. The idea here is simply to make vivid to ourselves the restrictions that it seems reasonable to impose on arguments for principles of justice, and therefore on these principles themselves. Thus it seems reasonable and generally acceptable that no one should be advantaged or disadvantaged by natural fortune or social circumstances in the choice of principles. It also seems widely agreed that it should be impossible to tailor principles to the circumstances of one's own case. We should insure further that particular inclinations and aspirations, and persons' conceptions of their good do not affect the principles adopted. The aim is to rule out those principles that it would be rational to propose for acceptance, however little the chance of success, only if one knew certain things that are irrelevant from the standpoint of justice. For example, if a man knew that he was wealthy, he might find it rational to advance the principle that various taxes for welfare measures be counted unjust; if he knew that he was poor, he would most likely propose the contrary principle. To represent the desired restrictions one imagines a situation in which everyone is deprived of this sort of information. One excludes the knowledge of those contingencies which sets men at odds and allows them to be guided by their prejudices. In this manner the veil of ignorance is arrived at in a natural way. This concept should cause no difficulty if we keep in mind the constraints on arguments that it is meant to express. At any time we can enter the original position, so to speak, simply by following a certain procedure, namely, by arguing for principles of justice in accordance with these restrictions.

It seems reasonable to suppose that the parties in the original position are equal. That is, all have the same rights in the procedure for choosing principles; each can make proposals, submit reasons for their acceptance, and so on. Obviously the purpose of these conditions is to represent equality between human beings as moral persons, as creatures having a conception of their good and capable of a sense of justice. The basis of equality is taken to be similarity in these two respects. Systems of ends are not ranked in value; and each man is presumed to have the requisite ability to understand and to act upon whatever principles are adopted. Together with the veil of ignorance, these conditions define the principles of justice as those which rational persons concerned to advance their interests would consent to as equals when none are known to be advantaged or disadvantaged by social and natural contingencies.

There is, however, another side to justifying a particular description of the original position. This is to see if the principles which would be chosen match our considered convictions of justice or extend them in an acceptable way. We can note whether applying these principles would lead us to make the same judgments about the basic structure of society which we now make intuitively and in which we have the greatest confidence; or whether, in cases where our present judgments are in doubt and given with hesitation, these principles offer a resolution which we can affirm on reflection. There are questions which we feel sure must be answered in a certain way. For example, we are confident that religious intolerance and racial discrimination are unjust. We think that we have examined these things with care and have reached what we believe is an impartial judgment not likely to be distorted by an excessive attention to our own interests. These convictions are provisional fixed points which we presume any conception of justice must fit. But we have much less assurance as to what is the correct distribution of wealth and authority. Here we may be looking for a way to remove our doubts. We can check an interpretation of the initial situation, then, by the capacity of its principles to accommodate our firmest convictions and to provide guidance where guidance is needed. . . .

A final comment. We shall want to say that certain principles of justice are justified because they would be agreed to in an initial situation of equality. I have emphasized that this original position is purely hypothetical. It is natural to ask why, if this agreement is never actually entered into, we should take any interest in these principles, moral or otherwise. The answer is that the conditions embodied in the description of the original position are ones that we do in fact accept. Or if we do not, then perhaps we can be persuaded to do so by philosophical reflection. Each aspect of the contractual situation can be given supporting grounds. Thus what we shall do is to collect together into one conception a number of conditions on principles that we are ready upon due consideration to recognize as reasonable. These constraints express what we are prepared to regard as limits on fair terms of social cooperation. One way to look at the idea of the original position, therefore, is to see it as an expository device which sums up the meaning of these conditions and helps us to extract their consequences. On the other hand, this conception is also an intuitive notion that suggests its own elaboration, so that led on by it we are drawn to define more clearly the standpoint from which we can best interpret moral relationships. We need a conception that enables us to envision our objective from afar: the intuitive notion of the original position is to do this for us. . . .

Two Principles of Justice

I shall now state in a provisional form the two principles of justice that I believe would be chosen in the original position. In this section I wish to make only the most general comments, and therefore the first formulation of these principles is tentative. As we go on I shall run through several formulations and approximate step by step the final statement to be given much later. I believe that doing this allows the exposition to proceed in a natural way.

The first statement of the two principles reads as follows.

First: each person is to have an equal right to the most extensive basic liberty compatible with a similar liberty for others.

Second: social and economic inequalities are to be arranged so that they are both (a) reasonably expected to be to everyone's advantage, and (b) attached to positions and offices open to all. . . .

By way of general comment, these principles primarily apply, as I have said, to the basic structure of society. They are to govern the assignment of rights and duties and to regulate the distribution of social and economic advantages. As their formulation suggests, these principles presuppose that the social structure can be divided into two more or less distinct parts, the first principle applying to the one, the second to the other. They distinguish between those aspects of the social system that define and secure the equal liberties of citizenship and those that specify and establish social and economic inequalities. The basic liberties of citizens are, roughly speaking, political liberty (the right to vote and to be eligible for public office) together with freedom of speech and assembly; liberty of conscience and freedom of thought; freedom of the person along with the right to hold (personal) property; and freedom from arbitrary arrest and seizure as defined by the concept of the rule of law. These liberties are all required to be equal by the first principle, since citizens of a just society are to have the same basic rights.

The second principle applies, in the first approximation, to the distribution of income and wealth and to the design of organizations that make use of differences in authority and responsibility, or chains of command. While the distribution of wealth and income need not be equal, it must be to everyone's advantage, and at the same time, positions of authority and offices of command must be accessible to all. One applies the second principle by holding positions open, and then, subject to this constraint, arranges social and economic inequalities so that everyone benefits.

These principles are to be arranged in a serial order with the first principle prior to the second. This ordering means that a departure from the institutions of equal liberty required by the first principle cannot be justified by, or compensated for, by greater social and economic advantages. The distribution of wealth and income, and the hierarchies of authority, must be consistent with both the liberties of equal citizenship and equality of opportunity.

It is clear that these principles are rather specific in their content, and their acceptance rests on certain assumptions that I must eventually try to explain and justify. A theory of justice depends upon a theory of society in ways that will become evident as we proceed. For the present, it should be observed that the two principles (and this holds for all formulations) are a special case of a more general conception of justice that can be expressed as follows.

> All social values—liberty and opportunity, income and wealth, and the bases of self-respect—are to be distributed equally unless an unequal distribution of any, or all, of these values is to everyone's advantage.

Injustice, then, is simply inequalities that are not to the benefit of all. Of course, this conception is extremely vague and requires interpretation.

As a first step, suppose that the basic structure of society distributes certain primary goods, that is, things that every rational man is presumed to want. These goods normally have a use whatever a person's rational plan of life. For simplicity, assume that the chief primary goods at the disposition of society are rights and liberties, powers and opportunities, income and wealth. (Later on in Part Three the primary good of self-respect has a central place.) These are the social primary goods. Other primary goods such as health and vigor, intelligence and imagination, are natural goods; although their possession is influenced by the basic structure, they are not so directly under its control. Imagine, then, a hypothetical initial arrangement in which all the social primary goods are equally distributed: everyone has similar rights and duties, and income and wealth are evenly shared. This state of affairs provides a benchmark for judging improvements. If certain inequalities of wealth and organizational powers would make everyone better off than in this hypothetical starting situation, then they accord with the general conception.

Now it is possible, at least theoretically, that by giving up some of their fundamental liberties men are sufficiently compensated by the resulting social and economic gains. The general conception of justice imposes no restrictions on what sort of inequalities are permissible; it only requires that everyone's position be improved. We need not suppose anything so drastic as consenting to a condition of slavery. Imagine instead that men forego certain political rights when the economic returns are significant and their capacity to influence the course of policy by the exercise of these rights would be marginal in any case. It is this kind of exchange which the two principles as stated rule out; being arranged in serial order they do not permit exchanges between basic liberties and economic and social gains. The serial ordering of principles expresses an underlying preference among primary social goods. When this preference is rational so likewise is the choice of these principles in this order. . . .

Another thing to bear in mind is that when principles mention persons, or require that everyone gain from an inequality, the reference is to representative persons holding the various social positions, or offices, or whatever, established by the basic structure. Thus in applying the second principle I assume that it is possible to assign an expectation of well-being to representative individuals holding these positions. This expectation indicates their life prospects as viewed from their social station. In general, the expectations of representative persons depend upon the distribution of rights and duties throughout the basic structure. When this changes, expectations change. I assume, then, that expectations are connected: by raising the prospects of the representative man in one position we presumably increase or decrease the prospects of representative men in other positions. Since it applies to institutional forms, the second principle (or rather the first part of it) refers to the expectations of representative individuals. As I shall discuss below, neither principle applies to distributions of particular goods to particular individuals who may be identified by their proper names. The situation where someone is considering how to allocate certain commodities to needy persons who are known to him is not within the scope of the principles. They are meant to regulate basic institutional arrangements. We must not assume that there is much similarity from the standpoint of justice between an administrative allotment of goods to specific persons and the appropriate design of society. Our common sense intuitions for the former may be a poor guide to the latter.

Now the second principle insists that each person benefit from permissible inequalities in the basic structure. This means that it must be reasonable for each relevant representative man defined by this structure, when he views it as a going concern, to prefer his prospects with the inequality to his prospects without it. One is not allowed to justify differences in income or organizational powers on the ground that the disadvantages of those in one position are outweighed by the greater advantages of those in another. Much less can infringements of liberty be counterbalanced in this. . . .

Democratic Equality and the Difference Principle

[Democratic equality] is arrived at by combining the principle of fair equality of opportunity with the difference principle. . . . Assuming the framework of institu-

tions required by equal liberty and fair equality of opportunity, the higher expectations of those better situated are just if and only if they work as part of a scheme
which improves the expectations of the least advantaged members of society. The
intuitive idea is that the social order is not to establish and secure the more attractive prospects of those better off unless doing so is to the advantage of those less
fortunate. . . .

To illustrate the difference principle, consider the distribution of income among
social classes. Let us suppose that the various income groups correlate with representative individuals by reference to whose expectations we can judge the distribution. Now those starting out as members of the entrepreneurial class in *property-
owning democracy*, say, have a better prospect than those who begin in the class
of unskilled laborers. It seems likely that this will be true even when the social
injustices which now exist are removed. What, then, can possibly justify this kind
of initial inequality in life prospects? According to the difference principle, it is
justifiable only if the difference in expectation is to the advantage of the representative man who is worse off, in this case the representative unskilled worker. The
inequality in expectation is permissible only if lowering it would make the working class even more worse off. Supposedly, given the rider in the second principle
concerning open positions, and the principle of liberty generally, the greater expectations allowed to entrepreneurs encourages them to do things which raise the
long-term prospects of the laboring class. Their better prospects act as incentives
so that the economic process is more efficient, innovation proceeds at a faster
pace, and so on. Eventually the resulting material benefits spread throughout the
system and to the least advantaged. I shall not consider how far these things are
true. The point is that something of this kind must be argued if these inequalities
are to be just by the difference principle. . . .

Fair Equality of Opportunity and Pure Procedural Justice

I should now like to comment upon the second part of the second principle, henceforth to be understood as the liberal principle of fair equality of opportunity. It
must not then be confused with the notion of careers open to talents. . . .

I should note that the reasons for requiring open positions are not solely, or
even primarily, those of efficiency. I have not maintained that offices must be
open if in fact everyone is to benefit from an arrangement. For it may be possible
to improve everyone's situation by assigning certain powers and benefits to positions despite the fact that certain groups are excluded from them. Although access
is restricted, perhaps these offices can still attract superior talent and encourage
better performance. But the principle of open positions forbids this. It expresses
the conviction that if some places were not open on a basis fair to all, those kept
out would be right in feeling unjustly treated even though they benefited from the
greater efforts of those who were allowed to hold them. They would be justified in
their complaint not only because they were excluded from certain external rewards
of office such as wealth and privilege, but because they were debarred from expe-

riencing the realization of self which comes from a skillful and devoted exercise of social duties. They would be deprived of one of the main forms of human good.

Now I have said that the basic structure is the primary subject of justice. This means, as we have seen, that the first distributive problem is the assignment of fundamental rights and duties and the regulation of social and economic inequalities and of the legitimate expectations founded on these. Of course, any ethical theory recognizes the importance of the basic structure as a subject of justice, but not all theories regard its importance in the same way. In justice as fairness society is interpreted as a cooperative venture for mutual advantage. The basic structure is a public system of rules defining a scheme of activities that leads men to act together so as to produce a greater sum of benefits and assigns to each certain recognized claims to a share in the proceeds. What a person does depends upon what the public rules say he will be entitled to, and what a person is entitled to depends on what he does. The distribution which results is arrived at by honoring the claims determined by what persons undertake to do in the light of these legitimate expectations. . . .

Primary Social Goods as the Basis of Expectations

The theory of the good adopted to account for primary goods . . . is a familiar one going back to Aristotle, and something like it is accepted by philosophers so different in other respects as Kant and Sidgwick. It is not in dispute between the contract doctrine and utilitarianism. The main idea is that a person's good is determined by what is for him the most rational long-term plan of life given reasonably favorable circumstances. A man is happy when he is more or less successful in the way of carrying out his plan. To put it briefly, the good is the satisfaction of rational desire. We are to suppose, then, that each individual has a rational plan of life drawn up subject to the conditions that confront him. This plan is designed to permit the harmonious satisfaction of his interests. It schedules activities so that various desires can be fulfilled without interference. It is arrived at by rejecting other plans that are either less likely to succeed or do not provide for such an inclusive attainment of aims. Given the alternatives available, a rational plan is one which cannot be improved upon; there is no other plan which, taking everything into account, would be preferable.

Now the assumption is that though men's rational plans do have different final ends, they nevertheless all require for their execution certain primary goods, natural and social. Plans differ since individual abilities, circumstances, and wants differ; rational plans are adjusted to these contingencies. But whatever one's system of ends, primary goods are necessary means. Greater intelligence, wealth and opportunity, for example, allow a person to achieve ends he could not rationally contemplate otherwise. The expectations of representative men are, then, to be defined by the index of primary social goods available to them. While the persons in the original position do not know their conception of the good, they do know, I assume, that they prefer more rather than less primary goods. And this information is sufficient for them to know how to advance their interests in the initial situation.

Relevant Social Positions

In applying the two principles of justice to the basic structure of society one takes the position of certain representative individuals and considers how the social system looks to them. The difference principle, for example, requires that the higher expectations of the more advantaged contribute to the prospects of the least advantaged. Or as I sometimes say more loosely, social and economic inequalities must be in the interest of the representative men in all relevant social positions. The perspective of those in these situations defines a suitably general point of view. But certainly not all social positions are relevant. For not only are there farmers, say, but dairy farmers, wheat farmers, farmers working on large tracts of land, and so on for other occupations and groups indefinitely. We cannot have a coherent and manageable theory if we must take such a multiplicity of positions into account. The assessment of so many competing claims is impossible. Therefore we need to identify certain positions as more basic than the others and as providing an appropriate standpoint for judging the social system. Thus the choice of these positions becomes part of the theory of justice. On what principle, though, are they to be identified?

To answer this question we must keep in mind the fundamental problem of justice and the manner in which the two principles cope with it. The primary subject of justice, as I have emphasized, is the basic structure of society. The reason for this is that its effects are so profound and pervasive, and present from birth. This structure favors some starting places over others in the division of the benefits of social cooperation. It is these inequalities which the two principles are to regulate. Once these principles are satisfied, other inequalities are allowed to arise from men's voluntary actions in accordance with the principle of free association. Thus the relevant social positions are, so to speak, the starting places properly generalized and aggregated. By choosing these positions to specify the general point of view one follows the idea that the two principles attempt to mitigate the arbitrariness of natural contingency and social fortune.

I suppose, then, that for the most part each person holds two relevant positions: that of equal citizenship and that defined by his place in the distribution of income and wealth. The relevant representative men, therefore, are the representative citizens and those who stand for the various levels of well-being. Since I assume that in general other positions are entered into voluntarily, we need not consider the point of view of men in these positions in judging the basic structure. Indeed, we are to adjust the whole scheme to suit the preferences of those in the so-called starting places. In judging the social system we are to disregard our more specific interests and associations and look at our situation from the standpoint of these representative men.

Now as far as possible the basic structure should be appraised from the position of equal citizenship. This position is defined by the rights and liberties required by the principle of equal liberty and the principle of fair equality of opportunity. When the two principles are satisfied, all are equal citizens, and so everyone holds this position. In this sense, equal citizenship defines a general point of view. The problems of adjudicating among the fundamental liberties are settled by reference to it. . . .

[A] serious difficulty is how to define the least fortunate group.

Here it seems impossible to avoid a certain arbitrariness. One possibility is to choose a particular social position, say that of the unskilled worker, and then to count as the least advantaged all those with the average income and wealth of this group, or less. The expectation of the lowest representative man is defined as the average taken over this whole class. Another alternative is a definition solely in terms of relative income and wealth with no reference to social position. Thus all persons with less than half of the median income and wealth may be taken as the least advantaged segment. This definition depends only upon the lower half of the distribution and has the merit of focusing attention on the social distance between those who have least and the average citizen. Surely this gap is an essential feature of the situation of the less favored members of society. I suppose that either of these definitions, or some combination of them, will serve well enough. . . .

The Tendency to Equality

. . . We see then that the difference principle represents, in effect, an agreement to regard the distribution of natural talents as a common asset and to share in the benefits of this distribution whatever it turns out to be. Those who have been favored by nature, whoever they are, may gain from their good fortune only on terms that improve the situation of those who have lost out. The naturally advantaged are not to gain merely because they are more gifted, but only to cover the costs of training and education and for using their endowments in ways that help the less fortunate as well. No one deserves his greater natural capacity nor merits a more favorable starting place in society. But it does not follow that one should eliminate these distinctions. There is another way to deal with them. The basic structure can be arranged so that these contingencies work for the good of the least fortunate. Thus we are led to the difference principle if we wish to set up the social system so that no one gains or loses from his arbitrary place in the distribution of natural assets or his initial position in society without giving or receiving compensating advantages in return. . . .

A further merit of the difference principle is that it provides an interpretation of the principle of fraternity. In comparison with liberty and equality, the idea of fraternity has had a lesser place in democratic theory. It is thought to be less specifically a political concept, not in itself defining any of the democratic rights but conveying instead certain attitudes of mind and forms of conduct without which we would lose sight of the values expressed by these rights. Or closely related to this, fraternity is held to represent a certain equality of social esteem manifest in various public conventions and in the absence of manners of deference and servility. No doubt fraternity does imply these things, as well as a sense of civic friendship and social solidarity, but so understood it expresses no definite requirement. We have yet to find a principle of justice that matches the underlying idea. The difference principle, however, does seem to correspond to a natural meaning of fraternity: namely, to the idea of not wanting to have greater advantages unless this is to the benefit of others who are less well off. The family, in its ideal conception and often in practice, is one place where the principle of maximizing the sum of advantages is rejected. Members of a family commonly do not wish to gain unless they can do so in ways that further the interests of the rest. Now wanting to act on the difference principle has precisely this consequence. Those better circumstanced are willing to have their greater advantages only under a scheme in which this works out for the benefit of the less fortunate.

Principles for Individuals: the Natural Duties

From the standpoint of justice as fairness, a fundamental natural duty is the duty of justice. This duty requires us to support and to comply with just institutions that exist and apply to us. It also constrains us to further just arrangements not yet established, at least when this can be done without too much cost to ourselves. Thus if the basic structure of society is just, or as just as it is reasonable to expect in the circumstances, everyone has a natural duty to do his part in the existing scheme. Each is bound to these institutions independent of his voluntary acts, performative or otherwise. Thus even though the principles of natural duty are derived from a contractarian point of view, they do not presuppose an act of consent, express or tacit, or indeed any voluntary act, in order to apply. The principles that hold for individuals, just as the principles for institutions, are those that would be acknowledged in the original position. These principles are understood as the outcome of a hypothetical agreement. If their formulation shows that no binding action, consensual or otherwise, is a presupposition of their application, then they apply unconditionally. The reason why obligations depend upon voluntary acts is given by the second part of the principle of fairness which states this condition. It has nothing to do with the contractual nature of justice as fairness. In fact, once the full set of principles, a complete conception of right, is on hand, we can simply forget about the conception of original position and apply these principles as we would any others.

The Original Position

The Nature of the Argument for Conceptions of Justice

The intuitive idea of justice as fairness is to think of the first principles of justice as themselves the object of an original agreement in a suitably defined initial situation. These principles are those which rational persons concerned to advance their interests would accept in this position of equality to settle the basic terms of their association. It must be shown, then, that the two principles of justice are the solution for the problem of choice presented by the original position. In order to do this, one must establish that, given the circumstances of the parties, and their knowledge, beliefs, and interests, an agreement on these principles is the best way for each person to secure his ends in view of the alternatives available. . . .

The Circumstances of Justice

The circumstances of justice may be described as the normal conditions under which human cooperation is both possible and necessary. Thus, as I noted at the outset, although a society is a cooperative venture for mutual advantage, it is typically marked by a conflict as well as an identity of interests. There is an identity of interests since social cooperation makes possible a better life for all than any would have if each were to try to live solely by his own efforts. . . .

When it is supposed that the parties are severally disinterested, and are not willing to have their interests sacrificed to the others, the intention is to express men's conduct and motives in cases where questions of justice arise. The spiritual ideals of saints and heroes can be as irreconcilably opposed as any other interests. Conflicts in pursuit of these ideals are the most tragic of all. Thus justice is the virtue of practices where there are competing interests and where persons feel entitled to press their rights on each other. In an association of saints agreeing on a common ideal, if such a community could exist, disputes about justice would not occur. Each would work selflessly for one end as determined by their common religion, and reference to this end (assuming it to be clearly defined) would settle every question of right. But a human society is characterized by the circumstances of justice. The account of these conditions involves no particular theory of human motivation. Rather, its aim is to include in the description of the original position the relations of individuals to one another which set the stage for questions of justice. . . .

The Veil of Ignorance

The idea of the original position is to set up a fair procedure so that any principles agreed to will be just. The aim is to use the notion of pure procedural justice as a basis of theory. Somehow we must nullify the effects of specific contingencies which put men at odds and tempt them to exploit social and natural circumstances to their own advantage. Now in order to do this I assume that the parties are situated behind a veil of ignorance. They do not know how the various alternatives will affect their own particular case and they are obliged to evaluate principles solely on the basis of general considerations.

It is assumed, then, that the parties do not know certain kinds of particular facts. First of all, no one knows his place in society, his class position or social status; nor does he know his fortune in the distribution of natural assets and abilities, his intelligence and strength, and the like. Nor, again, does anyone know his conception of the good, the particulars of his rational plan of life, or even the special features of his psychology such as his aversion to risk or liability to optimism or pessimism. More than this, I assume that the parties do not know the particular circumstances of their own society. That is, they do not know its economic or political situation, or the level of civilization and culture it has been able to achieve. The persons in the original position have no information as to which generation they belong. These broader restrictions on knowledge are appropriate in part because questions of social justice arise between generations as well as within them, for example, the question of the appropriate rate of capital saving and of the conservation of natural resources and the environment of nature. There is also, theoretically anyway, the question of a reasonable genetic policy. In these cases too, in order to carry through the idea of the original position, the parties must not know the contingencies that set them in opposition. They must choose principles the consequences of which they are prepared to live with whatever generation they turn out to belong to.

As far as possible, then, the only particular facts which the parties know is that their society is subject to the circumstances of justice and whatever this implies. It is taken for granted, however, that they know the general facts about human society. They understand political affairs and the principles of economic theory; they know the basis of social organization and the laws of human psychology. Indeed, the parties are presumed to know whatever general facts affect the choice of the principles of justice. . . .

Since the differences among the parties are unknown to them, and everyone is equally rational and similarly situated, each is convinced by the same arguments. Therefore, we can view the choice in the original position from the standpoint of one person selected at random. If anyone after due reflection prefers a conception of justice to another, then they all do, and a unanimous agreement can be reached. We can, to make the circumstances more vivid, imagine that the parties are required to communicate with each other through a referee as intermediary, and that he is to announce which alternatives have been suggested and the reasons offered in their support. He forbids the attempt to form coalitions, and he informs the parties when they have come to an understanding. But such a referee is actually superfluous, assuming that the deliberations of the parties must be similar.

Thus there follows the very important consequence that the parties have no basis for bargaining in the usual sense. No one knows his situation in society nor his natural assets, and therefore no one is in a position to tailor principles to his advantage. . . .

The Rationality of the Parties

I have assumed throughout that the persons in the original position are rational. In choosing between principles each tries as best he can to advance his interests. But

I have also assumed that the parties do not know their conception of the good. This means that while they know that they have some rational plan of life, they do not know the details of this plan, the particular ends and interests which it is calculated to promote. How, then, can they decide which conceptions of justice are most to their advantage? Or must we suppose that they are reduced to mere guessing? To meet this difficulty, I postulate that they accept the account of the good touched upon in the preceding chapter: they assume that they would prefer more primary social goods rather than less. Of course, it may turn out, once the veil of ignorance is removed, that some of them for religious or other reasons may not, in fact, want more of these goods. But from the standpoint of the original position, it is rational for the parties to suppose that they do want a larger share, since in any case they are not compelled to accept more if they do not wish to, nor does a person suffer from a greater liberty. Thus even though the parties are deprived of information about their particular ends, they have enough knowledge to rank the alternatives. They know that in general they must try to protect their liberties, widen their opportunities, and enlarge their means for promoting their aims whatever these are. Guided by the theory of the good and the general facts of moral psychology, their deliberations are no longer guesswork. They can make a rational decision in the ordinary sense.

The concept of rationality invoked here, with the exception of one essential feature, is the standard one familiar in social theory. Thus in the usual way, a rational person is thought to have a coherent set of preferences between the options open to him. He ranks these options according to how well they further his purposes; he follows the plan which will satisfy more of his desires rather than less, and which has the greater chance of being successfully executed. The special assumption I make is that a rational individual does not suffer from envy. He is not ready to accept a loss for himself if only others have less as well. . . .

The assumption of mutually disinterested rationality, then, comes to this: the persons in the original position try to acknowledge principles which advance their system of ends as far as possible. They do this by attempting to win for themselves the highest index of primary social goods, since this enables them to promote their conception of the good most effectively whatever it turns out to be. The parties do not seek to confer benefits or to impose injuries on one another; they are not moved by affection or rancor. Nor do they try to gain relative to each other; they are not envious or vain. Put in terms of a game, we might say: they strive for as high an absolute score as possible. They do not wish a high or a low score for their opponents, nor do they seek to maximize or minimize the difference between their successes and those of others. . . .

The Reasoning Leading to the Two Principles of Justice

. . . It will be recalled that the general conception of justice as fairness requires that all primary social goods be distributed equally unless an unequal distribution would be to everyone's advantage. No restrictions are placed on exchanges of these goods and therefore a lesser liberty can be compensated for by greater social and economic benefits. Now looking at the situation from the standpoint of one person selected arbitrarily, there is no way for him to win special advantages for himself. Nor, on the other hand, are there grounds for his acquiescing in special disadvantages. Since it is not reasonable for him to expect more than an equal share in the division of social goods, and since it is not rational for him to agree to less, the sensible thing for him to do is to acknowledge as the first principle of justice one requiring an equal distribution. Indeed, this principle is so obvious that we would expect it to occur to anyone immediately.

Thus, the parties start with a principle establishing equal liberty for all, including equality of opportunity, as well as an equal distribution of income and wealth. But there is no reason why this acknowledgment should be final. If there are inequalities in the basic structure that work to make everyone better off in comparison with the benchmark of initial equality, why not permit them? The immediate gain which a greater equality might allow can be regarded as intelligently invested in view of its future return. If, for example, these inequalities set up various incentives which succeed in eliciting more productive efforts, a person in the original position may look upon them as necessary to cover the costs of training and to encourage effective performance. One might think that ideally individuals should want to serve one another. But since the parties are assumed not to take an interest in one another's interests, their acceptance of these inequalities is only the acceptance of the relations in which men stand in the circumstances of justice. They have no grounds for complaining of one another's motives. A person in the original position would, therefore, concede the justice of these inequalities. Indeed, it would be shortsighted of him not to do so. He would hesitate to agree to these regularities only if he would be dejected by the bare knowledge or perception that others were better situated; and I have assumed that the parties decide as if they are not moved by envy. In order to make the principle regulating inequalities determinate, one looks at the system from the standpoint of the least advantaged representative man. Inequalities are permissible when they maximize, or at least all contribute to, the long-term expectations of the least fortunate group in society.

Now this general conception imposes no constraints on what sorts of inequalities are allowed, whereas the special conception, by putting the two principles in serial order (with the necessary adjustments in meaning), forbids exchanges between basic liberties and economic and social benefits.

. . . But roughly, the idea underlying this ordering is that if the parties assume that their basic liberties can be effectively exercised, they will not exchange a lesser liberty for an improvement in economic well-being. It is only when social conditions do not allow the effective establishment of these rights that one can concede their limitation; and these restrictions can be granted only to the extent that they are necessary to prepare the way for a free society. The denial of equal liberty can be defended only if it is necessary to raise the level of civilization so that in due course these freedoms can be enjoyed. Thus in adopting a serial order we are in effect making a special assumption in the original position, namely, that the parties know that the conditions of their society, whatever they are, admit the effective realization of the equal liberties. The serial ordering of the two principles of justice eventually comes to be reasonable if the general conception is consistently followed. This lexical ranking is the long-run tendency of the general view. . . .

It is useful as a heuristic device to think of the two principles as the maximin solution to the problem of social justice. There is an analogy between the two principles and the maximin rule for choice under uncertainty. This is evident from the fact that the two principles are those a person would choose for the design of a society in which his enemy is to assign him his place. The maximin rule tells us to rank alternatives by their worst possible outcomes: we are to adopt the alternative the worst outcome of which is superior to the worst outcomes of the others. The persons in the original position do not, of course, assume that their initial place in society is decided by a malevolent opponent. . . .

If the original position has been described so that it is rational for the parties to adopt the conservative attitude expressed by this rule, a conclusive argument can indeed be constructed for these principles. . . .

Equal Liberty

. . . Within the framework that justice establishes, moral conceptions with different principles, or conceptions representing a different balancing of the same principles, may be adopted by various parts of society. What is essential is that when persons with different convictions make conflicting demands on the basic structure as a matter of political principle, they are to judge these claims by the principles of justice. The principles that would be chosen in the original position are the kernel of political morality. They not only specify the terms of cooperation between persons but they define a pact of reconciliation between diverse religions and moral beliefs, and the forms of culture to which they belong. . . .

Political Justice and the Constitution

I now wish to consider political justice, that is, the justice of the constitution, and to sketch the meaning of equal liberty for this part of the basic structure. . . .

Political justice has two aspects arising from the fact that a just constitution is a case of imperfect procedural justice. First, the constitution is to be a just procedure satisfying the requirements of equal liberty; and second, it is to be framed so that of all the feasible just arrangements, it is the one more likely than any other to result in a just and effective system of legislation. The justice of the constitution is to be assessed under both headings in the light of what circumstances permit, these assessments being made from the standpoint of the constitutional convention.

The principle of equal liberty, when applied to the political procedure defined by the constitution, I shall refer to as the principle of (equal) participation. It requires that all citizens are to have an equal right to take part in, and to determine the outcome of, the constitutional process that establishes the laws with which they are to comply. Justice as fairness begins with the idea that where common principles are necessary and to everyone's advantage, they are to be worked out from the viewpoint of a suitably defined initial situation of equality in which each person is fairly represented. The principle of participation transfers this notion from the original position to the constitution as the highest-order system of social rules for making rules. If the state is to exercise a final and coercive authority over a certain territory, and if it is in this way to affect permanently men's prospects in life, then the constitutional process should preserve the equal representation of the original position to the degree that this is practicable.

For the time being I assume that a constitutional democracy can be arranged so as to satisfy the principle of participation. . . .

All sane adults, with certain generally recognized exceptions, have the right to take part in political affairs, and the precept one elector one vote is honored as far as possible. Elections are fair and free, and regularly held. Sporadic and un-predictable tests of public sentiment by plebiscite or other means, or at such times as may suit the convenience of those in office, do not suffice for a representative regime. There are firm constitutional protections for certain liberties, particularly freedom of speech and assembly, and liberty to form political associations. The principle of loyal opposition is recognized, the clash of political beliefs, and of the interests and attitudes that are likely to influence them, are accepted as a normal condition of human life. A lack of unanimity is part of the circumstances of jus-tice, since disagreement is bound to exist even among honest men who desire to follow much the same political principles. Without the conception of loyal opposi-tion, and an attachment to constitutional rules which express and protect it, the politics of democracy cannot be properly conducted or long endure. . . .

The principle of participation also holds that all citizens are to have an equal access, at least in the formal sense, to public office. Each is eligible to join politi-cal parties, to run for elective positions, and to hold places of authority. To be sure, there may be qualifications of age, residency, and so on. But these are to be reasonably related to the tasks of office; presumably these restrictions are in the common interest and do not discriminate unfairly among persons or groups in the sense that they fall evenly on everyone in the normal course of life.

. . . Turning now to the worth of political liberty, the constitution must take steps to enhance the value of the equal rights of participation for all members of society. It must underwrite a fair opportunity to take part in and to influence the political process. . . .

We may take for granted that a democratic regime presupposes freedom of speech and assembly, and liberty of thought and conscience. . . .

All citizens should have the means to be informed about political issues. They should be in a position to assess how proposals affect their well-being and which policies advance their conception of the public good. Moreover, they should have a fair chance to add alternative proposals to the agenda for political discussion. The liberties protected by the principle of participation lose much of their value whenever those who have greater private means are permitted to use their advan-tages to control the course of public debate. For eventually these inequalities will enable those better situated to exercise a larger influence over the development of legislation. In due time they are likely to acquire a preponderant weight in settling social questions, at least in regard to those matters upon which they normally agree, which is to say in regard to those things that support their favored circumstances.

Compensating steps must, then, be taken to preserve the fair value for all of the equal political liberties. A variety of devices can be used. For example, in a society allowing private ownership of the means of production, property and wealth must be kept widely distributed and government monies provided on a regular basis to encourage free public discussion. In addition, political parties are to be made independent from private economic interests by allotting them sufficient tax revenues to play their part in the constitutional scheme. (Their subventions might, for example, be based by some rule on the number of votes received in the last several elections, and the like.) What is necessary is that political parties be autonomous with respect to private demands, that is, demands not expressed in the public forum and argued for openly by reference to a conception of the public good. If society does not bear the costs of organization, and party funds need to be solicited from the more advantaged social and economic interests, the pleadings of these groups are bound to receive excessive attention. And this is all the more likely when the less favored members of society, having been effectively prevented by their lack of means from exercising their fair degree of influence, withdraw into apathy and resentment.

Historically one of the main defects of constitutional government has been the failure to insure the fair value of political liberty. The necessary corrective steps have not been taken, indeed, they never seem to have been seriously entertained. Disparities in the distribution of property and wealth that far exceed what is compatible with political equality have generally been tolerated by the legal system. Public resources have not been devoted to maintaining the institutions required for the fair value of political liberty. Essentially the fault lies in the fact that the democratic political process is at best regulated rivalry; it does not even in theory have the desirable properties that price theory ascribes to truly competitive markets. Moreover, the effects of injustices in the political system are much more grave and long lasting than market imperfections. Political power rapidly accumulates and becomes unequal; and making use of the coercive apparatus of the state and its law, those who gain the advantage can often assure themselves of a favored position. Thus inequities in the economic and social system may soon undermine whatever political equality might have existed under fortunate historical conditions. Universal suffrage is an insufficient counterpoise; for when parties and elections are financed not by public funds but by private contributions, the political forum is so constrained by the wishes of the dominant interests that the basic measures needed to establish just constitutional rule are seldom properly presented. . . .

Distributive Shares

In this chapter I take up the second principle of justice and describe an arrangement of institutions that fulfills its requirements within the setting of a modern state. I begin by noting that the principles of justice may serve as part of a doctrine of political economy. . . . I also emphasize that these principles have embedded in them a certain ideal of social institutions. . . . Throughout the choice between a private-property economy and socialism is left open; from the standpoint of the theory of justice alone, various basic structures would appear to satisfy its principles.

Justice as fairness is not at the mercy, so to speak, of existing wants and interests. It sets up an Archimedean point for assessing the social system without invoking a priori considerations. The long range aim of society is settled in its main lines irrespective of the particular desires and needs of its present members. And an ideal conception of justice is defined since institutions are to foster the virtue of justice and to discourage desires and aspirations incompatible with it. Of course, the pace of change and the particular reforms called for at any given time depend upon current conditions. But the conception of justice, the general form of a just society and the ideal of the person consistent with it are not similarly dependent.

Some Remarks about Economic Systems

It is essential to keep in mind that our topic is the theory of justice and not economics, however elementary. We are only concerned with some moral problems of political economy. . . .

I should like to conclude with a few comments about the extent to which economic arrangements may rely upon a system of markets in which prices are freely determined by supply and demand. Several cases need to be distinguished. All regimes will normally use the market to ration out the consumption goods actually produced. Any other procedure is administratively cumbersome, and rationing and other devices will be resorted to only in special cases. But in a free market system the output of commodities is also guided as to kind and quantity by the preferences of households as shown by their purchases on the market. Goods fetching a greater than normal profit will be produced in larger amounts until the excess is reduced. In a socialist regime planners' preferences or collective decisions often have a larger part in determining the direction of production. Both private-property and socialist systems normally allow for the free choice of occupation and of one's place of work. It is only under command systems of either kind that this freedom is overtly interfered with. . . .

It is evident, then, that there is no essential tie between the use of free markets and private ownership of the instruments of production. The idea that competitive prices under normal conditions are just or fair goes back at least to medieval times. While the notion that a market economy is in some sense the best scheme has been most carefully investigated by so-called bourgeois economists, this connection is a historical contingency in that, theoretically at least, a socialist regime can avail itself of the advantages of this system. One of these advantages is efficiency. Under certain conditions competitive prices select the goods to be produced and allocate resources to their production in such a manner that there is no way to improve upon either the choice of productive methods by firms, or the distribution of goods that arises from the purchases of households. There exists no rearrangement of the resulting economic configuration that makes one household better off (in view of its preferences) without making another worse off.

A further and more significant advantage of a market system is that, given the requisite background institutions, it is consistent with equal liberties and fair equality of opportunity. Citizens have a free choice of careers and occupations. There is no reason at all for the forced and central direction of labor. Indeed, in the absence of some differences in earnings as these arise in a competitive scheme, it is hard to see how, under ordinary circumstances anyway, certain aspects of a command society inconsistent with liberty can be avoided. Moreover, a system of markets decentralizes the exercise of economic power. Whatever the internal nature of firms, whether they are privately or state owned, or whether they are run by entrepreneurs or by managers elected by workers, they take the prices of outputs and inputs as given and draw up their plans accordingly. When markets are truly competitive, firms do not engage in price wars or other contests for market power. In conformity with political decisions reached democratically, the government regulates the economic climate by adjusting certain elements under its control, such as the overall amount of investment, the rate of interest, and the quantity of money, and so on. There is no necessity for comprehensive direct planning. Individual households and firms are free to make their decisions independently, subject to the general conditions of the economy.

In noting the consistency of market arrangements with socialist institutions, it is essential to distinguish between the allocative and the distributive functions of prices. The former is connected with their use to achieve economic efficiency, the latter with their determining the income to be received by individuals in return for what they contribute. It is perfectly consistent for a socialist regime to establish an interest rate to allocate resources among investment projects and to compute rental charges for the use of capital and scarce natural assets such as land and forests. Indeed, this must be done if these means of production are to be employed in the best way. For even if these assets should fall out of the sky without human effort, they are nevertheless productive in the sense that when combined with other factors a greater output results. It does not follow, however, that there need be private persons who as owners of these assets receive the monetary equivalents of these evaluations. Rather these accounting prices are indicators for drawing up an efficient schedule of economic activities. Except in the case of work of all kinds, prices under socialism do not correspond to income paid over to private individuals. Instead, the income imputed to natural and collective assets accrues to the state, and therefore their prices have no distributive function.

It is necessary, then, to recognize that market institutions are common to both private-property and socialist regimes, and to distinguish between the allocative and the distributive function of prices. Since under socialism the means of production and natural resources are publicly owned, the distributive function is greatly restricted, whereas a private-property system uses prices in varying degrees for both purposes. Which of these systems and the many intermediate forms most fully answers to the requirements of justice cannot, I think, be determined in advance. There is presumably no general answer to this question, since it depends in large part upon the traditions, institutions, and social forces of each country, and its particular historical circumstances. The theory of justice does not include these matters. But what it can do is to set out in a schematic way the outlines of a just economic system that admits of several variations. The political judgment in any given case will then turn on which variation is most likely to work out best in practice. A conception of justice is a necessary part of any such political assessment, but it is not sufficient. . . .

Background Institutions for Distributive Justice

The main problem of distributive justice is the choice of a social system. The principles of justice apply to the basic structure and regulate how its major institutions are combined into one scheme. Now, as we have seen, the idea of justice as fairness is to use the notion of pure procedural justice to handle the contingencies of particular situations. The social system is to be designed so that the resulting distribution is just however things turn out. To achieve this end it is necessary to set the social and economic process within the surroundings of suitable political and legal institutions. Without an appropriate scheme of these background institutions the outcome of the distributive process will not be just. Background fairness is lacking. I shall give a brief description of these supporting institutions as they might exist in a properly organized democratic state that allows private ownership of capital and natural resources. . . .

First of all, I assume that the basic structure is regulated by a just constitution that secures the liberties of equal citizenship (as described in the preceding chapter). Liberty of conscience and freedom of thought are taken for granted, and the fair value of political liberty is maintained. The political process is conducted, as far as circumstances permit, as a just procedure for choosing between governments and for enacting just legislation. I assume also that there is fair (as opposed to formal) equality of opportunity. This means that in addition to maintaining the usual kinds of social overhead capital, the government tries to insure equal chances of education and culture for persons similarly endowed and motivated either by subsidizing private schools or by establishing a public school system. It also enforces and underwrites equality of opportunity in economic activities and in the free choice of occupation. This is achieved by policing the conduct of firms and private associations and by preventing the establishment of monopolistic restrictions and barriers to the more desirable positions. Finally, the government guarantees a social minimum either by family allowances and special payments for sickness and employment, or more systematically by such devices as a graded income supplement (a so-called negative income tax).

In establishing these background institutions the government may be thought of as divided into four branches. Each branch consists of various agencies, or activities thereof, charged with preserving certain social and economic conditions.

These divisions do not overlap with the usual organization of government but are to be understood as different functions. The allocation branch, for example, is to keep the price system workably competitive and to prevent the formation of unreasonable market power. Such power does not exist as long as markets cannot be made more competitive consistent with the requirements of efficiency and the facts of geography and the preferences of households. The allocation branch is also charged with identifying and correcting, say by suitable taxes and subsidies and by changes in the definition of property rights, the more obvious departures from efficiency caused by the failure of prices to measure accurately social benefits and costs. To this end suitable taxes and subsidies may be used, or the scope and definition of property rights may be revised. The stabilization branch, on the other hand, strives to bring about reasonably full employment in the sense that those who want work can find it and the free choice of occupation and the deployment of finance are supported by strong effective demand. These two branches together are to maintain the efficiency of the market economy generally.

The social minimum is the responsibility of the transfer branch. . . . The essential idea is that the workings of this branch take needs into account and assign them an appropriate weight with respect to other claims. A competitive price system gives no consideration to needs and therefore it cannot be the sole device of distribution. There must be a division of labor between the parts of the social system in answering to the common sense precepts of justice. Different institutions meet different claims. Competitive markets properly regulated secure free choice of occupation and lead to an efficient use of resources and allocation of commodities to households. They set a weight on the conventional precepts associated with wages and earnings, whereas the transfer branch guarantees a certain level of well-being and honors the claims of need. . . .

The relevant point here is that certain precepts tend to be associated with specific institutions. It is left to the background system as a whole to determine how these precepts are balanced. Since the principles of justice regulate the whole structure, they also regulate the balance of precepts. In general, then, this balance will vary in accordance with the underlying political conception.

It is clear that the justice of distributive shares depends on the background institutions and how they allocate total income, wages and other income plus transfers. There is with reason strong objection to the competitive determination of total income, since this ignores the claims of need and an appropriate standard of life. From the standpoint of the legislative stage it is rational to insure oneself and one's descendants against these contingencies of the market. Indeed, the difference principle presumably requires this. But once a suitable minimum is provided by transfers, it may be perfectly fair that the rest of total income be settled by the price system, assuming that it is moderately efficient and free from monopolistic restrictions, and unreasonable externalities have been eliminated. Moreover, this way of dealing with the claims of need would appear to be more effective than trying to regulate income by minimum wage standards, and the like. It is better to assign to each branch only such tasks as are compatible with one another. Since the market is not suited to answer the claims of need, these should be met by a separate arrangement. Whether the principles of justice are satisfied, then, turns on whether the total income of the least advantaged (wages plus transfers) is such as to maximize their long-run expectations (consistent with the constraints of equal liberty and fair equality of opportunity).

Finally, there is a distribution branch. Its task is to preserve an approximate justice in distributive shares by means of taxation and the necessary adjustments in the rights of property. Two aspects of this branch may be distinguished. First of all, it imposes a number of inheritance and gift taxes, and sets restrictions on the rights of bequest. The purpose of these levies and regulations is not to raise revenue (release resources to government) but gradually and continually to correct the distribution of wealth and to prevent concentrations of power detrimental to the fair value of political liberty and fair equality of opportunity. For example, the progressive principle might be applied at the beneficiary's end. Doing this would encourage the wide dispersal of property which is a necessary condition, it seems, if the fair value of the equal liberties is to be maintained. The unequal inheritance of wealth is no more inherently unjust than the unequal inheritance of intelligence. It is true that the former is presumably more easily subject to social control; but the essential thing is that as far as possible inequalities founded on either should satisfy the difference principle. Thus inheritance is permissible provided that the resulting inequalities are to the advantage of the least fortunate and compatible with liberty and fair equality of opportunity. As earlier defined, fair equality of opportunity means a certain set of institutions that assures similar chances of education and culture for persons similarly motivated and keeps positions and offices open to all on the basis of qualities and efforts reasonably related to the relevant duties and tasks. It is these institutions that are put in jeopardy when inequalities of wealth exceed a certain limit; and political liberty likewise tends to lose its value, and representative government to become such in appearance only. The taxes and enactments of the distribution branch are to prevent this limit from being exceeded. Naturally, where this limit lies is a matter of political judgment guided by theory, good sense, and plain hunch, at least within a wide range. On this sort of question the theory of justice has nothing specific to say. Its aim is to formulate the principles that are to regulate the background institutions. . . .

. . . I now wish to give the final statement of the two principles of justice for institutions.

First Principle
    Each person is to have an equal right to the most extensive total system of equal basic liberties compatible with a similar system of liberty for all.
Second Principle
    Social and economic inequalities are to be arranged so that they are both:
        (a) to the greatest benefit of the least advantaged, consistent with the just savings principle, and
        (b) attached to offices and positions open to all under conditions of fair equality of opportunity.

First Priority Rule (The Priority of Liberty)

The principles of justice are to be ranked in lexical order and therefore liberty can be restricted only for the sake of liberty. There are two cases:

(a) a less extensive liberty must strengthen the total system of liberty shared by all;

(b) a less than equal liberty must be acceptable to those with the lesser liberty.

Second Priority Rule (The Priority of Justice over Efficiency and Welfare)

The second principle of justice is lexically prior to the principle of efficiency and to that of maximizing the sum of advantages; and fair opportunity is prior to the difference principle. There are two cases:

(a) an inequality of opportunity must enhance the opportunities of those with the lesser opportunity;

(b) an excessive rate of saving must on balance mitigate the burden of those bearing this hardship.

General Conception

All social primary goods—liberty and opportunity, income and wealth, and the bases of self-respect—are to be distributed equally unless an unequal distribution of any or all of these goods is to the advantage of the least favored.

42

Robert Nozick
Anarchy, State and Utopia

*Robert Nozick (1938–) is professor of philosophy at Harvard University. His
book* Anarchy, State and Utopia, *from which the following selection is taken,
won the National Book Award in 1975. In it he makes the case for* laissez-faire,
*arguing that only a minimal state is justifiable and legitimate. Among his other
works are* The Examined Life *(1989) and* Philosophical Explanations *(1981).*

From the Preface

Individuals have rights, and there are things no person or group may do to them
(without violating their rights). So strong and far-reaching are these rights that
they raise the question of what, if anything, the state and its officials may do.
How much room do individual rights leave for the state? The nature of the state,
its legitimate functions and its justifications, if any, is the central concern of this
book; a wide and diverse variety of topics intertwine in the course of our investigation.

Our main conclusions about the state are that a minimal state, limited to the
narrow functions of protection against force, theft, fraud, enforcement of contracts, and so on, is justified; that any more extensive state will violate persons'
rights not to be forced to do certain things, and is unjustified; and that the minimal
state is inspiring as well as right. Two note worthy implications are that the state
may not use its coercive apparatus for the purpose of getting some citizens to aid
others, or in order to prohibit activities to people for their *own* good or protection.

Despite the fact that it is only coercive routes toward these goals that are excluded, while voluntary ones remain, many persons will reject our conclusions
instantly, knowing they don't *want* to believe anything so apparently callous toward the needs and suffering of others. I know that reaction; it was mine when I
first began to consider such views. With reluctance, I found myself becoming
convinced of (as they are now often called) libertarian views, due to various considerations and arguments. . . .

On Moral Constraints and the State

Can behavior toward a person be constrained so that he is not to be used for any
end except as he chooses? This is an impossibly stringent condition if it requires
everyone who provides us with a good to approve positively of every use to which

we wish to put it. Even the requirement that he merely should not object to any use we plan would seriously curtail bilateral exchange, not to mention sequences of such exchanges. It is sufficient that the other party stands to gain enough from the exchange so that he is willing to go through with it, even though he objects to one or more of the uses to which you shall put the good. Under such conditions, the other party is not being used solely as a means, in that respect. Another party, however, who would not choose to interact with you if he knew of the uses to which you *intend* to put his actions or good, *is* being used as a means, even if he receives enough to choose (in his ignorance) to interact with you. ("All along, you were just *using* me" can be said by someone who chose to interact only because he was ignorant of another's goals and of the uses to which he himself would be put.) Is it morally incumbent upon someone to reveal his intended uses of an interaction if he has good reason to believe the other would refuse to interact if he knew? Is he *using* the other person, if he does not reveal this? And what of the cases where the other does not choose to be of use at all? In getting pleasure from seeing an attractive person go by, does one use the other solely as a means? Does someone so use an object of sexual fantasies? These and related questions raise very interesting issues for moral philosophy; but not, I think, for political philosophy.

Political philosophy is concerned only with *certain* ways that persons may not use others; primarily, physically aggressing against them. A specific side constraint upon action toward others expresses the fact that others may not be used in the specific ways the side constraint excludes. Side constraints express the inviolability of others, in the ways they specify. These modes of inviolability are expressed by the following injunction: "Don't use people in specified ways." An end-state view, on the other hand, would express the view that people are ends and not merely means (if it chooses to express this view at all), by a different injunction: "Minimize the use in specified ways of persons as means." Following this precept itself may involve using someone as a means in one of the ways specified. Had Kant held this view, he would have given the second formula of the categorical imperative as, "So act as to minimize the use of humanity simply as a means," rather than the one he actually used: "Act in such a way that you always treat humanity, whether in your own person or in the person of any other, never simply as a means, but always at the same time as an end."

Side constraints express the inviolability of other persons. But why may not one violate persons for the greater social good? Individually, we each sometimes choose to undergo some pain or sacrifice for a greater benefit or to avoid a greater harm: we go to the dentist to avoid worse suffering later; we do some unpleasant work for its results; some persons diet to improve their health or looks; some save money to support themselves when they are older. In each case, some cost is borne for the sake of the greater overall good. Why not, *similarly,* hold that some persons have to bear some costs that benefit other persons more, for the sake of the overall social good? But there is no *social entity* with a good that undergoes some sacrifice for its own good. There are only individual people, different individual people, with their own individual lives. Using one of these people for the benefit of others, uses him and benefits the others. Nothing more. What happens is that something is done to him for the sake of others. Talk of an overall social good covers this up. (Intentionally?) To use a person in this way does not sufficiently respect and take account of the fact that he is a separate person, that his is the only life he has. *He* does not get some overbalancing good from his sacrifice, and no one is entitled to force this upon him—least of all a state or government that claims his allegiance (as other individuals do not) and that therefore scrupulously must be *neutral* between its citizens. . . .

On Distributive Justice

The minimal state is the most extensive state that can be justified. Any state more extensive violates people's rights. Yet many persons have put forth reasons purporting to justify a more extensive state. It is impossible within the compass of this book to examine all the reasons that have been put forth. Therefore, I shall focus upon those generally acknowledged to be most weighty and influential, to see precisely wherein they fail. In this chapter we consider the claim that a more extensive state is justified, because necessary (or the best instrument) to achieve distributive justice; in the next chapter we shall take up diverse other claims.

The term "distributive justice" is not a neutral one. Hearing the term "distribution," most people presume that some thing or mechanism uses some principle or criterion to give out a supply of things. Into this process of distributing shares some error may have crept. So it is an open question, at least, whether *re*distribution should take place; whether we should do again what has already been done once, though poorly. However, we are not in the position of children who have been given portions of pie by someone who now makes last minute adjustments to rectify careless cutting. There is no *central* distribution, no person or group entitled to control all the resources, jointly deciding how they are to be doled out. What each person gets, he gets from others who give to him in exchange for something, or as a gift. In a free society, diverse persons control different resources, and new holdings arise out of the voluntary exchanges and actions of persons. There is no more a distributing or distribution of shares than there is a distributing of mates in a society in which persons choose whom they shall marry. The total result is the product of many individual decisions which the different individuals involved are entitled to make. Some uses of term "distribution," it is true, do not imply a previous distributing appropriately judged by some criterion (for example, "probability distribution"); nevertheless, despite the title of this chapter, it would be best to use a terminology that clearly is neutral. We shall speak of people's holdings; a principle of justice in holdings describes (part of) what justice tells us (requires) about holdings. . . .

The subject of justice in holdings consists of three major topics. The first is the *original acquisition of holdings,* the appropriation of unheld things. This includes the issues of how unheld things may come to be held, the process, or processes, by which unheld things may come to be held, the things that may come to be held by these processes, the extent of what comes to be held by a particular process, and so on. We shall refer to the complicated truth about this topic, which we shall not formulate here, as the principle of justice in acquisition. The second topic concerns the *transfer of holdings* from one person to another. By what processes may a person transfer holdings to another? How may a person acquire a holding from another who holds it? Under this topic come general descriptions of voluntary exchange, and gift and (on the other hand) fraud, as well as reference to particular conventional details fixed upon in a given society. The complicated truth about this subject (with placeholders for conventional details) we shall call the principle of justice in transfer. (And we shall suppose it also includes principles governing how a person may divest himself of a holding, passing it into an upheld state.)

If the world were wholly just, the following inductive definition would exhaustively cover the subject of justice in holdings.

   1. A person who acquires a holding in accordance with the principle of justice in acquisition is entitled to that holding.

   2. A person who acquires a holding in accordance with the principle of justice in transfer, from someone else entitled to the holding, is entitled to the holding.

   3. No one is entitled to a holding except by (repeated) applications of 1 and 2.

The complete principle of distributive justice would say simply that a distribution is just if everyone is entitled to the holdings they possess under the distribution.

A distribution is just if it arises from another just distribution by legitimate means. The legitimate means of moving from one distribution to another are specified by the principle of justice in transfer. The legitimate first "moves" are specified by the principle of justice in acquisition. Whatever arises from a just situation by just steps is itself just. The means of change specified by the principle of justice in transfer preserve justice. As correct rules of inference are truth-preserving, and any conclusion deduced via repeated application of such rules from only true premises is itself true, so the means of transition from one situation to another specified by the principle of justice in transfer are justice-preserving, and any situation actually arising from repeated transitions in accordance with the principle from a just situation is itself just. The parallel between justice-preserving transformations and truth-preserving transformations illuminates where it fails as well as where it holds. That a conclusion could have been deduced by truth-preserving means from premises that are true suffices to show its truth. That from a just situation a situation *could* have arisen via justice-preserving means does *not* suffice to show its justice. The fact that a thief's victims voluntarily *could* have presented him with gifts does not entitle the thief to his ill-gotten gains. Justice in holdings is historical; it depends upon what actually has happened. We shall return to this point later.

Not all actual situations are generated in accordance with the two principles of justice in holdings: the principle of justice in acquisition and the principle of justice in transfer. Some people steal from others, or defraud them, or enslave them, seizing their product and preventing them from living as they choose, or forcibly exclude others from competing in exchanges. None of these are permissible modes of transition from one situation to another. And some persons acquire holdings by means not sanctioned by the principle of justice in acquisition. The existence of past injustice (previous violations of the first two principles of justice in holdings) raises the third major topic under justice in holdings: the rectification of injustice in holdings. If past injustice has shaped present holdings in various ways, some identifiable and some not, what now, if anything, ought to be done to rectify these injustices? What obligations do the performers of injustice have toward those whose position is worse than it would have been had the injustice not been done? Or, than it would have been had compensation been paid promptly? How, if at all, do things change if the beneficiaries and those made worse off are not the direct parties in the act of injustice, but, for example, their descendants? Is an injustice done to someone whose holding was itself based upon an unrectified injustice? How far back must one go in wiping clean the historical slate of injustices? What may victims of injustice permissibly do in order to rectify the injustices being done to them, including the many injustices done by persons acting through their government? I do not know of a thorough or theoretically sophisticated treatment of such issues. Idealizing greatly, let us suppose theoretical investigation will produce a principle of rectification. This principle uses historical information about previous situations and injustices done in them (as defined by the first two principles of justice and rights against interference), and information about the actual course of events that flowed from these injustices, until the present, and it yields a description (or descriptions) of holdings in the society. The principle of rectification presumably will make use of its best estimate of subjective information about what would have occurred (or a probability distribution over what might have occurred, using the expected value) if the injustice had not taken place. If the actual description of holdings turns out not to be one of the descriptions yielded by the principle, then one of the descriptions yielded must be realized.

The general outlines of the theory of justice in holdings are that the holdings of a person are just if he is entitled to them by the principles of justice in acquisition and transfer, or by the principle of rectification of injustice (as specified by the first two principles). If each person's holdings are just, then the total set (distribution) of holdings is just. To turn these general outlines into a specific theory we would have to specify the details of each of the three principles of justice in holdings: the principle of acquisition of holdings, the principle of transfer of holdings, and the principle of rectification of violations of the first two principles. I shall not attempt that task here. . . .

Historical Principles and End-Result Principles

The general outlines of the entitlement theory illuminate the nature and defects of other conceptions of distributive justice. The entitlement theory of justice in distribution is *historical*; whether a distribution is just depends upon how it came about. In contrast, *current time-slice principles* of justice hold that the justice of a distribution is determined by how things are distributed (who has what) as judged by some *structural* principle(s) of just distribution. A utilitarian who judges between any two distributions by seeing which has the greater sum of utility and, if the sums tie, applies some fixed equality criterion to choose the more equal distribution, would hold a current time-slice principle of justice. As would someone who had a fixed schedule of trade-offs between the sum of happiness and equality. According to a current time-slice principle, all that needs to be looked at, in judging the justice of a distribution, is who ends up with what; in comparing any two distributions one need look only at the matrix presenting the distributions. No further information need be fed into a principle of justice. It is a consequence of such principles of justice that any two structurally identical distributions are equally just. (Two distributions are structurally identical if they present the same profile, but perhaps have different persons occupying the particular slots. My having ten and your having five, and my having five and your having ten are structurally identical distributions.) Welfare economics is the theory of current time-slice principles of justice. The subject is conceived as operating on matrices representing only current information about distribution. This, as well as some of the usual conditions (for example, the choice of distribution is invariant under relabeling of columns), guarantees that welfare economics will be a current time-slice theory, with all of its inadequacies.

Most persons do not accept current time-slice principles as constituting the whole story about distributive shares. They think it relevant in assessing the justice of a situation to consider not only the distribution it embodies, but also how that distribution came about. If some persons are in prison for murder or war crimes, we do not say that to assess the justice of the distribution in the society we must look only at what this person has, and that person has, and that person has, . . . at the current time. We think it relevant to ask whether someone did something so that he *deserved* to be punished, deserved to have a lower share. Most will agree to the relevance of further information with regard to punishments and penalties. Consider also desired things. One traditional socialist view is that workers are entitled to the product and full fruits of their labor; they have earned it; a distribution is unjust if it does not give the workers what they are entitled to. Such entitlements are based upon some past history. No socialist holding this view would find it comforting to be told that because the actual distribution A happens to coincide structurally with the one he desires D, A therefore is no less just than D; it differs only in that the "parasitic" owners of capital receive under A what the workers are entitled to under D, and the workers receive under A what the owners are entitled to under D, namely very little. This socialist rightly, in my view, holds onto the notions of earning, producing, entitlement, desert, and so forth, and he rejects current time-slice principles that look only to the structure of the resulting set of holdings. (The set of holdings resulting from what? Isn't it implausible that how holdings are produced and come to exist has no effect at all on who should hold what?) His mistake lies in his view of what entitlements arise out of what sorts of productive processes.

We construe the position we discuss too narrowly by speaking of *current* time-slice principles. Nothing is changed if structural principles operate upon a time sequence of current time-slice profiles and, for example, give someone more now to counterbalance the less he has had earlier. A utilitarian or an egalitarian or any mixture of the two over time will inherit the difficulties of his more myopic comrades. He is not helped by the fact that *some* of the information others consider relevant in assessing a distribution is reflected, unrecoverably, in past matrices. Henceforth, we shall refer to such unhistorical principles of distributive justice, including the current time-slice principles, and *end-result principles* or *end-state principles*.

In contrast to end-result principles of justice, *historical principles* of justice hold that past circumstances or actions of people can create differential entitlements or differential deserts to things. An injustice can be worked by moving from one distribution to another structurally identical one, for the second, in profile the same, may violate people's entitlements or deserts; it may not fit the actual history. The entitlement principles of justice in holdings that we have sketched are historical principles of justice. To better understand their precise character, we shall distinguish them from another subclass of the historical principles. Consider, as an example, the principle of distribution according to moral merit. This principle requires that total distributive shares vary directly with moral merit; no person should have a greater share than anyone whose moral merit is greater. (If moral merit could be not merely ordered but measured on an interval or ratio scale, stronger principles could be formulated.) Or consider the principle that results by substituting "usefulness to society" for "moral merit" in the previous principle. Or instead of "distribute according to moral merit," or "distribute according to usefulness to society," we might consider "distribute according to the weighted sum of moral merit, usefulness to society, and need," with the weights of the different dimensions equal. Let us call a principle of distribution *patterned* if it specifies that a distribution is to vary along with some natural dimension, weighted sum of natural dimensions, or lexicographic ordering of natural dimensions. And let us say a distribution is patterned if it accords with some patterned principle. (I speak of natural dimensions, admittedly without a general criterion for them, because for any set of holdings some artificial dimensions can be gimmicked up to vary along with the distribution of the set.) The principle of distribution in accordance with moral merit is a patterned historical principle, which specifies a patterned distribution. "Distribute according to I.Q." is a patterned principle that looks to information not contained in distributional matrices. It is not historical, however, in that it does not look to any past actions creating differential entitlements to evaluate a distribution; it requires only distributional matrices whose columns are labeled by I.Q. scores. The distribution in a society, however, may be composed of such simple patterned distributions, without itself being simply patterned. Different sectors may operate different patterns, or some combination of patterns may operate in different proportions across a society. A distribution composed in this manner, from a small number of patterned distributions, we also shall term "patterned." And we extend the use of "pattern" to include the overall designs put forth by combinations of end-state principles.

Almost every suggested principle of distributive justice is patterned: to each according to his moral merit, or needs, or marginal product, or how hard he tries, or the weighted sum of the foregoing, and so on. The principle of entitlement we have sketched is *not* patterned. There is no one natural dimension or weighted sum or combination of a small number of natural dimensions that yields the distributions generated in accordance with the principle of entitlement. The set of holdings that results when some persons receive their marginal products, others win at gambling, others receive a share of their mate's income, others receive gifts from foundations, others receive interest on loans, others receive gifts from admirers, others receive returns on investment, others make for themselves much of what they have, others find things, and so on, will not be patterned. Heavy strands of patterns will run through it; significant portions of the variance in holdings will be accounted for by pattern-variables. If most people most of the time choose to transfer some of their entitlements to others only in exchange for something from them, then a large part of what many people hold will vary with what they held that others wanted. More details are provided by the theory of marginal productivity. But gifts to relatives, charitable donations, bequests to children, and the like, are not best conceived, in the first instance, in this manner. Ignoring the strands of pattern, let us suppose for the moment that a distribution actually arrived at by the operation of the principle of entitlement is random with respect to any pattern. Though the resulting set of holdings will be unpatterned, it will not be incomprehensible, for it can be seen as arising from the operation of a small number of principles. These principles specify how an initial distribution may arise (the principle of acquisition of holdings) and how distributions may be transformed into others (the principle of transfer of holdings). The process whereby the set of holdings is generated will be intelligible, though the set of holdings itself that results from this process will be unpatterned.

The writings of F. A. Hayek focus less than is usually done upon what patterning distributive justice requires. Hayek argues that we cannot know enough about each person's situation to distribute to each according to his moral merit (but would justice demand we do so if we did have this knowledge?); and he goes on to say, "our objection is against all attempts to impress upon society a deliberately chosen pattern of distribution, whether it be an order of equality or of inequality." However, Hayek concludes that in a free society there will be distribution in accordance with value rather than moral merit; that is, in accordance with the perceived value of a person's actions and services to others. Despite his rejection of a patterned conception of distributive justice, Hayek himself suggests a pattern he thinks justifiable: distribution in accordance with the perceived benefits given to others, leaving room for the complaint that a free society does not realize exactly this pattern. Stating this patterned strand of a free capitalist society more precisely, we get "To each according to how much he benefits others who have the resources for benefiting those who benefit them." This will seem arbitrary unless some acceptable initial set of holdings is specified, or unless it is held that the operation of the system over time washes out any significant effects from the initial set of holdings. As an example of the latter, if almost anyone would have bought a car from Henry Ford, the supposition that it was an arbitrary matter who held the money than (and so bought) would not place Henry Ford's earnings under a cloud. In any event, *his* coming to hold it is not arbitrary. Distribution according to benefits to others *is* a major patterned strand in a free capitalist society, as Hayek correctly points out, but it is only a strand and does not constitute the whole pattern of a system of entitlements (namely, inheritance, gifts for arbitrary reasons, charity, and so on) or a standard that one should insist a society fit. Will people tolerate for long a system yielding distributions that they believe are unpatterned? No doubt people will not long accept a distribution they believe is *unjust*. People want their society to be and to look just. But must the look of justice reside in a resulting pattern rather than in the underlying generating principles? We are in no position to conclude that the inhabitants of a society embodying an entitlement conception of justice in holdings will find it unacceptable. Still, it must be granted that were people's reasons for transferring some of their holdings to others always irrational or arbitrary, we would find this disturbing. (Suppose people always determined what holdings they would transfer, and to whom, by using a random device.) We feel more comfortable upholding the justice of an entitlement system if most of the transfers under it are done for reasons. This does not mean necessarily that all deserve what holdings they receive. It means only that there is a purpose or point to someone's transferring a holding to one person rather than to another; that usually we can see what the transferrer thinks he's gaining, what cause he thinks he's serving, what goals he thinks he's helping to achieve, and so forth. Since in a capitalist society people often transfer holdings to others in accordance with how much they perceive these others benefiting them, the fabric constituted by the individual transactions and transfers is largely reasonable and intelligible. (Gifts to loved ones, bequests to children, charity to the needy also are nonarbitrary components of the fabric.) In stressing the large strand of distribution in accordance with benefit to others, Hayek shows the point of many transfers, and so shows that the system of transfer of entitlements is not just spinning its gears aimlessly. The system of entitlements is defensible when constituted by the individual aims of individual transactions. No overarching aim is needed, no distributional pattern is required.

To think that the task of a theory of distributive justice is to fill in the blank in "to each according to his _____" is to be predisposed to search for a pattern; and the separate treatment of "from each according to his _____" treats production and distribution as two separate and independent issues. On an entitlement view these are *not* two separate questions. Whoever makes something, having bought or contracted for all other held resources used in the process (transferring some of his holdings for these cooperating factors), is entitled to it. The situation is *not* one of something's getting made, and there being an open question of who is to get it. Things come into the world already attached to people having entitlements over them. From the point of view of the historical entitlement conception of justice in holdings, those who start afresh to complete "to each according to his _____" treat objects as if they appeared from nowhere, out of nothing. A complete theory of justice might cover this limit case as well; perhaps here is a use for the usual conceptions of distributive justice.

So entrenched are maxims of the usual form that perhaps we should present the entitlement conception as a competitor. Ignoring acquisition and rectification, we might say:

> From each according to what he chooses to do, to each according to what he makes for himself (perhaps with the contracted aid of others) and what others choose to do for him and choose to give him of what they've been given previously (under this maxim) and haven't yet expended or transferred.

This, the discerning reader will have noticed, has its defects as a slogan. So as a summary and greater simplification (and not as a maxim with any independent meaning) we have:

> *From each as they choose, to each as they are chosen.*

How Liberty Upsets Patterns

It is not clear how those holding alternative conceptions of distributive justice can reject the entitlement conception of justice in holdings. For suppose a distribution favored by one of these nonentitlement conceptions is realized. Let us suppose it is your favorite one and let us call this distribution D_1; perhaps everyone has an equal share, perhaps shares vary in accordance with some dimension you treasure. Now suppose that Wilt Chamberlain is greatly in demand by basketball teams, being a great gate attraction. (Also suppose contracts run only for a year, with players being free agents.) He signs the following sort of contract with a team: In each home game, twenty-five cents from the price of each ticket of admission goes to him. (We ignore the question of whether he is "gouging" the owners, letting them look out for themselves.) The season starts, and people cheerfully attend his team's games; they buy their tickets, each time dropping a separate twenty-five cents of their admission price into a special box with Chamberlain's name on it. They are excited about seeing him play; it is worth the total admission price to them. Let us suppose that in one season one million persons attend his home games, and Wilt Chamberlain winds up with $250,000, a much larger sum than the average income and larger even than anyone else has. Is he entitled to this income? Is this new distribution D_2, unjust? If so, why? There is *no* question about whether each of the people was entitled to the control over the resources they held in D_1; because that was the distribution (your favorite) that (for the purposes of argument) we assumed was acceptable. Each of these persons *chose* to give twenty-five cents of their money to Chamberlain. They could have spent it on going to the movies, or on candy bars, or on copies of *Dissent* magazine, or of *Monthly Review*. But they all, at least one million of them, converged on giving it to Wilt Chamberlain in exchange for watching him play basketball. If D_1 was a just distribution, and people voluntarily moved from it to D_2, transferring parts of their shares they were given under D_1 (what was it for if not to do something with?), isn't D_2 also just? If the people were entitled to dispose of the resources to which they were entitled (under D_1), didn't this include their being entitled to give it to, or exchange it with, Wilt Chamberlain? Can anyone else complain on grounds of justice? Each other person already has his legitimate share under D_1. Under D_1, there is nothing that anyone has that anyone else has a claim of justice against. After someone transfers something to Wilt Chamberlain, third parties *still* have their legitimate shares; *their* shares are not changed. By what process could such a transfer among two persons give rise to a legitimate claim of distributive justice on a portion of what was widely scattered information via prices, and coordinates persons' activities.

It puts things perhaps a bit too strongly to say that every patterned (or end-state) principle is liable to be thwarted by the voluntary actions of the individual parties transferring some of their shares they receive under the principle. For perhaps some *very* weak patterns are not so thwarted. Any distributional pattern with any egalitarian component is overturnable by the voluntary actions of individual persons over time; as is every patterned condition with sufficient content so as actually to have been proposed as presenting the central core of distributive justice. Still, given the possibility that some weak conditions or patterns may not be unstable in this way, it would be better to formulate an explicit description of the kind of interesting and contentful patterns under discussion, and to prove a theorem about their instability. Since the weaker the patterning, the more likely it is that the entitlement system itself satisfies it, a plausible conjecture is that any patterning either is unstable or is satisfied by the entitlement system. . . .

43

Jürgen Habermas
The Public Sphere

Jürgen Habermas (1929–), who teaches today in Frankfurt, Germany, is one of the leading political philosophers in Europe. His work extends and transforms the "Critical Theory" of the "Frankfurt School," whose leading figures, Max Horkeimer and Theodor Adorno, sought, in the 1930s and 1940s, to reconstruct Marxism as an open and nondeterministic theory. Habermas began with the attempt to develop a normative basis for Marxism, and this has taken him beyond Marxism to a theory which looks to communication to provide a model for community. He has also been a formidable critic of "post-modernist" theories. "The Public Sphere" is an encyclopedia article summarizing the key ideas of Habermas's important early book, The Structural Transformation of the Public Sphere *(1962). Among his many other works are* Knowledge and Human Interests *(1968) and* The Theory of Communicative Action *(1981).*

Concept

By "public sphere" we mean first of all a domain of our social life in which such a thing as public opinion can be formed. Access to the public sphere is open in principle to all citizens. A portion of the public sphere is constituted in every conversation in which private persons come together to form a public. They are then acting neither as business or professional people conducting their private affairs, nor as legal consociates subject to the legal regulations of a state bureaucracy and obligated to obedience. Citizens act as a public when they deal with matters of general interest without being subject to coercion; thus with the guarantee that they may assemble and unite freely, and express and publicize their opinions freely. When the public is large, this kind of communication requires certain means of dissemination and influence; today, newspapers and periodicals, radio and television are the media of the public sphere. We speak of a political public sphere (as distinguished from a literary one, for instance) when the public discussions concern objects connected with the practice of the state. The coercive power of the state is the counterpart, as it were, of the political public sphere, but it is not a part of it. State power is, to be sure, considered "public" power, but it owes the attribute of publicness to its task of caring for the public, that is, providing for the common good of all legal consociates. Only when the exercise of public authority has actually been subordinated to the requirement of democratic publicness does the political public sphere acquire an institutionalized influence on the government, by way of the legislative body. The term "public opinion" refers to the functions of criticism and control of organized state authority that the public exercises informally, as well as formally during periodic elections. Regulations concerning the publicness (or publicity [*Publizität*] in its original meaning) of state-related activities, as, for instance, the public accessibility required of legal proceedings, are also connected with this function of public opinion. To the public sphere as a sphere mediating between state and society, a sphere in which the public as the vehicle of public opinion is formed, there corresponds the principle of publicness—the publicness that once had to win out against the secret politics of monarchs and that since then has permitted democratic control of state activity.

It is no accident that these concepts of the public sphere and public opinion were not formed until the eighteenth century. They derive their specific meaning from a concrete historical situation. It was then that one learned to distinguish between opinion and public opinion, or *opinion publique*. Whereas mere opinions (things taken for granted as part of a culture, normative convictions, collective prejudices and judgments) seem to persist unchanged in their quasi-natural structure as a kind of sediment of history, public opinion, in terms of its very idea, can be formed only if a public that engages in rational discussion exists. Public discussions that are institutionally protected and that take, with critical intent, the exercise of political authority as their theme have not existed since time immemorial—they developed only in a specific phase of bourgeois society, and only by virtue of a specific constellation of interests could they be incorporated into the order of the bourgeois constitutional state.

History

It is not possible to demonstrate the existence of a public sphere in its own right, separate from the private sphere, in the European society of the High Middle Ages. At the same time, however, it is not a coincidence that the attributes of authority at that time were called "public." For a public representation of authority existed at that time. At all levels of the pyramid established by feudal law, the status of the feudal lord is neutral with respect to the categories "public" and "private"; but the person possessing that status represents it publicly; he displays himself, represents himself as the embodiment of a "higher" power, in whatever degree. This concept of representation has survived into recent constitutional history. Even today the power of political authority on its highest level, however much it has become detached from its former basis, requires representation through the head of state. But such elements derive from a pre-bourgeois social structure. Representation in the sense of the bourgeois public sphere, as in "representing" the nation or specific clients, has nothing to do with *representative publicness*, which inheres in the concrete existence of a lord. As long as the prince and the estates of his realm "are" the land, rather than merely "representing" it, they are capable of this kind of representation; they represent their authority "before" the people rather than for the people.

The feudal powers (the church, the prince, and the nobility) to which this representative publicness adheres disintegrated in the course of a long process of polarization; by the end of the eighteenth century they had decomposed into private elements on the one side and public on the other. The position of the church changed in connection with the Reformation; the tie to divine authority that the church represented, that is, religion, became a private matter. Historically, what is called the freedom of religion safeguarded the first domain of private autonomy; the church itself continued its existence as one corporate body under public law among others. The corresponding polarization of princely power acquired visible form in the separation of the public budget from the private household property of the feudal lord. In the bureaucracy and the military (and in part also in the administration of justice), institutions of public power became autonomous vis-à-vis the privatized sphere of the princely court. In terms of the estates, finally, elements from the ruling groups developed into organs of public power, into parliament (and in part also into judicial organs); elements from the occupational status groups, insofar as they had become established in urban corporations and in certain differentiations within the estates of the land, developed into the sphere of bourgeois society, which would confront the state as a genuine domain of private autonomy.

Representative publicness gave way to the new sphere of "public power" that came into being with the national and territorial states. Ongoing state activity (permanent administration, a standing army) had its counterpart in the permanence of relationships that had developed in the meantime with the stock market and the press, through traffic in goods and news. Public power became consolidated as something tangible confronting those who were subject to it and who at first found themselves only negatively defined by it. These are the "private persons" who are excluded from public power because they hold no office. "Public" no longer refers to the representative court of a person vested with authority; instead, it now refers to the competence-regulated activity of an apparatus furnished with a monopoly on the legitimate use of force. As those to whom this public power is addressed, private persons subsumed under the state form the public.

As a private domain, society, which has come to confront the state, as it were, is on the one hand clearly differentiated from public power; on the other hand, society becomes a matter of public interest insofar as with the rise of a market economy the reproduction of life extends beyond the confines of private domestic power. The *bourgeois public sphere* can be understood as the sphere of private persons assembled to form a public. They soon began to make use of the public sphere of informational newspapers, which was officially regulated, against the public power itself, using those papers, along with the morally and critically oriented weeklies, to engage in debate about the general rules governing relations in their own essentially privatized but publicly relevant sphere of commodity exchange and labor.

The Liberal Model of the Public Sphere

The medium in which this debate takes place—public discussion—is unique and without historical prototype. Previously the estates had negotiated contracts with their princes in which claims to power were defined on a case-by-case basis. As we know, this development followed a different course in England, where princely power was relativized through parliament, than on the Continent, where the estates were mediatized by the monarch. The "third estate" then broke with this mode of equalizing power, for it could no longer establish itself as a ruling estate. Given a commercial economy, a division of authority accomplished through differentiation of the rights of those possessing feudal authority (liberties belonging to the estates) was no longer possible—the power under private law of disposition of capitalist property is nonpolitical. The bourgeois are private persons; as such, they do not "rule." Thus their claims to power in opposition to public power are directed not against a concentration of authority that should be "divided" but rather against the principle of established authority. The principle of control, namely publicness, that the bourgeois public opposes to the principle of established authority aims at a transformation of authority as such, not merely the exchange of one basis of legitimation for another.

In the first modern constitutions the sections listing basic rights provide an image of the liberal model of the public sphere: they guarantee society as a sphere of private autonomy; opposite it stands a public power limited to a few functions; between the two spheres, as it were, stands the domain of private persons who have come together to form a public and who, as citizens of the state, mediate the state with the needs of bourgeois society, in order, as the idea goes, to thus convert political authority to "rational" authority in the medium of this public sphere. Under the presuppositions of a society based on the free exchange of commodities, it seemed that the general interest, which served as the criterion by which this kind of rationality was to be evaluated, would be assured if the dealings of private persons in the marketplace were emancipated from social forces and their dealings in the public sphere were emancipated from political coercion.

The political daily press came to have an important role during this same period. In the second half of the eighteenth century, serious competition to the older form of news writing as the compiling of items of information arose in the form of literary journalism. Karl Bücher describes the main outlines of this development: "From mere institutions for the publication of news, newspapers became the vehicles and guides of public opinion as well, weapons of party politics. The consequence of this for the internal organization of the newspaper enterprise was the insertion of a new function between the gathering of news and its publication: the editorial function. For the newspaper publisher, however, the significance of this development was that from a seller of new information he became a dealer in public opinion." Publishers provided the commercial basis for the newspaper without, however, commercializing it as such. The press remained an institution of the public itself, operating to provide and intensify public discussion, no longer a mere organ for the conveyance of information, but not yet a medium of consumer culture.

This type of press can be observed especially in revolutionary periods, when papers associated with the tiniest political coalitions and groups spring up, as in Paris in 1789. In the Paris of 1848 every halfway prominent politician still formed his own club, and every other one founded his own *journal*: over 450 clubs and more than 200 papers came into being there between February and May alone. Until the permanent legalization of a public sphere that functioned politically, the appearance of a political newspaper was equivalent to engagement in the struggle for a zone of freedom for public opinion, for publicness as a principle. Not until the establishment of the bourgeois constitutional state was a press engaged in the public use of reason relieved of the pressure of ideological viewpoints. Since then it has been able to abandon its polemical stance and take advantage of the earning potential of commercial activity. The ground was cleared for this development from a press of viewpoints to a commercial press at about the same time in England, France, and the United States, during the 1830s. In the course of this transformation from the journalism of writers who were private persons to the consumer services of the mass media, the sphere of publicness was changed by an influx of private interests that achieved privileged representation within it.

The Public Sphere in Mass Welfare-State Democracies

The liberal model of the public sphere remains instructive in regard to the normative claim embodied in institutionalized requirements of publicness; but it is not applicable to actual relationships within a mass democracy that is industrially advanced and constituted as a social-welfare state. In part, the liberal model had always contained ideological aspects; in part, the social presuppositions to which those aspects were linked have undergone fundamental changes. Even the forms in which the public sphere was manifested, forms which made its idea seem to a certain extent obvious, began to change with the Chartist movement in England and the February Revolution in France. With the spread of the press and propaganda, the public expanded beyond the confines of the bourgeoisie. Along with its social exclusivity the public lost the cohesion given it by institutions of convivial social intercourse and by a relatively high standard of education. Accordingly, conflicts which in the past were pushed off into the private sphere now enter the public sphere. Group needs, which cannot expect satisfaction from a self-regulating market, tend toward state regulation. The public sphere, which must now mediate these demands, becomes a field for competition among interests in the cruder form of forcible confrontation. Laws that have obviously originated under the "pressure of the streets" can scarcely continue to be understood in terms of a consensus achieved by private persons in public discussion; they correspond, in more or less undisguised form, to compromises between conflicting private interests. Today it is social organizations that act in relation to the state in the political public sphere, whether through the mediation of political parties or directly, in interplay with public administration. With the interlocking of the public and private domains, not only do political agencies take over certain functions in the sphere of commodity exchange and social labor; societal powers also take over political functions. This leads to a kind of "refeudalization" of the public sphere. Large-scale organizations strive for political compromises with the state and with one another, behind closed doors if possible; but at the same time they have to secure at least plebiscitarian approval from the mass of the population through the deployment of a staged form of publicity.

The political public sphere in the welfare state is characterized by a singular weakening of its critical functions. Whereas at one time publicness was intended to subject persons or things to the public use of reason and to make political decisions susceptible to revision before the tribunal of public opinion, today it has often enough already been enlisted in the aid of the secret policies of interest groups; in the form of "publicity" it now acquires public prestige for persons or things and renders them capable of acclamation in a climate of nonpublic opinion. The term "public relations" itself indicates how a public sphere that formerly emerged from the structure of society must now be produced circumstantially on a case-by-case basis. The central relationship of the public, political parties, and parliament is also affected by this change in function.

This existing trend toward the weakening of the public sphere, as a principle, is opposed, however, by a welfare-state transformation of the functioning of basic rights: the requirement of publicness is extended by state organs to all organizations acting in relation to the state. To the extent to which this becomes a reality, a no longer intact public of private persons acting as individuals would be replaced by a public of organized private persons. Under current circumstances, only the latter could participate effectively in a process of public communication using the channels of intra-party and intra-organizational public spheres, on the basis of a publicness enforced for the dealings of organizations with the state. It is in this process of public communication that the formation of political compromises would have to achieve legitimation. The idea of the public sphere itself, which signified a rationalization of authority in the medium of public discussions among private persons, and which has been preserved in mass welfare-state democracy, threatens to disintegrate with the structural transformation of the public sphere. Today it could be realized only on a different basis, as a rationalization of the exercise of social and political power under the mutual control of rival organizations committed to publicness in their internal structure as well as their dealings with the state and with one another.

44

Michel Foucault
Discipline and Punish

Michel Foucault (1926–1984) was born in Poitiers, France. Few thinkers have had as profound an effect on the thought of the last quarter-century as Foucault. He detailed in a wide array of studies his thesis that there was an "epistemological break" between the eighteenth and nineteenth centuries, and that it was during this point that the categories of modern thought came into existence. The modern bent for clearly separating ideas was, in his view, closely tied up with movements for clearly separating people. He studied these "enclosures" in psychology, penology, and medicine in his pioneering works, Madness and Civilization, Discipline and Punish, *and* Birth of the Clinic, *respectively. His idea that the genesis of categories of thought was bound up with power, that is, with strategies for social and political control, has given rise to a mode of historical analysis known as "genealogy" or "archeology," following his methodological theorizing in* The Order of Things. *Foucault's work is central to the development of "post-modernism." His last work,* The History of Sexuality, *has had a broad impact on the study of literature, culture, and politics.*

Docile Bodies

Let us take the ideal figure of the soldier as it was still seen in the early seventeenth century. To begin with, the soldier was someone who could be recognized from afar; he bore certain signs: the natural signs of his strength and his courage, the marks, too, of his pride; his body was the blazon of his strength and valour; and although it is true that he had to learn the profession of arms little by little—generally in actual fighting—movements like marching and attitudes like the bearing of the head belonged for the most part to a bodily rhetoric of honour; 'The signs for recognizing those most suited to this profession are a lively, alert manner, an erect head, a taut stomach, broad shoulders, long arms, strong fingers, a small belly, thick thighs, slender legs and dry feet, because a man of such a figure could not fail to be agile and strong'; when he becomes a pikebearer, the soldier 'will have to march in step in order to have as much grace and gravity as possible, for the pike is an honourable weapon, worthy to be borne with gravity and boldness.' By the late eighteenth century, the soldier has become something that can be made; out of a formless clay, an inapt body, the machine required can be constructed; posture is gradually corrected; a calculated constraint runs slowly through each part of the body, mastering it, making it pliable, ready at all times, turning silently into the automatism of habit; in short, one has 'got rid of the peasant' and given him 'the air of a soldier' (ordinance of 20 March 1764). Recruits become accustomed to 'holding their heads high and erect; to standing upright, without bending the back, to sticking out the belly, throwing out the chest and throwing back the shoulders; and, to help them acquire the habit, they are given this position while standing against a wall in such a way that the heels, the thighs, the waist and the shoulders touch it, as also do the backs of the hands, as one turns the arms outwards, without moving them away from the body . . . Likewise, they will be taught never to fix their eyes on the ground, but to look straight at those they pass . . . to remain motionless until the order is given, without moving the head, the hands or the feet . . . lastly to march with a bold step, with knee and ham taut, on the points of the feet, which should face outwards' (ordinance of 20 March 1764).

The classical age discovered the body as object and target of power. It is easy enough to find signs of the attention then paid to the body—to the body that is manipulated, shaped, trained, which obeys, responds, becomes skilful and increases its forces. The great book of Man-the-Machine was written simultaneously on two registers: the anatomico-metaphysical register, of which Descartes wrote the first pages and which the physicians and philosophers continued, and the technico-political register, which was constituted by a whole set of regulations and by empirical and calculated methods relating to the army, the school and the hospital, for controlling or correcting the operations of the body. These two registers are quite distinct, since it was a question, on the one hand, of submission and use and, on the other, of functioning and explanation: there was a useful body and an intelligible body. And yet there are points of overlap from one to the other. La Mettrie's *L'Homme-machine* is both a materialist reduction of the soul and a general theory of *dressage*, at the centre of which reigns the notion of 'docility,' which joins the analysable body to the manipulable body. A body is docile that may be subjected, used, transformed and improved. The celebrated automata, on the other hand, were not only a way of illustrating an organism, they were also political puppets, small-scale models of power: Frederick II, the meticulous king of small machines, well-trained regiments and long exercises, was obsessed with them.

What was so new in these projects of docility that interested the eighteenth century so much? It was certainly not the first time that the body had become the object of such imperious and pressing investments; in every society, the body was in the grip of very strict powers, which imposed on it constraints, prohibitions or obligations. However, there were several new things in these techniques. To begin with, there was the scale of the control: it was a question not of treating the body, *en masse*, 'wholesale,' as if it were an indissociable unity, but of working it 'retail,' individually; of exercising upon it a subtle coercion, of obtaining holds upon it at the level of the mechanism itself—movements, gestures, attitudes, rapidity: an infinitesimal power over the active body. Then there was the object of the control: it was not or was no longer the signifying elements of behaviour or the language of the body, but the economy, the efficiency of movements, their internal organization; constraint bears upon the forces rather than upon the signs; the only truly important ceremony is that of exercise. Lastly, there is the modality: it implies an uninterrupted, constant coercion, supervising the processes of the activity rather than its result and it is exercised according to a codification that partitions as closely as possible time, space, movement. These methods, which made possible the meticulous control of the operations of the body, which assured the constant subjection of its forces and imposed upon them a relation of docility-utility, might be called 'disciplines.' Many disciplinary methods had long been in existence—in monasteries, armies, workshops. But in the course of the seventeenth and eighteenth centuries the disciplines became general formulas of domination. They were different from slavery because they were not based on a relation of appropriation of bodies; indeed, the elegance of the discipline lay in the fact that it could dispense with this costly and violent relation by obtaining effects of utility at least as great. They were different, too, from 'service,' which was a constant, total, massive, non-analytical, unlimited relation of domination, established in the form of the individual will of the master, his 'caprice.' They were different from vassalage, which was a highly coded, but distant relation of submission, which bore less on the operations of the body than on the products of labour and the ritual marks of allegiance. Again, they were different from asceticism and from 'disciplines' of a monastic type, whose function was to obtain renunciations rather than increases of utility and which, although they involved obedience to others, had as their principal aim an increase of the mastery of each individual over his own body. The historical moment of the disciplines was the moment when an art of the human body was born, which was directed not only at the growth of its skills, nor at the intensification of its subjection, but at the formation of a relation that in the mechanism itself makes it more obedient as it becomes more useful, and conversely. What was then being formed was a policy of coercions that act upon the body, a calculated manipulation of its elements, its gestures, its behaviour. The human body was entering a machinery of power that explores it, breaks it down and rearranges it. A 'political anatomy,' which was also a 'mechanics of power,' was being born; it defined how one may have a hold over others' bodies, not only so that they may do what one wishes, but so that they may operate as one wishes, with the techniques, the speed and the efficiency that one determines. Thus discipline produces subjected and practised bodies, 'docile' bodies. Discipline increases the forces of the body (in economic terms of utility) and diminishes these same forces (in political terms of obedience). In short, it dissociates power from the body; on the one hand, it turns it into an 'aptitude,' a 'capacity,' which it seeks to increase; on the other hand, it reverses the course of the energy, the power that might result from it, and turns it into a relation of strict subjection. If economic exploitation separates the force and the product of labour, let us say that disciplinary coercion establishes in the body the constricting link between an increased aptitude and an increased domination.

The 'invention' of this new political anatomy must not be seen as a sudden discovery. It is rather a multiplicity of often minor processes, of different origin and scattered location, which overlap, repeat, or imitate one another, support one another, distinguish themselves from one another according to their domain of application, converge and gradually produce the blueprint of a general method. They were at work in secondary education at a very early date, later in primary schools; they slowly invested the space of the hospital; and, in a few decades, they restructured the military organization. They sometimes circulated very rapidly from one point to another (between the army and the technical schools or secondary schools), sometimes slowly and discreetly (the insidious militarization of the large workshops). On almost every occasion, they were adopted in response to particular needs: an industrial innovation, a renewed outbreak of certain epidemic diseases, the invention of the rifle or the victories of Prussia. This did not prevent them being total inscribed in general and essential transformations, which we must now try to delineate.

There can be no question here of writing the history of the different disciplinary institutions, with all their individual differences. I simply intend to map on a series of examples some of the essential techniques that most easily spread from one to another. These were always meticulous, often minute, techniques, but they had their importance: because they defined a certain mode of detailed political investment of the body, a 'new micro-physics' of power; and because, since the seventeenth century, they had constantly reached out to ever broader domains, as if they tended to cover the entire social body. Small acts of cunning endowed with a great power of diffusion, subtle arrangements, apparently innocent, but profoundly suspicious, mechanisms that obeyed economies too shameful to be acknowledged, or pursued petty forms of coercion—it was nevertheless they that brought about the mutation of the punitive system, at the threshold of the contemporary period. Describing them will require great attention to detail: beneath every set of figures, we must seek not a meaning, but a precaution; we must situate them not only in the inextricability of a functioning, but in the coherence of a tactic. They are the acts of cunning, not so much of the greater reason that works even in its sleep and gives meaning to the insignificant, as of the attentive 'malevolence' that turns everything to account. Discipline is a political anatomy of detail.

Before we lose patience we would do well to recall the words of Marshal de Saxe: 'Although those who concern themselves with details are regarded as folk of limited intelligence, it seems to me that this part is essential, because it is the foundation, and it is impossible to erect any building or establish any method without understanding its principles. It is not enough to have a liking for architecture. One must also know stone-cutting.' There is a whole history to be written about such 'stone-cutting'—a history of the utilitarian rationalization of detail in moral accountability and political control. The classical age did not initiate it; rather it accelerated it, changed its scale, gave it precise instruments, and perhaps found some echoes for it in the calculation of the infinitely small or in the description of the most detailed characteristics of natural beings. In any case, 'detail' had long been a category of theology and asceticism: every detail is important since, in the sight of God, no immensity is greater than a detail, nor is anything so small that it was not willed by one of his individual wishes. In this great tradition of the eminence of detail, all the minutiae of Christian education, of scholastic or military pedagogy, all forms of 'training' found their place easily enough. For the disciplined man, as for the true believer, no detail is unimportant, but not so much for the meaning that it conceals within it as for the hold it provides for the power that wishes to seize it. Characteristic is the great hymn to the 'little things' and to their eternal importance, sung by Jean-Baptiste de La Salle, in his *Traité sur les obligations des frères des Écoles chrétiennes*. The mystique of the everyday is joined here with the discipline of the minute. 'How dangerous it is to neglect little things. It is a very consoling reflection for a soul like mine, little disposed to great actions, to think that fidelity to little things may, by an imperceptible progress, raise us to the most eminent sanctity: because little things lead to greater . . . Little things; it will be said, alas, my God, what can we do that is great for you, weak and mortal creatures that we are. Little things; if great things presented themselves would we perform them? Would we not think them beyond our strength? Little things; and if God accepts them and wishes to receive them as great things? Little things; has one ever felt this? Does one judge according to experience? Little things; one is certainly guilty, therefore, if seeing them as such, one refuses them? Little things; yet it is they that in the end have made great saints! Yes, little things; but great motives, great feelings, great fervour, great ardour, and consequently great merits, great treasures, great rewards' (La Salle, *Traité* . . ., 238–9). The meticulousness of the regulations, the fussiness of the inspections, the supervision of the smallest fragment of life and of the body will soon provide, in the context of the school, the barracks, the hospital or the workshop, a laicized content, an economic or technical rationality for this mystical calculus of the infinitesimal and the infinite. And a History of Detail in the eighteenth century, presided over by Jean-Baptiste de La Salle, touching on Leibniz and Buffon, via Frederick II, covering pedagogy, medicine, military tactics and economics, should bring us, at the end of the century, to the man who dreamt of being another Newton, not the Newton of the immensities of the heavens and the planetary masses, but a Newton of 'small bodies,' small movements, small actions; to the man who replied to Monge's remark, 'there was only one world to discover': 'What do I hear? But the world of details, who has never dreamt of that other world, what of that world? I have believed in it ever since I was fifteen. I was concerned with it then, and this memory lives within me, as an obsession never to be abandoned. . . . That other world is the most important of all that I flatter myself I have discovered: when I think of it, my heart aches' (these words are attributed to Bonaparte in the Introduction to Saint-Hilaire's *Notions synthétiques et historiques de philosophie naturelle*). Napoleon did not discover this world; but we know that he set out to organize it; and he wished to arrange around him a mechanism of power that would enable him to see the smallest event that occurred in the state he governed; he intended, by means of the rigorous discipline that he imposed, 'to embrace the whole of this vast machine without the slightest detail escaping his attention.'

A meticulous observation of detail, and at the same time a political awareness of these small things, for the control and use of men, emerge through the classical age bearing with them a whole set of techniques, a whole corpus of methods and knowledge, descriptions, plans and data. And from such trifles, no doubt, the man of modern humanism was born.[1]

The Art of Distributions

In the first instance, discipline proceeds from the distribution of individuals in space. To achieve this end, it employs several techniques.

1. Discipline sometimes requires *enclosure*, the specification of a place hetero- geneous to all others and closed in upon itself. It is the protected place of disci- plinary monotony. There was the great 'confinement' of vagabonds and paupers; there were other more discreet, but insidious and effective ones. There were the *collèges*, or secondary schools: the monastic model was gradually imposed; board- ing appeared as the most perfect, if not the most frequent, educational régime; it became obligatory at Louis-le-Grand when, after the departure of the Jesuits, it was turned into a model school. There were the military barracks: the army, that vagabond mass, has to be held in place; looting and violence must be prevented; the fears of local inhabitants, who do not care for troops passing through their towns, must be calmed; conflicts with the civil authorities must be avoided; deser- tion must be stopped, expenditure controlled. The ordinance of 1719 envisaged the construction of several hundred barracks, on the model of those already set up in the south of the country; there would be strict confinements: 'The whole will be enclosed by an outer wall ten feet high, which will surround the said houses, at a distance of thirty feet from all the sides'; this will have the effect of maintaining the troops in 'order and discipline, so that an officer will be in a position to answer for them' (*L'Ordonnance militaire*, IXL, 25 September 1719). In 1745, there were barracks in about 320 towns; and it was estimated that the total capacity of the barracks in 1775 was approximately 200,000 men. Side by side with the spread of workshops, there also developed great manufacturing spaces, both ho- mogeneous and well defined: first, the combined manufactories, then, in the sec- ond half of the eighteenth century, the works or factories proper (the Chaussade ironworks occupied almost the whole of the Médine peninsula, between Nièvre and Loire; in order to set up the Indret factory in 1777, Wilkinson, by means of embankments and dikes, constructed an island on the Loire; Toufait built Le Creusot in the valley of the Charbonnière, which he transformed, and he had workers' accommodation built in the factory itself); it was a change of scale, but it was also a new type of control. The factory was explicitly compared with the monastery, the fortress, a walled town; the guardian 'will open the gates only on the return of the workers, and after the bell that announces the resumption of work has been rung'; a quarter of an hour later no one will be admitted; at the end of the day, the workshops' heads will hand back the keys to the Swiss guard of the factory, who will then open the gates. The aim is to derive the maximum advan- tages and to neutralize the inconveniences (thefts, interruptions of work, distur- bances and 'cabals'), as the forces of production become more concentrated; to protect materials and tools and to master the labour force: 'The order and inspec-

tion that must be maintained require that all workers be assembled under the same roof, so that the partner who is entrusted with the management of the manufactory may prevent and remedy abuses that may arise among the workers and arrest their progress at the outset.'

2. But the principle of 'enclosure' is neither constant, nor indispensable, nor sufficient in disciplinary machinery. This machinery works space in a much more flexible and detailed way. It does this first of all on the principle of elementary location or *partitioning*. Each individual has his own place; and each place its individual. Avoid distributions in groups; break up collective dispositions; analyse confused, massive or transient pluralities. Disciplinary space tends to be divided into as many sections as there are bodies or elements to be distributed. One must eliminate the effects of imprecise distributions, the uncontrolled disappearance of individuals, their diffuse circulation, their unusable and dangerous coagulation; it was a tactic of anti-desertion, anti-vagabondage, anti-concentration. Its aim was to establish presences and absences, to know where and how to locate individuals, to set up useful communications, to interrupt others, to be able at each moment to supervise the conduct of each individual, to assess it, to judge it, to calculate its qualities or merits. It was a procedure, therefore, aimed at knowing, mastering and using. Discipline organizes an analytical space.

And there, too, it encountered an old architectural and religious method: the monastic cell. Even if the compartments it assigns become purely ideal, the disciplinary space is always, basically, cellular. Solitude was necessary to both body and soul, according to a certain asceticism: they must, at certain moments at least, confront temptation and perhaps the severity of God alone. 'Sleep is the image of death, the dormitory is the image of the sepulchre . . . although the dormitories are shared, the beds are nevertheless arranged in such a way and closed so exactly by means of curtains that the girls may rise and retire without being seen' (*Règlement pour la communauté des filles du Bon Pasteur*). But this is still a very crude form.

3. *The rule of functional sites* would gradually, in the disciplinary institutions, code a space that architecture generally left at the disposal of several different uses. Particular places were defined to correspond not only to the need to supervise, to break dangerous communications, but also to create a useful space. The process appeared clearly in the hospitals, especially in the military and naval hospitals. In France, it seems that Rochefort served both as experiment and model. A port, and a military port is—with its circulation of goods, men signed up willingly or by force, sailors embarking and disembarking, diseases and epidemics—a place of desertion, smuggling, contagion: it is a crossroads for dangerous mixtures, a meeting-place for forbidden circulations. The naval hospital must therefore treat, but in order to do this it must be a filter, a mechanism that pins down and partitions; it must provide a hold over this whole mobile, swarming mass, by dissipating the confusion of illegality and evil. The medical supervision of diseases and contagions is inseparable from a whole series of other controls: the military control over deserters, fiscal control over commodities, administrative control over remedies, rations, disappearances, cures, deaths, simulations. Hence the need to

distribute and partition off space in a rigorous manner. The first steps taken at Rochefort concerned things rather than men, precious commodities, rather than patients. The arrangements of fiscal and economic supervision preceded the techniques of medical observation: placing of medicines under lock and key, recording their use; a little later, a system was worked out to verify the real number of patients, their identity, the units to which they belonged; then one began to regulate their comings and goings; they were forced to remain in their wards; to each bed was attached the name of its occupant; each individual treated was entered in a register that the doctor had to consult during the visit; later came the isolation of contagious patients and separate beds. Gradually, an administrative and political space was articulated upon a therapeutic space; it tended to individualize bodies, diseases, symptoms, lives and deaths; it constituted a real table of juxtaposed and carefully distinct singularities. Out of discipline, a medically useful space was born.

In the factories that appeared at the end of the eighteenth century, the principle of individualizing partitioning became more complicated. It was a question of distributing individuals in a space in which one might isolate them and map them; but also of articulating this distribution on a production machinery that had its own requirements. The distribution of bodies, the spatial arrangement of production machinery and the different forms of activity in the distribution of 'posts' had to be linked together. The Oberkampf manufactory at Jouy obeyed this principle. It was made up of a series of workshops specified according to each broad type of operation: for the printers, the handlers, the colourists, the women who touched up the design, the engravers, the dyers. The largest of the buildings, built in 1791, by Toussaint Barré, was 110 metres long and had three storeys. The ground floor was devoted mainly to block printing; it contained 132 tables arranged in two rows, the length of the workshop, which had eighty-eight windows; each printer worked at a table with his 'puller,' who prepared and spread the colours. There were 264 persons in all. At the end of each table was a sort of rack on which the material that had just been printed was left to dry. By walking up and down the central aisle of the workshop, it was possible to carry out a supervision that was both general and individual: to observe the worker's presence and application, and the quality of his work; to compare workers with one another, to classify them according to skill and speed; to follow the successive stages of the production process. All these serializations formed a permanent grid: confusion was eliminated:[2] that is to say, production was divided up and the labour process was articulated, on the one hand, according to its stages or elementary operations, and, on the other hand, according to the individuals, the particular bodies, that carried it out: each variable of this force—strength, promptness, skill, constancy—would be observed, and therefore characterized, assessed, computed and related to the individual who was its particular agent. Thus, spread out in a perfectly legible way over the whole series of individual bodies, the work force may be analysed in individual units. At the emergence of large-scale industry, one finds, beneath the division of the production process, the individualizing fragmentation of labour power; the distributions of the disciplinary space often assured both.

4. In discipline, the elements are interchangeable, since each is defined by the

place it occupies in a series, and by the gap that separates it from the others. The unit is, therefore, neither the territory (unit of domination), nor the place (unit of residence), but the *rank*: the place once occupies in a classification, the point at which a line and a column intersect, the interval in a series of intervals that one may traverse one after the other. Discipline is an art of rank, a technique for the transformation of arrangements. It individualizes bodies by a location that does not give them a fixed position, but distributes them and circulates them in a network of relations.

Take the example of the 'class.' In the Jesuit colleges, one still found an organization that was at once binary and unified; the classes, which might comprise up to two or three hundred pupils, were subdivided into groups of ten; each of these groups, with its 'decurion,' was placed in a camp, Roman or Carthaginian; each 'decury' had its counterpart in the opposing camp. The general form was that of war and rivalry; work, apprenticeship and classification were carried out in the form of the joust, through the confrontation of two armies; the contribution of each pupil was inscribed in this general duel; it contributed to the victory or the defeat of a whole camp; and the pupils were assigned a place that corresponded to the function of each individual and to his value as a combatant in the unitary group of his 'decury.' It should be observed moreover that this Roman comedy made it possible to link, to the binary exercises of rivalry, a spatial disposition inspired by the legion, with rank, hierarchy, pyramidal supervision. One should not forget that, generally speaking, the Roman model, at the Enlightenment, played a dual role: in its republican aspect, it was the very embodiment of liberty; in its military aspect, it was the ideal schema of discipline. The Rome of the eighteenth century and of the Revolution was the Rome of the Senate, but it was also that of the legion; it was the Rome of the Forum, but it was also that of the camps. Up to the empire, the Roman reference transmitted, somewhat ambiguously, the juridical ideal of citizenship and the technique of disciplinary methods. In any case, the strictly disciplinary element in the ancient fable used by the Jesuit colleges came to dominate the element of joust and mock warfare. Gradually—but especially after 1762—the educational space unfolds; the class becomes homogeneous, it is no longer made up of individual elements arranged side by side under the master's eye. In the eighteenth century, 'rank' begins to define the great form of distribution of individuals in the educational order: rows or ranks of pupils in the class, corridors, courtyards; rank attributed to each pupil at the end of each task and each examination; the rank he obtains from week to week, month to month, year to year; an alignment of age groups, one after another; a succession of subjects taught and questions treated, according to an order of increasing difficulty. And, in this ensemble of compulsory alignments, each pupil, according to his age, his performance, his behaviour, occupies sometimes one rank, sometimes another; he moves constantly over a series of compartments—some of these are 'ideal' compartments, marking a hierarchy of knowledge or ability, others express the distribution of values or merits in material terms in the space of the college or classroom. It is a perpetual movement in which individuals replace one another in a space marked off by aligned intervals.

The organization of a serial space was one of the great technical mutations of elementary education. It made it possible to supersede the traditional system (a pupil working for a few minutes with the master, while the rest of the heterogeneous group remained idle and unattended). By assigning individual places it made possible the supervision of each individual and the simultaneous work of all. It organized a new economy of the time of apprenticeship. It made the educational space function like a learning machine, but also as a machine for supervising, hierarchizing, rewarding. Jean-Baptiste de La Salle dreamt of a classroom in which the spatial distribution might provide a whole series of distinctions at once: according to the pupils' progress, worth, character, application, cleanliness and parents' fortune. Thus, the classroom would form a single great table, with many different entries, under the scrupulously 'classificatory' eye of the master: 'In every class there will be places assigned for all the pupils of all the lessons, so that all those attending the same lesson will always occupy the same place. Pupils attending the highest lessons will be placed in the benches closest to the wall, followed by the others according to the order of the lessons moving towards the middle of the classroom . . . Each of the pupils will have his place assigned to him and none of them will leave it or change it except on the order or with the consent of the school inspector.' Things must be so arranged that 'those whose parents are neglectful and verminous must be separated from those who are careful and clean; that an unruly and frivolous pupil should be placed between two who are well behaved and serious, a libertine either alone or between two pious pupils.'[3]

In organizing 'cells,' 'places' and 'ranks,' the disciplines create complex spaces that are at once architectural, functional and hierarchical. It is spaces that provide fixed positions and permit circulation; they carve out individual segments and establish operational links; they mark places and indicate values; they guarantee the obedience of individuals, but also a better economy of time and gesture. They are mixed spaces: real because they govern the disposition of buildings, rooms, furniture, but also ideal, because they are projected over this arrangement of characterizations, assessments, hierarchies. The first of the great operations of discipline is, therefore, the constitution of '*tableaux vivants*,' which transform the confused, useless or dangerous multitudes into ordered multiplicities. The drawing up of 'tables' was one of the great problems of the scientific, political and economic technology of the eighteenth century: how one was to arrange botanical and zoological gardens, and construct at the same time rational classifications of living beings; how one was to observe, supervise, regularize the circulation of commodities and money and thus build up an economic table that might serve as the principle of the increase of wealth; how one was to inspect men, observe their presence and absence and constitute a general and permanent register of the armed forces; how one was to distribute patients, separate them from one another, divide up the hospital space and make a systematic classification of diseases: these were all twin operations in which the two elements—distribution and analysis, supervision and intelligibility—are inextricably bound up. In the eighteenth century, the table was both a technique of power and a procedure of knowledge. It was a question of organizing the multiple, of providing oneself with an instrument to cover it and to master it; it was a question of imposing upon it an 'order.' Like the army general of whom Guibert spoke, the naturalist, the physician, the economist was 'blinded by the immensity, dazed by the multitude . . . the innumerable combinations that result from the multiplicity of objects, so many concerns together form a burden above his strength. In perfecting itself, in approaching true principles, the science of modern warfare might become simpler and less difficult'; armies 'with simple, similar tactics, capable of being adapted to every movement . . . would be easier to move and lead.' Tactics, the spatial ordering of men; taxonomy, and disciplinary space of natural beings; the economic table, the regulated movement of wealth.

But the table does not have the same function in these different registers. In the order of the economy, it makes possible the measurement of quantities and the analysis of movements. In the form of taxonomy, it has the function of characterizing (and consequently reducing individual singularities) and constituting classes (and therefore of excluding considerations of number). But in the form of the disciplinary distribution, on the other hand, the table has the function of treating multiplicity itself, distributing it and deriving from it as many effects as possible. Whereas natural taxonomy is situated on the axis that links character and category, disciplinary tactics is situated on the axis that links the singular and the multiple. It allows both the characterization of the individual as individual and the ordering of a given multiplicity. It is the first condition for the control and use of an ensemble of distinct elements: the base for a micro-physics of what might be called a 'cellular' power.

The Control of Activity

1. The *time-table* is an old inheritance. The strict model was no doubt suggested by the monastic communities. It soon spread. Its three great methods—establish rhythms, impose particular occupations, regulate the cycles of repetition—were soon to be found in schools, workshops and hospitals. The new disciplines had no difficulty in taking up their place in the old forms; the schools and poorhouses extended the life and the regularity of the monastic communities to which they were often attached. The rigours of the industrial period long retained a religious air; in the seventeenth century, the regulations of the great manufactories laid down the exercises that would divide up the working day: 'On arrival in the morning, before beginning their work, all persons shall wash their hands, offer up their work to God and make the sign of the cross'; but even in the nineteenth century, when the rural populations were needed in industry, they were sometimes formed into 'congregations', in an attempt to inure them to work in the workshops; the framework of the 'factory-monastery' was imposed upon the workers. In the Protestant armies of Maurice of Orange and Gustavus Adolphus, military discipline was achieved through a rhythmics of time punctuated by pious exercises; army life, Boussanelle was later to say, should have some of the 'perfections of the cloister itself.' For centuries, the religious orders had been masters of discipline:

they were the specialists of time, the great technicians of rhythm and regular activities. But the disciplines altered these methods of temporal regulation from which they derived. They altered them first by refining them. One began to count in quarter hours, in minutes, in seconds. This happened in the army, of course: Guibert systematically implemented the chronometric measurement of shooting that had been suggested earlier by Vauban. In the elementary schools, the division of time became increasingly minute; activities were governed in detail by orders that had to be obeyed immediately: 'At the last stroke of the hour, a pupil will ring the bell, and at the first sound of the bell all the pupils will kneel, with their arms crossed and their eyes lowered. When the prayer has been said, the teacher will strike the signal once to indicate that the pupils should get up, a second time as a sign that they should salute Christ, and a third that they should sit down.' In the early nineteenth century, the following time-table was suggested for the *Écoles mutuelles,* or 'mutual improvement schools': 8.45 entrance of the monitor, 8.52 the monitor's summons, 8.56 entrance of the children and prayer, 9.00 the children go to their benches, 9.04 first slate, 9.08 end of dictation, 9.12 second slate, etc. The gradual extension of the wage-earning class brought with it a more detailed partitioning of time: 'If workers arrive later than a quarter of an hour after the ringing of the bell . . .'; "if any one of the companions is asked for during work and loses more than five minutes . . .', 'anyone who is not at his work at the correct time. . . .' But an attempt is also made to assure the quality of the time used: constant supervision, the pressure of supervisors, the elimination of anything that might disturb or distract; it is a question of constituting a totally useful time: 'It is expressly forbidden during work to amuse one's companions by gestures or in any other way, to play at any game whatsoever, to eat, to sleep, to tell stories and comedies'; and even during the meal-break, 'there will be no telling of stories, adventures or other such talk that distracts the workers from their work'; 'it is expressly forbidden for any worker, under any pretext, to bring wine into the manufactory and to drink in the workshops.' Time measured and paid must also be a time without impurities or defects; a time of good quality, throughout which the body is constantly applied to its exercise. Precision and application are, with regularity, the fundamental virtues of disciplinary time. But this is not the newest thing about it. Other methods are more characteristic of the disciplines.

2. *The temporal elaboration of the act.* There are, for example, two ways of controlling marching troops. In the early seventeenth century, we have: 'Accustomed soldiers marching in file or in battalion to march to the rhythm of the drum. And to do this, one must begin with the right foot so that the whole troop raises the same foot at the same time.' In the mid-eighteenth century, there are four sorts of steps: 'The length of the the short step will be a foot, that of the ordinary step, the double step and the marching step will be two feet, the whole measured from one heel to the next; as for the duration, that of the small step and the ordinary step will last one second, during which two double steps would be performed; the duration of the marching step will be a little longer than one second. The oblique step will take one second; it will be at most eighteen inches from one heel to the next. . . . The ordinary step will be executed forwards, holding the head up high

and the body erect, holding oneself in balance successively on a single leg, and bringing the other forwards, the ham taut, the point of the foot a little turned outwards and low, so that one may without affectation brush the ground on which one must walk and place one's foot, in such a way that each part may come to rest there at the same time without striking the ground' ('Ordonnance du Ier janvier 1766, pour régler l'exercise de l'infanterie'). Between these two instructions, a new set of restraints had been brought into play, another degree of precision in the breakdown of gestures and movements, another way of adjusting the body to temporal imperatives.

What the ordinance of 1766 defines is not a time-table—the general framework for an activity; it is rather a collective and obligatory rhythm, imposed from the outside; it is a 'programme'; it assures the elaboration of the act itself; it controls its development and its stages from the inside. We have passed from a form of injunction that measured or punctuated gestures to a web that constrains them or sustains them throughout their entire succession. A sort of anatomo-chronological schema of behaviour is defined. The act is broken down into its elements; the position of the body, limbs, articulations is defined; to each movement are assigned a direction, an aptitude, a duration; their order of succession is prescribed. Time penetrates the body and with it all the meticulous controls of power.

3. Hence *the correlation of the body and the gesture*. Disciplinary control does not consist simply in teaching or imposing a series of particular gestures; it imposes the best relation between a gesture and the overall position of the body, which is its condition of efficiency and speed. In the correct use of the body, which makes possible a correct use of time, nothing must remain idle or useless: everything must be called upon to form the support of the act required. A well-disciplined body forms the operational context of the slightest gesture. Good handwriting, for example, presupposes a gymnastics—a whole routine whose rigorous code invests the body in its entirety, from the points of the feet to the tip of the index finger. The pupils must always 'hold their bodies erect, somewhat turned and free on the left side, slightly inclined, so that, with the elbow placed on the table, the shin can be rested upon the hand, unless this were to interfere with the view; the left leg must be somewhat more forward under the table than the right. A distance of two fingers must be left between the body and the table; for not only does one write with more alertness, but nothing is more harmful to the health than to acquire the habit of pressing one's stomach against the table; the part of the left arm from the elbow to the hand must be placed on the table. The right arm must be at a distance from the body of about three fingers and be about five fingers from the table, on which it must rest lightly. The teacher will place the pupils in the posture that they should maintain when writing, and will correct it either by sign or otherwise, when they change this position.' A disciplined body is the prerequisite of an efficient gesture.

4. *The body–object articulation*. Discipline defines each of the relations that the body must have with the object that it manipulates. Between them, it outlines a meticulous meshing. 'Bring the weapon forward. In three stages. Raise the rifle with the right hand, bringing it close to the body so as to hold it perpendicular

with the right knee, the end of the barrel at eye level, grasping it by striking it
with the right hand, the arm held close to the body at waist height. At the second
stage, bring the rifle in front of you with the left hand, the barrel in the middle
between the two eyes, vertical, the right hand grasping it at the small of the butt,
the arm outstretched, the trigger-guard resting on the first finger, the left hand at
the height of the notch, the thumb lying along the barrel against the moulding. At
the third stage, let go of the rifle with the left hand, which falls along the thigh,
raising the rifle with the right hand, the lock outwards and opposite the chest, the
right arm half flexed, the elbow close to the body, the thumb lying against the
lock, resting against the first screw, the hammer resting on the first finger, the
barrel perpendicular' ('Ordonnance du 1er janvier 1766 . . ., titre XI, article 2').
This is an example of what might be called the instrumental coding of the body. It
consists of a breakdown of the total gesture into two parallel series: that of the
parts of the body to be used (right hand, left hand, different fingers of the hand,
knee, eye, elbow, etc.) and that of the parts of the object manipulated (barrel,
notch, hammer, screw, etc.); then the two sets of parts are correlated together
according to a number of simple gestures (rest, bend); lastly, it fixes the canonical
succession in which each of these correlations occupies a particular place. This
obligatory syntax is what the military theoreticians of the eighteenth century called
'manoeuvre.' The traditional recipe gives place to explicit and obligatory prescriptions. Over the whole surface of contact between the body and the object it handles, power is introduced, fastening them to one another. It constitutes a body-
weapon, body-tool, body-machine complex. One is as far as possible from those
forms of subjection that demanded of the body only signs or products, forms of
expression or the result of labour. The regulation imposed by power is at the same
time the law of construction of the operation. Thus disciplinary power appears to
have the function not so much of deduction as of synthesis, not so much of exploitation of the product as of coercive link with the apparatus of production.

5. *Exhaustive use.* The principle that underlay the time-table in its traditional
form was essentially negative; it was the principle of non-idleness: it was forbidden to waste time, which was counted by God and paid for by men; the time-table
was to eliminate the danger of wasting it—a moral offence and economic dishonesty. Discipline, on the other hand, arranges a positive economy; it poses the
principle of a theoretically ever-growing use of time: exhaustion rather than use; it
is a question of extracting, from time, ever more available moments and, from
each moment, ever more useful forces. This means that one must seek to intensify
the use of the slightest moment, as if time, in its very fragmentation, were inexhaustible or as if, at least by an ever more detailed internal arrangement, one
could tend towards an ideal point at which one maintained maximum speed and
maximum efficiency. It was precisely this that was implemented in the celebrated
regulations of the Prussian infantry that the whole of Europe imitated after the
victories of Frederick II:[4] the more time is broken down, the more its subdivisions
multiply, the better one disarticulates it by deploying its internal elements under a
gaze that supervises them, the more one can accelerate an operation, or at least

regulate it according to an optimum speed; hence this regulation of the time of an action that was so important in the army and which was to be so throughout the entire technology of human activity: the Prussian regulations of 1743 laid down six stages to bring the weapon to one's foot, four to extend it, thirteen to raise it to the shoulder, etc. By other means, the 'mutual improvement school' was also arranged as a machine to intensify the use of time; its organization made it possible to obviate the linear, successive character of the master's teaching: it regulated the counterpoint of operations performed, at the same moment, by different groups of pupils under the direction of monitors and assistants, so that each passing moment was filled with many different, but ordered activities; and, on the other hand, the rhythm imposed by signals, whistles, orders imposed on everyone temporal norms that were intended both to accelerate the process of learning and to teach speed as a virtue;[5] 'the sole aim of these commands . . . is to accustom the children to executing well and quickly the same operations, to diminish as far as possible by speed the loss of time caused by moving from one operation to another.'

Through this technique of subjection a new object was being formed; slowly, it superseded the mechanical body—the body composed of solids and assigned movements, the image of which had for so long haunted those who dreamt of disciplinary perfection. This new object is the natural body, the bearer of forces and the seat of duration; it is the body susceptible to specified operations, which have their order, their stages, their internal conditions, their constituent elements. In becoming the target for new mechanisms of power, the body is offered up to new forms of knowledge. It is the body of exercise, rather than of speculative physics; a body manipulated by authority, rather than imbued with animal spirits; a body of useful training and not of rational mechanics, but one in which, by virtue of that very fact, a number of natural requirements and functional constraints are beginning to emerge. This is the body that Guibert discovered in his critique of excessively artificial movements. In the exercise that is imposed upon it and which it resists, the body brings out its essential correlations and spontaneously rejects the incompatible: 'On entering most of our training schools, one sees all those unfortunate soldiers in constricting and forced attitudes, one sees all their muscles contracted, the circulation of their blood interrupted . . . If we studied the intention of nature and the construction of the human body, we would find the position and the bearing that nature clearly prescribes for the soldier. The head must be erect, standing out from the shoulders, sitting perpendicularly between them. It must be turned neither to left nor to right, because, in view of the correspondence between the vertebrae of the neck and the shoulder-blade to which they are attached, none of them may move in a circular manner without slightly bringing with it from the same side that it moves one of the shoulders and because, the body no longer being placed squarely, the soldier can no longer walk straight in front of him or serve as a point of alignment. . . Since the hip-bone, which the ordinance indicates as the point against which the butt end should rest, is not situated the same in all men, the rifle must be placed more to the right for some, and more to the left for others. For the same reason of inequality of structure, the trigger-guard is more or less pressed against the body, depending on whether the outer parts of a man's shoulder is more or less fleshy.'

We have seen how the procedures of disciplinary distribution had their place among the contemporary techniques of classification and tabulation; but also how they introduced into them the specific problem of individuals and multiplicity. Similarly, the disciplinary controls of activity belonged to a whole series of researches, theoretical or practical, into the natural machinery of bodies; but they began to discover in them specific processes; behaviour and its organized requirements gradually replaced the simple physics of movement. The body, required to be docile in its minutest operations, opposes and shows the conditions of functioning proper to an organism. Disciplinary power has as its correlative an individuality that is not only analytical and 'cellular,' but also natural and 'organic.'

The Organization of Geneses

In 1667, the edict that set up the manufactory of the Gobelins envisaged the organization of a school. Sixty scholarship children were to be chosen by the superintendent of royal buildings, entrusted for a time to a master whose task it would be to provide them with 'upbringing and instruction,' then apprenticed to the various master tapestry makers of the manufactory (who by virtue of this fact received compensation deducted from the pupils' scholarships); after six years' apprenticeship, four years of service and a qualifying examination, they were given the right to 'set up and run a shop' in any town of the kingdom. We find here the characteristics of guild apprenticeship: the relation of dependence on the master that is both individual and total; the statutory duration of the training, which is concluded by a qualifying examination, but which is not broken down according to a precise programme; an overall exchange between the master who must give his knowledge and the apprentice who must offer his services, his assistance and often some payment. The form of domestic service is mixed with a transference of knowledge.[6] In 1737, an edict organized a school of drawing for the apprentices of the Gobelins; it was not intended to replace the training given by the master workers, but to complement it. It involved a quite different arrangement of time. Two hours a day, except on Sundays and feast days, the pupils met in the school. A roll-call was taken, from a list on the wall; the absentees were noted down in a register. The school was divided into three classes. The first for those who had no notion of drawing; they were made to copy models, which were more or less difficult according to the abilities of each pupil. The second 'for those who already have some principles,' or who had passed through the first class; they had to reproduce pictures 'at sight, without tracing,' but considering only the drawing. In the third class, they learnt clouring and pastel drawing, and were introduced to the theory and practice of dyeing. The pupils performed individual tasks at regular intervals; each of these exercises, signed with the name of its author and date of execution, was handed in to the teacher; the best were rewarded; assembled together at the end of the year and compared, they made it possible to establish the progress, the present ability and the relative place of each pupil; it was then decided which of them could pass into the next class. A general book, kept by the teachers and their assistants, recorded from day to day the behaviour of the pupils and everything that happened in the school; it was periodically shown to an inspector.

The Gobelins school is only one example of an important phenomenon: the development, in the classical period, of a new technique for taking charge of the time of individual existences; for regulating the relations of time, bodies and forces; for assuring an accumulation of duration; and for turning to ever-increased profit or use the movement of passing time. How can one capitalize the time of individuals, accumulate it in each of them, in their bodies, in their forces or in their abilities, in a way that is susceptible of use and control? How can one organize profitable durations? The disciplines, which analyse space, break up and rearrange activities, must also be understood as machinery for adding up and capitalizing time. This was done in four ways, which emerge most clearly in military organization.

1. Divide duration into successive or parallel segments, each of which must end at a specific time. For example, isolate the period of training and the period of practice; do not mix the instruction of recruits and the exercise of veterans; open separate military schools for the armed service (in 1764, the creation of the École Militaire in Paris, in 1776 the creation of twelve schools in the provinces); recruit professional soldiers at the youngest possible age, take children, 'have them adopted by the nation, and brought up in special schools'; teach in turn posture, marching, the handling of weapons, shooting, and do not pass to another activity until the first has been completely mastered: 'One of the principal mistakes is to show a soldier every exercise at once' ('Règlement de 1743 . . .'); in short, break down time into separate and adjusted threads. 2. Organize these threads according to an anaytical plan—successions of elements as simple as possible, combining according to increasing complexity. This presupposes that instruction should abandon the principle of analogical repetition. In the sixteenth century, military exercise consisted above all in copying all or part of the action, and of generally increasing the soldier's skill or strength;[7] in the eighteenth century, the instruction of the 'manual' followed the principle of the 'elementary' and not of the 'exemplary': simple gestures—the position of the fingers, the bend of the leg, the movement of the arms—basic elements for useful actions that also provide a general training in strength, skill, docility. 3. Finalize these temporal segments, decide on how long each will last and conclude it with an examination, which will have the triple function of showing whether the subject has reached the level required, of guaranteeing that each subject undergoes the same apprenticeship and of differentiating the abilities of each individual. When the sergeants, corporals, etc. 'entrusted with the task of instructing the others, are of the opinion that a particular soldier is ready to pass into the first class, they will present him first to the officers of their company, who will carefully examine him; if they do not find him sufficiently practised, they will refuse to admit him; if, on the other hand, the man

presented seems to them to be ready, the said officers will themselves propose him to the commanding officer of the regiment, who will see him if he thinks it necessary, and will have him examined by the senior officers. The slightest difference involves specific exercises. At the end of each series, others begin, branch off and subdivide in turn. Thus each individual is caught up in a temporal series which specifically defines his level or his rank. It is a disciplinary polyphony of exercises: 'Soldiers of the second class will be exercised every morning by sergeants, corporals, *anspessades*, lance-corporals. . . . The lance-corporals will be exercised every Sunday by the head of the section . . .; the corporals and *anspessades* will be exercised every Tuesday afternoon by the sergeants and their company and these in turn on the afternoons of every second, twelfth and twenty-second day of each month by senior officers.'

It is this disciplinary time that was gradually imposed on pedagogical practice—specializing the time of training and detaching it from the adult time, from the time of mastery; arranging different stages, separated from one another by graded examinations; drawing up programmes, each of which must take place during a particular stage and which involves exercises of increasing difficulty; qualifying individuals according to the way in which they progress through these series. For the 'initiatory' time of traditional training (an overall time, supervised by the master alone, authorized by a single examination), disciplinary time had substituted its multiple and progressive series. A whole analytical pedagogy was being formed, meticulous in its detail (it broke down the subject being taught into its simplest elements, it hierarchized each stage of development into small steps) and also very precocious in its history (it largely anticipated the genetic analyses of the *idéologues*, whose technical model it appears to have been). At the beginning of the eighteenth century, Demia suggested a division of the process of learning to read into seven levels: the first for those who are beginning to learn the letters, the second for those who are learning to spell, the third for those who are learning to join syllables together to make words, the fourth for those who are reading Latin in sentences or from punctuation to punctuation, the fifth for those who are beginning to read French, the sixth for the best readers, the seventh for those who can read manuscripts. But, where there are a great many pupils, further subdivisions would have to be introduced; the first class would comprise four streams: one for those who are learning the 'simple letters'; a second for those who are learning the 'mixed' letters; a third for those who are learning the abbreviated letters (*â, ê* . . .); a fourth for those who are learning the double letters (*ff, ss, tt, st*). The second class would be divided into three streams: for those who 'count each letter aloud before spelling the syllable, *D.O., DO*'; for those 'who spell the most difficult syllables, such as *bant, brand, spinx*', etc. Each stage in the combinatory of elements must be inscribed within a great temporal series, which is both a natural progress of the mind and a code for educative procedures.

The 'seriation' of successive activities makes possible a whole investment of duration by power: the possibility of a detailed control and a regular intervention (of differentiation, correction, punishment, elimination) in each moment of time; the possibility of characterizing, and therefore of using individuals according to the level in the series that they are moving through; the possibility of accumulating time and activity, of rediscovering them, totalized and usable in a final result, which is the ultimate capacity of an individual. Temporal dispersal is brought together to produce a profit, thus mastering a duration that would otherwise elude one's grasp. Power is articulated directly onto time; it assures its control and guarantees its use.

The disciplinary methods reveal a linear time whose moments are integrated, one upon another, and which is orientated towards a terminal, stable point; in short, an 'evolutive' time. But it must be recalled that, at the same moment, the administrative and economic techniques of control reveal a social time of a serial, oriented, cumulative type: the discovery of an evolution in terms of 'progress.' The disciplinary techniques reveal individual series: the discovery of an evolution in terms of 'genesis.' These two great 'discoveries' of the eighteenth century—the progress of societies and the geneses of individuals—were perhaps correlative with the new techniques of power, and more specifically, with a new way of administering time and making it useful, by segmentation, seriation, synthesis and totalization. A macro- and a micro-physics of power made possible, not the invention of history (it had long had no need of that), but the integration of a temporal, unitary, continuous, cumulative dimension in the exercise of controls and the practice of dominations. 'Evolutive' historicity, as it was then constituted—and so profoundly that it is still self-evident for many today—is bound up with a mode of functioning of power. No doubt it is as if the 'history-remembering' of the chronicles, genealogies, exploits, reigns and deeds had long been linked to a modality of power. With the new techniques of subjection, the 'dynamics' of continuous evolutions tends to replace the 'dynastics' of solemn events.

In any case, the small temporal continuum of individuality-genesis certainly seems to be, like the individuality-cell or the individuality-organism, an effect and an object of discipline. And, at the centre of this seriation of time, one finds a procedure that is, for it, what the drawing up of 'tables' was for the distribution of individuals and cellular segmentation, or, again, what *'manoeuvre'* was for the economy of activities and organic control. This procedure is 'exercise.' Exercise is that technique by which one imposes on the body tasks that are both repetitive and different, but always graduated. By bending behaviour towards a terminal state, exercise makes possible a perpetual characterization of the individual either in relation to this term, in relation to other individuals, or in relation to a type of itinerary. It thus assures, in the form of continuity and constraint, a growth, an observation, a qualification. Before adopting this strictly disciplinary form, exercise had a long history: it is to be found in military, religious and university practices either as initiation ritual, preparatory ceremony, theatrical rehearsal or examination. Its linear, continuously progressive organization, its genetic development in time were, at least in the army and the school, introduced at a later date— and were no doubt of religious origin. In any case, the idea of an educational 'programme' that would follow the child to the end of his schooling and which would involve from year to year, month to month, exercises of increasing complexity, first appeared, it seems, in a religious group, the Brothers of the Common

Life. Strongly inspired by Buysbroek and Rhenish mysticism, they transposed certain of the spiritual techniques to education—and to the education not only of clerks, but also of magistrates and merchants: the theme of a perfection towards the exemplary master guides the pupil; became with them that of an authoritarian perfection of the pupils by the teacher; the ever-increasing rigorous exercises that the ascetic life proposed became tasks of increasing complexity that marked the gradual acquisition of knowledge and good behaviour; the striving of the whole community towards salvation became the collective, permanent competition of individuals being classified in relation to one another. Perhaps it was these procedures of community life and salvation that were the first nucleus of methods intended to produce individually characterized, but collectively useful aptitudes.[8] In its mystical or ascetic form, exercise was a way of ordering earthly time for the conquest of salvation. It was gradually, in the history of the West, to change direction while preserving certain of its characteristics; it served to economize the time of life, to accumulate it in a useful form and to exercise power over men through the mediation of time arranged in this way. Exercise, having become an element in the political technology of the body and of duration, does not culminate in a beyond, but tends towards a subjection that has never reached its limit.

The Composition of Forces

'Let us begin by destroying the old prejudice, according to which one believed one was increasing the strength of a troop by increasing its depth. All the physical laws of movement become chimeras when one wishes to adapt them to tactics.'[9] From the end of the seventeenth century, the technical problem of infantry had been freed from the physical model of mass. In any army of pikes and muskets—slow, imprecise, practically incapable of selecting a target and taking aim—troops were used as a projectile, a wall or a fortress: 'the formidable infantry of the army of Spain'; the distribution of soldiers in this mass was carried out above all according to their seniority and their bravery; at the centre, with the task of providing weight and volume, of giving density to the body, were the least experienced; in front, at the angles and on the flanks, were the bravest or reputedly most skilful soldiers. In the course of the classical period, one passed over to a whole set of delicate articulations. The unit—regiment, battalion, section and, later, 'division'[10]—became a sort of machine with many parts, moving in relation to one another, in order to arrive at a configuration and to obtain a specific result. What were the reasons for this mutation? Some were economic: to make each individual useful and the training, maintenance, and arming of troops profitable; to give to each soldier, a precious unit, maximum efficiency. But these economic reasons could become determinant only with a technical transformation: the invention of the rifle:[11] more accurate, more rapid than the musket, it gave greater value to the soldier's skill; more capable of reaching a particular target, it made it possible to exploit fire-power at an individual level; and, conversely, it turned every soldier into a possible target, requiring by the same token greater mobility; it involved therefore the disappearance of a technique of masses in favour of an art that distributed units and men along extended, relatively flexible, mobile lines. Hence the need to find a whole calculated practice of individual and collective dispositions, movements of groups or isolated elements, changes of position, of movement from one disposition to another; in short, the need to invent a machinery whose principle would no longer be the mobile or immobile mass, but a geometry of divisible segments whose basic unity was the mobile soldier with his rifle;[12] and, no doubt, below the soldier himself, the minimal gestures, the elementary stages of actions, the fragments of spaces occupied or traversed.

The same problems arose when it was a question of constituting a productive force whose effect had to be superior to the sum of elementary forces that composed it: 'The combined working-day produces, relatively to an equal sum of working-days, a greater quantity of use-values, and, consequently, diminishes the labour-time necessary for the production of a given useful effect. Whether the combined working-day, in a given case, acquires this increased productive power, because it heightens the mechanical force of labour, or extends its sphere of action over a greater space, or contracts the field of production relatively to the scale of production, or at the critical moment sets large masses of labour to work . . . the special productive power of the combined working-day is, under all circumstances, the social productive power of labour, or the productive power of social labour. This power is due to cooperation itself.' On several occasions, Marx stresses the analogy between the problems of the division of labour and those of military tactics. For example: 'Just as the offensive power of a squadron of cavalry, or the defensive power of a regiment of infantry, is essentially different from the sum of the offensive or defensive powers of the individual cavalry or infantry soldiers taken separately, so the sum total of the mechanical forces exerted by isolated workmen differs from the social force that is developed, when many hands take part simultaneously in one and the same undivided operation.'

Thus a new demand appears to which discipline must respond: to construct a machine whose effect will be maximized by the concerted articulation of the elementary parts of which it is composed. Discipline is no longer simply an art of distributing bodies, of extracting time from them and accumulating it, but of composing forces in order to obtain an efficient machine. This demand is expressed in several ways.

1. The individual body becomes an element that may be placed, moved, articulated on others. Its bravery or its strength are no longer the principal variables that define it; but the place it occupies, the interval it covers, the regularity, the good order according to which it operates its movements. The soldier is above all a fragment of mobile space, before he is courage or honour. Guibert describes the soldier in the following way: 'When he is under arms, he occupies two feet along his greatest diameter, that is to say, taking him from one end to the other, and about one foot in his greatest thickness taken from the chest to the shoulders, to which one must add an interval of a foot between him and the next man; this gives two feet in all directions per soldier and indicates that a troop of infantry in battle occupies, either in its front or in its depth, as many steps as it has ranks.' This is a

functional reduction of the body. But it is also an insertion of this body-segment in a whole ensemble over which it is articulated. The soldier whose body has been trained to function part by part for particular operations must in turn form an element in a mechanism at another level. The soldiers will be instructed first 'one by one, then two by two, then in greater numbers. . . . For the handling of weapons, one will ascertain that, when the soldiers have been separately instructed, they will carry it out two by two, and then change places alternately, so that the one on the left may learn to adapt himself to the one on the right.' The body is constituted as a part of a multisegmentary machine.

2. The various chronological series that discipline must combine to form a composite time are also pieces of machinery. The time of each must be adjusted to the time of the others in such a way that the maximum quantity of forces may be extracted from each and combined with the optimum result. Thus Servan dreamt of a military machine that would cover the whole territory of the nation and in which each individual would be occupied without interruption but in a different way according to the evolutive segment, the genetic sequence in which he finds himself. Military life would begin in childhood, when young children would be taught the profession of arms in 'military manors'; it would end in these same manors when the veterans, right up to their last day, would teach the children, exercise the recruits, preside over the soldiers' exercises, supervise them when they were carrying out works in the public interest, and finally make order reign in the country, when the troops were fighting at the frontiers. There is not a single moment of life from which one cannot extract forces, providing one knows how to differentiate it and combine it with others. Similarly, one uses the labour of children and of old people in the great workshops; this is because they have certain elementary capacities for which it is not necessary to use workers who have many other aptitudes; furthermore, they constitute a cheap labour force; lastly, if they work, they are no longer at anyone's charge: 'Labouring mankind', said a tax collector of an enterprise at Angers, 'may find in this manufactory, from the age of ten to old age, resources against idleness and the penury that follows from it.' But it was probably in primary education that this adjustment of different chronologies was to be carried out with most subtlety. From the seventeenth century to the introduction, at the beginning of the nineteenth, of the Lancaster method, the complex clockwork of the mutual improvement school was built up cog by cog: first the oldest pupils were entrusted with tasks involving simple supervision, then of checking work, then of teaching; in the end, all the time of all the pupils was occupied either with teaching or with being taught. The school became a machine for learning, in which each pupil, each level and each moment, if correctly combined, were permanently utilized in the general process of teaching. One of the great advocates of the mutual improvement schools gives us some idea of this progress: 'In a school of 360 children, the master who would like to instruct each pupil in turn for a session of three hours would not be able to give half a minute to each. By the new method, each of the 360 pupils writes, reads or counts for two and a half hours.'

3. This carefully measured combination of forces requires a precise system of

command. All the activity of the disciplined individual must be punctuated and sustained by injunctions whose efficacy rests on brevity and clarity; the order does not need to be explained or formulated; it must trigger off the required behaviour and that is enough. From the master of discipline to him who is subjected to it the relation is one of signalization: it is a question not of understanding the injunction but of perceiving the signal and reacting to it immediately, according to a more or less artificial, prearranged code. Place the bodies in a little world of signals to each of which is attached a single, obligatory response: it is a technique of training, of *dressage*, that 'despotically excludes in everything the least representation, and the smallest murmur'; the disciplined soldier 'begins to obey whatever he is ordered to do; his obedience is prompt and blind; an appearance of indocility, the least delay would be a crime.' The training of school-children was to be carried out in the same way: few words, no explanation, a total silence interrupted only by signals—bells, clapping of hands, gestures, a mere glance from the teacher, or that little wooden apparatus used by the Brothers of the Christian Schools; it was called *par excellence* the 'Signal' and it contained in its mechanical brevity both the technique of command and the morality of obedience. 'The first and principal use of the signal is to attract at once the attention of all the pupils to the teacher and to make them attentive to what he wishes to impart to them. Thus, whenever he wishes to attract the attention of the children, and to bring the exercise to an end, he will strike the signal once. Whenever a good pupil hears the noise of the signal, he will imagine that he is hearing the voice of the teacher or rather the voice of God himself calling him by his name. He will then partake of the feelings of the young Samuel, saying with him in the depths of his soul: "Lord, I am here."' The pupil will have to have learnt the code of the signals and respond automatically to them. 'When prayer has been said, the teacher will strike the signal at once and, turning to the child whom he wishes to read, he will make the sign to begin. To make a sign to stop to a pupil who is reading, he will strike the signal once. . . To make a sign to a pupil to repeat when he has read badly or mispronounced a letter, a syllable or a word, he will strike the signal twice in rapid succession. If, after the sign had been made two or three times, the pupil who is reading does not find and repeat the word that he has badly read or mispronounced—because he has read several words beyond it before being called to order—the teacher will strike three times in rapid succession, as a sign to him to begin to read farther back; and he will continue to make the sign till the pupil finds the word which he has said incorrectly.' The mutual improvement school was to exploit still further this control of behaviour by the system of signals to which one had to react immediately. Even verbal orders were to function as elements of signalization: 'Enter your benches. At the word *enter*, the children bring their right hands down on the table with a resounding thud and at the same time put one leg into the bench; at the words *your benches* they put the other leg in and sit down opposite their slates . . . *Take your slates*. At the word *take*, the children, with their right hands, take hold of the string by which the slate is suspended from the nail before them, and, with their left hands, they grasp the slate in the middle; at the word *slates*, they unhook it and place it on the table'.[13]

To sum up, it might be said that discipline creates out of the bodies it controls four types of individuality, or rather an individuality that is endowed with four characteristics: it is cellular (by the play of spatial distribution), it is organic (by the coding of activities), it is genetic (by the accumulation of time), it is combinatory (by the composition of forces). And, in doing so, it operates four great techniques: it draws up tables; it prescribes movements; it imposes exercises; lastly, in order to obtain the combination of forces, it arranges 'tactics.' Tactics, the art of constructing, with located bodies, coded activities and trained aptitudes, mechanisms in which the product of the various forces is increased by their calculated combination are no doubt the highest form of disciplinary practice. In this knowledge, the eighteenth-century theoreticians saw the general foundation of all military practice, from the control and exercise of individual bodies to the use of forces specific to the most complex multiplicities. The architecture, anatomy, mechanics, economy of the disciplinary body: 'In the eyes of most soldiers, tactics are only a branch of the vast science of war; for me, they are the base of this science; they are this science itself, because they teach how to constitute troops, order them, move them, get them to fight; because tactics alone may make up for numbers, and handle the multitude; lastly, it will include knowledge of men, weapons, tensions, circumstances, because it is all these kinds of knowledge brought together that must determine those movements.' Or again: 'The term tactics . . . gives some idea of the respective position of the men who make up a particular troop in relation to that of the different troops that make up an army, their movements and their actions, their relations with one another.'

It may be that war as strategy is a continuation of politics. But it must not be forgotten that 'politics' has been conceived as a continuation, if not exactly and directly of war, at least of the military model as a fundamental means of preventing civil disorder. Politics, as a technique of internal peace and order, sought to implement the mechanism of the perfect army, of the disciplined mass, of the docile, useful troop, of the regiment in camp and in a field, on manoeuvres and on exercises. In the great eighteenth-century states, the army guaranteed civil peace no doubt because it was a real force, an ever-threatening sword, but also because it was a technique and a body of knowledge that could project their schema over the social body. If there is a politics-war series that passes through strategy, there is an army-politics series that passes through tactics. It is strategy that makes it possible to understand warfare as a way of conducting politics between states; it is tactics that makes it possible to understand the army as a principle for maintaining the absence of warfare in civil society. The classical age saw the birth of the great political and military strategy by which nations confronted each other's economic and demographic forces; but it also saw the birth of meticulous military and political tactics by which the control of bodies and individual forces were exercised within states. The *'militaire'*—the military institution, military science, the *militaire* himself, so different from what was formerly characterized by the term *'homme de guerre'*—was specified, during this period, at the point of junction between war and the noise of battle on the one hand, and order and silence, subservient to peace, on the other. Historians of ideas usually attribute the dream of a perfect society to the philosophers and jurists of the eighteenth century; but there was also a military dream of society; its fundamental reference was not to the state of nature, but to the meticulously subordinated cogs of a machine, not to the primal social contract, but to permanent coercions, not to fundamental rights, but to indefinitely progressive forms of training, not to the general will but to automatic docility.

'Discipline must be made national,' said Guibert. 'The state that I depict will have a simple, reliable, easily controlled administration. It will resemble those huge machines, which by quite uncomplicated means produce great effects; the strength of this state will spring from its own strength, its prosperity from its own prosperity. Time, which destroys all, will increase its power. It will disprove that vulgar prejudice by which we are made to imagine that empires are subjected to an imperious law of decline and ruin.' The Napoleonic régime was not far off and with it the form of state that was to survive it and, we must not forget, the foundations of which were laid not only by jurists, but also by soldiers, not only councillors of state, but also junior officers, not only the men of the courts, but also the men of the camps. The Roman reference that accompanied this formation certainly bears with it this double index: citizens and legionaries, law and manoeuvres. While jurists or philosophers were seeking in the pact a primal model for the construction or reconstruction of the social body, the soldiers and with them the technicians of discipline were elaborating procedures for the individual and collective coercion of bodies.

Notes

Editors' Note: The notes below are Foucault's. We have, however, eliminated some of his extensive citations that appear within the original text itself.

1. I shall choose examples from military, medical, educational and industrial institutions. Other examples might have been taken from colonization, slavery and child rearing.

2. Cf. what La Métherie wrote after a visit to Le Creusot: 'The buildings for so fine an establishment and so large a quantity of different work should cover a sufficient area, so that there will be no confusion among the workers during working time' (La Métherie, 66).

3. J.-B. de la Salle, *Conduite des écoles chrétiennes*, B.N. Ms. 11759, 248–9. A little earlier Batencour proposed that classrooms should be divided into three parts: 'The most honourable for those who are learning Latin. . . . It should be stressed that there are as many places at the tables as there will be writers, in order to avoid the confusion usually caused by the lazy.' In another, those who are learning to read: a bench for the rich and a bench for the poor 'so that vermin will not be passed on'. A third section for newcomers: 'When their ability has been recognized, they will be given a place' (M.I.D.B., 56–7).

4. The success of the Prussian troops can only be attributed to the 'excellence of their discipline and their exercise; the choice of exercise is not therefore a matter of indifference; in Prussia the subject has been studied for forty years with unremitting application' (Saxe, II, 249).

5. Writing exercise: '. . . 9: Hands on the knees. This command is conveyed by one ring on the bell; 10: hands on the table, head up; 11: clean the slates: everyone cleans his slate with a little saliva, or better still with a piece of rag; 12: show the slates; 13: monitors,

ct. They inspect the slates with their assistants and then those of their own bench. The ,stants inspect those of their own bench and everyone returns to his own place.'

6. This mixture appears clearly in certain classes of the apprenticeship contract: the ,naster is obliged to give his pupil—in exchange for his money and his labour—all his knowledge, without keeping any secret from him; otherwise, he is liable to a fine. Cf., for example, Grosrenaud, 62.

7. F. de la Noue recommended the creation of military academies at the end of the sixteenth century, suggesting that one should learn in them 'how to handle horses, to practise with the dagger, with and without shield, to fence, to perform on horseback, to jump; if swimming and wrestling were added, it would be to the good, for all this makes the person robust and more subtle' (Noue, 181–2).

8. Through the schools at Liège, Devenport, Zwolle, Wesel; and thanks also to Jean Sturm and his memorandun of 1538 for the organization of a *gymnasium* at Strasburg. Cf. *Bulletin de la société d'histoire du protestantisme*, XXV, 499–505.

It should be noted that the relations between the army, religious organization and education are very complex. The 'decury,' the unit of the Roman army, is to be found in Benedictine monasteries, as the unit of work and no doubt of supervision. The Brothers of the Common Life borrowed it and adapted it to their own education organization: the pupils were grouped in tens. It was this unit that the Jesuits took up in the scenography of their schools, thus reintroducing a military model. But the decury was replaced in turn by an even more military schema, with ranks, columns, lines.

9. Guibert, 18. In fact, this very old problem came into the forefront once more in the eighteenth century, for the economic and technical reasons that we are about to see; and the 'prejudice' in question had been discussed very often by others besides Guibert himself (followers of Folard, Pirch, Mesnil-Durand).

10. In the sense in which this term was used after 1759.

11. The movement that brought the rifle into widespread use may be roughly dated from the battle of Steinkirk, 1699.

12. On this importance of geometry, see J. de Beausobre: 'The science of war is essentially geometrical. . . The arrangement of a battalion and a squadron on a whole front and at so much height is alone the effect of an as yet unknown, but profound geometry' (Beausobre, 307).

13. *Journal pour l'instruction élémentaire*, April 1816. Cf. Tronchot, who has calculated that pupils must have been given over 200 commands a day (without counting exceptional orders); for the morning alone twenty-six commands communicated by the voice, twenty-three by signs, thirty-seven by rings of the bell, and twenty-four by whistle, which means a blow on the whistle or a ring on the bell every three minutes.

About the Editors

Mitchell Cohen is Professor of Political Science at Baruch College and the Graduate School of the City University of New York and coeditor of *Dissent* magazine. He is the author of *The Wager of Lucien Goldmann* (Princeton) and *Zion and State*. Nicole Fermon is Associate Professor of Political Science at Fordham University and the author of the forthcoming *The Political Education of Sentiment: Rousseau's Teaching on Women and the State*.